·SOUTH-WESTERN·
CENTURY 21
ACCOUNTING
ADVANCED

Kenton E. Ross, CPA
Professor Emeritus of Accounting
Texas A&M University–Commerce
Commerce, Texas

Mark W. Lehman, CPA
Associate Professor
School of Accountancy
Mississippi State University
Starkville, Mississippi

Claudia Bienias Gilbertson, CPA
Teaching Professor
North Hennepin Community College
Brooklyn Park, Minnesota

Robert D. Hanson
Late Associate Dean
College of Business Administration
Central Michigan University
Mount Pleasant, Michigan

THOMSON
SOUTH-WESTERN

SOUTH-WESTERN

THOMSON LEARNING

Century 21 Accounting, Advanced, Anniversary Edition
by Kenton E. Ross, Claudia Bienias Gilbertson, Mark W. Lehman, and Robert D. Hanson

Vice President/ Executive Publisher
Dave Shaut

Team Leader
Karen Schmohe

Acquisitions Editor
Marilyn Hornsby

Project Manager
Carol Sturzenberger

Sr. Marketing Manager
Nancy A. Long

Marketing Coordinator
Yvonne Patton-Beard

Production Manager
Patricia Matthews Boies

Manufacturing Coordinator
Kevin Kluck

Editorial Assistant
Stephanie White

Production Assistant
Nancy Stamper

Design Coordinator
Tippy McIntosh

Consulting Editor
Minta Berry

Cycle Opener Artwork
Marti Shohet

Cover Design
Tom Nikosey

Composition/Prepress
settingPace

Printer
R. R. Donnelley/Willard

For permission to use material from this text or product, contact us by

Tel (800) 730-2214
Fax (800) 730-2215
www.thomsonrights.com

For more information, contact South-Western, 5191 Natorp Boulevard, Mason, OH 45040; or find us on the World Wide Web at http://www.swep.com

About the Authors

Kenton E. Ross, Ed.D., C.P.A., is Professor Emeritus, Department of Accounting, at Texas A&M University—Commerce. He formerly served as Dean of the College of Business and Technology; Director of Business and Economic Research; and Head, Department of Accounting.

Claudia Bienias Gilbertson, M.B.A., C.P.A., is an experienced high school and community college instructor. She is currently a teaching professor at North Hennepin Community College.

Mark W. Lehman, Ph.D., C.P.A., is an Associate Professor in the School of Accountancy at Mississippi State University, where he teaches in the areas of microcomputers, accounting systems, and auditing. He regularly teaches continuing education classes on microcomputers and internal control.

The late **Robert D. Hanson,** Ph.D., was Professor of Business Education and Associate Dean of the College of Business Administration at Central Michigan University.

Ron Krug, C.P.A., is an Assistant Professor in the Business Economics Department at SUNY Oneonta. He has been teaching at the college level for 15 years.

Dan Passalacqua, M.A., has taught business education for over 24 years at the high school level and is an author, educational consultant, and district coordinator of occupational programs. Currently he is involved in total school restructuring at Oak Grove High School, San Jose, California.

REVIEWERS

Bruce J. (Ike) Bergeron
Business Instructor, Southeastern Vermont
Career Education Center
Brattleboro Union High School
Brattleboro, Vermont

Judith K. Berry
Business Services and Technology Consultant
Michigan Department of Education
East Lansing, Michigan

Margaret Chester
Instructor, Business Technology Department
Biloxi High School
Biloxi, Mississippi

Debbie Davidson
Accounting Instructor, Business Department
Ben Davis High School
Indianapolis, Indiana

Maurice Ellington
Chairperson, Business Education Department
John Marshall Metropolitan High School
Chicago, Illinois

Mary A. Gonzalez
Business Education Instructor
Weslaco High School
Weslaco, Texas

Cynthia A. Greene
Chairperson, Career Technology Department
Centennial High School
Fulton County Schools
Roswell, Georgia

James L. Knutson
Finance Director
City of Anoka
Anoka, Minnesota

Mary A. Lively
Business Technology Instructor
Great Oaks Institute of Technology and
Career Development
Cincinnati, Ohio

Maria Medina-Perez
Chairperson, Business Technology Education
Miami Palmetto Senior High School
Miami, Florida

Kelvin Meeks
Teacher, Business and Technology
Department
Raleigh-Egypt High School
Memphis, Tennessee

Lisa Olson
Chairperson, Business Education Department
Hartford Union High School
Hartford, Wisconsin

Ronald Romano
Chairperson, Business Education Department
Ogdensburg Free Academy
Ogdensburg, New York

Judith P. Sams
Chairperson, Business Department
Fuqua School
Farmville, Virginia

Patricia Samuels
Director, Academy of Finance
Withrow High School
Cincinnati, Ohio

William Sinai
Chairperson, Computerized Accounting
West Valley Occupational Center
Woodland, California

Linda L. White
Chairperson, Business Education Department
Accounting Teacher
Waynesboro Area Senior High School
Waynesboro, Pennsylvania

Vera M. White
Chairperson, Vocational Technology
Hallandale High School
Hallandale, Florida

INSTRUCTIONAL STRATEGIES

COMPLETE ACCOUNTING COVERAGE

Century 21 Accounting, Advanced Course expands on topics introduced in the first-year course while adding new topics about management accounting, cost accounting, not-for-profit accounting, and financial analysis. Accounting concepts are introduced using modern businesses to which students can relate.

COLORFUL, ATTRACTIVE PAGES

Bright, interesting colors throughout the text draw students in and get them excited about accounting! Imagine how eager students will be to read a bright and colorful textbook. Scattered throughout are eye-catching photos that represent the business featured in the part.

MANAGEABLE PEDAGOGY WITH SHORT, ACCESSIBLE LESSONS

Have you ever heard a student say, "Accounting is hard"? *Century 21 Accounting, Seventh Edition* has the answer. Chapters are divided into **short, accessible lessons** that cover one or two concepts.

The *Wraparound Teacher's Edition* contains comprehensive lesson plans for each lesson to help you plan your instructional time more easily.

- **Chart of Accounts** *used throughout the cycle is provided on the cycle opening pages for easy reference.*
- **Terms Preview** *displays all the key words introduced in the chapter.*
- **Objectives** *are listed at the beginning of each chapter to highlight lesson concepts and preview what students will learn.*

Illustrations are consistently placed directly above the corresponding text. No more flipping pages back and forth to find an illustration that appears on a different page from the explanatory text! Plus, students can quickly find the illustration they are looking for when reviewing or working problems.

Steps and call-outs are completely integrated into the illustrations. This makes it easy to understand and then apply the procedure being taught. Clear, concise, step-by-step instructions are directly linked to the specific part of the illustration where the work is recorded.

The **concentrated supporting text** covers one specific topic and motivates students to read each page. Students are not intimidated by pages of text, but are

encouraged to investigate the illustration and get further information by reading.

Many students are visual learners. Advanced accounting emphasizes learning step-by-step procedures and processes. With the combination of consistently placed, easy-to-locate illustrations, call-outs and instructions placed inside the illustrations, and step-by-step instructions, students can see how to complete accounting procedures and processes and can refer to **easy-to-read steps** for reinforcement and clarification.

LESSON PRACTICE

Each lesson ends with an activity page that provides immediate reinforcement of the lesson material. Instructors can use the end-of-lesson activities to make sure students fully understand all concepts and procedures before moving on to the next lesson.

- **Terms Review** *lists all the important new words learned in the lesson in the order they appear in the text.*
- **Audit Your Understanding** *asks two or more conceptual questions about the material covered in the lesson. The answers appear in Appendix D so students can check their understanding.*
- **Work Together** *provides guided practice through the students' first hands-on application of chapter procedures and concepts. Forms to complete the exercise are given in the Working Papers. Performing this exercise together with the instructor or in work teams gives students a basis for completing similar problems later.*
- **On Your Own** *mirrors and builds on the Work Together problem to give the student independent practice. Forms to complete the exercise are given in the Working Papers. Students work this problem to demonstrate proficiency, giving them a real sense of accomplishment. Instructors can informally assess whether students have mastered the basic concept covered in the lesson. Accounting isn't so hard after all!*
- *Students get further independent practice from an end-of-chapter* **Application Problem** *that mirrors or builds on the end-of-lesson problems.*

CHAPTER PRACTICE

Century 21 Accounting, Seventh Edition gives students **many short problems**. Students can now easily find and fix mistakes.

The **Summary** is a quick, short list of the topics covered in each lesson. Students can use the Summary to review their understanding of the material presented in the chapter. Instructors can ask questions based on the Summary as a fast way to verify student comprehension.

End-of-chapter exercises contain:

- ***Application problem***, at least one for each lesson.
- ***Mastery problem*** that tests overall comprehension of the entire chapter.
- ***Challenge problem*** that tests overall comprehension of the entire chapter.

Many end-of-chapter problems can be completed using Automated Accounting software.

- ***Reinforcement Activities*** at appropriate intervals.

And something new:

Most chapters contain one problem using real-life transaction statements.

APPENDICES

- ***Appendix A: Accounting Concepts*** lists in one place all of the accounting concepts that students encounter throughout the text.
- ***Appendix B: Using a Calculator and Computer Keypad*** provides important instruction in business calculator use and the ten-key touch system.
- ***Appendix C: Recycling Problems*** offers additional opportunities for student practice. There are one or more recycling problems for each chapter and these problems mirror the end-of-chapter mastery problems. Working papers are provided in the Study Guide and Recycling Problem Working Papers.
- ***Appendix D: Answers to Audit Your Understanding*** contains brief answers to Audit Your Understanding questions that appear at the end of each lesson. Students can use the questions and answers for self study.

FEATURES

Special features provide context for accounting learning and real-life information about business. Features provide cross-curricular material for the accounting classroom.

LESSON FEATURES

- **Cultural Diversity** shows students that many different cultures around the world and throughout history have contributed to the development of accounting and financial record keeping.
- **Professional Business Ethics** presents dilemmas that can arise in day-to-day business operations.
- **Small Business Spotlight** features information about how to become a successful entrepreneur.
- **Accounting at Work** introduces real-life businesspeople who tell their stories about how accounting helps in their careers.
- **Technology for Business** covers the interplay between technology and business life. Topics covered include spreadsheets, the Internet, and commercial accounting software.
- **Global Perspective** provides insight into working with international suppliers and customers. Most students will have some global business experience in their careers. This feature introduces students to some of the issues involved in global business.
- **Legal Issues in Accounting** covers the legal issues involved in forming and dissolving the different forms of business organization and touches on other legal aspects of business life.
- **Applied mathematics** boxes visually represent the intersection between accounting and mathematics and are strategically placed near relevant text to ensure optimum learning.
- **Remember** appears at the bottom of selected pages to reinforce critical accounting facts and procedures.
- **FYI** gives additional accounting and general business information related to the topics in a chapter.

CHAPTER FEATURES

- **Accounting in Your Career** features appear at the beginning of each chapter and entice students by showing how accounting is part of everyone's life. These scenarios answer the question, "Why should I learn this?" The Accounting in Your Career feature focuses your students' attention on the topics to be studied in the chapter.
- **Critical Thinking Questions** for Accounting in Your Career energize students with class discussions about accounting-related issues and can even be used as an informal pretest and posttest to demonstrate how much students have learned after studying a chapter. Suggested answers to each question are provided in the Wraparound Teacher's Edition.
- **Internet Activity** provides the Web address and instructions for accessing the Internet activity for each chapter.
- **Applied Communication** offers exercises for strengthening communication skills, a must for all students. Employers are expecting their business and accounting new hires to be able to communicate effectively, so get started here.
- **Cases for Critical Thinking** require students to carefully consider one or more questions, based on the accounting scenario being presented. An excellent opportunity for in-class discussion or group work!
- **Explore Accounting** includes opportunities for higher-level learning with Discussion, Research, and Required exercises directly related to the material presented in the feature. Topics include GAAP, fiscal periods, cash controls, and more.

AUTOMATED ACCOUNTING

- **Automated Accounting** sections conclude every chapter, and are a terrific opportunity for hands-on computer instruction with Automated Accounting. Now students see the connection between manual and automated accounting in every chapter.

CENTURY 21 ACCOUNTING
FAMILY OF PRODUCTS

South-Western Educational Publishing provides everything you and your students need to have a successful accounting classroom.

WRAPAROUND TEACHER'S EDITION

The *Wraparound Teacher's Edition* provides:

- **Overview** *of each accounting cycle and each chapter within a cycle.*

- **Teaching Strategies** *loaded with hints, tips, and suggestions for reaching students with different learning styles. Plus, a variety of instructional methods, such as cooperative learning, different media options, and more.*

- **Chapter Interleaf Charts** *that present concepts and skills covered in a chapter. Instructors can determine what will be new for students and what concepts and skills need reinforcement and emphasis. Also included is information about special features, technology and media, teaching strategies, and practice and assessment.*

- **Effective Teaching Model Lesson Plans** *that provide step-by-step instructional support for every lesson. Each Lesson Plan includes the headings Motivate, Explain, Demonstrate, Guided Practice, Independent Practice, Reteach, Enrich, and Close.*

- **Check Figures** *that can be provided to students as guideposts as students complete their work or that can be used by instructors for quick and easy grading.*

WORKING PAPERS

The *Working Papers* contain accounting forms and rulings for completing chapter problems and Reinforcement Activities. The *Working Papers* are carefully laid out so that forms for the next problem are available while the previous problem is being graded. Plenty of extra forms are provided for any necessary rework. The Teacher's Editions of the *Working Papers* provide solutions to the problems. A separate *Study Guide and Recycling Problem Working Papers* book is also available.

SIMULATIONS

Three new simulations are available for the advanced course. The first two are available in both manual and automated versions.

- **Blue Skies Outfitter** *is a departmentalized merchandising business organized as a corporation.*

- **Southgate Hardware** *is a merchandising business organized as a corporation.*

- **The Valley Fan Center** *is a manufacturer organized as a corporation using job order costing.*

TECHNOLOGY

- **Template disks** *are available for use with Automated Accounting 7.0, Windows; Automated Accounting 6.0, Windows; and Automated Accounting 6.0, Macintosh. Template files are available for many problems in the textbook, two of the comprehensive Reinforcement Activities, plus two of the simulations. Electronic Auditors are also available.*

- **Spreadsheet template disks** *correspond to selected textbook problems.*

ASSESSMENT BINDER PACKAGE

The *Assessment Binder Package* includes two separate versions of printed chapter and part tests, containing both objective questions and problems and a computerized testing program.

Other items available include
- **English and Spanish Dictionary**
- **Teacher's Resource Guide** in three-ring binder
- **Videotapes**

▶ **Features found in every chapter**
Explore Accounting
28, 55, 85, 125
Internet Activity
33, 59, 90, 131
Applied Communication
33, 59, 90, 131
Cases for Critical Thinking
33, 59, 90, 131

▶ **End of lesson review and practice**
Terms Review
11, 19, 27, 47, 54, 69, 77, 84, 100, 111, 118,
124
Audit Your Understanding
11, 19, 27, 47, 54, 69, 77, 84, 100, 111, 118,
124
Work Together
11, 19, 27, 47, 54, 69, 77, 84, 100, 111, 118,
124
On Your Own
11, 19, 27, 47, 54, 70, 78, 84, 100, 111, 118,
124

▶ **End of chapter
review and practice**
Chapter Summary
28, 55, 85, 125
Application Problems
29, 56, 86, 126
Mastery Problem
31, 58, 88, 129
Challenge Problem
32, 59, 90, 130

▶ **Reinforcement
Activity 1**
**Processing and Reporting
Departmentalized Accounting Data**
135

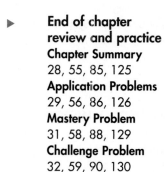

PART 2
Accounting Control Systems

Features

PART 4
Corporation Accounting

Features

PART 5
Management Accounting

Features

Table of Contents

PART 6
Cost Accounting

Features

PART 7
Other Accounting Systems

Features

► **Features found in every chapter**
Explore Accounting
594, 624, 653, 675
Internet Activity
599, 628, 657, 680
Applied Communication
599, 628, 657, 680
Cases for Critical Thinking
600, 628, 657, 680

End of lesson review and practice
Terms Review
► 586, 592, 618, 623, 640, 644, 651
Audit Your Understanding
586, 592, 608, 618, 623, 640, 644, 651, 667, 671, 674
Work Together
586, 592, 608, 618, 623, 640, 644, 651, 667, 671,674
On Your Own
586, 593, 609, 618, 623, 640, 644, 652, 667, 671,674

End of chapter review and practice
Chapter Summary
► 594, 624, 653, 675
Application Problems
595, 625, 654, 676
Mastery Problem
597, 627, 655, 677
Challenge Problem
598, 627, 656, 679

Introduction

Successful organizations depend on reliable financial information. To be successful, businesses must be able to achieve two objectives: (1) Provide the type and quality of merchandise or services their customers want. (2) Earn a reasonable profit. To achieve these objectives, business owners and managers use financial information to evaluate their current operations and to plan future operations.

Objectives of governmental and other not-for-profit organizations, such as schools, churches, and social clubs, differ from those of business organizations. Not-for-profit organizations seek to provide the best services possible for the least cost. Reliable financial information helps them achieve their goals.

Providing financial information that will assist managers in their decision making is an important function of accounting. In this book, you will explore accounting concepts and procedures used to provide reliable financial information.

Before you begin exploring these concepts and procedures, read this introduction. You will learn more about the accounting profession. You will also read about the many uses of accounting information and how the skills you learn in this course will be useful whether or not you choose accounting as a profession.

TERMS PREVIEW

accounting
accounting system
accounting records
financial accounting
managerial accounting
cost accounting
tax accounting
auditing
auditor
personal financial
    planning
management advisory
    services
ethics

ACCOUNTING
IN YOUR CAREER

CAREER CHOICES

Rob and Kendra have completed one accounting course and are beginning their second one. They are discussing their plans for the future. Rob is anxious to begin working. He plans to work full-time and continue his education part-time. He currently works after school for a recording studio. The studio specializes in voice-overs for radio commercials. Rob has enjoyed meeting many interesting people. He can continue working as a sound technician at the studio while he attends school. Recently, Rob visited a local community college. He was pleased to learn that the college has begun offering an associate degree in multimedia technology. The program appears to fit Rob's interests well. In fact, he would like to earn his degree, gain valuable work experience, and eventually open his own video/audio production studio.

Kendra enjoys sports. She plays several sports and earns money as a soccer official. Kendra plans to attend college in the fall. She will continue to officiate soccer games to earn money for college. Kendra has enjoyed her study of accounting and business. In fact, she has earned honors as one of the top business education students in her school. She has not yet decided what her major will be, but she is leaning toward business, possibly accounting. She has been accepted by two universities, both of which have excellent accounting programs. If she majors in accounting, she hopes to find a way to combine her interest in business and accounting with her love for sports.

Critical Thinking

1. What can Rob gain from his study of accounting that will help him with his future plans?
2. Is Kendra's goal of combining her interest in accounting and her interest in sports realistic? How can she accomplish her goal?

THE ACCOUNTING FRAMEWORK

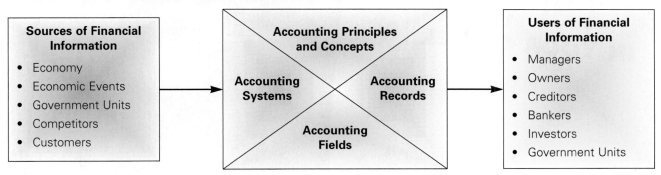

Figure I-1

As Kendra and Rob begin their second year of accounting, they review the basic purpose of accounting and accounting systems. Planning, recording, analyzing, and interpreting financial information is called **accounting**. The accounting framework in Figure I-1 presents the many sources and users of accounting information.

A successful business must understand the environment in which it operates. Information concerning the economy, economic events, government units, competitors, and customers is critical to effective business planning. Accounting records provide financial information about economic events, such as sales, collections on accounts receivable, or cash payments for operating and administrative expenses.

Accountants assist businesses in collecting, organizing, and interpreting financial information. A planned process for providing financial information that will be useful to management is called an **accounting system**. The accounting system varies due to the type and form of business organization.

Organized summaries of a business' financial activities are called **accounting records**. Many individuals and organizations need information about the financial activities of a business. An accounting system, therefore, produces a variety of accounting records. Users of accounting records include managers, owners, creditors, bankers, investors, and government units.

On the first day of class, the instructor asks students to form teams of three or four students. Each team is assigned to research the following topics and prepare a written report of their findings.

- Accounting as a profession.

- Professional certification needed for various accounting professionals.

- Employment opportunities.

- Skills learned in accounting that are transferable to other occupations.

- Accounting standards.

- Ethical standards maintained by the accounting profession.

Rob and Kendra have worked together before. They decide to work with two other students to prepare their report. Kendra is excited about working on the report, as she is interested in becoming an accountant. Rob does not desire a career in accounting, but hopes preparing the report teaches him how a course in accounting can help him succeed in any occupation. Working closely with other students on their team, they prepare the following report.

Accounting Fields

- Financial
- Managerial
- Cost
- Tax
- Accounting Systems
- Auditing
- Personal Financial Planning

Figure I-2

Accounting is a growing profession. Several accounting fields have emerged as a result of the varied uses of accounting information, as shown in Figure I-2. The demand for accountants remains strong because of the number, size, and complexity of businesses, governmental units, and other not-for-profit organizations. Continual change in government regulations and federal tax reporting requirements keeps the demand for accountants high.

Financial Accounting

The recording of a business' financial activities and the periodic preparation of financial reports is called **financial accounting**. Financial accounting reports are used primarily by persons outside the organization. External users of accounting information include creditors, investors, bankers, auditors, and personal financial planners.

Managerial Accounting

The analysis, measurement, and interpretation of financial accounting information is called **managerial accounting**. Managerial accounting provides information for internal decision making related to daily operations and the planning of future operations.

Cost Accounting

The determination and control of costs of a business enterprise is called **cost accounting**. Cost accounting provides information for *internal* decision making concerning the costs of operating merchandising and manufacturing businesses. Owners and managers use cost information for controlling current operations and planning for the future.

Tax Accounting

The preparation of tax returns as well as tax planning is called **tax accounting**. Tax accoun-

tants use financial statement information to prepare tax returns. Tax accountants must keep up-to-date on changes in tax regulations as well as court decisions on tax cases. This knowledge enables tax accountants to minimize a business' tax liability and ensure that the business or organization complies with tax laws.

Accounting Systems

Accounting systems create accounting reports containing financial, managerial, cost, and tax information. The systems accountant designs new accounting systems, adapts current systems, and assists in planning and implementing computerized accounting systems. Systems accountants explore ways to make accounting systems more efficient.

Auditing

The independent reviewing and issuing of an opinion on the reliability of accounting records is called **auditing**. A person who examines the records that support the financial records of a business to ensure that generally accepted accounting principles are being followed is called an **auditor**. The auditor's opinion is necessary for our economic system to operate efficiently. The auditor's opinion gives external users confidence in the financial statement information. With this confidence, individuals and businesses are more likely to enter into economic transactions.

Personal Financial Planning

Assisting individuals in managing their personal investments is called **personal financial planning**. Many people invest a portion of their income to pay for future expenditures, such as their retirement and their children's education. The increasing variety and complexity of investment opportunities cause many individuals to seek professional assistance. Accountants can assist their clients in interpreting financial information and determining which investments will maximize their investment income and meet their financial goals.

Professional Certification	Organization Granting Certification
• Certified Public Accountant (CPA) ⟶	American Institute of Certified Public Accountants (AICPA)
• Certified Management Accountant (CMA) ⟶	Institute of Management Accountants (IMA)
• Certified Internal Auditor (CIA) ⟶	Institute of Internal Auditors (IIA)
• Enrolled Agent (EA) ⟶	Internal Revenue Service (IRS)
• Certified Payroll Professional (CPP) ⟶	American Payroll Association (APA)
• Certified Credit Executive (CCE) ⟶	National Association of Credit Management (NACM)

Figure I-3

Certified Public Accountants

Figure I-3 lists some of the many professional accounting certifications available. The most widely recognized is the certified public accountant (CPA). Each state in the United States sets its own education and experience requirements for CPAs. The American Institute of Certified Public Accountants (AICPA) prepares and grades the examination for all states. Candidates are granted the CPA designation upon successfully completing the examination and meeting the requirements specified by the state in which they wish to practice. The CPA certificate signifies professional status in public accounting and is required before an accountant can issue an audit opinion.

Management Accountants

Private accountants who specialize in managerial and cost accounting are often referred to as management accountants. An accountant who has the required education and experience and passes a required examination is designated as a certified management accountant (CMA). The Institute of Management Accountants (IMA) grants the CMA certificate.

Certified Internal Auditor

Corporations whose shares of stock are publicly traded are required to hire public accountants to perform a yearly audit and issue an audit opinion. However, most large corporations also employ private accountants to assist the public accountants and to audit the operational efficiency of the business. These accountants are referred to as internal auditors. An accountant who has the required education and experience and passes a required examination is designated as a certified internal auditor (CIA). The Institute of Internal Auditors (IIA) grants the certificate.

Enrolled Agent

Some individuals specialize in the preparation of tax returns for others. Individuals completing the necessary training and passing an examination are designated as enrolled agents (EA) by the Internal Revenue Service (IRS).

Certified Payroll Professional

A certified payroll professional (CPP) designation indicates that an individual has demonstrated professional competence in payroll practices and understands applicable regulations. The American Payroll Association (APA) sponsors the required examination.

Certified Credit Executive

The National Association of Credit Management (NACM) offers the certified credit executive (CCE) designation. NACM is dedicated to the advancement of proper credit management and the promotion of good laws for the fair handling of credit transactions. Candidates must pass an examination and meet specific requirements for education and experience.

All of these certifications require continuing professional education. The specific requirements vary, but most accountants continue their accounting education throughout their careers.

Accounting firms	Environmental firms	Merchandising businesses
Advertising agencies	Federal government agencies	Military
Agricultural entities	Film companies	Publishers
Automotive manufacturers	Financial institutions	Recording studios
Automotive retailers	Foundations	Recreational facilities
Biotechnology firms	Franchised businesses	Restaurants
Bookstores	Grocers	Retail stores
Charitable organizations	Hospitals	Software developers
Colleges/Universities	Hotels/Motels	Sports arenas
Computer firms	Import/Export businesses	Sports franchises
Construction companies	Information systems businesses	State government agencies
Consulting companies	Law firms	Theme parks
Convention centers	Local government agencies	Travel agencies
Dental practices	Manufacturers	Veterinary practices
Entertainment enterprises	Medical practices	

Figure I-4

Accounting employment is usually in private accounting, public accounting, or governmental/not-for-profit accounting. In addition, individuals with strong accounting backgrounds have a wide range of employment opportunities that are not directly related to accounting. All organizations and businesses depend on reliable financial information. Employees who can establish and work within accounting guidelines and procedures are needed by businesses, large and small. Accounting expertise can be applied to most areas of interest. Employment opportunities exist in most types of businesses and organizations, such as the ones listed in Figure I-4.

Private Accounting

Persons employed in private accounting work for only one business. In small organizations, they may do all of the summarizing, analyzing, and interpreting of financial information for management. In large organizations, accountants typically specialize in one field of accounting, such as financial, managerial, cost, or tax.

Public Accounting

Persons employed in public accounting may work independently or as a member of a public accounting firm. Public accountants sell services

to individuals, businesses, governmental units, and not-for-profit organizations. Auditing and tax accounting have historically been the primary services provided by public accountants. As the business environment has become more complex, organizations have increasingly hired public accountants to solve a variety of business problems. Management advice provided to an organization by a public accountant is called **management advisory services**. Management advisory services represent the fastest-growing service provided by public accountants.

Governmental/Not-for-Profit Accounting

Some persons employed in governmental/not-for-profit accounting work for a governmental agency (federal, state, county, or city). The Internal Revenue Service is one governmental agency that employs large numbers of accountants. Accountants may also work for other not-for-profit organizations such as hospitals, churches, or foundations. The persons employed by these organizations perform duties similar to those performed in private accounting.

Other Accounting-Related Occupations

Not every company hires a full-time CPA to complete basic accounting functions. In fact, many businesses need individuals who can perform tasks requiring general accounting skills. For example, a small business might need an employee who can maintain accounts receivable and accounts payable. The same employee may communicate with clients, prepare billings, and answer the telephone. Medical offices often have a staff member who can process patient billings and payments. This staff member may also schedule appointments and handle routine office tasks.

In large businesses, employees frequently specialize in a single field such as accounts payable, accounts receivable, payroll, inventory, or purchasing. Although these jobs demand the use of many accounting skills, professional certification is not necessarily required. Experience, trustworthiness, a positive attitude, and a willingness to learn are often as important as certification.

Nonaccounting Occupations

In many companies, teams of employees make critical business decisions. The team may include a specialist in finance or accounting, but often each team member is expected to understand the team's financial results. In other companies, projects are handled by individuals representing different departments such as finance, engineering, research and development, manufacturing, marketing, and human resources. Many components of the projects discussed include accounting terminology and concepts. Owners of small businesses should have some knowledge of accounting, payroll processing, and tax requirements.

Personal Applications

In addition to being helpful on the job, an accounting background has many uses in one's personal life. An understanding of basic accounting concepts helps people use credit wisely, evaluate investment opportunities, plan for retirement, negotiate purchases of automobiles and homes, complete credit applications, and budget their resources. This knowledge assists individuals in making sound financial decisions throughout their lives.

TRANSFERABLE SKILLS

Analyzing	Group dynamics	Proving
Attending to details	Interpersonal relationships	Reading
Calculating	Interpreting	Scheduling
Clarifying	Listening	Speaking
Communicating	Mathematical reasoning	Spelling
Critical thinking	Organizing	Summarizing
Documenting	Planning	Technical expertise
Evaluating	Prioritizing	Time management
Explaining	Problem solving	Verifying
Following directions	Proofing	Writing

Figure I-5

In the process of developing specific accounting skills, a significant number of related skills may also be acquired. Many of these related skills are listed in Figure I-5. These related skills are used in a variety of employment areas and are readily transferable to other occupations. Individuals who do not enter the accounting profession use many of the skills they acquired in accounting courses in whatever occupation they choose.

Financial Accounting Standards Board (FASB)

Governmental Accounting Standards Board (GASB)

American Institute of Certified Public Accountants (AICPA)

Institute of Management Accountants (IMA)

Institute of Internal Auditors (IIA)

American Accounting Association (AAA)

Securities and Exchange Commission (SEC)

Internal Revenue Service (IRS)

Figure I-6

The accounting profession is guided by principles and concepts to provide standardization and consistency in the work performed. Figure I-6 lists several organizations that provide assistance and influence in the development of these principles and concepts.

The Financial Accounting Standards Board (FASB)

The FASB develops standards for financial accounting and reporting. When problems occur, the FASB studies the issues and forms recommended solutions. The solutions are reviewed by the various accounting organizations and individual accountants. Once accepted by the accounting profession, the FASB publishes statements of financial accounting standards and financial accounting concepts. These statements are recognized by accounting professionals as generally accepted accounting principles (GAAP) that accountants must follow in their work.

The Governmental Accounting Standards Board (GASB)

The GASB develops the standards used by state and municipal governments. Some of the GASB standards also apply to not-for-profit organizations. The GASB operates in a manner similar to the FASB in studying issues, developing recommended solutions, seeking industry review, and issuing governmental accounting standards.

The American Institute of Certified Public Accountants (AICPA)

The AICPA is the organization of practicing certified public accountants (CPAs). The AICPA

is the oldest and most influential of all organizations that guide the development of accounting principles and concepts. Administering and grading the uniform CPA examination is one of the primary roles of the AICPA.

The Institute of Management Accountants (IMA)

The IMA develops recommendations for using accounting information within an enterprise to direct business operations.

The Institute of Internal Auditors (IIA)

The IIA assists internal auditors in developing techniques useful in improving the accounting system of their business.

The American Accounting Association (AAA)

The AAA is composed primarily of accounting instructors. The AAA promotes the improvement of accounting education and publishes numerous journals that enable accounting instructors to share the results of their research.

The Securities and Exchange Commission (SEC)

The SEC is a government agency that regulates the issuance of stock by corporations and the trading of stock by the public. This agency issues regulations that must be followed in the preparation of financial statements and other reports filed with the Commission.

The Internal Revenue Service (IRS)

The IRS is a government agency that issues regulations defining income for federal income taxation. Accounting for income tax influences the development of accounting practices and concepts.

**American Institute of
Certified Public Accountants (AICPA)
Rules**

Rule 101—Independence

A member in public practice shall be independent in the performance of professional services.

Rule 102—Integrity and Objectivity

In the performance of any professional service, a member shall maintain objectivity and integrity, shall be free of conflicts of interest, and shall not knowingly misrepresent facts or subordinate his or her judgment to others.

Rule 201—General Standards

A. *Professional Competence.* Undertake only those professional services that the member or the member's firm can reasonably expect to be completed with professional competence.
B. *Due Professional Care.* Exercise due professional care in the performance of professional service.
C. *Planning and Supervision.* Adequately plan and supervise the performance of professional services.
D. *Sufficient Relevant Data.* Obtain sufficient relevant data to afford a reasonable basis for conclusions or recommendations in relation to any professional services performed.

Rule 202—Compliance with Standards

A member who performs auditing, management advisory, tax, or other professional services shall comply with standards issued by organizations approved by the Institute.

Rule 203—Accounting Principles

A member shall not express an opinion on financial statements that contain a departure from accounting principles issued by organizations approved by the Institute.

Rule 301—Confidential Client Information

A member in public practice shall not disclose any confidential client information without the specific consent of the client.

Rule 302—Contingent Fees

A member in public practice shall not perform an audit or prepare a tax return for a contingent fee. A contingent fee is an arrangement in which the fee to be charged is dependent upon a specific result being attained.

Rule 501—Acts Discreditable

A member shall not commit an act discreditable to the profession.

Rule 502—Advertising and Other Forms of Solicitation

A member in public practice shall not seek to obtain clients by advertising or other forms of solicitation in a manner that is false, misleading, or deceptive. Solicitation by the use of coercion, over-reaching, or harassing conduct is prohibited.

Rule 503—Commissions and Referral Fees

A. *Prohibited Commissions.* A member in public practice shall not for a commission recommend any product or service to an audit client.
B. *Disclosure of Permitted Commissions.* A member in public practice who is not prohibited by this rule from receiving a commission shall disclose that fact to his or her client.
C. *Referral Fees.* Any member who accepts a referral fee for recommending the services of another CPA to any person or entity shall disclose the referral fee to the client.

Rule 505—Form of Practice and Name

A member may practice public accounting only in the form of a proprietorship, a partnership, or a professional corporation. A member shall not practice public accounting under a firm name that is misleading. A firm may not designate itself as "Member of the American Institute of Certified Public Accountants" unless all of its partners are members of the Institute.

Adapted from the Code of Professional Conduct as amended May 20, 1991 (used and adapted with permission)

Figure I-7

All persons are faced daily with making decisions between right and wrong. The principles of right and wrong that guide an individual in making decisions are called **ethics**. A person's ethics are developed from relationships with family, friends, teachers, and other individuals who influence the person's life. The AICPA's Code of Professional Conduct, Figure I-7, provides guiding principles for ethical decision making by accountants.

CAUSES OF UNETHICAL BEHAVIOR

Unethical behavior occurs when an individual disregards his or her principles of right and wrong by choosing the wrong action. Six causes of unethical behavior in business are:

1. *Excessive emphasis on profits.* Managers' salaries may be based on their ability to increase profits. Managers may make decisions that will earn them a higher salary.

2. *Misplaced business loyalty.* Some individuals develop a misplaced dedication to their employer. They make decisions that benefit the business without considering others.

3. *Personal advancement.* Individuals sometimes develop a "whatever-it-takes" attitude toward their personal careers. They make decisions that advance their personal careers, regardless of the impact on others.

4. *Expectation of not getting caught.* Individuals can make unethical decisions because they know the chance of getting caught is small.

5. *Unethical business environment.* Managers who make ethical decisions are more likely to have employees who also make ethical decisions.

6. *Unwillingness to take a stand.* Individuals may not confront unethical behavior because they fear losing their jobs, missing a deserved promotion, or alienating other employees.

MAKING ETHICAL DECISIONS

Analyzing a situation is the first step in deciding whether an action is ethical. The following three-step checklist for making ethical decisions serves as a guide in collecting relevant information needed to make a wise decision.

1. *Is the action illegal?* An action should be immediately dismissed if it violates international, federal, state, or local laws.

2. *Does the action violate company or professional standards?* An action may be legal yet violate the standards of the business or profession. Violating these standards may affect the employee's job security and professional certification. The action may also have a negative effect on the business.

    Many professional accounting organizations have adopted codes of professional conduct to assist their members in making ethical decisions. These codes encourage the organizations' members to act and uphold the professional image of the accounting profession. The AICPA Code of Professional Conduct is summarized in Figure I-7.

3. *Who is affected, and how, by the action?* If an action is legal and complies with business and professional standards, the next step is to determine how the action will affect a variety of people. The people to be considered include employees and owners, customers, the local community, and society.

    When faced with an ethical dilemma, use the three-step checklist and the AICPA Code of Professional Conduct to help you determine whether any action demonstrates ethical or unethical behavior.

WRAP-UP

Kendra, Rob, and their teammates are pleased with their work and are surprised at what they have learned. They have begun to see that the accounting concepts and procedures they will examine this year will be useful to them no matter what education and career decisions they make. They submit their combined work to their instructor and are eager to continue their study of accounting.

The team is praised for its hard work and the quality of its report. The instructor challenges the four to use the ethics material to complete the Professional Business Ethics feature on the following pages.

Corey Bartlett, a certified public accountant, grew up in Grove City. After college, he returned to work in his mother's accounting firm. Last year he was appointed to the Grove City zoning board. The board is reviewing a request to rezone a large section of property on the outskirts of town. The zone change would permit The MarketPlace, a national discount retailer, to build a store. The MarketPlace would feature clothing and shoes, housewares and linens, appliances and electronics, lumber and hardware, health and beauty products, and lawn and garden supplies. The plans also include a pharmacy and a vision care center.

During the zoning board meeting, Corey listened as developers presented their vision of how the MarketPlace would improve the community and offer citizens quality merchandise at significantly lower prices than they are now paying. The land owners shared their concern about their ability to sell the property unless it is rezoned. They also reminded the board members that this is the only large piece of undeveloped land in Grove City. Local retail store owners expressed fears that a giant retailer would force them out of business. Other business owners and civic leaders pointed out that the closing of retail stores in the central business district would have a negative impact on other businesses and the community at large.

Corey knows most of the people who spoke during the meeting; many are clients. Understanding the possible negative impact the new store could have on many of the firm's small retail clients, Corey decided to vote against the rezoning. In a three to two vote, the zoning board denied the rezoning request.

Required:

Use the three-step checklist to analyze whether Corey's vote against the zoning change demonstrated ethical behavior. This first activity has been completed for you as follows.

1. Is the action illegal?

   No. Based on the information presented, the action is not illegal. In some cases government bodies have rules which address conflicts of interest and when a board member must abstain from voting.

2. Does the action violate company or professional standards?

   No. Corey faced a conflict between the interests of the community as a member of the zoning board and the interests of the business owners who are his clients. However, the CPA is not involved in providing professional services to a client in his role as a member of the zoning board.

3. Who is affected, and how, by the action?

   The table on the following page shows a useful way to organize your answer to 3. For each of the Professional Business Ethics features in this text, prepare a chart listing each person or group affected. Use the chart to list the positive and negative affects of the action.

COMMUNITY INVOLVEMENT, CONTINUED

Person(s) Affected	Negative Effect	Positive Effect
Corey Bartlett	Might cause Corey to lose current clients who disagree with his vote. Might cause potential clients to choose a different accountant.	Protects the income Corey earns from providing professional services to current clients.
CPA's clients	None	Protects Corey's clients from competition.
Grove City residents	Prevents residents from having access to lower cost merchandise. Limits tax revenues and employment opportunities.	Protects interests of current businesses and their employees.
The MarketPlace	Prohibits The MarketPlace from entering market and increasing sales/profits.	None.
Landowner	Prevents landowners from earning a profit from the sale of land.	None.

PROFESSIONAL BUSINESS ETHICS

SMALL BUSINESS SPOTLIGHT

The U.S. Commerce Department has recently increased the number of trade missions specifically designed for small businesses. These missions provide opportunities for representatives of small businesses to travel to foreign countries with Commerce officials. These trips are designed to put potential exporters in touch with local trade officials, prospective business partners, and potential customers.

Departmentalized Accounting

PART 1

MASTERSPORT CHART OF ACCOUNTS

Balance Sheet Accounts

(1000) Assets
1100	CURRENT ASSETS
1105	Cash
1110	Petty Cash
1115	Accounts Receivable
1120	Allowance for Uncollectible Accounts
1125-1	Merchandise Inventory—Golf
1125-2	Merchandise Inventory—Tennis
1130	Supplies—Office
1135	Supplies—Store
1140	Prepaid Insurance
1200	PLANT ASSETS
1205	Office Equipment
1210	Accumulated Depreciation—Office Equipment
1215	Store Equipment
1220	Accumulated Depreciation—Store Equipment

(2000) Liabilities
2105	Accounts Payable
2110	Employee Income Tax Payable—Federal
2115	Employee Income Tax Payable—State
2120	Federal Income Tax Payable
2125	Social Security Tax Payable
2128	Medicare Tax Payable
2130	Sales Tax Payable
2135	Unemployment Tax Payable—Federal
2140	Unemployment Tax Payable—State
2145	Health Insurance Premiums Payable
2150	Life Insurance Premiums Payable
2155	Dividends Payable

(3000) Stockholders' Equity
3105	Capital Stock
3110	Retained Earnings
3115	Dividends
3120-1	Income Summary—Golf
3120-2	Income Summary—Tennis
3125	Income Summary—General

Income Statement Accounts

(4000) Operating Revenue
4105-1	Sales—Golf
4105-2	Sales—Tennis
4110-1	Sales Discount—Golf
4110-2	Sales Discount—Tennis
4115-1	Sales Returns and Allowances—Golf
4115-2	Sales Returns and Allowances—Tennis

(5000) Cost of Merchandise
5105-1	Purchases—Golf
5105-2	Purchases—Tennis
5110-1	Purchases Discount—Golf
5110-2	Purchases Discount—Tennis
5115-1	Purchases Returns and Allowances—Golf
5115-2	Purchases Returns and Allowances—Tennis

(6000) Operating Expense
6100	SELLING EXPENSES
6105	Advertising Expense
6110	Credit Card Fee Expense
6115	Depreciation Expense—Store Equipment
6120-1	Salary Expense—Golf
6120-2	Salary Expense—Tennis
6125	Supplies Expense—Store
6200	ADMINISTRATIVE EXPENSES
6205	Depreciation Expense—Office Equipment
6210	Insurance Expense
6215	Miscellaneous Expense
6220	Payroll Taxes Expense
6225	Rent Expense
6230	Salary Expense—Administrative
6235	Supplies Expense—Office
6240	Uncollectible Accounts Expense

(7000) Income Tax
7105	Federal Income Tax Expense

The chart of accounts for MasterSport is illustrated above for ready reference as you study Part 1 of this textbook.

1

Recording Departmental Purchases and Cash Payments

AFTER STUDYING CHAPTER 1, YOU WILL BE ABLE TO:

1. Define accounting terms related to departmental purchases and cash payments.

2. Identify accounting concepts and practices related to departmental purchases and cash payments.

3. Perform file maintenance.

4. Journalize and post departmental purchases and purchases returns.

5. Journalize and post cash payments.

6. Reconcile a bank statement.

Financial information for a business can be recorded, summarized, and reported in a variety of ways. Accountants design accounting systems to meet the specific needs of the business. The way in which information is kept and reported in the accounting system is determined by the size, type, and complexity of the business. When designing financial records, the business should also consider the types of decisions that will be made based on the financial statements.

If managers want to use financial statements to assist in making decisions for individual departments, information for each department must be recorded separately. The types of information to be gathered by department include purchases, sales, cash payments and cash receipts. Payroll data may also be identified by department. Gathering information by department requires a somewhat different set of accounting procedures. Regardless of the accounting procedures used, the same accounting concepts and practices are followed.

If a business decides to record information by department, it must establish procedures to ensure that transactions are assigned to the correct department. Some businesses employ an accounting clerk for each department. The clerk's primary responsibility is to record day-to-day transactions for the department.

ACCOUNTING
IN YOUR CAREER

A NEW DEPARTMENT

Alonzo Guerra, CPA, has been consulted by The Book Place, a book retailer, concerning a planned expansion—the company wants to begin merchandising CDs and videos in addition to books. The company's senior accountant, Bill Dillon, has done some preliminary planning, but wants an expert to help plan the requirements of the accounting system for this expansion.

Bill has already determined that the chart of accounts and purchases and cash payments journals will need to be redesigned. In meeting with Alonzo, Bill explains that purchases are made from both large distributors and small independent publishers. Returns are frequent because the industry permits the return of merchandise that is not selling well after a certain period of time. Most vendors also offer cash discounts to encourage timely payment on account.

Bill further states that the store space will be doubled to make room for these new merchandise lines. However, he wants to keep the accounting system as simple as possible and suggests that the CDs and videos be combined into one department for accounting purposes. Office employees will process purchase orders for all three departments, but new sales associates will be hired to assist customers in the new areas. New store display fixtures will be needed to properly shelve the new merchandise. Alonzo promises to deliver a report on his recommendations by the end of the week.

Critical Thinking

1. Is Bill's goal to combine the two new lines into one department a good accounting practice? Why or why not?
2. From the information given, which accounts in the chart of accounts that are related to purchases and cash payments should be split into departmental accounts?
3. Should Alonzo recommend using a purchases returns and allowances journal or should returns be recorded in a general journal?

ACCOUNTING EQUATION

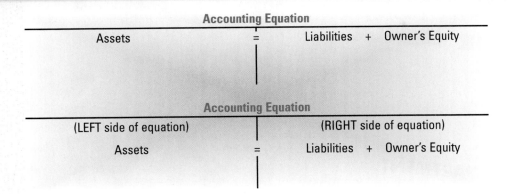

Accounting Equation

| Assets | = | Liabilities | + | Owner's Equity |

Accounting Equation

| (LEFT side of equation) | | (RIGHT side of equation) |
| Assets | = | Liabilities + Owner's Equity |

Figure 1-1

Anything of value that is owned is called an **asset**. An amount owed by a business is called a **liability**. Financial rights to the assets of a business are called **equities**. The amount remaining after the value of all liabilities is subtracted from the value of all assets is called **owner's equity**. In a corporation the value of the owner's equity is referred to as stockholders' equity.

An equation showing the relationship among assets, liabilities, and owner's equity is called an **accounting equation**. The accounting equation may be stated as assets = equities. More commonly the equation is stated as assets = liabilities + owner's equity.

The equation is often viewed as forming a "T." In Figure 1-1, assets are listed on the left side of the T account and equities (liabilities and owner's equity) on the right side of the T account. Total assets must always equal total liabilities plus owner's equity.

ACCOUNTING RECORDS

Accounting records show changes and the current account balance of each asset, liability, and owner's equity (or stockholders' equity) account. In the United States, the amounts are stated in dollars and cents. (CONCEPT: Unit of Measurement)

The unit of measurement concept states that business transactions are reported in numbers that have common values—that is, using a common unit of measurement. If part of the information in the accounting records is financial and part is nonfinancial, the financial statements will not be clear. For example, if MasterSport states its sales in number of units sold (nonfinancial) and its expenses in dollars (financial), net profit cannot be calculated.

The preceding concept reference indicates the application of a specific accounting concept. For a complete statement and explanation of the concepts, refer to Appendix A.

Information about business transactions is obtained from original business papers called **source documents**. Each journal entry must be supported by a source document proving that a transaction occurred.

F.Y.I.

The government's first regulation of accounting information occurred in 1917 with the Federal Reserve Board's publication of "Uniform Accounts."

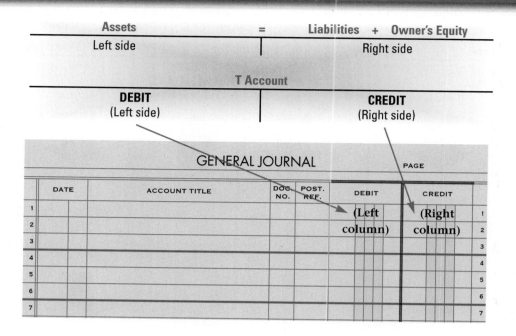

Figure 1-2

The recording of debit and credit parts of a transaction is called **double-entry accounting**. The accounting equation is the basis for all double-entry accounting. Two accounting principles are common to double-entry accounting. (1) The total value of things owned by a business (assets) equals the total value of claims of outsiders (liabilities) and claims of owners (owner's equity). (2) Debits equal credits for each business transaction recorded.

A form for recording transactions in chronological order is called a **journal**. A general journal may be used to record all business transactions. A general journal includes amount columns for recording the dollars and cents of a transaction. *(CONCEPT: Unit of Measurement)* The general journal has two amount columns. The left amount column is labeled Debit. The right amount column is labeled Credit. An entry recorded in the debit column is known as a debit. Likewise, an entry recorded in the credit column is known as a credit. The "T" previously described in the accounting equation is also pre-sent in a general journal's debit and credit amount columns as shown in Figure 1-2.

A journal used to record only one kind of transaction is called a **special journal**. A business with many daily transactions may use special journals. Special journals include amount columns used to record debits or credits to specific accounts. For example, a cash payments journal includes a Cash Credit amount column. MasterSport uses four special journals along with a general journal to record its transactions.

1. Purchases journal—for all purchases of merchandise on account

2. Cash payments journal—for all cash payments

3. Sales journal—for all sales of merchandise on account

4. Cash receipts journal—for all cash receipts

MasterSport uses a general journal to record all other transactions.

REMEMBER

Total assets must always equal total liabilities plus total owner's equity.

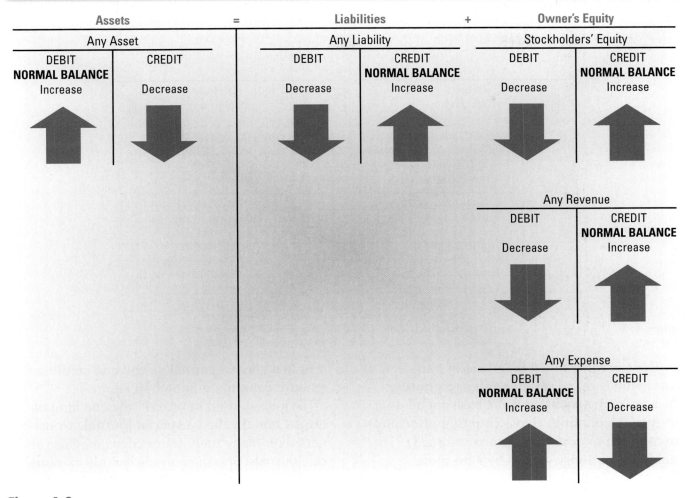

Figure 1-3

Transactions are journalized in chronological order. Periodically, information is sorted to summarize like kinds of information. A record summarizing all the information pertaining to a single item in the accounting equation is called an **account**.

The amount in an account is known as an account balance. Each business transaction causes a change in two or more account balances. Increases in an account balance are recorded in the same column as its normal balance. Decreases in an account balance are recorded in the column opposite its normal balance. The normal balances of different classifications of accounts are shown in Figure 1-3.

Asset account balances are increased by debits and decreased by credits. Liability and capital account balances as well as revenue account balances are increased by credits and decreased by debits. Expense account balances are increased by debits and decreased by credits.

REMEMBER

Increases in revenue accounts increase owner's equity. Therefore, the normal credit balance of revenue accounts is the same as the normal balance of owner's equity. Increases in expense accounts decrease owner's equity. Therefore the normal debit balance of expense accounts is opposite the normal balance of owner's equity.

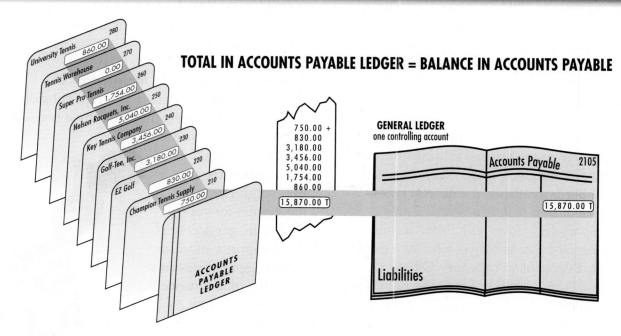

TOTAL IN ACCOUNTS PAYABLE LEDGER = BALANCE IN ACCOUNTS PAYABLE

Figure 1-4

A group of accounts is called a **ledger**. A ledger that contains all accounts needed to prepare financial statements is called a **general ledger**. A ledger that is summarized in a single general ledger account is called a **subsidiary ledger**. An account in a general ledger that summarizes all accounts in a subsidiary ledger is called a **controlling account**. Two subsidiary ledgers and two general ledger controlling accounts are commonly used.

Subsidiary Ledgers
    Accounts Receivable Ledger
    Accounts Payable Ledger

Controlling Accounts
    Accounts Receivable
    Accounts Payable

Accounts for customers who buy merchandise on account are kept in an accounts receivable ledger. The corresponding controlling account is Accounts Receivable. Separate accounts are kept in an accounts payable ledger for vendors to whom money is owed. The corresponding controlling account is Accounts Payable. The total of the subsidiary ledger accounts balances should equal the balance of the controlling account as shown in Figure 1-4.

GENERAL AND SUBSIDIARY LEDGER FILE MAINTENANCE

MasterSport uses a general ledger account numbering system that meets three needs. (1) A separate numeric listing is provided for each ledger division. (2) A predesigned arrangement of numbers is provided within each ledger division. (3) Enough account number digits are provided to allow the addition of new accounts. The procedure for arranging accounts in a general ledger, assigning account numbers, and keeping records current is called **file maintenance**.

The general ledger chart of accounts has seven divisions. The first digit of each four-digit account number shows the general ledger division in which the account is located. The accounts in some divisions, such as Assets, are divided into categories. The second digit of the account number shows the category in which the account is located. The last two digits show the location of a specific account with respect to other accounts in that division and category.

MasterSport uses a four-digit numbering system for general ledger accounts with each account number initially assigned sequentially by 5s. Assigning account numbers by 5s allows new accounts to be added easily between existing accounts.

Businesses add accounts as needed. A new account is assigned the unused middle number between two existing accounts. When no exact middle number is available, the nearest whole number is used.

MasterSport decided to add a new account Equipment Repair Expense between the two existing accounts Depreciation Expense—Office Equipment, 6205, and Insurance Expense, 6210. The unused middle number between 6205 and 6210 is 6207.5. The numbering system does not use decimals. Therefore, account number 6208, the nearest whole number, is used.

The rule for rounding states that decimals less than 5 are rounded down, and decimals 5 or greater are rounded up. Using this rule:

$$6207.5 \xrightarrow{\text{rounds to}} 6208$$

The new account is placed in the general ledger as follows.

6205   Depreciation Expense—Office Equipment (existing account)

6208   EQUIPMENT REPAIR EXPENSE (NEW ACCOUNT)

6210   Insurance Expense (existing account)

New accounts that are added after the last account in a division are assigned the next number in sequence. Dividends Payable, 2155, is the last existing account in the liabilities division. If MasterSport decides to add a new liability account after Dividends Payable, the number assigned would be 2160.

2155   Dividends Payable (existing account)
2160   NEW ACCOUNT

Subsidiary Ledger File Maintenance

The numbering system used for subsidiary ledger accounts meets the same three needs as the system for general ledger accounts. MasterSport uses a three-digit numbering system for subsidiary ledger accounts. MasterSport's subsidiary ledgers generally require more file maintenance than the general ledger. Therefore, subsidiary ledger account numbers are assigned by 10s to provide more numbers for adding new accounts between existing accounts. MasterSport uses the same file maintenance procedures for the subsidiary ledgers as for the general ledger.

Accounts in the accounts receivable subsidiary ledger use three-digit account numbers that begin with a 1. Accounts in the accounts payable subsidiary ledger use three-digit numbers that begin with a 2. This system corresponds to the system used for the general ledger, since asset accounts begin with a 1, and liability accounts begin with a 2.

Payment terms may vary among businesses. A good accounting system will include an easy way to identify the terms given by a specific vendor.

TERMS REVIEW

asset
liability
equities
owner's equity
accounting equation
source document
journal
special journal

double-entry accounting
account
ledger
general ledger
subsidiary ledger
controlling account
file maintenance

AUDIT YOUR UNDERSTANDING

1. How is the accounting equation most commonly stated?
2. What is the normal balance of an asset account? A revenue account?
3. What are the three needs met by MasterSport's account numbering system?

WORK TOGETHER

Performing file maintenance activities; adding general ledger accounts

A partial general ledger chart of accounts for M. Schmidt Distributors is shown below and provided in the *Working Papers*. Your instructor will guide you through the following examples.

	Liabilities	Accounts Added
2120	Federal Income Tax Payable	Medicare Tax Payable
2125	Social Security Tax Payable	
2130	Unemployment Tax Payable–State	Unemployment Tax Payable–Federal

4. Add the two new liability accounts to the general ledger chart of accounts using the unused middle number method.

ON YOUR OWN

Performing file maintenance activities; adding general ledger accounts

A partial general ledger chart of accounts for M. Schmidt Distributors is shown below and provided in the *Working Papers*. Work this problem independently.

	Administrative Expenses	Accounts Added
6205	Depreciation Expense—Office Equipment	Payroll Taxes Expense
6210	Rent Expense	Salary Expense—Administrative
6215	Supplies Expense—Office	Utilities Expense

5. Add the three new administrative expense accounts to the general ledger chart of accounts using the unused middle number method.

DEPARTMENTAL ACCOUNTING SYSTEM

Management decisions depend on accounting information about each phase of a business. When a business has two or more departments, accounting information should indicate how well each department is doing. Accounting information can determine the kinds of merchandise that produce the greatest or the least profit.

An accounting system showing accounting information for two or more departments is called a **departmental accounting system**. In a departmental accounting system, gross profit is calculated for each department. The general ledger, therefore, must include a number of separate departmental accounts. Shoe stores, furniture stores, computer stores, department stores, and sporting goods stores are examples of firms that commonly organize on a departmental basis.

A business that purchases and sells goods is called a **merchandising business**. MasterSport sells golf equipment and tennis equipment. The business is a corporation organized on a departmental basis.

Merchandising businesses may have two types of equipment: (1) equipment purchased for sale to customers and (2) equipment used in the operation of the business. MasterSport purchases and sells golf and tennis equipment. MasterSport uses office equipment and store equipment to operate the business.

MasterSport uses a departmental accounting system. Accounting information is recorded and reported for two departments: (1) Golf and (2) Tennis. The separate departmental accounts for MasterSport are in the chart of accounts, page 3. The accounts for the golf department are indicated by a *-1* after the account number. Accounts for the tennis department are indicated by a *-2* after the account number. For example, Merchandise Inventory—Golf is assigned number 1125-1 and Merchandise Inventory—Tennis is

assigned number 1125-2. The basic four digit account number for Merchandise Inventory is 1125. A fifth digit, -1 or -2, identifies departmental accounts.

Purchase invoices are used as the source document for all purchases on account. *(CONCEPT: Objective Evidence)*

The objective evidence concept states that a source document is prepared for each transaction. The source document is the original business paper indicating that the transaction did occur and that the amounts recorded in the accounting records are accurate and true. For example, a check is the original business paper for a cash payment. The original business paper for a purchase on account is the purchase invoice. When accounting information reported on the financial statements needs to be verified, an accountant will first check the accounting record. If the details of an entry need further checking, an accountant will then check the business papers as objective evidence that the transaction did occur.

All departmental purchases of merchandise on account are recorded in a purchases journal. A business with more than one department records a purchase on account in the same way as a business with a single department except for two differences. (1) Each purchase invoice has a notation placed on it showing to which department the purchase applies. (2) Each department has a separate Purchases Debit column in the purchases journal. MasterSport's purchases journal shown in Figure 1-5 has special Purchases Debit columns for each department—Golf and Tennis.

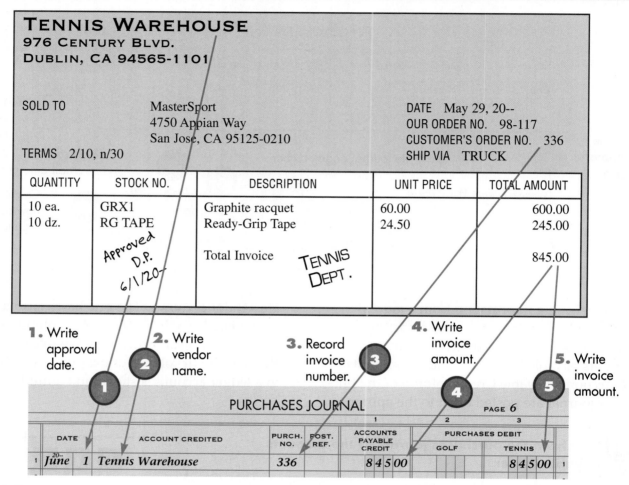

Figure 1-5

June 1. Purchased tennis equipment on account from Tennis Warehouse, $845.00. Purchase Invoice No. 336.

In the general ledger, Purchases—Tennis is increased by an $845.00 debit. Accounts Payable is increased by an $845.00 credit. In the accounts payable ledger, Tennis Warehouse is increased by an $845.00 credit.

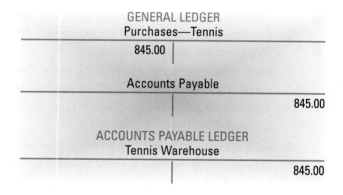

Journalize a purchase on account

1. Write the date, *June 1*, in the Date column of the purchases journal. Since this is the first entry on page 6, include the current year, *20--*.
2. Enter the vendor name, *Tennis Warehouse*, in the Account Credited column.
3. Record the invoice number, *336*, in the Purch. No. column. Since only purchase invoice numbers are recorded in the column, no identifying letter is necessary.
4. Write the credit amount, *845.00*, in the Accounts Payable Credit column.
5. Record the debit amount, *845.00*, in the Purchases Debit Tennis column.

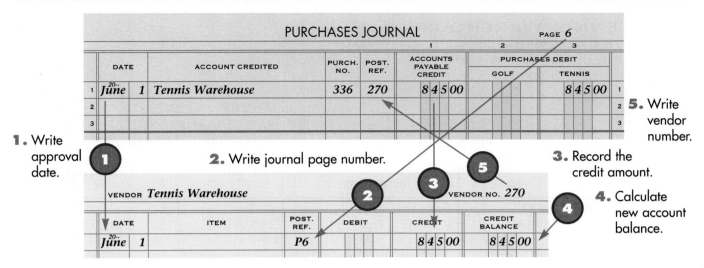

Figure 1-6

Transferring information from a journal entry to a ledger account is called **posting**. MasterSport keeps vendor accounts in an accounts payable ledger. Individual amounts in the Accounts Payable Credit column of the purchases journal are posted often to the appropriate vendor accounts. The purchases journal is abbreviated as P in the Post. Ref. column of the ledger accounts. Posting from the Accounts Payable Credit column of the purchases journal to a ledger account is shown in Figure 1-6.

S T E P S   **Post from the purchases journal to the accounts payable ledger**

1. Write the date of the transaction, *June 1*, in the Date column of the ledger account. Since this is the first ledger entry for Tennis Warehouse, include the current year, *20--*, in the Date column.
2. Enter the purchases journal page number, *P6*, in the Post. Ref. column of the ledger account.
3. Record the credit amount, *845.00*, in the Credit column of the account for Tennis Warehouse. All postings from the purchases journal to the ledger accounts will be to the Credit amount column of the ledger.
4. Add the amount in the Credit amount column to the previous balance in the Credit Balance column. Write the new account balance in the Credit Balance column. Since Tennis Warehouse has no balance, simply enter the amount, *845.00*, in the Credit amount column in the Credit Balance column.
5. Record the vendor number in the Post. Ref. column of the journal. The vendor number shows that the posting for this entry is complete.

REMEMBER

Purchases of merchandise on account are recorded in the purchases journal.

Purchases of merchandise for cash are recorded in the cash payments journal.

POSTING THE TOTALS OF A PURCHASES JOURNAL

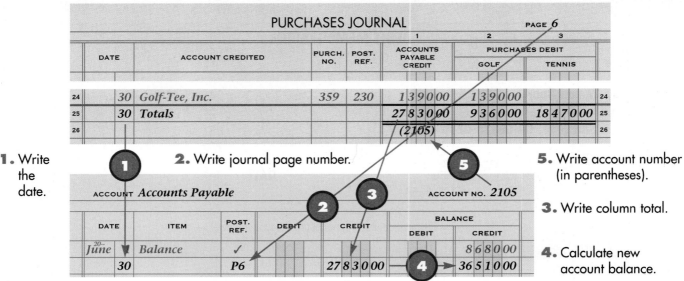

Figure 1-7

The purchases journal is proved and ruled at the end of each month. A purchases journal is proved by adding each column and then proving that the sum of the debit column totals equals the credit column total. Double lines are then ruled across the amount columns to show that the totals have been verified as correct. Each amount column total is posted to the general ledger account named in the column heading as shown in Figure 1-7.

S T E P S

Post the total of the Accounts Payable column to the general ledger

1. Write the date, *30*, in the Date column of the account.
2. Write the purchases journal page number, *P6*, in the Post. Ref. column of the account.
3. Write the column total, *27,830.00*, in the Credit amount column of the account.
4. Calculate and record the new account balance, *36,510.00*, in the Balance Credit column.
5. Write the general ledger account number in parentheses, *(2105)*, below the column total in the purchases journal.

PURCHASES JOURNAL WITH POSTING COMPLETED

PURCHASES JOURNAL   PAGE 6

	DATE	ACCOUNT CREDITED	PURCH. NO.	POST. REF.	ACCOUNTS PAYABLE CREDIT	PURCHASES DEBIT GOLF	PURCHASES DEBIT TENNIS	
1	June 1	Tennis Warehouse	336	270	8 4 5 00		8 4 5 00	1
23	30	EZ Golf	358	220	2 9 2 0 00	2 9 2 0 00		23
24	30	Golf-Tee, Inc.	359	230	1 3 9 0 00	1 3 9 0 00		24
25	30	Totals			27 8 3 0 00	9 3 6 0 00	18 4 7 0 00	25
26					(2105)	(5105-1)	(5105-2)	26
27								27

Figure 1-8

MasterSport's departmental purchases journal, Figure 1-8, is shown after all posting has been completed.

DEBIT MEMORANDUM

MasterSport
4750 Appian Way
San Jose, CA 95125-0210

TO   Key Tennis Company
2470 Wawona Drive
San Jose, CA 95125-5058

NO.   22
DATE   June 3, 20--

We have debited your account today as follows:

DESCRIPTION	UNIT PRICE		TOTAL	
2 aluminum junior tennis racquet Model #ALjr	27	25	54	50

Figure 1-9

Merchandise may be returned to a vendor for several reasons. The merchandise may be unsatisfactory. The merchandise may not be what was ordered. Also, merchandise may be received in damaged condition. When merchandise is returned, the vendor usually gives the buyer credit. Most vendors set some limits on returns and allowances. For example, many vendors specify that returns and requests for allowances must be made within 30 days of purchase.

A form prepared by the customer showing the price deduction taken by the customer for returns and allowances is called a **debit memorandum**. When returning merchandise or requesting an adjustment, MasterSport issues a debit memorandum like the one shown in Figure 1-9. The customer sends the debit memorandum to inform the vendor of the details of the purchases return or allowance. The debit memorandum is used as the source document for a purchases returns and allowances transaction. (CONCEPT: Objective Evidence)

An account that reduces a related account on a financial statement is called a **contra account**. Purchases—Tennis is a cost account. An account showing deductions from a purchases account is a contra cost account. **Purchases Returns and Allowances—Tennis** is one of MasterSport's contra cost accounts. Purchases returns and allowances are kept in a separate account and not deducted directly from the purchases account. This procedure helps the business see what proportion of the merchandise was returned to vendors.

REMEMBER

The normal balance of a contra account is opposite that of the related account.

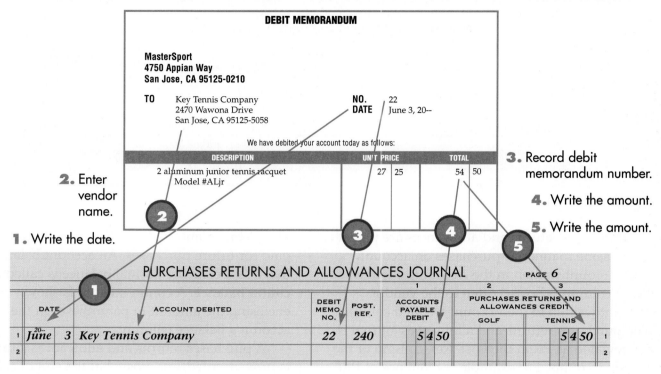

2. Enter vendor name.

1. Write the date.

3. Record debit memorandum number.

4. Write the amount.

5. Write the amount.

Figure 1-10

MasterSport records all purchases returns and allowances in a purchases returns and allowances journal. MasterSport's purchases returns and allowances journal is shown in Figure 1-10.

> *June 3. Returned tennis equipment to Key Tennis Company, $54.50, from Purchase Invoice No. 333. Debit Memorandum No. 22.*

In the general ledger, Accounts Payable is decreased by a $54.50 debit. Purchases Returns and Allowances—Tennis is increased by a $54.50

credit. In the accounts payable ledger, the vendor account, Key Tennis Company, is decreased by a $54.50 debit.

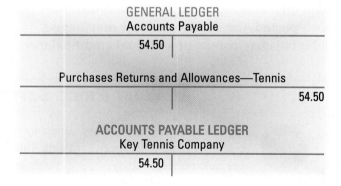

Journalize a purchases return

STEPS

1. Write the date, *June 3*, in the Date column of the purchases returns and allowances journal. Since this is the first entry on page 6 of the purchases returns and allowances journal, include the current year, *20--*.
2. Enter the vendor name, *Key Tennis Company*, in the Account Debited column.
3. Record the debit memorandum number, *22*, in the Debit Memo. No. column.
4. Write the debit amount, *54.50*, in the Accounts Payable Debit column.
5. Record the credit amount, *54.50*, in the Purchases Returns and Allowances Credit Tennis column.

	DATE	ACCOUNT DEBITED	DEBIT MEMO. NO.	POST. REF.	ACCOUNTS PAYABLE DEBIT	PURCHASES RETURNS AND ALLOWANCES CREDIT		
					1	2 GOLF	3 TENNIS	
1	June 3	Key Tennis Company	22	240	5 4 50		5 4 50	1
9	27	Super Pro Tennis	29	260	2 4 0 00		2 4 0 00	9
10	30	Totals			1 3 6 7 30	3 0 2 30	1 0 6 5 00	10
11					(2105)	(5115-1)	(5115-2)	11
12								12

PURCHASES RETURNS AND ALLOWANCES JOURNAL   PAGE 6

Figure 1-11

Purchases returns and allowances are posted in the same manner as purchases on account. Each amount written in the Accounts Payable Debit column is posted often to the vendor account written in the Account Debited column. The purchases returns and allowances journal is abbreviated as PR in the Post. Ref. column of the ledger accounts. For example, a reference of PR6 indicates that the posting came from page 6 of the purchases returns and allowances journal.

A purchases return or allowance may be made after a vendor has been paid in full. This situation might occur if an invoice is paid very soon after it is received. After the return has been posted, the vendor account may have a debit balance instead of a normal credit balance.

This debit balance reduces the amount to be paid for future purchases. An account balance that is opposite the normal balance is called a **contra balance**. A contra balance is shown by enclosing the amount in parentheses in the account's Balance column.

A purchases returns and allowances journal is proved, ruled, and posted at the end of each month. Each amount column total is posted to the general ledger account named in the column heading. The account number is written below the journal's column total to show that the amount has been posted. MasterSport's departmental purchases returns and allowances journal after posting is shown in Figure 1-11.

AT WHAT PRICE SAFETY?

Ziegler Industries assembles a safety system for passenger automobiles. This system substantially reduces severe injuries to drivers involved in accidents. In an effort to increase profits, Ziegler recently took steps to cut costs and increase production.

Instructions

Use the three-step checklist to help determine whether each of the following actions by Ziegler Industries demonstrates ethical behavior.

Situation 1. Ziegler has begun using some less expensive components. These components increase the system's estimated failure rate from 12 to 15 failures per 10,000 accidents. Despite this increase, the company continues to meet the government's safety standard of 20 failures per 10,000 accidents.

Situation 2. Ziegler saves $80 per system by purchasing less expensive components. As a result of this saving, they decide to reduce the unit sales price of the system by $25. Therefore, Ziegler increases the per unit profit by $55.

PROFESSIONAL BUSINESS ETHICS

TERMS REVIEW

departmental accounting system

merchandising business

posting

debit memorandum

contra account

contra balance

1. When MasterSport's tennis department purchases merchandise on account, what general ledger accounts are affected, and how?

2. What general ledger accounts are affected, and how, by a purchases return of tennis equipment?

WORK TOGETHER

Journalizing and posting purchases on account and purchases returns and allowances

Music Designs, Inc. has two departments: Compact Discs and Tapes. A purchases journal, purchases returns and allowances journal, partial general ledger, and accounts payable ledger are provided in the *Working Papers*. The balances are recorded as of March 1 of the current year. Your instructor will guide you through the following examples.

Mar. 1. Purchased tapes on account from Raymond Wholesalers, $1,350.00. P283.
2. Purchased compact discs on account from Artex Music, $965.00. P284.
5. Returned compact discs to Dade, Inc., $165.00, from P280. DM36.
6. Returned tapes to Raymond Wholesalers, $100.00, from P283. DM37.

3. Journalize each transaction. Source documents are abbreviated as follows: debit memorandum, DM; purchase invoice, P.

4. Post the items that are to be posted individually. Post from the journals in the following order: purchases journal and purchases returns and allowances journal. Save your work to complete the On Your Own below.

ON YOUR OWN

Journalizing and posting purchases on account and purchases returns and allowances

Use the working papers from the Work Together above. Work this problem independently.

Mar. 18. Purchased tapes on account from Quality Tapes, $268.00. P288.
20. Returned compact discs to Artex Music, $120.00, from P284. DM38.
23. Purchased tapes on account from Castle Records and Tapes, $993.00. P289.
31. Returned tapes to Castle Records and Tapes, $150.00, from P289. DM39.

5. Journalize each transaction.

6. Post the items that are to be posted individually. Prove and rule the journals. Post the totals.

DEPARTMENTAL CASH PAYMENTS

Most of MasterSport's cash payments are made by check. Therefore, checks are the source documents for most cash payments. *(CONCEPT: Objective Evidence)* All cash payments are recorded in a cash payments journal.

Cash Payment on Account

Purchases on account are expected to be paid within the stated credit period. A seller may encourage early payment by allowing a deduction from the invoice amount. A deduction that a vendor allows on the invoice amount to encourage prompt payment is called a **cash discount**. A cash discount on purchases taken by a customer is called a **purchases discount**.

A purchases discount is usually stated as a percentage. For example, the terms of an invoice may be written as *2/10, n/30*. The expression 2/10 means that 2% of the invoice amount may be deducted from the amount due if payment is made within 10 days of the invoice date. The expression n/30 means that payment of the total invoice amount must be made within 30 days of the invoice date. No discount can be deducted, however, if payment is made after 10 days from the invoice date. MasterSport takes advantage of all discounts allowed by vendors.

A purchases discount reduces the net amount of cash paid for a purchase. The account **Purchases Discount—Tennis** is in the cost of merchandise division of MasterSport's general ledger. Purchases discounts are kept in separate accounts and not deducted directly from the purchases accounts. This procedure helps the business see what proportion of purchases on account were allowed purchases discounts.

An account that reduces a related account on a financial statement is known as a contra account. The purchases discount accounts are contra cost accounts.

REMEMBER

The "n" in 2/10, n/30 represents the word *net*.

PROFESSIONAL ORGANIZATIONS

How do you meet other people in your profession? Join a professional organization. Several professional accounting organizations exist to serve the needs of various ethnic groups. Among these organizations are: The American Association of Hispanic Certified Public Accountants; The National Association of Black Accountants, Inc. (NABA); and The Association of Asian American Attorneys and Certified Public Accountants.

These associations maintain an informal network among members.

Such networks allow people in the profession to meet, to use services of other association members, and to share ideas and career opportunities. They also promote career opportunities for their members, work to expand representation of their ethnic groups in the workforce, and offer various forms of continuing education.

In addition to their national organizations, each has various chapters around the country. All three offer student memberships to college students who are studying accounting.

CULTURAL DIVERSITY

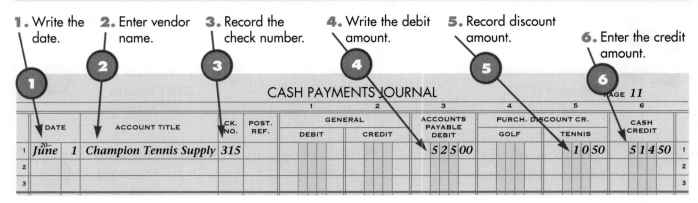

1. Write the date.
2. Enter vendor name.
3. Record the check number.
4. Write the debit amount.
5. Record discount amount.
6. Enter the credit amount.

Figure 1-12

MasterSport's cash payments journal, shown in Figure 1-12, has two debit columns—General Debit and Accounts Payable Debit. The journal also has four credit columns—General Credit, a Purchases Discount Credit column for each of the two departments, and Cash Credit.

June 1. Paid cash on account to Champion Tennis Supply, $514.50, covering Purchase Invoice No. 331 for tennis equipment for $525.00, less 2% discount, $10.50. Check No. 315.

The source document for this transaction is a check. *(CONCEPT: Objective Evidence)*

In the general ledger, Accounts Payable is decreased by a $525.00 debit. Cash is decreased

by a $514.50 credit. Purchases Discount—Tennis is increased by a $10.50 credit. In the accounts payable ledger, Champion Tennis Supply is decreased by a $525.00 debit.

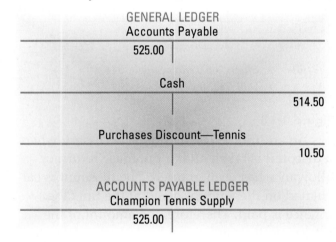

Journalize a cash payment that includes a purchases discount

1. Write the date, *June 1*, in the Date column of the cash payments journal. Since this is the first entry on page 11 of the cash payments journal, include the current year, *20--*.

2. Enter the vendor name, *Champion Tennis Supply*, in the Account Title column.

3. Record the check number, *315*, in the Ck. No. column.

4. Write the debit amount, *525.00*, in the Accounts Payable Debit column.

5. Record one credit amount, *10.50*, in the Purchases Discount Credit Tennis column.

6. Enter the other credit amount, *514.50*, in the Cash Credit column.

F.Y.I.

Some businesses organized by departments will have more than two departments. Additional columns will be added to the various journals to accommodate the number of departments in the business. For example, the cash payments journal for a business with four departments would have four Purchases Discount columns, one for each department.

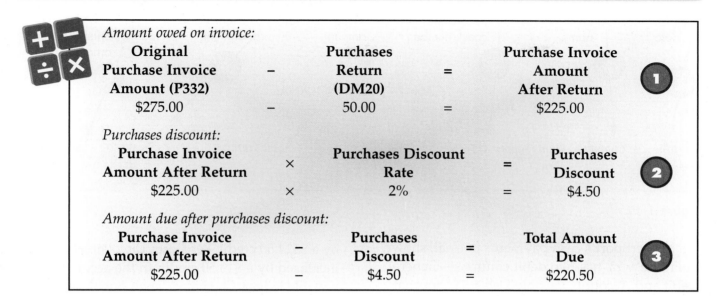

Amount owed on invoice:

Original Purchase Invoice Amount (P332)	–	Purchases Return (DM20)	=	Purchase Invoice Amount After Return	①
$275.00	–	50.00	=	$225.00	

Purchases discount:

Purchase Invoice Amount After Return	×	Purchases Discount Rate	=	Purchases Discount	②
$225.00	×	2%	=	$4.50	

Amount due after purchases discount:

Purchase Invoice Amount After Return	–	Purchases Discount	=	Total Amount Due	③
$225.00	–	$4.50	=	$220.50	

CASH PAYMENTS JOURNAL — PAGE 11

								1	2	3	4	5	6	
	DATE	ACCOUNT TITLE	CK. NO.	POST. REF.	GENERAL DEBIT	GENERAL CREDIT		ACCOUNTS PAYABLE DEBIT	PURCH. DISCOUNT CR. GOLF	PURCH. DISCOUNT CR. TENNIS	CASH CREDIT			
1	June 1	Champion Tennis Supply	315					525 00			10 50	514 50			1
2	1	Golf-Tee, Inc.	316					225 00	4 50		220 50				2

Figure 1-13

An additional calculation is necessary when a discount is taken after a purchase return or allowance has been granted. The discount is calculated on the amount owed at the time the invoice is paid. Therefore, the amount of the return or allowance must be deducted from the amount of the original purchase *before* the discount can be calculated.

> **June 1. Paid cash on account to Golf-Tee, Inc., $220.50, covering Purchase Invoice No. 332 for golf equipment for $275.00, less Debit Memorandum No. 20 for $50.00, and less 2% discount, $4.50. Check No. 316.**

The source document for this transaction is a check. *(CONCEPT: Objective Evidence)*

The total amount due for this purchase after the return and the discount is calculated as shown in Figure 1-13. This transaction is journalized the same way as a payment of cash when there is no purchases return or allowance. The only difference is the way in which the amounts are calculated.

GENERAL LEDGER
Accounts Payable
225.00 |

Cash
| 220.50

Purchases Discount—Golf
| 4.50

ACCOUNTS PAYABLE LEDGER
Golf-Tee, Inc.
225.00 |

S
T
E
P
S

Calculate a discount after a return or allowance is granted and journalize the cash payment

1. Calculate the amount owed on the invoice after the purchases return, *$225.00.*
2. Calculate the new purchases discount, *$4.50.*
3. Find the amount due after the purchases return and the purchases discount, *$220.50.*
4. Record the entry in the cash payments journal.

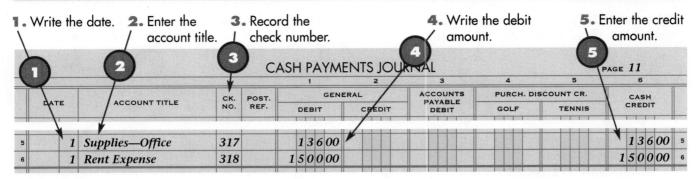

1. Write the date. **2.** Enter the account title. **3.** Record the check number. **4.** Write the debit amount. **5.** Enter the credit amount.

CASH PAYMENTS JOURNAL   PAGE 11

| DATE | ACCOUNT TITLE | CK. NO. | POST. REF. | GENERAL | | ACCOUNTS PAYABLE DEBIT | PURCH. DISCOUNT CR. | | CASH CREDIT |
				DEBIT	CREDIT		GOLF	TENNIS	
5	1 *Supplies—Office*	317		1 3 6 00					1 3 6 00	5
6	1 *Rent Expense*	318		1 5 0 0 00					1 5 0 0 00	6

Figure 1-14

June 1. Paid cash for office supplies, $136.00. Check No. 317.

Supplies—Office is increased by a $136.00 debit. Cash is decreased by a $136.00 credit.

The entry on line 5 of page 11 of the cash payments journal, Figure 1-14, shows the cash payment for supplies. Use the following steps to make the journal entry.

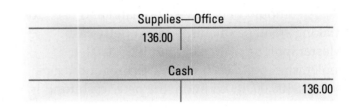

S T E P S **Journalize buying office supplies for cash**

1. Write the date, *1*, in the Date column.
2. Enter the account title, *Supplies—Office*, in the Account Title column.
3. Record the check number, *317*, in the Ck. No. column.
4. Write the debit amount, *136.00*, in the General Debit column.
5. Record the credit amount, *136.00*, in the Cash Credit column.

June 1. Paid cash for rent, $1,500.00. Check No. 318.

Rent Expense is increased by a $1,500.00 debit. Cash is decreased by a $1,500.00 credit.

The entry on line 6 of page 11 of the cash payments journal, Figure 1-13, shows the cash payment for an expense. Use the following steps to make the journal entry.

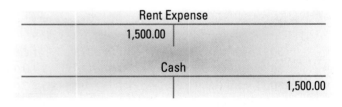

S T E P S **Journalize the cash payment of an expense**

1. Write the date, *1*, in the Date column.
2. Enter the account title, *Rent Expense*, in the Account Title column.
3. Record the check number, *318*, in the Ck. No. column.
4. Write the debit amount, *1,500.00*, in the General Debit column.
5. Record the credit amount, *1,500.00*, in the Cash Credit column.

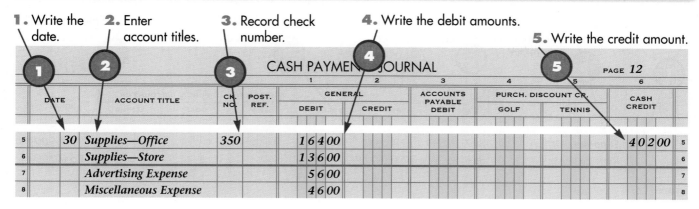

Figure 1-15

An amount of cash kept on hand and used for making small payments is called **petty cash**. MasterSport's petty cash fund is $500.00. It replenishes petty cash whenever the fund drops below $100.00. In addition, the petty cash fund is replenished on the last business day of each fiscal period, to assure that all expenses are recorded during the fiscal period in which they occurred. (CONCEPT: Matching Expenses with Revenue)

To replenish petty cash, a check is written for the amount spent from the fund. The check is cashed and the money placed back in the fund.

June 30. Paid cash to replenish the petty cash fund, $402.00: office supplies, $164.00; store supplies, $136.00; advertising, $56.00; miscellaneous expense, $46.00. Check No. 350.

The entry in Figure 1-15 shows the cash payment to replenish petty cash. The steps to record the entry are the same as the steps for other cash payment entries.

POSTING FROM A CASH PAYMENTS JOURNAL

CASH PAYMENTS JOURNAL
PAGE 12

DATE	ACCOUNT TITLE	CK. NO.	POST. REF.	GENERAL DEBIT	GENERAL CREDIT	ACCOUNTS PAYABLE DEBIT	PURCH. DISCOUNT CR. GOLF	PURCH. DISCOUNT CR. TENNIS	CASH CREDIT	
11	30	Miscellaneous Expense	M18	6215	1280					1280	11
12	30	Credit Card Fee Expense	M19	6110	3400 00					3400 00	12
13	30	Totals			1952000	173000	439300	14130	33150	612472 0	13
14					(✓)	(✓)	(2105)	(5110-1)	(5110-2)	(1105)	14

Figure 1-16

MasterSport posts often from the General Debit and General Credit columns to the general ledger. MasterSport also posts frequently from the Accounts Payable Debit column to the accounts payable ledger.

At the end of each month, the cash payments journal is proved and ruled. Totals of the special amount columns are posted to their respective accounts in the general ledger. The general ledger account number is written in parentheses immediately below the total. A check mark is recorded in parentheses below the totals of the General Debit and Credit columns to show that these totals are not posted. MasterSport's departmental cash payments journal, Figure 1-16, is shown after all posting has been completed.

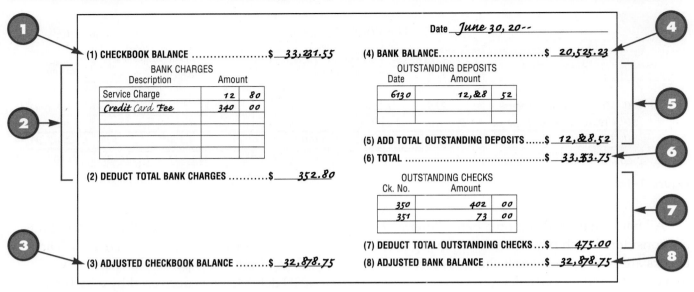

Figure 1-17

Banks keep detailed records of their depositors' checking accounts. Records are kept of all deposits received, all checks paid, and bank fees charged for maintaining an account. Bank charges include service charges and credit card fees.

A report of deposits, withdrawals, and bank balance sent to a depositor by a bank is called a **bank statement**. Bank statements are commonly sent to depositors monthly. Many banks include all canceled checks listed on the statement. Some banks do not return canceled checks with the statement. If the bank does not return canceled checks, the check numbers and amounts shown on the statement should be carefully compared to the check stubs.

A depositor should check the bank statement for accuracy as soon as it is received. Any errors found should be reported immediately to the bank. The bank balance is compared with the checkbook balance. Bringing information on a bank statement and a checkbook into agreement is known as reconciling a bank statement.

MasterSport uses the form shown in Figure 1-17 when reconciling the bank statement each month. The reconciliation indicates that the adjusted checkbook balance and the adjusted bank balance are the same, $32,878.75.

Reconciling a bank statement

1. Enter the checkbook balance as shown on check stub, *$33,231.55*.

2. Enter and add bank charges to obtain total bank charges, *$352.80*.

3. Deduct total bank charges from checkbook balance to obtain adjusted checkbook balance, *$32,878.75*.

4. Enter bank balance as shown on bank statement, *$20,525.23*.

5. Enter and add the amounts of any outstanding deposits recorded on the check stubs but not listed on the bank statement to obtain total outstanding deposits, *$12,828.52*.

6. Add total outstanding deposits to bank balance, *$33,353.75*.

7. Deduct total outstanding checks, *$475.00*.

8. Verify that the adjusted checkbook balance and the adjusted bank balance are the same, *$32,878.75*.

REMEMBER

Bank statements should be reconciled each month. Errors should be reported immediately to the bank.

	DATE	ACCOUNT TITLE	CK. NO.	POST. REF.	GENERAL		ACCOUNTS PAYABLE DEBIT	PURCH. DISCOUNT CR.		CASH CREDIT	
					DEBIT	CREDIT		GOLF	TENNIS		
11	30	Miscellaneous Expense	M18	6215	1 2 80					1 2 80	11
12	30	Credit Card Fee Expense	M19	6110	3 4 0 00					3 4 0 00	12
13	30	Totals			19 5 2 0 00	1 7 3 0 00	43 9 3 0 00	1 4 1 30	3 3 1 50	61 2 4 7 20	13
14					(✓)	(✓)	(2105)	(5110-1)	(5110-2)	(1105)	14

CASH PAYMENTS JOURNAL — PAGE *12*

Figure 1-18

All bank charges listed on a bank statement are considered cash payments. Even though no checks are issued, each bank charge is recorded in a cash payments journal.

MasterSport has two bank charges. One charge is a bank service charge for maintaining a checking account. The other charge is a credit card fee based on a percentage of the total of credit card sales deposited with the bank. Since no checks are available to serve as source documents, memorandums are prepared showing the details of each service charge. *(CONCEPT: Objective Evidence)*

> **June 30. Received bank statement showing June bank service charge, $12.80. Memorandum No. 18.**

The source document for this transaction is a memorandum. *(CONCEPT: Objective Evidence)*

Miscellaneous Expense is increased by a $12.80 debit. Cash is decreased by a $12.80 credit.

> **June 30. Recorded credit card fee expense for June, $340.00. Memorandum No. 19.**

The source document for this transaction is a memorandum. *(CONCEPT: Objective Evidence)*

Credit Card Fee Expense is increased by a $340.00 debit. Cash is decreased by a $340.00 credit.

The entry on lines 11 and 12 of page 12 of the cash payments journal, Figure 1-18, shows the entry for June's bank service charge and credit card fee expense. Use the following steps to make these journal entries.

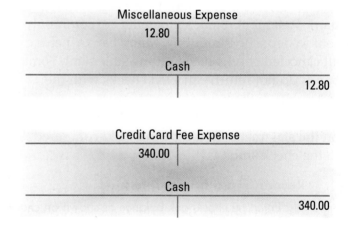

Journalize the cash payments for a bank service charge and credit card fee expense

1. Write the date, *30*, in the Date column.
2. Enter the account title in the Account Title column.
3. Record the memorandum number in the Ck. No. column and identify by the letter *M*.
4. Write the debit amount in the General Debit column.
5. Record the credit amount in the Cash Credit column.

TERMS REVIEW

cash discount

purchases discount

petty cash

bank statement

1. What general ledger accounts are affected, and how, by a cash payment on account for tennis equipment that includes a purchases discount?

2. Why is a petty cash fund always replenished on the last day of a fiscal period?

3. What source document does MasterSport use for each of the two bank charges shown on the bank statement?

WORK TOGETHER

Journalizing and posting departmental cash payments

Harmony Music has two departments: Guitars and Keyboards. A cash payments journal, partial general ledger, and accounts payable ledger are provided in the *Working Papers*. Source documents are abbreviated as follows: check, C; debit memorandum, DM; memorandum, M; and purchase number, P. Your instructor will guide you through the following examples.

Sept. 5. Paid cash on account for guitars from Peninsula Guitar covering P358 for $1,150.00. C241.
7. Paid cash for supplies, $120.00. C242.
9. Paid cash on account for keyboards from Magic Keyboard covering P360 for $2,210.00, less DM53 for $210.00, and less 2% discount. C243.

4. Journalize the transaction.

5. Post items that are to be posted individually. Save your work to complete the On Your Own below.

ON YOUR OWN

Journalizing and posting departmental cash payments

Use the working papers from the Work Together above. Work independently to complete the following problem.

Sept. 16. Paid cash on account for keyboards from Magic Keyboard covering P361 for $1,800.00, less 2% discount. C244.
19. Paid cash on account for guitars to Peninsula Guitar covering P359 for $1,680.00. C245.
30. Paid cash to replenish the petty cash fund, $64.00: supplies, $15.00; advertising expense, $22.00; miscellaneous expense, $27.00. C246.
30. Received bank statement showing September service charge, $10.00. M54.
30. Recorded credit card fee expense for September, $278.00. M55.

6. Journalize the transactions.

7. Post items that are to be posted individually. Prove and rule the journal. Post the totals.

CHAPTER UMMARY

After completing this chapter, you can

1. Define accounting terms related to departmental purchases and cash payments.
2. Identify accounting concepts and practices related to departmental purchases and cash payments.
3. Perform file maintenance.
4. Journalize and post departmental purchases and purchases returns.
5. Journalize and post cash payments.
6. Reconcile a bank statement.

EXPLORE ACCOUNTING

ACCOUNTING PROFESSIONALS

As a company grows, it can adopt two strategies to satisfy its need for accounting expertise. The company can add to its full-time accounting staff. Alternately, the company could hire independent consultants. Regardless of which strategy is adopted, the search for accounting professionals should include examining their professional certification.

The Certified Public Accountant (CPA) is the most widely recognized certification. To become a CPA, an individual must pass a certifying examination and meet the educational and experience requirements of the board of accountancy in the individual's state. A CPA is qualified to perform a variety of accounting functions, including processing accounting information, auditing financial state-

ments, preparing tax returns, and providing tax planning.

A partial list of additional certifications available in accounting and related areas follows.

Certified Management Accountant: Responsible for the accounting information system, assists managers to use accounting information in decision making, and works to provide the company with adequate financial resources to conduct business.

Certified Internal Auditor: Audits the accounting information system and other operational reporting systems.

Certified Information Systems Analyst: Designs computer information systems that provide timely accounting information while assuring that the information is accessible only to authorized personnel.

Certified Fraud Examiner: Investigates alleged fraudulent activities by examining account-

ing records and interviewing personnel; prepares evidence for admission into court.

Certified Financial Planner: Manages the company's employee benefits and assists employees to develop investment strategies to meet future needs.

Certified Contingency Planner: Develops plans that enable the company and its accounting information system to continue operations in the event of a natural disaster.

REQUIRED:

Identify an individual that has one of the certifications listed above. Ask the individual to describe how the certification has played a role in his or her professional career.

1-1 APPLICATION PROBLEM
Performing file maintenance activities; adding general ledger accounts

The following is CarMaster Detailing's partial general ledger chart of accounts.

	Assets	Accounts Added
1110	Cash	Petty Cash
1115	Accounts Receivable	Allowance for Uncollectible Accounts
1120	Merchandise Inventory	Supplies-Office
1125	Supplies-Store	Prepaid Insurance

Add the four new asset accounts to the general ledger chart of accounts using the unused middle number method. Assume Supplies-Store is currently the last account in the division.

1-2 APPLICATION PROBLEM
Journalizing and posting departmental purchases on account and purchases returns and allowances

LifeLine Communications has two departments: Cellular Phones and Pagers. A purchases journal, purchases returns and allowances journal, partial general ledger, and accounts payable ledger are provided in the *Working Papers*. The balances are recorded as of October 1 of the current year.

Transactions:

Oct. 1. Phones were purchased on account from CarPhone Wholesalers, $1,270.00. P183.
2. Pagers were purchased on account from PageMax, Inc., $970.00. P184.
5. Purchased phones on account from ExecuPhone, $2,100.00. P185.
6. The order from Western Distributors contained 5 defective pagers. Returned pagers, $205.00, from P180. DM40.
9. Purchased pagers on account from Cell Advantage, Inc., $945.00. P186.
13. Pagers were purchased on account from ComSystems, $2,240.00. P187.
17. Returned phones to CarPhone Wholesalers, $120.00, from P183. DM41.
 Posting. Post the items that are to be posted individually. Post from the journals in this order: purchases journal and purchases returns and allowances journal.
19. Purchased phones on account from Telecom Corporation, $450.00. P188.
20. Pagers were returned to PageMax, Inc., $90.00, from P184. DM42.
23. Issued P189 to purchase phones on account from ExecuPhone, $1,003.00.
30. Returned $75.00 of phones to Phone Solution, from P181. DM43.
 Posting. Post the items that are to be posted individually.

Instructions:

1. Journalize the transactions completed during October of the current year. Use page 11 of a purchases journal and page 3 of a purchases returns and allowances journal. Source documents are abbreviated as follows: debit memorandum, DM; purchase invoice, P.

2. Prove and rule the purchases journal. Post the totals.

3. Prove and rule the purchases returns and allowances journal. Post the totals.

APPLICATION PROBLEM
Journalizing and posting departmental cash payments

Los Gatos Nursery and Craft has two departments: Crafts and Plants. A partial general ledger and accounts payable ledger are given in the *Working Papers*. The balances are recorded as of November 1 of the current year.

Transactions:

Nov. 1. Paid cash for miscellaneous expense, $150.00. C303.
    2. Paid cash for rent, $1,300.00. C304.
    4. Paid cash on account to Wholesale Crafts, Inc. covering P287 for crafts for $885.00, less 2% discount. C305.
    5. Paid cash for advertising, $83.50. C306.
    8. Paid cash for supplies, $95.50. C307.
    10. Paid cash on account to Northtown Plants covering P288 for plants for $1,250.00, less 2% discount. C308.
    13. Paid cash on account to Century Crafts, Inc., covering P289 for crafts for $963.00, less 2% discount. C309.
    15. Paid cash for miscellaneous, $33.50. C310.
    Posting. Post the items that are to be posted individually.
    21. Paid cash for supplies, $52.00. C311.
    23. Paid cash on account to Evergreen Trees & Shrubs covering P290 for plants for $1,840.00, less 2% discount. C312.
    27. Paid cash on account to Evergreen Trees & Shrubs covering P292 for plants for $1,460.00, less 2% discount. C313.
    30. Paid cash to replenish the petty cash fund, $212.00: supplies, $89.00; advertising, $83.40; miscellaneous, $39.60. C314.
    30. Received bank statement showing November bank service charge, $14.30. M26.
    30. Recorded credit card fee expense for November, $488.20. M27.
    Posting. Post the items that are to be posted individually.

Instructions:

1. Journalize the transactions completed during November of the current year. Use page 21 of a cash payments journal. All of the vendors from which merchandise is purchased on account offer terms of 2/10, n/30. Source documents are abbreviated as follows: check, C; memorandum, M.

2. Prove and rule the cash payments journal. Post the totals.

APPLICATION PROBLEM
Reconciling a bank statement

On October 31 of the current year, San Jose Transmission Specialists, received a bank statement dated October 29. The following information is obtained from the bank statement and from the records of the business.

Bank statement balance	$31,820.00
Bank service charge	8.80

Bank credit card charge	325.20
Outstanding deposit:	
October 27	7,152.75
Outstanding checks:	
No. 361	89.50
No. 362	1,460.25
Checkbook balance on Check Stub No. 363	37,757.00

Prepare a bank statement reconciliation on a form similar to the one in this chapter. Use October 31 of the current year as the date.

MASTERY PROBLEM 1-5

Performing file maintenance activities; journalizing departmental purchases and cash payments; reconciling a bank statement

San Juan Camera has two departments: Cameras and Accessories. The following is San Juan Camera's partial general ledger chart of accounts.

6205   Depreciation Expense—Office Equipment
6210   Miscellaneous Expense
6215   Rent Expense
6220   Supplies Expense—Office
6225   Supplies Expense—Store

Transactions:

Nov. 1. Paid cash for advertising, $95.00. C273.
      1. Paid cash for rent, $1,250.00. C274.
      2. Purchased accessories on account from Standish Photo Supplies, $800.00. P262.
      3. Paid cash on account to National Camera Outlet covering P259 for cameras for $500.00, less 2% discount. C275.
      3. Purchased cameras on account from Jens Wholesale Cameras, $840.00. P263.
      5. Paid cash on account to Standish Photo Supplies covering P261 for accessories for $645.00, less 2% discount. C276.
      7. Returned cameras to Jens Wholesale Cameras, $88.00, from P263. DM28.
     10. Purchased cameras on account from Focal Camera Distributors, $388.00. P264.
     11. Paid cash for store supplies, $82.50. C277.
     14. Paid cash on account to Standish Photo Supplies covering P262 for accessories; no discount. C278.
     16. Returned accessories to Quality Film Company, $132.50, from P260. DM29.
     17. Purchased accessories on account from Farmer Camera Supply, Inc., $550.00. P265.
     17. Paid cash on account to Focal Camera Distributors covering P264 for cameras for $388.00, less 2% discount. C279.
     18. Paid cash on account to Jens Wholesale Cameras covering P263 for cameras for $840.00, less DM28 for $88.00; no discount. C280.
     18. Returned accessories to Farmer Camera Supply, Inc., $75.00, from P265. DM30.
     19. Purchased cameras on account from Jens Wholesale Cameras, $1,120.00. P266.
     21. Paid cash for office supplies, $62.30. C281.
     23. Purchased accessories on account from Quality Film Company, $336.00. P267.

continued

Nov. 24. Paid cash on account to Farmer Camera Supply, Inc. covering P265 for accessories for $550.00, less DM30 for $75.00, and less 2% discount. C282.

24. Purchased cameras on account from National Camera Outlet, $626.40. P268.

26. Paid cash on account to Jens Wholesale Cameras covering P266 for cameras for $1,120.00, less 2% discount. C283.

28. Paid cash for store supplies, $53.00. C284

30. Paid cash to replenish the petty cash fund, $221.00: office supplies, $57.10; advertising, $62.50; miscellaneous, $101.40. C285.

Instructions:

1. Add Insurance Expense and Uncollectible Accounts Expense to the general ledger chart of accounts using the unused middle number method described in this chapter. Assume the company lists expenses alphabetically.

2. Journalize the following transactions completed during November of the current year. Use page 11 of a purchases journal and a purchases returns and allowances journal and page 21 of a cash payments journal. All of the vendors from which merchandise is purchased on account offer terms of 2/10, n/30. Source documents are abbreviated as follows: check, C; debit memorandum, DM; purchase invoice, P.

3. Prepare a bank statement reconciliation. Use November 30 of the current year as the date. The bank statement is dated November 29. The following information is obtained from the bank statement and from the records of the business.

Bank statement balance	$16,578.00
Bank service charge	20.20
Bank credit card charge	382.80
Outstanding deposit:	
November 29	3,070.60
Outstanding checks:	
No. 283	1,097.60
No. 284	53.00
No. 285	221.00
Checkbook balance on Check Stub No. 286	18,680.00

4. Continue journalizing the following transactions.

Nov. 30. Received bank statement showing November bank service charge, $20.20. M31.

30. Recorded credit card fee expense for November, $382.80. M32.

5. Prove and rule the journals.

1-6 CHALLENGE PROBLEM
Journalizing purchases at net amount and using the account Discounts Lost

Introductory remarks: Some businesses record purchases at the net amount to be paid when the cash discount is taken. For example, merchandise is purchased for $1,000.00 with a 2% discount allowed if the account is paid within 10 days. The discount will reduce the price from $1,000.00 to $980.00. To record this purchase on account transaction, Purchases is debited for $980.00 and Accounts Payable is credited for $980.00. When the account is paid, Accounts Payable is debited for $980.00 and Cash is credited for $980.00. Purchases returns and allowances are also recorded at the discounted amount.

If the discount period expires before payment is made, the entry in the cash payments journal for the example above would be as follows: debit Accounts Payable for $980.00, debit Discounts Lost for $20.00, and credit Cash for $1,000.00. Because most cash discounts are taken, there are few entries involving the discounts lost account. For this reason, no special amount column is provided for the account in the cash payments journal. Instead, the amounts debited to this account are recorded in the General Debit column.

Instructions:

1. Journalize the transactions for Mastery Problem 1-5 following the method described above. Use page 11 of a purchases journal and a purchases returns and allowances journal and page 21 of a cash payments journal. All of the vendors from which merchandise is purchased on account offer terms of 2/10, n/30.

2. Prove and rule the journals.

INTERNET ACTIVITY

Point your browser to
http://accounting.swpco.com
Choose **Advanced Course**, choose **Activities**, and complete the activity for Chapter 1.

Applied Communication

A resume states your education, work experience, and qualifications. Your resume should be accurate, honest, and perfect in every respect. It is preferable to limit the resume to one typed page.

Required:

1. Research how to prepare an appropriate resume.
2. Prepare a personal resume that you could send to a prospective employer.

Cases for Critical Thinking

Case 1
Maria Hector manages a card and gift shop. The shop's general ledger includes a single sales account and a single purchases account. Periodically, Ms. Hector has an accountant review her accounting records and procedures. The accountant recommends that Ms. Hector change to a departmental accounting system. The accountant recommends that separate revenue and cost accounts be kept for the two types of merchandise sold—cards and gifts. Ms. Hector objects to the accountant's recommendation. She sees no advantage to complicating the accounting system by having separate departmental revenue and cost accounts. With whom do you agree? Why?

Case 2
Scott Pfeiffer manages a hardware store. He has found that his bank statement and checkbook reconcile without error month after month. In order to save the time spent reconciling his bank statement each month, Mr. Pfeiffer decides to make the reconciliation once every six months. His daughter, who helps with the business' accounting, disagrees with this practice. With whom do you agree? Why?

AUTOMATED ACCOUNTING

MAINTENANCE OF GENERAL LEDGER DATABASE AND AUTOMATED ENTRIES FOR PURCHASES AND CASH PAYMENTS

General Ledger Database

The general ledger database consists of a collection of accounts and the related account numbers needed for financial reporting. The ledger specifically lists accounts for assets, liabilities, capital, income and expenses.

Database

A pre-arranged file in which data can be entered and retrieved is known as a **database.** An example of a database in Automated Accounting is the general ledger. It contains general information about the business, a chart of accounts, and financial activity for each account. The database is designed so that, when you enter information, it updates the account balances and stores data in a designated area for creating reports. The general ledger database to be used for a problem is stored as a **template**. Templates can be used repeatedly. MasterSport stores its general ledger database as a template.

Ledger and General Ledger

A **ledger** is a group of accounts. A ledger that contains all accounts needed to prepare financial statements is called a **general ledger**. The name given to an account is known as an **account title**.

File Maintenance

A chart of accounts numbering system includes the account numbers that will be used to process transactions for various accounts. In this text, the numbering systems for manual and automated problems are the same. The process used to set up the chart of accounts, add new accounts, and change data for existing accounts is known as **file maintenance**. File maintenance includes arranging accounts in the general ledger and assigning the numbers.

Three steps are required to add an account or change an account number.

1. Create an account number or modify an existing number.

2. Enter it in the chart of accounts.

3. Check for accuracy by creating a revised chart of accounts list.

Adding an Account Within a Ledger

Adding a new account within a ledger may be necessary when an asset is purchased, a liability is incurred, or an additional expense category is added. A new account number is assigned the unused middle number between two existing accounts.

MasterSport added a new account, Equipment Repair Expense, between the two existing accounts Depreciation Expense—Office Equipment, 6205, and Insurance Expense, 6210. The unused middle number between 6205 and 6210 is 6207.5. The number 6207.5 contains five digits and cannot be assigned in a four-digit number system. Therefore, the nearest whole number, 6208, would be assigned. The new account, Equipment Repair Expense, is placed in the general ledger as follows:

6205 Depreciation Expense— Office Equipment (existing account)

6208 EQUIPMENT REPAIR EXPENSE (new account)

6210 Insurance Expense (existing account)

When adding a new account after the last account number in a division, assign the next number in the sequence. Sales Tax Payable, 2120, is the last existing account in the liabilities division. If MasterSport decides to add a new liability account after Sales Tax Payable, the new account number would be assigned number 2125.

MasterSport maintains a list of all vendors it uses. Vendors are stored in the system by name. Vendors may be added and deleted. MasterSport also maintains a list of its customers. The customer list is also stored by name.

Processing File Maintenance Data

In automated accounting, activities may be selected from the menu or from toolbar icons. In most cases, you will use the toolbar icons to process data. Figure AA1-1 shows the menu and toolbar for *Automated Accounting 7.0. Automated Accounting 8.0*

has additional menu options and toolbar buttons.

Figure AA1-1 also shows the Account Maintenance Window. The window is opened by clicking on the Accts. toolbar icon. To add an account, key the account number and account title in the appropriate columns and click the Add Account button. In the figure, Equipment Repair Expense has been added to the chart.

After file maintenance data have been keyed, a revised chart of accounts is displayed and checked for accuracy. The revised chart of accounts is printed and filed for future reference.

Recording Departmental Purchases and Cash Payments

MasterSport's accounting system has two departments: (1) Golf and (2) Tennis. MasterSport's departmental purchases and cash payments transactions are analyzed in Chapter 1.

Purchases on Account

MasterSport records all purchases on account transactions in the purchases journal.

> *June 1, 20--.*
> *Purchased tennis equipment on account from Tennis Warehouse, $845.00. Purchase Invoice No. 336.*

The journal entry to record this transaction includes entering the debit amount in the Purchases Tennis debit column on the purchases journal screen as shown in Figure AA1-2. The automated accounting software automatically records the credit to Accounts Payable for a purchases on account transaction. The vendor is then selected from the pull-down list.

Purchase Returns and Allowances

MasterSport records purchases returns and allowances in the general journal.

> *June 3, 20--.*
> *Returned tennis equipment to Key Tennis Company, $54.50, from Purchase Invoice No. 333. Debit Memorandum No. 22.*

The journal entry to record this transaction includes entering the debit amount in Accounts Payable for the specific vendor and the credit to the Purchases Returns and Allowances account on the general journal screen. For all general journal transactions, it is necessary to enter both the debit and credit amounts and to select the vendor name.

Cash Payment on Account

MasterSport records cash payments transactions in the cash payments journal.

> *June 1, 20--.*
> *Paid cash on account to Champion Tennis Supply, $514.50, covering Purchase Invoice No. 331 for stair master equipment for $525, less 2% discount, $10.50. Check No. 315.*

The journal entry to record this transaction includes entering a debit to the account to be paid on in the cash payments journal. The automated accounting software automatically records a credit to Cash for cash payment transactions.

An additional calculation is necessary when a discount is

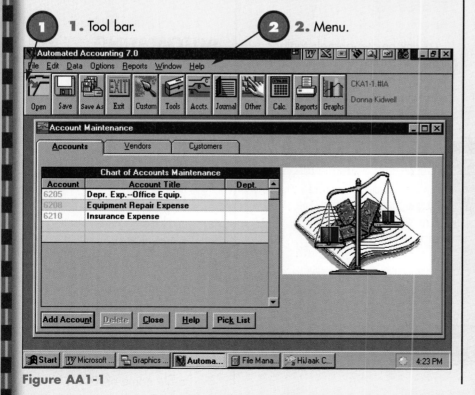

1. Tool bar.

2. Menu.

Figure AA1-1

taken after a purchase return or allowance has been granted. The amount of the return or allowance must be deducted from the amount of the original purchase *before* the discount can be calculated.

Buying Supplies for Cash

June 1, 20--.
Paid cash for office supplies, $136.00. Check No. 317.

The journal entry to record this transaction is entered on the cash payments journal screen. The transaction includes debiting the Supplies account. The automated accounting system will automatically credit Cash.

Cash Payment for an Expense

June 1, 20--.
Paid cash for rent, $1,500.00. Check No. 318.

The journal entry to record this transaction is entered on the cash payments journal screen. The transaction includes debiting the expense account. The automated accounting system will automatically credit Cash.

Cash Payment to Replenish Petty Cash

June 30, 20--.
Paid cash to replenish the petty cash fund, $402.00: office supplies, $164.00; store supplies, $136.00; advertising, $56; miscellaneous expense, $46.00. Check No. 350.

The journal entry to record this transaction is entered on the cash payments journal screen. The transaction includes debiting Office Supplies, Store Supplies, Advertising, and Miscellaneous.

The automated accounting system automatically credits the Cash account.

Processing Journal Entries

Click on the journals toolbar icon. Select the tab for the journal in which the transaction is to be recorded. Enter the transaction data. Use the Tab key to move among the columns. When you have entered all the transactions, click the Post button to post the data to the ledgers.

After all data for a problem have been entered into the journals and posted, journal reports are displayed, verified for accuracy, and printed. A report is printed for each journal in which data has been entered.

Reconciling a Bank Statement

In automated accounting, a data entry window is displayed on the monitor for entering bank reconciliation data. To reconcile a bank statement, bank charges, outstanding deposits and outstanding checks must be recorded. After the bank statement reconciliation data are keyed, the bank statement reconciliation report is printed.

AUTOMATING APPLICATION PROBLEM 1-1

Instructions:

1. Load *Automated Accounting 7.0* or higher software.

2. Select database A01-1 (Advanced Course Problem 1-1) from the accounting template disk.

3. Select File from the menu bar and choose the Save As menu command. Key the path to the drive and directory that contains your data files. Save the database with a file name of XXX011

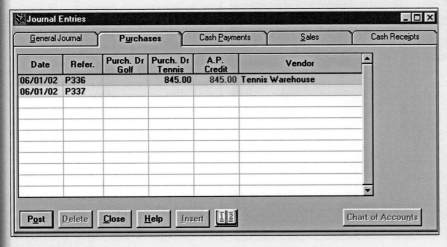

Figure AA1-2

(where XXX are your initials). (*Automated Accounting 8.0* allows long file names. Your instructor may direct you to use your full name when saving your files.)

4. Access Problem Instructions through the Help menu. Read the Problem Instruction screen. (In *Automated Accounting 8.0,* Problem Instructions are accessed by clicking the Browser toolbar button.)

5. Refer to page 29 for data used in this problem.

6. Exit the Automated Accounting software.

AUTOMATING APPLICATION PROBLEM 1-2

Instructions:

1. Load *Automated Accounting 7.0* or higher software.

2. Select database A01-2 (Advanced Course Problem 1-2) from the accounting template disk.

3. Select File from the menu bar and choose the Save As

menu command. Key the path to the drive and directory that contains your data files. Save the database with a file name of XXX012 (where XXX are your initials). (*Automated Accounting 8.0* allows long file names. Your instructor may direct you to use your full name when saving your files.)

4. Access Problem Instructions through the Help menu. Read the Problem Instruction screen. (In *Automated Accounting 8.0,* Problem Instructions are accessed by clicking the Browser toolbar button.)

5. Refer to page 29 for data used in this problem.

6. Exit the Automated Accounting software.

AUTOMATING MASTERY PROBLEM 1-5

Instructions:

1. Load *Automated Accounting 7.0* or higher software.

2. Select database A01-5 (Advanced Course Problem

1-5) from the accounting textbook template disk.

3. Select File from the menu bar and choose the Save As menu command. Key the path to the drive and directory that contains your data files. Save the database with a file name of XXX015 (where XXX are your initials). (*Automated Accounting 8.0* allows long file names. Your instructor may direct you to use your full name when saving your files.)

4. Access Problem Instructions through the Help menu. Read the Problem Instruction screen. (In *Automated Accounting 8.0,* Problem Instructions are accessed by clicking the Browser toolbar button.)

5. Key the transactions listed on page 31.

6. Exit the Automated Accounting software.

Recording Departmental Sales and Cash Receipts

AFTER STUDYING CHAPTER 2, YOU WILL BE ABLE TO:

1. Define terms related to departmental sales and cash receipts.

2. Identify concepts and practices related to departmental sales and cash receipts.

3. Journalize and post departmental sales on account and sales returns and allowances.

4. Journalize and post cash receipts.

Managers use departmental data to make decisions relating to business operations. A departmental accounting system used to record purchases and cash payments data provides valuable information. In order to have comprehensive departmental data, however, a business should record sales and cash receipts data separately for each department. For example, gross profit from operations for each department is one type of valuable information for management decision making. Departmental gross profit from operations helps business managers decide if each department is earning an appropriate profit. If not, departmental information can help managers determine which items are causing the problem. To determine departmental gross profit from operations, the business must keep records of sales and cost of merchandise sold by department.

ACCOUNTING
IN YOUR CAREER

PRODUCT CODING ERRORS

The Friday afternoon managers' meeting at Hardware Depot had just begun. The sales managers of the three departments—computers, software, and peripherals—were scanning their weekly sales reports. The CEO, Mariko Ishio, was waiting for controller Chad Billings to arrive, to begin the meeting. Chad rushed in and took the nearest chair. He opened his briefcase, retrieved his set of sales figures and said, "Sorry I'm late. Are we ready to begin?" At nods from around the table, he began his presentation. "Good news and bad news time, folks. Computer sales are up 25%, software is holding its own, and peripherals are down 25%."

Geneva Huber, the manager of the peripherals department, rose and said, "Chad, I just don't believe these figures. You know we have those new scanners and the new top speed modems. I've checked the inventory and they're so hot they're flying out the door. I can barely keep them in stock, and I don't see a decline in standard items either. I don't get it. Could there be something wrong with the reports?"

"I was surprised too, Geneva. Mariko, why don't you outline the new advertising campaign while I look over the inventory reports to see what's going on," said Chad.

Chad studied pages and pages of reports, frowning now and then, underlining a few items, and quickly making calculations on his calculator. At the close of the advertising presentation, Mariko asked, "Chad, have you found anything?"

"Yes, Mariko. Geneva is right. There is a problem with the sales report. Do you remember that we hurried to launch these new lines and skipped some of the audits? It looks like all of the new scanners and modems were coded as computer department items. I'll get these corrected and revise the reports. Shall we meet again Monday to continue with correct reports?"

Critical Thinking

1. Is it necessary to hold sales meetings as often as once a week?
2. What effect would the error in the product codes have on the company's income statement?
3. What other topics might be discussed at a weekly sales meeting?

DEPARTMENTAL SALES ON ACCOUNT

In Chapter 1, you learned to record purchases transactions for a departmental merchandising business. To have complete departmental data, MasterSport also records all sales transactions by department. MasterSport makes sales on account to individuals, clubs, leagues, and schools. It sells merchandise in two departments. The golf department sells golf equipment such as clubs, bags, balls, and carts. The tennis department sells tennis equipment including racquets, balls, bags, and nets.

MasterSport records all departmental sales on account in a sales journal. The sales journal has one debit column—Accounts Receivable Debit. The journal also has three credit columns—Sales Tax Payable Credit and special Sales Credit columns for Golf and Tennis.

The Sales Tax Payable Credit column is used to record all sales tax amounts that MasterSport collects. Most states require vendors to collect sales tax from their customers. The state in which MasterSport is located has a 5.0% sales tax. In most states, some customers are not required to pay a sales tax. Many agencies supported by local and state government and nonprofit educational institutions are exempt from paying a sales tax. For example, Swanville Schools is a tax-exempt customer of MasterSport.

MasterSport prepares sales invoices in duplicate for each sale on account. (CONCEPT: Objective Evidence) Each sales invoice shows the amount of merchandise sold by department. The customer receives the original copy of the sales invoice. The duplicate copy is the source document for journalizing the transaction. MasterSport records all departmental sales at the time of sale regardless of when payment is made. (CONCEPT: Realization of Revenue)

The realization of revenue concept states that revenue is recorded at the time goods or services are sold. A business may sell either goods or services. Cash may be received at the time of sale or an agreement may be made to receive payment at a later date. Regardless of when the business actually receives cash, the business records the sale amount in the accounting records at the time of sale. For example, a business sells office furniture for $2,000.00. The business agrees to an initial payment of $400.00 with the remaining balance to be divided in four monthly payments of $400.00 each. The business records the full $2,000.00 of revenue at the time of sale even though $1,600.00 will be paid later.

SMALL BUSINESS SPOTLIGHT

Most small businesses have the same kind of training needs as huge corporations. New employees, seasoned professionals, and executives all benefit from training throughout their careers. This includes everything from job-specific training to professional enrichment. While the needs may be the same, the budget and staffing might be quite different. Small businesses are finding solutions for their training needs within their own company and through outside sources. Small businesses frequently look to community colleges, trade groups, and professional associations for high-quality instruction. In many cases, small businesses are partnering with vendors for some of their training needs.

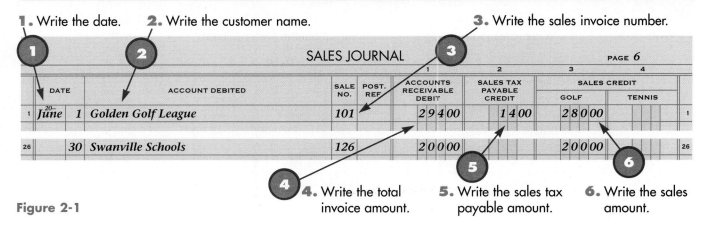

1. Write the date.   2. Write the customer name.   3. Write the sales invoice number.

4. Write the total invoice amount.   5. Write the sales tax payable amount.   6. Write the sales amount.

Figure 2-1

June 1. Sold golf equipment on account to Golden Golf League, $280.00, plus sales tax, $14.00; total, $294.00. Sales Invoice No. 101.

This transaction would be recorded in the departmental sales journal shown in Figure 2-1. The source document for this transaction is a sales invoice. *(CONCEPT: Objective Evidence)*

In the general ledger, Accounts Receivable is increased by a $294.00 debit. The amount that the customer owes represents the price of the merchandise plus the sales tax. All sales tax received is later remitted to the state in which MasterSport is located. Therefore, the liability account Sales Tax Payable is increased by a $14.00 credit. Sales—Golf is increased by a $280.00 credit. In the accounts receivable ledger, Golden Golf League is increased by a $294.00 debit.

The transaction on line 26 of the sales journal shows a transaction for a tax-exempt customer. Since Swanville Schools is an educational institution, it is not required by the state to pay sales tax.

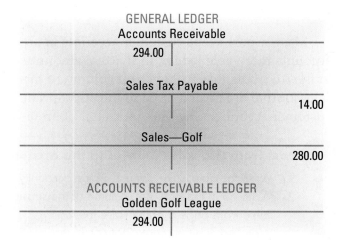

S T E P S

Record the sale in the sales journal

1. Write the date, *20--, June 1*, in the Date column.
2. Write the customer name, *Golden Golf League*, in the Account Debited column.
3. Write the sales invoice number, *101*, in the Sale No. column.
4. Write the total invoice amount, *294.00*, in the Accounts Receivable Debit column.
5. Write the credit amount, *14.00*, in the Sales Tax Payable Credit column.
6. Write the credit amount, *280.00*, in the Sales Credit Golf column.

F.Y.I.

All businesses and nonprofit entities that have employees must have a federal tax identification number. This number is used in much the same way that individuals use their social security numbers. The Internal Revenue Service identifies entities that are exempt from federal income tax by their federal identification numbers. States may require vendors to keep a written record of the federal tax identification numbers of their tax-exempt customers.

1. Write date.   **2.** Write sales journal page.   **3.** Enter amount in Debit column.

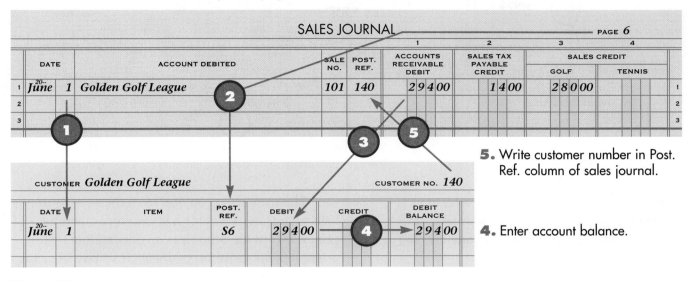

Figure 2-2

MasterSport keeps customer accounts in an accounts receivable ledger. Individual amounts in the Accounts Receivable Debit column of the sales journal are posted often to the appropriate customer accounts. The sales journal is abbreviated as S in the Post. Ref. column of the ledger accounts. Posting frequently keeps the customers' accounts up to date. Posting from the sales journal to the accounts receivable ledger is shown in Figure 2-2.

S T E P S

Post from the sales journal to the accounts receivable ledger

1. Write the date, *20--, June 1*, in the account's Date column.

2. Write *S6* in the Post. Ref. column of the subsidiary ledger account to indicate that the posting came from page 6 of the sales journal.

3. Write the debit amount, *294.00*, in the account's Debit column. This is the total amount due from the customer. It includes the price of the golf equipment and the sales tax.

4. Write the new account balance in the Debit Balance column. When the customer has an existing balance, add the amount in the Debit column to the previous balance in the Debit Balance column. Golden Golf League had no account balance before this transaction.

5. Write the customer number, *140*, in the Post. Ref. column of the sales journal to show that posting is completed for this line.

F.Y.I.

Sales taxes collected by businesses must be sent to the appropriate governmental agency. In many states, sales taxes are paid monthly. The payment is accompanied by a form that provides information such as total sales, sales tax collected, and sales exempt from sales tax.

			SALES JOURNAL							PAGE 6	
						1	2		3	4	
	DATE		ACCOUNT DEBITED	SALE NO.	POST. REF.	ACCOUNTS RECEIVABLE DEBIT	SALES TAX PAYABLE CREDIT		SALES CREDIT		
									GOLF	TENNIS	
1	June 1	Golden Golf League		101	140	2 9 4 00	1 4 00		2 8 0 00		1
2	1	Lawrence Bissell		102	110	2 3 5 2 00	1 1 2 00			2 2 4 0 00	2
3	1	Eastside Sports Center		103	120	9 0 3 00	4 3 00			8 6 0 00	3
25	30	Eastside Sports Center		125	120	2 6 2 50	1 2 50		2 5 0 00		25
26	30	Swanville Schools		126	170	2 0 0 00			2 0 0 00		26
27	30	Totals				1 9 3 3 6 50	9 0 5 55		8 9 9 0 65	9 4 4 0 30	27
28						(1115)	(2130)		(4105-1)	(4105-2)	28

1. **1.** Write date.

2. **2.** Write sales journal page.

3. **3.** Enter debit amount.

5. **5.** Write general ledger account number in parentheses

ACCOUNT **Accounts Receivable**   ACCOUNT NO. **1115**

	DATE	ITEM	POST. REF.	DEBIT	CREDIT	BALANCE	
						DEBIT	CREDIT
	June 1	Balance	✓			18 1 8 2 20	
	30		S6	1 9 3 3 6 50		37 5 1 8 70	

4. **4.** Enter account balance.

Figure 2-3

The sales journal is proved and ruled at the end of each month. Each amount column total is posted to the general ledger account named in the column heading. Posting a column total from the sales journal to a general ledger account is shown in Figure 2-3.

Post a column total from the sales journal to the general ledger

1. Write the date, *30*, in the account's Date column.

2. Write *S6* in the Post. Ref. column of the ledger account to indicate that the posting came from page 6 of the sales journal.

3. Write the amount, *19,336.50*, in the Debit column of the ledger account.

4. Add the amount in the Debit column, 19,336.50 to the previous balance of 18,182.20 to arrive at a new accounts receivable balance of *37,518.70*.

5. Write the general ledger account number, *1115*, in parentheses immediately below the column total in the sales journal to show that the amount has been posted.

REMEMBER

Proving a journal means verifying that the total debits equal the total credits. To prove a journal:

1. Add each amount column and write the total.

2. Add the column totals for all debit columns.

3. Add the column totals for all credit columns.

4. Verify that total debits and total credits are equal.

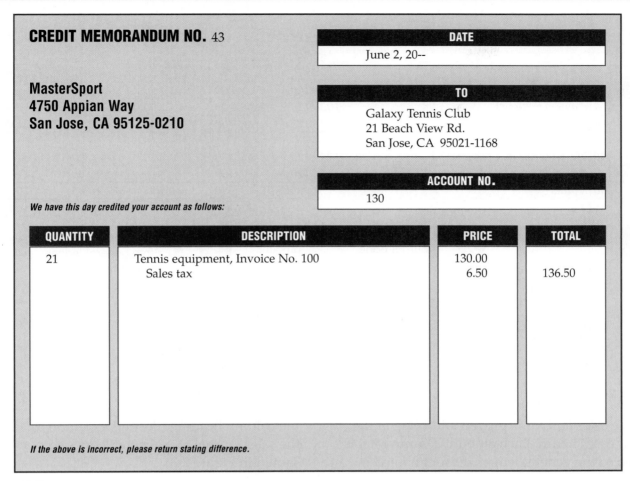

CREDIT MEMORANDUM NO. 43

MasterSport
4750 Appian Way
San Jose, CA 95125-0210

DATE
June 2, 20--

TO
Galaxy Tennis Club 21 Beach View Rd. San Jose, CA 95021-1168

ACCOUNT NO.
130

We have this day credited your account as follows:

QUANTITY	DESCRIPTION	PRICE	TOTAL
21	Tennis equipment, Invoice No. 100 Sales tax	130.00 6.50	 136.50

If the above is incorrect, please return stating difference.

Figure 2-4

Merchandising businesses normally have some merchandise returned. A customer may have received the wrong size, the wrong style, or damaged or unsatisfactory goods. The customer may return merchandise for a credit on account or a cash refund. Since the merchandise is usually returned before payment is made, the customer is generally granted credit on its account.

An allowance differs from a sales return in that credit is granted without the merchandise being returned. For example, an allowance may be given to a customer who receives less merchandise than it ordered. The allowance reduces the amount the customer has to pay.

A customer must request a sales return or allowance from the vendor. When a vendor accepts a sales return or grants an allowance, it prepares a written form stating the details of the return or allowance. The form prepared by the vendor showing the amount deducted for returns and allowances is called a **credit memorandum**. MasterSport issues a credit memorandum for each sales return it accepts and each sales allowance it grants. The credit memorandum form used by MasterSport is shown in Figure 2-4.

Many merchandising businesses also pay the shipping costs for returned merchandise. Some businesses issue special return shipping labels. In such cases, the freight company bills the shipping costs to the merchandising business. Other businesses require the customer to pay the shipping costs and then issue a credit to the customer for these costs.

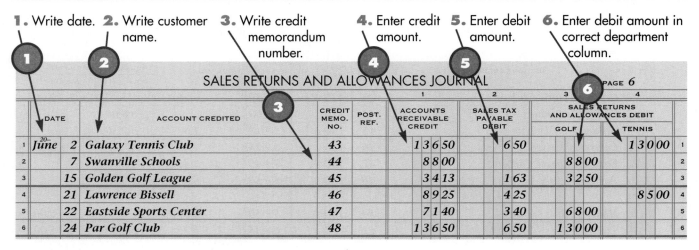

1. Write date.   2. Write customer name.   3. Write credit memorandum number.   4. Enter credit amount.   5. Enter debit amount.   6. Enter debit amount in correct department column.

SALES RETURNS AND ALLOWANCES JOURNAL PAGE 6

DATE		ACCOUNT CREDITED	CREDIT MEMO. NO.	POST. REF.	ACCOUNTS RECEIVABLE CREDIT	SALES TAX PAYABLE DEBIT	SALES RETURNS AND ALLOWANCES DEBIT GOLF	TENNIS	
June 2		Galaxy Tennis Club	43		136 50	6 50		130 00	1
	7	Swanville Schools	44		88 00		88 00		2
	15	Golden Golf League	45		34 13	1 63	32 50		3
	21	Lawrence Bissell	46		89 25	4 25		85 00	4
	22	Eastside Sports Center	47		71 40	3 40	68 00		5
	24	Par Golf Club	48		136 50	6 50	130 00		6

Figure 2-5

MasterSport records all sales returns and allowances in a sales returns and allowances journal. MasterSport's departmental sales returns and allowances journal includes a Sales Returns and Allowances Debit Golf column and a Sales Returns and Allowances Debit Tennis column.

An account that reduces a related account on a financial statement is known as a contra account. Sales—Tennis is a revenue account. Therefore, an account showing deductions from a sales account is a contra revenue account. Sales Returns and Allowances—Tennis is one of MasterSport's contra revenue accounts. Sales returns and allowances are kept in a separate account and not deducted directly from the sales account. This procedure helps the business see what proportion of the merchandise sold was returned by customers. (CONCEPT: Adequate Disclosure)

Galaxy Tennis Club for tennis equipment returned, $130.00, plus sales tax, $6.50, from Sales Invoice No. 100; total, $136.50. Credit Memorandum No. 43.

The source document for this transaction is a credit memorandum. (CONCEPT: Objective Evidence)

When a sales return is accepted or an allowance is granted, the sales tax amount is no longer due. In the general ledger, Sales Tax Payable is decreased by a $6.50 debit. Sales Returns and Allowances—Tennis is increased by a $130.00 debit. Accounts Receivable is decreased by a $136.50 credit. In the accounts receivable ledger, Galaxy Tennis Club is decreased by a $136.50 credit.

Details of the transaction involving Credit Memorandum No. 43 are recorded on line 1 of the sales returns and allowances journal shown in Figure 2-5.

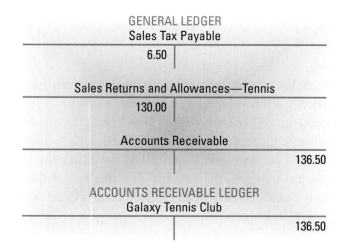

GENERAL LEDGER
Sales Tax Payable
6.50

Sales Returns and Allowances—Tennis
130.00

Accounts Receivable
136.50

ACCOUNTS RECEIVABLE LEDGER
Galaxy Tennis Club
136.50

R E M E M B E R

A contra account has a normal balance that is opposite its related account. For example, Sales—Tennis has a normal credit balance. Therefore, Sales Returns and Allowances—Tennis has a normal debit balance.

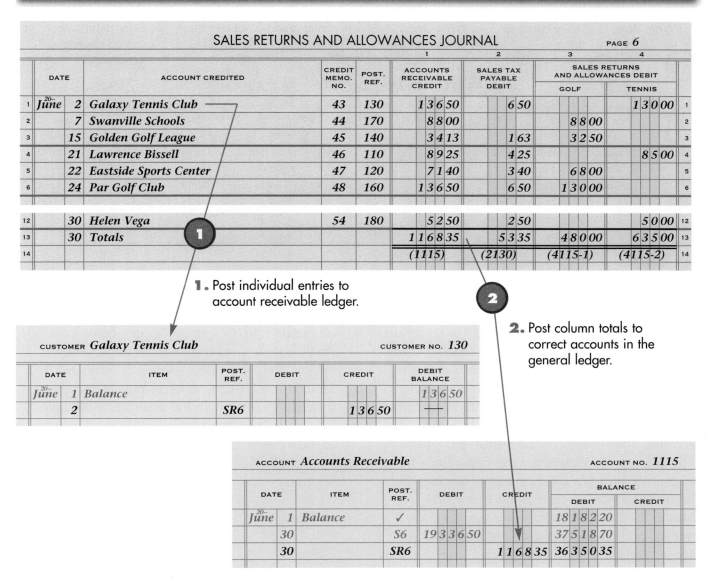

Figure 2-6

Sales returns and allowances are posted frequently to the customer's account in the accounts receivable ledger. This keeps the customer's accounts up to date. Specifically, a customer's account will be credited to reduce the amount owed to the vendor. The posting of the June 2 sales return from Galaxy Tennis Club is shown in Figure 2-6.

A sales returns and allowances journal is proved, ruled, and posted at the end of each month in the same manner as a sales journal. Each amount column total is posted to the general ledger account named in the column heading. For example, in Figure 2-6, the $1,168.35

total in the Accounts Receivable Credit column will be posted to accounts receivable in the general journal. The account number is written in parentheses below the column total in the journal to show that the amount has been posted.

When a sales return or allowance is granted after the customer has paid for the purchase, the customer account after posting may have a credit balance instead of a normal debit balance. The credit balance, a contra balance, reduces the amount to be received from a customer for future sales on account. When a three-column account form is used, a contra balance is shown by enclosing the amount in parentheses.

TERM REVIEW

credit memorandum

AUDIT YOUR UNDERSTANDING

1. What is a tax-exempt customer? Give an example.
2. For what purpose is a credit memorandum issued?

WORK TOGETHER

Journalizing and posting departmental sales on account and sales returns and allowances

The sales journal, sales returns and allowances journal, accounts receivable ledger, and partial general ledger for Hastings Beachware are provided in the *Working Papers*. Your instructor will guide you through the following examples.

3. Journalize each of the following sales on account and sales returns. The sales tax rate is 6%. Source documents are abbreviated as: sales invoice, S; credit memorandum, CM.

Sept. 1. Sold a bathing suit to Dana Brein for $30.00, plus sales tax. S012.
   10. Sold a beach umbrella to Kim Lockhart for $75.00, plus sales tax. S013.
   14. Sold bathing suits to Western High School Swim Team for $220.00. No sales tax. S014.
   15. Granted credit to Kim Lockhart for beach umbrella returned, $75.00, plus sales tax from sales invoice S013. Issued CM23.

4. Post the items that are to be posted individually.

ON YOUR OWN

Journalizing and posting departmental sales on account and sales returns and allowances

The sales journal, sales returns and allowances journal, accounts receivable ledger, and partial general ledger for Hastings Beachware are provided in the *Working Papers*. Work this problem independently.

5. Journalize each of the following sales on account and sales returns. The sales tax rate is 6%.

Sept. 18. Sold beach towel to John Muller for $12.00, plus sales tax. S015.
   24. Sold a beach umbrella to Dana Brein for $70.00, plus sales tax. S016.
   30. Granted credit to John Muller for beach towel returned, $12.00, plus sales tax from sales invoice S015. Issued CM24.

6. Post the items that are to be posted individually.
7. Prove and rule the sales journal and the sales returns and allowances journal. Post the totals to the general ledger.

DEPARTMENTAL CASH RECEIPTS

MasterSport keeps a record of all cash receipts. The sources of most cash receipts are (1) cash received from customer payments on account and (2) cash and credit card sales.

The amount of cash received when payment is made within a discount period is calculated as follows.

Sales discount:

Sales Invoice Amount	×	**Sales Discount Rate**	=	**Sales Discount**
$1,700.00	×	2%	=	$34.00

Sales tax liability reduction:

Sales Discount	×	**Sales Tax Rate**	=	**Sales Tax Reduction**
$34.00	×	5%	=	$1.70

Cash received:

Total Invoiced Amount	−	**Sales Discount**	−	**Sales Tax Reduction**	=	**Cash Received**
$1,785.00	−	$34.00	−	$1.70	=	$1,749.30

Cash Receipts on Account

Each customer is expected to pay the amount due within the credit terms agreed upon. To encourage early payment, a business may grant a deduction on the invoice amount. A deduction that a vendor allows on the invoice amount to encourage prompt payment is known as a cash discount. A cash discount on sales is called a **sales discount**. MasterSport sells on account using terms 2/10, n/30. These terms mean that a 2% sales discount may be deducted if sales on account are paid within 10 days of the invoice date. All sales on account must be paid within 30 days of the invoice date.

When a sale is made on account, the amount debited to Accounts Receivable reflects the total amount owed by the customer, including sales tax. Sales is credited only for the pre-tax selling price. An additional credit must be made to Sales Tax Payable for the sales tax liability on the total sales invoice amount. When payment is received within a discount period, the sales tax

liability is reduced by the amount of sales tax on the sales discount. Three amounts must be calculated when cash is received on account within a discount period:

1. sales discount

2. reduction in sales tax payable

3. cash received

When MasterSport receives cash on account, it prepares a receipt as the source document. (*CONCEPT: Objective Evidence*)

A percent is 1/100 of 1. Two percent can be written as 2%, .02, or 2/100.

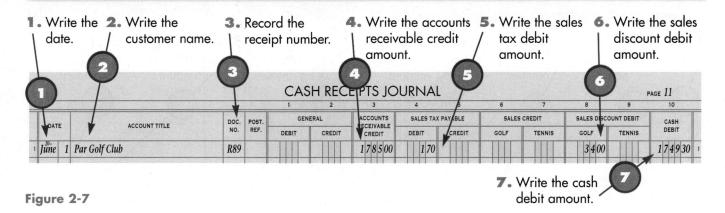

1. Write the date.

2. Write the customer name.

3. Record the receipt number.

4. Write the accounts receivable credit amount.

5. Write the sales tax debit amount.

6. Write the sales discount debit amount.

7. Write the cash debit amount.

Figure 2-7

MasterSport records all cash receipts in a cash receipts journal. The journal has five credit columns—General Credit, Accounts Receivable Credit, Sales Tax Payable Credit, Sales Credit Golf, and Sales Credit Tennis. The journal also has five debit columns—General Debit, Sales Tax Payable Debit, Sales Discount Debit Golf, Sales Discount Debit Tennis, and Cash Debit. Notice that both sales and sales discounts are recorded by department.

> June 1. Received cash on account from Par Golf Club, $1,749.30, covering Sales Invoice No. 96 for golf equipment for $1,785.00 ($1,700.00 plus sales tax, $85.00), less 2% discount, $34.00, and less sales tax, $1.70. Receipt No. 89.

Cash is increased by a $1,749.30 debit. Sales Tax Payable is decreased by a $1.70 debit, the sales tax on the sales discount amount. The contra revenue account, Sales Discount—Golf, is increased by a $34.00 debit. Using a separate account to record discounts allows the business to determine the proportion of available discounts that customers actually take. Accounts Receivable is decreased by a $1,785.00 credit. In the accounts receivable ledger, Par Golf Club is decreased by a $1,785.00 credit.

The customer's payment on account is shown in Figure 2-7. Use the following steps to make the journal entry.

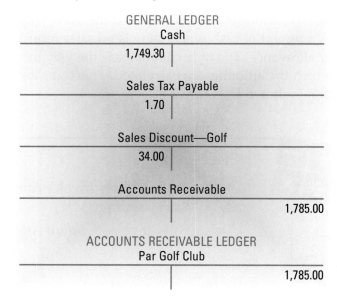

Recording the receipt of cash when the sales discount is taken

1. Write the date, 20--, June 1, in the Date column.

2. Write the customer name, Par Golf Club, in the Account Title column.

3. Record the document number, R89, in the Doc. No. column.

4. Write the credit amount, 1785.00, in the Accounts Receivable Credit column.

5. Write the debit amount, 1.70, in the Sales Tax Payable Debit column.

6. Write the debit amount, 34.00, in the Sales Discount Debit Golf column.

7. Write the debit amount, 1749.30, in the Cash Debit column.

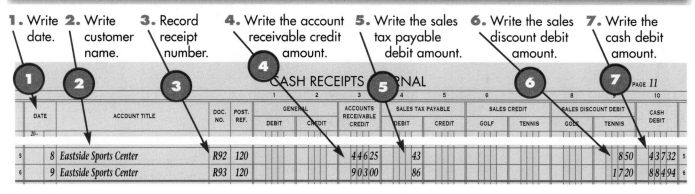

1. Write date. 2. Write customer name. 3. Record receipt number. 4. Write the account receivable credit amount. 5. Write the sales tax payable debit amount. 6. Write the sales discount debit amount. 7. Write the cash debit amount.

DATE	ACCOUNT TITLE	DOC. NO.	POST. REF.	GENERAL DEBIT	GENERAL CREDIT	ACCOUNTS RECEIVABLE CREDIT	SALES TAX PAYABLE DEBIT	SALES TAX PAYABLE CREDIT	SALES CREDIT GOLF	SALES CREDIT TENNIS	SALES DISCOUNT DEBIT GOLF	SALES DISCOUNT DEBIT TENNIS	CASH DEBIT	
20--														
8	Eastside Sports Center	R92	120			446 25	43					8 50	437 32	5
9	Eastside Sports Center	R93	120			903 00	86					17 20	884 94	6

Figure 2-8

June 8. Received cash on account from Eastside Sports Center, $437.32, covering Sales Invoice No. 97 for $525.00 ($500.00 plus sales tax, $25.00), less Credit Memorandum No. 42 for $78.75 ($75.00 plus sales tax, $3.75), less 2% discount, $8.50, and less sales tax, $0.43. Receipt No. 92.

This transaction is journalized the same way as a receipt of cash when there is no sales return or allowance. The only difference is the way in which the amounts are calculated. This transaction is shown in Figure 2-8.

Sales discounts are calculated on the amount owed at the time the invoice is paid. When a customer takes a discount after being granted a return or an allowance, the amount of the return or allowance must be deducted from the amount of the original sale *before* the discount can be calculated. To calculate the amount of cash received: (1) find the sales discount amount, (2) calculate the reduction in sales tax liability, and (3) determine the amount of cash to be received. The computation for each of these items is also shown below.

		Amount of Sale	Sales Tax	Total Receivable
	Original Sales Invoice Amount (S97)	$500.00	$25.00	$525.00
less	Sales Return (CM42)	− 75.00	− 3.75	− 78.75
equals	Sales Invoice Amount After Return	$425.00 +	$21.25 =	$446.25

Sales discount:

Sales Invoice Amount	×	**Sales Discount Rate**	=	**Sales Discount**
$425.00	×	2%	=	$8.50

Sales tax payable reduction:

Sales Discount	×	**Sales Tax Rate**	=	**Sales Tax Payable Reduction**
$8.50	×	5%	=	$0.43

Cash received:

Total Sales Amount After Return	−	**Sales Discount**	−	**Sales Tax Reduction**	=	**Cash Received**
$446.25	−	$8.50	−	$0.43	=	$437.32

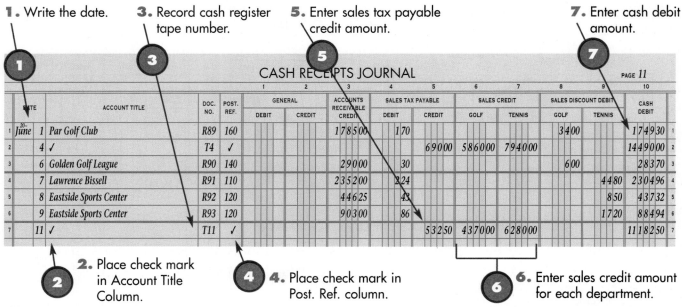

1. Write the date.

3. Record cash register tape number.

5. Enter sales tax payable credit amount.

7. Enter cash debit amount.

CASH RECEIPTS JOURNAL   PAGE 11

	DATE	ACCOUNT TITLE	DOC. NO.	POST. REF.	GENERAL DEBIT	GENERAL CREDIT	ACCOUNTS RECEIVABLE CREDIT	SALES TAX PAYABLE DEBIT	SALES TAX PAYABLE CREDIT	SALES CREDIT GOLF	SALES CREDIT TENNIS	SALES DISCOUNT DEBIT GOLF	SALES DISCOUNT DEBIT TENNIS	CASH DEBIT	
1	June 1	Par Golf Club	R89	160			1785 00	1 70				34 00		1749 30	1
2	4	√	T4	√					690 00	5860 00	7940 00			14490 00	2
3	6	Golden Golf League	R90	140			290 00	30				6 00		283 70	3
4	7	Lawrence Bissell	R91	110			2352 00	2 24					44 80	2304 96	4
5	8	Eastside Sports Center	R92	120			446 25	43					8 50	437 32	5
6	9	Eastside Sports Center	R93	120			903 00	86					17 20	884 94	6
7	11	√	T11	√					532 50	4370 00	6280 00			11182 50	7

2. Place check mark in Account Title Column.

4. Place check mark in Post. Ref. column.

6. Enter sales credit amount for each department.

Figure 2-9

MasterSport accepts cash or credit cards from its customers. An independent company or bank hired by MasterSport to process credit card sales automatically deposits the daily total of credit card sales to MasterSport's bank account. Because credit card sales result in an immediate increase in the bank account balance, credit card sales and cash sales are recorded together in the cash receipts journal.

Both cash and credit card sales are entered into a cash register. The cash register prints a receipt for the customer and internally accumulates data about total sales. At the end of each week, the cash register prints a summary of sales for the week. The summary, often referred to as a cash register tape, is identified with a T and the date. MasterSport uses the tape as the source document for cash and credit card sales. (CONCEPT: Objective Evidence)

> **June 11.** *Recorded cash and credit card sales, golf equipment, $4,370.00; tennis equipment, $6,280.00; plus sales tax, $532.50; total, $11,182.50. Cash Register Tape No. 11.*

Cash is increased by a $11,182.50 debit. Sales Tax Payable is increased by a $532.50 credit. Sales—Golf, is increased by a $4,370.00 credit and Sales—Tennis is increased by a $6,280.00 credit.

The details of Cash Register Tape No. 11 are recorded on line 7 of the cash receipts journal shown in Figure 2-9. The steps needed to record this transaction are similar to those required to record other cash receipts transactions.

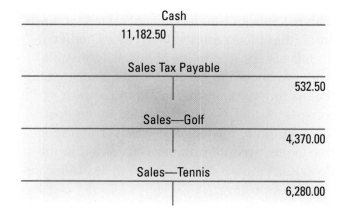

Cash	
11,182.50	

Sales Tax Payable	
	532.50

Sales—Golf	
	4,370.00

Sales—Tennis	
	6,280.00

REMEMBER

Sales transactions involving credit cards are recorded as cash sales.

CASH RECEIPTS JOURNAL PAGE 11

DATE	ACCOUNT TITLE	DOC. NO.	POST. REF.	GENERAL DEBIT	GENERAL CREDIT	ACCOUNTS RECEIVABLE CREDIT	SALES TAX PAYABLE DEBIT	SALES TAX PAYABLE CREDIT	SALES CREDIT GOLF	SALES CREDIT TENNIS	SALES DISCOUNT DEBIT GOLF	SALES DISCOUNT DEBIT TENNIS	CASH DEBIT
June 1	Par Golf Club	R89	160			1785 00	1 70				34 00		1749 30
4	✓	T4	✓					690 00	5860 00	7940 00			14490 00
6	Golden Golf League	R90	140			290 00	30				6 00		283 70
7	Lawrence Bissell	R91	110			2352 00	2 24					44 80	2304 96
8	Eastside Sports Center	R92	120			446 25	43					8 50	437 32
9	Eastside Sports Center	R93	120			903 00	86					17 20	884 94
11	✓	T11	✓					532 50	4370 00	6280 00			11182 50

CASH RECEIPTS JOURNAL PAGE 12

DATE	ACCOUNT TITLE	DOC. NO.	POST. REF.	GENERAL DEBIT	GENERAL CREDIT	ACCOUNTS RECEIVABLE CREDIT	SALES TAX PAYABLE DEBIT	SALES TAX PAYABLE CREDIT	SALES CREDIT GOLF	SALES CREDIT TENNIS	SALES DISCOUNT DEBIT GOLF	SALES DISCOUNT DEBIT TENNIS	CASH DEBIT
30	Swanville Schools	R108	170			399 00					7 98		391 02
30	✓	T30	✓					587 50	5620 00	6130 00			12337 50
30	Totals					19706 10	15 30	2621 50	24520 00	27910 00	147 00	169 00	74426 30
						(1115)	(2130)	(2130)	(4105-1)	(4105-2)	(4110-1)	(4110-2)	(1105)

1. Individual amounts are posted to the accounts receivable ledger.

2. Column totals are posted to the account named in the column heading.

Figure 2-10

Individual amounts are posted often from the cash receipts journal. Frequent postings are required to keep the customers' accounts up to date. MasterSport posts each amount written in the General Debit and Credit columns of the cash receipts journal to the general ledger. Each amount in the Accounts Receivable Credit column is also posted to the accounts receivable ledger as shown in Figure 2-10. To indicate that the posting came from page 11 of the cash receipts journal, *CR11* is recorded in the Post. Ref. column of the ledger account. The respective ledger account number is recorded in the Post. Ref. column of the journal to indicate completion of posting.

Transactions involving entries in the General Debit and Credit columns of a cash receipts journal are described in Chapter 9.

At the end of the month, the cash receipts journal is proved and ruled. Totals of the special amount columns are then posted to their respective accounts in the general ledger. The general ledger account number is written in parentheses immediately below the total. A check mark is placed in parentheses below the totals of the General Debit and Credit columns to show that the totals are not posted. MasterSport's departmental cash receipts journal, page 12, after all posting has been completed, is shown in Figure 2-10.

F.Y.I.

A growing number of businesses use computers to verify credit card transactions. This verification process protects consumers and helps prevent fraud.

Businesses post transactions affecting vendor and customer accounts often during the month so that balances of subsidiary ledger accounts are kept up to date. General ledger account balances are needed only when financial statements are prepared. Therefore, posting to general ledger accounts may be done less frequently than posting to subsidiary ledgers. However, all transactions, including special amount column totals, must be posted at the end of a fiscal period. The recommended order in which to post journals is listed as follows.

1. Sales journal

2. Sales returns and allowances journal

3. Purchases journal

4. Purchases returns and allowances journal

5. General journal

6. Cash receipts journal

7. Cash payments journal

This posting order generally places the debits and credits in the accounts in the order the transactions occurred.

GLOBAL PERSPECTIVE

INTERNATIONAL TERMS OF SALE

Terms of sale for international business are very similar to those used in the United States. However, it is important to make sure that all parties understand the terms before business is complete.

Selected international terms of sale are described below:

C.I.F. (Cost, Insurance, Freight) to the named port of import. Under this method, the seller quotes a price for the goods. The price includes insurance, all transportation, and all miscellaneous charges to the point of unloading the goods from the vessel.

F.A.S. (Free AlongSide a ship at the named U.S. port of export). Under this term, the seller quotes a price for goods that includes charges for delivery of the goods alongside a vessel at the port. The seller handles the cost of the unloading and wharf charges. All charges once goods are delivered to the vessel, including loading, ocean transportation, and insurance, are the responsibility of the buyer.

F.O.B. VESSEL (named port of export). The seller quotes a price that includes all expenses up to, and including, delivery of goods upon an overseas vessel that is provided by or for the buyer. Once the goods are loaded "on board," all subsequent charges are the sole responsibility of the buyer.

EX ("EX" means "from" the named point of origin) such as EX FACTORY. Under this term, the price quoted applies only at the point of origin, and the seller agrees to place the goods at the disposal of the buyer at the specified place on the date or within the period fixed. All other charges are the responsibility of the buyer.

Required:

Research the following terms of sale. Tell what the initials represent and what the actual terms involve.

1. F.O.B. (named port of exportation)
2. F.O.B. (named inland point of origin)
3. C. and F.

 **TERM REVIEW**

sales discount

 **AUDIT YOUR UNDERSTANDING**

1. What does 2/10, n/30 mean?

2. Why are credit card sales and cash sales recorded together in the sales journal?

 **WORK TOGETHER**

Journalizing and posting departmental cash receipts

The cash receipts journal, partial accounts receivable ledger, and partial general ledger for Shouk Imports are provided in the *Working Papers*. Shouk Imports offers credit terms of 2/10, n/30. The sales tax rate is 6%. Source documents are abbreviated as follows: receipt, R; cash register tape, T. Your instructor will guide you through the following examples.

Feb. 1. Received cash on account from Mona Andrews Design, $1,890.62 for six carpets, covering Sales Invoice No. 230 for $2,120.00 ($2,000 plus sales tax), less CM29 ($180 plus sales tax), less discount and less sales tax. R343.

7. Recorded cash and credit card sales for the week: carpeting, $2,468.00; furniture, $3,286.00; plus sales tax. T7.

12. Received a check from Bob Smits for furniture purchased on February 3. Sales invoice No. 231 had been written for $636.00 ($600.00 plus sales tax). His check was for $623.28. R344.

14. Recorded cash and credit card sales for the week: carpeting, $2,112.00; furniture, $2,653.00; plus sales tax. T14.

3. Journalize the cash receipts transactions made during February of the current year.

4. Post the items that are to be posted individually. Save your work to complete the On Your Own below.

 **ON YOUR OWN**

Journalizing and posting departmental cash receipts

Use the working papers from the Work Together above. Work this problem independently.

Feb. 19. Received a check from Joan Seymour for furniture purchased on February 12. Sales invoice No. 232 had been written for $742.00 ($700.00 plus sales tax). Her check was for $727.16. R345.

21. Recorded cash and credit card sales for the week: carpeting, $2,851.00; furniture, $3,057.00; plus sales tax. T21.

28. Recorded cash and credit card sales for the week: carpeting, $2,967.00; furniture, $2,803.00; plus sales tax. T28.

5. Journalize the cash receipts transactions made during February of the current year.

6. Post the items that are to be posted individually.

7. Prove and rule the cash receipts journal. Post the totals to the general ledger.

After completing this chapter, you can

1. Define accounting terms related to departmental sales and cash receipts.

2. Identify accounting concepts and practices related to departmental sales and cash receipts.

3. Journalize and post departmental sales on account and sales returns and allowances.

4. Journalize and post cash receipts.

EXPLORE ACCOUNTING

TRANSFER PRICING

Departmental accounting allows managers to evaluate the performance of individual departments. Some companies use departmental income from operations as a basis for rewarding effective managers. A management incentive plan could base a manager's salary on the amount of departmental income from operations, the percentage of income to net sales, or some other measure of profitability.

This type of incentive program becomes difficult to administer when a manager is responsible for a department in which the product is transferred to another department. Consider the following example.

Cement Art has two departments: design and casting. The design department creates molds used by the casting department to make a variety of cement statues, bird baths, and planters. The

casting department purchases its molds from the design department, pours cement in the molds, and sells the finished product to retail stores. The manager of each department receives a bonus equal to .05% of the department's profit on operations.

The incentive plan would seem to be a good idea. However, if the casting department is required to purchase molds from the design department at any price, the design department manager has no incentive to control production costs. Thus, management must establish policies to determine the prices of molds transferred between the departments. Setting prices for the transfer of products between the departments is known as transfer pricing. Several transfer pricing methods are available.

1. Set the price consistent with the prices charged by other suppliers of the same or similar products.

2. Set the price based on the price that the product could be sold to other companies.

3. If the product is unique, use a percentage markup. This method must include a provision for containing production costs.

REQUIRED:

With another student, assume the roles of the design and casting department managers. Assume the current cost of producing a mold is $20.00, and the mold is sold to the casting department for $25.00. The casting department adds $10.00 of other materials and labor to the product and sells the finished product to customers for $60.00. Negotiate a transfer pricing policy that provides an incentive salary for each manager. The policy should include a provision for the design manager to increase the price of a mold for an increase in production costs.

APPLICATION PROBLEM
Journalizing and posting departmental sales on account and sales returns and allowances

Breezy Outfitters is a retail shoe store with two departments: clothing and shoes. The general ledger and accounts receivable ledger are included in your *Working Papers*. The balances are recorded as of April 1 of the current year.

Transactions:

April 1. Sold shoes on account to Cherie Grecki, $93.00, plus sales tax. S63.
2. Sold clothing on account to Wade Thomas, $150.00, plus sales tax. S64.
5. Granted credit to Cherie Grecki for shoes returned, $93.00, plus sales tax from S63. CM12.
5. Sold shoes on account to Phil Kellerman, $74.00, plus sales tax. S65.
5. Sold shoes on account to Debbie Prosser, $180.00, plus sales tax. S66.
7. Sold clothing on account to Wade Thomas, $230.00, plus sales tax. S67.
10. Granted credit to Debbie Prosser for shoes returned, $80.00, plus sales tax from S66. CM13.
12. Sold clothing on account to Carole Tate, $275.00, plus sales tax. S68.
15. Granted credit to Wade Thomas for clothing returned, $140.00, plus sales tax from S67. CM14.
   Posting. Breezy Outfitters posts items individually to the accounts receivable ledger at mid-month and at the end of the month. Post the items accounted for through April 15. Post from the sales journal first and then from the sales returns and allowances journal.
17. Sold shoes on account to Cherie Grecki, $46.00, plus sales tax. S69.
19. Sold clothing on account to the Archibald School District, $463.00. No sales tax. S70.
24. Granted credit to Carole Tate for clothing returned, $58.00, plus sales tax from S68. CM15.
27. Sold clothing on account to Dana Eggers, $98.00, plus sales tax. S71.
30. Sold shoes on account to Ben Nesbitt, $124.00, plus sales tax. S72.
   Posting. Post the items individually to the accounts receivable ledger.

Instructions:

1. Journalize the transactions for April of the current year. Use page 4 of a sales journal and page 4 of a sales returns and allowances journal. The sales tax rate is 5%. Source documents are abbreviated as follows: credit memorandum, CM; sales invoice, S.

2. Prove and rule the sales journal. Post the totals to the general ledger.

3. Prove and rule the sales returns and allowances journal. Post the totals to the general ledger.

APPLICATION PROBLEM
Journalizing and posting departmental cash receipts

Chilleme, Inc., has two departments: tables and chairs. The general ledger and accounts receivable ledger are provided in your *Working Papers*. The balances are recorded as of June 1 of the current year.

Transactions:

June 1. Received payment from Wayne Miller for chairs purchased on account. Sales invoice No. 147 had been written for $157.50 ($150.00 plus sales tax). Because Miller paid within the discount period, his check was for $154.35 ($157.50 less discount and less sales tax). R110.

June 2. Amy Cannon sent a payment for two tables she had purchased on account. The payment was made within the discount period. Sales invoice No. 148 was written for $388.50 ($370.00 plus sales tax). Cannon's check was for $380.73 ($388.50 less discount and less sales tax). R111.

6. Bob Witt sent a check for $210.00 for chairs purchased on account. He did not pay within the discount period. Sales invoice number 135 had been written for $210.00 ($200.00 plus sales tax). R112.

6. The cash register tapes showed that cash and credit card sales for the week had been: tables, $6,240.00; chairs, $5,060.00; plus sales tax. (Assume sales tax was paid on all cash and credit card sales.) T6.

11. Dawn Sanzone sent a check for $514.50 for a table purchased on June 1. Sales invoice No. 149 had been written for $525.00 ($500.00 plus sales tax). She took the discount and accompanying sales tax. R113.

13. The cash register tapes showed that weekly cash and credit card sales had been: tables, $5,640.00; chairs, $3,570.00; plus sales tax. (Assume sales tax was paid on all cash and credit card sales.) T13.

    Posting. Chilleme, Inc., posts items individually to the accounts receivable ledger at mid-month and at the end of the month. Post the items accounted for through June 15.

17. Received payment from Amy Cannon for a table purchased on June 9. Sales invoice No. 150, written for $336.00 ($320.00 plus sales tax), was paid for with a $329.28 check ($336.00 less discount and less sales tax). R114.

18. David Ring sent a check for $442.47 for a table purchased on June 9. Sales invoice No. 151 was written for $451.50 ($430.00 plus sales tax). He subtracted the discount and accompanying sales tax. R115.

20. The cash register tapes showed that weekly cash and credit card sales had been: tables, $7,110.00; chairs, $4,850.00; plus sales tax. (Assume sales tax was paid on all cash and credit card sales.) T20.

24. A check for $771.75 was received from Joe Ricardo for eight chairs and a table purchased on June 15. Sales invoice No. 152 was written for $892.50 ($400.00 plus $20.00 sales tax for the chairs; and $450.00 plus $22.50 sales tax for the table). On June 16, Joe returned two chairs and received a credit memorandum for $100.00 plus $5.00 sales tax. He also took the discount of $15.00 and accompanying sales tax of $0.75. R116.

27. Cash and credit card sales for the week consisted of tables, $6,890.00; chairs, $5,150.00; plus sales tax. (Assume sales tax was paid on all cash and credit card sales.) T27.

30. Recorded cash and credit card sales on the last day of the month, even if a full week has not passed. Chilleme, Inc., recorded its cash and credit card sales for the period June 28–30: tables, $3,200.00; chairs, $2,980.00; plus tax. (Assume sales tax was paid on all cash and credit card sales.) T30.

    Posting. Post the items individually to the accounts receivable ledger.

Instructions:

1. Journalize the transactions for June of the current year. Use page 18 of a cash receipts journal. Chilleme, Inc., offers credit terms of 2/10, n/30. The sales tax rate is 5%. Source documents are abbreviated as follows: receipt, R; cash register tape, T.

2. Prove and rule the cash receipts journal. Post the totals to the general ledger.

MASTERY PROBLEM

Journalizing departmental sales, sales returns and allowances, and cash receipts

McKinney's Clothing Store has two departments: Men's Clothing and Women's Clothing.

Transactions:

June 1. Sold men's clothing on account to Jason Gunn, $660.00, plus sales tax. S134.
3. Sold men's clothing on account to Kara Wilder, $430.00, plus sales tax. S135.
4. Received cash on account from William Hodges, covering S132 for women's clothing ($360.00 plus sales tax), less discount and less sales tax. R83.
4. Recorded cash and credit card sales: men's clothing, $2,280.00; women's clothing, $2,520.00; plus sales tax. (Sales tax was paid on all cash and credit card sales.) T4.
6. Received cash on account from Robin Vaughn, covering S131 for men's clothing ($640.00 plus sales tax), less discount and less sales tax. R84.
8. Granted credit to Kara Wilder for men's clothing returned, $95.00, plus sales tax, from S135. CM28.
9. Kara Wilder sent a check covering S133 for women's clothing ($399.00 plus sales tax), less discount and less sales tax. R85.
11. Received cash on account from Jason Gunn, covering S134 for men's clothing ($660.00 plus sales tax), less discount and less sales tax. (Sales tax was paid on all cash and credit card sales.) R86.
11. Sold men's clothing on account to Paul Reed, $840.00, plus sales tax. S136.
11. Cash and credit card sales for the week consisted of men's clothing, $4,720.00; women's clothing, $5,030.00; plus sales tax. (Sales tax was paid on all cash and credit card sales.) T11.
13. Received cash on account from Kara Wilder, covering S135 for men's clothing ($430.00 plus sales tax), less CM28 ($95.00 plus sales tax), less discount and less sales tax. R87.
15. Linda Baron purchased women's clothing on account, $428.00, plus sales tax. S137.
17. Sold men's clothing on account to Robin Vaughn, $240.00, plus sales tax. S138.
18. Recorded cash and credit card sales: men's clothing, $5,130.00; women's clothing, $4,980.00; plus sales tax. (Sales tax was paid on all cash and credit card sales.) T18.
21. Received a check from Paul Reed, covering S136 for men's clothing ($840.00 plus sales tax), less discount and less sales tax. R88.
21. Granted credit to Linda Baron for women's clothing returned, $67.00, plus sales tax, from S137. CM29.
25. Cash and credit card sales for the week consisted of men's clothing, $4,750.00; women's clothing, $4,910.00; plus sales tax. T25.
28. Royalton Schools purchased women's clothing on account, $760.00; no sales tax. S139.
30. Recorded cash and credit card sales: men's clothing, $2,980.00; women's clothing, $3,110.00; plus sales tax. (Sales tax was paid on all cash and credit card sales.) T30.

Instructions:

1. Journalize the transactions completed during June of the current year. Use page 6 of a sales journal and a sales returns and allowances journal and page 11 of a cash receipts journal. McKinney's offers its customers terms of 2/10, n/30. The sales tax rate is 5%. Source documents are abbreviated as follows: credit memorandum, CM; receipt, R; sales invoice, S; cash register tape, T.

2. Prove and rule the sales journal and the sales returns and allowances journal.

3. Prove and rule the cash receipts journal.

CHALLENGE PROBLEM
Journalizing departmental sales, sales returns and allowances, and cash receipts

Assume that McKinney's Clothing Store, the business described in Mastery Problem 2-3, is located in a state that does not charge a retail sales tax. Also assume that McKinney's offers customers terms of 1/10, n/30. The journals with the proper headings are provided in your *Working Papers*.

Instructions:

1. Journalize the transactions given in Mastery Problem 2-3 without sales tax. Use page 6 of a sales journal and a sales returns and allowances journal and page 11 of a cash receipts journal.

2. Prove and rule the journals.

INTERNET ACTIVITY

Point your browser to
http://accounting.swpco.com
Choose **Advanced Course**,
choose **Activities**, and complete
the activity for Chapter 2.

Applied Communication

Research the sales tax laws in your state. Write a short report that answers the following questions:
1. What is the tax rate?
2. What goods and services are taxed?
3. Who is exempt from paying the sales tax?
4. How often is the sales tax liability paid to the state?

Cases for Critical Thinking

Case 1

Outdoor Adventures specializes in hiking, camping, and fishing gear. All accounting records are kept on a departmental basis. When a customer returns merchandise or receives an allowance, a journal entry is made debiting the appropriate sales account and crediting Accounts Receivable and the customer account. Do you agree or disagree with this accounting procedure? Why?

Case 2

Ogden's, Inc., sells a complete line of hardware products. To encourage early payment for sales on account, it offers a sales discount. When Ogden receives cash on account within a discount period, a sales discount amount and a sales tax on the discount amount are deducted from the invoice amount. The manager suggests that the business not record any sales tax for sales on account at the time of sale. Sales tax would be recorded only at the end of the fiscal period or when sales tax is due. The manager believes that this procedure would be easier and take less time because a sales tax would not need to be figured each time a sales discount is calculated. The accountant disagrees with the manager's suggestion. With whom do you agree? Why?

AUTOMATED ACCOUNTING

RECORDING ENTRIES FOR SALES AND CASH RECEIPTS USING SPECIAL JOURNALS

Recording Departmental Sales and Cash Receipts

Recording departmental sales are similar to recording any type of sale. The sales are recorded at the time of sale regardless of when payment is received. Departmental sales and cash receipts transactions are analyzed in this chapter.

Sales on Account

When recording departmental sales, each sales account will have a separate account based on the department. MasterSport uses a separate sales account for each of its two departments—golf and tennis. Sales on account transactions are recorded in a sales journal.

June 1, 20--.
Sold golf equipment on account to Golden Golf League, $280.00, plus tax, $14; total, $294.00. Sales Invoice No. 101.

The journal entry to record this transaction is entered on the sales

journal screen as shown in Figure AA2-1.

The transaction includes applying a credit to the sales—golf account. The automated accounting system automatically applies a debit to Accounts Receivable but you must specify the customer for which the sale was made. Other accounts may be affected.

Sales Returns and Allowances

Sales return and allowance transactions are recorded in the general journal.

June 2, 20--.
Granted credit to Galaxy Tennis Club for tennis equipment returned, $130.00, plus sales tax, $6.50, from Sales Invoice No. 100; total, $136.50. Credit Memorandum No. 43.

The journal entry to record this transaction is entered on the general journal screen. The transaction includes making a debit to

Sales Returns and Allowances and applying a credit to Accounts Receivable for the specific customer. Other accounts may be affected.

Cash Receipts on Account

Cash receipts transactions are recorded in a cash receipts journal.

June 1, 20--.
Received cash on account from Par Golf Club, $1,749.30, covering Sales Invoice No. 96 for golf equipment for $1,785.00 ($1,700.00 plus sales tax, $85.00), less 2% discount, $34, and less sales tax, $1.70. Receipt No. 89.

The journal entry to record this transaction is entered on the cash receipts journal screen. The transaction includes applying a credit entry to the Accounts Receivable account. An automatic debit is made to Cash by the automated accounting system. Other accounts may be affected. When there is a credit memorandum for a sales invoice, it is important to deduct this from the total amount of the invoice before calculating the discount.

Cash and Credit Card Sales

June 4, 20--.
Recorded cash and credit card sales: golf equipment, $5,860.00; tennis equipment, $7,940.00; plus sales tax, $690.00; total, $14,490.00. Cash Register Tape No. 4.

Journal Entries

General Journal	Purchases	Cash Payments	Sales	Cash Receipts

Date	Refer.	Sales Cr Golf	Sales Cr Tennis	Sales Tax Credit	A.R. Debit	Customer
06/01/02	S101	280.00		14.00	294.00	Golden Golf League
06/01/02	S102					

Post   Delete   Close   Help   Insert   Chart of Accounts

Figure AA2-1

AUTOMATED ACCOUNTING

The journal entry to record this transaction is entered in the cash receipts journal. The transaction includes applying a credit to the sales account. An automatic debit is made by the automated accounting system to Cash. Other accounts may be affected.

Processing Journal Entries

After all transactions have been recorded in the journals and posted to the ledgers, reports should be generated. A general journal report, sales journal report, and cash receipts journal report are displayed, verified for accuracy, printed, and filed for future reference.

AUTOMATING APPLICATION PROBLEM 2-1

Instructions:

1. Load *Automated Accounting* 7.0 or higher software.

2. Select database A02-1 (Advanced Course Problem 2-1) from the accounting template disk.

3. Select File from the menu bar and choose the Save As menu command. Key the path to the drive and directory that contains your data files. Save the database with a file name of XXX021 (where XXX are your initials).

4. Access Problem Instructions through the Help menu (7.0) or Browser tool (8.0). Read the Problem Instruction screen.

5. Key the transactions listed on page 56.

6. Exit the Automated Accounting software.

AUTOMATING APPLICATION PROBLEM 2-2

Instructions:

1. Load *Automated Accounting* 7.0 or higher software.

2. Select database A02-2 (Advanced Course Problem 2-2) from the accounting template disk.

3. Select File from the menu bar and choose the Save As menu command. Key the path to the drive and directory that contains your data files. Save the database with a file name of XXX022 (where XXX are your initials).

4. Access Problem Instructions through the Help menu (7.0) or Browser tool (8.0). Read the Problem Instruction screen.

5. Key the transactions listed on page 56.

6. Exit the Automated Accounting software.

AUTOMATING MASTERY PROBLEM 2-3

Instructions:

1. Load *Automated Accounting* 7.0 or higher software.

2. Select database A02-3 (Advanced Course Problem 2-3) from the accounting textbook template disk.

3. Select File from the menu bar and choose the Save As menu command. Key the path to the drive and directory that contains your data files. Save the database with a file name of XXX023 (where XXX are your initials).

4. Access Problem Instructions through the Help menu (7.0) or Browser tool (8.0). Read the Problem Instruction screen.

5. Key the transactions listed on page 58.

6. Exit the Automated Accounting software.

3

Calculating and Recording Departmental Payroll Data

AFTER STUDYING CHAPTER 3, YOU WILL BE ABLE TO:

1. Define accounting terms related to a departmental payroll system.

2. Identify accounting concepts and practices related to a departmental payroll system.

3. Maintain employee benefits records and calculate employee earnings.

4. Complete payroll records.

5. Journalize payroll transactions.

Employees are an essential element of the business world. Businesses depend on competent employees to operate successfully. Employees provide services to a business in exchange for money. The money paid for employee services is called a **salary**. Federal, state, and local laws require employers to keep accurate records of the money paid to employees and of other payments related to employee services. Payroll records are maintained for the business and for each employee. The actual payroll system used differs among businesses. A business protects itself by keeping complete and accurate payroll records of all required information.

The period covered by a salary payment is called a **pay period**. The total amount earned by all employees for a pay period is called **payroll**. In addition to salaries, a business must pay taxes based on the payroll. Taxes based on the payroll of a business are called **payroll taxes**. Employers are required by law to withhold certain payroll taxes from employee salaries each pay period.

Periodically, employers must pay government agencies all payroll taxes withheld from employee salaries as well as the employer payroll taxes. A business must also provide a yearly report to each employee showing the total salary earned and the total taxes withheld. The yearly report is provided to each employee on Form W-2. Businesses must distribute this form to their employees by January 31 reporting earnings and amounts withheld for the previous calendar year. Therefore, a business must keep records of each employee's earnings, amounts withheld, and net amount paid. Payroll records also must show the total amount of payroll taxes that a business must pay.

ACCOUNTING
IN YOUR CAREER

ARE COMMISSIONS AN INCENTIVE?

Fashion Furniture began as a small local furniture store. Over the years, however, the store has expanded its merchandise lines and added new departments for carpeting and computer and home entertainment furnishings. The founder and president of the company, Ben Altman, has always believed that commissions on sales provide an incentive to sell aggressively.

Today, sales associates are assigned to one of the three departments. All associates are paid a base salary of 150% of minimum wage plus 2% commission on the assigned department's total monthly sales. It is not unusual for a department to have more than $50,000 sales in a month. Associates are cross-trained for all departments' merchandise and spend as much as 40% of their time selling the merchandise of other departments.

Nancy Schirmer has just begun working for Fashion Furniture as a payroll and benefit analyst. When she met with the human resources department, she learned that the company experienced a great deal of employee turnover, even though benefits were very good and the commissions often provided employees with salaries higher than most retail furniture stores did. In meeting with the managers of the departments, she discovers that managers do not think that the sales associates work particularly hard at promoting sales for their assigned departments.

Nancy concludes that the compensation plan that worked so well for the one-department store when it was founded is no longer achieving its intended outcomes. As a result, she begins her analysis to prepare a recommendation for a new incentive plan.

Critical Thinking

1. Why don't the commissions encourage employees to promote the sales of their assigned departments?
2. How could the plan be changed to provide the desired incentives?
3. What would be the effect if commissions were to increase substantially under a new plan?

EMPLOYEE BENEFITS SCHEDULE

| | **MasterSport Employee Benefits Schedule** | | | |
| | **1** | **2** | **3** | **4** |
Benefits	**Earned After 12 Months**	**Biweekly After 12 Months**	**Minimum Time Blocks**	**Maximum Carry Over**
Vacation time hours	40	4	4	120
Sick leave time hours	0	2	1	80
Personal leave time hours	0	1	1	24

Figure 3-1

MasterSport's payroll system shows the amount of employee benefits, salaries, and withholdings for each employee and each department. Payments to employees for nonworking hours and to insurance and retirement programs are called **employee benefits**. Most businesses provide employee benefits as a reward for continuous service. Common benefits include vacation time, sick leave time, and personal leave time with pay after a period of continuous employment. Employee benefits may also include employer payments for health insurance and retirement. The number and type of employee benefits vary among businesses. Regardless of the type and number, records must show each employee's benefits earned, used, and available. MasterSport's employee benefits, shown in Figure 3-1, include vacation time, sick leave time, and personal leave time.

Vacation Time

MasterSport pays its employees every two weeks. A two-week pay period is referred to as a biweekly pay period. MasterSport's employees are entitled to one week (40 hours) of paid vacation time after completing one full year of employment. Beginning with the second year of employment, employees earn four paid vacation hours each biweekly pay period. Vacation time may be taken in blocks of at least four hours up to the maximum number of hours accumulated. Employees who do not use all of their accumu-

lated vacation hours in one year may carry over the unused hours to the next year. Each employee may accumulate up to three weeks (120 hours) of paid vacation time.

Sick Leave Time

Beginning with the second year of employment, MasterSport's employees accumulate two paid sick leave hours each biweekly pay period. Sick leave time must be taken in blocks of at least 1 hour up to the maximum number of hours accumulated. Sick leave time may accumulate to a maximum of 80 hours.

Personal Leave Time

Beginning with the second year of employment, MasterSport's employees accumulate one paid personal leave hour each biweekly pay period. Personal leave is to be used for required time away from business for personal reasons. Personal leave time must be taken in blocks of at least 1 hour and cannot exceed 8 hours at a time. Personal leave time may accumulate to a maximum of 24 hours.

Employee benefits, both financial and nonfinancial, add value to jobs. Companies often add employee benefits to compete for the best workers and to keep productive employees.

1. Write heading information.

2. Enter beginning hours available.

3. Record hours earned.

4. Enter hours used.

5. Compute accumulated hours available at end of pay period.

6. Carry hours available from previous pay period to the next pay period.

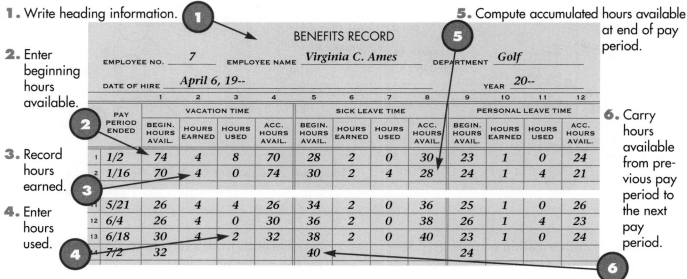

BENEFITS RECORD

EMPLOYEE NO. _7_   EMPLOYEE NAME _Virginia C. Ames_   DEPARTMENT _Golf_

DATE OF HIRE _April 6, 19--_   YEAR _20--_

		VACATION TIME				SICK LEAVE TIME				PERSONAL LEAVE TIME		
	1	2	3	4	5	6	7	8	9	10	11	12
PAY PERIOD ENDED	BEGIN. HOURS AVAIL.	HOURS EARNED	HOURS USED	ACC. HOURS AVAIL.	BEGIN. HOURS AVAIL.	HOURS EARNED	HOURS USED	ACC. HOURS AVAIL.	BEGIN. HOURS AVAIL.	HOURS EARNED	HOURS USED	ACC. HOURS AVAIL.
1 1/2	74	4	8	70	28	2	0	30	23	1	0	24
2 1/16	70	4	0	74	30	2	4	28	24	1	4	21
11 5/21	26	4	4	26	34	2	0	36	25	1	0	26
12 6/4	26	4	0	30	36	2	0	38	26	1	4	23
13 6/18	30	4	2	32	38	2	0	40	23	1	0	24
14 7/2	32				40				24			

Figure 3-2

Detailed information about each employee's benefits is maintained in a benefits record. A benefits record summarizes total benefits earned, used, and available at the end of each pay period. This summary information is used to prepare the benefits authorization form for the next pay period. A partial benefits record for Virginia Ames is shown in Figure 3-2.

MasterSport keeps its benefits records on printed sheets. One sheet is used for each employee. Each sheet covers a calendar year. Since a biweekly payroll system has 26 pay periods in a calendar year, each employee's benefits record has 26 lines. One line summarizes employee benefits for each pay period. Accumulated employee benefits available at the end of one calendar year are brought forward and recorded on the next year's benefits record.

S T E P S Prepare a benefits record

At the beginning of the year:

1. Write employee number, *7*; name, *Virginia C. Ames*; department, *Golf*; date of employment, *April 6, 19--*; and current year, *20--*.

2. Enter accumulated hours available from the last pay period of the previous year in the Begin. Hours Avail. columns 1, 5, and 9 for vacation, *74*; sick leave, *28*; and personal leave, *23*.

Each payroll period:

3. Enter the hours earned for each benefit in the Hours Earned columns 2, 6, and 10.

4. Record the hours used for each benefit in the Hours Used columns 3, 7, and 11. The benefits authorization form shown in Figure 3-3 is used to determine the hours used.

5. Compute the accumulated hours available at the end of a pay period for each benefit.

6. Carry forward accumulated hours available at the end of one pay period as the beginning hours available for the next pay period.

Vacation Time Beginning Hours Available	+	Vacation Time Hours Earned	−	Vacation Hours Used	=	Vacation Time Accumulated Hours Available
74	+	4	−	8	=	70

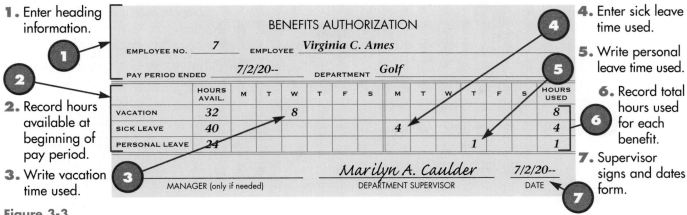

1. Enter heading information.

2. Record hours available at beginning of pay period.

3. Write vacation time used.

4. Enter sick leave time used.

5. Write personal leave time used.

6. Record total hours used for each benefit.

7. Supervisor signs and dates form.

Figure 3-3

A benefits authorization form is used to record and authorize employee benefits. MasterSport pays employee benefits biweekly for 80 hours of continuous work. Employee benefits are not paid for hours in excess of 80 hours per pay period.

At the beginning of the pay period, the accounting department records employee benefits in the Hours Avail. column of a benefits authorization form. The accounting department obtains this information from the Acc. Hours Avail. columns of the benefits record.

Each employee's benefits authorization form for the pay period is forwarded to the appropriate department supervisor or store manager. The benefits authorization form for Virginia Ames for the pay period ending 7/2/20-- is shown in Figure 3-3.

The department supervisor or store manager records employee benefits hours used on the benefits authorization form as they are used during each pay period. Sales clerks and accounting department employees must have their employee benefits authorized by their department supervisor. Department supervisors must have their employee benefits authorized by the store manager. At the end of the pay period, the completed benefits authorization forms are returned to the accounting department. The data from this form are used to update the benefits record.

S T E P S   Prepare a benefits authorization form

Steps completed by the accounting department:

1. Enter employee number, *7*; name, *Virginia C. Ames*; pay period ended, *7/2/20--*; and employee's department, *Golf*.

2. Record the number of hours of benefits available at the beginning of the pay period: *32* hours vacation, *40* hours sick leave, and *24* hours personal leave.

Steps completed by department supervisor or store manager:

3. Write vacation time used, *8* hours on Wednesday of the first week.

4. Enter sick leave used, *4* hours on Monday of the second week.

5. Write personal leave used, *1* hour on Thursday of the second week.

6. Record the total hours used for each benefit during the pay period, *8* hours vacation, *4* hours sick leave, and *1* hour personal leave.

7. Sign and date the form, *Marilyn A. Caulder, 7/2/20--*, and forward benefits authorization to the accounting department.

REMEMBER

For each benefit, beginning hours available plus hours earned minus hours used equals accumulated hours available.

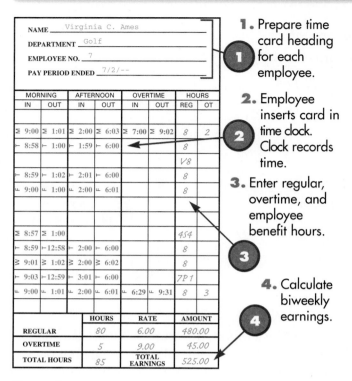

1. Prepare time card heading for each employee.

2. Employee inserts card in time clock. Clock records time.

3. Enter regular, overtime, and employee benefit hours.

4. Calculate biweekly earnings.

Figure 3-4

MasterSport pays an hourly salary biweekly to sales clerks and accounting department employees. MasterSport's biweekly pay period is 80 hours consisting of two regular 40-hour work weeks. The store is open six days a week. However, employees usually work only a five-day week of 40 hours. Days worked during a week vary so that enough employees are available each day. For example, one employee may work Monday through Friday while another employee may work Tuesday through Saturday.

Employee pay rates are usually stated as a rate per hour, day, week, month, or year. The pay rate may also be based on pieces produced per unit of time. The pay rate for MasterSport's sales clerks and accounting employees is stated as an hourly rate.

Sales clerks and accounting employees use a time clock to record their hours worked. The time card for Virginia Ames for the pay period ended July 2 is shown in Figure 3-4. All time worked in excess of 8 hours in any one day is considered overtime. Employees are paid 1-1/2 times the regular rate for overtime hours.

Prepare a payroll time card

Step completed by accounting department before the pay period begins:

1. Prepare payroll time card heading for each employee for each pay period. Heading includes employee name, department, employee number, and date of end of pay period.

Step completed by each employee:

2. Insert payroll time card in the time clock each time the employee arrives at work or leaves work. When the payroll time card is inserted, the time clock stamps the time on the card. At the end of the pay period, all time cards are taken to the accounting department.

Steps completed by accounting department at the end of the biweekly pay period:

3. Enter the regular hours, overtime hours, and authorized employee benefit hours on the payroll time cards. The employee benefits hours are shown by the first letter of the benefit written next to the hours. Ms. Ames' time card, shows *V8* written in the Hours Reg column for Wednesday of the first week. Ms. Ames gets credit for 8 regular hours for the day even though the hours represented vacation time. *S4* is written next to the 4 regular hours worked on Monday of the second week to show that 4 hours were used for sick leave time. *P1* is written next to the 7 regular hours worked on Thursday of the second week to show that 1 hour was used for personal leave time.

4. Calculate total biweekly earnings. Add the Hours Reg column and enter the total, *80*. Add the Hours OT column and enter the total, *5*. Add the regular and overtime hours and enter the total, *85*, as the Total Hours. Enter the pay rates, *6.00* per hour regular and *9.00* per hour overtime ($6.00 regular pay rate x 1.5). Calculate the regular salary, *480.00* (80 hours x $6.00 per hour), and the overtime, *45.00* (5 hours x $9.00 per hour). Add the regular and overtime amounts to determine total earnings, *525.00*.

COMMISSIONS RECORD

COMMISSIONS RECORD

EMPLOYEE NO. *3* EMPLOYEE NAME *Marilyn A. Caulder*

COMMISSION RATE *1%* MONTH *June* YEAR *20--*

DEPT. *Golf* REGULAR BIWEEKLY SALARY *$450.00*

Sales			
Sales on Account		$ *8,990.65*	
Cash and Credit Card Sales		*24,520.00*	
Total Sales		$ *33,510.65*	
Less: Sales Discounts	$ *147.00*		
Sales Returns and Allowances	*480.00*	*627.00*	
Net Sales			$ *32,883.65*
Commission on Net Sales			$ *328.84*

1. Record heading information.

2. Calculate employee commission.

Figure 3-5

The basic salary may be supplemented by other types of earnings. For example, an employee may receive commissions, cost-of-living adjustments, a share of profits, or a bonus.

STEPS: Prepare a commissions record

1. Record the employee number, employee name, commission rate, month, year, department, and regular biweekly salary at the top of the form.
2. Calculate the commission. June commissions for Marilyn A. Caulder are calculated as shown below.

At MasterSport, department supervisors are paid a regular biweekly salary. They are not paid for overtime hours. However, to encourage increased sales, the supervisors are paid a 1% commission on the department's monthly net sales.

The store manager is paid a regular biweekly salary and receives no salary for overtime hours. The store manager also earns an annual bonus based on the sales record for both departments.

Commissions for the previous month's net sales are included with the first biweekly pay period of a month. A commissions record, Figure 3-5, is used to calculate each department supervisor's commission.

A	Sales on account (from sales journal)		$ 8,990.65
+	Cash and credit card sales (from cash receipts journal)		24,520.00
=	Total sales		$33,510.65
	Total sales		$33,510.65
−	Sales Discount (from cash receipts journal)	$147.00	
−	Sales Returns & Allowances (from sales returns & allowances journal)	480.00	627.00
=	Net sales		$32,883.65
	Net sales		$32,883.65
×	Commission rate (1%)		.01
=	Commission		$ 328.84

TERMS REVIEW

salary

payroll

payroll taxes

pay period

employee benefits

1. Why are payroll taxes reported as separate items in accounting records and financial statements?
2. Why do most businesses provide employee benefits?
3. If an employee of MasterSport has a regular salary rate of $8.00 and works 5 hours of overtime during the biweekly period, what is the employee's overtime pay for the period?

WORK TOGETHER

Preparing a benefits record; calculating employee earnings; preparing a commissions record

A benefits record, employee earnings forms, and a commissions record used by Best Value Co., are provided in the *Working Papers*. Your instructor will guide you through the following examples.

4. Susan Fulton earns the following employee benefits each biweekly pay period: 4 hours of vacation, 2 hours of sick leave, and 1 hour of personal leave. Use the information below to prepare Susan's benefits record for the first two pay periods of the current year. Susan's employee number is 4, she works in the Hardware department, and she was hired on November 1, 20--.

Pay Period Ended	Regular Hours	Beginning Employee Benefits Available			Employee Benefits Used During Pay Period		
1/2	80	V96	S90	P15	V16	S0	P2
1/16	80	—	—	—	V8	S4	P0

V = Vacation time; S = Sick leave time; P = Personal leave time

5. The following information for two employees is taken from the time cards. On the employee earnings forms provided, calculate the amount of regular, overtime, and total earnings for each employee. Overtime hours are paid at 1-1/2 times the regular rate.

Employee Number	Hours Worked Regular	Overtime	Regular Rate
1	80	5	$8.75
2	80	4	7.00

6. Prepare a commissions record for John Balderas, Supervisor of the Hardware department, for January of the current year. Mr. Balderas, Employee No. 2, is paid a biweekly salary of $1,200.00 and receives a monthly commission of 1% of net sales. Commissions for the previous month are paid in the first pay period of the current month. Accounting records for the Hardware department for the month ended January 31 of the current year are as follows: sales on account, $10,348.00; cash and credit card sales, $15,523.00; sales discount, $179.00; sales returns and allowances, $2,039.00.

Preparing a benefits record; calculating employee earnings; preparing a commissions record

A benefits record, employee earnings forms, and a commissions record used by Best Value Co., are provided in the *Working Papers*. Work independently to complete the following instructions.

7. Keith Parker earns the following employee benefits each biweekly pay period: 4 hours of vacation, 2 hours of sick leave, and 1 hour of personal leave. Use the information below to prepare Keith's benefits record for the first two pay periods of the current year. Keith's employee number is 12, he works in the Paint department, and he was hired on June 1, 19--.

Pay Period Ended	Regular Hours	Beginning Employee Benefits Available			Employee Benefits Used During Pay Period		
1/2	80	V104	S96	P26	V24	S0	P4
1/16	80	—	—	—	V8	S8	P0

V = Vacation time; S = Sick leave time; P = Personal leave time

8. The following information for two employees is taken from the time cards. On the employee earnings forms provided, calculate the amount of regular, overtime, and total earnings for each employee. Overtime hours are paid at 1-1/2 times the regular rate.

Employee Number	Hours Worked Regular	Overtime	Regular Rate
3	80	6	$9.25
4	80	4	7.50

9. Prepare a commissions record for Anna Paden, Supervisor of the Paint department, for January of the current year. Ms. Paden, Employee No. 5, is paid a biweekly salary of $1,100.00 and receives a monthly commission of 1% of net sales. Commissions for the previous month are paid in the first pay period of the current month. Accounting records for the Paint department for the month ended January 31 of the current year are as follows: sales on account, $9,313.20; cash and credit card sales, $13,970.80; sales discount, $196.90; sales returns and allowances, $1,835.10.

PAYROLL DEDUCTIONS

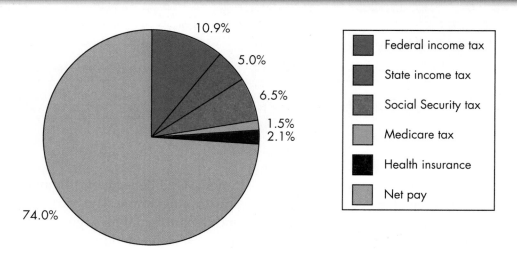

Legend:
- Federal income tax
- State income tax
- Social Security tax
- Medicare tax
- Health insurance
- Net pay

10.9%
5.0%
6.5%
1.5%
2.1%
74.0%

Figure 3-6

MasterSport is required by law to withhold federal income tax and two FICA taxes (social security tax and Medicare tax) from each employee's pay. FICA is the abbreviation for the Federal Insurance Contributions Act.

The total earnings, marital status, and number of withholding allowances claimed by an employee determine the federal income tax amount to be withheld. For each person supported, including the employee, an employee is entitled to a reduction in the amount on which income tax is calculated. A deduction from total earnings for each person legally supported by a taxpayer is called a **withholding allowance**.

The Federal Insurance Contributions Act (FICA) provides for a federal system of old-age, survivors, disability, and hospital insurance. The old-age, survivors, and disability insurance portion is financed by the social security tax. The hospital insurance portion is financed by the medicare tax. Each of these taxes is reported separately. Social security tax is calculated on employee earnings up to a maximum paid in a calendar year. The maximum amount of earnings on which a tax is calculated is called a **tax base**. Congress sets the tax base and the tax rates for social security tax. An act of Congress can change the tax base and tax rate at any time. The social security tax rate and base used in this text are 6.5% of earnings up to a maximum of $65,400.00 in each calendar year. Medicare does not have a tax base. Therefore, Medicare tax is calculated on total employee earnings. The medicare tax rate used in this text is 1.5% of total employee earnings.

Some cities and states also require that employers deduct amounts for income and other taxes from employee earnings. Laws for handling state, city, and county taxes vary.

Some businesses also make deductions from employee earnings for health insurance, life insurance, pension plans, and savings deposits. MasterSport makes deductions from its employee salaries for federal income tax, state income tax, social security tax, medicare tax, health insurance, and life insurance. The payroll components for Marilyn Caulder are shown in Figure 3-6.

REMEMBER

When an employee's earnings exceed the tax base, no more social security tax is deducted.

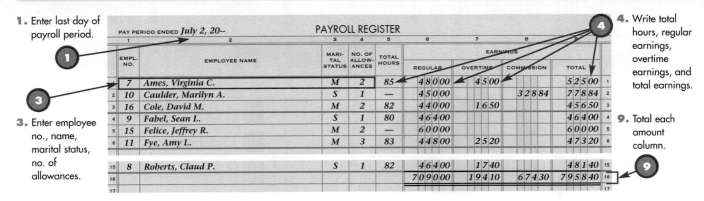

1. Enter last day of payroll period.

3. Enter employee no., name, marital status, no. of allowances.

4. Write total hours, regular earnings, overtime earnings, and total earnings.

9. Total each amount column.

Figure 3-7 (left side)

A business form used to record payroll information is called a **payroll register**. A payroll register summarizes the payroll for one pay period and shows total earnings, amounts withheld, and net pay for all employees. MasterSport prepares a separate payroll register for each biweekly payroll.

To provide better cost control, MasterSport separates employee earnings into three classifi-cations: Golf department, Tennis department, and administrative. The earnings of sales clerks and departmental managers are recorded in their respective departmental classification. The earnings of the store manager and accounting and office employees are recorded in the administrative classification.

Prepare a payroll register

For each pay period:

1. Enter the last day of the biweekly payroll period, *July 2, 20--,* at the top of the payroll register.

2. Record the date of payment, *July 9, 20--,* also at the top of the payroll register. The time between the end of a pay period and the date of payment is needed to prepare the payroll records and payroll checks.

For each employee:

3. Enter employee number, *7;* name, *Ames, Virginia C.;* marital status, *M;* and number of allowances, *2,* in columns 1, 2, 3, and 4. This information is taken from personnel records kept for each employee.

4. Write total hours, *85;* regular earnings, *480.00;* overtime earnings, *45.00;* and total earnings, *525.00,* in columns 5, 6, 7, and 9. This information is taken from Virginia Ames' time card.

5. Record total earnings, *525.00,* in the Golf Department column, column 10. Virginia Ames is a sales clerk in the golf department.

6. Enter the payroll deductions: federal income tax, *12.00;* state income tax, *26.25;* social security tax, *34.13;* medicare tax, *7.88;* health insurance, *16.00;* and life insurance, *12.80.* Federal income tax withholding is calculated using withholding tables, such as the ones shown in Figure 3-8, page 74. The state in which MasterSport operates calculates state income tax at 5% of total earnings. Virginia Ames' social security tax deduction for the biweekly pay period ended July 2 is calculated as follows:

	Total Earnings	×	Social Security Tax Rate	=	Social Security Tax Deduction
	$525.00	×	6.5%	=	$34.13

PREPARING A PAYROLL REGISTER (RIGHT PAGE)

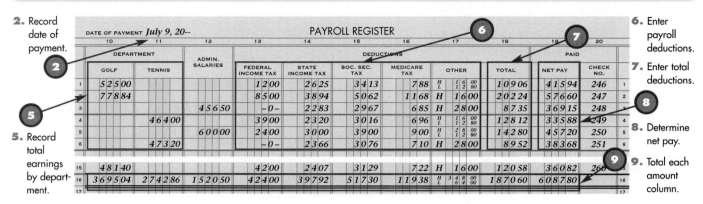

2. Record date of payment.

5. Record total earnings by department.

6. Enter payroll deductions.

7. Enter total deductions.

8. Determine net pay.

9. Total each amount column.

Figure 3-7 (right side)

Ms. Ames' medicare tax deduction for the biweekly pay period ended July 2 is calculated as follows:

Total Earnings	×	Medicare Tax Rate	=	Medicare Tax Deduction
$525.00	×	1.5%	=	$7.88

The health insurance deduction is $16.00 per biweekly pay period for each insured single employee claiming one allowance and each married employee who chooses single coverage. The deduction is $28.00 for all other married employees and single employees who claim more than one dependent. The health insurance deduction is identified by writing the letter *H* in front of the amount. The life insurance deduction is $12.80 per biweekly pay period for employees desiring life insurance. The deduction is identified by writing the letter *L* in front of the amount.

7. Add the amounts for deductions and enter the total, *109.06*, in column 18.

8. Subtract the total deductions from total earnings to determine net pay, *415.94*. The net pay for Virginia Ames is calculated as follows:

Total Earnings (column 9)	−	Total Deductions (column 18)	=	Net Pay (column 19)
$525.00	−	$109.06	=	$415.94

At the end of the payroll period:

9. When the net pay has been entered for all employees, total each payroll register amount column. Subtract the Total Deductions column from the Total Earnings column. The result should equal the total of the Net Pay column. If the totals do not agree, find and correct the errors. Prove and rule the payroll register. The proof of MasterSport's payroll register for the pay period ended July 2 is calculated as follows:

Total Earnings (column 9)	−	Total Deductions (column 18)	=	Net Pay (column 19)
$7,958.40	−	$1,870.60	=	$6,087.80

SINGLE Persons—BIWEEKLY Payroll Period

If the wages are—		And the number of withholding allowances claimed is—										
At least	But less than	0	1	2	3	4	5	6	7	8	9	10
		The amount of income tax to be withheld is—										
450	460	53	38	22	7							
460	470	54	39	24	9							
470	480	56	41	25	10							
480	490	57	42	27	12							
490	500	59	44	28	13							
500	520	61	46	31	15							
520	540	64	49	34	18	3						
540	560	67	52	37	21	6						
560	580	70	55	40	24	9						
580	600	73	58	43	27	12						
600	620	76	61	46	30	15						
620	640	79	64	49	33	18	3					
640	660	82	67	52	36	21	6					
660	680	85	70	55	39	24	9					
680	700	88	73	58	42	27	12					
700	720	91	76	61	45	30	15					
720	740	94	79	64	48	33	18	2				
740	760	97	82	67	51	36	21	5				
760	780	100	85	70	54	39	24	8				
780	800	103	88	73	57	42	27	11				
800	820	106	91	76	60	45	30	14				
820	840	109	94	79	63	48	33	17	2			
840	860	112	97	82	66	51	36	20	5			
860	880	115	100	85	69	54	39	23	8			
880	900	118	103	88	72	57	42	26	11			
900	920	121	106	91	75	60	45	29	14			
920	940	124	109	94	78	63	48	32	17	2		
940	960	127	112	97	81	66	51	35	20	5		
960	980	130	115	100	84	69	54	38	23	8		
980	1,000	133	118	103	87	72	57	41	26	11		

BIWEEKLY SINGLE PERSONS

MARRIED Persons—BIWEEKLY Payroll Period

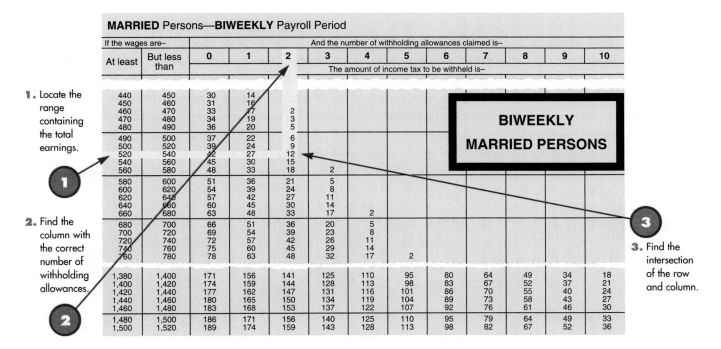

If the wages are—		And the number of withholding allowances claimed is—										
At least	But less than	0	1	2	3	4	5	6	7	8	9	10
		The amount of income tax to be withheld is—										
440	450	30	14									
450	460	31	16									
460	470	33	17	2								
470	480	34	19	3								
480	490	36	20	5								
490	500	37	22	6								
500	520	39	24	9								
520	540	42	27	12								
540	560	45	30	15								
560	580	48	33	18	2							
580	600	51	36	21	5							
600	620	54	39	24	8							
620	640	57	42	27	11							
640	660	60	45	30	14							
660	680	63	48	33	17	2						
680	700	66	51	36	20	5						
700	720	69	54	39	23	8						
720	740	72	57	42	26	11						
740	760	75	60	45	29	14						
760	780	78	63	48	32	17	2					
1,380	1,400	171	156	141	125	110	95	80	64	49	34	18
1,400	1,420	174	159	144	128	113	98	83	67	52	37	21
1,420	1,440	177	162	147	131	116	101	86	70	55	40	24
1,440	1,460	180	165	150	134	119	104	89	73	58	43	27
1,460	1,480	183	168	153	137	122	107	92	76	61	46	30
1,480	1,500	186	171	156	140	125	110	95	79	64	49	33
1,500	1,520	189	174	159	143	128	113	98	82	67	52	36

1. Locate the range containing the total earnings.

2. Find the column with the correct number of withholding allowances.

3. Find the intersection of the row and column.

BIWEEKLY MARRIED PERSONS

Figure 3-8

S T E P S

EXAMPLE: Virginia Ames is married and claims 2 withholding allowances. Her total earnings for the pay period are $525.00.

1. Use the left two columns of the Biweekly Married Persons tax table shown in Figure 3-8 to locate the range containing the total earnings—*At least 520 But less than 540.*

2. Find the column with the correct number of withholding allowances, *2.*

3. Find the intersection of the row and column. The amount of income tax to be withheld is *$12.00.*

For employees earning commissions, the amount of the commission is entered in column 8 of the payroll register shown in Figure 3-7. This information is taken from the employee's commission record. Department supervisors do not account for their hourly time on a time card. A line is therefore drawn through the Total Hours column, column 5, as shown on line 2 of the payroll register. Each department supervisor's salary remains the same for each biweekly pay period. Therefore, the salary amount is recorded in the Regular Earnings column, column 6. Commissions from the commissions records are entered in the Commission Earnings column, column 8. Regular earnings and commission earnings are added together to determine total earnings for the biweekly pay period.

The salaries of the store manager and non-sales employees, such as accounting department employees, are entered in the Admin. Salaries column, column 12 of the payroll register shown in Figure 3-7. Time cards and commission records show the department to be charged for each employee's total earnings.

REMEMBER

The Ck. No. column of the payroll register is not completed until the check has been written.

PATRICIA WYATT, PRESIDENT/CEO, COMMUNITY HOME HEALTH CARE, INC.

ACCOUNTING AT WORK

I feel very strongly that every high school student should successfully complete a course in accounting as the experience will prove invaluable when preparing for college or pursuing a career. Moreover, technological advances dictate that you must have a "numbers" mentality to compete in the 21st century. As a student, I was reluctant to even take accounting because I thought it was going to be boring. Quite to the contrary, I found it to be extremely challenging and exciting.

Accounting principles demand that you organize data, which can affect how you perform your daily activities. From my job as a clerk in a drug store as a teenager, where I had to close out the register and make bank deposits; to a successful career in the hospitality industry, accounting has always factored in. Consider tasks such as balancing cash, planning, structuring budgets, preparing payrolls, and other similar duties.

As I move forward now as a business person, serving on many different boards and committees, I wish I had taken more accounting classes. It would greatly enhance my ability to understand financial transactions, such as those represented on profit and loss statements, balance sheets, and other reports. My recommendation is that you seriously consider taking the "accounting plunge," even though you may not want to be an accountant. You will appreciate the results no matter what career path you choose.

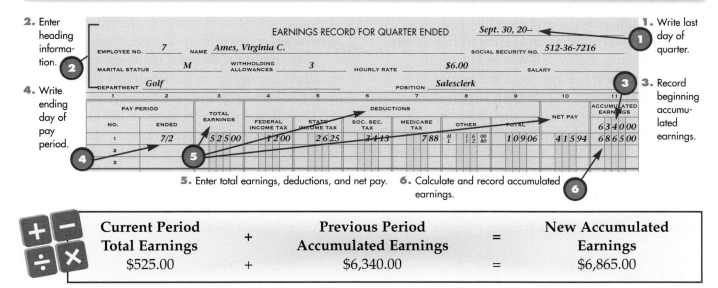

2. Enter heading information.

4. Write ending day of pay period.

1. Write last day of quarter.

3. Record beginning accumulated earnings.

5. Enter total earnings, deductions, and net pay.

6. Calculate and record accumulated earnings.

Current Period Total Earnings		Previous Period Accumulated Earnings		New Accumulated Earnings
$525.00	+	$6,340.00	=	$6,865.00

Figure 3-9

A business must send a quarterly report to federal and state governments showing employee taxable earnings and taxes withheld from employee earnings. Detailed information about each employee's earnings is summarized in a single record for each employee. A business form used to record details affecting payments made to an employee is called an **employee earnings record**. An employee's total earnings and deductions for each pay period are summarized on one line of the employee earnings record.

MasterSport prepares a new earnings record for each employee each quarter. Virginia Ames'

earnings record for the third quarter is shown in Figure 3-9.

Accumulated earnings are often referred to as year-to-date earnings. Accumulated earnings are needed for each employee because certain payroll taxes do not apply after an employee's earnings reach a specified amount. For example, employers pay federal and state unemployment taxes only on the first $7,000.00 of each employee's earnings during a calendar year. Social security taxes also are paid only on a maximum amount determined by law.

S T E P S Prepare an employee earnings record

1. Write the last day of the yearly quarter, *Sept. 30, 20--*, at the top of the earnings record.

2. Enter the employee's number, name, social security number, marital status, withholding allowances, hourly rate or salary, department, and position in the appropriate space. This information is taken from the employee's personnel records.

3. Record the fiscal year's accumulated earnings, *6,340.00*, for the beginning of the current quarter. This information is taken from the ending accumulated earnings for the previous quarters. The Accumulated Earnings column of the employee earnings record shows the accumulated earnings since the beginning of the fiscal year.

4. Write the ending date of the current pay period, *7/2*.

5. Enter the total earnings, deductions, and net pay in the assigned columns of the earnings record. This information is taken from the current pay period's payroll register.

6. Calculate and record the new accumulated earnings, *6,865.00*, on the same line as the other payroll information for the pay period ended July 2.

TERMS REVIEW

withholding allowance

tax base

payroll register

employee earnings record

AUDIT YOUR UNDERSTANDING

1. What three federal taxes are withheld from an employee's pay?

2. How is the amount of federal income tax withholding determined?

3. What is the formula for calculating net pay on the payroll register?

4. What amount is added to the accumulated earnings to get the new accumulated earnings to date?

WORK TOGETHER

Completing payroll records

Best Value Co.'s partial payroll register for the pay period ended July 3, 20-- and a blank earnings record form are provided in the *Working Papers*. Use the appropriate withholding tax tables shown in Figure 3-8 to determine the federal income tax. Deductions for all employees are 5% of total earnings for state income tax, 6.5% for social security tax, and 1.5% for medicare tax. Use *H* to indicate health insurance and *L* to indicate life insurance. Your instructor will guide you through the following examples.

5. Prepare the payroll register entries for the following two employees:

    a. On line 1: John Balderas, Employee No. 2, Hardware department supervisor, married, two allowances, regular salary of $1,200.00 per pay period plus 1% of net sales. Net sales for the period totaled $31,200.00. Health insurance premium is $56.00, and life insurance premium is $25.60.

    b. On line 4: Susan Fulton, Employee No. 4, Hardware department salesclerk, single, one allowance, regular salary of $10.00 per hour with overtime paid at 1-1/2 times the regular rate. Fulton worked 80 hours regular time and 8 hours overtime. Health insurance premium is $28.00.

6. Prove the payroll register totals for the pay period ended July 3, 20--. Prove the totals.

7. Prepare Susan Fulton's earnings record for the first pay period of the quarter ended September 30, 20--. Ms. Fulton's accumulated earnings as shown on the earnings record for quarter ended June 30, 20-- are $11,900.00. Save your work to complete the Work Together on page 84.

ON YOUR OWN

Completing payroll records

Best Value Co.'s partial payroll register for the pay period ended October 2, 20-- and a blank earnings record form are provided in the *Working Papers*. Use the appropriate withholding tax tables shown in Figure 3-8 to determine the federal income tax. Deductions for all employees are 5% of total earnings for state income tax, 6.5% for social security tax, and 1.5% for medicare tax. Use *H* to indicate health insurance and *L* to indicate life insurance. Work independently to complete the following instructions.

8. Prepare the payroll register entries for the following two employees:

   a. On line 11: Anna Paden, Employee No. 5, Paint department supervisor, married, one allowance, regular salary of $1,100.00 per pay period plus 1% of net sales. Net sales for the period totaled $30,500.00. Health insurance premium is $28.00, and life insurance premium is $25.60.

   b. On line 12: Keith Parker, Employee No. 12, Paint department salesclerk, single, one allowance, regular salary of $9.50 per hour with overtime paid at 1-1/2 times the regular rate. Parker worked 80 hours regular time and 10 hours overtime. Health insurance premium is $28.00.

9. Prove the payroll register totals for the pay period ended October 31, 20--. Prove the totals

10. Prepare Keith Parker's earnings record for the first pay period of the quarter ended December 31, 20--. Mr. Parker's accumulated earnings as shown on the earnings record for the quarter ended September 30, 20--, are $19,000.00. Save your work to complete the On Your Own on page 84.

EXERCISING STOCK OPTIONS

PROFESSIONAL BUSINESS ETHICS

Corporations often compensate executives with more than a salary. The compensation package often includes the right to purchase company stock at a specified price (this right is called a stock option). The option price is typically set higher than the current market price. If the stock price increases above the option price, the option enables the individual to purchase the stock at less than the market price. If the stock's market price never exceeds the option price, the option is worthless.

Required:

Use the three-step checklist to analyze whether the following use of stock options as executive compensation demonstrates ethical behavior.

Three years ago the board of directors of Sportzware, Inc. offered its new chief executive officer, Kayla Kwan, an annual salary or $185,000 plus 200,000 stock options at $30. The stock was selling for $18 at the time. Kayla successfully improved the corporation's profitability. As a result, the stock is currently selling for $35. Kayla exercised the stock options and purchased 200,000 shares of stock from Sportzware for $6 million. She immediately sold the stock on the stock exchange for $35 per share and realized a profit of $1 million.

3-3 Journalizing and Paying Payroll and Payroll Taxes

PAYROLL BANK ACCOUNT

MasterSport pays its employees biweekly by check. A special payroll checking account and special payroll checks are used. After a biweekly payroll register has been completed, a check is written on MasterSport's general checking account payable to *Payroll* for the total net pay. This check is deposited in a special payroll checking account against which payroll checks are written for each employee's net pay.

The amount of the biweekly deposit to the payroll account equals the sum of the biweekly salary payments. The special payroll account balance, therefore, is reduced to zero as soon as all employees have cashed their payroll checks. Because the special payroll bank account has a balance only until all payroll checks are cashed, no special account is needed in the general ledger.

AUTOMATIC CHECK DEPOSIT

Employees may authorize an employer to deposit payroll checks directly in their checking accounts at a specified bank. Depositing payroll checks directly to an employee's checking or savings account in a specific bank is called **automatic check deposit**. When automatic check deposit is used, the employer sends the check to the employee's bank for deposit.

In addition to automatic check deposit, employers may transfer payroll checks electronically. Transferring payroll amounts electronically from the employer's account directly to the employee's bank account is called **electronic funds transfer (EFT)**. Electronic funds transfer eliminates the need for preparing payroll checks. Under this system, each employee receives a statement of earnings and deductions similar to the detachable stub on a payroll check.

The use of automatic check deposit or electronic funds transfer for payroll does not change the accounting procedures for recording payroll. *(CONCEPT: Consistent Reporting)*

EMPLOYER PAYROLL TAXES

Payroll taxes represent business transactions with dollar amounts large enough to affect business decisions. Therefore, all payroll taxes are reported as separate items in accounting records and financial statements. *(CONCEPT: Materiality)* Most employers have four separate payroll taxes.

1. Employer social security tax

2. Medicare tax

3. Federal unemployment tax

4. State unemployment tax

Unemployment taxes are used to pay cash benefits to qualified workers for limited periods of unemployment.

A special payroll checking account for writing checks for individual net pay provides an internal control. Only payroll checks are written from this account.

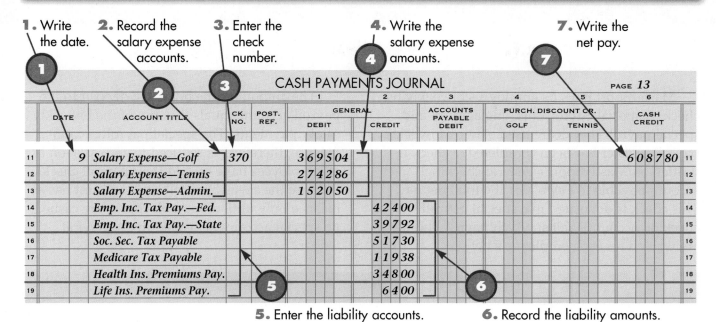

1. Write the date.

2. Record the salary expense accounts.

3. Enter the check number.

4. Write the salary expense amounts.

7. Write the net pay.

	DATE	ACCOUNT TITLE	CK. NO.	POST. REF.	GENERAL DEBIT	GENERAL CREDIT	ACCOUNTS PAYABLE DEBIT	PURCH. DISCOUNT CR. GOLF	PURCH. DISCOUNT CR. TENNIS	CASH CREDIT	
11	9	Salary Expense—Golf	370		3 6 9 5 04					6 0 8 7 80	11
12		Salary Expense—Tennis			2 7 4 2 86						12
13		Salary Expense—Admin.			1 5 2 0 50						13
14		Emp. Inc. Tax Pay.—Fed.				4 2 4 00					14
15		Emp. Inc. Tax Pay.—State				3 9 7 92					15
16		Soc. Sec. Tax Payable				5 1 7 30					16
17		Medicare Tax Payable				1 1 9 38					17
18		Health Ins. Premiums Pay.				3 4 8 00					18
19		Life Ins. Premiums Pay.				6 4 00					19

CASH PAYMENTS JOURNAL   PAGE 13

5. Enter the liability accounts.

6. Record the liability amounts.

Figure 3-10

MasterSport's payroll register, Figure 3-7, contains the information needed to journalize a payroll as shown in Figure 3-10. The source document for journalizing a payroll payment is the check written for the net payroll amount. (CONCEPT: *Objective Evidence*)

July 9.   Paid cash for biweekly payroll, $6,087.80 (total payroll: golf, $3,695.04; tennis, $2,742.86; administrative, $1,520.50; less deductions: employee income tax—federal, $424.00; employee income tax—state, $397.92; social security tax, $517.30; Medicare tax, $119.38; health insurance, $348.00; life insurance, $64.00). Check No. 370.

The T accounts below show the debits and credits to all affected accounts.

Salary Expense—Golf	
3,695.04	

Social Security Tax Payable	
	517.30

Salary Expense—Tennis	
2,742.86	

Medicare Tax Payable	
	119.38

Salary Expense— Administrative	
1,520.50	

Health Insurance Premiums Payable	
	348.00

Employee Income Tax Payable—Federal	
	424.00

Life Insurance Premiums Payable	
	64.00

Employee Income Tax Payable—State	
	397.92

Cash	
	6,087.80

S T E P S   **Journalize payment of a payroll**

1. Write the date, *9*, in the Date column of the cash payments journal.

2. Record the salary expense accounts, *Salary Expense—Golf, Salary Expense—Tennis, Salary Expense— Admin.*, in the Account Title column.

3. Enter the check number, *370*, in the Ck. No. column.

4. Write the salary expense amounts, *3,695.04, 2,742.86,* and *1,520.50*, in the General Debit column.

5. Enter the liability accounts, *Emp. Inc. Tax Pay.—Fed., Emp. Inc. Tax Pay.—State, Soc. Sec. Tax Pay., Medicare Tax Pay., Health Ins. Premiums Pay.,* and *Life Ins. Premiums Pay.*, in the Account Title column.

6. Record the liability amounts, *424.00, 397.92, 517.30, 119.38, 348.00,* and *64.00*, in the General Credit column.

7. Write the net pay, *6,087.80*, in the Cash Credit column.

JOURNALIZING EMPLOYER PAYROLL TAXES

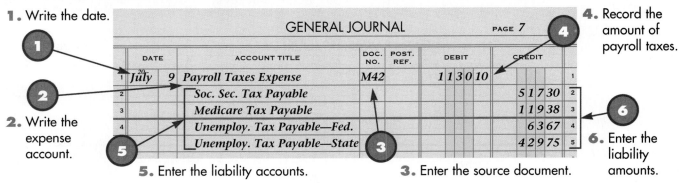

1. Write the date.

2. Write the expense account.

5. Enter the liability accounts.

3. Enter the source document.

4. Record the amount of payroll taxes.

6. Enter the liability amounts.

Figure 3-11

Employer payroll taxes expense is based on a percentage of employee earnings. The employer social security tax (6.5%) and Medicare tax (1.5%) rates are the same as the rates used for employees. The federal unemployment tax is 6.2% of the first $7,000.00 earned by each employee. An employer generally can deduct the amounts paid to state unemployment funds from federal unemployment payments. This deduction cannot be more than 5.4% of taxable earnings. The effective federal unemployment tax rate in most states is, therefore, 0.8% on the first $7,000.00 earned by each employee. (Federal 6.2% – deductible for state 5.4% = 0.8%.) The employer pays all of the unemployment tax on the first $7,000.00 of salary.

Employees in a few states have deductions from their earnings for state unemployment tax. Employees do not pay federal unemployment tax.

None of MasterSport's employees has earned $7,000.00 by the pay period ended July 2. Therefore, MasterSport's federal unemployment

tax is 0.8% of $7,958.40 total earnings, or $63.67. MasterSport's state unemployment tax is 5.4% of $7,958.40 total earnings, or $429.75.

Jeffrey Felice, manager, would have earned over $7,000.00 by July 2 had he worked since the beginning of the year. However, he started work at MasterSport on March 1 of the current year.

July 9. Recorded employer payroll taxes, $1,130.10, for the biweekly pay period ended July 2. Taxes owed are social security tax, $517.30; Medicare tax, $119.38; federal unemployment tax, $63.67; state unemployment tax, $429.75. Memorandum No. 42.

The journal entry to record the payroll taxes is shown in Figure 3-11.

Payroll Taxes Expense		Unemployment Tax Payable—Federal	
1,130.10			63.67
Social Security Tax Payable		**Unemployment Tax Payable—State**	
	517.30		429.75
Medicare Tax Payable			
	119.38		

Journalize employer payroll taxes

1. Write the date, *July 9*, in the Date column of the general journal.

2. Write the expense account, *Payroll Taxes Expense*, in the Account Title column.

3. Enter the source document, *M42*, in the Doc. No. column.

4. Record the amount of payroll taxes expense, *1,130.10*, in the debit column.

5. Enter the liability accounts, *Social Security Tax Payable, Medicare Tax Payable, Unemploy. Tax Payable—Fed.*, and *Unemploy. Tax Payable—State*, in the Account Title column.

6. Enter the liability amounts, *517.30, 119.38, 63.67,* and *429.75*, in the Credit column.

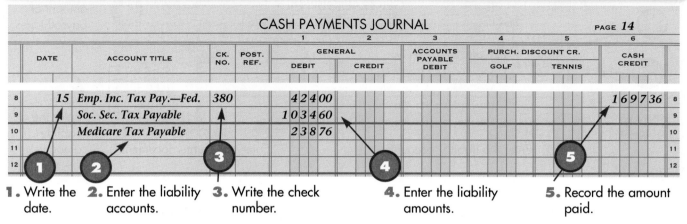

1. Write the date. **2.** Enter the liability accounts. **3.** Write the check number. **4.** Enter the liability amounts. **5.** Record the amount paid.

Figure 3-12

Employers must pay to federal, state, and local governments all payroll taxes withheld from employee earnings as well as the employer payroll taxes. The frequency of payments is determined by the amount owed.

Frequency and method of payment of withheld employees' federal income tax, social security tax, and medicare tax plus employer's social security tax and medicare tax are determined by the total amount of tax paid each year. If the total amount paid in the previous four quarters is $50,000.00 or less, a business is classified as a monthly schedule depositor. A monthly schedule depositor must pay the total amount due to an authorized financial institution by the 15th day of the following month accompanied by Form 8109, Federal Tax Deposit Coupon. A semiweekly schedule depositor must deposit amounts accumulated on salary payments made on Saturday, Sunday, Monday, or Tuesday by the following Friday. For salary payments made on Wednesday, Thursday, or Friday, payment must be made by the following Wednesday. Payment must be made directly to the Internal Revenue Service by the Electronic Federal Tax Payment System (EFTPS).

There are two exceptions to the standard tax payment schedules. (1) If less than $500 tax liability is accumulated during a three-month quarter, the deposit may be paid at the end of the month following the end of the quarter. (2) If a tax liability of $100,000 or more is accumulated

on any day, the amount must be deposited on the next banking day.

MasterSport is classified as a semiweekly schedule depositor. The biweekly pay day is Saturday. So the payroll taxes are deposited using the EFTPS on Friday following the Saturday pay day.

> *July 15. Paid cash for liability for employee federal income tax, $424.00, and for employees' and employer's social security tax, $1,034.60, and medicare tax, $238.76; total, $1,697.36. Check No. 380.*

MasterSport's federal income tax, social security tax, and medicare tax liabilities for the biweekly pay period ended July 2 and paid on July 9 are deposited on Friday, July 15 as shown in Figure 3-12. MasterSport's liability for state income tax withholding is paid at the end of each quarter.

F.Y.I.

Methods of paying payroll taxes described on this page were in effect when this textbook was written. Businesses with payroll tax liabilities of more than $20,000.00 in 1997 must pay electronically using the EFTPS System by 1999. At some future date, all businesses probably will be required to pay payroll taxes electronically.

JOURNALIZING PAYMENT OF FEDERAL UNEMPLOYMENT TAX LIABILITY

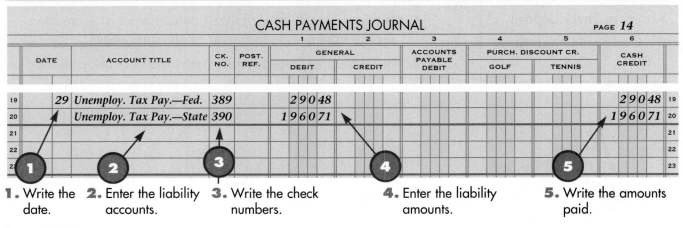

Figure 3-13

If the annual federal unemployment tax for a business is $100.00 or less, it must pay the tax in one payment by January 31 of the following year. If its annual tax is more than $100.00, the business must make quarterly payments in the month following the end of the quarter.

MasterSport's federal unemployment tax for the second quarter is $290.48. Therefore, it must make its payment during the first month of the following quarter, which is July, as shown in Figure 3-13.

July 29. *Paid cash for federal unemployment tax liability for quarter ended June 30, $290.48. Check No. 391.*

The T accounts below show the debits and credits to all affected accounts.

Unemployment Tax Payable—Federal	
290.48	

Cash	
	290.48

JOURNALIZING PAYMENT OF STATE UNEMPLOYMENT TAX LIABILITY

Requirements for paying state unemployment taxes vary from state to state. Usually, employers are required to pay the state unemployment tax during the month following each calendar quarter.

MasterSport's state unemployment tax for the second quarter is $1,960.71.

July 29. *Paid cash for state unemployment tax liability for quarter ended June 30, $1,960.71. Check No. 392.*

The T accounts below show the debits and credits to all affected accounts.

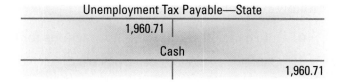

Unemployment Tax Payable—State	
1,960.71	

Cash	
	1,960.71

REMEMBER

Employees do not pay federal unemployment tax.

AUDIT YOUR UNDERSTANDING

1. When a payroll is journalized, which account is credited for the total net amount paid to all employees?

2. What four separate payroll taxes do most employers have?

WORK TOGETHER

Journalizing and paying payroll and payroll taxes

Use the working papers from the Work Together on page 77. A cash payments journal, page 15, and general journal, page 1, are provided in the *Working Papers*. Your instructor will guide you through the following examples.

3. Journalize the following transactions for July of the current year.

July 10. Paid July 3 payroll. Check No. 260.

10. Recorded employer's payroll taxes for the pay period ended July 3. Tax rates are 0.8% for federal unemployment tax and 5.4% for state unemployment tax. Social security and Medicare tax are the same as for employees. Memo. No. 33.

15. Paid employees' federal income tax withholding, the social security tax, and Medicare tax liabilities for the pay period ended July 3. Check No. 265.

29. Paid federal unemployment tax, $745.84, and state unemployment tax, $5,034.44, for the quarter ended June 30. Check No. 270.

ON YOUR OWN

Journalizing and paying payroll and payroll taxes

Use the working papers from the On Your Own on page 78. A cash payments journal, page 18, and general journal, page 10, are provided in the *Working Papers*. Work independently to complete the following problem.

4. Journalize the following transactions for October of the current year.

Oct. 9. Paid October 2 payroll. Check No. 335.

11. Recorded employer's payroll taxes for the pay period ended October 2. Tax rates are 0.8% for federal unemployment tax and 5.4% for state unemployment tax. Social security and Medicare tax are the same as for employees. Memo. No. 48.

14. Paid employees' federal income tax withholding, the social security tax, and Medicare tax liabilities for the pay period ended October 2. Check No. 339.

28. Paid federal unemployment tax, $783.65, and state unemployment tax, $5,289.62, for the quarter ended September 30. Check No. 344.

After completing this chapter, you can

1. Define accounting terms related to a departmental payroll system.

2. Identify accounting concepts and practices related to a departmental payroll system.

3. Maintain employee benefits records and calculate employee earnings.

4. Complete payroll records.

5. Journalize payroll transactions.

EXPLORE ACCOUNTING

PRETAX BENEFITS

Federal income tax is a major expense for most families. Current laws permit employers to set up retirement and cafeteria plans that allow employees to set aside a portion of their earnings on a pretax basis. Employees pay no taxes in that tax year on the amounts withheld.

Retirement Plans

For amounts placed in many qualified retirement accounts, income tax is "deferred" on earnings. Individuals will pay income taxes on the amounts withdrawn from their retirement accounts when they retire. Because of the income tax deferral, the amount available at retirement will be much larger.

The general requirements of most pretax retirement plans include:

1. The employer withholds the specified amount and deposits it in qualified investment vehicles, such as mutual funds.
2. The amount of earnings an employee can defer each year is limited.
3. Employees are assessed penalties if they withdraw amounts from their retirement account before the age of 59-1/2.
4. Withdrawals from retirement plan accounts must begin by the time the person reaches age 70-1/2.

Medical Savings Accounts and Cafeteria Plans

Medical savings accounts and cafeteria plans permit employees to have a portion of their pretax earnings deducted from their salaries. The amounts are used to reimburse out-of-pocket medical or childcare expenses. The advantage is that payment is made with pretax dollars. However, the amount of earnings withheld is available only for the purpose designated. For example, if an employee authorizes $50.00 a month to be withheld for medical costs but uses only $500.00 during the year, the remaining $100.00 that was withheld is NOT reimbursable to the employee.

REQUIRED:

1. Why would Congress allow employees to defer taxes?
2. Are there any disadvantages to participating in these tax deferral plans?

APPLICATION PROBLEM

Preparing a benefits record

Brumley's provides the same employee benefits as those described for MasterSport in Figure 3-1 in this chapter.

Instructions:

Prepare Monica Chaffee's benefits record for the first four biweekly pay periods of the current year. Use the following information.

Employee No.: 9   Employee Name: Monica A. Chaffee
Department: Sports Equip.   Date of Hire: April 1, 19--

Pay Period	Regular Hours	Employee Benefits Available			Employee Benefits Used		
1/2	80	V92	S100	P20	V16	S2	P2
1/16	80	___	___	___	V0	S4	P4
1/30	80	___	___	___	V0	S8	P0
2/13	80	___	___	___	V16	S0	P4

V = Vacation time; S = Sick leave time; P = Personal leave time

APPLICATION PROBLEM

Recording employee benefits and calculating earnings on time cards

Clark's has two departments, carpet and drapery. It uses a biweekly payroll system of 26 pay periods per year. It pays its salesclerks and employees in the accounting department on an hourly basis, and they receive 1-1/2 times the regular hourly pay rate for all hours worked in excess of 8 hours in one day. A time card is used for hourly employees to record hours worked.

Clark's provides the same employee benefits as those described for MasterSport in this chapter. The employee benefits provided are shown in Figure 3-1 in this chapter. Clark's also uses a benefits authorization form similar to the one shown in Figure 3-3.

Time cards and benefits authorization forms for selected employees of Clark's are provided in the *Working Papers*. The time cards and employee benefits authorizations are for the biweekly pay period ended March 12 of the current year.

Instructions:

1. Prepare an employee benefits record for each employee.

2. Record employee benefits hours on time cards for each employee.

3. Calculate regular, overtime, and total hours worked by each employee on the time cards.

4. Complete each time card by calculating regular, overtime, and total earnings. Save your work to complete Application Problem 3-4.

APPLICATION PROBLEM

Preparing departmental commissions records

Clark's employs a departmental supervisor for each of its two departments. Departmental supervisors receive a biweekly salary and monthly commissions of 1% of net sales. They receive their commissions for

the previous month in the first pay period of the current month. The following data are from the accounting records for the month ended February 28 of the current year.

a.   Carpet department: sales on account, $8,623.40; cash and credit card sales, $12,936.20; sales discount, $148.90; sales returns and allowances, $1,699.30.

b.   Drapery department: sales on account, $7,223.89; cash and credit card sales, $13,987.11; sales discount, $337.17; sales returns and allowances, $654.33.

Instructions:
Prepare February's commissions record for each of the following departmental supervisors. Save your work to complete Application Problem 3-4.

a.   Carpet department
     Employee name: Heidi Gowens
     Employee number: 9
     Regular salary: $540.00

b.   Drapery department
     Employee name: Dale Mantle
     Employee number: 14
     Regular salary: $520.00

APPLICATION PROBLEM
Completing a payroll register

Use the time cards from Application Problem 3-2 and the commissions records from Application Problem 3-3. Clark's partially completed payroll register for the biweekly pay period ended March 12 is provided in the *Working Papers*. Use the following additional data:

a.   A deduction for federal income tax is to be made from each employee's total earnings. Use the appropriate income tax withholding tables shown in Figure 3-8.

b.   A deduction of 5% for state income tax is to be made from each employee's total earnings.

c.   A deduction of 6.5% for social security and 1.5% for medicare tax is to be made from each employee's total earnings.

d.   All employees have dental insurance, $9.40, and health insurance, $13.20, deducted from their pay each biweekly pay period. These deductions are to be recorded in the Other Deductions column of the payroll register. Use *D* to indicate the dental insurance deduction. Use *H* to indicate the health insurance deduction. Both of these deductions are written on one line of the payroll register for each employee.

Instructions:
Complete the payroll register for the pay period ended March 12 and paid on March 19 of the current year. Save your work to complete Application Problems 3-5 and 3-6.

APPLICATION PROBLEM
Completing an employee earnings record

Use the payroll register from Application Problem 3-4. A partially completed employee earnings record for each of Clark's employees appears in the *Working Papers*.

Instructions:
Complete the employee earnings record for each employee. This pay period is the sixth of the first quarter of the current year.

APPLICATION PROBLEM
Journalizing payment of a departmental payroll

Use the payroll register from Application Problem 3-4.

Instructions:

1. Record the March 19 payroll payment on page 6 of a cash payments journal. The source document is Check No. 463.

2. Record the employer payroll taxes on page 6 of a general journal. Use March 19 of the current year as the date. The source document is Memorandum No. 41. Employer tax rates are social security tax, 6.5%; Medicare tax, 1.5%; federal unemployment, 0.8%; and state unemployment, 5.4%.

APPLICATION PROBLEM
Calculating and journalizing payment of payroll tax liabilities

Use the following payroll data for Walker's for the first quarter of the current year. Employer tax rates are social security, 6.5%; Medicare, 1.5%; federal unemployment, 0.8%; and state unemployment, 5.4%.

Period	Total Earnings	Social Security Tax Withheld	Medicare Tax Withheld	Federal Income Tax Withheld
Biweekly Period Ended March 28	$ 7,742.00	$503.23	$116.13	$911.00
First Quarter	46,452.00	–	–	–

Instructions:

1. Calculate the liability for federal income tax, social security tax, and Medicare tax for the biweekly pay period ended March 28. Include both the employees' tax withheld and the employer liability for social security and Medicare taxes. Record the payment of federal income tax withholding, social security tax, and Medicare tax on page 7 of a cash payments journal. The payment is made on April 3 using Check No. 492 as the source document.

2. Calculate the federal unemployment tax liability for the first quarter. Record the payment on page 8 of a cash payments journal. The payment is made on April 30 using Check No. 515 as the source document.

3. Calculate the state unemployment tax liability for the first quarter. Record the payment on page 8 of a cash payments journal. The payment is made on April 30 using Check No. 516 as the source document.

MASTERY PROBLEM
Completing payroll records, journalizing payment of a payroll, and journalizing payroll taxes

McCarron's Sewing Store has two departments, fabrics and supplies. It uses a biweekly payroll system of 26 pay periods per year. McCarron's pays salesclerks and employees in the accounting department on an

hourly basis, and they receive 1-1/2 times the regular hourly pay rate for all hours worked in excess of 8 hours in one day. Time cards are used for hourly employees to record the number of hours worked.

Department supervisors receive a biweekly salary and monthly commissions of 1% of net sales. Commissions for the previous month are paid in the first pay period of the next month.

McCarron's Sewing Store provides the same employee benefits as those described for MasterSport in this chapter. The employee benefits provided are in the employee benefits schedule shown in Figure 3-1 in this chapter. A benefits authorization form similar to the one shown in Figure 3-2 is also used.

McCarron's Sewing Store's partially completed payroll records for selected employees are provided in the *Working Papers*. The payroll records are for the pay period ended February 13 and are paid on February 20 of the current year.

Instructions:

1. Complete the benefits record for each employee and record employee benefits hours used on the time cards.

2. Calculate regular, overtime, and total hours worked by each employee.

3. Complete each time card by calculating regular, overtime, and total earnings.

4. Complete the commissions record for each departmental supervisor. The following data are from the accounting records for the month ended January 31 of the current year:
   a. Fabric department: sales on account, $5,443.89; cash and credit card sales, $8,017.02; sales discount, $85.86; sales returns and allowances, $296.66.
   b. Supplies department: sales on account, $5,209.33; cash and credit card sales, $9,903.55; sales discount, $156.67; sales returns and allowances, $1,302.31.

5. Complete the payroll register for the pay period ended February 13 and paid February 20 of the current year. Use the following additional data to complete the payroll register:
   a. A deduction for federal income tax is to be made from each employee's total earnings. Use the appropriate income tax withholding tables shown in Figure 3-8 in this chapter.
   b. A deduction of 5% for state income tax is to be made from each employee's total earnings.
   c. Deduction of 6.5% for social security tax and 1.5% for medicare tax are to be made from each employee's total earnings.
   d. All employees have health insurance, $14.80, and life insurance, $8.20, deducted from their pay each biweekly pay period. Use H to indicate the health insurance deduction. Use L to indicate the life insurance deduction.

6. Complete the employee earnings record for each employee. This pay period is the fourth of the first quarter of the current year.

7. Journalize the February 20 payroll payment on page 4 of a cash payments journal. The source document is Check No. 143.

8. Journalize the employer payroll taxes on page 4 of a general journal. Use February 20 of the current year as the date. The source document is Memorandum No. 14. Employer tax rates are social security, 6.5%; Medicare, 1.5%; federal unemployment, 0.8%; and state unemployment, 5.4%. The employee social security and Medicare taxes withheld and the employer share of social security and Medicare taxes will not be equal due to rounding differences.

CHALLENGE PROBLEM
Preparing a benefits record

Rancourt's uses a semimonthly payroll system. Three employee benefits are provided: vacation time, sick leave time, and personal leave time. The time available is outlined in the following employee benefits schedule.

RANCOURT'S EMPLOYEE BENEFITS

Benefits	Earned After 12 Months	Semimonthly After 12 Months	Minimum Time Blocks	Maximum Carry Over
Vacation time hours	40	3-1/3	4	120
Sick leave time hours	0	1-2/3	1	80
Personal leave time hours	0	1	1	24

Instructions:

Use the following information to prepare Arthur Delgado's benefits record for the first four semimonthly pay periods of the current year. V = Vacation time; S = Sick leave time; P = Personal leave time

Employee No.: 7
Department: Men's Shoes

Employee Name: Arthur J. Delgado
Date of Hire: June 5, 1986

Pay Period	Regular Hours	Employee Benefits Available			Employee Benefits Used		
1/15	80	V32-1/3	S25-2/3	P15	V0	S4	P2
1/31	80	___	___	___	V4	S0	P3
2/15	80	___	___	___	V8	S8	P0
2/29	80	___	___	___	V0	S0	P2

INTERNET ACTIVITY

Point your browser to
http://accounting.swpco.com
Choose **Advanced Course**, choose **Activities**, and complete the activity for Chapter 3.

Applied Communication

Write a letter to two local payroll processing companies. Request information about their services. When you receive the information, compare and contrast the services offered by the two companies.

Cases for Critical Thinking

Case 1

MasterSport uses one account, Payroll Taxes Expense, in which to record all of the expenses for social security tax, medicare tax, federal unemployment tax, and state unemployment tax. Sports Den uses four expense accounts—Social Security Tax Expense, Medicare Tax Expense, Federal Unemployment Tax Expense, and State Unemployment Tax Expense—when recording the business' four payroll tax expenses. Which system of recording taxes is more desirable? Explain your answer.

AUTOMATED ACCOUNTING

AUTOMATING PAYROLL ACCOUNTING DATA—PAYROLL PROCEDURES

Payroll procedures consist of maintaining the employee accounts and adding and deleting employee information. Payroll transactions are entered for each employee and taxes are calculated to determine payroll for employees and the employer's tax liability.

Payroll Transactions

Every pay period, employee payroll information is entered into the payroll system. The information needed for each employee includes the date, pay information, and employee's deductions. The employee taxes are entered or automatically calculated by the automated accounting program. Payroll transaction information is entered into the Payroll screen. The payroll register can be accessed on the Payroll tab of the Other Activities window. Figures AA3-1 and AA3-2 show the payroll register. Use the horizontal scroll bar at the bottom of the work area to move to the right and left.

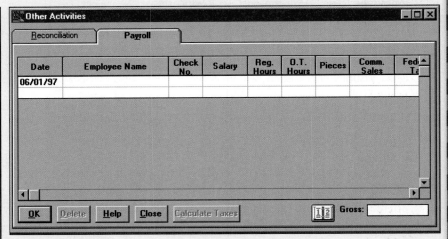

Figure AA3-1

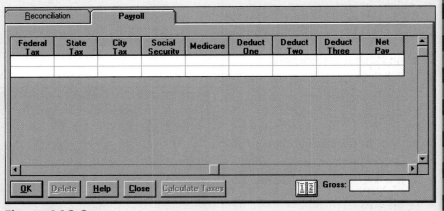

Figure AA3-2

Entering Payroll Transactions

For each employee, the information shown on the payroll screen is entered for each pay period. The employee's hours worked, regular and overtime, if any, tax deductions, and employee deductions. Accuracy is very important when entering this data in order to eliminate under or overpayments.

Employee transaction data is entered in the Payroll tab in the Other Activities window. Click on the Payroll tab to display the payroll screen. The following steps are used to enter payroll transactions.

1. Enter the date of the check.

2. Select the employee from the Employee drop-down list or key the first letter of the last name until the correct name appears.

3. Verify that the check number displayed in the Check No. cell is correct. If it is not correct, enter the correct check number.

4. Use the Tab key to enter salary information. If the employee is salaried, the salary amount will be displayed. If it is necessary to key a different salary, the salary amount cell can be changed. Entering a new amount will override the salary amount in the cell.

5. If the employee is paid by the hour, enter the regular hours worked in the Reg. Hours cell.

6. If the employee is paid hourly and has worked overtime, enter the overtime hours worked in the O.T. Hours cell.

7. Click on the Calculate Taxes button to have the software

automatically calculate the employee taxes. After the calculations are completed, the employee taxes are displayed in the various employee taxes cells. Visually check each cell to verify that an amount appears.

8. Enter all employee deductions.

9. Click OK. A display of the payroll check will be shown on the screen.

10. Click the Close button to continue or click Print to print the check.

Deleting Payroll Transactions

1. Select the transaction on the payroll screen you want to delete.

2. Click the Delete button to delete the payroll transaction. It is important to delete all fields of information related to the employee. If a check had already been written, it is important to mark it void.

Correcting Payroll Transactions

1. Select the payroll transaction you want to correct.

2. Enter the corrections. The employee's record will be updated and the previous check entered in error should be marked void.

3. Click OK.

Generating Payroll Journal Entries for the Period

The payroll journal entries can be generated automatically without any calculations by using the following steps:

1. Select the Current Payroll Journal Entry menu item from the Options menu.

2. When the confirmation box shown in Figure AA3-3 appears, click Yes.

3. The general journal window automatically appears, displaying the payroll journal entries that were posted. This entry appears as shown in Figure AA3-4. Click the Post button. Posting is done after verifying that the journal entry appears to be correct.

Generating Employer's Payroll Taxes

Generating employer's payroll taxes can be done by using the menu item for employer's payroll taxes.

Automated Accounting allows you to automatically generate the entry for the employer's portion of the payroll taxes.

To automatically generate the journal entry, use the following steps.

1. Choose Employer's Payroll Taxes from the Options menu.

2. When the confirmation box shown in Figure AA3-5 appears, click Yes.

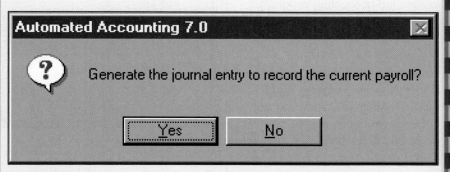

Figure AA3-3

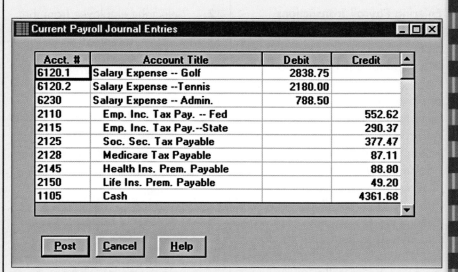

Figure AA3-4

3. The entry shown in Figure AA3-6 is automatically generated. Click the Post button.

4. Click the Close button of the general journal.

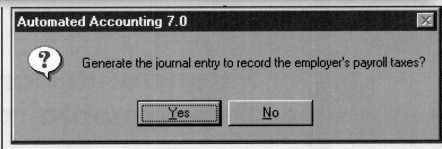

Figure AA3-5

AUTOMATING MASTERY PROBLEM 3-8

Instructions:

1. Load *Automated Accounting 7.0* or higher software.

2. Select database A03-8 (Advanced Course Problem 3-8) from the accounting text-book template disk.

3. Select File from the menu bar and choose the Save As menu command. Key the path to the drive and directory that contains your data files. Save the database with a file name of XXX038 (where XXX are your initials).

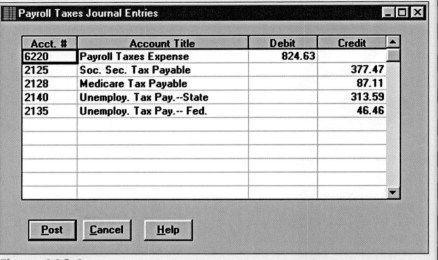

Figure AA3-6

4. Access Problem Instructions through the Help menu (7.0) or Browser tool (8.0). Read the Problem Instruction screen.

5. Refer to pages 88 and 89 for data used in this problem.

6. Exit the Automated Accounting software.

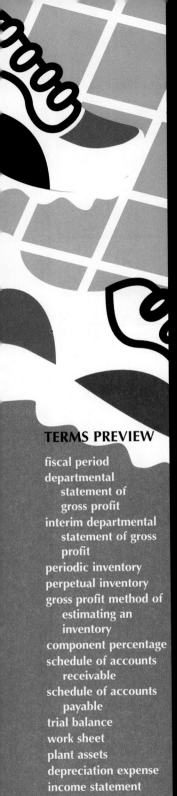

4

Financial Reporting for a Departmentalized Business

AFTER STUDYING CHAPTER 4, YOU WILL BE ABLE TO:

1. Define accounting terms related to financial reporting for a departmentalized business.

2. Identify accounting concepts and practices related to financial reporting for a departmentalized business.

3. Prepare interim departmental statement of gross profit.

4. Prepare a work sheet for a departmentalized business.

5. Prepare financial statements for a departmentalized business.

6. Analyze financial statements using selected component percentages.

7. Complete end-of-period work for a departmentalized business.

Financial statements summarize the financial information that a business records. These financial statements are then analyzed to evaluate the financial position and progress of the business. The managers of a business use the financial statements to make financial decisions for future operations. The financial statements are also used in preparing tax reports, which must be completed at least once a year. Therefore, financial statements are prepared at least once a year. The length of time for which a business summarizes and reports financial information is called a **fiscal period**. (CONCEPT: Accounting Period Cycle)

The accounting period cycle concept states that changes in financial information are reported for a specific period of time in the form of financial statements. The time period for which financial statements are prepared depends on the needs of the business. An accounting period may be one month, three months, six months, or one year. For tax purposes, every business prepares financial statements at the end of each year.

Each business determines the length of the fiscal period it uses. MasterSport uses a calendar-year fiscal period.

ACCOUNTING
IN YOUR CAREER

PROFITABLE ENOUGH TO CONTINUE?

Glamour Walls has two departments, paint and wallpaper in each of its stores. In recent years, the sales in all of the stores' paint departments have declined because customers find better pricing at the large home improvement discount stores. Consumers still prefer, however, to buy their wallpaper from stores like Glamour Walls, perhaps because of the availability of resident interior designers who advise on wallpaper selection.

Paul Somerville heads the accounting team of this multistore business. A dispute has arisen at the annual managers' meeting, and Paul has been asked for his input. The managers of the wallpaper departments are suggesting that the paint departments be dropped, since their sales are small and their gross profit percentages are only 20%. "We're carrying the paint department," they complain. These managers believe that if the paint departments were closed, they could use the space to carry additional lines of wallpaper. Paul Somerville anticipated that this issue would arise at the meeting. Therefore, he had prepared a transparency to illustrate the situation. The transparency showed the following information:

	Paint		Wallpaper	
Net Sales	$300,000	100%	$4,500,000	100%
Cost of Merchandise Sold	240,000	80%	2,475,000	55%
Gross Profit	60,000	20%	2,025,000	45%

Critical Thinking

1. What might Paul Somerville say to persuade the wallpaper department managers that the paint department should be kept?

2. Other than the financial information provided, are there other reasons the paint department should be maintained?

DEPARTMENTAL STATEMENT OF GROSS PROFIT

A departmentalized business prepares the same financial statements in the same form as a nondepartmentalized business. In addition, a departmentalized business usually prepares reports about how well each department is doing. A statement prepared at the end of a fiscal period showing the gross profit for each department is called a **departmental statement of gross profit**.

A departmental statement of gross profit provides revenue and cost information for each department. A review of this information may show a need to

1.   Change merchandise selling prices.

2.   Change suppliers of merchandise.

3.   Add, delete, or change products.

4.   Discontinue a department.

Gross profit information reflects changes between costs and selling prices. A departmental statement of gross profit also provides information that can be used to quickly determine potential profits. Therefore, a business often prepares a departmental statement of gross profit at the end of each month even though the fiscal period is longer than one month. A statement showing gross profit for each department for a portion of a fiscal period is called an **interim departmental statement of gross profit**. MasterSport prepares monthly interim departmental statements of gross profit.

Determining Ending Merchandise Inventory

To prepare an interim departmental statement of gross profit, both beginning and ending inventory amounts are needed. The ending inventory for one month becomes the beginning inventory for the next month.

Two principal methods are used to determine actual amounts of merchandise on hand. A merchandise inventory determined by counting, weighing, or measuring items of merchandise on hand is called a **periodic inventory**. A periodic inventory is sometimes referred to as a physical inventory. A merchandise inventory determined by keeping a continuous record of increases, decreases, and balance on hand is called a **perpetual inventory**. A perpetual inventory is sometimes referred to as a book inventory.

The cost of merchandise inventory is relatively easy to determine at any time when a perpetual inventory is kept. However, keeping a perpetual inventory for a merchandising business with many inventory items requires a good computer database system. Such systems are still not practical for many merchandising businesses.

For a periodic inventory, the business takes a physical count of merchandise. However, a periodic inventory on a monthly basis may not be practical. When a perpetual inventory is not kept and a monthly periodic inventory is not practical, a business may estimate merchandise inventory. Estimating inventory by using the previous year's percentage of gross profit on operations is called the **gross profit method of estimating an inventory**.

F. Y. I.

Interim financial statements provide managers timely information required to make decisions and to implement changes. Managers also use interim statements to spot trends and to evaluate the performance of the departments.

1. List beginning inventory.

2. Determine net purchases.

3. Calculate merchandise available for sale.

4. Determine net sales.

5. Calculate estimated gross profit.

6. Calculate the estimated cost of merchandise sold.

7. Calculate estimated ending inventory.

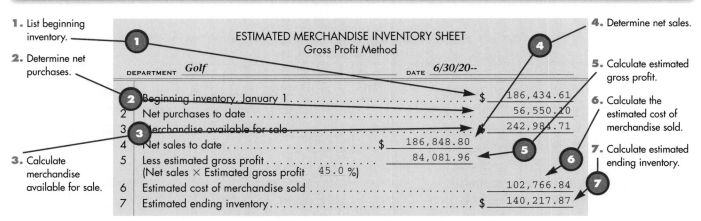

ESTIMATED MERCHANDISE INVENTORY SHEET
Gross Profit Method

DEPARTMENT *Golf*   DATE *6/30/20--*

1	Beginning inventory, January 1	$ 186,434.61
2	Net purchases to date	56,550.10
3	Merchandise available for sale	$ 242,984.71
4	Net sales to date	$ 186,848.80
5	Less estimated gross profit (Net sales × Estimated gross profit 45.0 %)	84,081.96
6	Estimated cost of merchandise sold	102,766.84
7	Estimated ending inventory	$ 140,217.87

Figure 4-1

MasterSport uses a periodic inventory system. It uses the gross profit method of estimating an inventory to determine monthly ending inventory. The golf department's estimated inventory sheet prepared on June 30 is shown in Figure 4-1. MasterSport used the following steps to prepare the estimated merchandise inventory sheet.

S T E P S Prepare an estimated merchandise inventory sheet

1. Obtain the beginning inventory, January 1, from the general ledger. The balance of Merchandise Inventory—Golf, *$186,434.61,* is the actual merchandise inventory on hand at the beginning of the fiscal period. The amount is the result of the periodic inventory count from December 31 of the previous year.

2. Determine net purchases to date, *$56,550.10,* as follows:

	Purchases—Golf	$59,430.60
−	Purchases Discount—Golf	− 1,090.20
		$58,340.40
−	Purchases Returns and Allowances—Golf	− 1,790.30
=	Net Purchases to Date (January 1–June 30)	$56,550.10

3. Add lines 1 and 2 to determine the merchandise available for sale, *$242,984.71.*

4. Determine net sales to date, *$186,848.80,* as follows.

	Sales—Golf	$190,540.20
−	Sales Discount—Golf	− 680.60
		$189,859.60
−	Sales Returns and Allowances—Golf	− 3,010.80
=	Net Sales to Date (January 1–June 30)	$186,848.80

5. Calculate the estimated gross profit, *$84,081.96,* by multiplying line 4 by 45.0%. The percentage used is a gross profit estimate based on records of previous years' operations.

6. Calculate the estimated cost of merchandise sold, *$102,766.84,* by subtracting line 5 from line 4.

7. Calculate the estimated ending inventory, *$140,217.87,* by subtracting line 6 from line 3. This estimate is used on the interim departmental statement of gross profit.

	Golf	*% of Net Sales	Tennis	*% of Net Sales	Total	*% of Net Sales
MasterSport Interim Departmental Statement of Gross Profit For Month Ended June 30, 20--						
Operating Revenue:						
Net Sales	$32,883.65	100.0	$36,546.30	100.0	$69,429.95	100.0
Cost of Merchandise Sold:						
Est. Mdse. Inv., June 1.	$149,387.48		$141,799.62		$291,187.10	
Net Purchases	8,916.40		17,073.50		25,989.90	
Mdse. Available for Sale.	$158,303.88		$158,873.12		$317,177.00	
Less Est. End. Inv., June 30. .	140,217.87		138,772.66		278,990.53	
Cost of Merchandise Sold . . .		18,086.01	55.0	20,100.46	55.0	38,186.47	55.0
Gross Profit on Operations	$14,797.64	45.0	$16,445.84	45.0	$31,243.48	45.0

*Rounded to nearest 0.1%

Figure 4-2

MasterSport's interim departmental statement of gross profit for the month ended June 30 is shown in Figure 4-2. The data are organized into three sections:

1. Operating revenue.

2. Cost of merchandise sold.

3. Gross profit on operations.

The beginning inventory for each department is the estimated ending inventory from the interim departmental statement of gross profit for the month ended May 31 of the current year.

Even when estimated inventory methods are used, a periodic inventory is usually taken at least once a year.

ANALYZING AN INTERIM DEPARTMENTAL STATEMENT OF GROSS PROFIT

To help a manager analyze financial information, relationships between items in a financial statement are calculated. The percentage relationship between one financial statement item and the total that includes that item is called a **component percentage**. Component percentages may be shown in a separate column on a financial statement. Four basic components are included in every sales dollar:

1. Cost of merchandise sold.

2. Gross profit on operations.

3. Total operating expenses.

4. Net income before federal income tax.

MasterSport analyzes its interim departmental statement of gross profit monthly by calculating a component percentage for cost of merchandise sold and gross profit on operations. The component percentages for operating expenses and net income are calculated and analyzed at the end of each fiscal period.

REMEMBER

Each department in a merchandising business has a merchandise inventory account and an income summary account.

	Total	*% of Net Sales
Operating Revenue:		
Net Sales	$69,429.95	100.0
Cost of Merchandise Sold:		
Est. Mdse. Inv., June 1.	$291,187.10	
Net Purchases	25,989.90	
Mdse. Available for Sale.	$317,177.00	
Less Est. End. Inv., June 30. .	278,990.53	
Cost of Merchandise Sold . . .	38,186.47	55.0
Gross Profit on Operations	$31,243.48	45.0

1. The cost of merchandise sold percentage:
$$\frac{\$38,186.47}{\$69,429.95} = .5499 \text{ or } 55\%$$

2. The gross profit percentage:
$$\frac{\$31,243.48}{\$69,429.95} = .45 \text{ or } 45\%$$

Figure 4-3

The cost of merchandise sold is a significant cost for all merchandising businesses. Management attempts to keep this cost as low as possible. The calculation of MasterSport's component percentage for total cost of merchandise sold is shown in Figure 4-3. Both the cost of merchandise sold percentage and the gross profit percentage use net sales in the denominator of the equation. From these percentages, we learn that for every $100 in sales, MasterSport spent $55 to obtain the goods sold. The remainder, $45, represents the gross profit on operations. Gross profit on operations must be large enough to cover total operating expenses and produce a net income.

Since MasterSport is a departmental business, similar calculations are made for each department. MasterSport uses the departmental component percentages to analyze the results of each department.

DETERMINING ACCEPTABLE LEVELS OF PERFORMANCE

For component percentages to be useful, a business must know acceptable levels of performance. Two sources are frequently used to determine acceptable performance. A business' historical records provide percentages that can be compared across time. The business should investigate significant changes in component percentages over time.

Industry performance standards are another source that businesses use for comparison. Industry trade organizations survey businesses and publish significant data such as component percentages. While these percentages represent industry averages, they allow useful comparisons to be made.

Based on these sources, MasterSport determines that the total cost of merchandise sold percentage should be 60.0% or less. As a result, total gross profit on operations should be 40.0% or more. MasterSport further determines that

these percentages are also good targets for each of the departments.

An analysis of the interim departmental statement of gross profit for the month ended June 30 indicates acceptable levels of performance. The component percentage for total cost of merchandise sold, 55.0%, is less than 60.0%. The component percentage for total gross profit on operations, 45.0%, is more than 40.0%. The component percentages for cost of merchandise sold and gross profit on operations for each department also indicate acceptable levels of performance.

Interim financial statements provide information for periods of time less than a year such as months, quarters, or semiannual periods.

fiscal period

departmental
statement of
gross profit

interim departmental
statement of gross
profit

periodic inventory

perpetual inventory

gross profit method
of estimating an
inventory

component
percentage

AUDIT YOUR **U**NDERSTANDING

1. In addition to regular financial statements, what other reports does a departmentalized business prepare?

2. What are the two principal methods for determining amounts of merchandise on hand?

3. What are the three sections of an interim departmental statement of gross profit?

WORK **TOGETHER**

Preparing an interim departmental statement of gross profit

The following data are obtained from the accounting records of Willow Glen Interior Design on May 31 of the current year. Estimated merchandise inventory forms and statement paper are provided in the *Working Papers*. Your instructor will guide you through the following examples.

	Kitchen	Bath
Beginning Inventory, January 1	$110,000.00	$84,000.00
Estimated Beginning Inventory, May 1	111,426.00	87,072.00
Net Purchases, January 1 to April 30	42,500.00	30,100.00
Net Sales, January 1 to April 30	78,600.00	52,300.00
Net Purchases for May	8,300.00	5,400.00
Net Sales for May	20,200.00	8,400.00
Estimated Gross Profit Percentage	48.0%	48.0%

4. Prepare an estimated merchandise inventory sheet for each department for the month ended May 31.

5. Prepare an interim departmental statement of gross profit for the month ended May 31. Calculate and record component percentages for cost of merchandise sold and gross profit on operations. Round percentage calculations to the nearest 0.1%.

ON YOUR **OWN**

Preparing an interim departmental statement of gross profit

The following data are obtained from the accounting records of Lassen Heating and Air Conditioning, Inc., on April 30 of the current year. Estimated merchandise inventory forms and statement paper are provided in the *Working Papers*. Work independently to complete the following problems.

	Commercial	Residential
Beginning Inventory, January 1	$280,000.00	$108,000.00
Estimated Beginning Inventory, April 1	287,894.00	118,884.00
Net Purchases, January 1 to March 31	120,500.00	62,300.00
Net Sales, January 1 to March 31	196,600.00	88,400.00
Net Purchases for April	66,200.00	13,400.00
Net Sales for April	71,100.00	14,400.00
Estimated Gross Profit Percentage	42.0%	42.0%

6. Prepare an estimated merchandise inventory sheet for each department for the month ended April 30.

7. Prepare an interim departmental statement of gross profit for the month ended April 30. Calculate and record component percentages for cost of merchandise sold and gross profit on operations. Round percentage calculations to the nearest 0.1%.

ACCOUNTING'S MYSTERY SOLVERS

A s the value of insurance claims have grown, so has the role of the forensic accountant. Forensic accountants are accounting's mystery solvers. They combine problem solving and analytical skills with their knowledge of accounting concepts and procedures.

Forensic accountants assist insurance companies in detecting fraud and inflated insurance claims. They may work alongside police detectives and fire and arson investigators. Often forensic accountants serve as expert witnesses in court. They testify to such things as the valuation of inventory, loss from business interruption, wrongful death claims, and product liability claims.

When a business experiences a loss from a fire or natural disaster, they may lose accounting records, as well as inventory and business assets. The business can call on a forensic accountant, or a team of forensic accountants, to help reconstruct its accounting records, and to determine the extent of its loss.

Other types of services offered by forensic accountants include appraisals; insurance coverage reviews; and litigation support for corporate liquidations, partnership dissolutions, and personal injury claims.

Accountants specializing in these investigative activities may belong to the National Association of Forensic Accountants (NAFA). The association is comprised of accounting firms specializing in professional investigations. The association serves all of North America. The association certifies its members and provides on-site training for new member firms.

LEGAL ISSUES IN ACCOUNTING

4-2 Preparing a Work Sheet for a Departmentalized Business

PROVING THE ACCURACY OF POSTING TO SUBSIDIARY LEDGERS

MasterSport
Schedule of Accounts Receivable
June 30, 20--

Lawrence Bissell	$ 950.60
Eastside Sports Center	644.70
Galaxy Tennis Club	1,785.00
Golden Golf League	1,592.50
Mary Lynch	245.70
Par Golf Club	1,391.25
Swanville Schools	775.25
Helen Vega	3,675.00
William Wenz	2,695.00
Total Accounts Receivable	$13,755.00

Figure 4-4

MasterSport prepares a report showing the total of all accounts receivable ledger accounts. A list of customer accounts, account balances, and total amount due from all customers is called a **schedule of accounts receivable**. The total of a schedule of accounts receivable must equal the balance of the general ledger controlling account, Accounts Receivable. MasterSport's schedule of accounts receivable is shown in Figure 4-4.

MasterSport also prepares a report showing the total of all accounts payable ledger accounts.

A list of vendor accounts, account balances, and total amount due all vendors is called a **schedule of accounts payable**. The total on a schedule of accounts payable must equal the balance of the controlling account, Accounts Payable. MasterSport's schedule of accounts payable is shown in Figure 4-5.

The balances of both controlling accounts, Accounts Receivable and Accounts Payable, agree with the totals shown on the two schedules. Therefore, posting to subsidiary ledgers is assumed to be correct.

MasterSport
Schedule of Accounts Payable
June 30, 20--

Champion Tennis Supply	$ 3,660.60
E-Z Golf	9,420.00
Golf Tee, Inc.	1,590.00
Key Tennis Company	1,514.30
Nelson Racquets, Inc.	10,840.00
Tennis Warehouse	3,610.40
University Tennis	725.00
Total Accounts Payable	$31,360.30

Figure 4-5

If debits equal credits in journals and if posting is done correctly, debits will equal credits in a general ledger. A proof of the equality of debits and credits in a general ledger is called a **trial balance**. A trial balance is most often prepared as part of the end-of-fiscal-period activities. MasterSport completes the end-of-fiscal-period work as of December 31 each year. *(CONCEPT: Accounting Period Cycle)*

Trial Balance on a Departmental Work Sheet

A columnar accounting form used to summarize the general ledger information needed to prepare financial statements is called a **work sheet**. A trial balance is prepared in the Trial Balance columns of the work sheet. General ledger accounts are listed in the Account Title column in the same order in which they appear in the general ledger. All accounts are listed regardless of whether there is a balance or not. MasterSport's trial balance for the current year ended December 31 is on the work sheet shown in Figure 4-6.

After all general ledger accounts and balances have been entered, the Trial Balance columns are totaled, checked for equality, and ruled. The two column totals, $1,302,612.99, are the same.

Adjustments on a Departmental Work Sheet

Some general ledger accounts are not up to date. For example, uncollectible accounts expense has not been recorded. The entries needed to bring accounts up to date are planned in the Adjustments columns of the work sheet.

Uncollectible Accounts Expense Adjustment. Merchandise is sometimes sold on account to customers who later are unable to pay the amounts owed. Amounts that cannot be collected from customers are business expenses. All expenses must be recorded in the fiscal period in which the expenses contribute to earning revenue. *(CONCEPT: Matching Expenses with Revenue)*

MasterSport has found from past experience that approximately 1% of the total sales on account will be uncollectible. Total sales on account for the current year are $210,940.00. Therefore, MasterSport's uncollectible accounts expense is calculated as follows.

Total Sales on Account	×	Percentage	=	Estimated Uncollectible Accounts Expense
$210,940.00	×	1%	=	$2,109.40

MasterSport estimates that of the $210,940.00 sales on account during the year, $2,109.40 will eventually be uncollectible.

Uncollectible Accounts Expense is increased by a $2,109.40 debit. **Allowance for Uncollectible Accounts**, a contra asset account, is increased by a $2,109.40 credit. The **Allowance for Uncollectible Accounts** balance represents the total estimated amount that MasterSport believes will not be collected from accounts receivable. This estimated amount is not deducted from the **Accounts Receivable** balance until MasterSport knows for sure which customers will not pay. The estimated uncollectible accounts amount, therefore, is recorded in a separate account titled **Allowance for Uncollectible Accounts**.

Entries related to uncollectible accounts expense are described in Chapter 7.

Uncollectible Accounts Expense	
Adj. *(a)* 2,109.40	

Allowance for Uncollectible Accounts	
	Dec. 31 Bal. 240.60
	Adj. *(a)* 2,109.40
	(New Bal. 2,350.00)

The **Uncollectible Accounts Expense** adjustment is recorded on the work sheet, lines 4 and 56, Figure 4-6. The adjustment is labeled *(a)* because it is the first adjustment recorded.

MasterSport

Work Sheet

For Year Ended December 31, 20--

	TRIAL BALANCE		ADJUSTMENTS		INCOME STATEMENT		BALANCE SHEET		
ACCOUNT TITLE	DEBIT	CREDIT	DEBIT	CREDIT	DEBIT	CREDIT	DEBIT	CREDIT	
1 Cash	4344000						4344000		1
2 Petty Cash	50000						50000		2
3 Accounts Receivable	1285500						1285500		3
4 Allowance for Uncoll. Accts.		24060		(a) 210940				235000	4
5 Merchandise Inventory—Golf	18643461		(b) 1842039				20485500		5
6 Merchandise Inventory—Tennis	19984460			(c) 936000			19048460		6
7 Supplies—Office	1270000			(d) 995000			275000		7
8 Supplies—Store	1433000			(e) 779000			654000		8
9 Prepaid Insurance	985000			(f) 565000			420000		9
10 Office Equipment	1690000						1690000		10
11 Accum. Depr.—Office Equipment		596000		(g) 149000				745000	11
12 Store Equipment	3890000						3890000		12
13 Accum. Depr.—Store Equipment		1800000		(h) 300000				2100000	13
14 Accounts Payable		3816030						3816030	14
15 Employee Income Tax Payable—Federal		268075						268075	15
16 Employee Income Tax Payable—State		111819						111819	16
17 Federal Income Tax Payable				(i) 119007				119007	17
18 Social Security Tax Payable		273057						273057	18
19 Medicare Tax Payable		63013						63013	19
20 Sales Tax Payable		313964						313964	20
21 Unemployment Tax Payable—Federal		2360						2360	21
22 Unemployment Tax Payable—State		15930						15930	22
23 Health Insurance Premiums Payable		226116						226116	23
24 Life Insurance Premiums Payable		35019						35019	24
25 Dividends Payable		3000000						3000000	25
26 Capital Stock		34000000						34000000	26
27 Retained Earnings		4221050						4221050	27
28 Dividends	3000000						3000000		28
29 Income Summary—Golf				(b) 1842039		1842039			29

Figure 4-6 (top half)

#	Account Title	Trial Balance Debit	Trial Balance Credit	Adjustments Debit	Adjustments Credit	Income Statement Debit	Income Statement Credit	Balance Sheet Debit	Balance Sheet Credit
30	Income Summary—Tennis								
31	Income Summary—General			(c) 9 360 00		9 360 00			
32	Sales—Golf		351 032 81				351 032 81		
33	Sales—Tennis		438 341 75				438 341 75		
34	Sales Discount—Golf	1 605 85				1 605 85			
35	Sales Discount—Tennis	2 005 25				2 005 25			
36	Sales Ret. and Allow.—Golf	4 950 50				4 950 50			
37	Sales Ret. and Allow.—Tennis	6 181 80				6 181 80			
38	Purchases—Golf	215 745 68				215 745 68			
39	Purchases—Tennis	231 766 62				231 766 62			
40	Purchases Discount—Golf		4 058 95				4 058 95		
41	Purchases Discount—Tennis		4 334 55				4 334 55		
42	Purchases Ret. and Allow.—Golf		8 282 48				8 282 48		
43	Purchases Ret. and Allow.—Tennis		8 897 52				8 897 52		
44	Advertising Expense	5 192 88				5 192 88			
45	Credit Card Fee Expense	5 950 00				5 950 00			
46	Depr. Expense—Store Equipment			(h) 3 000 00		3 000 00			
47	Salary Expense—Golf	90 924 19				90 924 19			
48	Salary Expense—Tennis	72 627 02				72 627 02			
49	Supplies Expense—Store			(e) 7 790 00		7 790 00			
50	Depr. Expense—Office Equipment			(x) 1 490 00		1 490 00			
51	Insurance Expense			(f) 5 650 00		5 650 00			
52	Miscellaneous Expense	5 958 48				5 958 48			
53	Payroll Taxes Expense	21 426 92				21 426 92			
54	Rent Expense	18 056 40				18 056 40			
55	Salary Expense—Admin.	43 667 19				43 667 19			
56	Supplies Expense—Office			(d) 9 950 00		9 950 00			
57	Uncollectible Accounts Expense			(a) 2 109 40		2 109 40			
58	Federal Income Tax Expense	10 800 00		(i) 1 190 07		11 990 07			
59		1 302 612 99	1 302 612 99	58 959 86	58 959 86	777 398 25	833 368 45	551 424 60	495 454 40
60	Net Income after Fed. Inc. Tax					55 970 20			55 970 20
61						833 368 45	833 368 45	551 424 60	551 424 60

Figure 4-6 (bottom half)

Merchandise Inventory Adjustments. The merchandise inventory account balance in the trial balance is the beginning inventory for a fiscal period. The amount of the ending inventory is determined by taking a periodic inventory at the end of a fiscal period.

The beginning golf merchandise inventory, $186,434.61, for MasterSport is shown on line 5 in the Trial Balance Debit column of the work sheet in Figure 4-6. The periodic inventory taken on December 31 shows that the cost of golf merchandise inventory is $204,855.00. To bring the golf merchandise inventory up to date, the balance of Merchandise Inventory—Golf needs to be increased by $18,420.39 ($204,855.00 ending inventory *less* $186,434.61 beginning inventory).

Merchandise Inventory—Golf	
Dec. 31 Bal.	186,434.61
Adj. *(b)*	18,420.39
(New Bal.	204,855.00)

Income Summary—Golf	
	Adj. *(b)* 18,420.39

The account Merchandise Inventory—Golf is debited for $18,420.39. Income Summary—Golf is credited for $18,420.39. The balance of Merchandise Inventory—Golf after this adjustment, $204,855.00, is equal to the actual ending inventory.

A similar adjustment is made for Merchandise Inventory—Tennis. The beginning tennis merchandise inventory, $199,844.60, is shown on line 6 in the Trial Balance Debit column of the work sheet. The periodic inventory taken on December 31 shows that the cost of tennis merchandise inventory is $190,484.60. Therefore, the balance of Merchandise Inventory—Tennis needs to be decreased by $9,360.00 ($199,844.60 beginning inventory *less* $190,484.60 ending inventory).

Income Summary—Tennis	
Adj. *(c)* 9,360.00	

Merchandise Inventory—Tennis	
Dec. 31 Bal. 199,844.60	Adj. *(c)* 9,360.00
(New Bal. 190,484.60)	

Income Summary—Tennis is debited for $9,360.00. Merchandise Inventory—Tennis is credited for $9,360.00. The balance of Merchandise Inventory—Tennis after this adjustment, $190,484.60, is equal to the actual ending inventory.

The two inventory adjustments are entered on the work sheet. The Merchandise Inventory—Golf adjustment is labeled *(b)*. The Merchandise Inventory—Tennis adjustment is labeled *(c)*.

Supplies Adjustments. A supplies inventory account balance in a trial balance includes two items. (1) The account balance on January 1. (2) The cost of supplies bought during the year. The account balance does not reflect the cost of any supplies used during the year, which is an operating expense. The amount of the ending inventory is determined by taking a periodic inventory at the end of a fiscal period.

MasterSport's office supplies account balance, $12,700.00, is shown on line 7 in the Trial Balance Debit column of the work sheet, Figure 4-6. The store supplies account balance, $14,330.00, is shown on line 8 in the Trial Balance Debit column of the work sheet.

The periodic inventory taken on December 31 shows that the cost of office supplies inventory is $2,750.00. To bring MasterSport's office supplies inventory up to date, the balance of Supplies—Office needs to be decreased by $9,950.00 (December 31 balance, $12,700.00, *less* ending inventory, $2,750.00).

Supplies Expense—Office	
Adj. *(d)* 9,950.00	

Supplies—Office	
Dec. 31 Bal. 12,700.00	Adj. *(d)* 9,950.00
(New Bal. 2,750.00)	

Supplies Expense—Office is increased by a $9,950.00 debit. Supplies—Office is decreased by a $9,950.00 credit. The balance of Supplies—Office after this adjustment, $2,750.00, is equal to the actual ending inventory.

A similar adjustment is made for store supplies inventory. The two supplies adjustments are entered on the work sheet. The Supplies—Office adjustment is labeled *(d)*. The Supplies—Store adjustment is labeled *(e)*.

Prepaid Insurance Adjustment. The prepaid insurance account balance includes two items. (1) The account balance on January 1. (2) The amount of insurance premiums paid during the year. The account balance does not reflect the amount of any insurance used during the year, which is an operating expense. The amount of unexpired insurance is determined at the end of a fiscal period.

MasterSport's prepaid insurance account balance, $9,850.00, is shown on line 9 in the Trial Balance Debit column of the work sheet, Figure 4-6. The actual unexpired prepaid insurance on December 31 is $4,200.00. To bring MasterSport's prepaid insurance account up to date, the balance of Prepaid Insurance must be decreased by $5,650.00 (December 31 balance, $9,850.00, *less* unexpired insurance, $4,200.00).

Insurance Expense			
Adj. *(f)*	5,650.00		

Prepaid Insurance			
Dec. 31 Bal.	9,850.00	Adj. *(f)*	5,650.00
(New Bal.	*4,200.00)*		

Insurance Expense is increased by a $5,650.00 debit. Prepaid Insurance is decreased by a $5,650.00 credit. The balance of Prepaid Insurance after this adjustment, $4,200.00, is equal to the actual unexpired prepaid insurance.

The Prepaid Insurance adjustment is entered on the work sheet. The adjustment is labeled *(f)*.

Depreciation Expense Adjustments. Assets that will be used for a number of years in the operation of a business are called **plant assets**. Plant assets are not bought for resale to customers in the normal course of business. Plant assets decrease in value because of use and because they become older with the passage of time and as new models become available. The portion of a plant asset's cost that is transferred to an expense account in each fiscal period during a plant asset's useful life is called **depreciation expense**. The decrease in the value of equipment because of use and passage of time is an operating expense. (*CONCEPT: Matching Expenses with Revenue*)

The matching expenses with revenue concept states that the revenue from business activities and the expenses associated with earning that revenue are recorded in the same accounting period. All revenue earned as a result of business operations must be reported. Likewise, all expenses incurred in producing the revenue during the accounting period must be reported. For example, a business had sales of $100,000.00 in December. Expenses before adjustments were $80,000.00. Adjustments for items such as uncollectible accounts expense, supplies expense, and depreciation expense totaled $5,000.00. Therefore, total expenses for December should be reported as $85,000.00. The matching of expenses with revenues results in an accurate report of net income of $15,000.00. By including all expenses, readers of the financial statements have a more complete picture of the financial condition of the business.

The amount of depreciation is an estimate. The actual decrease in equipment value is not known until equipment is disposed of or sold. For this reason, the *estimated* depreciation is recorded in a separate contra asset account for each type of equipment.

Calculating the amount of depreciation is described more fully in Chapter 8.

MasterSport estimates that the yearly depreciation on office equipment is $1,490.00. To adjust for the depreciation of office equipment, Depreciation Expense—Office Equipment is increased by a $1,490.00 debit. Accumulated Depreciation—Office Equipment is increased by a $1,490.00 credit.

Depreciation Expense—Office Equipment			
Adj. *(g)*	1,490.00		

Accumulated Depreciation—Office Equipment			
		Dec. 31 Bal.	5,960.00
		Adj. *(g)*	1,490.00
		(New Bal.	*7,450.00)*

A similar adjustment is made for Depreciation Expense—Store Equipment.

The two depreciation expense adjustments are entered on the work sheet, Figure 4-6. The Depreciation Expense—Office Equipment adjustment is labeled *(g)*. The Depreciation Expense—Store Equipment adjustment is labeled *(h)*.

Federal Income Tax Expense Adjustment.

Corporations anticipating federal income taxes of $500.00 or more are required to pay estimated taxes each quarter. The estimated tax is paid in quarterly installments in April, June, September, and December. Even though a corporation pays a quarterly estimated tax, the actual income tax must be calculated at the end of each fiscal year.

MasterSport estimated $10,800.00 federal income tax for the current year. Each quarterly income tax payment is recorded in a cash payments journal as a debit to Federal Income Tax Expense and a credit to Cash. At the end of the fiscal year, MasterSport determines that the federal income tax is $11,990.07. To bring its federal income tax expense account up to date, the balance of Federal Income Tax Expense must be increased by $1,190.07 (federal income tax amount, $11,990.07, *less* December 31 balance in Federal Income Tax Expense, $10,800.00).

Federal Income Tax Expense is increased by a $1,190.07 debit. Federal Income Tax Payable is

Federal Income Tax Expense		
Dec. 31 Bal.	10,800.00	
Adj. *(i)*	1,190.07	
(New Bal.	11,990.07)	

Federal Income Tax Payable		
	Adj. *(i)*	1,190.07

increased by a $1,190.07 credit. The balance of Federal Income Tax Expense after this adjustment, $11,990.07, is equal to the total federal income tax for the fiscal year.

The Federal Income Tax Expense adjustment, labeled *(i)*, is entered on the work sheet.

Calculating the actual federal income tax is described in more detail in Chapter 13.

After all adjustments have been entered on a work sheet, the Adjustments columns are totaled and checked for equality. The two column totals, $58,959.86, are the same. The work sheet's Adjustments columns are ruled as shown on line 58 of the work sheet.

BALANCE SHEET COLUMNS OF A WORK SHEET

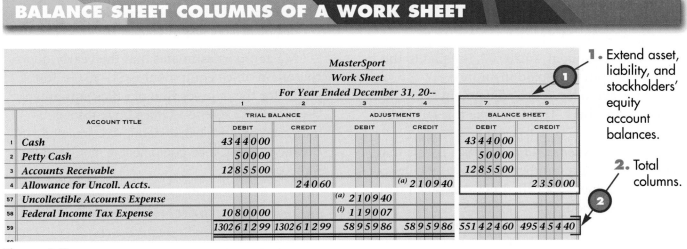

Figure 4-7

The asset, liability, and stockholders' equity account balances are extended to the Balance Sheet columns of a work sheet. For those accounts affected by adjustments, new balances are calculated and extended. For example, Allowance for Uncollectible Accounts, line 4 of the work sheet, Figure 4-6, has a Trial Balance Credit balance of $240.60. The Adjustments Credit column amount of $2,109.40 makes the new

account balance $2,350.00 ($240.60 *plus* $2,109.40). The new credit balance, $2,350.00, is extended to the Balance Sheet Credit column.

The two Balance Sheet columns are totaled, as shown in Figure 4-7. The totals are out of balance by the amount of change in stockholders' equity resulting from a net income or a net loss. MasterSport's two balance sheet column totals are shown on line 58 of the work sheet.

INCOME STATEMENT COLUMNS OF A WORK SHEET

	ACCOUNT TITLE	TRIAL BALANCE DEBIT	TRIAL BALANCE CREDIT	ADJUSTMENTS DEBIT	ADJUSTMENTS CREDIT	INCOME STATEMENT DEBIT	INCOME STATEMENT CREDIT
29	Income Summary—Golf				(b)1842039		1842039
30	Income Summary—Tennis			(c)936000		936000	
32	Sales—Golf		35103281				35103281
58	Federal Income Tax Expense	1080000		(i)119007		1199007	
59		130261299	130261299	5895986	5895986	77739825	83336845

1. Extend revenue, cost and expense accounts.
2. Total columns.

Figure 4-8

The balances of all revenue, cost, and expense accounts are extended to the Income Statement columns on a work sheet. The amounts in the Adjustments columns for Income Summary—Golf and Income Summary—Tennis are also extended to the Income Statement columns, as shown in Figure 4-8.

The two Income Statement columns are totaled, as shown on line 58 of the work sheet.

NET INCOME ON A WORK SHEET

1. Write difference between columns.
2. Add description.

	ACCOUNT TITLE	INCOME STATEMENT DEBIT	INCOME STATEMENT CREDIT	BALANCE SHEET DEBIT	BALANCE SHEET CREDIT
59		77739825	83336845	55142460	49545440
60	Net Income after Fed. Inc. Tax	5597020			5597020
		83336845	83336845	55142460	55142460

3. Write difference between columns.
4. Total columns.

Figure 4-9

The difference between the two Income Statement column totals on the work sheet is the net income or net loss for a fiscal period. If the Credit column total is larger than the Debit column total as shown in Figure 4-9, the difference is the net income. MasterSport's net income is calculated as follows.

	Income Statement Credit column total (line 58)	$833,368.45
−	Income Statement Debit Column total (line 58)	−777,398.25
=	Net income for the fiscal period	$ 55,970.20

The net income, $55,970.20, is written under the work sheet's Income Statement Debit column total to make the two Income Statement columns balance. The words *Net Income after Fed. Inc. Tax* are written in the Account Title column.

The difference between the two Balance Sheet column totals on the work sheet also represents the net income or net loss for a fiscal period. A net income increases stockholders' equity. Since stockholders' equity is increased with a credit, MasterSport's net income, $55,970.20, is written under the Balance Sheet

Credit column total to make the two Balance Sheet columns balance.

After the net income amount is written in the two work sheet columns, the last four columns are totaled again. The totals for each pair of columns must be the same. The two Income Statement totals are the same, $833,368.45. The two Balance Sheet totals are the same, $551,424.60. If columns do not balance, errors must be found and corrected before final ruling is done.

3. Write difference between columns.

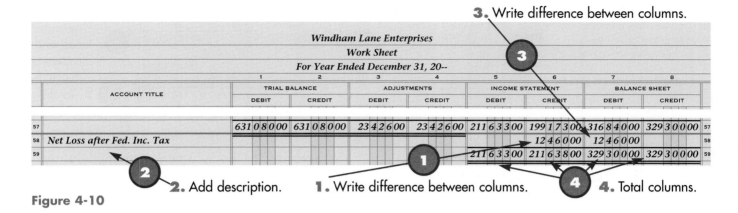

ACCOUNT TITLE	TRIAL BALANCE		ADJUSTMENTS		INCOME STATEMENT		BALANCE SHEET		
	DEBIT	CREDIT	DEBIT	CREDIT	DEBIT	CREDIT	DEBIT	CREDIT	
57	631 08 0 00	631 08 0 00	23 42 6 00	23 42 6 00	211 63 3 00	199 17 3 00	316 84 0 00	329 30 0 00	57
58 Net Loss after Fed. Inc. Tax						12 46 0 00	12 46 0 00		58
59					211 63 3 00	211 63 8 00	329 30 0 00	329 30 0 00	59

2. Add description.   **1.** Write difference between columns.   **4.** Total columns.

Figure 4-10

If the Income Statement Debit column total is larger than the Credit column total as shown in Figure 4-10, the difference represents a net loss. When a net loss occurs, the net loss amount is written on a work sheet in the Income Statement Credit and Balance Sheet Debit columns. The difference represents a decrease in stockholders' equity resulting from a net loss.

CULTURAL DIVERSITY

AFRICAN AMERICAN BUSINESSES

The Census Bureau's Survey of Minority-Owned Business Enterprises indicates that minority-owned enterprises are increasing in number and size. Firms owned by African Americans increased from 424,165 in 1987 to 620,912 in 1992. This represents a 46 percent increase. During the same period, total receipts increased by 63 percent from $19.8 billion to $32.2 billion.

About 94 percent of African American-owned firms operated as proprietorships in 1992. These businesses accounted for 50 percent of the gross receipts of Black-owned businesses.

The majority of businesses owned by African Americans operate in the service industries, such as health services, business services, and personal services. The retail trade accounted for the next largest concentration of Black-owned firms.

Black Enterprise magazine lists the nation's 100 largest black businesses in its B.E. 100. The list is comprised of industrial and service businesses that are at least 51 percent Black-owned. It maintains separate listings for the Auto Dealer 100, which lists the largest auto dealerships that are at least 51 percent Black-owned. From the 1997 B.E. 100, TLC Beatric International Holdings, Inc., located in New York, is listed as the largest employer with 4,700 employees. Spiral Inc./Power Line, located in Arizona, is listed as the top growth leader with a 215 percent increase in sales from 1995 to 1996.

TERMS REVIEW

schedule of accounts receivable

schedule of accounts payable

trial balance

work sheet

plant assets

depreciation expense

AUDIT YOUR UNDERSTANDING

1. What two reports are prepared to prove the accuracy of posting to subsidiary ledgers?

2. Why are adjustments made to certain accounts at the end of the fiscal period?

3. What account balances are extended to the Balance Sheet columns of a work sheet?

WORK TOGETHER

Analyzing adjusting entries

Selected information for Digital Car Stereo on December 31 of the current year is shown below. Selected T accounts with existing account balances are provided in the *Working Papers*. Your instructor will guide you through the following examples.

Account Title	Adjustment Information
Merchandise Inventory—Stereos	Actual Inventory, $49,430.00
Merchandise Inventory—Accessories	Actual Inventory, $4,630.00
Federal Income Tax Expense	Income Tax for Year, $13,110.00
Uncollectible Accounts Expense	2% of sales on account; total sales on account equal $175,000.00

4. Enter the required adjusting entries in the appropriate T accounts.

ON YOUR OWN

Analyzing adjusting entries

Selected information for Mission Laundry Supply on December 31 of the current year is shown below. Selected T accounts with existing account balances are provided in the *Working Papers*. Work independently to complete the following problem.

Account Title	Adjustment Information
Merchandise Inventory—Washers	Actual Inventory, $87,430.00
Merchandise Inventory—Dryers	Actual Inventory, $64,220.00
Depreciation Expense—Equipment	Estimated depreciation, $920.00
Uncollectible Accounts Expense	1% of sales on account; total sales on account equal $152,300.00

5. Enter the required adjusting entries in the appropriate T accounts.

DEPARTMENTAL STATEMENT OF GROSS PROFIT

MasterSport
Departmental Statement of Gross Profit
For Year Ended December 31, 20--

	Golf	*% of Net Sales	Tennis	*% of Net Sales	Total	*% of Net Sales
Operating Revenue:						
Net Sales	$344,476.46	100.0	$430,154.70	100.0	$774,631.16	100.0
Cost of Merchandise Sold:						
Mdse. Inventory, Jan. 1	$186,434.61		$199,844.60		$386,279.21	
Net Purchases	203,404.25		218,534.55		421,938.80	
Mdse. Available for Sale.	$389,838.86		$418,379.15		$808,218.01	
Less Ending Inv., Dec. 31. . . .	204,855.00		190,484.60		395,339.60	
Cost of Merchandise Sold . . .		184,983.86	53.7	227,894.55	53.0	412,878.41	53.3
Gross Profit on Operations		$159,492.60	46.3	$202,260.15	47.0	$361,752.75	46.7

*Rounded to nearest 0.1%

Figure 4-11

Financial statements are prepared to report the financial progress and condition of a business. (CONCEPT: *Adequate Disclosure*) MasterSport prepares four financial statements at the end of the annual fiscal period. (CONCEPT: *Accounting Period Cycle*)

1. Departmental statement of gross profit.

2. Income statement.

3. Statement of stockholders' equity.

4. Balance sheet.

The departmental statement of gross profit prepared at the end of a fiscal period is similar to the interim departmental statement of gross profit. However, interim departmental statements of gross profit use estimated ending inventories. The annual departmental statement of gross profit uses the actual ending periodic inventories. MasterSport's departmental statement of gross profit for the fiscal year ended December 31 is shown in Figure 4-11.

Data needed to complete the departmental statement of gross profit are taken from the Trial Balance, Income Statement, and Balance Sheet columns of the work sheet.

MasterSport analyzes the annual departmental statement of gross profit in the same way that it analyzes the interim departmental statement of gross profit. Component percentages for the total cost of merchandise sold and gross profit on operations are calculated. These percentages are also calculated for each department.

Income Statement Items	Acceptable Component Percentages	Actual Component Percentages
Net Sales	100.0%	100.0%
Cost of Merchandise Sold	60.0% or less	53.3%
Gross Profit on Operations	40.0% or more	46.7%
Total Operating Expenses	38.0% or less	37.9%
Net Income before Federal Income Tax	7.0% or more	8.8%

Figure 4-12

MasterSport uses the same performance standards for the annual departmental statement of gross profit as for the interim departmental statement of gross profit. For comparative purposes, MasterSport's acceptable and actual component percentages are shown in Figure 4-12.

The component percentage for total cost of merchandise sold should be 60% or less. The component percentage for total gross profit on operations should be 40% or more. The same performance standards are used for each department.

An analysis of the annual departmental statement of gross profit indicates acceptable levels of performance. The component percentage for total cost of merchandise sold, 53.3%, is less than 60.0%. The component percentage for total gross profit on operations, 46.7%, is more than 40.0%. The component percentages for total cost of merchandise sold and total gross profit on operations for each department also indicate acceptable levels of performance.

REMEMBER

A component percentage is usually carried to one decimal place.

SMALL BUSINESS SPOTLIGHT

There are over 600,000 franchises in the U.S. and they are responsible for 40% of all retail sales. In addition, they employ more than 8 million people. Some of the most familiar franchise businesses include fast food restaurants and auto care shops, but there is more to franchising than a quick lunch or an oil change. Other franchise businesses include dry cleaning, pet grooming, day care centers, bagel shops, coffee bars, business centers, housekeeping services, and interior decorators.

Every franchise starts with two players. First, there are entrepreneurs who franchise their businesses—franchisors. And then, there are franchisees who operate businesses.

The franchisor uses franchising to grow a successful business into a much larger enterprise. In most cases the franchisor, who owns things like the company name and trademarks, sells a license to a franchisee. The franchisee pays a license fee and monthly royalties to the franchisor. In exchange for the fee and royalties the franchisee gets help in setting up and running the franchise.

MasterSport
Income Statement
For Year Ended December 31, 20--

				% of Net Sales*
Operating Revenue:				
Sales............................			$789,374.56	
Less: Sales Discount		$ 3,611.10		
Sales Returns and Allow.		11,132.30	14,743.40	
Net Sales			$774,631.16	100.0
Cost of Merchandise Sold:				
Merchandise Inventory, Jan. 1, 20-- . .			$386,279.21	
Purchases.......................		$447,512.30		
Less: Purchases Discount	$ 8,393.50			
Purchases Returns and Allow...	17,180.00	25,573.50		
Net Purchases....................			421,938.80	
Total Cost of Mdse. Avail. for Sale . . .			$808,218.01	
Less Mdse. Inventory, Dec. 31, 20-- . .			395,339.60	
Cost of Merchandise Sold			412,878.41	53.3
Gross Profit on Operations..........			$361,752.75	46.7
Operating Expenses:				
Selling Expenses:				
Advertising Expense		$ 5,192.88		
Credit Card Fee Expense.........		5,950.00		
Depreciation Exp.—Store Equip....		3,000.00		
Salary Expense—Golf		90,924.19		
Salary Expense—Tennis		72,627.02		
Supplies Expense—Store		7,790.00		
Total Selling Expenses			$185,484.09	
Administrative Expenses:				
Depreciation Exp.—Office Equip. . . .		$ 1,490.00		
Insurance Expense		5,650.00		
Miscellaneous Expense		5,958.48		
Payroll Taxes Expense		21,426.92		
Rent Expense		18,056.40		
Salary Expense—Admin..........		43,667.19		
Supplies Expense—Office........		9,950.00		
Uncollectible Accounts Expense...		2,109.40		
Total Administrative Expenses			108,308.39	
Total Operating Expenses.........			293,792.48	37.9
Net Income before Federal Inc. Tax			$ 67,960.27	8.8
Less Federal Income Tax Exp.			11,990.07	1.5
Net Income after Federal Inc. Tax			$ 55,970.20	7.2

*Rounded to nearest 0.1%.

Figure 4-13

A financial statement showing the revenue and expenses for a fiscal period is called an **income statement**. An income statement reports the financial progress of a business for a fiscal period. MasterSport's income statement for the fiscal year ended December 31 is shown in Figure 4-13.

The data used to prepare MasterSport's income statement are obtained from the work sheet's Trial Balance, Income Statement, and Balance Sheet columns.

From this statement, MasterSport analyzes the component percentages for total operating expenses, net income before and after income tax, and federal income tax. Comparisons with previous performance and with published industry performance standards help determine acceptable levels of performance. From these sources, MasterSport determines that its component percentages for the end of the fiscal period, as shown in Figure 4-12, are acceptable.

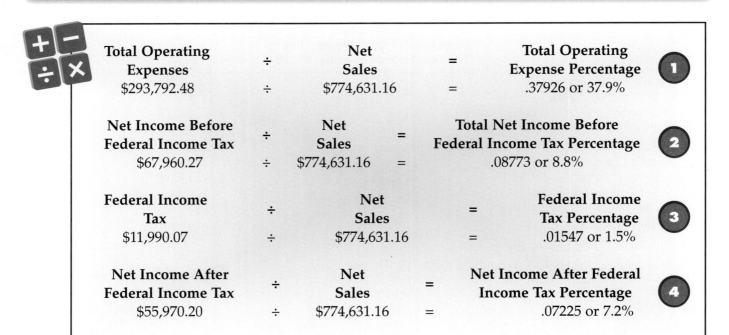

Total Operating Expenses	÷	Net Sales	=	Total Operating Expense Percentage	1
$293,792.48	÷	$774,631.16	=	.37926 or 37.9%	
Net Income Before Federal Income Tax	÷	Net Sales	=	Total Net Income Before Federal Income Tax Percentage	2
$67,960.27	÷	$774,631.16	=	.08773 or 8.8%	
Federal Income Tax	÷	Net Sales	=	Federal Income Tax Percentage	3
$11,990.07	÷	$774,631.16	=	.01547 or 1.5%	
Net Income After Federal Income Tax	÷	Net Sales	=	Net Income After Federal Income Tax Percentage	4
$55,970.20	÷	$774,631.16	=	.07225 or 7.2%	

Figure 4-14

Component percentages are shown in a separate column on the income statement. The percentages are calculated as shown in Figure 4-14. The percentages for total gross profit on operations and total cost of merchandise sold are obtained from the departmental statement of gross profit. The component percentage for total operating expenses is 37.9%.

The component percentage for net income before federal income tax is 8.8%. The last two items on the income statement, federal income tax expense and net income after federal income tax, are important. Since Congress sets the tax rate, MasterSport has limited control over these two items. However, MasterSport is interested in what portion of each sales dollar is paid to the federal government for income taxes. Therefore, the component percentages for federal income tax and net income after federal income tax are calculated.

The component percentage for federal income tax is 1.5%. The component percentage for net income after federal income tax is 7.2%. An analysis of MasterSport's income statement indicates acceptable levels of performance. The component percentages for cost of merchandise sold and gross profit on operations were analyzed on the departmental statement of gross profit. The component percentage for total operating expenses, 37.9%, is acceptable based on the performance standard of 38.0% or less. The component percentage for net income before federal income tax, 8.8%, is acceptable based on the performance standard of 7.0% or more.

S T E P S Calculating component percentage

1. Divide total operating expenses by net sales to determine the total operating expense percentage.
2. Divide net income before federal income tax by net sales to determine the total net income before federal income tax percentage.
3. Divide federal income tax by net sales to determine the federal income tax percentage.
4. Divide net income after federal income tax by net sales to determine the net income after federal income tax percentage.

MasterSport
Statement of Stockholders' Equity
For Year Ended December 31, 20--

Capital Stock:		
$170.00 Per Share		
January 1, 20--, 2,000 Shares Issued	$340,000.00	
Issued during Current Year, None	-0-	
Balance, December 31, 20--, 2,000 Shares Issued		$340,000.00
Retained Earnings:		
Balance, January 1, 20--	$ 42,210.50	
Net Income after Federal Income Tax for 20-- $55,970.20		
Less Dividends Declared during 20-- 30,000.00		
Net Increase during 20--	25,970.20	
Balance, December 31, 20--		68,180.70
Total Stockholders' Equity, December 31, 20--		$408,180.70

Figure 4-15

A financial statement that shows changes in a corporation's ownership for a fiscal period is called a **statement of stockholders' equity**. MasterSport's statement of stockholders' equity for the fiscal year ended December 31 is shown in Figure 4-15.

A statement of stockholders' equity contains two major sections.

1. Capital stock. Total shares of ownership in a corporation are called **capital stock**.

2. Retained earnings. An amount earned by a corporation and not yet distributed to stockholders is called **retained earnings**.

The first section shows that MasterSport started the fiscal year with $340,000.00 capital stock. This capital stock consisted of 2,000 shares of stock issued prior to January 1. During the year, MasterSport did not issue any additional stock. Thus, at the end of the fiscal year, MasterSport still had $340,000.00 capital stock. This information is obtained from the previous year's statement of stockholders' equity and the capital stock account.

The second section of MasterSport's statement of stockholders' equity shows that the business started the fiscal year with $42,210.50 retained earnings. This amount represents previous years' earnings that have been kept in the business. For the current fiscal year ended December 31, MasterSport earned net income after federal income tax of $55,970.20. This amount is obtained from line 59 of the work sheet, Figure 4-6.

Net income increases the retained earnings of a corporation. Some income may be retained by a corporation for business expansion. Some income may be distributed to stockholders as a return on their investment. Earnings distributed to stockholders are called **dividends**.

MasterSport's board of directors declared dividends of $30,000.00 during the year. The amount of dividends declared is obtained from line 27 of the Balance Sheet Debit column of the work sheet. The amount of dividends declared, $30,000.00, is subtracted from the amount of net income for the year, $55,970.20, to obtain the net increase in Retained Earnings for the year, $25,970.20. The net increase in Retained Earnings, $25,970.20, is added to the January 1 balance of Retained Earnings, $42,210.50, to obtain the December 31 balance, $68,180.70. MasterSport's capital stock, $340,000.00, plus retained earnings, $68,180.70, equals total stockholders' equity on December 31, $408,180.70.

Declaration and payment of dividends are described in Chapter 11.

MasterSport
Balance Sheet
December 31, 20--

ASSETS

Current Assets:

Cash		$ 43,440.00
Petty Cash		500.00
Accounts Receivable	$12,855.00	
Less Allowance for Uncollectible Accounts	2,350.00	10,505.00
Merchandise Inventory—Golf		204,855.00
Merchandise Inventory—Tennis		190,484.60
Supplies—Office		2,750.00
Supplies—Store		6,540.00
Prepaid Insurance		4,200.00
Total Current Assets			$463,274.60

Plant Assets:

Office Equipment	$16,900.00		
Less Accumulated Depreciation—Office Equipment	7,450.00	$ 9,450.00	
Store Equipment	$38,900.00		
Less Accumulated Depreciation—Store Equipment	21,000.00	17,900.00	
Total Plant Assets			27,350.00
Total Assets			$490,624.60

LIABILITIES

Current Liabilities:

Accounts Payable	$ 38,160.30	
Employee Income Tax Payable—Federal	2,680.75	
Employee Income Tax Payable—State	1,118.19	
Federal Income Tax Payable	1,190.07	
Social Security Tax Payable	2,730.57	
Medicare Tax Payable	630.13	
Sales Tax Payable	3,139.64	
Unemployment Tax Payable—Federal	23.60	
Unemployment Tax Payable—State	159.30	
Health Insurance Premiums Payable	2,261.16	
Life Insurance Premiums Payable	350.19	
Dividends Payable	30,000.00	
Total Liabilities		$ 82,443.90

STOCKHOLDERS' EQUITY

Capital Stock	$340,000.00	
Retained Earnings	68,180.70	
Total Stockholders' Equity		408,180.70
Total Liabilities and Stockholders' Equity		$490,624.60

Figure 4-16

A financial statement that reports assets, liabilities, and owner's equity on a specific date is called a **balance sheet**. A balance sheet reports the financial condition of a business on a specific date. MasterSport's balance sheet for December 31 is shown in Figure 4-16. Data used in preparing a balance sheet come from two sources.

1. Balance Sheet columns of the work sheet.

2. Statement of Stockholders' Equity.

On a balance sheet, the total assets must equal the total liabilities plus stockholders' equity. MasterSport's balance sheet shows total assets of $490,624.60 and total liabilities and stockholders' equity of the same amount. Therefore, MasterSport's balance sheet is in balance and is assumed to be correct.

Financial analysis of balance sheet items is described in Chapter 16.

TERMS REVIEW

income statement

statement of stockholders' equity

capital stock

retained earnings

dividends

balance sheet

AUDIT YOUR UNDERSTANDING

1. What four financial statements does MasterSport prepare at the end of its fiscal period?

2. What is the formula for calculating the component percentage for total operating expenses?

3. What are the two major sections of a statement of stockholders' equity?

WORK TOGETHER

Preparing an income statement with component percentages

Information from the Income Statement columns of Video Scene's work sheet of December 31 of the current year and a departmental statement of gross profit appear in the *Working Papers*. Statement paper is also provided in the *Working Papers*. Your instructor will guide you through the following example.

4. Prepare an income statement for the current year ending December 31. Record component percentages for cost of merchandise sold and gross profit on operations from the departmental statement of gross profit. Calculate and record component percentages for total operating expenses, net income before and after federal income tax, and federal income tax expense. Round percentage calculations to the nearest 0.1%.

ON YOUR OWN

Preparing an income statement with component percentages

Information from the income statement columns of Fremont Sign's work sheet of December 31 of the current year and a departmental statement of gross profit appear in the *Working Papers*. Statement paper is also provided in the *Working Papers*. Work independently to complete the following problem.

5. Prepare an income statement for the current year ending December 31. Record component percentages for cost of merchandise sold and gross profit on operations from the departmental statement of gross profit. Calculate and record component percentages for total operating expenses, net income before and after federal income tax, and federal income tax expense. Round percentage calculations to the nearest 0.1%.

JOURNALIZING ADJUSTING ENTRIES FOR A DEPARTMENTALIZED BUSINESS

1. Write Adjusting Entries in Account Title column.

2. Enter the adjusting entries without additional explanation.

		DATE		ACCOUNT TITLE	DOC. NO.	POST. REF.	DEBIT	CREDIT	
1				*Adjusting Entries*					1
2	Dec.²⁰⁻⁻		31	*Uncollectible Accounts Expense*			2 1 0 9 40		2
3				*Allowance for Uncoll. Accounts*				2 1 0 9 40	3
4			31	*Merchandise Inventory—Golf*			18 4 2 0 39		4
5				*Income Summary—Golf*				18 4 2 0 39	5
6			31	*Income Summary—Tennis*			9 3 6 0 00		6
7				*Merchandise Inventory—Tennis*				9 3 6 0 00	7
8			31	*Supplies Expense—Office*			9 9 5 0 00		8
9				*Supplies—Office*				9 9 5 0 00	9
10			31	*Supplies Expense—Store*			7 7 9 0 00		10
11				*Supplies—Store*				7 7 9 0 00	11
12			31	*Insurance Expense*			5 6 5 0 00		12
13				*Prepaid Insurance*				5 6 5 0 00	13
14			31	*Depreciation Exp.—Office Equip.*			1 4 9 0 00		14
15				*Accum. Depr.—Office Equip.*				1 4 9 0 00	15
16			31	*Depreciation Exp.—Store Equip.*			3 0 0 0 00		16
17				*Accum. Depr.—Store Equip.*				3 0 0 0 00	17
18			31	*Federal Income Tax Expense*			1 1 9 0 07		18
19				*Federal Income Tax Payable*				1 1 9 0 07	19

GENERAL JOURNAL — PAGE **8**

Figure 4-17

Account balances are changed only by posting journal entries. Journal entries recorded to update general ledger accounts at the end of a fiscal period are called **adjusting entries**. At the end of a fiscal period, the temporary account balances are transferred to an income summary account. This procedure summarizes, in one account, the effect of operating the business.

MasterSport's adjusting entries are shown in Figure 4-17. After the adjusting entries are posted, general ledger accounts will be up to date as of December 31.

**S
T
E
P
S** **Journalize adjusting entries**

1. Write the words *Adjusting Entries* in the Account Title column. This heading identifies the group of adjusting entries.

2. Enter each adjusting entry using information from the Adjustments column of the work sheet. The letters used to identify the adjustments provide the order for these entries. For example, adjustment *(a)* is the first adjusting entry to be recorded. No source document or explanation is written for each adjusting entry.

REMEMBER

Do not skip lines between adjusting entries.

1. Write "Closing Entries" in the Account Title column. ①

2. Record entry to close income statement accounts with credit balances. ②

3. Record entry to close income statement accounts with debit balances. ③

4. Record entry to close Income Summary to Retained Earnings. ④

5. Record entry for dividends. ⑤

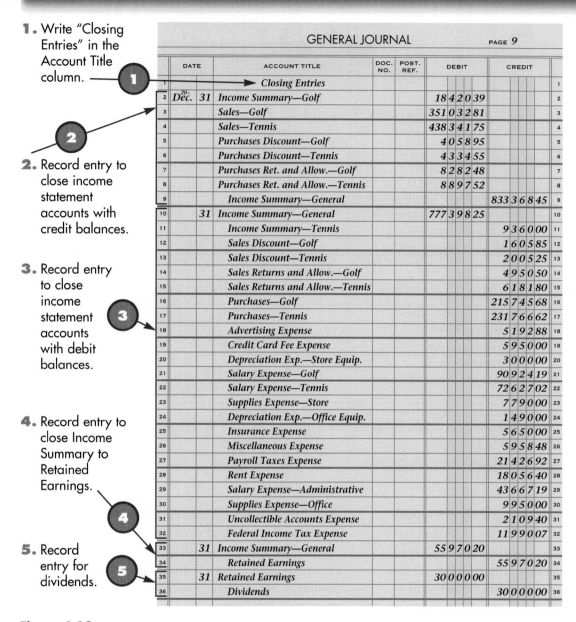

	DATE	ACCOUNT TITLE	DOC. NO.	POST. REF.	DEBIT	CREDIT	
1		Closing Entries					1
2	Dec. 31	Income Summary—Golf			18 4 2 0 39		2
3		Sales—Golf			351 0 3 2 81		3
4		Sales—Tennis			438 3 4 1 75		4
5		Purchases Discount—Golf			4 0 5 8 95		5
6		Purchases Discount—Tennis			4 3 3 4 55		6
7		Purchases Ret. and Allow.—Golf			8 2 8 2 48		7
8		Purchases Ret. and Allow.—Tennis			8 8 9 7 52		8
9		Income Summary—General				833 3 6 8 45	9
10	31	Income Summary—General			777 3 9 8 25		10
11		Income Summary—Tennis				9 3 6 0 00	11
12		Sales Discount—Golf				1 6 0 5 85	12
13		Sales Discount—Tennis				2 0 0 5 25	13
14		Sales Returns and Allow.—Golf				4 9 5 0 50	14
15		Sales Returns and Allow.—Tennis				6 1 8 1 80	15
16		Purchases—Golf				215 7 4 5 68	16
17		Purchases—Tennis				231 7 6 6 62	17
18		Advertising Expense				5 1 9 2 88	18
19		Credit Card Fee Expense				5 9 5 0 00	19
20		Depreciation Exp.—Store Equip.				3 0 0 0 00	20
21		Salary Expense—Golf				90 9 2 4 19	21
22		Salary Expense—Tennis				72 6 2 7 02	22
23		Supplies Expense—Store				7 7 9 0 00	23
24		Depreciation Exp.—Office Equip.				1 4 9 0 00	24
25		Insurance Expense				5 6 5 0 00	25
26		Miscellaneous Expense				5 9 5 8 48	26
27		Payroll Taxes Expense				21 4 2 6 92	27
28		Rent Expense				18 0 5 6 40	28
29		Salary Expense—Administrative				43 6 6 7 19	29
30		Supplies Expense—Office				9 9 5 0 00	30
31		Uncollectible Accounts Expense				2 1 0 9 40	31
32		Federal Income Tax Expense				11 9 9 0 07	32
33	31	Income Summary—General			55 9 7 0 20		33
34		Retained Earnings				55 9 7 0 20	34
35	31	Retained Earnings			30 0 0 0 00		35
36		Dividends				30 0 0 0 00	36

GENERAL JOURNAL   PAGE 9

Figure 4-18

Journal entries used to prepare temporary accounts for a new fiscal period are called **closing entries**. MasterSport's closing entries made on December 31 are shown in Figure 4-18. The information to journalize closing entries is obtained from the Income Statement columns of the work sheet. MasterSport records the following four closing entries:

1. Closing entry for income statement accounts with credit balances (revenue and contra cost accounts).

2. Closing entry for income statement accounts with debit balances (cost, contra revenue, and expense accounts).

3. Closing entry to record net income or net loss in the retained earnings account and to close the income summary account.

4. Closing entry for the dividends account.

Closing Entry for Income Statement Accounts with Credit Balances

The closing entry for MasterSport's income statement credit balance accounts on December 31 is shown on lines 1-9, Figure 4-18. Income statement credit balance accounts are the departmental income summary accounts with a credit balance (Income Summary—Golf), the revenue accounts (Sales—Golf and Sales—Tennis), and the contra cost accounts (Purchases Discount—Golf, Purchases Discount—Tennis, Purchases Returns and Allowances—Golf, and Purchases Returns and Allowances—Tennis).

Information needed for closing income statement credit balance accounts is obtained from the Income Statement Credit column of the work sheet, as shown in Figure 4-6.

MasterSport begins its closing entries on a new page of the general journal. Thus, all the closing entries are together on one page.

Closing Entry for Income Statement Accounts with Debit Balances

The closing entry for MasterSport's income statement debit balance accounts on December 31 is shown on lines 10-32, Figure 4-18. Income statement debit balance accounts are the departmental income summary accounts with a debit balance (Income Summary—Tennis), the contra revenue accounts (Sales Discount—Golf, Sales Discount—Tennis, Sales Returns and Allowances—Golf, and Sales Returns and Allowances—Tennis), the cost accounts (Purchases—Golf and Purchases—Tennis), and expense accounts.

Information needed for closing income statement debit balance accounts is obtained from the Income Statement Debit column of the work sheet, as shown in Figure 4-6.

Closing Entry to Record Net Income or Net Loss in the Retained Earnings Account and to Close the Income Summary Account

The closing entry to record MasterSport's net income in the retained earnings account and close the income summary account on December 31 is shown on lines 33-34, Figure 4-18.

The Income Summary—General account balance is equal to the net income (or net loss) for the fiscal period. A corporation's net income is recorded in the retained earnings account.

Information needed for this entry is obtained from line 59 of MasterSport's work sheet, as shown in Figure 4-6.

After the entry to record net income is posted, Income Summary has a zero balance. The net income, $55,970.20, has been recorded as a credit to Retained Earnings.

Closing Entry for the Dividends Account

The closing entry for MasterSport's dividends account on December 31 is shown on lines 35-36, Figure 4-18. The debit balance of a dividends account is the total amount of dividends declared during a fiscal period. Since dividends decrease the earnings that a corporation retains, the dividends account is closed to Retained Earnings.

Information needed for closing MasterSport's dividends account is obtained from line 28 of the Balance Sheet Debit column of the work sheet, as shown in Figure 4-6.

After the closing entry for the dividends account is posted, Dividends has a zero balance. The amount of the dividends, $30,000.00, has been recorded as a debit to Retained Earnings.

After closing entries are posted, all temporary accounts have zero balances and are prepared for a new fiscal period.

In most commercial, computerized accounting systems, year-end closing is performed by the computer. The accountant selects a menu item to close the accounting records for the year. The software automatically updates its database. In many systems, year-end closing cannot be undone.

MasterSport
Post-Closing Trial Balance
December 31, 20--

Account Title	Debit	Credit
Cash.	$ 43,440.00	
Petty Cash	500.00	
Accounts Receivable	12,855.00	
Allowance for Uncollectible Accounts		$ 2,350.00
Merchandise Inventory—Golf	204,855.00	
Merchandise Inventory—Tennis	190,484.60	
Supplies—Office	2,750.00	
Supplies—Store.	6,540.00	
Prepaid Insurance	4,200.00	
Office Equipment	16,900.00	
Accumulated Depreciation—Office Equipment		7,450.00
Store Equipment	38,900.00	
Accumulated Depreciation—Store Equipment		21,000.00
Accounts Payable		38,160.30
Employee Income Tax Payable—Federal		2,680.75
Employee Income Tax Payable—State		1,118.19
Federal Income Tax Payable		1,190.07
Social Security Tax Payable		2,730.57
Medicare Tax Payable		630.13
Sales Tax Payable		3,139.64
Unemployment Tax Payable—Federal		23.60
Unemployment Tax Payable—State		159.30
Health Insurance Premiums Payable.		2,261.16
Life Insurance Premiums Payable		350.19
Dividends Payable		30,000.00
Capital Stock		340,000.00
Retained Earnings		68,180.70
Totals	$521,424.60	$521,424.60

Figure 4-19

Debits must always equal credits in general ledger accounts. The trial balance recorded on the work sheet, Figure 4-6, proves that debits do equal credits before adjusting and closing entries are posted. After adjusting and closing entries are posted, equality of general ledger debits and credits is proved again. This procedure ensures that the equality of debits and credits has been maintained in preparation for a new fiscal period.

A trial balance prepared after the closing entries are posted is called a **post-closing trial balance**. MasterSport's post-closing trial balance prepared on December 31 is shown in Figure 4-19. The total of debit balances, $521,424.60, is the same as the total of credit balances. The equality of general ledger debits and credits is proved. MasterSport's general ledger is ready for the next fiscal period.

REMEMBER

Only temporary accounts are closed.

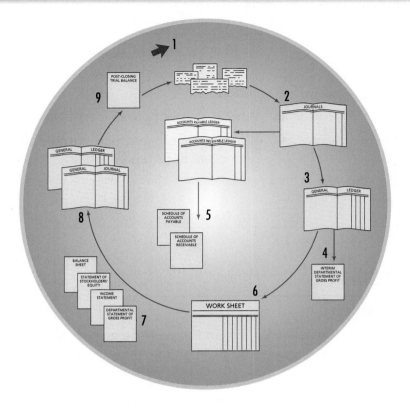

Figure 4-20

Accounting procedures used by MasterSport, a departmentalized merchandising business, are described in Chapters 1 through 4. The same procedures are used from year to year. *(CONCEPT: Consistent Reporting)* The series of accounting activities included in recording financial information for a fiscal period is called an **accounting cycle**. MasterSport's complete accounting cycle is shown in Figure 4-20. Accounting cycle procedures provide information for preparing interim and end-of-fiscal-period financial statements. *(CONCEPT: Accounting Period Cycle)*

S T E P S **In the accounting cycle for departmentalized business**

1. Verify source documents for accuracy. The source documents describe transactions and prove that the transaction did occur.
2. Record entries in journals using the information on the source documents.
3. Post journal entries to the ledgers.
4. Prepare interim departmental statement of gross profit. MasterSport prepares this statement monthly to assess the operating efficiency of each department.
5. Prepare schedules of accounts receivable and accounts payable from the subsidiary ledgers.
6. Prepare a trial balance on the work sheet. Complete the work sheet to summarize a business' financial condition.
7. Prepare financial statements using information on the work sheet and in the accounting records.
8. Journalize and post adjusting and closing entries using information from the work sheet.
9. Prepare a post-closing trial balance to check the equality of debits and credits in the general ledger. The accounting records for the fiscal period are complete and ready for the start of the next fiscal period.

UDIT YOUR
UNDERSTANDING

1. What is the purpose of adjusting entries?
2. Which accounts are closed at the end of an accounting period?
3. What is the purpose of a post-closing trial balance?
4. Which accounting activities in the accounting cycle are performed at the end of a fiscal period?

ORK
TOGETHER

Journalizing closing entries

The income statement columns of a work sheet and page 4 of a general journal are provided in the *Working Papers*. Your instructor will guide you through the following example.

5. Journalize the four closing entries to prepare Video Scene's general ledger for the next fiscal period. Dividends for the year equal $8,000.00.

N YOUR
OWN

Journalizing closing entries

The income statement columns of a work sheet and page 6 of a general journal are provided in the *Working Papers*. Work independently to complete the following problem.

6. Journalize the four closing entries to prepare Fremont Sign's general ledger for the next fiscal period. Dividends for the year equal $10,000.00.

After completing this chapter, you can

1. Define important accounting terms related to financial reporting for a departmentalized business.

2. Identify accounting concepts and practices related to financial reporting for a departmentalized business.

3. Prepare interim departmental statement of gross profit.

4. Prepare a worksheet for a departmentalized business.

5. Prepare financial statements for a departmentalized business.

6. Analyze financial statements using selected component percentages.

7. Complete end-of-period work for a departmentalized business.

EXPLORE ACCOUNTING

CONSOLIDATED FINANCIAL STATEMENTS

Departmental accounting enables a business to track the financial results of different portions of its business. Departments are commonly identified by type of services provided, products sold, or production methods used by a business in one geographic location.

Companies are constantly searching for ways to grow and increase their profitability. A business can expand its sales by introducing new, related products and selling those products in national or international regions. This new area of the business could be accounted for as a new department. But what if the business has already taken advantage of every growth opportunity in its industry? The next best growth opportunity is to purchase another business in

another industry. For example, Pacific Grocery, a national grocery store chain, might purchase the outstanding capital stock of Swing Video, a regional chain of video rental stores.

Should the video rental business be accounted for as a department of Pacific Grocery? If the video stores are physically relocated into the grocery stores, departmental accounting would be appropriate. But if the video stores continue to operate using the Swing Video name in their current locations, the accounting records should remain separate from the Pacific Grocery.

A company that purchases the capital stock of another company is known as a parent company. A company whose capital stock is purchased by another company is known as a subsidiary. When financial statements of a parent company are prepared, the statements should present the accounts of the

parent and all subsidiary companies. These financial statements are referred to as consolidated financial statements. Thus, when the consolidated financial statements of Pacific Grocery are prepared, the statements will include the account balances of both Pacific Grocery and Swing Video. The statements would include the heading Pacific Grocery and Subsidiary.

This method of accounting is similar to departmental accounting except that the accounting records are maintained independently.

REQUIRED:

Obtain the annual report of a corporation with consolidated financial statements. Identify information presented in the annual report that informs you that the company is consolidated. What information, if any, is provided about each subsidiary?

APPLICATION PROBLEM
Estimating ending merchandise inventory

Duckhorn Creek Golf Shop has two departments, equipment and accessories. The following data are obtained from the accounting records on January 31 of the current year.

	Equipment	Accessories
Beginning Inventory, January 1	$145,000.00	$153,000.00
Net Purchases for January	14,300.00	14,100.00
Net Sales for January	49,200.00	53,400.00
Gross Profit on Operations as a Percent of Sales	43.0%	43.0%

Instructions:

Prepare an estimated merchandise inventory sheet, similar to the one in this chapter, for each department for the month ended January 31.

APPLICATION PROBLEM
Preparing an interim departmental statement of gross profit; calculating component percentages

Allied Lighting has two departments, office and residential. The following data are obtained from the accounting records on March 31 of the current year.

	Office	Residential
Beginning Inventory, January 1	$154,640.00	$166,500.00
Estimated Beginning Inventory, March 1	131,344.00	135,660.00
Net Purchases, January 1 to February 28	23,360.00	24,840.00
Net Sales, January 1 to February 28	77,760.00	92,800.00
Net Purchases for March	13,497.20	9,978.40
Net Sales for March	29,200.00	33,600.00
Estimated Gross Profit Percentage	40.0%	40.0%

Instructions:

1. Prepare an estimated merchandise inventory sheet, similar to the one in this chapter, for each department for the month ended March 31 of the current year.

2. Prepare an interim departmental statement of gross profit. Calculate and record component percentages for departmental and total cost of merchandise sold and gross profit on operations. Round percentage calculations to the nearest 0.1%.

APPLICATION PROBLEM
Preparing subsidiary schedules

On December 31 of the current year, Gabriel's Gourmet Shop has the following vendor and customer accounts and balances.

Vendor	Account Balance	Customer	Account Balance
Barnett Co.	$2,250.40	Mary Anacker	$1,310.20
Gould Associates	1,520.30	Alice Conroy	820.70

Vendor	Account Balance	Customer	Account Balance
Hills Supply	936.80	Raymond Gaetz	826.10
Kroy Enterprises	1,262.50	John Klem	1,304.20
Swedberg, Inc.	826.10	Irma Musgrove	619.60
Williamson Products	2,270.60	Richard Wimer	2,026.40

Instructions:

1. Prepare a schedule of accounts payable. Compare the schedule total with the balance, $9,066.70, of the general ledger controlling account Accounts Payable. If the totals are not the same, find and correct the errors.

2. Prepare a schedule of accounts receivable. Compare the schedule total with the balance, $6,907.20, of the general ledger controlling account Accounts Receivable. If the totals are not the same, find and correct the errors.

APPLICATION PROBLEM
Calculating and analyzing component percentage for total operating expenses

The following data are obtained from the income statements of six businesses.

Business	Net Sales	Total Operating Expenses	Performance Standard— Not More Than
1	$148,000.00	$43,500.00	32.0%
2	175,500.00	51,750.00	30.0%
3	130,300.00	36,500.00	26.0%
4	145,600.00	35,930.00	25.0%
5	185,300.00	58,250.00	30.0%
6	163,900.00	44,980.00	28.0%

Use a form similar to the following.

1	2	3	4	5	6
Business	Net Sales	Total Operating Expenses	Performance Standard— Not More Than	Component Percentage	Performance Level
1	$148,000.00	$43,500.00	32.0%	29.4%	A

Instructions:

1. Calculate the component percentage for total operating expenses for each business. Round percentage calculations to the nearest 0.1%. Record the component percentage in Column 5.

2. Determine the performance level for each business by comparing the component percentage with the performance standard. If the performance level is acceptable, write an A in Column 6. If the performance level is unacceptable, write a U in Column 6. The component percentage and performance level for Business 1 are given as examples.

APPLICATION PROBLEM
Completing a work sheet for a departmentalized business

Regis Bookstore has two departments, teens and adults. The general ledger accounts and balances for December 31 of the current year are recorded on a work sheet in the *Working Papers*.

Instructions:

Complete the departmental work sheet for the year ended December 31 of the current year. Record the adjustments on the work sheet using the following information. Save your work to complete Application Problems 4-6 and 4-7.

Adjustment Information, December 31

Uncollectible accounts expense estimated as 1.0% of sales on account.

Sales on account for year	$125,910.00
Merchandise Inventory—Teens	168,820.10
Merchandise Inventory—Adults	173,450.80
Office Supplies Inventory	4,930.60
Store Supplies Inventory	5,720.40
Value of Prepaid Insurance	4,600.00
Annual Depreciation Expense—Office Equipment	1,280.00
Annual Depreciation Expense—Store Equipment	2,800.00
Federal Income Tax Expense for the Year	13,667.88

APPLICATION PROBLEM
Preparing financial statements for a departmentalized business

Instructions:

1. Use the worksheet from Application Problem 4-5. Prepare a departmental statement of gross profit for Regis Bookstore. Calculate and record component percentages for cost of merchandise sold and gross profit on operations. Round percentage calculations to the nearest 0.1%.

2. Prepare an income statement. Record the component percentages for cost of merchandise sold and gross profit on operations from the departmental statement of gross profit. Calculate and record the component percentages for total operating expenses and net income before and after federal income tax. Round percentage calculations to the nearest 0.1%.

3. Prepare a statement of stockholders' equity. Use the following additional information.

January 1 balance of capital stock account	$200,000.00
(2,000 shares issued for $100.00 per share)	
No additional capital stock issued.	
January 1 balance of retained earnings account	155,675.00
Dividends declared during the current year	30,000.00

4. Prepare a balance sheet.

4-7 APPLICATION PROBLEM
Journalizing adjusting and closing entries for a departmentalized business

Instructions:

1. Use the work sheet from Application Problem 4-5. Journalize the adjusting entries for Regis Bookstore. Use page 15 of a general journal.

2. Journalize the closing entries for Regis Bookstore. Continue using page 15 of a general journal. Dividends declared during the current year were $30,000.00.

4-8 MASTERY PROBLEM
Preparing end-of-fiscal-period work for a departmentalized business

Home Plate Sporting Goods has two departments, softball and baseball. The general ledger accounts and balances on December 31 of the current year are recorded on a work sheet in the *Working Papers*.

Instructions:

1. Complete the departmental work sheet for the year ended December 31 of the current year. Record the adjustments on the work sheet using the following information.

Adjustment Information, December 31	
Uncollectible accounts expense estimated as 1.0% of sales on account.	
Sales on account for year	$197,040.00
Merchandise Inventory—Softball	205,380.20
Merchandise Inventory—Baseball	236,520.80
Office Supplies Inventory	6,010.30
Store Supplies Inventory	4,220.50
Value of Prepaid Insurance	2,800.00
Annual Depreciation Expense—Office Equipment	1,200.00
Annual Depreciation Expense—Store Equipment	2,600.00
Federal Income Tax Expense for the Year	13,202.45

2. Prepare a departmental statement of gross profit. Calculate and record component percentages for cost of merchandise sold and gross profit on operations. Round percentage calculations to the nearest 0.1%.

3. Prepare an income statement. Record the component percentages for cost of merchandise sold and gross profit on operations from the departmental statement of gross profit. Calculate and record the component percentages for total operating expenses and net income before and after federal income tax. Round percentage calculations to the nearest 0.1%.

continued

4. Prepare a statement of stockholders' equity. Use the following additional information.

January 1 balance of capital stock account	$300,000.00
(1,500 shares issued for $200.00 per share)	
No additional capital stock issued.	
January 1 balance of retained earnings account	155,000.00
Dividends declared during the current year	30,000.00

5. Prepare a balance sheet.

6. Journalize the adjusting entries. Use page 18 of a general journal.

7. Journalize the closing entries. Continue using page 18 of a general journal. Do not skip a line between the adjusting and closing entries.

4-9 CHALLENGE PROBLEM
Preparing a 10-column work sheet for a departmentalized business

Introductory remarks:

Some businesses choose to use a work sheet that has 10 columns instead of the 8-column work sheet used by MasterSport. A 10-column work sheet has Adjusted Trial Balance Debit and Credit columns. These columns are used to recalculate account balances after the adjustments have been entered on the work sheet. If an account balance was not changed by the adjustments, the balance is transferred to the Adjusted Trial Balance column unchanged. If an account balance was adjusted, the new balance is transferred to the Adjusted Trial Balance columns. The Adjusted Trial Balance Debit and Credit columns are totaled. The total of the debit column must equal the total of the credit column. Once the columns are equal, the amounts in the Adjusted Trial Balance columns are transferred to either the Balance Sheet or Income Statement columns. The work sheet is completed as usual.

White Cliff Sport Clothing has two departments: Skiing and Snowboarding. The general ledger accounts and balances for December 31 of the current year are recorded on a work sheet in the *Working Papers.*

Instructions:

1. Complete the departmental work sheet for the year ended December 31 of the current year. Record the adjustments on the work sheet using the following information.

Adjustment Information, December 31

Uncollectible accounts expense estimated as 1.0% of sales on account.	
Sales on account for year	$ 35,000.00
Merchandise Inventory—Skiing	115,430.00
Merchandise Inventory—Snowboarding	97,680.00
Supplies Inventory	2,377.00
Value of Prepaid Insurance	500.00
Federal Income Tax Expense for the Year	4,795.18

2. Write a paragraph discussing the advantages and disadvantages of a 10-column work sheet. Use your experience in preparing the work sheet for this problem as the basis for your discussion.

INTERNET ACTIVITY

Point your browser to

http://accounting.swpco.com

Choose **Advanced Course**, choose **Activities**, and complete the activity for Chapter 4.

When sending your resume, a cover letter is your opportunity to introduce yourself to an employer and highlight your strongest qualifications.

The cover letter, or letter of application, consists of at least three paragraphs. In the first paragraph, introduce yourself, state the job for which your are applying, and express an interest in the job. The second paragraph should contain a description of your qualifications and related work experience. In the third paragraph, include an action statement. Request an interview, ask for a phone call, indicate how you will follow-up; and, most importantly, thank the reader for her or his time and consideration.

Required:

In a newspaper or similar publication, locate a job advertisement for a position for which you are qualified. Prepare a cover letter for the position you have selected.

Trade your cover letter with a classmate. Carefully proofread your classmate's cover letter. Mark errors in grammar and punctuation. Make any other suggestions for improvement.

Make the corrections to your cover letter before submitting it to your instructor.

Cases for Critical Thinking

Case 1

The following data are obtained from financial information for InfoTech for the month ended August 31 of the current year.

Beginning Inventory, Jan. 1	$98,000.00
Net Purchases for the Period, Jan. 1 to Aug. 31	42,500.00
Net Sales for the Period, Jan. 1 to Aug. 31	66,800.00

You are asked to report the estimated ending inventory on August 31 using the gross profit method for estimating inventory. What will you report?

Case 2

Cyber Graphics is a departmentalized business. An interim departmental statement of gross profit is prepared monthly. A departmental statement of gross profit is prepared at the end of each fiscal year. The manager suggests that the accountant extend the statements of gross profit by including a division of all expenses by department. The accountant indicates that the time required to divide the expenses by department would not add significantly to the information available for decision making. Do you agree or disagree with the accountant? Why?

AUTOMATED ACCOUNTING

COMPLETING END-OF-FISCAL-PERIOD WORK FOR A DEPARTMENTAL BUSINESS

During the fiscal period, many transactions are analyzed, journalized, and posted. When a transaction affects more than one accounting period, an adjusting entry may be needed to match revenues and expenses. To complete the accounting cycle, a trial balance is prepared. Adjusting entries are recorded, entered into the computer, and verified for accuracy. Financial statements are generated, and finally closing entries are generated and posted by the software. No work sheet is prepared in an automated accounting system.

Processing a Trial Balance

After all the usual transactions of the business are entered as journal entries, a preliminary trial balance is generated. A trial balance should be displayed and printed before adjusting entries are recorded. The trial balance indicates that debits equal credits. To display and print a trial balance:

1. Click the Reports button.

2. Select Ledger Reports from the Report Selection dialog box.

3. Choose Trial Balance from the Choose a Report to Display list as shown in Figure AA4-1.

4. Click the Print button to print a copy of the trial balance.

Adjusting Entries

This trial balance and period-end adjustment data are used as the basis for the adjusting entries. They include entries for assets that have been consumed or sold during the period and become expenses. For most asset accounts, such as Supplies and Insurance, the adjustment is made to the related expense account. The General Journal tab within the Journal Entries window is used to enter and post the adjusting entries. All of the adjusting entries are dated the last day of the fiscal period, and use *Adj. Ent.* as the reference.

Processing Financial Statements

The automated accounting system prepares financial statements from the information in the database. Financial statements can be displayed and printed at any time. They are always printed at the end of the fiscal period. The automated system does not prepare a departmental statement of gross profit. The following financial statements are prepared for the departmentalized business.

- Income statement

- Balance sheet

- Retained earnings statement

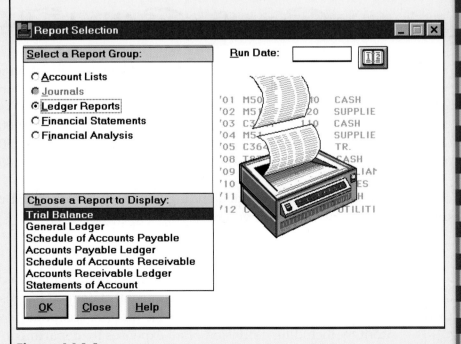

Figure AA4-1

AUTOMATED ACCOUNTING

To display and print the statements:

1. Click the Reports button.

2. Select Financial Statements from the Report Selection dialog box.

3. Choose the statement you want to print from the Choose a Report to Display list.

4. Click the Print button to print a copy of the statement.

Closing Entries for a Departmentalized Business

In an automated accounting system, closing entries are generated and posted by the software. The software automatically closes net income to the retained earnings account after closing the revenue and expense accounts. The dividends account is closed as well.

1. Choose Generate Closing Journal Entries from the Options menu.

2. Click Yes to generate the closing entries.

3. The general journal will appear, containing the journal entries.

4. Click the Post button.

5. Display a post-closing trial balance report.
   a. Click on the Reports toolbar button, or

choose the Reports Selection menu item from the Reports menu.
   b. Select the Ledger Reports option button from the Report Selection dialog box.
   c. Choose Trial Balance report.

AUTOMATING ACCOUNTING PROBLEM 4-6

Instructions:

1. Load *Automated Accounting 7.0* or higher software.

2. Select database A04-6 (Advanced Course Application Problem 4-6) from the accounting template disk.

3. Select File from the menu bar and choose the Save As menu command. Key the path to the drive and directory that contains your data files. Save the database with a file name of XXX046 (where XXX are your initials).

4. Access Problem Instructions through the Help menu (7.0) or Browser tool (8.0). Read the Problem Instruction screen.

5. Refer to page 128 for data used in this problem.

6. Exit the Automated Accounting software.

AUTOMATING ACCOUNTING PROBLEM 4-7

Instructions:

1. Load *Automated Accounting 7.0* or higher software.

2. Select database A04-7 (Advanced Course Application Problem 4-7) from the accounting template disk.

3. Select File from the menu bar and choose the Save As menu command. Key the path to the drive and directory that contains your data files. Save the database with a file name of XXX047 (where XXX are your initials).

4. Access Problem Instructions through the Help menu (7.0) or Browser tool (8.0). Read the Problem Instruction screen.

5. Refer to page 129 for data used in this problem.

6. Exit the Automated Accounting software.

AUTOMATING MASTERY PROBLEM 4-8

Instructions:

1. Load *Automated Accounting 7.0* or higher software.

2. Select database A04-8 (Advanced Course Mastery

Problem 4-8) from the accounting template disk.

3. Select File from the menu bar and choose the Save As menu command. Key the path to the drive and directory that contains your data files. Save the database with a file name of XXX048 (where XXX are your initials).

4. Access Problem Instructions through the Help menu (7.0) or Browser tool (8.0). Read the Problem Instruction screen.

5. Refer to page 129 for data used in this problem.

6. Exit the Automated Accounting software.

Processing and Reporting
Departmentalized Accounting Data

This activity reinforces selected learnings from Part 1, Chapters 1 through 4. The complete accounting cycle is for a departmentalized merchandising business organized as a corporation.

CAMPUS BOOKS, INC.

Campus Books, Inc., has two departments: Books and Supplies. Campus Books is open for business Monday through Saturday. A monthly rent is paid on the building. The business owns the office and store equipment.

Campus Books sells books and supplies to individuals and schools. Cash sales and sales on account are made. The business uses a national credit card service in addition to its own company credit card.

Campus Books' fiscal year is January 1 through December 31. During the fiscal year, a monthly interim departmental statement of gross profit is prepared.

Campus Books uses the chart of accounts shown on the following page. The journals and ledgers used by Campus Books are similar to those illustrated in Part 1. The journal and ledger forms are provided in the *Working Papers*. Beginning balances have been recorded in the ledgers.

PREPARING AN INTERIM DEPARTMENTAL STATEMENT OF GROSS PROFIT

Campus Books prepares an interim departmental statement of gross profit each month. The following data are obtained from the accounting records at the end of November of the current year.

	Books	Supplies
Beginning inventory, January 1	$164,164.20	$147,840.30
Estimated beginning inventory, November 1	180,205.05	157,195.78
Net purchases January 1 to October 31	133,839.60	130,449.20
Net sales, January 1 to October 31	214,179.55	220,170.40
Net purchases for November	13,007.20	14,162.58
Net sales for November	19,480.60	20,240.30
Gross profit on operation as a percent of sales	45.0%	45.0%

Instructions:

1. Use the gross profit method of estimating an inventory to prepare an estimated merchandise inventory sheet for each department for the month ended November of the current year.

2. Prepare an interim departmental statement of gross profit for the month ended November 30 of the current year. Calculate and record component percentages for departmental and total cost of merchandise sold and gross profit on operations. Round percentage calculations to the nearest 0.1%.

Balance Sheet Accounts

(1000) Assets

1100 CURRENT ASSETS
1105 Cash
1110 Petty Cash
1115 Accounts Receivable
1120 Allowance for Uncollectible Accounts
1125-1 Merchandise Inventory—Books
1125-2 Merchandise Inventory—Supplies
1130 Supplies—Office
1135 Supplies—Store
1140 Prepaid Insurance

1200 PLANT ASSETS
1205 Office Equipment
1210 Accumulated Depreciation—Office Equipment
1215 Store Equipment
1220 Accumulated Depreciation—Store Equipment

(2000) Liabilities

2105 Accounts Payable
2110 Employee Income Tax Payable—Federal
2115 Employee Income Tax Payable—State
2120 Federal Income Tax Payable
2125 Social Security Tax Payable
2128 Medicare Tax Payable
2130 Sales Tax Payable
2135 Unemployment Tax Payable—Federal
2140 Unemployment Tax Payable—State
2145 Health Insurance Premiums Payable
2150 Dividends Payable

(3000) Stockholders' Equity

3105 Capital Stock
3110 Retained Earnings
3115 Dividends
3120-1 Income Summary—Books
3120-2 Income Summary—Supplies
3125 Income Summary—General

Income Statement Accounts

(4000) Operating Revenue

4105-1 Sales—Books
4105-2 Sales—Supplies
4110-1 Sales Discount—Books
4110-2 Sales Discount—Supplies
4115-1 Sales Returns and Allowances—Books
4115-2 Sales Returns and Allowances—Supplies

(5000) Cost of Merchandise

5105-1 Purchases—Books
5105-2 Purchases—Supplies
5110-1 Purchases Discount—Books
5110-2 Purchases Discount—Supplies
5115-1 Purchases Returns and Allowances—Books
5115-2 Purchases Returns and Allowances—Supplies

(6000) Operating Expenses

6100 SELLING EXPENSES
6105 Advertising Expense
6110 Credit Card Fee Expense
6115 Depreciation Expense—Store Equipment
6120-1 Salary Expense—Books
6121-2 Salary Expense—Supplies
6125 Supplies Expense—Store

6200 ADMINISTRATIVE EXPENSES
6205 Depreciation Expense—Office Equipment
6210 Insurance Expense
6215 Miscellaneous Expense
6220 Payroll Taxes Expense
6225 Rent Expense
6230 Salary Expense—Administrative
6235 Supplies Expense—Office
6240 Uncollectible Accounts Expense

(7000) Income Tax

7105 Federal Income Tax Expense

Accounts Receivable Ledger

110 Marcella Amco
120 Matthew Barasso
130 Tanya Dockman
140 Brian Fadstad
150 Gilmore Public Schools
160 Belinda Judd
170 Janelle Kamschorr
180 Donald Lindgren
190 Renville Public Schools

Accounts Payable Ledger

210 A-1 Supplies
220 CBG Distributors
230 Grandway Products
240 H & B Books
250 Maryland Books & Supplies
260 Oliver Books, Inc.
270 Strup Supplies

RECORDING TRANSACTIONS

Instructions:

3. Journalize the following transactions completed during December of the current year. Calculate and record sales tax on all sales and sales returns and allowances as described in Chapter 3. The sales tax rate is 5.0%. No sales tax is charged on sales to schools. Campus Books offers its customers terms of 2/10, n/30. All of the vendors from which merchandise is purchased on account offer terms of 2/10, n/30. Source documents are abbreviated as follows: check, C; credit memorandum, CM; debit memorandum, DM; memorandum, M; purchase invoice, P; receipt, R; sales invoice, S; cash register tape, T.

Dec. 1. Paid cash for monthly payroll, $7,859.71 (total payroll: books, $4,522.20; supplies, $4,310.40; administrative, $2,630.25, less deductions: employee income tax—federal, $1,204.51; employee income tax—state, $537.60; Social Security tax, $745.09; Medicare tax, $171.94; health insurance, $944.00). C340.

1. Recorded employer payroll taxes, $964.38, for the monthly pay period ended November 30. Taxes owed are: Social Security tax, $745.09; Medicare tax, $171.94; federal unemployment tax, $6.11; state unemployment tax, $41.24. M40.

1. Paid cash for rent, $1,200.00. C341.

2. Paid cash for office supplies, $135.00. C342.

2. Granted credit to Gilmore Public Schools for supplies returned, $250.00, from S94. CM31.

2. Purchased books on account from Oliver Books, Inc., $1,933.00. P115.

3. Granted credit to Belinda Judd for books returned, $75.00, plus sales tax, from S95. CM32.

3. Recorded cash and credit card sales: books, $2,478.00; supplies, $2,588.50; plus sales tax. T3.
   Posting. Post the items that are to be posted individually. Post from the journals in this order: sales journal, sales returns and allowances journal, purchases journal, purchases returns and allowances journal, general journal, cash receipts journal, cash payments journal.

5. Returned books to H & B Books, $1,435.00, from P112. DM58.

5. Sold books on account to Matthew Barasso, $880.00, plus sales tax. S97.

5. Received cash on account from Tanya Dockman, $493.92, covering S92 for supplies for $504.00 ($480.00 plus sales tax), less discount, and less sales tax. R139.

6. Paid cash on account to CBG Distributors, $2,185.50, covering P111 for books for $2,230.10, less discount. C343.

7. Paid cash on account to H & B Books, $3,915.25, covering P112 for books for $5,430.15, less DM58, and less discount. C344.

7. Returned books to Oliver Books, Inc., $300.00, from P115. DM59.

8. Received cash on account from Gilmore Public Schools, $5,870.40, covering S94 for supplies for $6,240.20, less CM31, and less discount. R140.

8. Received cash on account from Belinda Judd, $180.07, covering S95 for books for $262.50 ($250.00 plus sales tax), less CM32, less discount, and less sales tax. R141.

Dec. 8. Received cash on account from Renville Public Schools, $9,389.87, covering S96 for books for $9,581.50, less discount. R142.

8. Paid cash on account to Maryland Books & Supplies, $554.09, covering P113 for supplies for $565.40, less discount. C345.

9. Paid cash on account to Oliver Books, Inc., $4,821.80, covering P114 for books for $4,920.20, less discount. C346.

9. Granted credit to Matthew Barasso for books returned, $100.00, plus sales tax, from S97. CM33.

10. Recorded cash and credit card sales: books, $4,946.50; supplies, $3,650.00; plus sales tax. T10.
Posting. Post the items that are to be posted individually.

12. Paid cash on account to Oliver Books, Inc., $1,600.34, covering P115 for books for $1,933.00, less DM59, and less discount. C347.

13. Sold supplies on account to Marcello Amco, $450.00, plus sales tax. S98.

15. Paid cash for liability for federal employee income tax, $1,240.80, and for Social Security tax, $1,286.11; Medicare tax, $296.79; total, $2,823.70. C348.

15. Paid cash for quarterly federal income tax estimate, $1,200.00. C349. (Debit Federal Income Tax Expense; credit Cash.)

15. Received cash on account from Matthew Barasso, $802.62, covering S97 for books for $924.00 ($880.00 plus sales tax), less CM33, less discount, and less sales tax. R143.

17. Recorded cash and credit card sales: books, $3,820.60; supplies, $3,240.50; plus sales tax. T17.
Posting. Post the items that are to be posted individually.

22. Sold supplies on account to Renville Public Schools, $4,750.00; no sales tax. S99.

22. Purchased supplies on account from Strup Supplies, $1,647.00. P116.

22. Purchased supplies on account from A-1 Supplies, $1,278.50. P117.

23. Sold books on account to Brian Fadstad, $1,720.00, plus sales tax, S100.

23. Sold supplies on account to Janelle Kamschorr, $920.00, plus sales tax. S101.

23. Received cash on account from Marcello Amco, $463.05, covering S98 for supplies for $472.50 ($450.00 plus sales tax), less discount, and less sales tax. R144.

24. Purchased books on account from CBG Distributors, $1,500.00. P118.

24. Recorded cash and credit card sales: books, $4,160.10; supplies, $3,420.50; plus sales tax. T24.
Posting. Post the items that are to be posted individually.

26. Sold supplies on account to Donald Lindgren, $540.00, plus sales tax. S102.

26. Returned supplies to A-1 Supplies, $265.00, from P117. DM60.

27. Purchased books on account from Maryland Books & Supplies, $2,440.50. P119.

27. Purchased supplies on account from Grandway Products, $3,157.99. P120.

28. Sold books on account to Donald Lindgren, $650.00, plus sales tax. S103.

4. Prepare a bank statement reconciliation. Use December 29 of the current year as the date. The following information is obtained from the bank statement and from the records of the business.

Bank statement balance	$48,363.56
Bank service charge	11.40
Bank credit card charge	354.20
Outstanding deposit: December 29	7,959.63
Outstanding checks:	
No. 348	2,823.70
No. 349	1,200.00
Checkbook balance on Check Stub No. 349	52,665.09

5. Continue journalizing the following transactions.

Dec. 30. Received bank statement showing December bank service charge, $11.40. M41.

30. Recorded credit card fee expense for December, $354.20. M42.

31. Granted credit to Renville Public Schools for supplies returned, $1,500.00, from S99. CM34.

31. Sold books on account to Gilmore Public Schools, $6,200.00; no sales tax. S104.

31. Paid cash to replenish petty cash fund, $415.00: store supplies, $145.00; advertising, $160.00; miscellaneous, $110.00. C350.

31. Recorded cash and credit card sales: books, $3,580.40; supplies, $2,480.00; plus sales tax. T31.
   Posting. Post the items that are to be posted individually.

COMPLETING JOURNALS

Instructions:

6. Prove and rule the sales journal and the sales returns and allowances journal. Post the totals of the special columns.

7. Prove and rule the purchases journal and the purchases returns and allowances journal. Post the totals of the special columns.

8. Prove the cash receipts journal and the cash payments journal.

9. Prove cash. The balance on the next unused check stub is $61,397.91.

10. Rule the cash receipts journal. Post the totals of the special columns.

11. Rule the cash payments journal. Post the totals of the special columns.

END-OF-FISCAL-PERIOD WORK

Instructions:

12. Prepare a schedule of accounts receivable and a schedule of accounts payable. Compare each schedule total with the balance of the controlling account in the general ledger. The total and the balance should be the same.

13. Prepare a trial balance on a work sheet.

14. Complete the work sheet. Record the adjustments on the work sheet using the information on the following page.

Adjustment Information, December 31

Uncollectible accounts expense estimated as 1.0% of sales on account.

Sales on account for year, $241,257.00.

Merchandise inventory—books	$174,469.25
Merchandise inventory—supplies	151,439.85
Office supplies inventory	4,635.00
Store supplies inventory	3,960.00
Value of prepaid insurance	4,400.00
Annual depreciation expense—office equipment	870.00
Annual depreciation expense—store equipment	940.00
Federal income tax expense for the year	5,013.75

15. Prepare a departmental statement of gross profit. Calculate and record component percentages for cost of merchandise sold and gross profit on operations. Round percentage calculations to the nearest 0.1%.

16. Prepare an income statement. Record the component percentages for cost of merchandise sold and gross profit on operations from the departmental statement of gross profit. Calculate and record the component percentages for total operating expenses and net income before and after federal income tax. Round component percentage calculations to the nearest 0.1%.

17. Prepare a statement of stockholders' equity. Use the following additional information.

January 1 balance of capital stock account	$300,000.00
(3,000 shares issued for $100.00 per share)	
No additional capital stock issued.	
January 1 balance of retained earnings account	97,525.70

18. Prepare a balance sheet.

19. Use page 13 of a general journal. Journalize and post the adjusting entries.

20. Continue using page 13 of a general journal. Journalize and post the closing entries. Do not skip a line between the adjusting and closing entries.

21. Prepare a post-closing trial balance.

A BUSINESS SIMULATION
Blue Skies Outfitter

Activities in
Blue Skies Outfitter:

1. Recording transactions in special journals and a general journal.

2. Calculating and recording departmental payroll data.

3. Preparing a bank reconciliation.

4. Posting items to be posted individually to a general ledger and subsidiary ledgers.

5. Proving and ruling journals.

6. Posting column totals to a general ledger.

7. Preparing schedules of accounts receivable and accounts payable.

8. Preparing a trial balance on a work sheet.

9. Planning adjustments and completing a work sheet.

10. Preparing financial statements.

11. Journalizing and posting adjusting entries.

12. Journalizing and posting closing entries.

13. Preparing a post-closing trial balance.

Blue Skies Outfitter is a departmentalized merchandising business organized as a corporation. This business simulation covers the realistic transactions completed by Blue Skies Outfitter, which has two departments: Equipment and Supplies. The activities included in the accounting cycle for Blue Skies Outfitter are listed at left.

This simulation is available from the publisher in either manual or automated versions.

Accounting Control Systems

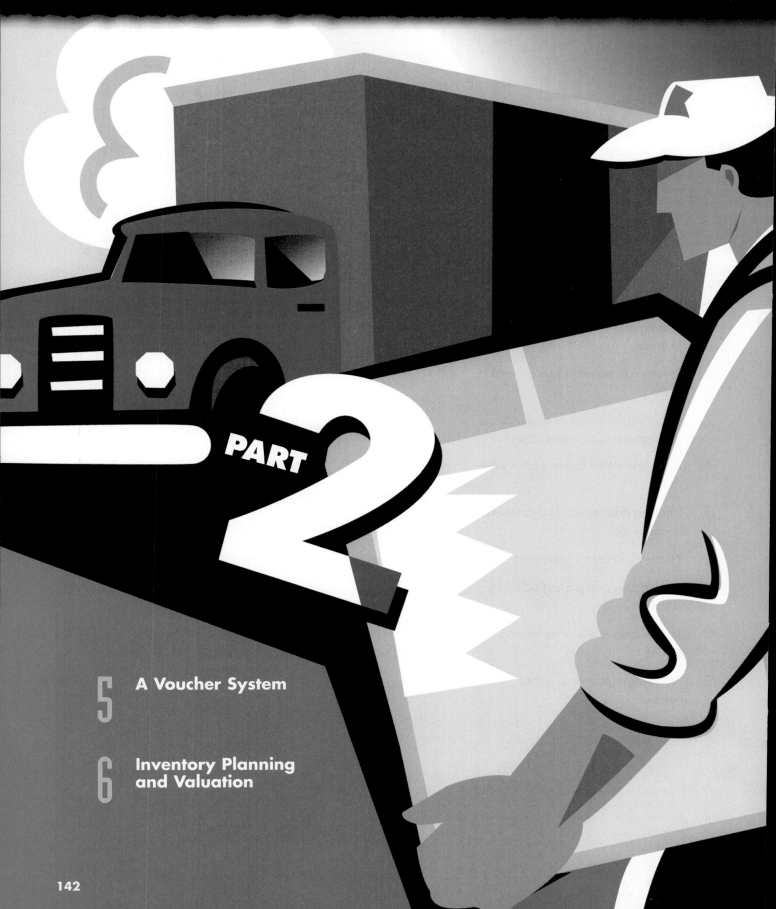

PART **2**

OFFICEMART, INC. CHART OF ACCOUNTS

Balance Sheet Accounts

(1000) Assets
1100	CURRENT ASSETS
1105	Cash
1110	Petty Cash
1115	Accounts Receivable
1120	Allowance for Uncollectible Accounts
1125	Merchandise Inventory
1130	Supplies—Sales
1135	Supplies—Administrative
1140	Prepaid Insurance
1200	PLANT ASSETS
1205	Delivery Equipment
1210	Accumulated Depreciation—Delivery Equipment
1215	Office Equipment
1220	Accumulated Depreciation—Office Equipment
1225	Store Equipment
1230	Accumulated Depreciation—Store Equipment

(2000) Liabilities
2100	CURRENT LIABILITIES
2105	Vouchers Payable
2110	Employee Income Tax Payable—Federal
2115	Employee Income Tax Payable—State
2120	Federal Income Tax Payable
2125	Social Security Tax Payable
2128	Medicare Tax Payable
2130	Sales Tax Payable
2135	Unemployment Tax Payable—Federal
2140	Unemployment Tax Payable—State
2145	Dividends Payable

(3000) Stockholders' Equity
3105	Capital Stock
3110	Retained Earnings
3115	Dividends
3120	Income Summary

Income Statement Accounts

(4000) Operating Revenue
4105	Sales
4110	Sales Discount
4115	Sales Returns and Allowances

(5000) Cost of Merchandise
5105	Purchases
5110	Purchases Discount
5115	Purchases Returns and Allowances

(6000) Operating Expenses
6100	SELLING EXPENSES
6105	Advertising Expense
6110	Delivery Expense
6115	Depreciation Expense—Delivery Equipment
6120	Depreciation Expense—Store Equipment
6125	Miscellaneous Expense—Sales
6130	Salary Expense—Sales
6135	Supplies Expense—Sales
6200	ADMINISTRATIVE EXPENSES
6205	Depreciation Expense—Office Equipment
6210	Insurance Expense
6215	Miscellaneous Expense—Administrative
6220	Payroll Taxes Expense
6225	Rent Expense
6230	Salary Expense—Administrative
6235	Supplies Expense—Administrative
6240	Uncollectible Accounts Expense
6245	Utilities Expense

(7000) Income Tax Expense
7105	Federal Income Tax Expense

The chart of accounts for OfficeMart, Inc. is illustrated above for ready reference as you study Part 2 of this textbook.

5 A Voucher System

AFTER STUDYING CHAPTER 5, YOU WILL BE ABLE TO:

1. Define accounting terms related to a voucher system.

2. Identify accounting concepts and practices related to a voucher system.

3. Prepare a voucher.

4. Journalize data from vouchers in a voucher register.

5. Journalize voucher payment transactions in a check register.

6. Journalize purchases returns and allowances and payroll transactions in a voucher system.

An accounting system includes procedures for recording and reporting accurate and up-to-date financial information. An accounting system should also include procedures to assist management in controlling a company's daily operations. Management is particularly concerned with procedures and records to control and protect assets. One asset that should be controlled and protected is cash. Cash is the asset most likely to be misused because its ownership is easily transferred. Also, transactions generally affect the cash account more often than other general ledger accounts. Many businesses, therefore, use specific cash control procedures.

Among the procedures used to control cash are storing it in a safe place, making bank deposits regularly, and approving all cash payments. Cash payments should be approved before being paid to ensure that the goods or services were ordered, have been received, and the amounts due are correct. In small businesses, the owner or manager usually approves cash payments. In large businesses, several persons may have authority to approve cash payments. A business form used to show an authorized person's approval for a cash payment is called a **voucher**. A set of procedures for controlling cash payments by preparing and approving vouchers before payments are made is called a **voucher system**. In a voucher system, NO check can be issued without a properly authorized voucher.

TERMS PREVIEW

voucher
voucher system
voucher register
voucher check
check register

ACCOUNTING
IN YOUR CAREER

PAYING UNSIGNED VOUCHERS

Atchison Company uses a voucher system that requires preparation of a voucher and its approval for payment before a check can be issued. Each day LaWanda Lewis signs onto the computerized accounting system to get a list of checks that should be prepared for the day. She then checks each invoice to be paid against the voucher jacket to make sure that payment has been approved.

Todd Ehrlinger is responsible for approving all vouchers and when he is not available, Nancy Tackett is the backup. Today, however, Todd Ehrlinger is in the hospital for emergency surgery, and Nancy Tackett is on vacation rock climbing in a remote location where she cannot be reached by phone. In checking the vouchers, LaWanda discovers that two items have not been approved for payment by either Todd or Nancy. One is the weekly payroll. The other is an invoice for $10,500 with terms of 2/10, n/30.

LaWanda is a conscientious employee who always gets good performance reviews. She has sometimes been criticized, however, for lacking initiative. She knows that vouchers are not to be paid until an authorized person has approved the voucher, so she is not sure what to do about the two unapproved items. Finally, she decides to go ahead and issue the checks for the two unapproved items. As she is preparing the checks for mailing, a delivery arrives and the messenger insists that the $15.00 messenger fee be paid immediately before leaving the message.

Critical Thinking

1. LaWanda did not follow established procedures when she prepared the checks for the two unapproved items. What is your opinion about the action that she took?
2. Should LaWanda also issue a check to the messenger service for the $15.00 fee without having an approved voucher?

5-1 Vouchers and Voucher Registers

VERIFYING AN INVOICE

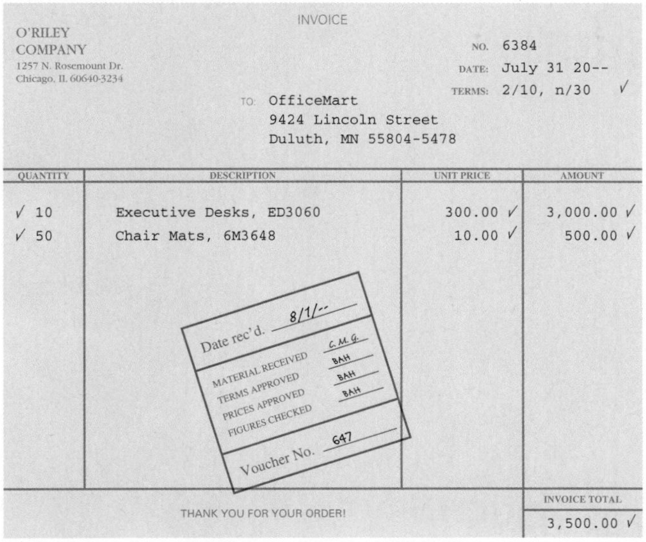
INVOICE

O'RILEY COMPANY
1257 N. Rosemount Dr.
Chicago, IL 60640-3234

NO. 6384
DATE: July 31 20--
TERMS: 2/10, n/30 ✓

TO: OfficeMart
9424 Lincoln Street
Duluth, MN 55804-5478

QUANTITY	DESCRIPTION	UNIT PRICE	AMOUNT
✓ 10	Executive Desks, ED3060	300.00 ✓	3,000.00 ✓
✓ 50	Chair Mats, 6M3648	10.00 ✓	500.00 ✓

Date rec'd. 8/1/--
MATERIAL RECEIVED C.M.G.
TERMS APPROVED BAH
PRICES APPROVED BAH
FIGURES CHECKED BAH
Voucher No. 647

THANK YOU FOR YOUR ORDER!

INVOICE TOTAL 3,500.00 ✓

Figure 5-1

OfficeMart, a merchandising business, sells office furniture and supplies. When OfficeMart receives an invoice, a verification form is stamped on the invoice, as shown in Figure 5-1.

OfficeMart's receiving clerk verifies that the items were received in the correct quantities. A clerk in OfficeMart's purchasing department verifies that the terms and prices are correct. The calculations on the invoice are also verified. Each person doing a part of the work places a check mark next to the items verified and initials the verification form to show responsibility for that part.

A VOUCHER

After an invoice is checked for accuracy, a voucher is prepared for each invoice received from a vendor.

August 1. Purchased merchandise on account from O'Riley Company, $3,500.00. Voucher No. 647.

When a voucher system is used, the source document for an approved cash payment is the voucher. The source document for this transaction is Voucher No. 647. *(CONCEPT: Objective Evidence)*

In a voucher system, the general ledger liability account, Vouchers Payable, is used instead of Accounts Payable. Accounts Payable has been used to record only amounts of items bought on account. In a voucher system, Vouchers Payable is used to record *ALL* amounts to be paid by check. Since Vouchers Payable is a liability account, the normal balance is on the credit side of the account. With a voucher system, an accounts payable ledger is not kept. Instead, vouchers needing to be paid are kept in an unpaid vouchers file. The unpaid vouchers file shows all amounts owed and to whom they are owed.

Purchases	
3,500.00	

Vouchers Payable	
	3,500.00

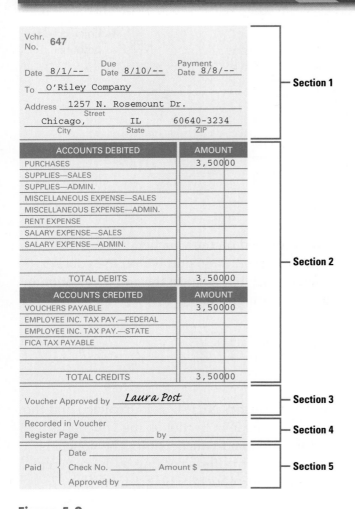

Figure 5-2

A form is printed on the outside of a voucher to summarize the contents and provide space for approving payments, as shown in Figure 5-2. After the invoice is summarized on the voucher, the voucher is folded so that related documents can be placed inside. For this reason a voucher is sometimes known as a voucher jacket.

OfficeMart uses prenumbered voucher forms and must account for all voucher numbers. Therefore, the prenumbered vouchers serve as an additional control within OfficeMart's voucher system.

The outside of OfficeMart's voucher has five sections for recording information: (1) Information about the payee. (2) Information about the accounts affected. (3) Approval of the voucher. (4) Information about where the voucher is recorded. (5) Information about the payment of the voucher.

Sections 1, 2, and 3 of the voucher are completed at the time it is prepared. Sections 4 and 5 are completed as described later in this chapter.

Section 1—Payee Information

OfficeMart's accounting clerk uses the verified invoice shown in Figure 5-1 to enter information about the payee in Section 1 of the voucher.

The voucher's due date is calculated using information on the invoice. The invoice is dated July 31, with terms of 2/10, n/30. Therefore, to take the discount, the invoice must be paid no later than August 10.

From experience, OfficeMart has learned that most checks are received within two days. Therefore, OfficeMart writes and mails checks for cash payments two days before the due date. Thus, the payment date for Voucher No. 647 is August 8.

After Section 1 of the voucher is completed, the voucher number, 647, is recorded on the invoice's verification stamp, as shown in Figure 5-1.

Section 2—Accounts Affected

Two accounts are affected by this transaction: the cost account, **Purchases**, is debited, and the liability account, **Vouchers Payable**, is credited. Section 2 of the voucher lists preprinted account titles for accounts most often affected by cash payments. **Purchases** is preprinted under the heading Accounts Debited. **Vouchers Payable** is preprinted under the heading Accounts Credited. Therefore, only the amount of the invoice, *$3,500.00*, must be entered in Section 2. Total Debits and Total Credits are also calculated and entered. If additional account titles are needed, they are entered on the blank lines in Section 2.

Section 3—Voucher Approval

As a double check, many businesses authorize one person, sometimes more, to approve vouchers before they are journalized. Laura Post, accountant, is authorized to approve vouchers for OfficeMart. When Laura verifies that the voucher is correct, she approves it by signing her name in Section 3.

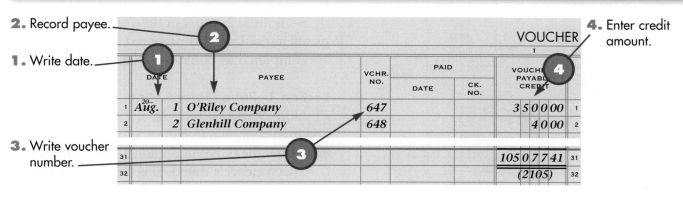

2. Record payee.

1. Write date.

4. Enter credit amount.

3. Write voucher number.

Figure 5-3 (left side)

After it has been approved, a voucher is recorded, as shown in Figure 5-3. A journal used to record vouchers is called a **voucher register**. A voucher register is similar to and replaces a purchases journal. Since OfficeMart's vouchers are prenumbered, all vouchers can be accounted for. A missing voucher number shows that a voucher has not been recorded.

Journalizing a Voucher in a Voucher Register's Special Columns

OfficeMart's voucher register has special columns for Vouchers Payable Credit, Purchases Debit, Supplies—Sales Debit, and Supplies—Administrative Debit. For accounts with no special amount columns, information is recorded in the General columns. Voucher 647 is recorded on line 1 of the voucher register.

Section 4 of a Voucher—Where the Voucher Is Recorded

The person who records the voucher in the voucher register also completes Section 4 of the voucher. The person makes a notation indicating the page on which the information is recorded in the voucher register. The person also initials the

space provided on the voucher. Placing the voucher register page number on the voucher provides easy reference to the entry's location in the voucher register.

Recorded in Voucher Register Page _____ 21 _____ by _____ G. R. S. _____

After Voucher No. 647 is journalized and the notation is made in Section 4, the voucher is filed in an unpaid vouchers file. The vouchers are placed in this file according to the payment date. Filing the vouchers by payment date makes it easier to determine which vouchers need to be paid each day. This method helps ensure payment of invoices within the discount period. Thus, Voucher No. 647 is filed under the date on which it is to be paid, August 8.

Payment of a voucher is described later in this chapter.

S T E P S **Journalizing a voucher in the special columns of a voucher register**

1. Write the date of the voucher, *Aug. 1, 20--*, in the Date column.
2. Record the name of the payee, *O'Riley Company*, in the Payee column.
3. Write the voucher number, *647*, in the Vchr. No. column.
4. Enter the credit amount, *3,500.00*, in the Vouchers Payable Credit column.
5. Record the debit amount, *3,500.00*, in the appropriate debit column. Since this is a purchase transaction, the debit is made to Purchases.

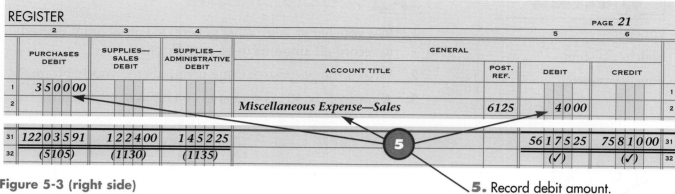

	PURCHASES DEBIT	SUPPLIES—SALES DEBIT	SUPPLIES—ADMINISTRATIVE DEBIT	GENERAL				
	2	3	4	ACCOUNT TITLE	POST. REF.	DEBIT (5)	CREDIT (6)	
1	3 5 0 0 00							1
2				*Miscellaneous Expense—Sales*	6125	4 0 00		2
31	122 0 3 5 91	1 2 2 4 00	1 4 5 2 25			56 1 7 5 25	75 8 1 0 00	31
32	(5105)	(1130)	(1135)			(✓)	(✓)	32

Figure 5-3 (right side)

5. Record debit amount.

Journalizing a Voucher in the General Columns of a Voucher Register

OfficeMart's voucher register has special debit amount columns for Purchases Debit, Supplies—Sales Debit, and Supplies—Administrative Debit. When an account other than these four is affected, the information is recorded in the General columns.

> **August 2.** **Received invoice for sales miscellaneous expense from Glenhill Company, $40.00. Voucher No. 648.**

Voucher No. 648 is prepared in the same manner as Voucher No. 647. Voucher No. 648 is recorded on line 2 of the voucher register.

A notation is made on Voucher No. 648 in Section 4 to show where the voucher was recorded and by whom.

Miscellaneous Expense—Sales	
40.00	

Vouchers Payable	
	40.00

Proving, Ruling, and Posting a Voucher Register

Separate amounts recorded in the General Debit and General Credit columns of a voucher register are posted individually during the month. As each amount is posted, the account number is written in the Post. Ref. column of the voucher register.

At the end of each month, OfficeMart's voucher register is proved and ruled. The procedures for proving and ruling a voucher register are the same as those previously described for special journals.

As previously described for special journals, totals of special amount columns are posted to the general ledger accounts listed in the column headings. Totals of General Debit and General Credit amount columns are not posted.

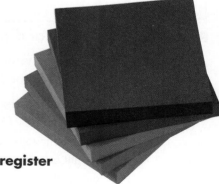

S T E P S **Journalizing a voucher in the general columns of a voucher register**

1. Write the date of the voucher, *Aug. 2*, in the Date column.
2. Record the name of the payee, *Glenhill Company*, in the Payee column.
3. Enter the voucher number, *648*, in the Vchr. No. column.
4. Record the credit amount, *40.00*, in the Vouchers Payable Credit column.
5. Record the debit amount, *40.00*, in the General Debit column. Write the title of the account to be debited, *Miscellaneous Expense—Sales*, in the General Account Title column.

AUDIT YOUR
UNDERSTANDING

1. In a voucher system, what general ledger account is used to record all amounts to be paid by check?

2. What is the purpose of using prenumbered voucher forms?

3. A voucher register is similar to and replaces what journal?

WORK
TOGETHER

Preparing a voucher and journalizing vouchers in a voucher register

A voucher and page 10 of a voucher register for Cloverleaf Crafts is provided in the *Working Papers*. Your instructor will guide you through the following examples. The abbreviation for voucher is *V*.

Oct. 1. Purchased merchandise on account from Dickens Company, 11200 Irving Street, Minneapolis, MN 55411, terms 2/10, n/30, $600.00. V152.

2. Received invoice for October rent from Land Development Co., $1,300.00. V153.

4. Bought sales supplies on account from University Supplies, $350.00. V154.

8. Received invoice for delivery service from City Delivery Co., $25.00. V155.

4. Prepare Voucher 152 for the October 1 transaction.

5. Journalize the transactions completed during October of the current year.

6. Prove and rule the voucher register. Save your work to complete the Work Together on page 154.

ON YOUR
OWN

Preparing a voucher and journalizing vouchers in a voucher register

A voucher and page 8 of a voucher register for Trails End are provided in the *Working Papers*. Work independently to complete the following problem. The abbreviation for voucher is *V*.

Aug. 1. Purchased merchandise on account from Darst Corporation, 7020 Niles Lane, Centuria, WI 54824, terms 2/10, n/30, $300.00. V89.

3. Received invoice for miscellaneous expense from G & G Company, $75.00. V90.

5. Bought administrative supplies on account from Heartland Supplies, $200.00. V91.

8. Received invoice for advertising from City News, $225.00. V92.

7. Prepare Voucher 89 for the August 1 transaction.

8. Journalize the transactions completed during August of the current year.

9. Prove and rule the voucher register. Save your work to complete the On Your Own on page 154.

5-2 Voucher Check and Check Registers

PREPARING A VOUCHER CHECK

1. Enter voucher no.

2. Enter payee's invoice no.

6. Prepare check to payee for net amount of invoice.

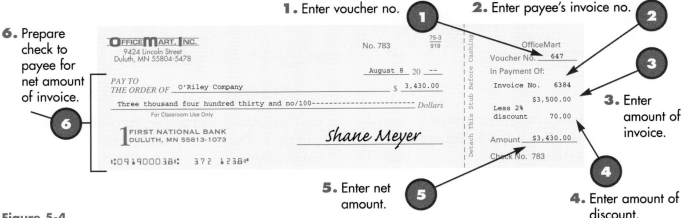

Figure 5-4

3. Enter amount of invoice.

5. Enter net amount.

4. Enter amount of discount.

OfficeMart pays each voucher by check as shown in Figure 5-4. It prepares a check for the amount of each voucher less any purchases discount. The check and voucher are presented to a person authorized to approve payment. A check with space for writing details about a cash payment is called a **voucher check**. OfficeMart prepares voucher checks in duplicate. The original is given to the payee and OfficeMart keeps the duplicate. The duplicate check is used as the source document for a cash payment transaction. (*CONCEPT: Objective Evidence*)

On August 8, vouchers to be paid on that day are removed from the unpaid vouchers file. Included in this group is Voucher No. 647. OfficeMart's cash payments clerk prepares the voucher checks.

OfficeMart uses the detachable section at the right of the voucher check to record details about the cash payment. On Check No. 783, the information includes the following items:

1. OfficeMart's voucher number, 647.

2. Payee's invoice number, 6384.

3. Amount of invoice, $3,500.00.

4. Amount of discount, $70.00.

5. Net amount for which check is written, $3,430.00.

Before a payee deposits or cashes a voucher check, the detachable section showing details of the transaction is removed. It is kept by the payee as a record of the check.

Section 5 of a Voucher—Payment of a Voucher

The person who prepares the check also completes part of Section 5 of the voucher by noting the date paid, the check number, and the amount. The manager, Shane Meyer, verifies that the information on the check and on the voucher agrees and is accurate. After verification, he signs the check and initials Section 5 of the voucher.

Paid { Date *Aug. 8, 20--*
Check No. *783* Amount $ *3,430.00*
Approved by *S.M.*

Information about this payment must also be recorded in the voucher register. The person who prepares the check usually makes this notation. The date on which this voucher is paid, Aug. 8, and the check number, 783, are written in the Paid columns of the voucher register. This information is written on the same line as the original entry for Voucher No. 647.

The check is given or sent to the payee, and the voucher is filed in the paid vouchers file according to the name of the vendor.

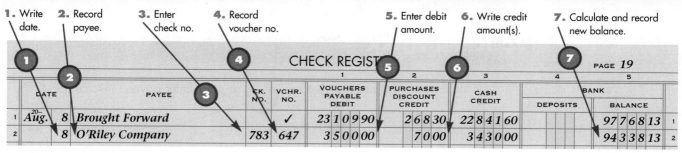

Figure 5-5

A journal used in a voucher system to record cash payments is called a **check register**. The check register is similar to and replaces a cash payments journal.

Maintaining Bank Columns in a Check Register

OfficeMart uses a check register to maintain the checking account balance as shown in Figure 5-5. OfficeMart's check register has two Bank columns, Deposits and Balance. Using these two Bank columns, OfficeMart keeps an up-to-date record of cash in the checking account. The Bank Deposits column is used to record the amounts deposited in the checking account. The Bank Balance column shows the checking account balance after each check and each deposit are recorded in the check register.

Journalizing Checks in a Check Register

OfficeMart prepares a voucher for each approved cash payment. Therefore, each check is issued in payment of a voucher. Checks are recorded in the check register in the order they are written.

In OfficeMart's voucher system, only three general ledger accounts are affected by a cash

payment: Vouchers Payable, Purchases Discount, and Cash. Therefore, OfficeMart's check register has only three special amount columns: Vouchers Payable Debit, Purchases Discount Credit, and Cash Credit. Each check is recorded in a check register as a debit to the liability account, Vouchers Payable, and a credit to the asset account, Cash. If a discount is taken for prompt payment, the discount amount is recorded as a credit to the contra cost account, Purchases Discount.

> August 8. Paid cash to O'Riley Company, $3,430.00, covering Voucher No. 647 for $3,500.00, less 2% discount, $70.00. Check No. 783.

The liability account, Vouchers Payable, is debited for $3,500.00. The contra cost account, Purchases Discount, is credited for $70.00. Cash is credited for the net amount paid, $3,430.00.

Vouchers Payable		
3,500.00	Vchr. 647	3,500.00

Purchases Discount	
	70.00

Cash	
	3,430.00

Journalizing checks in a check register

1. Write the date of the payment, *8*, in the Date column.
2. Record the name of the payee, *O'Riley Company*, in the Payee column.
3. Enter the check number, *783*, in the Ck. No. column.
4. Record the number of the voucher being paid, *647*, in the Vchr. No. column.
5. Enter the debit amount, *3,500.00*, in the Vouchers Payable Debit column.
6. Write the credit amounts, *70.00* and *3,430.00*, in the Cash and the Purchases Discount Credit columns.
7. Calculate and record the new cash balance, *94,338.13*, in the Bank Balance column.

	DATE	PAYEE	CK. NO.	VCHR. NO.	VOUCHERS PAYABLE DEBIT 1	PURCHASES DISCOUNT CREDIT 2	CASH CREDIT 3	BANK DEPOSITS 4	BANK BALANCE 5	
1	Aug. 8	Brought Forward		✓	23 1 0 9 90	2 6 8 30	22 8 4 1 60		97 7 6 8 13	1
2	8	O'Riley Company	783	647	3 5 0 0 00	7 0 00	3 4 3 0 00		94 3 3 8 13	2
3	11	Jacobs Equipment	784	649	9 7 3 91	1 9 48	9 5 4 43		93 3 8 3 70	3
4	14	Petty Cash Cust., OfficeMart	785	656	2 1 2 50		2 1 2 50		93 1 7 1 20	4
5	14	Deposit		✓				18 7 6 7 15	111 9 3 8 35	5
22	31	Payroll	800	694	4 3 3 1 96		4 3 3 1 96		95 3 7 3 21	22
23	31	Deposit		✓				19 2 9 4 78	114 6 6 7 99	23
24	31	Totals			103 4 5 2 22	5 6 6 88	102 8 8 5 34			24
25					(2105)	(5110)	(1105)			25

Figure 5-6

At the end of each month, the special amount columns of the check register are proved, ruled, and posted.

OfficeMart's procedures for posting from its check register are the same as those previously described for special journals. However, no separate amounts are posted individually because the check register does not have a General Debit or General Credit column. The three special amount column totals are posted to the general ledger accounts listed in the column headings. After each total is posted, the account number is written in parentheses below the column total.

The two Bank columns are used to summarize the status of the checking account balance. These two columns are neither ruled nor posted.

A deposit in the checking account is shown on line 5 of Figure 5-6. The Deposits column does not need to be totaled and posted because each cash receipt is recorded in the cash receipts journal and posted from that journal. At the end of each month, cash is proved by comparing the last amount in the Balance column of the check register with the balance in the general ledger cash account. Cash is proved if the two amounts are the same.

STARTING A NEW PAGE OF A CHECK REGISTER

	DATE	PAYEE	CK. NO.	VCHR. NO.	VOUCHERS PAYABLE DEBIT 1	PURCHASES DISCOUNT CREDIT 2	CASH CREDIT 3	BANK DEPOSITS 4	BANK BALANCE 5	
1	Sept. 1	Brought Forward		✓					114 6 6 7 99	1

Figure 5-7

A new page of a check register may be needed either during a month or at the start of a new month. When a new page is started during a month, the totals of the Vouchers Payable Debit, Purchases Discount Credit, and Cash Credit columns are brought forward from the previous page. The balance of the Bank Balance column is also brought forward. No amount is brought forward for the Bank Deposits column.

OfficeMart begins a new page of the check register at the beginning of each month, as shown in Figure 5-7. Only the balance of the Bank Balance column is brought forward. The totals of the special amount columns are not brought forward because they were posted at the end of the previous month.

TERMS REVIEW

voucher check

check register

AUDIT YOUR UNDERSTANDING

1. A check register is similar to and replaces what journal?
2. In what order are paid vouchers filed?
3. What account is debited for each check recorded in a check register?

WORK TOGETHER

Journalizing cash payments and deposits in a check register

Use the working papers from the Work Together on page 150. Page 10 of a check register for Cloverleaf Crafts is provided in the *Working Papers*. Your instructor will guide you through the following examples. Source documents are abbreviated as follows: check, C; voucher, V.

Oct. 8. Paid cash to Dickens Company, $588.00, covering V152 for $600.00, less 2% discount, $12.00. C309.
    9. Paid cash to University Supplies, $350.00, covering V154. C310.
   11. Paid cash to Land Development Co., $1,300.00, covering V153. C311.
   16. Made a deposit in the checking account, $3,775.09.

4. Record the bank balance brought forward on October 1 of the current year, $18,765.55.

5. Journalize the transactions completed during October of the current year. As each cash payment is journalized, make the appropriate notation in the voucher register.

6. Prove and rule the check register.

ON YOUR OWN

Journalizing cash payments and deposits in a check register

Use the working papers from the On Your Own on page 150. Page 8 of a check register for Trails End is provided in the *Working Papers*. Work this problem independently. Source documents are abbreviated as follows: check, C; voucher, V.

Aug. 8. Paid cash to Darst Corp., $294.00, covering V89 for $300.00, less 2% discount, $6.00. C222.
    9. Paid cash to Heartland Supplies, $200.00, covering V91. C223.
   11. Paid cash to C & G Company, $75.00, covering V90. C224.
   15. Made a deposit in the checking account, $1,388.12.

7. Record the bank balance brought forward on August 1 of the current year, $5,422.67.

8. Journalize the transactions completed during August of the current year. As each cash payment is journalized, make the appropriate notation in the voucher register.

9. Prove and rule the check register.

PURCHASES RETURNS AND ALLOWANCES

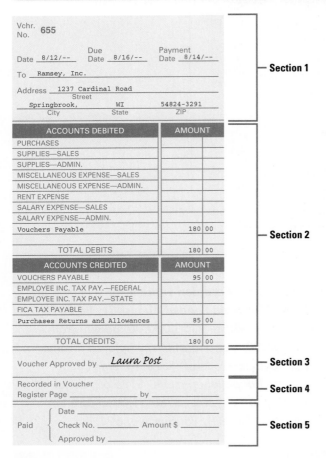

Figure 5-8

Using a voucher system requires that some transactions follow different procedures. Two examples are purchases returns and allowances and payroll transactions.

A purchases returns and allowances transaction reduces the total amount owed for an invoice. Therefore, the voucher record for that invoice must be changed to show the reduction in the amount owed.

August 12.   Issued Debit Memorandum No. 98 to Ramsey, Inc. for return of merchandise purchased, $85.00. Cancel Voucher No. 652. Voucher No. 655.

Voucher No. 655 is prepared for this transaction, as shown in Figure 5-8, and is the source document for the entry (CONCEPT: *Objective Evidence*)

The liability account, **Vouchers Payable**, is debited for $180.00 to cancel Voucher No. 652. **Vouchers Payable** is credited for $95.00, the difference between Voucher No. 652 ($180.00) and Debit Memorandum No. 98 ($85.00). The contra cost account, **Purchases Returns and Allowances**, is credited for $85.00, the amount of merchandise returned.

OfficeMart follows five steps in changing the original amount owed for Voucher No. 652 because of the purchases return. The entry recording this voucher is on lines 6 and 9 of the voucher register in Figure 5-9 on the next page.

Changing the original amount of a voucher because of a purchase return

1. Remove the original voucher, No. 652, from the unpaid vouchers file. Write *Canceled* across Section 5.

2. Prepare a new voucher, No. 655. Place the canceled voucher and the debit memorandum inside.

3. In the voucher register, on the same line as the original voucher, write *See Vchr. 655,* in the Paid columns. The number indicates the new voucher number.

4. Record the new voucher on the next available line of the voucher register. Enter the new credit amount, 95.00, in the Vouchers Payable Credit column. Write the title of the account debited, *Vouchers Payable,* in the General Account Title column. Write the amount of the canceled voucher, *180.00,* in the General Debit column. On the next line of the register, write the other account title, *Purchases Returns and Allowances,* in the General Account Title column. Enter the amount of the return, *85.00,* in the General Credit column.

5. File the new voucher by its payment date in the unpaid vouchers file. The payment date is based on the terms of the original invoice. Therefore, the new voucher has the same payment date as the original voucher.

RECORDING PAYROLL IN A VOUCHER REGISTER (LEFT SIDE)

VOUCHER

	DATE		PAYEE	VCHR. NO.	PAID DATE	PAID CK. NO.	VOUCHERS PAYABLE CREDIT 1	
1	20-- Aug.	1	O'Riley Company	647	Aug. 8	783	3 500 00	1
2		2	Glenhill Company	648			40 00	2
3		4	Jacobs Equipment	649	Aug. 11	784	973 91	3
4		5	Salem Wholesale Instruments	650			451 00	4
5		7	Bob's Delivery Service	651	Aug. 17	786	63 00	5
6		7	Ramsey, Inc.	652	See Vchr. 655		180 00	6
7		10	Superior Office Supplies	653			87 00	7
8		12	Kuker Company	654	Aug. 19	788	276 00	8
9		12	Ramsey, Inc.	655			95 00	9
10								10
11		14	Petty Cash Custodian, OfficeMart	656	Aug. 14	785	212 50	11
12								12
26		31	Payroll	694	Aug. 31	800	4 331 96	26
27								27
28								28
29								29
30								30
31								31

Figure 5-9 (left side)

OfficeMart pays its employees semimonthly. A payroll register showing details for each payroll is prepared. The payroll register is prepared in a way similar to the description in Chapter 3. Information from a payroll register is used in preparing a voucher for payroll.

August 31. Recorded voucher for semimonthly payroll for period ended August 31, $4,331.96 (total payroll: sales, $3,000.00; administrative, $2,854.00; less deductions: employee income tax payable—federal, $878.10; employee income tax payable—state, $175.62; social security tax payable, $380.51; Medicare tax payable, $87.81). Voucher No. 694.

A PAYROLL VOUCHER

VOUCHER Vchr. No. 694

Payment Date August 31 20 --

Date August 31 20 -- Terms ____ Due August 31 20 --

To Payroll

Address

City ____ State ____ ZIP ____

For the following: Enclose all invoices or other papers.

DATE	VOUCHER DETAILS		AMOUNT
Aug. 31	Payroll for period ended 8/31/--		
	Salary Expense--Sales		$3,000.00
	Salary Expense--Administrative		2,854.00
	Deductions:		
	Employee Inc. Tax Pay.--Federal	$878.10	
	Employee Inc. Tax Pay.--State	175.62	
	Social Security Tax Payable	380.51	
	Medicare Tax Payable	87.81	1,522.04
	Net cash payment		$4,331.96

OFFICEMART, INC.

Figure 5-10

A payroll register is needed for several purposes, as described in Chapter 3. Therefore, the payroll register cannot be placed inside a voucher for payroll. For this reason, information from the payroll register is summarized on the inside of Voucher No. 694 as shown in Figure 5-10.

The inside of the voucher allows additional space so that more detailed information about the transaction can be noted.

The outside of a payroll voucher is completed in a manner similar to the completion of other vouchers.

	PURCHASES DEBIT	SUPPLIES— SALES DEBIT	SUPPLIES— ADMINISTRATIVE DEBIT	GENERAL ACCOUNT TITLE	POST. REF.	DEBIT	CREDIT	
1	3 5 0 0 00							1
2				Miscellaneous Expense—Sales	6125	4 0 00		2
3	9 7 3 91							3
4	4 5 1 00							4
5		6 3 00						5
6	1 8 0 00							6
7			8 7 00					7
8	2 7 6 00							8
9				Vouchers Payable	2105	1 8 0 00		9
10				Purchases Returns and Allowances	5115		8 5 00	10
11		4 0 00	5 5 25	Advertising Expense	6105	4 7 00		11
12				Miscellaneous Expense—Administrative	6215	7 0 25		12
26				Salary Expense—Sales	6130	3 0 0 0 00		26
27				Salary Expense—Administrative	6230	2 8 5 4 00		27
28				Employee Income Tax Payable—Federal	2110		8 7 8 10	28
29				Employee Income Tax Payable—State	2115		1 7 5 62	29
30				Social Security Tax Payable	2125		3 8 0 51	30
31				Medicare Tax Payable	2128		8 7 81	31

REGISTER · PAGE 21

Figure 5-9 (right side)

The voucher register entry to record Voucher No. 694 is shown on lines 26 to 31 of Figure 5-9. An entry is made in OfficeMart's general journal for the employer's payroll taxes. This entry is the same as the one described in Chapter 3. Later, when payroll taxes are due, vouchers are prepared, approved, and paid. One voucher is prepared for total payroll taxes owed to the federal government. Another voucher is prepared for total payroll taxes owed to the state government.

ADVANTAGES OF A VOUCHER SYSTEM

A voucher system has the following advantages for businesses that make many cash payments.

1. Only a few people can authorize and approve all cash payments. This procedure helps protect and control cash.

2. A voucher jacket provides a convenient way to file invoices and related business papers for future reference. This is especially true when invoices received from vendors are of different sizes.

3. Unpaid vouchers are filed by their payment dates to help ensure payment of invoices within the discount periods.

4. An unpaid vouchers file and a paid vouchers file eliminate posting to an accounts payable ledger.

5. A paid vouchers file provides three different and easy ways to find information about a paid voucher:
   a. *If only the voucher number is known,* look in the voucher register for that number and find the payee's name on the same line. The voucher will be in the paid vouchers file under the name of the payee.
   b. *If only the check number used to pay the voucher is known,* look in the check register for the check number. The payee's name is on the same line. The voucher will be in the paid vouchers file under the name of the payee.
   c. *If only the name of the payee is known,* look in the paid vouchers file where vouchers are filed under the name of the payee.

1. What accounts are affected, and how, when a debit memorandum is issued for the return of merchandise purchased and the original voucher is canceled?

2. What is the first step in canceling a voucher?

3. Where is the information obtained for preparing a voucher for payroll?

Journalizing purchases returns and allowances and payroll in a voucher register

A voucher register for Gille Company is provided in the *Working Papers*. Source documents are abbreviated as follows: debit memorandum, DM; voucher, V. Your instructor will guide you through the following examples.

May 1. Purchased merchandise on account from Casey Corporation, $1,500.00. V75.

4. Issued DM4 to Casey Corporation for return of merchandise purchased, $300.00. Cancel V75. V76.

15. Recorded voucher for semimonthly payroll for period ended May 15, $3,308.18 (total payroll: sales, $2,780.52; administrative, $1,690.00, less deductions: employee income tax payable—federal, $670.58; employee income tax payable—state, $134.12; social security tax payable, $290.58; Medicare tax payable, $67.06). V77.

4. Journalize the transactions completed during May of the current year. Use page 5 of a voucher register. When a voucher is canceled, make appropriate notations in the voucher register.

Journalizing purchases returns and allowances and payroll in a voucher register

A voucher register for Geist Company is provided in the *Working Papers*. Source documents are abbreviated as follows: debit memorandum, DM; voucher, V. Work independently to complete the following problem.

June 1. Purchased merchandise on account from Prickett Corporation, $900.00. V110.

4. Issued DM56 to Prickett Corporation for return of merchandise purchased, $300.00. Cancel V110. V111.

15. Recorded voucher for semimonthly payroll for period ended June 15, $4,778.63 (total payroll: sales, $3,957.61; administrative, $2,500.00, less deductions: employee income tax payable—federal, $968.64; employee income tax payable—state, $193.73; social security tax payable, $419.75; Medicare tax payable, $96.86). V112.

5. Journalize the transactions completed during June of the current year. Use page 6 of a voucher register. When a voucher is canceled, make appropriate notations in the voucher register.

CHAPTER 5 SUMMARY

After completing this chapter, you can

1. Define accounting terms related to a voucher system.
2. Identify accounting concepts and practices related to a voucher system.
3. Prepare a voucher.
4. Journalize data from vouchers in a voucher register.
5. Journalize voucher payment transactions in a check register.
6. Journalize purchases returns and allowances and payroll transactions in a voucher system.

EXPLORE ACCOUNTING

INTERNAL CONTROL SYSTEMS

A company should establish policies and procedures to protect the assets of the company and to insure the reliability of the company's accounting records. Such a set of policies and procedures is known as an internal control system. The American Institute of Certified Public Accountants defines an internal control structure as "the policies and procedures established to provide reasonable assurance that specific entity objectives will be achieved." A reliable internal control structure requires that *all*
employees follow the policies and procedures established.

An accurate accounting system is an important part of a reliable internal control structure. Accounting controls must support internal controls. This chapter introduced one such accounting control, the voucher system.

A widely used internal control is "separation of duties." This means that no one employee is given authority to totally control an asset. For example, in this chapter's discussion, one employee prepared the voucher, another employee approved the voucher, and a third employee
approved the check payment. Without this control mechanism, an employee has a better chance of stealing from the employer.

REQUIRED:

In-Class Assignment: In groups of 3 or 4, determine why internal controls are important. Who are they designed to protect?

Research Assignment: Contact at least one business in your community. Ask what internal controls have been established to protect the company's assets. Summarize and present your findings to your class.

APPLICATION PROBLEM
Preparing a voucher and journalizing vouchers in a voucher register

TeleTronics uses a voucher register similar to the one described in this chapter.

Transactions:

Sept. 1. Purchased merchandise on account from Eastern Company, 9424 Denison Pkwy., Corning, NY, 14830, terms: 2/10, n/30, $3,100.00. V87.
2. Post Real Estate Developers sent an invoice for $1,150.00 for September's rent. V88.
5. Bought sales supplies on account from Supra Supply Company, $258.00. V89.
8. Received invoice for advertising from Newport News, $87.50. V90.
11. Purchased merchandise on account from Hoyer Company, $3,347.75. V91.
18. Received invoice for delivery service from Rapid Rabbit, $235.15. V92.
19. Purchased $1,973.00 of merchandise on account from Beggen Company. V93.
23. Bought office equipment on account from Syracuse Company, $1,315.00. V94.
25. Received invoice for utilities from Northside Electric Cooperative, $185.00. V95.
29. Bought administrative supplies on account from Northern Supply, $317.00. V96.
30. Manley Maintenance Company sent an invoice for $25.00. The amount was for a miscellaneous sales expense. V97.

Instructions:

1. Prepare Voucher 87 for the September 1 transaction.

2. Journalize the transactions completed during September of the current year. Use page 9 of a voucher register. The abbreviation for voucher is V.

3. Prove and rule the voucher register.

The voucher register prepared in Problem 5.1 is needed to complete Problem 5.2.

APPLICATION PROBLEM
Journalizing cash payments and deposits in a check register

TeleTronics uses a check register similar to the one described in this chapter.

Transactions:

Sept. 2. Paid cash to Post Real Estate Developers, $1,150.00, covering V88. C83.
8. Paid cash to Newport News, $87.50, covering V90. C84.
9. Paid cash to Eastern Company, $3,038.00, covering V87 for $3,100.00, less 2% discount, $62.00. C85.
13. Paid cash to Supra Supply Company, $258.00, covering V89. C86.
18. Paid cash to Rapid Rabbit, $235.15, covering V92. C87.
19. Paid cash to Hoyer Company, $3,280.79, covering V91 for $3,347.75, less 2% discount, $66.96. C88.
24. Made a deposit in the checking account, $5,684.54.
25. Paid cash to Northside Electric Cooperative, $185.00, covering V95. C89.
30. Paid cash to Manley Maintenance Company, $25.00, covering V97. C90.

Instructions:

1. Use page 9 of a check register. Record the bank balance brought forward on September 1 of the current year, $19,443.13.

2. Continue using page 9 of the check register. Journalize the cash payments and deposits completed during September of the current year. As each cash payment is journalized, make the appropriate notation in the voucher register. Source documents are abbreviated as follows: check, C; voucher, V.

3. Prove and rule the check register.

APPLICATION PROBLEM
Journalizing purchases returns and allowances in a voucher register

Nygren Supply Company uses a voucher register similar to the one described in this chapter.

Transactions:

Feb. 1. Purchased merchandise on account from Hamline Corporation, $2,700.00. V10.
   4. Issued DM2 to Hamline Corporation for return of merchandise purchased, $200.00. Cancel V10. V11.
   15. Purchased merchandise on account from Moorhead, Inc., $1,778.00. V12.
   17. Issued DM3 to Moorhead, Inc., for return of merchandise purchased, $350.00. Cancel V12. V13.

Instructions:

Journalize the transactions completed during February of the current year. Use page 2 of a voucher register. When a voucher is canceled, make appropriate notations in the voucher register. Source documents are abbreviated as follows: debit memorandum, DM; voucher, V.

APPLICATION PROBLEM
Preparing and journalizing a voucher for payroll

Bowman Service Center uses a voucher form and a voucher register similar to the ones described in this chapter. Bowman Service Center's payroll register for May 15 of the current year shows the following information. The abbreviation for voucher is V.

Transactions:

May 15. Recorded voucher for semimonthly payroll for period ended May 15, $3,120.97 (total payroll: sales, $2,530.53; administrative, $1,687.00, less deductions: employee income tax payable—federal, $632.63; employee income tax payable—state, $126.53; social security tax payable, $274.14; Medicare tax payable, $63.26). V51.

Instructions:

1. Prepare a voucher for the payroll on May 15 of the current year.

2. Use page 5 of a voucher register. Journalize the voucher for the payroll. Assume that the voucher has been approved. After the voucher is journalized, complete Section 4 of the voucher.

MASTERY PROBLEM

Journalizing transactions in a voucher system

Jameson Company uses a voucher register and a check register similar to the ones described in this chapter.

Transactions:

Nov. 1. Purchased merchandise on account from Georgia Company, $975.00. V68.
2. Bought $216.80 of administrative supplies on account from Supply World. V69.
4. Bought store equipment on account from Equipment Plus, $1,998.00. V70.
8. Purchased merchandise on account from North Heights Corporation, $1,695.15. V71.
8. Paid $955.50 to Georgia Company covering V68 for $975.00, less 2% discount, $19.50. C57.
10. Made a deposit in the checking account, $3,579.00.
14. Received invoice for delivery service from Quick Delivery, $24.10. V72.
14. Paid cash to Quick Delivery, $24.10, covering V72. C58.
14. Issued DM10 to North Heights Corporation for return of merchandise purchased, $225.00. Cancel V71. V73.
15. Paid cash to North Heights Corporation, $1,440.75, covering V73 for $1,470.15, less 2% discount, $29.40. C59.
16. Recorded voucher for semimonthly payroll for period ended November 15, $1,459.64 (total payroll: sales, $1,183.50; administrative, $789.00; less deductions: employee income tax payable—federal, $295.88; employee income tax payable—state, $59.18; social security tax payable, $128.21; Medicare tax payable, $29.59). V74.
16. Paid cash for semimonthly payroll, $1,459.64, covering V74. C60.
22. Paid cash to Supply World, $216.80, covering V69. C61.
25. Issued Voucher No. 75 to buy office equipment on account from Fischer Equipment, $2,350.00.
29. Deposited $1,170.15 in the checking account.
30. Purchased merchandise on account from Georgia Company, $2,258.50. V76.

Instructions:

1. Use page 20 of a check register. Record the bank balance brought forward on November 1 of the current year, $11,676.77.

2. Journalize the transactions completed during November of the current year. Use page 22 of a voucher register and page 20 of a check register. When a voucher is paid or canceled, make appropriate notations in the voucher register. Source documents are abbreviated as follows: check, C; debit memorandum, DM; voucher, V.

3. Prove and rule both the voucher register and the check register.

CHALLENGE PROBLEM

Journalizing purchases invoices at the net amount in a voucher system

Cayman Company uses a voucher system. All of the vendors with whom Cayman Company does business offer terms of 2/10, n/30. Cayman has a policy of paying all invoices within the discount period. The business records invoice vouchers at the net amount (invoice total less a 2% discount). Thus, a $1,000.00 invoice, allowing a 2% discount of $20.00, is recorded at the net amount, $980.00. Purchases is debited and Vouchers Payable is credited for $980.00. A purchases discount account is not used.

If an invoice *is not* paid within the discount period, Cayman Company loses the discount. This loss is recorded in an account titled Discounts Lost. Thus, if the $1,000.00 invoice described above *is not* paid within the discount period, the business must pay the full $1,000.00. However, one of the controls in a voucher system is that no check can be written for more than the voucher amount. Therefore, for a check to be written for the full $1,000.00, the original voucher must be canceled. A new voucher for $1,000.00 must be prepared, approved, and recorded.

This new voucher would include a debit to Discounts Lost of $20.00, a debit to Vouchers Payable of $980.00 (the amount of the original voucher), and a credit to Vouchers Payable of $1,000.00. Once this voucher is approved, a check can be written for $1,000.00 to pay the full amount due.

If an invoice is recorded at its net amount, all purchases returns and allowances are recorded at net amounts. A $1,000.00 invoice recorded at net with a 2% discount has a $100.00 purchase return and allowance. Thus, the $100.00 return is discounted by 2% and recorded as $98.00. For the return, Vouchers Payable is debited $980.00 (the amount of original voucher), Purchases Returns and Allowances is credited for $98.00, and Vouchers Payable is credited for $882.00 (the amount of the new voucher).

Cayman's voucher register is similar to the one described for OfficeMart in this chapter. However, the third amount column is titled Discounts Lost. There is only one Supplies Debit column because there is only one supplies account. Cayman's check register has two special amount columns: Vouchers Payable Debit and Cash Credit.

Transactions:

Dec. 11. Purchased merchandise on account from Knotts Company, $2,000.00.
15. Made a deposit in the checking account, $1,000.00.
15. Bought supplies on account from Fairgate Supply Company, $200.00.
18. Bought store equipment on account from Hightop Company, $1,000.00.
18. Paid cash to Knotts Company covering V109. C80.
19. Purchased merchandise on account from Neal Company, $500.00.
22. Made a deposit in the checking account, $2,000.00.
25. Paid cash to Hightop Company covering V111. C81.
26. Paid cash to Fairgate Supply Company covering V110. C82.
28. Bought supplies on account from Peerless Supply Company, $300.00.
28. Issued DM30 to Neal Company for return of merchandise purchased, $50.00. Cancel V112.
29. Made a deposit in the checking account, $1,000.00.
31. Paid cash to Neal Company covering V115. C83.

Instructions:

1. Use page 20 of a check register. Record the amounts brought forward on December 11 of the current year.

Vouchers Payable Debit	$1,395.00
Cash Credit	1,395.00
Bank Balance	8,500.00

2. Journalize the transactions completed during December of the current year. Use page 25 of a voucher register. Assume that for all purchases of merchandise, equipment, or supplies, the invoice terms are 2/10, n/30. When a voucher is paid or canceled, make appropriate notations in the voucher register. Number vouchers consecutively starting with Voucher No. 109. Source documents are abbreviated as follows: check, C; debit memorandum, DM; voucher, V.

3. Prove and rule both the voucher register and the check register.

INTERNET ACTIVITY

Point your browser to

http://accounting.swpco.com

Choose **Advanced Course**, choose **Activities**, and complete the activity for Chapter 5.

Information is the key to a successful business. The loss of information can inhibit the ability of accountants to prepare reports and managers to make business decisions. Computer viruses can cause the information in computer files to be destroyed and, therefore, are a serious problem for businesses of all sizes.

Required:

1. Go to the library and research computer viruses.
2. Write a short report about computer viruses. Include the following items:
   a. A description of one particular computer virus.
   b. The origin of the virus.
   c. Ways to prevent your computer from getting a virus.
   d. The action to take if you detect a virus.

Cases for Critical Thinking

Case 1

Kelly White, the bookkeeper for Greenfield, Inc., is setting up the company's voucher system. As she plans, she is trying to decide how many columns to use in the voucher register. She is also trying to decide what headings to use for the special columns in the voucher register. What should Ms. White consider in making her decision about these special columns?

Case 2

Harper Company uses a voucher system for cash payments. Jonathan Bartell, the bookkeeper, receives and verifies the invoices. He then prepares the voucher and enters the voucher in the voucher register. When the voucher is due, Mr. Bartell prepares and signs the check and enters the payment in the check register. What is your opinion of the procedure that Harper Company follows for its voucher system? Explain.

Case 3

Review the entries you made for the Challenge Problem. Compare these entries with the entries for purchases on account made in the Mastery Problem. What is your opinion of recording purchases invoices at the net amount?

SAFETY TIPS TO MAINTAIN YOUR COMPUTER AND DISKS

Electrical Equipment

The following rules protect the operator of the equipment, other persons in the environment, and the equipment itself.

1. Do not unplug equipment by pulling on the electrical cord. Instead, grasp the plug at the outlet and remove it.

2. Do not stretch electrical cords across an aisle where someone might trip over them.

3. Avoid food and beverages near equipment where a spill might result in an electrical short.

4. Do not attempt to remove the cover of equipment for any reason while the power is turned on.

5. Do not attempt to repair equipment while it is plugged in. To avoid damage most repairs should be done by an authorized service technician.

6. Always turn the power off when finished using equipment.

7. Do not overload extension cords.

8. Follow manufacturer recommendations for safe use.

9. Replace frayed electrical cords immediately.

Computers

1. To avoid damage to the drives, do not insert pencils or other implements in floppy disk or CD-ROM drives.

2. To prevent overheating, avoid blocking air vents.

3. Position keyboards to prevent bumping or dropping them off the work surface.

4. Take care not to spill food or liquid on or in any computer component. If you do, turn off the computer immediately; unplug it; and notify your instructor before cleaning up the spill or turning on the equipment.

5. Avoid jolting or jostling your computer if it becomes necessary to move it.

6. Do NOT attempt to open or repair any part of the computer or monitor unless directed to do so by your instructor.

Monitors

1. Most manufacturers advise repair by authorized service technicians only.

2. Adjust brightness and focus for comfortable viewing.

3. Reposition computer or use glare visors to avoid glare on the monitor screen.

4. Do not leave fingerprints on the screen. Keep the screen clear of dust. Only use a soft cloth for cleaning the screen.

Printers

1. Do not let jewelry, ties, scarves, loose sleeves, or other clothing get caught in the machinery. This could result in damage to the machinery and could cause personal injury.

2. Exercise caution when using toxic chemicals such as toner in order to avoid spills.

Disks and Disk Drives

1. Do not bend disks.

2. Do not touch exposed surfaces of disks.

3. Be sure the disk drive is not running when you insert or remove a disk.

4. Keep disks away from extreme hot or cold temperatures. Do not leave disks in a car during very hot or cold weather.

5. Keep disks away from magnetic fields such as transformers and magnets.

6. Keep disks away from smoke, ashes, and dust, including chalk dust.

7. Be sure to make back-up copies.

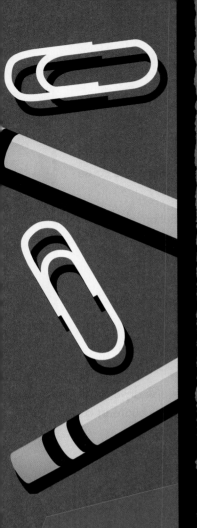

6

Inventory Planning and Valuation

AFTER STUDYING CHAPTER 6, YOU WILL BE ABLE TO:

1. Define accounting terms related to planning and costing inventory.

2. Identify accounting concepts and practices related to planning, counting, and costing inventory.

3. Describe the nature of merchandise inventory.

4. Determine the cost of merchandise inventory using selected costing methods.

5. Estimate the cost of merchandise inventory using selected estimating methods.

6. Calculate merchandise inventory turnover ratio and average number of days' sales in merchandise inventory.

TERMS PREVIEW

consignment
consignee
consignor
stock record
stock ledger
purchase order
inventory record
first-in, first-out
    inventory costing
    method
last-in, first-out
    inventory costing
    method
weighted-average
    inventory costing
    method
lower of cost or market
    inventory costing
    method
retail method of
    estimating inventory
merchandise inventory
    turnover ratio
average number of
    days' sales in
    merchandise
    inventory

For most merchandising businesses, merchandise inventory is the largest asset. Merchandising businesses implement good control measures in managing their inventory. A successful business must maintain an adequate amount of merchandise inventory that customers are willing to buy. A business may fail if it keeps too much or too little merchandise inventory on hand.

Business managers frequently analyze sales and inventory transactions to assist them in planning future inventory purchases. From this analysis, managers can determine the items of inventory that are selling well and the items that are not selling well. Managers also examine sales and inventory transactions to identify any seasonal trends in sales. This information allows managers to order the right kinds of merchandise at the right time.

Many businesses now maintain their inventory records on computer. Computerized inventory systems can keep more accurate records of the amount of inventory on hand than other systems can. Computerized systems also provide more frequent inventory information to managers. Managers use this information to make effective business decisions.

ACCOUNTING
IN YOUR CAREER

JUGGLING THE INVENTORY

Logan Controls Corporation and Prism Video, Inc., are both located in a state that levies a tax on inventory. The tax is a property tax that is payable on all inventory on hand on the last day of the fiscal year. The managers of the two companies take different approaches to managing the inventory and the tax liability on the inventory.

Margaret Price manages the assets of Logan Controls and has been charged with minimizing the inventory by the end of the year to reduce the taxes. She has a friend who has a vacant warehouse just over the state line in the next state. She plans to arrange for all the company trucks to haul the most expensive items of inventory to the warehouse in the next state to evade the tax on that part of the inventory.

Thomas Reynolds is the tax accountant at Prism Video. Two months before the end of the year, he called all the department managers to a meeting to explain the difficulty with the inventory. He said that the inventory was at one of its highest levels and requested that extra sales efforts be made to sell as much inventory as possible by the end of the year. He proposed a year-end sale with deep sales discounts to lower the inventory. One of the managers asked, "You want us to sell at bargain basement prices to reduce the inventory so we don't have to pay taxes on it. Isn't that tax evasion? And isn't that illegal?"

Thomas Reynolds replied, "There's a big difference between tax avoidance and tax evasion."

Critical Thinking

1. What is the difference between tax avoidance and tax evasion?
2. Are the companies planning tax avoidance or tax evasion?
3. What are the ethical implications of the two inventory plans?

6-1 The Nature of Merchandise Inventory

FLOW OF INVENTORY COSTS

Figure 6-1

Merchandise is continually being purchased and sold. A business' actual merchandise inventory changes from day to day. The flow of inventory costs through the records of a business is shown in Figure 6-1. The cost of the merchandise available for sale consists of:

1. The cost of the beginning merchandise inventory.

2. The cost of the net purchases added to the inventory during the fiscal period.

At the end of each fiscal period, the cost of the merchandise available for sale is divided into:

1. The cost of the ending merchandise inventory. The ending merchandise inventory represents a *current* asset that will be charged as costs in *future* fiscal periods.

2. The cost of the merchandise sold during the *current* fiscal period. This cost materially affects the amount of net income reported for the fiscal period. (*CONCEPT: Adequate Disclosure*)

EFFECTS OF ERRORS IN COSTING AN INVENTORY

The cost of both beginning and ending merchandise inventory affects items on an income statement, a statement of stockholders' equity, and a balance sheet. The effects are shown in Figure 6-2.

An accurate merchandise inventory cost must be determined to adequately report the financial progress and condition of a merchandising business. (*CONCEPT: Adequate Disclosure*) If the ending inventory is understated, the cost of merchandise sold will be overstated. Consequently, the net income will be understated. As a result, total assets and total stockholders' equity will be understated. If the ending inventory is overstated, the reverse will be true, and additional income tax must be paid on the overstated income. In neither situation will financial statements report accurate information. (*CONCEPT: Adequate Disclosure*)

Reports and Items Affected	If Ending Inventory is	
	Understated	Overstated
Income Statement:		
Cost of Merchandise Sold..........	Overstated	Understated
Gross Profit.....................	Understated	Overstated
Net Income.....................	Understated	Overstated
Statement of Stockholders' Equity:		
Net Income.....................	Understated	Overstated
Retained Earnings................	Understated	Overstated
Stockholders' Equity..............	Understated	Overstated
Balance Sheet:		
Merchandise Inventory............	Understated	Overstated
Total Assets....................	Understated	Overstated
Stockholders' Equity..............	Understated	Overstated

Figure 6-2

Items in the merchandise inventory of a merchandising business are frequently referred to as *goods*. Typically, a business counts as part of its inventory all goods that it legally owns. The cost of these goods includes:

1. The price paid to vendors for the merchandise. This price includes the purchase invoice amount less discounts, returns, and allowances granted by the vendors.

2. The cost involved in getting the goods to the place of business and ready for sale. This cost includes transportation charges paid by the buyer.

Merchandising businesses must know both the cost of the goods and the number of goods in inventory. Businesses use two methods to determine the number of goods in inventory:

1. Taking a physical count of the individual items in inventory. All goods in inventory as of a given date are included in a physical inventory count.

2. Keeping a continuous record for each merchandise item showing the number purchased and the number sold. Using this method, a business can determine the number of goods in inventory at any point in time.

Goods in Transit

Merchandising businesses purchase goods from suppliers. The suppliers ship the goods to the businesses. For goods in transit at the time of a physical count of inventory, the business must determine who holds title to the goods. When title to goods in transit passes from the supplier to the buyer, the goods become part of the buyer's inventory regardless of where they are physically located.

A vendor's terms of sale may include the provision *FOB shipping point*. FOB is an abbreviation for the phrase *Free On Board*. FOB shipping point means that the buyer pays the transportation charges. Under FOB shipping point terms, the title to the goods passes to the buyer as soon as the vendor delivers the goods to a transportation business. These goods in transit, but not yet received by the buyer, are part of the *buyer's* inventory.

If the terms of sale are *FOB destination*, the vendor pays the transportation charges. Title to the goods passes to the buyer when the buyer receives the goods. These goods in transit, but not yet received by the buyer, are part of the *vendor's* inventory. The buyer does not include these goods in the cost of inventory.

Goods on Consignment

Goods that are given to a business to sell but for which title remains with the vendor, are called a **consignment**. The person or business that receives goods on consignment is called the **consignee**. The person or business that gives goods on consignment is called the **consignor**.

The consignee agrees to receive, care for, and attempt to sell the consigned goods. If the goods are sold, the consignee deducts a commission from the sale amount and sends the remainder to the consignor. In a consignment, title to the goods does not pass to the consignee. The goods on consignment are part of the consignor's inventory. The consignee does not include consigned goods in the cost of its inventory.

A consignee agrees to care for the goods on consignment and to make adequate attempts to sell them. Therefore, a consignee has implied liabilities if anything should happen to the goods before they are sold. A consignee often reports the cost of consigned goods as an attachment or footnote to its balance sheet.

F.Y.I.

Inventory management consists of determining the quantity of goods on hand and developing procedures for ordering, receiving, and maintaining the inventory.

1. Record the description information.

4. Enter all purchase transactions.

2. Write the beginning quantity.

3. Record all sales transactions.

STOCK RECORD

Description _3½" Computer Diskettes (boxes)_   Stock No. _F106_

Reorder _1,000_   Minimum _300_   Location _Bin 26_

	1	2	3	4	5	6	7
	INCREASES			DECREASES			BALANCE
	DATE	PURCHASE INVOICE NO.	QUANTITY	DATE	SALES INVOICE NO.	QUANTITY	QUANTITY
	Jan. 1 20--						700
				Jan. 16	1761	120	580
				Feb. 21	1923	310	270
				Mar. 6	2071	230	40
	Mar. 7	669	1,000				1,040
				Oct. 31	2967	160	670

Figure 6-3

A continuous record of merchandise inventory increases, decreases, and balance on hand is known as a perpetual inventory. OfficeMart, Inc., sells office furniture, equipment, and supplies. It maintains a perpetual inventory.

A perpetual inventory provides day-to-day records about the quantity of merchandise on hand. Based on the records, management knows when an item of inventory is low and needs to be reordered. For each inventory item, the record shows the number on hand, the number purchased, and the number sold. A form used to show the type of merchandise, quantity received, quantity sold, and balance on hand is called a **stock record**. A file of stock records for all merchandise on hand is called a **stock ledger**.

OfficeMart's stock record for the diskettes is shown in Figure 6-3. It includes a notation of the minimum balance at which a reorder is to be placed. For example, OfficeMart determines that

two weeks are required to order and to receive a shipment of boxes of 3 1/2" diskettes from a vendor. In a two-week period, OfficeMart will sell an average of 300 boxes of diskettes. Therefore, OfficeMart reorders diskettes when the inventory reaches 300 boxes, or units. Each reorder is for 1,000 units. On February 21, the inventory balance falls below the reorder point. An order is immediately placed for 1,000 boxes. The order is received on March 7.

A completed form authorizing a seller to deliver goods with payment to be made later is called a **purchase order**. OfficeMart prepares purchase orders for all purchases.

During the year, sales are recorded on the stock record when the sale is made. Purchases are recorded on the stock record when the goods are received. Unit prices are not recorded on the stock records. They are obtained from copies of the purchase invoices.

S T E P S   Maintaining a stock record

1. Record the description of the inventory item, _3-1/2" Computer Diskettes (boxes)_, the stock number, _F106_, the reorder quantity, _1,000_, the minimum number, _300_, and the warehouse location, _Bin 26_.
2. Write the beginning quantity. On _Jan. 1, 20--_, the quantity on hand was _700_.
3. Record all sales transactions in the Decreases columns of the stock record. After each sale, enter the new quantity in column 7. For the sale on January 16, write _Jan. 16_ in column 4, the sales invoice number, _1761_, in column 5, and the quantity sold, _120_, in column 6. In column 7, record the new balance of inventory, _580_.
4. Enter all purchase transactions in the Increases columns of the stock record when the goods are received. Enter the date, purchase invoice number, quantity, and balance.

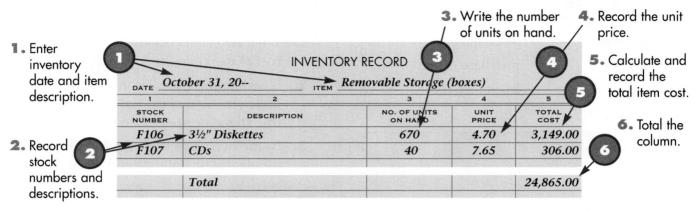

Figure 6-4

A merchandise inventory determined by counting, weighing, or measuring items of merchandise on hand is known as a periodic inventory. Counting, weighing, or measuring merchandise on hand for a periodic inventory is commonly referred to as "taking an inventory." For businesses with a large quantity of merchandise on hand, taking an inventory count is expensive. Therefore, businesses usually take a periodic inventory only once each fiscal period.

When only a periodic inventory is used, the low quantity of a merchandise item can be overlooked. When this happens, the business may not have the merchandise when customers want it. For this reason, OfficeMart uses the perpetual inventory method. Errors can occur, however, even when the perpetual inventory method is used. Therefore, OfficeMart takes a periodic inventory once each year to check the accuracy of the perpetual inventory.

A form used during a periodic inventory to record information about each item of merchandise on hand is called an **inventory record**. One inventory record is used for each item or category of items in inventory. When taking an inventory, OfficeMart uses an inventory record for categories of merchandise as shown in Figure 6-4.

The periodic inventory count is compared to the perpetual inventory. Any differences are adjusted on the stock records. In the case of stock item F106, the physical count of boxes of the 3-1/2" diskettes matched the quantity listed on the stock record. Therefore, no adjustment was needed. If large differences are found, the business should review its recording and control procedures to ensure that the inventory and the inventory records are being properly maintained.

S T E P S Complete the inventory record

1. Enter the date of the periodic inventory, *October 31, 20--*, and the item description, *Removable Computer Storage (boxes)*.
2. Record the stock number, *F106*, and description, *3 1/2"-Diskettes*.
3. Write the actual number of units on hand, *670*.
4. Record the unit price, *4.70*. The unit price data are obtained from purchase invoices. In this case, all 3-1/2" diskettes in inventory were purchased at the same price. Additional lines of the record are used to record units purchased at a different unit price.
5. Calculate and record the total cost, *3,149.00*. Total cost for each item is calculated by multiplying the unit price, column 4, by the number of items on hand, column 3.
6. Determine the total cost for these inventory items, *24,865.00*. The total of all inventory records is the total cost of the ending merchandise inventory.

TERMS REVIEW

consignment

consignee

consignor

stock record

stock ledger

purchase order

inventory record

AUDIT YOUR UNDERSTANDING

1. What two elements are included in the cost of merchandise available for sale?

2. If ending merchandise inventory is understated, will the net income be overstated or understated?

3. Name two ways to determine the number of inventory items on hand.

WORK TOGETHER

Completing a stock record for a perpetual inventory system

A stock record form and an inventory record form for Tower Television are provided in the *Working Papers*. Your instructor will guide you through the following examples.

4. Fill in the top portion of the stock record form with the following information: Description, 19" color television set; Stock No., K087; Reorder, 80; Minimum, 20; and Location, Bin 12.

5. Record the following information. Save your work to complete the On Your Own below.

Date	Purchase Invoice No.	Sales Invoice No.	Quantity	Balance
Sept. 1				62
Sept. 12		475	40	
Sept. 16		508	8	
Sept. 17	183		80	
Sept. 20		653	15	

ON YOUR OWN

Completing a stock record for a perpetual inventory system and comparing it to an inventory record

Use the working papers from the Work Together above. Work independently to complete the following problem.

6. Record the remaining information for product number K087 on the stock record.

Date	Purchase Invoice No.	Sales Invoice No.	Quantity	Balance
Sept. 23		714	40	
Sept. 25		761	22	
Sept. 26	255		80	
Sept. 30		850	12	

7. Compare the ending balance in units from the stock record with the number of units on hand for product K087 in the inventory record. Make sure they are equal.

6-2 Inventory Costing

FIRST-IN, FIRST-OUT INVENTORY COSTING METHOD

FIFO Inventory Costing Method

Purchase			Ending Inventory	
Date	**Units**	**Unit Price**	**Units**	**Total Cost**
January, beginning inventory....	500	$1.00	0	0.00
June	500	1.20	200	$240.00
November	500	1.25	500	625
Totals.....................			700	$865.00

3. Multiply ending inventory units by unit price.

1. Assign units from most recent purchase.

700	Units in ending inventory
= 500	From Nov. purchase
200	Units to be assigned
− 200	From June purchase
0	Units to be assigned

4. Total the ending inventory columns.   **2.** Assign units from next most recent purchase.

Figure 6-5

Once OfficeMart takes a periodic inventory, it determines a dollar cost for each item. *(CONCEPT: Unit of Measurement)* The unit prices are obtained from purchase invoices. For example, in Figure 6-4, the 670 F106 boxes of diskettes have a unit price of $4.70 and a total cost of $3,149.00.

Various methods may be used to determine the cost of merchandise inventory. A business selects the method that best matches the revenue and costs for that business. *(CONCEPT: Matching Expenses with Revenue)*

Using the price of merchandise purchased first to calculate the cost of merchandise sold first is called the **first-in, first-out inventory costing method**. FIFO is an abbreviation for first in, first out. The FIFO method of determining

the cost of merchandise on hand assumes that the merchandise purchased first (first in) is the merchandise sold first (first out). Thus, the FIFO method uses the most recent purchase prices to determine the cost of merchandise inventory remaining. For example, OfficeMart has an inventory of 700 three-ring binders on November 30. If OfficeMart used the FIFO method, the binders would be costed as shown in Figure 6-5.

Using the FIFO method, the remaining 300 units from the June purchase and the 500 units in beginning inventory are designated as the units that were sold. These binders are *first in*. Therefore, the business assumes that they are also the *first out*, or first sold.

Calculate inventory costs using the FIFO method

1. Assign ending inventory units from the most recent purchase. The number of units in ending inventory is 700. All *500* units from the November purchase are assigned to ending inventory.

2. If all units of ending inventory have not been assigned, assign units from the next most recent purchase. In Figure 6-5, 200 units have not been assigned. The next most recent purchase, June, includes 500 units. Therefore, all 200 units to be assigned will come from the June purchase. All 700 units in ending inventory have now been assigned.

3. Multiply the units in the Ending Inventory Units column by the unit prices. Enter the results, *$240.00* and *625.00*, in the Total Cost column.

4. Total the two Ending Inventory columns. The total number of units, *700*, is equal to the number of units on hand as determined by the periodic inventory. The total cost assigned to the ending inventory using the FIFO method is *$865.00*.

LAST-IN, FIRST-OUT INVENTORY COSTING METHOD

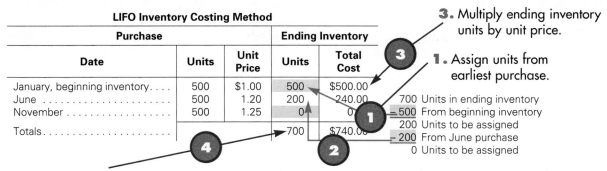

LIFO Inventory Costing Method

Purchase			Ending Inventory	
Date	Units	Unit Price	Units	Total Cost
January, beginning inventory....	500	$1.00	500	$500.00
June	500	1.20	200	240.00
November	500	1.25	0	0
Totals.....................			700	$740.00

3. Multiply ending inventory units by unit price.

1. Assign units from earliest purchase.

700	Units in ending inventory
− 500	From beginning inventory
200	Units to be assigned
− 200	From June purchase
0	Units to be assigned

4. Total the ending inventory columns.   **2.** Assign units from next earliest purchase.

Figure 6-6

Using the price of merchandise purchased last to calculate the cost of merchandise sold first is called the **last-in, first-out inventory costing method**. LIFO is an abbreviation for last in, first out. The LIFO method assumes that the merchandise purchased last (last in) is the merchandise sold first (first out). Thus, the LIFO method uses the earliest purchase prices to determine the cost of merchandise inventory. If OfficeMart used the LIFO method, the 700 binders would be costed as shown in Figure 6-6.

Of the 700 units on hand, 500 units are assumed to be the units in the beginning inventory at $1.00 per unit. The remaining 200 units are assumed to have been purchased on the next earliest date, June, at $1.20 each. None is considered to be part of the 500 units purchased on the most recent date, November. The total cost, using the LIFO method, is $740.00.

Using the LIFO method, the remaining 300 units from the June purchase and the 500 units from the November purchase are designated as the units that were sold. These binders are *last in*. Therefore, the business assumes that they are also the *first out*, or first sold.

WEIGHTED-AVERAGE INVENTORY COSTING METHOD

Weighted-Average Inventory Costing Method
Quantity on Hand, 700 units

Purchase			Total Cost
Date	Units	Unit Price	
January, beginning inventory....	500	$1.00	$ 500.00
June	500	1.20	600.00
November	500	1.25	625.00
Totals.....................	1,500		$1,725.00

Total of Beginning Inventory and Purchases	÷	Total Units	=	Weighted-Average Price per Unit
$1,725.00	÷	1,500	=	$1.15

Units in Ending Inventory	×	Weighted-Average Price per Unit	=	Cost of Ending Inventory
700	×	$1.15	=	$805.00

Figure 6-7

REMEMBER

FIFO uses the most recent purchase prices to determine the cost of merchandise inventory.

Using the average cost of beginning inventory plus merchandise purchased during a fiscal period to calculate the cost of merchandise sold is called the **weighted-average inventory costing method**. This method is based on the assumption that the cost is an average of the price paid for similar items purchased during the fiscal period. If OfficeMart used the weighted-average method, the 700 binders would be costed as shown in Figure 6-7.

The total cost, $1,725.00, is divided by the total units purchased, 1,500, to calculate the weighted-average cost per unit, $1.15. The 700 units currently on hand are assumed to have been purchased at an average cost of $1.15 each. Therefore, the total cost of ending merchandise inventory using the weighted-average method is

$805.00. If OfficeMart used the weighted-average method, it would use the same weighted-average cost per unit, $1.15, to determine the cost of merchandise sold.

COSTING INVENTORY DURING PERIODS OF INCREASING PRICES

Summary of Three Methods of Costing Inventory of 700 units of Ring Binders during a Period of Increasing Prices

Purchase		FIFO Method		LIFO Method		Weighted-Average Method
Date	Unit Price	Units	Cost	Units	Cost	
Jan., begin. inv.	$1.00	0	0.00	500	$500.00	Average Cost $1.15
June	1.20	200	$240.00	200	240.00	
Nov.	1.25	500	625.00	0	0.00	
Totals		700	$865.00	700	$740.00	$805.00

If prices are rising:

	FIFO	LIFO	Weighted-Average
Ending inventory valuation	Highest	Lowest	Always falls
Cost of merchandise sold	Lowest	Highest	between
Reported net income	Highest	Lowest	FIFO and LIFO

Figure 6-8

In the inventory costing situations described for the ring binders, prices increased from $1.00 to $1.25 per unit. Three ways of costing the inventory of 700 ring binders during a period of increasing prices are summarized in Figure 6-8.

The cost of the ending inventory affects the cost of merchandise sold amount on the income statement. The higher the ending inventory, the lower the cost of merchandise sold amount, and vice versa. Therefore, during a period of *increasing prices*, the FIFO method usually results in the lowest cost of merchandise sold. The LIFO method usually results in the highest cost of merchandise sold.

The higher the cost of merchandise sold, the lower the net income reported on financial statements, and vice versa. Therefore, during a period of *increasing prices*, the FIFO method usually results in the highest reported net income. The LIFO method usually results in the lowest reported net income.

To reiterate: During a period of rising prices, the FIFO method shows a higher ending inventory than the other methods do. This results in a lower cost of merchandise sold, which in turn yields a higher reported net income. The opposite holds true for the LIFO method.

Summary of Three Methods of Costing Inventory of 700 units of Ring Binders during a Period of Decreasing Prices

Purchase		FIFO Method		LIFO Method		Weighted-Average Method
Date	Unit Price	Units	Cost	Units	Cost	
Jan., begin. inv.	$1.25	0	0.00	500	$625.00	Average Cost $1.15
June	1.20	200	$240.00	200	240.00	
Nov.	1.00	500	500.00	0	0.00	
Totals		700	$740.00	700	$865.00	$805.00

Figure 6-9

Prices for inventory items may also decrease. If OfficeMart determined the cost of inventory during a period of decreasing prices, the three inventory costing methods would be summarized as shown in Figure 6-9.

During a period of *decreasing prices*, as shown in Figure 6-9, the FIFO method usually results in the lowest merchandise inventory cost. This lower inventory cost results in a higher cost of merchandise sold and a lower net income. During a period of *decreasing prices*, the LIFO method usually results in the highest merchandise inventory cost. This higher inventory cost results in a lower cost of merchandise sold and a higher net income.

RESULTS OF THE THREE INVENTORY COSTING METHODS COMPARED

Comparison of Three Methods of Costing Inventory during Periods of Increasing or Decreasing Prices

Prices are	Total Inventory Cost Using		
	FIFO Method	LIFO Method	Weighted-Average Method
Increasing	$865.00	$740.00	$805.00
Decreasing	$740.00	$865.00	$805.00

Figure 6-10

A comparison of three methods of costing inventory during periods of increasing and decreasing prices is shown in Figure 6-10.

The weighted-average method usually results in a total cost between the FIFO and LIFO total costs in both periods of increasing and decreasing prices. For businesses that purchase items with frequent fluctuations in price, the weighted-average method results in more consistent reporting of merchandise inventory costs.

Each business selects the method of costing merchandise inventory that best fits its policies and goals. A business selects one method of costing merchandise inventory and uses it for a number of years. In this way, the information on a series of financial statements can be compared easily. (*CONCEPT: Consistent Reporting*)

F.Y.I.

The goal of the Japanese concept, the just-in-time (JIT) system, is to minimize inventory. Materials should be received only when they are needed for production; they should not be kept in inventory. The JIT system works well when vendors and buyers work together as a team to plan inventory levels.

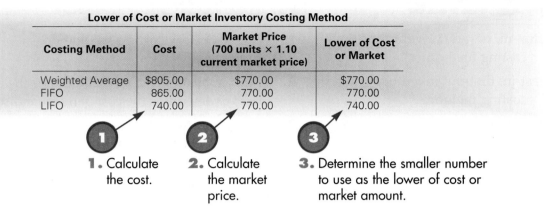

Lower of Cost or Market Inventory Costing Method

Costing Method	Cost	Market Price (700 units × 1.10 current market price)	Lower of Cost or Market
Weighted Average	$805.00	$770.00	$770.00
FIFO	865.00	770.00	770.00
LIFO	740.00	770.00	740.00

1. Calculate the cost.

2. Calculate the market price.

3. Determine the smaller number to use as the lower of cost or market amount.

Figure 6-11

Using the lower of cost or market price to calculate the cost of ending merchandise inventory is called the **lower of cost or market inventory costing method**. In this context, *market* refers to the current replacement cost of the merchandise item. For example, OfficeMart may currently have to pay a vendor $1.10 to purchase a ring binder. The market price, therefore, is $1.10. When merchandise is purchased, the unit price is used to record inventory costs. (*CONCEPT: Historical Cost*)

The historical cost concept states that the actual amount paid for merchandise or other items bought is recorded. OfficeMart purchased a delivery truck valued at $20,000.00 and advertised at a sale price of $18,000.00. OfficeMart negotiated to purchase the delivery truck for $17,000.00. The amount recorded in accounting records for the delivery truck is the historical cost, $17,000.00—the actual amount paid.

Six months later, OfficeMart sells the delivery truck to Flowers by Giverney for $15,000.00. For Flowers by Giverney, the historical cost of the delivery truck is $15,000.00.

If the unit price is higher than the market price at the end of a fiscal period, the inventory cost is reduced to the current market price. However, if the unit price is lower than the market price, the inventory cost is maintained at the unit price.

Two amounts are needed to apply the lower of cost or market method:

1. The cost of the inventory using the FIFO, LIFO, or weighted-average method.

2. The current market price of the inventory.

These two amounts are then compared, and the lower of the two is used to cost the inventory. For example, OfficeMart uses the weighted-average method of costing inventory. The weighted-average cost and the current market price for 700 ring binders are shown in Figure 6-11. The weighted-average cost is $805.00, and the current market price is $770.00. Using the lower of cost or market method, the market price of the binders is lower than the weighted-average cost. Therefore, the market value of $770.00 is used as the cost of the binders.

If OfficeMart used the FIFO method, the FIFO cost would be $865.00. The $770.00 market price is lower than the FIFO cost, so the market price would be used instead of the FIFO cost. If OfficeMart used the LIFO method, the LIFO cost would be $740.00. The LIFO cost is lower than the market price, so the LIFO cost would be used to cost the inventory.

F.Y.I.

New models of computers tend to drive down the market prices of existing models. In this case, the market prices of the existing models may be less than the cost of the computers. Good inventory management attempts to minimize inventory for which the market price is lower than the cost.

ERMS
REVIEW

first-in, first-out inventory costing method

last-in, first-out inventory costing method

weighted-average inventory costing method

lower of cost or market inventory costing method

UDIT YOUR
UNDERSTANDING

1. What inventory costing method does a business usually use?

2. Which inventory costing method uses the earliest purchase prices to determine the cost of merchandise inventory?

3. During a period of increasing prices, what inventory costing method will result in the highest reported net income?

4. What two amounts are needed to apply the lower of cost or market inventory costing method?

ORK
TOGETHER

Costing ending inventory using FIFO, LIFO, and weighted average

Forms for calculating inventory costs for Cassie's Kitchen are provided in the *Working Papers*. Your instructor will guide you through the following examples.

5. Cassie's Kitchen had the following beginning inventory and purchases for a salad maker, stock number T1150. At the end of the year, 140 units remained in ending inventory. Determine the cost of the ending inventory using the FIFO, LIFO, and weighted-average inventory costing methods.

	Units	Unit Price
January, Beginning Inventory	120	$20.00
July, Purchase	100	$22.00
October, Purchase	100	$27.60

N YOUR
OWN

Costing ending inventory using FIFO, LIFO, and weighted average

Forms for calculating inventory costs for Cassie's Kitchen are provided in the *Working Papers*. Work independently to complete the following problem.

6. Cassie's Kitchen had the following beginning inventory and purchases for a frying pan, stock number M1030. At the end of the year, 75 units remained in ending inventory. Determine the cost of the ending inventory using the FIFO, LIFO, and weighted-average inventory costing methods.

	Units	Unit Price
January, Beginning Inventory	50	$4.20
March, Purchase	70	$4.50
November, Purchase	60	$5.05

6-3 Estimating the Inventory

GROSS PROFIT METHOD OF ESTIMATING INVENTORY

ESTIMATED MERCHANDISE INVENTORY SHEET
Gross Profit Method

COMPANY *OfficeMart, Inc.*   DATE *10/31/--*

1	Beginning inventory, January 1	$ 158,930.00
2	Net purchases to date	762,440.00
3	Merchandise available for sale	$ 921,370.00
4	Net sales to date . . . . $ 1,296,000.00	
5	Less estimated gross profit 550,800.00	
	(Net sales × Estimated gross profit *42.5* %)	
6	Estimated cost of merchandise sold	745,200.00
7	Estimated ending inventory	$ 176,170.00

1. Write beginning inventory amount.

2. Determine net purchases.

3. Calculate merchandise available for sale.

4. Enter net sales.

5. Estimate gross profit.

6. Calculate estimated cost of merchandise sold.

7. Determine estimated ending inventory.

Figure 6-12

A business that keeps periodic inventory records and prepares monthly interim financial statements needs a cost to use for monthly ending merchandise inventory. Taking a monthly periodic inventory is usually too expensive. Therefore, monthly ending inventories may be estimated. Merchandisers who use perpetual inventory can take monthly ending inventory amounts from stock records (see Figure 6-3), so they usually don't need to make estimates.

Estimating inventory by using the previous years' percentage of gross profit on operations is known as the gross profit method of estimating inventory. This method assumes that a continuing relationship exists between gross profit and net sales. Based on experience in previous fiscal periods, a gross profit to net sales percentage is calculated. On October 31, OfficeMart estimates its ending merchandise inventory using the gross profit method as shown in Figure 6-12.

An ending merchandise inventory amount calculated using the gross profit method is an estimate and is not absolutely accurate. However, for monthly interim financial statements, the estimated amount is sufficiently accurate without taking a periodic inventory.

STEPS Estimate ending merchandise inventory using the gross profit method

1. Write the January 1 beginning inventory, *158,930.00*, from the merchandise inventory account in the general ledger.

2. Determine net purchases to date, *762,440.00*. Using amounts from the general ledger, subtract purchases discounts and purchases returns and allowances from purchases.

3. Calculate merchandise available for sale, *921,370.00*, by adding lines 1 and 2.

4. Enter net sales to date, *1,296,000.00*. Using amounts from the general ledger, subtract sales discount and sales returns and allowances from sales.

5. Multiply the amount on line 4 by 42.5% to calculate estimated gross profit, *550,800.00*. The percentage, 42.5%, is an average of the gross profit percentages from OfficeMart's income statements for the past three years.

6. Calculate estimated cost of merchandise sold, *745,200.00*, by subtracting line 5 from line 4.

7. Determine estimated ending inventory, *176,170.00*, by subtracting line 6 from line 3.

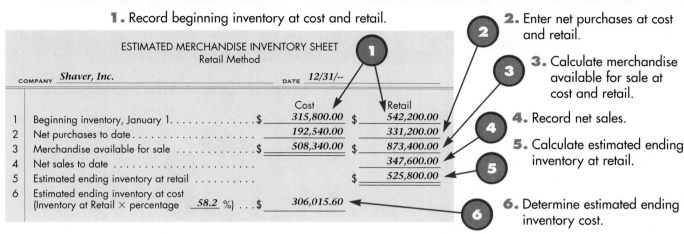

1. Record beginning inventory at cost and retail.

2. Enter net purchases at cost and retail.

3. Calculate merchandise available for sale at cost and retail.

4. Record net sales.

5. Calculate estimated ending inventory at retail.

6. Determine estimated ending inventory cost.

Figure 6-13

Estimating inventory by using a percentage based on both cost and retail prices is called the **retail method of estimating inventory**. The retail method may be used instead of the gross profit method. To use the retail method, a business must keep separate records of both cost and retail prices for net purchases, net sales, and beginning merchandise inventory. Figure 6-13 shows an estimated ending merchandise inventory, using the retail method, for Shaver, Inc.

STEPS   Estimate ending merchandise inventory using the retail method

1. Record the January 1 beginning inventory at cost, *315,800.00*, from the merchandise inventory account in the general ledger. Enter the beginning inventory at retail, *542,200.00*, which is obtained from the separate record of retail prices that must be maintained to use the retail method.

2. Enter net purchases to date at cost, *192,540.00*. Using amounts from the general ledger, subtract purchases discounts and purchases returns and allowances from purchases. Enter net purchases to date at retail, *331,200.00*, from the separate record of retail prices.

3. Calculate merchandise available for sale at cost, *508,340.00*, and at retail, *873,400.00*, by adding lines 1 and 2.

4. Record net sales to date at retail, *347,600.00*. Using amounts from the general ledger, subtract sales discount and sales returns and allowances from sales. Recall that a merchandising business always records sales at retail.

5. Calculate estimated ending inventory at retail, *525,800.00*, by subtracting line 4 from line 3.

6. Determine estimated ending inventory at cost, *306,015.60*, by multiplying line 5 by 58.2%. The percentage of merchandise available for sale at cost to merchandise available for sale at retail, 58.2%, is calculated from the amounts on line 3.

	Merchandise Available for Sale at Cost	÷	Merchandise Available for Sale at Retail	=	Percentage
	$508,340.00	÷	$873,400.00	=	58.2%

Many businesses that need to estimate ending merchandise inventory use the gross profit method rather than the retail method. The gross profit method does not require separate records for cost and retail prices. Since OfficeMart uses a perpetual inventory, monthly ending inventories are available from the stock records without estimating or taking a monthly inventory.

MERCHANDISE INVENTORY TURNOVER

The more rapidly a business sells merchandise, the more chance it has to make a satisfactory net income. For example, more revenue results from selling 100 ring binders per day than from selling 60 binders per day. Two measures of the speed with which merchandise inventory is sold are:

1. Merchandise inventory turnover ratio.

2. Average number of days' sales in merchandise inventory.

Merchandise Inventory Turnover Ratio

The number of times the average amount of merchandise inventory is sold during a specific period of time is called the **merchandise inventory turnover ratio**. A merchandise inventory turnover ratio expresses a relationship between an average inventory and the cost of merchandise sold. Merchandise inventory represents a large investment for most merchandising businesses. Therefore, a low merchandise inventory turnover ratio usually indicates a low return on investment.

OfficeMart's merchandise inventory turnover ratio for the current fiscal year is calculated as follows.

January 1 Merchandise Inventory	+	December 31 Merchandise Inventory	÷	2	=	Average Merchandise Inventory
($168,365.00	+	$173,325.00)	÷	2	=	$170,845.00

Cost of Merchandise Sold	÷	Average Merchandise Inventory		=	Merchandise Inventory Turnover Ratio
$925,368.00	÷	$170,845.00		=	5.4 times

A 5.4 merchandise inventory turnover ratio means that the business sold the average merchandise inventory 5.4 times during the current year. National trade associations publish this ratio and others. OfficeMart can compare its ratio with the ratio for similar businesses which have an average merchandise inventory turnover ratio of 7.0 times. OfficeMart's turnover ratio of 5.4 is below the industry standard of 7.0. To correct this situation, OfficeMart's managers should consider taking action to better control the quantity of merchandise inventory on hand.

Average Number of Days' Sales in Merchandise Inventory

The period of time needed to sell an average amount of merchandise inventory is called the **average number of days' sales in merchandise inventory**. The average number of days' sales in merchandise inventory based on a 5.4 merchandise inventory turnover ratio is calculated as shown below.

Days in Year	÷	Merchandise Inventory Turnover Ratio	=	Average Number of Days' Sales in Merchandise Inventory
365	÷	5.4	=	68 days

The average number of days' sales in merchandise inventory is rounded to the nearest day. This level of accuracy provides managers with adequate information to make sound business decisions.

An average of 68 days means that, on average, each item in merchandise inventory is sold 68 days after it is purchased. Published averages from trade associations show that businesses similar to OfficeMart have an average number of days' sales in merchandise inventory of 53. OfficeMart's management should seek ways to increase its turnover of merchandise inventory.

The higher the number of days in merchandise inventory, the longer merchandise tends to remain unsold. A business can reduce the merchandise inventory turnover ratio and the number of days' sales in merchandise inventory by reducing the size of the inventory kept on hand. However, a lower inventory level may not allow a business to meet customers' demands. A business also can improve its turnover ratio and the number of days' sales in merchandise inventory by increasing the amount of merchandise sold during a month or a year.

TECHNOLOGY FOR BUSINESS

SPREADSHEET ACTIVITY—VALUATION OF INVENTORY

Front Porch, a small retail store, sells hand-crafted wooden porch furniture. Front Porch uses the weighted-average inventory costing method. Front Porch currently carries three items in its inventory: high-back chairs, rocking chairs, and porch swings.

The following inventory data are available for high-back chairs for the first six months of the year:

High-back Chairs

Purchases	Units	Unit Price
January, beginning inventory	18	$35.00
February	75	40.00
April	10	45.00
June	5	50.00
June 30, physical inventory	26	

Required:

1. Create a spreadsheet to calculate the June 30 inventory for high-back chairs. Use Figure 6-7 as a model for creating the spreadsheet. Create formulas for the total cost of each purchase and for the column totals. Save the spreadsheet as HIGHBACK. (Hint: The weighted-average cost of the ending inventory should be $1,042.41.)

2. Make copies of the spreadsheet you created in 1 to calculate the value of other inventory items for Front Porch. Use the information below.

Rocking Chairs

Purchases	Units	Unit Price
January, beginning inventory	2	$42.00
February	18	42.00
March	6	50.00
April	3	57.00
June 30, physical inventory	11	

Porch Swings

Purchases	Units	Unit Price
January, beginning inventory	1	$80.00
January	8	85.00
March	6	88.00
May	2	92.00
June 30, physical inventory	3	

retail method of estimating inventory

merchandise inventory turnover ratio

average number of days' sales in merchandise inventory

AUDIT YOUR UNDERSTANDING

1. On what assumptions is the gross profit method of estimating inventory based?
2. To use the retail method of estimating inventory, what records must be kept?
3. Explain a merchandise inventory turnover ratio of 5.0.
4. How is the average number of days' sales in merchandise inventory calculated?

WORK TOGETHER

Estimating inventory using the gross profit and retail methods

The following information is available for Handy Hardware for the month of April. Estimated merchandise inventory sheets are provided in the *Working Papers*. Your instructor will guide you through the following examples.

	Cost	Retail
Beginning Inventory, April 1	$124,850	$193,400
Net Purchases	73,230	110,340
Net Sales		138,500

Gross Profit Percentage: 37%

Percentage of merchandise available for sale at cost to merchandise available at retail: 65.2%

5. Estimate the ending inventory using the gross profit method.
6. Estimate the ending inventory using the retail method.

ON YOUR OWN

Estimating inventory using the gross profit and retail methods

The following information is available for Handy Hardware for the month of October. Estimated merchandise inventory sheets are provided in the *Working Papers*. Work independently to complete the following problem.

	Cost	Retail
Beginning Inventory, October 1	$182,570	$276,380
Net Purchases	115,440	190,730
Net Sales		204,340

Gross Profit Percentage: 37%

Percentage of merchandise available for sale at cost to merchandise available at retail: 63.8%

7. Estimate the ending inventory using the gross profit method.
8. Estimate the ending inventory using the retail method.

CHAPTER 6 SUMMARY

After completing this chapter, you can

1. Define accounting terms related to planning and costing inventory.
2. Identify accounting concepts and practices related to planning, counting, and costing inventory.
3. Describe the nature of merchandise inventory.
4. Determine the cost of merchandise inventory using selected costing methods.
5. Estimate the cost of merchandise inventory using selected estimating methods.
6. Calculate merchandise inventory turnover ratio and average number of days' sales in merchandise inventory.

EXPLORE ACCOUNTING

COMPUTERIZED PURCHASING SYSTEMS

The traditional method for purchasing inventory requires many documents and manual steps to complete. The process involves many employees, requires several days to place an order, and is subject to many clerical errors.

A modern, computerized purchasing system might work as follows: The company's computer continually monitors stock levels against minimum quantities established by management. When the quantity of any inventory item falls below its reorder point, the computer automatically sends a message to a vendor's computer with the order information. (Management frequently enters into long-term contracts with selected vendors that govern prices and delivery schedules.) The vendor's computer immediately informs its warehouse to ship the items. When the items are received, the company's computer sends a message to its bank's computer instructing the bank to transfer funds to the vendor's account.

The direct transfer of information between computers of two or more companies is called electronic data interchange (EDI). EDI reduces the cost of placing an order by reducing paperwork and labor costs. The most important advantage, however, results from improved delivery times. The traditional manual ordering system required several days or weeks to process an order. An EDI system can have the order in transit on the same day the order is placed. Improved delivery time allows companies to reduce inventory levels, which results in substantial cost savings.

REQUIRED:

Contact your local bank and inquire if its computer system uses EDI to support its customers' purchasing systems.

APPLICATION PROBLEM
6-1
Keeping perpetual inventory records

Bowman Lawn and Garden sells lawn and garden equipment to a variety of customers. For many years the business used a periodic inventory system. However, it switched to a perpetual merchandise inventory system two years ago. The perpetual system gives the company better control of its inventory.

Instructions:

1. Complete the heading of a stock record for each of the following two inventory items. Also record the balance on April 1 of the current year for each item.

    Lawn mower:
        Stock number R263
        Reorder, 60
        Minimum, 15
        Location, bin 41
        Number on hand April 1, 32

    Hedge trimmer:
        Stock number J184
        Reorder, 35
        Minimum, 8
        Location, bin 49
        Number on hand April 1, 17

2. Record on the stock records the merchandise items received and sold during April of the current year. Source documents are abbreviated as follows: sales invoice, S; purchase invoice, P.

Transactions:

April 2. Sold 9 lawn mowers to Rogers Lawn and Garden, S211.

     3. Sold 5 hedge trimmers to Besotral, Inc., S212.

     6. Lawn Haven bought 6 lawn mowers and 6 hedge trimmers, S213.

    10. Received 35 hedge trimmers from Hughes Manufacturing, P742.

    11. Gilbert Co. bought 10 hedge trimmers, S214.

    15. Five more lawn mowers were sold to Rogers Lawn and Garden, S215.

    16. Lawn King Manufacturing shipped 60 lawn mowers, P743.

    19. Sold 30 lawn mowers to Christie's Landscaping, S216.

    20. Home Beautiful bought 20 lawn mowers and 15 hedge trimmers, S217.

    24. Twelve more lawn mowers were sold to Lawn Haven, S218.

    25. Received 60 lawn mowers from Lawn King Manufacturing, P744.

    28. Sold 10 hedge trimmers to Greene, Inc., S219.

    29. Hughes Manufacturing shipped 35 hedge trimmers, P745.

    30. Sold 7 lawn mowers to Movin' Mowers, S220.

APPLICATION PROBLEM
Determining inventory cost using FIFO, LIFO, weighted average, and lower of cost or market

Accounting records at Wayne, Inc., show the following purchases, periodic inventory counts, and market prices.

Stock No.	January 1 Inventory		First Purchase		Second Purchase		Third Purchase		Fourth Purchase		December 31 Inventory	December 31 Market Price
	No.	Unit Price	No.	Unit Price	No.	Unit Price	No.	Unit Price	No.	Unit Price		
A30	15	$8.00	15	$10.00	15	$12.00	20	$14.00	20	$10.00	35	$12.00
B18	10	9.00	10	9.00	12	9.00	12	8.00	12	8.00	30	7.50
C45	22	5.00	30	6.00	30	6.00	30	7.00	30	8.00	64	8.00
D12	12	7.00	5	7.00	5	9.00	10	8.00	5	7.00	20	7.50

Instructions:

1. Calculate the inventory costs using the FIFO, LIFO, and weighted average inventory costing methods. Assume that the lower of cost or market method is applied to each inventory item separately. Use a form similar to the following. The inventory cost for Stock No. A30 is given as an example.

Stock No.	Dec. 31 Inventory	Market Price	Inventory Costing Method								
			FIFO			LIFO			Weighted Average		
			Unit Price	Total Cost	Lower of Cost or Market	Unit Price	Total Cost	Lower of Cost or Market	Unit Price	Total Cost	Lower of Cost or Market
A30	35	35 @ $12.00 = $420.00	20 @ $10.00 15 @ 14.00	$410.00	$410.00	15 @ $8.00 15 @ 10.00 5 @ 12.00	$330.00	$330.00	35 @ $10.94	$382.90	$382.90

2. Total the three Lower of Cost or Market columns.

3. Which of the three methods of costing inventory results in the highest inventory cost for Wayne, Inc.? Which results in the lowest inventory cost?

6-3

APPLICATION PROBLEM
Estimating cost of merchandise inventory using estimating methods

The records of Walker, Inc., show the following on December 31 of the current year.

Item	Cost	Retail
Beginning merchandise inventory..........	$ 42,400.00	$ 70,000.00
Net purchases to date...................	136,000.00	227,400.00
Net sales to date......................	—	208,800.00
Gross profit percentage.................	40%	

Instructions:

1. Calculate the corporation's estimated ending inventory using the gross profit method of estimating inventory. Round the percentages to the nearest 0.1%.

2. Calculate the corporation's estimated ending inventory using the retail method of estimating inventory. Round the percentages to the nearest 0.1%.

APPLICATION PROBLEM

6-4

Calculating merchandise inventory turnover ratio and average number of days' sales in merchandise inventory

Selected information for three corporations follows.

	Corporation		
Item	A	B	C
Beginning Merchandise Inventory	$ 15,800.00	$ 80,500.00	$ 64,300.00
Ending Merchandise Inventory	21,200.00	78,900.00	54,600.00
Cost of Merchandise Sold	167,700.00	848,000.00	567,400.00

Instructions:

1. For each corporation, calculate the merchandise inventory turnover ratio. Round the ratio to the nearest 0.1%.

2. For each corporation, calculate the average number of days' sales in merchandise inventory. Round the amount to the nearest day.

3. Which corporation has the best merchandise inventory turnover ratio?

MASTERY PROBLEM

6-5

Determining cost of merchandise inventory; estimating cost of merchandise inventory using estimating methods; calculating merchandise inventory turnover ratio and average number of days' sales in merchandise inventory

On December 31 of the current year, Sowell, Inc., took a periodic inventory. The following information is obtained from Sowell's records.

Stock No.	January 1 Inventory		First Purchase		Second Purchase		December 31 Inventory	Market Price
	No.	Unit Price	No.	Unit Price	No.	Unit Price		
R46	14	$ 7.00	15	$ 8.00	15	$ 9.00	18	$ 9.50
S10	16	5.00	10	5.00	10	8.00	26	4.75
T76	8	12.00	15	11.00	15	11.00	25	10.00
U92	7	8.00	7	8.00	7	8.00	10	8.00
V17	5	4.00	10	6.00	10	7.00	5	6.00

Instructions:

1. Calculate the inventory costs using the FIFO, LIFO, and weighted-average inventory costing methods. Use the form in the *Working Papers*.

2. Total the three Total Cost columns.

3. Sowell uses the LIFO inventory costing method to determine the cost of inventory. Use the market price given in the form at the beginning of the problem to determine the cost of inventory using the lower of cost or market. Total the Lower of Cost or Market column. Use the form in the *Working Papers*.

continued

4. Calculate the corporation's estimated ending inventory using the gross profit method of estimating inventory. The corporation's records show the following on December 31 of the current year.

Item	Cost	Retail
Beginning merchandise inventory.	$21,200.00	$ 35,000.00
Net purchases to date.	68,000.00	113,700.00
Net sales to date.	—	103,700.00
Gross profit percentage.		40%

5. Calculate the corporation's estimated ending inventory using the retail method of estimating inventory. Round the percentage to the nearest 0.1%.

6. Use the information and the estimated inventory calculated in Instruction 4. Calculate the corporation's merchandise inventory turnover ratio. Round the ratio to the nearest 0.1%.

7. Calculate the corporation's average number of days' sales in merchandise inventory. Round the amount to the nearest day.

6-6

CHALLENGE PROBLEM
Determining the unit price of merchandise inventory purchases

Minder, Inc., recently received a shipment of merchandise inventory. Minder maintains a perpetual inventory using unit prices including freight and cash discounts. The following information is from the purchase invoice for the shipment.

Stock No.	Quantity	Unit Price	Total Cost
A69	50	$2.00	$100.00
V56	15	6.00	90.00
X28	30	4.00	120.00
W12	20	3.00	60.00
S92	5	8.00	40.00
Subtotal			$410.00
Freight			20.50
Cash Discount			(8.20)
Total Cost			$422.30

Instructions:

1. Divide the total cost by the subtotal. Round the percentage to the nearest 0.1%

2. Calculate the adjusted unit price of each item by multiplying the percentage calculated in Instruction 1 by the unit price of the item.

3. Calculate the adjusted total cost for each item by multiplying the quantity by the adjusted unit price.

INTERNET ACTIVITY

Point your browser to

http://accounting.swpco.com

Choose **Advanced Course**, choose **Activities**, and complete the activity for Chapter 6.

Applied Communication

Each year, retail businesses lose millions of dollars to theft and fraud. As consumers, we all pay for these illegal actions in the form of higher prices.

Required:

1. Research the actions that retail businesses take to control theft and fraud. Write a short report about your findings.
2. Explain why businesses must charge higher prices for their goods as a result of theft and fraud.
3. Discuss in class what actions you would take if you were with a friend who was shoplifting.

Cases for Critical Thinking

Case 1
Quitman, Inc., keeps a perpetual merchandise inventory. A new member of the board of directors notices that two employees work full time keeping the inventory records. The director suggests that the corporation stop using the perpetual inventory system and take a periodic inventory once a year when information is needed for financial statements. The director also suggests that the salaries saved by eliminating the positions of the two inventory employees will be more than the cost of an annual periodic inventory. What is your opinion of this suggestion? Explain your answer.

Case 2
Hastings, Inc., sells many different items of sports equipment. The corporation takes a periodic inventory once every three months for use in preparing quarterly financial statements. A newly employed accountant suggests that the corporation change over to a perpetual inventory. What would you recommend? Explain your recommendation.

AUTOMATED ACCOUNTING

INVENTORY PLANNING AND VALUATION

Inventory planning and valuation is necessary to accurately account for inventory and report asset values in financial statements. Merchandise inventory is usually the largest current asset of a merchandising business. Therefore, it is important to select an inventory system that provides the most accurate and up-to-date inventory valuations. Inventory planning and valuation may be accomplished by using either a manual or an automated inventory system. Today, most businesses use automated inventory systems.

Inventory Processing

Inventory processing includes recording items sold, ordered, and received in the inventory records. The inventory records are stored in a database that is separate from the general ledger database. To update the inventory records:

1. Click the Other Activities toolbar button.

2. Select the Inventory tab to display the data entry window.

3. Enter the data for items sold, ordered, and received.

4. Click OK.

Automated Accounting 8.0 has a more complete inventory system:

1. When inventory items are ordered, a purchase order is recorded in the Purch. Order tab of the Other Activities window.

2. When an order is received, a purchase invoice is issued and recorded in the Purch. Invoice tab of the Other Activities window.

3. When merchandise is sold, the sales invoice is entered in the Sales Invoice tab of the Other Activities window.

After all inventory processing data have been keyed, an Inventory Transaction report should be displayed, verified for accuracy, and printed. To print the Inventory Transaction report:

1. Click the Reports toolbar button.

2. Choose Inventory Reports from Select a Report Group.

3. Select Inventory Transactions from the Choose a Report to Display list.

4. Click OK.

5. Enter the Start and End date for the report.

6. Click OK.

The inventory transactions report is checked for accuracy by comparing the report totals with the totals on the inventory source documents or forms.

Inventory Exceptions

Inventory exceptions are those inventory items that require close monitoring. When inventory levels are low or there are no stock items, management will need to reorder or take action. The software provides an option for generating an exception report. This report lists items that are out of stock and items that are at or below the reorder point. To generate the report, select Inventory Exceptions from the list of inventory reports.

Inventory Valuation

Automated Accounting 7.0 or higher allows users to determine inventory costs using the average cost, LIFO, or FIFO costing methods. Reports can be generated to see the valuations using each of the inventory cost methods mentioned.

1. Click the Reports toolbar button.

2. Choose the Inventory Reports option button from the Select a Report Group list.

3. Select a valuation option from the Choose a Report to Display list.

Yearly Sales

The yearly sales report accumulates total sales throughout the year for each stock item. Therefore, a yearly sales report showing total sales for January, generated at month end, would include only sales for January. February's month-end report would show the accumulation of

AUTOMATED ACCOUNTING

AUTOMATING ACCOUNTING PROBLEM 6-1

Instructions:

1. Load *Automated Accounting* 7.0 or higher software.

2. Select database A06-1 (Advanced Course Application Problem 6-1) from the accounting template disk.

3. Select File from the menu bar and choose the Save As menu command. Key the path to the drive and directory that contains your data files. Save the database with a file name of XXX061 (where XXX are your initials).

4. Access Problem Instructions through the Help menu. Read the Problem Instruction screen.

5. Refer to page 184 for data used in this problem.

6. Exit the Automated Accounting software.

AUTOMATING ACCOUNTING PROBLEM 6-2

Instructions:

1. Load *Automated Accounting* 7.0 or higher software.

2. Select database A06-2 (Advanced Course Application Problem 6-2) from the accounting template disk.

3. Select File from the menu bar and choose the Save As menu command. Key the path to the drive and directory that contains your data files. Save the database with a file name of XXX062 (where XXX are your initials).

4. Access Problem Instructions through the Help menu. Read the Problem Instruction screen.

5. Refer to page 185 for data used in this problem.

6. Exit the Automated Accounting software.

PART 3

7 **Accounting for Uncollectible Accounts**

8 **Accounting for Plant Assets**

9 **Accounting for Notes Payable, Prepaid Expenses, and Accrued Expenses**

10 **Accounting for Notes Receivable, Unearned Revenue, and Accrued Revenue**

APPLIANCE CENTER, INC. CHART OF ACCOUNTS

Balance Sheet Accounts

(1000) Assets
1100	CURRENT ASSETS
1105	Cash
1110	Petty Cash
1115	Notes Receivable
1120	Interest Receivable
1125	Accounts Receivable
1130	Allowance for Uncollectible Accounts
1135	Merchandise Inventory
1140	Supplies—Administrative
1145	Supplies—Sales
1150	Supplies—Warehouse
1155	Prepaid Insurance
1160	Prepaid Interest
1200	PLANT ASSETS
1205	Land
1215	Building
1220	Accumulated Depreciation—Building
1225	Office Equipment
1230	Accumulated Depreciation—Office Equipment
1235	Store Equipment
1240	Accumulated Depreciation—Store Equipment
1245	Warehouse Equipment
1250	Accumulated Depreciation—Warehouse Equipment

(2000) Liabilities
2100	CURRENT LIABILITIES
2105	Notes Payable
2110	Interest Payable
2115	Accounts Payable
2120	Employee Income Tax Payable
2125	Federal Income Tax Payable
2130	Social Security Tax Payable
2133	Medicare Tax Payable
2135	Salaries Payable
2140	Sales Tax Payable
2145	Unearned Rent
2150	Unemployment Tax Payable—Federal
2155	Unemployment Tax Payable—State
2200	LONG-TERM LIABILITY
2205	Mortgage Payable

(3000) Stockholders' Equity
3105	Capital Stock
3110	Retained Earnings
3115	Income Summary

Income Statement Accounts

(4000) Operating Revenue
4105	Sales
4110	Sales Discount
4115	Sales Returns and Allowances

(5000) Cost of Merchandise
5105	Purchases
5110	Purchases Discount
5115	Purchases Returns and Allowances

(6000) Operating Expense
6100	ADMINISTRATIVE EXPENSES
6105	Depreciation Expense—Building
6110	Depreciation Expense—Office Equipment
6115	Insurance Expense
6120	Miscellaneous Expense—Administrative
6125	Payroll Taxes Expense
6130	Property Tax Expense
6135	Salary Expense—Administrative
6140	Supplies Expense—Administrative
6145	Uncollectible Accounts Expense
6200	SELLING EXPENSES
6205	Advertising Expense
6210	Credit Card Fee Expense
6215	Depreciation Expense—Store Equipment
6220	Miscellaneous Expense—Sales
6225	Salary Expense—Sales
6230	Supplies Expense—Sales
6300	WAREHOUSE EXPENSES
6305	Depreciation Expense—Warehouse Equipment
6310	Miscellaneous Expense—Warehouse
6315	Salary Expense—Warehouse
6320	Supplies Expense—Warehouse

(7000) Other Revenue
7105	Gain on Plant Assets
7110	Interest Income
7115	Rent Income

(8000) Other Expenses
8105	Interest Expense
8110	Loss on Plant Assets

(9000) Income Tax
9105	Federal Income Tax Expense

The chart of accounts for Appliance Center, Inc., is illustrated above for ready reference as you study Part 3 of this textbook.

7

Accounting for Uncollectible Accounts

AFTER STUDYING CHAPTER 7, YOU WILL BE ABLE TO:

1. Define accounting terms related to uncollectible accounts.

2. Identify accounting concepts and practices related to uncollectible accounts.

3. Calculate and record estimated uncollectible accounts expense using the direct write-off method.

4. Calculate and record estimated uncollectible accounts expense using the allowance method.

5. Calculate and analyze accounts receivable turnover ratios.

Many business transactions are completed on account rather than for cash. Businesses offer credit terms to attract new customers, increase sales to current customers, and encourage customer loyalty. Before a business sells merchandise on account, it should investigate the customer's credit rating to ensure that the customer will pay promptly.

Regardless of the care taken in granting credit, some customers will not pay when payment is due. Accounts receivable that cannot be collected are called **uncollectible accounts**. Uncollectible accounts are sometimes referred to as bad debts.

When a business makes a sale on account to a customer, it records the amount in a general ledger account titled Accounts Receivable. The amount remains recorded in this asset account until it is paid or until it is specifically known to be uncollectible.

When a customer account is believed to be uncollectible, the account is no longer an asset. An uncollectible account should be canceled and removed from the assets of the business. Canceling the balance of a customer account because the customer is not expected to pay is called **writing off an account**.

Occasionally an account that has been written off is collected. The account balance is restored and the receipt of cash is recorded. A complete history of the transactions for each customer is maintained.

ACCOUNTING
IN YOUR CAREER

PERILS OF RAPID GROWTH

SuperMicro Development Corporation has been growing rapidly. The company started when two college roommates began to do programming for local companies on special projects. The partners were talented, accurate, and fast and soon had more work than they could handle. Each month they hired more programmers to help until they finally formed a corporation.

Today the company has a special group of developers who work only on Internet web site design and another group who solve problems related to the date function conversion from the 1900s to the 2000s. Business is booming. The original partners have added some support staff, but until now have used outside services for their accounting. It is not unusual for accounts receivable to be more than $1,000,000 at any one time. One of the staff assistants sends out monthly invoices and marks accounts paid when payments are received. However, not much other attention has been paid to the accounts receivable.

As do many companies that experience rapid growth, the company is beginning to have difficulty meeting its cash obligations. Rent for office space increases as development personnel are added and, of course, the payroll expands as well. Equipment and office furnishings for new personnel also drain cash. Anthony Galina, the newly hired controller, needs to solve the cash crisis. He notices that the large balance of accounts receivable and a schedule of aging accounts receivable show a large number of accounts 60, 90, and more days past due. In addition, the allowance for uncollectible accounts account has a $50,000 debit balance.

Critical Thinking

1. How can the allowance account have a debit balance? What are the implications for the financial statements?
2. What recommendations should Anthony Galina make regarding accounts receivable to improve the cash flow?
3. What recommendations should Anthony Galina make to correct the debit balance in the allowance account?

RECORDING UNCOLLECTIBLE ACCOUNTS EXPENSE

	GENERAL JOURNAL					PAGE 11	
	DATE	ACCOUNT TITLE	DOC. NO.	POST. REF.	DEBIT	CREDIT	
1	Nov. 20-- 15	**Uncollectible Accounts Expense**	M21		5 0 00		1
2		**Accounts Rec./James Nordquist**				5 0 00	2

Figure 7-1

An amount owed by a specific customer is part of the accounts receivable account balance until it is paid or is written off as uncollectible. An uncollectible account is closed by transferring the balance to a general ledger account titled **Uncollectible Accounts Expense**.

Northwest Cleaners dry cleans clothing for its customers. Most of the business' sales are made for cash or are paid with a credit card. The business does make a few sales on account. The business has a small number of accounts receivable and very few of these accounts become uncollectible. Therefore, Northwest Cleaners records uncollectible accounts expense only when a specific account is actually known to be uncollectible. Recording uncollectible accounts expense only when an amount is actually known to be uncollectible is called the **direct write-off method of recording losses from uncollectible accounts**.

On November 15, Northwest Cleaners learned that James Nordquist is unable to pay his account. Northwest Cleaners decides that James Nordquist's account is uncollectible. The entry to record the write-off is made in the general journal as shown in Figure 7-1.

> **November 15. Wrote off James Nordquist's past due account as uncollectible, $50.00. Memorandum No. 21.**

After this entry is journalized and posted, the balance of **Accounts Receivable** no longer includes the $50.00 as part of the business' assets. Also, James Nordquist's account has a zero balance and is written off.

GENERAL LEDGER
Uncollectible Accounts Expense

Write off	50.00	

Accounts Receivable

Bal.	54,789.05	Write off	50.00
(New Bal.	54,739.05)		

ACCOUNTS RECEIVABLE LEDGER
James Nordquist

Bal.	50.00	Write off	50.00
(New Bal. zero)			

A credit rating is an evaluation of the willingness and ability of an individual or business to pay debts on a timely basis. Credit ratings are maintained by a variety of organizations.

REMEMBER

Uncollectible accounts are also referred to as bad debts. Thus, the accounts used could be titled Bad Debt Expense and Collection of Bad Debts.

1. Make an entry to reopen the account.

2. Make an entry to record the cash receipt.

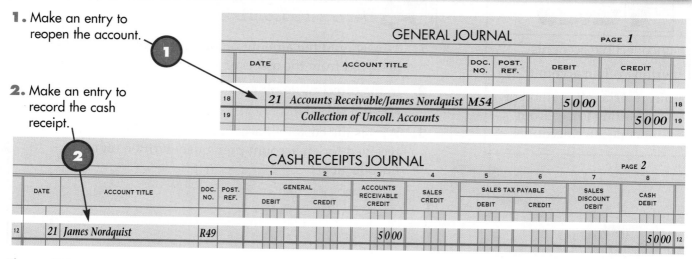

GENERAL JOURNAL PAGE 1

DATE	ACCOUNT TITLE	DOC. NO.	POST. REF.	DEBIT	CREDIT
21	Accounts Receivable/James Nordquist	M54		5000	
	Collection of Uncoll. Accounts				5000

CASH RECEIPTS JOURNAL PAGE 2

					1	2	3	4	5	6	7	8
DATE		ACCOUNT TITLE	DOC. NO.	POST. REF.	GENERAL DEBIT	GENERAL CREDIT	ACCOUNTS RECEIVABLE CREDIT	SALES CREDIT	SALES TAX PAYABLE DEBIT	SALES TAX PAYABLE CREDIT	SALES DISCOUNT DEBIT	CASH DEBIT
21		James Nordquist	R49				5000					5000

Figure 7-2

Sometimes a customer's written-off account is later collected. When the account is written off, the balance is recorded as an expense. When the account is later collected, the amount is recorded as other revenue.

January 21. Received cash in full payment of James Nordquist's account, previously written off as uncollectible, $50.00. Memorandum No. 54 and Receipt No. 49.

Northwest Cleaners needs a complete history of each customer's credit activities. Therefore, two journal entries are recorded for the collection of a written-off account receivable as shown in Figure 7-2.

1. A general journal entry to reopen the customer account.

2. A cash receipts journal entry to record the cash received on account.

The account Collection of Uncollectible Accounts is used for recording collection of pre-viously written-off accounts. The account is closed to Income Summary at the end of a fiscal period and is reported on an income statement as part of Other Revenue.

GENERAL LEDGER

Cash

Received	50.00		

Accounts Receivable

| Bal. | 54,789.05 | Write off | 50.00 |
| Reopen | 50.00 | Received | 50.00 |

Collection of Uncollectible Accounts

| | | Reopen | 50.00 |

ACCOUNTS RECEIVABLE LEDGER

James Nordquist

Bal.	50.00	Write off	50.00
Reopen	50.00	Received	50.00
(New Bal. zero)			

S T E P S

Collecting a written-off account using the direct write-off method

1. Record an entry in the general journal to debit *Accounts Receivable/James Nordquist* and credit *Collection of Uncollectible Accounts* for the amount of the receipt, *50.00.*

2. Record an entry on the cash receipts journal to debit *Cash* and credit *Accounts Receivable* for the amount of the receipt, *50.00.*

F Y I

Uncollectible accounts are also referred to as bad debts. Thus, the accounts used could be titled Bad Debts Expense and Collection of Bad Debts.

TERMS REVIEW

uncollectible accounts

writing off an account

direct write-off method of recording losses from uncollectible accounts

AUDIT YOUR UNDERSTANDING

1. Why should the amount of an uncollectible account be removed from the assets of a business?

2. In the direct write-off method, how is an uncollectible account closed?

3. Why is the customer account reopened when cash is received for an account previously written off as uncollectible?

WORK TOGETHER

Journalizing entries to write off uncollectible accounts—direct write-off method

Cracker, Inc., uses the direct write-off method of recording uncollectible accounts expense. A general journal and a cash receipts journal are provided in the *Working Papers*. Source documents are abbreviated as follows: memorandum, M; receipt, R. Your instructor will guide you through the following examples.

4. Journalize the following transactions completed during the current year.

Jan. 10. Wrote off Melinda Sanford's past due account as uncollectible, $261.54. M13.

Mar. 12. Wrote off Mark Polk's past due account as uncollectible, $45.00. M24.

Apr. 13. Received cash in full payment of Andrew Leslie's account, previously written off as uncollectible, $67.42. M31 and R158.

Nov. 15. Received cash in full payment of Melinda Sanford's account, previously written off as uncollectible, $261.54. M84 and R313.

ON YOUR OWN

Journalizing entries to write off uncollectible accounts—direct write-off method

Kelley, Inc., uses the direct write-off method of recording uncollectible accounts expense. A general journal and a cash receipts journal are provided in the *Working Papers*. Source documents are abbreviated as follows: memorandum, M; receipt, R. Work this problem independently.

5. Journalize the following transactions completed during the current year.

Jan. 20. Wrote off Belinda Rafferty's past due account as uncollectible, $265.48. M15.

Feb. 15. Wrote off Ervin Bond's past due account as uncollectible, $52.00. M21.

Apr. 10. Received cash in full payment of Stephanie Byrd's account, previously written off as uncollectible, $178.43. M34 and R89.

Oct. 5. Received cash in full payment of Belinda Rafferty's account, previously written off as uncollectible, $265.48. M104 and R135.

ESTIMATING UNCOLLECTIBLE ACCOUNTS EXPENSE

Some businesses use the direct write-off method and record uncollectible accounts expense only when a specific customer account is determined to be uncollectible. However, when the direct write-off method is used, the expense may be recorded in a fiscal period different from the fiscal period of the sale. Uncollectible accounts expense should be recorded in the same fiscal period in which the sales revenue is received. (CONCEPT: Matching Expenses with Revenue)

At the time sales on account are made, a business has no way to know for sure which customer will not pay an amount due. Therefore, the business makes an estimate based on its past history of uncollectible accounts. Crediting the estimated value of uncollectible accounts to a contra account is called the **allowance method of recording losses from uncollectible accounts**. Two methods are commonly used to estimate uncollectible accounts expense:

1. Percentage of sales method.

2. Percentage of accounts receivable method.

The *percentage of sales method* assumes that a percentage of each sales dollar will become an uncollectible account. The *percentage of accounts receivable method* assumes that a percentage of accounts receivable at the fiscal year-end will become uncollectible. Regardless of the method used, the estimated amount is charged to Uncollectible Accounts Expense.

LEGAL ISSUES IN ACCOUNTING

REPRESENTATIVE PAYEES FOR SOCIAL SECURITY BENEFITS

Retirees receive Social Security benefits. Supplemental Security Income (SSI) is received by disabled individuals and children of deceased workers. For those who need assistance managing their money, the Social Security Administration (SSA) allows a friend, relative, or other interested party to be appointed as a representative payee. The representative payee receives the Social Security or SSI payment on behalf of the beneficiary.

Before the SSA allows an individual to serve as a representative payee, it carefully investigates the individual's trustworthiness and ability to carefully manage the beneficiary's benefits. Among a representative payee's duties are:

- Regular contact with the beneficiary to determine how benefits can be used for his or her personal care or well-being.
- Good recordkeeping of how the funds were spent. Periodically, the SSA requires representative payees to complete a Representative Payee Report accounting for the funds received on behalf of the beneficiary.

All monies received from the SSA must be used for the personal care and well-being of the beneficiary. There is no specific list of approved expenditures; however, the SSA requires that the money first be used to ensure that the beneficiary's day-to-day needs for food and shelter are met.

Net Sales	×	Percentage	=	Estimated Uncollectible Accounts Expense	
$113,285.75	×	0.5%	=	$566.43	

1. Compute the estimated uncollectible accounts expense.

Morgan, Inc.

Work Sheet

For Year Ended December 31, 20--

	ACCOUNT TITLE	TRIAL BALANCE		ADJUSTMENTS		INCOME STATEMENT		BALANCE SHEET		
		DEBIT	CREDIT	DEBIT	CREDIT	DEBIT	CREDIT	DEBIT	CREDIT	
4	Allowance for Uncoll. Accounts		25 87		(a) 566 43					4
49	Uncollectible Accounts Expense			(a) 566 43						49

Figure 7-3

2. Record an adjustment on a worksheet.

Past experience of Morgan, Inc., indicates that approximately 0.5% of its net sales will prove to be uncollectible. On December 31, Morgan estimated that 0.5% of its $113,285.75 net sales, $566.43, eventually will prove to be uncollectible. Morgan does not yet know which customer accounts in the accounts receivable ledger will become uncollectible. Therefore, the amount cannot be recorded directly in accounts receivable.

Before the adjustment is made, Morgan's general ledger shows Allowance for Uncollectible Accounts with a $25.87 credit balance. This balance is what remains of estimates made in previous fiscal periods but not yet specifically identified by customer. The new balance, $592.30, is an estimate of the accounts receivable that will become uncollectible.

At the end of a fiscal period, an adjustment for uncollectible accounts expense is planned on a work sheet as shown in Figure 7-3.

The balance of Allowance for Uncollectible Accounts may increase from year to year. A large increase may indicate that an incorrect percentage is being used to calculate the uncollectible amount. When this occurs, a new percentage should be calculated based on actual experience for the past two or three years.

Uncollectible Accounts Expense	
Adj.	566.43

Allowance for Uncollectible Accounts	
Bal.	25.87
Adj.	566.43
(New Bal.	592.30)

S T E P S

Estimating uncollectible accounts expense by using the percentage of sales method

1. Compute the estimated uncollectible accounts expense by multiplying net sales, *113,285.75*, by the percentage estimate, *0.5%*, which totals *566.43*.

2. Record an adjustment on the worksheet, recording a debit to Uncollectible Accounts Expense and a credit to Allowance for Uncollectible Accounts.

Customer	Account Balance	Not Yet Due	Days Account Balance Past Due			
			1–30	31–60	61–90	Over 90
Louise Asmus	$ 735.51	$ 735.51				
Mark Darby	132.58		132.58			
⋮	⋮	⋮	⋮	⋮	⋮	⋮
Ann Gabriel	99.55					99.55
Kathy Quay	238.00	200.00	38.00			
Thomas Yost	133.67				133.67	
Totals	$12,891.97	$8,734.08	$2,952.90	$749.54	$238.45	$217.00
Percentages	—	0.1%	0.2%	0.4%	10.0%	80.0%

Figure 7-4

The *percentage of accounts receivable method* assumes that a percentage of the accounts receivable account balance is uncollectible. Therefore, emphasis is placed on estimating a percentage of accounts receivable that will not be collected. An amount that will bring the balance of Allowance for Uncollectible Accounts up to the estimated amount is recorded in that account.

Analyzing accounts receivable according to when they are due is called **aging accounts receivable**. Rosedale, Inc., ages accounts receivable at the end of each fiscal period, as shown in Figure 7-4, to provide information for the uncollectible accounts expense adjustment. Rosedale sells on terms of 2/10, n/30. Rosedale expects customers to pay in full within 30 days. If Rosedale has not received cash within 30 days, it mails reminders to the customers. If it has not received cash after 60 days, the company makes special attempts to collect the amount due. If the business has not collected an amount from a customer after 90 days, it may stop selling on account to that customer until collection has been made.

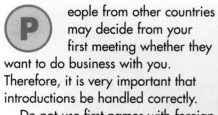

BUSINESS INTRODUCTIONS

People from other countries may decide from your first meeting whether they want to do business with you. Therefore, it is very important that introductions be handled correctly.

Do not use first names with foreign business associates until invited to do so.

In Japan and India, address a person by adding Mr. or Mrs. to their last name. Use a title such as Dr. if appropriate. Address people from the Middle East as their name appears on their business card. Usually Mr. or Sheik will be used. If they are members of a royal family, use Your Excellency.

Chinese names appear in the reverse order of names in the United States. The family name or "last" name precedes the first name. For example, Mr. Wu Ho is called Mr. Wu because Ho is his given name.

In Latin America, address a person as Señor, Señora, or Señorita, followed by the last name. If they have a title such as doctor, be sure to use it.

Required:

Research foreign business introductions. Find the appropriate introduction for meeting someone from Germany, South Africa, and England.

GLOBAL PERSPECTIVE

Age Group	Amount	Percentage	Uncollectible
Not Yet Due	$ 8,734.08	0.1%	$ 8.73
1–30 Days	2,952.90	0.2%	5.91
31–60 Days	749.54	0.4%	3.00
61–90 Days	238.45	10.0%	23.85
Over 90 Days	217.00	80.0%	173.60
Totals	$12,891.97	—	$215.09

Current Balance of Allowance for Uncollectible Accounts	40.78
Estimated Addition to Allowance for Uncollectible Accounts	$174.31

1. Compute an estimate for each age group.

2. Compute the total estimate.

3. Compute the addition to the allowance account.

Figure 7-5

Based on past records, Rosedale determines that a percentage of each accounts receivable age group will become uncollectible in the future. For example, 0.4% of the accounts receivable overdue 31–60 days will probably become uncollectible. Also, 80.0% of the accounts overdue more than 90 days probably will become uncollectible.

Using these percentages, Rosedale calculates the total amount of estimated uncollectible accounts receivable, as shown in Figure 7-5. Of the total accounts receivable on December 31, $12,891.97, the business estimates that $215.09 will prove to be uncollectible in the future.

Rosedale's general ledger shows that **Allowance for Uncollectible Accounts** has a $40.78 credit balance. This balance is what remains of estimates made in previous fiscal periods but not yet specifically identified by customer. The allowance account is increased by a $174.31 credit. The new balance of the allowance

account, $215.09 (previous balance, $40.78, *plus* adjustment, $174.31), equals the estimate of uncollectible accounts.

Uncollectible Accounts Expense	
Adj. 174.31	

Allowance for Uncollectible Accounts	
	Bal. 40.78
	Adj. 174.31
	(New Bal. 215.09)

F.Y.I.

An estimate of the amount of uncollectible accounts expense can also be computed by using a single percentage of the total accounts receivable account balance. Although this method is easier to compute, a method using age group information typically yields a better estimate of the expense.

S **Estimating the balance of uncollectible accounts expense using the percentage of accounts receivable method**

T
E   **1.** Compute the estimate for each age group. Multiply the amount of each age group by the percentage estimate.
P   **2.** Compute the total, *$215.09*, of the uncollectible estimates.
S   **3.** Subtract the current balance, *40.78*, from the total estimate to determine the addition to the allowance account, *$174.31*. (If the allowance account has a debit balance, add the current balance to the total estimate.)

	DATE	ACCOUNT TITLE	DOC. NO.	POST. REF.	DEBIT	CREDIT	
4	5	*Allowance for Uncollectible Accts.*	*M71*		4 2 80		4
5		*Accounts Rec./Candace Rhode*		/		4 2 80	5
6							6

GENERAL JOURNAL   PAGE *1*

Figure 7-6

The procedures for writing off an account are the same regardless of the allowance method used to calculate the estimated uncollectible accounts expense. When a specific customer account is thought to be uncollectible, the account balance is written off as shown in Figure 7-6. Appliance Center determined that Candace Rhode will probably not pay the amount she owes, $42.80. The balance is no longer *estimated* to be uncollectible; it is *actually determined* to be uncollectible.

January 5. Wrote off Candace Rhode's past due account as uncollectible, $42.80. Memorandum No. 71.

After this entry is journalized and posted, Candace Rhode's account has a zero balance, and the account is written off.

Appliance Center did not notify Candace Rhode that it wrote off her account. Although Appliance Center believes the account is probably uncollectible, it may continue its attempts to collect the account. In some cases, customers do subsequently pay accounts that have been written off.

In a previous fiscal period, an adjusting entry was recorded for estimated uncollectible accounts expense resulting in an **Allowance for Uncollectible Accounts** balance of $1,363.88. This balance is the estimated amount of uncollectible accounts. The $42.80 debit entry in this account removes an amount that is no longer estimated but is actual.

Uncollectible Accounts Expense is not affected when a business writes off an account using the allowance method. The expense is recorded in an adjusting entry at the end of a previous fiscal period.

GENERAL LEDGER
Allowance for Uncollectible Accounts

Write off	42.80	Bal.	1,363.88

Accounts Receivable

Bal.	45,462.79	Write off	42.80

ACCOUNTS RECEIVABLE LEDGER
Candace Rhode

Bal.	42.80	Write off	42.80
(New Bal. zero)			

F.Y.I.

Businesses extend credit to encourage sales. Restricting customers' ability to purchase on account may have a negative impact on both sales and net income. Managers must carefully balance the goals of maximizing sales while limiting uncollectible accounts expense. Although every business can determine its own credit terms, managers must consider competitors' credit terms. Having more restrictive credit terms than competitors could have a negative impact on sales.

F.Y.I.

Proper internal control requires that the custody, recording, and authority for a transaction be segregated. The employee responsible for writing off an account should not also have access to the cash received from customers paying their accounts.

1. Reopen the account.

2. Record the cash receipt.

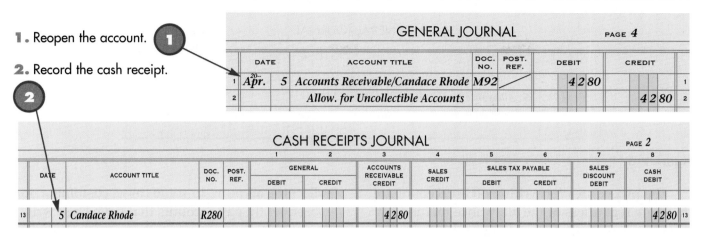

Figure 7-7

Later in the year, Appliance Center received a check in full payment of the amount owed by Candace Rhode.

April 5. Received cash in full payment of Candace Rhode's account, previously written off as uncollectible, $42.80. Memorandum No. 92 and Receipt No. 280.

Appliance Center's records must show a complete history of Ms. Rhode's credit dealings. The collection of a written-off account receivable involves two journal entries as shown in Figure 7-7.

A general journal entry is recorded to reopen the customer account. The $42.80 debit increases Accounts Receivable and Candace Rhode's account in the accounts receivable ledger. The account balances now appear as they were

before Ms. Rhode's account was written off as uncollectible.

The cash received from Ms. Rhode is then recorded in the cash receipts journal. The $42.80 credit decreases Accounts Receivable and Ms. Rhode's account in the accounts receivable ledger.

GENERAL LEDGER
Cash

Received	42.80	

Accounts Receivable

| Bal. | 45,462.79 | Write off | 42.80 |
| Reopen | 42.80 | Received | 42.80 |

Allowance for Uncollectible Accounts

| Write off | 42.80 | Bal. | 1,363.88 |
| | | Reopen | 42.80 |

ACCOUNTS RECEIVABLE LEDGER
Candace Rhode

Bal.	42.80	Write off	42.80
Reopen	42.80	Received	42.80
(New Bal. zero)			

S T E P S

Journalizing the collection of a written-off account—allowance method

1. Reopen the account by debiting Accounts Receivable and crediting Allowance for Doubtful Accounts for the amount of the receipt, *42.80*.

2. Record an entry in the cash receipts journal to debit Cash and credit Accounts Receivable for the amount of the receipt, *42.80*.

R E M E M B E R

Entries for the collection of a written-off account present evidence of the customer's credit history. Managers can use this information to make informed decisions about extending credit to the customer in the future.

TERMS
REVIEW

allowance method of
recording losses from
uncollectible accounts

aging accounts receivable

AUDIT YOUR
UNDERSTANDING

1. What are the two methods commonly used to estimate uncollectible accounts expense?

2. What is the formula for estimating uncollectible accounts expense based on net sales?

3. How is the addition to allowance for uncollectible accounts calculated using the percentage of accounts receivable method?

Estimating amount of uncollectible accounts expense; journalizing the adjusting entry

General journal pages are provided in the *Working Papers*. Your instructor will guide you through the following independent examples.

4. Lynum, Inc., had net sales of $245,321.09 during the current year. It estimates that the amount of uncollectible accounts expense is equal to 0.5% of net sales. Journalize the adjusting entry for uncollectible accounts expense on December 31 of the current year.

5. The aging of accounts receivable for Kersten, Inc., as of December 31 of the current year and estimated percentages of uncollectible accounts by age group are presented in the *Working Papers*. Calculate the estimated balance of Allowance for Uncollectible Accounts. Then journalize the adjusting entry for uncollectible accounts expense. The balance of Allowance for Uncollectible Accounts on December 31 before adjusting entries are recorded is $63.24.

Estimating amount of uncollectible accounts expense; journalizing the adjusting entry

General journal pages are provided in the *Working Papers*. Work this problem independently.

6. Hillcrest, Inc., had net sales of $685,409.50 during the current year. It estimates that the amount of uncollectible accounts expense is equal to 0.8% of net sales. Journalize the adjusting entry for uncollectible accounts expense on December 31 of the current year.

7. The aging of accounts receivable for Malloy, Inc., as of December 31 of the current year and estimated percentages of uncollectible accounts by age group are presented in the *Working Papers*. Calculate the estimated balance of Allowance for Uncollectible Accounts. Then journalize the adjusting entry for uncollectible accounts expense. The balance of Allowance for Uncollectible Accounts on December 31 before adjusting entries are recorded is $391.75.

CHAPTER 7 Accounting for Uncollectible Accounts **205**

CALCULATING THE ACCOUNTS RECEIVABLE TURNOVER RATIO

	Total Accounts Receivable	−	Allowance for Uncollectible Accounts	=	Book Value of Accounts Receivable	
Beginning	$50,329.14	−	$1,416.83	=	$48,912.31	**1.** Compute the beginning and ending book value.
Ending	$45,462.79	−	$1,363.88	=	$44,098.91	

Beginning Book Value of Accounts Receivable	+	Ending Book Value of Accounts Receivable	÷	2	=	Average Book Value of Accounts Receivable	
($48,912.31	+	$44,098.91)	÷	2	=	$46,505.61	**2.** Compute the average book value.

Net Sales on Account	÷	Average Book Value of Accounts Receivable	=	Accounts Receivable Turnover Ratio	
$330,312.85	÷	$46,505.61	=	7.1 times	**3.** Compute the accounts receivable turnover.

Days in Year	÷	Accounts Receivable Turnover Ratio	=	Average Number of Days for Payment	
365	÷	7.1	=	51	**4.** Compute the average number of days for payment.

Figure 7-8

Appliance Center needs cash to purchase additional merchandise to sell to customers and to pay for operating expenses. If it does not collect amounts due from customers promptly, too large a share of the assets of the business will be in accounts receivable and not immediately usable. All businesses selling on account need prompt collection from credit customers.

Appliance Center analyzes how frequently customers make payments on account. If customers are not paying promptly, the business will adopt new procedures to speed collections. One way to analyze the collection efficiency of a business is to calculate the accounts receivable turnover ratio as shown in Figure 7-8. The number of times the average amount of accounts receivable is collected during a specified period is called the **accounts receivable turnover ratio**. The accounts receivable turnover ratio is calculated by dividing net sales on account by the average book value of accounts receivable.

Businesses may calculate this ratio monthly, quarterly, or yearly.

The difference between the balance of **Accounts Receivable** and its contra account, **Allowance for Uncollectible Accounts**, is called the **book value of accounts receivable**.

An accounts receivable turnover ratio of 7.1 times means that Appliance Center turns over (or collects) its average accounts receivable about seven times a year. The number of days in a year, 365, divided by the accounts receivable turnover ratio, 7.1, yields the average number of days required to pay. Appliance Center's customers are taking an average of 51 days to pay their accounts in full.

S
T
E
P
S

Calculating the accounts receivable turnover ratio and the average number of days for payment

1. Compute the beginning and ending book value of accounts receivable. The book values are computed by subtracting the allowance for doubtful accounts from the total accounts receivable.

2. Compute the average book value of accounts receivable, $46,505.61, by adding the beginning book value, $48,912.31, to the ending book value, $44,098.91, and dividing the total by 2.

3. Compute the accounts receivable turnover ratio by dividing net sales on account, $330,312.85, by the average book value of accounts receivable, $46,505.61.

4. Compute the average number of days for payment , 51, by dividing 365 days by the accounts receivable turnover ratio, 7.1.

ANALYZING ACCOUNTS RECEIVABLE TURNOVER RATIOS

Appliance Center, Inc.—Accounts Receivable Turnover Ratios

Year	20X1	20X2	20X3	20X4	20X5	20X6	20X7
Ratio	6.2	6.4	6.0	6.4	6.8	6.8	7.1
Days for Payment	59	57	61	57	54	54	51

Figure 7-9

Most of Appliance Center's customers do pay their accounts, but many customers take much longer than the expected 30 days.

From 20X1 through 20X7, the accounts receivable turnover ratio rose from 6.2 to 7.1 times as shown in Figure 7-9. In 20X1, customers took an average of 59 days to pay their accounts in full. In 20X7, customers took an average of 51 days to pay their accounts in full, 8 fewer days than in 20X1.

With the exception of 20X3, the turnover ratio has been steadily increasing. On the average, customers have been paying their accounts in full in a fewer number of days each year. Appliance Center wants this favorable trend to continue.

Appliance Center needs to plan additional ways to encourage customers to pay their accounts in less time. With n/30 credit terms, the goal should be to have a turnover ratio of 12.0 times (365 days / 12.0 accounts receivable turnover ratio = 30 average number of days for payment).

The business might take several steps to create a more favorable accounts receivable turnover ratio.

1. Send statements of account to customers more often, including a request for prompt payment.

2. Not sell on account to any customer who has an account for which payment is overdue more than 30 days.

3. Encourage more cash sales and fewer sales on account.

4. Conduct a more rigorous credit check on new customers before extending credit to them.

Sometimes the demand for quicker payment can result in a loss of business. Some customers might start buying from competitors. A business must weigh a change in credit policies against the effect the change will have on total sales.

F Y I

A business that does not record sales on account separately from cash sales uses total net sales to compute the accounts receivable turnover ratio.

accounts receivable
  turnover ratio

book value of accounts
  receivable

AUDIT YOUR UNDERSTANDING

1. What is the formula for calculating the accounts receivable turnover ratio?

2. How would you interpret the situation of a business that desires an accounts receivable turnover ratio of 12.0 times but actually has a turnover ratio of 6.0 times?

3. How can extremely restrictive credit terms have a negative impact on a business?

WORK TOGETHER

Calculating accounts receivable turnover ratios

Millikin Industries offers its customers n/30 credit terms. The turnover ratio for the prior year was 8.7. The following account balances were obtained from Millikin Industries' records for the current year. Your instructor will guide you through the following examples.

Account	January 1	December 31
Accounts Receivable	$264,483.18	$275,486.58
Allowance for Uncollectible Accounts	$8,234.22	$10,723.36
Net Sales on Account		$2,396,656.10

4. Calculate the accounts receivable turnover ratio for the current year.

5. Calculate the average number of days for payment.

6. Is Millikin Industries effective in collecting its accounts receivable?

ON YOUR OWN

Calculating accounts receivable turnover ratios

Stokes Building Supply offers its customers n/45 credit terms. The turnover ratio for the prior year was 5.8. The following account balances were obtained from the records of Stokes Building Supply for the current year. Work independently to complete the following problem.

Account	January 1	December 31
Accounts Receivable	$163,874.05	$186,383.48
Allowance for Uncollectible Accounts	$6,544.83	$7,745.86
Net Sales on Account		$872,895.94

7. Calculate the accounts receivable turnover ratio for the current year.

8. Calculate the average number of days for payment.

9. Is Stokes Building Supply effective in collecting its accounts receivable?

After completing this chapter, you can

1. Define accounting terms related to uncollectible accounts.
2. Identify accounting concepts and practices related to uncollectible accounts.
3. Calculate and record estimated uncollectible accounts expense using the direct write-off method.
4. Calculate and record estimated uncollectible accounts expense using the allowance method.
5. Calculate and analyze accounts receivable turnover ratios.

EXPLORE ACCOUNTING

CREDIT SCORING SYSTEMS

To help reduce the amount of uncollectible accounts, a business should evaluate the credit worthiness of potential customers before granting credit. The traditional credit evaluation involves a credit analyst manually evaluating financial information to determine if the customer has the financial resources to pay the account.

The benefit of reducing bad debt expenses should exceed the costs of performing credit evaluations. A business must consider the cost, in both the time and money, involved in credit evaluations. A business should not, for example, spend $70,000 in salaries and other expenses to evaluate credit if the business can only reduce its annual bad debt expense by $50,000. In addition, customers may be unwilling to wait for a business to perform a

traditional credit evaluation, favoring to purchase goods from another business.

A more cost-effective method for evaluating credit worthiness is available. A statistical method used to predict a customer's willingness to pay its account on a timely basis is called a credit scoring system. In addition to considering financial information, a credit scoring system considers other factors that have been shown to be predictors of credit worthiness, such as: frequency of delinquent accounts, length of credit history, types of credit, available credit, frequency of credit applications, number of credit inquiries, industry comparative data, number of employees, management problems, and prior bankruptcies.

A score is assigned to each factor. The higher the score, the more creditworthy the customer. An effective credit scoring system

will utilize information obtained from a credit application or available from public sources. A company can maintain its own system or use systems maintained by independent credit rating companies.

Credit scoring systems are optimally used for routine credit decisions that must be made quickly on relatively low-dollar sales on account. For sales on account that are relatively large, the credit decisions should involve the human decision of the traditional credit evaluation.

Regardless of how credit is evaluated, a company must assure that its decisions are consistent. Federal laws exist to assure that individuals and businesses have equal access to credit.

REQUIRED:

Research the Fair Credit Reporting Act. How does this act protect the rights of the consumer?

APPLICATION PROBLEM

Journalizing entries to write off uncollectible accounts—direct write-off method

Stallworth uses the direct write-off method of recording uncollectible accounts expense.

Instructions:
Journalize the following transactions completed during the current year. Use page 3 of a general journal and page 4 of a cash receipts journal. Source documents are abbreviated as follows: memorandum, M; receipt, R.

Transactions:
Feb. 16. Wrote off William Rose's past due account as uncollectible, $215.64. M18.
Mar. 23. Received cash in full payment of Emma Peden's account, previously written off as uncollectible, $175.00. M43 and R215.
May 7. Wrote off Tom Ming's past due account as uncollectible, $187.32. M61.
Aug. 10. Received cash in full payment of William Rose's account, previously written off as uncollectible, $215.64. M78 and R341.

APPLICATION PROBLEM

Estimating amount of uncollectible accounts expense by using a percentage of net sales—allowance method; journalizing the adjusting entry

Jacobs Market had net sales of $863,245.32 during the current year. The corporation estimates that the amount of uncollectible accounts expense is equal to 0.6% of net sales.

Instructions:
Journalize the adjusting entry for uncollectible accounts expense on December 31 of the current year. Use page 24 of a general journal.

APPLICATION PROBLEM

Estimating the balance of Allowance for Uncollectible Accounts by aging accounts receivable—allowance method; journalizing the adjusting entry

The following information has been taken from the records of Rosetta Company as of December 31 of the current year.

Customer	Account Balance	Not Yet Due	Days Account Balance Past Due			
			1–30	31–60	61–90	Over 90
Acorn & Karr	$623.74			$623.74		
Base Industries	723.22	$723.22				
⋮	⋮	⋮	⋮	⋮	⋮	⋮
Wright Stores	612.67					612.67
Yui Co.	1,723.33	1,048.99	$674.34			
Totals	$89,363.45	$44,434.51	$25,623.64	$10,535.20	$5,235.40	$3,534.70
Percentages	—	0.2%	0.5%	1.0%	5.0%	60.0%

Instructions:

1. Calculate the estimated balance of Allowance for Uncollectible Accounts.

2. Journalize the adjusting entry for uncollectible accounts expense on December 31 of the current year. Use page 12 of a general journal. The balance of Allowance for Uncollectible Accounts on December 31 before adjusting entries are recorded is $589.63.

7-4 APPLICATION PROBLEM
Journalizing entries to write off uncollectible accounts and collect written-off accounts—allowance method

McCafferty, Inc., uses the allowance method of recording uncollectible accounts expense.

Instructions:

Journalize the following transactions completed during the current year. Use page 3 of a general journal and page 8 of a cash receipts journal. Source documents are abbreviated as follows: memorandum, M; receipt, R.

Transactions:

Feb. 14. Wrote off Peggy King's past due account as uncollectible, $357.00. M16.

Apr. 25. Wrote off Mel Kober's past due account as uncollectible, $84.98. M34.

May 12. Received cash in full payment of Carolyn Kelly's account, previously written off as uncollectible, $74.00. M43 and R264.

Aug. 2. Wrote off Lynn Hartman's past due account as uncollectible, $74.93. M71.

Oct. 6. Received cash in full payment of Peggy King's account, previously written off as uncollectible, $357.00. M92 and R484.

7-5 APPLICATION PROBLEM
Calculating the accounts receivable turnover ratio

Fleming Company offers its customers n/30 credit terms. The turnover ratio for the prior year was 4.5. The following account balances were obtained from the records of Fleming Company for the current year:

Account	January 1	December 31
Accounts Receivable	$584,348.48	$604,285.25
Allowance for Doubtful Accounts	$20,153.35	$23,485.62
Net Sales		$3,848,348.27

Instructions:

1. Calculate the accounts receivable turnover ratio for the current year.

2. Calculate the average number of days for payment.

3. Is Fleming Company effective in collecting its accounts receivable?

7-6 APPLICATION PROBLEM
Accounts receivable transactions using the allowance method

Cofield Engineering uses the allowance method of recording uncollectible accounts expense.

Instructions:
Journalize the following transactions completed during the current year. Use page 4 of a general journal and page 10 of a cash receipts journal. Source documents are abbreviated as follows: memorandum, M; receipt, R.

Transactions:

Mar. 23. A phone call to Larry Wade, president of Wade Supply, confirmed that the company is intending to file bankruptcy. Mr. Wade stated that no money would likely be available to pay its creditors. The Wade account of $4,000.00 is over 180 days past due. M32.

Apr. 4. Last year you wrote off the $3,200.00 balance of Creative Decor. The account was over 180 days past due and collection seemed doubtful. Today you received a $3,200.00 check from Creative Decor along with a letter stating that the company had just received a large contract and they wished to reestablish a credit account with your company. M45 and R156.

May 14. Received a reply to a collection request letter sent to Raymond Fisher. Mr. Fisher refuses to pay the remaining $75.00 of his bill, stating that the original bill was larger than the agreed-upon price. Although your records clearly indicate the $75.00 was an appropriate charge, your manager believes that further efforts to collect this account are pointless. M54.

Oct. 10. Today you received an $800.00 check from Wade Supply. In the enclosed letter, Mr. Wade stated that the bankruptcy court ordered the company to pay 20 cents for every dollar owed to its creditors. Thus, the $800.00 is the only amount that Wade Supply would ever be able to pay of its original account balance of $4,000.00. M72 and R348.

Nov. 21. A letter sent to Mary Crawford was returned in the mail, with a U.S. Postal Service stamp stating that the party no longer lives at the address and has left no forwarding address. Ms. Crawford owed $600.00 from an invoice dated January 24. M89.

7-7 MASTERY PROBLEM
Journalizing entries for uncollectible accounts—allowance method; calculating and journalizing the adjusting entry for uncollectible accounts expense

Northern, Inc., uses the allowance method of recording uncollectible accounts expense. The following information was obtained from Northern's records for the current year.

Account	January 1	December 31
Accounts Receivable	$49,576.17	$62,791.30
Allowance for Doubtful Accounts	$1,463.89	$3,813.98
Net Sales on Account		$349,562.10

Transactions:

Jan. 9. Wrote off Jane Martinez' past due account as uncollectible, $634.65. M20.

Mar. 4. Wrote off Jason Young's past due account as uncollectible, $782.50. M29.

Mar. 28. Received cash in full payment of Jane Martinez' account, previously written off as uncollectible, $634.65. M40 and R24.

June 20. Wrote off Allison Aanerud's past due account as uncollectible, $617.16. M58.

Oct. 7. Wrote off Meredith Darst's past due account as uncollectible, $808.15. M74.

Dec. 11. Received cash in full payment of Jason Young's account, previously written off as uncollectible, $782.50. M82 and R92.

Instructions:

1. Journalize the transactions above that were completed during the current year. Use page 1 of a general journal and page 1 of a cash receipts journal. Source documents are abbreviated as follows: memorandum, M; receipt, R.

2. Journalize the adjusting entry for uncollectible accounts expense on December 31 of the current year. Northern estimates that the amount of uncollectible accounts expense is equal to 1% of its net sales of $377,539.58.

3. Compute the accounts receivable turnover and average days for payment.

7-8 CHALLENGE PROBLEM
Estimating and journalizing uncollectible accounts expense by aging accounts receivable—allowance method; calculating and journalizing the adjusting entry for uncollectible accounts expense

A complete list of the accounts receivable of Wind Refrigeration follows:

Account	Amount	Invoice Date
Atkins Co.	$2,523.64	May 16
Bankhead Supply	2,435.75	December 13
Coffman Distributing	943.74	November 30
Fleet Trucking	2,643.23	December 23
Griffin Industries	7,896.54	October 16
Miskelly & Sons	2,754.48	November 15
Oswalt, Inc.	8,723.54	December 4
Rice Shipping Co.	4,363.27	August 25
Smith Stores	1,324.76	September 20

Instructions:

1. Age the accounts receivable by determining the age group for each invoice and totaling the invoice amounts in each age group category.

2. Calculate the estimated balance of Allowance for Uncollectible Accounts using the following percentages: not yet due, 0.3%; 1–30 days past due, 1.0%; 31–60 days, 4.0%; 61–90 days, 20%; and over 90 days, 60%.

3. Journalize the adjusting entry for uncollectible accounts expense on December 31 of the current year. Use page 12 of a general journal. The Allowance for Uncollectible Accounts has a debit balance of $692.16 on December 31 of the current year before adjusting entries are recorded.

Applied Communication

Stegall Company had experienced no growth in sales or net income for several years. At your suggestion, the company changed its credit terms on January 1, 20X4, from n/60 to 2/10, n/30. In addition, the company loosened its requirements to extend credit to new customers. All sales are on account. Selected information, in thousands of dollars, taken from the December 31 financial statements for the past four years follows.

Item	20X1	20X2	20X3	20X4
Accts. Receivable	$496	$492	$514	$384
Allow. for Doubtful Accts.	17	17	18	42
Net Sales	2,653	2,676	2,689	2,945
Uncollectible Accts. Exp.	26	26	27	58
Net Income	253	259	262	284

Alice Shirley, a member of the board of directors, has suggested that the company return to its previous credit policies, citing the significant rise in the uncollectible accounts expense.

Required:

Write a memorandum to Alice supporting the new credit policy.

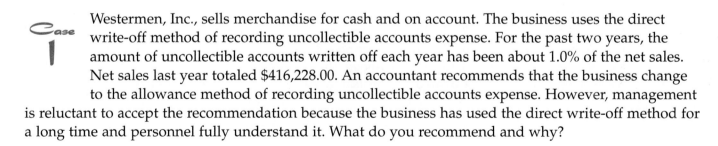

Cases for Critical Thinking

Case 1

Westermen, Inc., sells merchandise for cash and on account. The business uses the direct write-off method of recording uncollectible accounts expense. For the past two years, the amount of uncollectible accounts written off each year has been about 1.0% of the net sales. Net sales last year totaled $416,228.00. An accountant recommends that the business change to the allowance method of recording uncollectible accounts expense. However, management is reluctant to accept the recommendation because the business has used the direct write-off method for a long time and personnel fully understand it. What do you recommend and why?

Case 2

The following entries were made in each of the years shown. What effect will the entries in each of these years have on the financial statements of the business?

20X1   Adjusting entry: debit Uncollectible Accounts Expense, credit Allowance for Uncollectible Accounts, $2,000.00.

20X2   Wrote off Gerald Garland's account as uncollectible, $550.00.

20X3   Reopened Gerald Garland's account; received payment in full for the account, $550.00.

AUTOMATED ACCOUNTING

AUTOMATED ENTRIES FOR UNCOLLECTIBLE ACCOUNTS AND WRITE-OFFS

Recording Uncollectible Accounts

Using the direct write-off method, Uncollectible Accounts Expense and Accounts Receivable are used to write off an uncollectible account.

Using the allowance method, an allowance for uncollectible accounts is maintained. Manual calculations are required to determine the amount of the allowance to be recorded as an adjusting entry at the end of the accounting period. The process is described in Chapter 7.

When an account is determined to be uncollectible, it is written off using the general ledger accounts: Allowance for Uncollectible Accounts and Accounts Receivable. In *Automated Accounting 7.0*, the journal entries should be entered after the amounts have been calculated.

Reinstating a Written-Off Account

Occasionally a customer will make payment on an account that has been written off. When this occurs, the account receivable is reinstated and the payment is recorded as described in the chapter.

Other Computerized Accounting Systems

The automated accounting systems used in many businesses today will calculate the amounts that should be posted and will also do the posting based on how the system is set up to handle uncollectible accounts expenses and write-offs. In these cases, it is important to verify that the amounts posted to the accounts are accurate.

AUTOMATING APPLICATION PROBLEM 7-1

Instructions:

1. Load *Automated Accounting 7.0* or higher software.

2. Select database A07-1 (Advanced Course Application Problem 7-1) from the accounting template disk.

3. Select File from the menu bar and choose the Save As menu command. Key the path to the drive and directory that contains your data files. Save the database with a file name of XXX071 (where XXX are your initials).

4. Access Problem Instructions through the Help menu. Read the Problem Instruction screen.

5. Key the data listed on page 210.

6. Exit the Automated Accounting software.

AUTOMATING APPLICATION PROBLEM 7-4

Instructions:

1. Load *Automated Accounting 7.0* or higher software.

2. Select database A07-4 (Advanced Course Application Problem 7-4) from the accounting template disk.

3. Select File from the menu bar and choose the Save As menu command. Key the path to the drive and directory that contains your data files. Save the database with a file name of XXX074 (where XXX are your initials).

4. Access Problem Instructions through the Help menu. Read the Problem Instruction screen.

5. Key the data listed on page 211.

6. Exit the Automated Accounting software.

AUTOMATING MASTERY PROBLEM 7-7

Instructions:

1. Load *Automated Accounting 7.0* or higher software.

2. Select database A07-7 (Advanced Course Mastery Problem 7-7) from the accounting template disk.

3. Select File from the menu bar and choose the Save As menu command. Key the path to the drive and directory that contains your data files. Save the database with a file name of XXX077 (where XXX are your initials).

4. Access Problem Instructions through the Help menu. Read the Problem Instruction screen.

5. Key the data listed on page 212.

6. Exit the Automated Accounting software.

8

Accounting for Plant Assets

AFTER STUDYING CHAPTER 8, YOU WILL BE ABLE TO:

1. Define accounting terms related to plant assets and depreciation.

2. Identify accounting concepts and practices related to accounting for plant assets and depreciation.

3. Journalize entries for buying plant assets.

4. Calculate and record property tax expense.

5. Calculate and record depreciation expense for a plant asset using straight-line depreciation.

6. Journalize entries disposing of plant assets.

7. Calculate depreciation expense using other methods.

A business owns a variety of assets, all of which are used to help it earn a profit. Some assets such as cash, accounts receivable, and supplies are exchanged for cash or consumed within a year. Cash and other assets expected to be exchanged for cash or consumed within a year are known as current assets. Other assets, such as land, buildings, and equipment, are expected to help the business earn a profit for more than one year. Assets that will be used for a number of years in the operation of a business are known as plant assets. Plant assets are sometimes referred to as fixed assets or long-term assets.

Since businesses expect to remain in business indefinitely, the accounting records must be kept up-to-date as plant assets are bought and used. *(CONCEPT: Going Concern)*

The going concern concept states that financial statements are prepared with the expectation that a business will remain in operation indefinitely. A business bought store equipment for $30,000.00. The store equipment is expected to last 10 years. Yearly depreciation, therefore, is recorded and reported based on the expected life of the equipment. After six years of the expected 10-year life, the equipment's book value (cost less accumulated depreciation) is $13,200.00. If the business ended operations and the equipment had to be sold, the amount received may be less than the $13,200.00. However, accounting records are maintained with the expectation that the business will remain in operation indefinitely and that the cost will be allocated over the useful life of the equipment.

ACCOUNTING
IN YOUR CAREER

TECHNICAL OBSOLESCENCE

Tamara Thompson is the plant assets manager for Athex Systems, Inc., which designs and implements databases for corporate clients. The company is noted in the industry and the financial community for its integrity. Tamara heads a company committee that is studying the effect of the accounting methods used for plant assets on the company income statement and tax liability.

The fact-finding phase of the study has just been completed and several relevant facts have become evident. The company owns 10,000 individual microcomputer workstations, many costing more than $3,000 each. As many as 30% of these microcomputers are replaced each year. The straight-line depreciation method is used for these computers, and most of them have an estimated five-year life and $1,000 salvage value.

The committee met for a morning brainstorming session. One of the procedures of brainstorming is to list all ideas mentioned, even those that seem ridiculous or impossible at the time. Even the "wild" ideas sometimes result in effective, imaginative solutions to problems. After an exhaustive session of brainstorming, a final list of possible recommendations was compiled. All of the recommendations would result in increased depreciation expense being reported. The final list suggested: (1) using a three-year useful life for the microcomputers; (2) using an accelerated declining-balance depreciation method; and (3) using a zero salvage value and giving retired computers to employees for home use. The committee then suggested that Tamara discuss these recommendations with the controller before the committee writes its report.

Critical Thinking

1. What effect does the depreciation method have on net income? On corporate income tax?
2. How closely do the three recommendations presented match actual experiences with microcomputers?

PLANT ASSET RECORD

1. Complete when asset is purchased. **1**

2. Complete when asset is disposed of. **2**

3. Complete each year to record annual depreciation expense. **3**

PLANT ASSET RECORD, No. _72_	General Ledger Account No. _1225_
Description _Copying Machine_	General Ledger Account _Office Equipment_

Date Bought _January 2, 20--_	Serial Number _X3492D194_	Original Cost _$1,680.00_
Estimated Useful Life _5 years_	Estimated Salvage Value _$230.00_	Depreciation Method _Straight-Line_

Disposed of: Discarded _____ Sold _____ Traded _____
Date _____ Disposal Amount _____

YEAR	ANNUAL DEPRECIATION EXPENSE	ACCUMULATED DEPRECIATION	ENDING BOOK VALUE

Figure 8-1

A business keeps a separate record of each plant asset it owns. An accounting form on which a business records information about each plant asset is called a **plant asset record**. Appliance Center uses a printed card as its plant asset record as shown in Figure 8-1.

Appliance Center's plant asset record has three sections. Section 1 is prepared when the company buys a plant asset. Information in this section shows a description of the item, the general ledger account title and number, date bought, serial number, and information needed to calculate annual depreciation expense for the plant asset. Section 2 provides space for recording the disposition of the plant asset. Section 3 provides space for recording annual depreciation expense.

Calculating depreciation and disposing of plant assets are described later in this chapter.

S T E P S **Prepare a plant asset record**

1. When an asset is bought, enter the general information about the asset in the top section of the plant asset record.
2. The center section will be completed when the asset is discarded, sold, or traded.
3. At the end of each year, record the annual depreciation expense, the accumulated depreciation, and the ending book value.

REMEMBER

A building and the land it is located on are typically purchased together for a single price. Separate values must be assigned to each asset. If a sales contract does not specify separate amounts for the land and building, a professional appraisal may be used to determine separate amounts.

BUYING A PLANT ASSET FOR CASH

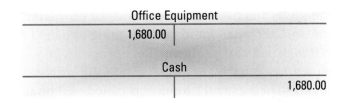

	DATE	ACCOUNT TITLE	CK. NO.	POST. REF.	GENERAL DEBIT	GENERAL CREDIT	ACCOUNTS PAYABLE DEBIT	PURCHASES DISCOUNT CREDIT	CASH CREDIT	
1	20-- Jan. 2	Office Equipment	62		1 6 8 0 00				1 6 8 0 00	1

CASH PAYMENTS JOURNAL — PAGE 1

Figure 8-2

Appliance Center needs a new copying machine. Because this plant asset is to be used in the office, it is classified as office equipment.

> **January 2. Paid cash for new copying machine, $1,680.00. Check No. 62.**

The entry is recorded in the cash payments journal as shown in Figure 8-2. Appliance Center has three kinds of plant assets: office equipment,

store equipment, and warehouse equipment. A separate general ledger account is used for each of these plant assets.

```
            Office Equipment
     1,680.00 |


                  Cash
                |          1,680.00
```

BUYING A PLANT ASSET ON ACCOUNT

	DATE	ACCOUNT TITLE	DOC. NO.	POST. REF.	DEBIT	CREDIT	
1	20-- Jan. 2	Office Equipment	M70		3 3 0 0 00		1
2		Accts. Pay./Discount Computers		/		3 3 0 0 00	2

GENERAL JOURNAL — PAGE 1

Figure 8-3

Not all plant assets are bought for cash. Appliance Center sometimes buys a plant asset on one date and pays for it on a later date.

> **January 2. Bought an office computer on account from Discount Computers, $3,300.00. Memorandum No. 70.**

This transaction does not involve the purchase of merchandise. Therefore, the entry is not recorded in a purchases journal. It is recorded in the general journal as shown in Figure 8-3. The entry is posted to both the general ledger and the accounts payable ledger.

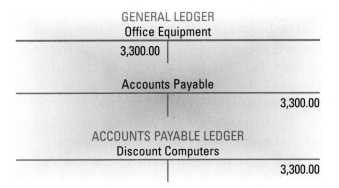

```
GENERAL LEDGER
Office Equipment
  3,300.00 |


Accounts Payable
          |          3,300.00


ACCOUNTS PAYABLE LEDGER
Discount Computers
          |          3,300.00
```

An office equipment business may sell such things as desks, chairs, file cabinets, and typewriters. These items are for sale to customers and are not used in the operation of the office equipment business. Therefore, equipment purchased to sell to customers is classified as merchandise rather than as plant assets.

CASH PAYMENTS JOURNAL										PAGE 23	
					1		2	3	4	5	
DATE		ACCOUNT TITLE	CK. NO.	POST. REF.	GENERAL			ACCOUNTS PAYABLE DEBIT	PURCHASES DISCOUNT CREDIT	CASH CREDIT	
					DEBIT		CREDIT				
1	Feb. 20-- 1	Property Tax Expense	122		3 2 5 0 00					3 2 5 0 00	1
2											2

Figure 8-4

In most states, businesses have to pay taxes on plant assets. For tax purposes, state and federal governments define two kinds of property: real and personal. Land and anything attached to it is called **real property**. Real property is sometimes referred to as real estate. All property not classified as real property is called **personal property**.

Assessed Value of Property

The value of an asset determined by tax authorities for the purpose of calculating taxes is called the **assessed value**. Assessed value is usually based on the judgment of persons referred to as assessors. Assessors are elected by citizens or are specially trained employees of a governmental unit.

An asset's assessed value may not be the same as the book value on the business' or individual's records. The assessed value is assigned to an asset for tax purposes only. Often the assessed value is only a part of the true value of the asset. However, many persons and businesses use the assessed value to estimate the market value of an asset.

Calculating Property Tax on Plant Assets

Most governmental units with taxing power have a tax based on the value of real property. The real property tax is used on buildings and land. Some governmental units also tax personal property such as cars, boats, trailers, and airplanes.

A governmental taxing unit determines a tax rate to use in calculating taxes. The tax rate is multiplied by an asset's *assessed* value, not the book value recorded on a business' records.

Appliance Center's buildings and land have been assessed for a total of $65,000.00. The city tax rate is 5%.

Assessed Value	×	Tax Rate	=	Annual Property Tax
$65,000.00	×	5%	=	$3,250.00

Paying Property Tax on Plant Assets

On February 1, Appliance Center paid its property tax as shown in Figure 8-4.

Feb 1. Paid cash for property tax, $3,250.00. Check No. 122.

Payment of property taxes is necessary if a firm is to continue in business. Therefore, Appliance Center classifies property tax as an operating expense.

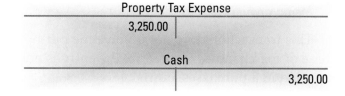

Property Tax Expense
3,250.00 |

Cash
| 3,250.00

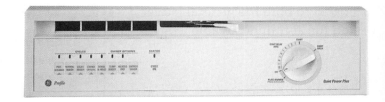

TERMS REVIEW

plant asset record
real property
personal property
assessed value

AUDIT YOUR UNDERSTANDING

1. What are the three sections of a plant asset record?
2. Why are asset purchases not recorded in a purchases journal?
3. What accounts are affected, and how, by an entry to pay property tax?

WORK TOGETHER

Journalizing asset purchase and property tax transactions

Depreciate all plant assets using the straight-line method. Plant asset records, a general journal, and a cash payments journal are provided in the *Working Papers*. Source documents are abbreviated as: check, C; memorandum, M. Your instructor will guide you through the following examples.

Jan. 3. Paid cash for scanner (plant asset no. 162), $600.00: no estimated salvage value; estimated useful life, three years; serial no. V2GR34. C310.

Jan. 5. Bought freight scale (plant asset no. 163) on account from Trent, Inc., $2,800.00: estimated salvage value, $400.00; estimated useful life, five years; serial no. GY52232B. M61.

Feb. 27. Paid property taxes on real property with an assessed value of $215,000.00. The tax rate in the city where the property is located is 3.5% of assessed value. C389.

4. Journalize the transactions completed during 20X1. General ledger accounts are: Office Equipment, 1225 and Warehouse Equipment, 1245.

5. Complete section 1 of a plant asset record for new asset purchases. Save your work to complete the Work Together on page 226.

ON YOUR OWN

Journalizing asset purchase and property tax transactions

Depreciate all plant assets using the straight-line method. Plant asset records, a general journal, and a cash payments journal are provided in the *Working Papers*. Source documents are abbreviated as: check, C; memorandum, M. Work independently to complete the following problem.

Jan. 2. Bought a cash register (plant asset no. 416) on account from JP Enterprises, $800.00: estimated salvage value, $200.00; estimated useful life, five years; serial no. G3HR644. M35.

Jan. 6. Paid cash for an office chair, (plant asset no. 417), $500.00: estimated salvage value, $10.00; estimated useful life, seven years; serial no. FB1523. C415.

Feb. 26. Paid property taxes on real property with an assessed value of $280,000.00. The tax rate in the city where the property is located is 4.2% of assessed value. C489.

6. Journalize the transactions completed during 20X1. General ledger accounts are: Office Equipment, 1225 and Store Equipment, 1235.

7. Complete section 1 of a plant asset record for new asset purchases. Save your work to complete the On Your Own on page 226.

FACTORS USED TO CALCULATE DEPRECIATION

Plant assets may wear out, may no longer be needed in the operation of a business, or may become outdated by new models. To match revenue with the expenses incurred to earn it, the cost of a plant asset should be allocated to an expense account over the useful life of the plant asset. (CONCEPT: *Matching Expenses with Revenue*) The portion of a plant asset's cost that is transferred to an expense account in each fiscal period during a plant asset's useful life is known as depreciation expense.

Because of its permanent nature, land is not subject to depreciation. Increases or decreases in land value are usually recorded only when land is sold or otherwise disposed of.

Three factors are used to calculate a plant asset's annual depreciation expense:

1. Original cost.

2. Estimated salvage value.

3. Estimated useful life.

Original Cost

The original cost of a plant asset includes all costs paid to make the asset usable to a business. These costs include the purchase price, delivery costs, and any necessary installation costs. (CONCEPT: *Historical Cost*)

Estimated Salvage Value

When a plant asset is disposed of, some part of its original value may remain. When a plant asset is bought, its final value can only be estimated. The estimated salvage value is the amount an owner expects to receive when a plant asset is removed from use. Salvage value is also referred to as residual value, scrap value, or trade-in value.

Until a plant asset is disposed of, most businesses have difficulty determining its *exact* salvage value. Thus, until actually disposed of, a plant asset's salvage value can only be *estimated*. Because salvage value is used to calculate a plant asset's annual depreciation, the most accurate estimate possible is made when a plant asset is bought.

Estimated Useful Life

The estimated useful life of a plant asset is the number of years it is expected to be useful to a business. A plant asset's useful life differs from one situation to another. Most businesses use past experience as the basis for estimating a plant asset's useful life. If a calculator usually lasts five years for a specific business, then the business uses five years as the estimated useful life of a new calculator. Sometimes, however, a business has difficulty estimating a plant asset's useful life. In these cases, it may use the Internal Revenue Service's guidelines that give the estimated useful life for many plant assets.

Depreciation Methods

Various depreciation methods are illustrated in this chapter. A business should select the depreciation method that provides the best financial information. A business typically uses the same depreciation method for all assets within a plant asset category.

REMEMBER

Two of the three values used to compute depreciation are estimates.

STRAIGHT-LINE DEPRECIATION

Plant asset: Computer
Depreciation method: Straight-line

Original cost: $2,000.00
Estimated salvage value: $175.00
Estimated useful life: 5 years

Year	Beginning Book Value	Annual Depreciation	Ending Book Value
1	$2,000.00	$ 365.00	$1,635.00
2	1,635.00	365.00	1,270.00
3	1,270.00	365.00	905.00
4	905.00	365.00	540.00
5	540.00	365.00	175.00
Total Depreciation	—	$1,825.00	—

Figure 8-5

Charging an equal amount of depreciation expense for a plant asset in each year of useful life is called the **straight-line method of depreciation**.

On January 2, 20X1, Appliance Center bought a computer for $2,000.00 with an estimated salvage value of $175.00 and an estimated useful life of five years. Figure 8-5 shows the details of the purchase and the depreciation amounts for each year of the asset's estimated useful life.

The estimated total depreciation expense is divided by the estimated useful life to compute the annual depreciation expense. The annual depreciation expense is the same for each year if the asset is used for the entire year.

−	Original Cost	$2,000.00
	Estimated Salvage Value	− 175.00
=	Estimated Total Depreciation Expense	$1,825.00
÷	Years of Estimated Useful Life	÷ 5
=	Annual Depreciation Expense	$ 365.00

The annual depreciation expense is subtracted from the beginning book value to compute the ending book value. The beginning book value for a year is the ending book value of the prior year.

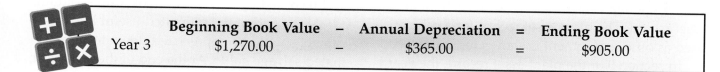

	Beginning Book Value	−	Annual Depreciation	=	Ending Book Value
Year 3	$1,270.00	−	$365.00	=	$905.00

Annual depreciation expense also may be calculated using an annual percentage rate. In the preceding example, the plant asset has an estimated useful life of five years. Therefore, the annual depreciation rate is 20% (100% divided by 5 equals .20, or 20%). Estimated total depreciation expense, $1,825.00, times depreciation rate, 20%, equals annual depreciation expense, $365.00.

1. Calculate annual depreciation expense.

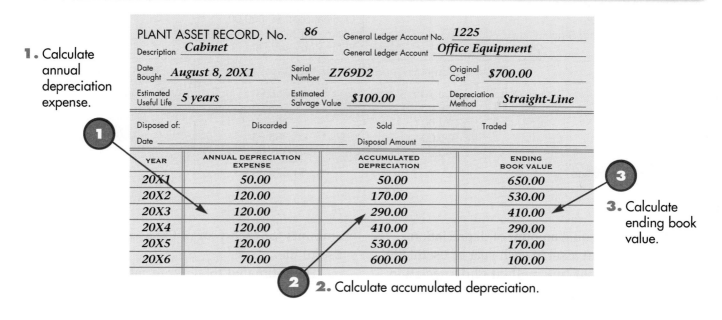

PLANT ASSET RECORD, No. _86_   **General Ledger Account No.** _1225_

Description _Cabinet_   **General Ledger Account** _Office Equipment_

Date Bought _August 8, 20X1_   **Serial Number** _Z769D2_   **Original Cost** _$700.00_

Estimated Useful Life _5 years_   **Estimated Salvage Value** _$100.00_   **Depreciation Method** _Straight-Line_

Disposed of: Discarded _____   Sold _____   Traded _____

Date _____   Disposal Amount _____

YEAR	ANNUAL DEPRECIATION EXPENSE	ACCUMULATED DEPRECIATION	ENDING BOOK VALUE
20X1	50.00	50.00	650.00
20X2	120.00	170.00	530.00
20X3	120.00	290.00	410.00
20X4	120.00	410.00	290.00
20X5	120.00	530.00	170.00
20X6	70.00	600.00	100.00

3. Calculate ending book value.

2. Calculate accumulated depreciation.

	20X3 Depreciation Expense	+	**20X2** Accumulated Depreciation	=	**20X3** Accumulated Depreciation
20X3	$120.00	+	$170.00	=	$290.00

	Original Cost	–	**Accumulated Depreciation**	=	**Ending Book Value**
20X3	$700.00	–	$290.00	=	$410.00

Figure 8-6

Appliance Center records annual depreciation expense in two places for each plant asset:

1. On the plant asset record.

2. As part of the adjusting entries that are posted to general ledger accounts.

On December 31, Appliance Center recorded the annual depreciation expense on each plant asset record. The plant asset record for a cabinet used as office equipment is shown in Figure 8-6.

In section 3 of the plant asset record, the year is recorded in the Year column. The depreciation expense for the plant asset is recorded in the Annual Depreciation Expense column. The amount recorded in the Annual Depreciation Expense column is $50.00, the depreciation expense for the months that the cabinet was used in 20X1. For a full year, the annual depreciation expense is $120.00. The amount of accumulated depreciation is recorded in the

Accumulated Depreciation column. The accumulated depreciation is the sum of the previous year's accumulated depreciation and the annual depreciation expense for the current year.

The original cost of a plant asset minus accumulated depreciation is called the **book value of a plant asset**. A new book value is calculated and recorded in the Ending Book Value column.

At the end of the estimated useful life, the cabinet should be depreciated down to its estimated salvage value. At the end of the sixth year, the ending book value is equal to the estimated salvage value, $100.00. The calculation for depreciation uses an *estimated* useful life. The cabinet's *actual* useful life may exceed the estimate made when the asset was put into use. If a plant asset is used longer than the estimated useful life, depreciation is *not* recorded once the book value equals the estimated salvage value.

	DATE	ACCOUNT TITLE	DOC. NO.	POST. REF.	DEBIT	CREDIT	
1		*Adjusting Entries*					1
22	31	*Depr. Exp.—Office Equipment*			11 5 7 1 00		22
23		*Accum. Depr.—Office Equipment*				11 5 7 1 00	23

GENERAL JOURNAL　　PAGE *13*

Figure 8-7

After depreciation expense is recorded on the plant asset records, depreciation amounts for the year are totaled.

An adjusting entry is made to record the total depreciation expense for the fiscal year for each category of plant assets. Appliance Center records separate adjusting entries for office equipment, store equipment, warehouse equipment, and building. The adjusting entry for office equipment is shown in Figure 8-7.

Depreciation Expense—Office Equipment

Dec. 31 Adj.	11,571.00	

Accumulated Depreciation—Office Equipment

	Jan. 1 Bal.	37,434.00
	Dec. 31 Adj.	11,571.00
	Dec. 31 Bal.	*49,005.00*

CALCULATING DEPRECIATION EXPENSE FOR PART OF A YEAR

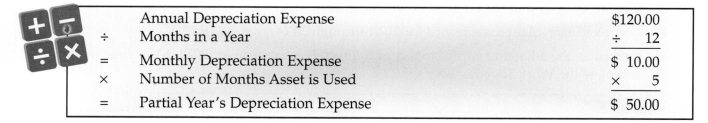

÷	Annual Depreciation Expense	$120.00
	Months in a Year	÷ 12
=	Monthly Depreciation Expense	$ 10.00
×	Number of Months Asset is Used	× 5
=	Partial Year's Depreciation Expense	$ 50.00

A calendar month is the smallest unit of time used to calculate depreciation. A plant asset may be placed in service at a date other than the first day of a fiscal period. In such cases, depreciation expense is calculated to the nearest first of a month. To calculate depreciation expense for part of a year, the annual depreciation expense is divided by 12 to determine depreciation expense for a month. The monthly depreciation is then multiplied by the number of months the plant asset was used that year.

Appliance Center bought a cabinet on August 8, 20X1. The annual straight-line depreciation expense is $120.00. The depreciation

expense for the part of the year that Appliance Center used the cabinet (August through December equals 5 months) is $50.00.

F.Y.I.

Calculating depreciation expense for part of a year also is used when a plant asset is discarded or sold during a fiscal year. The partial year's depreciation expense is computed for the period from the start of the fiscal year to the date the asset is discarded or sold.

straight-line method of
    depreciation
book value of a plant
    asset

UDIT YOUR
UNDERSTANDING

1. To match revenue with the expenses incurred to earn it, the cost of a plant asset should be allocated to an expense over what period of time?

2. Which accounting concept is being applied when depreciation expense is recorded for plant assets?

3. Why is annual depreciation for land not recorded?

4. What three factors are used to calculate a plant asset's annual depreciation expense?

5. What is the smallest unit of time used to calculate depreciation?

ORK
TOGETHER

Calculating and journalizing depreciation

Use the plant asset records from the Work Together on page 221. Depreciation tables and a general journal are provided in the *Working Papers*. Your instructor will guide you through the following examples.

6. Complete the depreciation table for each asset using the straight-line depreciation method. If the asset was not purchased at the beginning of 20X1, compute the depreciation expense for the part of 20X1 that the company owned the asset.

7. Complete each plant asset record for 20X1 through 20X4.

8. Journalize the adjusting entries to record depreciation expense for 20X1. Save your work to complete the Work Together on page 233.

N YOUR
OWN

Calculating and journalizing depreciation

Use the plant asset records from the On Your Own on page 221. Depreciation tables and a general journal are provided in the *Working Papers*. Work this problem independently.

9. Complete the depreciation table for each asset using the straight-line depreciation method. If the asset was not purchased at the beginning of 20X1, compute the depreciation expense for the part of 20X1 that the company owned the asset.

10. Complete each plant asset record for 20X1 through 20X4.

11. Journalize the adjusting entries to record depreciation expense for 20X1. Save your work to complete the On Your Own on page 233.

8-3 Disposing of Plant Assets

DISCARDING A PLANT ASSET WITH NO BOOK VALUE

1. Record entry to remove plant asset from accounts. **(1)**

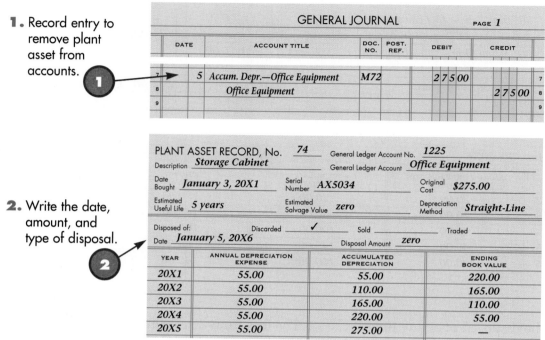

2. Write the date, amount, and type of disposal. **(2)**

Figure 8-8

Appliance Center usually disposes of plant assets in one of three ways:

1. The plant asset is discarded because no useful life remains.

2. The plant asset is sold because it is no longer needed even though it might still be usable.

3. The plant asset is traded for another plant asset of the same kind.

If a plant asset has a salvage value of zero and its total accumulated depreciation is equal to the original cost value, the plant asset has no book value. When a plant asset with no book value is discarded, a journal entry is recorded that removes the original cost of the plant asset and its related accumulated depreciation as shown in Figure 8-8.

January 5, 20X6. Discarded storage cabinet: original cost, $275.00; total accumulated depreciation through December 31, 20X5, $275.00. Memorandum No. 72.

Accumulated Depreciation—Office Equipment	
275.00	Bal. 275.00

Office Equipment	
Bal. 275.00	275.00

(S) **Discarding a plant asset with no book value**

(T) **1.** Record an entry on the general journal to remove the original cost, *275.00*, from Office Equipment and Accumulated Depreciation—Office Equipment. When this entry is posted, all amounts for the discarded cabinet are removed from the two accounts.

(E) **2.** Check the type of disposal, *Discarded*, and write the date, *Jan. 5, 20X6*, and disposal amount, *zero*, on the plant asset record. These notations complete the history of the plant asset.

(P)

(S)

1. Record a partial year's depreciation expense.

GENERAL JOURNAL   PAGE 6

	DATE	ACCOUNT TITLE	DOC. NO.	POST. REF.	DEBIT	CREDIT	
4	30	Depr. Exp.—Office Equipment	M92		20 00		4
5		Accum. Depr.—Office Equipment				20 00	5
6	30	Accum. Depr.—Office Equipment	M92		1 60 00		6
7		Loss on Plant Assets			40 00		7
8		Office Equipment				2 00 00	8
9							9

3. Write the date, amount, and type of disposal.

2. Record the partial year's depreciation.

Disposed of: Discarded ✓   Sold _____   Traded _____

Date **June 30, 20X6**   Disposal Amount **zero**

YEAR	ANNUAL DEPRECIATION EXPENSE	ACCUMULATED DEPRECIATION	ENDING BOOK VALUE
20X2	20.00	20.00	180.00
20X3	40.00	60.00	140.00
20X4	40.00	100.00	100.00
20X5	40.00	140.00	60.00
20X6	20.00	160.00	40.00

4. Record entry to remove plant asset from accounts.

Figure 8-9

A plant asset may be disposed of at any time during its useful life. When a plant asset is disposed of, its depreciation expense from the beginning of the current fiscal year to the date of disposal is recorded as shown in Figure 8-9.

When an asset with a book value is discarded, a journal entry is recorded to: (1) Remove the original cost of the plant asset and its related accumulated depreciation. (2) Recognize the loss on disposal of the asset.

June 30, 20X6. Discarded office table: original cost, $200.00; total accumulated depreciation through December 31, 20X5, $140.00; additional depreciation to be recorded through June 30, 20X6, $20.00. Memorandum No. 92.

The loss from discarding a plant asset with a book value is equal to the asset's book value. The loss is not an operating expense. Therefore, **Loss on Plant Assets** is classified as an Other Expense.

Depreciation Expense—Office Equipment

Add. Depr.	20.00		

Accumulated Depreciation—Office Equipment

		Bal.	140.00
Disposal	160.00	Add. Depr.	20.00

Loss on Plant Assets

Disposal	40.00		

Office Equipment

Bal.	200.00	Disposal	200.00

S T E P S   **Discarding an asset with a book value**

1. Record a partial year's depreciation expense, *20.00*, by debiting Depreciation Expense—Office Equipment and crediting Accumulated Depreciation—Office Equipment.

2. Record the depreciation in section 3 of the plant asset record.

3. Check the type of disposal, *Discarded*, and write the date, *June 30, 20X6*, and the disposal amount, *zero*, on the plant asset record. These notations complete the history of the plant asset.

4. Record an entry to remove the original cost, *200.00*, from Office Equipment and *160.00* from Accumulated Depreciation—Office Equipment. Record the loss on disposal, *40.00*, as a debit to Loss on Plant Assets.

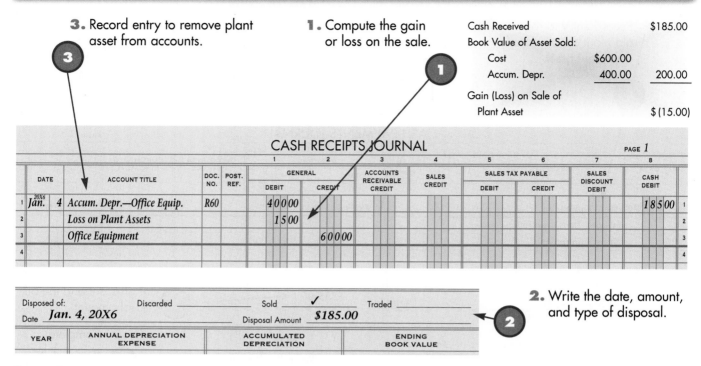

3. Record entry to remove plant asset from accounts.

1. Compute the gain or loss on the sale.

Cash Received		$185.00
Book Value of Asset Sold:		
Cost	$600.00	
Accum. Depr.	400.00	200.00
Gain (Loss) on Sale of Plant Asset		$ (15.00)

CASH RECEIPTS JOURNAL   PAGE 1

					1	2	3	4	5	6	7	8
	DATE	ACCOUNT TITLE	DOC. NO.	POST. REF.	GENERAL DEBIT	GENERAL CREDIT	ACCOUNTS RECEIVABLE CREDIT	SALES CREDIT	SALES TAX PAYABLE DEBIT	SALES TAX PAYABLE CREDIT	SALES DISCOUNT DEBIT	CASH DEBIT
1	20X6 Jan. 4	Accum. Depr.—Office Equip.	R60		400 00							185 00	1
2		Loss on Plant Assets			15 00								2
3		Office Equipment				600 00							3
4													4

2. Write the date, amount, and type of disposal.

Disposed of:	Discarded _____	Sold ✓	Traded _____
Date **Jan. 4, 20X6**		Disposal Amount **$185.00**	

YEAR	ANNUAL DEPRECIATION EXPENSE	ACCUMULATED DEPRECIATION	ENDING BOOK VALUE

Figure 8-10

When a plant asset is sold, a journal entry is recorded to:

1. Remove the original cost of the plant asset and its related accumulated depreciation.

2. Recognize the cash received.

3. Recognize the gain or loss on disposal of the asset.

> *January 4, 20X6. Received cash from sale of fax machine, $185.00: original cost, $600.00; total accumulated depreciation through December 31, 20X5, $400.00. Receipt No. 60.*

S **Selling a plant asset**

T **1.** Compute the gain or loss, *15.00 loss*, by subtracting the book value of the asset, *200.00*, from the cash received, *185.00*.

E **2.** Check the type of disposal, *Sold*, and write the date, *January 4, 20X6*, and the disposal amount,

P $185.00, on the plant asset record. These notations complete the history of the plant asset.

S **3.** Record an entry on the cash receipts journal to remove the original cost, *600.00*, from Office Equipment and *400.00* from Accumulated Depreciation—Office Equipment. Record the loss on sale, *15.00*, as a debit to Loss on Plant Assets.

The amount of gain or loss is calculated by subtracting the book value from the cash received. The $15.00 loss on disposal is recorded as a debit to **Loss on Plant Assets** as shown in Figure 8-10.

The sale of plant assets is not a normal operating activity of Appliance Center. A loss from the sale of plant assets is classified as Other Expense.

Cash	
185.00	

Accumulated Depreciation—Office Equipment	
	400.00 Bal. 400.00

Loss on Plant Assets	
15.00	

Office Equipment	
Bal. 600.00	600.00

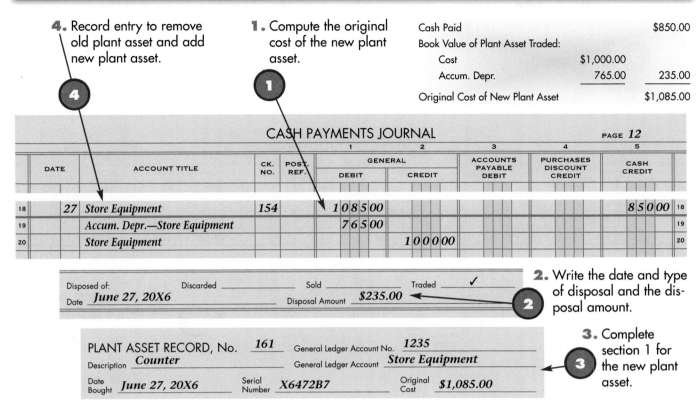

4. Record entry to remove old plant asset and add new plant asset.

1. Compute the original cost of the new plant asset.

Cash Paid		$850.00
Book Value of Plant Asset Traded:		
Cost	$1,000.00	
Accum. Depr.	765.00	235.00
Original Cost of New Plant Asset		$1,085.00

CASH PAYMENTS JOURNAL

PAGE 12

	DATE	ACCOUNT TITLE	CK. NO.	POST. REF.	GENERAL DEBIT	GENERAL CREDIT	ACCOUNTS PAYABLE DEBIT	PURCHASES DISCOUNT CREDIT	CASH CREDIT	
18	27	Store Equipment	154		1 0 8 5 00				8 5 0 00	18
19		Accum. Depr.—Store Equipment			7 6 5 00					19
20		Store Equipment				1 0 0 0 00				20

Disposed of: Discarded _____ Sold _____ Traded ✓
Date **June 27, 20X6** _____ Disposal Amount **$235.00**

2. Write the date and type of disposal and the disposal amount.

PLANT ASSET RECORD, No. **161** General Ledger Account No. **1235**
Description **Counter** General Ledger Account **Store Equipment**
Date Bought **June 27, 20X6** Serial Number **X6472B7** Original Cost **$1,085.00**

3. Complete section 1 for the new plant asset.

Figure 8-11

Appliance Center needed a new store counter. The vendor agreed to take cash and an old store counter in trade. The new plant asset's original cost equals the cash *actually* paid plus the book value of the asset traded. (*CONCEPT: Historical Cost*)

When an old plant asset is traded for a new plant asset, the journal entry:

1. Removes the original cost of the old plant asset and its related accumulated depreciation.

2. Recognizes the cash paid.

3. Records the new plant asset at its original cost.

June 27, 20X6. Paid cash, $850.00, plus old counter for new store counter: original cost of old counter, $1,000.00; total accumulated depreciation through June 27, 20X6, $765.00. Memorandum No. 130 and Check No. 154.

Store Equipment			
Bal.	1,000.00	Trade-in	1,000.00
New Equip.	1,085.00		

Accumulated Depreciation—Store Equipment			
	765.00	Bal.	765.00

Cash			
			850.00

S Trading a plant asset

T **1.** Compute the original cost of the new asset, *$1,085.00*, by adding the book value of the asset traded, *$235.00*, and the cash paid, *$850.00*.

E **2.** Check the type of disposal, *Traded*, and write the date, *June 27, 20X6*, and the disposal amount, *$235.00*, on the plant asset record of the traded asset.

P **3.** Complete section 1 of the plant asset record for the new asset.

S **4.** Record the journal entry to reflect the trade of plant assets.

2. Write the date, type, and amount of disposal.

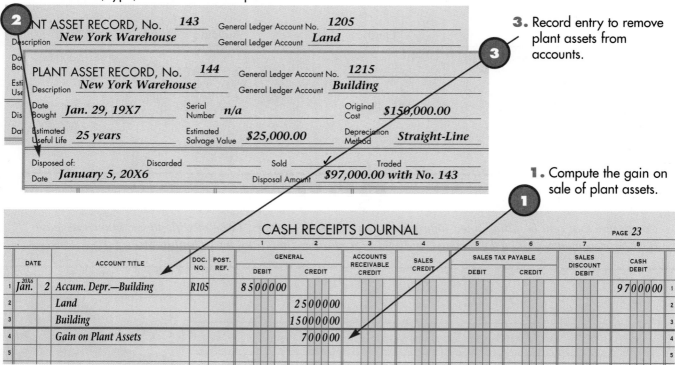

3. Record entry to remove plant assets from accounts.

1. Compute the gain on sale of plant assets.

Figure 8-12

Land is considered to be a permanent plant asset. Therefore, its useful life is not estimated, and annual depreciation is not recorded for it. The book value of land is the original cost. (*CONCEPT: Historical Cost*)

Land is seldom discarded (abandoned). Usually land is sold at the same time that the buildings on it are sold. Figure 8-12 indicates that a separate plant record is maintained for the land and the building. Each record is updated when a sale is made.

January 2, 20X6. Fidelity Company sold land with a building for $97,000.00 cash; original

cost of land, $25,000.00; original cost of building, $150,000.00; total accumulated depreciation on building through December 31, 20X5, $85,000.00. Receipt No. 105.

The journal entry:

1. Removes the original cost of the land and building and the building's related accumulated depreciation.

2. Recognizes the cash received.

3. Recognizes the gain on disposal of the plant assets.

S T E P S Selling land and buildings

1. Compute the gain on the sale of plant assets, *$7,000.00*, by subtracting the book value of the land and buildings, *$90,000.00*, from the cash received, *$97,000.00*.

2. Check the type of disposal, *Sold*, and write the date, *Jan. 2, 20X6*, and the disposal amount, *$97,000.00*, on each plant asset record. Include a reference to the other plant asset included in the sale.

3. Record an entry on the cash receipts journal to remove the original cost of land, *25,000.00*, and buildings, *150,000.00*, and to remove *85,000.00* from Accumulated Depreciation—Building. Record the gain on sale, *7,000.00*, as a credit to Gain on Plant Assets.

The amount of the gain is the cash received less the book value of the assets sold.

	Land	Building	Total
Cash Received			$97,000.00
Cost of Assets	$25,000.00	$150,000.00	
Accumulated Depreciation		85,000.00	
Book Values of Assets Sold	25,000.00	65,000.00	90,000.00
Gain on Sale of Plant Assets			$ 7,000.00

F. Y. I.

Companies that rent buildings often improve and modify their interiors. These modifications, known as lease-hold improvements, can be depreciated and sold in a manner similar to other plant assets.

MICHAEL C. FASSINO, CPA

ACCOUNTING AT WORK

You remember the story of the elephant and everybody touching the elephant in a different place? And each had a different idea of what the elephant looked like? In business, each department has its own view of its importance in the operation.

Sales says, "If we didn't sell it, you wouldn't be able to make it." Manufacturing says, "If we didn't make it, you wouldn't have anything to sell." What the accountant says is, "If we didn't measure performance, nobody would know what they were doing or what the business was doing."

Numbers are the language of business.

I was a Marine Corps officer with a history degree. Served in Viet Nam. The only jobs I could get when I came out were as a shift supervisor or foreman.

I looked into grad school and saw an opening for a graduate assistant.

I needed that stipend, so I planned to interview in several areas. The only guy in the office was about my dad's age, dressed casually, friendly, outgoing. I was very impressed by him.

He said to me, "I'll bet you can't tell what I do here, can you?" I didn't know. "I'm the chairman of the accounting department."

Wow. He didn't look like what I thought accountants looked like. He had his Ph.D. and CPA, and was a great teacher.

He showed me that the modern accountant is not a mere "numbers cruncher." Some people see only a page of numbers; an accountant can look at those numbers and see trends, can see where the business is going, can see the future. Accounting lets you see the bigger picture, and discover where something may need fixed while there's still time.

AUDIT YOUR UNDERSTANDING

1. What is recorded on a plant asset record for a plant asset that has been discarded?

2. When an asset is disposed of after the beginning of the fiscal year, what entry may need to be recorded before an entry is made for a discarded plant asset?

3. What is the formula to compute the gain or loss on the sale of a plant asset?

4. When cash is paid and old store equipment is traded for new store equipment, what is the formula for calculating the new equipment's original cost?

WORK TOGETHER

Recording the disposal of plant assets

Use the plant asset records from the Work Together on page 226. The following transactions occurred in 20X5. A general journal, cash receipts journal, and plant asset records are provided in the *Working Papers*. Source documents are abbreviated as follows: check, C; memorandum, M; receipt, R. Your instructor will guide you through the following examples.

Jan.	3.	Discarded scanner, no. 162. M65.
Mar.	30.	Received cash for sale of freight scale, no.163, $600.00. M125 and R145.
June	26.	Received cash for sale of a desk, no. 127, $500.00. M151 and R273.
Dec.	28.	Paid cash, $30,000.00, plus old truck, no. 116, for new truck, no. 172. M222 and C671.
Dec.	30.	Sold land, no. 105, and a building, no.106, for $110,000.00. M224 and R663.

5. Journalize additional depreciation, if needed. Journalize the disposal of each plant asset.

6. Make appropriate notations in the plant asset records.

ON YOUR OWN

Recording the disposal of plant assets

Use the plant asset records from the Work Together on page 226. The following transactions occurred in 20X5. A general journal, cash receipts journal, and plant asset records are provided in the *Working Papers*. Source documents are abbreviated as follows: check, C; memorandum, M; receipt, R. Work this problem independently.

Jan.	4.	Discarded office chair, no. 417. M5.
May	28.	Received cash for sale of cash register, no. 416, $100.00. M52 and R243.
June	30.	Sold land, no. 390, and a building, no. 391, for $106,000.00. M63 and R283.
Oct.	2.	Discarded office file cabinet, no. 369. M121.
Dec.	29.	Paid cash, $1,200.00, plus old computer, no. 428, for new computer, no. 439. M153 and C775.

7. Journalize additional depreciation, if needed. Journalize the disposal of each plant asset.

8. Make appropriate notations in the plant asset records.

DECLINING-BALANCE METHOD OF DEPRECIATION

	Total Depreciation Expense	100%
÷	Estimated Useful Life	÷ 5 years
=	Straight-Line Rate	20%
×	Double the Rate	× 2
=	Declining-Balance Rate	40%

1. Calculate the declining-balance rate.

1

Plant asset: Computer
Depreciation method: Declining balance

Original cost: $2,000.00
Estimated salvage value: $175.00
Estimated useful life: 5 years

Year	Beginning Book Value	Declining-Balance Rate	Annual Depreciation	Ending Book Value
1	$2,000.00	40%	$ 800.00	$1,200.00
2	1,200.00	40%	480.00	720.00
3	720.00	40%	288.00	432.00
4	432.00	40%	172.80	259.20
5	259.20	40%	84.20	175.00
Total Depreciation		—	$1,825.00	—

2

	Beginning Book Value	×	Depreciation Rate	=	Annual Depreciation Expense
Year 3	$720.00	×	40%	=	$288.00

2. Calculate the annual depreciation.

Figure 8-13

Many plant assets depreciate more in the early years of useful life than in the later years. Charging more depreciation expense in the early years of a plant asset may be more accurate than charging the same amount each year.

Multiplying the book value at the end of each fiscal period by a constant depreciation rate is called the **declining-balance method of depreciation**. Although the depreciation rate is the same each year, the annual depreciation expense declines from year to year as shown in Figure 8-13.

The declining-balance depreciation rate is based on the straight-line rate. A declining-balance rate that is twice the straight-line rate is commonly used. This method of depreciation is referred to as the double declining-balance method. For example, a plant asset with an estimated useful life of five years would have a depreciation rate of 40%.

When using the declining-balance method, the annual depreciation expense is calculated using the beginning book value for each year. The beginning book value is the same as the ending book value from the previous year. In the asset's first year of service, the beginning book value equals its original cost.

A plant asset is never depreciated below its estimated salvage value. Therefore, in the last year, only enough depreciation expense is recorded to reduce the book value of the plant asset to its salvage value. Thus, the depreciation expense in the fifth year is limited to $84.20 ($259.20 – $175.00).

REMEMBER

The declining-balance method does not use the estimated salvage value to compute annual depreciation. The estimated salvage value is used only to limit the last year's depreciation expense.

Years' Digits	Fraction
1	5/15
2	4/15
3	3/15
4	2/15
5	1/15
Total	15

1. Calculate the fraction.

Plant asset: Computer
Depreciation method: Sum-of-the-years-digits

Original cost: $2,000.00
Estimated salvage value: $175.00
Estimated useful life: 5 years

Year	Beginning Book Value	Fraction	Total Depreciation	Annual Depreciation	Ending Book Value
1	$2,000.00	5/15	$1,825.00	$ 608.33	$1,391.67
2	1,391.67	4/15	$1,825.00	486.67	905.00
3	905.00	3/15	$1,825.00	365.00	540.00
4	540.00	2/15	$1,825.00	243.33	296.67
5	296.67	1/15	$1,825.00	121.67	175.00
Total Depreciation				$1,825.00	

Original Cost	$2,000.00
Estimated Salvage Value	− 175.00
Estimated Total Depreciation Expense	$1,825.00
Year's Fraction	× 5/15
Annual Depreciation Expense	$608.33

2. Calculate the annual depreciation.

Figure 8-14

Another method of calculating depreciation is based on a fraction derived from the years' digits for the useful life of a plant asset. Using fractions based on the number of years of a plant asset's useful life is called the **sum-of-the-years-digits method of depreciation**.

The fractions are determined as follows: The years' digits are added (1 + 2 + 3 + 4 + 5 = 15). Then, using the sum of the years' digits, a fraction is created for each year with the years' digits in reverse order. Year 1 has a fraction of 5/15. Year 5 has a fraction of 1/15.

The depreciation expense for each year is calculated by multiplying the total depreciation expense times the fraction for that year.

The sum-of-the-years-digits method results in a last year ending book value equal to the plant asset's salvage value as shown in Figure 8-14.

F Y I

A company can select any generally accepted depreciation method. Once it has selected a method, however, the company cannot change the method unless it can show that the new method would better report the company's financial activities.

REMEMBER

Like the straight-line method, the estimated salvage value is subtracted from the original cost to compute an estimated total depreciation expense. Thus, the estimated salvage value is used to compute each year's annual depreciation expense.

COMPARISON OF THREE METHODS OF DEPRECIATION

Plant asset: Computer
Depreciation method: Comparison

Original cost: $2,000.00
Estimated salvage value: $175.00
Estimated useful life: 5 years

Year	Straight-Line Method	Double Declining-Balance Method	Sum-of-the-Years-Digits Method
1	$ 365.00	$ 800.00	$ 608.33
2	365.00	480.00	486.67
3	365.00	288.00	365.00
4	365.00	172.80	243.33
5	365.00	84.20	121.67
Total Depreciation	$1,825.00	$1,825.00	$1,825.00

Figure 8-15

Regardless of the depreciation method used, the total depreciation expense over the useful life of an asset is the same as that shown in Figure 8-15.

Each of these depreciation methods conforms to generally accepted accounting principles. The straight-line method is easy to calculate. The same amount of depreciation expense is recorded for each of the five years of estimated life.

The double declining-balance method is relatively easy to calculate. This method records a larger depreciation expense in the early years than the straight-line method does.

The sum-of-the-years-digits method is not as easy to use as the straight-line or declining-balance methods. This method also records a higher depreciation expense in the early years than the straight-line method does. Both the declining-balance method and the sum-of-the-years-digits method are known as accelerated depreciation methods.

SPREADSHEET ACTIVITY—DEPRECIATION SCHEDULE

B riarwood Center, an executive conference center, uses a spreadsheet to calculate depreciation. The following information is available for a high-volume photocopy machine:

Original cost	$22,700
Estimated salvage value	$4,500
Estimated useful life, in years	5

Required:

1. Create a depreciation schedule spreadsheet. Use Figure 8-5 as a model. Write formulas to calculate annual depreciation, ending book value, and total depreciation.
2. Make copies of the spreadsheet you created in 1 to calculate the depreciation for the display equipment. Use the information below.

Original cost	$6,800
Estimated salvage value	$1,200
Estimated useful life, in years	3

TECHNOLOGY FOR BUSINESS

PRODUCTION-UNIT METHOD OF DEPRECIATION

	Original cost	$18,200.00
−	Estimated Salvage Value	− 2,000.00
=	Estimated Total Depreciation Expense	$16,200.00
÷	Estimated Useful Life	÷ 90,000 miles
=	Depreciation Rate	$0.18/mile

1. Calculate the depreciation rate.

Plant asset: Truck
Depreciation method: Production-unit
Original cost: $18,200.00
Estimated salvage value: $2,000.00

Estimated total depreciation: $16,200.00
Estimated useful life: 90,000 miles
Depreciation rate: $0.18 per mile driven

Year	Beginning Book Value	Miles Driven	Annual Depreciation	Ending Book Value
1	$18,200.00	9,000	$ 1,620.00	$16,580.00
2	16,580.00	23,000	4,140.00	12,440.00
3	12,440.00	25,000	4,500.00	7,940.00
4	7,940.00	22,000	3,960.00	3,980.00
5	3,980.00	8,000	1,440.00	2,540.00
Totals		87,000	$15,660.00	

2. Calculate the annual depreciation.

	Total Miles Driven	×	Depreciation Rate	=	Annual Depreciation Expense
Year 1	9,000	×	$0.18	=	$1,620.00

Figure 8-16

Sometimes the useful life of a plant asset depends on how much the asset is used. For example, an automobile will wear out faster if it is driven 80,000 miles a year rather than 60,000 miles. Calculating estimated annual depreciation expense based on the amount of production expected from a plant asset is called the **production-unit method of depreciation**.

Mariah Delivery Service owns a small truck. The truck originally cost $18,200.00, and had an estimated salvage value of $2,000.00 and an estimated useful life of 90,000 miles. The depreciation rate for the truck is calculated by dividing the estimated total depreciation expense by the estimated useful life.

Depreciation expense for each year of the truck's estimated useful life is calculated at 18 cents per mile driven. The annual depreciation expense for the truck is calculated by multiplying the total number of miles driven by the depreciation rate. After five years, $15,660.00 of depreciation has been expensed, as shown in Figure 8-16. Additional depreciation expense will be recorded in future years as the truck approaches its 90,000 miles of useful life.

Although relatively easy to compute, the production-units method of depreciation significantly increases the work required to compute depreciation. The company must collect the production units for each asset. For large companies with many locations, the collection of this information can be a difficult task.

REMEMBER

The accounts used to record depreciation expense are the same regardless of the depreciation method used.

Plant asset: Printer	Original cost: $2,000.00	
Depreciation method: MACRS	Property class: 5 year	

Year	Depreciation Rate	Annual Depreciation
1	20.00%	$400.00
2	32.00%	640.00
3	19.20%	384.00
4	11.52%	230.40
5	11.52%	230.40
6	5.76%	115.20
Totals	100.00%	$2,000.00

Figure 8-17

Most businesses use one of the generally accepted accounting methods to calculate depreciation for financial reporting purposes. A depreciation method required by the Internal Revenue Service to be used for income tax calculation purposes for most plant assets placed in service after 1986 is called the **Modified Accelerated Cost Recovery System**. This depreciation system is generally referred to as MACRS, the initials of its full name.

MACRS is a depreciation method with prescribed periods for nine classes of useful life for plant assets. A property is assigned to a specified class based on its characteristics and general life expectancy. The two most common classes, other than real estate, are the five-year and the seven-year property classes. The five-year property class includes cars, general-purpose trucks, computers, manufacturing equipment, and office machinery. The seven-year property class includes office furniture and fixtures. The depreciation for these two property classes approximates the use of the double declining-balance method.

To calculate depreciation using MACRS, the Internal Revenue Service has prescribed methods that use annual percentage rates to determine depreciation for each class of plant asset. These rates are applied to the total cost of the plant asset without considering a salvage value. All plant assets are assumed to be placed in service in the middle of the year and taken out of service in the middle of the year. For example, the five-year property class depreciation is spread over six years, as shown in Figure 8-17.

Annual depreciation is calculated by multiplying the plant asset's original cost times the depreciation rate for its specific class. A printer is classified as five-year property.

	Original Cost	×	Depreciation Rate	=	Annual Depreciation Expense
Year 3	$2,000.00	×	19.20%	=	$384.00

	Original Cost	$100,000.00
−	Estimated Salvage Value	− $12,250.00
=	Estimated Total Value of Coal	$87,750.00
÷	Estimated Tons of Recoverable Coal	÷ 50,000
=	Depletion Rate per Ton of Coal	$1.755

1. Calculate the depletion rate.

Plant asset: Coal mine
Depletion method: Production-unit
Original cost: $100,000.00
Estimated salvage value: $12,250.00

Estimated total depletion: $87,750.00
Estimated tons of recoverable coal: 50,000 tons
Depletion rate: $1.755 per ton

Year	Beginning Book Value	Tons Recovered	Annual Depletion	Ending Book Value
1	$100,000.00	6,000	$10,530.00	$89,470.00
2	89,470.00	12,000	21,060.00	68,410.00
3	68,410.00	13,000	22,815.00	45,595.00
4	45,595.00	9,000	15,795.00	29,800.00
5	29,800.00	6,000	10,530.00	19,270.00
Totals		46,000	$80,730.00	

Tons of Coal Removed	×	Depletion Rate	=	Annual Depletion Expense
Year 1 6,000	×	$1.755	=	$10,530.00

2. Calculate the annual depletion.

Figure 8-18

Some plant assets decrease in value because part of these plant assets is physically removed in the operation of a business. For example, a lumber business owns land on which many trees grow. The business removes the trees to use for lumber. The land with the trees still growing on it is more valuable than the land from which the trees have been removed. The decrease in the value of a plant asset because of the removal of a natural resource is called **depletion**.

McGladden Company owns land on which a coal mine is located. The land with the coal has an original cost of $100,000.00. The company's experts estimate that the land contains 50,000 tons of recoverable coal. The estimated value of the remaining land after the coal is removed is $12,250.00. Therefore, each ton of coal taken

from the land decreases the land's value by $1.755.

In the first year of operation, the business removed 6,000 tons of coal. The depletion expense for the first year is $10,530.00 as shown in Figure 8-18. McGladden uses the general ledger accounts Mine, Accumulated Depletion—Mine, and Depletion Expense—Mine to record depletion.

F.Y.I.

Depletion is used to charge the cost of a variety of natural resources, including oil, gas, coal, gravel, minerals, and timber.

REMEMBER

The method used to compute depletion is the same as the production-unit method of depreciation. A rate per unit of production is multiplied by the amount of production to compute depletion.

 **TERMS REVIEW**

declining-balance method
of depreciation

sum-of-the-years-digits
method of depreciation

production-unit method
of depreciation

Modified Accelerated
Cost Recovery System

depletion

 **AUDIT YOUR UNDERSTANDING**

1. Which depreciation method does not use the estimated salvage value to compute annual depreciation?

2. What is the basis for the production-unit method of calculating depreciation?

3. How does a mining company calculate the amount of depletion for a year?

 **WORK TOGETHER**

Computing depreciation using various depreciation methods and calculating depletion

The following information relates to a delivery truck purchased on January 2, 20X1. Depreciation tables are provided in the *Working Papers*. Your instructor will guide you through the following examples.

		Miles Driven	
Original Cost	$90,000.00	20X1	34,600
Estimated Salvage Value	$6,000.00	20X2	47,300
Estimated Useful Life	3 years or 200,000 miles	20X3	52,800
MACRS Property Class	5-year	20X4	36,900

4. Complete depreciation tables showing depreciation expense calculated using the double declining-balance, sum-of-the-years-digits, production-unit, and MACRS methods of depreciation.

The following data relate to a mineral mine owned by Kellogg, Inc. A depletion table is provided in the *Working Papers*.

		Tons Mined	
Original Cost	$260,000.00	20X1	3,500
Estimated Salvage Value	$60,000.00	20X2	12,500
Estimated Tons of Recoverable Minerals	60,000 tons	20X3	15,600

5. Complete a table showing depletion expense calculated using the production-unit method.

ON YOUR OWN

Computing depreciation using various depreciation methods and calculating depletion

The following information relates to a machine purchased on January 3, 20X1. Work independently to complete the following problem.

		Year	Hours
Original Cost	$13,500.00	20X1	600
Estimated Salvage Value	$1,500.00	20X2	1,200
Estimated Useful Life	5 years or 5,000 hours	20X3	900
MACRS Property Class	5 year	20X4	1,000
		20X5	800

6. Complete tables showing depreciation expense calculated using the double declining-balance, sum-of-the-years-digits, production-unit, and MACRS methods of depreciation.

The following data relate to a gas well owned by JH Enterprises.

		Year	MCF Recovered
Original Cost	$920,000.00	20X1	30,000
Estimated Salvage Value	$20,000.00	20X2	90,000
Estimated MCF of Recoverable Gas	600,000 MCF	20X3	100,000
		20X4	120,000

7. Complete a depletion table for this well; show depletion expense calculated using the production-unit method.

CAUGHT IN THE MIDDLE

PROFESSIONAL BUSINESS ETHICS

As an employee, there are times when you must decide whether to do what you are told or do what you think is right. There are many situations where you can end up "caught in the middle."

Required:

Use the three-step checklist to help determine whether the actions of the people in the following situations demonstrate ethical behavior.

Situation 1. Quest Video is under contract with the federal government to produce training videos for the Environmental Protection Agency. The contract entitles Quest Video to charge its cost plus 15 percent. A government document specifically out-lines which expenditures qualify as "contract costs." Company picnics do not qualify as a contract expense, salaries do. After the annual company picnic, the company president told Jared Stern, who is a CPA, to record the expenditure as a salary expense.

Situation 2. Naomi Grant recently started working in the accounting department of a small manufacturing firm. When she tries to record the payment of premiums for flood insurance she realizes that the chart of accounts does not include an account for prepaid flood insurance. Her supervisor, a CPA, told her to record the premium as an expense and said, "That's the way we have always done it."

CHAPTER 8 SUMMARY

After completing this chapter, you can

1. Define accounting terms related to plant assets and depreciation.
2. Identify accounting concepts and practices related to accounting for plant assets
3. Journalize entries for buying plant assets.
4. Calculate and record property tax expense.
5. Calculate and record depreciation expense for a plant asset using straight-line depreciation.
6. Journalize entries for disposing of plant assets.
7. Calculate depreciation expense using other methods.

EXPLORE ACCOUNTING

TAX LAWS ENCOURAGE PLANT ASSETS PURCHASES

Tax law and generally accepted accounting principles (GAAP) often have conflicting objectives. Tax law is enacted to generate tax revenues. In contrast, GAAP are designed to report the results of operations.

The primary purpose of federal income tax laws is to guide the government's collection of tax revenue. However, Congress also uses income tax law to influence businesses. To promote economic development, Congress has periodically passed tax laws that provide businesses with financial incentives to purchase plant assets.

A business that purchases plant assets will likely hire more employees, purchase additional raw materials, and earn a higher net income—all resulting in increasing economic activity and income tax revenues.

Congress has used the following three tax laws to enable businesses to recover a larger portion of their plant asset purchases in the first year than would be permitted by simply using straight-line depreciation.

Accelerated Depreciation: To spur the economy after World War II, Congress modified the tax laws in 1954 to permit the use of accelerated depreciation methods.

Investment Tax Credit: In 1962, President Kennedy proposed a tax credit for certain purchases of plant assets. Congress has periodically changed the percentage credits, purchase limitations, and qualifying assets. Unlike a tax deduction, a tax credit is a reduction in the tax paid. For example, a company purchasing an 8% qualifying asset for $50,000 could reduce its tax liability by $4,000.

Section 179 Property: In 1986, the rising federal debt motivated Congress to reduce the investment

tax credit in favor of a tax law that enabled a business to expense up to $17,500 of plant asset purchases each year. For example, a company purchasing $50,000 of equipment could expense $17,500 of the equipment in the year of purchase and depreciate the remaining $32,500 using the current tax rates.

GAAP allow the use of accelerated depreciation methods. However, neither the investment tax credit nor Section 179 property rules can be used for financial reporting.

REQUIRED:

Obtain a copy of IRS Form 4562, Depreciation and Amortization. Identify the parts of the form used to report Section 179 property and MACRS depreciation. Prepare a list of amounts and other information that is required to prepare the form.

APPLICATION PROBLEM 8-1
Journalizing entries to record buying plant assets

Mannings, Inc. uses three plant asset accounts: Office Equipment, Store Equipment, and Warehouse Equipment.

Transactions:

Jan. 2. Paid cash for office file cabinet (plant asset no. 1), $500.00: estimated salvage value, $50.00; estimated useful life, five years; serial no. FC2467. C130.

Jan. 3. Bought office word processor (plant asset no. 2) on account from Darst, Inc., $400.00: no estimated salvage value; estimated useful life, five years; serial no. X4672Y101. M11.

Apr. 4. Bought hand truck (plant asset no. 3) for warehouse on account from Boeser, Inc., $100.00: estimated salvage value, $25.00; estimated useful life, five years; serial no. 23D4689. M24.

May 1. Paid cash for used truck (plant asset no. 4) to be used between warehouses, $8,500.00: estimated salvage value, $1,000.00; estimated useful life, five years; serial no. 45J3257XF29. C210.

July 1. Paid cash for store shelving (plant asset no. 5), $500.00: estimated salvage value, $25.00; estimated useful life, 10 years; no serial no. C250.

Instructions:

1. Journalize the transactions completed during the current year. Use page 1 of a general journal and page 1 of a cash payments journal. General ledger accounts are: Office Equipment, 1225; Store Equipment, 1235; and Warehouse Equipment, 1245. Source documents are abbreviated as follows: check, C; memorandum, M.

2. Complete Section 1 of a plant asset record for each plant asset. Save the plant asset records from Application Problem 8-1 to complete Application Problems 8-3, 8-4, and 8-5.

APPLICATION PROBLEM 8-2
Calculating and journalizing property tax

Dependable Deliveries, Inc., has real property with an assessed value of $350,000.00. The annual tax rate in the city where the property is located is 4.5% of assessed value. Half of the annual tax is collected every six months.

Instructions:

1. Calculate Dependable Deliveries' total annual property tax.

2. Journalize the payment of the tax on February 26 with check No. 124. Use page 3 of a cash payments journal.

APPLICATION PROBLEM 8-3
Calculating depreciation using the straight-line method

Use the plant asset record from Application Problem 8-1. Complete a depreciation table for each of the plant assets bought by Mannings, Inc. Save the depreciation tables from Application Problem 8-3 to complete Application Problem 8-4.

APPLICATION PROBLEM 8-4
Journalizing annual depreciation expense

Use the plant asset records from Application Problem 8-1 and the depreciation tables from Application Problem 8-3.

Instructions:

1. Use the plant asset records prepared in Application Problem 8-1. For each plant asset, record depreciation for 20X1 in section 3 of the plant asset record.

2. Use page 12 of a general journal and the depreciation tables prepared in Application Problem 8-3. Journalize the three adjusting entries for office, store, and warehouse depreciation expense on December 31, 20X1.

3. For each plant asset, record depreciation for 20X2, 20X3, and 20X4 in section 3 of the plant asset record.

4. Journalize the three adjusting entries for December 31, 20X2. Save the plant asset records from Application Problem 8-4 to complete Application Problem 8-5.

APPLICATION PROBLEM 8-5
Recording disposal of plant assets

Use the plant asset records from Application Problem 8-4. Mannings, Inc., completed the following transactions. Use the appropriate plant asset records from Application Problem 8-4 for additional information needed. Use page 1 of a general journal, page 6 of a cash receipts journal, and page 12 of a cash payments journal. Source documents are abbreviated as follows: check, C; memorandum, M; receipt, R.

Transactions:

Jan. 21, 20X5.	An office word processor, plant asset no. 2, was no longer being used. It was discarded. M522.
Jan. 28, 20X5.	Discarded office file cabinet, plant asset no. 1. M523.
Mar. 29, 20X6.	Received cash for sale of hand truck, $10.00, plant asset no. 3. M575 and R645.
Dec. 31, 20X6.	Received cash for sale of store shelving, $250.00, plant asset no. 5. M631 and R733.
Dec. 31, 20X6.	Paid $8,000.00 in cash plus old truck, plant asset no. 4, for new truck, plant asset no. 29. M632 and C815.

Instructions:

1. For each transaction in 20X5, do the following.
   a. Journalize an entry for additional depreciation if needed.
   b. Journalize the disposal of the plant asset.
   c. Make appropriate notations in the plant asset record.

2. Complete each plant asset record for the year.

3. Repeat instructions 1 and 2 for 20X6.

APPLICATION PROBLEM
8-6
Recording the sale of land and building

On January 2, 20X6, Jamestown, Inc., sold land and a company operations building it is no longer using. The following data relating to the land and building are obtained from the accounting records of Jamestown:

Cash Received	$73,000.00
Original Cost of Land	20,000.00
Original Cost of Building	100,000.00
Accumulated Depreciation on Building to 12/31/X5	61,200.00

Instructions:

1. Journalize the sale of the land and building. Use page 12 of a cash receipts journal. The source document is receipt no. 125.

2. Make appropriate notations in the plant asset records.

APPLICATION PROBLEM
8-7
Calculating depreciation expense using the straight-line, declining-balance, and sum-of-the-years-digits methods

The following data relating to an office desk are obtained from the accounting records of Byrum, Inc.

Original Cost	$2,400.00
Estimated Salvage Value	200.00
Estimated Useful Life	4 years

Instructions:

Prepare a depreciation table showing depreciation expense calculated using the straight-line, declining-balance, and sum-of-the-years-digits methods.

APPLICATION PROBLEM
8-8
Calculating depreciation expense using the production-unit method

The following data relating to a truck are obtained from the accounting records of Marcotte, Inc.:

Original Cost	$10,000.00
Estimated Salvage Value	1,000.00
Estimated Useful Life	120,000 miles

Instructions:

1. Calculate the depreciation rate.

2. Prepare a depreciation table for this truck showing depreciation expense calculated using the production-unit method.

APPLICATION PROBLEM 8-9
Calculating depreciation expense using MACRS

The following data relating to a computer are obtained from the accounting records of Caesar Company.

Original Cost $3,300.00
Property Class 5-year property

Instructions:
Prepare a depreciation table showing depreciation expense calculated using MACRS.

APPLICATION PROBLEM 8-10
Calculating depletion expense using production-unit method

The following data relating to a coal mine are obtained from the accounting records of Geist, Inc.

Original Cost $45,000.00
Estimated Salvage Value   1,000.00
Estimated Tons of Recoverable Coal   50,000 tons

Instructions:
Prepare a depletion table for this mine showing depletion expense calculated using the production-unit method.

MASTERY PROBLEM 8-11
Recording entries for plant assets

Western, Inc., uses the straight-line method of calculating depreciation expense. Western uses one plant asset account, Office Equipment, account no. 1230. The plant asset records for Western are given in the *Working Papers.*

Transactions:
Jan. 2. Paid cash for new computer, plant asset no. 172, $1,900.00: estimated salvage value, $400.00; estimated useful life, five years; serial no. SD345J267. C122.
Jan. 2. Discarded desk, serial no. D3481, plant asset no. 167. M47.
Mar. 29. Discarded table, serial no. T3929, plant asset no. 168. M52.
Mar. 30. Received cash from sale of word processor, $100.00: serial no. TM48194H32, plant asset no. 170. M54 and R191.
June 29. Received cash from sale of filing cabinet, $150.00: serial no. FC125, plant asset no. 169. M62 and R224.
July 2. Paid cash, $500.00, plus old copying machine, serial no. C56M203, plant asset no. 171, for new copying machine: estimated salvage value of new machine, $100.00; estimated useful life of new machine, five years; serial no., C35194, plant asset no. 173. M70 and C239.

Instructions:
1. Journalize the transactions completed during 20X9. Journalize an entry for additional depreciation expense if needed. Use page 1 of a general journal, page 6 of a cash receipts journal, and page 8 of a cash payments journal. Source documents are abbreviated as follows: check, C; memorandum, M; receipt, R.
2. Make needed notations on plant asset records or prepare new records.

8-12

CHALLENGE PROBLEM
Recording entries for plant assets

McNeilley, Inc., uses the straight-line method to calculate depreciation expense. McNeilley uses two plant asset accounts, Office Equipment and Delivery Equipment.

Transactions:

Jan. 1, 20X1.   Paid cash for new office word processor, plant asset no. 1, $600.00: estimated salvage value, $100.00; estimated useful life, eight years; serial no. T45M3409. C130.

Mar. 1, 20X1.   Paid cash for office desk, plant asset no. 2, $700.00: estimated salvage value, $150.00; estimated useful life, five years; serial no. D345. C190.

June 30, 20X1.   Paid cash for office chair, plant asset no. 3, $125.00: estimated salvage value, $10.00; estimated useful life, five years; no serial no. C200.

July 1, 20X1.   Paid cash for delivery truck, plant asset no. 4, $10,000.00: estimated salvage value, $1,000.00; estimated useful life, five years; serial no. 345X32LD54. C220.

Jan. 2, 20X3.   Paid cash, $400.00, plus old word processor, serial no. T45M3409, for new word processor: estimated salvage value of new word processor, $100.00; estimated useful life of new word processor, plant asset no. 5, five years; new word processor serial no. T64M4391. M50 and C300.

July 1, 20X3.   Discarded office chair bought on June 30, 20X1. M66.

Sept. 1, 20X3.   Paid cash, $5,500.00, plus old delivery truck, serial no. 345X32LD54, for new delivery truck: estimated salvage value of new truck, $2,000.00; estimated useful life of new truck, plant asset no. 6, five years; new truck serial no. 432XY30LE25. M70 and C310.

Instructions:

Journalize the transactions. Use page 7 of a general journal and page 12 of a cash payments journal. Source documents are abbreviated as follows: check, C; memorandum, M; receipt, R.

INTERNET ACTIVITY

Point your browser to
http://accounting.swpco.com
Choose **Advanced Course**, choose **Activities**, and complete the activity for Chapter 8.

Applied Communication

Examine the comparison of depreciation methods in Figure 8-15. Although the amount of depreciation recorded each year varies, the total depreciation over the asset's full life is the same.

Required:
Prepare a graph comparing the three depreciation methods. Make sure the graph is clearly labeled. The declining-balance method and the sum-of-the-years-digits method are often referred to as accelerated depreciation methods. Use the graph to explain what is meant by accelerated depreciation.

Cases for Critical Thinking

Case 1
A corporation's plant assets include office equipment, a building, and the land on which the building is located. The corporation's general ledger includes a single account, Plant Assets and a single account, Accumulated Depreciation—Plant Assets. The corporation's accountant suggests that the plant assets be divided into three accounts, Office Equipment, Building, and Land. The corporation's president does not think this is a good idea. With whom do you agree and why?

Case 2
A corporation owns land on which there are both an active coal mine and timber. The corporation also owns an office building and the land on which it is located. The corporation uses three plant asset accounts: (1) Land and Buildings (depreciation calculated using the straight-line method). (2) Timber (depreciation calculated using the declining-balance method). (3) Coal Mine (depreciation calculated using the declining-balance method). Do you agree with the accounting procedures being used? Explain your answers.

Case 3
A corporation currently uses straight-line depreciation for all plant assets. Its balance sheet reports accumulated depreciation and its income statement reports the depreciation expense for the current period. When the corporation's tax accountant prepares the corporate income tax return, all depreciation is reported using MACRS. Assume that all of the company's assets are one or two years old. Further assume that all the assets are in the 5-year property class. Will the net income reported on the tax return be greater than or less than the net income reported on the income statement? Explain your reasoning.

Case 4
The city in which a corporation is located has a business property tax. This tax is 1% of all business property over $50,000. The corporation is a small service business. Its assets that are subject to the tax are only $10,000. The law states that all businesses must file a return even if they owe no tax. The penalty for not filing is $100. The corporation's accountant has attempted to complete the tax return. However, some parts of the return are very technical. The accountant gets an estimate from a tax specialist to prepare the return. The estimate is $125 for the first year and $75 for the second and third years. What should the accountant do?

AUTOMATED ACCOUNTING

AUTOMATED DEPRECIATION AND CREATING DEPRECIATION SCHEDULES

In *Automated Accounting 7.0*, depreciation schedules can be maintained using the following methods: straight-line (SL), double-declining-balance (DDB), and sum-of-the-years-digits (SYD).

Adding Plant Asset Data

Complete plant asset information is required for each plant asset. The information is entered in the Plant Assets tab of the Account Maintenance window. To add a new asset, enter all the requested information on a new line. Then click the Add Asset button.

Plant asset data can also be changed by clicking on the cell containing the data to be changed. The Add Asset button changes to the Change Asset button.

Displaying or Printing Plant Asset Reports

A plant asset list and depreciation schedules can be displayed and printed by selecting the appropriate report. When selecting the depreciation schedules report, select the asset or range of assets for the depreciation schedules you want to generate.

Generating Depreciation Adjusting Entries

Choose Depreciation Adjusting Entries from the Option menu. Click Yes to generate the depreciation adjusting entries. The software will analyze the plant asset records, calculate an amount based on the period, and generate the depreciation adjusting entries. The journal entries will display on the screen for your review and confirmation. Verify the accuracy of the entries, then click the Post button.

AUTOMATING APPLICATION PROBLEM 8-7

Instructions:

1. Load *Automated Accounting 7.0* or higher software.

2. Select database A08-07 (Advanced Course Application Problem 8-7) from the accounting template disk.

3. Select File from the menu bar and choose the Save As menu command. Key the path to the drive and directory that contains your data files. Save the database with a file name of XXX087 (where XXX are your initials).

4. Access Problem Instructions through the Help menu. Read the Problem Instruction screen.

5. Refer to page 245 for data used in this problem.

6. Exit the Automated Accounting software.

AUTOMATING MASTERY PROBLEM 8-11

Instructions:

1. Load *Automated Accounting 7.0* or higher software.

2. Select database A08-11 (Advanced Course Mastery Problem 8-11) from the accounting template disk.

3. Select File from the menu bar and choose the Save As menu command. Key the path to the drive and directory that

contains your data files. Save the database with a file name of XXX0811 (where XXX are your initials).

4. Access Problem Instructions through the Help menu. Read the Problem Instruction screen.

5. Key the data listed on page 246.

6. Exit the Automated Accounting software.

AUTOMATING CHALLENGE PROBLEM 8-12

Instructions:

1. Load *Automated Accounting 7.0* or higher software.

2. Select database A08-12 (Advanced Course Challenge Problem 8-12) from the accounting template disk.

3. Select File from the menu bar and choose the Save As menu command. Key the path to the drive and directory that contains your data files. Save the database with a file name of XXX0812 (where XXX are your initials).

4. Access Problem Instructions through the Help menu. Read the Problem Instruction screen.

5. Key the data listed on page 247.

6. Exit the Automated Accounting software.

9

Accounting for Notes Payable, Prepaid Expenses, and Accrued Expenses

AFTER STUDYING CHAPTER 9, YOU WILL BE ABLE TO:

1. Define accounting terms related to notes payable, prepaid expenses, and accrued expenses.

2. Identify accounting concepts and practices related to notes payable, prepaid expenses, and accrued expenses.

3. Journalize transactions for notes payable.

4. Journalize adjusting and reversing entries for prepaid expenses initially recorded as expenses.

5. Journalize adjusting and reversing entries for accrued expenses.

Business transactions occur throughout a fiscal period. Some transactions begin in one accounting period and are completed in a different accounting period. Accounting records for each period, however, must show all information needed to prepare the financial statements of a business. *(CONCEPT: Adequate Disclosure)* Therefore, some financial activities require the use of special accounting procedures.

Most expenses occur in the same period in which a cash payment is made for the expense. Some expenses, such as insurance and advertising, require cash payment before the benefit is received. Thus, a cash payment for these expenses may occur in the fiscal period before the related expense should be recognized. In addition, a business may borrow money in one period and repay it in another period. Interest owed in the current period must be included in the financial statements of the current period. *(CONCEPT: Matching Expenses with Revenue)*

ACCOUNTING
IN YOUR CAREER

NEW PRODUCT LAUNCH

Meekin Industries produces frozen foods. The company enjoys sales of $25,000,000 per year, employs 250 people, and is well known and popular in its region. The frozen food industry is very competitive. The competition keeps prices down, so the company just manages to pay its expenses from current cash flow. For the past two years, the company has been researching a new technology that will produce better-tasting microwavable frozen entrees and desserts that are unlike anything currently on the market. Taste testers in the region have rated the product very favorably.

Meekin has a well-planned advertising campaign for launching the new line of products and believes that the new line can double the company's sales within two years. The company faces one large hurdle, the $2,000,000 cash investment needed to launch the new product. In its current financial situation, the company does not have $2,000,000 cash for the launch. Toby Jenkins, finance manager, has approached several area banks to arrange loans to launch the new product. Most of the loan managers were reluctant to take the risk. However, Toby finally obtained two different loan proposals.

The first loan, from First State Bank, is for six months at 14% interest. Commonwealth Bank has offered a one-year, 16% loan. The finance committee is considering the effects of each of the two loan packages. The general reaction is disappointment that the interest rates are higher than the prevailing rates in the industry.

Critical Thinking

1. What is the interest cost of the two loans?
2. Why do you think the interest rates are higher than normal?
3. In addition to the interest cost, what should the finance committee consider in making its decision?

BORROWING MONEY WITH A NOTE PAYABLE

CASH RECEIPTS JOURNAL   PAGE 5

	DATE	ACCOUNT TITLE	DOC. NO.	POST. REF.	GENERAL DEBIT	GENERAL CREDIT	ACCOUNTS RECEIVABLE CREDIT	SALES CREDIT	SALES TAX PAYABLE DEBIT	SALES TAX PAYABLE CREDIT	SALES DISCOUNT DEBIT	CASH DEBIT	
1	Mar. 2	Notes Payable	R143			1 5 0 0 00						1 5 0 0 00	1
2													2
3													3

Figure 9-1

A written and signed promise to pay a sum of money at a specified time is called a **promissory note**. Promissory notes signed by a business and given to a creditor are called **notes payable**. The day a note is issued is called the **date of a note**. The original amount of a note is called the **principal of a note**. The date a note is due is called the **maturity date of a note**. An amount paid for the use of money for a period of time is called **interest**. The percentage of the principal that is paid for use of the money is called the **interest rate of a note**.

Appliance Center occasionally borrows money from a bank. It signs a note payable with the bank as evidence of the debt.

March 2. Signed a 180-day, 10% note, $1,500.00. R143.

Upon signing the note, Appliance Center receives the $1,500.00. It records the transaction in the cash receipts journal as shown in Figure 9-1. Appliance Center issues a receipt that is used as the source document for the transaction. *(CONCEPT: Objective Evidence)*

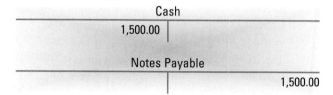

Cash	
1,500.00	

Notes Payable	
	1,500.00

F.Y.I.

A note payable that will be repaid during the next fiscal year should be recorded in an account classified as a current liability. A note payable scheduled to mature in later fiscal periods should be classified as a long-term liability. When borrowing money for five or more years, many companies issue written promises referred to as bonds. The accounting for bonds is presented in Chapter 12.

SMALL BUSINESS SPOTLIGHT

Finding new markets is a key to growing any business. For many small businesses those new markets span the globe. It is not unusual to find new markets as close to home as Canada and Mexico and as far away as Africa and the Pacific Rim. With the number of small businesses on the increase, the U.S. Commerce Department has developed and expanded programs aimed at helping small businesses export their products.

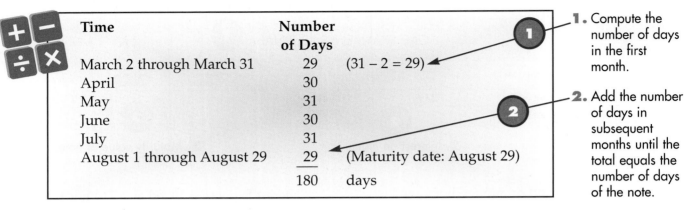

Time	Number of Days		
March 2 through March 31	29	(31 – 2 = 29)	**1.** Compute the number of days in the first month.
April	30		
May	31		**2.** Add the number of days in subsequent months until the total equals the number of days of the note.
June	30		
July	31		
August 1 through August 29	29	(Maturity date: August 29)	
	180	days	

Figure 9-2

The number of days in each month during the term of the note impacts the maturity date. The maturity date for Appliance Center's 180-day, March 2 note payable is August 29. The maturity date is determined as shown in Figure 9-2.

S T E P S **Calculating the maturity date**

1. Compute the number of days in the first month, *29*, by subtracting the date of the note, *2*, from the number of days in the month the note was signed, *31*.
2. Continue adding the number of days in each of the following months until the total equals the number of days of the note, *180*.

F.Y.I.

The term of a note can be stated in months or years. Thus, a six-month note dated March 2 matures on September 2. The number of days between March 2 and September 2 must be determined to use in interest calculations.

Principal	×	Interest Rate	×	Time as Fraction of Year	=	Interest for Fraction of Year
$1,500.00	×	10%	×	$\dfrac{180}{360}$	=	$75.00

Figure 9-3

The interest rate of the note is stated as an annual rate. The interest paid on the note is calculated by applying the annual rate for the portion of the year that the note is outstanding as shown in Figure 9-3. For ease of calculation, most banks use 360 rather than 365 as the number of days in a year.

F.Y.I.

Agencies of the federal government generally use a 365-day year when calculating interest. Consumer interest also is generally calculated on a 365-day year. However, most banks use a 360-day year when calculating interest. Therefore, the interest calculations in this textbook use a 360-day year.

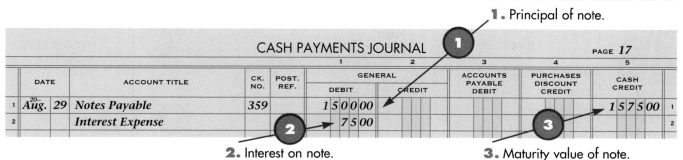

1. Principal of note.

	DATE		ACCOUNT TITLE	CK. NO.	POST. REF.	GENERAL		ACCOUNTS PAYABLE DEBIT	PURCHASES DISCOUNT CREDIT	CASH CREDIT	
						DEBIT	CREDIT				
1	Aug.	29	Notes Payable	359		1500 00					1
2			Interest Expense			75 00				1575 00	2

CASH PAYMENTS JOURNAL   PAGE 17

2. Interest on note.

3. Maturity value of note.

Figure 9-4

The interest accrued on money borrowed is called **interest expense**. On the maturity date, the borrower pays both the principal of the note payable and the interest expense. The payment of the note is recorded in the cash payments journal as shown in Figure 9-4. The amount that is due on the maturity date of a note is called the **maturity value**. Appliance Center pays the maturity value of its note on the maturity date.

> *August 29. Paid cash for the maturity value of the Mar. 2 note: principal, $1,500.00, plus interest, $75.00; total, $1,575.00. Check No. 359.*

Interest Expense is listed as an Other Expense on Appliance Center's chart of accounts. Expenses that are not a part of the normal operating expenses of a business are classified as other expenses.

Notes Payable	
1,500.00	Bal. 1,500.00

Interest Expense	
75.00	

Cash	
	1,575.00

TERMS REVIEW

promissory note

notes payable

date of a note

principal of a note

maturity date of a note

interest

interest rate of a note

interest expense

maturity value

AUDIT YOUR UNDERSTANDING

1. What formula does Appliance Center use to calculate interest on notes?
2. How is the interest rate on a note stated?
3. The borrower pays what two amounts at the note's maturity?

WORK TOGETHER

Journalizing notes payable transactions

A cash receipts journal and a cash payments journal are provided in the *Working Papers*. Source documents are abbreviated as: check, C; receipt, R. Your instructor will guide you through the following examples.

4. Using the current year, journalize the following transactions in the cash receipts journal.
   May 14.   Signed a 90-day, 12% note with First National Bank, $5,000.00. R145.
   June 5.   Signed a 180-day, 10% note with American Bank, $8,000.00. R213.
5. Calculate the maturity date of each note and the total amount of interest due at maturity for each note.
6. Journalize the following transactions in the cash payments journal. Use the maturity dates and interest amounts calculated in the previous steps.
   Paid cash for the maturity value of the $5,000.00 note. C345.
   Paid cash for the maturity value of $8,000.00 note. C652.

ON YOUR OWN

Journalizing notes payable transactions

A cash receipts journal and a cash payments journal are provided in the *Working Papers*. Source documents are abbreviated as: check, C; receipt, R. Work this problem independently.

7. Using the current year, journalize the following transactions in the cash receipts journal.
   Mar. 23.   Signed a 180-day, 10% note with Commerce Bank, $6,000.00. R84.
   July 12.   Signed a 60-day, 12% note with Farmers National Bank, $12,000.00. R151.
8. Calculate the maturity date for each note and the total amount of interest due at maturity for each note.
9. Journalize the following transactions on page 14 of a cash payments journal. Use the maturity dates and interest amounts calculated in the previous steps.
   Paid cash for the maturity value of the $12,000.00 note. C455.
   Paid cash for the maturity value of $6,000.00 note. C464.

DESCRIPTION OF PREPAID EXPENSES

Expenses paid in one fiscal period but not reported as expenses until a later fiscal period are called **prepaid expenses**. Prepaid expenses include items such as supplies, insurance, advertising, and income taxes. Only that portion of cash payment for expenses that have been used in the current fiscal period should be reported as an expense in that fiscal period. *(CONCEPT: Matching Expenses with Revenue)*

Prepaid expenses may be recorded initially as assets or as expenses. MasterSport, described in Part 1, initially records cash payments for supplies and insurance as assets. Appliance Center, in contrast, initially records these payments as expenses. Both methods are acceptable provided that the company consistently applies its chosen method from year to year.

Prepaid expenses are assets until they are actually used. For example, Appliance Center has a quantity of sales supplies on hand on any given day during the year. The company will use these sales supplies in the current and future fiscal periods. The amount recorded in the account Supplies Expense—Sales prior to the fiscal year-end adjustments represents a mixture of an expense (supplies already used) and an asset (supplies not yet used).

Appliance Center records an adjusting entry to recognize as an expense only those sales supplies used during the fiscal year. An adjusting entry could be made each day to recognize the sales supplies used that day. However, as a practical accounting procedure, this adjusting entry is made only when financial statements need to be prepared. *(CONCEPT: Adequate Disclosure)* Appliance Center records adjustments on December 31, the end of its fiscal year.

ADDRESSING SAFETY CONCERNS

Attention to workplace safety creates a more friendly work environment. A safe workplace can reduce the risk of lawsuits, avoid government fines and penalties, and increase productivity. Workers need to feel safe to work productively. Even workers who perform dangerous jobs need to know that their employers have taken reasonable precautions to insure their safety.

The Occupational Safety and Health Administration (OSHA) is the government agency responsible for enforcing federal workplace safety laws and regulations. OSHA has been given the legal authority to inspect most businesses for compliance with the law. OSHA imposes civil penalties up to $70,000 for violations. The amount of the penalty is determined by the severity of the violation. Willful or repeated violations incur the largest penalties.

OSHA offers a free consultation service to help businesses identify potential hazards at their worksites. The consultants will work with the business to develop and improve occupational safety and health management systems.

Good safety practices can also reduce workers' compensation insurance premiums. Businesses that experience many workplace injuries or illnesses will pay a higher premium than other businesses in the same industry.

Thinking about safety before injuries occur saves money and legal difficulties for businesses.

LEGAL ISSUES IN ACCOUNTING

1. Debit the expense account.

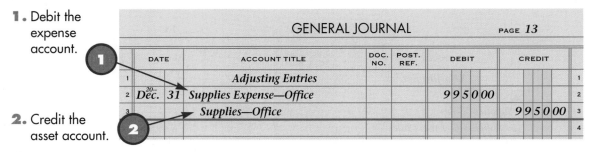

	DATE	ACCOUNT TITLE	DOC. NO.	POST. REF.	DEBIT	CREDIT	
		GENERAL JOURNAL				PAGE *13*	
1		*Adjusting Entries*					1
2	Dec. 31	*Supplies Expense—Office*			9 9 5 0 00		2
3		*Supplies—Office*				9 9 5 0 00	3
4							4

2. Credit the asset account.

Figure 9-5

When MasterSport, described in Part 1, buys office supplies, the asset Supplies—Office is debited and Cash is credited. MasterSport recorded adjusting entries for supplies at the end of a fiscal period as shown in Figure 9-5. Adjusting entries are recorded so that the supplies used during a fiscal period are reported as expenses and the supplies not used are reported as assets. (CONCEPT: Matching Expenses with Revenue)

MasterSport initially recorded the prepaid supplies in the asset account Supplies—Office. The $12,700.00 debit balance represents the beginning inventory of supplies plus the total amount of all office supplies bought during the fiscal period. Nothing has been recorded in MasterSport's office supplies expense account during the fiscal period.

MasterSport determined that the actual amount of office supplies inventory was $2,750.00. An adjusting entry of $9,950.00 ($12,700.00 – $2,750.00) is necessary.

After recording the adjustment, the new balance of Supplies—Office, $2,750.00, is the ending office supplies inventory on December 31. The new balance of Supplies Expense—Office, $9,950.00, represents supplies used during the current year.

Supplies—Office			
12/31 Bal.	12,700.00	12/31 Adj.	9,950.00
(New Bal.	2,750.00)		

Supplies Expense—Office	
12/31 Adj.	9,950.00

Closing Entries

To prepare a general ledger for the next fiscal period, closing entries are journalized and posted.

After its closing entries have been posted, MasterSport's general ledger accounts are ready for the next fiscal period. On December 31, the amount of the office supplies inventory, $2,750.00, is recorded in the account in which it can be added to the amount of supplies that will be bought in the next fiscal period.

Income Summary			
12/31 Clos.	9,950.00		

Supplies Expense—Office			
12/31 Adj.	9,950.00	12/31 Clos.	9,950.00
(New Bal. zero)			

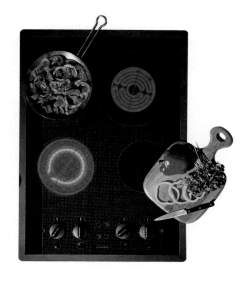

REMEMBER

Similar entries are made for each supply account, such as Supplies—Administrative and Supplies—Warehouse.

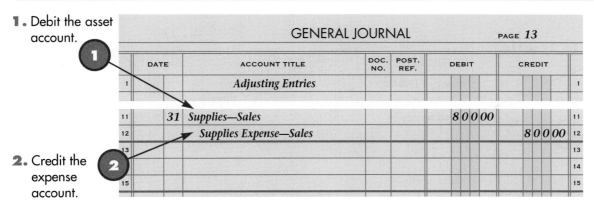

1. Debit the asset account.

2. Credit the expense account.

GENERAL JOURNAL — PAGE 13

	DATE	ACCOUNT TITLE	DOC. NO.	POST. REF.	DEBIT	CREDIT	
1		Adjusting Entries					1
11	31	Supplies—Sales			8 0 0 00		11
12		Supplies Expense—Sales				8 0 0 00	12
13							13
14							14
15							15

Figure 9-6

When Appliance Center buys sales supplies, Supplies Expense—Sales is debited and Cash is credited. The $2,000.00 debit balance of Supplies Expense—Sales represents the amount of the beginning sales supplies inventory plus the total amount of all sales supplies bought during the fiscal period. Nothing has been recorded in Appliance Center's sales supplies account during the fiscal period.

On December 31, Appliance Center takes a physical count of the sales supplies on hand. It determines that the sales supplies ending inventory is $800.00 and records the necessary adjusting entry as shown in Figure 9-6.

The new balance of Supplies—Sales, *$800.00*, represents the ending sales supplies inventory on December 31. The new balance of Supplies Expense—Sales, *$1,200.00*, recognizes the amount of sales supplies used during the current year.

Supplies—Sales			
12/31 Adj.	800.00		

Supplies Expense—Sales			
12/31 Bal.	2,000.00	12/31 Adj.	800.00
(New Bal.	1,200.00)		

Closing Entry for Supplies Expense

To prepare a general ledger for the next fiscal period, closing entries are journalized and posted. After the closing entry is recorded, the Supplies Expense—Sales account balance is zero. The debit balance of $800.00 in Supplies—Sales represents the amount of sales supplies on hand on December 31.

Income Summary		
12/31 Clos.	1,200.00	

Supplies Expense—Sales		
12/31 Bal.	2,000.00	12/31 Adj.	800.00
(New Bal. zero)		12/31 Clos.	1,200.00

REMEMBER

Although MasterSport and Appliance Center use different procedures, both correctly separate and record the asset and expense portions of the cost of supplies. Both procedures meet the requirements of the *Matching Expenses with Revenue* concept.

REVERSING ENTRY—SUPPLIES INITIALLY RECORDED AS AN EXPENSE

1. Debit the expense account.

2. Credit the asset account.

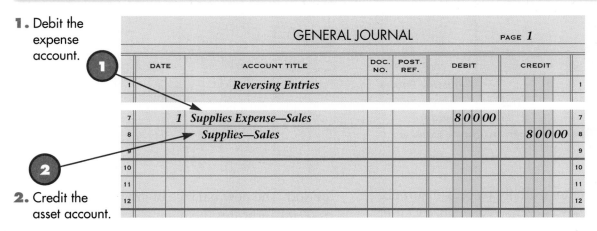

Figure 9-7

After the closing entries have been posted, MasterSport's general ledger accounts are ready for the next fiscal period. However, Appliance Center's general ledger accounts are not ready for the next fiscal period.

Appliance Center initially records the amount of all supplies bought in an expense account. On December 31, the amount of Appliance Center's sales supplies inventory, *$800.00*, is the debit balance of **Supplies—Sale**s. On January 1, the $800.00 should be returned as a debit in **Supplies Expense—Sales**. The $800.00 debit can then be added to the amount of sales supplies bought during the next year.

Some businesses that initially record prepaid items as expenses reverse the adjusting entries for prepaid expenses at the beginning of each fiscal period. An entry made at the beginning of one fiscal period to reverse an adjusting entry made in the previous fiscal period is called a **reversing entry**. Thus, a reversing entry is the exact opposite of the related adjusting entry.

Appliance Center initially records supplies as expenses and therefore needs to record reversing entries. Accountants use the following rule of thumb to determine whether a reversing entry is needed: If an adjusting entry *creates* a balance in an asset or a liability account, the adjusting entry is reversed.

Because Appliance Center's adjusting entry for sales supplies created a balance in **Supplies—Sales**, a reversing entry is needed. The reversing entry is shown in Figure 9-7.

After the reversing entry is posted, the cost of the sales supplies inventory, *$800.00*, is recorded in the account where it can be added to the amount of supplies bought in the next fiscal period. The balance of **Supplies—Sales** is zero as it was before the adjusting entry.

Supplies Expense—Sales

12/31 Bal.	2,000.00	12/31 Adj.	800.00
1/1 Rev.	800.00	12/31 Clos.	1,200.00
(New Bal.	800.00)		

Supplies—Sales

| 12/31 Adj. | 800.00 | 1/1 Rev. | 800.00 |
| (New Bal. zero) | | | |

REMEMBER

MasterSport initially records supplies as assets but *does not* record reversing entries. On December 31, the amount of the office supplies inventory, $2,750.00, is recorded in the account where it can be added to the amount of supplies bought in the next fiscal period.

Although MasterSport and Appliance Center use different accounting procedures, both correctly separate and record the asset and expense portions of supply costs.

PREPAID INSURANCE INITIALLY RECORDED AS AN EXPENSE

1. Debit the asset account.

2. Credit the expense account.

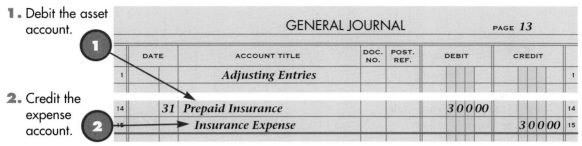

Figure 9-8

Appliance Center initially records insurance premiums as expenses. When Appliance Center pays insurance premiums, Insurance Expense is debited and Cash is credited.

On December 31, Appliance Center determines that the amount of the unexpired insurance premiums totals $300.00 and records the necessary adjusting entry as shown in Figure 9-8.

The new balance of Prepaid Insurance, $300.00, represents the amount of unexpired insurance premiums at the end of the fiscal period. The new balance of Insurance Expense $600.00, indicates the insurance expense for the fiscal period.

Prepaid Insurance		
12/31 Adj.	300.00	

Insurance Expense			
12/31 Adj.	900.00	12/31 Adj.	300.00
(New Bal.	600.00)		

REVERSING ENTRY FOR PREPAID INSURANCE

1. Debit the expense account.

2. Credit the asset account.

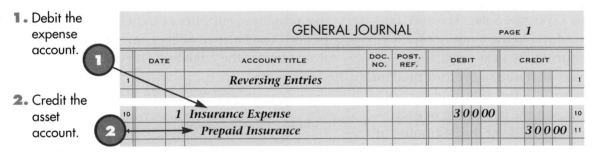

Figure 9-9

Insurance Expense is closed as part of Appliance Center's closing entries.

Appliance Center's adjusting entry for insurance expense created a balance in the asset account Prepaid Insurance. Therefore, on January 1, Appliance Center needs a reversing entry for insurance expense. The reversing entry is shown in Figure 9-9.

The new balance of Insurance Expense, $300.00, can now be added to the amount of insurance premiums paid during the next fiscal period. The new balance of Prepaid Insurance is zero as it was before the adjusting entry.

Insurance Expense			
12/31 Bal.	900.00	12/31 Adj.	300.00
(New Bal. zero)		12/31 Clos.	600.00
1/1 Rev.	300.00		
(New Bal.	300.00)		

Prepaid Insurance			
12/31 Adj.	300.00	1/1 Rev.	300.00
(New Bal. zero)			

REMEMBER

No reversing entry is required when expenses are initially charged to a prepaid expense account.

TERMS REVIEW

prepaid expenses

reversing entry

AUDIT YOUR UNDERSTANDING

1. Which accounting concept is being applied when an adjusting entry is recorded for prepaid expenses?

2. Why is an adjusting entry made for supplies at the end of a fiscal period?

3. What rule of thumb can accountants follow to determine whether a reversing entry is needed?

WORK TOGETHER

Journalizing adjusting and reversing entries for prepaid expenses initially recorded as expenses

Janson, Inc., has the following general ledger balances on December 31 of the current year before it records adjusting entries. A general journal is provided in the *Working Papers*. Your instructor will guide you through the following examples.

Supplies Expense—Administrative	$3,200.00	Insurance Expense	$2,000.00
Supplies Expense—Sales	1,500.00		

4. Using the following adjustment information, journalize the adjusting entries for supplies and insurance on December 31 of the current year.

Administrative Supplies Inventory	$500.00	Value of Prepaid Insurance	$600.00
Sales Supplies Inventory	400.00		

5. Journalize the reversing entries on January 1 of the next year.

ON YOUR OWN

Journalizing adjusting and reversing entries for prepaid expenses initially recorded as expenses

Wren Industries has the following general ledger balances on December 31 of the current year before it records adjusting entries. A general journal is provided in the *Working Papers*. Work this problem independently.

Supplies Expense—Administrative	$4,600.00	Insurance Expense	$6,000.00
Supplies Expense—Sales	4,800.00		

6. Using the following adjustment information, journalize the adjusting entries for supplies and insurance on December 31 of the current year.

Administrative Supplies Inventory	$800.00	Value of Prepaid Insurance	$900.00
Sales Supplies Inventory	600.00		

7. Journalize the reversing entries on January 1 of the next year.

9-3 Accrued Expenses

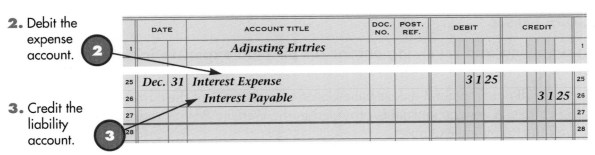

	Principal	×	Interest Rate	×	Time as Fraction of Year	=	Interest for 15 Days		**1.** Determine the amount of accrued interest.
	$7,500.00	×	10%	×	$\frac{15}{360}$	=	$31.25	**1**	

2. Debit the expense account. **2**

3. Credit the liability account. **3**

	DATE	ACCOUNT TITLE	DOC. NO.	POST. REF.	DEBIT	CREDIT	
1		*Adjusting Entries*					1
25	Dec. 31	*Interest Expense*			31 25		25
26		*Interest Payable*				31 25	26
27							27
28							28

Figure 9-10

Expenses incurred in one fiscal period but not paid until a later fiscal period are called **accrued expenses**. In any fiscal period, Appliance Center may need to account for four types of accrued expenses.

1. Accrued interest expense.

2. Accrued salary expense.

3. Accrued employer payroll taxes expense.

4. Accrued federal income tax expense.

On December 31, Appliance Center has a 60-day, 10% note payable for $7,500.00, dated December 16, on which interest has accrued.

On December 31, Appliance Center owes 15 days worth of accrued interest on the note, *$31.25*. The accrued interest expense for this note should be reported in the current fiscal period. *(CONCEPT: Matching Expenses with Revenue)* The adjusting entry shown in Figure 9-10 records the accrued interest adjustment.

Interest Expense	
12/31 Bal.	2,142.50
12/31 Adj.	31.25
(New Bal.	2,173.75)

Interest Payable	
	12/31 Adj. 31.25

S T E P S

Recording the adjusting entry for accrued interest expense

1. Determine the interest expense for the current period, $31.25.

2. Record the debit to *Interest Expense*, 31.25. The debit increases the expense in the current period.

3. Record the credit to *Interest Payable*, 31.25. The credit increases the liability in the current period.

REMEMBER

Any adjustment that creates an asset or liability should be reversed.

REVERSING ENTRY FOR ACCRUED INTEREST

1. Debit the liability account.

2. Credit the expense account.

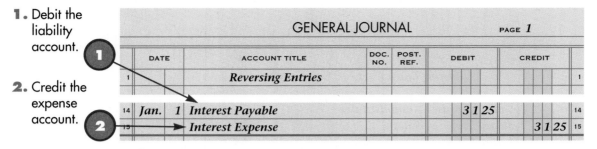

	DATE		ACCOUNT TITLE	DOC. NO.	POST. REF.	DEBIT	CREDIT	
1			*Reversing Entries*					1
14	Jan.	1	*Interest Payable*			3 1 25		14
15			*Interest Expense*				3 1 25	15

GENERAL JOURNAL   PAGE *1*

Figure 9-11

Appliance Center's adjusting entry for accrued interest expense creates a balance in a liability account. After preparing its financial statements, Appliance Center journalizes and posts closing entries. To prepare the accounts for the next year, Appliance Center records a reversing entry for accrued interest expense, as shown in Figure 9-11.

When Appliance Center pays the note on February 14 of the following year, the total interest expense payment is *$125.00*. The total interest expense should be divided between the two fiscal periods. Interest for the prior year, *$31.25*, is charged for the 15 days the note was outstanding in that year. Interest for the current period, *$93.75*, relates to the 45 days from the start of the fiscal year to the maturity date.

Interest Payable

1/1 Rev.	31.25	12/31 Adj.	31.25
		(New Bal. zero)	

Interest Expense

12/31 Bal.	2,142.50	12/31 Clos.	2,173.75
12/31 Adj.	31.25		
(New Bal. zero)			
		1/1 Rev.	31.25

PAYMENT OF NOTE AT MATURITY

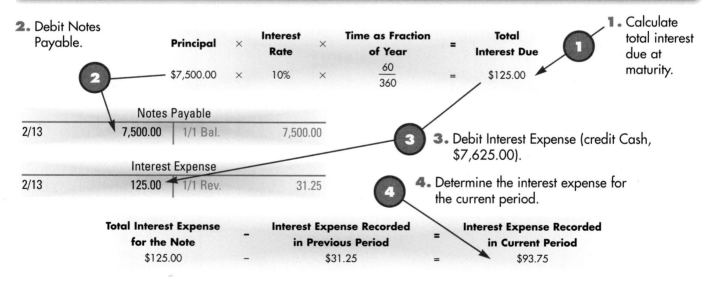

2. Debit Notes Payable.

1. Calculate total interest due at maturity.

Principal	×	Interest Rate	×	Time as Fraction of Year	=	Total Interest Due
$7,500.00	×	10%	×	$\frac{60}{360}$	=	$125.00

Notes Payable

2/13	7,500.00	1/1 Bal.	7,500.00

Interest Expense

2/13	125.00	1/1 Rev.	31.25

3. Debit Interest Expense (credit Cash, $7,625.00).

4. Determine the interest expense for the current period.

Total Interest Expense for the Note	–	Interest Expense Recorded in Previous Period	=	Interest Expense Recorded in Current Period
$125.00	–	$31.25	=	$93.75

Figure 9-12

On the maturity date, Appliance Center writes a check for the maturity value of $7,625.00. This decreases Notes Payable by a $7,500.00 debit. The $125.00 debit to Interest Expense, less the $31.25 credit balance created by the reversing entry, equals the $93.75 interest expense for the current period.

1. Debit the expense accounts.

1

2. Credit the liability accounts.

2

	DATE	ACCOUNT TITLE	DOC. NO.	POST. REF.	DEBIT	CREDIT	
		GENERAL JOURNAL				PAGE *13*	
1		*Adjusting Entries*					1
28	31	*Salary Expense—Administrative*			7 5 0 00		28
29		*Salary Expense—Sales*			8 5 0 00		29
30		*Salary Expense—Warehouse*			4 5 0 00		30
31		*Salaries Payable*				1 5 6 0 00	31
32		*Employee Income Tax Payable*				3 2 6 00	32
33		*Social Security Tax Payable*				1 3 3 25	33
34		*Medicare Tax Payable*				3 0 75	34

Figure 9-13

Appliance Center pays its employees each Friday for the time they worked during the previous week. On December 31, Appliance Center owes, but has not paid, the employees for Monday through Friday of the previous week. On Friday, January 5, the employees will receive a paycheck that includes five days' pay from the previous fiscal period.

On December 31, even though the employees have not been paid, salaries for five days are reported as an expense of the current fiscal period. (CONCEPT: *Matching Expenses with Revenue*) The financial statements must show all the business expenses for a fiscal period. (CONCEPT: *Adequate Disclosure*)

On December 31, Appliance Center owes $1,560.00 of salaries to employees who work in its three departments. To determine the adjusting entry, Appliance Center must prepare the payroll register. However, the checks are not prepared or distributed to employees until the normal payment date, January 5. The adjusting entry to record the accrued salary expense is shown in Figure 9-13.

Salary Expense—Administrative

12/31 Bal.	37,062.50		
12/31 Adj.	750.00		
(New Bal.	37,812.50)		

Salary Expense—Sales

12/31 Bal.	45,075.00		
12/31 Adj.	850.00		
(New Bal.	45,925.00)		

Salary Expense—Warehouse

12/31 Bal.	22,037.50		
12/31 Adj.	450.00		
(New Bal.	22,487.50)		

Salaries Payable

		12/31 Adj.	1,560.00

Employee Income Tax Payable

		12/31 Adj.	326.00

Social Security Tax Payable

		12/31 Bal.	402.59
		12/31 Adj.	133.25
		(New Bal.	535.84)

Medicare Tax Payable

		12/31 Bal.	92.91
		12/31 Adj.	30.75
		(New Bal.	123.66)

REMEMBER

When a company incurs a salary expense, it must recognize this expense as a liability in the period in which employees provide their services to the company.

1. Debit the liability accounts.

1

2. Credit the expense accounts.

2

	DATE		ACCOUNT TITLE	DOC. NO.	POST. REF.	DEBIT	CREDIT	
1			*Reversing Entries*					1
14								14
15		1	*Salaries Payable*			1 5 6 0 00		15
16			*Employee Income Tax Payable*			3 2 6 00		16
17			*Social Security Tax Payable*			1 3 3 25		17
18			*Medicare Tax Payable*			3 0 75		18
19			*Salary Expense—Administrative*				7 5 0 00	19
20			*Salary Expense—Sales*				8 5 0 00	20
21			*Salary Expense—Warehouse*				4 5 0 00	21
22								22
23								23
24								24
13								12
14								13

GENERAL JOURNAL   PAGE *14*

Figure 9-14

After Appliance Center records closing entries for payroll, the three payroll expense accounts have zero balances. The salaries payable account reflects the $1,560.00 salaries to be paid on January 5.

The entry to reverse the payroll adjustment removes the adjusting entry amounts from the four payroll liability accounts, as shown in Figure 9-14. The three salary expense accounts have contra (credit) balances after the reversing entry. When Appliance Center pays the payroll in January, the amount debited in each account is offset by the credit contra balance.

Fiscal years often end in the middle of payroll periods. Therefore, payroll expense must be accrued for the number of days of the payroll period in the current fiscal year. Estimates of the tax liabilities, based on previous payroll periods, are used to prepare the adjusting entry.

F.Y.I.

Reversing entries eliminate the need to remember that the payroll liability accounts reflect an expense from the previous accounting period.

Salaries Payable

1/1 Rev.	1,560.00	12/31 Adj.	1,560.00
		(New Bal. zero)	

Employee Income Tax Payable

1/1 Rev.	326.00	12/31 Adj.	326.00
		(New Bal. zero)	

Social Security Tax Payable

1/1 Rev.	133.25	12/31 Bal.	535.84
		12/31 Adj.	133.25
		(New Bal.	*535.84)*

Medicare Tax Payable

1/1 Rev.	30.75	12/31 Bal.	123.66
		12/31 Adj.	30.75
		(New Bal.	*123.66)*

Salary Expense—Administrative

12/31 Bal.	37,062.50	12/31 Clos.	37,812.50
12/31 Adj.	750.00	1/1 Rev.	750.00
		(New Bal.	*750.00)*

Salary Expense—Sales

12/31 Bal.	45,075.00	12/31 Clos.	45,925.00
12/31 Adj.	850.00	1/1 Rev.	850.00
		(New Bal.	*850.00)*

Salary Expense—Warehouse

12/31 Bal.	22,037.50	12/31 Clos.	22,487.50
12/31 Adj.	450.00	1/1 Rev.	450.00
		(New Bal.	*450.00)*

1. Debit the expense account.

2. Credit the liability accounts.

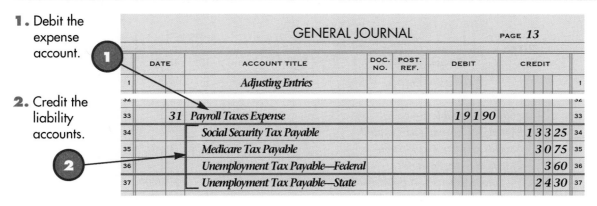

GENERAL JOURNAL   PAGE *13*

	DATE	ACCOUNT TITLE	DOC. NO.	POST. REF.	DEBIT	CREDIT	
1		*Adjusting Entries*					1
32							32
33	31	*Payroll Taxes Expense*			1 9 1 90		33
34		*Social Security Tax Payable*				1 3 3 25	34
35		*Medicare Tax Payable*				3 0 75	35
36		*Unemployment Tax Payable—Federal*				3 60	36
37		*Unemployment Tax Payable—State*				2 4 30	37

Figure 9-15

Employer payroll taxes for accrued salaries must be recorded at the end of a fiscal period. Appliance Center has four employer payroll taxes:

1. Social security tax.

2. Medicare tax.

3. Federal unemployment tax

4. State unemployment tax.

The entry to record the accrued employer payroll taxes on December 31 of the current year is shown in Figure 9-15.

1. Debit the liability accounts.

2. Credit the expense account.

GENERAL JOURNAL   PAGE *16*

	DATE	ACCOUNT TITLE	DOC. NO.	POST. REF.	DEBIT	CREDIT	
1		*Reversing Entries*					1
17							17
18	1	*Social Security Tax Payable*			1 3 3 25		18
19		*Medicare Tax Payable*			3 0 75		19
20		*Unemployment Tax Payable—Federal*			3 60		20
21		*Unemployment Tax Payable—State*			2 4 30		21
22		*Payroll Taxes Expense*				1 9 1 90	22

Figure 9-16

After Appliance Center records closing entries for payroll taxes, the payroll taxes expense account has a zero balance. The four payroll tax liability accounts reflect the tax payments to be made during the next fiscal year.

The entry to reverse the payroll taxes adjustment removes the adjusting entry amounts from the four payroll tax liability accounts, as shown in Figure 9-16. The payroll tax expense account has a contra (credit) balance after the reversing entry. When the payroll taxes are paid, the amount debited to **Payroll Taxes Expense** will be offset by the credit contra balance. Thus, the transaction recorded is the same as other payroll tax payments during the fiscal year.

1. Debit the expense account.

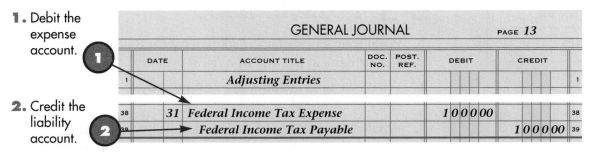

	DATE	ACCOUNT TITLE	DOC. NO.	POST. REF.	DEBIT	CREDIT	
1		*Adjusting Entries*					1
38	31	*Federal Income Tax Expense*			1 0 0 0 00		38
39		*Federal Income Tax Payable*				1 0 0 0 00	39

GENERAL JOURNAL   PAGE *13*

2. Credit the liability account.

Figure 9-17

Corporations must pay federal income tax on net income. At the beginning of each year, Appliance Center makes an estimate of its federal income tax obligation. It pays the estimated amount in four quarterly payments. At the end of a year, Appliance Center revises its income tax estimate for the year. Any unpaid federal income tax is an accrued expense for which an adjusting entry must be made.

On December 31, Appliance Center's records show that quarterly income tax payments have been made for a total of $9,000.00. On December 31, Appliance Center estimates that its income tax will be $10,000.00. Thus, the accrued federal income tax remaining to be paid is $1,000.00 (total tax, $10,000.00, *minus* amount paid, $9,000.00). The adjusting entry for the accrual is shown in Figure 9-17.

Federal Income Tax Payable is a current liability account. **Federal Income Tax Expense** is an expense account located in the general ledger division titled *Income Tax*.

During the year, cash will be paid for accrued income tax expense for the previous year plus periodic payments for the current year's income tax expense. To avoid confusing the amount of tax expense recorded for each of these years and to provide year-to-date income tax expense information for each year, Appliance Center does not reverse this adjusting entry.

HISPANIC AMERICAN BUSINESSES

T he Census Bureau's Survey of Minority-Owned Business Enterprises indicates that minority-owned enterprises are increasing in number and size. One of the fastest growing segments of U.S. business population during the period from 1987 to 1992 was businesses owned by Hispanic Americans. During this period, the number of Hispanic-owned businesses increased from 422,373 to 771,708. In addition, their total receipts more than tripled, from $24.7 billion to $72.8 billion.

With the impressive growth in Hispanic-owned businesses, *Hispanic Business* magazine has created lists of successful Hispanic-owned businesses, including the Hispanic Business 500, the Hispanic Business High Tech 50, and the Fast-Growing 100. The 1997 Hispanic Business 500 gives the honor of largest Hispanic-owned corporation to Burt Automotive Network of Englewood, Colorado. Its chief executive office (CEO) is Lloyd G. Chavez. This automotive sales and service company was started in 1939, employs over 800, and had total revenue in 1996 of about $813 million.

CULTURAL DIVERSITY

1. What four kinds of accrued expenses might Appliance Center have at the end of a fiscal period?

2. What accounts are affected, and how, by an adjusting entry for accrued interest expense?

3. What accounts are affected, and how, by a reversing entry for accrued salary expense?

Journalizing adjusting and reversing entries for accrued expenses

Selected information relating to accruals for December 31 of the current year is given in the *Working Papers*. General journal pages are provided in the *Working Papers*. Your instructor will guide you through the following examples.

4. Journalize the adjusting entries for accrued interest, accrued payroll, accrued employer payroll taxes, and accrued federal income tax on December 31 of the current year.

5. Journalize the appropriate reversing entries on January 1 of the next year.

Journalizing adjusting and reversing entries for accrued expenses

Selected information relating to accruals for December 31 of the current year is given in the *Working Papers*. General journal pages are provided in the *Working Papers*. Work independently to complete the following problem.

6. Journalize the adjusting entries for accrued interest, accrued payroll, accrued employer payroll taxes, and accrued federal income tax on December 31 of the current year.

7. Journalize the appropriate reversing entries on January 1 of the next year.

After completing this chapter, you can

1. Define accounting terms related to notes payable, prepaid expenses, and accrued expenses.
2. Identify accounting concepts and practices related to notes payable, prepaid expenses, and accrued expenses.
3. Journalize transactions for notes payable.
4. Journalize adjusting and reversing entries for prepaid expenses initially recorded as expenses.
5. Journalize adjusting and reversing entries for accrued expenses.

EXPLORE ACCOUNTING

ACCOUNTING FOR WARRANTY EXPENSES

Sunset Pools offers its customers a two-year warranty on its swimming pools. Sunset Pools makes all repairs resulting from defective parts free of charge to the customer.

When Sunset Pools sells a swimming pool, it does not know how much repair will be required during the warranty period. Some pools have no problems; other pools, called "lemons," require extensive repairs. Sunset Pools estimates that it spends an average of $150 on warranty repairs for each pool.

Applying the matching concept, expenses associated with earning revenue should be recorded in the same accounting period. Thus, the cost of

repairing a pool during the warranty period should be recorded in the same period as the pool sale. For each pool sold, Sunset Pools records the following entry:

Warranty Exp.	150.00	
Accrued Warranty Exp.		150.00

When costs are incurred to repair a pool under warranty, Sunset Pools records the following entry:

Accrued Warranty Exp.	45.00	
Cash		45.00

Accountants must periodically analyze the accrued warranty expense account. If the actual costs incurred are significantly more or less than the $150 per pool charge, a new warranty expense estimate is computed.

Warranty expenses demonstrate the impact of accounting estimates on financial statements. Companies must hire accountants with the proper training to ensure that these estimates are as accurate as possible.

REQUIRED:

Sunset Pools is starting to sell outdoor spas. It will maintain warranty expenses in a separate accrual account. Industry publications report that the average spa requires $50 of repairs during its one-year warranty period. After seven sales, Sunset Pools incurs a $500 repair. What is the balance in Accrued Spa Warranty Expense? Does the balance indicate that the $50 estimate is inaccurate? Explain.

9-1 APPLICATION PROBLEM
Journalizing notes payable transactions

Raecker, Inc., completed the following transactions during the current year. Source documents are abbreviated as follows: check, C; receipt, R.

Transactions:

Aug. 1. Signed a 90-day, 11% note with City National Bank for $1,100.00. R143.

Sept. 12. Signed a 60-day, 12% note with First American Bank for $1,200.00. R176.

Oct. 21. Signed a 60-day, 10% note with Commercial State Bank for $800.00. R203.

Instructions:

1. Journalize the transactions on page 15 of a cash receipts journal.

2. Calculate the maturity dates for each note.

3. Calculate the total amount of interest due at maturity for each note.

4. Journalize the following transactions on page 21 of a cash payments journal. Use the maturity dates and the interest amounts calculated in the preceding steps.

   Paid cash for the maturity value of the City National Bank note. C245.

   Paid cash for the maturity value of the First American Bank note. C352.

   Paid cash for the maturity value of Commercial State Bank note. C459.

9-2 APPLICATION PROBLEM
Journalizing adjusting and reversing entries for prepaid expenses initially recorded as expenses

Dupre, Inc., has the following general ledger balances on December 31 of the current year before adjusting entries are recorded.

Supplies Expense—Administrative	$1,500.00
Supplies Expense—Sales	2,500.00
Insurance Expense	3,000.00

Instructions:

1. Use the following adjustment information. Journalize the adjusting entries for supplies and insurance on December 31 of the current year. Use page 13 of a general journal.

Administrative Supplies Inventory	$450.00
Sales Supplies Inventory	800.00
Value of Prepaid Insurance	720.00

2. Journalize the reversing entries on January 1 of the next year. Use page 1 of a general journal.

APPLICATION PROBLEM 9-3
Journalizing adjusting and reversing entries for accrued expenses

Auxbury, Inc., has gathered the following information relating to accrued interest, accrued payroll, accrued employer payroll taxes, and accrued federal income tax on December 31 of the current year.

a.   One note payable is outstanding on December 31: 180-day, 12% note with First National Bank, $15,000, dated October 22.

b.   Payroll information from the December 31 payroll is as follows:

Payroll and Employee Payroll Taxes		Employer Payroll Taxes	
Salaries—Administrative	$600.00	Social Security Tax	$71.50
Salaries—Sales	500.00	Medicare Tax	16.50
Federal Income Tax Withheld	240.00	Federal Unemployment Tax	8.80
Social Security Tax Withheld	71.50	State Unemployment Tax	59.40
Medicare Tax Withheld	16.50		

c.   Estimated federal income tax quarterly payment, $1,300.00.

Instructions:

1.   Journalize the adjusting entries for accrued interest, accrued payroll, accrued employer payroll taxes, and accrued federal income tax on December 31 of the current year. Use page 13 of a general journal.

2.   Journalize the appropriate reversing entries on January 1 of the next year. Use page 1 of a general journal.

MASTERY PROBLEM 9-4
Journalizing adjusting and reversing entries for prepaid expenses initially recorded as expenses and for accrued expenses

Sass, Inc., completed the following transactions during the current year. Sass initially records prepaid expenses as expenses. Source documents are abbreviated as follows: check, C; receipt, R.

Transactions:

July   1.   Signed a 60-day, 12% note with Southern Bank for $700.00. R123.
Oct.   10.   Signed a 45-day, 10% note with American Bank for $1,500.00. R149.
Nov.   1.   Signed a 90-day, 11% note with Commercial Bank for $1,000.00. R152.

Instructions:

1.   Journalize the transactions on page 15 of a cash receipts journal.

2.   Calculate the maturity dates for each note.

3.   Journalize the following transactions on page 21 of a cash payments journal. Use the maturity dates calculated in the prior step.

Paid cash for the maturity value of the Southern Bank note. C105.

Paid cash for the maturity value of the American Bank note. C195.

continued

4. Sass, Inc., has the following general ledger balances on December 31 of the current year before adjusting entries are recorded.

Supplies Expense—Administrative	$400.00
Supplies Expense—Sales	600.00
Insurance Expense	900.00

Use the following information to journalize adjusting entries for prepaid expenses and accrued expenses on December 31 of the current year. The estimated federal income tax is $800.00. Use page 13 of a general journal.

Administrative Supplies Inventory	$200.00
Sales Supplies Inventory	300.00
Value of Prepaid Insurance	350.00

Payroll and Employee Payroll Taxes		Employer Payroll Taxes	
Salaries—Administrative	$350.00	Social Security Tax	$49.73
Salaries—Sales	415.00	Medicare Tax	11.47
Federal Income Tax Withheld	120.00	Federal Unemployment Tax	6.12
Social Security Tax Withheld	49.73	State Unemployment Tax	41.31
Medicare Tax Withheld	11.47		

5. Journalize the appropriate reversing entries on January 1 of the next year. Use page 1 of a general journal.

9-5 CHALLENGE PROBLEM
Journalizing entries for notes payable and prepaid insurance when no reversing entries are recorded

Reversing entries eliminate the balance of an asset or liability created by an adjusting entry. Unlike the Appliance Center's accounting procedures illustrated in this chapter, Baird Company has elected not to record reversing entries. Instead, Baird's accounting personnel must assign different accounts and amounts to subsequent transactions to correctly eliminate the asset or liability account balances.

The following transactions occurred related to a note payable.

Transactions:

Nov. 1, 20X1.	Signed a 180-day, 12% note payable with First National Bank for $10,000.00. R142
Dec. 31, 20X1.	Accrued interest expense.
Dec. 31, 20X1.	Closed the interest expense account.
Apr. 30, 20X2.	Paid the maturity value of the First National Bank note. C154

Instructions:

1. Journalize the transactions and record them in T accounts. Record the first three transactions correctly. Record the April 30 transaction, assuming that an accounting clerk fails to recognize that the transaction relates to a December 31 adjusting entry. Describe the error resulting from the accounting clerk's failure.

2. Create another set of T accounts and journalize the transactions again. Determine the correct accounts and amounts for the April 30 transaction to ensure that the final account balances are correct.

INTERNET ACTIVITY

Point your browser to
http://accounting.swpco.com

Choose **Advanced Course**, choose **Activities**, and complete the activity for Chapter 9.

Applied Communication

As the financial vice president of Mason Co., you are responsible for ensuring that an adequate supply of cash exists to pay operating expenses. The marketing department has secured a huge order that will require funds for increased inventory and employee levels. A budget analysis reveals that a $100,000, 270-day note will be required to adequately fund the production of the order.

Over the past three years, Mason Co. has signed seven notes totaling $200,000 with First National Bank. Each note was for 90 days or less, was issued at prime plus 2-1/2, and was repaid on the due date.

Assume that the class is the bank loan committee of First National Bank. Make an oral presentation to persuade the loan committee to approve the $100,000, 270-day note at prime plus 2%. Recognize that the committee will be hesitant because of the amount of the note, the term of the note, and the lower interest rate. The following facts about Mason Co.'s five-year history may be used to support your request:

- 120% sales growth
- double number of items produced
- 20% annual increase in net income
- 100% increase in employment
- stable upper management
- 20% reduction in customer complaints
- increased market share from 25% to 33%
- 10% increase in dividends
- liabilities declined from 45% to 25% of assets

Cases for Critical Thinking

Case 1

Roberta Wagner owns Wagner Books. At the end of each month, Wagner Books borrows money from a bank and uses the proceeds to pay all of its outstanding accounts payable. The business signs a 15-day, 12.5% note payable for each loan. Each month to date, Wagner Books has been able to pay the notes payable when due. Mrs. Wagner uses this procedure to maintain good credit ratings with vendors. Is her reasoning sound? Explain your answer.

Case 2

Jennifer Pier, owner and manager of Pier, Inc., does not record adjusting or reversing entries for accrued payroll. Ms. Pier says that the matter is taken care of when the first payroll is recorded in the next month. The CPA who advises Ms. Pier suggests that the adjusting and reversing entries should be made. He states that omission of these entries affects the information reported on the business' financial statements. With whom do you agree? Explain your answer.

AUTOMATED ACCOUNTING

CALCULATING NOTES AND INTEREST USING PLANNING TOOLS

Planning Tools

Planning tools are easy-to-use applications for producing results for different types of financial investments. There are five different tabs included on the Planning Tools screen:

- College Planner
- Savings Planner
- Loan Planner
- Retirement Plan
- Notes and Interest

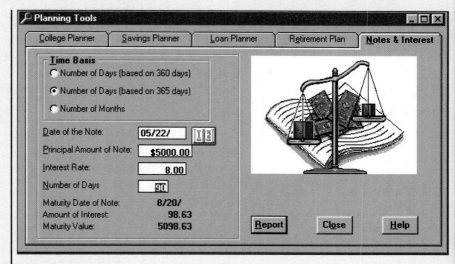

Figure AA9-1

Notes and Interest

In this section, the Notes and Interest planning tool will be explored. As discussed in Chapter 9, a written and signed promise to pay a sum of money at a specified time is called a **promissory note**. Promissory notes signed by a business and given to a creditor are called **notes payable**. The day a note is issued is called the **date of the note**. The original amount of a note is called the **principal of a note**. The date a note is due is called the **maturity date of a note**.

The Notes and Interest planning tool is located on the Notes & Interest tab on the Planning Tools screen, as shown in Figure AA9-1. The tool is used to:

- Determine the maturity date of the note
- Calculate the amount of interest
- Calculate the maturity value of the note

Entering Note Data in the Notes and Interest Planning Tool

To use the tool, you must know the date of the note, the principal amount of the note, the interest rate, and the number of days (months) for which the note will be outstanding. The following steps are used for any note.

1. Click on the Tools toolbar button.

2. Select the Notes & Interest tab.

3. Select the time basis by clicking on the appropriate radio button. There are three time basis options: number of days (based on 360 days); number of days (based on 365 days); and number of months.

4. Enter the date of the note, which is the date the note was issued.

5. Enter the principal amount of the note.

6. Enter the interest rate.

7. Enter the number of days (time period for which the note is outstanding). If you select Number of Months as the time basis, you enter the number of months, rather than the number of days.

Once all the data are entered, the results are displayed at the bottom on the planner's screen.

Displaying or Printing the Note Analysis Report

A sample Notes Analysis report is shown in Figure AA9-2. To display or print the report, use the following steps:

1. Click the Report button on the Notes & Interest screen.

2. Choose the Print button if you wish to print the report. (You

AUTOMATED ACCOUNTING

Note Analysis

Note Analysis
05/22/

Date of the Note	05/22/
Time of the Note	90 Days
Principal of the Note	5000.00
Interest Rate of the Note	8.00
Amount of Interest	98.63
Maturity Date of the Note	8/20/
Maturity Value of the Note	5098.63

[Print]   [Help]   [Close]   [Copy]

Figure AA9-2

may choose to view the report, instead of printing it.)

3. Click the Close button. You also have the option to copy the report to the clipboard so that you may include the note data in a separate document.

AUTOMATING APPLICATION PROBLEM 9-1

Instructions:

1. Load *Automated Accounting* 7.0 or higher software.

2. Select database A09-1 (Advanced Course Application Problem 9-1) from the accounting template disk.

3. Select File from the menu bar and choose the Save As menu command. Key the path to the drive and directory that contains your data files. Save the database with a file name of XXX091 (where XXX are your initials).

4. Access Problem Instructions through the Help menu. Read the Problem Instruction screen.

5. Key the data listed on page 270.

6. Exit the Automated Accounting software.

AUTOMATING MASTERY PROBLEM 9-4

Instructions:

1. Load *Automated Accounting* 7.0 or higher software.

2. Select database A09-4 (Advanced Course Mastery Problem 9-4) from the accounting template disk.

3. Select File from the menu bar and choose the Save As menu command. Key the path to the drive and directory that contains your data files. Save the database with a file name of XXX094 (where XXX are your initials).

4. Access Problem Instructions through the Help menu. Read the Problem Instruction screen.

5. Key the data listed on page 271.

6. Exit the Automated Accounting software.

10

Accounting for Notes Receivable, Unearned Revenue, and Accrued Revenue

AFTER STUDYING CHAPTER 10, YOU WILL BE ABLE TO:

1. Define accounting terms related to notes receivable, unearned revenue, and accrued revenue.

2. Identify accounting concepts and practices related to notes receivable, unearned revenue, and accrued revenue.

3. Journalize transactions for notes receivable.

4. Journalize adjusting and reversing entries for unearned revenue initially recorded as revenue.

5. Journalize adjusting and reversing entries for accrued revenue.

A business entity must report accurate and up-to-date information about notes receivable and accrued revenue on its financial statements at the end of a fiscal period. *(CONCEPT: Adequate Disclosure)* Because of the nature of notes receivable and some types of revenue, special accounting procedures may be required at the end of a fiscal period. For example, a note receivable issued in one fiscal period with a maturity date in the following fiscal period requires special accounting procedures. Special accounting procedures also are required for two types of revenue:

1. Revenue received in one fiscal period but not earned until the next fiscal period.

2. Revenue earned in one fiscal period but not received until the next fiscal period.

The special accounting procedures are designed so that the correct amount of revenue earned in the fiscal period is recognized in the financial statements. *(CONCEPT: Matching Expenses with Revenue)*

ACCOUNTING
IN YOUR CAREER

SIX MONTHS SAME AS CASH

Electronic World sells sound systems, televisions, satellite dishes, and computers through its electronic equipment department. The company also has a department for large household appliances. Few of Electronic World's sales are for cash. For lower-priced products, some buyers use credit cards. However, buyers of the more expensive systems and appliances purchase on credit.

Electronic World carries its own accounts, but customers must sign a note. The appliance industry experiences a great deal of competition, and profit margins are low. Companies compete on price and on the credit terms they offer. The largest companies can usually offer the lowest prices because their quantity buying enables them to purchase merchandise to sell at a low cost. Most of Electronic World's competitors offer terms of 90 days same as cash. This means that a customer signs a note, but pays no interest if the principal is paid within 90 days.

Electronic World's sales are down as the fourth quarter begins. In the monthly management meeting, Gina Morgan, the sales manager, says, "It's clear to me that we have to take dramatic action if we want to increase our sales. First, we need to offer better terms than the competition. What if we extend our same-as-cash terms to 180 days? That would knock the socks off the competition. Then the second thing we need to do is loosen up the credit approval process. We are turning customers down."

Some of the managers agree with Gina's proposals. But Ted Matthews, the accounting manager, particularly disagrees with loosening the credit approvals. "We already have defaults on 5% of our notes as it is," he says, "We should be tightening the approvals, not loosening them."

"But, Ted," says Gina, "we have to get more sales if we're going to stay in business."

Critical Thinking
1. What are the advantages and disadvantages of offering terms of 180 days?
2. What is your opinion of loosening the credit approval process?

ISSUING A NOTE RECEIVABLE FOR AN ACCOUNT RECEIVABLE

	GENERAL JOURNAL				PAGE 4	
DATE	ACCOUNT TITLE	DOC. NO.	POST. REF.	DEBIT	CREDIT	
1	20-- Apr. 3	Notes Receivable	NR11		3 0 0 00		1
2		Accounts Rec./Duane Jansen				3 0 0 00	2

Figure 10-1

Promissory notes that a business accepts from customers are called **notes receivable**. Notes receivable are usually due within a year. Therefore, notes receivable are classified as current assets.

Notes receivable can be issued to customers who need an extension of time to pay on account.

April 3. Accepts a 30-day, 12% note from Duane Jansen for an extension of time on his account, $300.00. Note Receivable No. 11.

The amount to be received is changed from an account receivable to a note receivable, as shown in Figure 10-1. In the accounts receivable ledger, the customer account, Duane Jansen, is decreased by a $300.00 credit. The balance of Mr. Jansen's accounts receivable account is zero.

GENERAL LEDGER
Notes Receivable

| 4/3 | 300.00 | |

Accounts Receivable

| | | 4/3 | 300.00 |

ACCOUNTS RECEIVABLE LEDGER
Duane Jansen

| Bal. | 300.00 | 4/3 | 300.00 |
| | | (New Bal. zero) | |

ISSUING A NOTE FOR A SALE

	GENERAL JOURNAL				PAGE 4	
DATE	ACCOUNT TITLE	DOC. NO.	POST. REF.	DEBIT	CREDIT	
3	4	Notes Receivable	NR12		4 5 0 00		3
4		Sales				4 5 0 00	4

Figure 10-2

Most sales on account assume that the customer will pay within 30 days or less. To promote sales, a company may allow its customers to sign a note extending payment over a longer period of time. If no cash is received, the sale is recorded on a general journal, as shown in Figure 10-2. If a cash down payment is received, the transaction could be recorded in a cash receipts journal.

April 4. Accepts a 90-day, 12% note from Mark Carver for the sale of an appliance, $450.00. Note Receivable No. 12.

Notes Receivable

| 4/4 | 450.00 | |

Sales

| | | 4/4 | 450.00 |

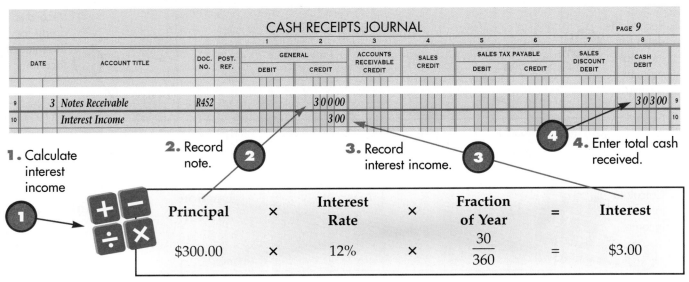

Figure 10-3

Interest is earned for the period of time a note is outstanding. Because the interest rate is stated as an annual rate, the actual interest earned must be computed as a fraction of a year. For ease of calculation, most companies use a 360-day year to calculate interest. The calculation of interest and the receipt of cash in payment of the note receivable are shown in Figure 10-3.

Whether a note is accepted for the extension of time for an account receivable or for a sale, the transaction to record the receipt of cash on the maturity date is the same.

> **May 3. Received cash for the maturity value of Note Receivable No. 11: principal, $300.00, plus interest, $3.00; total, $303.00. Receipt No. 452.**

Interest Income is classified as Other Revenue, as shown on Appliance Center's chart of accounts.

Cash

5/3 303.00	

Notes Receivable

Bal. 300.00	5/3 300.00
(New Bal. zero)	

Interest Income

	5/3 3.00

REMEMBER

The interest rate on a note is stated as an annual rate. To compute the interest for a period of time, the interest rate must be multiplied by the fraction of a year that the note was outstanding.

RECORDING A DISHONORED NOTE RECEIVABLE

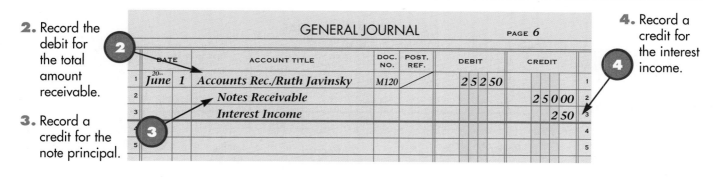

2. Record the debit for the total amount receivable.

3. Record a credit for the note principal.

4. Record a credit for the interest income.

1. Calculate interest income

Principal	×	Interest Rate	×	Fraction of Year	=	Interest
$250.00	×	12%	×	$\frac{30}{360}$	=	$2.50

Figure 10-4

A note that is not paid when due is called a **dishonored note**. The notes receivable account balance should include only the amount of notes receivable that a business expects to collect. Otherwise, Notes Receivable will be reported incorrectly on a balance sheet. *(CONCEPT: Adequate Disclosure)*

On June 1, the maturity date of Note Receivable No. 8, Ruth Javinsky owes the principal, *$250.00*, plus accrued interest. Interest is accrued for the 30-day term of the note.

Although the note is dishonored, Ruth still owes the money to Appliance Center. A journal entry is recorded to transfer the maturity value of the note to accounts receivable, as shown in Figure 10-4.

> *June 1. Ruth Javinsky dishonored Note Receivable No. 8, a 30-day, 12% note, maturity value due today: principal, $250.00; interest, $2.50; total, $252.50. Memorandum No. 120.*

The journal entry for a dishonored note receivable does not cancel the debt. Appliance Center does not inform Ruth Javinsky that the note's maturity value was transferred to Accounts Receivable. Appliance Center continues to try to collect the account. However, the debt is transferred to Accounts Receivable and carried on the records until Ruth pays the amount or her account is declared uncollectible.

GENERAL LEDGER

Accounts Receivable

| 6/1 | 252.50 | |

Notes Receivable

| 5/1 | 250.00 | 6/1 | 250.00 |

Interest Income

| | | 6/1 | 2.50 |

ACCOUNTS RECEIVABLE LEDGER

Ruth Javinsky

| 6/1 | 252.50 | |

REMEMBER

The accounting for uncollectible accounts was presented in Chapter 7. Dishonored notes receivable, when added to the balance of Accounts Receivable, are considered when computing adjustments to Allowance for Uncollectible Accounts. If the dishonored note, after being transferred to Accounts Receivable, is deemed uncollectible, the account is written off using the procedures discussed in Chapter 7.

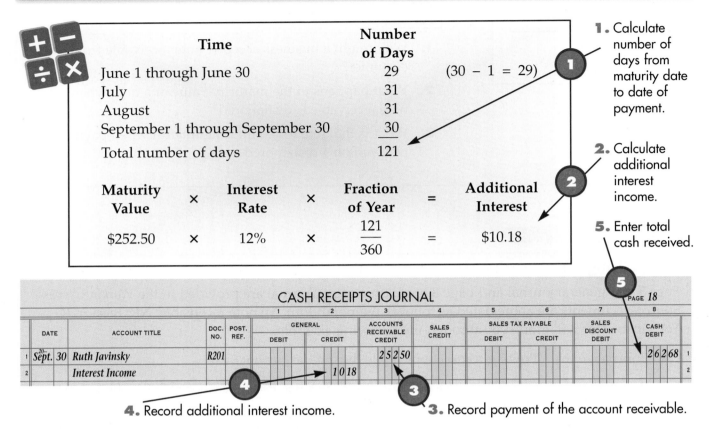

Figure 10-5

Sometimes payment may be received on a previously dishonored note. Additional interest is charged from maturity date to payment date.

On September 30, Ruth Javinsky paid Appliance Center the maturity value of her note plus interest. The time for computing additional interest begins when the note is dishonored and ends on the day cash is received. The number of days for which interest is owed is calculated using the same method as determining the due date of a note. Instead of adjusting the date of the last month to equal a predetermined number of days, the payment date is used to determine the number of days in the final month, as shown in Figure 10-5.

The interest rate is adjusted for the fraction of the year from the date the note was dishonored to the payment date. The additional interest is based on the maturity value of the note on the date the note was dishonored, *$252.50.*

September 30. Received cash from Ruth Javinsky for dishonored Note Receivable No. 8: *maturity value, $252.50, plus additional interest, $10.18; total, $262.68. Receipt No. 201.*

Ruth Javinsky's account in the accounts receivable ledger provides a complete history of the transactions. Management should use this information when making any future decisions to extend credit to this customer.

GENERAL LEDGER
Cash

| 9/30 | 262.68 | |

Accounts Receivable

| Bal. | 252.50 | 9/30 | 252.50 |

Interest Income

| | | 9/30 | 10.18 |

ACCOUNTS RECEIVABLE LEDGER
Ruth Javinsky

| Bal. | 252.50 | 9/30 | 252.50 |
| (New Bal. zero) | | | |

TERMS REVIEW

notes receivable

dishonored note

AUDIT YOUR UNDERSTANDING

1. Why might a business accept a note receivable from a customer?
2. What happens to the maturity value of a note when a note receivable is dishonored?
3. What is the time for computing interest when payment is received on a dishonored note?

WORK TOGETHER

Journalizing notes receivable transactions

Page 5 of a general journal and page 8 of a cash receipts journal are provided in the *Working Papers*. Source documents are abbreviated as follows: memorandum, M; note receivable, NR; receipt, R. Your instructor will guide you through the following example.

4. Journalize the following transactions made during the current year.

May 1.	Accepted a 60-day, 15% note from Patrick Sampson for an extension of time on his account, $400.00. NR1.
June 1.	Accepted a 180-day, 18% note from Sandy Adams for the sale of equipment, $700.00. NR2.
June 30.	Patrick Sampson dishonored NR1; maturity value, $400.00 plus interest. M142.
Nov. 28.	Received cash for the maturity value of NR2: principal, $700.00 plus interest. R310.
Dec. 12.	Received cash from Patrick Sampson for dishonored NR1, $410.00 plus additional interest. R432.

ON YOUR OWN

Journalizing notes receivable transactions

Page 6 of a general journal and page 9 of a cash receipts journal are provided in the *Working Papers*. Source documents are abbreviated as follows: memorandum, M; note receivable, NR; receipt, R. Work this problem independently.

5. Journalize the following transactions made during the current year.

May 14.	Accepted a 90-day, 18% note from Pamula Yates for an extension of time on her account, $320.00. NR19.
June 1.	Accepted a 120-day, 18% note from Walt Harrison for the sale of furniture, $1,500.00. NR20.
Aug. 12.	Pamula Yates dishonored NR19; maturity value, $320.00 plus interest. M82.
Oct. 26.	Received cash for the maturity value of NR20, $1,500.00 plus interest. R430.
Dec. 22.	Received cash on account from Pamula Yates for dishonored NR19, $334.40 plus additional interest. R753.

10-2 Unearned and Accrued Revenue

ADJUSTING ENTRY FOR UNEARNED REVENUE INITIALLY RECORDED AS A REVENUE

1. Debit the revenue account.

2. Credit the liability account.

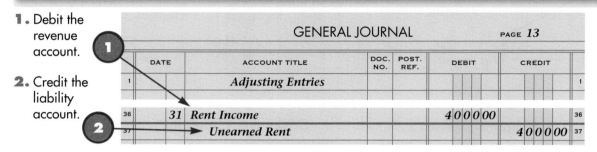

	DATE	ACCOUNT TITLE	DOC. NO.	POST. REF.	DEBIT	CREDIT	
		Adjusting Entries					1
36	31	*Rent Income*			4 0 0 0 00		36
37		*Unearned Rent*				4 0 0 0 00	37

GENERAL JOURNAL — PAGE 13

Figure 10-6

Some revenue is received during a fiscal period but is not actually earned until the next fiscal period. Revenue received in one fiscal period but not earned until the next fiscal period is called **unearned revenue**. Unearned revenue is also known as deferred revenue.

Unearned revenue may be recorded initially as a liability or as revenue. Appliance Center rents part of its building to Pace Delivery and initially records rent receipts as revenue.

On December 1, Appliance Center received $6,000.00 from Pace Delivery, $2,000.00 per month for December, January, and February rent. The receipt was recorded as rent income and is included in the $28,000.00 balance of Rent Income.

Only that part of rent actually earned should be recorded as revenue in a fiscal period. An adjusting entry is recorded to separate the earned and unearned portions of the rent

recorded in Rent Income, as shown in Figure 10-6. The January and February rent is unearned and should be reported in Unearned Rent.

The $4,000.00 balance of Unearned Rent, a liability account, represents the value of two months of rent owed to Pace Delivery. The new balance of Rent Income, $24,000.00, correctly reflects 12 months of rent at $2,000.00 per month.

Unearned Rent is classified as a Current Liability and Rent Income is classified as Other Revenue, as shown on Appliance Center's chart of accounts.

Unearned Rent		
	Adj.	4,000.00

Rent Income		
Adj.	4,000.00	Dec. 31 Bal. 28,000.00
		(New Bal. 24,000.00)

1. Debit the liability account.

2. Credit the revenue account.

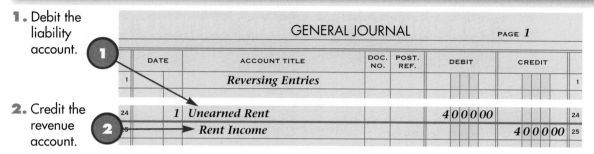

GENERAL JOURNAL					PAGE 1	
DATE	ACCOUNT TITLE	DOC. NO.	POST. REF.	DEBIT	CREDIT	
	Reversing Entries					1
24	1 *Unearned Rent*			4 0 0 0 00		24
	Rent Income				4 0 0 0 00	25

Figure 10-7

On December 31, Rent Income is closed as part of Appliance Center's closing entries. After closing entries are posted, the balance in Rent Income is zero and ready to record transactions in the next fiscal period.

Reversing entries for prepaid and accrued expenses are described in Chapter 9. If an adjusting entry *creates* a balance in an asset or liability account, the adjusting entry is reversed. Reversing entries for unearned revenue are made for the same reason as for prepaid expenses. The amount of unearned revenue must be returned to the account in which it was initially recorded.

Appliance Center's adjusting entry created a balance in the liability account, Unearned Rent. Therefore, Appliance Center needs to make a reversing entry for unearned rent on January 1, as shown in Figure 10-7.

On January 1, after the reversing entry is posted, the new balance of Unearned Rent is zero as it was before the adjusting entry. Rent Income has a $4,000.00 credit balance. The rent received in advance for January and February, $4,000.00, is part of the rent revenue earned in the new fiscal period.

Unearned Rent			
Rev.	4,000.00	Adj.	4,000.00
		(New Bal. zero)	

Rent Income			
Adj.	4,000.00	Dec. 31 Bal.	28,000.00
Clos.	24,000.00	*(New Bal. zero)*	
		Rev.	4,000.00
		(New Bal.	*4,000.00)*

THE FEDERAL GOVERNMENT IS LEARNING TO SHOP AT ELECTRONIC STORES

The federal government purchases billions of dollars of goods and services every year. Various government agencies have developed Web-based electronic stores. The Government Services Administration (GSA) administers GSA Advantage, the largest of these electronic stores. GSA Advantage supplies more than 4 million items to other government agencies. Other departments and agencies, including NASA and the various branches of the Armed Services, operate smaller electronic stores.

Authorized federal employees can make purchases from these electronic stores. Currently, purchases are made by "credit cards" with various purchasing limits. Eventually, the credit cards will be replaced by smart cards.

The Web-based electronic stores reduce the purchasing cycle by more than 50 percent. Substantial cost savings result from lower inventory levels and reduced paperwork.

TECHNOLOGY FOR BUSINESS

Note	Principal	×	Interest Rate	×	Fraction of Year	=	Accrued Interest Income
12	$500.00	×	10%	×	$\frac{30}{360}$	=	$4.17
13	$700.00	×	10%	×	$\frac{15}{360}$	=	2.92
			Total accrued interest income, December 31....				$7.09

1. Calculate interest earned on the notes.

1

2. Record entry to accrue interest income.

2

	GENERAL JOURNAL				PAGE 13		
	DATE	ACCOUNT TITLE	DOC. NO.	POST. REF.	DEBIT	CREDIT	
1		*Adjusting Entries*					1
2	Dec. 31	*Interest Receivable*			7 09		2
3		*Interest Income*				7 09	3

Figure 10-8

Revenue earned in one fiscal period but not received until a later fiscal period is called **accrued revenue**. For example, a business accepts a 30-day note on December 15. During December, the business earned interest for 16 days. However, the business will not receive any of the interest until the note's maturity in January. Interest for the first 16 days must be recorded in the current fiscal period. *(CONCEPT: Matching Expenses with Revenue)*

On December 31, Appliance Center has two notes receivable outstanding.

Note Receivable No. 12, a 60-day, 10% note dated December 1, $500.00.

Note Receivable No. 13, a 30-day, 10% note dated December 16, $700.00.

Accrued interest for each note is calculated from the date of the note through the end of the fiscal year, as shown in Figure 10-8.

The accrued interest for all notes is totaled to compute the adjusting entry amount. The adjusting entry increases the balance of Interest Income to include interest that has been earned but not received in cash.

The amount of interest owed to the company is reported as Interest Receivable. Interest

Receivable is classified as a Current Asset, as shown on Appliance Center's chart of accounts.

Interest Receivable	
Adj. 7.09	

Interest Income	
	Dec. 31 Bal. 65.70
	Adj. 7.09
	(New Bal. 72.79)

F.Y.I.

A company that accepts a large number of notes might benefit from using a ledger system similar to an accounts receivable ledger. The ledger enables management to identify the total amount of notes outstanding with any single customer. Thus, management could make more informed decisions about extending additional credit to a particular customer.

	DATE		ACCOUNT TITLE	DOC. NO.	POST. REF.	DEBIT	CREDIT	
1			*Reversing Entries*					1
2	20-- Jan.	1	*Interest Income*			7 09		2
3			*Interest Receivable*				7 09	3

GENERAL JOURNAL   PAGE 1

Figure 10-9

Interest Income is closed as part of Appliance Center's closing entries. After closing entries are posted, Interest Income has a zero balance. The $7.09 balance in Interest Receivable represents interest that Appliance Center has earned but has not yet received in cash.

The adjusting entry for accrued interest income created a balance in the asset account Interest Receivable. Therefore, on January 1, Appliance Center needs to reverse the adjusting entry that created the balance in Interest Receivable, as shown in Figure 10-9.

The new balance of Interest Receivable is zero, as it was before the adjusting entry. The new debit balance, $7.09, in Interest Income is a contra balance. When cash is received on the maturity date of each note, a credit to Interest Income will offset the debit balance.

Interest Income			
Clos.	72.79	Dec. 31 Bal.	65.70
		Adj.	7.09
Rev.	7.09		
(New Bal.	*7.09)*		

Interest Receivable			
Adj.	7.09	Rev.	7.09
(New Bal. zero)			

REMEMBER

Reversing entries eliminate the need for accounting personnel to remember to apply different account distributions to selected transactions. Without reversing entries, accounting personnel need to determine whether each interest payment was part of a prior year-end adjusting entry. If previously adjusted, the interest payment needs to be divided between Interest Receivable and Interest Income. With reversing entries, however, accounting personnel can simply record all interest payments to Interest Income.

COLLECTION OF DEBTS

T he Fair Debt Collection Practices Act defines the steps collectors may use to collect money owed to a creditor. A debt collector may contact the debtor in person, by mail, telephone, telegram, or fax. The collector may not:
- Contact the debtor at unreasonable times or places.
- Threaten or harass the debtor.
- Use false statements such as a threat of arrest or the threat of

legal action, unless legal action can be taken and is intended to be taken.
- Send the debtor official-looking documents from a court or government agency.
- Collect an amount greater than the debt, unless allowed by law.
- Force a debtor to accept collect calls.
- Take or threaten to take property, unless allowed by law.

LEGAL ISSUES IN ACCOUNTING

TERMS **R**EVIEWS

unearned revenue

accrued revenue

AUDIT YOUR **U**NDERSTANDING

1. What accounts are affected, and how, when rent received in advance is initially recorded as a revenue?
2. What is the rule for determining whether an adjusting entry should be reversed?
3. What accounts are affected, and how, by a reversing entry for rent revenue when rent receipts are initially recorded as a revenue?
4. What accounts are affected, and how, by an adjusting entry for accrued interest income?
5. What accounts are affected, and how, by a reversing entry for accrued interest income?

WORK **T**OGETHER

Journalizing adjusting and reversing entries for unearned revenue initially recorded as revenue and for accrued revenue

Valentine, Inc., is preparing its December 31 financial statements for the current year. On December 1, the company received a $2,100.00 rent payment from Owens & Nolen, LLP. The payment is the $700.00 per month rent for December of the current year through February of the next year. Valentine initially records rent receipts as revenue. General journal pages are provided in the *Working Papers*. Your instructor will guide you through the following examples.

6. Journalize the adjusting entry for unearned rent. Use page 13 of a general journal.
7. Journalize the reversing entry for unearned rent. Use page 14 of a general journal.

Valentine, Inc., has two notes receivable outstanding on December 31 of the current year.

Note No.	Interest Rate	Term	Principal	Date
14	15%	60-days	$2,000.00	November 14
15	16%	60-days	$3,000.00	December 6

8. Journalize the adjusting entry for accrued interest income. Use page 13 of a general journal.
9. Journalize the reversing entry for accrued interest income. Use page 14 of a general journal.

Journalizing adjusting and reversing entries for unearned revenue initially recorded as revenue and for accrued revenue

Parker Discount Stores is preparing its December 31 financial statements for the current year. On October 30, the store paid $1,500.00 to K-98.1 Radio for advertising. The advertising contract requires K-98.1 to provide Parker with $500.00 of advertising time per month for November of the current year through January of the next year. K-98.1 initially records advertising receipts as revenue. General journal pages are provided in the *Working Papers*. Work this problem independently.

10. Journalize the adjusting entry for unearned advertising. Use page 19 of a general journal.

11. Journalize the reversing entry for unearned advertising. Use page 20 of a general journal.

Parker Discount Stores has two notes receivable outstanding on December 31 of the current year.

Note No.	Interest Rate	Term	Principal	Date
26	18%	90-days	$4,000.00	November 8
29	16%	60-days	$1,500.00	December 12

12. Journalize the adjusting entry for accrued interest income. Use page 19 of a general journal.

13. Journalize the reversing entry for accrued interest income. Use page 20 of a general journal.

SUMMARY

After completing this chapter, you can

1. Define accounting terms related to notes receivable, unearned revenue, and accrued revenue.

2. Identify accounting concepts and practices related to notes receivable, unearned revenue, and accrued revenue.

3. Journalize transactions for notes receivable.

4. Journalize adjusting and reversing entries for unearned revenue initially recorded as revenue.

5. Journalize adjusting and reversing entries for accrued revenue.

EXPLORE ACCOUNTING

FACTORING ACCOUNTS RECEIVABLE

New businesses must have an adequate amount of working capital to purchase inventory, rent or buy fixed assets, and pay employees during the planning, construction, and opening periods. Access to independent sources of working capital, such as bank loans, is often limited until a business proves it can maintain profitability.

Accounts receivable can become a significant drain on working capital. Inventory sold on account does not immediately provide cash to purchase new inventory. Customers unable to purchase out-of-stock items shop elsewhere. The more successful a business is at selling inventory on account, the greater its need for working capital.

A solution to this problem is that a business can sell its accounts receivable to another company for cash. Assigning the rights to accounts receivable to an independent company in exchange for cash is known as factoring. The factoring company pays 85% to 95% of the value of the accounts receivable sold. The factoring company assumes the responsibility and cost of collecting the accounts.

Factoring costs the business 5% to 15% of sales on account. However, the immediate cash received allows the business to continue operations. In addition, management can focus its attention on more important aspects of the business than on the collection of accounts receivable.

REQUIRED:

Accounting equations are provided in the *Working Papers*.

Record transactions using the following assumptions for eight weeks, with and without factoring. Would you recommend that Chism Company factor accounts receivable at 90% of value?

1. All cash was used to purchase $10,000 of inventory.
2. Disregard other operating expenses.
3. With a complete inventory, sales are $2,000 per week ($1,000 cost). If the inventory levels drop below $10,000, however, sales for out-of-stock items are lost. Chism can still sell 20% of available inventory each week.
4. All sales are on account with n/30 terms. Cash collected is used to restock inventory up to $10,000.
5. Accounts receivable are factored at 90% of value.

APPLICATION PROBLEM 10-1
Journalizing transactions for notes receivable

Bellingham, Inc., completed the following transactions during the current year.

Transactions:

Aug. 1. Bellingham agreed to an extension of time on James Huber's account by accepting a 60-day, 10% note from him, $200.00. NR1.

Aug. 1. Accepted a 60-day, 12% note from Frank Otto for a sale on account, $300.00. NR2.

Sept. 30. The 60-day, 10% note from James Huber (NR1) was dishonored; $200.00 plus interest. M12.

Sept. 30. Accepted a 60-day, 10% note from Melissa Carr for an extension of time on her account, $500.00. NR3.

Sept. 30. Received cash for the maturity value of NR2, $300.00 plus interest. R10.

Nov. 30. Principal, $500.00, plus interest was received for the maturity value of NR3. R32.

Dec. 1. James Huber sent a check for dishonored NR1, $203.33 plus additional interest. R33.

Instructions:

Use page 8 of a general journal and page 15 of a cash receipts journal to journalize the transactions. Source documents are abbreviated as follows: memorandum, M; note receivable, NR; receipt, R.

APPLICATION PROBLEM 10-2
Journalizing adjusting and reversing entries for unearned revenue initially recorded as revenue

On November 1 of the current year, Billies, Inc., received a $2,700.00 rent payment from Simms & Ulman. The payment covers rent of office space for November through April, $450.00 per month. Billies initially records rent payments as revenue.

Instructions:

1. Journalize the adjusting entry for unearned rent on December 31 of the current year. Use page 13 of a general journal.

2. Journalize the reversing entry for unearned rent on January 1 of the next year. Use page 1 of a general journal.

APPLICATION PROBLEM 10-3
Journalizing adjusting and reversing entries for accrued revenue

On December 31 of the current year, McNeilson, Inc., has two notes receivable.

Note Receivable No. 1, a 90-day, 10% note dated November 1, $200.00.
Note Receivable No. 2, a 60-day, 10% note dated December 1, $300.00.

Instructions:

1. Calculate the accrued interest on the notes as of December 31.

2. Journalize the adjusting entry for accrued interest income on December 31 of the current year. Use page 13 of a general journal.

3. Journalize the reversing entry for accrued interest income on January 1 of the next year. Use page 1 of a general journal.

10-4

MASTERY PROBLEM
Journalizing notes receivable, unearned revenue, and accrued revenue initially recorded as revenue transactions

Marier, Inc., completed the following transactions during the current year. Marier initially records prepaid and unearned items as revenue.

Transactions:

July 1. Accepted a 90-day, 10% note from Timothy Johnson for a sale on account, $500.00. NR12.

July 5. Accepted a 90-day, 12% note from Gerald Kammer for an extension of time on his account, $600.00. NR13.

Sept. 29. Timothy Johnson dishonored NR12, a 90-day, 10% note, $500.00 plus interest. M32.

Oct. 3. Received cash for the maturity value of NR13, $600.00 plus interest. R65.

Nov. 1. Received cash for November through January rent, $500.00 per month, in advance from Centuria, Inc., $1,500.00. R70.

Dec. 1. Received cash from Timothy Johnson for dishonored NR12, $512.50 plus additional interest. R81.

Dec. 4. Accepted a 90-day, 12% note from Jackie Webb for sale on account, $900.00. NR14.

Instructions:

1. Use page 7 of a general journal and page 19 of a cash receipts journal to journalize the transactions. Source documents are abbreviated as follows: memorandum, M; note receivable, NR; receipt, R.

2. Continue using page 7 of the general journal. Journalize the necessary adjusting entries.

3. Journalize the reversing entries on January 1 of the next year. Use page 1 of a general journal.

10-5

CHALLENGE PROBLEM
Journalizing accounts and notes receivable

Hillsdale, Inc., sells on account with n/30 terms. If the account is not paid within 30 days, Hillsdale begins charging customers 18% interest on their outstanding balance. At 120 days past due, Hillsdale asks customers to sign a 60-day, 18% note for the original amount of the sale plus 90 days of accrued interest. During the year, Hillsdale accrues interest income when notes are issued or payments on account are made.

Unfortunately, customers are not always willing to pay all or any of the interest charges. Because the amounts are often small, Hillsdale must consider the negative impact that attempting to collect these amounts may have on its image. Thus, it writes off many interest charges as uncollectible.

Transactions:

July 4. Accepted a 60-day, 18% note from Steven Bozeman for an extension of time, $500.00 plus accrued interest. NR26.

July 12. Received $618.00 cash from Pierre Black on payment of NR18, a $627.00 note ($600.00 plus $27.00 accrued interest) issued 60 days ago. Mr. Black included a letter stating that he would pay interest only on the note and only for the original sale amount. R70.

July 15. Received $250.00 cash in payment of John Hamilton's account. The account balance resulted from a sale on account of $250.00 on May 16. R71.

July 31. Hillsdale's credit manager decided not to attempt to collect the interest charges on the accounts of Pierre Black and John Hamilton. M46.

INTERNET ACTIVITY

Point your browser to
http://accounting.swpco.com
Choose **Advanced Course**, choose **Activities**, and complete the activity for Chapter 10.

Applied Communication

You have just been hired as the new credit manager for Harrell and Company, a chain of lumber stores. While evaluating the accounting system, you notice that many of the credit accounts are 120 to 180 days past due. Although these customers ultimately pay their accounts, they do not abide by the n/30 terms specified on the sales invoice.

At your suggestion, management has approved a plan to change the credit terms to 2/10, n/30, with 18% interest charged on overdue accounts. In addition, you will require a note receivable to be signed for accounts over 90 days past due as a condition for the customer to receive additional credit.

Required:
Prepare a letter to send to current credit customers informing them of the new credit terms.

Cases for Critical Thinking

Case 1

Farmland, Inc., issued a 60-day, 12%, $600.00 note receivable to a customer. The customer dishonored the note at maturity. The accounting clerk recorded the dishonored note receivable by debiting Accounts Receivable and crediting Notes Receivable for the maturity value, $612.00. Thirty days later, the customer paid $618.12 for the dishonored note. The accounting clerk recorded this amount by debiting Cash and crediting Notes Receivable. Farmland's bookkeeper checked the work and decided that the journal entries were both incorrect. Do you agree? Explain your answer.

Case 2

At the beginning of December, Maxim Floral, Inc., received three months' rent in advance. Maxim initially records rent payment as a revenue. On December 31, Maxim does not make an adjusting entry for unearned rent. What effect will this have on the firm's financial statements?

AUTOMATED ACCOUNTING

CORRECTION OF ERRORS

When entering data into journals it is very easy to make errors unless you are careful. It is important to check your work as you enter transactions into the accounting system. People use different methods in order to lessen the likelihood of entering incorrect transactions and amounts, and entering transactions into the wrong journal.

Sometimes it may be necessary to locate and correct journal entries that have already been posted to the ledgers. The same procedure is used to locate and correct errors in all journals.

Finding a Journal Entry

Use the following steps to find a journal entry:

1. Click on the special journal tab to which the journal entry was made (General, Purchases, Cash Payments, Sales, Cash Receipts).

2. Choose the Find menu item from the Edit menu.

3. Enter the date, reference, vendor name, or amount of the transaction you want to find in the Find What text box. Then click OK.

4. If a matching transaction is found, it will be displayed onscreen so that it may be changed or deleted.

Changing Transactions

When changing or deleting journal transactions:

1. Click the journal tab in which you want to make a change.

2. Select the specific transaction that you wish to change.

3. Enter the correct journal entry and click the Post command button.

Accounting systems can be very efficient in processing data but it is the responsibility of the individual entering data to make accuracy a high priority. When producing a business' financial reports from an accounting system, if transactions were entered with errors, the reports will not represent the true financial position of the company. An error can cause management to make business decisions based on inaccurate information which could have serious consequences for a business.

AUTOMATING APPLICATION PROBLEM 10-1

Instructions:

1. Load *Automated Accounting 7.0* or higher software.

2. Select database A10-1 (Advanced Course Application Problem 10-1) from the accounting template disk.

3. Select File from the menu bar and choose the Save As menu command. Key the path to the drive and directory that contains your data files. Save the database with a file name of XXX101 (where XXX are your initials).

4. Access Problem Instructions through the Help menu. Read the Problem Instruction screen.

5. Key the data listed on page 290.

6. Exit the Automated Accounting software.

AUTOMATING MASTERY PROBLEM 10-4

Instructions:

1. Load *Automated Accounting 7.0* or higher software.

2. Select database A10-4 (Advanced Course Mastery Problem 10-4) from the accounting template disk.

3. Select File from the menu bar and choose the Save As menu command. Key the path to the drive and directory that contains your data files. Save the database with a file name of XXX104 (where XXX are your initials).

4. Access Problem Instructions through the Help menu. Read the Problem Instruction screen.

5. Key the data listed on page 291.

6. Exit the Automated Accounting software.

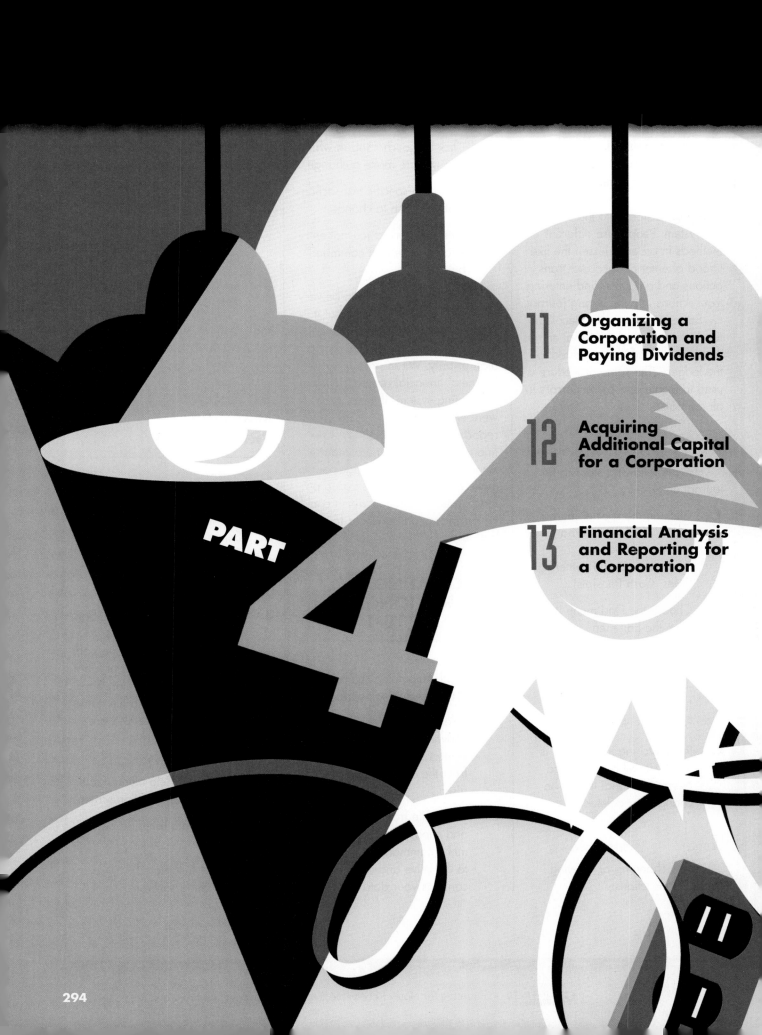

PART 4

LAMPLIGHT, INC. CHART OF ACCOUNTS

Balance Sheet Accounts

(1000) Assets

1100 CURRENT ASSETS
1105   Cash
1110   Petty Cash
1115   Notes Receivable
1120   Interest Receivable
1125   Accounts Receivable
1130   Allowance for Uncollectible Accounts
1135   Subscriptions Receivable
1140   Merchandise Inventory
1145   Supplies—Store
1150   Supplies—Administrative
1155   Prepaid Insurance
1160   Prepaid Interest

1200 LONG-TERM INVESTMENT
1205   Bond Sinking Fund

1300 PLANT ASSETS
1305   Store Equipment
1310   Accumulated Depreciation—Store Equipment
1315   Building
1320   Accumulated Depreciation—Building
1325   Office Equipment
1330   Accumulated Depreciation—Office Equipment
1335   Land

1400 INTANGIBLE ASSET
1405   Organization Costs

(2000) Liabilities

2100 CURRENT LIABILITIES
2105   Interest Payable
2110   Accounts Payable
2115   Employee Income Tax Payable
2120   Federal Income Tax Payable
2125   Social Security Tax Payable
2130   Medicare Tax Payable
2135   Salaries Payable
2140   Sales Tax Payable
2145   Unemployment Tax Payable—Federal
2150   Unemployment Tax Payable—State
2155   Health Insurance Premiums Payable
2160   Dividends Payable

2200 LONG-TERM LIABILITY
2205   Bonds Payable

(3000) Stockholders' Equity
3105   Capital Stock—Common
3110   Stock Subscribed—Common
3115   Paid-in Capital in Excess of Stated Value—Common
3120   Capital Stock—Preferred
3125   Stock Subscribed—Preferred
3130   Paid-in Capital in Excess of Par Value—Preferred
3135   Discount on Sale of Preferred Stock
3140   Treasury Stock
3145   Paid-in Capital from Sale of Treasury Stock
3150   Retained Earnings
3155   Dividends—Common
3160   Dividends—Preferred
3165   Income Summary

Income Statement Accounts

(4000) Operating Revenue
4105   Sales
4110   Sales Discount
4115   Sales Returns and Allowances

(5000) Cost of Merchandise
5105   Purchases
5110   Purchases Discount
5115   Purchases Returns and Allowances

(6000) Operating Expenses

6100 SELLING EXPENSES
6105   Advertising Expense
6110   Credit Card Fee Expense
6115   Depreciation Expense—Store Equipment
6120   Miscellaneous Expense—Sales
6125   Salary Expense—Sales
6130   Supplies Expense—Sales

6200 ADMINISTRATIVE EXPENSES
6205   Depreciation Expense—Building
6210   Depreciation Expense—Office Equipment
6215   Insurance Expense
6220   Miscellaneous Expense—Administrative
6225   Payroll Taxes Expense
6230   Property Tax Expense
6235   Salary Expense—Administrative
6240   Supplies Expense—Administrative
6245   Uncollectible Accounts Expense
6250   Utilities Expense

(7000) Other Revenue
7105   Gain on Plant Assets
7110   Interest Income

(8000) Other Expenses
8105   Interest Expense
8110   Loss on Plant Assets
8115   Organization Expense

(9000) Income Tax
9105   Federal Income Tax Expense

The chart of accounts for LampLight, Inc. is illustrated above for ready reference as you study Part 4 of this textbook.

11
Organizing a Corporation and Paying Dividends

AFTER STUDYING CHAPTER 11, YOU WILL BE ABLE TO:

1. Define accounting terms related to corporate accounting.

2. Identify accounting concepts and practices related to corporate accounting.

3. Journalize transactions related to starting a corporation.

4. Journalize transactions related to stock subscriptions.

5. Prepare a balance sheet for a newly formed corporation.

6. Calculate dividends for a corporation.

7. Journalize transactions of a corporation related to declaring and paying dividends.

Selecting the form of business ownership is an important decision of new business owners. An organization with the legal rights of a person and that may be owned by many persons is called a **corporation**. *(CONCEPT: Business Entity)* A corporation is organized by law to exist separately and apart from its owners. Corporations differ from other forms of businesses principally in the nature of ownership and management.

A corporation's ownership is divided into units. Each unit of ownership is known as a share of stock. Total shares of ownership in a corporation are known as capital stock. An owner of one or more shares of a corporation is known as a stockholder.

Stockholders share a corporation's earnings. Earnings distributed to stockholders are known as dividends. Corporations may retain some or all of their earnings to finance future business expansion and improvement. However, most corporations distribute a portion of their earnings to stockholders.

TERMS PREVIEW

corporation
board of directors
articles of
    incorporation
charter
common stock
preferred stock
stock certificate
par value
par-value stock
no-par-value stock
stated-value stock
subscribing for capital
    stock
organization costs
intangible assets
declaring a dividend
date of declaration
date of record
date of payment

ACCOUNTING
IN YOUR CAREER

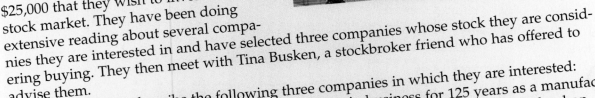

INVESTING IN THE STOCK MARKET

Bob and Marie Schneider have saved $25,000 that they wish to invest in the stock market. They have been doing extensive reading about several companies they are interested in and have selected three companies whose stock they are considering buying. They then meet with Tina Busken, a stockbroker friend who has offered to advise them.

Bob and Marie describe the following three companies in which they are interested:

Smith-Kent Industries. This company has been in business for 125 years as a manufacturer of household furnishings. It has kept up with the times and pays a 4% dividend on common stock nearly every year. The market price of the stock is $27.50, and has remained at that level for the past 10 years.

InFoData Technology Corporation. InFoData has not paid any dividends on either common or preferred stock for the past five years. However, it makes a generous profit each year that it invests back into research. The market price of the stock has increased about 25% each year for the past five years.

Benton, Inc. Benton, Inc., has missed paying the 10% dividend on preferred stock only once in the last 20 years. There is generally little change in the market price of the stock.

Tina tells the Schneiders that all the companies they have chosen have merit, but they will have to decide what their investment goals are before she can help them choose among the companies. She says that they might consider either growth or income and that they also need to decide how much risk they can bear.

Critical Thinking

1. What does Tina Busken mean by the goals of "growth" and "income"?
2. Evaluate the investment potential of the three companies.

ARTICLES OF INCORPORATION

1. Nature of business.

2. Types of stock authorized.

3. Initial directors.

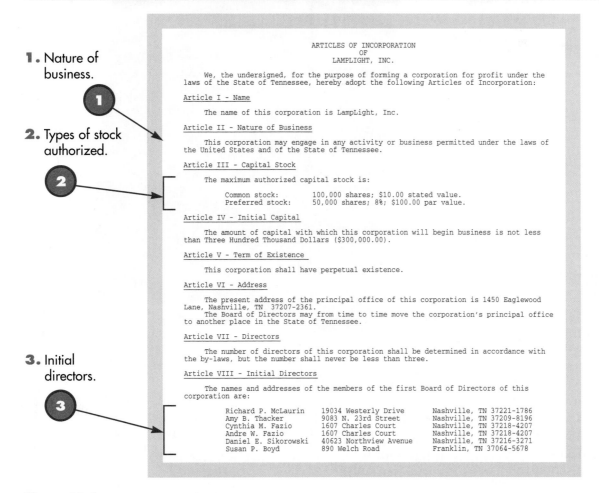

```
                        ARTICLES OF INCORPORATION
                                  OF
                            LAMPLIGHT, INC.

        We, the undersigned, for the purpose of forming a corporation for profit under the
    laws of the State of Tennessee, hereby adopt the following Articles of Incorporation:

    Article I - Name

        The name of this corporation is LampLight, Inc.

    Article II - Nature of Business

        This corporation may engage in any activity or business permitted under the laws of
    the United States and of the State of Tennessee.

    Article III - Capital Stock

        The maximum authorized capital stock is:

            Common stock:         100,000 shares; $10.00 stated value.
            Preferred stock:       50,000 shares; 8%; $100.00 par value.

    Article IV - Initial Capital

        The amount of capital with which this corporation will begin business is not less
    than Three Hundred Thousand Dollars ($300,000.00).

    Article V - Term of Existence

        This corporation shall have perpetual existence.

    Article VI - Address

        The present address of the principal office of this corporation is 1450 Eaglewood
    Lane, Nashville, TN  37207-2361.
        The Board of Directors may from time to time move the corporation's principal office
    to another place in the State of Tennessee.

    Article VII - Directors

        The number of directors of this corporation shall be determined in accordance with
    the by-laws, but the number shall never be less than three.

    Article VIII - Initial Directors

        The names and addresses of the members of the first Board of Directors of this
    corporation are:

            Richard P. McLaurin    19034 Westerly Drive      Nashville, TN 37221-1786
            Amy B. Thacker         9083 N. 23rd Street        Nashville, TN 37209-8196
            Cynthia M. Fazio       1607 Charles Court         Nashville, TN 37218-4207
            Andre W. Fazio         1607 Charles Court         Nashville, TN 37218-4207
            Daniel E. Sikorowski   40623 Northview Avenue     Nashville, TN 37216-3271
            Susan P. Boyd          890 Welch Road             Franklin, TN 37064-5678
```

Figure 11-1

A corporation may have many owners. Most owners do not participate in the management of the business. Instead, they elect a small group to represent their combined interests and to be responsible for management of the corporation. A group of persons elected by the stockholders to manage a corporation is called a **board of directors**. A board of directors determines corporate policies and selects corporate officers to supervise the day-to-day management of the corporation.

Legal Requirements for Forming a Corporation

Persons seeking to form a corporation must submit an application to the state in which the company is to be incorporated. A written application requesting permission to form a corporation is called the **articles of incorporation**. Some articles of incorporation are submitted to the federal government, but most are submitted to a state government. When the articles of incorporation are approved, a corporation comes into existence. The approved articles of incorporation are called a **charter**. A charter is also referred to as a certificate of incorporation.

LampLight, Inc. is a corporation that sells lighting fixtures. The articles of incorporation submitted for LampLight, Inc. are shown in Figures 11-1 and 11-2.

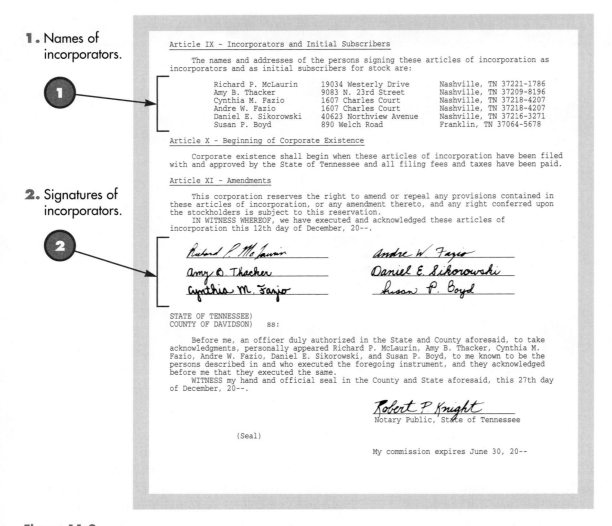

1. Names of incorporators.

2. Signatures of incorporators.

Article IX - Incorporators and Initial Subscribers

The names and addresses of the persons signing these articles of incorporation as incorporators and as initial subscribers for stock are:

```
Richard P. McLaurin      19034 Westerly Drive      Nashville, TN 37221-1786
Amy B. Thacker           9083 N. 23rd Street       Nashville, TN 37209-8196
Cynthia M. Fazio         1607 Charles Court        Nashville, TN 37218-4207
Andre W. Fazio           1607 Charles Court        Nashville, TN 37218-4207
Daniel E. Sikorowski     40623 Northview Avenue    Nashville, TN 37216-3271
Susan P. Boyd            890 Welch Road            Franklin, TN 37064-5678
```

Article X - Beginning of Corporate Existence

Corporate existence shall begin when these articles of incorporation have been filed with and approved by the State of Tennessee and all filing fees and taxes have been paid.

Article XI - Amendments

This corporation reserves the right to amend or repeal any provisions contained in these articles of incorporation, or any amendment thereto, and any right conferred upon the stockholders is subject to this reservation.

IN WITNESS WHEREOF, we have executed and acknowledged these articles of incorporation this 12th day of December, 20--.

Richard P. McLaurin   *Andre W. Fazio*

Amy B. Thacker   *Daniel E. Sikorowski*

Cynthia M. Fazio   *Susan P. Boyd*

STATE OF TENNESSEE)
COUNTY OF DAVIDSON)   ss:

Before me, an officer duly authorized in the State and County aforesaid, to take acknowledgments, personally appeared Richard P. McLaurin, Amy B. Thacker, Cynthia M. Fazio, Andre W. Fazio, Daniel E. Sikorowski, and Susan P. Boyd, to me known to be the persons described in and who executed the foregoing instrument, and they acknowledged before me that they executed the same.

WITNESS my hand and official seal in the County and State aforesaid, this 27th day of December, 20--.

Robert P. Knight
Notary Public, State of Tennessee

(Seal)

My commission expires June 30, 20--

Figure 11-2

As stated, LampLight is organized as a corporation to sell lighting fixtures and accessories. However, Article II of its articles of incorporation describes the nature of the business in broad, general terms. This broad purpose enables LampLight to expand into other kinds of business activities, if it desires, without applying for a new charter.

Rights of Stockholders

Most stockholders have three basic rights.

1. To vote at stockholders' meetings unless an exception is made for holders of a particular kind of stock.

2. To share in a corporation's earnings.

3. To share in the distribution of the assets of the corporation if it ceases operations and sells all its assets.

Capital Stock of a Corporation

Corporations may issue two basic kinds of stock: common and preferred. Stock that does not give stockholders any special preferences is called **common stock**. Stock that gives stockholders preference in earnings and other rights is called **preferred stock**. LampLight is authorized to issue both common and preferred stock as described in Article III, Figure 11-1.

REMEMBER

Although the format of the articles of incorporation varies from one corporation to another, the articles usually address similar items.

CERTIFICATE OF STOCK

LAMPLIGHT, INC.

COMMON STOCK

This Certifies that

Fiona Washington

is the owner of

One Hundred Shares

without par

Issued April 30, 20--   Certificate Number LLI-321D9

Figure 11-3

Written evidence of the number of shares that each stockholder owns in a corporation is called a **stock certificate**. A corporation issues a stock certificate when it receives full payment for the stock. A stock certificate, such as the one shown in Figure 11-3, usually states the issue date, certificate number, number of shares, and name of the stockholder.

A corporation keeps a record of stock issued to each stockholder. A stockholder may later decide to sell some or all shares of stock owned. Changing ownership of stock is referred to as a stock transfer. Some corporations handle the issuing and transferring of stock certificates as well as the record of stock ownership. Most corporations, however, engage a transfer agent, such as a bank, to issue certificates and keep stock ownership records.

Value of Stock

Shares of stock are frequently assigned a value. A value assigned to a share of stock and printed on the stock certificate is called **par value**. A share of stock that has an authorized value printed on the stock certificate is called **par-value stock**.

A share of stock that has no authorized value printed on the stock certificate is called **no-par-value stock**. Some states require that no-par-value stock be assigned a stated or specific value. No-par-value stock that is assigned a value by a corporation is called **stated-value stock**. Stated-value stock is similar to par-value stock except that the value is not printed on the stock certificates.

Common Stock

If a corporation issues only one type of stock, that stock is common stock. If a corporation issues only common stock, the common stockholders are entitled to all of the dividends. In most corporations, only owners of common stock have a right to vote on matters brought before the stockholders. LampLight is authorized to issue no-par-value common stock with a stated value of $10.00.

Most stock sold today is common stock.

Preferred Stock

To attract more investors, a corporation may offer preferred stock with preferences as to some of the basic stockholders' rights. Preferred stockholders usually do not have voting rights and cannot influence when and how much is paid in dividends. Therefore, a typical preference given to preferred stockholders is to receive dividends before common stockholders. Other preferences granted preferred stockholders may include the following:

1. Unpaid dividends may accumulate from one year to another. In years that dividends are not paid, the preferred dividends accumulate and are paid in a later year. Accumulated preferred dividends must be paid before any common stock dividends are paid.

2. Dividends may be shared with common stockholders above a stated percentage or amount. Once the dividend to common stockholders equals the stated percentage of the preferred stock, additional dividends may be shared between preferred and common stockholders.

Every preference granted to preferred stockholders comes at the expense of common stockholders. For example, if preferred stockholders share in dividends above a stated percentage, common stockholders give up a right to some dividends. However, regardless of the type of stock issued, no stockholder is entitled to dividends until a corporation's board of directors votes to pay dividends.

Preferred stock dividends may be stated as a percentage of par value or as an amount per share. For example, LampLight has authorized the issuance of 8%, $100.00 par-value preferred stock.

INTERNATIONAL PACKAGES AND CUSTOMS INSPECTIONS

 hen sending a package overseas, appropriate documentation must accompany the package to verify its contents. Customs officials will read the documentation and may open the package to verify its contents.

All major trading nations use the Harmonized Commodity Description and Coding System (HS). HS establishes a single ten-digit code for each type of commodity. This code may be obtained from the Census Bureau's Foreign Trade Division.

Shipping restrictions apply to certain commodities. The Food and Drug Administration (FDA) regulates the import of items such as foods, pharmaceuticals, medical devices, and cosmetics. These restrictions protect American citizens from improperly tested items that could cause physical harm.

The U. S. Department of Agriculture (USDA) regulates the import of items such as meat and meat products, insects, plants, fruits, and vegetables. Restrictions on shipments protect domestic horticulture from infection by disease or insects.

The Federal Communications Commission (FCC) regulates the import of such items as cordless telephones, video games, microwave ovens, and radio transmitters. By regulating such items, the quality of consumer products can be protected.

Required:

Obtain a guide from a carrier that provides the guidelines for sending a package internationally. Select a foreign country and assume that you are sending a package that contains a ten page legal document. The package weighs less than two pounds.

1. Which forms must be completed to send the document?
2. How should you package the document?
3. How much will it cost?
4. When will it be delivered?

GLOBAL PERSPECTIVE

1. Write the date.   **2.** Enter the account title.

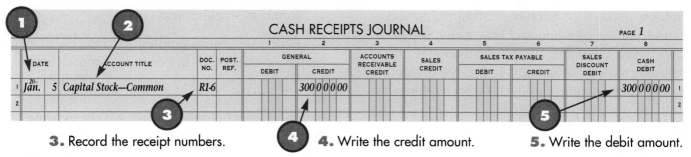

3. Record the receipt numbers.   **4.** Write the credit amount.   **5.** Write the debit amount.

Figure 11-4

LampLight's charter is its legal authorization to begin business in the name of the corporation. The corporation needs assets to operate. It obtains its initial capital by selling stock to the incorporators.

Capital Accounts of a Corporation

Because of the number of owners, a corporation does not keep a separate capital account for each stockholder. Instead, it maintains a single summary general ledger capital account for each kind of stock issued. When a corporation issues only common stock, the value of all stock issued is recorded in a single capital stock account. When a corporation issues both common and preferred stock, separate capital stock accounts are used for common and preferred stock.

A corporation's net income is recorded in the capital account **Retained Earnings**. Using this account keeps the net income separate from the recorded values of issued capital stock. A net income is credited and a net loss is debited to Retained Earnings.

Issuing Capital Stock When Forming a Corporation

When the corporation is formed, each of LampLight's six incorporators agrees to buy 5,000 shares of common stock at the stated value. Thus, a total of 30,000 shares of common stock, stated value $10.00, is issued for a total of $300,000.00.

January 5. Received cash from six incorporators for 30,000 shares of $10.00 stated-value common stock, $300,000.00. Receipt Nos. 1–6.

Cash is debited for $300,000.00. Capital Stock—Common is credited for $300,000.00, the value of the issued common stock. The journal entry to record this transaction is shown in Figure 11-4.

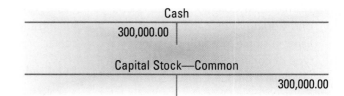

(S)(T)(E)(P)(S) **Journalize the entry to record cash received for common stock**

    1. Write the current year and the date in the Date column of the cash receipts journal.

    2. Enter *Capital Stock—Common* in the Account Title column.

    3. Record the receipt numbers, *R1–6*, in the Doc. No. column.

    4. Write the credit amount, *300,000.00*, in the General Credit column.

    5. Record the debit amount, *300,000.00*, in the Cash Debit column.

F.Y.I.

A debit balance in Retained Earnings is often referred to as a deficit.

ORGANIZATION COSTS OF A CORPORATION

	DATE	ACCOUNT TITLE	CK. NO.	POST. REF.	GENERAL		ACCOUNTS PAYABLE DEBIT	PURCHASES DISCOUNT CREDIT	CASH CREDIT	
					DEBIT	CREDIT				
1	Jan. 5	Organization Costs	1		2 4 0 0 00				2 4 0 0 00	1
2										2
3										3
4										4

CASH PAYMENTS JOURNAL — PAGE 1

Figure 11-5

Fees and other expenses of organizing a corporation are called **organization costs**. Organization costs may include the following:

1. An incorporation fee paid to the state when the articles of incorporation are submitted.

2. Attorney fees for legal services during the process of incorporation.

3. Other incidental expenses incurred prior to receiving a charter.

A corporation cannot be formed without organization costs. Until it receives a charter, a corporation does not exist to pay the organization costs. The planning required to start a new corporation often takes months. Therefore, one of the incorporators usually agrees to pay these costs until the charter is granted. The incorporator or incorporators who agree to pay the organization cost should keep accurate and complete records of all amounts paid on behalf of the corporation. After it receives a charter, a corporation reimburses the incorporator for the organization costs.

If substantial organization costs were recorded as an expense in a corporation's first year, net income could be reduced unreasonably during that first year. Furthermore, benefits derived from these expenditures extend over many years. Therefore, these costs are recorded in an asset account, **Organization Costs**, until charged as an expense. (CONCEPT: *Matching Expenses with Revenue*)

Adjusting entries to record portions of the organization costs as an expense each year are described in Chapter 13.

Amy Thacker agreed to pay the organization costs for LampLight until the company receives its charter. On January 5, Amy submitted a statement of organization costs, $2,400.00, that she had incurred prior to the receipt of the charter.

January 5. Paid cash to Amy Thacker as reimbursement for organization costs, $2,400.00. Check No. 1.

Organization Costs is debited for $2,400.00. Cash is credited for $2,400.00. The journal entry to record this transaction is shown in Figure 11-5.

Organization Costs	
Jan. 5 2,400.00	

Cash	
	Jan. 5 2,400.00

corporation

board of directors

articles of
   incorporation

charter

common stock

preferred stock

stock certificate

par value

par-value stock

no-par-value stock

stated-value stock

organization costs

1. What are the responsibilities of a corporation's board of directors?

2. What three basic rights do stockholders usually have?

3. What two basic kinds of stock may a corporation issue?

4. In place of a general ledger capital account for each owner, how does a corporation show stock ownership?

5. What accounts are affected, and how, when a corporation initially sells and issues common stock to incorporators?

6. What three items may be included in the organization costs of a corporation?

Journalizing transactions for starting a corporation

Presidential Limousine, Inc., received its corporate charter on April 2 of the current year. The corporation is authorized to issue 50,000 shares of $20.00 stated-value stock. A cash receipts journal and a cash payments journal are provided in the *Working Papers*. Source documents are abbreviated as follows: check, C; receipt, R. Your instructor will guide you through the following examples.

7. Journalize the following transactions. Save your work to complete the Work Together on page 309.

   Apr. 3. Received cash from four incorporators for 30,000 shares of $20.00 stated-value common stock, $600,000.00. R1–4.

   4. Paid cash to Julie Albrecht as reimbursement for organization costs, $10,000.00. C1.

ON YOUR OWN

Journalizing transactions for starting a corporation

Sierra Corporation received its corporate charter on June 3 of the current year. The corporation is authorized to issue 80,000 shares of $10.00 stated-value stock. A cash receipts journal and a cash payments journal are provided in the *Working Papers*. Source documents are abbreviated as follows: check, C; receipt, R. Work this problem independently.

8. Journalize the following transactions. Save your work to complete the On Your Own on page 309.

June 3. Received cash from three incorporators for 40,000 shares of $10.00 stated-value common stock, $400,000.00. R1–3.

5. Paid cash to Raul Mendoza as reimbursement for organization costs, $15,000.00. C1.

BUSINESSES OWNED BY ASIAN AMERICANS AND OTHER RELATED GROUPS

CULTURAL DIVERSITY

The Census Bureau's Survey of Minority-Owned Business Enterprises indicates that minority-owned enterprises are increasing in number and size. The Census Bureau groups together its statistics about businesses owned by Asian Americans, American Indians, Alaskan Natives, and Pacific Islanders. For this discussion, such businesses will be referred to API/AIAN-owned businesses. Firms owned by this segment of the population increased from 376,711 in 1987 to 606,438 in 1992. This represents a 61 percent increase. During the same period, total receipts increased by 194 percent from $34 billion to $100 billion. These increases represent the fastest growing segment of the minority-enterprise business groups.

About 83 percent of API/AIAN-owned firms operated as proprietorships in 1992. These businesses accounted for 35.4 percent of the gross receipts of API/AIAN-owned businesses. During the period from 1987 to 1992, there was a large increase in both partnerships and Subchapter S corporations owned by Asian Americans, American Indians, Alaskan Natives, and Pacific Islanders.

Forty-five percent of API/AIAN-owned businesses operated in the service industries, primarily in business, personal, and health services. Another 22 percent of the API/AIAN-owned firms operated in the retail trades. Average receipts of API/AIAN-owned businesses were $165,000, compared with $193,000 for all U.S. firms. Average receipts of API/AIAN-owned companies exceeded those for all U.S. firms in the construction and service industries.

JOURNALIZING A STOCK SUBSCRIPTION

1. Write the date.

2. Enter the account debited.

3. Record memorandum number.

4. Enter debit amount.

5. Enter the account credited.

6. Enter credit amount.

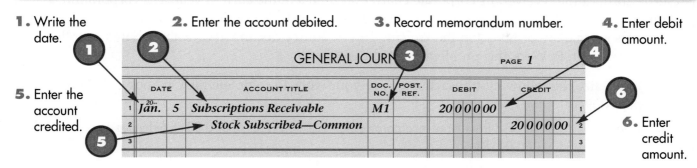

	DATE		ACCOUNT TITLE	DOC. NO.	POST. REF.	DEBIT	CREDIT	
1	20-- Jan.	5	Subscriptions Receivable	M1		20 00 0 00		1
2			Stock Subscribed—Common				20 00 0 00	2
3								3

GENERAL JOURNAL   PAGE 1

Figure 11-6

Corporations frequently contract with investors to sell capital stock with payment to be received at a later date. Future payment for the stock may be made all at one time or on an installment plan. Entering into an agreement with a corporation to buy capital stock and pay at a later date is called **subscribing for capital stock**.

On January 5, Daniel Herring subscribed for 2,000 shares of LampLight's common stock at $10.00 a share. He agreed to pay $10,000.00 on March 1 and $10,000.00 not later than July 1.

January 5. Received a subscription from Daniel Herring for 2,000 shares of $10.00 stated-value common stock, $20,000.00. Memorandum No. 1.

The journal entry to record this transaction is shown in Figure 11-6. Subscriptions Receivable is debited for $20,000.00. The asset account Subscriptions Receivable shows the unpaid amount of all subscriptions. Stock Subscribed—Common is credited for $20,000.00. The capital account Stock Subscribed—Common shows the total amount of stock subscribed but not issued. This capital account is used because stock certificates are issued only when the stock is fully paid for. The amounts are recorded in Capital Stock—Common only when stock is fully paid for and stock certificates are issued.

Subscriptions Receivable	
20,000.00	

Stock Subscribed—Common	
	20,000.00

S **Journalize the entry to record a stock subscription**

T **1.** Write the current year and the date in the Date column of the general journal.

E **2.** Enter the title of the account debited, *Subscriptions Receivable*, on line 1 in the Account Title column.

P **3.** Record memorandum number, *M1*, in the Doc. No. column.

P **4.** Write the debit amount, *20,000.00*, in the Debit column.

S **5.** Enter the title of the account credited, *Stock Subscribed—Common*, in the Account Title column.

   6. Write the credit amount, *20,000.00*, in the Credit column.

REMEMBER

Holders of subscribed stock have no voting rights.

				CASH RECEIPTS JOURNAL								PAGE 3	
				1	2	3	4	5	6	7	8		
DATE	ACCOUNT TITLE	DOC. NO.	POST. REF.	GENERAL		ACCOUNTS RECEIVABLE CREDIT	SALES CREDIT	SALES TAX PAYABLE		SALES DISCOUNT DEBIT	CASH DEBIT		
				DEBIT	CREDIT			DEBIT	CREDIT				
1	Mar. 1	Subscriptions Receivable	R45		10 0 0 0 00						10 0 0 0 00		1

Figure 11-7

On March 1, LampLight received cash from Daniel Herring in payment of half of his stock subscription. The journal entry to record this transaction is shown in Figure 11-7.

March 1. Received cash from Daniel Herring in partial payment of stock subscription, $10,000.00. Receipt No. 45.

Cash is debited for $10,000.00. Subscriptions Receivable is credited for $10,000.00. The new balance of this account, $10,000.00, is the amount

that Daniel still owes for his stock subscription. A similar journal entry is made on July 1 when Daniel pays the second installment of the stock subscription.

Cash	
Mar. 1 10,000.00	

Subscriptions Receivable	
Jan. 5 20,000.00	Mar. 1 10,000.00
(New Bal. 10,000.00)	

			GENERAL JOURNAL		PAGE 7	
DATE		ACCOUNT TITLE	DOC. NO.	POST. REF.	DEBIT	CREDIT
1	July 1	Stock Subscribed—Common	M67		20 0 0 0 00		1
2		Capital Stock—Common				20 0 0 0 00	2

Figure 11-8

When a stock subscription is fully paid for, a stock certificate is issued to the stockholder. The journal entry to record the issuance of stock to Daniel is shown in Figure 11-8.

July 1. Issued Stock Certificate No. 7 to Daniel Herring for 2,000 shares of $10.00 stated-value common stock. Memorandum No. 67.

Stock Subscribed—Common is debited for $20,000.00. Capital Stock—Common is credited for $20,000.00. The new balance of this account, $320,000.00, is the value of all common stock issued by LampLight.

LampLight records the issuance of stock only to the original stockholder. A stockholder may later

decide to sell shares of stock. LampLight does not journalize such stock transfers because these transactions do not generate additional capital for the corporation. However, the name of the new stockholder must be entered in LampLight's stock ownership records so that future dividend payments will be made to the correct person.

Stock Subscribed—Common	
July 1 20,000.00	Jan. 5 20,000.00
	(New Bal. zero)

Capital Stock—Common	
	Jan. 5 300,000.00
	July 1 20,000.00
	(New Bal. 320,000.00)

1. List intangible assets as the last category of assets.

①

2. List sources of paid-in capital.

②

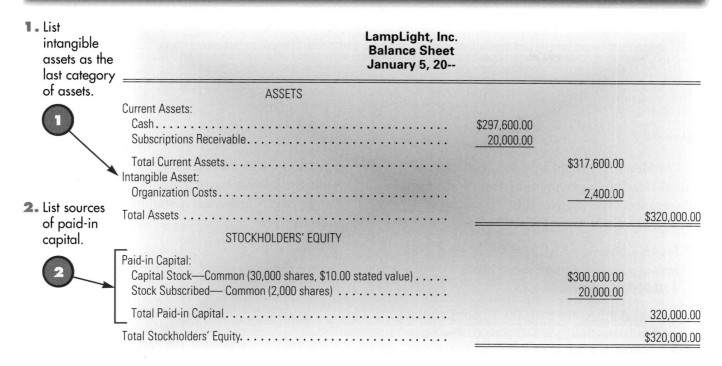

LampLight, Inc.
Balance Sheet
January 5, 20--

ASSETS

Current Assets:		
Cash.	$297,600.00	
Subscriptions Receivable.	20,000.00	
Total Current Assets.		$317,600.00
Intangible Asset:		
Organization Costs.		2,400.00
Total Assets		$320,000.00

STOCKHOLDERS' EQUITY

Paid-in Capital:		
Capital Stock—Common (30,000 shares, $10.00 stated value)	$300,000.00	
Stock Subscribed— Common (2,000 shares)	20,000.00	
Total Paid-in Capital.		320,000.00
Total Stockholders' Equity.		$320,000.00

Figure 11-9

LampLight's balance sheet at the end of business on January 5 is shown in Figure 11-9.

LampLight's cash on hand, January 5, is the original $300,000.00 paid by the incorporators *minus* the $2,400.00 paid for organization costs. The subscriptions receivable on January 5 is the amount due from Daniel Herring.

Assets of a nonphysical nature that have value for a business are called **intangible assets**. The heading, Intangible Asset, is listed on the balance sheet as the last subdivision in the Assets section. The asset account Organization Costs is presented in the intangible assets section. A corporation with long-term investments and plant assets shows them on a balance sheet before intangible assets.

Paid-in capital is a subdivision of the stockholders' equity section of a balance sheet. LampLight's paid-in capital on January 5

consists of $300,000.00 in issued common stock plus $20,000.00 in common stock subscribed. LampLight has not yet issued any preferred stock. Therefore, no amount for preferred stock is shown on the balance sheet.

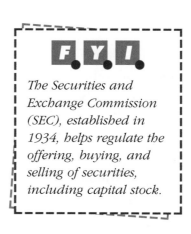

F.Y.I.

The Securities and Exchange Commission (SEC), established in 1934, helps regulate the offering, buying, and selling of securities, including capital stock.

REMEMBER

To publicly sell large issues of stock, a corporation must have the approval of the Securities and Exchange Commission (SEC) to certify that information about the business is not being concealed.

TERMS REVIEW

subscribing for capital stock

intangible assets

AUDIT YOUR UNDERSTANDING

1. What accounts are affected, and how, when subscribed stock is issued?

2. How are assets of a nonphysical nature reported on the balance sheet?

WORK TOGETHER

Journalizing transactions for stock subscriptions and preparing a balance sheet

Use the working papers from the Work Together on page 304. A general journal and statement paper are provided in the *Working Papers*. Source documents are abbreviated as follows: memorandum, M; receipt, R. Your instructor will guide you through the following examples.

3. Journalize the following transactions.
   Apr. 7. Received a subscription from Robert Companari for 5,000 shares of $20.00 stated-value common stock, $100,000.00. M1.
   24. Received cash from Robert Companari in payment of stock subscription, $100,000.00. R5.
   25. Issued Stock Certificate No. 5 to Robert Companari for 5,000 shares of $20.00 stated-value common stock, $100,000.00. M2.

4. Prepare a balance sheet for Presidential Limousine as of April 30 of the current year.

ON YOUR OWN

Journalizing transactions for stock subscriptions and preparing a balance sheet

Use the working papers from the On Your Own on page 305. A general journal and statement paper are provided in the *Working Papers*. Source documents are abbreviated as follows: memorandum, M; receipt, R. Work this problem independently.

5. Journalize the following transactions.
   June 11. Received a subscription from Jan Lee for 1,000 shares of $10.00 stated-value common stock, $10,000.00. M1.
   19. Received a subscription from Bill Ackermann for 3,000 shares of $10.00 stated-value common stock, $30,000.00. M2.
   24. Received cash from Jan Lee in payment of stock subscription, $10,000.00. R4.
   25. Issued Stock Certificate No. 4 to Jan Lee for 1,000 shares of $10.00 stated-value common stock, $10,000.00. M3.

6. Prepare a balance sheet for Sierra Corporation as of June 30 of the current year.

DIVIDENDS

Once operations begin, a new corporation usually retains a portion of net income to finance future business expansion and improvement. However, most corporations distribute a portion of the earnings to stockholders.

Corporate earnings distributed to stockholders are known as dividends. Action by a board of directors to distribute corporate earnings to stockholders is called **declaring a dividend**. The board determines when and what amount of the retained earnings will be distributed. A corporation has no obligation to distribute money to stockholders until the board of directors has declared a dividend.

Three important dates are involved in distributing a dividend:

1. Date of declaration. The date on which a board of directors votes to distribute a dividend is called the **date of declaration**.

2. Date of record. The date that determines which stockholders are to receive dividends is called the date of record. Stockholders may buy and sell stock at any time. However, only persons listed as stockholders on the date of record will receive dividends.

3. Date of payment. The date on which dividends are actually to be paid to stockholders is called the **date of payment**.

Ordinarily, the date of payment occurs several weeks after the date of record. Thus, a corporation has time to determine who is entitled to receive dividends and to prepare dividend checks to mail on the date of payment.

Transactions are recorded in a corporation's accounts on two of the three dates: (1) date of declaration and (2) date of payment.

Calculating a Dividend

When a board of directors declares a dividend, the corporation is obligated to pay it. At the date of declaration, the corporation incurs a liability that must be recorded.

The board of directors of CompuForm, Inc. has decided to declare an annual dividend of $24,000.00. On the date of record, the corporation has issued 1,000 shares of 8%, $100.00 par-value preferred stock and 16,000 shares of $20.00 stated-value common stock. The value of the preferred and common stock is calculated as follows.

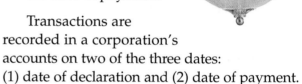

	Number of Preferred Shares	×	Par Value	=	Value of Preferred Stock
	1,000	×	$100.00	=	$100,000.00
	Number of Common Shares	×	Stated Value	=	Value of Common Stock
	16,000	×	$20.00	=	$320,000.00

REMEMBER

No stockholder is guaranteed a dividend.

The value of preferred stock is used to calculate the dividend on preferred stock. The distribution of the $24,000.00 dividend between preferred and common stock is calculated as follows:

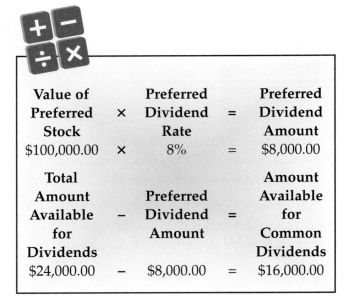

Value of Preferred Stock	×	Preferred Dividend Rate	=	Preferred Dividend Amount
$100,000.00	×	8%	=	$8,000.00

Total Amount Available for Dividends	−	Preferred Dividend Amount	=	Amount Available for Common Dividends
$24,000.00	−	$8,000.00	=	$16,000.00

The dividend rate for common stock is calculated as follows:

Common Dividend Amount	÷	Value of Common Stock	=	Common Dividend Rate
$16,000.00	÷	$320,000.00	=	5%

A summary of CompuForm's dividends follows.

	Amount	Rate
Preferred Stock Dividends	$ 8,000.00	8%
Common Stock Dividends	16,000.00	5%

In subsequent years, CompuForm may elect to increase its annual dividend. CompuForm's preferred stock dividend rate will never exceed 8%. Therefore, additional dividends will be distributed to common stock, increasing the common stock dividend rate. The common stock dividend rate may be less than, equal to, or more than the preferred stock dividend rate.

ACCOUNTING AT WORK

ALFREDA MOORE, BUSINESS MANAGER

As the college's Business Manager, I work closely with our CPA. I am responsible for payroll, financial statements, managing student accounts, and so on. Our accountant does the audit.

The most rewarding part of my work is seeing a student graduate whom I have helped, especially when it is someone who thought he or she could never afford to get through school. As the graduate walks across the stage and receives the diploma, I remember the day I helped make arrangements for tuition payments.

The most difficult part of my work is when a student does not want to open up about his or her finances. The student will make promises he or she cannot keep, and eventually drop out of school. Sometimes I wonder if I did something wrong. It's hard to work with those who will not communicate with you. If I know that someone has a problem, then I may be able to help.

I've been with the college five years. At first, I volunteered in the Financial Office and did bookkeeping. I suggested some changes, which worked, and they hired me. I have taken us from a manual system of bookkeeping to our present computerized setup.

When I was in high school, I never planned to go into this field. Then I went to a community college and earned an Associate Degree in Accounting. Prior to working at the college, I worked for fifteen years in banking and insurance.

I am glad I studied accounting. It has opened many doors for me.

	DATE		ACCOUNT TITLE	DOC. NO.	POST. REF.	DEBIT	CREDIT	
1	Dec.²⁰⁻	15	Dividends—Common	M132		16 0 0 0 00		1
2			Dividends—Preferred			8 0 0 0 00		2
3			Dividends Payable				24 0 0 0 00	3

GENERAL JOURNAL — PAGE 12

Figure 11-10

The journal entry to record the transaction needed when the dividends are declared is shown in Figure 11-10.

December 15. CompuForm's board of directors declared an annual dividend of $24,000.00. Preferred stock issued is $100,000.00 of 8%, $100.00 par-value preferred stock. Common stock issued is $320,000.00 of $20.00 stated-value common stock. Date of payment is January 15. Memorandum No. 132.

Dividends—Common is debited for $16,000.00. Dividends—Preferred is debited for $8,000.00. Dividends Payable is credited for $24,000.00.

CASH PAYMENTS JOURNAL — PAGE 1

		DATE		ACCOUNT TITLE	CK. NO.	POST. REF.	GENERAL DEBIT	GENERAL CREDIT	ACCOUNTS PAYABLE DEBIT	PURCHASES DISCOUNT CREDIT	CASH CREDIT	
							1	2	3	4	5	
18			15	Dividends Payable	432		24 0 0 0 00				24 0 0 0 00	18

Figure 11-11

On January 15, CompuForm issued a single check for $24,000.00, the total amount of the dividends to be paid. The check is deposited in a special dividend checking account. A separate check to each eligible stockholder is written against the special checking account. This procedure avoids a large number of entries in CompuForm's cash payments journal. The special dividend checking account also reserves cash specifically for paying the dividends.

CompuForm's dividend check is given to an agent who handles the details of preparing and mailing stockholders' checks. CompuForm's agent is the bank with which the corporation has its checking account.

January 15. Paid cash for annual dividend declared December 15, $24,000.00. Check No. 432.

Dividends Payable is debited and Cash is credited for $24,000.00. The journal entry to record this transaction is shown in Figure 11-11.

REMEMBER

Dividends may be paid in additional capital stock, known as a stock dividend, instead of cash. Dividends Payable is debited and Capital Stock is credited when the stock is issued on the date of payment.

ORK TOGETHER

Calculating and journalizing the dividends for a corporation

On January 10 of the current year, the board of directors of Eagle Express, Inc. declared an annual dividend of $60,000.00. On the date of record, the corporation had issued 2,000 shares of 6%, $100.00 par-value preferred stock and 30,000 shares of $22.00 stated-value common stock.

Page 4 of a general journal and page 11 of a cash payments journal are provided in the *Working Papers*. Source documents are abbreviated as follows: check, C; memorandum, M. Your instructor will guide you through the following examples.

4. Calculate the value of preferred stock.
5. Calculate the amount of dividends for the current year to be paid to preferred and common shareholders.
6. Journalize the entry to record the declaration of a dividend on January 10. M29.
7. Journalize the entry to record the payment of the dividend on January 30. C124.

N YOUR OWN

Calculating and journalizing the dividends for a corporation

On July 2 of the current year, the board of directors of StarVideo Corporation declared an annual dividend of $90,000.00. On the date of record, the corporation had issued 3,500 shares of 8%, $80.00 par-value preferred stock and 60,000 shares of $12.00 stated-value common stock.

Page 7 of a general journal and page 14 of a cash payments journal are provided in the *Working Papers*. Source documents are abbreviated as follows: check, C; memorandum, M. Work this problem independently.

8. Calculate the value of preferred stock.
9. Calculate the amount of dividends for the current year to be paid to preferred and common shareholders.
10. Journalize the entry to record the declaration of a dividend on July 2. M87.
11. Journalize the entry to record the payment of the dividend on August 2. C326.

After completing this chapter, you can

1. Define important accounting terms related to organizing a corporation and paying dividends.

2. Identify accounting concepts and practices related to corporate accounting.

3. Journalize transactions for starting a corporation.

4. Journalize transactions related to stock subscriptions.

5. Prepare a balance sheet for a newly formed corporation.

6. Calculate dividends for a corporation.

7. Journalize transactions for declaring and paying dividends for a corporation.

EXPLORE ACCOUNTING

STOCK SPLITS

Most stock purchases are made in multiples of 100 shares. A stock trade of 100 shares is called a round lot. A stock trade in an amount other than a multiple of 100 shares is called an odd lot. Because brokerage firms typically charge additional fees for odd lot trades, investors have a financial incentive to trade stock only in round lots.

As the market price per share rises, the total cost of a round lot can exceed the financial resources of the average individual investor. For example, a round lot of a stock trading at $60 per share would cost $6,000 plus brokerage fees. The demand for the stock declines when individual investors become unable to purchase the stock.

This decline in demand has a negative effect on the stock's market value.

One solution to this problem is to reduce the stock's market price to a reasonable amount. To reduce the market price, a corporation can increase the number of shares outstanding by dividing each outstanding share into two or more shares. Dividing a share of stock into a larger number of shares is called a stock split. In a 2-for-1 stock split, the company doubles the number of shares and reduces each share's par value by half. Thus, an investor holding 100 shares of $10 par value stock then owns 200 shares of $5 par value stock. More important, the market price of the stock, once at $60 per share, immediately drops to $30 per share.

Some investors mistakenly think that a stock split increases their ownership in the company and the value of their investment. Before the stock split, the investor owned 100 shares of $60 stock valued at $6,000. After the stock split, the investor owns 200 shares of $30 stock, also valued at $6,000. Because all stockholders now own twice the number of shares, each investor's percentage ownership in the corporation remains the same.

REQUIRED:

Explain the concept of stock splits using a pizza as a symbol for the total value of the corporation.

APPLICATION PROBLEM
Journalizing transactions for starting a corporation

Pacific Technologies Corporation received its charter on January 4 of the current year. The corporation is authorized to issue 200,000 shares of $10.00 stated-value common stock and 50,000 shares of 12%, $100.00 par-value preferred stock.

Transactions:

Jan. 4. Received cash from three incorporators for 48,000 shares of $10.00 stated-value common stock, $480,000.00. R1–3.

     4. Paid cash to Joseph Garza as reimbursement for organization costs, $2,000.00. C1.

Instructions:

Journalize the transactions. Use page 1 of a cash receipts journal, a cash payments journal, and a general journal. Source documents are abbreviated as follows: check, C; receipt, R. Save your work to complete Application Problem 11-2.

APPLICATION PROBLEM
Journalizing transactions for stock subscriptions and preparing a balance sheet

Use the working papers for Application Problem 11-1.

Transactions:

Jan. 5. Received a subscription from Karen Yoshihara for 2,000 shares of $10.00 stated-value common stock, $20,000.00. M1.

    16. Received a subscription from Tyronne Carter for 10,000 shares of $10.00 stated-value common stock, $100,000.00. M2.

Feb. 1. Received cash from Karen Yoshihara in payment of stock subscription, $20,000.00. R4.

     1. Issued Stock Certificate No. 4 to Karen Yoshihara for 2,000 shares of $10.00 stated-value common stock, $20,000.00. M3.

     8. Received cash from Tyronne Carter in partial payment of stock subscription, $50,000.00. R5.

    15. Received a subscription from Cindy Coburn for 300 shares of $10.00 stated-value common stock, $3,000.00. M4.

Mar. 1. Received cash from Tyronne Carter in final payment of stock subscription, $50,000.00. R6.

     1. Issued Stock Certificate No. 5 to Tyronne Carter for 10,000 shares of $10.00 stated-value common stock, $100,000. M5.

Instructions:

1. Journalize the transactions. Source documents are abbreviated as follows: memorandum, M; receipt, R.

2. Prepare a balance sheet for Pacific Technologies Corporation as of March 2 of the current year.

APPLICATION PROBLEM
Calculating dividends for a corporation

The information shown on page 316 is available from the accounting records of two different corporations.

Instructions:

1. Calculate the value of preferred stock.

2. Calculate the amount of dividends to be paid each year to preferred and common shareholders.

continued

	Corporations	
	Edison	Carmac
Preferred Stock:		
Description	$100.00 par-value	$50.00 par-value
Dividend Rate	10%	8%
Shares Issued	2,000	10,000
Common Stock:		
Description	$2.00 stated-value	$1.00 stated-value
Shares Issued	300,000	200,000
Annual Dividend:		
Year 1	$25,000.00	$50,000.00
Year 2	$30,000.00	$60,000.00
Year 3	$35,000.00	$75,000.00

APPLICATION PROBLEM
Journalizing transactions for declaring and paying dividends

PlasticTech, Inc. completed the following transactions during the current year.

Transactions:

Aug. 12. PlasticTech's board of directors declared an annual dividend of $180,000.00. Preferred stock issued is $500,000.00 of 10%, $100.00 par-value preferred stock. Common stock issued is $1,000,000.00 of $1,000.00 stated-value common stock. Date of payment is November 15. M65.

Nov. 15. Paid $180,000.00 cash for annual dividend declared August 12. C139.

Instructions:

Journalize the transactions. Use page 8 of a general journal and page 21 of a cash payments journal. Source documents are abbreviated as follows: check, C; memorandum, M.

MASTERY PROBLEM
Journalizing transactions for starting a corporation, declaring and paying dividends, and preparing a balance sheet

SkyPark, Inc. received its charter on August 1 of the current year. The corporation is authorized to issue 150,000 shares of $5.00 stated-value common stock and 50,000 shares of 10%, $100.00 par-value preferred stock.

Transactions:

20X2

Aug. 4. Ten incorporators pay cash for 50,000 shares of $5.00 stated-value common stock, $250,000.00. R1–10.

     4. Dan O'Brien was reimbursed for organization costs, $6,500.00. C1.

     6. Diane Scalacci subscribed to purchase 500 shares of $5.00 stated-value common stock, $2,500.00. M1.

    21. McCabe Daniels subscribed to purchase 3,000 shares of $5.00 stated-value common stock, $15,000.00. M2.

Sept. 16. Diane Scalacci made full payment on stock subscription, $2,500.00. R11.

16. Issued Stock Certificate No. 11 to Diane Scalacci for 500 shares. M3.

Oct. 1. McCabe Daniels made a partial payment on stock subscription, $7,500.00. R12.

15. Kay Mehta subscribed to purchase 6,000 shares of $5.00 stated-value common stock, $30,000.00. M4.

Nov. 1. McCabe Daniels made final payment on stock subscription, $7,500.00. R13.

1. Issued Stock Certificate No. 12 to McCabe Daniels for 3,000 shares. M5.

Instructions:

1. Journalize the transactions. Use page 1 of a cash receipts journal, a cash payments journal, and a general journal. Source documents are abbreviated as follows: check, C; memorandum, M; receipt, R.

2. Prepare a balance sheet for SkyPark, Inc. as of November 2 of the current year.

3. Journalize the following additional transactions completed during the following two years to record the declaration and payment of the dividends. Continue using page 1 of the general journal and the cash payments journal.

Additional Transactions:

20X3

Nov. 15. SkyPark's board of directors declared an annual dividend of $40,000.00. Preferred stock issued is $100,000.00 of 10%, $100.00 par-value preferred stock. Common stock issued is $400,000.00 of $5.00 stated-value common stock. Date of payment is January 15. M206.

20X4

Jan. 15. Paid cash for annual dividend declared November 15, $40,000.00. C339.

11-6 CHALLENGE PROBLEM
Journalizing transactions for a corporation

On January 1, 20X1, Atlantic Semiconductor Corporation had issued the following stock:

250,000 shares of $10.00 stated-value common stock.
20,000 shares of 12%, $100.00 par-value preferred stock.

Transactions:

20X1

June 7. A subscription was received from Grace Young for 2,000 shares of $10.00 stated-value common stock, $20,000.00. M234.

Oct. 15. Grace Young paid cash in partial payment of stock subscription, $10,000.00. R245.

Nov. 1. Atlantic Semiconductor's board of directors declared an annual dividend of $400,000.00. Date of payment is January 15, 20X2. M245.

20X2

Jan. 15. The annual dividend declared November 1, $400,000.00, was paid. C1489.

Feb. 21. Grace Young paid cash in final payment of stock subscription, $10,000.00. R296.

21. Issued Stock Certificate No. 132 to Grace Young for 2,000 shares of $10.00 stated-value common stock, $20,000.00. M262.

Oct. 12. A subscription was received from James Richards for 1,000 shares of $100.00 par-value preferred stock, $100,000.00. M289.

Nov. 1. Atlantic Semiconductor's board of directors declared an annual dividend of $450,000.00. Date of payment is January 15, 20X3. M292.

continued

20X3

Jan. 15. Paid annual dividend declared November 1, $450,000.00. C1654.

May 12. Cash was received from James Richards in full payment for 1,000 shares of $100.00 par-value preferred stock, $100,000.00. R312.

May 12. Stock Certificate No. 87 was issued to James Richards for 1,000 shares. M324.

Nov. 1. Atlantic Semiconductor's board of directors declared an annual dividend of $450,000.00. Date of payment is January 15, 20X4. M364.

Instructions:

Journalize the transactions. Use page 12 of a cash receipts journal, page 14 of a cash payments journal, and page 6 of a general journal. Source documents are abbreviated as follows: check, C; memorandum, M; receipt, R.

INTERNET ACTIVITY

Point your browser to

http://accounting.swpco.com

Choose **Advanced Course**, choose **Activities**, and complete the activity for Chapter 11.

Applied Communication

Most accountants actively participate in professional organizations. The organizations have periodic dinner meetings at which guest speakers make presentations regarding current accounting topics. As a member of a professional organization, you may be asked to introduce a guest speaker.

Required:

Prepare an introduction for a business professional you know personally. Identify the individual's most significant professional qualifications that allow him or her to speak on the topic. Include information regarding the speaker's community service and personal information to highlight his or her personal qualities.

Cases for Critical Thinking

Case 1 Jennifer Hester is considering whether she should buy stock as an investment. She asks you whether it would be better to buy common stock or preferred stock. How would you answer her? Explain your suggestions.

Case 2 Salvatoro, 22 years old, recently inherited $5,000.00. He has decided to invest the money in the stock market. He wants his investment to grow quickly. A friend recommended mutual funds as a good way to invest in the stock market. Salvatoro has asked you to research the types of mutual funds available and recommend how he should proceed.

AUTOMATED ACCOUNTING

USING THE LOAN PLANNER

Planning Tools

Planning tools are easy-to-use applications within an accounting system that provide fast and easy ways of making calculations that are commonly needed for journal entries and reports. Five planning tools have been included in *Automated Accounting 7.0* and higher.

The Automated Accounting section in Chapter 9, pages 274 and 275, introduced the notes and interest planning tool. When a business uses notes receivable or notes payable to finance transactions, information about interest amounts, payment amounts, and due dates may be calculated using the appropriate planner. Planning tools are also efficient and easy-to-use tools to use for what-if scenarios.

Loan Planner

The Loan Planner is similar to the Notes and Interest tool. It is used to calculate the amount of a loan, the loan payment amount, and the number of payments. A common use of this tool is to compute the monthly payment when a loan is made using the stated interest rate. The loan planner may then be used to generate an amortization schedule that will show the amount of principal and interest associated with each payment. To use the Loan Planner:

1. Click on the *Tools* toolbar button or select Planning Tools from the Data menu.

2. Click the *Loan Planner* tab.

3. Select the Loan Amount, Loan Payment Amount, or the Number of Payments option button in the Calculate option group. The unknown amount to be calculated text box will be dimmed, based upon the option selected.

4. Enter the data in the text boxes and press the Tab key. The calculated results will appear at the bottom of the Planning dialog box.

5. Click on the *Report* command button to produce a Loan Amortization Schedule. Once displayed, the report may be printed or copied to the clipboard for entering into a spreadsheet or word processor.

6. Click on *Close* to exit the report and return to the planner. Steps 3–5 may then be repeated for different calculation options, or for different data sets.

7. Click on Close, or press ESC, to exit the planner.

Displaying or Printing the Loan Amortization Schedule

The Loan Amortization Schedule can be generated by following these steps:

1. Click on the Reports button on the Loan Planner screen after entering the data.

2. Choose the Print button if you wish to print the report or you may choose to view only.

3. Click the Close button. You also have the option to copy the report to the clipboard so that you may include the loan data on a separate document.

USING SPECIAL TOOLS: THE LOAN PLANNER

Instructions:

1. Load *Automated Accounting 7.0* or higher software.

2. Select New from the File menu.

3. Click on the Tools toolbar button.

4. Click on the Loan Planner tab. Select Loan Payment Amount from the Calculate box. Enter a loan amount of $14,000.00, an interest rate of 8.00%, and 36 payments. The payment amount will be automatically calculated.

5. Click on the Report command button from within the Loan Planner tab. Print the report, or copy it to the clipboard for entering into a word processor or spreadsheet application.

6. Click Close to return to the planner. Steps 4 and 5 may then be repeated for different calculation options, or for different data sets.

7. Click Close or press ESC to exit the planner. Upon exiting a planning tool, your data will not be saved. Be sure to print a report, or copy it to a word processor or spreadsheet and save it in that application.

8. Exit the Automated Accounting software.

12

Acquiring Additional Capital for a Corporation

AFTER STUDYING CHAPTER 12, YOU WILL BE ABLE TO:

1. Define accounting terms related to acquiring capital for a corporation.

2. Identify accounting concepts and practices related to acquiring capital for a corporation.

3. Journalize entries for issuing additional capital stock.

4. Journalize entries for buying and selling treasury stock.

5. Journalize entries for bonds payable.

As a corporation grows, it may require additional capital to finance its expansion. The portion of a corporation's net income not paid to stockholders as dividends is a primary source of additional capital. Retained earnings may not, however, provide an adequate source of capital for a corporation. Both new and existing corporations may require a large increase in capital to finance rapid expansion. Thus, a corporation can acquire additional capital by selling stock to investors or borrowing money.

Articles of incorporation are usually written to permit a corporation to issue more shares of stock than it sold to initial investors. As the need arises for more capital, a corporation can issue some of the remaining authorized stock. LampLight, Inc. is authorized by its charter to issue a total of 100,000 shares of common stock and 50,000 shares of preferred stock. (CONCEPT: Business Entity) However, LampLight initially issued only 32,000 shares of common stock during its first year as described in Chapter 11. Thus, LampLight may sell some of the remaining shares of common or some shares of preferred stock to raise additional capital.

Once capital stock has been issued it may be reacquired by the company. Special procedures are required to account for such shares.

ACCOUNTING
IN YOUR CAREER

CHOOSING BETWEEN STOCKS AND BONDS

Video Technology Corporation has a new invention that will deliver Internet access to most homes in the country. A $25 million investment in a new manufacturing facility is required to produce the equipment. The finance committee, headed by Roger Peterson, has explored two options for financing this expansion: issuing preferred stock and issuing bonds. The committee was unable to find a bank willing to lend this amount on a note or mortgage.

At the board of directors meeting, the two alternatives are being discussed. Roger presents the analysis of the options to the finance committee as follows:

1. Issue 25,000 shares of 6%, $1,000 par value cumulative preferred stock. The company is popular with investors, and Roger anticipates no difficulty in selling the entire stock issue at or above par value.

2. Issue 20-year, 11%, $1,000 par value bonds. Roger also expects to sell the complete issue without difficulty because of the company's excellent credit history.

The board decides to consider the following factors before voting on the alternative financing plans: (1) the effect on corporate income taxes and retained earnings, (2) the annual cost, and (3) the amount to be paid at the end of the 20 years.

Roger has anticipated these questions and begins his presentation using overhead transparencies that show the calculations involved.

Critical Thinking

1. Assuming a 30% corporate income tax rate, what will be the effect of the two alternatives on the corporation's income tax and retained earnings if income before bond interest expense and income taxes is $15,000,000?

2. What is the annual cost of the two plans?

3. What amount is to be paid at the end of the 20 years?

12-1 Capital Stock Transactions

ISSUING PREFERRED STOCK AT PAR VALUE

1. Calculate the amounts to be recorded.

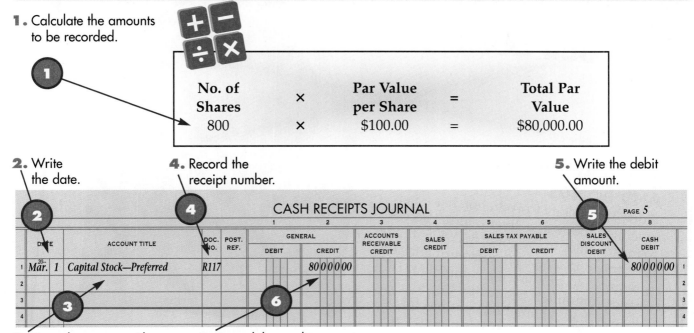

1

No. of Shares	×	Par Value per Share	=	Total Par Value
800	×	$100.00	=	$80,000.00

2. Write the date.

4. Record the receipt number.

5. Write the debit amount.

CASH RECEIPTS JOURNAL — PAGE 5

					1 GENERAL DEBIT	2 GENERAL CREDIT	3 ACCOUNTS RECEIVABLE CREDIT	4 SALES CREDIT	5 SALES TAX PAYABLE DEBIT	6 SALES TAX PAYABLE CREDIT	7 SALES DISCOUNT DEBIT	8 CASH DEBIT
DATE	ACCOUNT TITLE	DOC. NO.	POST. REF.									
Mar. 1	Capital Stock—Preferred	R117				80 000 00						80 000 00

3. Enter the account title.

6. Record the credit amount.

Figure 12-1

LampLight decided to issue preferred stock to raise additional capital. Brenda Henson paid par value, $100.00, for 800 shares of preferred stock, as shown in Figure 12-1.

> **March 1. Received cash from Brenda Henson for 800 shares of $100.00 par value preferred stock at $100.00 per share, $80,000.00. Receipt No. 117.**

Cash is debited for $80,000.00. Capital Stock—Preferred is credited for $80,000.00, the total par value of the issued preferred stock.

Cash	
80,000.00	

Capital Stock—Preferred	
	80,000.00

F.Y.I.
Par value is not directly related to market value.

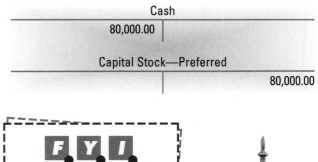

S T E P S Journalize preferred stock issued at par value

1. Calculate the amounts to be recorded for the sale of 800 shares of preferred stock at par.
2. Write the date in the Date column of the cash receipts journal. Since this is the first entry on page 5 of the cash receipts journal, record the current year in the Date column.
3. Enter the account title, *Capital Stock—Preferred*, in the Account Title column.
4. Record the receipt number, *R117*, in the Doc. No. column.
5. Write the debit amount, *80,000.00*, in the Cash Debit column.
6. Record the credit amount, *80,000.00*, in the General Credit column.

ISSUING PREFERRED STOCK FOR MORE THAN PAR VALUE

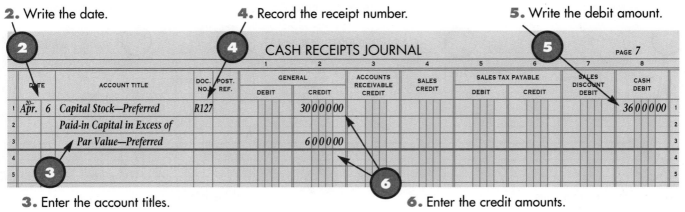

1. Calculate the amounts to be recorded.

	No. of Shares	×	Value per Share	=	Value
Total received	300	×	$120.00	=	$36,000.00
Par value	300	×	100.00	=	30,000.00
Amount received in excess of par value					$ 6,000.00

2. Write the date.

4. Record the receipt number.

5. Write the debit amount.

3. Enter the account titles.

6. Enter the credit amounts.

Figure 12-2

Sometimes preferred stock is issued for more than its par value. LampLight sold 300 shares of preferred stock at $120.00 per share to Adam Kellogg, as shown in Figure 12-2.

> *April 6. Received cash from Adam Kellogg for 300 shares of $100.00 par value preferred stock at $120.00 per share, $36,000.00. Receipt No. 127.*

Cash is debited for $36,000.00, the total amount received. Capital Stock—Preferred is credited for $30,000.00, the total par value of the preferred stock issued. Paid-in Capital in Excess of Par Value—Preferred is credited for $6,000.00, the amount received in excess of the par value.

Regardless of the amount received, the credit to the capital stock account always equals the par or stated value of the stock issued.

Cash	
Apr. 6 36,000.00	

Capital Stock—Preferred	
	Balance 80,000.00
	Apr. 6 30,000.00
	(New Bal. 110,000.00)

Paid-in Capital in Excess of Par Value—Preferred	
	Apr. 6 6,000.00

Journalize preferred stock issued for more than par value

1. Calculate the amounts to be recorded for 300 shares of preferred stock sold at more than par value.

2. Write the date in the Date column of the cash receipts journal.

3. Enter the account titles, *Capital Stock—Preferred* and *Paid-in Capital in Excess of Par Value—Preferred*, on separate lines in the Account Title column.

4. Record the receipt number, *R127*, in the Doc. No. column.

5. Write the debit amount, *36,000.00*, in the Cash Debit column.

6. Enter the appropriate credit amounts, *30,000.00* and *6,000.00*, on separate lines in the General Credit column.

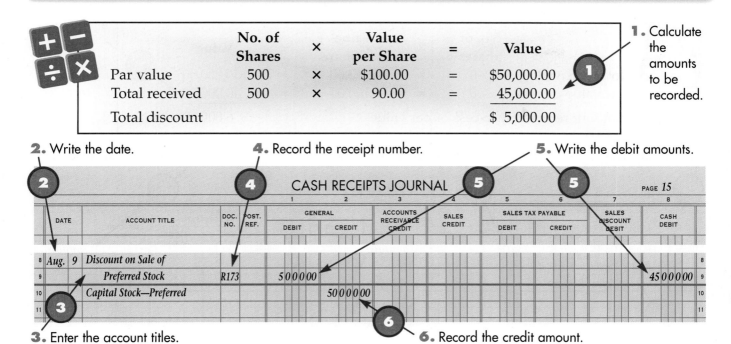

2. Write the date. **4.** Record the receipt number. **5.** Write the debit amounts.

3. Enter the account titles. **6.** Record the credit amount.

Figure 12-3

An amount less than par or stated value at which capital stock is sold is called a **discount on capital stock**. The legal treatment of discounts on capital stock varies from state to state. In some states, a stockholder may be liable for the amount of discount on par value stock if a corporation is unable to pay creditors. In other states, a stockholder is not liable for the amount of the discount.

LampLight sold 500 shares of $100.00 par value preferred stock to Hazel Deloach at a price of $90.00 per share, as shown in Figure 12-3.

> *August 9. Received cash from Hazel Deloach for 500 shares of $100.00 par value preferred stock at $90.00 per share, $45,000.00. Receipt No. 173.*

Cash is debited for $45,000.00, the amount of cash received. Discount on Sale of Preferred Stock is debited for $5,000.00, the discount amount. Capital Stock—Preferred is credited for $50,000.00, the par value of the 500 shares of preferred stock.

Cash	
Aug. 9	45,000.00

Discount on Sale of Preferred Stock	
Aug. 9	5,000.00

Capital Stock—Preferred	
	Balance 110,000.00
	Aug. 9 50,000.00
	(New Bal. 160,000.00)

F.Y.I.

Discount on Sale of Preferred Stock is a contra owner's equity account; hence, it is increased with a debit.

F.Y.I.

The credit to the capital stock account always equals the par or stated value of the stock issued regardless of the amount received.

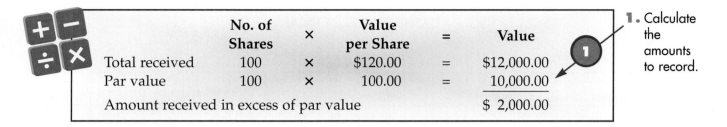

	No. of Shares	×	Value per Share	=	Value
Total received	100	×	$120.00	=	$12,000.00
Par value	100	×	100.00	=	10,000.00
Amount received in excess of par value					$ 2,000.00

1. Calculate the amounts to record.

2. Write the date.

3. Enter the account titles.

4. Record the memorandum number.

5. Write the debit amount.

GENERAL JOURNAL   PAGE **10**

	DATE		ACCOUNT TITLE	DOC. NO.	POST. REF.	DEBIT	CREDIT	
1	20-- Oct.	7	Office Equipment	M246		12 0 0 0 00		1
2			Capital Stock—Preferred				10 0 0 0 00	2
3			Paid-in Capital in Excess of					3
4			Par Value—Preferred				2 0 0 0 00	4
5								5

6. Record the credit amounts.

Figure 12-4

Occasionally, corporations issue capital stock in exchange for assets other than cash. When other assets are used to pay for capital stock, the investor and corporation must agree on the value of the assets and the capital stock.

LampLight issued 100 shares of preferred stock to Steven McBee in exchange for office equipment. The office equipment was accepted in full payment of the 100 shares of preferred stock. The agreed upon total value of the equipment is $12,000.00. Therefore, the equipment fully pays for the 100 shares of preferred stock, as shown in Figure 12-4.

October 7. Received office equipment from Steven McBee at an agreed value of $12,000.00 for 100 shares of $100.00 par value preferred stock. Memorandum No. 246.

Office Equipment is debited for $12,000.00. Capital Stock—Preferred is credited for $10,000.00, the total par value of the preferred stock issued. Paid-in Capital in Excess of Par Value—Preferred is credited for $2,000.00, the amount received in excess of the par value.

Office Equipment	
Oct. 7 12,000.00	

Capital Stock—Preferred	
	Balance 160,000.00
	Oct. 7 10,000.00
	(New Bal. 170,000.00

Paid-in Capital in Excess of Par Value—Preferred	
	Balance 6,000.00
	Oct. 7 2,000.00
	(New Bal. 8,000.00

F.Y.I.

Occasionally, a firm acquires a company by issuing stock in exchange for the company's assets.

ISSUING COMMON STOCK WITH NO PAR VALUE

	DATE	ACCOUNT TITLE	DOC. NO.	POST. REF.	GENERAL		ACCOUNTS RECEIVABLE CREDIT	SALES CREDIT	SALES TAX PAYABLE		SALES DISCOUNT DEBIT	CASH DEBIT	
					DEBIT	CREDIT			DEBIT	CREDIT			
12	July 8	Capital Stock—Common	R148			14 0 0 0 00						14 0 0 0 00	12
13													13

CASH RECEIPTS JOURNAL   PAGE *13*

Figure 12-5

Common stock often has no par value assigned to it or printed on the stock certificates. With no-par value stock, the entire amount paid by an investor is recorded in the capital stock account. Wheeler, Inc., sells no-par value common stock. The journal entry to record the transaction is shown in Figure 12-5.

July 8. Received cash from Elizabeth Griffin for 1,000 shares of no-par value common stock at $14.00 per share, $14,000.00. Receipt No. 148.

Cash is debited for $14,000.00, the total amount received. Capital Stock—Common is credited for $14,000.00, the total amount received for the 1,000 shares of stock.

ISSUING COMMON STOCK WITH A STATED VALUE

CASH RECEIPTS JOURNAL   PAGE *19*

	DATE	ACCOUNT TITLE	DOC. NO.	POST. REF.	GENERAL		ACCOUNTS RECEIVABLE CREDIT	SALES CREDIT	SALES TAX PAYABLE		SALES DISCOUNT DEBIT	CASH DEBIT	
					DEBIT	CREDIT			DEBIT	CREDIT			
1	20- Oct. 10	Capital Stock—Common	R181			1 0 0 0 00						1 2 0 0 00	1
2		Paid-in Capital in Excess of											2
3		Stated Value—Common				2 0 0 00							3
4													4

Figure 12-6

Corporations may assign a value to no-par value common stock. The value is known as the stated value. A stated value to no-par value shares serves the same function as par value. Therefore, no-par value common stock with a stated value is recorded using the same procedures as par value stock. An entry for issuing common stock at stated value is shown in Figure 11-4, page 302. An entry for issuing common stock at more than stated value is shown in Figure 12-6.

LampLight's articles of incorporation shown in Figures 11-1 and 11-2 on pages 298 and 299, specify that the company's common stock has a stated value of $10.00. LampLight sold 100

shares of common stock to Alice Blake for $12.00 a share, as shown in Figure 12-6.

October 10. Received cash from Alice Blake for 100 shares of $10.00 stated value common stock at $12.00 per share, $1,200.00. Receipt No. 181.

Cash is debited for $1,200.00, the total amount received. Capital Stock—Common is credited for $1,000.00, the total stated value of the 100 shares. Paid-in Capital in Excess of Stated Value—Common is credited for $200.00, the amount received in excess of the stated value.

1. To finance rapid expansion, how can a corporation acquire additional capital?

2. What accounts are affected, and how, when LampLight receives cash for preferred stock sold at par value?

3. What accounts are affected, and how, when LampLight receives cash for preferred stock sold for more than par value?

4. What accounts are affected, and how, when LampLight receives cash for preferred stock sold for less than par value?

5. What is the function of stated value?

Journalizing capital stock transactions

Page 4 of a cash receipts journal and page 2 of a general journal are provided in the *Working Papers*. Your instructor will guide you through the following examples.

May 2. Received cash from Kari Kovaleski for 200 shares of $50.00 par value preferred stock at $60.00 per share, $12,000.00. Receipt No. 234.

3. Received cash from Phil Mullins for 100 shares of $50.00 par value preferred stock at $45.00 per share, $4,500.00. Receipt No. 235.

5. Received office equipment from Laura Nguyen at an agreed upon value of $5,000.00 for 100 shares of $50.00 par value preferred stock. Memorandum No. 103.

5. Received cash from Arbus Kleinhoffer for 300 shares of $8.00 stated value common stock at $10.00 per share, $3,000.00. Receipt No. 236.

7. Received cash from Jenny Wasito for 100 shares of $8.00 stated value common stock at $8.00 per share, $800.00. Receipt No. 237.

6. Journalize each transaction completed during the current year.

ON YOUR OWN

Journalizing capital stock transactions

Page 5 of a cash receipts journal and page 3 of a general journal are provided in the *Working Papers*. Work independently to complete the following problem.

June 3. Received cash from George Lyding for 200 shares of $80.00 par value preferred stock at $85.00 per share, $17,000.00. Receipt No. 174.

6. Received cash from Blanca Echauri for 200 shares of $80.00 par value preferred stock at $78.00 per share, $15,600.00. Receipt No. 175.

8. Received land from Asghar Ebadat at an agreed upon value of $32,000.00 for 400 shares of $80.00 par value preferred stock. Memorandum No. 223.

9. Received cash from Barbara Parisot for 100 shares of $15.00 stated value common stock at $15.00 per share, $1,500.00. Receipt No. 176.

11. Received cash from Jin Myoung for 100 shares of $15.00 stated value common stock at $16.00 per share, $1,600.00. Receipt No. 177.

12. Received cash from Bernadine Barthel for 200 shares of $80.00 par value preferred stock at $80.00 per share, $16,000.00. Receipt No. 178.

14. Received office furniture from Rita Gomez at an agreed upon value of $8,000.00 for 100 shares of $80.00 par value preferred stock. Memorandum No. 224.

7. Journalize each transaction completed during the current year.

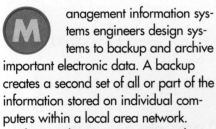

ELECTRONIC BACKUPS

TECHNOLOGY FOR BUSINESS

Management information systems engineers design systems to backup and archive important electronic data. A backup creates a second set of all or part of the information stored on individual computers within a local area network.

Three techniques are commonly used. First is a complete backup. All the information on the system is backed up to a storage device such as a tape or an optical disk. Complete backup requires the most time to complete, but ensures that all information is stored in another location.

The second backup method is incremental backups. Using this method, only the files that have been changed or created since the last backup are saved to the storage device. The time to complete the backup is less than a total backup. However, if a system failure occurs, restoring the files will take longer. The complete backup is restored first, then each incremental backup is restored.

The most complex method of backup is known as dynamic backup. Each time a file is saved, a backup is created. Thus, if a system failure occurs, virtually no data is lost. The technology for dynamic backups is more complex and more costly than the other two methods.

Whichever method is used, backing up files is an important part of any quality management information system.

BUYING TREASURY STOCK

1. Write the date. **3.** Record the check number. **5.** Record the credit amount.

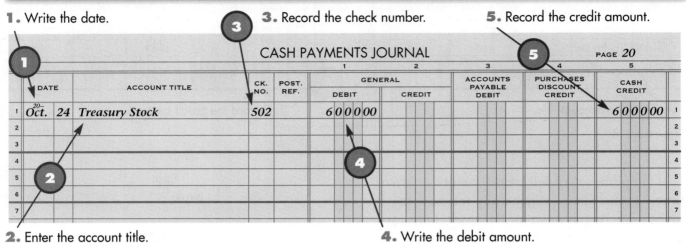

2. Enter the account title. **4.** Write the debit amount.

Figure 12-7

A corporation's own stock that has been issued and reacquired is called **treasury stock**. When a corporation buys treasury stock, it reduces the number of shares outstanding. However, treasury stock is still considered to be issued stock. A corporation usually intends to use the treasury stock for a specific purpose. For example, a corporation may acquire treasury stock to be given to employees as bonus payments.

Treasury stock is not an asset of a corporation. Since treasury stock is not owned by a stockholder, the stock does not involve voting rights. Dividends are not paid on treasury stock. Once treasury stock is given or sold to a stockholder, it ceases to be treasury stock and is again capital stock outstanding. A corporation records treasury stock at the price paid regardless of the stock's par or stated value. *(CONCEPT: Historical Cost)*

October 24. Paid cash to Francis Burns for 500 shares of $10.00 stated value common stock at $12.00 per share, $6,000.00. Check No. 502.

Treasury Stock is debited for $6,000.00, the amount paid for the 500 shares of treasury stock. Cash is credited for $6,000.00. The journal entry to record this transaction is shown in Figure 12-7.

Capital stock accounts have normal credit balances. Treasury Stock is a contra capital stock account and therefore has a normal debit balance.

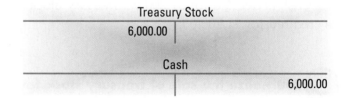

S
T
E
P
S

Journalize the purchase of treasury stock

1. Write the date in the Date column of the cash payments journal.
2. Enter the account title, *Treasury Stock*, in the Account Title column.
3. Record the check number, *502*, in the Check Number column. Since only check numbers are recorded in the column, no identifying letter is necessary.
4. Write the debit amount, *6,000.00*, in the General Debit column.
5. Record the credit amount, *6,000.00*, in the Cash Credit column.

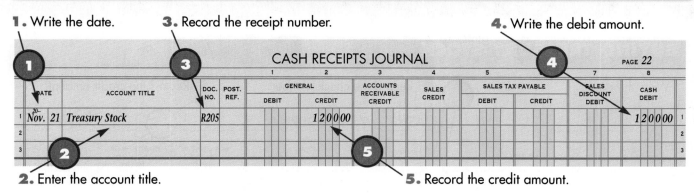

1. Write the date. **3.** Record the receipt number. **4.** Write the debit amount.

CASH RECEIPTS JOURNAL   PAGE 22

	DATE	ACCOUNT TITLE	DOC. NO.	POST. REF.	GENERAL DEBIT	GENERAL CREDIT	ACCOUNTS RECEIVABLE CREDIT	SALES CREDIT	SALES TAX PAYABLE DEBIT	SALES TAX PAYABLE CREDIT	SALES DISCOUNT DEBIT	CASH DEBIT	
1	Nov. 21	Treasury Stock	R205			1 2 0 0 00						1 2 0 0 00	1
2													2
3													3

2. Enter the account title. **5.** Record the credit amount.

Figure 12-8

Companies may sell treasury stock at any time. Treasury stock is generally reissued to investors who pay cash for the stock. Investors pay the current market price for the stock.

The market price of stock will be explained in Chapter 13.

The current value of stock in the marketplace may be the same as the original cost of the treasury stock. Assume LampLight sold some of its treasury stock at the $12.00 original cost, as shown in Figure 12-8.

November 21. Received cash from Lisa Vance for 100 shares of treasury stock at $12.00 per share, $1,200.00. Treasury stock was originally bought by LampLight on October 24 at $12.00 per share. Receipt No. 205.

Cash is debited for $1,200.00. Treasury Stock is credited for $1,200.00.

	Cash	
	1,200.00	

	Treasury Stock	
Balance	6,000.00	1,200.00
(New Bal.	4,800.00)	

S T E P S **Journalize the sale of treasury stock for original cost**

1. Write the date in the Date column of the cash receipts journal.
2. Enter the account title, *Treasury Stock*, in the Account Title column.
3. Record the receipt number identified by the letter R, *R205*, in the Doc. No. column.
4. Write the debit amount, *1,200.00*, in the Cash Debit column.
5. Record the credit amount, *1,200.00*, in the General Credit column.

SMALL BUSINESS SPOTLIGHT

There are many challenges associated with starting a new business or growing an existing one. Over 3.5 million small business owners and aspiring entrepreneurs have looked to SCORE to help them meet these challenges. SCORE (Service Corps of Retired Executives) includes over 12,000 trained volunteer business counselors dedicated to sharing real-world business experience with their clients. SCORE business counselors provide advice in areas such as writing a business plan, managing cash flow, assessing capital needs, starting or operating a business, and buying or selling a business. With almost 400 local chapters, SCORE provides face-to-face counseling along with low-cost workshops and seminars. Program topics are often tailored to meet the specific needs of a community.

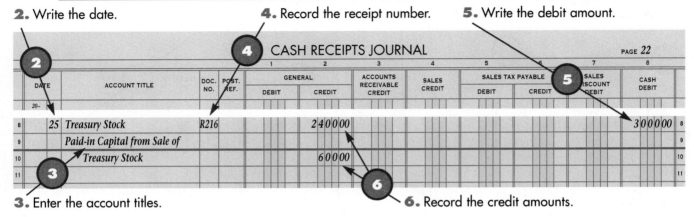

	No. of Shares	×	Value per Share	=	Value
Total received	200	×	$15.00	=	$3,000.00
Original cost	200	×	12.00	=	2,400.00
Amount received in excess of original cost					$ 600.00

1. Calculate the amounts to be recorded.

2. Write the date.   **4.** Record the receipt number.   **5.** Write the debit amount.

Figure 12-9

3. Enter the account titles.   **6.** Record the credit amounts.

LampLight sold 200 shares of treasury stock to Mary Long for $15.00 per share, as shown in Figure 12-9.

> **November 25.** Received cash from Mary Long for 200 shares of treasury stock at $15.00 per share, $3,000.00. Treasury stock was bought on October 24 at $12.00 per share. Receipt No. 216.

Cash is debited for $3,000.00, the total amount received from the sale of the treasury stock. Treasury Stock is credited for $2,400.00, the original cost of the 200 shares of treasury stock.

Paid-in Capital from Sale of Treasury Stock is credited for $600.00, the amount received in excess of the treasury stock's original cost.

Cash	
3,000.00	

Treasury Stock	
Balance 4,800.00	2,400.00
(New Bal. 2,400.00)	

Paid-in Capital from Sale of Treasury Stock	
	600.00

S
T
E
P
S

Journalize the sale of treasury stock for more than original cost

1. Calculate the amounts to be recorded for the sale of 200 shares of treasury stock at more than the original cost.

2. Write the date in the Date column of the cash receipts journal.

3. Enter the account titles in the Account Title column.

4. Record the receipt number, *R216*, in the Doc. No. column.

5. Write the debit amount in the Cash Debit column.

6. Record the credit amounts in the General Credit column.

F.Y.I.

A corporation may acquire treasury stock to regain control or to have additional stock to use for specific purposes such as stock dividends.

SELLING TREASURY STOCK FOR LESS THAN ORIGINAL COST

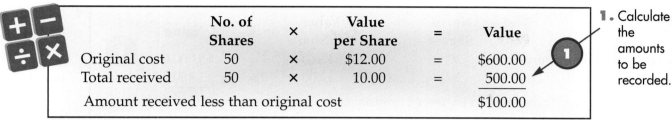

	No. of Shares	×	Value per Share	=	Value	
Original cost	50	×	$12.00	=	$600.00	**1.** Calculate the amounts to be recorded.
Total received	50	×	10.00	=	500.00	
Amount received less than original cost					$100.00	

2. Write the date. **4.** Record the receipt number. **5.** Write the debit amounts.

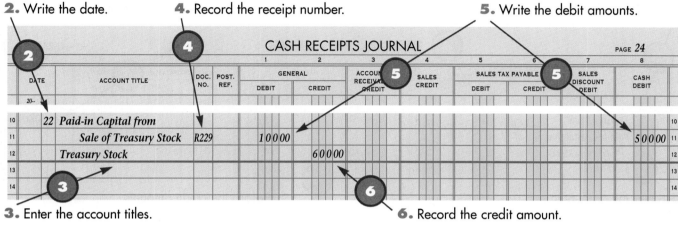

3. Enter the account titles. **6.** Record the credit amount.

Figure 12-10

LampLight sold 50 shares of treasury stock to Frank Demetz for $10.00 per share, as shown in Figure 12-10.

> ***December 22. Received cash from Frank Demetz for 50 shares of treasury stock at $10.00 per share, $500.00. Treasury stock was originally bought October 24 at $12.00 per share. Receipt No. 229.***

Cash is debited for $500.00, the total amount of cash received. Paid-in Capital from Sale of Treasury Stock is debited for $100.00, the amount received that is less than the treasury stock's original cost. Treasury Stock is credited for $600.00, the original cost.

When treasury stock transactions occur, no entry is made in Capital Stock—Common or Capital Stock—Preferred. Treasury stock is

Cash	
500.00	

Paid-in Capital from Sale of Treasury Stock			
	100.00	Balance	600.00
		(New Bal.	*500.00)*

Treasury Stock			
Balance	2,400.00		600.00
(New Bal.	*1,800.00)*		

considered to be issued stock. The difference between the balances of the capital stock accounts and the treasury stock account is the value of outstanding stock. After the entry on December 22 for the sale of treasury stock, the number of LampLight's outstanding shares of capital stock is calculated as follows:

	No. of Shares Issued	−	No. of Shares of Treasury Stock	=	No. of Shares Outstanding
Preferred	1,700	–	0	=	1,700
Common	32,100	–	150	=	31,950

332   CHAPTER 12 Acquiring Additional Capital for a Corporation

TERM REVIEW

treasury stock

AUDIT YOUR UNDERSTANDING

1. What is treasury stock?
2. What accounts are affected, and how, when treasury stock is sold for more than its original cost?
3. What accounting concept is being applied when a corporation records the purchase of treasury stock at the price paid regardless of the stock's par or stated value?

WORK TOGETHER

Journalizing treasury stock transactions

Page 11 of a cash receipts journal and page 8 of a cash payments journal are provided in the *Working Papers.* Your instructor will guide you through the following examples.

Mar. 9. Paid cash to Dana O'Brien for 300 shares of $20.00 stated value common stock at $22.00 per share, $6,600.00. Check No. 753.

12. Received cash from Doug Johnston for 100 shares of treasury stock at $24.00 per share, $2,400.00. Treasury stock was purchased on March 9 at $22.00 per share. Receipt No. 409.

13. Received cash from Ida Mann for 100 shares of treasury stock at $22.00 per share, $2,200.00. Treasury stock was purchased on March 9 at $22.00 per share. Receipt No. 410.

16. Received cash from Kathy Milhouse for 100 shares of treasury stock at $21.00 per share, $2,100.00. Treasury stock was purchased on March 9 at $22.00 per share. Receipt No. 411.

4. Journalize each transaction completed during the current year.

ON YOUR OWN

Journalizing treasury stock transactions

Page 7 of a cash receipts journal and page 6 of a cash payments journal are provided in the *Working Papers.* Work independently to complete the following problem.

Aug. 22. Paid cash to Tai Arriaga for 500 shares of $15.00 stated value common stock at $15.00 per share, $7,500.00. Check No. 172.

23. Received cash from Joyce Cariel for 250 shares of treasury stock at $14.00 per share, $3,500.00. Treasury stock was purchased on August 22 at $15.00 per share. Receipt No. 85.

25. Received cash from Stan Gavin for 250 shares of treasury stock at $15.00 per share, $3,750.00. Treasury stock was purchased on August 22 at $15.00 per share. Receipt No. 86.

26. Paid cash to Cindy Hopper for 750 shares of $15.00 stated value common stock at $16.00 per share, $12,000.00. Check No. 173.

27. Received cash from Tim Coburn for 100 shares of treasury stock at $17.00 per share, $1,700.00. Treasury stock was purchased on August 26 at $16.00 per share. Receipt No. 87.

5. Journalize each transaction completed during the current year.

CORPORATE BONDS PAYABLE

For a growing business, the capital needed to expand may come from three sources:

1. Using retained earnings.

2. Selling additional capital stock.

3. Borrowing the funds.

A business' management team may find that capital needed for expansion could be accumulated from retained net income during the next 5 to 10 years. However, the business may need the additional capital within the next year. A corporation's board of directors must decide whether to raise the needed capital by selling additional stock or borrowing the money.

An advantage of selling stock is that the additional capital becomes part of a corporation's permanent capital. Permanent capital does not have to be returned to stockholders as long as the business continues to operate. Another advantage is that dividends do not have to be paid to stockholders unless the earnings are sufficient to warrant such payments. A disadvantage of selling more stock to raise additional capital is that the ownership is spread over more shares and more owners.

An advantage of borrowing the additional capital is that stockholders' equity is not spread over additional shares of stock. A disadvantage is that interest must be paid on the loan, which decreases the net income. This decrease in net income decreases the amount available for dividends. Another disadvantage of borrowing additional capital is that the amount borrowed must be repaid in the future.

Large loans are sometimes difficult to obtain for short periods. Corporations frequently borrow needed capital with the provision that the loan be repaid several years in the future. Therefore, the loan can be paid out of future earnings accumulated over several years.

Large loans may also be difficult to obtain from one bank or one individual. A printed, long-term promise to pay a specified amount on a specified date and to pay interest at stated intervals is called a **bond**. Bonds are similar to notes payable because both are written promises to pay. However, most notes payable are for one year or less, but bonds generally run for a long period of time, such as 5, 10, or 20 years. Also, bonds payable tend to be issued for larger amounts than notes payable.

All bonds representing the total amount of a loan are called a **bond issue**. A corporation usually sells an entire bond issue to a securities dealer who sells individual bonds to the public.

1. Record the issuance of the bonds.

Figure 12-11

On July 1, 20X0, LampLight borrowed $250,000.00 to expand its building. LampLight issued 250, 12%, $1,000.00 par value bonds. The bonds are scheduled to mature in five years. Annual interest on the bonds is to be paid on July 1 of each year. The bond issue was sold at par value to a securities dealer. The journal entry to record the sale of the bonds is shown in Figure 12-11.

July 1, 20X0. Received cash for the face value of a five-year, 12%, $1,000.00 par value bond issue, $250,000.00. Receipt No. 246.

Cash is debited for $250,000.00. Bonds Payable is credited for $250,000.00.

Cash	
250,000.00	

Bonds Payable	
	250,000.00

PAYING INTEREST ON BONDS

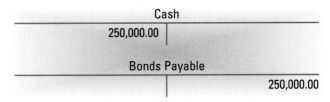

1. Calculate the annual interest.

Balance Owed on Bond Issue	×	Bond Interest Rate	=	Annual Interest
$250,000.00	×	12%	=	$30,000.00

2. Record the payment of interest.

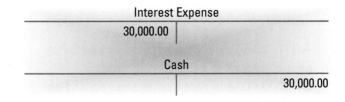

Figure 12-12

A year's interest is paid to each bondholder on July 1 of each year until the bond's maturity date. A person or institution, usually a bank, given legal authorization to administer property for the benefit of property owners is called a **trustee**. LampLight pays the interest amount to a bond trustee who in turn handles the details of paying each individual bondholder.

July 1, 20X1. Paid cash to bond trustee for annual interest on bond issue, $30,000.00. Check No. 562.

Interest Expense is debited for $30,000.00. Cash is credited for $30,000.00. The journal entry to record this transaction is shown in Figure 12-12.

Interest Expense	
30,000.00	

Cash	
	30,000.00

DEPOSITING CASH IN A BOND SINKING FUND

1. Record the initial payment to the bond sinking fund.

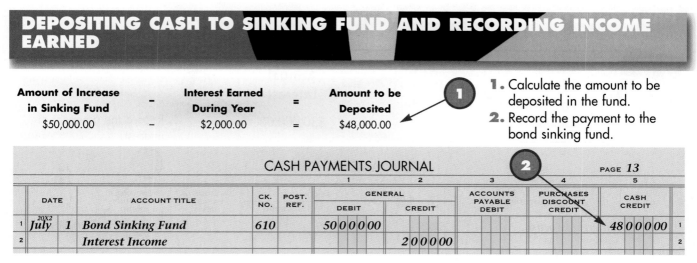

	DATE	ACCOUNT TITLE	CK. NO.	POST. REF.	GENERAL DEBIT	GENERAL CREDIT	ACCOUNTS PAYABLE DEBIT	PURCHASES DISCOUNT CREDIT	CASH CREDIT	
	20X1									
2	1	Bond Sinking Fund	563		50 00 00 00				50 00 00 00	2

Figure 12-13

To assure bondholders that the bond issue will be paid at maturity, LampLight annually deposits a portion of the loan value with the bond trustee. An amount set aside to pay a bond issue when due is called a **bond sinking fund**. LampLight spreads the $250,000.00 amount over the five years that the bond issue is outstanding. The bond sinking fund is increased each year by $50,000.00, one-fifth of the total principal. On the bond issue's maturity date, a total of $250,000.00 will be available in the bond sinking fund to pay the bondholders.

July 1, 20X1. Paid cash to bond trustee for annual deposit to bond sinking fund, $50,000.00. Check No. 563.

Bond Sinking Fund is debited for $50,000.00. Cash is credited for $50,000.00. The entry to record the deposit for 20X1 is shown in Figure 12-13.

DEPOSITING CASH TO SINKING FUND AND RECORDING INCOME EARNED

Amount of Increase in Sinking Fund	–	Interest Earned During Year	=	Amount to be Deposited
$50,000.00	–	$2,000.00	=	$48,000.00

1. Calculate the amount to be deposited in the fund.
2. Record the payment to the bond sinking fund.

CASH PAYMENTS JOURNAL — PAGE 13

	DATE	ACCOUNT TITLE	CK. NO.	POST. REF.	GENERAL DEBIT	GENERAL CREDIT	ACCOUNTS PAYABLE DEBIT	PURCHASES DISCOUNT CREDIT	CASH CREDIT	
1	20X2 July 1	Bond Sinking Fund	610		50 00 00 00				48 00 00 00	1
2		Interest Income				2 00 00 00				2

Figure 12-14

The bond trustee invests the sinking fund. The interest earned reduces the deposit that LampLight must make. For example, the trustee reports to LampLight that the sinking fund investment earned $2,000.00. Thus, on July 1, 20X2, LampLight pays only $48,000.00 to the trustee.

July 1, 20X2. Paid cash to bond trustee for annual deposit to bond sinking fund, $48,000.00, and recorded interest earned on bond sinking fund, $2,000.00. Check No. 610.

Bond Sinking Fund is debited for $50,000.00. Cash is credited for $48,000.00, the actual amount deposited. Interest Income is credited for $2,000.00, the amount of interest earned. The journal entry to record the deposit for 20X2 is shown in Figure 12-14.

As the bond sinking fund balance increases, the amount of interest earned in a year usually increases. Thus, the amount LampLight must deposit each year decreases.

GENERAL JOURNAL					PAGE 6	
	DATE	ACCOUNT TITLE	DOC. NO.	POST. REF.	DEBIT	CREDIT
1	20X4 July 1	Bonds Payable	M600		250 00 0 00		1
2		Bond Sinking Fund				250 00 0 00	2
3							3

Figure 12-15

A bond sinking fund is an asset to LampLight until the trustee makes payment to the bondholders. When LampLight's bonds are due, the bond trustee uses the bond sinking fund to pay the bondholders. Paying the amounts owed to bondholders for a bond issue is called **retiring a bond issue**. The journal entry to retire the bonds is shown in Figure 12-15.

July 1, 20X4. Received notice from bond trustee that bond issue was retired using bond sinking fund, $250,000.00. Memorandum No. 600.

Bonds Payable is debited for $250,000.00, the total amount of the bond issue. Bond Sinking Fund is credited for $250,000.00, the amount in the fund used to retire the bond issue. After this entry is posted, both Bonds Payable and Bond Sinking Fund will have zero balances.

All of LampLight's bond issue matures on the same date. Bonds that all mature on the same date are called **term bonds**. Sometimes portions of a bond issue mature on different dates. Portions of a bond issue that mature on different dates are called **serial bonds**. For example, a 10-year bond issue with one-tenth of the bonds maturing every year is a serial bond issue. An advantage of serial bonds is that interest does not have to be paid on the total bond issue for the total 10 years.

> **F.Y.I.**
>
> *A limited liability company (LLC) and a limited liability partnership (LLP) provide the flexibility of a partnership by allowing earnings to flow through to its partners as personal income. This feature eliminates the double-taxation penalty of a corporation.*

> **F.Y.I.**
>
> *If a bond is sold for less than its face value, it is said to be sold at a "discount." Cash and Discount on Bonds Payable are debited and Bonds Payable is credited.*

Bonds Payable			
Retired	250,000.00	Balance (New Bal. zero)	250,000.00

Bonds Sinking Fund			
Balance (New Bal. zero)	250,000.00	Retired	250,000.00

COMPARISON OF CAPITAL STOCK AND BONDS AS A SOURCE OF CORPORATE CAPITAL

Capital Stock

1. Stockholders are corporate owners.
2. Capital Stock is a stockholders' equity account.
3. Stockholders have a secondary claim against corporate assets.
4. Dividends are paid to stockholders out of corporate net income.
5. Dividends are not fixed costs and do not have to be paid if net income is insufficient.
6. Amount received from sale of stock is relatively permanent capital; amount invested by stockholders does not have to be returned to them in foreseeable future.

Bonds

1. Bondholders are corporate creditors.
2. Bonds Payable is a liability account.
3. Bondholders have a primary, or first, claim against corporate assets.
4. Interest paid to bondholders is a corporate expense.
5. Interest on bonds is a fixed expense; the expense must be paid when due; payment does not depend on amount of net income.
6. Amount received from sale of bonds is not permanent; amount invested by bondholders must be returned to them on bonds' maturity date.

Figure 12-16

PROFESSIONAL BUSINESS ETHICS

CONFIDENTIALITY

Certified public accountants routinely see and hear confidential information while providing professional services to clients. The AICPA Rules of the Code of Professional Conduct prohibit disclosure of confidential information without the specific consent of the client.

Instructions

Use the three-step checklist to help determine whether the actions described in the following situations demonstrate ethical behavior.

Situation 1. Sierra Jamison, who recently passed the CPA examination, had lunch with a friend from high school. While talking about their jobs, Sierra told her friend about working on an audit of a large local company. She shared information about the salaries and bonuses of the company officers.

Situation 2. DataPlus, a company in serious financial trouble, is a client of Anthony Sherman, a CPA. While playing golf, a friend said she was thinking about investing in DataPlus and asked Anthony if he knew anything about the company. Anthony said he didn't want to talk about business while on the links.

Situation 3. Brianna Nelson runs a successful catering business. Lauren Ortiz, a CPA, is Brianna's accountant. During routine meetings with Lauren the caterer talks about her catering clients' marital problems, plastic surgeries, and unusual eating habits. Lauren considers Brianna a great source of stories and routinely repeats things Lauren tells her to friends and relatives.

TERMS REVIEW

bond

bond issue

trustee

bond sinking fund

retiring a bond issue

term bonds

serial bonds

AUDIT YOUR UNDERSTANDING

1. What are two advantages of raising needed capital by selling stock?

2. What is an advantage of raising additional capital by borrowing?

3. What is a disadvantage of borrowing additional capital?

4. What accounts are affected, and how, when cash is deposited in a bond sinking fund in the second year of a bond issue?

WORK TOGETHER

Journalizing bonds payable transactions

On February 1, 20X1, Cyrotech, Inc., received $300,000.00 cash for a bond issue. The bond agreement provides that a bond sinking fund is to be increased annually by $37,500.00 for the next eight years. The bond trustee has guaranteed Cyrotech an interest rate of 4% on its sinking fund investment. A cash receipts journal, cash payments journal, and general journal are provided in the *Working Papers*. Your instructor will guide you through the following examples.

Feb. 1, 20X1. Received cash for face value of an 8-year, 10%, $500.00 par value bond issue, $300,000.00. Receipt No. 135.

1, 20X2. Paid cash to bond trustee for annual interest on bond issue, $30,000.00. Check No. 201.

1, 20X2. Paid cash to bond trustee for first annual deposit to bond sinking fund. Check No. 202.

1, 20X3. Paid cash to bond trustee for annual interest on bond issue, $30,000.00. Check No. 313.

1, 20X3. Paid cash to bond trustee for annual deposit to bond sinking fund and recorded interest earned on bond sinking fund. Check No. 314. (Interest earned equals 4% of the bond sinking fund deposit made on February 1, 20X2.)

3, 20X9. Received notice from bond trustee that bond issue was retired using bond sinking fund, $300,000.00. Memorandum 87.

4. Journalize the transactions.

ON YOUR OWN

Journalizing bonds payable transactions

On May 1, 20X1, Biotech, Inc., received $500,000.00 cash for a bond issue. The bond agreement provides that a bond sinking fund is to be increased annually by $100,000.00 for the next five years. The bond trustee has guaranteed Biotech an interest rate of 5% on its sinking fund investment. A cash receipts journal, cash payments journal, and general journal are provided in the *Working Papers*. Work independently to complete the following problem.

May	1, 20X1.	Received cash for face value of a 5-year, 8%, $1,000.00 par value bond issue, $500,000.00. Receipt No. 63.
	1, 20X2.	Paid cash to bond trustee for annual interest on bond issue, $40,000.00. Check No. 71.
	1, 20X2.	Paid cash to bond trustee for annual deposit to bond sinking fund. Check No. 72.
	1, 20X3.	Paid cash to bond trustee for annual interest on bond issue. Check No. 173.
	1, 20X3.	Paid cash to bond trustee for annual deposit to bond sinking fund and recorded interest earned on bond sinking fund. Check No. 174. (Interest earned equals 5% of the bond sinking fund deposit made on May 1, 20X2.)
	2, 20X6.	Received notice from bond trustee that bond issue was retired using bond sinking fund, $500,000.00. Memorandum 33.

5. Journalize the transactions.

STOCKHOLDER RIGHTS

wnership of stock normally entitles the shareholder to numerous rights including:

1. The right to sell shares owned, known as the right of transfer.
2. The preemptive right to maintain proportionate ownership in the corporation.
3. The right to a share of all profits distributed in the form of dividends.
4. The right to review the accounting records of a corporation.
5. The right to attend shareholder meetings.
6. The right to vote for directors and for other issues that come before the stockholders.

Voting rights give the shareholder one vote for each share owned. In some states, shareholders are entitled to cumulative voting. Under cumulative voting, a shareholder is entitled to one vote per share times the number of directors being elected. For example, Devon Eagle owns 100 shares of the Adler Corporation. Three directors are to be elected. Devon is entitled to 300 votes (100 shares x 3 directors = 300 votes). The votes may be cast for one director or any combination of the candidates. Cumulative voting helps protect the interests of stockholders who own less than 50 percent of the outstanding shares.

LEGAL ISSUES IN ACCOUNTING

CHAPTER 12 *S UMMARY*

After completing this chapter, you can

1. Define accounting terms related to acquiring capital for a corporation.

2. Identify accounting concepts and practices related to acquiring capital for a corporation.

3. Journalize entries for issuing additional capital stock.

4. Journalize entries for buying and selling treasury stock.

5. Journalize entries for bonds payable.

EXPLORE ACCOUNTING

CONVERTIBLE BONDS

Corporations often use long-term bonds to raise the investment capital required to expand operations. A bond is a contract between the corporation and the bondholder. The corporation promises to pay the bondholder interest during the life of the bond and the bond principle at the maturity date.

A corporation can add a variety of provisions to a bond contract. One such provision is referred to as a conversion option. A bond that can be exchanged for a specified number of capital stock is called a **convertible bond.** At the bondholder's request, the bond can be traded, or converted, for a specified number of shares of the corporation.

Assume that Chris Harrison purchased a 10%, 20-year, $1,000 convertible bond from Castle Corporation. The bond is convertible to 40 shares of

Castle's capital stock. Castle's stock is traded at $12 per share on the bond issuance date. Chris can elect to convert the bond any time during the life of the bond.

Chris has no incentive to convert the bond to stock until the market value of the stock climbs above the $25 conversion price ($1,000 bond/40 shares = $25 per share). The market price of the stock in the future will determine whether Chris elects to convert his bond.

Suppose the market price climbs to $20 per share but is not expected to increase. Chris would not convert his bond to stock, since the converted stock would only be worth $800 ($20 x 40 shares). Thus, Chris would hold the bond to maturity and receive the $1,000 maturity value.

If the market price climbs to $30 per share, Chris can convert his bond and receive 40 shares of stock. The stock is immediately worth $1,200 ($30 x 40 shares).

Chris can either sell his stock, earning an instant $200 gain. However, Chris can also hold the stock in hope that the stock price will continue to rise.

Why would a corporation issue convertible bonds? When purchasing the bond, Chris knew that there was the potential to earn money in addition to the interest income if the stock rose above $25. Thus, Chris accepted a 12% interest rate on the bond instead of the 13% market rate for bonds with no conversion feature. Thus, Castle Corporation's interest expense was reduced due to the conversion feature.

REQUIRED:

Assume Chris converted his stock and immediately sold the stock for a $200 gain. Research how this $200 gain should be recorded in the corporation's financial statements. Do you agree with the findings of your research?

APPLICATION PROBLEM
Journalizing capital stock transactions

PC Design, Inc., is authorized to issue 200,000 shares of $5.00 stated value common stock and 50,000 shares of 12%, $100.00 par value preferred stock. PC Design has 25,000 shares of common stock outstanding.

Transactions:

Feb. 8. Andre Cashman sent a check for 5,000 shares of $5.00 stated value common stock at $5.00 per share, $25,000.00. R398.

26. Jason Gutto exchanged a parcel of land at an agreed value of $30,000.00 for 300 shares of $100.00 par value preferred stock. M67.

Apr. 15. Jacquelyn Parker sent a $40,000.00 check for 400 shares of $100.00 par value preferred stock at $100.00 per share. R518.

Aug. 25. Received a $48,000.00 check from Lynn Kruschke for 500 shares of $100.00 par value preferred stock at $96.00 per share. R601.

Dec. 11. Received cash from Behrooz Behzadi for 200 shares of $100.00 par value preferred stock at $102.00 per share, $20,400.00. R698.

Instructions:

Journalize the transactions completed during the current year. Use page 2 of a cash receipts journal and a general journal. Source documents are abbreviated as follows: memorandum, M; receipt, R.

APPLICATION PROBLEM
Journalizing treasury stock transactions

Advanced Laser, Inc., is authorized to issue 150,000 shares of $10.00 stated value common stock. Advanced Laser has 50,000 shares of stock outstanding.

Transactions:

Feb. 21. Paid cash to Corey Fiske for 400 shares of $10.00 stated value common stock at $10.00 per share, $4,000.00. C87.

27. Received cash from Aurelia Gillien for 125 shares of treasury stock at $10.00 per share, $1,250.00. Treasury stock was bought on February 21 at $10.00 per share. R126.

Mar. 22. Paid cash to Leona Metzger for 750 shares of $10.00 stated value common stock at $11.00 per share, $8,250.00. C138.

Apr. 15. Received cash from Efren Merrill for 275 shares of treasury stock at $12.00 per share, $3,300.00. Treasury stock was bought on February 21 at $10.00 per share. R151.

July 30. Received cash from Susan Matsuda for 300 shares of treasury stock at $10.00 per share, $3,000.00. Treasury stock was bought on March 22 at $11.00 per share. R203.

Instructions:

Journalize the transactions completed during the current year. Use page 2 of a cash receipts journal and page 3 of a cash payments journal. Source documents are abbreviated as follows: check, C; receipt, R.

APPLICATION PROBLEM
Journalizing bonds payable transactions

On January 1, 20X1, Security Communications, Inc., received cash, $200,000.00, for a bond issue. The bond agreement provides that a bond sinking fund is to be increased by $20,000.00 every six months for the next five years.

Transactions:

Jan. 1, 20X1. Received cash for the face value of a 5-year, 9%, $1,000.00 par value bond issue, $200,000.00. R104.

July 1, 20X1. Paid cash to bond trustee for semiannual interest on bond issue, $9,000.00. C294.

July 1, 20X1. Paid cash to bond trustee for semiannual deposit to bond sinking fund, $20,000.00. C295.

Jan. 1, 20X2. Paid cash to bond trustee for semiannual interest on bond issue, $9,000.00. C504.

Jan. 1, 20X2. Paid cash to bond trustee for semiannual deposit to bond sinking fund, $19,200.00, and recorded interest earned on bond sinking fund, $800.00. C505.

Jan. 4, 20X6. Received notice from bond trustee that bond issue was retired using bond sinking fund, $200,000.00. M290.

Instructions:

Journalize the transactions. Use page 1 of a cash receipts journal, page 8 of a cash payments journal, and page 1 of a general journal. Source documents are abbreviated as follows: check, C; memorandum, M; receipt, R.

MASTERY PROBLEM
Journalizing stock and bond transactions

On January 1, 20X1, Sentry VideoLink, Inc., received cash, $50,000.00, for a bond issue. The bond agreement provides that Sentry VideoLink is to increase a bond sinking fund by $5,000.00 every six months for the next five years.

Transactions:

Jan. 1, 20X1. Received cash for the face value of a 5-year, 12%, $1,000.00 par value bond issue, $50,000.00. R198.

Jan. 12, 20X1. Received cash from Stuart Peterson for 1,000 shares of $10.00 stated value common stock at $10.00 per share. R210.

Feb. 21, 20X1. Paid cash to Ruben Mendoza for 900 shares of $10.00 stated value common stock at $12.00 per share. C97.

Feb. 28, 20X1. Received cash from Tai Banh for 500 shares of treasury stock at $12.00 per share. Treasury stock was bought on February 21 at $12.00 per share. R215.

Mar. 13, 20X1. Received cash from Rebecca Munson for 200 shares of $10.00 stated value common stock at $15.00 per share. R220.

Mar. 22, 20X1. Paid cash to Dermot Concannon for 2,000 shares of $10.00 stated value common stock at $16.00 per share. C138.

Apr. 8, 20X1. Received cash from Rachel Kaplan for 100 shares of $100.00 par value preferred stock at $101.00 per share. R226.

Apr. 15, 20X1. Received cash from Blake Kenefick for 300 shares of treasury stock at $18.00 per share. Treasury stock was bought on February 21 at $12.00 per share. R231.

May 15, 20X1. Received cash from Paige Anderson for 800 shares of $100.00 par value preferred stock at $97.50 per share. R232.

July 1, 20X1. Paid cash to bond trustee for semiannual interest on bond issue, $3,000.00. C200.

July 1, 20X1. Paid cash to bond trustee for semiannual deposit to bond sinking fund, $5,000.00. C201.

July 14, 20X1. Received delivery equipment from Travis Kimball at an agreed on value of $20,000.00 for 200 shares of $100.00 par value preferred stock. M148.

July 23, 20X1. Received cash from Brad Manning for 300 shares of treasury stock at $14.00 per share. Treasury stock consisted of 100 shares bought on February 21 at $12.00 per share and 200 shares bought on March 22 at $16.00 per share. R353.

Jan. 1, 20X2. Paid cash to bond trustee for semiannual interest on bond issue, $3,000.00. C504.

Jan. 1, 20X2. Paid cash to bond trustee for semiannual deposit to bond sinking fund, $4,600.00, and recorded interest earned on bond sinking fund, $400.00. C505.

Jan. 1, 20X6. Received notice from bond trustee that bond issue was retired using bond sinking fund, $50,000.00. M491.

Instructions:

Journalize the transactions. Use page 1 of a cash receipts journal, page 8 of a cash payments journal, and page 1 of a general journal. Source documents are abbreviated as follows: check, C; memorandum, M; receipt, R.

12-5 CHALLENGE PROBLEM
Journalizing stock and bond transactions

Interspan Technologies, Inc., is authorized to issue 100,000 shares of $1.00 stated value common stock and 25,000 shares of 10%, $100.00 par value preferred stock. On January 1, 20X1, Interspan has the following outstanding stock: common stock, 40,000 shares; preferred stock, 10,000 shares. Provisions of a bond issue, January 1, 20X1, include (a) payment of interest on the bond issue on July 1 and January 1 of each year and (b) assurance by Interspan of an increase of $20,000.00 in a bond sinking fund on July 1 and January 1 of each year.

Transactions:

Jan. 1, 20X1. Cash was received for the face value of a 10-year, 10%, $1,000.00 par value bond issue, $200,000.00. R51.

Feb. 5, 20X1. Paid John Salas for 5,000 shares of $1.00 stated value common stock at $1.60 per share. C120.

Feb. 12, 20X1. Cash was received from Michael Donato for 15,000 shares of $1.00 stated value common stock at $1.20 per share. R64.

Feb. 20, 20X1. Carmen Romero paid cash for 500 shares of $100.00 par value preferred stock at $100.00 per share. R105.

Mar. 14, 20X1. Office equipment was received from Elaine Zaballos at an agreed on value of $7,000.00 for 5,000 shares of $1.00 stated value common stock. M195.

Apr. 3, 20X1. Jennifer Chapman paid cash for 1,000 shares of treasury stock at $1.50 per share, $1,500.00. Treasury stock was bought on February 5 at $1.60 per share. R210.

May 10, 20X1 Deana Maxson paid cash for 300 shares of $100.00 par value preferred stock at $99.00 per share. R387.

July 1, 20X1. Paid semiannual interest to bond trustee on bonds payable. C389.

July	1, 20X1.	Paid cash to bond trustee for semiannual deposit to bond sinking fund, $20,000.00. C390.
Sept.	18, 20X1.	Cash was received from Perry McCarthy for 2,500 shares of treasury stock at $2.00 per share. Treasury stock was bought on February 5 at $1.60 per share. R561.
Oct.	14, 20X1.	Raj Vaudagna paid cash for 150 shares of $100.00 par value preferred stock at $103.00 per share. R600.
Jan.	1, 20X2.	Paid cash to bond trustee for semiannual interest on bonds payable. C634.
Jan.	1, 20X2.	Paid cash to bond trustee for semiannual deposit to bond sinking fund. Interest earned on money in sinking fund since last payment on July 1, $800.00. C635.
Jan.	2, 20X6.	Received notice from bond trustee that bond issue was retired using bond sinking fund, $200,000.00. M428.

Instructions:
Journalize the transactions. Use page 1 of a cash receipts journal, page 2 of a cash payments journal, and page 1 of a general journal. Source documents are abbreviated as follows: check, C; memorandum, M; receipt, R.

INTERNET ACTIVITY

Point your browser to
http://accounting.swpco.com
Choose **Advanced Course**, choose **Activities**, and complete the activity for Chapter 12.

Applied Communication

The most important step in the employment process is the interview. During the interview, an employer will ask you a variety of questions about your abilities, qualifications, and attitudes. You must be thoroughly prepared to answer a prospective employer's questions. Two of the most frequently asked interview questions involve your qualifications for the job and your interest in working for the company.

Required:
1. Find a job advertisement in the newspaper or other source for a position for which you are qualified. Write several paragraphs discussing your qualifications for the job. (You may use the same advertisement you selected for the Applied Communications activity in Chapter 4. Review your resume to make a list of your skills, qualifications, education, work experience, and accomplishments.)
2. Research the company identified in the job advertisement. Write several paragraphs explaining your interest in working for the company, using specific facts about it.

Cases for Critical Thinking

Case 1

Cecil Thomas pays $12,000.00 for 2,000 shares of $5.00 stated value common stock of Datkins, Inc. A year later, Mr. Thomas sells the 2,000 shares of stock to Sally Gilliam for a total of $14,000.00. Ms. Gilliam sends a notice to Datkins so that ownership can be changed on the corporation's stock records. An accounting clerk at Datkins is not sure of the correct journal entry. What advice would you give the accounting clerk?

AUTOMATED ACCOUNTING

UNDERSTANDING GRAPHS

Using Graphs and Charts

Graphs and charts are pictorial representations of data that may be used to effectively communicate summary information. Graphs and charts can be produced by the computer, displayed on the monitor, and printed to a printer. Graphs and charts are used to clarify the meanings of the words and numbers that appear in the financial statements. They are commonly used to enhance presentations, track sales, monitor expenses, identify trends, and make forecasts.

Graphs and charts can be used to enhance written or oral presentations. In reports, graphs and charts add a visual break for the reader. The reader will often review the graphs and charts to get a quick summary of written material or numerical data. Speakers may use electronic presentation software or overhead transparencies to illustrate important points. Graphs and charts are often an important part of these presentations.

Many accounting software packages are capable of producing graphs and charts of data contained within their files. *Automated Accounting 7.0* and higher can generate two- and three-dimensional pie and bar charts and line graphs from data used in the following reports:

- Balance sheet
- Income statement
- Sales
- Expense distribution
- Actual versus budget

Creating a Graph

To prepare a graph based on financial data:

1. Choose the Graph Selection menu item from the Reports menu or click the Graphs toolbar button.

2. When the Graph Selection dialog box appears, as shown in Figure AA12-1, select an option from the Data to Graph list.

3. Select an option from the Type of Graph list. (Menu items that are grayed out are unavailable, since they are inappropriate for the selected type of report.)

4. Click the OK button to produce the graph. A 3-D bar graph is shown in Figure AA12-2. (The graphing function in *Automated Accounting 8.0* is slightly different. However, it prepares a variety of

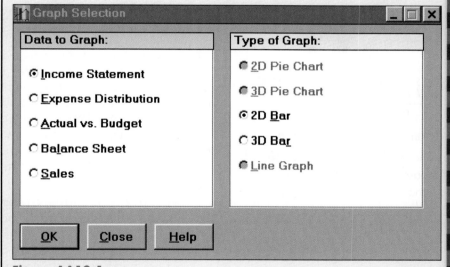

Figure AA12-1

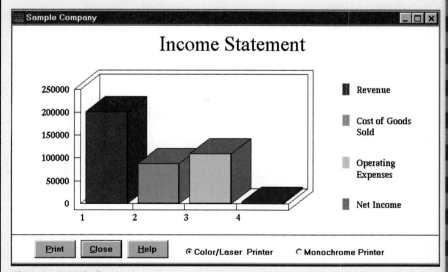

Figure AA12-2

graphs, depending on the type of data available.)

Choosing a Graph Style

Different styles of graphs are used to display different types of financial information. Use the following descriptions to help you choose the correct type of graph.

1. Pie graphs may be used to illustrate parts of a whole. For example, a pie graph could be used to show the percentages of cost of goods sold, operating expenses, and net income. The percentages represent the values part of net sales.

2. Bar graphs may be used to show the relative size of related items, such as expenses.

3. Line graphs may be used to illustrate trends, such as net sales or net income over a period of years.

Both 2-D and 3-D graphs are available. The information shown in these two types of graphs are identical. Although the information is the same, 3-D graphs are sometimes more difficult to interpret. When selecting the type of graph, consider how your reader will use the information.

Printing Graphs

Graphs created in *Automated Accounting 7.0* or higher can be printed in black and white or in color, depending on the capabilities of your printer. Select one of the radio buttons at the bottom of the graph to indicate the type of printer you will use to print the graph. Use the Monochrome option if your printer only prints in black and white. (In *Automated Accounting* 8.0, you do not need to specify the capabilities of your printer.)

13

Financial Analysis and Reporting for a Corporation

AFTER STUDYING CHAPTER 13, YOU WILL BE ABLE TO:

1. Define terms related to financial analysis and reporting for a corporation.

2. Identify concepts and practices related to financial analysis and reporting for a corporation.

3. Prepare a work sheet for a corporation.

4. Calculate federal income tax for a corporation.

5. Prepare and analyze financial statements for a corporation.

6. Prepare selected end-of-fiscal-period work for a corporation.

Corporations prepare three important financial statements at the end of each fiscal period to report their financial progress and condition. (*CONCEPT: Adequate Disclosure*)

1. Income statement.

2. Statement of stockholders' equity.

3. Balance sheet.

Corporations normally provide an analysis of the financial statements to help interested persons understand and use the information. Information on the income statement is used to analyze component percentages and earnings per share. Information on the statement of stockholders' equity is used to analyze equity per share and determine price-earnings ratio. Balance sheet information is used to determine accounts receivable turnover ratio, the rate earned on average stockholders' equity, and the rate earned on average total assets.

A corporation's board of directors uses the information on the financial statements for making management decisions. The board of directors also uses the information to determine whether to distribute earnings to stockholders. Stockholders and other investors use the information to determine whether to begin or continue investing in the corporation. Creditors use the information to determine whether the corporation will be able to meet its credit obligations.

TERMS PREVIEW

amortization
earnings per share
equity per share
market value
price-earnings ratio
rate earned on average
    stockholders' equity
rate earned on average
    total assets

ACCOUNTING
IN YOUR CAREER

FULL DISCLOSURE

Electricon Corporation plans to introduce a new line of products next year, beginning in January. Many of the activities needed to introduce these new products have taken place during the current fiscal year and therefore impact this year's financial statements. Management has already taken action to shift as many of the costs as possible to the next year so that expenses and revenue match. However, some costs could not be shifted.

Myra Smathers, the chair of the board of directors, is concerned that the additional costs will negatively affect the income statement to the extent that investors will not be as interested in Electricon stock. She is especially concerned about the addition of 50 new sales representatives, which will increase Sales Salary Expense from $6 million to $8 million a year. In addition, inventory on hand has increased from $16 to $24 million to have the new products ready to ship. Training for the new representatives has cost $0.5 million, and $2 million has already been spent on a saturation advertising campaign.

Addressing the board and Electricon senior management, Myra says, "We have already spent $12.5 million dollars on these new products and don't have any sales to offset these expenses. Our new costs are 30% of current sales. We had better be very successful with these new products next year." Donald Wyndham, CEO, explains, "This is not so unusual. The saying is that you have to spend money to make money, and I have to say that this is the most carefully planned introduction we have ever done. I am confident that at this time next year you will be very happy with our numbers. So will the investors."

Critical Thinking

1. The new sales representatives are on the payroll only for the last three months of the year. What is the amount of increase in Sales Salary Expense for the current year?
2. How will the cost of merchandise sold component percentage be affected by the increase in ending inventory?
3. Should some explanation of the increased costs be given in the annual report, or should the new product launch be kept a secret from competitors?

13-1 Work Sheet for a Corporation

ORGANIZATION EXPENSE ADJUSTMENT

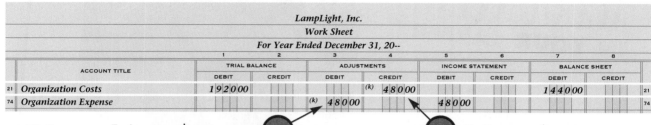

LampLight, Inc.
Work Sheet
For Year Ended December 31, 20--

	ACCOUNT TITLE	TRIAL BALANCE DEBIT	TRIAL BALANCE CREDIT	ADJUSTMENTS DEBIT	ADJUSTMENTS CREDIT	INCOME STATEMENT DEBIT	INCOME STATEMENT CREDIT	BALANCE SHEET DEBIT	BALANCE SHEET CREDIT	
21	Organization Costs	1 9 2 0 00			(k) 4 8 0 00			1 4 4 0 00		21
74	Organization Expense			(k) 4 8 0 00		4 8 0 00				74

Figure 13-1 **1.** Increase the expense. **1**   **2** **2.** Decrease the asset.

LampLight prepares a work sheet at the end of fiscal period. Most of its adjustments are similar to those described for MasterSport in Part 1. LampLight also records adjustments for organization expense and federal income tax expense.

Corporate organization costs are intangible assets. A common accounting practice is to write off intangible assets over a period of years. Recognizing a portion of an expense in each of several years is called **amortization**.

LampLight incurred total organization costs of $2,400.00. LampLight spreads the $2,400.00 expense over five years. Thus, one-fifth of this amount, $480.00, is amortized in each of the first five years. In the first year, $480.00 was amortized as an expense. An adjustment is planned

on the work sheet for the second year's amortization, as shown in Figure 13-1.

Organization Expense is debited for $480.00. **Organization Costs** is credited for $480.00. The new balance of **Organization Costs**, $1,440.00, is the amount to be amortized in the next three years.

> ### F.Y.I.
>
> *A recent FASB rule change requires many companies to write off organization costs in the company's first fiscal year. This change will effectively eliminate the amortization of organization costs. However, amortization continues to apply to other intangible assets, such as patents and copyrights owned by a company.*

FEDERAL INCOME TAX EXPENSE ADJUSTMENT

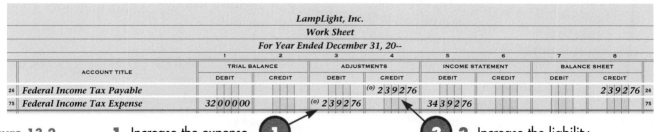

LampLight, Inc.
Work Sheet
For Year Ended December 31, 20--

	ACCOUNT TITLE	TRIAL BALANCE DEBIT	TRIAL BALANCE CREDIT	ADJUSTMENTS DEBIT	ADJUSTMENTS CREDIT	INCOME STATEMENT DEBIT	INCOME STATEMENT CREDIT	BALANCE SHEET DEBIT	BALANCE SHEET CREDIT	
26	Federal Income Tax Payable				(o) 2 3 9 2 76				2 3 9 2 76	26
75	Federal Income Tax Expense	3 2 0 0 0 00		(o) 2 3 9 2 76		3 4 3 9 2 76				75

Figure 13-2 **1.** Increase the expense. **1**   **2** **2.** Increase the liability.

At the beginning of the year, LampLight *estimated* its federal income tax for the year to be $32,000.00. LampLight paid the estimated tax to the federal government in four equal quarterly installments of $8,000.00 each. As of December

31, LampLight calculated its *actual* federal income tax to determine whether it owes additional income tax. An adjustment is planned on the work sheet for the additional amount owed, as shown in Figure 13-2.

CALCULATING FEDERAL INCOME TAX EXPENSE

S
T
E
P
S

Calculating federal income tax expense

1. Complete the work sheet's Adjustments columns except for the federal income tax expense adjustment. Do not total the Adjustments columns at this time.
2. Extend all amounts, except Federal Income Tax Expense, to the work sheet's Income Statement columns.
3. Determine the work sheet's Income Statement column totals using a calculator. Do not record the column totals on the work sheet. Calculate the difference between the two totals. The difference is the net income before federal income tax. LampLight's net income before federal income tax is:

Income Statement Credit Column Total	−	Income Statement Debit Column Total before Federal Income Tax	=	Net Income before Federal Income Tax
$883,782.75	−	$752,647.48	=	$131,135.27

4. Calculate the amount of federal income tax using a tax rate table furnished by the Internal Revenue Service. The Internal Revenue Service distributes corporate tax rate tables each year. LampLight's actual federal income tax is calculated as shown using the following tax rate table:

15% of net income before taxes, zero to $50,000.00
Plus 25% of net income before taxes, $50,000.00 to $75,000.00
Plus 34% of net income before taxes, $75,000.00 to $100,000.00
Plus 39% of net income before taxes, $100,000.00 to $335,000.00
Plus 34% of net income before taxes over $335,000.00

Net Income before Taxes	×	Tax Rate	=	Federal Income Tax Amount
$50,000.00	×	15%	=	$ 7,500.00
Plus 25,000.00	×	25%	=	6,250.00
Plus 25,000.00	×	34%	=	8,500.00
Plus 31,135.27	×	39%	=	12,142.76
$131,135.27				$34,392.76

5. Calculate the amount of accrued federal income tax expense as follows:

Total Federal Income Tax Expense	−	Estimated Federal Income Tax Already Paid	=	Accrued Federal Income Tax Expense
$34,392.76	−	$32,000.00	=	$2,392.76

6. Record the federal income tax expense adjustment, as shown in Figure 13-2.
7. Extend the new balance of Federal Income Tax Payable, *2,392.76*, to the Balance Sheet Credit column.
8. Extend the new balance of Federal Income Tax Expense, *34,392.76*, to the Income Statement Debit column.
9. Total the work sheet's Adjustments, Income Statement, and Balance Sheet columns as shown in Figure 13-3.

Federal Income Tax Expense is debited for $2,392.76. Federal Income Tax Payable is credited for $2,392.76. The new balance of **Federal Income** Tax Expense, $34,392.76, is the total amount of federal income tax due based on the net income before federal income tax.

LampLight, Inc.
Work Sheet
For Year Ended December 31, 20--

| | TRIAL BALANCE | | ADJUSTMENTS | | INCOME STATEMENT | | BALANCE SHEET | |
ACCOUNT TITLE	DEBIT	CREDIT	DEBIT	CREDIT	DEBIT	CREDIT	DEBIT	CREDIT
1 Cash	2543640						2543640	
2 Petty Cash	25000						25000	
3 Notes Receivable	1000000						1000000	
4 Interest Receivable			(a)100000				100000	
5 Accounts Receivable	13523454						13523454	
6 Allow. for Uncoll. Accts.		42013		(b)627750				669763
7 Subscriptions Receivable								
8 Merchandise Inventory	26745309			(c)869790			25875519	
9 Supplies—Sales	1431567			(d)586904			844663	
10 Supplies—Administrative	2261370			(e)1445640			815730	
11 Prepaid Insurance	1690000			(f)591131			1098869	
12 Prepaid Interest			(g)1047				1047	
13 Bond Sinking Fund	5000000						5000000	
14 Store Equipment	14298334						14298334	
15 Accum. Depr.—Store Equip.		1512300		(h)1675300				3187600
16 Building	16500000						16500000	
17 Accum. Depr.—Building		825000		(i)825000				1650000
18 Office Equipment	7392823						7392823	
19 Accum. Depr.—Office Equip.		765200		(j)973413				1738613
20 Land	13300000						13300000	
21 Organization Costs	192000			(k)48000			144000	
22 Interest Payable				(l)1500000				1500000
23 Accounts Payable		30585540						30585540
24 Employee Income Tax Pay.		123890						123890
25 Federal Income Tax Pay.				(o)239276				239276
26 Social Security Tax Payable		62480		(n)4119				66599
27 Medicare Tax Payable		14410		(n)951				15361
28 Salaries Payable				(m)633373				633373
29 Sales Tax Payable		215474						215474
30 Unemploy. Tax Pay.—Federal		8745		(n)120				8865
31 Unemploy. Tax Pay.—State		59029		(n)810				59839
32 Health Ins. Premiums Payable		42800						42800
33 Dividends Payable		29575500						29575500
34 Bonds Payable		250000000						250000000
35 Capital Stock—Common		321000000						321000000
36 Stock Subscribed—Common								

Figure 13-3 (top half)

#	Account	Trial Balance Dr	Trial Balance Cr	Adjustments Dr	Adjustments Cr	Income Statement Dr	Income Statement Cr	Balance Sheet Dr	Balance Sheet Cr
37	Pd.-in Cap. in Exc. of St. Val.—Com.		20000						20000
38	Capital Stock—Preferred		170000000						170000000
39	Stock Subscribed—Preferred								
40	Pd.-in Cap. in Exc. of Par Val.—Pref.		800000						800000
41	Disc. on Sale of Preferred Stock	500000						500000	
42	Treasury Stock	180000						180000	
43	Pd.-in Cap. from Sale of Tr. Stock		50000						50000
44	Retained Earnings		5858835						5858835
45	Dividends—Common	1597500						1597500	
46	Dividends—Preferred	1360000						1360000	
47	Income Summary			(c) 869790		869790			
48	Sales		87295240				87295240		
49	Sales Discount	869512				869512			
50	Sales Ret. and Allow.	290056				290056			
51	Purchases	45539648				45539648			
52	Purchases Discount		671035				671035		
53	Purchases Ret. and Allow.		267000				267000		
54	Advertising Expense	1778200				1778200			
55	Credit Card Fee Expense	628500				628500			
56	Depr. Exp.—Store Equip.			(b) 1675300		1675300			
57	Miscellaneous Exp.—Sales	940612				940612			
58	Salary Expense—Sales	6322600		(m) 45789		6368389			
59	Supplies Expense—Sales			(d) 586904		586904			
60	Depr. Expense—Building			(i) 825000		825000			
61	Depr. Exp.—Office Equip.			(j) 973413		973413			
62	Insurance Expense			(f) 591131		591131			
63	Miscellaneous Exp.—Admin.	1257068				1257068			
64	Payroll Taxes Expense	990240		(n) 6000		996240			
65	Property Tax Expense	670000				670000			
66	Salary Expense—Admin.	2364333		(m) 17584		2381917			
67	Supplies Expense—Admin.			(e) 1445640		1445640			
68	Uncollectible Accounts Exp.			(b) 627750		627750			
69	Utilities Expense	2872725				2872725			
70	Gain on Plant Assets				(a) 100000				
71	Interest Income		45000				145000		
72	Interest Expense	1530000		(g) 1047		3028953			
73	Loss on Plant Assets								
74	Organization Expense			(k) 48000		48000			
75	Federal Inc. Tax Expense	3200000		(o) 239276		3439276			
76		1787944491	1787944491	9552624	9552624	78704024	88378275	1061005079	96426328
77	Net Inc. after Fed. Inc. Tax					9674251			9674251
78						88378275	88378275	1061005079	1061005079

Figure 13-3 (bottom half)

**ERM**
REVIEW

amortization

**UDIT YOUR**
UNDERSTANDING

1. What is amortization?

2. How often is estimated federal income tax paid?

**ORK**
TOGETHER

Calculating federal income tax expense, recording the adjustment, and completing a work sheet

A work sheet for Provident Electronics, Inc., for the current year is provided in the *Working Papers*. Your instructor will guide you through the following examples.

3. Calculate net income before federal income tax.

4. Calculate the amount of federal income tax using the following rates:

15% of net income before taxes, zero to $50,000.00
Plus 25% of net income before taxes, $50,000.00 to $75,000.00
Plus 34% of net income before taxes, $75,000.00 to $100,000.00
Plus 39% of net income before taxes, $100,000.00 to $335,000.00
Plus 34% of net income before taxes over $335,000.00

5. Calculate the accrued federal income tax expense.

6. Record the adjustment on the work sheet.

7. Complete the work sheet. Save your work to complete the Work Together on page 369.

**N YOUR**
OWN

Calculating federal income tax expense, recording the adjustment, and completing a work sheet

A work sheet for BRE Corporation for the current year is provided in the *Working Papers*. Work this problem independently.

8. Calculate net income before federal income tax.

9. Calculate the amount of federal income tax using the tax rates given in 4. above.

10. Calculate the accrued federal income tax expense.

11. Record the adjustment on the work sheet.

12. Complete the work sheet. Save your work to complete the On Your Own on page 369.

354 CHAPTER 13 Financial Analysis and Reporting for a Corporation

INCOME STATEMENT FOR A CORPORATION

LampLight, Inc.
Income Statement
For Year Ended December 31, 20--

				Percentage of Net Sales*
Operating Revenue:				
Sales			$872,952.40	
Less: Sales Discount	$ 8,695.12			
Sales Returns and Allowances	2,900.56	11,595.68		
Net Sales			$861,356.72	100.0
Cost of Merchandise Sold:				
Merchandise Inventory, Jan. 1, 20--			$267,453.09	
Purchases		$455,396.48		
Less: Purchases Discount	$6,710.35			
Purchases Returns and Allowances	2,670.00	9,380.35		
Net Purchases			446,016.13	
Total Cost of Merchandise Available for Sale			$713,469.22	
Less Merchandise Inventory, Dec. 31, 20--			258,755.19	
Cost of Merchandise Sold			454,714.03	52.8
Gross Profit on Operations			$406,642.69	47.2
Operating Expenses:				
Selling Expenses:				
Advertising Expense	$ 17,782.00			
Credit Card Fee Expense	6,285.00			
Depreciation Expense—Store Equipment	16,753.00			
Miscellaneous Expense—Sales	9,406.12			
Salary Expense—Sales	63,683.89			
Supplies Expense—Sales	5,869.04			
Total Selling Expenses		$119,779.05		13.9
Administrative Expenses:				
Depreciation Expense—Building	$ 8,250.00			
Depreciation Expense—Office Equipment	9,734.13			
Insurance Expense	5,911.31			
Miscellaneous Expense—Administrative	12,570.68			
Payroll Taxes Expense	9,962.40			
Property Tax Expense	6,700.00			
Salary Expense—Administrative	23,819.17			
Supplies Expense—Administrative	14,456.40			
Uncollectible Accounts Expense	6,277.50			
Utilities Expense	28,727.25			
Total Administrative Expenses		126,408.84		14.7
Total Operating Expenses			246,187.89	28.6
Income from Operations			$160,454.80	18.6
Other Revenue:				
Interest Income		$ 1,450.00		
Other Expenses:				
Interest Expense	$ 30,289.53			
Organization Expense	480.00			
Total Other Expenses		$ 30,769.53		
Net Deduction			29,319.53	3.4
Net Income before Federal Income Tax			$131,135.27	15.2
Less Federal Income Tax Expense			34,392.76	4.0
Net Income after Federal Income Tax			$ 96,742.51	11.2

*Rounded to nearest 0.1%

Figure 13-4

LampLight uses net sales as the basis for calculating component percentages on its income statement as shown in Figure 13-4.

Income Statement Items	Acceptable Component Percentages	Actual Component Percentages
Cost of Merchandise Sold	Not more than 55.0%	52.8%
Gross Profit on Operations	Not less than 45.0%	47.2%
Total Selling Expenses	Not more than 12.0%	13.9%
Total Administrative Expenses	Not more than 18.0%	14.7%
Total Operating Expenses	Not more than 30.0%	28.6%
Income from Operations	Not less than 15.0%	18.6%
Net Deduction from Other Expenses	Not more than 4.0%	3.4%
Net Income before Federal Income Tax	Not less than 11.0%	15.2%

Figure 13-5

The percentage relationship between one financial statement item and the total that includes that item is known as a component percentage. LampLight determines acceptable component percentages for each major item of cost, expense, and income as shown in Figure 13-5. Like MasterSport in Chapter 4, LampLight does not analyze component percentages for federal income tax expense or net income after federal income tax.

For the current year, LampLight has achieved acceptable percentages for most items. However, the component percentage for total selling expenses, 13.9%, is higher than the maximum acceptable percentage, 12.0%, a negative result. Thus, LampLight's managers further analyze the expense accounts that compose selling expenses. The managers' investigation reveals a sharp increase in the price of television advertising, one component of selling expenses. To correct this situation for the next fiscal period, LampLight's managers can do the following:

1. Reduce advertising costs and continue using 12.0% as the maximum acceptable component percentage.

2. Increase the maximum acceptable component percentage to recognize the increased advertising cost.

SHARE OF NET INCOME ASSIGNED TO PREFERRED AND COMMON STOCK

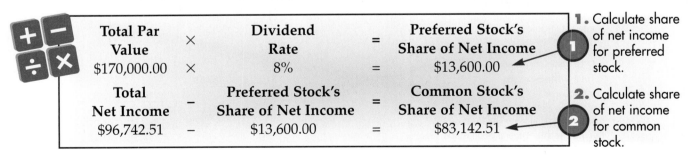

Figure 13-6

The total earnings for outstanding preferred stock equals the 8% dividend specified on the stock certificates. The total share of net income for common stock is the remainder of the net income after the preferred stock's share is deducted. These amounts are calculated as shown in Figure 13-6.

Share of Net Income	÷	Shares of Stock Outstanding	=	Earnings per Share
$83,142.51	÷	31,950	=	$2.60

Figure 13-7

The amount of net income belonging to a single share of stock is called **earnings per share**. Earnings per share is typically calculated only on the number of common shares outstanding. For example, LampLight has 32,100 shares of common stock issued. However, 150 of these shares are treasury stock and, therefore, are not outstanding stock. LampLight has 31,950 shares of outstanding common stock (32,100 shares *less* 150 shares *equals* 31,950).

For the year ended December 31, LampLight's earnings per share on common stock is calculated as shown in Figure 13-7.

STATEMENT OF STOCKHOLDERS' EQUITY FOR A CORPORATION

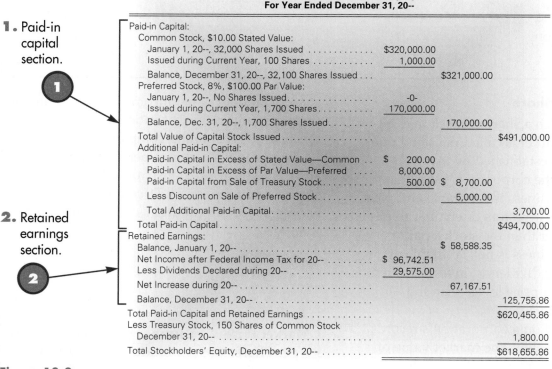

1. Paid-in capital section.

2. Retained earnings section.

LampLight, Inc.
Statement of Stockholders' Equity
For Year Ended December 31, 20--

Paid-in Capital:
Common Stock, $10.00 Stated Value:
January 1, 20--, 32,000 Shares Issued $320,000.00
Issued during Current Year, 100 Shares 1,000.00
Balance, December 31, 20--, 32,100 Shares Issued ... $321,000.00
Preferred Stock, 8%, $100.00 Par Value:
January 1, 20--, No Shares Issued................. -0-
Issued during Current Year, 1,700 Shares......... 170,000.00
Balance, Dec. 31, 20--, 1,700 Shares Issued......... 170,000.00
Total Value of Capital Stock Issued.................. $491,000.00
Additional Paid-in Capital:
Paid-in Capital in Excess of Stated Value—Common .. $ 200.00
Paid-in Capital in Excess of Par Value—Preferred 8,000.00
Paid-in Capital from Sale of Treasury Stock.......... 500.00 $ 8,700.00
Less Discount on Sale of Preferred Stock........... 5,000.00
Total Additional Paid-in Capital..................... 3,700.00
Total Paid-in Capital............................... $494,700.00
Retained Earnings:
Balance, January 1, 20-- .... $ 58,588.35
Net Income after Federal Income Tax for 20--.......... $ 96,742.51
Less Dividends Declared during 20-- 29,575.00
Net Increase during 20--............................ 67,167.51
Balance, December 31, 20--.......................... 125,755.86
Total Paid-in Capital and Retained Earnings $620,455.86
Less Treasury Stock, 150 Shares of Common Stock
December 31, 20-- 1,800.00
Total Stockholders' Equity, December 31, 20-- $618,655.86

Figure 13-8

A statement of stockholders' equity shows changes occurring in the stockholders' equity for a fiscal period. LampLight's statement of stockholders' equity has two major sections as shown in Figure 13-8.

Some businesses prepare a statement of retained earnings instead of a statement of stockholders' equity. A statement of retained earnings includes information only about the changes in retained earnings during a fiscal period. The remainder of the information about changes in paid-in capital is placed on the corporation's balance sheet.

As of December 31, LampLight has issued $321,000.00 in common stock and $170,000.00 in preferred stock. LampLight also has $1,800.00 in treasury stock. Therefore, the total stock outstanding is $489,200.00. The total stockholders' equity, *$618,655.86*, is shown on the last line of the statement of stockholders' equity. LampLight uses information on its statement of stockholders' equity to analyze (1) equity per share, (2) market value per share, and (3) price-earnings ratio.

Equity per Share

The amount of total stockholders' equity belonging to a single share of stock is called **equity per share**. The equity of preferred stock is equal to its total par value, *$170,000.00*, or $100.00 per share. The remainder of the total stockholders' equity is the equity of the common stock, calculated as shown below. Common stock equity should at least equal its stated value to be acceptable. LampLight's common stock equity per share is higher than its stated value of $10.00 per share and therefore is acceptable.

	Total Stockholders' Equity	÷	Shares of Capital Stock Outstanding	=	Equity per Share
Preferred	$170,000.00	÷	1,700	=	$100.00
Common	448,655.86	÷	31,950	=	14.04
Total	$618,655.86				

Market Value per Share

The price at which a share of stock may be sold on the stock market is called **market value**. The market value is established by investors' buying and selling the corporation's stock on the stock market. If a business is profitable and pays adequate dividends, investors often offer to pay a market price higher than the stock's par or stated value. If a business is not profitable or does not pay regular dividends, investors often offer to pay a market price lower than the stock's par or stated value.

Stock is recorded on a corporation's records at the par or stated value. The market value of stock is not recorded on corporate records.

Price-Earnings Ratio

The relationship between the market value per share and earnings per share of a stock is called the **price-earnings ratio**. Investors usually want to buy stock in companies that are earning a reasonable amount of net income. One way to determine whether a company is earning a reasonable amount of net income is to calculate the price-earnings ratio. The ratio is then compared to standards for similar companies.

LampLight's earnings per share on common stock is $2.60 as previously described. Using stock market reports on December 31, the price-earnings ratio for common stock is calculated as follows:

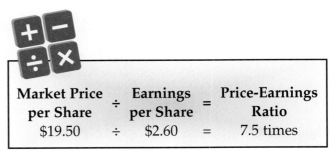

Market Price per Share	÷	Earnings per Share	=	Price-Earnings Ratio
$19.50	÷	$2.60	=	7.5 times

The common stock price-earnings ratio, 7.5 times, means that the stock is selling for 7.5 times its share of the earnings. For businesses similar to LampLight, a common stock price-earnings ratio between 6.0 and 10.0 times is considered acceptable. LampLight's price-earnings ratio for common stock is acceptable.

LampLight, Inc.
Balance Sheet
December 31, 20--

ASSETS

Current Assets:		
Cash		$ 25,436.40
Petty Cash		250.00
Notes Receivable		10,000.00
Interest Receivable		1,000.00
Accounts Receivable	$135,234.54	
Less Allowance for Uncollectible Accounts	6,697.63	128,536.91
Merchandise Inventory		258,755.19
Supplies—Sales		8,446.63
Supplies—Administrative		8,157.30
Prepaid Insurance		10,988.69
Prepaid Interest		10.47
Total Current Assets		$451,581.59
Long-Term Investment:		
Bond Sinking Fund		50,000.00
Plant Assets:		
Store Equipment	$142,983.34	
Less Accumulated Depreciation—Store Equipment	31,876.00	$111,107.34
Building	$165,000.00	
Less Accumulated Depreciation—Building	16,500.00	148,500.00
Office Equipment	$ 73,928.23	
Less Accumulated Depreciation—Office Equipment	17,386.13	56,542.10
Land		133,000.00
Total Plant Assets		449,149.44
Intangible Assets:		
Organization Costs		1,440.00
Total Assets		$952,171.03

LIABILITIES

Current Liabilities:		
Interest Payable	$ 15,000.00	
Accounts Payable	30,585.40	
Employee Income Tax Payable	1,238.90	
Federal Income Tax Payable	2,392.76	
Social Security Tax Payable	665.99	
Medicare Tax Payable	153.61	
Salaries Payable	633.73	
Sales Tax Payable	2,154.74	
Unemployment Tax Payable—Federal	88.65	
Unemployment Tax Payable—State	598.39	
Health Insurance Premiums Payable	428.00	
Dividends Payable	29,575.00	
Total Current Liabilities		$ 83,515.17
Long-Term Liability:		
Bonds Payable		250,000.00
Total Liabilities		$333,515.17

STOCKHOLDERS' EQUITY

Total Stockholders' Equity		618,655.86
Total Liabilities and Stockholders' Equity		$952,171.03

Figure 13-9

A corporate balance sheet reports assets, liabilities, and stockholders' equity on a specific date. LampLight's December 31 balance sheet is shown in Figure 13-9. LampLight calculates three ratios based on information from the balance sheet: (1) accounts receivable turnover ratio, (2) rate earned on stockholders' equity, and (3) rate earned on total assets.

The number of times the average amount of accounts receivable is collected annually is known as the accounts receivable turnover ratio. LampLight calculates this ratio as described in the steps below.

LampLight's terms of sales are 2/10, n/30. Therefore, LampLight expects payment within 30 days. The expected accounts receivable turnover ratio is 12.2 times (365 days in a year ÷ 30 days). LampLight's average number of days for payment, 53, is higher than the expected level of 30 days. Therefore, LampLight's accounts receivable turnover ratio, 6.9 times, is unacceptable. LampLight needs to consider ways to encourage customers to pay their accounts within the credit period.

STEPS Calculating accounts receivable turnover ratio

1. Calculate the average book value of accounts receivable. Beginning balances are obtained from the financial statements of the prior year. Ending balances are obtained from the work sheet for the current year.

Accounts Receivable Beginning Balance	−	Allowance for Uncollectible Accounts Beginning Balance	=	Beginning Book Value
$124,983.89	−	$4,362.18	=	$120,621.71

Accounts Receivable Ending Balance	−	Allowance for Uncollectible Accounts Ending Balance	=	Ending Book Value
$135,234.54	−	$6,697.63	=	$128,536.91

(Beginning Book Value of Accounts Receivable	+	Ending Book Value of Accounts Receivable)	÷ 2	=	Average Book Value of Accounts Receivable
($120,621.71	+	$128,536.91)	÷ 2	=	$124,579.31

2. Calculate the accounts receivable turnover ratio. Some businesses use separate accounts to record the amount of cash sales and net sales on account. Net sales as reported on the income statement should be used as net sales on account if the business does not record this information.

Net Sales on Account	÷	Average Book Value of Accounts Receivable	=	Accounts Receivable Turnover Ratio
$861,356.72	÷	$124,579.31	=	6.9 times

3. Calculate the average number of days for payment.

Days in Year	÷	Accounts Receivable Turnover Ratio	=	Average Number of Days for Payment
365	÷	6.9	=	53

RATE EARNED ON AVERAGE STOCKHOLDERS' EQUITY

1. Calculate average stockholders' equity. **1**

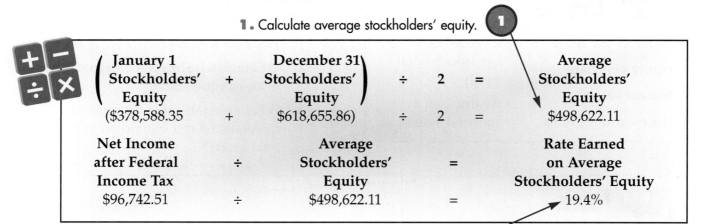

Figure 13-10

2. Calculate the rate earned. **2**

The relationship between net income and average stockholders' equity is called the **rate earned on average stockholders' equity**. The rate earned on average stockholders' equity for LampLight is calculated as shown in Figure 13-10.

For each dollar that stockholders have invested, LampLight is earning $0.194 in net income. The best investment is in a corporation with the highest rate earned on average stockholders' equity. For example, Midtown, Inc., has a rate earned on average stockholders' equity of 14.2% compared to LampLight's rate of 19.4%. Based on this one analysis, an investor would choose to invest in LampLight's stock rather than Midtown's.

RATE EARNED ON AVERAGE TOTAL ASSETS

1. Calculate average total assets. **1**

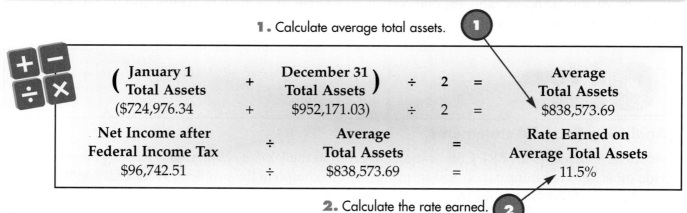

Figure 13-11

2. Calculate the rate earned. **2**

The relationship between net income and average total assets is called **rate earned on average total assets**. This rate for LampLight is calculated as shown in Figure 13-11.

For each dollar of assets that the corporation owns, the business has earnings of $0.115 after it pays federal income tax. Information published by trade organizations shows that businesses similar to LampLight tend to have a rate earned on average total assets between 10.0% and 14.0%. LampLight's rate, 11.5%, is acceptable.

Other methods to analyze corporate financial statement items are described in Chapter 16.

earnings per share

equity per share

market value

price-earnings ratio

rate earned on average stockholders' equity

rate earned on average total assets

1. What does earnings per share represent?
2. What relationship is represented by the price-earnings ratio?
3. What amounts must be known to calculate the rate earned on average total assets?

WORK TOGETHER

Analyzing financial statements

Financial statements for Provident Electronics, Inc., are given in the *Working Papers*. The *Working Papers* provide other selected information and forms needed to complete the problem. Your instructor will guide you through the following examples.

4. Calculate and record on the income statement the component percentages for the indicated items. Round the percentage calculations to the nearest 0.1%.
5. Calculate earnings per share. Round calculations to the nearest cent.
6. Use the statement of stockholders' equity and the additional information supplied to calculate: (a) equity per share of stock and (b) the price-earnings ratio.
7. Use the balance sheet and the additional information supplied to calculate the: (a) accounts receivable turnover ratio, (b) rate earned on average stockholders' equity, and (c) rate earned on average total assets.

ON YOUR OWN

Analyzing financial statements

Financial statements for BRE Corporation are given in the *Working Papers*. The *Working Papers* provide other selected information and forms needed to complete the problem. Work independently to complete the following problem.

8. Calculate and record on the income statement the component percentages for the indicated items. Round the percentage calculations to the nearest 0.1%.
9. Calculate earnings per share. Round calculations to the nearest cent.
10. Use the statement of stockholders' equity and the additional information supplied to calculate: (a) equity per share of stock and (b) the price-earnings ratio.
11. Use the balance sheet and the additional information supplied to calculate the: (a) accounts receivable turnover ratio, (b) rate earned on average stockholders' equity, and (c) rate earned on average total assets.

13-3 Other End-of-Fiscal-Period Work

ADJUSTING ENTRIES

	DATE		ACCOUNT TITLE	DOC. NO.	POST. REF.	DEBIT	CREDIT	
1			*Adjusting Entries*					1
2	Dec.²⁰⁻⁻	31	Interest Receivable			1 0 0 0 00		2
3			Interest Income				1 0 0 0 00	3
4		31	Uncollectible Accounts Expense			6 2 7 7 50		4
5			Allowance for Uncoll. Accts.				6 2 7 7 50	5
6		31	Income Summary			8 6 9 7 90		6
7			Merchandise Inventory				8 6 9 7 90	7
8		31	Supplies Expense—Sales			5 8 6 9 04		8
9			Supplies—Sales				5 8 6 9 04	9
10		31	Supplies Expense—Admin.			14 4 5 6 40		10
11			Supplies—Admin.				14 4 5 6 40	11
12		31	Insurance Expense			5 9 1 1 31		12
13			Prepaid Insurance				5 9 1 1 31	13
14		31	Prepaid Interest			1 0 47		14
15			Interest Expense				1 0 47	15
16		31	Depreciation Exp.—Store Equip.			16 7 5 3 00		16
17			Accum. Depr.—Store Equip.				16 7 5 3 00	17
18		31	Depreciation Exp.—Building			8 2 5 0 00		18
19			Accum. Depr.—Building				8 2 5 0 00	19
20		31	Depreciation Exp.—Office Equip.			9 7 3 4 13		20
21			Accum. Depr.—Office Equip.				9 7 3 4 13	21
22		31	Organization Expense			4 8 0 00		22
23			Organization Costs				4 8 0 00	23
24		31	Interest Expense			15 0 0 0 00		24
25			Interest Payable				15 0 0 0 00	25
26		31	Salary Expense—Sales			4 5 7 89		26
27			Salary Expense—Admin.			1 7 5 84		27
28			Salaries Payable				6 3 3 73	28
29		31	Payroll Taxes Expense			6 0 00		29
30			Social Security Tax Payable				4 1 19	30
31			Medicare Tax Payable				9 51	31
32			Unemploy. Tax Pay.—Federal				1 20	32
33			Unemploy. Tax Pay.—State				8 10	33
34		31	Federal Income Tax Expense			2 3 9 2 76		34
35			Federal Income Tax Payable				2 3 9 2 76	35
36								36
37								37
38								38

GENERAL JOURNAL   PAGE 13

Figure 13-12

In addition to a work sheet and financial statements, LampLight prepares adjusting entries, closing entries, a post-closing trial balance, and reversing entries. LampLight's December 31 adjusting entries are shown in Figure 13-12.

	DATE		ACCOUNT TITLE	DOC. NO.	POST. REF.	DEBIT	CREDIT	
1			*Closing Entries*					1
2	Dec.²⁰⁻⁻	31	Sales			872 95 2 40		2
3			Purchases Discount			6 7 10 35		3
4			Purchases Returns and Allowances			2 6 70 00		4
5			Interest Income			1 4 50 00		5
6			Income Summary				883 78 2 75	6
7		31	Income Summary			778 34 2 34		7
8			Sales Discount				8 69 5 12	8
9			Sales Returns and Allowances				2 90 0 56	9
10			Purchases				455 39 6 48	10
11			Advertising Expense				17 78 2 00	11
12			Credit Card Fee Expense				6 28 5 00	12
13			Depreciation Exp.—Store Equip.				16 75 3 00	13
14			Miscellaneous Exp.—Sales				9 40 6 12	14
15			Salary Expense—Sales				63 68 3 89	15
16			Supplies Expense—Sales				5 86 9 04	16
17			Depreciation Exp.—Building				8 25 0 00	17
18			Depreciation Exp.—Office Equip.				9 73 4 13	18
19			Insurance Expense				5 91 1 31	19
20			Miscellaneous Exp.—Admin.				12 57 0 68	20
21			Payroll Taxes Expense				9 96 2 40	21
22			Property Tax Expense				6 70 0 00	22
23			Salary Expense—Admin.				23 81 9 17	23
24			Supplies Expense—Admin.				14 45 6 40	24
25			Uncollectible Accounts Expense				6 27 7 50	25
26			Utilities Expense				28 72 7 25	26
27			Interest Expense				30 28 9 53	27
28			Organization Expense				4 80 00	28
29			Federal Income Tax Expense				34 39 2 76	29
30		31	Income Summary			96 74 2 51		30
31			Retained Earnings				96 74 2 51	31
32		31	Retained Earnings			29 57 5 00		32
33			Dividends—Common				15 97 5 00	33
34			Dividends—Preferred				13 60 0 00	34
35								35

GENERAL JOURNAL — PAGE 14

Figure 13-13

LampLight records four closing entries at the end of a fiscal period.

1. Closing entry for income statement accounts with credit balances (revenue and contra cost accounts).

2. Closing entry for income statement accounts with debit balances (cost, contra revenue, and expense accounts).

3. Closing entry to record net income or net loss in the retained earnings account and close the income summary account.

4. Closing entry for the dividends accounts.

LampLight's December 31 closing entries are shown in Figure 13-13. LampLight's closing entries are similar to those described for MasterSport in Chapter 5.

LampLight, Inc.
Post-Closing Trial Balance
December 31, 20--

Account Title	Debit	Credit
Cash	$ 25,436.40	
Petty Cash	250.00	
Notes Receivable	10,000.00	
Interest Receivable	1,000.00	
Accounts Receivable	135,234.54	
Allowance for Uncollectible Accounts		$ 6,697.63
Subscriptions Receivable		
Merchandise Inventory	258,755.19	
Supplies—Sales	8,446.63	
Supplies—Administrative	8,157.30	
Prepaid Insurance	10,988.69	
Prepaid Interest	10.47	
Bond Sinking Fund	50,000.00	
Store Equipment	142,983.34	
Accumulated Depreciation—Store Equipment		31,876.00
Building	165,000.00	
Accumulated Depreciation—Building		16,500.00
Office Equipment	73,928.23	
Accumulated Depreciation—Office Equipment		17,386.13
Land	133,000.00	
Organization Costs	1,440.00	
Interest Payable		15,000.00
Accounts Payable		30,585.40
Employee Income Tax Payable		1,238.90
Federal Income Tax Payable		2,392.76
Social Security Tax Payable		665.99
Medicare Tax Payable		153.61
Salaries Payable		633.73
Sales Tax Payable		2,154.74
Unemployment Tax Payable—Federal		88.65
Unemployment Tax Payable—State		598.39
Health Insurance Premiums Payable		428.00
Dividends Payable		29,575.00
Bonds Payable		250,000.00
Capital Stock—Common		321,000.00
Stock Subscribed—Common		
Paid-in Capital in Excess of Stated Value—Common		200.00
Capital Stock—Preferred		170,000.00
Stock Subscribed—Preferred		
Paid-in Capital in Excess of Par Value—Preferred		8,000.00
Discount on Sale of Preferred Stock	5,000.00	
Treasury Stock	1,800.00	
Paid-in Capital from Sale of Treasury Stock		500.00
Retained Earnings		125,755.86
Totals	$1,031,430.79	$1,031,430.79

Figure 13-14

LampLight's December 31 post-closing trial balance is shown in Figure 13-14.

REMEMBER

If the totals on the post-closing trial balance are the same, the accounting records are ready for the next fiscal period.

	DATE		ACCOUNT TITLE	DOC. NO.	POST. REF.	DEBIT	CREDIT	
1			*Reversing Entries*					1
2	Jan.²⁰⁻⁻	1	Interest Income			1 0 0 0 00		2
3			Interest Receivable				1 0 0 0 00	3
4		1	Interest Expense			1 0 47		4
5			Prepaid Interest				1 0 47	5
6		1	Interest Payable			15 0 0 0 00		6
7			Interest Expense				15 0 0 0 00	7
8		1	Salaries Payable			6 3 3 73		8
9			Salary Expense—Sales				4 5 7 89	9
10			Salary Expense—Administrative				1 7 5 84	10
11		1	Social Security Tax Payable			4 1 19		11
12			Medicare Tax Payable			9 51		12
13			Unemploy. Tax Pay.—Federal			1 20		13
14			Unemploy. Tax Pay.—State			8 10		14
15			Payroll Taxes Expense				6 0 00	15

GENERAL JOURNAL — PAGE 15

Figure 13-15

If an adjusting entry creates a balance in an asset or liability account, LampLight reverses the adjusting entry. Like most corporations, however, LampLight does not reverse the adjusting entry that records federal income tax. LampLight's reversing entries recorded on January 1 are shown in Figure 13-15.

ART DiMARTILE, MANAGEMENT INFORMATION SYSTEMS

I work in the Management Systems Division of Procter and Gamble Company. I am responsible for planning and developing computerized information systems for a segment of Research and Development at P & G. In my job I manage people, budgets, and projects.

We have many technical centers in North America, Europe, Asia, and Latin America. Our Senior Vice President of R & D has announced that our stated goal is to have people in these centers work together as if they were all in the same building. I am responsible for helping to develop the Information Systems strategy to achieve that goal.

I have an undergraduate business degree from Cornell University and a masters in Business Administration from Penn State University. I took two accounting classes at Cornell. I then took advanced accounting and financial management at Penn State.

My accounting classes gave me the training to manage budgets and to develop financial proposals for new projects. Accounting also helps me understand how the business works, so we can develop systems that our people can use in their jobs to make our company more efficient and profitable.

I don't know of any career path that doesn't require a good dose of accounting.

ACCOUNTING AT WORK

Form **1120** Department of the Treasury Internal Revenue Service	**U.S. Corporation Income Tax Return** For calendar year 20-- or tax year beginning ...., 20--, ending ...., 20 ... ▶ Instructions are separate. See page 1 for Paperwork Reduction Act Notice.	OMB No. 1545-0123 **20--**

A Check if a:
(1) Consolidated return (attach Form 851) ☐
(2) Personal holding co. (attach Sch. PH) ☐
(3) Personal service corp. (as defined in Temporary Regs. sec. 1.441-4T—see instructions) ☐

Use IRS label. Other-wise, please print or type.	Name LampLight, Inc.	**B** Employer identification number 74-1334457
	Number, street, and room or suite no. (If a P.O. box, see page 6 of instructions.) 1450 Eaglewood Lane	**C** Date incorporated 12/26/--
	City or town, state, and ZIP code Nashville, TN 37207-2361	**D** Total assets (see Specific Instructions) $ 952,171 | 03

E Check applicable boxes: (1) ☐ Initial return (2) ☐ Final return (3) ☐ Change in address

Income

1a	Gross receipts or sales 864,257|28 **b** Less returns and allowances 2,900|56 **c** Bal ▶	**1c**	861,356 72
2	Cost of goods sold (Schedule A, line 8)	**2**	454,714 03
3	Gross profit. Subtract line 2 from line 1c	**3**	406,642 69
4	Dividends (Schedule C, line 19)	**4**	-0-
5	Interest	**5**	1,450 00
6	Gross rents	**6**	-0-
7	Gross royalties	**7**	-0-
8	Capital gain net income (attach Schedule D (Form 1120))	**8**	-0-
9	Net gain or (loss) from Form 4797, Part II, line 20 (attach Form 4797)	**9**	-0-
10	Other income (see instructions—attach schedule)	**10**	-0-
11	**Total income.** Add lines 3 through 10 ▶	**11**	408,092 69

Deductions (See instructions for limitations on deductions.)

12	Compensation of officers (Schedule E, line 4)	**12**	28,432 50
13a	Salaries and wages 59,070|56 **b** Less jobs credit -0- **c** Balance ▶	**13c**	59,070 56
14	Repairs	**14**	-0-
15	Bad debts	**15**	6,277 50
16	Rents	**16**	-0-
17	Taxes	**17**	16,662 40
18	Interest	**18**	30,289 53
19	Charitable contributions (see instructions for 10% limitation)	**19**	-0-
20	Depreciation (attach Form 4562) . . **20** 34,737|13		
21	Less depreciation claimed on Schedule A and elsewhere on return . . **21a** -0-	**21b**	34,737 13
22	Depletion	**22**	-0-
23	Advertising	**23**	17,782 00
24	Pension, profit-sharing, etc., plans	**24**	-0-
25	Employee benefit programs	**25**	-0-
26	Other deductions (attach schedule)	**26**	83,705 80
27	**Total deductions.** Add lines 12 through 26 ▶	**27**	276,957 42
28	Taxable income before net operating loss deduction and special deductions. Subtract line 27 from line 11	**28**	131,135 27
29	**Less: a** Net operating loss deduction (see instructions) . . . . **29a** -0-		
	b Special deductions (Schedule C, line 20) . . . . . **29b** -0-	**29c**	-0-

Tax and Payments

30	**Taxable income.** Subtract line 29c from line 28	**30**	131,135 27
31	**Total tax** (Schedule J, line 10)	**31**	34,392 76
32	**Payments: a** 20-- overpayment credited to 20-- **32a** -0-		
b	20-- estimated tax payments **32b** 32,000 00		
c	Less 20-- refund applied for on Form 4466 **32c** (-0-) **d** Bal ▶ **32d** 32,000 00		
e	Tax deposited with Form 7004 **32e** -0-		
f	Credit from regulated investment companies (attach Form 2439) . . . . **32f** -0-		
g	Credit for Federal tax on fuels (attach Form 4136). See instructions . . **32g** -0-	**32h**	32,000 00
33	Estimated tax penalty (see instructions). Check if Form 2220 is attached ▶ ☐	**33**	-0-
34	**Tax due.** If line 32h is smaller than the total of lines 31 and 33, enter amount owed	**34**	2,392 76
35	**Overpayment.** If line 32h is larger than the total of lines 31 and 33, enter amount overpaid . . .	**35**	
36	Enter amount of line 35 you want: **Credited to** 19-- **estimated tax** ▶ **Refunded** ▶	**36**	

Please Sign Here

Under penalties of perjury, I declare that I have examined this return, including accompanying schedules and statements, and to the best of my knowledge and belief, it is true, correct, and complete. Declaration of preparer (other than taxpayer) is based on all information of which preparer has any knowledge.

▶ *Susan P. Boyd* | Date 3/15/-- | ▶ Title Treasurer
Signature of officer

Paid Preparer's Use Only

Preparer's signature ▶	Date	Check if self-employed ☐	Preparer's social security number
Firm's name (or yours if self-employed) and address ▶		E.I. No. ▶	
		ZIP code ▶	

Figure 13-16

LampLight must file a federal income tax return and pay income taxes. Page 1 of LampLight's Form 1120, U.S. Corporation Income Tax Return, is shown in Figure 13-16.

Some amounts reported on a corporation's income statement must be modified to complete the tax return. For example, LampLight presents both payroll tax expense and property tax expense on its income statement. LampLight's managers require this information to make sound business decisions. However, the tax form requires LampLight to report only the total of all taxes.

When a corporation is dissolved, it must meet legal requirements and follow correct accounting procedures. However, corporations are rarely dissolved. When an owner (stockholder) decides not to participate in the corporation, the stockholder merely sells all shares of stock owned. The corporation is not dissolved.

The dissolution of a corporation involves many legal procedures and documents. Documents that must be filed include a notice to the state in which the business was incorporated and a notice to all creditors of the corporation. Since the dissolution of a corporation is complex, the board of directors should seek legal advice.

Once a corporation is dissolved, the liquidation process can begin. The procedure for selling noncash assets is similar to that for proprietorships and partnerships. However, since a corporation is a taxable entity, the gains and losses on the sale of noncash assets are subject to taxation. Therefore, additional tax reports for the corporation must be filed. The accounting aspects of actually liquidating a corporation are extremely complex. Therefore, obtaining professional accounting services to assist in the liquidation of a corporation is recommended.

GLOBAL PERSPECTIVE

INTERNATIONAL ORGANIZATIONS

There are many international organizations that establish trade regulations and standards to facilitate conducting business among the various countries in the world. The United States is a member of several trade-related organizations.

The United Nations plays an important role in foreign trade and has many organizations that make contributions. For example, The International Court of Justice (ICJ) decides disputes between nations, The International Monetary Fund (IMF) promotes international monetary cooperation and currency stabilization among member nations, The Universal Postal Union (UPU) promotes international cooperation in postal service, and the United Nations Children's Fund (UNICEF) provides aid to children and mothers in developing countries.

The International Chamber of Commerce (ICC) serves traders in over 100 countries. Its most important function is to issue rules on international trade practices. It is not a government agency and confines its activities to business issues rather than national policy issues.

The General Agreement on Tariffs and Trade (GATT) promotes economic growth by liberalizing world trade through requiring its member governments to reduce artificial trade restraints. There are 90 members of GATT, and the U.S. is a charter member.

The European Union (EU) is a group of 15 European democracies—Austria, Belgium, Denmark, Finland, France, Germany, Greece, the Republic of Ireland, Italy, Luxembourg, the Netherlands, Portugal, Spain, Sweden, and the United Kingdom. The EU has a short-term goal to integrate member nations' economies so members will act as a single nation for trade purposes. The EU's long-term goal is to unite member nations into a political union.

There are a number of smaller organizations throughout the world that promote cooperative trade.

Required:

Select one international trade organization and research the organization's creation, policies, and accomplishments.

AUDIT YOUR UNDERSTANDING

1. What four closing entries are recorded at the end of the period?
2. What form is used to file the federal income tax return for a corporation?
3. How does the liquidation of a corporation differ from the liquidation of a proprietorship or partnership?

WORK TOGETHER

End-of-fiscal period work for a corporation

Use the work sheet for Provident Electronics, Inc. from the Work Together on page 354. Statement paper and pages 14, 15, and 16 of a general journal are provided in the *Working Papers*. Your instructor will guide you through the following examples.

4. Journalize the adjusting entries on page 14 of the general journal.
5. Journalize the closing entries on page 15 of the general journal.
6. Prepare a post-closing trial balance as of December 31 of the current year.
7. Journalize the reversing entries on page 16 of the general journal.

End-of-fiscal period work for a corporation

Use the work sheet for BRE Corporation from the On Your Own on page 354. Statement paper and pages 8, 9, and 10 of a general journal are provided in the *Working Papers*. Your instructor will guide you through the following problem.

8. Journalize the adjusting entries on page 8 of the general journal.
9. Journalize the closing entries on page 9 of the general journal.
10. Prepare a post-closing trial balance as of December 31 of the current year.
11. Journalize the reversing entries on page 10 of the general journal.

CHAPTER 13 SUMMARY

After completing this chapter, you can

1. Define important accounting terms related to financial analysis and reporting for a corporation.

2. Identify accounting concepts and practices related to financial analysis and reporting for a corporation.

3. Prepare a work sheet for a corporation.

4. Calculate federal income tax for a corporation.

5. Prepare and analyze financial statements for a corporation.

EXPLORE ACCOUNTING

NOTES TO FINANCIAL STATEMENTS

As today's business world becomes increasingly complex, investors' need for accounting information also continues to grow. Much of the information investors need goes beyond the general ledger account balances presented on financial statements. For example, the Financial Accounting Standards Board has determined that investors should have the scheduled payments on long-term debt for the next five years.

A complete set of financial statements includes four basic statements: income statement, balance sheet, statement of stockholders' equity, and statement of cash flows. The financial state-

ments also include a variety of disclosures, called notes, that present additional information regarding amounts presented in the basic financial statements.

Each note begins with a heading that contains a number and title. The first note is typically a statement of significant account principles used to prepare the financial statements. This note would include the methods used to cost inventory, depreciate assets, and other principles where management can select among acceptable alternatives.

Subsequent notes can cover a variety of topics, depending upon the individual characteristics of the company. For example, an oil company would explain how it values its crude oil reserves.

Other notes might include information on inventory, fixed assets, income taxes, etc. Other significant events affecting the corporation, such as mergers, discontinued operations, and lawsuits, are also disclosed in the notes to financial statements.

REQUIRED:

Obtain the annual reports of three public corporations. What reference on each financial statement directs you to examine the notes to financial statements? Compare the titles of each note contained in each annual report. Which notes were presented in more than one annual report? Which notes were unique to one of the corporations?

APPLICATION PROBLEM
Preparing a work sheet for a corporation

General ledger account titles and balances for Trexler, Inc., are recorded on a work sheet in the *Working Papers* accompanying this textbook.

Instructions:
Complete the work sheet for the current year ended December 31. Record the adjustments on the work sheet using the following information. Save your work to complete Application Problems 13-3 and 13-4.

Adjustment Information, December 31

Accrued Interest Income	$160.17
Uncollectible Accounts Expense (estimated as 1.0% of sales on account)	
Sales on Account for Year	126,405.00
Merchandise Inventory	51,450.23
Sales Supplies Inventory	1,202.70
Administrative Supplies Inventory	959.85
Value of Prepaid Insurance	1,436.58
Prepaid Interest	1.85
Annual Depreciation Expense—Store Equipment	1,294.57
Annual Depreciation Expense—Building	2,900.00
Annual Depreciation Expense—Office Equipment	3,018.64
Organization Expense	50.00
Accrued Interest Expense	4,002.57
Accrued Salaries—Sales	153.97
Accrued Salaries—Administrative	593.49
Accrued Payroll Taxes—Social Security Tax	48.59
Accrued Payroll Taxes—Medicare	11.21
Accrued Payroll Taxes—Federal Unemployment Tax	1.72
Accrued Payroll Taxes—State Unemployment Tax	11.61

Federal income taxes are based on the tax rate table in this chapter.

APPLICATION PROBLEM
Calculating federal income taxes

During the past year, three corporations earned the following net income before federal income taxes:

Corporation A $73,932.56
Corporation B $467,032.45
Corporation C $38,296.44

Instructions:
Calculate the amount of federal income tax expense for each of the three corporations. Use the tax rate table in this chapter.

APPLICATION PROBLEM
Preparing financial statements for a corporation

Use the work sheet prepared in Application Problem 13-1.

continued

Instructions:

1. Prepare an income statement for the current year ended December 31.

2. Calculate and record the following component percentages: (a) cost of merchandise sold, (b) gross profit on operations, (c) total selling expenses, (d) total administrative expenses, (e) total operating expenses, (f) income from operations, (g) net addition or deduction resulting from other revenue and expenses, (h) net income before federal income tax, (i) federal income tax expense, and (j) net income after federal income tax. Round the percentage calculations to the nearest 0.1%.

3. Use the Income Statement Analysis table given in the *Working Papers.* Analyze Trexler's income statement by determining whether component percentages are within acceptable levels. If any component percentage is not within an acceptable level, suggest steps that the company should take.

4. Calculate earnings per share. Round the calculation to the nearest cent. Trexler has 10,900 shares of $10.00 stated-value common stock issued and 420 shares of $100.00 par-value preferred stock issued. Treasury stock consists of 70 shares of common stock. The dividend rate on preferred stock is 10%.

5. Prepare a statement of stockholders' equity for the current year ended December 31. Use the following additional information.

	January 1 Balance	Issued During the Year	December 31 Balance
Common Stock:			
No. of Shares	8,000	2,900	10,900
Amount	$80,000.00	$29,000.00	$109,000.00
Preferred Stock:			
No. of Shares	150	270	420
Amount	$15,000.00	$27,000.00	$ 42,000.00

Treasury stock consists of 70 shares of common stock.
The January 1 balance of Retained Earnings was $13,411.26.

6. Calculate the following items: (a) equity per share of stock and (b) price-earnings ratio. The market price of common stock on December 31 is $24.00.

7. Prepare a balance sheet for December 31 of the current year.

8. Calculate the following items:
   (a) Accounts receivable turnover ratio. Net sales on account are $126,405.00. Accounts receivable and allowance for uncollectible accounts on January 1 were $26,495.72 and $1,142.37, respectively.
   (b) Rate earned on average stockholders' equity. Total stockholders' equity on January 1 was $106,951.26.
   (c) Rate earned on average total assets. Total assets on January 1 were $233,699.75.

APPLICATION PROBLEM
Completing other end-of-fiscal-period work

Use the work sheet prepared in Application Problem 13-1.

Instructions:

1. Journalize the adjusting entries. Use page 13 of a general journal.

2. Journalize the closing entries. Use page 14 of a general journal.

3. Journalize the reversing entries. Use page 15 of a general journal. Use January 1 of the year following the current year as the date.

MASTERY PROBLEM
Completing end-of-fiscal-period work for a corporation

The general ledger account titles and balances for Lander, Inc., are recorded on a work sheet in the *Working Papers*.

Instructions:

1. Complete the work sheet for December 31 of the current year. Record the adjustments on the work sheet using the following information.

Adjustment Information, December 31

Accrued Interest Income	$277.18
Uncollectible Accounts Expense (estimated as 1.0% of sales on account)	
Sales on Account for Year	213,441.00
Merchandise Inventory	86,876.38
Sales Supplies Inventory	9,808.79
Administrative Supplies Inventory	3,620.75
Value of Prepaid Insurance	2,363.94
Prepaid Interest	3.12
Annual Depreciation Expense—Store Equipment	9,746.00
Annual Depreciation Expense—Building	2,400.00
Annual Depreciation Expense—Office Equipment	2,185.95
Organization Expense	75.00
Accrued Interest Expense	7,004.34
Accrued Salaries—Sales	375.65
Accrued Salaries—Administrative	1,002.13
Accrued Payroll Taxes—Social Security Tax	89.55
Accrued Payroll Taxes—Medicare	20.67
Accrued Payroll Taxes—Federal Unemployment Tax	1.27
Accrued Payroll Taxes—State Unemployment Tax	8.59

Federal income taxes are based on the tax rate table in this chapter.

2. Prepare an income statement. Calculate and record the following component percentages: (a) cost of merchandise sold, (b) gross profit on operations, (c) total selling expenses, (d) total administrative expenses, (e) total operating expenses, (f) income from operations, (g) net addition or deduction resulting from other revenue and expenses, (h) net income before federal income tax, (i) federal income tax expense, and (j) net income after federal income tax. Round percentage calculations to the nearest 0.1%.

3. Use the Income Statement Analysis table given in the *Working Papers*. Analyze Lander's income statement by determining whether component percentages are within acceptable levels. If any component percentage is not within an acceptable level, suggest steps that the company should take.

4. Calculate earnings per share. Round the calculation to the nearest cent. Lander has 18,400 shares of $10.00 stated-value common stock issued and 720 shares of $100.00 par-value preferred stock issued. Treasury stock consists of 90 shares of common stock. The dividend rate on preferred stock is 10%.

continued

5. Prepare a statement of stockholders' equity for the current year ended December 31. Use the following additional information.

	January 1 Balance	Issued During the Year	December 31 Balance
Common Stock:			
No. of Shares	18,000	400	18,400
Amount	$180,000.00	$ 4,000.00	$184,000.00
Preferred Stock:			
No. of Shares	600	120	720
Amount	$ 60,000.00	$12,000.00	$ 72,000.00

The January 1 balance of Retained Earnings was $22,645.60.

6. Calculate the following items based on information on the statement of stockholders' equity: (a) equity per share of stock and (b) price-earnings ratio. The market price of common stock on December 31 is $30.00.

7. Prepare a balance sheet for December 31 of the current year.

8. Calculate the following items based on information from the balance sheet.
   (a) Accounts receivable turnover ratio. Net sales on account were $213,441.00. Accounts receivable and allowance for doubtful accounts on January 1 were $49,435.32 and $2,146.40, respectively.
   (b) Rate earned on average stockholders' equity. Total stockholders' equity on January 1 was $290,485.60.
   (c) Rate earned on average total assets. Total assets on January 1 were $392,691.70.

9. Journalize the adjusting entries. Use page 13 of a general journal.

10. Journalize the closing entries. Use page 14 of a general journal.

11. Journalize the reversing entries. Use page 1 of a general journal. Use January 1 of the year following the current year as the date.

13-6 CHALLENGE PROBLEM
Preparing a Form 1120, U.S. Corporation Income Tax Return

Goldstein, Inc., has completed its work sheet and financial statements for the fiscal year ending on December 31 of the current year. The income statement for Goldstein is in the *Working Papers*.
   The following information required to prepare the tax return is obtained from company records.

Employer identification number: 65-074738
Date incorporated: January 5
Address: 7834 Industrial Road, Oxford, MS 38655-1500
Total assets: $786,986.50
Compensation of officers: $7,217.60
Estimated tax payments: $42,000.00

Instructions:

1. Complete the company name and address in the spaces provided on the tax form.

2. Use the information provided to complete lines D–F. Write the amount of compensation of officers on line 12. Write the estimated tax payments on line 32b.

3. Use the amounts on the income statement to complete the following lines of the tax form.

Tax Form

Line	Income Statement Account(s)
1a	Sales less Sales Discount
1b	Sales Returns and Allowances
2	Cost of Merchandise Sold
5	Interest Income
13a	Salary Expense—Sales plus Salary Expense—Administrative less Compensation of officers
15	Uncollectible Accounts Expense
17	Payroll Taxes Expense plus Property Taxes
18	Interest Expense
20	The sum of the three depreciation expense accounts
23	Advertising Expense
26	All other expenses not reported on other lines
31	Federal Income Tax Expense

4. Calculate the amounts on lines 1c, 3, 11, 13c, 21b, 27, 30, 32h, and 34 using the instructions provided on the tax form.

5. Check the accuracy of the completed tax form by comparing the amount on line 30 of the tax form to Net Income before Federal Income Tax on the income statement.

6. Write -0- on the remaining blank lines on the tax form.

INTERNET ACTIVITY

Point your browser to

http://accounting.swpco.com

Choose **Advanced Course**, choose **Activities**, and complete the activity for Chapter 13.

Applied Communication

The market price of a stock may change daily as its shares are traded on a stock exchange. Research and write a brief report about one of the stock exchanges. Describe such things as how a company is listed on the exchange, how shares are traded, and how an individual can find the current market price of a stock listed on the exchange.

Cases for Critical Thinking

Case 1
A corporation president suggests to the accounting department that the statement of stockholders' equity be dropped from the end-of-fiscal-period work. The president's reason is that the same information is reported on the corporation's balance sheet. The accounting department wants to continue using the statement. Which would you recommend? Why?

Case 2
Kevin Edwards has $20,000.00 in a savings account that is earning 6% interest. He is thinking of investing the money in stock that has a stated value and a current market price of $100.00 per share. For the past three years, the stock dividends have amounted to $9.00 per share per year. Mr. Edwards asks your advice. What would you recommend? Explain your answer.

AUTOMATED ACCOUNTING

END-OF-PERIOD WORK FOR A CORPORATION

During the fiscal period, numerous transactions are analyzed, journalized, and posted. When a transaction affects more than one accounting period, an adjusting entry may be needed to match revenues and expenses with the appropriate accounting period. To complete the accounting cycle, adjusting entries are entered into the computer and verified for accuracy. The financial statements are generated, and then closing entries are generated and posted by the software.

Trial Balance

Before adjusting entries are recorded, a trial balance is displayed and printed. The trial balance proves the equality of debits and credits in the general ledger. To display the trial balance:

1. Click the Reports toolbar button, or choose the Report Selection menu item from the Reports menu.

2. When the Report Selection dialog appears, choose the Ledger Reports option button from the Select a Report Group list.

3. Select Trial Balance from the Choose a Report to Display list.

4. Click the OK button.

From the Trial Balance display window, the report can be printed or copied to the Clipboard in spreadsheet or word processing format.

Adjusting Entries

The trial balance and period-end adjustment data are used as the basis for the adjusting entries. Adjusting entries are used to:

1. Transfer to expense the amount of assets consumed. For example, office supplies and prepaid insurance.

2. Update the merchandise inventory account.

3. Recognize accrued revenues and accrued expenses.

To record adjusting entries, use the following steps:

1. Click the Journal toolbar button, or choose the Journal Entries menu item from the Data menu.

2. Select the General Journal tab from the Journal Entries window, if necessary.

3. Key the adjusting entries. All adjusting entries are dated the last day of the fiscal period. Adj. Ent. is used as the reference for all adjusting entries.

4. Click the Post button.

Financial Statements

The reports that summarize information from the ledgers are known as financial statements. The most common financial statements for a business organized as a corporation are the balance sheet and the income statement. *Automated Accounting 7.0* or higher can also display a retained earnings statement.

After adjusting entries have been posted, financial statements are prepared. To display financial statements:

1. Click the Reports toolbar button, or choose the Report Selection menu item from the Reports menu. The Report Selection window displays.

2. Choose the Financial Statements option button from the Select a Report Group list.

3. Choose the financial statement report you would like to display from the Choose a Report to Display list.

4. Click the OK button.

The up-to-date account balances stored by the software are used to calculate and display the current financial statements.

Closing Entries

In an automated accounting system, closing entries are generated and posted by the software. The software automatically closes net income to Retained Earnings after closing the revenue and expense accounts. The dividend account is closed as well. The steps required are as follows:

1. Choose Generate Closing Journal Entries from the Options menu.

AUTOMATED ACCOUNTING

2. Click Yes to generate the closing entries.

3. The general journal will appear, containing the journal entries. Verify the accuracy of the transactions.

4. Click the Post button.

AUTOMATING MASTERY PROBLEM 13-5

Instructions:

1. Load *Automated Accounting* 7.0 or higher software.

2. Select database AA13-5 (Advanced Course Mastery Problem 13-5) from the accounting template disk.

3. Select File from the menu bar and choose the Save As menu command. Key the path to the drive and directory that contains your data files. Save the database with a file name of XXX135 (where XXX are your initials).

4. Access Problem Instructions through the Help menu. Read the Problem Instruction screen.

5. Refer to page 373 for data used in this problem.

6. Exit the Automated Accounting software.

Processing and Reporting
Accounting Data for a Corporation

This activity reinforces selected learnings from Parts 2 through 4, Chapters 5 through 13.

WHITEHURST, INC.

The accounting activities are for Whitehurst, Inc., a merchandising business organized as a corporation. Whitehurst sells plumbing and related products to building contractors, homeowners, and other consumers. Whitehurst's fiscal year is from January 1 through December 31.

PART A: JOURNALIZING TRANSACTIONS

In Part A of this reinforcement activity, selected transactions for Whitehurst, Inc., completed during December of the current year, are journalized.

Whitehurst uses the chart of accounts shown on page 379. The journals used by Whitehurst are similar to those illustrated in Parts 2 through 4.

RECORDING TRANSACTIONS

Instructions:

1. Journalize the following transactions completed during December of the current year. Use page 23 of a cash receipts journal, page 23 of a cash payments journal, and page 12 of a general journal. Whitehurst records prepaid interest expense initially as an expense and rent received in advance as revenue. Other prepaid and unearned items are recorded initially as assets and liabilities. Source documents are abbreviated as follows: check, C; memorandum, M; note payable, NP; note receivable, NR; receipt, R.

Dec. 1. Whitehurst's board of directors declared an annual dividend of $15,820.00. Preferred stock issued is $40,400.00 of 10%, $100.00 par-value preferred stock. Common stock issued is $11,780.00 of $10.00 stated-value common stock. Date of payment is December 30. M316.

1. Wrote off Susan Vine's past-due account as uncollectible, $427.50. M317.

1. Received cash for three months' rent in advance from Woodcrest, Inc., $2,400.00. R126.

1. Discarded a store fixture: original cost, $1,050.00; total accumulated depreciation through December 31 of last year, $840.00; additional depreciation to be recorded through December 1 of the current year, $210.00. M318.

1. Received a subscription from Delmar Adams for 30 shares of $100.00 par-value preferred stock, $3,000.00. M319.

2. Paid cash for office equipment, $2,650.00. C476.

4. Patrick Carson dishonored NR4, a 30-day, 10% note, maturity value due today: principal, $150.00; interest, $1.25; total, $151.25. M320.

4. Discarded an office table: original cost, $250.00; total accumulated depreciation through December 31 of last year, $150.00; additional depreciation to be recorded through December 4 of the current year, $50.00. M321.

WHITEHURST, INC. CHART OF ACCOUNTS

Balance Sheet Accounts

(1000) Assets
1100 CURRENT ASSETS
- 1105 Cash
- 1110 Petty Cash
- 1115 Notes Receivable
- 1120 Interest Receivable
- 1125 Accounts Receivable
- 1130 Allowance for Uncollectible Accounts
- 1135 Subscriptions Receivable
- 1140 Merchandise Inventory
- 1145 Supplies—Sales
- 1150 Supplies—Administrative
- 1155 Prepaid Insurance
- 1160 Prepaid Interest

1200 LONG-TERM INVESTMENT
- 1205 Bond Sinking Fund

1300 PLANT ASSETS
- 1305 Store Equipment
- 1310 Accumulated Depreciation—Store Equipment
- 1315 Building
- 1320 Accumulated Depreciation—Building
- 1325 Office Equipment
- 1330 Accumulated Depreciation—Office Equipment
- 1335 Land

1400 INTANGIBLE ASSET
- 1405 Organization Costs

(2000) Liabilities
2100 CURRENT LIABILITIES
- 2105 Notes Payable
- 2110 Interest Payable
- 2115 Accounts Payable
- 2120 Employee Income Tax Payable
- 2125 Federal Income Tax Payable
- 2130 Social Security Tax Payable
- 2133 Medicare Tax Payable
- 2135 Salaries Payable
- 2140 Sales Tax Payable
- 2145 Unearned Rent
- 2150 Unemployment Tax Payable—Federal
- 2155 Unemployment Tax Payable—State
- 2160 Health Insurance Premiums Payable
- 2165 Dividends Payable

2200 LONG-TERM LIABILITY
- 2205 Bonds Payable

(3000) Stockholders' Equity
- 3105 Capital Stock—Common
- 3110 Stock Subscribed—Common
- 3115 Paid-in Capital in Excess of Stated Value—Common
- 3120 Capital Stock—Preferred
- 3125 Stock Subscribed—Preferred
- 3130 Paid-in Capital in Excess of Par Value—Preferred
- 3135 Treasury Stock
- 3140 Paid-in Capital from Sale of Treasury Stock
- 3145 Retained Earnings
- 3150 Dividends—Common
- 3155 Dividends—Preferred
- 3160 Income Summary

Income Statement Accounts

(4000) Operating Revenue
- 4105 Sales
- 4110 Sales Discount
- 4115 Sales Returns and Allowances

(5000) Cost of Merchandise
- 5105 Purchases
- 5110 Purchases Discount
- 5115 Purchases Returns and Allowances

(6000) Operating Expenses
6100 SELLING EXPENSES
- 6105 Advertising Expense
- 6110 Credit Card Fee Expense
- 6115 Depreciation Expense—Store Equipment
- 6120 Miscellaneous Expense—Sales
- 6125 Salary Expense—Sales
- 6130 Supplies Expense—Sales

6200 ADMINISTRATIVE EXPENSES
- 6205 Depreciation Expense—Building
- 6210 Depreciation Expense—Office Equipment
- 6215 Insurance Expense
- 6220 Miscellaneous Expense—Administrative
- 6225 Payroll Taxes Expense
- 6230 Property Tax Expense
- 6235 Salary Expense—Administrative
- 6240 Supplies Expense—Administrative
- 6245 Uncollectible Accounts Expense
- 6250 Utilities Expense

(7000) Other Revenue
- 7105 Gain on Plant Assets
- 7110 Interest Income
- 7115 Rent Income

(8000) Other Expenses
- 8105 Interest Expense
- 8110 Loss on Plant Assets
- 8115 Organization Expense

(9000) Income Tax
- 9105 Federal Income Tax Expense

Dec. 4. Received a 60-day, 10% note from Leigh Calhoun for an extension of time on her account, $500.00. NR5.

5. Issued a 6-month, 10% note, $10,000.00. NP6.

5. Paid cash to bond trustee for annual interest on bond issue, $24,000.00. C482.

5. Paid cash to bond trustee for annual deposit to bond sinking fund, $18,400.00, and recorded interest earned on bond sinking fund, $1,600.00. C487.

6. Received cash from Leslie Johns for 700 shares of $10.00 stated-value common stock at $11.00 per share, $7,700.00. R134.

7. Received cash for the maturity value of NR1, principal, $150.00, plus interest, $2.47; total, $152.47. R136.

11. Received cash from sale of office equipment, $70.00: original cost, $700.00; total accumulated depreciation through December 31 of last year, $500.00; additional depreciation to be recorded through December 11 of the current year, $100.00. M322 and R138.

11. Paid cash to Marlin Pratt for 60 shares of $10.00 stated-value common stock at $9.00 per share, $540.00. C502.

12. Paid cash for the maturity value of NP4: principal, $300.00, plus interest, $6.00; total, $306.00. C503.

13. Received cash from Robert Shull for 200 shares of $10.00 stated-value common stock at $10.00 per share, $2,000.00. R140.

14. Received cash for the maturity value of NR2: principal, $247.50, plus interest; $4.07; total $251.57. R141.

16. Paid cash for the maturity value of NP3: principal, $1,000.00, plus interest, $16.44; total, $1,016.44. C509.

19. Received office equipment from Valerie DeLong at an agreed value of $1,000.00 for 10 shares of $100.00 par-value preferred stock. M323.

20. Received cash in full payment of Susan Vine's account, previously written off as uncollectible, $427.50. M324 and R143.

21. Paid cash, $2,000.00, plus an office microcomputer, for a new microcomputer: original cost of old microcomputer, $3,500.00; total accumulated depreciation through December 31 of last year, $2,100.00; additional depreciation to be recorded through December 21 of the current year, $700.00. M325 and C515.

27. Discounted at 12% a 60-day non-interest-bearing note, $5,000.00; proceeds, $4,900.00; interest, $100.00. NP7.

28. Received cash from James Dier for 10 shares of treasury stock at $13.00 per share, $130.00. Treasury stock was bought on December 11 at $9.00 per share. R146.

29. Received cash from sale of an old cash register used in sales, $800.00: original cost, $1,600.00; total accumulated depreciation through December 31 of last year, $896.00; additional depreciation to be recorded through December 29 of the current year, $144.00. M326 and R147.

29. Received cash from Patrick Carson for dishonored NR4: principal, $151.25, plus additional interest, $1.05; total, $152.30. R148.

29. Received cash from Delmar Adams in payment of stock subscription, $3,000.00. R149.

29. Issued Stock Certificate No. 14 to Delmar Adams for 30 shares of $100.00 par-value preferred stock, $3,000.00. M327.

30. Paid cash for annual dividend declared December 1, $15,820.00. C519.

2. Prove and rule the cash receipts and cash payments journals.

PART B: END-OF-FISCAL-PERIOD WORK

In Part B, Whitehurst's end-of-fiscal-period work is completed. This work is similar to activities described in Chapter 14. The December 31 trial balance is recorded on a work sheet in the *Working Papers* accompanying this textbook.

Instructions:

3. Complete the work sheet for the year ended December 31 of the current year. Record the adjustments on the work sheet using the following additional information.

Adjustment Information, December 31

Accrued interest income	$ 95.70
Uncollectible accounts expense estimated as 0.1% of net sales on account.	
Net sales on account for year, $343,472.60.	
Merchandise inventory	206,618.63
Sales supplies inventory	1,456.06
Administrative supplies inventory	730.00
Value of prepaid insurance	970.00
Prepaid interest	93.33
Annual depreciation expense—store equipment	8,300.00
Annual depreciation expense—building	1,500.00
Annual depreciation expense—office equipment	1,150.00
Organization expense	300.00
Accrued interest expense	2,025.00
Accrued salaries—sales	3,232.04
Accrued salaries—administrative	716.50
Accrued payroll taxes—Social Security tax	256.65
Accrued payroll taxes—Medicare tax	59.23
Accrued payroll taxes—federal unemployment tax	15.79
Accrued payroll taxes—state unemployment tax	106.58
Rent received in advance and still unearned	1,200.00

Federal income tax expense for the year is calculated at the following rates:

15% of net income before taxes, zero to $50,000.00.

Plus 25% of net income before taxes, $50,000.00 to $75,000.00.

Plus 34% of net income before taxes, $75,000.00 to $100,000.00.

Plus 39% of net income before taxes, $100,000.00 to $335,000.00.

Plus 34% of the net income before taxes over $335,000.00.

4. Prepare an income statement. Calculate and record the following component percentages. (a) Cost of merchandise sold. (b) Gross profit on operations. (c) Total selling expenses. (d) Total administrative expenses. (e) Total operating expenses. (f) Income from operations. (g) Net addition or deduction resulting from other revenue and expenses. (h) Net income before federal income tax. (i) Federal income tax expense. (j) Net income after federal income tax. Round percentage calculations to the nearest 0.1%.

5. Analyze Whitehurst's income statement by determining if component percentages are within acceptable levels. If any component percentage is not within an acceptable level, suggest steps that the company should take. Acceptable component percentages are given in the *Working Papers*.

6. Calculate earnings per share. Round the calculation to the nearest cent. Whitehurst has 12,680 shares of $10.00 stated-value common stock issued and 444 shares of 10%, $100.00 par-value preferred stock issued. Treasury stock consists of 50 shares of common stock.

7. Prepare a statement of stockholders' equity. Use the following additional information.

	January 1 Balance	Issued During the Year	December 31 Balance
Common stock:			
No. of shares	11,780	900	12,680
Amount	$117,800.00	$9,000.00	$126,800.00
Preferred stock:			
No. of shares	404	40	444
Amount	$ 40,400.00	$4,000.00	$ 44,400.00

The January 1 balance of Retained Earnings was $26,759.39.

8. Calculate the following items based on information on the statement of stockholders' equity. (a) Equity per share of stock. (b) Price-earnings ratio. The market price of common stock on December 31 is $13.50.

9. Prepare a balance sheet for December 31 of the current year.

10. Calculate the following items based on information from the balance sheet. (a) Accounts receivable turnover ratio. Accounts receivable and allowance for uncollectible accounts on January 1 were $36,785.45 and $698.35, respectively. (b) Rate earned on average stockholders' equity. Total stockholders' equity on January 1 was $186,459.39. (c) Rate earned on average total assets. Total assets on January 1 were $458,204.24.

11. Use pages 13 and 14 of a general journal. Journalize the adjusting entries.

12. Use pages 14 and 15 of a general journal. Do not skip a line. Journalize the closing entries.

13. Use page 1 of a general journal. Journalize the reversing entries. Use January 1 of the year following the current year as the date.

A BUSINESS SIMULATION
Southgate Hardware

Activities in
Southgate Hardware:

1. Recording transactions in special journals and a general journal.

2. Posting items to be posted individually to a general ledger and subsidiary ledgers.

3. Proving and ruling journals.

4. Posting column totals to a general ledger.

5. Preparing schedules of accounts receivable and accounts payable.

6. Preparing a trial balance on a work sheet.

7. Planning adjustments and completing a work sheet.

8. Preparing financial statements.

9. Journalizing and posting adjusting entries.

10. Journalizing and posting closing entries.

11. Preparing a post-closing trial balance.

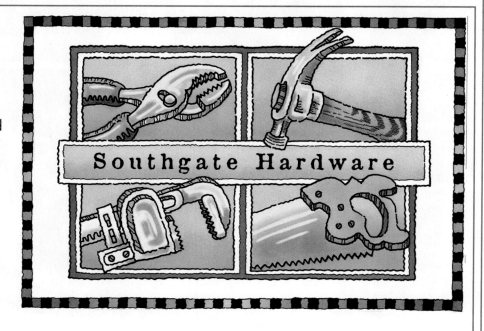

Southgate Hardware is a merchandising business organized as a corporation. This business simulation covers the realistic transactions completed by Southgate Hardware, which sells a broad range of hardware. The activities included in the accounting cycle for Southgate Hardware are listed at left.

This simulation is available from the publisher in either manual or automated versions.

REFLECTION, INC. CHART OF ACCOUNTS

Balance Sheet Accounts

(1000) Assets
1100 CURRENT ASSETS
1105   Cash
1110   Petty Cash
1115   Notes Receivable
1120   Interest Receivable
1125   Accounts Receivable
1130   Allowance for Uncollectible Accounts
1135   Merchandise Inventory
1140   Supplies—Sales
1145   Supplies—Administrative
1150   Prepaid Insurance

1200 PLANT ASSETS
1205   Equipment—Delivery
1210   Accumulated Depreciation—Delivery Equipment
1215   Equipment—Office
1220   Accumulated Depreciation—Office Equipment
1225   Equipment—Warehouse
1230   Accumulated Depreciation—Warehouse Equipment
1235   Building
1240   Accumulated Depreciation—Building
1245   Land

(2000) Liabilities
2100 CURRENT LIABILITIES
2105   Notes Payable
2110   Interest Payable
2115   Accounts Payable
2120   Employee Income Tax Payable
2125   Federal Income Tax Payable
2128   Social Security Tax Payable
2130   Medicare Tax Payable
2135   Sales Tax Payable
2140   Unemployment Tax Payable—Federal
2145   Unemployment Tax Payable—State
2150   Dividends Payable

2200 LONG-TERM LIABILITY
2205   Mortgage Payable

(3000) Capital
3105   Capital Stock
3110   Retained Earnings
3115   Dividends
3120   Income Summary

Income Statement Accounts

(4000) Operating Revenue
4105   Sales
4110   Sales Discount
4115   Sales Returns and Allowances

(5000) Cost of Merchandise
5105   Purchases
5110   Purchases Discount
5115   Purchases Returns and Allowances

(6000) Operating Expenses
6100 SELLING EXPENSES
6105   Advertising Expense
6110   Delivery Expense
6115   Depreciation Expense—Delivery Equipment
6120   Depreciation Expense—Warehouse Equipment
6125   Miscellaneous Expense—Sales
6130   Salary Expense—Commissions
6135   Salary Expense—Regular
6140   Supplies Expense—Sales

6200 ADMINISTRATIVE EXPENSES
6205   Depreciation Expense—Office Equipment
6210   Insurance Expense
6215   Miscellaneous Expense—Administrative
6220   Payroll Taxes Expense
6225   Rent Expense
6230   Salary Expense—Administrative
6235   Supplies Expense—Administrative
6240   Uncollectible Accounts Expense
6245   Utilities Expense

(7000) Other Revenue
7105   Gain on Plant Assets
7110   Interest Income

(8000) Other Expenses
8105   Interest Expense
8110   Loss on Plant Assets

(9000) Income Tax
9105   Federal Income Tax Expense

The chart of accounts for Reflection, Inc. is illustrated above for ready reference as you study Part 5 of this textbook.

14

Budgetary Planning and Control

AFTER STUDYING CHAPTER 14, YOU WILL BE ABLE TO:

1. Define accounting terms related to budgetary planning and control.

2. Identify accounting concepts and practices related to preparing and analyzing budgeted income statements and cash budgets.

3. Gather information to prepare a budget.

4. Prepare a budgeted income statement.

5. Prepare a cash budget and performance report.

Business managers make a variety of business decisions each day. The quality of these decisions has a direct impact on the business' ability to improve profitability. Financial planning is one tool managers use to improve profitability. A business must earn a net income to continue in existence. (CONCEPT: Going Concern)

Planning the financial operations of a business is called **budgeting**. A written financial plan of a business for a specific period of time, expressed in dollars, is called a **budget**. (CONCEPT: Unit of Measurement) A business prepares a variety of budgets. Each budget provides managers with detailed information about a specific area of the business' operations.

A budget is a view into the future—a financial estimate of future business activities. Budget preparation begins with identifying company goals. Company goals might be to increase sales, reduce cost of merchandise sold, or increase net income. All of these goals affect budget preparation because the budget is a business' financial plan.

Two budgets commonly prepared in businesses are the budgeted income statement and the cash budget. The budgeted income statement is a projection of a business' sales, costs, expenses, and net income for a fiscal period. It is similar to a regular income statement and is sometimes known as an operating budget. The cash budget is a projection of a business' cash receipts and payments for a fiscal period. It is used to manage estimated cash shortages and overages.

ACCOUNTING
IN YOUR CAREER

PREPARING BUDGETS

Lionel Destino has been the manager of the marketing department at Training Systems, Inc., for two months. He just came from the first meeting on the budget for the coming year. Since this is his first time to prepare the budget for the marketing department, he is apprehensive about it. At the budget meeting, he and the other department managers were given printed copies of the current year's budget for their departments and a spreadsheet model for preparing next year's budget estimates. They were also told the sales forecast for the new year. Stephanie Lao, who manages the human resources department, is a good friend and has mentored Lionel in his career with Training Systems. At lunch after the meeting, Lionel expresses his concerns about preparing the budget. Stephanie volunteers to help him with the budget if he will help her to learn the spreadsheet software. They agree to meet in the morning.

"Lionel, preparing the budget is very time consuming, but it isn't that hard; you just have to pay attention to the details," Stephanie says. "Most of us take the new sales projections they've given us and apply the percentage increase in sales to each of the items in our current budget to come up with the figures for the new budget. Then we adjust individual amounts for any additional plans we have."

Lionel responds, "Stephanie, I had that figured out, but someone told me I should also ask for more than I need because the management committee will always cut some of my estimates. All of my people need new computers, and I'm going to ask for more expensive computers than they need so we'll have what we really need after my proposal is cut." Stephanie replies, "My experience has been that if you can justify your requests, you usually get them. The committee is pretty good at detecting inflated figures."

Critical Thinking

1. What is your opinion of Stephanie's explanation of the budget process at Training Systems?
2. Evaluate Lionel's idea for getting approval for the new computers he wants.

14-1 Budget Planning

BUDGET FUNCTIONS

Budgets are projections or estimates of what will happen in the future expressed in financial terms. A carefully prepared budget reflects the best projections possible by those persons who prepare it. A completed budget shows the projected course of action for a business. A budget serves three important business functions.

1. **Planning**. In preparing a budget, managers project what will happen in the future. This view of the future helps a manager plan actions that will meet desired goals. The budgeting process forces a manager to decide which actions should be emphasized to achieve the desired goals.

2. **Operational control**. A budget projects the accomplishments of a business. It specifies the type and the amount of projected activities. By comparing actual performance with projected performance, management can judge how well a business is achieving its goals. For example, managers compare actual expenses with budgeted expenses to identify differences. By identifying actual expense items that are higher than budgeted, a business can act to reduce these amounts.

3. **Department coordination**. Profitable business growth requires all managers to be aware of the company's plans. A budget reflects these plans. Each phase of a business operation must be coordinated with all related phases. For example, to achieve projected sales, the purchasing department must know when and how much merchandise to purchase. Therefore, all management personnel must help plan and use a budget as a guide to control and coordinate sales, costs, and expenses.

BUDGET PERIOD

The length of time covered by a budget is called the **budget period**. Usually this period is one year. Some companies also prepare a long-range budget of five years or more for special projects and plant and equipment purchases. However, the annual budget is the one used to compare current financial performance with budget plans.

An annual budget is normally prepared for a company's fiscal year. The annual budget is commonly divided into quarterly and monthly budgets. Such budget subdivisions provide frequent opportunities to evaluate how actual operations compare with budgeted operations.

A budget must be prepared in sufficient time to be communicated to the appropriate managers prior to the beginning of a budget period.

Large and complex companies start gathering budget information long before the beginning of a new budget year. Gathering information, performing analysis, making decisions, preparing the budget, and approving and communicating the budget take considerable time.

F.Y.I.

Most budgets are based on forecasts of increases or decreases over previous years' performances. In zero-based budgeting, however, the data are prepared each year as though operations were being started for the first time.

Figure 14-1

Budgets cannot be exact since they show only projected sales, costs, and expenses. However, a company should project future operations as accurately as possible. A company uses many information sources such as those shown in Figure 14-1.

Company Records

The accounting and sales records of a business contain much of the information needed to prepare budgets. Accounting information about previous years' operations is used to determine trends in sales, purchases, and operating expenses. Expected price changes, sales promotion plans, and market research studies also are important in projecting activity for a budget period.

General Economic Information

A general slowdown or speedup in the national economy may affect budget decisions. Unusually high inflation rates affect budgeted amounts. A labor strike may affect some related industries and thus affect company operations. New product development, changes in consumer buying habits, availability of merchandise, international trade, and general business conditions all must be considered when preparing budgets.

Company Staff and Managers

Sales personnel estimate the amount of projected sales. Considering projected sales for the new budget period, other department managers project budget items for their areas of responsibility of the business.

Good Judgment

Good judgment by the individuals preparing the budgets is essential to realistic budgets. Even after evaluating all available information, answers to many budget questions are seldom obvious. Since some information will conflict with other information, final budget decisions are based on good judgment.

REMEMBER

National magazines and newspapers are a good source of information regarding general economic conditions.

Reflection, Inc.
Comparative Income Statement
For Years Ended December 31, 20X1 and 20X2

	20X2	20X1	Increase (Decrease) Amount	Increase (Decrease) Percentage*
Operating Revenue:				
Net Sales	$1,880,000	$1,700,000	$180,000	10.6
Cost of Merchandise Sold	1,231,720	1,105,000	126,720	11.5
Gross Profit on Operations	$ 648,280	$ 595,000	$ 53,280	9.0
Operating Expenses:				
Selling Expenses:				
Advertising Expense	$ 45,120	$ 37,800	$ 7,320	19.4
Delivery Expense	150,410	140,640	9,770	6.9
Depr. Expense—Delivery Equipment	7,200	7,000	200	2.9
Depr. Expense—Warehouse Equipment	10,800	10,800	0	0.0
Miscellaneous Expense—Sales	11,490	11,960	(470)	(3.9)
Salary Expense—Commissions	75,200	68,000	7,200	10.6
Salary Expense—Regular	34,160	28,320	5,840	20.6
Supplies Expense—Sales	11,280	10,850	430	4.0
Total Selling Expenses	$ 345,660	$ 315,370	$ 30,290	9.6
Administrative Expenses:				
Depr. Expense—Office Equipment	$ 14,400	$ 12,000	$ 2,400	20.0
Insurance Expense	4,800	4,500	300	6.7
Miscellaneous Expense—Administrative	38,770	33,640	5,130	15.2
Depr. Expense—Warehouse Equipment	19,200	19,200	0	0.0
Payroll Taxes Expense	22,540	20,590	1,950	9.5
Rent Expense	30,000	30,000	0	0.0
Salary Expense—Administrative	77,830	75,240	2,590	3.4
Supplies Expense—Administrative	13,620	14,600	(980)	(6.7)
Uncollectible Accounts Expense	11,280	10,230	1,050	10.3
Utilities Expense	10,080	7,320	2,760	37.7
Total Administrative Expenses	$ 242,520	$ 227,320	$ 15,200	6.7
Total Operating Expenses	$ 588,180	$ 542,690	$ 45,490	8.4
Income from Operations	$ 60,100	$ 52,310	$ 7,790	14.9
Other Expenses:				
Interest Expense	$ 3,000	$ 6,500	($ 3,500)	(53.8)
Net Income before Federal Income Tax	$ 57,100	$ 45,810	$ 11,290	24.6
Federal Income Tax Expense	9,280	6,870	2,410	35.1
Net Income after Federal Income Tax	$ 47,820	$ 38,940	$ 8,880	22.8
Units (sq. ft.) of Mirror Sold	376,000	340,000	36,000	10.6

*Percentages rounded to the nearest 0.1%.

Figure 14-2

Preparation for planning a budget involves analyzing available financial information. An analysis of previous years' sales, cost, and expense amounts is an important part of budget preparation. An income statement containing sales, cost, and expense information for two or more years is called a **comparative income statement**.

Reflection, Inc., is a corporation that sells custom-cut mirrors. A comparative income statement provides the information for Reflection's analysis of previous years' sales, costs, and expenses. This statement shows trends that may be taking place in these items. The statement also highlights items that may be increasing or decreasing at a higher rate than other items on the statement. Reflection's comparative income statement is shown in Figure 14-2.

INTERPRETING THE COMPARATIVE INCOME STATEMENT

Compare the percentage change in expenses or costs to the percentage change in sales.	Effect on net income
If the % increase ↑ in expenses or costs > the % increase ↑ in sales, net income ↓ decreases.	Unfavorable
If the % increase ↑ in expenses or costs < the % increase ↑ in sales, net income ↑ increases.	Favorable
If the % decrease ↓ in expenses or costs > the % decrease ↓ in sales, net income ↑ increases.	Favorable
If the % decrease ↓ in expenses or costs < the % decrease ↓ in sales, net income ↓ decreases.	Unfavorable

Figure 14-3

The first column of Reflection's comparative income statement shows actual sales, costs, and expenses for 20X2, the current year. The second column shows actual amounts for 20X1, the prior year. The third column shows the amount of increase or decrease from the prior year, 20X1, to the current year, 20X2. (For example, 20X2 cost of merchandise sold, $1,231,720, *less* 20X1 cost of merchandise sold, $1,105,000, *equals* the increase, $126,720.) The fourth column shows the percentage by which the current year amount increased or decreased from the prior year amount. (For example, the cost of merchandise sold increase, $126,720, *divided* by the 20X1 amount, $1,105,000, *equals* the percentage of increase, 11.5%.) Reflection rounds percentages to the nearest 0.1%.

Managers review each increase or decrease amount on the comparative income statement. The percentage of increase or decrease indicates whether the change is favorable, unfavorable, or normal compared with net sales. If a cost or expense item increase is a higher percentage than the net sales increase, net income is unfavorably affected. However, if the net sales increase is a higher percentage than cost and expense items, net income is favorably affected. Decreases have the opposite effect. If a cost or expense item decrease is a higher percentage than the net sales decrease, net income is favorably affected. If the net sales decrease is a higher percentage than cost and expense items, net income is unfavorably affected. Figure 14-3 summarizes the effect of changes in expenses or costs on net income.

Unfavorable results require further inquiry to determine the cause. Reflection's net sales increased 10.6% over 20X1. The goal for 20X2 was to increase sales volume by 10.0%. The actual 10.6% increase resulted from an increase in units sold from 340,000 to 376,000 square feet of mirrors. The unit sales price remained at $5.00. Management attributed the increase to two factors. (1) A more intensive advertising campaign increased market share from 42.0% to 45.0%. (2) Favorable economic conditions spurred new home building and created a greater demand for mirrors.

Reflection, Inc., analyzes each cost and expense amount and percentage. For example, the cost of merchandise sold increased 11.5% over 20X1. Most of the increase resulted from the 10.6% increase in the number of units sold. In addition, the purchase price per square foot of mirrors increased during 20X2 from $3.25 per square foot to $3.30. Advertising expense increased 19.4% over 20X1. The increase is consistent with the successful effort to expand market share. Management believes that more expensive television advertising resulted in a significant increase in third and fourth quarter unit sales.

During the annual budget process, Reflection also does the following:

1. Analyzes general and industry economic conditions to determine probable changes in sales volume for the coming year.

2. Sets company goals for costs and expenses as a percentage of sales.

REMEMBER

Comparative financial statements may be prepared for a fiscal year or a month.

budgeting

budget

budget period

comparative income
  statement

1. How does the budgeting process help control expenses?

2. What is the length of time generally covered by a company's budget?

3. Will net income increase or decrease if the percentage change in expenses is less than the percentage change in net sales? Explain.

ORK
TOGETHER

Analyzing a comparative income statement

The comparative income statement for San Francisco Sourdough Baking Company shows a percentage increase for net sales of 14.2%. A table is provided in the *Working Papers*. Your instructor will guide you through the following examples.

4. Indicate whether the following percentage change in cost and expense items is favorable or unfavorable:

Cost/Expense Item	Percentage of Increase (Decrease)
Cost of Merchandise Sold	11.0%
Advertising Expense	15.1%
Salary Expense	12.5%
Utilities Expense	(1.2%)

N YOUR
OWN

Analyzing a comparative income statement

The comparative income statement for Precision Racing Components, Inc., indicates a percentage increase in net sales of 8.3%. A table is provided in the *Working Papers*. Work the following problem independently.

5. Indicate whether the following percentage change in cost and expense items is favorable or unfavorable:

Cost/Expense Item	Percentage of Increase (Decrease)
Cost of Merchandise Sold	11.0%
Advertising Expense	7.3%
Insurance Expense	(4.5%)
Rent Expense	2.0%

ANNUAL OPERATIONAL PLANS AND GOALS

Goals for 20X3:
1.   The economy is projected to remain strong throughout 20X3. Therefore, the sales goal is to increase unit sales to 400,000 units, about a 6.4% increase. The unit sales price will be increased in the second quarter from $5.00 to $5.25 per square foot to recover merchandise cost increases in 20X2 and projected increases in the budget year.
2.   Sales distribution by quarters is projected to be consistent with prior quarters.
3.   The unit cost of merchandise is projected to rise from $3.30 to $3.40 in the first quarter, a 3.0% increase.
4.   An automated cutting machine has been ordered. It will cost $20,000 and is projected to save approximately $10,000 per year in salary expense.
5.   All employees on salary will receive a 5.0% increase in wage rate.
6.   Rigid controls on all expenditures will be exercised.

Figure 14-4

After previous years' records have been analyzed, a business sets goals, develops operational plans, and prepares projection of sales, costs, and expenses for the coming year. Annual company goals establish targets that the company will work toward in the coming year. Goals help a company coordinate the efforts of all areas toward a common direction. An operational plan provides general guidelines for achieving the company's goals. Operational plans and goals generally are determined by a planning group consisting of the company's executive officers and department managers.

At Reflection, the planning group includes the president and all department managers. The planning group reviews the analysis of the previous years' comparative income statement and considers possible changes in economic conditions that may affect the company. From these discussions, the company's operational plan and goals for the coming year are determined. After reviewing company records and considering general economic conditions, Reflection's planning group develops the planning guidelines shown in Figure 14-4.

The operational plan is converted into a more precise plan expressed in dollars by preparing a budgeted income statement. Reflection prepares separate schedules for the major parts of the budgeted income statement. Separate schedules are prepared for sales, purchases, selling expenses, administrative expenses, and other revenue and expenses. To permit more frequent comparisons with budgeted amounts, schedules for the budget are separated into quarterly projections.

At Reflection, the accounting department is responsible for coordinating budget preparation. The sales manager is responsible for preparing the sales, purchases, and selling expenses budget schedules. The administrative manager is responsible for preparing the administrative expenses budget and the other revenue and expenses budget schedules. The accounting department then prepares the budgeted income statement from these schedules. The completed budget, with attached schedules, is submitted to the budget committee for approval. The budget committee consists of the president and two members of Reflection's board of directors.

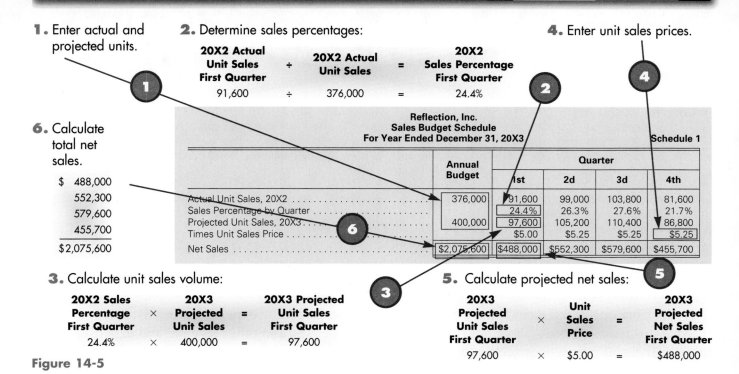

Figure 14-5

A statement that shows the projected net sales for a budget period is called a **sales budget schedule**. The sales budget schedule is prepared first because the other schedules are affected by the projected net sales. Projected net sales are used to estimate the amount of merchandise to purchase and the amount that may be spent for salaries, advertising, and other selling and administrative expenses.

Reflection's sales manager, with knowledge of the budget guidelines and with the assistance of sales representatives, prepares the sales budget schedule shown in Figure 14-5. Based on the planning group's goal of a 6.4% increase in unit sales, the budget reflects an increase from 376,000 to 400,000 units. The sales manager plans to increase the unit sales price from $5.00 to $5.25 in the second quarter. The timing of the increase was planned after reviewing competitors' selling prices and analyzing projected costs of merchandise.

Accurate projections are important for effective budgeting. However, since budgets are based on estimates, most businesses round the projected amounts to simplify the budgeting process. Reflection Inc., rounds unit projections to the nearest hundred units and dollar projections to the nearest $10.

Preparing a sales budget schedule

1. Enter the number of actual units, *376,000*, and projected units, *400,000*, in the Annual Budget column.

2. Determine the sales percentages by quarter. Dividing the annual budget into quarterly segments provides more frequent opportunities to compare actual with budgeted operations.

3. Calculate the unit sales volume for each quarter. Reflection's planning group believes that quarterly sales percentages will remain the same. Therefore, 24.4% of annual sales are expected to occur in the first quarter.

4. Enter the unit sales prices for each quarter.

5. Calculate projected net sales for each quarter.

6. Calculate total net sales for 20X3.

1. Calculate ending inventory for each quarter:

20X3 Unit Sales Second Quarter	×	Ending Inventory Unit Sales Percentage	=	20X3 Ending Inventory First Quarter
105,200	×	40.0%	=	42,080 rounded to 42,100

5. Determine purchases.

139,700 units
− 39,200
100,500 units

4. Enter beginning inventory.

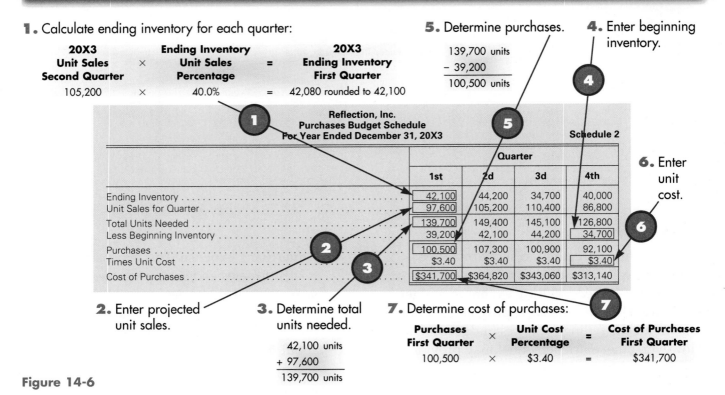

6. Enter unit cost.

Reflection, Inc.
Purchases Budget Schedule
For Year Ended December 31, 20X3

Schedule 2

	Quarter			
	1st	2d	3d	4th
Ending Inventory	42,100	44,200	34,700	40,000
Unit Sales for Quarter	97,600	105,200	110,400	86,800
Total Units Needed	139,700	149,400	145,100	126,800
Less Beginning Inventory	39,200	42,100	44,200	34,700
Purchases	100,500	107,300	100,900	92,100
Times Unit Cost	$3.40	$3.40	$3.40	$3.40
Cost of Purchases	$341,700	$364,820	$343,060	$313,140

2. Enter projected unit sales.

3. Determine total units needed.

42,100 units
+ 97,600
139,700 units

7. Determine cost of purchases:

Purchases First Quarter	×	Unit Cost Percentage	=	Cost of Purchases First Quarter
100,500	×	$3.40	=	$341,700

Figure 14-6

After the planning group approves the sales budget schedule, the remaining budget schedules are prepared. A statement prepared to show the projected amount of purchases that will be required during a budget period is called a **purchases budget schedule**. The following factors are considered when planning a purchases budget schedule:

1. Projected unit sales.

2. The quantity of merchandise on hand at the beginning of the budget period.

3. The quantity of merchandise needed to fill projected sales orders without having excessive inventory.

4. The price trends of merchandise to be purchased.

The sales manager prepares the purchases budget schedule shown in Figure 14-6. The sales manager determines that the number of units in ending inventory should be about 40.0% of the number of units projected to be sold in the subsequent quarter.

S T E P S Preparing a purchases budget schedule

1. Calculate ending inventory for each quarter. Round estimates to the nearest hundred. Use *40,000* units for the fourth quarter's ending inventory (100,000 projected to be sold in the first quarter of 20X4 x 40%).

2. Enter projected unit sales for the quarter from the sales budget schedule.

3. Add ending inventory units and projected sales units to determine total units needed per quarter.

4. Enter beginning inventory, which is the same as ending inventory for the preceding quarter. Reflection's ending inventory of 39,200 units on December 31, 20X2, becomes its January 1 beginning inventory.

5. Subtract beginning inventory from total units needed to determine total unit purchases for the quarter.

6. Enter the unit cost for each quarter. Reflection's planning group has projected that material costs will rise from $3.30 to $3.40 per unit in the first quarter of 20X3.

7. Multiply the unit purchases each quarter by the unit cost to determine the cost of purchases.

	Annual Budget	Quarter			
		1st	2d	3d	4th
Advertising Expense	$ 49,820	$11,710	$13,260	$ 13,910	$10,940
Delivery Expense	160,000	39,040	42,080	44,160	34,720
Depr. Expense—Delivery Equipment	7,200	1,800	1,800	1,800	1,800
Depr. Expense—Warehouse Equipment	13,800	2,700	3,700	3,700	3,700
Miscellaneous Expense—Sales	10,380	2,440	2,760	2,900	2,280
Salary Expense—Commissions	83,020	19,520	22,090	23,180	18,230
Salary Expense—Regular	25,370	6,190	6,670	7,000	5,510
Supplies Expense—Sales.............................	12,450	2,930	3,310	3,480	2,730
Total Selling Expenses	$362,040	$86,330	$95,670	$100,130	$79,910

Reflection, Inc.
Selling Expenses Budget Schedule
For Year Ended December 31, 20X3
Schedule 3

Figure 14-7

A statement prepared to show projected expenditures related directly to the selling operations is called a **selling expenses budget schedule**. The sales manager projects the information for the selling expenses budget schedule. However, other sales personnel may provide specific information. For example, the advertising manager supplies much of the advertising expense information. After selling expenses information has been projected, a selling expenses budget schedule is prepared.

Some selling expense items are relatively stable and require little budget planning. For example, depreciation expenses for delivery and warehouse equipment are reasonably stable from year to year unless new equipment is bought. On the other hand, several selling expenses increase and decrease in relation to sales increases and decreases. Reflection has a seasonal business with higher sales during the second and third quarters. The company hires more personnel and spends more for advertising and sales supplies during the heavy sales season. All of these factors are considered when making a selling expenses budget schedule. Reflection's selling expenses budget schedule is shown in Figure 14-7.

Reflection's sales manager uses a number of approaches to project the various selling expenses. Most selling expenses are linked closely to the amount of quarterly net sales. Reflection's management uses the following projection guides to prepare its selling expenses budget schedule.

1. **Advertising expense.** This expense is closely related to sales and sales promotions for the year. Advertising expense for 20X2 was 2.4% ($45,120 ÷ $1,880,000) of net sales. Sales promotion emphasis will be maintained at about the same level this year. Thus, 2.4% of each quarter's projected net sales will be allocated to advertising expense. First quarter projected advertising expense is $11,710 (2.4% × $488,000 = $11,712, rounded to $11,710).

2. **Delivery expense.** This expense is closely related to the number of units sold and delivered. The previous year's delivery expense increased significantly because an external freight company was used for increased deliveries until Reflection could acquire an additional truck. Rigid cost control measures will be applied to reduce future unit delivery expenses. Delivery expense is projected to be $0.40 per unit (sq. ft.) sold times each quarter's projected unit sales. First quarter projected delivery expense is $39,040 ($0.40 × 97,600 units).

3. **Depreciation expense—delivery equipment.** No new delivery equipment will be added. Thus, depreciation expense will remain the same as for the previous year ($1,800 per quarter).

4. **Depreciation expense—warehouse equipment.** A new automated cutter will be acquired at the beginning of the second quarter, increasing quarterly depreciation expense in the second, third, and fourth quarters from $2,700 to $3,700 per quarter.

5. **Miscellaneous expense—sales.** Miscellaneous expense was 0.6% ($11,490 ÷ $1,880,000) of net sales in 20X2. Management is committed to reducing miscellaneous expense to 0.5% of net sales in 20X3. First quarter miscellaneous expense is projected as $2,440 (0.5% × $488,000).

6. **Salary expense—commissions.** Salespersons will continue to earn a 4.0% commission on net sales. First quarter commissions are projected as $19,520 (4.0% × $488,000).

7. **Salary expense—regular.** Regular salary expense is determined by salary increases and changes in activity that affect the number of people employed. The new automated cutter will reduce regular salary expense by $10,000. A 5.0% raise will be added to remaining salaries. Thus, the projected annual amount is calculated as shown below.

Salary Expense: 20X2 Comparative Income Statement	$ 34,160
Less Reduction from Automated Cutter	– 10,000
Total	$ 24,160
Plus 5.0% Rate Increase	+ 1,210
Projected Salary Expense—Regular	$ 25,370

The projected amount is allocated among the four quarters in relation to the sales percentage from the sales budget schedule. First quarter regular salaries are projected as $6,190 (24.4% × $25,370).

8. **Supplies expense—sales.** Supplies expense was 0.6% ($11,280 ÷ $1,880,000) of net sales in 20X2. The same percentage relationship is expected in 20X3. First quarter supplies expense is projected as $2,930 (0.6% × $488,000 = $2,928, rounded to $2,930).

After the quarterly amounts have been calculated and entered, the annual budget amounts are determined by totaling the quarterly amounts.

WHO OWNS THIS SMALL BUSINESS?

In the 21st century, the answers to the question, "Who owns this small business?" is likely to be "A woman." In 1992, there were about 6 million women-owned firms. During the period of 1987 to 1992, the number of women-owned firms increased about 43 percent. The 1992 receipts of women-owned businesses were $1.574 trillion.

Women entrepreneurs start businesses at the rate of more than 4,000 per month. In 1996, women represented 36 percent of all small business owners. With the astonishing rate at which women are starting businesses, they will own a majority of all small businesses early in the 21st century.

Many of these "small businesses" employ over 100 people. Women-owned businesses are creating jobs at a faster rate than job growth in the overall economy. In fact, one out of four workers is employed in a woman-owned business.

Women-owned businesses are likely to be good community citizens. Many actively participate in their community, contribute to community projects, and provide a flexible work environment for their work force.

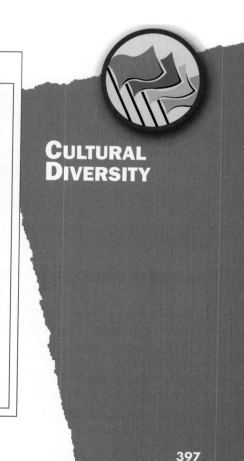

CULTURAL DIVERSITY

Reflection, Inc.
Administrative Expenses Budget Schedule
For Year Ended December 31, 20X3   Schedule 4

	Annual Budget	Quarter			
		1st	2d	3d	4th
Depr. Expense—Office Equipment	$ 14,400	$ 3,600	$ 3,600	$ 3,600	$ 3,600
Insurance Expense...........................	5,600	1,400	1,400	1,400	1,400
Miscellaneous Expense—Administrative	36,760	9,190	9,190	9,190	9,190
Payroll Taxes Expense	22,810	5,540	5,900	6,070	5,300
Rent Expense	30,000	7,500	7,500	7,500	7,500
Salary Expense—Administrative	81,720	20,430	20,430	20,430	20,430
Supplies Expense—Administrative..................	14,540	3,420	3,870	4,060	3,190
Uncollectible Accounts Expense	12,450	2,930	3,310	3,480	2,730
Utilities Expense	10,980	4,870	1,470	1,610	3,030
Total Administrative Expenses......................	$229,260	$58,880	$56,670	$57,340	$56,370

Figure 14-8

A statement that shows the projected expenses for all operating expenses not directly related to selling operations is called an **administrative expenses budget schedule**. The administrative manager prepares this budget schedule using information from these sources:

1. Past records.

2. Company plans.

3. Sales and selling expenses budget schedules.

4. Discussions with other managers.

After the administrative expenses have been projected, the administrative expenses budget schedule is prepared. Reflection's administrative expenses budget schedule is shown in Figure 14-8.

Most administrative expenses are known and remain the same each period. Some administrative expenses need to be budgeted as a percentage of another amount from another budget. The following information was used to prepare the administrative expenses budget schedule.

1. **Depreciation expense—office equipment.** Recently purchased office equipment increased annual depreciation to $14,400. Annual depreciation is divided equally over the four quarters.

2. **Insurance expense.** Annual insurance is projected to increase to $5,600 primarily because of added coverage for the new automated cutting machine. An equal amount is paid each quarter.

3. **Miscellaneous expense—administrative.** Closely related to administrative salaries, miscellaneous expense was 49.8% ($38,770 ÷ $77,830) of administrative salaries in 20X2. Management is committed to reducing miscellaneous expense to 45.0% of projected administrative salaries in 20X3. First quarter miscellaneous expense is projected as $9,190 (45.0% × $20,430 = $9,194, rounded to $9,190).

4. **Payroll taxes expense.** Based on current payroll tax rates, payroll taxes expense is 12.0% of all salaries each quarter. First quarter salaries are projected as $46,140 ($19,520 + 6,190 + 20,430). Thus, payroll taxes expense is projected as $5,540 (12.0% × $46,140 = $5,537, rounded to $5,540).

5. **Rent expense.** Reflection leases the building for a known rental fee of $2,500 per month. Thus, rent expense can be projected accurately at $7,500 each quarter.

6. **Salary expense—administrative.** No new administrative personnel will be hired. Salary expense is projected as $81,720, equal to the 20X2 amount, $77,830, adjusted for a 5.0% salary rate increase. An equal amount is paid each quarter. Thus, each quarter's salary expense is projected as $20,430 ($81,720 ÷ 4).

7. **Supplies expense—administrative.** Supplies expense was 0.7% ($13,620 ÷ $1,880,000) of net sales for 20X2. The same percentage will be used in 20X3. First quarter supplies expense is projected as $3,420 (0.7% × $488,000 = $3,416, rounded to $3,420).

8. **Uncollectible accounts expense.** Closely related to net sales, uncollectible accounts expense was 0.6% ($11,280 ÷ $1,880,000) of net sales in 20X2. First quarter uncollectible accounts expense is projected as $2,930 (0.6% × $488,000 = $2,928, rounded to $2,930).

9. **Utilities expense.** Utilities expense is based on the amount of power, heat, telephone, and other utilities used in 20X2. Costs are projected to increase by 9.0%, consisting of a 5.0% projected increase in activity and a 4.0% increase in rates. Utilities expense by quarter in 20X2 is multiplied by 109% (100.0% + 9.0%) to calculate 20X3's projected utilities expense as follows:

	20X2 Actual Utilities Expense	× 109% =	20X3 Projected Utilities Expense
1st Quarter	$ 4,470	× 109% =	$ 4,870
2d Quarter	1,350	× 109% =	1,470
3d Quarter	1,480	× 109% =	1,610
4th Quarter	2,780	× 109% =	3,030
Total	$10,080	× 109% =	$10,980

OTHER REVENUE AND EXPENSES BUDGET SCHEDULE

Reflection, Inc.
Other Revenue and Expenses Budget Schedule
For Year Ended December 31, 20X3

Schedule 5

	Annual Budget	Quarter			
		1st	2d	3d	4th
Other Expenses:					
Interest Expense	$2,250	$750	$750	$750	

Figure 14-9

Budgeted revenue and expenses from activities other than normal operations are shown in a statement called **other revenue and expenses budget schedule**. Typical items in this budget are interest income, interest expense, and gains or losses on the sale of plant assets. Reflection's other revenue and expenses budget schedule is shown in Figure 14-9. Reflection has only one other expense item and no other revenue items.

Reflection's administrative manager is responsible for projecting the information in the other revenue and expenses budget schedule. Projected interest expense, the only item in the budget, is based on the interest due on a $20,000 loan used to acquire the automated cutter. Since Reflection plans to repay the $20,000 loan at the beginning of the fourth quarter, the budget schedule shows interest expense for only three quarters.

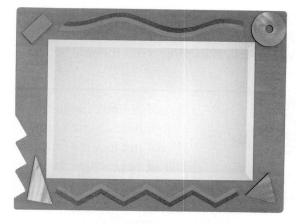

	Annual Budget	Quarter			
		1st	2d	3d	4th
Operating Revenue:					
Net Sales (Schedule 1)	$2,075,600	$488,000	$552,300	$579,600	$455,700
Cost of Merchandise Sold:					
Beginning Inventory	$ 129,360	$129,360	$143,140	$150,280	$117,980
Purchases (Schedule 2)	1,362,720	341,700	364,820	343,060	313,140
Total Merchandise Available	$1,492,080	$471,060	$507,960	$493,340	$431,120
Less Ending Inventory	136,000	143,140	150,280	117,980	136,000
Cost of Merchandise Sold	$1,356,080	$327,920	$357,680	$375,360	$295,120
Gross Profit on Operations	$ 719,520	$160,080	$194,620	$204,240	$160,580
Operating Expenses:					
Selling Expenses (Schedule 3)	$ 362,040	$ 86,330	$ 95,670	$100,130	$ 79,910
Administrative Expenses (Schedule 4)	229,260	58,880	56,670	57,340	56,370
Total Operating Expenses	$ 591,300	$145,210	$152,340	$157,470	$136,280
Income from Operations	$ 128,220	$ 14,870	$ 42,280	$ 46,770	$ 24,300
Net Deduction (Schedule 5)	$ 2,250	$ 750	$ 750	$ 750	
Net Income before Federal Income Tax	$ 125,970	$ 14,120	$ 41,530	$ 46,020	$ 24,300
Federal Income Tax Expense	32,380	8,100	8,100	8,100	8,080
Net Income after Federal Income Tax	$ 93,590	$ 6,020	$ 33,430	$ 37,920	$ 16,220

Reflection, Inc.
Budgeted Income Statement
For Year Ended December 31, 20X3

1. Beginning inventory:
39,200 units × $3.30 =
$129,360

1

2. Ending inventory:
42,100 units × $3.40 =
$143,140

2

Figure 14-10

A statement that shows a company's projected sales, costs, expenses, and net income is called a **budgeted income statement**. Since the five budget schedules contain detailed items, Reflection prepares a shortened budgeted income statement and attaches the budget schedules. Reflection's budgeted income statement is shown in Figure 14-10.

The first quarter beginning inventory is calculated using the 20X2 unit cost, $3.30. Other inventory amounts are calculated using the unit cost for 20X3, $3.40.

Amounts from the five budget schedules allow Reflection to project net income before federal income tax. Federal income taxes are estimated using a tax rate table furnished by the Internal Revenue Service. Reflection uses the tax rate table shown below. Using these rates, Reflection calculates its federal income tax.

Quarterly income tax payments are *$8,100* ($32,380 ÷ 4 = $8,095, rounded to $8,100). Thus, Reflection's payments equal $24,300 ($8,100 × 3 quarters) through the third quarter. The fourth quarter amount equals the unpaid amount of federal income taxes, *$8,080* ($32,380 − $24,300).

15% of net income before taxes, zero to $50,000.00.
25% of net income before taxes less $5,000.00, $50,001.00 to $75,000.00.
34% of net income before taxes less $11,750.00, $75,001.00 to $100,000.00.
39% of net income before taxes less $16,750.00, $100,001.00 to $335,000.00.

Net Income Before Federal Income Tax	×	Tax Rate	=	Federal Income Tax Expense
$125,970	×	39% less $16,750	=	$32,378.30 rounded to $32,380

TERMS REVIEW

sales budget schedule
purchases budget schedule
selling expenses budget schedule
administrative expenses budget schedule
other revenue and expenses budget schedule
budgeted income statement

AUDIT YOUR UNDERSTANDING

1. How do annual goals help a company?
2. What factors are considered in preparing a sales budget schedule?

WORK TOGETHER

Planning for a budgeted income statement

Actual unit sales for 20X1 were 230,000. Sterling Circuits, Inc., anticipates a 10.8% increase in unit sales for the upcoming year, 20X2. It projects that 18% of all yearly sales will occur during the first quarter. Sterling rounds unit projections to the nearest hundred units and dollar projections to the nearest $10. Your instructor will guide you through the following problem. Show your work.

3. How many units are projected to be sold during the first quarter of 20X2? If the unit sales price is $7.50, calculate the projected sales amount for the first quarter of 20X2.

4. If the desired ending inventory for the first quarter of 20X2 is 11,100 units, determine the number of units needed to meet the ending inventory and sales goals for the first quarter.

5. If the beginning inventory for the first quarter of 20X2 equals 9,400 units, how many units should be purchased to meet the inventory and sales goals for the first quarter?

6. Material costs per unit are projected to be $4.10. Compute the projected cost of purchases.

ON YOUR OWN

Planning for a budgeted income statement

Actual unit sales for 20X1 were 90,000. Graphite Co. forecasts a 6.1% increase in unit sales for the upcoming year, 20X2. It projects that 20% of all yearly sales will occur during the first quarter. Graphite rounds unit projections to the nearest hundred units and dollar projections to the nearest $10. Work independently to complete the following problem. Show your work.

7. How many units are projected to be sold during the first quarter of 20X2? If the unit sales price is $16.00, calculate the projected sales amount for the first quarter of 20X2.

8. If the desired ending inventory for the first quarter of 20X2 is 4,700 units, determine the number of units needed to meet the ending inventory and sales goals for the first quarter.

9. If the beginning inventory for the first quarter of 20X2 equals 3,400 units, how many units should be purchased to meet the inventory and sales goals for the first quarter?

10. Material costs per unit are expected to be $7.80. Compute the projected cost of purchases.

CASH RECEIPTS BUDGET SCHEDULE

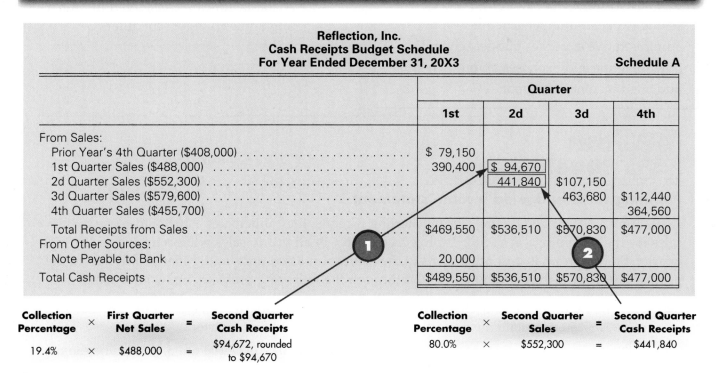

Reflection, Inc.
Cash Receipts Budget Schedule
For Year Ended December 31, 20X3   Schedule A

| | Quarter | | | |
	1st	2d	3d	4th
From Sales:				
Prior Year's 4th Quarter ($408,000)	$ 79,150			
1st Quarter Sales ($488,000)	390,400	$ 94,670		
2d Quarter Sales ($552,300)		441,840	$107,150	
3d Quarter Sales ($579,600)			463,680	$112,440
4th Quarter Sales ($455,700)				364,560
Total Receipts from Sales	$469,550	$536,510	$570,830	$477,000
From Other Sources:				
Note Payable to Bank	20,000			
Total Cash Receipts	$489,550	$536,510	$570,830	$477,000

Collection Percentage	×	First Quarter Net Sales	=	Second Quarter Cash Receipts
19.4%	×	$488,000	=	$94,672, rounded to $94,670

Collection Percentage	×	Second Quarter Sales	=	Second Quarter Cash Receipts
80.0%	×	$552,300	=	$441,840

Figure 14-11

Good cash management requires planning and controlling cash so that it will be available to meet obligations when they come due. Reflection prepares a cash budget to help analyze cash inflows and cash outflows. The treasurer prepares Reflection's cash budget in consultation with the budget committee. A corporation treasurer is an officer of the corporation who is usually responsible for planning the corporation's requirement for and use of cash. The treasurer analyzes

1. Projected receipts from cash sales, customers on account, and other sources.

2. Projected cash payments for ordinary expenses such as rent, payroll, and payments to vendors on account.

3. Other cash payments such as to buy plant assets or supplies.

Projected cash receipts for a budget period are reported on a statement called a **cash receipts**

budget schedule. Reflection's cash receipts budget schedule is shown in Figure 14-11. To prepare a cash receipts budget schedule, projections are composed of the following:

1. Quarterly cash sales.

2. Quarterly collections on account from customers. The amounts received from customers will not be the same as the amount of sales on account. Normally, cash is received for sales on account made during the previous one or two months. In addition, some sales returns and allowances and uncollectible accounts are likely.

3. Cash to be received quarterly from other sources.

REMEMBER

Many budget items are based on the budgeted estimate of sales. Therefore, the budget is only as accurate as the sales forecast.

An analysis of Reflection's sales for previous years shows the following pattern of net sales per quarter:

1. About 60.0% of all net sales are cash sales.

2. About 20.0% are sales on account collected in the same quarter. Thus, 80.0% of a quarter's net sales are collected during the same quarter.

3. About 19.4% are collected in the following quarter.

4. About 0.6% of net sales prove to be uncollectible.

Cash receipts in the first quarter include $79,150 from 20X2's fourth quarter sales on account (19.4% × $408,000 = $79,152, rounded to $79,150).

Cash sales and collections on account provide most of the cash receipts. If additional cash is needed, other sources of cash should be planned. After making a preliminary plan of projected cash receipts and cash payments, the treasurer determines that cash on hand will be reduced in the first quarter to an unusually low level. This condition could prevent the company from making timely payments for its expenditures. Therefore, the treasurer arranges to borrow $20,000 during the first quarter.

TECHNOLOGY FOR BUSINESS

NUMERICAL FORMAT OPTIONS

Columns of data in a spreadsheet may include several different types of data. In columns E and F of the spreadsheet below, numbers are shown as currency amounts, percentage amounts, ratios, and a general whole numbers.

Use of the numerical format options available on electronic spreadsheets makes the data easier to read and understand. For example, the rate earned on net sales in cells E7 and F7 are shown as percentages. In addition to numerous formatting options, the number of decimal places displayed may also be specified. Good spreadsheet design includes proper numerical formatting.

	A	B	C	D	E	F
1	Financial Statement Analysis					
2					Current	Prior
3					Year	Year
4	Rate Earned on Net Sales:					
5		Net Income after Federal Income Tax			$42,322	$38,976
6		Net Sales			514,560	465,430
7		Rate Earned on Net Sales			8.2%	8.4%
8	Earnings per Share:					
9		Net Income after Federal Income Tax			$42,322	$38,976
10		Shares of Stock Outstanding			10,000	10,000
11		Earnings per Share			$4.23	$3.90
12	Price-Earnings Ratio:					
13		Market Price per Share			$25.00	$22.00
14		Earnings per Share			$4.23	$3.90
15		Price-Earnings Ratio			5.9	5.6

Reflection, Inc.
Cash Payments Budget Schedule
For Year Ended December 31, 20X3

Schedule B

	Quarter			
	1st	2d	3d	4th
For Merchandise:				
Prior Year's 4th Quarter Purchases ($212,500)	$ 63,750			
1st Quarter Purchases ($341,700)	239,190	$102,510		
2d Quarter Purchases ($364,820)		255,370	$109,450	
3d Quarter Purchases ($343,060)			240,140	$102,920
4th Quarter Purchases ($313,140)				219,200
Total Cash Payments for Purchases	$302,940	$357,880	$349,590	$322,120
For Operating Expenses:				
Cash Selling Expenses	$ 81,830	$ 90,170	$ 94,630	$ 74,410
Cash Administrative Expenses	52,350	49,760	50,260	50,040
Total Cash Operating Expenses	$134,180	$139,930	$144,890	$124,450
For Other Cash Payments:				
Federal Income Tax Expense	$ 8,100	$ 8,100	$ 8,100	$ 8,080
Automated Cutting Machine	20,000			
Cash Dividend		50,000		50,000
Investment				25,000
Note Payable and Interest				22,250
Total Other Cash Payments	$ 28,100	$ 58,100	$ 8,100	$105,330
Total Cash Payments	$465,220	$555,910	$502,580	$551,900

Figure 14-12

Projected cash payments for a budget period are reported on a statement called a **cash payments budget schedule**. Reflection's cash payments budget schedule is shown in Figure 14-12. To prepare the schedule, the accountant and treasurer make the following projections:

1. Quarterly cash payments for accounts payable or notes payable to vendors.

2. Quarterly cash payments for each expense item. This projection requires an analysis of the selling expenses, administrative expenses, and other revenue and expenses budget schedules.

3. Quarterly cash payments for buying equipment and other assets.

4. Quarterly cash payments for dividends.

5. Quarterly cash payments for investments.

Reflection's accountant and treasurer use the following projection guides to prepare the cash payments budget schedule.

1. **Cash payments for merchandise.** An analysis of past records for payments to vendors on account shows the following cash payment pattern:
   a. About 10.0% of all purchases are cash purchases.
   b. About 60.0% are purchases on account paid for in the quarter. Thus, 70.0% (10.0% + 60.0%) of a quarter's purchases are paid for during the same quarter.
   c. The remaining 30.0% are purchases on account paid for in the following quarter.

Cash payments are calculated using the same procedure used for cash receipts. Purchase amounts are from the purchases budget schedule. First quarter cash payments for first quarter purchases are $239,190 (70.0% × $341,700).

2. **Cash payments for operating expenses.**
Cash payments for most operating expenses are made in the quarter the expense is incurred. However, the selling expenses budget schedule, Figure 14-7, and the administrative expenses budget schedule, Figure 14-8, include some projected items for which cash will not be paid. For example, cash is not paid for depreciation and uncollectible accounts expenses. Therefore, these amounts are not included in the cash payments budget schedule. The first quarter's cash payments for selling expenses and for administrative expenses are calculated as follows:

Selling Expenses		$86,330
Less: Depr. Exp.—Deliv. Equip.	$1,800	
Depr. Exp.—Ware. Equip.	2,700	4,500
Cash Payment for Selling Exp.		$81,830
Administrative Expenses		$58,880
Less: Depr. Exp.—Office Equip.	$3,600	
Uncollectible Accts. Exp.	2,930	6,530
Cash Payment for Admin. Exp.		$52,350

3. **Other cash payments.** Reflection also plans for cash payments other than for merchandise, selling expenses, and administrative expenses. Federal income tax

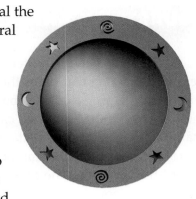

payments equal the quarterly federal income tax expense amounts on the budgeted income statement. Reflection also plans to buy a new automated cutting machine for $20,000 at the end of the first quarter. The company expects to pay a $50,000 cash dividend to stockholders in the second and fourth quarters. Since a large cash balance is projected for the third quarter, Reflection plans a $25,000 interest-earning investment in the fourth quarter. Also, plans call for repaying the promissory note plus interest, *$22,250,* at the beginning of the fourth quarter.

The last line of the cash payments budget schedule shows the total cash payments projected each quarter. This total indicates the minimum amount of cash that must be available each quarter.

CASH BUDGET

Reflection, Inc.
Cash Budget
For Year Ended December 31, 20X3

	Quarter			
	1st	**2d**	**3d**	**4th**
Cash Balance—Beginning	$ 21,780	$ 46,110	$ 26,710	$ 94,960
Cash Receipts (Schedule A)	489,550	536,510	570,830	477,000
Cash Available	$511,330	$582,620	$597,540	$571,960
Less Cash Payments (Schedule B)	465,220	555,910	502,580	551,900
Cash Balance—Ending	$ 46,110	$ 26,710	$ 94,960	$ 20,060

Figure 14-13

A statement that shows for each month or quarter a projection of a company's beginning cash balance, cash receipts, cash payments, and ending cash balance is called a **cash budget**. Reflection's cash budget, shown in Figure 14-13

is prepared from the information in the cash receipts budget schedule and the cash payments budget schedule. The first quarter beginning cash balance is taken from the balance sheet on December 31, 20X2.

At the end of each quarter of a budget period, Reflection compares the actual cash balance with the projected cash balance shown on the cash budget. If the actual cash balance is less than the projected balance, the reasons for the decrease are determined and action is taken to correct the problem. One reason may be that some customers are not paying their accounts when they should. Another may be that expenses are exceeding budget projections. If the decrease continues, the company could have a quarter in which there is not enough cash to make all the required cash payments. If this shortage does occur, the business will have to borrow money until receipts and payments are brought into balance.

PERFORMANCE REPORT

Reflection, Inc.
Performance Report
For Quarter Ended March 31, 20X3

	Budget	Actual	Increase (Decrease) Amount	Increase (Decrease) Percentage*
Unit Sales (sq. ft.)	97,600	98,500	900	0.9
Operating Revenue:				
Net Sales	$488,000	$492,500	$4,500	0.9
Cost of Merchandise Sold	327,920	330,680	2,760	0.8
Gross Profit on Operations	$160,080	$161,820	$1,740	1.1
Operating Expenses:				
Selling Expenses:				
Advertising Expense	$ 11,710	$ 12,050	$ 340	2.9
Delivery Expense	39,040	38,735	(305)	(0.8)
Depr. Expense—Delivery Equipment	1,800	1,800		
Depr. Expense—Warehouse Equipment	2,700	2,700		
Miscellaneous Expense—Sales	2,440	2,530	90	3.7
Salary Expense—Commissions	19,520	19,620	100	0.5
Salary Expense—Regular	6,190	6,190		
Supplies Expense—Sales	2,930	2,900	(30)	(1.0)
Total Selling Expenses	$ 86,330	$ 86,525	$ 195	0.2
Administrative Expenses:				
Depr. Expense—Office Equipment	$ 3,600	$ 3,600		
Insurance Expense	1,400	1,400		
Miscellaneous Expense—Administrative	9,190	9,350	$ 160	1.7
Payroll Taxes Expense	5,540	5,550	10	0.2
Rent Expense	7,500	7,500		
Salary Expense—Administrative	20,430	20,430		
Supplies Expense—Administrative	3,420	3,490	70	2.0
Uncollectible Accounts Expense	2,930	2,800	(130)	(4.4)
Utilities Expense	4,870	5,180	310	6.4
Total Administrative Expenses	$ 58,880	$ 59,300	$ 420	0.7
Total Operating Expenses	$145,210	$145,825	$ 615	0.4
Income from Operations	14,870	15,995	$1,125	7.6
Net Deduction	$ 750	$ 750	0	0.0
Net Income before Federal Income Tax	$ 14,120	$ 15,245	$1,125	8.0
Federal Income Tax Expense	8,100	8,100	0	0.0
Net Income after Federal Income Tax	$ 6,020	$ 7,145	$1,125	18.7

*Percentages rounded to the nearest 0.1%.

Figure 14-14

At the end of each quarter, a business prepares an income statement that compares actual amounts with the budgeted income statement for the same period. This comparison shows variations between actual and projected items. A report showing a comparison of projected and actual amounts for a specific period of time is called a **performance report**.

Each quarter, Reflection prepares a quarterly performance report like the one shown in Figure 14-14. This report is sent to the sales manager and the administrative manager. Knowing about significant differences between projected and actual income statement amounts helps the managers identify areas that need to be reviewed. By identifying large variations early, managers may be able to make changes that will correct negative effects on net income for the year. If conditions change significantly, the budget for the remainder of the year can be revised.

Preparation of a performance report is similar to preparation of a comparative income statement. However, a performance report compares actual amounts with projected amounts for the same fiscal period. A comparative income statement compares actual amounts of one fiscal period with actual amounts of a prior fiscal period.

The first amount column of the performance report shows the amounts projected for the first quarter. The second amount column shows the actual sales, costs, and expenses for the quarter. The third amount column shows how much the actual amount varies from the projected amount. For example, actual net sales, $492,500, *less* projected net sales, $488,000, *equals* the increase, $4,500. The fourth column shows the percentage, the actual amount increased or decreased from the projected amount. For example, the net sales increase, $4,500, *divided by* projected net sales, $488,000, *equals* the percentage of increase, 0.9%. Percentages are rounded to the nearest 0.1%.

An analysis is made of all significant differences to determine why the differences occurred. Normally, Reflection only considers changes of 5.0% or more to be significant. However, because the items influencing gross profit are large dollar amounts, small percentage changes affect net income significantly. Therefore, Reflection's sales manager reviews changes in net sales and cost of merchandise sold regardless of the amount of change.

Reflection's performance report indicates that three items should be reviewed:

1. Net sales.

2. Cost of merchandise sold.

3. Utilities expense.

Managers should determine what actions, if any, can correct the unfavorable situations such as the 6.4% increase in utilities expense. If the utility service cost has increased, the manager cannot change that. However, if power is being wasted, procedures may need to be changed to avoid the waste.

Managers should also determine what actions caused favorable results, such as the 0.9% increase in net sales, and encourage a continuation of those favorable actions.

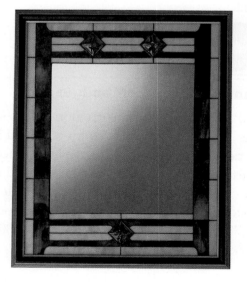

REMEMBER

Actual performance must be compared with budgeted estimates in order for a business to evaluate its budgeting procedures.

cash receipts budget schedule

cash payments budget schedule

cash budget

performance report

1. Why is a cash budget important?

2. What information is reported in a cash budget?

3. How does a performance report differ from a comparative income statement?

ORK
TOGETHER

Planning for a cash budget

MicroVision's sales for previous years show that of total net sales, approximately 50% are cash sales, 30% are sales on account collected in the same quarter, 18% are sales on account collected in the next quarter, and 2% prove to be uncollectible. For the current year, net sales for the first quarter are $425,000.00 and for the second quarter, $360,500.00.

    The cash payment budget schedule shows the following cash payments during the second quarter: total purchases, $289,000.00; total operating expenses, $97,840; federal income tax expense, $9,210.00; and notes payable and interest, $7,240.00. MicroVision rounds dollar projections to the nearest $10. Your instructor will guide you through the following examples.

4. Determine the total amount of cash received during the second quarter.

5. Calculate the total cash payments for the second quarter.

6. The beginning cash balance for the second quarter equals $61,560. Compute the ending cash balance for the second quarter.

N YOUR
OWN

Planning for a cash budget

MediaNet's sales for the previous years show that of total net sales, approximately 45% are cash sales, 40% are sales on account collected in the same quarter, 14% are sales on account collected in the next quarter, and 1% prove to be uncollectible. For the current year, net sales for the second quarter are $518,000.00 and for the third quarter, $670,250.00.

    The cash payment budget schedule shows the following cash payments during the third quarter: total purchases, $410,000.00; total operating expenses, $101,630; federal income tax expense, $11,780.00; and cash dividend, $80,000.00. MediaNet rounds dollar projections to the nearest $10. Work the problem independently.

7. Determine the total amount of cash received during the third quarter.

8. Calculate the total cash payments for the third quarter.

9. The beginning cash balance for the third quarter equals $24,860.00. Compute the ending cash balance for the third quarter.

CHAPTER 14 *Summary*

After completing this chapter, you can

1. Define important accounting terms related to budgetary planning and control.

2. Identify accounting concepts and practices related to preparing and analyzing budgeted income statements and cash budgets.

3. Gather information to prepare a budget.

4. Prepare a budgeted income statement.

5. Prepare a cash budget and a performance report.

EXPLORE ACCOUNTING

SPREADSHEET BUDGETING TOOLS

Budgeting has been a popular use for electronic spreadsheet programs since these software programs became readily available in the early 1980s. By entering labels for accounts and accounting periods in cells, the structure of the budget can quickly be tailored to the nature of the business. Users create formulas to compute total revenues, expenses, and net income. Thus, with a knowledge of budgeting concepts, spreadsheet users can create a budget with a limited amount of effort.

Newer electronic spreadsheets have made budget creation even easier. These programs contain tools to assist the user in designing the budget and creating the formulas. The budget tools are especially useful for individuals with a limited knowledge of budgeting concepts. For most budgeting tools, the starting point is selecting the type and design of the budget.

Personal or Business

The budget tool suggests revenue and expense accounts commonly used in personal or business budgets. The user may add and delete accounts to customize the budget to the individual's needs.

Budget or Budget vs. Actual Analysis

The budget can be created to provide space for actual information to be entered at the end of each accounting period. The spreadsheet can be used to compute the amount or percentage difference between budget and actual amounts.

Number of Periods

The user identifies the starting period and the number of periods. A period can consist of a month, a quarter, or a year.

Quarterly and Yearly Totals

For a monthly budget, the budget tool can compute quarterly and yearly totals. With this information, the budget tool automatically creates the budget, including all labels and formulas. Format techniques, such as bolded text, numeric formats, and shaded cells, are applied to improve understanding.

REQUIRED:

Use the budget tool of your electronic spreadsheet program to prepare a personal budget for your first year after high school.

14-1 APPLICATION PROBLEM
Preparing a sales budget schedule and a purchases budget schedule

PhotoMax, Inc., plans to prepare a sales budget schedule and a purchases budget schedule for 20X3. Management has set a sales goal of 250,000 units. After reviewing price trends, the sales manager projects that PhotoMax will need to increase its unit sales price from $12.50 to $14.00 in the first quarter.

The sales manager, after checking with the company's merchandise suppliers, projects that the cost of merchandise will increase from $7.00 to $7.50 per unit in the first quarter of 20X3.

Quarterly unit sales for 20X2 are as follows:

1st quarter	58,500 units	3d quarter	68,900 units
2d quarter	62,700 units	4th quarter	43,900 units

After considering the time required to reorder merchandise, the sales manager requests that 30.0% of the next quarter's unit sales be available in the prior quarter's ending inventory. Ending inventory for 20X2 is 27,700 units. Management projects that 65,000 units will be sold in the first quarter of 20X4.

Instructions:

1. Prepare a sales budget schedule (Schedule 1) for the four quarters ended December 31, 20X3. PhotoMax rounds unit amounts to the nearest hundred units, dollar amounts to the nearest $10, and percentage amounts to the nearest 0.1%.

2. Prepare a purchases budget schedule (Schedule 2) for the four quarters ended December 31, 20X3.

14-2 APPLICATION PROBLEM
Preparing a budgeted income statement

The sales manager and administrative manager of Coffee Oasis have made the following projections to be used in preparing a budgeted income statement.

a. Total net sales for 20X3 are projected to be $1,400,000. In each quarter the following percentages of total net sales were made:

1st quarter	20.0%	3d quarter	25.0%
2d quarter	25.0%	4th quarter	30.0%

b. Purchases and merchandise ending inventories are projected as follows. Ending inventory for 20X2 was $88,250.

	Purchases	Ending Inventory
1st quarter	$201,000	$111,500
2d quarter	242,500	110,500
3d quarter	283,000	132,500
4th quarter	246,250	99,250

c. Expenses for 20X3 are projected as follows. Except where noted, percentages are based on projected net sales. For these items, calculate each quarter's amount by multiplying the percentage times that quarter's net sales. Calculate the annual total by adding the four quarterly amounts. When a dollar amount is given, the total amount should be divided equally among the four quarters.

Selling Expenses		Administrative Expenses	
Advertising Expense	1.5%	Depreciation Expense—Office Equipment	$4,800
Delivery Expense	2.7%	Insurance Expense	$6,000
Depreciation Expense—		Miscellaneous Expense—	
Delivery Equipment	$3,400	Administrative	$5,600
Depreciation Expense—		Payroll Taxes Expense	13.2% of salaries
Store Equipment	$4,200	Rent Expense	$12,800
Miscellaneous Expense—Sales	$15,800	Salary Expense—Administrative	$46,000
Salary Expense—Sales	6.0%	Supplies Expense—Administrative	$4,240
Supplies Expense—Sales	2.0%	Uncollectible Accounts Expense	0.8%
		Utilities Expense	$18,400

Federal income taxes are calculated using the tax rate table shown in this chapter. Equal quarterly income tax payments are based on the projected annual federal income tax expense.

Instructions:

1. Prepare a selling expenses budget schedule (Schedule 3) for the four quarters ended December 31, 20X3. Coffee Oasis rounds all amounts to the nearest $10.

2. Prepare an administrative expenses budget schedule (Schedule 4) for the four quarters ended December 31, 20X3.

3. Prepare a budgeted income statement for the four quarters ended December 31, 20X3.

APPLICATION PROBLEM
Preparing a cash budget with supporting schedules

The following table shows SeaWest Fabrication's projected net sales, purchases, and cash payments for expenses for 20X3.

			Cash Payments for Expenses	
Quarter	Net Sales	Purchases	Selling	Administrative
1st	$646,300	$558,300	$32,100	$38,600
2d	674,900	571,600	36,200	38,900
3d	661,800	561,200	42,400	39,700
4th	681,600	582,300	36,800	39,800

Additional information is as follows:

  a. Actual amounts for the fourth quarter of 20X2: sales, $639,200; purchases, $548,240.

  b. The balance of cash on hand on January 1, 20X3, is $35,720.

  c. In each quarter, cash sales are 10.0% and collections of accounts receivable are 50.0% of the projected net sales for the current quarter. Collections from the preceding quarter's net sales are 39.5% of that quarter. Uncollectible accounts expense is 0.5% of net sales.

  d. In each quarter, cash payments for cash purchases are 10.0% and for accounts payable 30.0% of the purchases for the current quarter. Cash payments for purchases of the preceding quarter are 60.0% of that quarter.

  e. Record only total projected cash payments for expenses as shown in the table above.

continued

f. In the second quarter, SeaWest will borrow $35,000 on a promissory note and will purchase equipment costing $31,600 for cash. In the third quarter dividends of $30,000 will be paid in cash. In the fourth quarter, the promissory note plus interest will be paid in cash, $37,500.

g. Equal quarterly income tax payments are based on projected annual federal income tax expense of $7,720.

Instructions:

1. Prepare a cash receipts budget schedule (Schedule A) for the four quarters ended December 31, 20X3. Round all amounts to the nearest $10.

2. Prepare a cash payments budget schedule (Schedule B) for the four quarters ended December 31, 20X3.

3. Prepare a cash budget for the four quarters ended December 31, 20X3.

MASTERY PROBLEM
Preparing a budgeted income statement and a cash budget with supporting budget schedules

On December 31, 20X2, the accounting records of Zylar, Inc., show the following unit sales for 20X2.

1st quarter	22,000 units	3d quarter	34,800 units
2d quarter	34,400 units	4th quarter	28,800 units

The following are additional actual amounts for the 4th quarter of 20X2.

Sales (28,800 units @ $5.60)	$161,280
Purchases (26,400 units @ $4.00)	105,600
Ending inventory	12,500 units

Management has established a unit sales goal of 130,000 units for 20X3 and 24,000 units for the first quarter of 20X4. The sales manager, after reviewing price trends and checking with the company's merchandise suppliers, projects that the unit cost of merchandise will increase from $4.00 to $4.25 in the first quarter of 20X3. Because of the increase in costs, the company will need to increase its unit sales price from $5.60 to $6.00 in the first quarter of 20X3.

After considering the time required to reorder merchandise, the sales manager requests that 40.0% of each quarter's unit sales be available in the prior quarter's ending inventory.

Expenses are projected as shown on the following page. Except where noted, percentages are based on quarterly projected net sales. For these items, calculate each quarter's amount by multiplying the percentage times that quarter's net sales. Calculate the annual total by adding the four quarterly amounts. When a dollar amount is given, the total amount should be divided equally among the four quarters.

Interest expense for each quarter is projected to be $1,250.

Federal income taxes are calculated using the tax rate table shown in this chapter. Equal quarterly income tax payments are based on the projected annual federal income tax expense.

Additional information is as follows:

a. The balance of cash on hand on January 1, 20X3, is $41,600.

b. In each quarter, cash sales are 10.0% and collections of accounts receivable are 40.0% of the projected net sales for the current quarter. Collections from the preceding quarter's net sales are 49.4% of that quarter. Uncollectible accounts expense is 0.6% of net sales.

Selling Expenses		Administrative Expenses	
Advertising Expense	1.2%	Depreciation Expense—Office Equipment	$3,600
Delivery Expense	0.6%	Insurance Expense	$4,200
Depreciation Expense—		Miscellaneous Expense—	
Delivery Equipment	$2,400	Administrative	$3,000
Depreciation Expense—		Payroll Taxes Expense	12.0% of salaries
Store Equipment	$6,680	Rent Expense	$9,600
Miscellaneous Expense—Sales	0.4%	Salary Expense—Administrative	$25,200
Salary Expense—Sales	5.0%	Supplies Expense—Administrative	$2,800
Supplies Expense—Sales	0.8%	Uncollectible Accounts Expense	0.6%
		Utilities Expense	1.8%

c. In each quarter, cash payments for cash purchases are 10.0% and for accounts payable 55.0% of the purchases for the current quarter. Cash payments for purchases of the preceding quarter are 35.0% of that quarter.

d. In the first quarter, $40,000 will be borrowed on a promissory note, and equipment costing $30,000 will be purchased for cash. In each quarter, dividends of $10,000 will be paid in cash. In the fourth quarter, the promissory note plus interest will be paid in cash, $45,000.

Instructions:

Prepare the following budget schedules for the year ended December 31, 20X3. Round percentage amounts to the nearest 0.1%, unit amounts to the nearest 100 units, and dollar amounts to the nearest $10.

a. Prepare a sales budget schedule (Schedule 1).
b. Prepare a purchases budget schedule (Schedule 2).
c. Prepare a selling expenses budget schedule (Schedule 3).
d. Prepare an administrative expenses budget schedule (Schedule 4).
e. Prepare an other revenue and expenses budget schedule (Schedule 5).
f. Prepare a budgeted income statement.
g. Prepare a cash receipts budget schedule (Schedule A).
h. Prepare a cash payments budget schedule (Schedule B).
i. Prepare a cash budget.

14-5 CHALLENGE PROBLEM
Preparing a performance report

A partially completed performance report for Quasar Robotics, Inc., is in the *Working Papers.*

Quasar Robotics, Inc., has just completed its first quarter of the fiscal year ended December 31, 20X3. Management is interested in identifying significant favorable and unfavorable differences between projected and actual amounts. Quasar Robotics only considers changes of 5.0% or more to be significant. Management reviews changes in net sales and cost of merchandise regardless of the amount of change.

Instructions:

1. Complete the performance report by calculating the increase (decrease) from budget and percentage increase (decrease) from budget.

2. Place an asterisk (*) in the right margin by every item that is significant.

INTERNET ACTIVITY

Point your browser to

http://accounting.swpco.com

Choose **Advanced Course**, choose **Activities**, and complete the activity for Chapter 14.

Applied Communication

People often think that only accountants need to know accounting. Many students may not consider taking accounting because they have no interest in being an accountant. Whether students aspire to be doctors, teachers, lawyers, scientists, florists, or artists, they will need to use accounting to control the financial resources of their business or organization.

Required:

Create a presentation that could be made to your high school counselor, student body, or incoming students to persuade the audience that everyone needs accounting. Use the following guidelines.

1. Prepare a list of skills learned in accounting that can be used in everyday life.

2. Elaborate by writing a paragraph to discuss each skill and how advantageous it is for a person to gain the skill.

3. Prepare graphic aids such as transparency masters that could be used to present the material.

Cases for Critical Thinking

Case 1
Thomas Baker, president of Brundage Corporation, says he has observed that an increase in sales almost always results in an increase in net income. Therefore, he is considering recommending that the company set a sales goal increase of 15.0% for next year and "spare no expense" to achieve this goal. Thomas asks for your opinion regarding his recommendation. How would you respond?

Case 2
Camille Stibbe is general manager of Alden Corporation. She suggests that the budgeted income statement and the cash budget seem to show the same information. Therefore, she recommends that one of the statements be eliminated to reduce accounting costs. What response would you make to Camille?

AUTOMATED ACCOUNTING

PREPARING A PERFORMANCE REPORT

A budget is a financial plan for the future. It can be used to plan revenue and expenses. A performance report is a type of financial statement that compares budgeted and actual amounts. Once budgeted data have been entered into the accounting system, a performance report can be generated.

Entering and Changing Budget Amount Data

When the Other Activities menu item is chosen from the Data menu or the Other toolbar button is clicked, the Other Activities window containing the Budgets tab will appear. The Budgets tab allows you to enter the budgeted amounts for income statement accounts. To enter budget amounts:

1. Enter the budgeted amount for the first account (or highlight an amount you wish to change and enter a new amount).

2. Press the Tab key to move to the next account. The accounts are scrollable. When you have entered the amount for the last account visible, the accounts will scroll up so that you can enter the next budget amount.

3. When all budget amounts have been entered, click OK.

Preparing a Performance Report

Once the budgeted amounts have been entered, a performance report may be displayed or printed. Use the following steps to display the report:

1. Click the Reports toolbar button, or choose the Reports Selection menu item from the Reports menu.

2. When the Report Selection dialog appears, choose Financial Statements from the Select a Report Group list.

3. Choose Performance Report from the Choose a Report to Display list.

4. Click OK.

The report will be displayed in the scrollable Report Viewer Window. The report may be printed and/or copied for inclusion in another application, such as a spreadsheet or word processor.

AUTOMATING CHALLENGE PROBLEM 14-5

Instructions:

1. Load *Automated Accounting 7.0* or higher software.

2. Select database A14-5 (Advanced Course Challenge Problem 14-5) from the accounting template disk.

3. Select File from the menu bar and choose the Save As menu command. Key the path to the drive and directory that contains your data files. Save the database with a file name of XXX145 (where XXX are your initials).

4. Access Problem Instructions through the Help menu. Read the Problem Instruction screen.

5. Refer to page 413 for data used in this problem.

6. Exit the Automated Accounting software.

15
Accounting Information for Management Decisions

AFTER STUDYING CHAPTER 15, YOU WILL BE ABLE TO:

1. Define terms related to accounting information for management decisions.

2. Identify accounting concepts and practices related to preparing accounting information for management decisions.

3. Prepare an income statement reporting contribution margin.

4. Calculate the contribution margin rate.

5. Calculate the breakeven point.

6. Calculate the sales dollars and sales units required to earn a planned amount of net income.

7. Determine the effect of changes in sales volume, unit costs, and unit sales prices on net income.

8. Calculate a sales mix.

Managers use financial statements to make good business decisions. An income statement is one source of information on which a manager can base decisions. An income statement includes information about operating revenue, cost of merchandise sold, gross profit on operations, operating expenses, and net income or net loss. By analyzing the income statement, managers can gain an understanding of the relationship among sales, costs, and expenses.

Managers can increase net income by increasing sales and/or decreasing costs and expenses. Managers, with the advice and assistance of accountants, analyze the relationships among sales, costs, and expenses to:

1. Determine the level of sales necessary to achieve planned net income.

2. Evaluate the impact of changes in sales volume, unit sales prices, and unit costs on net income.

3. Identify the strengths and weaknesses of a company.

ACCOUNTING
IN YOUR CAREER

DESIGNER DENIM

Wildfire, Inc., makes denim apparel and works closely with fashion designers to take advantage of new styles, trends, and fads. The company is known in the industry for quickly taking advantage of emerging trends in clothing. To be profitable, the company's management team has been extensively trained in financial analysis so that team members can make decisions quickly but with careful study of the effect on company profits.

A new style of denim shirt has been proposed. Its quarterly sales are estimated to be 5,000 units. Don Martino, cost accountant, states that unit manufacturing costs for the shirts will be $6.50 and other variable costs will be $7.50. He proposes a selling price of $25.00 for the shirts. "At a $25.00 price level," Don tells the managers, "we'll have a contribution margin of $55,000. If you remember from our seminar last month, the contribution margin is the total variable costs subtracted from the total sales. So at 5,000 units, we'll sell $125,000 and have variable costs of $14.00 times 5,000 units." Don further explains that the shirts will be manufactured in the Pennsylvania plant that has fixed costs of $25,000 per quarter. The profit on the new line, after all fixed and variable costs are paid, will be $30,000.

Deborah Anderson, the Pennsylvania plant manager, says, "Don, that's a good analysis, and it sounds like this new line will be profitable. But we just got a major new order for the denim work shirts we produce in the plant and sell at the same price as the new line. Our contribution margin rate is 40%, and this order will use all our excess capacity. We'll have to bring on some extra labor and new equipment to produce the new shirts. I think we had better go back to the spreadsheets for some more analysis."

Critical Thinking

1. What is the contribution margin rate on the new designer shirts? If no other labor or equipment can be added, which shirt will be more profitable to manufacture?

2. If more labor and equipment are added to produce the new shirts, how does that affect the financial analysis?

ABBREVIATED INCOME STATEMENT

Reflection, Inc.
Income Statement
For Month Ended July 31, 20--

Operating Revenue:		
Net Sales		$180,000.00
Cost of Merchandise Sold		118,800.00
Gross Profit on Operations		$ 61,200.00
Operating Expenses:		
Selling Expenses	$31,930.00	
Administrative Expenses	20,820.00	
Total Operating Expenses		52,750.00
Income from Operations		$ 8,450.00
Other Expenses		2,450.00
Net Income		$ 6,000.00

Figure 15-1

Total Costs Versus Unit Cost

All costs for a specific period of time are called **total costs**. The abbreviated income statement in Figure 15-1 shows that the total cost of the merchandise sold by Reflection, Inc. during July was $118,800.00. Total selling expenses were $31,930.00. These totals show how much money was spent for these activities during a specific period of time. *(CONCEPT: Accounting Period Cycle)*

An amount spent for one unit of a specific product or service is called a **unit cost**. Reflection sold 36,000 square feet of mirrors during July at a total cost of $118,800.00. The unit cost of each square foot of mirrors is calculated as follows:

Cost of Merchandise Sold Total Cost	÷	Units Sold	=	Cost of Merchandise Sold Unit Cost
$118,800.00	÷	36,000	=	$3.30

Units may be expressed in many different terms. However, units should be expressed in terms that are meaningful to the people who are responsible for the costs. Some examples of other unit terms are gallons, liters, pounds, kilograms, inches, yards, meters, and hours. Knowing unit costs can be helpful to a manager in setting unit selling prices and in planning cost control.

F Y I

Spreadsheet software is often used to perform what-if analyses. Managers use what-if analyses to examine the financial results of various assumptions. For example, managers can project the net income for the next fiscal period if variable costs increase.

VARIABLE COST CHARACTERISTICS

Month	Units Purchased	Unit Cost per sq. ft.	Total Cost
January	27,300	$3.30	$ 90,090.00
February	26,100	3.30	86,130.00
March	29,200	3.30	96,360.00
April	33,500	3.30	110,550.00
May	30,400	3.30	100,320.00
June	35,100	3.30	115,830.00
July	36,000	3.30	118,800.00

Reflection, Inc.
Mirror Purchases
For Period January 1–July 31, 20--

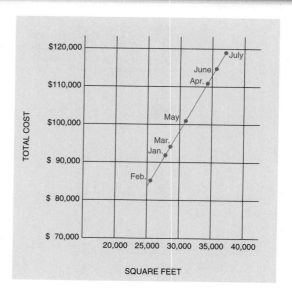

Figure 15-2

Costs may be separated into two parts: variable and fixed. Total costs that change in direct proportion to a change in the number of units are called **variable costs**. The *total* variable cost *varies* with a change in the number of units. Specifically, it increases. The *unit* variable cost *remains the same* regardless of the number of units.

For example, a business buys 1 hour of radio advertising for $150.00. Later the business buys 10 more hours of advertising for $1,500.00 (10 × $150.00 = $1,500.00). Regardless of the number of hours purchased, the unit cost of an hour of advertising is $150.00 per hour. Thus, radio advertising is a variable cost.

Reflection's mirror purchases for the months January through July are shown in Figure 15-2. The volume of mirrors purchased ranges from a low of 26,100 square feet in February to a high of 36,000 square feet in July. However, the price paid per square foot (unit cost) remained at $3.30 throughout the seven-month period. Therefore, these costs have the characteristics of variable costs.

Reflection's monthly costs for mirror purchases are plotted on the graph in Figure 15-2. The line between the plotted points indicates the relationship between the number of square feet of mirrors purchased and the total cost of mirrors. The straight, upward sloped line shows that as the quantity of mirrors increases, the total cost also increases. The line is straight because Reflection's unit cost per square foot remained the same although the number of units purchased per month varied.

FIXED COSTS

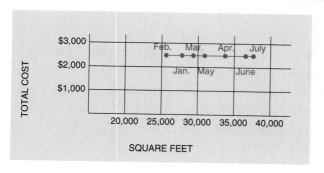

Figure 15-3

Total costs that remain constant regardless of change in business activity are called **fixed costs**. For example, Reflection's rent is $2,500.00 per month. Rent is *fixed* because the amount has been set at $2,500.00 per month regardless of how many square feet of mirrors are purchased. If each monthly rental cost is plotted on a graph and points are connected, the chart will appear as shown in Figure 15-3. The fixed cost line is a straight line parallel to the base of the graph.

Reflection, Inc.
Income Statement
For Month Ended July 31, 20--

Operating Revenue:		
Net Sales (36,000 sq. ft. @ $5.00)		$180,000.00
Cost of Merchandise Sold (36,000 sq. ft. @ $3.30)		118,800.00
Gross Profit on Operations		$ 61,200.00
Operating Expenses:		
Selling Expenses:		
Sales Commission (36,000 sq. ft. @ $.20)	$ 7,200.00	
Delivery Costs (36,000 sq. ft. @ $.40)	14,400.00	
Other Variable Costs (36,000 sq. ft. @ $.15)	5,400.00	
Other Fixed Costs	4,930.00	$31,930.00
Administrative Expenses:		
Rent	$ 2,500.00	
Insurance	400.00	
Other Variable Costs (36,000 sq. ft. @ $.20)	7,200.00	
Other Fixed Costs	10,720.00	20,820.00
Total Operating Expenses		52,750.00
Income from Operations		$ 8,450.00
Other Expenses		2,450.00
Net Income		$ 6,000.00

Reflection, Inc.
Income Statement
For Month Ended July 31, 20--

Operating Revenue:		
Net Sales (36,000 sq. ft. @ $5.00)		$180,000.00
Variable Costs:		
Cost of Merchandise Sold (36,000 sq. ft. @ $3.30)	$118,800.00	
Sales Commission (36,000 sq. ft. @ $.20)	7,200.00	
Delivery Costs (36,000 sq. ft. @ $.40)	14,400.00	
Other Selling Costs (36,000 sq. ft. @ $.15)	5,400.00	
Other Administrative Costs (36,000 sq. ft. @ $.20)	7,200.00	
Total Variable Costs		153,000.00
Contribution Margin		$ 27,000.00
Fixed Costs:		
Rent	$ 2,500.00	
Insurance	400.00	
Other Selling Costs	4,930.00	
Other Administrative Costs	10,720.00	
Other Expenses	2,450.00	
Total Fixed Costs		21,000.00
Net Income		$ 6,000.00

Figure 15-4

An income statement reports operating revenue, cost of merchandise sold, gross profit on operations, operating expenses, and net income or net loss. Gross profit is determined by subtracting cost of merchandise sold from net sales. On a typical income statement, as shown in the top portion of Figure 15-4, costs are shown as cost of merchandise sold, selling expenses, and administrative expenses.

Income determined by subtracting all variable costs from net sales is called **contribution margin**. Reflection's income statement shown in the bottom portion of Figure 15-4 reports contribution margin and net income by grouping costs into two categories: variable costs and fixed costs.

The concept of contribution margin is important to managers because it allows them to determine the income available to cover fixed costs and provide a profit. Reflection's managers can determine from this income statement that the total contribution margin in July was $27,000.00. The contribution margin per unit is calculated as follows.

Total Contribution Margin	÷	Units Sold	=	Contribution Margin per Unit
$27,000.00	÷	36,000	=	$0.75

Thus, Reflection determined that it will earn a $0.75 contribution margin for each square foot of mirrors sold. The managers also know that the company will have $21,000.00 of fixed costs each month regardless of the number of square feet of mirrors sold. Therefore, in July Reflection earned net income of $6,000.00.

GONZALO FLORES, PROFESSOR

I studied business administration in high school, and took additional work in accounting in college. In 1984, I took a job as administrator of a charitable corporation providing social services to children and young teens. There was a need to structure a sound bookkeeping system, and I took the initiative.

We had to be accountable to both the federal and state governments, to our trustees, and to those for whom we were providing our services. I set up their books, and maintained them for eight years.

I moved to Eagle Pass, Texas, to accept a post as college professor. My wife became manager of the college bookstore some six years later. She realized the need for bookkeeping, and I agreed to help. We see this as a team effort. I have an office at the school, but do most of the bookkeeping on my computer at home.

My knowledge of accounting has benefitted me in two ways. First, I have been able to manage my finances. Knowing how to keep a budget, to keep track of expenditures, and to plan for future purchases has helped me manage my resources. It's not a matter of making a lot of money, but of how you manage the money you do make.

Second, in my professional life I have found that understanding and learning accounting has expanded my possibilities. Whether in the business world, or starting your own business, or even interrelating with the business community; accounting has helped me in all these.

ACCOUNTING AT WORK

total costs

unit cost

variable costs

fixed costs

contribution margin

1. If total monthly fixed costs for a company were plotted on a graph for seven months, would the line drawn between the plotted points be parallel to the base or sloped? Explain why.

2. How does contribution margin differ from gross profit?

WORK **TOGETHER**

Preparing an income statement with contribution margin

An income statement for Wightman's Lumber is included in the *Working Papers*. Your instructor will guide you through the following examples.

3. Use the following information to prepare Wightman Lumber's *January* income statement reporting contribution margin. The February information will be used to complete the On Your Own below.

	January	February
Net Sales	52,000 square feet	47,000 square feet
Unit Sales Price	$7.50 per square foot	$7.50 per square foot
Cost of Merchandise Sold	$4.60 per square foot	$4.80 per square foot
Selling Expenses:		
Sales Commission	$.32 per square foot	$.32 per square foot
Delivery Cost	$.50 per square foot	$.55 per square foot
Other Variable Selling Expenses	$.35 per square foot	$.35 per square foot
Other Fixed Selling Expenses	$7,120.00	$7,120.00
Administrative Expenses:		
Rent	$3,800.00	$3,800.00
Insurance	$450.00	$450.00
Other Variable Administrative Expenses	$.30 per square foot	$.33 per square foot
Other Fixed Administrative Expenses	$12,540.00	$12,540.00

ON YOUR **OWN**

Preparing an income statement with contribution margin

Use the February information from the Work Together above. An income statement for Wightman Lumber is included in the *Working Papers*. Work independently to complete this problem.

4. Prepare Wightman Lumber's *February* income statement reporting contribution margin.

15-2 Determining Breakeven

CALCULATING THE BREAKEVEN POINT

Contribution Margin $27,000.00	÷ ÷	**Net Sales** $180,000.00	= =	**Contribution Margin Rate** .15 or 15%	**1**
Total Fixed Costs $21,000.00	÷ ÷	**Contribution Margin Rate** .15 or 15%	= =	**Sales Dollar Breakeven Point** $140,000.00	**2**
Sales Dollar Breakeven Point $140,000.00	÷ ÷	**Unit Sales Price** $5.00	= =	**Unit Sales Breakeven Point** 28,000 units	**3**

Figure 15-5

If a manager is to make decisions that yield a favorable net income for a company, the manager needs two important types of information. (1) The amount of merchandise or services the company must sell to earn a favorable net income. (2) The factors that contribute most to net income.

The amount of sales at which net sales is equal to total costs is called the **breakeven point**. At the breakeven point, neither a net income nor a net loss occurs. At sales levels above the breakeven point, net income occurs. Conversely, at sales levels below the breakeven point, net loss occurs. Knowing the breakeven point allows managers to determine the amount of sales needed to start earning a profit. The breakeven point can be stated in sales dollars or unit sales as shown in Figure 15-5.

The amounts required to calculate a breakeven point are obtained from an income statement prepared to report contribution margin, such as the income statement in Figure 15-4.

S T E P S Calculating a breakeven point

1. Calculate the contribution margin rate by dividing the total contribution margin by net sales. The amounts are taken from historical financial statements, which are often used to project future sales and costs. Reflection uses total amounts rounded to the nearest $10 in breakeven point calculations. This rate means that for every $1.00 of revenue, $0.15 is contribution margin. The contribution rate is available to pay for fixed costs and provide net income. Variable costs change in direct proportion to changes in sales activity. Therefore, for every $1.00 of revenue, $0.85 is required for variable costs.

2. Calculate the sales dollar breakeven point by dividing total fixed costs by the contribution margin rate. The sales dollar breakeven point is the amount of sales at which the entire contribution margin is used to pay for fixed costs. Reflection must have total sales of $140,000.00 just to recover the fixed costs of doing business. More than $140,000.00 in sales must be made if the company is to earn a net income. At a sales level of exactly $140,000, total costs are $140,000 (fixed costs are $21,000 and variable costs are $119,000 [$140,000 x .85]), and Reflection achieves no net income. Any sales level less than $140,000 results in a net loss.

3. Calculate the unit sales breakeven point by dividing the sales dollar breakeven point by the unit sales price. The unit sales breakeven point indicates the number of square feet of mirrors that Reflection must sell at $5.00 per square foot to achieve breakeven sales.

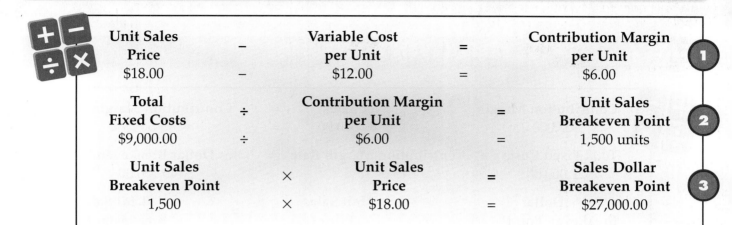

Unit Sales Price	−	Variable Cost per Unit	=	Contribution Margin per Unit	1
$18.00	−	$12.00	=	$6.00	
Total Fixed Costs	÷	Contribution Margin per Unit	=	Unit Sales Breakeven Point	2
$9,000.00	÷	$6.00	=	1,500 units	
Unit Sales Breakeven Point	×	Unit Sales Price	=	Sales Dollar Breakeven Point	3
1,500	×	$18.00	=	$27,000.00	

Figure 15-6

When a business plans to introduce a new product, management is interested in knowing how many units the company must sell to break even. Unfortunately, no financial statements exist from which sales and cost information can be obtained. Therefore, an alternative method to calculate the breakeven point using the *contribution margin per unit* rather than the *contribution margin rate* is necessary.

Reflection is considering selling desk lamps at $18.00 per unit. Management expects variable costs of $12.00 per unit with fixed costs of $9,000.00 per month. From the analysis, Reflection determines that it must sell more than 1,500 desk lamps per month before the company begins to make a net income. Thus, management will begin selling desk lamps if it believes it can sell more than 1,500 per month.

This alternative method is also useful for calculating the breakeven point for existing products when complete financial statements are not available.

F.Y.I.

The nature of some businesses requires a large investment in fixed costs. Businesses such as airlines, public utilities, and railroads have large fixed costs. These businesses may be considered riskier because much of their revenue is devoted to paying these fixed costs.

S **Calculating a breakeven point for a new product**

T
E
P
S

1. Calculate the contribution margin per unit by subtracting the variable cost per unit from the unit sales price. The contribution margin per unit represents the amount available per unit to cover fixed costs and earn a profit.

2. Calculate the unit sales breakeven point by dividing the total fixed costs by the contribution margin per unit. The unit sales breakeven point indicates the number of units that must be sold at the projected unit sales price to cover all variable and fixed costs. If Reflection sells exactly 1,500 units, it will earn no net income, nor will it incur a net loss.

3. Calculate the sales dollar breakeven point by multiplying the unit sales breakeven point by the unit sales price. This calculation gives the revenue earned by selling 1,500 units at the projected sales price, $18.00 per unit.

Reflection, Inc.
Breakeven Income Statement
For Month Ended July 31, 20--

Operating Revenue:		
Net Sales (28,000 sq. ft. @ $5.00)		$140,000.00
Variable Costs:		
Cost of Merchandise Sold (28,000 sq. ft. @ $3.30)	$92,400.00	
Sales Commission (28,000 sq. ft. @ $.20)	5,600.00	
Delivery Costs (28,000 sq. ft. @ $.40)	11,200.00	
Other Selling Costs (28,000 sq. ft. @ $.15)	4,200.00	
Other Administrative Costs (28,000 sq. ft. @ $.20)	5,600.00	
Total Variable Costs		119,000.00
Contribution Margin		$ 21,000.00
Fixed Costs:		
Rent	$ 2,500.00	
Insurance	400.00	
Other Selling Costs	4,930.00	
Other Administrative Costs	10,720.00	
Other Expenses	2,450.00	
Total Fixed Costs		21,000.00
Net Income		$ –0–

Figure 15-7

The breakeven income statement in Figure 15-7 shows the proof for Reflection's breakeven point for mirror sales. If the breakeven point is accurate, net income is zero.

The breakeven income statement is a projection of sales and costs under specific assumptions. Reflection reports projected amounts to the nearest $10. Total sales, $140,000.00, is equal to the sales dollar breakeven point. Each variable cost is calculated by multiplying the unit sales breakeven point, *28,000 units*, by the unit variable cost of each cost item. The amount of each fixed cost is taken from the July income statement. The contribution margin, *$21,000.00*, is 15% of net sales, *$140,000.00*. This verifies Reflection's contribution margin rate of 15%.

CONFIDENTIALITY

Certified public accountants routinely see and hear confidential information relating to their clients. The AICPA Rules of the Code of Professional Conduct prohibit disclosure of confidential information without the specific consent of the client.

Required:

Use the three-step checklist to help determine whether the actions described in the following situation demonstrates ethical behavior.

Paxton Plastics manufactures molded plastic backyard play systems. Paxton is involved in several lawsuits as the result of children being injured while playing on Paxton's Slide by Slide double-wide sliding board. During a recent audit Justin Portero, a CPA, learns that the company knew about structural problems with the sliding board and continued to manufacture and sell the products. Several company officers told Justin that they expect the company to lose the lawsuits and there is talk of criminal charges. They fear that stock prices will plummet in the near future. Justin knows that his cousin owns Paxton stock. Without providing any details, he suggested his cousin sell his stock before the price falls.

PROFESSIONAL BUSINESS ETHICS

 **TERM REVIEW**

breakeven point

 **AUDIT YOUR UNDERSTANDING**

1. In what two ways can the breakeven point be stated?
2. How is the contribution margin per unit used?
3. What is the simplest way to verify the accuracy of a breakeven calculation?

 **WORK TOGETHER**

Calculating breakeven in sales dollars and unit sales and preparing a breakeven income statement

An income statement for Cherie's Pizza is included in the *Working Papers*. Your instructor will guide you through the following examples.

4. Use the following information to calculate the breakeven point in sales dollars and unit sales for *July*. The August information will be used to complete the On Your Own below.

	July	August
Net Sales	$60,000.00	$80,000.00
Unit Sales Price	$8.00	$8.00
Contribution Margin	$12,000.00	$10,000.00
Total Fixed Costs	$8,000.00	$8,000.00
Unit Variable Cost	$6.40	$7.00

5. Prepare a breakeven income statement for July of the current year. Save your work to complete the Work Together on page 434.

 **ON YOUR OWN**

Calculating breakeven in sales dollars and unit sales and preparing a breakeven income statement

Use the August information from the Work Together above. An income statement for Cherie's Pizza is included in the *Working Papers*. Work independently to complete this problem.

6. Calculate the breakeven point in sales dollars and unit sales for *August*.

7. Prepare a breakeven income statement for August of the current year. Save your work to complete the On Your Own on page 434.

CALCULATING SALES TO EARN PLANNED NET INCOME

Total Fixed Costs	+	Planned Net Income	=	Required Contribution Margin	1
$21,000.00	+	$1,500.00	=	$22,500.00	
Required Contribution Margin	÷	Contribution Margin Rate	=	Sales Dollars	2
$22,500.00	÷	.15 or 15%	=	$150,000.00	

Figure 15-8

Determining the breakeven point provides management with important information about the relationship of sales, variable costs, and fixed costs. Businesses do not, however, operate merely to break even. Managers need information that will assist them in achieving planned net income. The breakeven analysis can be used to calculate the dollar and unit sales needed to earn a specified amount of planned net income.

F.Y.I

Fixed costs for your school might include the depreciation on the building and the principal's salary. These costs are the same no matter how many students are enrolled.

Variable costs for your school might include the cost of computers, cafeteria lunches, and textbooks. These costs will increase or decrease depending on the number of students enrolled.

Identify other costs involved with your school. Are they fixed or variable?

S T E P S — Calculating sales to earn planned net income

1. Calculate the required contribution margin. The sum of total fixed costs and the planned net income is the contribution margin necessary both to cover fixed costs and to earn the planned amount of net income. Reflection's managers want to know the amount of total sales required to earn $1,500.00 of net income.

2. Calculate the amount of sales dollars by dividing the required contribution margin by the contribution margin rate. Thus, Reflection must sell 30,000 square feet of mirrors ($150,000.00 total sales *divided by* the unit sales price of $5.00) to earn $1,500.00 of net income.

The required contribution margin, *$22,500.00*, can be divided by the contribution margin per unit, *$0.75*, to calculate the number of units to be sold ($22,500.00/$0.75 = 30,000).

		1	2	3	4	5
		Per Unit	**Number of Units**			
				26,000	**28,000**	**30,000**
Net Sales		$5.00	$130,000.00	$140,000.00	$150,000.00
Variable Costs		4.25	110,500.00	119,000.00	127,500.00
Contribution Margin		$0.75	$ 19,500.00	$ 21,000.00	$ 22,500.00
Fixed Costs			21,000.00	21,000.00	21,000.00
Net Income (Loss)			$ (1,500.00)	$ —0—	$ 1,500.00

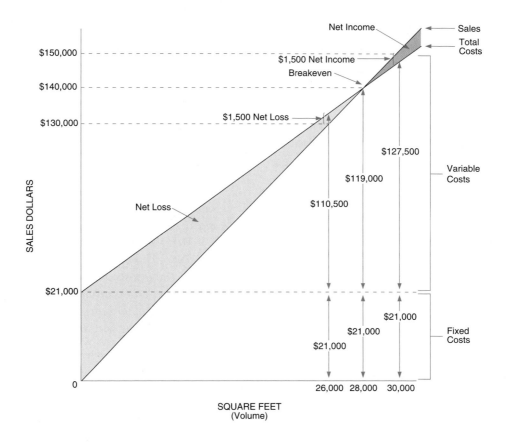

Figure 15-9

Businesses must be able to determine the change in net income that would result from changes in the relationship of sales, variable costs, and fixed costs. Reflection's managers desire answers to questions such as these: What would net income be if sales increase or decrease? Would it be profitable to change production methods? What would be the effect on net income of a decrease in unit sales price and an increase in sales volume?

Reflection has calculated its unit sales breakeven point to be 28,000 square feet. The table in Figure 15-9 shows how net income

changes for a decrease or an increase of 2,000 units. For each square foot of mirrors Reflection sells, $0.75 of contribution margin is available for fixed costs and net income. At the 28,000 unit breakeven point, the $21,000.00 contribution margin pays for fixed costs, leaving no remaining amount for net income. For each square foot of mirrors above 28,000 units sold, the $0.75 per square foot contribution margin increases net income. Therefore, when 30,000 square feet of mirrors are sold, net income is expected to be $1,500.00 (2,000 square feet × $0.75 contribution margin per unit).

If only 26,000 square feet of mirrors are sold during the month, the contribution margin of $19,500.00 would not cover the fixed costs of $21,000.00. At this sales volume, a net loss of $1,500.00 would result.

The graph in Figure 15-9 shows the relationship of sales, costs, and net income as the volume changes. The sales line, beginning at zero, represents unit sales price times number of units sold. The total cost line starting at $21,000.00 (total fixed costs) represents the total fixed and variable costs for the number of units sold. No matter what the sales volume is, the fixed costs remain constant. The variable cost area represents 85% of sales regardless of volume.

At the breakeven point, the sales and total costs lines intersect, indicating that neither a net income nor a net loss will occur. If 30,000 square feet of mirrors are sold, the sales line is above the total cost line. At this sales volume, $150,000.00 of sales is higher than the sum of fixed costs ($21,000.00) and variable costs ($127,500.00), resulting in net income of $1,500.00. If sales volume is below 28,000 square feet, the total cost line is above the sales line indicating a net loss.

EFFECT OF COST CHANGES AT AVERAGE VOLUME

	Alternative 1 Manual Cutting			Alternative 2 Automated Cutting		
	Per Unit	Units Sold	Total	Per Unit	Units Sold	Total
Net Sales	$5.00	30,000	$150,000.00	$5.00	30,000	$150,000.00
Variable Costs	4.25	30,000	127,500.00	4.00	30,000	120,000.00
Contribution Margin	$0.75	30,000	$ 22,500.00	$1.00	30,000	$ 30,000.00
Fixed Costs			21,000.00			28,500.00
Net Income (Loss)			$ 1,500.00			$ 1,500.00

Figure 15-10

Two types of costs, variable and fixed, influence the decisions a company may make. Total variable costs increase or decrease as sales increase or decrease. Total fixed costs remain constant regardless of sales amount.

Reflection's management is concerned that the relatively low contribution margin rate makes increasing net income difficult for the company. Reflection is searching for ways to improve its percentage of net income per sales dollar. An alternate production method is being considered. The new method would automate the cutting of mirrors. A cost comparison of the two methods, Alternative 1 and Alternative 2, is shown in Figure 15-10 and is described below.

- *Alternative 1: Manual Cutting.* Variable costs per square foot of mirrors are $4.25. Reflection currently pays a crew to cut mirrors to dimensions ordered by its customers. Of the total variable costs, $0.25

per square foot represents the cost of this crew. Fixed costs are $21,000.00 per month.

- *Alternative 2: Automated Cutting.* The company buys an automated cutter and assigns the cutting crew to process orders of new product lines. The variable costs of the mirrors decrease by $0.25 per square foot to $4.00 per square foot. However, the new method requires buying the automated cutter and employing an experienced cutter at a fixed salary. Thus, fixed costs increase by $7,500.00 per month to $28,500.00.

Sales have been averaging about 30,000 square feet of mirrors per month. At a 30,000-unit sales level, net income is the same for both alternatives. With Alternative 2, the contribution margin is higher, but fixed costs also are higher. Thus, the higher fixed costs cancel the higher contribution margin.

	Alternative 1 Manual Cutting			Alternative 2 Automated Cutting		
	Per Unit	Units Sold	Total	Per Unit	Units Sold	Total
Net Sales	$5.00	32,000	$160,000.00	$5.00	32,000	$160,000.00
Variable Costs	4.25	32,000	136,000.00	4.00	32,000	128,000.00
Contribution Margin	$0.75	32,000	$ 24,000.00	$1.00	32,000	$ 32,000.00
Fixed Costs			21,000.00			28,500.00
Net Income (Loss)			$ 3,000.00			$ 3,500.00

Figure 15-11

Reflection is planning to increase unit sales. A cost comparison with a sales volume of 32,000 units is shown in Figure 15-11. With the increased sales volume, Alternative 2 earns a higher net income. If Reflection expects a permanent sales increase, Alternative 2 would be more profitable than Alternative 1.

EFFECT OF CHANGES IN COSTS ON CONTRIBUTION MARGIN RATE

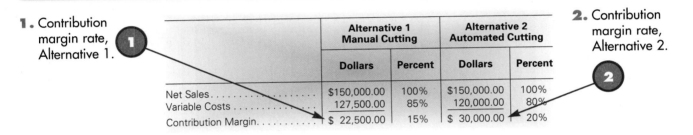

1. Contribution margin rate, Alternative 1.

2. Contribution margin rate, Alternative 2.

	Alternative 1 Manual Cutting		Alternative 2 Automated Cutting	
	Dollars	Percent	Dollars	Percent
Net Sales	$150,000.00	100%	$150,000.00	100%
Variable Costs	127,500.00	85%	120,000.00	80%
Contribution Margin	$ 22,500.00	15%	$ 30,000.00	20%

Figure 15-12

As long as sales increase as expected, Alternative 2 will be favored. However, if sales do not increase, the results will be much different. If the number of units actually sold falls below 30,000, the results will favor Alternative 1.

What is the reason for the change in favorable alternatives? The contribution margin rate favors Alternative 2. Figure 15-12 shows that the contribution margin rate for Alternative 1 is 15% versus 20% for Alternative 2. This means that for every $1.00 of sales from Alternative 1, $0.15 is available for fixed costs and net income. But for every $1.00 of sales from Alternative 2, $0.20 is available for fixed costs and net income.

A higher contribution margin rate is usually desirable. However, fixed costs must also be reasonable since the contribution margin must cover the fixed costs before any net income is earned. The contribution margin rate, 20%, for the automated cutting method is more favorable. But fixed costs are $28,500.00—$7,500.00 more than fixed costs for the manual cutting method. If sales volume declines, the increased contribution margin is not enough to recover the increased fixed costs. Therefore a reduction in net income occurs.

A logical conclusion is "everything else being equal, the activity with the higher contribution margin rate is more profitable." If "everything else" is equal, selecting the more profitable choice is very simple. However, alternatives are seldom that simple because fixed costs probably differ for each alternative. Therefore, an effective business looks for the best combination of fixed and variable costs.

	Current Price			Price Reduction and Sales Volume Increase		
	Per Unit	Units Sold	Total	Per Unit	Units Sold	Total
Net Sales..................	$5.00	30,000	$150,000.00	$4.75	36,000	$171,000.00
Variable Costs..............	4.25	30,000	127,500.00	4.25	36,000	153,000.00
Contribution Margin...........	$0.75	30,000	$ 22,500.00	$0.50	36,000	$ 18,000.00
Fixed Costs.................			21,000.00			21,000.00
Net Income (Loss)............			$ 1,500.00			$ (3,000.00)

Figure 15-13

Setting the sales price of a product is extremely important. If the price is set too high, potential customers will buy from another business. If the price is set too low, the company may not earn enough money to cover costs and may suffer a loss. The objective is to set sales prices that provide a reasonable amount of net income while keeping prices competitive.

Reflection earned record net income in July, selling 36,000 units. Unfortunately, Reflection's managers believe that a price reduction is necessary to sustain this sales volume. Management is considering a plan to reduce unit sales price by 5% (from $5.00 to $4.75). Management projects that the price decrease will result in a 20% increase in the average number of units sold

(from 30,000 to 36,000 units). Should Reflection implement this price reduction? Figure 15-13 shows the effect of this price change on sales volume and net income.

Price cutting can be dangerous. In July, Reflection had a $0.75 contribution margin per square foot of mirrors sold. Average sales of 30,000 units resulted in $22,500.00 total contribution margin. A unit sales price reduction of 5% ($0.25 per unit) to $4.75 per unit reduces the contribution margin to $0.50, a 33-1/3% reduction. The potential results of a price cut can be calculated. The unit sales required to maintain the net income using the new contribution margin is calculated as follows.

Contribution Margin	÷	New Contribution Margin per Unit	=	Unit Sales Required to Maintain Planned Net Income
$22,500.00	÷	$0.50	=	45,000 units

A decrease in unit sales price from $5.00 to $4.75 is projected to increase average sales from 30,000 to 36,000 units. However, at $4.75, the company would have to sell a total of 45,000 units to maintain the same net income as current sales at the $5.00 price. Reducing the unit sales price by $0.25 would not be a profitable decision if the company can sell only 36,000 units.

F.Y.I.

Spreadsheet software is an ideal tool to use for calculating breakeven and for analyzing the effect of price, cost, and sales mix changes. An effective spreadsheet identifies the variables used in an analysis, for example units sold, price per unit, variable costs, and fixed costs. The analysis is built by creating formulas that reference these variables. When the amounts of the variables are changed, the spreadsheet instantly recalculates the analysis and displays the results.

VideoPort, Inc.
Income Statement
For Month Ended November 30, 20--

Operating Revenue:		
Net Sales		
Televisions (150 units @ $350)	$52,500.00	
VCRs (90 units @ $250)	22,500.00	$75,000.00
Variable Costs:		
Televisions (150 units @ $210)	$31,500.00	
VCRs (90 units @ $150)	13,500.00	45,000.00
Contribution Margin		$30,000.00
Fixed Costs		24,000.00
Net Income		$ 6,000.00

	Product Sales	÷	Net Sales	=	Sales Mix	
Television	$52,500.00	÷	$75,000.00	=	70%	**1**
VCR	$22,500.00	÷	$75,000.00	=	30%	

Contribution Margin	÷	Net Sales	=	Contribution Margin Rate	
$30,000.00	÷	$75,000.00	=	.40 or 40%	**2**

Total Fixed Costs	+	Planned Net Income	=	Required Contribution Margin Rate	
$24,000.00	+	$10,000.00	=	$34,000.00	**3**

Required Contribution Margin	÷	Contribution Margin Rate	=	Total Sales Dollars	
$34,000.00	÷	.40 or 40%	=	$85,000.00	**4**

	Sales Mix	×	Total Sales Dollars	=	Product Sales Dollars	
Television	70%	×	$85,000.00	=	$59,500.00	**5**
VCR	30%	×	$85,000.00	=	$25,500.00	

	Product Sales Dollars	÷	Unit Sales Price	=	Product Unit Sales	
Television	$59,500.00	÷	$350.00	=	170 units	**6**
VCR	$25,500.00	÷	$250.00	=	102 units	

Figure 15-14

Businesses that sell two or more products can also use breakeven point calculations to assist managers in planning. Relative distribution of sales among various products is called **sales mix**. The sales mix must be calculated to determine the breakeven point for a company that sells more than one product. VideoPort, Inc. sells televisions and videocassette recorders (VCRs). The income statement in Figure 15-14 reports VideoPort's sales and cost information for the month ended November 30.

VideoPort expects the relationship of television to VCR sales to remain relatively stable in future months. However, management has indicated its objective to improve monthly net income to $10,000.00. How many televisions and VCRs should VideoPort plan to purchase and sell?

The procedures used to calculate sales to earn a planned net income are similar to those previously described in this chapter. Six steps are used to calculate sales of more than one product to earn a planned net income.

Managers of the television and VCR departments can now plan to accomplish these sales objectives. For example, the television department manager knows that the department must sell 20 more televisions (170 – 150 = 20) each month. Thus, the manager can plan to increase purchases and devise new sales promotion and advertising campaigns to sell the increased number of televisions.

TECHNOLOGY FOR BUSINESS

USING A SPREADSHEET TO PERFORM BREAKEVEN ANALYSIS

Micron, Inc., a large wholesaler, plans to introduce a new product line next year. Three lines are being considered. Micron performs extensive market research on potential new product lines. The three lines being considered have tested well.

To make the final decision among the three product lines, management has decided that the line with the lowest breakeven point will be added. The following data are available for the three product lines:

Required:

1. Create a spreadsheet that calculates the breakeven point for the three product lines. Use descriptive column headings and row titles. [Hint: Develop the breakeven formula for the Line A. Use the Copy command to copy the formula for Lines B and C.]

2. From your analysis, which line should Micron add next year?

	Line A	Line B	Line C
Sales price per unit	$42.00	$48.00	$46.00
Variable costs per unit	18.00	26.00	14.00
Fixed costs	$14,600.00	$11,800.00	$27,200.00

AUDIT YOUR UNDERSTANDING

1. What two types of costs influence management's decisions?
2. To earn a planned net income, the required contribution margin must equal what two amounts?

WORK TOGETHER

Calculating sales to earn a planned net income, calculating the effect of volume changes on net income, and calculating the effect of changes in selling price

Use the working papers and data from the Work Together on page 426. Forms for completing this Work Together are provided in the *Working Papers*. Your instructor will guide you through the following examples.

3. Assume that Cherie's Pizza wants a net income for July of $3,000. Calculate the amount of sales dollars needed to achieve this net income.

4. Determine the net income or loss if: (a) 4,000 units are sold; (b) 5,000 units are sold; (c) 6,000 units are sold.

5. Assume Cherie's Pizza normally sells 7,500 pizzas in July. If the selling price is reduced by $.50, Cherie's expects to sell 9,000 pizzas. Calculate the effect on net income of this change.

ON YOUR OWN

Calculating sales to earn a planned net income, calculating the effect of volume changes on net income, and calculating the effect of changes in selling price

Use the working papers and data from the On Your Own on page 426. Forms for completing this On Your Own are provided in the *Working Papers*. Work independently to complete this problem.

6. Assume Cherie's Pizza wants a net income for August of $3,000. Calculate the amount of sales dollars needed to achieve this net income.

7. Determine the net income or loss if: (a) 7,000 units are sold; (b) if 8,000 units are sold; (c) 9,000 units are sold.

8. Assume Cherie's Pizza normally sells 10,000 pizzas in August. If the selling price is increased by $.50, Cherie's expects to sell 9,500 pizzas. Calculate the effect on net income of this change.

After completing this chapter, you can

1. Define important terms related to accounting information for management decisions.

2. Identify accounting concepts and practices related to preparing accounting information for management decisions.

3. Prepare an income statement reporting contribution margin.

4. Calculate the contribution margin rate.

5. Calculate the breakeven point.

6. Calculate the sales dollars and sales units required to earn a planned amount of net income.

7. Determine the effect of changes in sales volume, unit costs, and unit sales prices on net income.

8. Calculate a sales mix.

EXPLORE ACCOUNTING

MIXED COSTS

A cost having both fixed and variable characteristics is called a mixed cost. For example, Mason Castings uses natural gas to operate a casting furnace. Even if the company processes no castings, keeping the furnace heated incurs a cost—a fixed cost. The gas required to maintain a constant furnace temperature increases with the number of castings produced—a variable cost. Thus, natural gas expense is a mixed cost.

A statistical method used to determine the fixed and variable costs of a mixed cost is called regression analysis. Natural gas expense for the past six months can be used to estimate the fixed and variable costs.

Units	Temperature	Expense
4,653	28	$5,507
4,657	34	5,869
5,423	43	6,791
6,754	47	7,697
5,876	58	7,918
6,137	78	9,249

Using the number of units produced and the average outdoor temperature in the multiple regression equation allows management to estimate that the fixed cost is $1,500 and that variables costs are $60 for every degree of temperature and $.50 for every unit produced. With this information, management can accurately estimate future expenses.

REQUIRED:

Use the multiple regression tool of an electronic spreadsheet and the following six-month actual cost information to determine the fixed and variable amounts of labor costs. Assume that the number of units produced and the number of production days have an impact on labor costs. (Hint: Identify the cost as the dependent, y, variable and the units and days as independent, x, variables.)

Units	Days	Cost
675	15	$10,025
867	18	11,801
768	20	12,304
978	22	13,728
965	20	12,895
875	18	11,825

APPLICATION PROBLEM
Preparing an income statement reporting contribution margin

Milford Pump Company's income statement has been prepared for November of the current year.

Milford Pump Company
Income Statement
For Month Ended November 30, 20--

Operating Revenue:			
Net Sales (8,700 units @ $210.00)			$1,827,000.00
Cost of Merchandise Sold (8,700 units @ $145.00)			1,261,500.00
Gross Profit on Operations			$ 565,500.00
Operating Expenses:			
Selling Expenses:			
Sales Commission (8,700 units @ $6.00)	$52,200.00		
Delivery Costs (8,700 units @ $4.80)	41,760.00		
Other Variable Costs (8,700 units @ $2.75)	23,925.00		
Other Fixed Costs	76,510.00	$194,395.00	
Administrative Expenses:			
Rent	$15,000.00		
Insurance	9,750.00		
Other Variable Costs (8,700 units @ $5.50)	47,850.00		
Other Fixed Costs	45,290.00	117,890.00	
Total Operating Expenses			312,285.00
Income from Operations			$ 253,215.00
Other Expenses			12,000.00
Net Income			$ 241,215.00

Instructions:

1. Prepare Milford Pump Company's November income statement reporting contribution margin.

2. Calculate the contribution margin per unit.

3. Calculate variable cost per unit. Plot variable costs and fixed costs on a graph.

APPLICATION PROBLEM
Calculating contribution margin and breakeven point

Farris Electronics is considering expanding its product line to include portable radios. Management projects that radios would sell for $60.00 each. Variable costs are projected to be $25.00 with total fixed costs of $42,000.00 per month.

Instructions:

1. Calculate the contribution margin per unit.

2. Calculate the unit sales breakeven point.

3. Calculate the sales dollar breakeven point.

4. Farris has projected that it could sell 1,000 units per month. Should the company expand its product line to sell the portable radios? Support your answer.

APPLICATION PROBLEM
Calculating plans for net income

Dennis Williams is projecting the coming year's net income potential for Williams Paint. The paint is sold for $15.00 a gallon. Variable costs per gallon are $10.00, and annual fixed costs are $135,000.00. Complete each of the following instructions independently of the others.

Instructions:

1. Calculate the (a) unit sales and (b) sales dollar breakeven points.

2. If a $50,000.00 annual net income is planned, calculate the required (a) number of gallons of paint to be sold and (b) sales dollars.

3. Dennis plans to purchase a new paint mixing machine that would reduce the cost of paint by $0.50 per gallon but increase annual fixed costs by $52,000.00. Calculate the (a) unit sales and (b) sales dollar breakeven points. Should Dennis purchase the mixing machine? Explain your answer.

APPLICATION PROBLEM
Calculating the effects on net income of changes in unit sales price, variable costs, fixed costs, and volume

The following information pertains to a product sold by Gomez Company:

Unit Sales Price	$12.00
Unit Variable Costs	$9.60
Unit Contribution Margin	$2.40
Fixed Costs	$48,000.00

Instructions:

1. Determine the net income or loss
   a. if 17,000 units are sold.
   b. if 20,000 units are sold.
   c. if 23,000 units are sold.

2. Gomez Company is considering purchasing equipment that would reduce the unit variable cost to $8.50. However, fixed costs would increase to $58,000.
   a. If 20,000 units were expected to be sold, would Gomez Company's net income increase if the new equipment were purchased and used?
   b. If only 17,000 units were expected to be sold, would Gomez Company's net income increase if the new equipment were purchased and used?

3. Gomez Company believes that a 10% reduction in the unit sales price would result in a 30% increase in the number of units sold. Assume that normal sales volume before any price reduction was 20,000 units. Assume also that the equipment described in instruction 2 was not purchased, so that the fixed costs and unit variable costs were $48,000.00 and $9.60, respectively. Would the reduction in sales price increase or decrease net income?

APPLICATION PROBLEM 15-5
Calculating sales mix

Schenk, Inc., sells desk lamps and desks. The following information is from the June income statement. Schenk's management is interested in knowing the number of lamps and desks it must sell to earn $10,000.00 of net income.

Schenk, Inc. Income Statement For Month Ended June 30, 20--		
Net Sales:		
Lamps (1,000 @ $40.00)	$40,000.00	
Desks (240 @ $250.00)	60,000.00	
Total Net Sales		$100,000.00
Variable Costs:		
Lamps (1,000 @ $30.00)	$30,000.00	
Desks (240 @ $125.00)	30,000.00	
Total Variable Costs		60,000.00
Contribution Margin		$ 40,000.00
Fixed Costs		38,000.00
Net Income		$ 2,000.00

Instructions:
Schenk's managers need sales information assuming that the company earns $10,000.00 of monthly net income. Calculate the following amounts to achieve the $10,000.00 planned net income.

a. Sales mix.
b. Contribution margin rate.
c. Total sales dollars.
d. Product sales dollars.
e. Product unit sales.

MASTERY PROBLEM 15-6
Calculating contribution margin and breakeven point; calculating sales dollars and unit sales for planned net income

Ratliff Corporation produces lawn fertilizer spreaders. Ratliff's income statement shown on the next page has been prepared for August of the current year.

Instructions:

1. Prepare Ratliff's August income statement reporting contribution margin.

2. Calculate the contribution margin rate.

3. Calculate the sales dollar breakeven point.

4. Calculate the unit sales breakeven point.

5. If a $15,000.00 monthly net income is planned, calculate the required (a) sales dollars and (b) unit sales.

6. Ratliff is considering using computer-based machines to increase the productivity of the manufacturing process. The new machines would reduce variable costs by $4.20 per unit but increase monthly fixed costs by $10,000.00. Calculate the projected net income assuming that Ratliff sells 3,000 units. Should Ratliff purchase the machines? Explain your answer.

Ratliff Corporation
Income Statement
For Month Ended August 31, 20--

Operating Revenue:			
Net Sales (3,000 units @ $25.00)			$75,000.00
Cost of Merchandise Sold (3,000 units @ $16.00)			48,000.00
Gross Profit on Operations			$27,000.00
Operating Expenses:			
Selling Expenses:			
Sales Commission (3,000 units @ $0.60)	$1,800.00		
Delivery Costs (3,000 units @ $0.75)	2,250.00		
Other Variable Costs (3,000 units @ $1.15)	3,450.00		
Other Fixed Costs	3,590.00	$11,090.00	
Administrative Expenses:			
Rent	$1,000.00		
Insurance	600.00		
Other Variable Costs (3,000 units @ $0.25)	750.00		
Other Fixed Costs	5,610.00	7,960.00	
Total Operating Expenses			19,050.00
Income from Operations			$ 7,950.00
Other Expenses			800.00
Net Income			$ 7,150.00

15-7 CHALLENGE PROBLEM
Calculating the effects on net income of changes in unit sales price, variable costs, and fixed costs

Millard, Inc., sold 68,000 computer printers last year with the following results.

Millard, Inc.
Income Statement
For Year Ended December 31, 20--

Net Sales (68,000 units @ $250.00)	$17,000,000.00
Less Variable Costs (68,000 units @ $200.00)	13,600,000.00
Contribution Margin	$ 3,400,000.00
Less Fixed Costs	2,980,000.00
Net Income	$ 420,000.00

Complete each of the following instructions independently of the others.

Instructions:

1. Millard projects that it can sell 75,000 printers next year at the current $250.00 unit sales price. However, management believes that it can increase net income by selling its printer below the unit sales price of its competitors. Millard's marketing department projects that it could sell 100,000 printers at a unit sales price of $230.00. Calculate the projected net income. Should Millard reduce the unit sales price to $230.00? Explain your answer.

2. Millard currently purchases the power cable from another manufacturer at a cost of $7.00 per unit. The company is considering producing the cable. Millard projects that it can produce the cable for $2.00 each plus annual fixed costs of $240,000.00. Calculate the projected net income assuming a sales volume of 75,000 printers. Should Millard produce the power cables? Explain your answer.

Applied Communication

Charts and graphs are often used to help people understand numbers. To be helpful, charts and graphs must be clearly labeled.

Required:

1. Use the data from Application Problem 15-4, Instruction 1, to prepare a graph similar to the one in Figure 15-9. Label the graph clearly.
2. Prepare a brief written explanation of the graph.

INTERNET ACTIVITY

Point your browser to
http://accounting.swpco.com
Choose **Advanced Course**, choose **Activities**, and complete the activity for Chapter 15.

Cases for Critical Thinking

Case 1

George Edmonds, the new accountant for Zigler Company, has recommended the preparation of income statements reporting contribution margin rather than statements reporting gross profit. He states that the income statement with contribution margin provides better information. Kimberly Johnson, the manager, disagrees that one statement is better than the other. She says gross profit is the same as contribution margin, so it does not make any difference which statement is prepared. Which person is correct? Explain.

Case 2

Denise Young, an accountant for Chiles Corporation, has been asked to prepare an income statement that reports contribution margin. Miss Young has asked you to prepare an analysis of three months' costs. Provide Miss Young with an analysis of these data that include the unit cost of variable costs and monthly costs of fixed costs. Explain to Miss Young how you prepared your analysis.

	May	June	July
Unit Sales	400	500	600
Cost of Merchandise Sold	$8,000.00	$10,000.00	$12,000.00
Advertising Expense	2,300.00	2,300.00	2,300.00
Depreciation Expense	1,000.00	1,000.00	1,000.00
Payroll Taxes Expense	640.00	800.00	960.00
Rent Expense	2,000.00	2,000.00	2,000.00
Salary Expense	3,200.00	4,000.00	4,800.00
Supplies Expense	1,200.00	1,200.00	1,200.00
Utilities Expense	600.00	750.00	900.00

AUTOMATED ACCOUNTING

USING COMPUTERIZED REPORTS FOR MANAGEMENT DECISIONS

The accounting department of a business is responsible for generating financial reports. Managers use these reports to make informed business decisions. Individuals working as sales managers, production managers, purchasing managers, or in any other department of the business must be able to interpret accounting information to plan for and organize their business. Financial reports are also used for decision making by owners, investors, and lenders.

A computerized accounting system can provide a variety of timely reports to managers. These reports help managers compare and analyze the differences between the financial data for the current fiscal period and the previous fiscal period. Two types of financial analysis available are:

- Horizontal trend analysis

- Vertical trend analysis

Horizontal trend analysis compares the ending balance for the current fiscal period with the ending balance of the previous fiscal period for each item on the statement. The difference is reported as a percentage change. This type of analysis may be generated for both the balance sheet and the income statement.

Vertical trend analysis shows the relationship of the component parts to the total. On the income statement, total revenue (or sales) is expressed as 100%, and the other items are expressed as a percentage of total revenue. On the balance sheet, assets are expressed as a percentage of total assets, while liabilities and stockholders' equity items are expressed as a percentage of total liabilities and stockholders' equity. In *Automated Accounting 7.0* or higher, vertical analysis is included for both current and previous fiscal periods.

Preparing a Financial Analysis Report

Use the following steps to display the horizontal and vertical trend analysis reports:

1. Click the Reports toolbar button, or choose the Reports Selection menu item from the Reports menu.

2. When the Report Selection dialog appears, choose Financial Analysis from the Select a Report Group list.

3. Choose one of the vertical or horizontal analysis reports from the Choose a Report to Display list.

4. Click OK.

The report will be displayed in the scrollable Report Viewer Window. The report may be printed and/or copied for inclusion in another application, such as a spreadsheet or word processor.

1. To print the report, click the Print button.

2. To copy the report, click the Copy button and select the format for the report. The data are copied to the Clipboard in either the spreadsheet format or the word processing format.

Financial Statement Analysis

AFTER STUDYING CHAPTER 16, YOU WILL BE ABLE TO:

1. Define accounting terms related to financial statement analysis.

2. Identify accounting concepts and practices related to financial statement analysis.

3. Analyze financial statements.

4. Calculate earnings performance.

5. Perform efficiency analysis.

6. Analyze the long-term financial strength of a business.

Financial statements report the financial progress and condition of a business for a fiscal period. *(CONCEPT: Adequate Disclosure)*

The adequate disclosure concept states that financial statements contain the information necessary to understand a business' financial condition. Owners, managers, lenders, and investors rely on financial statements to make informed decisions. All relevant financial information must be adequately and completely disclosed on financial statements.

A business reports only the total liabilities of $200,000.00 on its balance sheet. However, the total liabilities include $75,000.00 in current liabilities and $125,000.00 in long-term liabilities. Therefore, the balance sheet does not adequately disclose the nature of the liabilities. The critical information not disclosed is that $75,000.00 is current and due within a few months.

Managers use financial information to identify areas for improving profitability. Banks and lending agencies use the information to decide whether to loan money to a business. Owners and potential owners use the information to decide whether to buy, sell, or keep their investment. Each group uses the financial information in a different way to assist with decision making.

Although financial statements provide useful information, they can be difficult to understand. For example, is a significant increase in the cost of merchandise sold an unfavorable trend? This question cannot be answered without considering information in other financial statement items, such as net sales. Financial statement analysis provides this information, since it calculates the relationships among financial statement items.

TERMS PREVIEW

ratio
trend analysis
rate earned on net
   sales
working capital
current ratio
quick assets
acid-test ratio
debt ratio
equity ratio

ACCOUNTING
IN YOUR CAREER

PERSUADING THE BOARD OF DIRECTORS

Technicom's senior management team, headed by Jack Dennison, CEO, and Marguerite Devere, controller, is meeting in late December to discuss the anticipated operating results for the year. Much of the discussion focuses on the presentation of the financial statements to the board of directors at its January meeting. Jack has worked with the current board for several years and understands how the board operates and what its preferences are. Marguerite is relatively new to the company, and this will be her first board meeting.

Marguerite has prepared preliminary financial statements and a full complement of analysis ratios, rates, and percentages. Jack asks what the current ratio is, and Marguerite reports that it is 1.8. Jack asks Marguerite, "Is there anything we can do to push this rate up to 2.0? That's what the board prefers to see, and if we can get them past that figure, then we can concentrate on the more important issues for the coming year."

"Jack, we have current assets of $1.8 million and current liabilities of $1.0 million. If we pay off $200,000 of accounts payable, we'll have a 2.0 current ratio. Do you think that will satisfy them?"

"Yes, thanks, Marguerite. That would help. The board usually pays attention only to the current financial statements. You know that we have not hit our sales or net income targets for the year. But we have performed much better than last year. How can we get the board to see this year's performance in that perspective?"

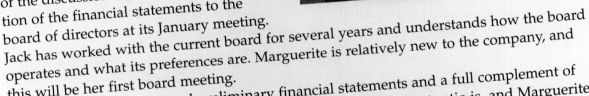

Critical Thinking

1. Why will the $200,000 payment increase the current ratio to 2.0?
2. Is it ethical to manipulate cash payments to improve financial statement analysis?
3. How could comparison with previous years' results be presented on the financial statements?
4. What is your opinion of how the board of directors looks at the financial statements?

FINANCIAL ANALYSIS OBJECTIVES

Financial analysis objectives are determined by a business' characteristics and achievements that are important to the person making the analysis. Information is analyzed to obtain more knowledge about the business' strengths and weaknesses. Common objectives for analyzing financial information are to determine (1) profitability, (2) efficiency, (3) short-term financial strength, and (4) long-term financial strength.

Financial statements, with supporting schedules, are the primary information sources to be analyzed. A statement showing two or more years' information permits a reader to compare year-to-year differences. Financial statements providing information for each of two or more fiscal periods are known as comparative financial statements. Thus, consistent preparation and reporting of financial information are essential. (CONCEPT: Consistent Reporting)

The consistent reporting concept states that the same accounting procedures must be followed in the same way in each accounting period. Some business decisions require a comparison of current financial statements with previous financial statements. If accounting information is recorded and reported differently each accounting period, comparisons from one accounting period to another may not be possible. For example, in one period a business reports $170,000.00 for total operating expenses and in the next period it reports $120,000 as cost of merchandise sold and $50,000 as operating expenses. A user of this information cannot adequately compare the two accounting periods. Therefore, unless a change is necessary to make information more easily understood, accounting information is reported in a consistent way for each accounting period.

RATIO ANALYSIS

a. | **Net Sales** | ÷ | **Net Income** | = | **Stated Ratio** |
$2,000,000.00 ÷ $200,000.00 = 10 times (often stated as 10 to 1 or 10:1)

The stated ratio means net sales is 10 times net income. Another way of stating this ratio is 10:1, or for every $10.00 of net sales, the business earns $1.00 of net income.

b. **Net Income** ÷ **Net Sales** = **Percentage Ratio**
$200,000.00 ÷ $2,000,000.00 = .10 or 10%

Net income is 10% of net sales.

c. **Net Income** ÷ **Net Sales** = **Fractional Ratio**
$200,000.00 ÷ $2,000,000.00 = 1/10

Net income is one-tenth of net sales.

Figure 16-1

A comparison between two numbers showing how many times one number exceeds the other is called a **ratio**. A ratio may be expressed as a stated ratio, percentage, or fraction. For a business with net sales of $2,000,000.00 and net income of $200,000.00, the relationship may be

stated as any of the ratios calculated in Figure 16-1. All three methods of calculating and expressing ratios are correct and essentially the same. The method selected is usually determined by the statement user's preference.

Hamilton Corporation
Comparative Income Statement
For Years Ended December 31, 20-- and 20--

	Current Year	Prior Year	Increase (Decrease) Amount	Increase (Decrease) Percentage*
Operating Revenue:				
Net Sales................................	$4,767,200	$3,633,000	$1,134,200	31.2
Cost of Merchandise Sold:				
Merchandise Inv., Jan. 1..................	$ 423,800	$ 232,300	$ 191,500	82.4
Net Purchases...........................	2,726,900	2,226,900	500,000	22.5
Total Cost of Mdse. Avail. for Sale	$3,150,700	$2,459,200	$ 691,500	28.1
Less Mdse. Inventory, Dec. 31...............	547,900	423,800	124,100	29.3
Cost of Merchandise Sold...................	$2,602,800	$2,035,400	$ 567,400	27.9
Gross Profit on Operations.................	$2,164,400	$1,597,600	$ 566,800	35.5
Operating Expenses:				
Selling Expenses:				
Advertising Expense	$ 46,700	$ 30,100	$ 16,600	55.1
Delivery Expense......................	74,600	55,200	19,400	35.1
Salary Expense—Sales.................	912,400	696,800	215,600	30.9
Supplies Expense	81,600	63,800	17,800	27.9
Other Selling Expenses.................	102,900	78,700	24,200	30.7
Total Selling Expenses	$1,218,200	$ 924,600	$ 293,600	31.8
Administrative Expenses:				
Salary Expense—Administrative	$ 290,200	$ 229,600	$ 60,600	26.4
Uncollectible Accounts Expense..........	27,700	19,100	8,600	45.0
Other Administrative Expenses...........	229,500	189,200	40,300	21.3
Total Administrative Expenses	$ 547,400	$ 437,900	$ 109,500	25.0
Total Operating Expenses..............	$1,765,600	$1,362,500	$ 403,100	29.6
Income from Operations....................	$ 398,800	$ 235,100	$ 163,700	69.6
Other Expenses:				
Interest Expense.......................	$ 62,000	$ 52,000	$ 10,000	19.2
Net Income before Fed. Inc. Tax	$ 336,800	$ 183,100	$ 153,700	83.9
Less Federal Income Tax Exp.	114,500	54,700	59,800	109.3
Net Income after Fed. Inc. Tax.............	$ 222,300	$ 128,400	$ 93,900	73.1

*Rounded to nearest 0.1%

1	Current Year Net Sales	$4,767,200.00
2	− Prior Year Net Sales	3,633,000.00
3	= Increase or Decrease in Net Sales	$1,134,200.00
	÷ Prior Year Net Sales	3,633,000.00
4	= % Increase or Decrease in Net Sales	31.2%

Figure 16-2

F.Y.I.

The prior year is always used as the base year to calculate the percentage increase or decrease.

Trends in a business' financial condition and operating results will not be apparent from a review of a single year's financial information. Comparison of information for two or more fiscal periods is needed to determine whether a business is making satisfactory progress. A comparison of the relationship between one item on a financial statement and the same item on a previous fiscal period's financial statement is called **trend analysis**. Trend analysis is sometimes referred to as horizontal analysis. A comparative income statement with trend analysis is shown in Figure 16-2. The calculation of the favorable trend in net sales is included in the figure.

	Current Year	Prior Year	Increase (Decrease)	
			Amount	Percentage*
Hamilton Corporation **Comparative Statement of Stockholders' Equity** **For Years Ended December 31, 20-- and 20--**				
Capital Stock:				
$10.00 Per Share				
Balance, January 1	$ 500,000	$500,000	$ –0–	0.0
Additional Capital Stock Issued.....................	100,000	–0–	100,000	—
Balance, December 31	$ 600,000	$500,000	$100,000	20.0
Retained Earnings:				
Balance, January 1	$ 349,300	$320,900	$ 28,400	8.9
Net Income after Federal Income Tax	222,300	128,400	93,900	73.1
Total	$ 571,600	$449,300	$122,300	27.2
Less Dividends Declared	120,000	100,000	20,000	20.0
Balance, December 31	$ 451,600	$349,300	$102,300	29.3
Total Stockholders' Equity, December 31...............	$1,051,600	$849,300	$202,300	23.8
Capital Stock Shares Outstanding	60,000	50,000	10,000	20.0

*Rounded to nearest 0.1%

Figure 16-3

The trend in stockholders' equity can be determined from information on Hamilton Company's comparative statement of stockholders' equity, Figure 16-3. Total stockholders' equity increased 23.8% from the prior year. Further review shows the increase in stockholders' equity was caused by an increase in both capital stock and net income. Management believes that the prior year's stockholders' equity was unsatisfactorily low; thus, the trend is favorable.

A percentage increase (decrease) cannot be calculated if the amount divided by is zero. Therefore, a dash (—) is recorded in the percentage column.

PRODUCT LIABILITY

A contingent liability is a liability that may occur if a certain set of future events occur. The amount of the liability is not yet known, and may or may not be reasonably estimated. Product liability claims are examples of contingent liabilities for many companies. Product liability claims result from injuries or other losses caused by a defective product.

Based on the breach of warranty laws, product liability was limited to claims by the buyer of a product against the seller. However, most courts now apply strict liability to product liability claims. Under strict liability, manufacturers and whole-salers, as well as retailers, can be held responsible for defective products.

Corporations are required to report certain contingent liabilities in their financial statements. If the amount of the contingent liability can be reasonably estimated, the estimated amount is reported in the liabilities section of the balance sheet. If the amount cannot be reasonably estimated, the contingent liability is disclosed in the notes to the financial statements.

LEGAL ISSUES IN ACCOUNTING

Hamilton Corporation
Comparative Balance Sheet
December 31, 20-- and 20--

	Current Year	Prior Year	Increase (Decrease) Amount	Percentage*
ASSETS				
Current Assets:				
Cash	$ 206,100	$ 104,300	$101,800	97.6
Accounts Receivable (net)............	474,000	569,200	(95,200)	(16.7)
Merchandise Inventory.............	547,900	423,800	124,100	29.3
Other Current Assets	26,100	21,300	4,800	22.5
Total Current Assets	$1,254,100	$1,118,600	$135,500	12.1
Total Plant Assets (net)............	813,600	641,100	172,500	26.9
Total Assets	$2,067,700	$1,759,700	$308,000	17.5
LIABILITIES				
Current Liabilities:				
Notes Payable	$ 222,200	$ 241,600	$ (19,400)	(8.0)
Interest Payable	12,900	20,700	(7,800)	(37.7)
Accounts Payable	344,300	413,300	(69,000)	(16.7)
Federal Income Tax Payable............	11,300	3,300	8,000	242.4
Other Current Liabilities	5,400	6,500	(1,100)	(16.9)
Total Current Liabilities	$ 596,100	$ 685,400	$ (89,300)	(13.0)
Long-Term Liability:				
Mortgage Payable................	$ 420,000	$ 225,000	$195,000	86.7
Total Liabilities	$1,016,100	$ 910,400	$105,700	11.6
STOCKHOLDERS' EQUITY				
Capital Stock	$ 600,000	$ 500,000	$100,000	20.0
Retained Earnings	451,600	349,300	102,300	29.3
Total Stockholders' Equity	$1,051,600	$ 849,300	$202,300	23.8
Total Liabilities and Stockholders' Equity	$2,067,700	$1,759,700	$308,000	17.5

*Rounded to nearest 0.1%

Figure 16-4

Changes in Hamilton's balance sheet accounts are shown in Figure 16-4. Accounts Receivable and Plant Assets are reported at book value. Information on this statement shows that total assets increased 17.5% during the current year. This increase was caused by an 11.6% increase in total liabilities and a 23.8% increase in total stockholders' equity. This trend is considered favorable because assets are increasing and the increase came more from the significant increase in stockholders' equity than the increase in liabilities.

Comparative financial statements report a business' current and past activity. However, most financial statement readers are also interested in how well a business will do in the future. Trend analysis is one method of financial analysis used to help predict how well a busi-

ness will perform in the future. *(CONCEPT: Adequate Disclosure)* Trend analysis is often performed using financial statements for a three-to-five year period. Lenders and investors are very interested in how well a business will perform in the long term. Favorable trends over a period of several years often indicate that management is making good decisions.

Financial statements are beneficial only to the extent that they are analyzed and used by the corporation to measure progress.

Hamilton Corporation
Comparative Income Statement
For Years Ended December 31, 20-- and 20--

	Current Year		Prior Year	
	Amount	Percentage*	Amount	Percentage*
Operating Revenue:				
Net Sales	$4,767,200	100.0	$3,633,000	100.0
Cost of Merchandise Sold:				
Merchandise Inv., Jan. 1	$ 423,800	8.9	$ 232,300	6.4
Net Purchases	2,726,900	57.2	2,226,900	61.3
Total Cost of Mdse. Avail. for Sale.	$3,150,700	66.1	$2,459,200	67.7
Less Mdse. Inventory, Dec. 31	547,900	11.5	423,800	11.7
Cost of Merchandise Sold	$2,602,800	54.6	$2,035,400	56.0
Gross Profit on Operations	$2,164,400	45.4	$1,597,600	44.0
Operating Expenses:				
Selling Expenses:				
Advertising Expense.	$ 46,700	1.0	$ 30,100	0.8
Delivery Expense	74,600	1.6	55,200	1.5
Salary Expense—Sales.	912,400	19.1	696,800	19.2
Supplies Expense	81,600	1.7	63,800	1.8
Other Selling Expenses	102,900	2.2	78,700	2.2
Total Selling Expenses	$1,218,200	25.6	$ 924,600	25.5
Administrative Expenses:				
Salary Expense—Administrative	$ 290,200	6.1	$ 229,600	6.3
Uncollectible Accounts Expense	27,700	0.6	19,100	0.5
Other Administrative Expenses	229,500	4.8	189,200	5.2
Total Administrative Expenses	$ 547,400	11.5	$ 437,900	12.1
Total Operating Expenses	$1,765,600	37.0	$1,362,500	37.5
Income from Operations	$ 398,800	8.4	$ 235,100	6.5
Other Expenses:				
Interest Expense	$ 62,000	1.3	$ 52,000	1.4
Net Income before Fed. Inc. Tax	$ 336,800	7.1	$ 183,100	5.0
Less Federal Income Tax Exp.	114,500	2.4	54,700	1.5
Net Income after Fed. Inc. Tax	$ 222,300	4.7	$ 128,400	3.5

*Rounded to nearest 0.1%.
Percentage totals may not equal sum of parts because of rounding.

Figure 16-5

The percentage relationship between one financial statement item and the total that includes that item is known as a component percentage. Component percentage analysis is also referred to as vertical analysis. Component percentages for items on an income statement are normally calculated as a percentage of net sales. The component percentage is shown in a separate percentage column. Hamilton's income statement with component percentages is shown in Figure 16-5. This statement is similar to the one shown for MasterSport in Chapter 4 and for LampLight in Chapter 13.

Component percentages on comparative statements show changes in a specific item from year to year. For example, Hamilton's cost of merchandise sold decreased from 56.0% to 54.6% of net sales. These percentages show a favorable trend since the cost of merchandise sold took a smaller part of each sales dollar in the current year. Similar comparisons can be made for each item on the comparative income statement. The cause of significant unfavorable changes should be investigated so that corrective action can be taken.

Hamilton Corporation
Comparative Statement of Stockholders' Equity
For Years Ended December 31, 20-- and 20--

	Current Year		Prior Year	
	Amount	Percentage*	Amount	Percentage*
Capital Stock:				
$10.00 Per Share				
Balance, January 1	$ 500,000	47.5	$500,000	58.9
Additional Capital Stock Issued	100,000	9.5	0	0.0
Balance, December 31	$ 600,000	57.1	$500,000	58.9
Retained Earnings:				
Balance, January 1	$ 349,300	33.2	$320,900	37.8
Net Income after Federal Income Tax	222,300	21.1	128,400	15.1
Total	$ 571,600	54.4	$449,300	52.9
Less Dividends Declared	120,000	11.4	100,000	11.8
Balance, December 31	$ 451,600	42.9	$349,300	41.1
Total Stockholders' Equity, December 31	$1,051,600	100.0	$849,300	100.0
Capital Stock Shares Outstanding	60,000		50,000	

*Rounded to nearest 0.1%.
Percentage totals may not equal sum of parts because of rounding.

Figure 16-6

Component percentages for items on a comparative statement of stockholders' equity are normally calculated as a percentage of total stockholders' equity. As shown in Figure 16-6, capital stock represents 57.1% of Hamilton's stockholders' equity for the current year. The remaining 42.9% is retained earnings. Respective percentages for the prior year are 58.9% and 41.1%. Thus, little change has occurred in the component makeup of total equity. However, the percentage of dividends declared decreased slightly from 11.8% to 11.4%, an unfavorable trend for stockholders.

Acceptable Levels of Financial Performance

For financial analysis to be useful, a company must define acceptable levels of performance for each type of analysis. For example, Wiseman Grocery considers a component percentage of 3.0% for income from operations to be very good. However, Mitchell Manufacturing Co. considers a 12.0% component percentage for income from operations the minimum acceptable result. The difference is due to the different financial characteristics of the two businesses.

The grocery company has a low investment in plant assets and sells its inventory quickly. The manufacturing company has a high investment in plant assets and holds its inventory much longer. The manufacturing company's larger investment per sales dollar means that the company must earn a higher rate on sales. Each company's management team must determine the acceptable levels of performance for each financial analysis made.

Many businesses use two major guides to determine acceptable levels of performance: (1) prior company performance and (2) comparison with published trade performance standards.

Other sources of performance guides include (1) financial and credit-reporting companies such as Dun and Bradstreet, (2) the company's planned financial objectives (budget schedules), (3) current interest rates that could be earned by investing capital elsewhere, and (4) financial information available on the Internet.

Each company's management team should determine the acceptable performance level for each financial analysis made by the company.

Hamilton Corporation
Comparative Balance Sheet
December 31, 20-- and 20--

	Current Year		Prior Year	
	Amount	**Percentage***	**Amount**	**Percentage***
ASSETS				
Current Assets:				
Cash	$ 206,100	10.0	$ 104,300	5.9
Accounts Receivable (book value)	474,000	22.9	569,200	32.3
Merchandise Inventory	547,900	26.5	423,800	24.1
Other Current Assets	26,100	1.3	21,300	1.2
Total Current Assets	$1,254,100	60.7	$1,118,600	63.6
Total Plant Assets (book value)	813,600	39.3	641,100	36.4
Total Assets	$2,067,700	100.0	$1,759,700	100.0
LIABILITIES				
Current Liabilities:				
Notes Payable	$ 222,200	10.7	$ 241,600	13.7
Interest Payable	12,900	0.6	20,700	1.2
Accounts Payable	344,300	16.7	413,300	23.5
Federal Income Tax Payable	11,300	0.5	3,300	0.2
Other Current Liabilities	5,400	0.3	6,500	0.4
Total Current Liabilities	$ 596,100	28.8	$ 685,400	38.9
Long-Term Liability:				
Mortgage Payable	$ 420,000	20.3	$ 225,000	12.8
Total Liabilities	$1,016,100	49.1	$ 910,400	51.7
STOCKHOLDERS' EQUITY				
Capital Stock	$ 600,000	29.0	$ 500,000	28.4
Retained Earnings	451,600	21.8	349,300	19.8
Total Stockholders' Equity	$1,051,600	50.9	$ 849,300	48.3
Total Liabilities and Stockholders' Equity	$2,067,700	100.0	$1,759,700	100.0

*Rounded to nearest 0.1%.
Percentage totals may not equal sum of parts because of rounding.

Figure 16-7

Component percentages for asset amounts on a comparative balance sheet are normally calculated as a percentage of total assets. Liabilities and stockholders' equity amounts are calculated as a percentage of total liabilities and stockholders' equity. Information on Hamilton's comparative balance sheet, Figure 16-7, shows that current liabilities were 28.8% of total liabilities and stockholders' equity, down from 38.9% in the prior year.

Since current liabilities were at a high percentage in the prior year, Hamilton considers the reduction from 38.9% to 28.8% as a very favorable change. Hamilton's investors and lenders would also be pleased with this result. Similar comparisons can be made for each item on the comparative balance sheet.

F.Y.I.

An unfavorable ratio in one year may be balanced by previous actual positive results and future expected positive results. The trend in a ratio may be more important than the ratio for a particular year.

TERMS REVIEW

ratio

trend analysis

AUDIT YOUR UNDERSTANDING

1. Why do managers, banks, lending agencies, owners, and potential owners need the financial information for a business?

2. What are four common objectives for analyzing a business' financial information?

3. Which accounting concept is being applied when comparative financial statements are prepared to provide useful information for statement users?

4. What two major guides do businesses use to determine acceptable levels of performance?

WORK TOGETHER

Analyzing comparative financial statements

Baycom Corporation's comparative income statement is provided in the *Working Papers*. Your instructor will guide you through the following examples.

5. Complete the partial income statement using trend analysis. Round percentage calculations to the nearest 0.1%.

6. Complete the income statement using component percentage analysis. Round percentage calculations to the nearest 0.1%.

ON YOUR OWN

Analyzing comparative financial statements

Baycom Corporation's comparative balance sheet is provided in the *Working Papers*. Work independently to complete the following problem.

7. Complete the comparative balance sheet using trend analysis. Round percentage calculations to the nearest 0.1%.

8. Complete the balance sheet using component percentage analysis. Round percentage calculations to the nearest 0.1%.

EARNINGS PERFORMANCE ANALYSIS

The amount and consistency of earnings are important measures of a business' success. The earnings of a business must be satisfactory to continue operations. (CONCEPT: Going Concern) Consequently, managers, owners, and creditors are interested in an analysis of earnings performance. Hamilton calculates five earnings performance ratios for the two most recent years. (1) Rate earned on average total assets. (2) Rate earned on average stockholders equity. (3) Rate earned on net sales. (4) Earnings per share. (5) Price-earnings ratio.

RATE EARNED ON AVERAGE TOTAL ASSETS

Hamilton Corporation
Comparative Balance Sheet
December 31, 20-- and 20--

	Current Year		Prior Year	
	Amount	Percentage*	Amount	Percentage*
ASSETS				
Current Assets:				
Cash	$ 206,100	10.0	$ 104,300	5.9
Accounts Receivable (book value)	474,000	22.9	569,200	32.3
Merchandise Inventory	547,900	26.5	423,800	24.1
Other Current Assets	26,100	1.3	21,300	1.2
Total Current Assets	$1,254,100	60.7	$1,118,600	63.6
Total Plant Assets (book value)	813,600	39.3	641,100	36.4
Total Assets	$2,067,700	100.0	$1,759,700	100.0

*Rounded to nearest 0.1%.

1 → January 1 Total Assets + December 31 Total Assets ÷ 2 = Average Total Assets

(1,759,700.00 + $2,067,700.00 ÷ 2 = $1,913,700.00

2 → Net Income after Federal Income Tax ÷ Average Total Assets = Rate Earned on Average Total Assets

$222,300.00 ÷ $1,913,700.00 = 11.6%

Hamilton Corporation
Comparative Income Statement
For Years Ended December 31, 20-- and 20--

	Current Year		Prior Year	
	Amount	Percentage*	Amount	Percentage*
Other Expenses:				
Interest Expense	$ 62,000	1.3	$ 52,000	1.4
Net Income before Fed. Inc. Tax	$ 336,800	7.1	$ 183,100	5.0
Less Federal Income Tax Exp.	114,500	2.4	54,700	1.5
Net Income after Fed. Inc. Tax	$ 222,300	4.7	$ 128,400	3.5

*Rounded to nearest 0.1%.

Figure 16-8

A business uses its assets to earn net income. If a business uses all assets as efficiently as possible, it should earn the best possible net income. The rate found by dividing net income after federal income tax by average total assets is known as the rate earned on average total assets. The rate earned on average total assets shows how well a business is using its assets to earn net income. Hamilton's rate of return on average total assets is calculated as shown in Figure 16-8 using income statement and balance sheet information.

S T E P S

Calculating the rate of return on average total assets

1. Calculate average total assets. Average total assets is the average amount of assets held during a year.
   a. Add January 1 total assets and December 31 total assets. (Total assets for January 1 are the same as the total assets on the prior year's December 31 balance sheet.)
   b. Divide the total by 2.
2. Divide net income after federal income taxes by average total assets to determine the rate earned on average total assets.

An 11.6% rate earned on average total assets means that for each $1.00 of assets, the business earned 11.6 cents. A table comparing this result to the rate for the prior year is shown below. (Some information for the prior year is taken from financial statements that are not illustrated.)

	Current Year	Prior Year
Net Income after Federal Income Tax	$ 222,300.00	$ 128,400.00
January 1 Total Assets	1,759,700.00	1,437,600.00
December 31 Total Assets	2,067,700.00	1,759,700.00
Average Total Assets	1,913,700.00	1,598,650.00
Rate Earned on Average Total Assets	11.6%	8.0%

Hamilton compares this rate to rates of return on alternative investments. Hamilton's goal is to earn a rate of return that is at least as high as other types of investments. For example, if Hamilton can earn more by placing extra cash in government bonds, the company is not meeting its earnings goal.

Investment sources available to Hamilton are earning 10.0%. Although the prior year's investments fell below this goal, the trend in the rate earned improved significantly from 8.0% to 11.6%. Therefore, Hamilton believes that a rate earned on total assets of 11.6% is satisfactory.

Publications such as Dun and Bradstreet *list various ratios for a variety of businesses.*

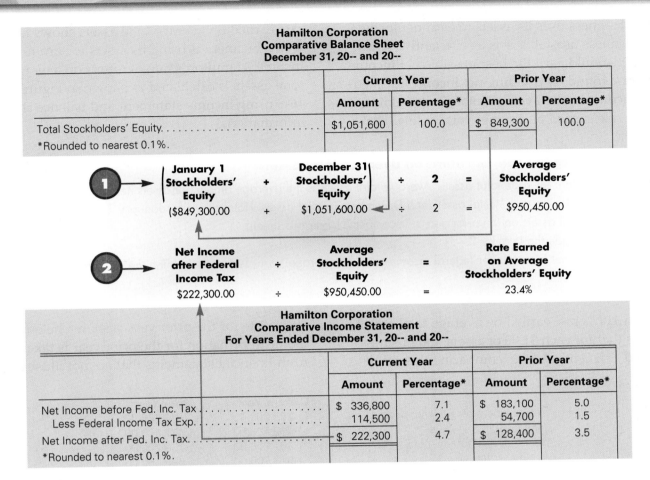

Figure 16-9

Investors compare the rate earned on stockholders' equity for several businesses to determine the best investment. Hamilton's rate earned on average stockholders' equity is calculated as shown in Figure 16-9.

The following table compares the current year's rate to the rate for the prior year. (Some information for the prior year is taken from financial statements that are not illustrated.)

Hamilton's rate earned fell well below industry standards in the prior year. However, its rate of earnings has increased significantly from 15.4% to 23.4%. Based on the trend and a

S T E P S Calculating the rate of return on average stockholders' equity

1. Calculate average stockholders' equity. (January 1 total stockholders' equity is the same as the total stockholders' equity on the prior year's December 31 balance sheet.)

2. Divide net income after federal income taxes by average total stockholders' equity to determine the rate earned on average total assets.

comparison with industry standards, Hamilton achieved a satisfactory rate earned on average stockholders' equity.

	Current Year	Prior Year	Industry Standard (2 yrs.)
Net Income after Federal Income Tax	$ 222,300.00	$128,400.00	
January 1 Stockholders' Equity	849,300.00	820,900.00	
December 31 Stockholders' Equity	1,051,600.00	849,300.00	
Average Stockholders' Equity	950,450.00	835,100.00	
Rate Earned on Average Stockholders' Equity	23.4%	15.4%	20%

Hamilton Corporation Comparative Income Statement For Years Ended December 31, 20-- and 20--				
	Current Year		Prior Year	
	Amount	Percentage*	Amount	Percentage*
Operating Revenue:				
Net Sales	$4,767,200	100.0	$3,633,000	100.0
Other Expenses:				
Interest Expense	$ 62,000	1.3	$ 52,000	1.4
Net Income before Fed. Inc. Tax	$ 336,800	7.1	$ 183,100	5.0
Less Federal Income Tax Exp.	114,500	2.4	54,700	1.5
Net Income after Fed. Inc. Tax	$ 222,300	4.7	$ 128,400	3.5
*Rounded to nearest 0.1%.				

1 → **Net Income after Federal Income Tax** ÷ **Net Sales** = **Rate Earned on Net Sales**

$222,300.00 ÷ $4,767,200.00 = 4.7%

Figure 16-10

A business that carefully controls costs should earn a consistent rate on net sales from year to year. The rate found by dividing net income after federal income tax by net sales is called the **rate earned on net sales**. However, if costs suddenly change, the rate earned on net sales also changes.

Hamilton's rate earned on net sales for the current year is calculated as shown in Figure 16-10 using information from the income statement.

The following table compares the current rate to the rate from the prior year.

	Current Year	Prior Year
Net Income after Federal Income Tax	$ 222,300.00	$ 128,400.00
Net Sales	4,767,200.00	3,633,000.00
Rate Earned on Net Sales	4.7%	3.5%

The component percentage for net income after federal income tax, Figure 16-10, is the same percentage as the rate earned on net sales. In both calculations, net income is calculated as a percentage of net sales.

When determining an acceptable rate earned on net sales, Hamilton considers what is normal for similar businesses and the company's own past experience. Businesses similar to Hamilton have been earning about a 4.0% rate on net sales for the last two or three years. Based on a comparison of similar businesses, Hamilton's rate earned on net sales of 3.5% in the prior year was unsatisfactory. The trend in rate earned increased to 4.7% in the current year, a satisfac-

tory rate. This trend should be watched closely for any future declines. When the rate earned on net sales declines, the company must increase sales or reduce costs to maintain an acceptable rate.

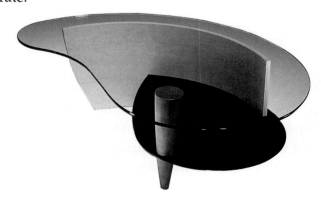

Hamilton Corporation
Comparative Income Statement
For Years Ended December 31, 20-- and 20--

	Current Year		Prior Year	
	Amount	Percentage*	Amount	Percentage*
Net Income before Fed. Inc. Tax	$ 336,800	7.1	$ 183,100	5.0
Less Federal Income Tax Exp.	114,500	2.4	54,700	1.5
Net Income after Fed. Inc. Tax.	$ 222,300	4.7	$ 128,400	3.5
*Rounded to nearest 0.1%.				

Hamilton Corporation
Comparative Balance Sheet
December 31, 20-- and 20--

	Current Year		Prior Year	
	Amount	Percentage*	Amount	Percentage*
Total Stockholders' Equity.	$1,051,600	100.0	$ 849,300	100.0
Capital Stock Shares Outstanding	60,000		50,000	
*Rounded to nearest 0.1%.				

1 → | Net Income after Federal Income Tax | ÷ | Shares of Capital Stock Outstanding | = | Earnings per Share |
| $222,300.00 | ÷ | 60,000 | = | $3.71 |

Figure 16-11

The amount of net income earned on one share of common stock during a fiscal period is known as earnings per share. Stockholders and management frequently use earnings per share as a measure of success. As earnings per share increase, more people become interested in buying stock. This demand for stock causes stock prices to go up. The company then finds it easier to issue stock or borrow money.

Hamilton's earnings per share for the current year is calculated as shown in Figure 16-11 using information from the income statement and statement of stockholders' equity.

The earnings per share is calculated for the current and prior years as shown below.

	Current Year	Prior Year
Net Income after Federal Income Tax	$222,300.00	$128,400.00
Shares of Capital Stock Outstanding	60,000	50,000
Earnings Per Share	$3.71	$2.57

Increases in earnings per share signal stockholders that the company is continuing to increase the net income earned for each share. Hamilton knows that a positive trend is important to the company. Earnings per share increased significantly from $2.57 to $3.71, a very favorable trend.

Earnings per share is one of the most widely recognized financial ratios.

Market Price per share	÷	Earnings per Share	=	Price-Earnings Ratio
$43.50	÷	$3.71	=	11.7 times

Figure 16-12

Investors want to buy stock in companies that will earn a reasonable return on their investment. The relationship between the market value per share of stock and the earnings per share is known as the price-earnings ratio. As described in Chapter 13, the price-earnings ratio of a company's stock relates profitability to the amount that the investors currently pay for the stock. The price-earnings ratio is usually expressed as a stated ratio.

Hamilton's capital stock sold for $43.50 per share on December 31 of the current year. Hamilton's price-earnings ratio for the current year is calculated as shown in Figure 16-12.

The following price-earnings ratios are calculated for the current and prior years:

	Current Year	Prior Year
Market Price per Share	$43.50	$24.50
Earnings per Share	3.71	2.57
Price-Earnings Ratio	11.7 times	9.5 times

The market price of a share of stock is determined by the amount that investors are willing to pay for it. If investors think that a company's profitability is increasing, they are usually willing to pay more for the stock. Thus, the market price of a company's stock is influenced strongly by what potential investors think the company's earnings will be in the future. Hamilton's price-earnings ratio increased from 9.5 to 11.7. This change indicates that investors considered the stock more valuable and were willing to pay more for the stock per dollar earned by the corporation in the current year. This increased demand is a favorable trend for Hamilton.

INTERNATIONAL MAIL

When sending documents internationally, there are three categories of mail:

1. LC mail (initials for the French *lettres* and *cartes postale*—meaning "letters" and "postcards"). LC mail consists mainly of letters, letter packages, and postcards.
2. AO mail (initials for the French *Autres Objets*—meaning "other things"). AO mail usually consists of items considered printed materials, such as books, periodicals, and braille publications. This service is usually by ship and is slower than airmail.
3. CP mail (initials for the French *par Colis Postal*—meaning "by parcel

post"). CP mail is the equivalent of American parcel post. CP mail resembles fourth class domestic mail. It is the only class of mail that can be insured. This service is also usually by ship.

Special services are also offered.

Required:

Contact the local United States Postal Service or another mail service to obtain information about:
1. Express mail.
2. International Priority Airmail.
3. Registered mail.

Write a brief report about your findings.

GLOBAL PERSPECTIVE

The profitability and continued growth of a business are influenced by how efficiently the business utilizes its assets. The operating cycle of a merchandising business consists of three phases. (1) Purchase merchandise. (2) Sell merchandise, frequently on account. (3) Collect the accounts receivable. Much of a business' assets are in accounts receivable and merchandise inventory. The faster a business can convert these assets to cash and begin another operating cycle, the more efficient and profitable the business will be.

ACCOUNTS RECEIVABLE TURNOVER RATIO

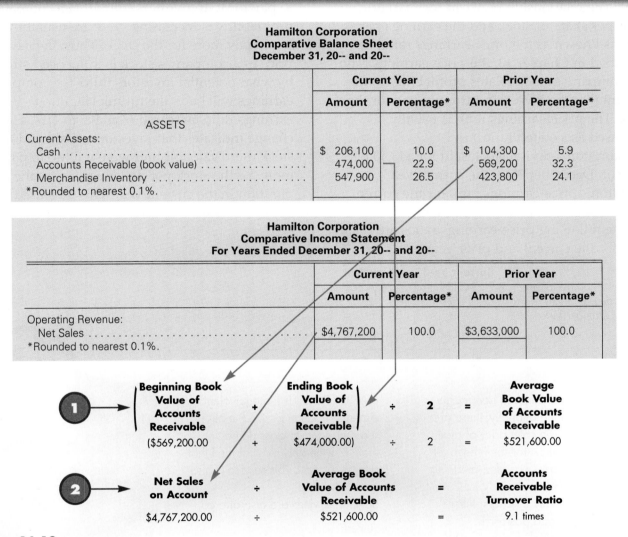

Hamilton Corporation
Comparative Balance Sheet
December 31, 20-- and 20--

	Current Year		Prior Year	
	Amount	Percentage*	Amount	Percentage*
ASSETS				
Current Assets:				
Cash	$ 206,100	10.0	$ 104,300	5.9
Accounts Receivable (book value)	474,000	22.9	569,200	32.3
Merchandise Inventory	547,900	26.5	423,800	24.1
*Rounded to nearest 0.1%.				

Hamilton Corporation
Comparative Income Statement
For Years Ended December 31, 20-- and 20--

	Current Year		Prior Year	
	Amount	Percentage*	Amount	Percentage*
Operating Revenue:				
Net Sales	$4,767,200	100.0	$3,633,000	100.0
*Rounded to nearest 0.1%.				

1 Beginning Book Value of Accounts Receivable + Ending Book Value of Accounts Receivable ÷ 2 = Average Book Value of Accounts Receivable

($569,200.00 + $474,000.00) ÷ 2 = $521,600.00

2 Net Sales on Account ÷ Average Book Value of Accounts Receivable = Accounts Receivable Turnover Ratio

$4,767,200.00 ÷ $521,600.00 = 9.1 times

Figure 16-13

A business accepts accounts receivable to encourage sales. However, the earnings process is not complete until the business receives cash for sales on account. Thus, an efficient company closely monitors the length of time required to collect its receivables. The number of times the average amount of accounts receivable is collected annually is known as the accounts receivable turnover ratio. This ratio monitors a business' accounts receivable collection efficiency.

Hamilton's accounts receivable turnover ratio for the current year is calculated as shown in Figure 16-13, using the information from the balance sheet and income statement.

Hamilton's turnover ratio indicates that accounts are being collected 9.1 times a year. The average number of days for customers to pay their accounts is calculated:

Days in Year	÷	Accounts Receivable Turnover Ratio	=	Average Number of Days for Payment
365	÷	9.1	=	40 days

The accounts receivable turnover ratio for the prior year was 7.0 times. The average number of days for payment was 52 days. Hamilton's credit terms are n/30. Thus, the company's goal is to collect accounts receivable in 30 days or less. Neither year's results meet that goal. However, the ratio improved from 7.0 to 9.1. This favorable trend means the company is becoming more efficient in its collection efforts by reducing collection of its accounts receivable from 52 to 40 days.

MERCHANDISE INVENTORY TURNOVER RATIO

Step 1:	January 1 Merchandise Inventory	+	December 31 Merchandise Inventory	÷	2	=	Average Merchandise Inventory
	($423,800.00	+	$547,900.00	÷	2	=	$485,850.00

Step 2:	Cost of Merchandise Sold	÷	Average Merchandise Inventory	=	Merchandise Inventory Turnover Ratio
	$2,602,800.00	÷	$485,850.00	=	5.4 times

Figure 16-14

A company earns income when it sells merchandise. The faster it sells its merchandise inventory, the more efficient and generally more profitable the business. The number of times the average amount of merchandise inventory is sold annually is known as the merchandise inventory turnover ratio. This ratio can be used to monitor merchandise inventory efficiency.

Hamilton's merchandise inventory turnover ratio is calculated as shown in Figure 16-14, using information from the income statement (Figure 16-5). The turnover ratio of 5.4 indicates that the inventory is being sold 5.4 times in a year. The average number of days' sales in merchandise inventory is 68 days (365 days ÷ 5.4 turnover ratio = 68 days). Last year, Hamilton had a merchandise turnover ratio of 6.2 times, resulting in an average number of days' sales in merchandise inventory of 59 days.

An optimum merchandise inventory turnover ratio is determined by two factors. (1) Amount of sales. (2) Number of days needed to replenish inventory. Previous experience indicates that Hamilton needs to maintain an inventory turnover ratio of about 6.0. This 6.0 ratio equates to an average number of days' sales in merchandise inventory of 61 days. Last year, Hamilton's days' sales in inventory was 59 days. This lower than desired level of inventory resulted in lost sales because some items were out of stock before new inventory arrived. However, the current year inventory level, 68 days, is satisfactory.

TERM REVIEW

rate earned on net sales

WORK TOGETHER

Calculating earnings performance and efficiency analysis ratios

Information from TeleNet Corporation's financial statements for the current year is provided in the *Working Papers*. Your instructor will guide you through the following examples.

4. Calculate the following earnings performance and efficiency ratios for the current year. Round percentage calculations to the nearest 0.1%, dollar amounts to the nearest $.01, and the price-earnings ratio to the nearest .1 (tenth).
   a. Rate earned on average total assets
   b. Rate earned on average stockholders' equity
   c. Rate earned on net sales
   d. Earnings per share
   e. Price-earnings ratio
   f. Accounts receivable turnover ratio
   g. Average number of days for accounts receivable payment
   h. Merchandise inventory turnover ratio
   i. Average number of days' sales in merchandise inventory

ON YOUR OWN

Calculating earnings performance and efficiency analysis ratios

Information from Razure Adventures Company's financial statements for the current year are provided in the *Working Papers*. Work independently to complete the following problem.

5. Calculate the following earnings performance and efficiency ratios for the current year. Round percentage calculations to the nearest 0.1%, dollar amounts to the nearest $.01, and the price-earnings ratio to the nearest .1 (tenth).
   a. Rate earned on average total assets
   b. Rate earned on average stockholders' equity
   c. Rate earned on net sales
   d. Earnings per share
   e. Price-earnings ratio
   f. Accounts receivable turnover ratio
   g. Average number of days for accounts receivable payment
   h. Merchandise inventory turnover ratio
   i. Average number of days' sales in merchandise inventory

16-3 Calculating Financial Strength Analysis

SHORT-TERM FINANCIAL STRENGTH ANALYSIS

A successful business needs adequate capital. A business gets capital from two sources. (1) Owners' investments and retained earnings. (2) Loans. Some capital, either owned or borrowed, is to be used for long periods of time. Some capital is borrowed for short periods of time. A business can invest capital in assets (such as equipment and buildings) for long periods of time. A business also invests in assets (such as merchandise) that will be converted back to cash in a short period of time. Short-term assets are referred to as current assets because they are consumed in a business' daily activities or exchanged for cash. Long-term assets are referred to as plant assets and are used over a long period of time.

Hamilton uses three measures to analyze short-term financial strength. (1) Working capital. (2) Current ratio. (3) Acid-test ratio.

WORKING CAPITAL

	Total Current Assets	−	Total Current Liabilities	=	Working Capital
Current Year	$1,254,100.00	−	$596,100.00	=	$658,000.00
Prior Year	$1,118,600.00	−	$685,400.00	=	$433,200.00

Figure 16-15

The amount of total current assets less total current liabilities is called **working capital**. Working capital, stated in dollars, is the amount of current assets available to the business after current liabilities are paid. It is not the amount of cash available to the business. The amount of working capital can be compared from year to year to look for a trend. However, working capital cannot be used easily to compare Hamilton with other companies in the industry.

Hamilton's working capital for December 31 of the current year and December 31 of the prior year is calculated as shown in Figure 16-15, using information from the balance sheet (Figure 16-7).

Hamilton's working capital increased from $433,200.00 to $658,000.00, a favorable trend. A review of other financial information suggests that part of the reason for the prior year's lower working capital was the company's fast expansion. Frequently, when a business expands rapidly, it borrows money to buy more inventory and pay more employees. The rate of increased costs for merchandise and payroll may be initially greater than the rate of increase in sales and net income. In the current year, Hamilton lowered its current liabilities by issuing more capital stock and increasing long-term liabilities.

The **Wall Street Journal** *and many local newspapers report price-earnings ratios in their stock quotations.*

	Total Current Assets	÷	Total Current Liabilities	=	Current Ratio
Current Year	$1,254,100.00	÷	$596,100.00	=	2.1 times
Prior Year	$1,118,600.00	÷	$685,400.00	=	1.6 times

Figure 16-16

A ratio that shows the numeric relationship of current assets to current liabilities is called the **current ratio**. Normally, current liabilities are expected to be paid from cash on hand plus cash soon to be received from other current assets.

The current ratio is calculated by dividing total current assets by total current liabilities. Hamilton's current ratio for the current year and the prior year are calculated as shown in Figure 16-16, using information from the balance sheet.

The current ratio of 2.1 means that Hamilton owns $2.10 in current assets for each $1.00 needed to pay current liabilities.

Businesses similar to Hamilton try to maintain a current ratio of 2.0 times. Industry experience has shown that a business with a current ratio of less than 2.0 times has difficulty raising ready cash to pay current liabilities on time. At the same time, industry experience shows that a current ratio can be too high. If the current ratio is 3.0 times or higher, the business has more capital invested in current assets than is needed to run the business.

In the prior year, Hamilton's current ratio, 1.6, was significantly below the desired ratio. However, the current year's ratio, 2.1, is at a satisfactory level. A review of financial information suggests that part of the reason for the prior year's lower current ratio was the company's fast expansion. In the current year, Hamilton lowered its current liabilities by issuing more capital stock and increasing long-term liabilities.

	Total Quick Assets (Cash + Accounts Receivable)	÷	Total Current Liabilities	=	Acid-Test Ratio
Current Year	($206,100.00 + $474,000.00)	÷	$596,100.00	=	1.1 times
Prior Year	($104,300.00 + $569,200.00)	÷	$685,400.00	=	1.0 times

Figure 16-17

Those current assets that are cash or that can be quickly turned into cash are called **quick assets**. Quick assets include cash, accounts receivable, and marketable securities, but not merchandise inventory or prepaid expenses. A ratio that shows the numeric relationship of quick assets to current liabilities is called the **acid-test ratio**. This ratio shows the ability of a business to pay all current liabilities almost immediately if necessary.

Hamilton's acid-test ratio for the current year and prior year is calculated as shown in Figure 16-17. The current year's ratio of 1.1 indicates that for each $1.00 needed to pay current liabilities, Hamilton has $1.10 available in quick assets. For companies similar to Hamilton, the desired industry standard for an acid-test ratio is between 0.9 and 1.3.

Hamilton's acid-test ratio has increased from 1.0 to 1.1, a favorable trend. Part of the cash received from the sale of capital stock and the increase in long-term liabilities was used to reduce the level of current liabilities and improve the acid-test ratio.

Businesses that are successful and are able to continue operating through both strong and weak economic periods usually have long-term financial strength. Long-term financial strength requires a balance between stockholders' capital and borrowed capital. A profitable business can be even more profitable by using borrowed capital wisely. However, borrowed capital must be repaid with interest. Continuing operation of a business with a large percentage of borrowed capital may be jeopardized if net income declines and it cannot make loan payments. Also, creditors are reluctant to loan additional money to companies with a high level of liabilities. A well-managed company monitors its long-term financial strength to ensure that a reasonable balance between stockholders' capital and borrowed capital is maintained.

Hamilton uses three measures to analyze long-term financial strength: (1) debt ratio, (2) equity ratio, and (3) equity per share.

DEBT RATIO

	Total Liabilities	÷	Total Assets	=	Debt Ratio
Current Year	$1,016,100.00	÷	$2,067,700.00	=	49.1%
Prior Year	$ 910,400.00	÷	$1,759,700.00	=	51.7%

Figure 16-18

The ratio found by dividing total liabilities by total assets is called the **debt ratio**. This ratio shows the percentage of assets that are financed with borrowed capital (liabilities).

Hamilton's debt ratio for the current year and the prior year are calculated as shown in Figure 16-18, using information from the balance sheet (Figure 16-7).

The current year ratio, 49.1%, indicates that for each $1.00 of assets owned by Hamilton, the company has borrowed 49.1 cents.

The average debt ratio for companies similar to Hamilton is 43.0%. Hamilton's ratios are above the industry average, an unfavorable condition. Rapid growth over the past two or three years, financed primarily through borrowed capital, has caused the unfavorable liabilities level. However, the additional capital stock that Hamilton issued this year helped lower the debt ratio from 51.7% to 49.1%. The company should consider issuing more capital stock to reduce the total liabilities to an industry average of 43.0%.

	Total Stockholders' Equity	÷	Total Assets	=	Equity Ratio
Current Year	$1,051,600.00	÷	$2,067,700.00	=	50.9%
Prior Year	$ 849,300.00	÷	$1,759,700.00	=	48.3%

Figure 16-19

The ratio found by dividing stockholders' equity by total assets is called the **equity ratio**. This ratio shows the percentage of assets that are provided by stockholders' equity.

Hamilton's equity ratio for the current year and the prior year are calculated as shown in Figure 16-19, using information from the statement of stockholders' equity (Figure 16-6) and the balance sheet (Figure 16-7).

Hamilton's ratio for the current year, 50.9%, indicates that for each $1.00 of assets owned by the company, 50.9 cents' worth was acquired with stockholders' capital. The average equity ratio for companies similar to Hamilton is 57.0%. Hamilton's ratios are below the industry average, an unfavorable condition.

The debt and equity ratios show the mix of capital provided by capital borrowed and capital provided by stockholders. The sum of the two ratios equals 100%, as shown here:

	Current Year	Prior Year
Debt Ratio	49.1%	51.7%
Equity Ratio	50.9%	48.3%
Totals	100.0%	100.0%

The totals always equal 100% because the total liabilities and stockholders' equity represent the source of all asset ownership. Due to rapid expansion, Hamilton's prior year's equity ratio declined to an unfavorable level. In the current year, Hamilton increased the percentage of ownership provided by stockholders' equity by issuing more capital stock. Hamilton plans to continue its efforts to increase the equity ratio by reducing its liabilities and issuing additional stock.

EQUITY PER SHARE

	Total Stockholders' Equity	÷	Shares of Capital Stock Outstanding	=	Equity per Share
Current Year	$1,051,600.00	÷	60,000	=	$17.53
Prior Year	$ 849,300.00	÷	50,000	=	$16.99

Figure 16-20

The amount of total stockholders' equity belonging to a single share of stock is known as equity per share. Hamilton's equity per share for the current year and the prior year are calculated as shown in Figure 16-20, using information from the statement of stockholders' equity (Figure 16-6).

Hamilton's equity per share in the current year, $17.53, indicates that on December 31, each share of capital stock represents ownership in $17.53 of the assets.

Equity per share tells stockholders how much ownership of the company each share represents. For example, the stockholders of Hamilton know that each share represents $17.53 ownership of the total company assets. This ownership has increased from $16.99 per share in the prior year, a favorable trend.

TERMS REVIEW

working capital

current ratio

quick assets

acid-test ratio

debt ratio

equity ratio

1. What are two sources from which a business gets capital?

2. What three measures can be used to analyze short-term financial strength?

3. What is the major difference between current assets and quick assets?

4. What is the formula for the acid-test ratio?

5. Why does a well-managed company monitor its long-term financial strength?

6. What is the formula for calculating debt ratio?

7. What is the formula for calculating equity per share?

WORK TOGETHER

Analyzing short-term and long-term financial strength

Information taken from Applied Technology's comparative balance sheet is provided in the *Working Papers*. Your instructor will guide you through the following problem.

8. Calculate the following short-term financial strength analysis ratios for the current year and prior year. Round ratios to the nearest .1 (tenth). Your instructor will guide you through the examples.

   a. Working capital
   b. Current ratio
   c. Acid-test ratio

   d. Debt ratio
   e. Equity ratio
   f. Equity per share

ON YOUR OWN

Analyzing short-term and long-term financial strength

Information taken from Online Office Supply's comparative balance sheet is provided in the *Working Papers*. Work independently to complete the following problem.

9. Calculate the following short-term financial strength analysis ratios for the current year and prior year. Round ratios to the nearest .1 (tenth). Work independently to complete the following problem.

   a. Working capital
   b. Current ratio
   c. Acid-test ratio

   d. Debt ratio
   e. Equity ratio
   f. Equity per share

After completing this chapter, you can

1. Define accounting terms related to financial statement analysis.

2. Identify accounting concepts and practices related to financial statement analysis.

3. Analyze financial statements.

4. Calculate earnings performance.

5. Perform efficiency analysis.

6. Analyze the long-term financial strength of businesses.

EXPLORE ACCOUNTING

DETAILED INFORMATION ON FINANCIAL STATEMENTS

Many of the financial statements used in this text report the balance of every account in the chart of accounts. These example companies have a relatively small number of accounts. Thus, every account balance can easily be reported on the financial statements. As companies grow, it becomes impractical for them to report every account. A company with hundreds of locations, for example, is likely to have a cash account for each location. Rather than reporting each cash account balance, the company combines all cash accounts and report a single amount on the financial statements. The same method is used to report all accounts on the

financial statements. For most users of the financial statements, a single cash amount provides adequate information. Most investors do not need to know the balance of each of the company's hundreds of cash accounts. Instead, the total cash amount is adequate for financial statement analysis. Detailed account information has rarely been available to individuals outside of the company. The cost of providing this information was not considered worth the benefit that a few individuals might gain. However, computer technology has made the distribution of this detailed information significantly less expensive. Accountants are starting to recognize that the detailed information can be made available at a low cost using the Internet. The traditional finan-

cial statements are likely to remain as the primary method that companies use to report their financial information. The number of users accessing the detailed information is likely to increase, however, as users become more comfortable using the Internet and learn how to evaluate detailed information to improve business decisions.

REQUIRED:

Examine the annual report of a corporation and identify the balance in the inventory account. Why would you expect the amount to be the total of many inventory accounts? Suggest reasons that management might need many inventory accounts. Why might you, as a potential investor, want to know the inventory balance of a particular location?

APPLICATION PROBLEM

16-1

Analyzing comparative financial statements using trend analysis

The comparative financial statements for CyberOptic Corporation are in the *Working Papers*. The financial statements have been completed up to the trend analysis section. The following information is taken from the financial records of CyberOptic for two consecutive fiscal years ended December 31.

	Current Year	Prior Year
Accounts Receivable (book value), January 1	$ 76,820.00	$ 69,450.00
Total Assets, January 1	670,670.00	544,200.00
Market Price per Share of Stock, December 31	23.50	16.50

Instructions:

1. Complete the following comparative financial statements using trend analysis. Round percentage calculations to the nearest 0.1%.
   - a. Comparative income statement
   - b. Comparative stockholders' equity statement
   - c. Comparative balance sheet

2. Use the financial statements' trend analysis to determine whether the trend from the prior to the current year for each of the following items appears to be favorable or unfavorable. Give reasons for these trends. Save your work to complete Application Problems 16-3, 16-4, 16-5, and 16-6.
   - a. Net sales
   - b. Net income
   - c. Total stockholders' equity
   - d. Total assets

APPLICATION PROBLEM

16-2

Analyzing comparative financial statements using component percentage analysis

The comparative financial statements for CyberOptic Corporation are in the *Working Papers*. The financial statements have been completed up to the comparative analysis section.

Instructions:

1. Complete the following comparative financial statements using component percentage analysis. Round percentage calculations to the nearest 0.1%.
   - a. Comparative income statement
   - b. Comparative stockholders' equity statement
   - c. Comparative balance sheet

2. Use the financial statements' component percentage analysis to determine whether the current year's results for the following items, compared with those for the prior year, appear to be favorable or unfavorable. Give reasons for your responses.
   - a. As a percentage of net sales:
     - (1) Cost of merchandise sold
     - (2) Gross profit on operations
     - (3) Total operating expenses
     - (4) Net income after federal income tax

continued

b. As a percentage of total stockholders' equity:
   (1) Retained earnings
   (2) Capital stock
c. As a percentage of total assets or total liabilities and stockholders' equity:
   (1) Current assets
   (2) Current liabilities

APPLICATION PROBLEM
Analyzing earnings performance from comparative financial statements

Use the comparative statements from Application Problem 16-1 to complete this problem.

Instructions:

1. Based on CyberOptic's comparative financial statements prepared in Application Problem 16-1 and the information given in the text for Application Problem 16-1, calculate the following for each year.
   a. Rate earned on average total assets
   b. Rate earned on average stockholders' equity
   c. Rate earned on net sales
   d. Earnings per share
   e. Price-earnings ratio

2. For each analysis, indicate whether a favorable or an unfavorable trend occurred from the prior to the current year. Give reasons for these trends.

APPLICATION PROBLEM
Analyzing efficiency from comparative financial statements

Use the comparative statements from Application Problem 16-1 to complete this problem.

Instructions:

1. Based on CyberOptic's comparative financial statements prepared in Application Problem 16-1 and the information given in the text for Application Problem 16-1, calculate the following for each year. All of CyberOptic's sales are on account.
   a. Accounts receivable turnover ratio
   b. Average number of days for payment
   c. Merchandise inventory turnover ratio
   d. Average number of days' sales in merchandise inventory

2. For each analysis, indicate whether a favorable or an unfavorable trend occurred from the prior to the current year. Give reasons for these trends.

APPLICATION PROBLEM
Analyzing short-term financial strength from a comparative balance sheet

Use the comparative balance sheet from Application Problem 16-1 to complete this problem.

Instructions:

1. Based on CyberOptic's comparative balance sheet prepared in Application Problem 16-1, calculate the following for each year.

a. Working capital
b. Current ratio
c. Acid-test ratio

2. For each analysis, indicate whether a favorable or an unfavorable trend occurred from the prior to the current year. Give reasons for these trends.

16-6 APPLICATION PROBLEM
Analyzing long-term financial strength from a comparative balance sheet

Use the comparative balance sheet from Application Problem 16-1 to complete this problem.

Instructions:
1. Based on CyberOptic's comparative balance sheet prepared in Application Problem 16-1, calculate the following for each year:
   a. Debt ratio
   b. Equity ratio
   c. Equity per share

2. For each analysis, indicate whether a favorable or an unfavorable trend occurred from the prior to the current year. Give reasons for these trends.

16-7 MASTERY PROBLEM
Analyzing comparative financial statements

The comparative financial statements for Advanced Auto Technology, Inc., are in the *Working Papers*. The financial statements have been completed up to the financial analysis section. The following information is taken from the financial records of Advanced Auto Technology for two fiscal years ended December 31:

	Current Year	Prior Year
Accounts Receivable (book value), January 1	$242,890.00	$236,580.00
Merchandise Inventory, January 1	172,890.00	53,760.00
Total Assets, January 1	762,860.00	693,200.00
Stockholders' Equity, January 1	413,160.00	306,780.00
Shares of Capital Stock Outstanding	48,000	40,000
Market Price per Share of Stock, December 31	42.50	30.00

Instructions:
1. Complete the following comparative financial statements using trend analysis. Round percentage calculations to the nearest 0.1%.
   a. Comparative income statement
   b. Comparative stockholders' equity statement
   c. Comparative balance sheet

2. Use the financial statements' trend analysis to determine whether the trend from the prior to the current year for each of the following items appears to be favorable or unfavorable. Give reasons for these trends.
   a. Net sales
   b. Net income
   c. Total stockholders' equity
   d. Total assets

continued

3. Complete the comparative income statement using component percentage analysis. Round percentage calculations to the nearest 0.1%.

4. Record from the statement prepared in Instruction 3 or calculate the component percentages for each of the following. Determine whether the current year's results, compared with those for the prior year, appear to be favorable or unfavorable. Give reasons for your responses.
   a. As a percentage of net sales:
      (1) Cost of merchandise sold
      (2) Gross profit on operations
      (3) Total operating expenses
      (4) Net income after federal income tax
   b. As a percentage of total stockholders' equity:
      (1) Retained earnings
      (2) Capital stock
   c. As a percentage of total assets or total liabilities and stockholders' equity:
      (1) Current assets
      (2) Current liabilities

5. Based on Advanced Auto Technology's comparative financial statements, calculate the following ratios for each year.
   a. Profitability ratios:
      (1) Rate earned on average total assets
      (2) Rate earned on average stockholders' equity
      (3) Rate earned on net sales
      (4) Earnings per share
      (5) Price-earnings ratio
   b. Efficiency ratios:
      (1) Accounts receivable turnover ratio
      (2) Merchandise inventory turnover ratio
   c. Short-term financial strength ratios:
      (1) Working capital
      (2) Current ratio
      (3) Acid-test ratio
   d. Long-term financial strength ratios:
      (1) Debt ratio
      (2) Equity ratio
      (3) Equity per share

6. For each of the items in Instruction 5, indicate whether a favorable or an unfavorable trend occurred from the prior to the current year. Give reasons for these trends.

16-8 CHALLENGE PROBLEM
Analyzing comparative financial statements

The comparative financial statements for CompuCircuit Corporation are in the *Working Papers*. The financial statements have been completed up to the financial analysis section. The following information is taken from the financial records of CompuCircuit for two fiscal years ended December 31:

	Current Year	Prior Year
Accounts Receivable (book value), January 1	$105,500.00	$126,400.00
Total Assets, January 1	979,660.00	1,052,400.00
Market Price per Share of Stock, December 31	7.50	29.50

Instructions:

1. Prepare the following comparative financial statements using trend analysis. Round percentage calculations to the nearest 0.1%.
   a. Comparative income statement
   b. Comparative stockholders' equity statement
   c. Comparative balance sheet

2. Use the financial statements' trend analysis to determine whether the trend from the prior to the current year for each of the following items appears to be favorable or unfavorable. Give reasons for these trends.
   a. Net sales
   b. Net income
   c. Total stockholders' equity
   d. Total assets

3. Complete the comparative income statement using component percentage analysis. Round percentage calculations to the nearest 0.1%.

4. Record from the statement prepared in Instruction 3 or calculate the component percentages for each of the following. Determine whether the current year's results, compared with those for the prior year, appear to be favorable or unfavorable. Give reasons for your responses.
   a. As a percentage of net sales:
      (1) Cost of merchandise sold
      (2) Gross profit on operations
      (3) Total operating expenses
      (4) Net income after federal income tax
   b. As a percentage of total stockholders' equity:
      (1) Retained earnings
      (2) Capital stock
   c. As a percentage of total assets or total liabilities and stockholders' equity:
      (1) Current assets
      (2) Current liabilities

5. Based on CompuCircuit's comparative financial statements, calculate the following ratios for each year:
   a. Profitability ratios:
      (1) Rate earned on average total assets
      (2) Rate earned on average stockholders' equity
      (3) Rate earned on net sales
      (4) Earnings per share
      (5) Price-earnings ratio
   b. Efficiency ratios:
      (1) Accounts receivable turnover ratio
      (2) Merchandise inventory turnover ratio

continued

c. Short-term financial strength ratios:
       (1) Working capital
       (2) Current ratio
       (3) Acid-test ratio
   d. Long-term financial strength ratios:
       (1) Debt ratio
       (2) Equity ratio
       (3) Equity per share

6. For each of the items in Instruction 5, indicate whether a favorable or an unfavorable trend occurred from the prior to the current year. Give reasons for these trends.

INTERNET ACTIVITY

Point your browser to
http://accounting.swpco.com
Choose **Advanced Course**, choose **Activities**, and complete the activity for Chapter 16.

Applied Communication

Corporate annual reports include a letter from the chief executive officer (CEO). The letter highlights achievements and positive results from the past year. If necessary, it delivers news of negative results with an explanation of the steps being taken to correct the problems.

Required:

Select one of the companies from the problems: CyberOptic Corporation, Advanced Auto Technology, Inc., or CompuCircuit Corporation. Assume that you are the CEO of the company. Using the information from your problem solutions, write a letter to stockholders that will appear in the company's annual report. You may add any details you would like, as long as the details are consistent with the financial analysis.

Cases for Critical Thinking

Case 1

Alpha Network Solutions has had declining net income the past four years. The company president employs you as a consultant to review the company's operations in an effort to identify the reason for the decline. As part of your analysis, you make a component percentage analysis of the company's four most recent income statements. A part of that analysis is shown below. What are the implications from the information? What are the problems or potential problems evident from this analysis? What are your suggestions to the company?

	20X4	20X3	20X2	20X1
Cost of Merchandise Sold	62.1%	58.4%	55.2%	52.5%
Total Selling Expenses	12.1%	14.6%	15.7%	18.9%

Case 2

Minta Perry has received year-end information, including financial statements, from her accountant. Among the information is a report that the accounts receivable turnover ratio in the prior year was 8.7 and for the current year is 6.2. Ms. Perry is overjoyed at the trend of the accounts receivable turnover ratio. Do you agree with her reaction? Explain your answer.

AUTOMATED ACCOUNTING

ANALYZING AUTOMATED FINANCIAL STATEMENTS AND RATIO ANALYSIS

One method of evaluating relationships within the financial statements is the use of ratio analysis. Ratios obtained from numbers in the financial statements may be compared to the ratios of previous years, to those of companies in similar industries, or to industry averages computed by companies such as Dow Jones or Standard & Poor's. Ratio analysis is one of the tools managers, investors, and lenders use to predict how well a business will do in the future.

Ratios used by business are commonly grouped by their objectives:

- The evaluation of short-term financial strength

- The evaluation of long-term financial strength

- Efficiency

- Earnings performance

Most of the data needed to compute the common ratios are available within the database maintained by accounting software. Additional information that the accountant may need to input to complete the analysis include the number of shares of stock outstanding and the current market price per share.

Performing Ratio Analysis

Use the following steps to display the ratio analysis report:

1. Click the Reports toolbar button, or choose the Reports Selection menu item from the Reports menu.

2. When the Report Selection dialog appears, choose Financial Analysis from the Select a Report Group list.

3. Choose Ratio Analysis from the Choose a Report to Display list.

4. Click OK.

5. Enter the number of shares of stock outstanding and the market price per share.

6. Click OK.

The report will be displayed in the scrollable Report Viewer Window. The report may be printed and/or copied for inclusion in another application, such as a spreadsheet or word processor.

AUTOMATING MASTERY PROBLEM 16-7

Instructions:

1. Load *Automated Accounting 7.0* or higher software.

2. Select database AA16-7 (Advanced Course Mastery Problem 16-7) from the accounting template disk.

3. Select File from the menu bar and choose the Save As menu command. Key the path to the drive and directory that contains your data files. Save the database with a file name of XXX167 (where XXX are your initials).

4. Access Problem Instructions through the Help menu. Read the Problem Instruction screen.

5. Refer to page 469 for data used in this problem.

6. Exit the Automated Accounting software.

17 Statement of Cash Flows

AFTER STUDYING CHAPTER 17, YOU WILL BE ABLE TO:

1. Define accounting terms related to cash flow analysis.

2. Identify accounting concepts and practices related to cash flow analysis.

3. Describe operating, investing, and financing activities and provide examples of each.

4. Prepare the operating activities section of a statement of cash flows.

5. Prepare the investing activities and financing activities sections of a statement of cash flows.

6. Prepare a statement of cash flows.

The information presented on the income statement, balance sheet, and statement of stockholders' equity provides individuals insight into the financial condition of a business. Managers, investors, and other interested parties use this information to improve profitability, determine operating efficiency, and make informed managerial decisions. The accounting method that records revenues when they are earned and expenses when they are incurred is called the **accrual basis of accounting**. Generally accepted accounting principles (GAAP) require that most businesses use the accrual basis of accounting for their financial statements.

The accounting method that records revenues when they are received and expenses when they are paid is called the **cash basis of accounting**. Some small businesses use this method of accounting because it is easy to use and less expensive to maintain. However, cash-basis financial statements do not provide enough information about the financial condition of the business to satisfy most investors and creditors.

Accrual-based financial statements give a complete picture of the financial condition of a business. However, managers and investors may need additional information about the cash flows of a business. By analyzing cash flows, individuals can determine whether a company has enough cash to continue operating. Firms short on cash may experience problems paying expenses, purchasing new merchandise, replacing worn equipment, repaying debts, and providing owners with a return on their investment. It is critical that financial statement analysis include a study of a company's ability to produce and manage cash.

ACCOUNTING
IN YOUR CAREER

WHERE'S THE CASH?

Heather Baxter is the CEO and majority stockholder of Dynamic Products, Inc., a company she started. The company sells industrial supplies. The company began as a proprietorship. Heather and a few other investors incorporated the company several years ago. Jay Thompson is the accounting analyst who prepares the daily cash projections. Heather insists on having this cash report prepared daily because she learned as a proprietor of a small business that managing the cash was key to succeeding in business.

The daily cash projection report shows all cash payments due on a single date, the beginning cash balance, and cash receipts for the day. When there is not sufficient cash to make the payments that are due, cash is borrowed from a standing line of credit at the bank. When there is a large surplus of cash, such as when payment on a large contract is received, the surplus is invested. By managing cash so tightly, the company is assured of making timely payments to take advantage of all discounts for early payments. Large cash balances are put to work to earn interest. The company's credit rating is one of the highest in the industry.

Jay prepares a monthly statement of cash flows. In addition, he prepares the same statement for each quarter, and another at the end of each fiscal year. In reviewing procedures, Heather questions why the statement of cash flows is prepared at all, since the daily cash projection report is always available. She thinks the time used to prepare the statement could be better used to encourage timely payments by accounts receivable or to explore new investment opportunities.

Critical Thinking

1. Would time spent encouraging timely payments by accounts receivable or exploring new investment opportunities be a better use of Jay Thompson's time?
2. What does the statement of cash flows show that the daily cash projection report does not?
3. Is it necessary to prepare a statement of cash flows as often as is currently being done?

CASH FLOW ANALYSIS

Case Study

Two years ago, in January, Gina and Kevin Harnley formed Snow Creek Corporation for the purpose of selling ski equipment, snowboards, and related accessories. During the first year, the company produced sales of over $300,000 and earned a net income of approximately $60,000. Last year was equally impressive. Assets increased, sales exceeded $500,000, and a net income of more than $100,000 was earned. Two months into the current year, however, Snow Creek Corporation lacked the amount of cash necessary to pay its current bills. If Snow Creek was growing and profits were rising, how does one explain the company's shortage of cash and inability to pay bills?

One of the main reasons for Snow Creek's financial problems was its generous credit policy, which created a large volume of accounts receivable. Snow Creek's credit policy of "no payments for six months" definitely attracted buyers. However, problems arose when a large number of Snow Creek's customers did not make their payments on time.

Another reason for Snow Creek's difficulties was a large increase in inventory. Snow Creek required a greater level of inventory to assure that it had an adequate selection of items for a growing number of customers. It paid for the merchandise within the 30-day credit terms, but it had not yet sold much of the inventory. The company ran out of money to pay its bills. Cash was going out to purchase inventory and not enough was coming in to pay expenses.

The Harnleys, who manage the company, failed to foresee their problems because they prepared their income statements using the accrual basis of accounting. Sale amounts were recognized when snow equipment and accessories left the store, not when cash was received. Consequently, Snow Creek Corporation showed strong sales and profits. However, an analysis of the company's cash receipts and cash payments shows a different picture.

Some investors and financial analysts rely heavily on an examination of income statements and balance sheets to judge a company's performance. However, impressive profits are not always a guarantee of success in the future. For example, despite reporting a substantial net income for the year, a business may experience a cash shortage and have difficulty paying its bills. Cash flow analysis helps owners, creditors, and other interested parties:

1. Determine a company's potential to produce cash in the future.

2. Judge a company's ability to pay bills and repay debts.

3. Explain changes in the cash account balance.

4. Evaluate a company's investment and equity transactions.

SMALL BUSINESS SPOTLIGHT

The U.S. Small Business Administration (SBA) is an independent agency of the federal government. Created by an act of Congress in 1953, the SBA is dedicated to helping Americans start and operate successful small enterprises. Today, the SBA is involved in financing, training, and advocacy for small firms.

Snow Creek Corporation
Statement of Cash Flows
For Year Ended December 31, 20X2

Cash Flows from Operating Activities:			
Net Income		$100,344.00	
Adjustments to Net Income:			
Depreciation Expense	$ 11,605.00		
Changes in current assets and liabilities:			
Increase in accounts receivable	(110,530.00)		
Decrease in supplies	399.00		
Increase in merchandise inventory	(116,640.00)		
Increase in notes payable	38,990.00		
Increase in accounts payable	54,924.00		
Total adjustments to net income		($121,252.00)	
Cash used for operating activities			($20,908.00)
Cash Flows from Investing Activities:			
Addition to equipment		($20,680.00)	
Proceeds from sale of property		30,000.00	
Cash provided by investing activities			$9,320.00
Cash Flows from Financing Activities:			
Repayment of mortgage		($547.00)	
Proceeds from issuance of common stock		40,000.00	
Dividend payment		(32,000.00)	
Cash provided by financing activities			$7,453.00
Net Decrease in Cash			($4,135.00)
Cash Balance, Beginning of Period			12,540.00
Cash Balance, End of Period			$8,405.00

Figure 17-1

The cash receipts and cash payments of a company are called **cash flows**. A statement that summarizes cash receipts and cash payments resulting from business activities during a fiscal period is called a **statement of cash flows**. The statement, as shown in Figure 17-1, explains the change in Cash during a fiscal period by reporting the sources (inflows or receipts) and uses (outflows or payments) of a company's cash.

By studying a company's cash flows, a manager can analyze why there were profits and yet not enough cash to pay bills. No other financial statement provides this important information.

The Harnleys made business decisions based on information reported on the income statement and balance sheet. They failed to realize that the revenues reported on the income statement rarely match cash receipts. If a company reports sales on account of $100,000.00, it is unlikely that the company had $100,000.00 in actual cash receipts. Not all customers pay in a timely manner.

The income statement and balance sheet are prepared using an accrual basis of accounting. The statement of cash flows is prepared using the cash basis of accounting. The cash basis of accounting recognizes revenue when cash is received and expenses when cash is paid out.

REMEMBER

The cash inflows and outflows of a business are identified using the information presented on a company's financial statements.

Accrual Basis	vs.	Cash Basis
Revenue recognized at the time it is *earned*		Revenue recognized at the time cash is *received*

Accrual Basis				Cash Basis	
Revenues	$25,000.00		Revenues	$	0.00
Expenses	0.00		Expenses		0.00
Net Income	$25,000.00		Net Income	$	0.00

Figure 17-2

Assume that Flomax Corporation has sales on account during the year and no expenses. Under the accrual basis for accounting, revenue is recognized at the time it is earned.

Accounts Receivable	
25,000.00	

Sales	
	25,000.00

Assume the account receivable remains outstanding at the end of the fiscal year. Using the accrual basis of accounting, Flomax reports revenues as shown in Figure 17-2. However, the income calculation prepared under the cash basis shows no revenue for the period, hence, no net income. Under the cash basis of accounting, revenue is not recognized until cash is received.

Accrual Basis	vs.	Cash Basis
Expense recognized at the time it is *incurred*		Expense recognized at the time cash is *paid*

Accrual Basis				Cash Basis	
Revenues	$25,000.00		Revenues	$	0.00
Expenses	3,000.00		Expenses		0.00
Net Income	$22,000.00		Net Income	$	0.00

Figure 17-3

Similarly, the recognition of expenses does not always match the payments of cash. For example, Flomax Corporation recognizes one week of salaries earned by employees before the close of the current fiscal year. The salary expense will not be paid until the next fiscal period. Using the accrual basis, Flomax recognizes the

Salaries Expense	
3,000.00	

Salaries Payable	
	3,000.00

expense during the current fiscal year as shown in the T accounts.

Assume that this is Flomax Corporation's only expense of the year. Using the accrual basis of accounting, Flomax's net income is $22,000.00, as shown in Figure 17-3. The accrual basis of accounting recognizes an expense at the time it is incurred. Using the cash basis of accounting, Flomax has no expenses to report in the current period. The cash basis recognizes an expense when cash is paid. Since no cash was received and no cash was paid, a net income of $0.00 is reported.

Operating Activities

Cash Inflows (sources of cash)
Cash sales of merchandise
Cash sales of services
Interest income
Dividends received from the ownership of stock in other
  companies
Cash received from charge customers

Cash Outflows (uses of cash)
Advertising
Credit card fees
Insurance expense
Interest payments
Payroll expenses
Property tax
Utility expenses
Income tax

Figure 17-4

The statement of cash flows is divided into three sections: cash flows from *operating activities*, cash flows from *investing activities*, and cash flows from *financing activities*. The cash flows for each of these sections are calculated by analyzing the information presented on the income statement, the balance sheet, and the statement of stockholders' equity.

The cash receipts and payments necessary to operate a business on a day-to-day basis are called **operating activities**. For example, a list of common cash inflows and cash outflows from operating activities is presented in Figure 17-4. Snow Creek Corporation uses cash to add merchandise and to pay the daily expenses required to operate the business and earn a profit.

CASH FLOWS FROM INVESTING ACTIVITIES

Investing Activities

Cash Inflows (sources of cash)
Sale of property
Sale of equipment
Sale of building
Collections of long-term loans

Cash Outflows (uses of cash)
Purchase of land
Purchase of equipment
Purchase of building
Purchase of patents or special licenses
Loans to other companies
Purchase of stock in other companies
Purchase of bonds in other companies

Figure 17-5

Cash receipts and cash payments involving the sale or purchase of assets used to earn revenue over a period of time are called **investing activities**. A list of common cash inflows and cash outflows involving investing activities is shown in Figure 17-5.

Creditors, owners, and potential investors examine the investing activities to assess the future financial strength and profitability of a business. Financial analysts know that investment activities are necessary if the business is to remain profitable. If a company sells buildings and equipment to raise cash for operations, there would soon be no buildings and equipment to produce or store the goods.

REMEMBER

Sources of cash represent cash inflows and are added on the statement of cash flows. Uses of cash represent cash outflows and are subtracted on the statement of cash flows.

Financing Activities

Cash Inflows (sources of cash)
Capital stock issue
Mortgage issue
Bond issue
Long-term loans

Cash Outflows (uses of cash)
Purchase of treasury stock
Payment of cash dividends
Repayment of loan/note principal
Retirement of bond principal

Figure 17-6

F.Y.I.

The Financial Accounting Standards Board (FASB), in Statement No. 95, classifies the interest paid on borrowed money as an operating activity. The reason for this classification is that the payment of interest expense on a loan is considered to have a direct impact on a firm's net income.

When Gina and Kevin Harnley decided to form Snow Creek Corporation, they had to obtain the necessary funding to carry out their plan. The Harnleys decided to sell common stock to acquire the financing they needed. Cash receipts and payments involving debt or equity transactions are called **financing activities**. These activities usually involve borrowing money from creditors and repaying the principal or acquiring capital from owners and providing a return on their investment.

Financing activities are often used to ensure that an adequate balance exists in the cash account. If a firm's business activities use more cash than it receives, it must obtain additional financing.

Some financing activities reduce the cash balance. This occurs when cash is used to pay dividends, repay the principal of a loan, or purchase treasury stock. These payments of cash decrease the amount available for operating and investing activities. A list of common cash inflows and cash outflows related to financing activities is shown in Figure 17-6.

KEEPING FINANCIAL TRANSACTIONS SAFE

Each day, millions of financial transactions are electronically transmitted. Many of these transactions are made using the Internet. Several technologies exist to safeguard these transactions from electronic theft and fraud. Among the oldest of these technologies is encryption. Before data are transmitted, they are disguised through encryption. If the transmitted data are stolen, the thief cannot access the data. When the data reach the proper destination, the receiving party will decrypt the information. Two keys, or sets of codes, are needed. One is used to encrypt the information; the other is used to decrypt it.

A further safeguard for electronic data transmission is the use of digital certificates. These certificates are used to link the encryption key and the decryption key. Digital certificates are issued by third-party vendors. They link the encryption and decryption keys and prevent unauthorized parties from possessing the decryption key. Before digital certificates are issued, the identity of the business or individual is verified. This verification provides another level of security.

TECHNOLOGY FOR BUSINESS

TERMS REVIEW

accrual basis of accounting

cash basis of accounting

cash flows

statement of cash flows

operating activities

investing activities

financing activities

AUDIT YOUR UNDERSTANDING

1. Using the accrual accounting basis, when are revenues and expenses recognized?

2. Using the cash accounting basis, when are revenues and expenses recognized?

3. Identify the three categories of business activities reported on the statement of cash flows.

WORK TOGETHER

Classifying cash flows

The following business transactions represent selected cash receipts (cash inflows) and cash payments (cash outflows) of Los Altos Cyclery. A blank form is provided in the *Working Papers*. Your instructor will guide you through the following problem.

4. Identify each transaction as (1) a cash inflow or cash outflow and (2) as an operating, investing, or financing activity.
   - a. Receipts from the issue of capital stock.
   - b. Cash purchase of office furniture.
   - c. Dividend payment.
   - d. Advertising expense.
   - e. Receipts from the sale of merchandise.
   - f. Cash received from the issue of a mortgage.
   - g. Repayment of loan principal.
   - h. Purchase of another company's stock.

ON YOUR OWN

Classifying cash flows

The following business transactions represent selected cash receipts (cash inflows) and cash payments (cash outflows) of Burlingame Tuxedo. A blank form is provided in the *Working Papers*. Work independently to complete this problem.

5. Identify each transaction as (1) a cash inflow or cash outflow and (2) as an operating, investing, or financing activity.
   - a. Receipts from the issue of bonds.
   - b. Cash purchase of office furniture.
   - c. Salary expense.
   - d. Receipts from tuxedo rentals.
   - e. Receipts from the issue of a mortgage.
   - f. Cash receipt from sale of equipment.
   - g. Cash purchase of treasury stock.
   - h. Payment of property taxes.

DETERMINING CASH FLOWS FROM OPERATING ACTIVITIES

The operating activity section of the statement of cash flows reports the cash inflows and cash outflows resulting from the operation of a business. These cash flows can be indirectly determined by identifying the net income for the period and making several adjustments.

Net Income

Net income presented on an income statement summarizes revenues and expenses generated by the operating activities of a business during the fiscal period. For this reason, net income is a good starting point for calculating the cash flows from operating activities. Since a net income eventually brings additional money into a firm, net income is viewed as a source of cash. A net loss reduces the amount of money available for expenditures and is considered to be a use of cash.

Since the income statement is prepared using the accrual basis of accounting and the statement of cash flows is prepared using the cash basis of accounting, the recognition of revenues and expenses occurs at different times. Adjustments are made to net income to recognize the timing differences.

ADJUSTING NET INCOME FOR DEPRECIATION

Depreciation Expense		
Dec. 31	500.00	

◄—— Effect on cash: None; add amount to net income

Accumulated Depreciation—Equipment		
	Dec. 31	500.00

Figure 17-7

Depreciation expense is recognized on the income statement. However, it does not involve an outflow of cash. Since depreciation expense does not use cash, the amount is added back to the net income amount.

At the end of the fiscal year, Centaur Corporation expenses an appropriate amount of the original cost of equipment using the straight-line method of depreciation. Depreciation for the year is recorded by debiting Depreciation Expense and crediting Accumulated Depreciation—Equipment as shown in Figure 17-7.

Notice that the credit for this transaction is Accumulated Depreciation—Equipment, not Cash. Depreciation expense does not affect the balance in the cash account. However, depreciation expense is deducted from company revenues to determine net income. Since no cash is paid out, the amount of depreciation expense reported on the income statement must be added back to net income to determine the actual cash generated from operating activities. The amount of depreciation expense added back to net income is one of the adjustments to net income to determine the actual source of cash from operations.

> **F.Y.I.**
>
> *Determine if the increase or decrease in an account represents a source of cash or a use of cash. If a change in an account represents a source of cash, it is always added on the statement of cash flows. If a change represents a use of cash, it is always subtracted.*

Cash	
Dec. 15	80,000.00

Sales	
Nov. 15	100,000.00

Accounts Receivable			
Nov. 15	100,000.00	Dec. 15	80,000.00
Dec. 31 Bal.	20,000.00		

Increase in noncash current asset is a use of cash. ⟶

Figure 17-8

The second adjustment to net income involves changes in *noncash current assets* (current assets other than cash). Increases and decreases in noncash current assets impact cash flows and require an adjustment to net income. For example, an increase in the current asset Accounts Receivable indicates that not all of the sales on account reported for a fiscal period were collected. Consequently, an increase in accounts receivable means that cash received from sales is less than the sales amount reported on the income statement.

On November 1, Heritage Corporation began business. Figure 17-8 shows a T account analysis of the following transactions.

Nov. 15. Heritage Corporation makes its only sale on account, $100,000.00.

Dec. 15. Heritage receives $80,000.00 as a partial payment on the account. No other collections occur during the year.

The $20,000.00 increase in accounts receivable represents cash that has not yet been received and, therefore, must be deducted from net income to determine cash flow. This adjustment to net income informs analysts that the cash inflows from sales on account during the year were $80,000.00 ($100,000.00 – $20,000.00) and not the full $100,000.00 reported as sales on the income statement. An increase in a noncash current asset is considered to be a *use of cash*. This use of cash supports the company's daily operations by allowing the business to offer customers the option to buy now and pay later. A use of cash means a specified sum of money is no longer available for other business activities.

Noncash current assets may also decrease during a fiscal period. A decrease in a noncash current asset represents a *source of cash* and is added back to the net income amount. This concept is illustrated through the continued use of the previous example involving Heritage Corporation.

At the end of its second year in business, Heritage Corporation has a $10,000.00 balance in Accounts Receivable. From an analysis of the T account, we learn that:

1. The balance in *Accounts Receivable* at the beginning of the year was $20,000.00.

2. Sales on account of $130,000.00 were made during the year.

3. Payments on account of $140,000.00 were received.

4. The Accounts Receivable balance at the end of the year is $10,000.00.

How can a company collect $140,000.00 of receivables if sales on account for the year are only $130,000.00? In this instance, Heritage collected a portion of the $20,000.00 balance in accounts receivable due from the previous year. The balance in Accounts Receivable declined from $20,000.00 on January 1 to $10,000.00 on December 31. This decrease is added to net income to determine cash flow.

Each noncash current asset is analyzed in a similar manner to accounts receivable.

Accounts Receivable			
Jan. 1 Bal.	20,000.00	Cash received	140,000.00
Credit sales	130,000.00		
Dec. 31 Bal.	10,000.00		

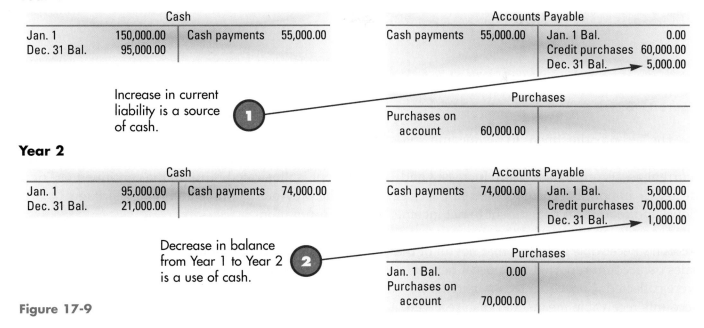

Figure 17-9

The third adjustment to net income involves changes in current liabilities. During the operating activities of a business, increases and decreases in current liabilities occur as debts are added and paid off in the process of generating revenues. For instance, an increase in accounts payable indicates that not all of the purchases on account made during a fiscal period were paid in full. An increase in current liabilities has a positive impact on cash flows as shown for the Fairtex Corporation in Figure 17-9.

The $5,000.00 increase in accounts payable at the end of the first year means the actual cash outflow for purchases on account was $55,000.00 and not the full $60,000.00 reported as purchases on the income statement. For this reason, net income is adjusted by adding back $5,000.00 for

the increase in a current liability. Since the company has use of the $5,000.00, the increase in a current liability represents a *source of cash*.

During the second year of operation, Fairtex Corporation was extremely aggressive in paying off its debts. In fact, the company paid off $74,000.00 of accounts payable, $4,000.00 more than the total purchases on account of $70,000.00. Why would a company pay more than it owes? In this instance, Fairtex paid a portion of the $5,000.00 accounts payable balance owed for the previous year. A decrease in a current liability represents a *use of cash* and is subtracted from the net income figure.

Each current liability is analyzed in a similar manner to accounts payable.

SUMMARY

- Depreciation expense is *added* back to net income since it is a noncash expense
- Increases in noncash current assets (assets other than cash) and decreases in current liabilities represent *uses of cash* and are *deducted* from net income
- Decreases in noncash current assets and increases in current liabilities represent *sources of cash* and are *added* to net income

The operating activities section of the statement of cash flows shows the amount of cash actually received and paid as a result of operating a business. The adjustments to net income required to determine the cash flows from operating activities are reviewed in Figure 17-10.

Figure 17-10

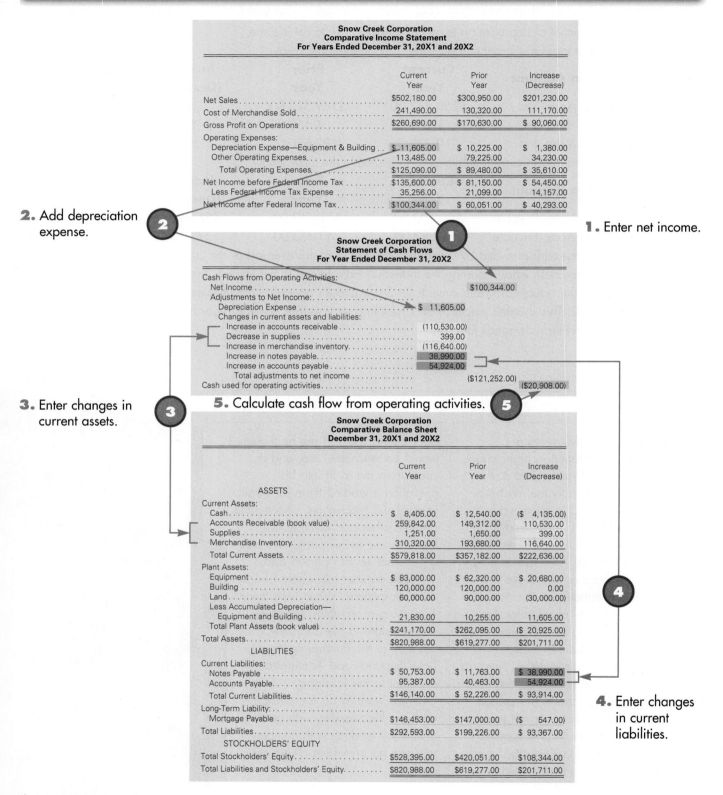

2. Add depreciation expense.

1. Enter net income.

3. Enter changes in current assets.

5. Calculate cash flow from operating activities.

4. Enter changes in current liabilities.

Snow Creek Corporation
Comparative Income Statement
For Years Ended December 31, 20X1 and 20X2

	Current Year	Prior Year	Increase (Decrease)
Net Sales	$502,180.00	$300,950.00	$201,230.00
Cost of Merchandise Sold	241,490.00	130,320.00	111,170.00
Gross Profit on Operations	$260,690.00	$170,630.00	$ 90,060.00
Operating Expenses:			
Depreciation Expense—Equipment & Building	$ 11,605.00	$ 10,225.00	$ 1,380.00
Other Operating Expenses	113,485.00	79,225.00	34,230.00
Total Operating Expenses	$125,090.00	$ 89,480.00	$ 35,610.00
Net Income before Federal Income Tax	$135,600.00	$ 81,150.00	$ 54,450.00
Less Federal Income Tax Expense	35,256.00	21,099.00	14,157.00
Net Income after Federal Income Tax	$100,344.00	$ 60,051.00	$ 40,293.00

Snow Creek Corporation
Statement of Cash Flows
For Year Ended December 31, 20X2

Cash Flows from Operating Activities:		
Net Income		$100,344.00
Adjustments to Net Income:		
Depreciation Expense	$ 11,605.00	
Changes in current assets and liabilities:		
Increase in accounts receivable	(110,530.00)	
Decrease in supplies	399.00	
Increase in merchandise inventory	(116,640.00)	
Increase in notes payable	38,990.00	
Increase in accounts payable	54,924.00	
Total adjustments to net income	($121,252.00)	
Cash used for operating activities		($20,908.00)

Snow Creek Corporation
Comparative Balance Sheet
December 31, 20X1 and 20X2

	Current Year	Prior Year	Increase (Decrease)
ASSETS			
Current Assets:			
Cash	$ 8,405.00	$ 12,540.00	($ 4,135.00)
Accounts Receivable (book value)	259,842.00	149,312.00	110,530.00
Supplies	1,251.00	1,650.00	399.00
Merchandise Inventory	310,320.00	193,680.00	116,640.00
Total Current Assets	$579,818.00	$357,182.00	$222,636.00
Plant Assets:			
Equipment	$ 83,000.00	$ 62,320.00	$ 20,680.00
Building	120,000.00	120,000.00	0.00
Land	60,000.00	90,000.00	(30,000.00)
Less Accumulated Depreciation—			
Equipment and Building	21,830.00	10,255.00	11,605.00
Total Plant Assets (book value)	$241,170.00	$262,095.00	($ 20,925.00)
Total Assets	$820,988.00	$619,277.00	$201,711.00
LIABILITIES			
Current Liabilities:			
Notes Payable	$ 50,753.00	$ 11,763.00	$ 38,990.00
Accounts Payable	95,387.00	40,463.00	54,924.00
Total Current Liabilities	$146,140.00	$ 52,226.00	$ 93,914.00
Long-Term Liability:			
Mortgage Payable	$146,453.00	$147,000.00	($ 547.00)
Total Liabilities	$292,593.00	$199,226.00	$ 93,367.00
STOCKHOLDERS' EQUITY			
Total Stockholders' Equity	$528,395.00	$420,051.00	$108,344.00
Total Liabilities and Stockholders' Equity	$820,988.00	$619,277.00	$201,711.00

Figure 17-11

The first section of the statement of cash flows shows the cash flows from operating activities as shown in Figure 17-11.

Reporting cash flows from operating activities

STEPS

1. Enter net income, *$100,344.00* as shown on Snow Creek's comparative income statement.
2. Add the amount of depreciation expense, *$11,605.00*, to net income.
3. Enter the changes in current assets as indicated in the table below.

Change in Account	Current Year	Prior Year	Increase (Decrease)	Source or use of cash
Increase in Accts. Rec.	$259,842.00	$149,312.00	$110,530.00	use of cash
Decrease in Supplies	1,251.00	1,650.00	(399.00)	source of cash
Increase in Mdse. Inv.	310,320.00	193,680.00	116,640.00	use of cash

4. Enter the changes in current liabilities as indicated in the table below.

Change in Account	Current Year	Prior Year	Increase (Decrease)	Source or use of cash
Increase in Notes Payable	$50,753.00	$11,763.00	$38,990.00	source of cash
Increase in Accts. Payable	95,387.00	40,463.00	54,924.00	source of cash

5. Determine the cash provided by operating activities (if cash increases) or the cash used by operating activities (if cash decreases). After reporting the individual adjustments to net income, the statement of cash flows shows that the actual cash requirements for Snow Creek's operating activities exceeded net income by $20,908.00. This shortfall places Snow Creek in a very serious position regarding the company's ability to meet its short-term demands for cash.

ROBIN L. OLIVER, ADMINISTRATIVE ASSISTANT ACCOUNTANT

ACCOUNTING AT WORK

I took two years of accounting in high school, and I really liked it. It was fun; it's probably the most interesting class I took. In some ways it was challenging. I never liked history; I was not a big science buff, either. But I made A's in accounting. It's only as hard as you make it. A lot of it is common sense.

I never actually planned for the accounting field to be my career. I worked in libraries from seventh grade through college. While I was in college, I actually combined two card catalogs for my school. The college bought another library and it was my job to put the two libraries together. When we moved to Kentucky, I tried to get a job in the library field but there were no openings.

An employment agency sent me for an interview, and the man hired me. He saw my accounting background. He told me he thought I would be teachable, too, and he could train me to fit into his operation. I worked there for three years. I did receivables, phone sales, counter sales, and commissions. I learned how to sell parts, and was a customer service person also.

I took another job where I began as a receptionist. When I left there I was doing receivables, payables, was assistant to the Controller, assistant to the Purchasing Agent, Sales Support, and Administrative Assistant to the President.

If you want to do something, and you like working with people, and enjoy working with numbers, you can go anywhere. There are no limits.

I look at a career as like going to school, but getting paid for it. I don't ever want to stop learning.

AUDIT YOUR UNDERSTANDING

1. Although depreciation expense is recognized on the income statement under the accrual basis of accounting, it does not involve an outflow of cash. Why?

2. What does an increase in the balance of accounts receivable indicate?

3. What does an increase in the balance of accounts payable indicate?

4. What is the starting point for calculating the cash flow from operating activities?

WORK TOGETHER

Preparing the operating activity section for a statement of cash flows

A comparative balance sheet for Zephyr Corporation is provided in the *Working Papers*. The income statement for the current year indicates that net income was $10,160.00 and the depreciation expense was $27,300.00. Statement paper and a form for analyzing changes in accounts are also provided in the *Working Papers*. Your instructor will guide you through the following examples.

5. For each item listed on the form, record the appropriate December 31 balances for the current and prior years.

6. For each item listed on the form, classify it as a current asset or current liability.

7. Compute the amount of increase or decrease from the prior year.

8. Indicate if the increase or decrease represents a source of cash or a use of cash.

9. Prepare the operating activity section of the statement of cash flows for the current year ended December 31. Save your work to complete the Work Together on page 493.

ON YOUR OWN

Preparing the operating activity section for a statement of cash flows

A comparative balance sheet for Cirrus Corporation is provided in the *Working Papers*. The income statement for the current year indicates that net income was $20,900.00 and the depreciation expense was $4,900.00. Statement paper and a form for analyzing changes in accounts are also provided in the *Working Papers*. Work independently to complete the following problem.

10. For each item listed on the form, record the appropriate December 31 balances for the current and prior years.

11. For each item listed on the form, classify it as a current asset or current liability.

12. Compute the amount of increase or decrease from the prior year.

13. Indicate if the increase or decrease represents a source of cash or a use of cash.

14. Prepare the operating activity section of the statement of cash flows for the current year ended December 31. Save your work to complete the On Your Own on page 493.

PREPARING THE INVESTING ACTIVITIES SECTION

Snow Creek Corporation
Comparative Balance Sheet
December 31, 20X1 and 20X2

	Current Year	Prior Year	Increase (Decrease)
ASSETS			
Plant Assets:			
Equipment	$ 83,000.00	$ 62,320.00	$ 20,680.00
Building	120,000.00	120,000.00	0.00
Land	60,000.00	90,000.00	(30,000.00)
Less Accumulated Depreciation—			
Equipment and Building	21,830.00	10,255.00	11,605.00
Total Plant Assets (book value)	$241,170.00	$262,095.00	$(20,925.00)

1. Enter changes in long-term assets.

Snow Creek Corporation
Statement of Cash Flows
For Year Ended December 31, 20X2

Cash Flows from Investing Activities:		
Increase in equipment	$(20,680.00)	
Decrease in land	30,000.00	
Cash provided by investing activities		$9,320.00

2. Determine the effect on cash from investing activities.

Figure 17-12

Responsible investing activities are critical to the long-term success of a company. Cash flows resulting from a company's investing activities are identified by analyzing the changes in long-term assets (plant assets) presented on the comparative balance sheet. Snow Creek's investing activities section for the statement of cash flows is shown in Figure 17-12.

S **Reporting cash flows from investing activities**

T
E **1.** Analyze changes in long-term assets. The $20,680.00 increase in equipment represents a cash outflow. The
P increase in a long-term asset is a use of cash. During the year, Snow Creek Corporation sold a parcel of land
S for $30,000, the same amount paid for the land one year earlier. The $30,000.00 decrease in the long-term
asset, Land, represents a cash inflow and is a source of cash. The following table summarizes the changes.

Change in Account	Current Year	Prior Year	Increase (Decrease)	Source or use of cash
Increase in Equipment	$83,000.00	$62,320.00	$20,680.00	use of cash
Decrease in Land	60,000.00	90,000.00	($30,000.00)	source of cash

2. Determine the cash provided by investing activities (if cash increases) or the cash used by investing activities (if cash decreases). Snow Creek's investing activities provided $9,320.00 in cash during the current year.

The increase in accumulated depreciation for equipment and building ($11,605.00) can be ignored. This increase matches the depreciation expense that was recorded on the income statement. The effect on cash flows was already accounted for under operating activities.

When calculating the cash flows from investing activities, it is useful to remember that:

- Increases in long-term assets generally result in cash outflows (*uses of cash*) that are subtracted on the statement of cash flows.

- Decreases in long-term assets generally result in cash inflows (*sources of cash*) that are added on the statement of cash flows.

PREPARING THE FINANCING ACTIVITY SECTION

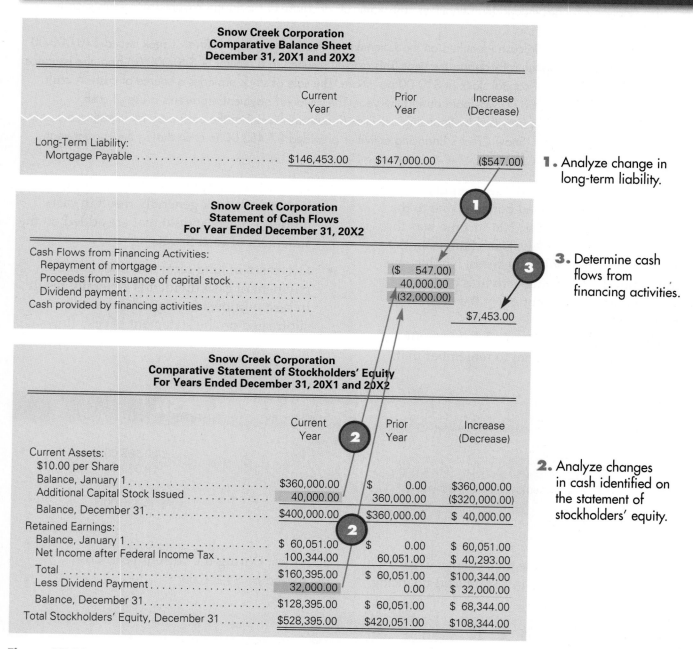

Snow Creek Corporation
Comparative Balance Sheet
December 31, 20X1 and 20X2

	Current Year	Prior Year	Increase (Decrease)
Long-Term Liability:			
Mortgage Payable	$146,453.00	$147,000.00	($547.00)

1. Analyze change in long-term liability.

Snow Creek Corporation
Statement of Cash Flows
For Year Ended December 31, 20X2

Cash Flows from Financing Activities:	
Repayment of mortgage	($ 547.00)
Proceeds from issuance of capital stock	40,000.00
Dividend payment	(32,000.00)
Cash provided by financing activities	$7,453.00

3. Determine cash flows from financing activities.

Snow Creek Corporation
Comparative Statement of Stockholders' Equity
For Years Ended December 31, 20X1 and 20X2

	Current Year	Prior Year	Increase (Decrease)
Current Assets:			
$10.00 per Share			
Balance, January 1	$360,000.00	$ 0.00	$360,000.00
Additional Capital Stock Issued	40,000.00	360,000.00	($320,000.00)
Balance, December 31	$400,000.00	$360,000.00	$ 40,000.00
Retained Earnings:			
Balance, January 1	$ 60,051.00	$ 0.00	$ 60,051.00
Net Income after Federal Income Tax	100,344.00	60,051.00	$ 40,293.00
Total	$160,395.00	$ 60,051.00	$100,344.00
Less Dividend Payment	32,000.00	0.00	$ 32,000.00
Balance, December 31	$128,395.00	$ 60,051.00	$ 68,344.00
Total Stockholders' Equity, December 31	$528,395.00	$420,051.00	$108,344.00

2. Analyze changes in cash identified on the statement of stockholders' equity.

Figure 17-13

Financing activities are often used to maintain an adequate balance in the cash account. These activities usually involve borrowing money from creditors and repaying the principal or acquiring capital from owners and providing a return on their investment. Cash flows originating from a company's financing activities are identified by examining the changes in long-term liabilities reported on the balance sheet and the changes in stockholders' equity reported on the statement of stockholders' equity. This analysis is shown in Figure 17-13.

S T E P S — Reporting cash flows from financing activities

1. Analyze changes in long-term liabilities. The $547.00 decrease in Mortgage Payable represents a cash outflow.

2. Analyze changes in cash identified on the statement of stockholders' equity. Snow Creek issued $40,000.00 of additional capital stock during the year. This activity resulted in a receipt of $40,000.00 from the issuance of 4,000 shares of capital stock at $10.00 per share. The sale of stock provides a source of cash. A cash dividend of $32,000.00 was paid during the year. The dividend payment represents a use of cash.

3. Determine the cash provided by financing activities (if cash increases) or the cash used by investing activities (if cash decreases). Snow Creek's financing activities provided $7,453.00 in cash during the current year.

The statement of stockholders' equity also shows a change in **Retained Earnings** due to the net income of the business. Net income was the starting point for the analysis of changes in the operating activities of the business. Net income results from the operating activities of the business. Net income does not affect the financing activities of the business.

When calculating the cash flows from financing activities, it is beneficial to remember that:

- Increases in long-term liabilities and the issuance of stock generally result in cash inflows (*sources of cash*) that are added on the statement of cash flows.

- Decreases in long-term liabilities and the payment of cash dividends generally result in cash outflows (*uses of cash*) that are subtracted on the statement of cash flows.

CALCULATE THE NET INCREASE OR DECREASE IN CASH

Cash used for operating activities (Figure 17-11)	$(20,908.00)
Cash provided by investing activities (Figure 17-12)	9,320.00
Cash provided by financing activities (Figure 17-13)	7,453.00
Net change in cash	$ (4,135.00)

Figure 17-14

Figure 17-14 shows the total change in cash resulting from operating, investing, and financing activities. During the current year, Cash decreased by $4,135.00.

REMEMBER

Financing activities involve debt or equity transactions.

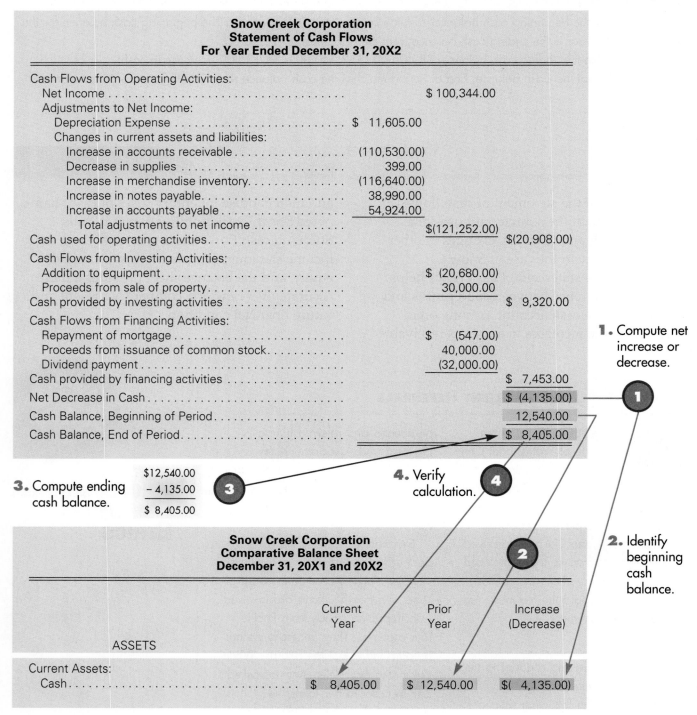

Snow Creek Corporation
Statement of Cash Flows
For Year Ended December 31, 20X2

Cash Flows from Operating Activities:			
Net Income		$ 100,344.00	
Adjustments to Net Income:			
Depreciation Expense	$ 11,605.00		
Changes in current assets and liabilities:			
Increase in accounts receivable.................	(110,530.00)		
Decrease in supplies	399.00		
Increase in merchandise inventory..............	(116,640.00)		
Increase in notes payable.....................	38,990.00		
Increase in accounts payable	54,924.00		
Total adjustments to net income	$(121,252.00)		
Cash used for operating activities.................		$(20,908.00)	
Cash Flows from Investing Activities:			
Addition to equipment............................	$ (20,680.00)		
Proceeds from sale of property....................	30,000.00		
Cash provided by investing activities		$ 9,320.00	
Cash Flows from Financing Activities:			
Repayment of mortgage	$ (547.00)		
Proceeds from issuance of common stock..........	40,000.00		
Dividend payment	(32,000.00)		
Cash provided by financing activities		$ 7,453.00	
Net Decrease in Cash..............................		$ (4,135.00)	
Cash Balance, Beginning of Period.................		12,540.00	
Cash Balance, End of Period.......................		$ 8,405.00	

1. Compute net increase or decrease.

3. Compute ending cash balance.

$12,540.00
– 4,135.00
$ 8,405.00

4. Verify calculation.

2. Identify beginning cash balance.

Snow Creek Corporation
Comparative Balance Sheet
December 31, 20X1 and 20X2

	Current Year	Prior Year	Increase (Decrease)
ASSETS			
Current Assets:			
Cash......................................	$ 8,405.00	$ 12,540.00	$(4,135.00)

Figure 17-15

The completed statement of cash flows is shown in Figure 17-15. The Cash balances at the beginning and end of the period shown on the statement of cash flows must match the amounts shown on the comparative balance sheet.

Completing the statement of cash flows

1. Compute the net increase or decrease in Cash resulting from operating, investing, and financing activities.

2. Identify the beginning cash balance from the comparative balance sheet. The beginning cash balance for the current year is the ending cash balance from the prior year, $12,540.00.

3. Compute the ending cash balance, $8,405.00 ($12,540.00 − $4,135.00 decrease in cash).

4. Verify that the Cash Balance, End of Period matches the cash balance shown on the comparative balance sheet.

CASH FLOW ANALYSIS SUMMARY

The intent of the statement of cash flows is to report and explain the sources and uses of a company's cash and to clarify changes in other account balances. In the case of Snow Creek Corporation, the statement of cash flows helps explain the difference between solid profits and a decrease in the cash account. Among other things, the large increases in accounts receivable and merchandise inventory (uses of cash) hampered Snow Creek's ability to pay its bills. Studying cash flows along with analyzing the income statement, statement of stockholders' equity, and the balance sheet provides a more accurate overview of a company's present and future financial condition.

CLIENT REFERRALS

The AICPA Rules of the Code of Professional Conduct require members to disclose the receipt or payment of a referral fee. If a CPA receives a fee for referring a person or business to another CPA, the CPA who received the fee must disclose the acceptance of the fee to the client. In addition, the CPA who paid the fee must also disclose the payment.

Required:

Use the three-step checklist to help determine whether the actions described in the following situations demonstrate ethical behavior.

Situation 1. Kizzy Anderson is a sole practitioner. A friend contacted Kizzy about representing his company, DecKits, in a complex business merger. Kizzy told him that she did not have the expertise that he needed and referred him to Navarro and Associates. Kizzy received a referral fee from Navarro and Associates. She immediately sent a letter to DecKits disclosing the referral fee.

Situation 2. Zachary Harris is a partner in the firm Arita and Harris, Certified Public Accountants. Most of Arita and Harris' clients are involved with importing goods from Pacific Rim countries. They generally do not prepare individual tax returns. When Zak's neighbor Helen Anastos asked Zak to prepare her taxes, he suggested she contact Kizzy Anderson. After meeting with Helen, Kizzy sent Zak a thank you note for the referral.

PROFESSIONAL BUSINESS ETHICS

AUDIT YOUR UNDERSTANDING

1. How are the cash flows resulting from a company's investing activities identified?

2. Why is an increase in accumulated depreciation on the balance sheet ignored when analyzing the cash flows from investing activities?

3. How are the cash flows originating from a company's financing activities identified?

4. How does an individual know if all cash transactions have been properly accounted for on the statement of cash flows?

WORK TOGETHER

Preparing the investing and financing activities sections for the statement of cash flows; completing the statement of cash flows

Use the working papers from the Work Together on page 487. A comparative balance sheet and forms for analyzing changes in long-term assets, long-term liabilities, and stockholders' equity are provided in the *Working Papers*. Your instructor will guide you through the following examples.

5. Complete the changes in long-term assets and long-term liabilities form.

6. Prepare the investing activities section of the statement of cash flows.

7. Complete the changes in stockholders' equity form.

8. Prepare the financing activities section of the statement of cash flows.

9. Complete the statement of cash flows.

ON YOUR OWN

Preparing the investing and financing activities sections for the statement of cash flows; completing the statement of cash flows

Use the working papers from the On Your Own on page 487. A comparative balance sheet and forms for analyzing changes in long-term assets, long-term liabilities, and stockholders' equity are provided in the *Working Papers*. Work independently to complete the following problem.

10. Complete the changes in long-term assets and long-term liabilities form.

11. Prepare the investing activities section of the statement of cash flows.

12. Complete the changes in stockholders' equity form.

13. Prepare the financing activities section of the statement of cash flows.

14. Complete the statement of cash flows.

After completing this chapter, you can

1. Define important accounting terms related to cash flow analysis.

2. Identify accounting concepts and practices related to cash flow analysis.

3. Describe and provide examples of operating, investing, and financing activities.

4. Prepare the operating activities section of a statement of cash flows.

5. Prepare the investing activities and financing activities sections of a statement of cash flows.

6. Complete a statement of cash flows.

EXPLORE ACCOUNTING

FASB STATEMENT NO. 95

The development of generally accepted accounting principles (GAAP) is a political process. After researching an accounting issue, the Financial Accounting Standards Board (FASB) issues a proposal for new principle in a Discussion Memorandum (DM). Interested individuals and companies submit comments about the DM to the FASB. The FASB considers their comments in producing its final statement.

A good example of this political process is FASB Statement No. 95, Statement of Cash Flows. The statement allows companies to use two methods to report cash flows from operating activities. Although the FASB recommends the direct method, most companies use the alternative indirect method. The indirect method, as illustrated in this textbook, begins with net income and

makes adjustments for changes in current assets and liabilities. In contrast, the direct method reports each major class of cash receipts and cash payments, as illustrated below.

If the FASB encourages the use of the direct method, why do most companies use the indirect method? First, the indirect method was used for many years for preparing a similar statement that was required prior to FASB No. 95. Second, the direct method requires more effort to obtain the information. Most of the information for an indirect method statement can be obtained from other financial

statements. The direct method requires the company to obtain more detailed information directly from the general ledger.

REQUIRED:

Obtain a copy of FASB No. 95. Read the portion of the statement (paragraph 106-121) that presents the FASB's reasons for allowing companies to use either the indirect or direct methods. Do you agree with the FASB's reasons? Identify other accounting principles where two or more methods are allowed. Should alternative methods be allowed to report the same accounting information?

Cash flows from operating activities:	
Cash received from customers	$ 670,000.00
Cash paid to suppliers and employees	(540,000.00)
Interest paid	(34,000.00)
Income taxes paid	(29,000.00)
Net cash provided by operating activities	$ 67,000.00

APPLICATION PROBLEM
Classifying cash flows

The following business transactions represent selected cash receipts (cash inflows) and cash payments (cash outflows) of Ridge Development Corporation.

a.	dividend payment	e.	cash purchase of computer equipment
b.	payment of insurance premium	f.	sale of treasury stock
c.	receipts from the signing of a note payable	g.	receipts from consulting services
d.	payment of payroll taxes		

Instructions:
Use the form provided in the *Working Papers* to identify each transaction as (1) a cash inflow or cash outflow and (2) as an operating, investing, or financing activity.

APPLICATION PROBLEM
Calculating the cash flows from operating activities

The following information was taken from the financial statements of Flexcor Corporation on December 31 of the current year. The comparative income statement of Flexcor Corporation reveals the following net income and depreciation expense for the current year.

Net income	$91,460.00
Depreciation expense	12,500.00

The comparative balance sheet of Flexcor Corporation lists the following current assets and current liabilities and their ending balances for the current and prior years.

	Current Year	Prior Year
Accounts Receivable (book value)	$ 55,515.00	$ 48,000.00
Merchandise Inventory	118,316.00	121,000.00
Supplies	6,148.00	5,500.00
Accounts Payable	49,762.00	44,000.00

Instructions:

1. In the forms provided in the *Working Papers*, record the appropriate amount for net income. Indicate if this item represents a source of cash or use of cash.

2. Record the appropriate amount for depreciation expense. Indicate if this item represents a source of cash or use of cash.

3. For each current asset and current liability, write the balances for the current year and prior year. Classify each account as a current asset or current liability. Compute the amount of increase or decrease from the prior year. Indicate if the increase or decrease represents a source of cash or a use of cash.

4. Using the information collected, prepare the cash flows from operating activities section of the statement of cash flows for the current year ending December 31. Save your work to complete Application Problem 17-3.

APPLICATION PROBLEM
Calculating the cash flows from investing activities

Use the statement of cash flows started in Application Problem 17-1. The comparative balance sheet of Flexcor Corporation lists the following long-term assets and their ending balances for the current and prior years.

	Current Year	Prior Year
Office equipment	$ 22,800.00	$ 12,500.00
Office furniture	12,210.00	9,000.00
Land (decrease due to sale)	100,000.00	140,000.00

Instructions:

1. For each account, write the balances for the current year and prior year. Compute the amount of increase or decrease from the prior year. Indicate if the increase or decrease represents a source of cash or a use of cash.

2. Using the statement of cash flows started in Application Problem 17-1, prepare the Cash Flows from Investing Activities section of the statement of cash flows. Save your work to complete Application Problem 17-4.

APPLICATION PROBLEM
Calculating the cash flows from financing activities and completing a statement of cash flows

Use the statement of cash flows started in Application Problem 17-1. The comparative balance sheet of Flexcor Corporation lists the following long-term liability and its ending balance for the current and prior years.

	Current Year	Prior Year
Mortgage payable	$80,100.00	$92,000.00

The comparative statement of stockholders' equity of Flexcor Corporation reveals the following stock and dividend information for the current year.

Sale of additional common stock	20,000.00
Payment of cash dividend	50,000.00

Instructions:

1. For the long-term liability, record the amount of increase or decrease from the prior year. Indicate if the increase or decrease represents a source of cash or a use of cash.

2. For each amount taken from the comparative statement of stockholders' equity, record the appropriate amount. Indicate if these activities represent a source of cash or use of cash.

3. Using the statement of cash flows started in Application Problem 17-1, prepare the cash flows from financing activities section of the statement of cash flows.

4. Compute the net increase or decrease resulting from operating, investing, and financing activities.

5. Record the cash balance for the beginning of the period in the form provided. Flexcor started the year with a beginning cash balance of $67,930.00.

6. Compute the cash balance for the end of the fiscal period by adding the amount of increase or decrease in cash and the beginning cash amount.

7. Complete the statement of cash flows for Flexcor Corporation by entering the net increase or decrease in cash, the beginning cash balance, and the ending cash balance.

8. Verify the accuracy of the statement of cash flows by comparing the statement's ending cash balance with the cash balance of $156,763.00 listed for the current year on Flexcor's comparative balance sheet.

MASTERY PROBLEM
Preparing a statement of cash flows

Use the abbreviated comparative financial statements for West Coast Construction, Inc. in the *Working Papers*.

Instructions:

1. Review the comparative income statement and identify the amounts of net income (or net loss) and depreciation expense for the period. Indicate if each item represents a source of cash or use of cash.

2. Analyze the comparative balance sheet and complete the following steps:
   a. Prepare a list of current assets and current liabilities.
   b. Write the balances for the current year and prior year.
   c. Classify each account as a current asset or current liability.
   d. Compute the amount of increase or decrease from the prior year.
   e. Indicate if the increase or decrease represents a source of cash or a use of cash.

3. Analyze the comparative balance sheet and complete the following steps:
   a. Prepare a list of long-term assets.
   b. Write the balances for the current year and prior year.
   c. Compute the amount of increase or decrease from the prior year.
   d. Indicate if the increase or decrease represents a source of cash or a use of cash.

4. Reexamine the comparative balance sheet and complete the following steps:
   a. Prepare a list of long-term liabilities.
   b. Compute the amount of increase or decrease from the prior year.
   c. Indicate if the increase or decrease represents a source of cash or a use of cash.

5. Review the comparative statement of stockholders' equity and (1) identify the amounts of any additional stock issued or cash dividends paid and (2) indicate if each item represents a source of cash or use of cash.

6. Prepare the operating, investing, and financing activities sections of a statement of cash flows.

7. Enter the cash balance at the beginning of the year as shown on the comparative balance sheet.

8. Compute the cash balance for the end of the period to complete the statement of cash flows.

9. Verify the accuracy of the statement of cash flows by comparing the statement's ending cash balance with the cash balance listed for the current year on West Coast's comparative balance sheet.

17-6 CHALLENGE PROBLEM
Preparing a statement of cash flows

Use the abbreviated comparative financial statements for Pacific Digital Corporation in the *Working Papers*. The comparative balance sheet for Pacific Digital Corporation lists an intangible asset, Patents. The patents were granted in the first year of the business' existence. Intangible assets like Patents are written off as an expense over a period of years. Although the expense is recognized on the income statement under the accrual basis of accounting, it does not involve an outflow of cash. The cash was actually spent in an earlier period. Since the amortized patent expense shown on Pacific Digital's comparative income statement does not use cash, it is handled the same way as depreciation expense. Both patents and depreciation expense are adjustments to net income (or net loss) and presented before changes in current assets and liabilities.

Instructions:
Prepare a statement of cash flows for the current year for Pacific Digital Corporation.

INTERNET ACTIVITY
Point your browser to
http://accounting.swpco.com
Choose **Advanced Course**, choose **Activities**, and complete the activity for Chapter 17.

Applied Communication

You are the President of a non-profit organization that has grown quickly over the last few years. For the first time, you have had an independent accountant audit your financial records. Upon the recommendation of the accountant, your staff has begun preparing a statement of cash flows.

The organization is overseen by a volunteer board of directors. They meet monthly to review the financial stability of the organization and to assist management in developing long-range plans. At each meeting, you present the financial statements from the previous month.

Required:
Since most of the members of your board are not familiar with the statement of cash flows, prepare a short explanation of the purpose and use of the statement.

Cases for Critical Thinking

Case 1

Techmart Corporation is a young start-up firm that produces components for high-resolution televisions. During the last two years, sales have grown dramatically. Currently, Techmart is experiencing a cash shortage and is having difficulty purchasing manufacturing supplies and meeting its weekly payroll. Lately, the company has not been very successful in collecting its accounts receivable. The company offers its clients 90 days to pay on all receivables and does not understand why there is a shortage of cash. What suggestions can you offer the president of Techmart regarding its collection policy? Explain your recommendations. What can Techmart do during the short run to overcome its shortage of cash?

USING THE SAVINGS PLANNER

Planning Tools

Planning tools are easy-to-use applications for producing results for different types of financial investments. *Automated Accounting 7.0* and higher includes five such tools located on the different tabs included on the Planning Tools screen.

Savings Planner

The Savings Planner is similar to the loan planner introduced in the Automated Accounting section of Chapter 11, page 319. The Savings Planner is used to perform one of three calculations:

1. The monthly contribution required to meet a target ending savings balance

2. The ending savings balance of a series of contributions

3. The number of months required to meet a specified ending savings balance

One of the calculations is chosen from the Calculate box. The item to be calculated appears grayed (or dimmed). Enter the other items and the planner will make the calculation. For example, Andrew Ruiz is saving money to pay for his living expenses at college. He places $500.00 in a money market account. He plans to add $50.00 a month. Interest is earned on the account at the rate of 6.5%. How much will Andrew have at the end of three years (36 months)? Using the Savings Planner to make the calculation, Andrew will have $2,588.92 at the end of three years, as shown in Figure AA17-1.

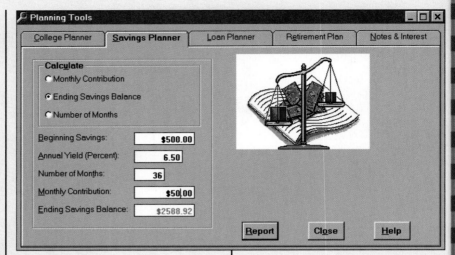

Figure AA17-1

The Savings Planner Report

A report of the findings may be displayed or printed. Click the Report button to display the report. Click the Print button from the Savings Plan report display to print it.

USING SPECIAL TOOLS: THE SAVINGS PLANNER

Instructions:

1. Load *Automated Accounting 7.0* or higher software.

2. Select New from the File menu.

3. Click on the Tools toolbar button.

4. Click on the Savings Planner tab. Select Number of Months from the Calculate box. Enter a beginning balance of $250.00. Enter an Annual Yield of 7%. Enter a Monthly Contribution of $100.00 and an Ending Savings Balance of $2,000.00. How many months are required for the savings balance to reach $2,000.00?

5. Click on the Report command button from within the Savings Planner tab. Print the report, or copy it to the clipboard for entering into a word processor or spreadsheet application.

6. Click Close or press ESC to return to the planner. Steps 4 and 5 may then be repeated for different calculation options, or for different data sets.

7. Click Close or press ESC to exit the planner. Upon exiting a planning tool, your data will not be saved. Be sure to print a report, or copy it to a word processor or spreadsheet and save it in that application.

8. Exit the Automated Accounting software.

Cost Accounting

AQUACRUISER, INC. CHART OF ACCOUNTS

Balance Sheet Accounts

(1000) Assets
1100 CURRENT ASSETS
1105   Cash
1110   Accounts Receivable
1115   Allowance for Uncollectible Accounts
1120   Merchandise Inventory—Accessories
1125   Merchandise Inventory—Boats
1130   Supplies
1135   Prepaid Insurance

1200 PLANT ASSETS
1205   Delivery Equipment—Boats
1210   Accumulated Depreciation—Delivery Equipment, Boats
1215   Office Equipment
1220   Accumulated Depreciation—Office Equipment
1225   Store Equipment—Accessories
1230   Accumulated Depreciation—Store Equipment, Accessories
1235   Store Equipment—Boats
1240   Accumulated Depreciation—Store Equipment, Boats

(2000) Liabilities
2100 CURRENT LIABILITIES
2105   Accounts Payable
2110   Employee Income Tax Payable
2115   Federal Income Tax Payable
2120   Social Security Tax Payable
2123   Medicare Tax Payable
2125   Salaries Payable
2130   Sales Tax Payable
2135   Unemployment Tax Payable—Federal
2140   Unemployment Tax Payable—State
2145   Dividends Payable

(3000) Stockholders' Equity
3105   Capital Stock
3110   Retained Earnings
3115   Dividends
3120   Income Summary—Accessories
3125   Income Summary—Boats
3130   Income Summary—General

Income Statement Accounts

(4000) Operating Revenue
4105   Sales—Accessories
4110   Sales Discount—Accessories
4115   Sales Returns and Allowances—Accessories
4120   Sales—Boats
4125   Sales Discount—Boats
4130   Sales Returns and Allowances—Boats

(5000) Cost of Merchandise
5105   Purchases—Accessories
5110   Purchases Discount—Accessories
5115   Purchases Returns and Allowances—Accessories
5120   Purchases—Boats
5125   Purchases Discount—Boats
5130   Purchases Returns and Allowances—Boats

(6000) Direct Expenses
6100 DIRECT EXPENSES—ACCESSORIES
6105   Advertising Expense—Accessories
6110   Depreciation Expense—Store Equipment, Accessories
6115   Insurance Expense—Accessories
6120   Payroll Taxes Expense—Accessories
6125   Salary Expense—Accessories
6130   Supplies Expense—Accessories

6200 DIRECT EXPENSES—BOATS
6205   Advertising Expense—Boats
6210   Delivery Expense—Boats
6215   Depreciation Expense—Delivery Equipment, Boats
6220   Depreciation Expense—Store Equipment, Boats
6225   Insurance Expense—Boats
6230   Payroll Taxes Expense—Boats
6235   Salary Expense—Boats
6240   Supplies Expense—Boats
6245   Uncollectible Accounts Expense—Boats

(7000) Indirect Expenses
7105   Credit Card Fee Expense
7110   Depreciation Expense—Office Equipment
7115   Insurance Expense—Administrative
7120   Miscellaneous Expense
7125   Payroll Taxes Expense—Administrative
7130   Rent Expense
7135   Salary Expense—Administrative
7140   Supplies Expense—Administrative
7145   Utilities Expense

(8000) Income Tax
9105   Federal Income Tax Expense

The chart of accounts for AquaCruiser, Inc. is illustrated above for ready reference as you study Chapter 18 of this textbook.

18

Cost Accounting for a Merchandising Business

AFTER STUDYING CHAPTER 18, YOU WILL BE ABLE TO:

1. Define accounting terms related to cost accounting for a departmentalized merchandising business.

2. Identify accounting concepts and practices related to cost accounting for a departmentalized merchandising business.

3. Journalize entries for direct and indirect expenses.

4. Prepare a work sheet for a departmentalized merchandising business.

5. Prepare a departmental margin statement and income statement with departmental margin.

Businesses make many different products available to meet the many needs of consumers. To meet these needs efficiently, businesses normally specialize in a part of the total process necessary to make and deliver these products to consumers. Manufacturing businesses make the products. Each manufacturing business normally concentrates on making only a few similar types of products. Merchandising businesses purchase and display products from many different manufacturers to provide consumers a selection of products in one location. Regardless of the type of business, a company needs accurate, timely statements of revenue, costs, and expenses to operate a profitable business. *(CONCEPT: Adequate Disclosure)*

SMALL BUSINESS SPOTLIGHT

The Small Business Administration maintains an elaborate, but easy to use, web site to help small business owners access information about programs and services. The site includes an online library, calendar of events, and information about starting, financing, and expanding a business. For more information, visit the SBA online at www.sba.gov

ACCOUNTING
IN YOUR CAREER

WHO IS RESPONSIBLE?

Holly Fogel, the manager of the mail order division of Specialty Retail, is preparing for her annual performance review. Her annual raise will be based on the results of the performance review. To prepare for the review, she uses her spreadsheet software to create a departmental margin statement for the mail order division. In the statement, she lists all the costs that are directly attributed to her division and therefore under her control. These include the cost of merchandise sold and all the expenses associated with her division. The expenses directly connected to her division include equipment depreciation, advertising, uncollectible accounts, building rent, delivery expense, and the salary and payroll taxes expenses of her employees. Her departmental margin after all costs and expenses are deducted from her sales revenue is $120,000.

Holly is pleased with this figure because it is a 20% increase over last year's margin and a 10% increase over the budget forecast. She is looking forward to a good review and is already dreaming about how she will spend her raise. She is proud of the increase in margin too because her sales jumped due to a special promotion she planned.

Ron Dolan conducts the review and begins by saying how disappointed he is in the division's results. He offers his copy of the departmental margin statement and says, "Holly, you haven't improved margin over last year's figures." Holly quickly compares Mr. Dolan's statement with hers and sees that her division has been charged with part of the cost of the $40,000 renovation to corporate headquarters and a share of the costs of the accounting and human resources office. "Mr. Dolan," Holly begins, "look at my figures. I've included only the costs that I am responsible for. It isn't fair to evaluate me based on items over which I have no control."

Critical Thinking

1. Which departmental margin statement is properly prepared? Why?
2. Is Holly correct in maintaining that she should not be evaluated based on costs she cannot control?
3. What do you think about the way this performance review has been handled?

FEATURES OF A RESPONSIBILITY ACCOUNTING SYSTEM

1. Each manager is assigned responsibility for only those revenues, costs, and expenses for which the manager can make decisions and affect the outcome.

2. The revenues, costs, and expenses for which a manager is responsible must be readily identifiable with the manager's unit. For example, if a manager is responsible for supplies expense, that manager should make decisions about the use of supplies. Also, a separate record should be kept for the manager's supplies expense. Thus, responsibility accounting traces revenues, costs, and expenses to the individual managers who are responsible for making decisions about those revenues, costs, and expenses.

Figure 18-1

Controlling costs is essential to a business' success. However, who should control a business' costs? Good management practices require that each manager be responsible for controlling all costs incurred by the manager's business unit. Assigning control of business revenues, costs, and expenses as a responsibility of a specific manager is called **responsibility accounting**.

Merchandising businesses with effective cost controls generally use some kind of responsibility accounting. Figure 18-1 describes the two important features of a successful responsibility accounting system.

A typical merchandising business income statement reports net income earned during a fiscal period. (CONCEPT: Accounting Period Cycle) However, the statement usually does not report specific information that a department manager can use to control departmental costs. Therefore, merchandising businesses often prepare departmental statements to show each department's contribution to net income.

In responsibility accounting, operating expenses are classified as either direct or indirect expenses. An operating expense identifiable with and chargeable to the operation of a specific department is called a **direct expense**. The cost of supplies used by a specific department is an example of a direct expense. An operating expense chargeable to overall business operations and not identifiable with a specific department is called an **indirect expense**. The cost of electricity used by a business' overall operation is an example of an indirect expense.

The revenue earned by a department less its cost of merchandise sold and less its direct expenses is called **departmental margin**. A statement that reports departmental margin for a specific department is called a **departmental margin statement**.

AquaCruiser, Inc., uses responsibility accounting to help control costs and expenses. AquaCruiser has two merchandising departments, accessories and boats. Each department's revenue, cost of merchandise sold, and direct expenses are recorded in separate departmental general ledger accounts as shown in AquaCruiser's chart of accounts.

Each business develops a chart of accounts to best meet its needs. MasterSport, in Part 1, adds a -1 and -2 to identify its departmental accounts. AquaCruiser, another departmentalized business, groups by type, such as revenue, cost of merchandise, direct expenses, and indirect expenses. For example, Direct Expenses—Accessories are 6100 numbers. Direct Expenses—Boats are 6200 numbers.

F.Y.I.

A typical income statement does not show costs broken down by department. Departmental margin statements show revenues and expenses for a department. Therefore, department managers use departmental margin statements for planning and analysis.

	DATE	ACCOUNT TITLE	CK. NO.	POST. REF.	GENERAL 1 DEBIT	GENERAL 2 CREDIT	ACCOUNTS PAYABLE 3 DEBIT	PURCH. DISCOUNT CR. 4 ACCESS.	PURCH. DISCOUNT CR. 5 BOATS	CASH 6 CREDIT	
1	Apr. 1	Advertising Exp.—Access.	610		40000					40000	1

CASH PAYMENTS JOURNAL — PAGE 16

Figure 18-2

Procedures for recording revenue, cost, and expense transactions are similar for most merchandising businesses. The journalizing procedures used by MasterSport in Chapters 1 and 2 are similar to the procedures used by AquaCruiser. AquaCruiser has separate accounts, as does MasterSport for each department's merchandise inventory, sales, and purchases. In addition to these accounts, AquaCruiser has separate accounts in the general ledger for each department's direct expenses, such as advertising, salaries, and supplies. Separate departmental accounts for sales, merchandise inventory, purchases, and direct expenses provide information needed to prepare departmental margin statements.

A journal entry prepared by AquaCruiser to record a direct expense is shown in Figure 18-2. AquaCruiser's accessories department manager decided to buy the advertising services. The advertising promotes the department's sale of boat accessories. Since the department manager controls the advertising expense and the department receives the benefits, the expense is classified as a direct expense. To ensure that such expenses are recorded as direct expenses, the account title also includes the department's name, Advertising Expense—Accessories.

	DATE	ACCOUNT TITLE	CK. NO.	POST. REF.	GENERAL 1 DEBIT	GENERAL 2 CREDIT	ACCOUNTS PAYABLE 3 DEBIT	PURCH. DISCOUNT CR. 4 ACCESS.	PURCH. DISCOUNT CR. 5 BOATS	CASH 6 CREDIT	
2	1	Rent Expense	611		600000					600000	2

CASH PAYMENTS JOURNAL — PAGE 16

Figure 18-3

A journal entry prepared by AquaCruiser to record an indirect expense is shown in Figure 18-3. The accessories department uses a portion of the space rented by AquaCruiser. However, the decision to rent the specific facility was made by the company president, not the accessories department manager. In addition, rent expense is not separated by departments but is one payment for the entire facility used by all departments. Since this expense is not separated by departments, the expense is recorded as an indirect expense. Indirect expenses are reported in the company's income statement but not in departmental margin statements. Direct and indirect expenses are reported in the same way each fiscal period. (CONCEPT: Consistent Reporting)

Indirect expenses are not reported in departmental margin statements.

AquaCruiser, Inc.

Work Sheet

For Month Ended April 30, 20--

ACCOUNT TITLE	TRIAL BALANCE DEBIT	TRIAL BALANCE CREDIT	ADJUSTMENTS DEBIT	ADJUSTMENTS CREDIT	DEPT. MARGIN — ACCESSORIES DEBIT	ACCESSORIES CREDIT	BOATS DEBIT	BOATS CREDIT	INCOME STATEMENT DEBIT	INCOME STATEMENT CREDIT	BALANCE SHEET DEBIT	BALANCE SHEET CREDIT
1 Cash	10431500										10431500	
2 Accounts Receivable	6820400										6820400	
3 Allow. for Uncoll. Accts.		13400		(a) 75000								88400
4 Mdse. Inv.—Accessories	15583800		(b)1246800								16830600	
5 Mdse. Inv.—Boats	20336400		(c)1627000								21963400	
6 Supplies	627600			(d)332200							295400	
7 Prepaid Insurance	235000			(e)29400							205600	
8 Delivery Equip.—Boats	3396000										3396000	
9 Accum. Depr.—Del. Equip., Boats		1020000		(f)57000								1077000
10 Office Equipment	1199000										1199000	
11 Accum. Depr.—Office Equipment		180000		(g)20000								200000
12 Store Equipment—Access.	3027000										3027000	
13 Accum. Depr.—Store Equip., Access.		908000		(h)50600								958600
14 Store Equipment—Boats	760000										760000	
15 Accum. Depr.—Store Equip., Boats		228000		(i)12500								240500
16 Accounts Payable		9851000										9851000
17 Employee Income Tax Payable		539000										539000
18 Federal Income Tax Payable				(j)1146000								1146000
19 Social Security Tax Payable		780000										780000
20 Medicare Tax Payable		180000										180000
21 Salaries Payable												
22 Sales Tax Payable		1688000										1688000
23 Unemploy. Tax Pay.—Federal		38400										38400
24 Unemploy. Tax Pay.—State		259200										259200
25 Dividends Payable												
26 Capital Stock		30000000										30000000
27 Retained Earnings		18658200										18658200
28 Dividends	3000000										3000000	
29 Income Summary—Access.			(b)1246800			1246800						
30 Income Summary—Boats				(c)1627000				1627000				
31 Income Summary—General												
32 Sales—Accessories		13180000				13180000						
33 Sales Discount—Accessories	44000				44000							

Figure 18-4 (top half)

#	Account	Adjustments	Dept. Margin—Accessories Dr	Dept. Margin—Accessories Cr	Dept. Margin—Boats Dr	Dept. Margin—Boats Cr	Income Statement Dr	Income Statement Cr	Balance Sheet Dr	Balance Sheet Cr
34	Sales Ret. and Allow.—Access.		110000							
35	Sales—Boats					15151000				
36	Sales Discount—Boats				75700					
37	Sales Ret. and Allow.—Boats				72500					
38	Purchases—Accessories		8831300							
39	Purch. Discount—Accessories			44100						
40	Purch. Ret. and Allow.—Access.			39000						
41	Purchases—Boats				8976500					
42	Purch. Discount—Boats					54000				
43	Purch. Ret. and Allow.—Boats					36300				
44	Advertising Exp.—Access.		165000							
45	Depr. Exp.—Store Equip., Access.	(h) 50600	50600							
46	Insurance Exp.—Access.	(e) 11400	11400							
47	Payroll Taxes Exp.—Access.		252100							
48	Salary Expense—Access.		1950000							
49	Supplies Expense—Access.	(d) 127900	127900							
50	Advertising Expense—Boats				233500					
51	Delivery Expense—Boats				475000					
52	Depr. Exp.—Del. Equip., Boats	(f) 57000			57000					
53	Depr. Exp.—Store Equip., Boats	(l) 12500			12500					
54	Insurance Expense—Boats	(e) 15200			15200					
55	Payroll Taxes Exp.—Boats				233900					
56	Salary Expense—Boats				1800000					
57	Supplies Expense—Boats	(d) 112100			112100					
58	Uncollect. Accts. Expense—Boats	(a) 75000			75000					
59	Credit Card Fee Expense						368500			
60	Depr. Exp.—Office Equip.	(g) 20000					20000			
61	Insurance Expense—Admin.	(e) 2800					2800			
62	Miscellaneous Expense						504700			
63	Payroll Taxes Exp.—Admin.						291600			
64	Rent Expense						600000			
65	Salary Expense—Admin.						2250000			
66	Supplies Expense—Admin.	(d) 92200					92200			
67	Utilities Expense						295600			
68			11443300	14509900	12138900	16868300				
69	Dept. Margin—Access.		3066600					3066600		
70	Dept. Margin—Boats				4729400			4729400		
71				14509900 / 14509900		16868300 / 16868300				
72	Federal Income Tax Expense	(i) 1146000					1146000			
73		4596500 / 4596500	92847600	92847600			5571400	7796000	65704300	67928900
74							2224600			2224600
75	Net Income after Fed. Inc. Tax						7796000 / 7796000		67928900 / 67928900	

Figure 18-4 (bottom half)

AquaCruiser uses an expanded work sheet to sort information needed for departmental margin statements. The 12-column work sheet prepared by AquaCruiser on April 30 is shown in Figure 18-4 on pages 506 and 507. Eight amount columns on the work sheet are the same as those described previously. AquaCruiser uses four additional columns: Departmental Margin Statement—Accessories Debit and Credit and Departmental Margin Statement—Boats Debit and Credit. Information in these four additional columns is used to prepare departmental margin statements.

Trial Balance on a Work Sheet

AquaCruiser prepares a trial balance in the same way as previously described for other types of businesses. AquaCruiser's April 30 trial balance is on the work sheet, Figure 18-4. All general ledger accounts are listed even if they have no balance. Three income summary accounts are used. Two are used for adjusting inventory accounts related to separate departments, Income Summary—Accessories and Income Summary—Boats. They are also used to close the revenue, cost, and direct expense accounts of both departments. Income Summary—General is used for other closing entries.

AquaCruiser writes the account Federal Income Tax Expense on the work sheet two lines below Departmental Margin—Boats. This location simplifies subtotaling the income statement columns and calculating additional income tax expense. Procedures for calculating corporate income tax are described in Chapter 13.

Adjustments on a Work Sheet with Departmental Margins

The information below is needed for adjusting AquaCruiser's general ledger accounts for the month ended April 30 of the current year.

AquaCruiser's adjustments are in the work sheet's Adjustments columns, Figure 18-4. The departmental merchandise inventory adjustments are recorded in each department's appropriate income summary account.

Adjustments are made for uncollectible accounts expense, changes in departmental merchandise inventory, supplies used, insurance expired, depreciation, and estimated federal income tax expense.

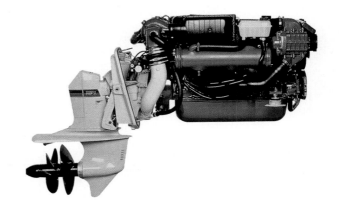

Adjustment Information, April 30	
Uncollectible Accounts Expense—Boats Estimated as 1.0% of Sales on Account	
Sales on Account for Year	$ 75,000.00
Merchandise Inventory—Accessories	168,306.00
Merchandise Inventory—Boats	219,634.00
Supplies Used—Accessories	1,279.00
Supplies Used—Boats	1,121.00
Supplies Used—Administrative	922.00
Insurance Expired—Accessories	114.00
Insurance Expired—Boats	152.00
Insurance Expired—Administrative	28.00
Depreciation Expense—Delivery Equipment, Boats	570.00
Depreciation Expense—Office Equipment	200.00
Depreciation Expense—Store Equipment, Accessories	506.00
Depreciation Expense—Store Equipment, Boats	125.00
Federal Income Tax Expense for April	11,460.00

Uncollectible Accounts Expense is included in the direct expenses section of AquaCruiser's departmental margin statement—boats because only boats are sold on credit. Therefore, uncollectible accounts expense is charged only to this department. In some companies uncollectible accounts expense is divided among various departments. In other companies uncollectible accounts expense is considered an administrative expense and is listed in the indirect expenses section of the income statement.

AquaCruiser keeps a record of supplies used by each department so that supplies expense can be charged to the appropriate department. The effect of the supplies adjustment for April is shown in the T accounts.

Supplies Expense—Accessories

Adj. (d)	1,279.00

Supplies Expense—Boats

Adj. (d)	1,121.00

Supplies Expense—Administrative

Adj. (d)	922.00

Supplies

Apr. 1 Bal.	6,276.00	Adj. (d)	3,322.00

Notice that a separate expense account is maintained for each department and for administrative uses. The administrative account records the use of supplies by any staff person who does not work in one of the departments. For example, the use of supplies by the accounting staff would be recorded in the administrative account.

AquaCruiser also analyzes insurance records each month to determine how much insurance expense each department has incurred. Insurance is maintained on the equipment, the space occupied, and the inventory. The insurance that can be identified with equipment used by a department or inventory held by a department is assigned to that department. All other insurance is considered administrative. The effect of the adjustment to record insurance expired for each department is shown in the T accounts.

These adjustments record expenses associated with producing revenue for a fiscal period. (CONCEPT: Matching Expenses with Revenue)

Insurance Expense—Accessories

Adj. (e)	114.00

Insurance Expense—Boats

Adj. (e)	152.00

Insurance Expense—Administrative

Adj. (e)	28.00

Prepaid Insurance

Apr. 1 Bal.	2,350.00	Adj. (e)	294.00

STEPS Completing a work sheet with departmental margin columns

1. Extend balance sheet items to the Balance Sheet Debit and Credit columns. (Lines 1-28 of Figure 18-4). The procedure for extending the balance sheet amounts is the same as previously described in this textbook. When an account is not affected by an adjustment, the amount in the Trial Balance Debit or Credit column is extended to either the Balance Sheet Debit or Credit column. When an account is affected by an adjustment, the new balance is calculated and extended to either the Balance Sheet Debit or Credit column.

2. Extend revenue, cost, and direct expense items for the accessories department to the Departmental Margin—Accessories Debit and Credit columns (Lines 29, 32—34, 38—40, and 44—49). The procedure for extending these income statement amounts is the same as previously described. The difference is that the amounts are extended to the Departmental Margin Statements—Accessories Debit and Credit columns.

3. Extend the revenue, cost, and direct expense items for the boats department to the Departmental Margin Statements—Boats Debit and Credit columns (Lines 30, 35—37, 41—43, and 50—58). The procedure for extending these income statement amounts is the same as that for the accessories department amounts described in Step 2.

4. Extend the indirect expense items to the Income Statement Debit column (Lines 59—67).

5. Calculate the departmental margin for each department (Lines 69 and 70).

   a. Rule a single line across the Departmental Margin Statements—Accessories Debit and Credit columns on the line with the last expense account, line 67. Add each column and write the totals under the ruled line. Subtract the smaller total from the larger total ($145,099.00 − $114,433.00 = $30,666.00). Write the difference, *$30,666.00*, in the Departmental Margin Statements—Accessories Debit column on the next line, line 69. Write the same amount in the Income Statement Credit column on the same line. Write the words *Dept. Margin—Access.* on the same line in the Account Title column. The amount written on this line, $30,666.00, is the departmental margin for the accessories department for the month ended April 30 of the current year.

   b. The same procedure is followed to calculate departmental margin for the boats department. The totals for the Boats Debit and Credit columns are written on the same line as the totals of the Accessories columns. This departmental margin is recorded in the work sheet's Departmental Margin Statements—Boats Debit column and in the Income Statement Credit column. The amounts are written on the line below the departmental margin for the accessories department, line 70.

   c. The Departmental Margin Statements columns for the two departments are totaled and ruled as shown on line 71.

6. Calculate the federal income tax expense and record it on the work sheet. The procedure for calculating estimated federal income tax expense is the same as that described in Chapter 13 except AquaCruiser estimates the amount for one month. The monthly net income before federal income tax is multiplied by 12 to determine estimated annual net income before federal income tax. Estimated tax is calculated on annual net income using the procedure described in Chapter 13. The federal income tax amount is divided by 12 to obtain the estimated federal income tax expense for the month. AquaCruiser calculated the estimated federal income tax expense for April as follows.

April net income before federal income tax	$ 33,706.00
Multiplied by 12	× 12
Estimated annual net income before federal income tax	$404,472.00
Federal income tax	$137,520.48
Divided by 12	÷ 12
Estimated federal income tax expense for April	$ 11,460.04*

*Since amount is an estimate, AquaCruiser rounds the amount to the nearest dollar.

7. Total the Adjustments, Income Statement, and Balance Sheet columns. Calculate and record net income after federal income tax. Rule the work sheet as shown on lines 73–75.

TERMS REVIEW

responsibility accounting

direct expense

indirect expense

departmental margin

departmental margin statement

AUDIT YOUR UNDERSTANDING

1. What two features are required if responsibility accounting is to be successful?
2. For what type of accounts does AquaCruiser have separate departmental accounts in the general ledger?
3. Which financial statements are prepared from information in the four additional columns of AquaCruiser's work sheet?

WORK TOGETHER

Preparing a work sheet with departmental margins

Callostay Co. has two departments, books and music. The trial balance and adjustment information for Callostay are provided in the *Working Papers*. Your instructor will guide you through the following examples. Save your work to complete the Work Together on page 516.

4. Record the adjustments on the work sheet and total the adjustments columns.
5. Extend amounts to the proper debit and credit columns for the Departmental Margin Statement—Books, Departmental Margin Statement—Music, Income Statement, and Balance Sheet. Accounts on trial balance lines 55–63 are classified as indirect expenses. Total and rule the work sheet.

ON YOUR OWN

Journalizing direct and indirect expenses

Franklin Shoppes, Inc., has two departments: crafts and fabrics. Franklin completed the following transactions during October of the current year. Page 8 of a cash payments journal is provided in the *Working Papers*. Source documents are abbreviated as: check, C. Work independently to complete this problem.

Oct. 1. Paid cash for utilities bill, $225.00. C435. (Utilities are used by all departments.)

Oct. 8. Paid cash for advertising in a craft fair program, $150.00. C485. The ad was prepared by the craft department and includes craft products only.

Oct. 12. Paid cash for rush delivery on a special order of fabric for a regular customer, $35.00. C491.

Oct. 15. Paid cash for bimonthly payroll. Craft Department: $1,258.51 (total payroll, $1,562.00, less deductions: employee income tax, $184.00; social security tax, $96.84; Medicare tax, $22.65). Fabric Department: $1,469.70 (total payroll, $1,850.00, less deductions: employee income tax, $212.00; social security tax, $141.50; Medicare tax, $26.80). C502.

6. Journalize the transactions. Expenses not identified with a specific department are recorded as indirect expenses.

DEPARTMENTAL MARGIN STATEMENT—ACCESSORIES

1. Determine net sales for department.

2. Determine cost of merchandise sold for department.

3. Calculate gross profit.

4. Record direct expenses of the department.

5. Calculate the departmental margin.

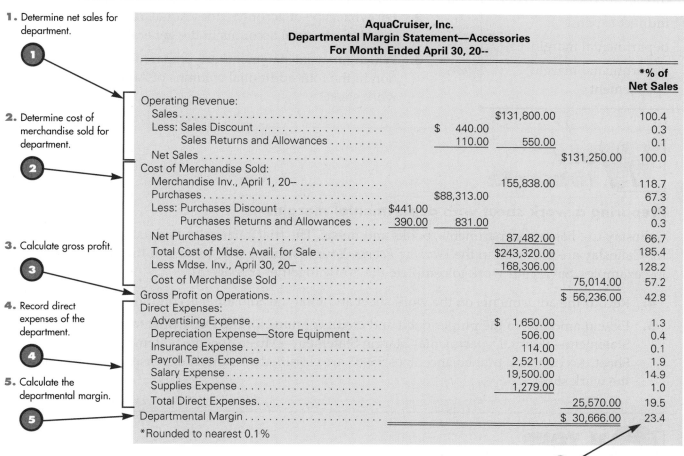

AquaCruiser, Inc.
Departmental Margin Statement—Accessories
For Month Ended April 30, 20--

			*% of Net Sales
Operating Revenue:			
Sales....................		$131,800.00	100.4
Less: Sales Discount..................	$ 440.00		0.3
Sales Returns and Allowances.........	110.00	550.00	0.1
Net Sales.....................		$131,250.00	100.0
Cost of Merchandise Sold:			
Merchandise Inv., April 1, 20--..............		155,838.00	118.7
Purchases........................	$88,313.00		67.3
Less: Purchases Discount................	$441.00		0.3
Purchases Returns and Allowances.....	390.00	831.00	0.3
Net Purchases.....................		87,482.00	66.7
Total Cost of Mdse. Avail. for Sale...........		$243,320.00	185.4
Less Mdse. Inv., April 30, 20--.............		168,306.00	128.2
Cost of Merchandise Sold.................		75,014.00	57.2
Gross Profit on Operations..................		$ 56,236.00	42.8
Direct Expenses:			
Advertising Expense....................	$ 1,650.00		1.3
Depreciation Expense—Store Equipment.....	506.00		0.4
Insurance Expense.....................	114.00		0.1
Payroll Taxes Expense..................	2,521.00		1.9
Salary Expense......................	19,500.00		14.9
Supplies Expense.....................	1,279.00		1.0
Total Direct Expenses..................		25,570.00	19.5
Departmental Margin.....................		$ 30,666.00	23.4

*Rounded to nearest 0.1%

Figure 18-5

6. Calculate the component percentages.

Financial statements reporting revenue, costs, and direct expenses under a specific department's control are called **responsibility statements**. AquaCruiser prepares the usual end-of-fiscal-period financial statements: income statement, statement of stockholders' equity, and balance sheet. In addition, AquaCruiser prepares two responsibility statements: (1) departmental margin statement—accessories and (2) departmental margin statement—boats. *(CONCEPT: Adequate Disclosure)*

Major responsibility for improving AquaCruiser's financial condition rests with management, including the department managers. The departmental margin statements assist in decision making. These provide information about the two departments' progress.

AquaCruiser's departmental margin statement—accessories for the month ended April 30 is shown in Figure 18-5. Information for this statement is obtained from the Departmental Margin Statements—Accessories columns of the work sheet, Figure 18-4.

The departmental margin statement includes information about operating revenue, cost of merchandise sold, and the direct expenses that can be identified with AquaCruiser's accessories department. The format of the statement is similar to an income statement. However, only direct expenses for the accessories department are included on the departmental margin statement.

Departmental Margin	÷	Net Sales	=	Component Percentage for Departmental Margin
$30,666.00	÷	$131,250.00	=	23.4%

	Component Percentages		
	April	March	February
Departmental Margin	23.4%	22.5%	22.2%

Figure 18-6

AquaCruiser calculates component percentages on departmental margin statements to help management interpret the information. The component percentages are calculated by dividing the amount on each line by the amount of departmental net sales. For the departmental margin statement—accessories, the departmental margin component percentage is calculated as shown in Figure 18-6.

A company may set departmental margin goals for each of its departments to encourage and determine acceptable performance by each department. AquaCruiser has set a minimum departmental margin goal of 22.0% for the accessories department. Departmental goals are determined by reviewing the department's previous achievements and evaluating changes in selling prices and department costs.

Component percentages for the current fiscal period also are compared to component percentages for previous fiscal periods. The accessories department's departmental margin component percentages for the current and two preceding months are also shown in Figure 18-6.

Since a department has control of and can affect its departmental margin by specific departmental action, this component percentage is an excellent measure of a department's performance. AquaCruiser's accessories department manager can determine whether the department is performing satisfactorily by making two comparisons. (1) Current period's departmental margin component percentage compared with the company-assigned goal of at least 22.0% depart-

mental margin. (2) Current period's departmental margin component percentage compared with previous periods' departmental margin component percentages. During February through April, the department exceeded the company-assigned goal, a favorable result. The accessories department increased its departmental margin component percentage from 22.2% to 23.4% in two months, a favorable trend.

When changes in component percentages occur for an item on the departmental margin statement, the department manager seeks the reasons for the changes. If changes are positive, the policies resulting in favorable changes are continued. If changes are negative, the manager seeks to change policies to prevent further declines.

Departmental revenue may increase because of special sales and advertising programs. The cost of merchandise may change because lower prices are obtained when merchandise is purchased. Other component percentages may change because of an increase or decrease in direct expenses. Without the information on the departmental margin statement, a department manager will not know which policies to continue and which to change. (CONCEPT: Adequate Disclosure)

Thus, departmental margin statements provide information to help managers identify unusual changes in revenue and cost amounts. The statements also provide information to assist company officers as well as department managers in evaluating departmental performance.

1. Determine net sales for department.

①

2. Determine cost of merchandise sold for department.

②

3. Calculate gross profit.

③

4. Record direct expenses of the department.

④

5. Calculate the departmental margin.

⑤

AquaCruiser, Inc.
Departmental Margin Statement—Boats
For Month Ended April 30, 20--

			*% of Net Sales
Operating Revenue:			
Sales		$151,510.00	101.0
Less: Sales Discount	$ 757.00		0.5
Sales Returns and Allowances	725.00	1,482.00	0.5
Net Sales		$150,028.00	100.0
Cost of Merchandise Sold:			
Merchandise Inv., April 1, 20–		$203,364.00	135.6
Purchases	$89,765.00		59.8
Less: Purchases Discount	$540.00		0.4
Purchases Returns and Allowances	363.00	903.00	0.2
Net Purchases		88,862.00	59.2
Total Cost of Mdse. Avail. for Sale		$292,226.00	194.8
Less Mdse. Inv., April 30, 20–		219,634.00	146.4
Cost of Merchandise Sold		72,592.00	48.4
Gross Profit on Operations		$ 77,436.00	51.6
Direct Expenses:			
Advertising Expense	$ 2,335.00		1.6
Delivery Expense	4,750.00		3.2
Depreciation Expense—Delivery Equipment	570.00		0.4
Depreciation Expense—Store Equipment	125.00		0.1
Insurance Expense	152.00		0.1
Payroll Taxes Expense	2,339.00		1.6
Salary Expense	18,000.00		12.0
Supplies Expense	1,121.00		0.7
Uncollectible Accounts Expense	750.00		0.5
Total Direct Expenses		30,142.00	20.1
Departmental Margin		$ 47,294.00	31.5

*Rounded to nearest 0.1%

Figure 18-7

6. Calculate the component percentages. **⑥**

AquaCruiser prepares a departmental margin statement for both the boats and accessories departments. The departmental margin state- ment—boats for the month ended April 30 is shown in Figure 18-7.

HISPANIC FIRM WINS CONTRACTING AWARD

Vista Technologies, a Hispanic-owned business, received the 1997 Prime Contractor of the Year award from the Small Business Administration. Vista was selected from a competitive pool of more than 300 businesses. The award recognizes Vista's superior overall quality in management, technical capabilities, delivery, and performance. The Small Business Administration's criteria for the award include financial health, labor rela- tions, cost performance, and special achievements.

The environmental engineering firm offers state-of-the-art capabilities in environmental technologies and weapons systems acquisition support. It employs more than 180 and had revenues of $16 million in 1996. The company was founded in 1989 by its president, Armando De La Paz. Its phenomenal revenue growth in the early 1990s landed it on the Fastest Growing 100 list of Hispanic businesses.

CULTURAL DIVERSITY

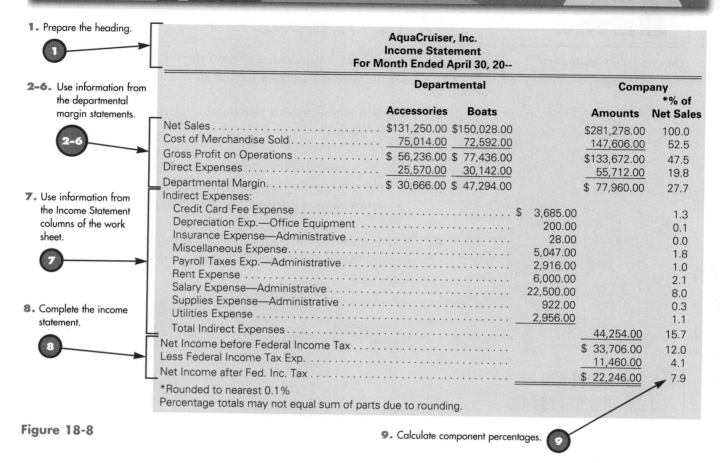

1. Prepare the heading.

1

2–6. Use information from the departmental margin statements.

2–6

7. Use information from the Income Statement columns of the work sheet.

7

8. Complete the income statement.

8

AquaCruiser, Inc.
Income Statement
For Month Ended April 30, 20--

| | Departmental | | Company | |
	Accessories	Boats	Amounts	*% of Net Sales
Net Sales	$131,250.00	$150,028.00	$281,278.00	100.0
Cost of Merchandise Sold	75,014.00	72,592.00	147,606.00	52.5
Gross Profit on Operations	$ 56,236.00	$ 77,436.00	$133,672.00	47.5
Direct Expenses	25,570.00	30,142.00	55,712.00	19.8
Departmental Margin	$ 30,666.00	$ 47,294.00	$ 77,960.00	27.7
Indirect Expenses:				
Credit Card Fee Expense		$ 3,685.00		1.3
Depreciation Exp.—Office Equipment		200.00		0.1
Insurance Expense—Administrative		28.00		0.0
Miscellaneous Expense		5,047.00		1.8
Payroll Taxes Exp.—Administrative		2,916.00		1.0
Rent Expense		6,000.00		2.1
Salary Expense—Administrative		22,500.00		8.0
Supplies Expense—Administrative		922.00		0.3
Utilities Expense		2,956.00		1.1
Total Indirect Expenses			44,254.00	15.7
Net Income before Federal Income Tax			$ 33,706.00	12.0
Less Federal Income Tax Exp.			11,460.00	4.1
Net Income after Fed. Inc. Tax			$ 22,246.00	7.9

*Rounded to nearest 0.1%
Percentage totals may not equal sum of parts due to rounding.

Figure 18-8

9. Calculate component percentages. **9**

AquaCruiser's income statement for the month ended April 30 is shown in Figure 18-8. The income statement is prepared with five columns: two for departmental amounts and three for company amounts and component percentages.

Preparing an income statement

1. Write the heading. Use the same format as for income statements previously described.

2. Prepare the net sales section. Totals are obtained from the departmental margin statements.

3. Prepare the cost of merchandise sold section. Totals are obtained from the departmental margin statements, Figures 18-5 and 18-7.

4. Prepare the gross profit section. Totals are obtained from the departmental margin statements.

5. Prepare the direct expenses section. Totals are obtained from the departmental margin statements. Details about direct expenses are not listed. Managers can refer to departmental margin statements for the details.

6. Prepare the departmental margin section. Information is obtained from the departmental margin statements. Company amounts in steps 2 through 6 are totals of departmental amounts.

7. Prepare the indirect expenses section. Account titles and balances are obtained from the Income Statement columns of the work sheet, Figure 18-4.

8. Complete the income statement. The procedure is the same as for income statements previously described. AquaCruiser has no Other Revenue or Other Expenses. However, if these items were included, the same procedure as previously described would be followed.

9. Calculate the component percentages. The procedure is the same as calculating the percentages of net sales on departmental margin statements. However, the percentages are based on company net sales.

TERM REVIEW

responsibility statements

AUDIT YOUR UNDERSTANDING

1. Where does AquaCruiser obtain the information to prepare the direct expenses section of the income statement?

2. How is the component percentage for departmental margin calculated?

3. What two comparisons can be made using the component percentage for departmental margin to determine if a department is performing satisfactorily?

4. Where does AquaCruiser obtain the information to prepare the indirect expenses section of the income statement?

WORK TOGETHER

Departmental margin statement

Use the work sheet from the Work Together on page 511. Statement paper is provided in the *Working Papers*. Your instructor will guide you through the following example.

5. Prepare a departmental margin statement for the books department. Calculate and record the component percentages for each item on the statement. Round percentage calculations to the nearest 0.1%.

ON YOUR OWN

Departmental margin statement

Use the work sheet from the Work Together on page 511. Statement paper is provided in the *Working Papers*. Work independently to complete the following problem.

6. Prepare a departmental margin statement for the music department. Calculate and record the component percentages for each item on the statement. Round percentage calculations to the nearest 0.1%.

CHAPTER UMMARY

After completing this chapter, you can

1. Define accounting terms related to cost accounting for a departmentalized merchandising business.

2. Identify accounting concepts and practices related to cost accounting for a departmentalized merchandising business.

3. Journalize entries for direct and indirect expenses.

4. Prepare a work sheet for a departmental merchandising business.

5. Prepare a departmental margin statement and an income statement with departmental margin.

EXPLORE ACCOUNTING

EXCEPTION REPORTS

The amount of financial information available to managers can become overwhelming. Responsibility accounting is one way that managers focus accounting information on one aspect of the business. A departmental margin statement, for example, focuses on the revenue and expenses controlled by the manager of a single department. Even departmental margin statements can be overwhelming for a large company with hundreds of departments. How does an upper-level manager examine all of these statements to identify problems?

Rather than reviewing every line of every departmental statement, a manager can instruct the computer system to prepare a report of only those accounts for which the actual results differ significantly from expected results.

These reports, often called exception reports, should identify both positive and negative situations. For example, an exception report could identify those accounts that differ by more than 10% from departmental budgets. This shorter report would allow the manager to quickly focus on areas that deserve attention.

Managers must gather information and be objective when investigating the reasons for excessive expenses. Does wages expense exceeding budget by 20% indicate that workers lack discipline? Although this explanation is possible, other factors could cause even the best employees to be unproductive, such as these:

- Workers have not received adequate training.
- Equipment is obsolete and often broken.
- Parts are frequently out of stock.

It is natural for managers to focus on negative situations. The manager can work with the department manager to correct the problem. Too often managers neglect to investigate the reasons for positive performances. If a department has generated sales 20% more than its budget, the manager should investigate what strategies and methods can account for the successful results. This information can then be shared with other departments to improve sales throughout the company.

REQUIRED:

A manager of Summertime Furniture receives an exception report showing that lumber costs of its picnic table department are 32% above the budget. List possible explanations for the apparent problem in the purchase and use of lumber.

APPLICATION PROBLEM
Journalizing direct and indirect expenses

Wall Designs, a paint and wallpaper merchandising business, uses an accounting system that provides information needed to prepare departmental margin statements as well as an income statement. The company has two departments, paint and wallpaper. Source documents are abbreviated as: check, C.

Transactions:

Mar. 1. Paid cash for March rent, $5,000.00. C234. (Used by all departments.)
    4. Paid cash for paint department advertising, $50.00. C262.
  11. Paid cash for wallpaper department delivery expense, $84.00. C316.
  16. Paid cash for telephone bill, $124.00. C331. (A miscellaneous expense used by all departments.)
  23. Paid cash for wallpaper department advertising, $73.00. C394.
  30. Paid cash for electric bill, $2,840.00. C437. (Amount used cannot be identified with each department.)
  31. Paid cash for wallpaper department's monthly payroll, $3,888.00 (total payroll, $4,800.00, less deductions: employee income tax, $528.00; social security tax, $313.92; Medicare tax, $70.08). C486.

Instructions:

Journalize the transactions completed during March of the current year. Use page 5 of a cash payments journal. Expenses not identified with a specific department are recorded as indirect expenses.

APPLICATION PROBLEM
Preparing a work sheet with departmental margins

AllSports Center is a merchandising business that sells sports clothing and equipment. The company uses a monthly fiscal period. AllSports Center's July 31 trial balance is recorded on a 12-column work sheet in the *Working Papers*. The following adjustment information is available.

Adjustment Information, July 31

Uncollectible Accounts Expense—Equipment Estimated as 1.0% of Sales on Account

Sales on Account for the Month	$20,520.00
Merchandise Inventory—Clothing	37,821.30
Merchandise Inventory—Equipment	55,978.80
Supplies Used—Clothing	298.40
Supplies Used—Equipment	370.80
Supplies Used—Administrative	164.80
Insurance Expired—Clothing	60.30
Insurance Expired—Equipment	115.60
Insurance Expired—Administrative	20.10
Depreciation Expense—Delivery Equipment, Equipment	198.00
Depreciation Expense—Office Equipment	28.00
Depreciation Expense—Store Equipment, Clothing	185.50
Depreciation Expense—Store Equipment, Equipment	32.00
Federal Income Tax Expense for the Month	2,156.00

Instructions:

1. Complete a work sheet for the month ended July 31 of the current year. Record the adjustments on the work sheet using the adjustment information on the preceding page.

2. Extend amounts to the proper debit and credit columns for Departmental Margin Statement—Clothing, Departmental Margin Statement—Equipment, Income Statement, and Balance Sheet. Accounts on trial balance lines 58—66 are classified as indirect expenses. Save your work to complete Application Problems 18-3 and 18-4.

APPLICATION PROBLEM
Preparing departmental margin statements

Use the work sheet from Application Problem 18-2 to complete this problem.

Instructions:

Prepare departmental margin statements for AllSports Center's clothing department and equipment department. Calculate and record the component percentages for each item on the statements. Round percentage calculations to the nearest 0.1%. Save your work to complete Application Problem 18-4.

APPLICATION PROBLEM
Preparing an income statement with departmental margins

Use the work sheet from Application Problem 18-2 and statements from Application Problem 18-3 to complete this problem.

Instructions:

Prepare an income statement for AllSports Center. Calculate and record the component percentages for each item on the statements. Round the percentage calculations to the nearest 0.1%.

MASTERY PROBLEM
Completing end-of-fiscal-period work for a merchandising business using departmental margins

Furniture DeCor, Inc., is a merchandising business that specializes in custom furniture and accessories. The company uses a yearly fiscal period. Furniture DeCor's December 31 trial balance is recorded on a 12-column work sheet in the *Working Papers*. The adjustment information on the next page is available.

Instructions:

1. Complete a work sheet for the year ended December 31 of the current year. Record the adjustments using the information on the next page.

2. Extend amounts to the proper debit and credit columns for Departmental Margin Statement—Furniture, Departmental Margin Statement—Accessories, Income Statement, and Balance Sheet. Accounts on trial balance lines 54—62 are classified as indirect expenses.

continued

3. Prepare departmental margin statements for each department. Calculate and record the percentages for each item on the statements. Round percentage calculations to the nearest 0.1%.

4. Prepare an income statement for Furniture DeCor, Inc. Calculate and record the component percentages for each item on the statement. Round percentage calculations to the nearest 0.1%.

Adjustment Information, December 31

Uncollectible Accounts Expense—Furniture Estimated as 1.0% of Sales on Account

Sales on Account for Year	$ 10,160.00
Merchandise Inventory—Furniture	112,460.00
Merchandise Inventory—Accessories	46,543.80
Supplies Used—Furniture	1,409.00
Supplies Used—Accessories	896.30
Supplies Used—Administrative	422.70
Insurance Expired—Furniture	1,395.00
Insurance Expired—Accessories	1,395.00
Insurance Expired—Administrative	325.00
Depreciation Expense—Office Equipment	529.50
Depreciation Expense—Store Equipment, Furniture	2,131.30
Depreciation Expense—Store Equipment, Accessories	981.70
Federal Income Tax Expense for the Year	2,958.60

18-6 CHALLENGE PROBLEM
Analyzing a departmental margin statement

The departmental margin statement for the camcorder department of Ultra Video, Inc., for the years 20X6 and 20X7 is provided in the *Working Papers*. The company has set a goal for the camcorder department to contribute a minimum of 25.0% departmental margin. For the years 20X1 through 20X6, the departmental margin for the camcorder department has varied from 25.5% to 29.0% of net sales.

Instructions:

1. Calculate and record the component percentages for each item on the 20X7 departmental margin statement. Round percentage calculations to the nearest 0.1%.

2. Calculate the changes in percentage of Net Sales from 20X6 to 20X7 for the following items: (a) cost of merchandise sold, (b) gross profit, (c) total direct departmental expenses, and (d) departmental margin.

3. From an analysis of the departmental margin statement and the amounts obtained from Instructions 1 and 2, answer the following questions:
   a. Is the departmental margin for the camcorder department at a satisfactory percentage of sales? Explain why it is or is not satisfactory.
   b. Is the trend of the cost of merchandise sold percentage favorable or unfavorable? Explain why it is or is not favorable. Suggest some possible reasons for the change in cost of merchandise sold from 20X6 to 20X7.
   c. Is the trend of the total direct departmental expenses percentage favorable or unfavorable? Explain why the trend is or is not favorable.

INTERNET ACTIVITY

Point your browser to
http://accounting.swpco.com

Choose **Advanced Course**,
choose **Activities**, and complete
the activity for Chapter 18.

You manage a department that has not had a good month. One of your best employees became manager of another department. Another good employee had to take an extended medical leave. Some merchandise planned for a seasonal promotion was delayed due to bad weather. As a result, customers went to a competing store to make their purchases. All direct expenses were as planned. These factors all contributed to your department's failure to achieve its sales goals for the month.

Your manager, Wilma Knight, asks you to prepare a written explanation detailing the reasons the department did not perform well during the past month. She also expects you to explain the changes you plan to make in the coming month to get the department back on track.

Required:

Prepare a memo in which you accept responsibility for the performance of the department. Briefly explain the problems you encountered and what you did about them. End the memo by listing several steps you are taking to improve next month's results.

Cases for Critical Thinking

Superior Corporation prepares departmental margin statements for each of its four departments. A new company accountant listed the sum of the departmental margins as the company's net income on the tax return. Is the accountant's procedure correct? Explain.

Kelley's Hardware has three departments. The departmental margins reported for the three departments for the year ended December 31 are:

Plumbing	$51,400.00
Electrical	$54,300.00
Household	$ 1,780.00

These amounts are similar to the departmental margins reported for the past four years. The owner is considering closing the household department because of the consistently low departmental margin. Before taking action, he asks for your recommendation. What is your reply? What factors should be considered before a decision is made to close the department?

AUTOMATED ACCOUNTING

DEPARTMENT MARGIN STATEMENTS FOR A MERCHANDISING BUSINESS

The typical income statement reports information for all the activities of business taken as a whole. This type of financial statement is prepared primarily for external users. Department managers require statements that show more detail. For example, a departmental margin statement shows revenues and costs for a specific department.

An expense traceable to the operation of a specific department is called a direct expense. The revenue earned by a department less its cost of goods sold and its direct expenses is called department margin. Responsibility accounting assigns control of the departmental margin to the department manager. Since a manager is held accountable for the results of his or her department, departmental margin statements allow the manager to analyze the results of the department without being concerned about the revenues, costs, and expenses of other departments.

To produce departmental margin statements in *Automated Accounting 7.0* or higher, the company must be set up as a departmentalized business. In addition, the chart of accounts must contain separate accounts for each department for accounts that require departmental information.

Specifying Company Information

Certain data are required for each company that is set up for use with *Automated Accounting 7.0* or higher. This information is entered when the problem template is set up, and the information is rarely changed. This company set up information is entered in the Customize Accounting System window. The window can be viewed by clicking on the Custom button on the toolbar or by selecting the Customize Accounting System menu item from the Data menu. The number of departments is specified on the Company Info. tab. The Company Info. tab is used to identify and specify various characteristics about the company being set up. To begin to set up a departmentalized company:

1. Enter the Company Name and Problem Name. The name of the company and problem name are printed as part of the heading for each report.

2. Click on the Departments drop-down list and select the number of departments.

3. Select the appropriate Business Organization option button.

4. Click on each Feature check box to indicate the accounting system setup data that is to be included in set up.

5. Select the appropriate Type of Business option button.

6. Click OK.

Adding and Changing Accounts

In addition to specifying the number of departments in the company setup, the chart of accounts must contain a department identifier for each account that will be maintained by department. Click on the Accts. toolbar button or select Maintain Accounts from the Data menu to display the Account Maintenance window. The Accounts tab allows you to add new accounts, change account titles, and identify departments.

To add an account:

1. Enter the account number in the Account column at the end of the existing list of accounts.

2. Enter the title for the new account.

3. For a departmentalized business, enter the department number for all accounts that are maintained by department. These accounts include Sales, Sales Returns and Allowances, Sales Discounts, Purchases, Purchases Returns and Allowances, Purchases Discounts, Income Summary, and any direct expenses charged to a specific department.

4. Click on the Add Account command button. The new account will be inserted into

the chart of accounts in account number sequence.

Notice that *Automated Accounting 7.0* requires more than an account number to identify the accounts by department. MasterSport, in Part 1 of this text, used a -1 and -2 to identify departmental accounts. The software uses a similar system, although the 1 or 2 is entered in the Dept. column of the Accounts tab of the Accounts Maintenance window.

Preparing Departmental Gross Profit Statements

When a company has been set up as a departmentalized business and the sales, cost of goods sold, and direct expense accounts have been set up by department, the software will produce a departmental gross profit statement for each department.

1. Click the Reports toolbar button or choose the Report Selection menu item from the Report menu.

2. Click on the Financial Statements option from the Select Report Group list. The reports available for that group will be listed.

3. Select Gross Profit Statements from the Choose a Report to Display list, as shown in Figure AA18-1.

4. Click OK.

The reports for all departments will be displayed in the scrollable

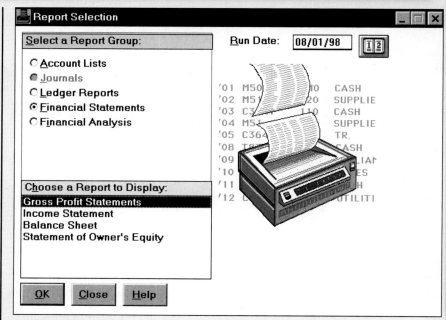

Figure AA18-1

Report Viewer window, from which they may be printed and/or copied for inclusion in another application, such as a spreadsheet or a word processor.

AUTOMATING MASTERY PROBLEM 18-5

Instructions:

1. Load *Automated Accounting 7.0* or higher software.

2. Select database AA18-5 (Advanced Course Mastery Problem 18-5) from the accounting template disk.

3. Select File from the menu bar and choose the Save As menu command. Key the path to the drive and directory that contains your data files. Save

the database with a file name of XXX185 (where XXX are your initials).

4. Access Problem Instructions through the Help menu. Read the Problem Instruction screen.

5. Refer to page 519 for data used in this problem.

6. Exit the Automated Accounting software.

19

Cost Accounting for a Manufacturing Business

AFTER STUDYING CHAPTER 19 YOU WILL BE ABLE TO:

1. Define accounting terms related to cost accounting for a manufacturing business.

2. Identify accounting concepts and practices related to cost accounting for a manufacturing business.

3. Identify the elements of manufacturing costs: (1) direct materials, (2) direct labor, and (3) factory overhead.

4. Identify the flow of costs through the manufacturing process.

5. Prepare selected ledgers and cost sheets for a manufacturing business.

The three general types of businesses are service, merchandising, and manufacturing. Service businesses provide a needed service for their customers. Examples of service business are accounting firms, law firms, and medical practices.

Merchandising businesses sell products to customers. A merchandising business purchases products and, without changing the products' forms, sells those products to customers. Department stores and grocery stores are examples of merchandising businesses.

A manufacturing business buys materials and uses labor and machinery to change the materials into a finished product. A manufacturing business generally sells the finished product to a merchandising business, which then sells the product to customers.

FaxaVision, Inc., a facsimile manufacturing business, buys modems, print motors, cutter assemblies, document sensors, and other materials. Using labor and machinery, FaxaVision combines the materials to make facsimile machines, commonly referred to as fax machines. Merchandising businesses buy the fax machines from FaxaVision for resale to customers.

A service business needs to know the cost of providing services to be able to calculate net income. A merchandising business needs to know the cost of merchandise sold to calculate net income. For the same reason, a manufacturing company needs to know the costs required to produce finished products that it sells. To know how much finished products cost, FaxaVision keeps records of all costs involved in making the products.

TERMS PREVIEW

direct materials
direct labor
factory overhead
indirect materials
indirect labor
work in process
finished goods
materials ledger
cost ledger
finished goods ledger
applied overhead

ACCOUNTING
IN YOUR CAREER

TRACKING COSTS ACCURATELY

Durable Manufacturing uses a cost accounting system. Factory workers complete a time sheet on which they record the number of minutes they work on each job during a day. Workers shift around to different jobs during the day and have resisted keeping accurate time records. They maintain that it takes too much time away from the manufacturing work to stop and complete the time sheet each time they shift to another job.

Materials are disbursed from a central supply warehouse, and materials requisitions forms are completed for each disbursement. A new clerk in the supply warehouse is careless in completing the materials requisitions and often neglects to record the job number, particularly when one disbursement is for several jobs.

The cost accounting department analyzes and summarizes the time sheets and materials requisitions. No one in the department has much knowledge about how the company's products are manufactured, and the accuracy of the information is rarely questioned. It is assumed that as long as the total hours and total materials are recorded correctly, the distribution of time and materials to specific products will average out correctly at the end of the fiscal period.

The products manufactured are all very different. Some have low sales quantities and high manufacturing costs. Others are inexpensive to manufacture and have high sales volume. The company's sales revenue continues to increase each quarter, but net income is declining.

Critical Thinking

1. How can a company with increasing sales revenue also have decreasing net income?
2. How should the company be setting the prices it charges for its products?
3. What would you recommend to improve the operations of this company?

THREE COST ELEMENTS

The manufacturing cost of any finished product includes three cost elements: (1) direct materials, (2) direct labor, and (3) factory overhead.

Direct Materials

Materials that are of significant value in the cost of a finished product and that become an identifiable part of the product are called **direct materials**. Direct materials include all items used in the manufacturing process that have sufficient value to justify charging the cost directly to the product. (CONCEPT: Materiality)

The materiality concept states that business activities creating dollar amounts large enough to affect business decisions should be recorded and reported as separate items in accounting records and financial statements. Dollar amounts that are small and not considered important in decision making may be combined with other amounts in the accounting records and financial statements. For example, modems and print motors used to manufacture fax machines are considered direct materials and accounted for separately. Connectors and gears used in the manufacture of fax machines are parts with a small enough dollar value that they are grouped together and only their total value is recorded in the accounting records.

Direct Labor

Salaries of factory workers who make a product are called **direct labor**. Direct labor includes salaries only of persons working directly on a product. Salaries of supervisors, maintenance workers, and others whose efforts do not apply directly to the manufacture of a product are not considered to be direct labor.

Factory Overhead

All expenses other than direct materials and direct labor that apply to making products are called **factory overhead**. Some materials used in manufacturing a product cost a very small amount for each unit produced. Materials used in the completion of a product that are of insignificant value to justify accounting for separately are called **indirect materials**. Indirect materials may include items such as glue, solder, bolts, and rivets. Materials and supplies used by the factory such as cleaning supplies and lubricants for the machinery are also classified as indirect materials.

Some factory workers devote their time to supervisory, clerical, and maintenance tasks necessary to operate the factory. Such workers include time clerks, supervisors, maintenance people, receiving clerks, and inspectors. Salaries paid to factory workers who are not actually making products are called **indirect labor**.

Other costs are also incurred in the manufacturing process. (1) Depreciation of factory buildings and equipment. (2) Repairs to factory buildings and equipment. (3) Insurance on building, equipment, and stock. (4) Taxes on property owned. (5) Heat, light, and power. All of these expenses, along with indirect materials and indirect labor, make up factory overhead.

INVENTORIES FOR A MANUFACTURING BUSINESS

A merchandising business normally has one general ledger account for merchandise inventory. However, a manufacturing business has three inventory accounts related to the products manufactured. (1) Materials. (2) Work in Process. (3) Finished Goods. These accounts as classified as current assets of FaxaVision, Inc.

CHART OF ACCOUNTS FOR FAXAVISION, INC.

Balance Sheet Accounts

(1000) Assets
1100 CURRENT ASSETS
1105	Cash
1110	Petty Cash
1115	Accounts Receivable
1120	Allowance for Uncollectible Accounts
1125	Materials
1130	Work in Process
1135	Finished Goods
1140	Supplies—Factory
1145	Supplies—Sales
1150	Supplies—Administrative
1155	Prepaid Insurance

1200 PLANT ASSETS
1205	Factory Equipment
1210	Accumulated Depreciation—Factory Equipment
1215	Office Equipment
1220	Accumulated Depreciation—Office Equipment
1225	Store Equipment
1230	Accumulated Depreciation—Store Equipment
1235	Building
1240	Accumulated Depreciation—Building
1245	Land

(2000) Liabilities
2100 CURRENT LIABILITIES
2105	Accounts Payable
2110	Employee Income Tax Payable
2115	Federal Income Tax Payable
2120	Social Security Tax Payable
2123	Medicare Tax Payable
2125	Salaries Payable
2130	Unemployment Tax Payable—Federal
2135	Unemployment Tax Payable—State
2140	Dividends Payable

2200 LONG-TERM LIABILITY
2205	Mortgage Payable

(3000) Stockholders' Equity
3105	Capital Stock
3110	Retained Earnings
3115	Dividends
3120	Income Summary

Income Statement Accounts

(4000) Operating Revenue
4105	Sales

(5000) Cost of Sales
5105	Cost of Goods Sold

(5500) Manufacturing Costs
5505	Factory Overhead
5510	Depreciation Expense—Factory Equipment
5515	Depreciation Expense—Building
5520	Heat, Light, and Power Expense
5525	Insurance Expense—Factory
5530	Miscellaneous Expense—Factory
5535	Payroll Taxes Expense—Factory
5540	Property Tax Expense—Factory
5545	Supplies Expense—Factory

(6000) Operating Expenses
6100 SELLING EXPENSES
6105	Advertising Expense
6110	Delivery Expense
6115	Depreciation Expense–Store Equipment
6120	Miscellaneous Expense—Sales
6125	Salary Expense—Sales
6130	Supplies Expense—Sales

6200 ADMINISTRATIVE EXPENSES
6205	Depreciation Expense—Office Equipment
6210	Insurance Expense—Administrative
6215	Miscellaneous Expense—Administrative
6220	Payroll Taxes Expense—Administrative
6225	Property Tax Expense—Administrative
6230	Salary Expense—Administrative
6235	Supplies Expense—Administrative
6240	Uncollectible Accounts Expense
6245	Utilities Expense—Administrative

(7000) Other Revenue
7105	Gain on Plant Assets
7110	Miscellaneous Revenue

(8000) Other Expenses
8105	Interest Expense
8110	Loss on Plant Assets

(9000) Income Tax
9105	Federal Income Tax Expense

The chart of accounts for FaxaVision, Inc., is illustrated above for ready reference as you study Chapters 19 and 20 of this textbook.

Figure 19-1

A materials inventory account shows the costs of materials on hand that have not yet been used in making a product. Products that are being manufactured but are not yet complete are called **work in process**. A work in process inventory account, therefore, shows all costs that have been spent on products that are not yet complete. Manufactured products that are fully completed are called **finished goods**. A finished goods inventory account, therefore, shows the cost of completed products still on hand and unsold.

Manufacturing costs are grouped together in the chart of accounts as shown in Figure 19-1. All of these expenses relate directly to the costs of producing the products.

Manufacturing businesses keep detailed cost records for three purposes. (1) To determine accurate costs for each product made. (2) To provide specific cost information to managers who must identify high cost areas so that corrective action can be taken. (3) To provide cost summary information for journal entries.

Subsidiary Cost Ledgers

Three subsidiary ledgers provide the detailed cost information for the three manufacturing inventory accounts.

1. **Materials Ledger**. FaxaVision uses a perpetual inventory system for direct and indirect materials. A perpetual inventory record provides detailed cost information about each type of material. A ledger containing all records of materials is called a **materials ledger**.

2. **Cost Ledger**. FaxaVision keeps a record of all charges for direct materials, direct labor, and factory overhead for each job. The record is known as a cost sheet. A cost sheet is maintained for each manufacturing job. A ledger containing all cost sheets for products in the process of being manufactured is called a **cost ledger**.

3. **Finished Goods Ledger**. The company keeps a record of each kind of finished good to provide a perpetual inventory of each product produced and its cost. A ledger containing records of all finished goods on hand is called a **finished goods ledger.** This ledger is similar to a materials ledger.

Journal entries for job costs are described in Chapter 20.

MANUFACTURING COST FLOWS

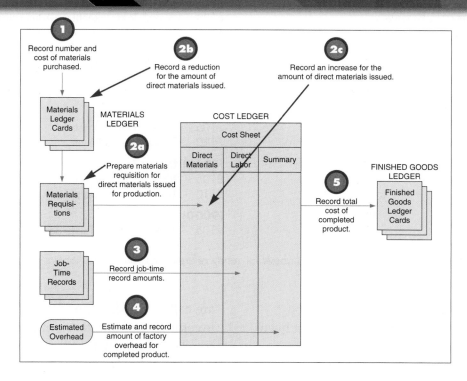

Figure 19-2

Manufacturing costs are recorded on cost forms as costs occur. The forms used and the sequence of steps followed for recording

FaxaVision's manufacturing costs are shown in Figure 19-2.

Recording manufacturing costs

STEPS

1. Record the number and cost of each kind of material purchased on materials ledger cards. This step is performed for both direct and indirect materials.

2. Prepare a materials requisition to use when direct materials are issued for use in the factory. The amount of direct materials issued is recorded as a reduction on the materials ledger card and an increase in the Direct Materials column of the cost sheet.

3. Prepare job-time records when direct labor is used. Time record amounts are recorded in the Direct Labor column of the cost sheet.

4. Estimate and record the amount of factory overhead when a product is completed. The amount of factory overhead is recorded in the Summary column of the cost sheet. Estimating factory overhead is described later in this chapter.

5. Total all costs on the cost sheet when a product is completed. Transfer the total to a finished goods ledger card.

ACCOUNTING AT WORK

DON LASKOWSKI, FOUNDER, WOOD-MIZER PRODUCTS, INC.

There is absolutely no question that the knowledge of accounting is necessary for us to survive in today's world, both from a personal and a business standpoint.

I took accounting as a freshman in high school because it was required. Had I known what a critical role it would play in my life, I would have applied myself much more, as it is a basic building block to structuring and organizing life experiences.

In personal life, it is needed to develop a budget to help live within one's income means and to keep records for accurate tax reporting. Many in our society are struggling with finances and end up in bankruptcy because of inadequate understanding of basic accounting.

From a business standpoint, a lack of accounting knowledge will severely limit career opportunities. I am not an accountant but I have needed accounting knowledge in every job I've had. It is almost impossible to start one's own business without a clear understanding of the relationship of costs and income. This is true whether that business is a small garage, restaurant, beauty parlor, service company, or manufacturer.

At age 47, I started my own company working in my garage and on our kitchen table. Today, we have 650 employees building portable saw mills which we sell to 98 countries throughout the world. This involves the handling of currency from all these countries, dealing with exchange rates, transportation, salaries and benefits, tariffs, and so on. I would not have been able to make the business decisions that I must make daily without a good basic understanding of accounting.

Accounting begins with our personal lives. We must understand the basics of accounting in order to succeed both personally and professionally.

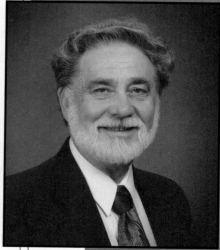

TERMS REVIEW

direct materials

direct labor

factory overhead

indirect materials

indirect labor

work in process

finished goods

materials ledger

cost ledger

finished goods
  ledger

AUDIT YOUR UNDERSTANDING

1. What are the three manufacturing cost elements of a finished product?

2. What term is used to describe products that are being manufactured but are not yet complete?

3. What is the purpose of a cost sheet?

Classifying manufacturing costs; specifying the ledger used for initial recording

An analysis sheet for Gutman's Gutters, a firm that manufactures aluminum and steel gutters, is included in the *Working Papers*. Your instructor will guide you through the following examples.

4. For each of the following costs, determine whether the cost should be classified as direct materials, direct labor, or factory overhead.

5. Specify the subsidiary ledger (materials ledger, cost ledger, finished goods ledger) in which the cost is first recorded. Save your work to complete the On Your Own below.
   a. Wages earned by an employee working on the production of gutters.
   b. Aluminum used in the production of gutters.
   c. The rent expense of the factory in which the gutters are made.
   d. A cleaning solvent used to clean production machinery.
   e. Fringe benefits received by an employee working on the production of gutters.

Classifying manufacturing costs; specifying the ledger used for initial recording

Use the working papers from the Work Together above. Work independently to complete the following problem.

6. For each of the following costs, determine whether the cost should be classified as direct materials, direct labor, or factory overhead.

7. Specify the subsidiary ledger (materials ledger, cost ledger, finished goods ledger) in which the cost is first recorded.
   a. Rivets used in the production of gutters.
   b. Wages earned by a maintenance employee.
   c. The property taxes of the factory.
   d. Fringe benefits of the factory supervisor.
   e. Wages earned by an employee who inspects finished gutters before they leave the factory.

RECORDS FOR MATERIALS

1. Open a materials ledger card.   **2.** Record orders placed.   **4.** Record the new balance.

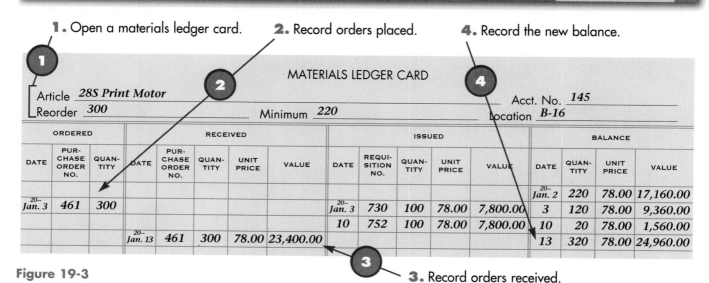

Figure 19-3

3. Record orders received.

A manufacturing business keeps a record of materials used in the manufacturing process. The business should have on hand sufficient materials so that the manufacturing process will not be interrupted. However, too large a stock of materials requires needless investment in inven- tory. To provide a perpetual inventory and detailed cost information about materials, FaxaVision keeps a materials ledger card for each type of material. A materials ledger card is shown in Figure 19-3.

S T E P S **Opening a materials ledger card and recording materials ordered**

1. Open a materials ledger card for each type of material kept in the storeroom.
   a. Enter the name and account number of the item.
   b. Determine and record the reorder quantity and minimum quantities to be kept in stock. When the number on hand equals the minimum, the materials clerk notifies the purchasing agent to place a new order.
2. Record the date of an order, *Jan. 3*, the purchase order number, *461*, and the quantity ordered, *300*, in the Ordered columns. The data are recorded from a purchase order. The purchase order authorizes a seller to deliver goods with payment to be made later. The order was placed because the quantity on hand, 220 units, equaled the minimum level at which a new order is placed. Note that the quantity ordered equals the reorder quantity shown at the top of the ledger card.
3. When the items ordered are received, record the date, *Jan. 13*, the purchase order number, *461*, the quantity, *300*, the unit price, *78.00*, and the total value of the order, *23,400.00*, in the Received columns of the materials ledger card. The total value is the quantity, 300, multiplied by the unit price, $78.00.
4. Add the quantity and value to the previous balances and extend the amounts to the Balance columns.

Notice that the materials ledger card in Figure 19-3 also shows items that have been issued. The issuing of materials will be dis- cussed later in the chapter. The total value for all the materials ledger cards equals the balance of the materials general ledger account.

The relationship of the general ledger accounts to the forms and ledgers described in this chapter is explained in Chapter 20.

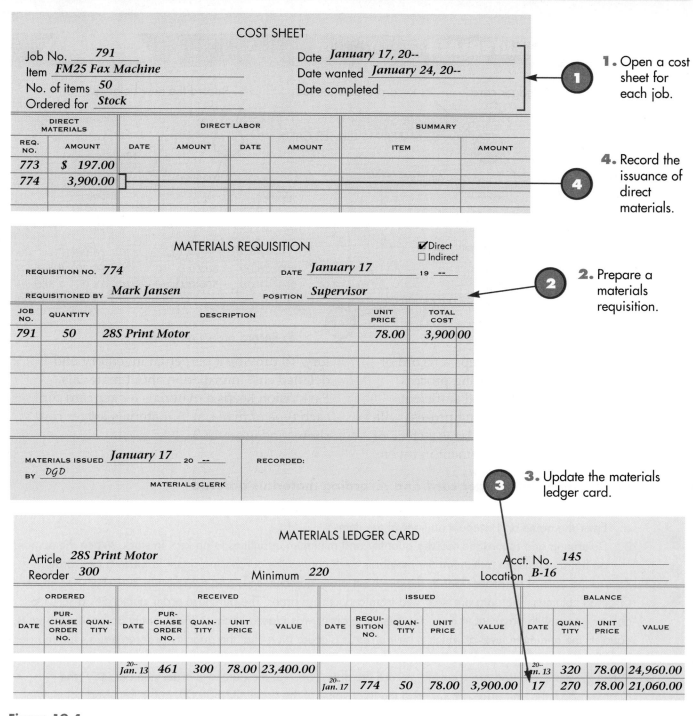

Figure 19-4

During the manufacturing process, all costs of making a product must be recorded. All charges for direct materials, direct labor, and factory overhead for a particular job are recorded on a cost sheet, such as the one shown in Figure 19-4.

When direct materials are needed for a job, they are requested from the storeroom using a materials requisition form. A materials requisition form is used to authorize transfer of items from the storeroom to the factory. When materials are issued to the factory from the storeroom, the materials ledger card is updated.

S) Recording direct materials on a cost sheet

1. Open a new cost sheet for each job started. When the cost accounting department receives a request from the factory department supervisor for a job number, it assigns the number and prepares a new job cost sheet. To open a new job cost sheet:

   a. Enter the Job No., *791*.

   b. Enter the stock number and the description of the product, *FM25 Fax Machine*.

   c. Enter the number of items to be manufactured, *50*.

   d. Enter the customer that ordered the item. In this case, the product will replenish FaxaVision's stock of the fax machine. Therefore, *Stock* is entered on the Ordered for line.

   e. Enter the date the job number is assigned, *January 17, 20--*.

   f. Enter the date the item is wanted, *January 24, 20--*.

2. Prepare a materials requisition in triplicate. One copy of a materials requisition is kept in the factory. Two copies are sent to the materials storeroom.

   a. Enter the requisition number, *774*. Requisitions are numbered in order. The next available number is assigned.

   b. Enter the name of the person who is making the requisition, *Mark Jansen*.

   c. Check the appropriate box to indicate whether the requisition is for direct or indirect materials. In this case, a motor is a major part of the finished product. Therefore, the Direct box is checked.

   d. Enter the date of the requisition, *January 17, 20--*.

   e. Enter the position of the person making the requisition, *Supervisor*. Usually, a supervisor or a manager has the authority to make the requisition.

   f. Enter the job number to which the materials are being issued, *791*.

   g. Enter the quantity requisitioned, *50*.

   h. Enter the stock number and description, *28S Print Motor*.

   i. Enter the unit price of the materials, *78.00*.

   j. Enter the total cost of the materials being issued to the factory, *3,900.00*. The total cost is determined by multiplying the quantity by the unit price (50 × $78.00 = $3,900.00).

   k. Record the date on which the materials are issued to the factory, *January 17, 20--*.

   l. The materials clerk initials the requisition to show that the materials have been issued. One copy of the completed materials requisition is kept in the storeroom. The original requisition is sent to the cost accounting department.

3. Update the materials ledger card. When the materials requisition is received by the cost accounting department, an entry is made in the materials ledger.

   a. Enter the date the materials are issued to the factory, *January 17, 20--*, in the Date column of the Issued section of the materials ledger card.

   b. Enter the requisition number, *774*.

   c. Enter the quantity issued, *50*.

   d. Enter the unit price, *78.00*.

   e. Enter the total value of the materials issued, *3,900.00*.

   f. Enter the date in the Balance Date column.

   g. Enter the new quantity of the material, *270*, in the Balance Quantity column. Subtract the quantity issued from the current quantity in inventory (320 − 50 = 270) to determine the new quantity.

   h Enter the unit price, *78.00*.

   i. Enter the total value of the material, *21,060.00* (270 units × $78.00 = $21,060.00).

4. Record the issuance of direct materials on the cost sheet. When the cost accounting department receives the materials requisition, an entry is made on the cost sheet.

   a. Enter the requisition number, *774*, in the Req. No. column.

   b. Enter the total value of the materials issued, *3,900.00*, in the Direct Materials Amount column.

JOB – TIME RECORD

Employee Number __20__   Job Number __791__

Date __1/17/--__

Time started __1 p.m.__

Time finished __5 p.m.__

Total time spent on job . . . . __4.0 hrs.__

1. Each employee prepares a job-time record for each job worked on.

COST SHEET

Job No. __791__   Date _January 17, 20--_
Item __FM25 Fax Machine__   Date wanted _January 24, 20--_
No. of items __50__   Date completed _____
Ordered for __Stock__

2. Record the total of all the job-time records for the job.

DIRECT MATERIALS		DIRECT LABOR				SUMMARY	
REQ. NO.	AMOUNT	DATE	AMOUNT	DATE	AMOUNT	ITEM	AMOUNT
773	$ 197.00	Jan. 17	$ 556.00				
774	3,900.00						

Figure 19-5

Factory employees may work on a number of different jobs each day. Therefore, a job-time record is kept to indicate the amount of time spent on each job. At the end of each day, all job-time records are summarized. The total direct labor cost for each job is recorded on each job's cost sheet.

A job-time record for one FaxaVision employee working 4 hours on Job No. 791 is shown in Figure 19-5. All the direct labor costs for Job No. 791 are recorded in the Direct Labor columns of the cost sheet shown in Figure 19-5.

S T E P S Assigning direct labor to jobs

Each factory employee:

1. Prepares a job-time record for each job worked on during the day. The record includes employee number, job number, date, time started and time finished. The employee calculates and records the total time spent on the job.

Accounting department:

2. Totals the time on job-time records for each job and records the cost in the Direct Labor column of the cost sheet.

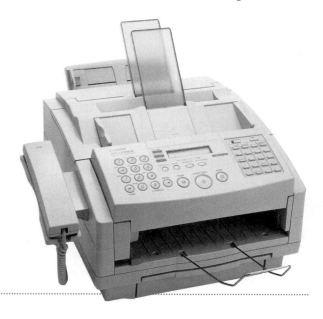

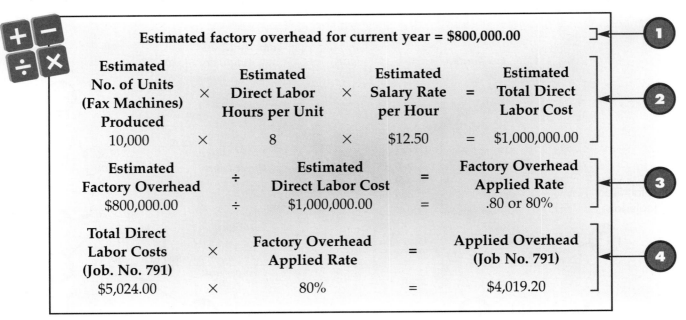

Estimated factory overhead for current year = $800,000.00 ⟶ ①

Estimated No. of Units (Fax Machines) Produced		Estimated Direct Labor Hours per Unit		Estimated Salary Rate per Hour		Estimated Total Direct Labor Cost	
10,000	×	8	×	$12.50	=	$1,000,000.00	⟵ ②

Estimated Factory Overhead		Estimated Direct Labor Cost		Factory Overhead Applied Rate	
$800,000.00	÷	$1,000,000.00	=	.80 or 80%	⟵ ③

Total Direct Labor Costs (Job. No. 791)		Factory Overhead Applied Rate		Applied Overhead (Job No. 791)	
$5,024.00	×	80%	=	$4,019.20	⟵ ④

Figure 19-6

Some factory overhead expenses occur regularly throughout a fiscal period, and others occur irregularly. Many factory overhead expenses are not known until the end of a fiscal period. Therefore, factory overhead expenses normally are charged to jobs by using an application rate based on a known cost such as direct labor. This method applies factory overhead expenses to all jobs and permits a company to record overhead on a cost sheet when a job is completed. The estimated amount of factory overhead recorded on cost sheets is called **applied overhead**. The applied overhead is calculated for Job No. 791 as shown in Figure 19-6.

Applied overhead is recorded on cost sheets during the fiscal period and before all factory overhead for the current period is known. *(CONCEPT: Matching Expenses with Revenue)* Therefore, the factory overhead applied rate is calculated before the fiscal periods begins.

S T E P S **Determining a factory overhead applied rate**

1. Estimate the amount of factory overhead costs for the next fiscal period. Generally, three factors are considered in estimating factory overhead. (a) Amount of factory overhead for the past several fiscal periods. (b) Number of products the factory expects to produce in the next fiscal period. (c) Expected change in unit costs of factory overhead items. FaxaVision expects to produce 10,000 fax machines during the coming year. Considering this volume, previous years' overhead, and anticipated cost increases, FaxaVision estimates factory overhead as $800,000.00.

2. Estimate the number of base units that will be used in the next fiscal period. Base units are usually cost items that can be identified easily. Direct labor cost, direct labor hours, and direct materials cost are common bases. A base unit should be selected that most closely relates to actual overhead costs. FaxaVision uses direct labor cost as a base unit because there is a close relationship between the amount of direct labor cost and factory overhead costs. FaxaVision estimates next year's direct labor cost as $1,000,000.00.

3. Calculate the factory overhead applied rate. Divide estimated factory overhead costs by the estimated base unit. FaxaVision's factory overhead applied rate is 80% of direct labor cost.

4. Calculate and record the amount of applied overhead, *4,019.20*, on the cost sheet for Job No. 791 (total direct labor for Job No. 791, $5,024.00, multiplied by the factory overhead rate, 80%).

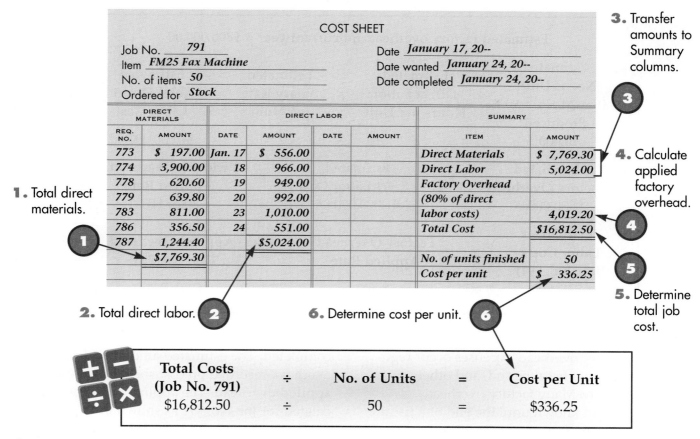

Figure 19-7

The completed cost sheet for Job No. 791 is shown in Figure 19-7. When a job is completed, its total costs are calculated and recorded in the Summary columns of the cost sheet. Direct Materials and Direct Labor columns on the cost sheet are totaled and the totals are recorded in the Summary columns. Then factory overhead is applied to the job. A cost per unit is determined for each job.

Job No. 791 was completed on January 24, as indicated in Figure 19-7. At the end of a fiscal period, cost sheets will also exist for jobs that have not been completed. The total value for all cost sheets for work still in process equals the balance of the work in process account in the general ledger. Thus, at the end of a fiscal period, cost sheets for work in process are totaled to determine ending inventory for the general ledger account Work in Process.

S T E P S Completing a cost sheet

1. Total the Direct Materials Amount column, *$7,769.30*.
2. Total the Direct Labor Amount column, *$5,024.00*.
3. Transfer the direct materials and direct labor amounts to the Summary columns.
4. Calculate and record the applied overhead, *$4,019.20*, in the Summary columns. Remember that factory overhead is applied at the rate of 80% of direct labor cost ($5,024.00 x 80% = $4,019.20).
5. Total the three cost elements in the cost sheet's Summary columns, *$16,812.50*. This is the total cost of the job.
6. Determine the cost per unit, *$336.25* ($16,812.50 total cost ÷ 50 units = $336.25).

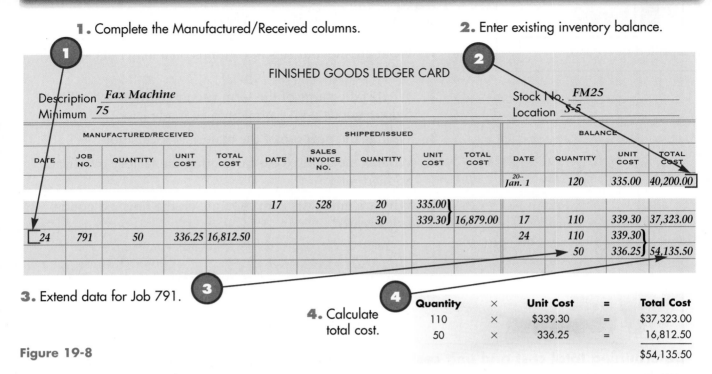

1. Complete the Manufactured/Received columns.   **2.** Enter existing inventory balance.

FINISHED GOODS LEDGER CARD

Description _Fax Machine_   Stock No. _FM25_
Minimum _75_   Location _S-5_

| MANUFACTURED/RECEIVED | | | | | SHIPPED/ISSUED | | | | | | BALANCE | | | |
DATE	JOB NO.	QUANTITY	UNIT COST	TOTAL COST	DATE	SALES INVOICE NO.	QUANTITY	UNIT COST	TOTAL COST		DATE	QUANTITY	UNIT COST	TOTAL COST
											20-- Jan. 1	120	335.00	40,200.00
					17	528	20	335.00⎫						
							30	339.30⎭	16,879.00		17	110	339.30	37,323.00
24	791	50	336.25	16,812.50							24	110	339.30⎫	
												50	336.25⎭	54,135.50

3. Extend data for Job 791.   **4.** Calculate total cost.

Quantity	×	Unit Cost	=	Total Cost
110	×	$339.30	=	$37,323.00
50	×	336.25	=	16,812.50
				$54,135.50

Figure 19-8

When a job is completed, the finished goods are placed in the finished goods stock area. At this time, summary information from the cost sheet is recorded on the completed product's finished goods ledger card. The entry for the completed Job No. 791 is recorded on the finished goods ledger card shown in Figure 19-8.

The total value for all finished goods ledger cards equals the finished goods inventory account balance in the general ledger. After FaxaVision's Job No. 791 is completed and recorded, the company has 160 FM25 Fax Machines on hand at a total cost of $54,135.50. This amount will be added to the total costs of all other finished goods still on hand to determine the balance of finished goods inventory in the general ledger.

S T E P S **Completing a finished goods ledger card**

1. Complete the Manufactured/Received columns of the finished goods ledger card.
   a. Record the date the finished goods are transferred to the finished goods inventory, _24_.
   b. Enter the Job No., _791_.
   c. Enter the quantity, _50_.
   d. Enter the unit cost, _336.25_.
   e. Enter the total cost, _16,812.50_.
2. Enter the existing inventory in the Balance columns.
   a. Enter the date, _24_.
   b. Enter the previous quantity of fax machines in inventory, _110_, and the unit cost, _339.30_. Units costs for each job may differ since the amount of direct materials and direct labor used may vary. Therefore, the unit costs for each job are kept separate.
3. Extend the quantity, _50_, and the unit cost, _336.25_, for Job 791.
4. Calculate the total cost of all goods in inventory, _54,135.50_. Although unit costs are kept separate, the total cost balance is combined for all units in the finished goods inventory. FaxaVision uses the first-in, first-out inventory method. Thus, the cost recorded first is the cost removed from inventory first when units are sold.

TERM REVIEW

applied overhead

AUDIT YOUR UNDERSTANDING

1. What are the four sets of columns on a materials ledger card?

2. What is the name of the form used to authorize a seller to deliver goods with payment to be made later?

3. What is the purpose of the materials requisition?

4. What is the formula for calculating the factory overhead applied rate?

5. Why are unit costs kept separate on the finished goods ledger card?

WORK TOGETHER

Determining total cost and unit cost for a job and determining total cost for a finished item

A cost sheet and partial finished goods ledger card for Leather Originals, a manufacturer of leather furniture, are provided in the *Working Papers*. Your instructor will guide you through the following examples.

6. Complete the cost sheet for Job No. 657 by filling in the Summary columns. Factory overhead is applied based on direct labor hours. Estimated factory overhead for the period was $3,000,000. The number of estimated direct labor hours was 200,000. A total of 530 direct labor hours was used on Job No. 657.

7. Calculate a new balance for item K-39 sofa on the partial finished goods ledger card.

ON YOUR OWN

Determining total cost and unit cost for a job and determining total cost for a finished item

A cost sheet and partial finished goods ledger card for Leather Originals, a manufacturer of leather furniture, are provided in the *Working Papers*. Work independently to complete the following problem.

8. Complete the cost sheet for Job No. 711 by filling in the Summary columns. Factory overhead is applied based on direct labor hours. Estimated factory overhead for the period was $3,000,000. The number of estimated direct labor hours was 200,000. A total of 743 direct labor hours was used on Job No. 711.

9. Calculate a new balance for item S-68 chair on the partial finished goods ledger card.

CHAPTER SUMMARY

After completing this chapter, you can

1. Define accounting terms related to cost accounting for a manufacturing business.

2. Identify accounting concepts and practices related to cost accounting for a manufacturing business.

3. Identify the elements of manufacturing costs: (1) direct materials, (2) direct labor, and (3) factory overhead.

4. Identify the flow of costs through the manufacturing process.

5. Prepare selected ledgers and cost sheets for a manufacturing business.

EXPLORE ACCOUNTING

EQUIVALENT UNITS OF PRODUCTION

Two general manufacturing costing methods exist: job order costing illustrated in this chapter and process costing.

Process costing is useful when a single production process uses a continuous flow of inputs to produce the same product. To illustrate process costing, assume that Hubble Inc. began the month with 200 televisions in production. Each unit is estimated to be 20% complete as to labor. During the month, Hubble began 1,000 units and completed 800 units. At the end of the month, the 400 units in production were 70% complete. Management budgeted $40.00 of direct labor per unit. During May, the company incurred $40,000 of direct labor. If the 800 com-

pleted units are used as a measure, it would appear that the laborers have not been efficient ($40,000 ÷ 800 = $50.00 per unit).

A better number would recognize the work performed on units incomplete at the end of the month. An estimate of the number of units that could be started and completed during a period is known as the equivalent units of production (EUP). Hubble calculates EUP as shown below.

The workers were actually more efficient than projected in the budget ($40,000 ÷ 1,040 EUP = $38.46).

REQUIRED:

Determine the equivalent cost per unit of labor for the following problem. Nelson Company began the month with 600 units in production, each unit 60% complete as to labor. During the current month, these units were completed. During the month, Nelson also started 2,000 units and completed 1,800 units. At the end of the month, the 200 units in production were 10% complete. Labor costs, estimated to be $9.00 per unit, were actually $20,000.

Beginning Inventory	200 units	×	80%	=	160 EUP
Started and Completed	600 units	×	100%	=	600 EUP
Started and in Process	400 units	×	70%	=	280 EUP
Total EUP					1,040 EUP

APPLICATION PROBLEM
Classifying manufacturing costs and determining which ledger to use for initial recording

Krasnoy Tire, a maker of tires for cars, trucks, and tractors, is trying to determine how to account for various factory costs. The costs include the following:

a. Wages earned by a factory supervisor.
b. Fringe benefits of the factory supervisor.
c. The rent expense of company headquarters, which is located 10 miles from the factory.
d. Rubber used in the production of tires.
e. The property taxes of the factory.
f. Wages earned by an employee working on the production of tires.
g. Inexpensive glue used sparingly in the production of tires.
h. A cleaning solvent used to clean production machinery.
i. Wages earned by an employee who inspects finished tires before they leave the factory.
j. Wages earned by a marketing manager at company headquarters.

Instructions:

1. For each of the costs above, determine whether the cost should be classified as direct materials, direct labor, factory overhead, or none. Hint: Only costs related to the factory or to production should be included as manufacturing costs.

2. Specify the subsidiary ledger (materials ledger, cost ledger, finished goods ledger) in which the cost is first recorded.

APPLICATION PROBLEM
Classifying manufacturing costs and determining which ledger to use for initial recording

Wilmington, Inc., manufactures heating systems. The company maintains a materials ledger for all direct materials.

Transactions:

Oct. 1. Ordered 500 T-5 thermostats. Purchase Order No. 83.
3. Issued 110 T-5 thermostats. Materials Requisition No. 196.
4. Issued 45 T-5 thermostats. Materials Requisition No. 200.
7. Received 500 T-5 thermostats; unit price $39.50. Purchase Order No. 83.
12. Issued 220 T-5 thermostats. Materials Requisition No. 207.
17. Issued 85 T-5 thermostats. Materials Requisition No. 218.
29. Issued 55 T-5 thermostats. Materials Requisition No. 231.
29. Ordered 500 T-5 thermostats. Purchase Order No. 88.

Instructions:

1. Prepare a materials ledger card for T-5 thermostats. The thermostat is Account No. 76. Reorder quantity is set at 500 thermostats, minimum at 175 thermostats. Inventory location is Area A18.

2. Record the beginning balance on October 1 of the current year of 175 T-5 thermostats at a unit price of $39.50.

3. Record the transactions.

APPLICATION PROBLEM
Calculating factory overhead applied rate

AutoAnswer, Inc., a manufacturer of telephone answering machines, uses a factory overhead applied rate to charge overhead costs to its manufactured products.

The company manager estimates that AutoAnswer will manufacture 30,000 units next year. For this amount of production, the cost accountant estimates total factory overhead costs to be $336,000.00. Estimated direct labor cost for next year is $420,000.00.

Instructions:
Calculate AutoAnswer's factory overhead applied rate for next year as a percentage of direct labor cost.

APPLICATION PROBLEM
Preparing a cost sheet

On July 1, Esquire Tables, Inc., began work on Job No. 309. The order is for 45 No. ET42 game tables for stock; date wanted is July 10.

Transactions:

July   1.   Direct material, $641.25. Materials Requisition No. 432.
      1.   Direct labor, $465.00. Daily summary of job-time records.
      2.   Direct materials, $345.00. Materials Requisition No. 438.
      2.   Direct labor, $364.50. Daily summary of job-time records.
      3.   Direct labor, $301.50. Daily summary of job-time records.
      5.   Direct materials, $261.00. Materials Requisition No. 447.
      5.   Direct labor, $285.00. Daily summary of job-time records.
      8.   Direct labor, $201.00. Daily summary of job-time records.

Instructions:
1. Open a cost sheet and record the transactions.
2. Complete the cost sheet, recording factory overhead at the applied rate of 75% of direct labor costs.

APPLICATION PROBLEM
Recording entries in a finished goods ledger

Decatur Industries, Inc., maintains a finished goods ledger for all of its manufactured products.

Transactions:

Apr.   2.   Received from production department 210 C45 bats at a unit cost of $8.80. Job No. 315.
      8.   Mike's Place, a store selling baseball equipment, cards, and memorabilia, ordered 90 C45 bats. Sales Invoice No. 511.
      9.   Production department completed 140 C45 bats and sent them to finished goods inventory. The unit cost for Job No. 334 was $9.00.
    14.   Sports Unlimited, a wholesale distributor of sports equipment, purchased 75 C45 bats. Sales Invoice No. 521.

continued

16. Job No. 339 was completed, with 100 C45 bats sent to finished goods inventory. The unit cost was $8.60.
23. Mike's Place purchased 300 C45 bats. Sales Invoice No. 536.
27. Sold 75 bats to The Grand Old Game, a baseball retailer. Sales Invoice No. 543.
28. Received from production department 120 C45 bats at a unit cost of $8.85. Job No. 363.

Instructions:

1. Prepare a finished goods ledger card for stock no. C45 baseball bats. Minimum quantity is set at 250 units. Inventory location is Area R-12.

2. Record the beginning balance on April 1 of the current year for 280 C45 baseball bats at a unit cost of $8.70. Decatur Industries uses the first-in, first-out method to record inventory costs.

3. Record the transactions.

MASTERY PROBLEM
Preparing cost records

Gemini manufactures athletic shoes. The company records manufacturing costs by job number and uses a factory overhead applied rate to charge overhead costs to its products.

The company estimates Gemini will manufacture 50,000 shoes next year. For this amount of production, total factory overhead is estimated to be $398,800.00. Estimated direct labor costs for next year are $498,500.00

Instructions:

1. Calculate Gemini's factory overhead applied rate for next year as a percentage of direct labor cost.

On May 3, Gemini began work on Job No. 283. The order is for 150 pairs of No. 52L athletic shoes for stock; date wanted May 13.

2. Open a cost sheet for Job No. 283 and record the following items.

May 3. Direct materials, $862.50. Materials Requisition No. 392.
3. Direct labor, $129.00. Daily summary of job-time records.
4. Direct labor, $248.00. Daily summary of job-time records.
5. Direct materials, $472.50. Materials Requisition No. 399.
5. Direct labor, $175.00. Daily summary of job-time records.
6. Direct labor, $192.00. Daily summary of job-time records.
7. Direct labor, $295.00. Daily summary of job-time records.
10. Direct materials, $360.00. Materials Requisition No. 428.
10. Direct labor, $165.00. Daily summary of job-time records.
11. Direct labor, $152.00. Daily summary of job-time records.
12. Direct labor, $124.00. Daily summary of job-time records.

3. Complete the cost sheet, recording factory overhead at the rate calculated in Instruction 1.

4. Prepare a finished goods ledger card for Stock No. 52L athletic shoes. Minimum quantity is set at 100. Inventory location is Area C-50.

5. Record on the finished goods ledger card the beginning balance on May 1. The May 1 balance of 52L athletic shoes is 140 units at a unit cost of $30.45. Gemini uses the first-in, first-out method to record inventory costs.

6. Record the following transactions on the finished goods ledger card for 52L athletic shoes.

May 5. Sold 60 pairs of 52L athletic shoes. Sales Invoice No. 633.
12. Received 150 pairs of 52L athletic shoes. Record cost from cost sheet for Job No. 283.
18. Sold 30 pairs of 52L athletic shoes. Sales Invoice No. 652.

19-7 CHALLENGE PROBLEM
Preparing cost records

Sea Explor manufactures deep-sea diving suits. The company records manufacturing costs by job number and uses a factory overhead applied rate to charge overhead costs to its products.

Sea Explor estimates they will manufacture 10,000 diving suits next year. For this amount of production, total factory overhead is estimated to be $600,000.00. Estimated direct materials costs for next year are $80.00 for each suit manufactured. Estimated direct labor for next year is 4 labor hours for each suit at $12.50 per hour.

Instructions:
1. Calculate Sea Explor's factory overhead applied rate for next year for each of the following three bases. (a) Direct materials cost. (b) Direct labor cost. (c) Direct labor hours.

On May 9, Sea Explor began work on Job No. 365. The order is for 55 SE80 diving suits for stock; date wanted May 19.

2. Open a cost sheet for Job No. 365 and record the following items.

May 9. Direct materials, $1,160.50. Materials Requisition No. 421.
9. Direct labor, $274.75. Daily summary of job-time records.
10. Direct labor, $441.00. Daily summary of job-time records.
11. Direct materials, $2,321.00. Materials Requisition No. 430.
11. Direct labor, $392.00. Daily summary of job-time records.
12. Direct labor, $423.00. Daily summary of job-time records.
13. Direct labor, $440.00. Daily summary of job-time records.
16. Direct materials, $1,017.50. Materials Requisition No. 438.
16. Direct labor, $370.00. Daily summary of job-time records.
17. Direct labor, $352.00. Daily summary of job-time records.
18. Direct labor, $181.00. Daily summary of job-time records.

3. Complete the cost sheet, recording factory overhead at the direct materials cost rate calculated in Instruction 1.

4. Prepare a finished goods ledger card for Stock No. SE80 diving suit. Minimum quantity is set at 30. Inventory location is Area J16.

5. Record on the finished goods ledger card the beginning balance on May 1. The May 1 balance of SE80 diving suits is 40 units at a unit cost of $191.50. Sea Explor uses the last-in, first-out method to record inventory costs.

6. Record the following transactions on the finished goods ledger card for SE80 diving suits.

May 11. Sold 10 SE80 diving suits. Sales Invoice No. 450.
18. Received 55 SE80 diving suits. Record cost from cost sheet for Job No. 365.
23. Sold 30 SE80 diving suits. Sales Invoice No. 494.
25. Sold 25 SE80 diving suits. Sales Invoice No. 523.

Applied Communication

You are appointed to participate on a time-efficiency team. The team includes factory workers, supervisors, and a representative from the accounting department. Currently the factory workers record their time on job-time sheets. They also calculate the total time worked on each job. A worker may work on three or four jobs each day. The accounting department receives about 200 job-time sheets each day. A clerk verifies the workers' calculations on the job-time records. Any changes to the total time must be initialed by a supervisor.

Required:

The company has appointed your team to explore ways to automate the time recording process. Your job on the team is to explore bar code technology. Write a report on bar code technology. Make a recommendation to the team indicating whether bar codes could be used to replace the job-time sheets.

Cases for Critical Thinking

Case 1

Century Fan Company manufactures ceiling fans. During the current year, payments were made for the following items. A new clerk classified the cost items. Are the cost items classified correctly? If not, give the correct classification and explain the reason for your corrected classification.

1. Wood to be used for fan blades. (Factory Overhead)
2. Insurance premium on the factory building. (Direct Materials)
3. Salary of factory workers assembling fans. (Factory Overhead)
4. Bolts used in assembling the fans. (Direct Materials)
5. Salary of factory supervisor. (Direct Labor)
6. Brooms used to sweep the factory floors. (Direct Materials)
7. Salary of packer who packs fan crates for shipping. (Direct Labor)
8. Paint and stain to be used on the fans. (Direct Materials)

Case 2

Astro Company has found that total factory overhead is usually about 60% of direct labor cost. The business manufactures one product that is processed in three different manufacturing departments: A, B, and C. In Department A, much expensive machinery is used. In Department B, some machinery is used. In Department C, virtually no machinery is used, all the work being manual work. There is a great difference in the amount of time required to process various jobs in the different departments. Under these circumstances do you believe that the company should charge factory overhead to each job at the rate of 60% of direct labor? If not, what would you recommend?

AUTOMATED ACCOUNTING

DEPARTMENT MARGIN STATEMENTS FOR A MANUFACTURING BUSINESS

Manufacturing businesses, as well as merchandising and service businesses, prepare external financial statements reporting information for all activities of business taken as a whole. The primary financial statements prepared for a manufacturing business are the income statement and the balance sheet. Manufacturing businesses also need information reported on a product or department basis if they produce multiple products. Managers use these reports in making decisions. To prepare such reports, computerized accounting systems require a chart of accounts with separate accounts for departmental revenues, costs, and expenses.

When a departmentalized accounting system is used, account balance information for revenues, cost of goods manufactured and sold, and direct expenses (those traceable to the operation of a specific department) can be transferred to a spreadsheet and used to prepare reports in a variety of formats. Departmental margin reports similar to those prepared for merchandising businesses can be generated by the spreadsheet. In addition, supplementary schedules used to simplify the preparation of the balance sheet and the income statement may be prepared.

The ABC Company has three products for which it wishes to track departmental revenues and expenses. It uses a spreadsheet program to prepare the following supplemental schedules:

- Cost of goods manufactured

- Cost of goods sold

By preparing supplemental schedules before preparing the margin statement, accountants can include detail from the ledger accounts while still maintaining the clarity of the individual statements. The cost of goods manufactured statement details information about:

- Direct materials

- Direct labor

- Applied overhead used in the production of each of the company's products

- Beginning work in process inventory

- Ending work in process inventory

The total costs calculated on this schedule are then included in the cost of goods sold schedule.

After the supplemental schedules have been prepared, the departmental margin statement, like the one prepared for a merchandising business is completed. It includes direct revenues and expenses (both product costs and operating expenses) for each product, unit, or department that is being tracked individually.

When a computerized spreadsheet program is used in preparing reports and schedules, formulas are incorporated in the spreadsheet. Formulas for totals and subtotals allow monthly changes to be made to the report without having to recreate the entire form. The first time a spreadsheet report is created, it is a good idea to manually check all formulas for accuracy. Once the formulas have been verified, the spreadsheet may be used repeatedly with confidence that the formulas are accurate. The spreadsheet schedule is saved. In subsequent months, the spreadsheet is opened, renamed, and new data entered.

20

Accounting Transactions and Financial Reporting for a Manufacturing Business

AFTER STUDYING CHAPTER 20, YOU WILL BE ABLE TO:

1. Define accounting terms related to accounting transactions and financial reporting for a manufacturing business.

2. Identify accounting concepts and practices related to accounting transactions and financial reporting for a manufacturing business.

3. Journalize transactions for a manufacturing business.

4. Prepare selected financial statements for a manufacturing business.

TERMS PREVIEW

underapplied overhead
overapplied overhead
statement of cost of
  goods
  manufactured

Managing a manufacturing business requires more elaborate planning and control than managing a merchandising business. In addition to sales and administrative activities required of both types of businesses, a manufacturing business must provide the knowledge and resources needed to make the product.

Accounting for a manufacturing business is more complex than accounting for a merchandising business. To provide usable financial information for a manufacturing business, detailed cost records must be maintained throughout the manufacturing process. These detailed manufacturing cost records provide a business with information needed to price its product, analyze manufacturing costs, and make other important management decisions. Procedures for maintaining detailed manufacturing cost records are described in Chapter 19.

In addition to detailed cost records, a manufacturing business also needs accurate financial statements. To provide financial statements, it must make journal entries to reflect cost transactions in general ledger accounts.

Manufacturing cost data are generally recorded daily to provide up-to-date cost information for managers. However, most manufacturing costs are recorded for financial reporting purposes only when up-to-date account balances are needed to prepare financial statements. These end-of-fiscal-period journal entries update the general ledger manufacturing accounts before financial statements are prepared.

ACCOUNTING
IN YOUR CAREER

REPORTING MANUFACTURING COSTS

Sudbury Home Products manufactures two product lines. Each product line has several different products. Some of the products require extensive labor with relatively low materials costs. Others involve expensive materials but are produced on an automated, high-speed assembly line with such high volume sales that unit labor costs are low.

At the end of each fiscal period, the financial statements include a statement of costs of goods manufactured for each product line, as well as an income statement and balance sheet for the whole company's operations. The income statement shows cost of goods manufactured, but the direct materials, direct labor, and applied factory overhead for each product line are shown only on the statement of cost of goods manufactured for each product line.

In a department meeting, William Turman questioned the purpose of the statement of cost of goods manufactured. He asked why these statements are never included in the annual report mailed to stockholders. He said, "I am not an experienced accountant by any means, but I have taken an accounting course. I thought the accounting concept of adequate disclosure would require us to publish all the financial statements. If we're not going to share this information, why do we even prepare it?"

Critical Thinking
1. Why does a manufacturing company prepare a statement of cost of goods manufactured?
2. Why does Sudbury prepare a statement of cost of goods manufactured for each product line?
3. How would you respond to Mr. Turman's question?
4. Which published financial statement would include the cost of goods manufactured?
5. Which published financial statement would include the amount of work in process inventory?

FLOW OF MANUFACTURING COSTS

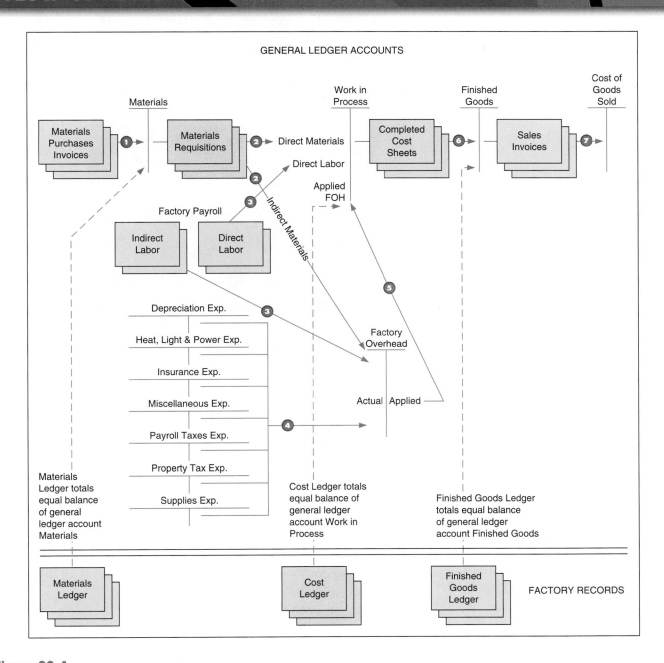

Figure 20-1

All manufacturing costs flow through the manufacturing accounts. FaxaVision uses cost sheets to record direct materials, direct labor, and overhead costs of each job. This method permits the company to determine the unit costs of completed jobs. The unit costs are recorded in the company's perpetual inventory of finished goods. Therefore, these costs are recorded through each phase of the manufacturing process. Summary journal entries update general ledger accounts for costs incurred in completing jobs, as shown in Figure 20-1. Thus, end-of-fiscal-period inventory adjustments are not required.

Recording journal entries for manufacturing accounts

1. Record materials purchased by debiting Materials and crediting Accounts Payable.
2. Record direct materials transferred to the factory by crediting Materials and debiting Work in Process. Record indirect materials transferred to the factory by crediting Materials and debiting Factory Overhead.
3. Record factory payroll by debiting direct labor to Work in Process, debiting indirect labor to Factory Overhead, crediting payroll liability accounts (e.g. Accounts Payable), and crediting Cash.
4. Close individual manufacturing expense accounts by debiting Factory Overhead and crediting each manufacturing expense account for its balance.
5. Record applied overhead by debiting Work in Process and crediting Factory Overhead for the total overhead amount applied during the fiscal period.
6. Record cost of products completed by crediting Work in Process and debiting Finished Goods.
7. Record cost of products sold by crediting Finished Goods and debiting Cost of Goods Sold.

JOURNAL ENTRIES TO RECORD FACTORY PAYROLL FOR A MONTH

CASH PAYMENTS JOURNAL   PAGE 2

	DATE	ACCOUNT TITLE	CK. NO.	POST. REF.	GENERAL DEBIT	GENERAL CREDIT	ACCOUNTS PAYABLE DEBIT	PURCHASES DISCOUNT CREDIT	CASH CREDIT	
1	Jan. 15	Work in Process	1194		39 245 00				41 325 38	1
2		Factory Overhead			11 774 00					2
3		Employee Income Tax Payable				5 612 10				3
4		Social Security Tax Payable				3 336 64				4
5		Medicare Tax Payable				7 44 88				5
21	31	Work in Process	1211		44 255 00				46 600 12	21
22		Factory Overhead			13 276 00					22
23		Employee Income Tax Payable				6 328 40				23
24		Social Security Tax Payable				3 762 53				24
25		Medicare Tax Payable				8 39 95				25

1. Debit the factory accounts.

2. Credit the three tax withholding accounts.

3. Credit cash for the next payroll.

Figure 20-2

FaxaVision pays all factory employees twice each month. A separate payroll register is prepared for factory employees. A cash payments journal entry is prepared for each factory payroll. The journal entries for the January 15 and January 31 factory payroll for FaxaVision are shown in Figure 20-2.

Recording factory payroll

1. Debit Work in Process for direct labor and Factory Overhead for indirect labor.
2. Credit Employee Income Tax Payable, Social Security Tax Payable, and Medicare Tax Payable for the amounts withheld from employees.
3. Credit Cash for the net pay.

Work in Process

Bal. 82,579.00	
1/15 39,245.00	
1/31 44,255.00	

Factory Overhead

1/15 11,774.00	
1/31 13,276.00	

Employee Income Tax Payable

	1/15 5,612.10
	1/31 6,328.40

Social Security Tax Payable

	1/15 3,336.64
	1/31 3,762.53

Medicare Tax Payable

	1/15 744.88
	1/31 839.95

Cash

	1/15 41,325.38
	1/31 46,600.12

	DATE		ACCOUNT CREDITED	PURCH. NO.	POST. REF.	MATERIALS DR. ACCTS. PAY. CR.	
1	Jan.²⁰⁻⁻	4	Oakley Electronics	621		7 0 9 7 80	1
24		31	Total			168 6 4 2 60	24

MATERIALS PURCHASES JOURNAL   PAGE *1*

Figure 20-3

FaxaVision records the amount of direct and indirect materials purchased and issued in the general ledger account **Materials**. FaxaVision uses a perpetual inventory in the factory that permits the company to charge cost of materials to a job as materials are issued. (*CONCEPT: Matching Expenses with Revenue*)

FaxaVision uses a special materials purchases journal to record all materials purchases. Purchases are made on account; therefore, the journal has a single amount column. An entry in the materials purchases journal is shown in Figure 20-3.

At the end of a month, the total of the materials purchases journal is posted to **Materials** and **Accounts Payable** in the general ledger.

In the materials account, the January 1 debit balance, *$121,231.20*, is the materials inventory at the beginning of the month. The January 31 debit, *$168,642.60*, is the total posted from the materials purchases journal. This represents the total cost of direct and indirect materials purchased during the month.

Materials	
Jan. 1 Bal. 121,231.20	
Jan. 31 168,642.60	

Accounts Payable	
	Jan. 31 168,642.60

	DATE		ACCOUNT TITLE	DOC. NO.	POST. REF.	DEBIT	CREDIT	
1	Jan.²⁰⁻⁻	31	Work in Process	M240		156 4 7 7 00		1
2			Factory Overhead			11 4 4 7 50		2
3			Materials				167 9 2 4 50	3

GENERAL JOURNAL   PAGE *1*

Figure 20-4

A materials requisition is prepared for direct materials issued for a specific job. After materials are issued, the requisition amount is recorded on a cost sheet and the requisition is filed. At the end of a month, the total value of all direct materials issued to specific jobs must be transferred from **Materials** to **Work in Process**.

A materials requisition is also prepared for indirect materials used in the factory. After the

indirect materials are issued to the factory, the requisition is filed. At the end of the month, the total value of all indirect materials issued is transferred from **Materials** to **Factory Overhead**.

FaxaVision prepares a memorandum with monthly summary information of the direct materials requisitions and the indirect materials totals. The general journal entry to transfer these amounts is shown in Figure 20-4.

The balance in the Work in Process account, *$82,579.00*, is the beginning inventory of **Work in Process**. The other debits represent the total amounts of direct labor and direct materials used for all jobs during the month.

The debits to **Factory Overhead** represent the total amounts of indirect labor used and indirect materials issued during the month.

Work in Process	
Bal.	82,579.00
Jan. 15 Dir. Lab.	39,245.00
Jan. 31 Dir. Lab.	44,255.00
Jan. 31 Dir. Mat.	156,477.00

Factory Overhead	
Jan. 15 Ind. Lab.	11,774.00
Jan. 31 Ind. Lab.	13,276.00
Jan. 31 Ind. Mat.	11,447.50

	DATE	ACCOUNT TITLE	DOC. NO.	POST. REF.	DEBIT	CREDIT	
4	31	Factory Overhead	M241		30 4 5 6 00		4
5		Depr. Exp.—Factory Equip.				2 5 0 0 00	5
6		Depr. Exp.—Building				1 3 0 0 00	6
7		Heat, Light, and Power Exp.				6 1 5 8 50	7
8		Insurance Exp.—Factory				6 2 0 00	8
9		Miscellaneous Exp.—Factory				7 8 4 40	9
10		Payroll Taxes Exp.—Factory				15 4 1 4 10	10
11		Property Tax Exp.—Factory				1 4 6 3 60	11
12		Supplies Exp.—Factory				2 2 1 5 40	12

GENERAL JOURNAL — PAGE 1

Figure 20-5

Factory overhead includes various indirect factory expenses such as indirect labor, indirect materials, taxes, depreciation, and insurance. Actual factory overhead expenses are summarized in an account titled **Factory Overhead**.

Indirect labor and indirect materials are posted directly to the factory overhead account from the entries shown in Figures 20-2 and 20-4. Other indirect expenses are recorded throughout the month in other manufacturing expense accounts. At the end of each month, these indirect expense account balances are transferred to the factory overhead account. The actual factory overhead can then be compared with the estimated amount of factory overhead recorded on the job cost sheets. Recall from Chapter 19 that factory overhead is estimated (applied) so that a company can record overhead on a cost sheet as

soon as a job is completed.

Adjusting entries are made at the end of a fiscal period. These adjusting entries include debits to the depreciation expense, insurance expense, and supplies expense accounts. The closing entry to transfer actual overhead expenses to the factory overhead account is shown in Figure 20-5.

After postings are completed, all actual factory overhead expense accounts are summarized in the factory overhead account.

Factory Overhead	
Jan. 15 Ind. Lab.	11,774.00
Jan. 31 Ind. Lab.	13,276.00
Jan. 31 Ind. Mat.	11,447.50
Jan. 31 Act. OH	30,456.00
(New Bal.	66,953.50)

RECORDING APPLIED OVERHEAD

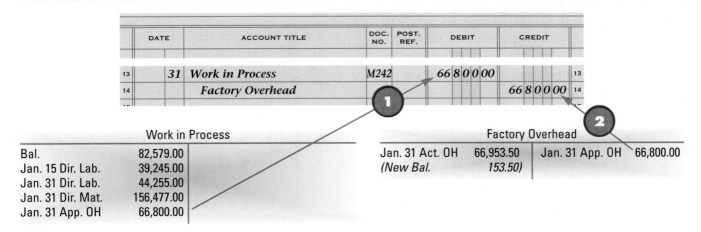

	DATE	ACCOUNT TITLE	DOC. NO.	POST. REF.	DEBIT	CREDIT	
13	31	*Work in Process*	M242		66 80 0 00		13
14		*Factory Overhead*				66 80 0 00	14

Work in Process

Bal.	82,579.00
Jan. 15 Dir. Lab.	39,245.00
Jan. 31 Dir. Lab.	44,255.00
Jan. 31 Dir. Mat.	156,477.00
Jan. 31 App. OH	66,800.00

Factory Overhead

Jan. 31 Act. OH	66,953.50	Jan. 31 App. OH	66,800.00
(New Bal.	*153.50)*		

Figure 20-6

FaxaVision applies factory overhead to each job at the rate of 80% of direct labor charges. At the end of each month, FaxaVision totals the applied factory overhead recorded on all job cost sheets. Its applied factory overhead for January is *$66,800.00*. The journal entry to record applied factory overhead is shown in Figure 20-6.

The factory overhead account debit, *$66,953.50*, is the actual factory overhead

expense for the month. The credit, *$66,800.00*, is the applied factory overhead for the month. The account's $153.50 debit ending balance results from recording less applied factory overhead than the amount of actual factory overhead expenses.

DISPOSING OF OVERAPPLIED AND UNDERAPPLIED FACTORY OVERHEAD BALANCES

	DATE	ACCOUNT TITLE	DOC. NO.	POST. REF.	DEBIT	CREDIT	
15	31	*Income Summary*	M243		1 5 3 50		15
16		*Factory Overhead*				1 5 3 50	16

Figure 20-7

The rate used to calculate applied factory overhead is only an estimate. Therefore, the factory overhead account may have an ending balance. The amount by which applied factory overhead is less than actual factory overhead is called **underapplied overhead**. The debit balance, *$153.50*, in FaxaVision's account indicates underapplied overhead for January. The journal entry to close the factory overhead account at the end of January is shown in Figure 20-7.

A credit balance indicates that applied factory overhead is more than actual factory overhead. The amount by which applied factory

overhead is more than actual factory overhead is called **overapplied overhead**. If the factory overhead account has a credit balance, Factory Overhead is debited and Income Summary is credited for the overapplied overhead amount.

Overhead may be overapplied or underapplied for two reasons. (1) Actual expenses may be higher or lower than normal, an event that requires closer control over expenditures. (2) The factory overhead applied rate may be inaccurate. If the rate is found to be inaccurate, a revised rate is determined. The revised rate is used in the next fiscal period.

RECORDING FINISHED GOODS TRANSACTIONS

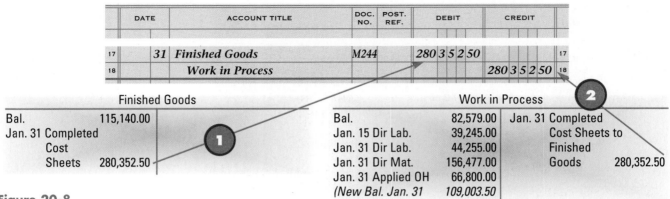

Figure 20-8

FaxaVision totals the cost sheets for all jobs completed during the month. Its January total, $280,352.50, is the cost of work finished during the month. This amount is transferred from Work in Process to Finished Goods. The journal entry to record this transaction is shown in Figure 20-8.

The balance in the finished goods account, $115,140.00, represents beginning inventory. The

January 31 debit to Finished Goods and credit to Work in Process, $280,352.50, represents the cost of finished goods transferred from the factory to the stockroom. The work in process account balance, $109,003.50, is the total amount of direct materials, direct labor, and applied factory overhead charged to the jobs in the ending inventory of work in process.

RECORDING SALES AND COST OF GOODS SOLD

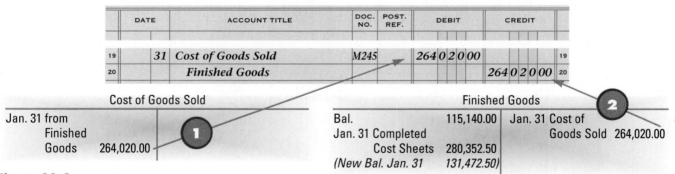

Figure 20-9

FaxaVision records sales using the procedure described in Chapter 2. Since FaxaVision uses a perpetual inventory, a different procedure is used to determine and record cost of goods sold. For each sale, the number of products shipped, the unit cost, and the total amounts of products sold are recorded on the sales invoice.

At the end of the month, cost information on all sales invoices is totaled. The total costs recorded for FaxaVision's January sales, $264,020.00, is the cost of goods sold for the month. This number represents the total *cost* of

products sold, not the revenue derived from sales (which is determined by selling price). This total cost is transferred from the inventory account Finished Goods to the cost account Cost of Goods Sold, as shown in Figure 20-9.

The debit to Cost of Goods Sold, $264,020.00, is the cost of goods sold during the month. The credit to Finished Goods, $264,020.00, is the cost of finished goods sold during the month and removed from inventory. The finished goods account balance, $131,472.50, is the ending inventory of finished goods.

ACCOUNT *Materials* ACCOUNT NO. *1125*

DATE		ITEM	POST. REF.	DEBIT	CREDIT	BALANCE DEBIT	BALANCE CREDIT
Jan. 20--	1	Balance	✓			121 231 20	
	31		MP1	168 642 60		289 873 80	
	31		G1		167 924 50	121 949 30	

ACCOUNT *Work in Process* ACCOUNT NO. *1130*

DATE		ITEM	POST. REF.	DEBIT	CREDIT	BALANCE DEBIT	BALANCE CREDIT
Jan. 20--	1	Balance	✓			82 579 00	
	15		CP2	39 245 00		121 824 00	
	31		CP2	44 255 00		166 079 00	
	31		G1	156 477 00		322 556 00	
	31		G1	66 800 00		389 356 00	
	31		G1		280 352 50	109 003 50	

ACCOUNT *Finished Goods* ACCOUNT NO. *1135*

DATE		ITEM	POST. REF.	DEBIT	CREDIT	BALANCE DEBIT	BALANCE CREDIT
Jan. 20--	1	Balance	✓			115 140 00	
	31		G1	280 352 50		395 492 50	
	31		G1		264 020 00	131 472 50	

ACCOUNT *Cost of Goods Sold* ACCOUNT NO. *5105*

DATE		ITEM	POST. REF.	DEBIT	CREDIT	BALANCE DEBIT	BALANCE CREDIT
Jan. 20--	31		G1	264 020 00		264 020 00	

ACCOUNT *Factory Overhead* ACCOUNT NO. *5505*

DATE		ITEM	POST. REF.	DEBIT	CREDIT	BALANCE DEBIT	BALANCE CREDIT
Jan. 20--	15		CP2	11 774 00		11 774 00	
	31		CP2	13 276 00		25 050 00	
	31		G1	11 447 50		36 497 50	
	31		G1	30 456 00		66 953 50	
	31		G1		66 800 00	153 50	
	31		G1		153 50	—	—

Figure 20-10

The effect of posting the entries described in this chapter is shown in Figure 20-10.

1. Where are direct materials, direct labor, and overhead costs for each job initially recorded?

2. After factory overhead has been applied to work in process, what does a credit balance in Factory Overhead indicate?

3. Explain the difference between actual factory overhead and applied factory overhead.

ORK
TOGETHER

Preparing manufacturing journal entries

A materials purchases journal, a cash payments journal, and a general journal for Vanyo, Inc., a manufacturer of cardboard boxes, are provided in the *Working Papers*. Your instructor will guide you through the following examples.

4. Prepare journal entries for each of the following transactions or events.

May 3. Purchased $15,400.00 of materials on account from Bushnell Corrugated.

5. Requisitioned $2,650.00 of direct materials and $350.00 of indirect materials for the production department.

15. Paid employees their semimonthly pay. Gross (pretax) direct labor costs were $11,200. Gross indirect labor costs were $1,600.00. Employee income tax was $1,480.00. Social security tax was 6.2% and Medicare tax was 1.45% of gross wages.

21. Requisitioned $4,700.00 of direct materials and $2,100.00 of indirect materials for the production department.

31. Obtained factory costs for the month: depreciation on building, $750.00; depreciation on equipment, $1,200.00; insurance, $325.00; property taxes, $545.00; utilities, $1,880.00. Assume that these expenses have already been properly accounted for and now need to be closed.

31. Paid employees their semimonthly pay. Gross (pretax) direct labor costs were $10,150.00. Gross indirect labor costs were $1,370.00. Employee income tax was $1,220.00. Social security tax was 6.2% and Medicare tax was 1.45% of gross wages.

31. Applied overhead at the rate of 50% of direct labor costs.

31. Transferred cardboard boxes costing $29,920 to finished goods during the month.

31. Sold cardboard boxes costing $24,760 during the month.

ON YOUR OWN

Preparing manufacturing journal entries

A materials purchases journal, a cash payments journal, and a general journal for Vanyo, Inc., a manufacturer of cardboard boxes, are provided in the *Working Papers*. Work independently to complete the following problem.

5. Prepare journal entries for each of the following transactions or events.

June 4. Purchased $8,100.00 of materials on account from Fresno, Inc.

7. Requisitioned $3,770.00 of direct materials and $730.00 of indirect materials for the production department.

15. Paid employees their semimonthly pay. Gross (pretax) direct labor costs were $12,590.00. Gross indirect labor costs were $1,940.00. Employee income tax was $1,780.00. Social security tax was 6.2% and Medicare tax was 1.45% of gross wages.

15. Requisitioned $2,300.00 of direct materials and $1,530.00 of indirect materials for the production department.

30. Obtained factory costs for the month: depreciation on building, $750.00; depreciation on equipment, $1,200.00; insurance, $325.00; property taxes, $570.00; utilities, $1,960.00. Assume that these expenses have already been properly accounted for and now need to be closed.

30. Paid employees their semimonthly pay. Gross (pretax) direct labor costs were $10,860.00. Gross indirect labor costs were $1,785.00. Employee income tax was $1,615.00. Social security tax was 6.2% and Medicare tax was 1.45% of gross wages.

30. Applied overhead at the rate of 50% of direct labor costs.

30. Transferred cardboard boxes costing $35,500.00 to finished goods during the month.

30. Sold cardboard boxes costing $32,160.00 during the month.

GLOBAL PERSPECTIVE

INTERNATIONAL BANKING

International business transactions usually require the use of international services from a commercial bank. More than 300 U.S. banks have international banking departments to assist customers with international business.

Some specific services that are offered by commercial banks are: exchange of currency; assistance in financing exports; and collection of invoices, drafts, letters of credit, and other foreign receivables.

Required:

Contact a local bank that has an international department. Find out the following information.
1. With what countries does the bank have specialized relationships?
2. Does the bank handle letters of credit? If so, what is the procedure to negotiate a letter of credit?
3. Is financial assistance available to exporters? If so, what are the guidelines.

PREPARING THE WORK SHEET

The primary purpose of cost accounting information is to help managers make better decisions. However, some of this information is also used to prepare financial statements, which may be important not only to managers inside the firm but also to investors, creditors, and others outside the organization.

Several of the procedures used to prepare a manufacturing business' work sheet and financial statements are similar to the procedures used for a merchandising business.

A work sheet is used to plan a manufacturing business' financial information for fiscal period statements just as it is for merchandising businesses. However, a manufacturing business' work sheet includes three inventory accounts and a cost of goods sold account. FaxaVision's work sheet for January is shown in Figure 20-11.

FaxaVision's work sheet, similar to the work sheets of other manufacturing businesses using the perpetual inventory method, has several unique characteristics:

1. The entries to record direct materials, work in process, and finished goods bring manufacturing inventory accounts up to date on January 31. Thus, the balances of **Materials, Work in Process,** and **Finished Goods** are brought up to date before a work sheet is prepared. Adjustments for these inventory accounts do not need to be planned on a work sheet.

2. The factory keeps perpetual inventory subsidiary ledgers and detailed cost records. Based on these subsidiary records, summary journal entries are made to record the flow of costs through the manufacturing process to the cost of goods sold account. Since all manufacturing costs flow toward the account **Cost of Goods Sold,** no manufacturing cost accounts on the work sheet have balances. Amounts in these accounts have been transferred to either one of the inventory accounts or the cost of goods sold account. The cost of goods sold amount, *$264,020.00,* is extended to the Income Statement Debit column.

3. **Income Summary** has a debit balance of $153.50. This balance resulted from closing the underapplied overhead to **Income Summary.** The amount represents additional manufacturing costs that are not already in the inventory or cost of goods sold account. The amount is extended to the Income Statement Debit column.

Extending other accounts to the Income Statement and Balance Sheet columns and calculating net income are similar to the procedures described for corporations in Chapter 13.

FaxaVision, Inc.
Work Sheet
For Month Ended January 31, 20--

	ACCOUNT TITLE	TRIAL BALANCE DEBIT	TRIAL BALANCE CREDIT	ADJUSTMENTS DEBIT	ADJUSTMENTS CREDIT	INCOME STATEMENT DEBIT	INCOME STATEMENT CREDIT	BALANCE SHEET DEBIT	BALANCE SHEET CREDIT	
1	Cash	18263360						18263360		1
2	Petty Cash	30000						30000		2
3	Accounts Receivable	22420750						22420750		3
4	Allow. for Uncoll. Accts.		454160		(a) 205660				659820	4
5	Materials	12194930						12194930		5
6	Work in Process	10900350						10900350		6
7	Finished Goods	13147250						13147250		7
8	Supplies—Factory	725870						725870		8
9	Supplies—Sales	953120			(b) 185020			768100		9
10	Supplies—Administrative	242580			(c) 46840			195740		10
11	Prepaid Insurance	419860			(d) 13060			406800		11
12	Factory Equipment	18200000						18200000		12
13	Accum. Depr.—Factory Equipment		5461000						5461000	13
14	Office Equipment	2526000						2526000		14
15	Accum. Depr.—Office Equipment		620000		(e) 53000				673000	15
16	Store Equipment	2290000						2290000		16
17	Accum. Depr.—Store Equipment		677000		(f) 49000				726000	17
18	Building	39700000						39700000		18
19	Accum. Depr.—Building		5950000						5950000	19
20	Land	17700000						17700000		20
21	Accounts Payable		18969850						18969850	21
22	Employee Income Tax Payable		1187140						1187140	22
23	Federal Income Tax Payable				(g) 2099500				2099500	23
24	Social Security Tax Payable		1397906						1397906	24
25	Medicare Tax Payable		322594						322594	25
26	Salaries Payable									26
27	Unemploy. Tax Payable—Federal		126840						126840	27
28	Unemploy. Tax Payable—State		856170						856170	28
29	Dividends Payable									29
30	Mortgage Payable		10000000						10000000	30
31	Capital Stock		60000000						60000000	31

Figure 20-11 (top half)

#	Account	Trial Balance Dr	Trial Balance Cr	Adjustments Dr	Adjustments Cr	Income Statement Dr	Income Statement Cr	Balance Sheet Dr	Balance Sheet Cr
32	Retained Earnings		469 638 80						469 638 80
33	Dividends	153 50						153 50	
34	Income Summary								
35	Sales		411 480 00				411 480 00		
36	Cost of Goods Sold	264 020 00				264 020 00			
37	Factory Overhead								
38	Depr. Expense—Factory Equipment								
39	Depr. Expense—Building								
40	Heat, Light, and Power Expense								
41	Insurance Expense—Factory								
42	Miscellaneous Exp.—Factory								
43	Payroll Taxes Exp.—Factory								
44	Property Tax Exp.—Factory								
45	Supplies Expense—Factory								
46	Advertising Expense	4 784 40				4 784 40			
47	Delivery Expense	11 058 60				11 058 60			
48	Depr. Expense—Store Equipment			(f) 490 00		490 00			
49	Miscellaneous Expenses—Sales	1 554 50				1 554 50			
50	Salary Expense—Sales	28 078 00				28 078 00			
51	Supplies Expense—Sales			(b) 1 850 20		1 850 20			
52	Depr. Expense—Office Equipment			(e) 530 00		530 00			
53	Insurance Expense—Admin.			(d) 130 60		130 60			
54	Miscellaneous Exp.—Admin.	2 184 20				2 184 20			
55	Payroll Taxes Exp.—Admin.	7 100 00				7 100 00			
56	Property Tax Exp.—Admin.	159 80				159 80			
57	Salary Expense—Admin.	21 922 00				21 922 00			
58	Supplies Expense—Admin.			(c) 468 40		468 40			
59	Uncollectible Accounts Expense			(a) 2 056 60		2 056 60			
60	Utilities Expense—Admin.	1 543 80				1 543 80			
61	Gain on Plant Assets								
62	Miscellaneous Revenue								
63	Interest Expense	1 500 00				1 500 00			
64	Loss on Plant Assets	145 90				145 90			
65	Federal Income Tax Expense			@ 20 995 00		20 995 00			
66		1 941 345 40	1 941 345 40	26 520 80	26 520 80	370 725 50	411 480 00	1 594 691 50	1 553 937 00
67	Net Income after Fed. Inc. Tax					40 754 50			40 754 50
68						411 480 00	411 480 00	1 594 691 50	1 594 691 50

Figure 20-11 (bottom half)

FaxaVision, Inc.
Statement of Cost of Goods Manufactured
For Month Ended January 31, 20--

Direct Materials.	$156,477.00
Direct Labor	83,500.00
Factory Overhead Applied	66,800.00
Total Cost of Work Placed in Process.	$306,777.00
Work in Process Inventory, Jan. 1, 20--	82,579.00
Total Cost of Work in Process During January	$389,356.00
Less Work in Process Inventory, Jan. 31, 20--	109,003.50
Cost of Goods Manufactured	$280,352.50

1. Enter direct materials, direct labor, and factory overhead applied.

2. Total the cost of work placed in process.

3. Add beginning work in process inventory.

4. Subtract ending work in process inventory.

Figure 20-12

A manufacturing business prepares an income statement, a statement of stockholders' equity, and a balance sheet. These statements are similar to those previously described for other kinds of businesses. A statement showing details about the cost of finished goods is called a **statement of cost of goods manufactured**. This statement shows the details of the cost ele-ments—materials, direct labor, and factory over-head—spent on the goods completed in a fiscal period. A statement of cost of goods manufac-tured supplements the income statement. FaxaVision's statement of cost of goods manu-factured is shown in Figure 20-12.

S T E P S Preparing a statement of cost of goods manufactured

1. Enter direct materials, *$156,477.00*. This is the amount debited to Work in Process in the general journal, Figure 20-4. Enter direct labor, *$83,500.00*, from the cash payments journal, Figure 20-2. Enter factory overhead applied, *$66,800.00*. The amount of factory overhead is the total of the applied factory overhead recorded on cost sheets. The journal entry to record applied factory overhead was shown in Figure 20-6.

2. Total the cost of work placed in process by adding direct materials, direct labor, and factory overhead applied.

3. Add beginning work in process inventory, *$82,579.00*, to determine the total cost of work in process during the month.

4. Subtract ending work in process inventory, *$109,003.50*, to determine the cost of goods manufactured during the month.

SOURCES OF INCOME STATEMENT INFORMATION

FaxaVision's income statement for the month of January is shown in Figure 20-13. Information for FaxaVision's income statement comes from three sources:

1. Beginning and ending finished goods inventories, *$115,140.00* and *$131,472.50*, come from the general ledger account, Figure 20-10.

2. Cost of goods manufactured, *$280,352.50*, comes from the statement of cost of goods manufactured, Figure 20-12.

3. All other amounts come from the Income Statement columns of the work sheet, Figure 20-11.

FaxaVision, Inc.
Income Statement
For Month Ended January 31, 20--

			*% of Net Sales
Operating Revenue:			
Sales		$411,480.00	100.0
Cost of Goods Sold:			
Finished Goods Inventory, Jan. 1, 20--	$115,140.00		
Cost of Goods Manufactured	280,352.50		
Total Cost of Finished Goods Available for Sale	$395,492.50		
Less Finished Goods Inventory, Jan. 31, 20--	131,472.50		
Cost of Goods Sold	$264,020.00		
Underapplied Overhead	153.50		
Net Cost of Goods Sold		264,173.50	64.2
Gross Profit on Operations		$147,306.50	35.8
Operating Expenses:			
Selling Expenses:			
Advertising Expense	$ 4,784.40		
Delivery Expense	11,058.60		
Depreciation Expense—Store Equipment	490.00		
Miscellaneous Expense—Sales	1,554.50		
Salary Expense—Sales	28,078.00		
Supplies Expense—Sales	1,850.20		
Total Selling Expenses		$ 47,815.70	
Administrative Expenses:			
Depreciation Expense—Office Equipment	$ 530.00		
Insurance Expense—Administrative	130.60		
Miscellaneous Expense—Administrative	2,184.20		
Payroll Taxes Expense—Administrative	7,100.00		
Property Tax Expense—Administrative	159.80		
Salary Expense—Administrative	21,922.00		
Supplies Expense—Administrative	468.40		
Uncollectible Accounts Expense	2,056.60		
Utilities Expense—Administrative	1,543.80		
Total Administrative Expenses		$ 36,095.40	
Total Operating Expenses		83,911.10	20.4
Net Income from Operations		$ 63,395.40	15.4
Other Expenses:			
Interest Expense	$ 1,500.00		
Loss on Plant Assets	145.90		
Net Deduction		1,645.90	0.4
Net Income before Federal Income Tax		$ 61,749.50	15.0
Less Federal Income Tax Expense		20,995.00	5.1
Net Income after Federal Income Tax		$ 40,754.50	9.9

*Rounded to nearest 0.1%

Figure 20-13

This income statement differs in two ways from the income statements of merchandising businesses shown in previous chapters:

1. Cost of goods manufactured is used instead of purchases. Details of the cost of goods manufactured are given on the statement of cost of goods manufactured.

2. The amount of underapplied overhead, *$153.50*, is added to the cost of goods sold. The amount is added because applied overhead is less than the actual overhead.

The cost of goods manufactured in Figure 20-12 includes the applied overhead amount rather than the actual amount. The income statement must be adjusted to reflect actual factory overhead costs. Theoretically, the underapplied or overapplied overhead should be apportioned among the work in process inventory, finished goods inventory, and cost of goods sold accounts. However, since the amount is small, it is charged entirely to cost of goods sold.

FaxaVision, Inc.
Balance Sheet
January 31, 20--

ASSETS

Current Assets:			
Cash		$182,633.60	
Petty Cash		300.00	
Accounts Receivable	$224,207.50		
Less Allowance for Uncollectible Accounts	6,598.20	217,609.30	
Materials		121,949.30	
Work in Process		109,003.50	
Finished Goods		131,472.50	
Supplies—Factory		7,258.70	
Supplies—Sales		7,681.00	
Supplies—Administrative		1,957.40	
Prepaid Insurance		4,068.00	
Total Current Assets			$ 783,933.30
Plant Assets:			
Factory Equipment	$182,000.00		
Less Accumulated Depreciation—Factory Equipment	54,610.00	$127,390.00	
Office Equipment	$ 25,260.00		
Less Accumulated Depreciation—Office Equipment	6,730.00	18,530.00	
Store Equipment	$ 22,900.00		
Less Accumulated Depreciation—Store Equipment	7,260.00	15,640.00	
Building	$397,000.00		
Less Accumulated Depreciation—Building	59,500.00	337,500.00	
Land		177,000.00	
Total Plant Assets			676,060.00
Total Assets			$1,459,993.30

LIABILITIES

Current Liabilities:			
Accounts Payable		$189,698.50	
Employee Income Tax Payable		11,871.40	
Federal Income Tax Payable		20,995.00	
Social Security Tax Payable		13,979.06	
Medicare Tax Payable		3,225.94	
Unemployment Tax Payable—Federal		1,268.40	
Unemployment Tax Payable—State		8,561.70	
Total Current Liabilities			$ 249,600.00
Long-Term Liability:			
Mortgage Payable			100,000.00
Total Liabilities			$ 349,600.00

STOCKHOLDERS' EQUITY

Capital Stock		$600,000.00	
Retained Earnings		510,393.30	
Total Stockholders' Equity			1,110,393.30
Total Liabilities and Stockholders' Equity			$1,459,993.30

Figure 20-14

The balance sheet prepared by FaxaVision on January 31, of the current year is shown in Figure 20-14.

Except for the list of inventories, the balance sheet of a manufacturing business is similar to the balance sheet of a merchandising business. In a manufacturing business, the current assets section of the balance sheet lists three types of inventories: (1) materials, (2) work in process, and (3) finished goods.

A statement of stockholders' equity for a manufacturing business is similar to that of a merchandising business described in Chapter 14. The statement of stockholders' equity for FaxaVision is not illustrated.

TERM REVIEW

statement of cost of goods manufactured

AUDIT YOUR UNDERSTANDING

1. To which work sheet column is the debit balance of Cost of Goods Sold extended?

2. How is underapplied overhead accounted for on an income statement?

3. In which section of the balance sheet are the three inventory accounts of a manufacturing business listed?

WORK TOGETHER

Preparing statement of cost of goods manufactured, income statement, and balance sheet

Work sheets for Bedthings, Inc., a manufacturing firm, are included in the *Working Papers*. Additional information for Bedthings for the months of March and April follow. Your instructor will guide you through the following examples.

	March	April
Cost of Direct Materials Used to Produce Finished Goods	$110,950.00	$123,490.00
Cost of Direct Labor Used to Produce Finished Goods	82,165.00	88,205.00
Actual Factory Overhead	61,150.00	64,320.00
Applied Factory Overhead	62,310.00	63,730.00
Beginning Finished Goods Inventory	102,845.00	118,520.00
Beginning Work in Process Inventory	78,100.00	78,360.00

4. Prepare a statement of cost of goods manufactured for March of the current year.

5. Prepare an income statement for March of the current year.

6. Prepare a balance sheet as of March 31 of the current year.

ON YOUR OWN

Preparing statement of cost of goods manufactured, income statement, and balance sheet

Work sheets for Bedthings, Inc., a manufacturing firm, are included in the *Working Papers*. Use the information for April from the Work Together above. Work independently to complete the following problems.

7. Prepare a statement of cost of goods manufactured for April of the current year.

8. Prepare an income statement for April of the current year.

9. Prepare a balance sheet as of April 30 of the current year.

CHAPTER  20 SUMMARY

After completing this chapter, you can

1. Define accounting terms related to accounting transactions and financial reporting for a manufacturing business.

2. Identify accounting concepts and practices related to accounting transactions and financial reporting for a manufacturing business.

3. Journalize transactions for a manufacturing business.

4. Prepare selected financial statements for a manufacturing business.

EXPLORE ACCOUNTING

ISO 9000 CERTIFICATION

Downhill Cycle assembles mountain bikes from components manufactured by other companies. Rather than personally examining each supplier's manufacturing process, the managers of Downhill Cycle require its suppliers to be ISO 9000 certified. ISO 9000 certification assures customers that the company has an effective quality management system that continually evaluates and improves the production process.

The ISO certification program was developed by the International Organization of Standards (ISO), a worldwide federation of national standards organizations. ISO's role includes programs that certify the manufacturing process. To become ISO 9000 certified, a company must follow the ISO's standards for various phases of the production process, including design, development, production, inspection, and servicing. The company must maintain an information system to record its compliance with ISO standards. Finally, the company must hire an independent organization to audit its initial and continuing compliance with ISO standards. ISO 9000 certification does not assure or guarantee the production of quality products. However, ISO 9000 certification does make a positive statement about a company's commitment to quality.

Other than helping to control costs, how does ISO 9000 certification impact accounting? Accountants assist in designing and operating the information systems necessary to collect ISO 9000 compliance data. Accountants in public accounting firms are also involved in ISO 9000 certification. These firms can either assist a client to prepare for the ISO 9000 certification process or be the independent organization that audits the client and awards ISO 9000 certification.

REQUIRED:

Research answers to the following questions:

1. How is ISO 9000 certification similar to financial statement audits?

2. Several types of ISO certification are available. Explain the purpose of ISO 14000 standards.

3. An acronym for the International Organization of Standardization would logically be IOS. Explain why the ISO title is used for the organization and its certifications.

20-1 APPLICATION PROBLEMS
Journalizing cost accounting transactions for a manufacturing company

Perry, Inc., completed the following factory cost transactions during August of the current year:

Transactions:

Aug. 4. Purchased $6,152.80 of materials from Sharon Company on account. P047.
   7. Paid cash for machinery used for production, $3,458.00. C651.
   15. Bought supplies for use in the factory by paying $583.83 cash. C658.
   21. Had machinery repaired. Made cash payment of $1,123.00 to repairer. C667. (Miscellaneous Expense—Factory)
   24. Purchased materials on account from Hubbard Company, $3,510.72. P048. Monthly factory payroll was paid in cash, $7,599.32 (direct labor, $7,200.00, and indirect labor, $1,920.00; less deductions: employee income tax, $823.00; Social security tax, $566.87; Medicare tax, $130.81). C679.

Instructions:

1. Journalize the following transactions. Use page 4 of a materials purchases journal and page 8 of a cash payments journal. Source documents are abbreviated as follows: check, C; purchase invoice, P.

2. Total and rule the materials purchases journal.

3. Prove and rule the cash payments journal.

20-2 APPLICATION PROBLEM
Journalizing and posting entries that summarize cost records at the end of a fiscal period

The following information is taken from the records of Cramer Corporation on March 31 of the current year. The accounts and balances needed to complete this problem are provided in the *Working Papers*.

a. The total factory payroll for the month from the payroll register is $122,530.00, distributed as follows:

Work in Process	$102,570.00	Employee Income Tax Payable	13,478.50
Factory Overhead	19,960.00	Social Security Tax Payable	7,964.45
Cash	99,249.10	Medicare Tax Payable	1,837.95

b. The total of all requisitions of direct materials issued during the month is $139,419.80. The total of all requisitions of indirect materials issued during the month is $4,505.00.
c. The factory overhead to be charged to Work in Process is 68% of the direct labor cost.
d. The total of all cost sheets completed during the month is $294,313.50.
e. The total of costs recorded on all sales invoices for March is $395,800.00.

Instructions:

1. Journalize the factory payroll entry on page 6 of a cash payments journal. C371. Post the general debit and general credit amounts.

2. Journalize the following entries on page 3 of a general journal. Post the entries.
   a. An entry to transfer the total of all direct materials requisitions to Work in Process and indirect materials to Factory Overhead. M34.
   b. An entry to close all individual manufacturing expense accounts to Factory Overhead. M35.
   c. An entry to record applied factory overhead to Work in Process. M36.

continued

3. Continue using page 3 of the general journal. Journalize and post the entry to close the balance of the factory overhead account to Income Summary. M37.

4. Journalize and post the entry to transfer the total of all cost sheets completed from Work in Process to Finished Goods. M38.

5. Journalize and post the entry to transfer the cost of products sold from Finished Goods to Cost of Goods Sold. M39. Save your work to complete Application Problem 20-3.

APPLICATION PROBLEM
Preparing a statement of cost of goods manufactured

Use the working papers from Application Problem 20-2 to complete this problem.

Instructions:
Prepare a statement of cost of goods manufactured for Cramer Corporation. The statement is for the month ended March 31 of the current year.

MASTERY PROBLEM
Journalizing entries that summarize cost records at the end of a fiscal period

The following information is taken from the records of Simmons Corporation on May 31 of the current year. The accounts and balances needed to complete this problem are provided in the *Working Papers*.

a. The total factory payroll for the month according to the payroll register is $77,430.00, distributed as follows.

Work in Process	$58,160.00	Employee Income Tax Payable	8,627.50
Factory Overhead	19,270.00	Social Security Tax Payable	5,032.95
Cash	62,608.10	Medicare Tax Payable	1,161.45

b. The total of all requisitions of direct materials issued during the month is $64,344.00. The total of all requisitions of indirect materials issued during the month is $5,835.00.

c. The factory overhead to be charged to Work in Process is 80% of the direct labor cost.

d. The total of all cost sheets completed during the month is $166,425.00.

e. The total of costs recorded on all sales invoices for May is $258,705.00.

Instructions:

1. Journalize the factory payroll entry on page 10 of a cash payments journal. C711. Post the general debit and general credit amounts.

2. Journalize the following entries on page 5 of a general journal. Post the debit and credit amounts.
   a. An entry to transfer the total of all direct materials requisitions to Work in Process and indirect materials to Factory Overhead. M211.
   b. An entry to close all individual manufacturing expense accounts to Factory Overhead. M212.
   c. An entry to record applied factory overhead to Work in Process. M213.

3. Continue using page 5 of the general journal. Journalize and post the entry to close the balance of the factory overhead account to Income Summary. M214.

4. Journalize and post the entry to transfer the total of all cost sheets completed from Work in Process to Finished Goods. M215.

5. Journalize and post the entry to transfer the cost of products sold from Finished Goods to Cost of Goods Sold. M216.

6. Prepare a statement of cost of goods manufactured for the month ended May 31 of the current year.

20-5 CHALLENGE PROBLEM
Journalizing entries that summarize cost records at the end of a fiscal period; preparing financial statements

The following information is taken from the records of Cozart Company on July 31 of the current year. The accounts and balances needed to complete this problem are provided in the *Working Papers*.

a. The total factory payroll for the month from the payroll register is $63,000.00, distributed as follows.

Work in Process	$46,600.00	Employee Income Tax Payable	6,930.00
Factory Overhead	16,400.00	Social Security Tax Payable	4,095.00
Cash	51,030.00	Medicare Tax Payable	945.00

b. The total of all requisitions of direct materials issued during the month is $67,760.00. The total of all requisitions of indirect materials issued during the month is $6,990.00.

c. The factory overhead to be charged to Work in Process is 95% of the direct labor cost.

d. The total of all cost sheets completed during the month is $140,984.00.

e. The total of costs recorded on all sales invoices for July is $112,176.83.

Instructions:

1. Journalize the factory payroll entry on page 14 of a cash payments journal. C341. Post the general debit and general credit amounts.

2. Journalize the following entries on page 7 of a general journal. Post the entries.
   a. An entry to transfer the total of all direct materials requisitions to Work in Process and indirect materials to Factory Overhead. M698.
   b. An entry to close all individual manufacturing expense accounts to Factory Overhead. M699.
   c. An entry to record applied factory overhead to Work in Process. M700.

3. Continue using page 7 of the general journal. Journalize and post the entry to close the balance of the factory overhead account to Income Summary. M701.

4. Journalize and post the entry to transfer the total of all cost sheets completed from Work in Process to Finished Goods. M702.

5. Journalize and post the entry to transfer the cost of products sold from Finished Goods to Cost of Goods Sold. M703.

6. Prepare a statement of cost of goods manufactured for the month ended July 31 of the current year.

Cozart's general ledger accounts and their balances on July 31 of the current year are given on the work sheet in the *Working Papers*. (The Employee Income Tax Payable, Social Security Tax Payable, and Medicare Tax Payable balances differ from your ledger account balances due to additional postings completed for payroll taxes and sales and administrative salaries.)

7. Prepare an 8-column work sheet for the month ended July 31 of the current year. Record the adjustments on the work sheet using the following information.

continued

Uncollectible Accounts Expense Estimated as 1.0% of Total Sales on Account.

Sales on Account for Year	$76,275.00
Sales Supplies Inventory	1,762.50
Administrative Supplies Inventory	520.74
Value of Prepaid Administrative Insurance	1,383.30
Monthly Depreciation Expense—Office Equipment	68.51
Monthly Depreciation Expense—Store Equipment	61.88
Federal Income Tax Expense Estimated for the Month	7,807.00

8. Prepare an income statement for the month ended July 31 of the current year. Calculate and record the following component percentages: (a) net cost of goods sold, (b) gross profit on operations, (c) total operating expenses, (d) income from operations, (e) net addition or deduction resulting from other revenue and expenses, (f) net income before federal income tax, (g) federal income tax expense, and (h) net income after federal income tax. Round percentage calculations to the nearest 0.1%.

9. Prepare a balance sheet for July 31 of the current year. A statement of stockholders' equity is not prepared. Therefore, add the amount of net income after federal income tax to the beginning balance of Retained Earnings to obtain the ending balance.

Applied Communication

A new clerk has been hired at the company for which you work. You have been asked to explain the flow of materials from ordering through issuing to the factory.

Required:

Prepare a chart and a brief written explanation of the flow of materials.

INTERNET ACTIVITY

Point your browser to

http://accounting.swpco.com

Choose **Advanced Course**, choose **Activities**, and complete the activity for Chapter 20.

Cases for Critical Thinking

Case 1

Kingston Corp., a manufacturing company, uses the perpetual inventory method for all inventory accounts. Direct materials, direct labor, and applied overhead are recorded on cost sheets similar to FaxaVision's. At the end of each month, general journal entries are made to update the general ledger manufacturing accounts. Overapplied or Underapplied Overhead is closed to Income Summary and reported on the income statement as an adjustment to the cost of goods sold.

A new accountant suggests that the company could save considerable time if a number of accounting changes are made: (1) use the periodic inventory method, (2) drop the use of applied overhead, and (3) close all manufacturing accounts to Income Summary similar to the procedure used by merchandising businesses. The accountant indicates that these new procedures would provide adequate information to prepare the income statement with a substantial time and cost saving.

Should the changes in accounting procedures be made? Will the changes provide adequate information? How will the changes affect the information now provided?

AUTOMATED ACCOUNTING

FINANCIAL STATEMENTS FOR A MANUFACTURING BUSINESS

Manufacturing businesses, as well as merchandising businesses, prepare external financial statements reporting information for all the activities of the business taken as a whole. These statements include a balance sheet, an income statement, and a statement of stockholders' equity. The statement of stockholders' equity does not differ from that prepared for a corporation operating a merchandising business, but there are differences between the balance sheet and the income statement.

The asset section of the balance sheet for a manufacturing business will include the three types of inventory:

- Materials
- Work in process
- Finished goods

The partial balance sheet below shows the inventory accounts in the currents assets section.

The liabilities and stockholders' sections of the balance sheet do not differ from the financial statements of a merchandising business. The income statement of a manufacturing company may be presented in a number of ways. Like that of a merchandising company, the statement must include cost of goods sold information. Some companies include cost of goods sold as a section of the income statement. Many large corporations prefer to use supplemental schedules prepared with a spreadsheet program to present information about the cost of goods manufactured and the cost of goods sold. By preparing supplemental schedules before preparing the income statement, accounts can include detail from the ledger accounts while still maintaining the clarity of the individual statements.

Good spreadsheet design includes formulas and clear columns and row labels. Schedules prepared on a spreadsheet will resemble manual statements and schedules. Formulas will be used for all subtotals and totals. Formulas should be manually verified when the spreadsheet is created.

Many businesses create spreadsheet templates for frequently used schedules. The template is a skeleton design with a heading, titles, and formatting in place. Formulas are placed in the subtotal and total cells. Each month, the template is opened and saved with a name to identify the report and month, such as COGS_March. The data for the current month are entered and verified. Then the report is printed.

ABC Manufacturing
Partial Balance Sheet
Month Ended March 31, 20--

Assets
Current Assets

Cash	$182,650
Accounts receivable, net	216,600
Materials	121,950
Work in process	108,400
Finished goods	131,475
Supplies	14,740
Total Current Assets	$775,815

Processing and Reporting Cost Accounting Data for a Manufacturing Business

This activity reinforces selected learnings from Chapters 19 and 20. Job cost accounting processing and reporting is emphasized for a manufacturing company organized as a corporation.

FURNITURE DECOR, INC.

Furniture Decor, Inc., is a corporation that manufactures office furniture. Furniture Decor uses a job cost accounting system to record manufacturing costs. The fiscal year is from January 1 through December 31. Monthly financial statements are prepared.

PART A: RECORDING COST ACCOUNTING ACTIVITIES

In Part A of this reinforcement activity, Furniture Decor's daily cost accounting activities for one month will be recorded.

Furniture Decor uses the chart of accounts shown on the following page. The journals and ledgers used by Furniture Decor are similar to those illustrated in Chapters 19 and 20. The job cost sheets, selected general ledger accounts, and other accounting records or forms needed to do the cost accounting activities are provided in the *Working Papers*. Beginning balances have been recorded.

The January 31 general ledger balances are the result of posting completed during the month of January. Note that **Accounts Payable** has a debit balance for this reason. Also, the balances of the payroll liability accounts are the amounts posted for sales and administrative salaries for January.

CALCULATING FACTORY OVERHEAD APPLIED RATE

Instructions:

1. Calculate the factory overhead applied rate based on direct labor costs. Estimated annual factory overhead costs for the current year are $306,000.00. Estimated direct labor hours to be used during the current year are 17,000 hours at an estimated rate of $15.00 per hour. Retain the calculations for use later in this reinforcement activity.

RECORDING TRANSACTIONS

Instructions:

2. Record the following transactions completed during January of the current year in the appropriate cost records and journals. Use page 1 of a materials purchases journal, general journal, and cash payments journal. Recording instructions are provided only for the first occurrence of each kind of transaction. Source documents are abbreviated as follows: check, C; memorandum, M; materials requisition, MR; purchase order, PO; sales invoice, S.

FURNITURE DECOR, INC. CHART OF ACCOUNTS

Balance Sheet Accounts

(1000) Assets

1100 CURRENT ASSETS
1105 Cash
1110 Petty Cash
1115 Accounts Receivable
1120 Allowance for Uncollectible Accounts
1125 Materials
1130 Work in Process
1135 Finished Goods
1140 Supplies—Factory
1145 Supplies—Sales
1150 Supplies—Administrative
1155 Prepaid Insurance

1200 PLANT ASSETS
1205 Factory Equipment
1210 Accumulated Depreciation—Factory Equipment
1215 Office Equipment
1220 Accumulated Depreciation—Office Equipment
1225 Store Equipment
1230 Accumulated Depreciation—Store Equipment
1235 Building
1240 Accumulated Depreciation—Building
1245 Land

(2000) Liabilities

2100 CURRENT LIABILITIES
2105 Accounts Payable
2110 Employee Income Tax Payable
2115 Federal Income Tax Payable
2120 Social Security Tax Payable
2123 Medicare Tax Payable
2125 Salaries Payable
2130 Unemployment Tax Payable—Federal
2135 Unemployment Tax Payable—State
2140 Dividends Payable

2200 LONG-TERM LIABILITY
2205 Mortgage Payable

(3000) Stockholders' Equity

3105 Capital Stock
3110 Retained Earnings
3115 Dividends
3120 Income Summary

Income Statement Accounts

(4000) Operating Revenue

4105 Sales

(5000) Cost of Sales

5105 Cost of Goods Sold

(5500) Manufacturing Costs

5505 Factory Overhead
5510 Depreciation Expense—Factory Equipment
5515 Depreciation Expense—Building
5520 Heat, Light, and Power Expense
5525 Insurance Expense—Factory
5530 Miscellaneous Expense—Factory
5535 Payroll Taxes Expense—Factory
5540 Property Tax Expense—Factory
5545 Supplies Expense—Factory

(6000) Operating Expenses

6100 SELLING EXPENSES
6105 Advertising Expense
6110 Delivery Expense
6115 Depreciation Expense—Store Equipment
6120 Miscellaneous Expense—Sales
6125 Salary Expense—Sales
6130 Supplies Expense—Sales

6200 ADMINISTRATIVE EXPENSES
6205 Depreciation Expense—Office Equipment
6210 Insurance Expense—Administrative
6215 Miscellaneous Expense—Administrative
6220 Payroll Taxes Expense—Administrative
6225 Property Tax Expense—Administrative
6230 Salary Expense—Administrative
6235 Supplies Expense—Administrative
6240 Uncollectible Accounts Expense
6245 Utilities Expense—Administrative

(7000) Other Revenue

7105 Gain on Plant Assets
7110 Miscellaneous Revenue

(8000) Other Expenses

8105 Interest Expense
8110 Loss on Plant Assets

(9000) Income Tax

9105 Federal Income Tax Expense

Jan. 3. Opened a cost sheet for Job No. 232, 250 C200 computer desks ordered for stock. Date wanted, January 12.

3. Issued direct materials to factory for Job No. 232, $5,100.00. MR750.
   Materials list: 6,000 square feet base wood @ $0.20 per square foot
   6,000 square feet laminate @ $0.60 per square feet
   187.5 pounds adhesive @ $1.60 per pound
   Record the direct materials in the materials ledger and the cost ledger.

5. Opened a cost sheet for Job No. 233, 200 P150 printer tables ordered for stock. Date wanted, January 17.

5. Issued direct materials to factory for Job No. 233, $3,400.00. MR751.
   Materials list: 4,000 square feet base wood @ $0.20 per square foot
   4,000 square feet laminate @ $0.60 per square foot
   125 pounds adhesive @ $1.60 per pound

5. Ordered 30,000 square feet base wood. PO520.
   Record the purchase order in the materials ledger.

5. Ordered 20,000 square feet laminate. PO521.

7. Ordered 1,600 casters. PO522.

7. Ordered direct materials to factory for Job No. 232, $1,250.00. MR752.
   Materials list: 1,000 casters @ $1.25 each

7. Ordered 1,000 sets hinges. PO523.

7. Recorded weekly summary of job-time records to cost ledger.
   Job No. 232 $3,300.00
   Job No. 233   1,125.00

7. Ordered 1,000 pounds adhesive. PO524.

10. Issued direct materials to factory for Job No. 233, $1,200.00. MR753.
    Materials list: 800 casters @ $1.25 each
    200 sets metal glides @ $1.00 per set

10. Ordered 300 sets of metal glides. PO525.

10. Sold 100 C200 computer desks to Office Mart. S323.
    Record only the cost in the finished goods ledger. Furniture Decor uses the first-in, first-out inventory method. Thus, the cost recorded first is the cost removed from inventory first when units are sold.

10. Ordered 1,000 fasteners. PO526.

10. Received at materials stockroom 20,000 square feet of laminate @ $0.60 per square foot. Materials were purchased on account from Plastics Unlimited, $12,000.00. PO521.
    Record all receipts of materials in the materials ledger and purchases journal.

11. Completed Job No. 232. Apply factory overhead to job. Use the rate calculated in Instruction 1. Complete the cost sheet. Interim summary of job-time records for Job No. 232, $1,387.50.
    When jobs are completed in the middle of a week, Furniture Decor makes a special interim summary of job-time records for these jobs. Therefore, direct labor costs will be complete. Record the finished goods in the finished goods ledger.

12. Opened a cost sheet for Job No. 234, 120 E400 entertainment centers ordered for stock. Date wanted, January 18.

12. Issued direct materials to factory for Job No. 234, $5,100.00. MR754.
    Materials list: 6,000 square feet base wood @ $0.20 per square foot
    6,000 square feet laminate @ $0.60 per square foot
    187.5 pounds adhesive @ $1.60 per pound

Jan. 12. Received at materials stockroom 30,000 square feet of base wood @ $0.20 per square foot. Materials were purchased on account from Wood Craft, Inc., $6,000.00. P0520.

12. Received at materials stockroom 1,600 casters @ $1.25 each. Materials were purchased on account from Wheels Galore, $2,000.00. P0522.

12. Received at materials stockroom 300 sets of metal glides @ $1.00 per set. Materials were purchased on account from Simpson Company, $300.00. P0525.

14. Opened a cost sheet for Job No. 235, 150 V110 video tape cabinets for stock. Date wanted, January 27.

14. Issued direct materials to factory for Job No. 235, $2,040.00. MR755.
   Materials list: 2,400 square feet base wood @ $0.20 per square foot
   2,400 square feet laminate @ $0.60 per square foot
   75 pounds adhesive @ $1.60 per pound

14. Recorded weekly summary of job-time records to cost ledger.
   Job No. 233 $1,875.00
   Job No. 234   1,800.00
   Job No. 235   225.00

14. Completed Job No. 233.

17. Paid cash for semimonthly factory payroll, $11,080.80 (direct labor, $9,712.50, and indirect labor, $3,967.50, less deductions: employee income tax, $1,504.80; Social security tax, $889.20; Medicare, $205.20). C782.
   Record the payroll entry in the cash payments journal. Post the general debit and general credit amounts.

17. Recorded employer factory payroll taxes, $1,942.56, for the semimonthly pay period ended January 15. Taxes owed are Social security tax, $889.20; Medicare, $205.20; federal unemployment tax, $109.44; state unemployment tax, $738.72. M308.
   Record the entry in the general journal. Post the amounts.

17. Sold 150 P150 printer tables to CompuFurnishings. S324.

18. Issued direct materials to factory for Job No. 234, $420.00. MR756.
   Materials list: 240 sets of hinges @ $1.00 per set
   240 fasteners @ $0.75 each

18. Opened a cost sheet for Job No. 236, 200 B160 bookcases ordered for stock. Date wanted, January 28.

18. Issued direct materials to factory for Job No. 236, $6,800.00. MR757.
   Materials list: 8,000 square feet base wood @ $0.20 per square foot
   8,000 square feet laminate @ $0.60 per square foot
   250 pounds adhesive @ $1.60 per pound

19. Completed Job No. 234. Interim summary of job-time record for Job No. 234, $1,800.00.

20. Sold 60 T120 TV carts to Office Mart. S325.

21. Issued direct materials to factory for Job No. 235, $825.00. MR758.
   Materials list: 300 sets metal glides @ $1.00 per set
   300 sets hinges @ $1.00 per set
   300 fasteners @ $0.75 each

21. Received at materials stockroom 1,000 pounds adhesive @ $1.60 per pound. Materials were purchased on account from Cal Adhesives, $1,600.00. P0524.

21. Received at materials stockroom 1,000 fasteners @ $0.75 each. Materials were purchased on account from Simpson Company, $750.00. P0526.

Jan. 21. Ordered 300 sets metal glides. PO527.
  21. Posted weekly summary of job-time records to cost ledger.
    Job No. 235 $1,125.00
    Job No. 236   2,250.00
  24. Ordered 20,000 square feet laminate. PO528.
  24. Received at materials stockroom 1,000 sets of hinges @ $1.00 per set. Materials were purchased on account from Simpson Company, $1,000.00. PO523.
  25. Issued direct materials to factory for Job No. 236, $700.00. MR759.
    Materials list: 400 sets of hinges @ $1.00 per set
          400 fasteners @ $0.75 each
  25. Opened a cost sheet for Job No. 237, 160 T120 TV carts ordered for stock. Date wanted, January 31.
  25. Issued direct materials to factory for Job No. 237, $1,904.00. MR760.
    Materials list: 2,240 square feet base wood @ $0.20 per square foot
          2,240 square feet laminate @ $0.60 per square foot
          70 pounds adhesive @ $1.60 per pound
  26. Sold 90 E400 entertainment centers to BizFurn. S326.
  27. Completed Job No. 235. Interim summary of job-time records for Job No. 235, $900.00.
  27. Sold 200 V110 video tape cabinets to CompuFurnishings. S327.
  28. Issued direct materials to factory for Job No. 237, $800.00. MR761.
    Materials list: 640 casters @ $1.25 each
  28. Opened a cost sheet for Job No. 238, 200 C200 computer desks ordered for stock. Date wanted, February 8.
  28. Issued direct materials to factory for Job No. 238, $4,080.00. MR762.
    Materials list: 4,800 square feet base wood @ $0.20 per square foot
          4,800 square feet laminate @ $0.60 per square foot
          150 pounds adhesive @ $1.60 per pound
  28. Posted weekly summary of job-time records to cost ledger.
    Job No. 236 $2,250.00
    Job No. 237   1,440.00
    Job No. 238   630.00
  28. Completed Job No. 236.
  28. Sold 120 B160 bookcases to Office Mart. S328.
  31. Received at materials stockroom 300 metal glides @ $1.00 per set. Materials were purchased on account from Simpson Company, $300.00. PO527.
  31. Received at materials stockroom indirect materials (bolts, screws, and nails). Materials were purchased on account from Grant Hardware Supplies, $1,200.00. PO519.
    Record indirect materials purchases only in the materials purchases journal.
  31. Posted summary of job-time records for January 31 to cost ledger.
    Job No. 237 $360.00
    Job No. 238   630.00
  31. Sold 200 C200 computer desks to Straight Arrow, Inc. S329.
  31. Completed Job No. 237.
  31. Paid cash for semimonthly factory payroll, $12,988.20 (direct labor, $11,385.00, and indirect labor, $4,650.00, less deductions: employee income tax, $1,764.00; Social Security tax, $1,042,28; Medicare tax, $240.52). C856.
  31. Recorded employer factory payroll taxes, $2,276.97, for the semimonthly pay period ended January 31. Taxes owed are Social Security tax, $1,042,28;

Medicare tax, $240.52; federal unemployment tax, $128.28; state unemployment tax, $865.89. M345.

COMPLETING COST RECORDS

Instructions:

3. Jobs not completed on January 31 are work in process. The factory overhead for the month of January on work in process must be recorded. Apply the factory overhead rate to the direct labor costs recorded on the cost sheet for work in process. Record this amount in the Summary column with the item description *Factory Overhead for January* and the explanation of how this was calculated.

4. Total and rule the materials purchases journal. Post the total. Do not post the individual amounts. The abbreviation for the materials purchases journal is MP.

5. Prove and rule the cash payments journal. Do not post the total of the Cash Cr. column.

6. Record the following entries. Continue using page 1 of the general journal. Use January 31 as the date. Post after journalizing each entry.
   a. An entry to transfer the total of all direct materials requisitions to Work in Process and indirect materials to Factory Overhead. The total of all requisitions of direct materials issued during January is $33,619.00. The total of all requisitions of indirect materials issued is $1,181.00. M346.
   b. An entry to close all individual manufacturing expense accounts to Factory Overhead. M347.
   c. An entry to record applied factory overhead to Work in Process. (Sum of factory overhead applied to cost sheets for the month.) M348.

7. Continue using page 1 of the general journal. Journalize and post the entry to close the balance of the factory overhead account to Income Summary. M349.

8. Journalize and post the entry to transfer the total of all cost sheets completed from Work in Process to Finished Goods. M350.

9. Journalize and post the entry to transfer the cost of products sold from Finished Goods to Cost of Goods Sold. The total cost recorded on all sales invoices for January is $61,137.50. M351.

10. Prove the subsidiary ledgers as follows.
   a. Add the ending balances in the materials ledger. The ending balance of the indirect materials is $1,369.00. The total of the materials ledger must equal the ending balance of Materials in the general ledger.
   b. Add the costs recorded on all cost sheets in the cost ledger that have not been completed. This total must equal the ending balance of Work in Process in the general ledger.
   c. Add the ending balances in the finished goods ledger. This total must equal the ending balance of Finished Goods in the general ledger.

11. Prepare a statement of cost of goods manufactured for Furniture Decor, Inc. for the month ended January 31 of the current year.

PART B: COMPLETING END-OF-FISCAL-PERIOD ACTIVITIES

In Part B of this reinforcement activity, all accounting activities have been completed up to, but not including, a trial balance for the month of January.

The January 31 balances of the general ledger accounts not provided in Part A are recorded on an 8-column work sheet in the *Working Papers*.

Instructions:

12. Record the January 31 balances from the general ledger accounts used in Part A on the work sheet for Furniture Decor, Inc. Complete the Trial Balance columns of the work sheet.

13. Complete the work sheet for the month ended January 31 of the current year. Record the adjustments on the work sheet using the following information.

Adjustment Information, January 31

Uncollectible accounts expense estimated as 1.0% of sales on account.
  Sales on account for month, $27,000.00.

Sales supplies inventory	$1,111.35
Administrative supplies inventory	302.47
Value of prepaid administrative insurance	257.40
Monthly depreciation expense—office equipment	34.25
Monthly depreciation expense—store equipment	31.00
Federal income tax expense estimated for the month	3,682.38

14. Prepare an income statement for the month ended January 31 of the current year. Calculate and record the following component percentages. (a) Cost of goods sold. (b) Gross profit on operations. (c) Total operating expenses. (d) Income from operations. (e) Net addition or deduction resulting from other revenue and expenses. (f) Net income before federal income tax. (g) Federal income tax. (h) Net income after federal income tax. Round percentage calculations to the nearest 0.1%.

15. Prepare a balance sheet for January 31 of the current year. A statement of stockholders' equity is not prepared. Therefore, add the amount of net income after federal income taxes to the beginning balance of Retained Earnings to obtain the ending balance.

Activities in
The Valley Fan Center:

1. Recording transactions in special journals and a general journal.

2. Recording items in materials ledgers, cost sheets, and finished goods ledgers.

3. Posting items to be posted individually to a general ledger and subsidiary ledgers.

4. Proving and ruling journals.

5. Recording and posting general journal entries that summarize cost records.

6. Proving the subsidiary ledgers.

7. Preparing a trial balance on a work sheet.

8. Planning adjustments and completing a work sheet.

9. Preparing financial statements.

10. Journalizing and posting adjusting entries.

11. Journalizing and posting closing entries.

12. Preparing a post-closing trial balance.

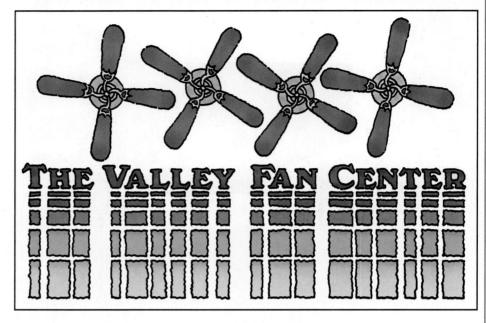

The Valley Fan Center is a manufacturing business organized as a corporation. This business simulation covers the realistic transactions completed by The Valley Fan Center, which manufactures ceiling fans for specialty retailing. The activities included in the accounting cycle for The Valley Fan Center are listed at the left.

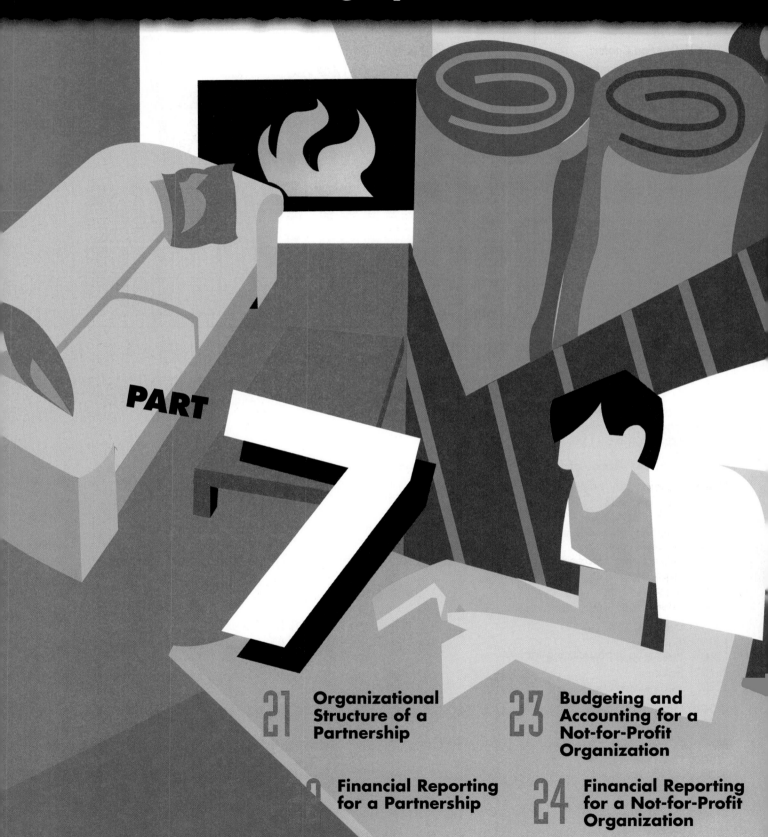

Other Accounting Systems

7

Organizational Structure of a Partnership

23 **Budgeting and Accounting for a Not-for-Profit Organization**

Financial Reporting for a Partnership

24 **Financial Reporting for a Not-for-Profit Organization**

MALIN CARPET DESIGN CHART OF ACCOUNTS

Balance Sheet Accounts

(1000) Assets
1100 CURRENT ASSETS
1105   Cash
1110   Petty Cash
1115   Accounts Receivable
1120   Allowance for Uncollectible Accounts
1125   Supplies—Carpet
1130   Supplies—Office
1135   Prepaid Insurance

1200 PLANT ASSETS
1205   Equipment
1210   Accumulated Depreciation—Equipment
1215   Truck
1220   Accumulated Depreciation—Truck

(2000) Liabilities
2100 CURRENT LIABILITIES
2105   Accounts Payable

(3000) Owners' Equity
3105   May Baker, Capital
3110   May Baker, Drawing
3115   Lindel Mattingly, Capital
3120   Lindel Mattingly, Drawing
3125   Income Summary

Income Statement Accounts

(4000) Operating Revenue
4105   Sales

(5000) Operating Expenses
5105   Advertising Expense
5110   Depreciation Expense—Equipment
5115   Depreciation Expense—Truck
5120   Insurance Expense
5125   Miscellaneous Expense
5130   Rent Expense
5135   Supplies Expense—Carpet
5140   Supplies Expense—Office
5145   Truck Expense
5150   Uncollectible Accounts Expense
5155   Utilities Expense

The chart of accounts for MaLin Carpet Design is illustrated above for ready reference as you study Chapters 21 and 22 of this textbook.

21

Organizational Structure of a Partnership

AFTER STUDYING CHAPTER 21, YOU WILL BE ABLE TO:

1. Define accounting terms related to forming and expanding a partnership.

2. Identify accounting concepts and practices related to forming and expanding a partnership.

3. Journalize transactions related to forming a partnership.

4. Journalize transactions related to expanding a partnership.

A corporation is one form of business that may be owned by many persons. Large corporations may have thousands of owners. These owners are known as shareholders because they own shares of stock.

Another form of business may also have more than one owner. A business in which two or more persons combine their assets and skills is known as a partnership. Each member of a partnership is known as a partner. Partnerships generally have only a few owners (partners). Partnerships do not issue shares of stock. Each partner has an equity account. Except for recording owners' equity and income taxes, accounting procedures for a partnership are similar to those for a corporation.

Unlike a corporation, however, a partnership does not have an unlimited life. Any change in the number of partners terminates an existing partnership. When a new partner is admitted, the partners sign a new partnership agreement. The old partnership's accounting records are often continued for the new partnership. As a result, initial investment journal entries for all partners are not always needed. Journal entries are needed, however, to show clearly how the partners' equity has changed. One or both of the following journal entries may be needed:

1. To show how much the new partner invests.

2. To show how the new partner's admission affects existing partners' capital accounts.

TERMS PREVIEW

partnership agreement
mutual agency
goodwill

ACCOUNTING
IN YOUR CAREER

PARTNERSHIP DISAGREEMENTS

Maria Degas and Thomas Shiveley have been working together for five years as landscapers. Maria meets with the clients and designs the landscapes. Thomas buys the plants and materials and hires and supervises the work crews. The business has been very successful and has a number of corporate clients that require monthly maintenance and new designs. The business has also earned an outstanding reputation with a number of wealthy individual clients from whom it receives many referrals.

Thomas, however, has a serious health problem. Increasingly, his daughter Connie has been doing most of the buying. Due to her inexperience, plants and materials are often not available when the work crews need them. Furthermore, Connie is buying from the most expensive dealers and is not grouping purchases in large quantities to take advantage of quantity discounts.

Maria notices that profit margins are declining and the work crews are complaining. Thomas finally tells Maria that he will have to have surgery that will make him unable to continue working in the business. He suggests that Maria replace him with Connie as her new partner. However, Maria has never gotten along with Connie and does not want to work with her. Thomas, however, refuses to dissolve the partnership except to form a new one with his daughter as partner in his place. There is no formal partnership agreement.

Critical Thinking

1. In this scenario, what is the most serious cause of the problems Maria has in deciding the future of the partnership?

2. Maria is prepared to mortgage the business to pay Thomas half the equity of the partnership so he can start a new business for himself and his daughter. Will this kind of loan be easy for Maria to obtain from her bank based on the business' reputation?

3. If a new partner has the cash to buy a 50% interest in the business, should the new partner pay Maria, Thomas, or the partnership?

PARTNERSHIP AGREEMENT

PARTNERSHIP AGREEMENT

THIS CONTRACT is made and entered into this thirty-first day of December, 20--, by and between May Baker and Lindel Mattingly, of Petersburg, VA.

WITNESSETH: That the said parties have this date formed a partnership to engage in and conduct a business under the following stipulations which are a part of this contract. The partnership will begin operation January 1, 20--.

FIRST: The business shall be conducted under the name of MaLin Carpet Design, located initially at 1910 South Crater Road, Petersburg, VA 23801-2343.

SECOND: The investment of each partner is: May Baker: Equity in a business located at 1910 South Crater Road, Petersburg, VA 23801-2343, and as shown in a balance sheet to be provided by Ms. Baker on December 31, 20--. Total investment, $22,880.00. Lindel Mattingly: Cash equal to one-half of the initial investment of Ms. Baker. Total investment, $11,440.00.

THIRD: Both partners are to (a) participate in all general policy-making decisions, (b) devote full time and attention to the partnership business, and (c) engage in no other business enterprise without the written consent of the other partner. Ms. Baker is to be general manager of the business' operations.

FOURTH: Neither partner is to become a surety or bonding agent for anyone without the written consent of the other partner.

FIFTH: The partners' shares in earnings and losses of the partnership are: Ms. Baker: 5% interest on equity as of January 1 of each year; salary, $5,000.00 per year; remaining income or loss, 50%. Mr. Mattingly: 5% interest on equity as of January 1 of each year; salary, $3,000.00 per year; remaining income or loss, 50%.

SIXTH: No partner is to withdraw assets in excess of the agreed upon interest and salary without the other partner's written consent.

SEVENTH: All partnership transactions are to be recorded in accordance with standard and generally accepted accounting procedures and concepts. The partnership records are to be open at all times for inspection by either partner.

EIGHTH: In case of either partner's death or legal disability, the equity of the partners is to be determined as of the time of the death or disability of the one partner. The continuing partner is to have first option to buy the deceased/disabled partner's equity at recorded book value.

NINTH: This partnership agreement is to continue indefinitely unless (a) terminated by death of one partner, (b) terminated by either partner by giving the other partner written notice at least ninety (90) days prior to the termination date, or (c) terminated by written mutual agreement signed by both partners.

TENTH: At the termination of this partnership agreement, the partnership's assets, after all liabilities are paid, will be distributed according to the balance in partners' capital accounts.

IN WITNESS WHEREOF, the parties to this contract have set their hands and seals on the date and year written.

Signed ___May Baker___ (Seal) Date ___December 31, 20--___

Signed ___Lindel Mattingly___ (Seal) Date ___December 31, 20--___

Figure 21-1

A partnership is created when two or more persons agree orally or in writing to form a business using the partnership form of organization. As in other forms of business, a partnership's financial records are kept separate from those of the partners. (CONCEPT: Business Entity)

May Baker and Lindel Mattingly agree to form a partnership called MaLin Carpet Design. Prior to forming the partnership, May owned a similar business and Lindel was employed as a carpet installer.

MaLin Carpet Design provides carpet installation services to homeowners, housing developers, and businesses. The business does not sell merchandise. For this reason, it does not need general ledger accounts for merchandise inventory, purchases, purchases discount, and purchases returns and allowances. The partners, who provide all the services to customers, are not employees of the partnership. The Internal Revenue Service does not consider the money that partners receive from a partnership to be salaries. Therefore, the business does not need accounts for recording salaries and payroll taxes.

A written agreement setting forth the conditions under which a partnership is to operate is called a **partnership agreement**. A partnership's life is limited to the length of time agreed on by the partners. A partnership is terminated by the partners' mutual agreement, death of a partner, withdrawal of one partner, or admission of a new partner. In comparison, a corporation has unlimited life.

Each partner can bind a partnership to any contract. The right of all partners to contract for a partnership is called **mutual agency**. Each partner is an agent of the partnership unless restricted by agreement.

Legally, a partnership agreement may be either written or oral. However, to avoid misunderstandings, a partnership agreement should be in writing. Some but not all states require that a partnership agreement be in writing.

With an attorney's assistance, Ms. Baker and Mr. Mattingly prepare their partnership agreement, shown in Figure 21-1. Both partners sign three copies of the partnership agreement. Each partner receives a copy for personal records, and the third copy becomes part of the partnership's records.

PARTNERSHIP CAPITAL ACCOUNTS

The owners' equity division of a partnership's general ledger has two capital accounts for each partner.

1. An account in which to record a partner's equity includes the word *capital* in the title. The two equity accounts in MaLin's general ledger are May Baker, Capital and Lindel Mattingly, Capital.

2. An account in which the earnings taken out of the partnership during the fiscal period are recorded includes the word *drawing* in the title. Assets taken out of a business for the owner's personal use are known as withdrawals. The two accounts in MaLin's general ledger used to record withdrawals are titled May Baker, Drawing and Lindel Mattingly, Drawing.

Partners' withdrawals can be a cause of misunderstandings. For this reason, most partnership agreements include a statement controlling withdrawals. MaLin's partnership agreement has a controlling statement in item 6 of the partnership agreement.

PARTNERS' INITIAL INVESTMENTS

Ms. Baker invests the assets of her existing business in the new partnership. According to item 2 of the partnership agreement, Ms. Baker will provide a December 31 balance sheet for her existing business.

The two partners agree on a value for all invested assets on the date the partnership begins, January 1. Ms. Baker's initial investment is $22,880.00, the agreed upon value of her equity in her previous business. Mr. Mattingly's initial investment is cash of $11,440.00.

A partnership can have an unlimited number of partners.

JOURNAL ENTRIES TO RECORD PARTNERS' INITIAL INVESTMENTS

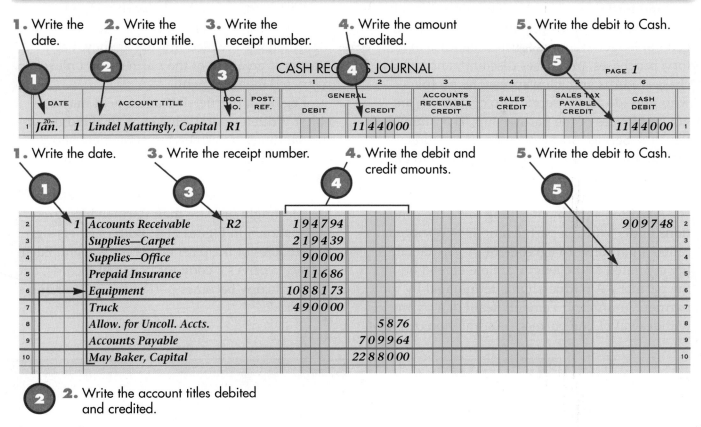

1. Write the date.

2. Write the account title.

3. Write the receipt number.

4. Write the amount credited.

5. Write the debit to Cash.

1. Write the date.

3. Write the receipt number.

4. Write the debit and credit amounts.

5. Write the debit to Cash.

2. Write the account titles debited and credited.

Figure 21-2

A separate journal entry is made for each partner's initial investment as shown in Figure 21-2.

January 1, 20--. Received cash from partner, Lindel Mattingly, as an initial investment, $11,440.00. Receipt No. 1.

Cash is debited for $11,440.00. Lindel Mattingly, Capital is credited for $11,400.00.

January 1, 20--. Accepted assets and liabilities of May Baker's existing business as an initial investment, $28,880.00. Receipt No. 2.

All asset amounts on the balance sheet are debited. Allowance for Uncollectible Accounts and Accounts Payable are credited.

Ⓢ Journalizing receipt of partners' initial investments

Ⓣ Ⓔ Ⓟ Ⓢ

1. Write the date, 20--, Jan 1, in the Date column.
2. Write the account titles in the Account Title column. For Lindel Mattingly's investment, write the account to be credited, *Lindel Mattingly, Capital*. For May Baker's investment, write the accounts to be debited, *Accounts Receivable, Supplies—Carpet, Supplies—Office, Prepaid Insurance, Equipment,* and *Truck.* Also write the accounts to be credited, *Allowance for Uncollectible Accounts, Accounts Payable,* and *May Baker, Capital.*
3. Write the receipt numbers, *R1* and *R2*, in the Doc. No. column.
4. Write the amounts in the General Debit and Credit columns. The only credit amount for Lindel Mattingly is *11,440.00* for the cash investment. For May Baker's investment, debit the asset accounts, *1,947.94, 2,194.39, 900.00, 116.86, 10,881.73,* and *4,900.00.* Credit the contra asset, liability, and capital accounts, *58.76, 7,099.64,* and *22,800.00.*
5. Write the debits to Cash, *11,440.00* and *9,097.48* in the Cash Debit column.

Baker's Carpet Design
Balance Sheet
December 31, 20--

ASSETS

Current Assets:

Cash		$ 9,097.48
Accounts Receivable	$1,947.94	
Less Allowance for Uncollectible Accounts	58.76	1,889.18
Supplies—Carpet		2,194.39
Supplies—Office		900.00
Prepaid Insurance		116.86
Total Current Assets		$14,197.91

Plant Assets:

Equipment	$10,881.73	
Truck	4,900.00	
Total Plant Assets		15,781.73
Total Assets		$29,979.64

LIABILITIES

Accounts Payable	$ 7,099.64

OWNER'S EQUITY

May Baker, Capital	22,880.00
Total Liabilities and Owner's Equity	$29,979.64

Figure 21-3

Ms. Baker's investment includes cash, other assets, and liabilities from her prior existing business. Both partners agree to any estimates shown on the balance sheet. For example, **Allowance for Uncollectible Accounts** is an estimate. After reviewing the accounts, Lindel and May agree that the $58.76 is a fair estimate of the amount that may become uncollectible.

A copy of the balance sheet from May Baker's previous business, Figure 21-3, is attached to a receipt to provide needed details for the journal entry. *(CONCEPT: Objective Evidence)*

MINORITY RECRUITING

Companies today are very interested in achieving a balance in their work force. They recognize that there are advantages in a work force that has the same ethnic and cultural composition as their customers. This attitude creates opportunity for minorities.

Many cities have annual "work force diversity" job fairs in which those looking for jobs meet employers looking for employees. At these minority job fairs, a wide range of jobs may be available. Companies are especially interested in minority hiring in sales, marketing, customer service, and technical and administrative positions.

Business interest in recruiting minorities grew in the 1990s and is expected to continue to grow in the 21st century.

CULTURAL DIVERSITY

1. Why should a partnership agreement be in writing?
2. What happens to an existing partnership if a partner dies?
3. What does mutual agency mean?

WORK
TOGETHER

Forming a partnership

A cash receipts journal is provided in the *Working Papers*. Your instructor will guide you through the following examples.

Betty Jensen and Glen Chau agree to form a partnership on April 1 of the current year. The partnership assumes the assets and liabilities of Ms. Jensen's existing business. Mr. Chau invests cash equal to Ms. Jensen's investment. Partners share equally in all changes in equity. The March 31 balance sheet for Ms. Jensen's existing business is shown in the *Working Papers*. Source documents are abbreviated as follows: memorandum, M; receipt, R.

Apr. 1. Received cash from partner, Glen Chau, as an initial investment, $42,000.00. R1.
 1. Accepted assets and liabilities of Betty Jensen's existing business as an initial investment, $42,000.00. R2.

4. Journalize the transactions in a cash receipts journal on April 1 of the current year.

ON YOUR
OWN

Forming a partnership

A cash receipts journal is provided in the *Working Papers*. Work independently to complete the following problem.

David Rice and Tanya Taylor agree to form a partnership on July 1 of the current year. The partnership assumes the assets and liabilities of Mr. Rice's existing business. Ms. Taylor invests cash equal to Mr. Rice's investment. Partners share equally in all changes in equity. The June 30 balance sheet for Mr. Rice's existing business is shown in the *Working Papers*. Source documents abbreviated as follows: receipt, R.

July 1. Received cash from partner, Tanya Taylor, as an initial investment, $32,000.00. R1.
 1. Accepted assets and liabilities of David Rice's existing business as an initial investment, $32,000.00. R2.

5. Journalize the transactions in a cash receipts journal on July 1 of the current year.

ADMITTING A PARTNER WITH NO CHANGE IN TOTAL EQUITY

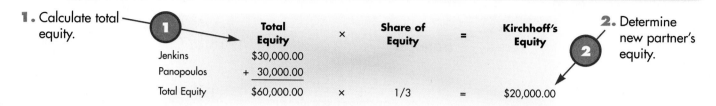

1. Calculate total equity.

1

	Total Equity	×	Share of Equity	=	Kirchhoff's Equity
Jenkins	$30,000.00				
Panopoulos	+ 30,000.00				
Total Equity	$60,000.00	×	1/3	=	$20,000.00

2. Determine new partner's equity.

2

3. Record the entry to redistribute the capital.

3

GENERAL JOURNAL   PAGE 6

	DATE		ACCOUNT TITLE	DOC. NO.	POST. REF.	DEBIT	CREDIT	
1	20-- June	1	Elaine Jenkins, Capital	M23		10 0 0 0 00		1
2			Anna Panopoulos, Capital			10 0 0 0 00		2
3			Fred Kirchhoff, Capital				20 0 0 0 00	3

Figure 21-4

Elaine Jenkins and Anna Panopoulos are partners in an existing business. The partners agree to admit Fred Kirchhoff as a new partner. However, the business does not need additional capital at the present time. Therefore, Elaine and Anna agree to sell part of their existing equity to Fred.

The existing partners each have $30,000.00 equity in the existing partnership. The three partners agree that Fred is to pay $20,000.00 for a one-third equity in the new partnership. Elaine and Anna receive cash from Fred for equity in the partnership. The partnership does not receive the cash from the sale of equity.

The two existing partners are each entitled to one-half of the price Fred pays for one-third of the equity of the partnership. Therefore, Fred pays $10,000.00 to Elaine and Anna. Also, $20,000.00 of the existing equity is transferred to Fred on the partnership's records, as shown in Figure 21-4.

The receipt of cash, a personal transaction among Elaine, Anna, and Fred, is not recorded on the partnership's records. However, the redistribution of capital is a partnership entry and is journalized.

S T E P S Admitting a partner with no change in total equity

1. Calculate the total equity of the business, $60,000.00.

2. Determine the new partner's equity in the partnership, $20,000.00 ($60,000.00 × 1/3).

3. Record the entry in the general journal to transfer a portion of the existing equity to the new partner.

REMEMBER

If partners agree to sell part of their existing equity to a new partner, the receipt of cash is a personal transaction that is not recorded on the partnership's records.

ADMITTING A PARTNER WITH EQUITY EQUAL TO NEW PARTNER'S INVESTMENT

1. Calculate total equity.

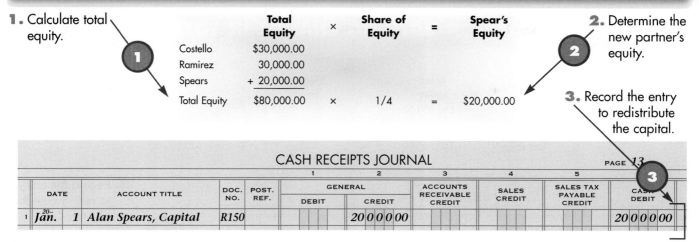

	Total Equity	×	Share of Equity	=	Spear's Equity
Costello	$30,000.00				
Ramirez	30,000.00				
Spears	+ 20,000.00				
Total Equity	$80,000.00	×	1/4	=	$20,000.00

2. Determine the new partner's equity.

3. Record the entry to redistribute the capital.

CASH RECEIPTS JOURNAL   PAGE 13

	DATE	ACCOUNT TITLE	DOC. NO.	POST. REF.	GENERAL DEBIT	GENERAL CREDIT	ACCOUNTS RECEIVABLE CREDIT	SALES CREDIT	SALES TAX PAYABLE CREDIT	CASH DEBIT
1	Jan. 1	Alan Spears, Capital	R150			20 0 0 0 00				20 0 0 0 00

Figure 21-5

Partnerships often seek to increase their total equity to allow the business to grow. Partnerships may seek to expand their current markets, move into new markets, or sell new types of merchandise. Additional capital gives partnerships added financial strength as the business grows.

John Costello and Juliet Ramirez are partners in an existing partnership. Each partner's equity is $30,000.00 for a total equity of $60,000.00. The existing partners agree to admit Alan Spears as a partner with a one-fourth interest for a $20,000.00 cash investment. Alan Spears' equity is calculated as shown in Figure 21-5. Alan's investment does not change John or Juliet's equity.

July 1, 20--. Received cash from new partner, Alan Spears, for a one-fourth equity in the business, $20,000.00. Receipt No. 150.

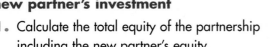

S T E P S Admitting a partner with equity equal to new partner's investment

1. Calculate the total equity of the partnership including the new partner's equity.

2. Determine the new partner's equity.

3. Record the entry to admit the new partner.

F.Y.I.

The use of several individuals' names in the name of a business is often an indication of a partnership.

REMEMBER

The balance sheet for a partnership includes an equity account for each partner.

ADMITTING A PARTNER WITH EQUITY GREATER THAN NEW PARTNER'S INVESTMENT

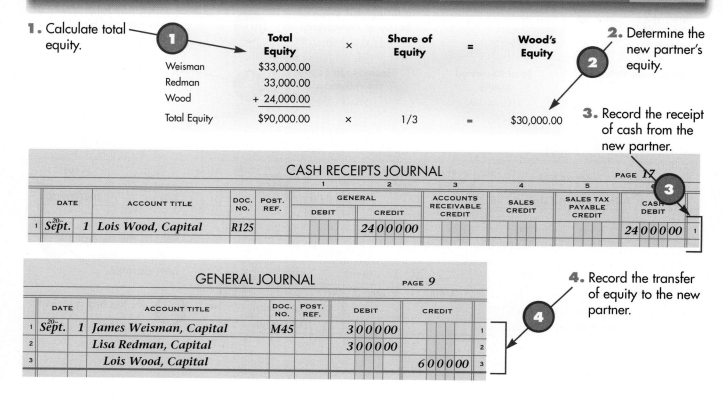

1. Calculate total equity.

1

	Total Equity	×	Share of Equity	=	Wood's Equity
Weisman	$33,000.00				
Redman	33,000.00				
Wood	+ 24,000.00				
Total Equity	$90,000.00	×	1/3	=	$30,000.00

2. Determine the new partner's equity.

2

3. Record the receipt of cash from the new partner.

CASH RECEIPTS JOURNAL — PAGE 17

	DATE	ACCOUNT TITLE	DOC. NO.	POST. REF.	GENERAL DEBIT	GENERAL CREDIT	ACCOUNTS RECEIVABLE CREDIT	SALES CREDIT	SALES TAX PAYABLE CREDIT	CASH DEBIT	
1	Sept. 1	Lois Wood, Capital	R125			24 0 0 0 00				24 0 0 0 00	1

3

GENERAL JOURNAL — PAGE 9

	DATE	ACCOUNT TITLE	DOC. NO.	POST. REF.	DEBIT	CREDIT	
1	Sept. 1	James Weisman, Capital	M45		3 0 0 0 00		1
2		Lisa Redman, Capital			3 0 0 0 00		2
3		Lois Wood, Capital				6 0 0 0 00	3

4. Record the transfer of equity to the new partner.

4

Figure 21-6

James Weisman and Lisa Redman both have equity of $33,000.00 in an existing partnership. The existing partners agree to admit Lois Wood as a partner with a one-third interest for a $24,000.00 cash investment. Lois's equity is calculated as shown in Figure 21-6.

September 1, 20--. Received cash from new partner, Lois Wood, for a one-third equity in the business, $24,000.00. Existing equity is redistributed as follows: from James Weisman, $3,000.00; from Lisa Redman, $3,000.00. Receipt No. 125 and Memorandum No. 45.

Two journal entries are required to record this transaction. (1) Receipt of cash is recorded. (2) Redistribution of existing equity is recorded. These entries are shown in Figure 21-6.

S T E P S

Admitting a partner with equity greater than new partner's investment

1. Calculate the total equity, including the new partner's investment of cash.

2. Determine the new partner's equity. In this case, the cash investment by the new partner is less than the equity that will be assigned to her.

3. Record the receipt of cash from the new partner in the cash receipts journal.

4. Record the transfer of equity to Lois Wood from James Weisman and Lisa Redman. After the entry, each partner's capital account has a $30,000.00 balance.

F.Y.I.

One reason for admitting a new partner with greater equity than investment is when a celebrity joins the partnership, bringing name recognition and increased sales.

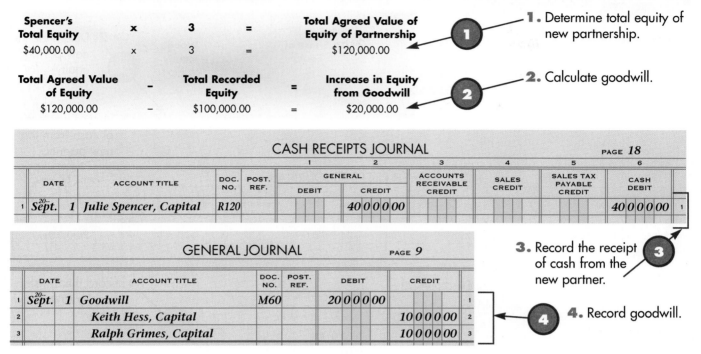

Figure 21-7

Keith Hess and Ralph Grimes are partners in an existing business. Each partner's equity is $30,000.00, for a total equity of $60,000.00. The existing partners agree to admit Julie Spencer as a partner with a one-third interest for a $40,000.00 cash investment. Julie is willing to pay $40,000.00 for a one-third equity. She believes the total equity value is worth $120,000.00 after her investment.

The value of a business in excess of the total investment of owners is called **goodwill**. The partners agree that Julie's willingness to pay $40,000.00 for a one-third interest is evidence that goodwill exists. The value of goodwill is calculated as shown in Figure 21-7.

September 1, 20--. Received cash from new partner, Julie Spencer, for a one-third equity in the business, $40,000.00. Goodwill, $20,000.00, is distributed as follows: Keith Hess, $10,000.00; Ralph Grimes, $10,000.00. Receipt No. 120 and Memorandum No. 60.

Two journal entries are required for this transaction. (1) Receipt of cash is recorded. (2) Distribution of goodwill is recorded. The $20,000.00 amount of equity in excess of the total recorded investment of the three partners is the value of goodwill.

S T E P S Admitting a partner when goodwill is recognized

1. Determine the total equity of the new partnership by multiplying her investment, $40,000.00, by 3. The total, $120,000.00, will be the total agreed value of equity of the new partnership.
2. Subtract the total recorded equity, $30,000.00 + $30,000.00 + $40,000.00 = $100,000.00 from the total agreed value of equity calculated in Step 1.
3. Record the cash investment by the new partner in a cash receipts journal.
4. Record the recognition of goodwill in the general journal.

Cash		
Sept. 1	40,000.00	

Goodwill		
Sept. 1	20,000.00	

Keith Hess, Capital

		Bal.	30,000.00
		Sept. 1	10,000.00
		(New Bal.	*40,000.00)*

Ralph Grimes, Capital

		Bal.	30,000.00
		Sept. 1	10,000.00
		(New Bal.	*40,000.00)*

Julie Spencer, Capital

		Sept. 1	40,000.00

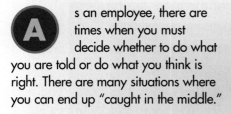

	Previous Equity	+	Share of Goodwill	=	New Equity
Hess	$ 30,000.00	+	$10,000.00	=	$ 40,000.00
Grimes	30,000.00	+	10,000.00	=	40,000.00
Spencer	+ 40,000.00	+	—	=	40,000.00
Total	$100,000.00	+	$20,000.00	=	$120,000.00

Figure 21-8

The analysis of the investment of cash by Julie Spencer and the distribution of goodwill is shown in the T accounts in Figure 21-8. None of the goodwill is recorded in Julie Spencer's capital account. She invested $40,000.00 for a one-third share of the business. One-third of the total equity, *$120,000.00,* equals the current balance of Ms. Spencer's capital account, *$40,000.00.*

Goodwill may be recorded only at the time of a change in ownership of business. An ongoing business may be worth more than the equity value stated in the accounting records. However, goodwill may not be recorded without some evidence of its value. This evidence is provided by the willingness of an investor to pay a premium for an ownership interest in the business.

When used, the account **Goodwill** is located in a general ledger's Intangible Assets section. Intangible assets are nonphysical assets that have value to a business.

PROFESSIONAL BUSINESS ETHICS

CAUGHT IN THE MIDDLE

As an employee, there are times when you must decide whether to do what you are told or do what you think is right. There are many situations where you can end up "caught in the middle."

Required:

Use the three-step checklist to help determine whether the actions of employer and employee in the following situation demonstrate ethical behavior.

Nicholas Chou is the bookkeeper for the Berkshire Bed and Breakfast. Last month cash was tight, so the owner told Nicholas to write out the checks to pay suppliers, but not to mail them until there was enough money in the checking account to cover the checks.

1. What happens to an existing partnership when a new partner is admitted?

2. When admitting a new partner, how is the new partner's equity calculated?

3. What accounts are debited and credited to record the distribution of goodwill when a new partner is admitted?

Admitting partners to existing partnerships

Four independent situations are given below. Assume partners of the existing partnership are Maria Heath and Lisa Curtis. The new partner is Wade Torres. For each situation, prepare the appropriate journal entries to admit the new partner. Page 12 of a cash receipts journal and page 6 of a general journal are provided in the *Working Papers*. Source documents are abbreviated as follows: memorandum, M; receipt, R. Your instructor will guide you through the following examples.

4. Maria Heath and Lisa Curtis have equity of $24,000.00 each in an existing partnership. On April 1 of the current year, the two partners agree to admit Wade Torres as a third partner. Each partner agrees to sell Mr. Torres $8,000.00 of her equity and to give him a one-third share of ownership. Mr. Torres is to pay the money directly to the two original partners.

Apr. 1. Journalized personal sale of equity to new partner, Wade Torres, $16,000.00, distributed as follows: from Maria Heath, $8,000.00; from Lisa Curtis, $8,000.00. M32.

5. Maria Heath and Lisa Curtis have equity of $80,000.00 each in the partnership. Partners share equally in all changes in equity. On April 1 of the current year, the two partners agree to admit Wade Torres as a partner with a one-third share of the total equity.

Apr. 1. Received cash from new partner, Wade Torres, for a one-third equity in the business, $80,000.00. R101.

6. Maria Heath and Lisa Curtis have equity of $50,000.00 each in an existing partnership. The partners share equally in all changes in equity. On April 1 of the current year, the existing partners agree to admit Wade Torres with a one-third share of the total equity.

Apr. 1. Received cash from new partner, Wade Torres, for a one-third equity in the business, $35,000. Existing equity is redistributed as follows: from Maria Heath, $5,000.00; from Lisa Curtis, $5,000.00. R125 and M31.

7. Maria Heath and Lisa Curtis have equity of $34,000.00 each in an existing business. The partners share equally in all changes in equity. On April 1 of the current year, Wade Torres is admitted as a new partner with a one-third share of the total equity.

Apr. 1. Received cash from new partner, Wade Torres, for a one-third equity in the business, $40,000.00. Goodwill, $12,000.00, is distributed as follows: Maria Heath, $6,000.00; Lisa Curtis, $6,000.00. R89 and M22.

Admitting partners to existing partnerships

Four independent situations are given below. Assume that partners of the existing partnership are Kyle Bowen and Susan Wong. The new partner is Angie Mills. For each situation, prepare the appropriate journal entries to admit the new partner. Page 18 of a cash receipts journal and page 9 of a general journal are provided in the *Working Papers*. Work independently to complete the following problem.

8. Kyle Bowen and Susan Wong have equity of $36,000.00 each in an existing partnership. On June 1 of the current year, the two partners agree to admit Angie Mills as a one-third partner. Each partner agrees to sell Ms. Mills $12,000.00 equity and to give her a one-third share of ownership. Ms. Mills is to pay the money directly to the two original partners.

June   1.   Journalized personal sale of equity to new partner, Angie Mills, $24,000.00, distributed as follows: from Kyle Bowen, $12,000.00; from Susan Wong, $12,000.00. M36.

9. Kyle Bowen and Susan Wong have equity of $75,000.00 each in the partnership. Partners share equally in all changes in equity. On June 1 of the current year, the two partners agree to admit Angie Mills as a partner with a one-third share of the total equity.

June   1.   Received cash from new partner, Angie Mills, for a one-third equity in the business, $75,000.00. R142.

10. Kyle Bowen and Susan Wong have equity of $36,000.00 each in an existing partnership. The partners share equally in all changes in equity. On June 1 of the current year, the existing partners agree to admit Angie Mills with a one-third share of the total equity.

June   1.   Received cash from new partner, Angie Mills, for a one-third equity in the business, $30,000.00. Existing equity is redistributed as follows: from Kyle Bowen, $2,000.00; from Susan Wong, $2,000.00. R130 and M40.

11. Kyle Bowen and Susan Wong each have $52,000.00 equity in an existing business. The partners share equally in all changes in equity. On June 1 of the current year, Angie Mills is admitted as a new partner with a one-third share of the total equity.

June   1.   Received cash from new partner, Angie Mills, for a one-third equity in the business, $60,000.00. Goodwill, $16,000.00, is distributed as follows: Kyle Bowen, $8,000.00; Susan Wong, $8,000.00. R160 and M46.

After completing this chapter, you can

1. Define accounting terms related to forming and expanding a partnership.

2. Identify accounting concepts and practices related to forming and expanding a partnership.

3. Journalize transactions related to forming a partnership.

4. Journalize transactions related to expanding a partnership.

EXPLORE ACCOUNTING

LIMITED LIABILITY PARTNERSHIPS

The organizational structure of a corporation differs from a partnership in four ways.

1. Continuity of life. A partnership ends upon the death or withdrawal of an owner. Stockholders of a corporation buy and sell stock without affecting the life of the corporation.

2. Centralization of management. A partnership generally is managed by one or more of its partners. A corporation generally is managed by professional managers employed by the stockholders.

3. Limited liability. All partners are liable for contracts and liabilities incurred by the partnership. A corporation is treated as a separate legal entity. Thus the stockholders are not liable for the contracts or liabilities of the corporation.

4. Free transferability of interest. Generally, a partnership ends if a partner dies or withdraws. In addition, other partners must agree before a partner can sell his/her share to another person. Stockholders can buy and sell shares of a corporation without consulting other stockholders.

Because a corporation is a legal entity, a corporation must pay income taxes on its net income.

Most states allow a special kind of partnership, called a limited liability partnership and frequently referred to as an LLP. An LLP must file articles of organization with the state. The operating agreement is similar to a traditional partnership agreement. The LLP must be managed by the members or a group of managers who are elected by the members. To qualify to be taxed as a partnership, the partnership can have

no more than two of the characteristics of a corporation. Most LLPs retain the two characteristics, centralization of management and limited liability.

The attractiveness of an LLP is twofold. (1) Partners can be taxed as a partnership (net income reported on individual partner's tax return). (2) Partners have limited liability for the actions of the partnership much like stockholders of a corporation. For these reasons, many partnerships have changed to an LLP.

REQUIRED:

1. Make a list of the types of businesses that would be most appropriate organized as an LLP.

2. Through additional reading about LLPs or interviewing local partners of an LLP, determine other advantages and disadvantages of an LLP.

21-1 APPLICATION PROBLEM
Forming a partnership

Carmen Estrada and Paula Jeter agree to form a partnership on June 1 of the current year. The partnership assumes the assets and liabilities of Carmen's existing business. Paula invests cash equal to Carmen's investment. Partners share equally in all changes in equity. The May 31 balance sheet for Carmen's existing business is as follows.

Carmen's Crafts			
Balance Sheet			
May 31, 20--			
ASSETS			
Current Assets:			
Cash		$14,532.00	
Accounts Receivable	$3,746.47		
Less Allowance for Uncollectible Accounts	74.92	3,671.55	
Merchandise Inventory		26,298.34	
Supplies		670.59	
Total Current Assets		$45,172.48	
Plant Assets:			
Equipment		9,481.12	
Total Assets		$54,653.60	
LIABILITIES			
Accounts Payable		$ 8,653.60	
OWNER'S EQUITY			
Carmen Estrada, Capital		46,000.00	
Total Liabilities and Owner's Equity		$54,653.60	

Transactions:

June 1. Received cash from partner, Paula Jeter, as an initial investment, $46,000.00. R1.
 1. Accepted assets and liabilities of Carmen Estrada's existing business as an initial investment, $46,000.00. R2.

Instructions:

Journalize the transactions using page 1 of a cash receipts journal. Source documents are abbreviated as follows: memorandum, M; receipt, R.

21-2 APPLICATION PROBLEM
Admitting a partner with no change in total equity

Steven Myer and William Riggs are partners in an existing business. Each partner has equity of $30,000.00. On October 1 of the current year, the two partners agree to admit Sandra DeVito as a third partner. Each of the partners agrees to personally sell Sandra $10,000.00 of his equity and to give her a one-third share of ownership. Sandra is to pay the money directly to the two original partners.

Transaction:

Oct. 1. Journalized personal sale of equity to new partner, Sandra DeVito, $20,000.00, distributed as follows: from Steven Myer, $10,000.00; from William Riggs, $10,000.00. M24.

Instructions:

Journalize the transaction using page 12 of a general journal.

APPLICATION PROBLEM
Admitting a partner with equity equal to new partner's investment

Susan Wang and Lelah Burch are partners in an existing business. Each partner has $60,000.00 equity in the partnership. Partners share equally in all changes in equity. On April 1 of the current year, the two partners agree to admit Daryl Wetzel as a partner with a one-third share of the total equity.

Transaction:
Apr. 1. Received cash from new partner, Daryl Wetzel, for a one-third equity in the business, $60,000.00. R95.

Instructions:
Journalize the transaction using page 13 of a cash receipts journal.

APPLICATION PROBLEM
Admitting a partner with equity greater than new partner's investment

Stanley Neal and Helen Jobe each have equity of $40,000.00 in an existing partnership. The partners share equally in all changes in equity. On August 1 of the current year, the existing partners agree to admit Greg Talbot with a one-third share of the total equity.

Transaction:
Aug. 1. Received cash from new partner, Greg Talbot, for a one-third equity in the business, $22,000.00. Existing equity is redistributed as follows: from Stanley Neal, $6,000.00; from Helen Jobe, $6,000.00. R116 and M25.

Instructions:
Journalize the transaction using page 14 of a cash receipts journal and page 7 of a general journal.

APPLICATION PROBLEM
Admitting a partner when goodwill is recognized

Arthur Jansky and Edward Thayer are partners, each with $27,000.00 equity in an existing business. The partners share equally in all changes in equity. On March 1 of the current year, Dean McGee is admitted as a new partner with a one-third share of the total equity.

Transaction:
Mar. 1. Received cash from new partner, Dean McGee, for a one-third equity in the business, $36,000.00. Goodwill, $18,000.00, is distributed as follows: Arthur Jansky, $9,000.00; Edward Thayer, $9,000.00. R67 and M10.

Instructions:
Journalize the transaction using page 5 of a cash receipts journal and page 3 of a general journal.

MASTERY PROBLEM
Forming and expanding a partnership

21-6

On July 1 of the current year, Roy Hatfield and Michelle Allen form a partnership. The partners share equally in all changes in equity. The partnership assumes the assets and liabilities of Roy's existing business. Michelle invests cash equal to Roy's investment. The June 30 balance sheet for Roy's existing business is as follows.

Hatfield Financial Services
Balance Sheet
June 30, 20--

ASSETS			
Current Assets:			
Cash		$4,291.23	
Accounts Receivable	$3,303.60		
Less Allowance for Uncollectible Accounts	35.79	3,267.81	
Supplies		290.19	
Total Current Assets			$ 7,849.23
Plant Assets:			
Equipment			4,378.14
Total Assets			$12,227.37
LIABILITIES			
Accounts Payable			$ 227.37
OWNER'S EQUITY			
Roy Hatfield, Capital			12,000.00
Total Liabilities and Owner's Equity			$12,227.37

Transactions:

July 1. Received cash from partner, Michelle Allen, as an initial investment, $12,000.00. R1.

1. Accepted assets and liabilities of Roy Hatfield's existing business as an initial investment, $12,000.00. R2.

Aug. 1. Journalized personal sale of equity to new partner, Frank Boyd, $8,000.00, distributed as follows: from Michelle Allen, $4,000.00; from Roy Hatfield, $4,000.00. M8.

Oct. 1. Received cash from new partner, Danita McGrew, for a one-fourth equity in the business, $8,000.00. R80.

Oct. 20. Received cash from new partner, Donna Wells, for a one-fifth equity in the business, $7,000.00. Existing equity is redistributed as follows: from Michelle Allen, $200.00; from Roy Hatfield, $200.00; from Frank Boyd, $200.00; from Danita McGrew, $200.00. R92 and M18.

Dec. 5. Received cash from new partner, Pearl Morgan, for a one-sixth equity in the business, $8,200.00. Goodwill, $2,000.00, is distributed as follows: Roy Hatfield, $400.00; Michelle Allen, $400.00; Frank Boyd, $400.00; Danita McGrew, $400.00; Donna Wells, $400.00. R118 and M24.

Instructions:

Journalize the transactions using page 1 of a cash receipts journal and page 1 of a general journal.

CHALLENGE PROBLEM
Forming and expanding a partnership

On May 1 of the current year, Marsha Huerta and John Ward form a partnership. The partnership assumes the assets and liabilities of the two partners' existing businesses. Partners share equally in all changes in equity. The May 1 balance sheets for the existing businesses are as follows.

Marsha's Party Planner
Balance Sheet
May 1, 20--

ASSETS

Current Assets:

Cash		$4,258.32
Accounts Receivable	$2,280.56	
Less Allowance for Uncollectible Accounts	35.43	2,245.13
Merchandise Inventory		6,237.29
Total Current Assets		$12,740.74
Plant Assets:		
Office Equipment		2,943.49
Total Assets		$15,684.23

LIABILITIES

Accounts Payable		$ 3,684.23

OWNER'S EQUITY

Marsha Huerta, Capital		12,000.00
Total Liabilities and Owner's Equity		$15,684.23

Ward's Wedding Chapel
Balance Sheet
May 1, 20--

ASSETS

Current Assets:

Cash	$4,323.49	
Supplies	2,075.21	
Merchandise Inventory	6,342.04	
Total Current Assets		$12,740.74
Plant Assets:		
Office Equipment		2,959.88
Total Assets		$15,700.62

LIABILITIES

Accounts Payable		$ 3,700.62

OWNER'S EQUITY

John Ward, Capital		12,000.00
Total Liabilities and Owner's Equity		$15,700.62

Transactions:

May 1. Accepted assets and liabilities of Marsha Huerta's existing business as an initial investment. R1.
      1. Accepted assets and liabilities of John Ward's existing business as an initial investment. R2.

July 1. Accepted assets of Dan Ogden's existing business as an investment of new partner for a one-third equity in the business. M80. Mr. Ogden's July 1 balance sheet is as follows.

Dan Ogden Balance Sheet July 1, 20--	
ASSETS	
Merchandise Inventory.	$12,000.00
OWNER'S EQUITY	
Dan Ogden, Capital	$12,000.00

July 20. Received cash from new partner, Pam Wise, for a one-fourth equity in the business, $15,000.00. R24 and M85.

Nov. 5. Accepted assets of Rodney Stein's existing business as an investment of new partner for a one-fifth equity in the business. Goodwill, $1,000.00, is distributed as follows: Marsha Huerta, $250.00; John Ward, $250.00; Dan Ogden, $250.00; Pam Wise, $250.00. R92 and M105. Mr. Stein's November 5 balance sheet is as follows.

Stein Supplies Balance Sheet November 5, 20--	
ASSETS	
Cash	$ 5,000.00
Merchandise Inventory	8,000.00
Total Assets	$13,000.00
OWNER'S EQUITY	
Rodney Stein, Capital	$13,000.00

Instructions:
Journalize the transactions using page 8 of a cash receipts journal and page 4 of a general journal.

INTERNET ACTIVITY

Point your browser to
http://accounting.swpco.com
Choose **Advanced Course**, choose **Activities**, and complete the activity for Chapter 21.

Applied Communication

Partnerships have operating expenses each month. Advertising, depreciation, and rent expense are examples of those operating expenses. Controlling these expenses affects the net income of the business.

Required:

Identify the operating expenses for MaLin Carpet Design in this chapter. Prepare a brief report, including a pie graph, that depicts the operating expenses for the year ended December 31. Do you think MaLin is controlling its operating expenses?

Cases for Critical Thinking

Case 1
Partner A contracted with a vendor to buy a computer for the partnership. Partner A did not discuss the transaction with Partner B or get Partner B's approval. Partner B refused to approve payment for the computer when it was delivered, claiming that the vendor cannot force payment because all partners did not agree to buy the computer. The vendor claims that the transaction is valid, and the partnership must pay for the computer. Is Partner B or the vendor correct? Explain.

Case 2
Helen Cole, her husband, and her son were partners in a business. Mrs. Cole's husband died, leaving his equity in the partnership to Mrs. Cole. Mrs. Cole and her son plan to form a new partnership and continue the business. Mrs. Cole's brother owns a similar business. The brother suggests that they combine the two businesses into a corporation. What questions do you suggest Mrs. Cole answer before she decides whether to form a partnership with her son or a corporation with her son and brother?

SMALL BUSINESS SPOTLIGHT

Look at the figures below and you decide—how big is small business?

Small businesses:
- provide virtually all of the net new jobs
- represent 99.7% of all employers
- employ 53% of the private workforce
- provide 47% of receipts (sales)
- provide 55% of innovations
- account for 35% of federal contract dollars
- account for 28% of jobs in high technology sectors
- account for 51% of private sector output

Source: *Small Business Answer Card 1997*, U.S. Small Business Administration, Office of Advocacy

AUTOMATED ACCOUNTING

SETTING UP AUTOMATED ACCOUNTING SYSTEMS FOR PARTNERSHIPS

Accounting software packages can be tailored to the needs of various types of businesses. Before accounting data can be entered, information about the company must be entered. The Customize Accounting System window is used to enter company information.

Company Info Tab

General information about a new company is specified on this tab. The company name and problem number are printed as part of the header for every report. Other information required includes business organization, features, type of business, type of income statement, and which checks will be printed from the accounting system.

Classify Accounts Tab

For most businesses, the default account classifications will be used. However, the classification numbers can be edited if necessary.

Required Accts. Tab

To prepare reports and perform period-ending closing tasks, certain accounts are required. Based upon the information specified on the Company Information tab, the computer will automatically search the chart of accounts to determine and list the accounts it requires. Accounts that cannot automatically be determined must be keyed.

AUTOMATING APPLICATION PROBLEM 21-1

Instructions:

1. Load *Automated Accounting* 7.0 or higher software.

2. Select database A21-1 (Advanced Course Application Problem 21-1) from the accounting template disk.

3. Select File from the menu bar and choose the Save As menu command. Key the path to the drive and directory that contains your data files. Save the database with a file name of XXX211 (where XXX are your initials).

4. Access Problem Instructions through the Help menu. Read the Problem Instruction screen.

5. Key the data listed on page 595.

6. Exit the Automated Accounting software.

AUTOMATING MASTERY PROBLEM 21-6

Instructions:

1. Load *Automated Accounting* 7.0 or higher software.

2. Select database A21-6 (Advanced Course Application Problem 21-6) from the accounting template disk.

3. Select File from the menu bar and choose the Save As menu command. Key the path to the drive and directory that contains your data files. Save the database with a file name of XXX216 (where XXX are your initials).

4. Access Problem Instructions through the Help menu. Read the Problem Instruction screen.

5. Key the data listed on page 597.

6. Exit the Automated Accounting software.

22 Financial Reporting for a Partnership

AFTER STUDYING CHAPTER 22, YOU WILL BE ABLE TO:

1. Define accounting terms related to distributing earnings and completing end-of-fiscal-period work for a partnership.

2. Identify accounting concepts and practices related to distributing earnings and completing end-of-fiscal-period work for a partnership.

3. Calculate the distribution of partnership earnings.

4. Journalize entries for withdrawal of partnership earnings.

5. Complete end-of-fiscal-period work for a partnership.

6. Prepare a distribution of net income statement for a partnership.

7. Journalize entries for liquidating a partnership.

Most end-of-fiscal-period work is similar for corporations, proprietorships, and partnerships. Two major procedures are different. (1) A corporation calculates and pays income tax on its net income, but partnerships and proprietorships do not. (2) A corporation maintains separate accounts for contributed capital (Capital Stock) and earned capital (Retained Earnings). Partnerships and proprietorships combine contributed and earned capital in one account for each owner.

A corporation may distribute some, but usually not all, of its earnings to stockholders as dividends. However, partnerships, like proprietorships, distribute all earnings of the business to the owners' capital accounts. The owners may then withdraw the earnings or leave them in the business.

TERMS PREVIEW

distribution of net
    income statement
deficit
owners' equity
    statement
liquidation of a
    partnership
realization

ACCOUNTING
IN YOUR CAREER

SHARING PARTNERSHIP INCOME

John Salera and Mallory Thompson are talented computer programmers. Both have excellent jobs in the computer software industry but want to be in business for themselves. They have outlined an idea for a new computer game that they believe is unlike any other available today. They are meeting with the manager of one of these funds next week to seek financing to start a business to produce this new game. They believe that they can afford to resign from their current positions and devote full time to launching this new game software. They need outside financing, however, because neither has more than $5,000 to invest in the business.

John and Mallory prepare a detailed proposal, including all estimated costs and sales, and meet with the fund manager, Donald West. He likes their presentation and says that he will recommend their proposal to the board. They then discuss the financial terms. Mr. West proposes that a partnership be formed with John, Mallory, and the fund as partners. He proposes that John and Mallory draw frugal annual salaries of $25,000, just enough to meet minimal living expenses. The venture fund, he insists, will demand a 40% interest on its initial investment of $250,000, to be paid in quarterly installments beginning after the next year. John and Mallory may then divide remaining net income in any way they prefer. After they leave the meeting, Mallory says to John, "It sounds like they're going to get all the money while we do all the work. That's not fair."

Critical Thinking

1. Do you agree with Mallory that the proposed distribution of earnings is unfair?
2. Should John and Mallory reject this proposal and contact banks for a business loan?

DISTRIBUTION OF PARTNERSHIP EARNINGS

All earnings of a partnership are distributed to the partners. Five methods are commonly used for calculating the distribution of partnership earnings.

1. Fixed percentage.

2. Percentage of total equity.

3. Interest on equity.

4. Salaries.

5. Combination of methods.

FIXED PERCENTAGE

	Total Net Income	×	Fixed Percentage	=	Share of Net Income
Costa	$20,000.00	×	60%	=	$12,000.00
McKee	$20,000.00	×	40%	=	8,000.00
Total					$20,000.00

Figure 22-1

The basis on which a partnership's earnings are distributed is usually stated in the partnership agreement. If a partnership agreement does not indicate how to divide the earnings, most state laws stipulate that partners share the earnings equally. For example, the earnings of two partners are shared on a fixed percentage of 50% and 50%. The law applies regardless of differences in the partners' investments, abilities, or time devoted to partnership business.

Scott Costa and Gary McKee are partners. On January 1, the partners' equities are Scott, $50,000.00 and Gary, $30,000.00. The net income for the year ended December 31 is $20,000.00. The partnership agreement states that Scott is to receive 60% and Gary is to receive 40% of the net income or net loss. The distribution of net income is calculated as shown in Figure 22-1.

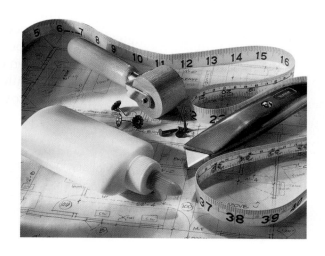

F.Y.I.

Limited partnerships include owners who have limited liability and limited operating responsibilities. Limited partnerships are sometimes formed for special projects such as Broadway plays.

PERCENTAGE OF TOTAL EQUITY

	Partner's Equity	÷	Total Equity	=	Percentage of Total Equity
Costa	$50,000.00	÷	$80,000.00	=	62.5%
McKee	30,000.00	÷	$80,000.00	=	37.5%
Total	$80,000.00				

	Total Net Income	×	Percentage of Total Equity	=	Share of Net Income
Costa	$20,000.00	×	62.5%	=	$12,500.00
McKee	$20,000.00	×	37.5%	=	7,500.00
Total					$20,000.00

Figure 22-2

Partners often agree to use capital account balances on the first day of a fiscal year as the basis for calculating the distribution of partnership earnings. If Scott and Gary had agreed to use this method, referred to as the *percentage of total equity method*, the percentages would be calculated as shown in Figure 22-2.

INTEREST ON EQUITY

	Partner's Equity	×	Interest Rate	=	Interest on Equity
Baker	$22,880.00	×	5%	=	$1,144.00
Mattingly	$11,440.00	×	5%	=	$ 572.00

Figure 22-3

Interest on equity is often used as a method to distribute earnings when partners invest different amounts in a partnership. Partners often agree to use capital account balances on the first day of a fiscal year as the basis for this income distribution method. The partnership agreement states the interest rate.

MaLin Carpet Design's partnership agreement, Item Five, shown in Figure 21-1, stipulates that each partner is to receive 5% interest on equity. On January 1, May Baker's equity is $22,880.00 and Lindel Mattingly's equity is $11,440.00. The interest on equity is calculated as shown in Figure 22-3.

When the interest on equity method is used, the remaining net income or net loss is distributed using another income distribution method as described later in this chapter.

The rate of interest on equity is often related to the current bank prime lending rate.

SALARIES

Salaries are often used as a method to distribute earnings when partners contribute different amounts of personal service or bring different prior experience to a partnership. The amount of salary for each partner is stated in the partnership agreement.

MaLin's partnership agreement states that salaries are to be paid as follows: May Baker, $5,000.00; Lindel Mattingly, $3,000.00. When salaries are used, the remaining net income or net loss is distributed using a combination of methods described in the following paragraphs.

COMBINATION OF METHODS

	Interest on Equity	Salary	Distribution of Remaining Net Income or Net Loss
Baker	5%	$5,000.00	50%
Mattingly	5%	$3,000.00	50%

	Baker	Mattingly	Distribution
Total Net Income			$37,400.00
Interest on Equity	$ 1,144.00	$ 572.00	
Salary	5,000.00	3,000.00	
Total	$ 6,144.00	$ 3,572.00	9,716.00
Remaining Net Income			$27,684.00
Distribution of Remaining Net Income	13,842.00	13,842.00	
Total Distribution	$19,986.00	$17,414.00	$37,400.00

Figure 22-4

A combination of income distribution methods may be used for distributing partnership earnings. MaLin's partnership agreement states the earnings distribution as shown in Figure 22-4. The distribution of MaLin's net income, *$37,400.00,* is calculated as shown in Figure 22-4.

WITHDRAWAL OF PARTNERSHIP EARNINGS

A partner often needs a portion of the annual net income before the end of a fiscal year when the actual net income is known. Thus, during a fiscal year, partners take assets out of the partnership in anticipation of the net income for the year. Assets taken out of a business for the owner's personal use are known as withdrawals. Usually the partnership agreement indicates limits on the amount of assets that may be withdrawn.

REMEMBER

A partner may have a large capital balance yet be unable to withdraw any assets from the partnership. Cash or other assets must be available for a partner to make a withdrawal.

A partner's salary is not an expense to the business.

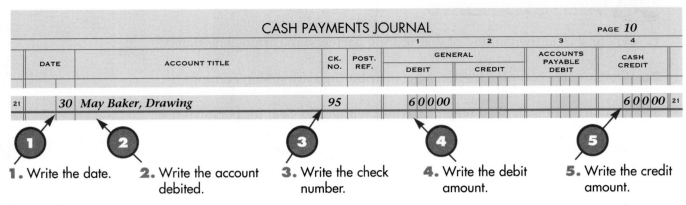

Figure 22-5

1. Write the date. **2.** Write the account debited. **3.** Write the check number. **4.** Write the debit amount. **5.** Write the credit amount.

May 30, 20--. May Baker, partner, withdrew cash for personal use, $600.00. Check No. 95.

May Baker, Drawing is debited for $600.00. Cash is credited for $600.00. The entry is made in the cash payments journal as shown in Figure 22-5.

S T E P S

Partner's withdrawal of cash

1. Write the date, *30*, in the Date column.
2. Write the title of the account debited, *May Baker, Drawing*, in the Account Title column.
3. Write the check number, *95*, in the Ck. No. column.
4. Write the debit amount, *600.00*, in the General Debit column.
5. Write the credit amount, *600.00*, in the Cash Credit column.

```
May Baker, Drawing
600.00  |

           Cash
        |  600.00
```

1. Write the date.

2. Write the account debited.

4. Write the debit amount.

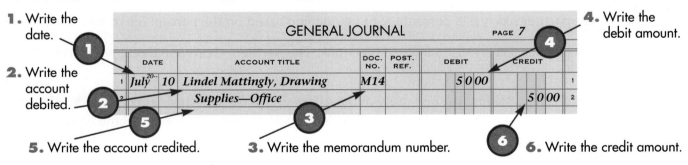

5. Write the account credited.   **3.** Write the memorandum number.   **6.** Write the credit amount.

Figure 22-6

July 10, 20--. Lindel Mattingly, partner, withdrew office supplies for personal use, $50.00. Memorandum No. 14.

Office supplies withdrawn for personal use are not a business expense. This transaction reduces the partnership's office supplies inventory and, therefore, Supplies—Office is credited.

Lindel Mattingly, Drawing is debited for $50.00. Supplies—Office is credited for $50.00.

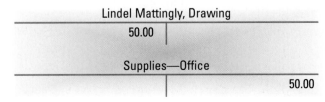

```
Lindel Mattingly, Drawing
50.00  |

        Supplies—Office
      |  50.00
```

AUDIT YOUR UNDERSTANDING

1. Where should the method of distributing partnership earnings be stated?

2. What are five common methods for distributing partnership earnings?

3. What account is debited when a partner withdraws cash for personal use?

4. What account is debited when a partner withdraws supplies for personal use?

WORK TOGETHER

Calculating partnership earnings and journalizing partnership withdrawals

Scott Badger and Maxine Giesen are partners in a business. On December 31 of the current year, the partners' equities are Scott, $60,000.00 and Maxine, $90,000.00. The net income for the year is $60,000.00. A work sheet for calculating distribution of partners' earnings, a cash payments journal, and a general journal are provided in the *Working Papers*. Your instructor will guide you through the following examples.

5. For each of the following independent cases, calculate how the $60,000.00 net income will be distributed to the two partners.

   a. Each partner receives a fixed percentage of 50% of net income.

   b. Each partner receives a percentage of net income based on the percentage of total equity.

   c. Each partner receives 10% interest on equity. The partners share remaining net income equally.

   d. Scott receives 8% interest on equity and a salary of $18,000.00. Maxine receives 8% interest on equity and a salary of $22,500.00. The partners share remaining net income equally.

6. Record the following transactions in the appropriate journal.

   June 20, 20--.   Scott Badger, partner, withdrew cash for personal use, $750.00. Check No. 133.

   July 1, 20--.   Maxine Giesen, partner, withdrew office supplies for personal use, $45.00. Memorandum No. 23.

ON YOUR OWN

Calculating partnership earnings and journalizing partnership withdrawals

Rose Nabors and Sam Ives are partners in a business. On December 31 of the current year, the partners' equities are Rose, $50,000 and Sam, $75,000.00. The net income for the year is $50,000.00. A work sheet for calculating distribution of partners' earnings, a cash payments journal, and a general journal are provided in the *Working Papers*. Work independently to complete the following problem.

7. For each of the following independent cases, calculate how the $50,000.00 net income will be distributed to the two partners.
   a. Each partner receives a fixed percentage of 50% of net income.
   b. Each partner receives a percentage of net income based on the percentage of total equity.
   c. Each partner receives 8% interest on equity. The partners share remaining net income equally.
   d. Rose receives 10% interest on equity and a salary of $16,000.00. Sam receives 10% interest on equity and a salary of $14,000.00. The partners share remaining net income equally.

8. Record the following transactions in the appropriate journal.
   Apr.15, 20--.   Rose Nabors, partner, withdrew cash for personal use, $800.00. Check No. 126.
   Oct. 3, 20--.   Sam Ives, partner, withdrew store supplies for personal use, $120.00. Memorandum No. 18.

LEGAL ISSUES IN ACCOUNTING

THE FTC FRANCHISE RULE

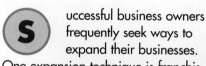

uccessful business owners frequently seek ways to expand their businesses. One expansion technique is franchising. A franchise is a contractual arrangement in which the owner of a trademark, trade name, or copyright licenses others, under specified conditions or limitations, to use the trademark, trade name, or copyright to sell goods or services. The person or business entity granting the franchise is known as the franchisor. The person or business entity to whom the franchise is granted is known as the franchisee.

The Federal Trade Commission (FTC) Franchise Rule requires the franchisor to make a written disclosure of important information about the franchisor, the franchised business, and the franchise relationship. The disclo-

sure should state information about the total cost, the amount of control the franchisor will have over the operations of the franchisee, the plan for termination of the franchise, and the conditions for renewal of the franchise. A franchisor must allow the potential franchisee at least 10 business days to review the disclosure document before asking the person to invest in the franchise.

Since the Franchise Rule is a trade regulation, it is enforced by the FTC. If the FTC finds that the rule has been violated, it may issue injunctions, freeze the assets of the franchisor, enact fines up to $10,000 per violation, and require that monetary compensation be given to those harmed by the actions of the franchisor.

ADJUSTMENTS ON A WORK SHEET

End-of-fiscal-period work for a partnership is similar to that for a corporation. In preparing partnership financial statements, accountants apply accounting principles in the same way during each fiscal period. *(CONCEPT: Consistent Reporting)*

All accounts in MaLin's general ledger are listed in a work sheet's Account Title column as shown in Figure 22-7 on the next page. Adjustments are planned on a partnership work sheet in the same manner as on a corporate work sheet, with one exception. No adjustment for accrued federal income tax is *ever* planned on a partnership work sheet because partnerships do not pay federal income tax.

As described later in this chapter, partnership net income is reported to the Internal Revenue Service on the partners' personal tax returns.

Because MaLin Carpet Design does not sell merchandise, it does not need to make an adjustment for merchandise inventory. Adjustments for uncollectible accounts, supplies, insurance, and depreciation are planned on the work sheet.

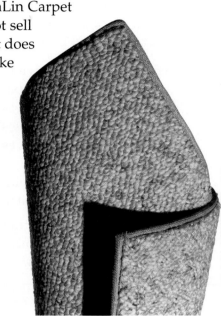

INCOME STATEMENT

MaLin Carpet Design Income Statement For Year Ended December 31, 20--		
		% of Sales*
Operating Revenue:		
Sales.	$72,020.27	100.0
Operating Expenses:		
Advertising Expense	$ 985.00	
Depreciation Expense—Equipment	1,250.50	
Depreciation Expense—Truck	918.75	
Insurance Expense.	503.20	
Miscellaneous Expense	2,869.21	
Rent Expense	8,400.00	
Supplies Expense—Carpet	7,676.50	
Supplies Expense—Office	1,420.00	
Truck Expense	8,477.56	
Uncollectible Accounts Expense	119.55	
Utilities Expense	2,000.00	
Total Operating Expenses	34,620.27	48.1
Net Income	$37,400.00	51.9
*Rounded to the nearest 0.1%.		

Figure 22-8

MaLin Carpet Design

Work Sheet

For Year Ended December 31, 20--

	ACCOUNT TITLE	TRIAL BALANCE DEBIT	TRIAL BALANCE CREDIT	ADJUSTMENTS DEBIT	ADJUSTMENTS CREDIT	INCOME STATEMENT DEBIT	INCOME STATEMENT CREDIT	BALANCE SHEET DEBIT	BALANCE SHEET CREDIT	
1	Cash	4280247						4280247		1
2	Petty Cash	20000						20000		2
3	Accounts Receivable	1199251						1199251		3
4	Allow. for Uncollectible Accts.		1992		(a) 11955				13947	4
5	Supplies—Carpet	930500			(b) 767650			162850		5
6	Supplies—Office	184500			(c) 142000			42500		6
7	Prepaid Insurance	134970			(d) 50320			84650		7
8	Equipment	1250497						1250497		8
9	Accum. Depr.—Equipment				(e) 125050				125050	9
10	Truck	490000						490000		10
11	Accum. Depr.—Truck				(f) 91875				91875	11
12	Accounts Payable		852123						852123	12
13	May Baker, Capital		2288000						2288000	13
14	May Baker, Drawing	450000						450000		14
15	Lindel Mattingly, Capital		1144000						1144000	15
16	Lindel Mattingly, Drawing	275000						275000		16
17	Income Summary									17
18	Sales		7202027				7202027			18
19	Advertising Expense	98500				98500				19
20	Depr. Expense—Equipment			(e) 125050		125050				20
21	Depr. Expense—Truck			(f) 91875		91875				21
22	Insurance Expense			(d) 50320		50320				22
23	Miscellaneous Expense	286921				286921				23
24	Rent Expense	840000				840000				24
25	Supplies Expense—Carpet			(b) 767650		767650				25
26	Supplies Expense—Office			(c) 142000		142000				26
27	Truck Expense	847756				847756				27
28	Uncollectible Accounts Expense			(a) 11955		11955				28
29	Utilities Expense	200000				200000				29
30		11488142	11488142	1188850	1188850	3462027	7202027	8254995	4514995	30
31	Net Income					3740000			3740000	31
32						7202027	7202027	8254995	8254995	32

Figure 22-7

A partnership income statement is similar to a corporation income statement with one exception. Federal income tax expense is *not* reported on a partnership income statement because a partnership does not pay federal income tax.

MaLin calculates two component percentages on its income statement as shown in Figure 22-8.

1. *Operating expenses component percentage.* MaLin expects a component percentage not more than 55.0%. Therefore, MaLin's operating expenses component percentage of 48.1% is acceptable. (Operating Expenses, $34,620.27 ÷ Sales, $72,020.27 = Operating Expense Component Percentage, 48.1%).

2. *Net income component percentage.* MaLin expects a component percentage not less than 45.0%. Therefore, MaLin's net income component percentage of 51.9% is acceptable. (Net Income, $37,400.00; Sales, $72,020.27 = Net Income Component Percentage, 51.9%).

The net income component percentage is often high for partnerships that sell only services because they have no cost of merchandise sold. Also, the partners' salaries are not expenses of the partnership.

F.Y.I.

Fields of accounting become extremely specialized as technical requirements increase. For example, some accountants specialize in accounting only for the gas and oil industry.

DISTRIBUTION OF NET INCOME STATEMENT SHOWING A NET INCOME

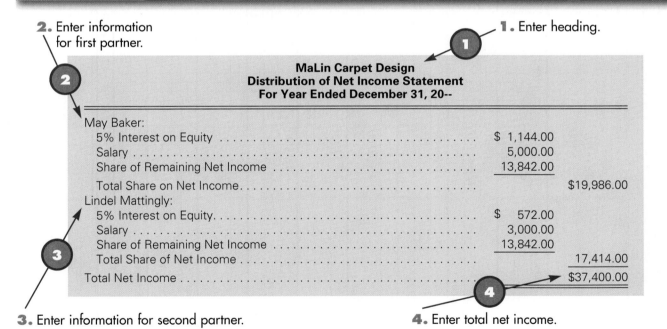

2. Enter information for first partner.

1. Enter heading.

MaLin Carpet Design
Distribution of Net Income Statement
For Year Ended December 31, 20--

May Baker:		
5% Interest on Equity	$ 1,144.00	
Salary	5,000.00	
Share of Remaining Net Income	13,842.00	
Total Share on Net Income		$19,986.00
Lindel Mattingly:		
5% Interest on Equity	$ 572.00	
Salary	3,000.00	
Share of Remaining Net Income	13,842.00	
Total Share of Net Income		17,414.00
Total Net Income		$37,400.00

3. Enter information for second partner.

4. Enter total net income.

Figure 22-9

A partnership financial statement showing distribution of net income or net loss to partners is called a **distribution of net income statement**.

MaLin's distribution of partnership earnings for the current year was calculated as shown in

Figure 22-4. The amounts calculated are reported on the Distribution of Net Income Statement shown in Figure 22-9.

Preparing a distribution of net income statement

1. Enter the 3-line heading, *MaLin Carpet Design, Distribution of Net Income Statement, For Year Ended December 31, 20--*.

2. Enter the information for *May Baker*. List the distribution methods, *5% Interest on Equity, Salary,* and *Share of Remaining Net Income*. Enter the amounts of distribution for each method, *$1,144.00, $5,000.00,* and *$13,842.00*, respectively. Finally, enter the *Total Share of Net Income, $19,986.00*.

3. Enter the information for *Lindel Mattingly*. List the distribution methods, *5% Interest on Equity, Salary,* and *Share of Remaining Net Income*. Enter the distribution amounts for each method, *$572.00, $3,000.00,* and *$13,842.00*, respectively. Finally, enter the *Total Share of Net Income, $17,414.00*.

4. Enter *Total Net Income, $37,400.00*.

DISTRIBUTION OF NET INCOME STATEMENT SHOWING A DEFICIT

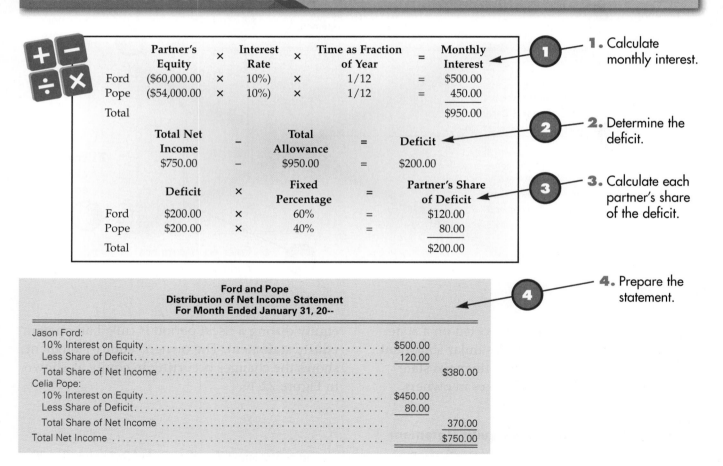

1. Calculate monthly interest.

2. Determine the deficit.

3. Calculate each partner's share of the deficit.

4. Prepare the statement.

Figure 22-10

When salaries or interest on equity are stipulated, the amounts are allowed whether sufficient net income is available. The amount by which allowances to partners exceed net income is called a **deficit**. Partners share deficits according to the partnership agreement.

On January 1, the equity of two partners is as follows: Jason Ford, $60,000.00 and Celia

Pope, $54,000.00. Each partner receives a 10% annual interest on equity and shares any remaining income or deficit on a fixed percentage of 60% and 40%, respectively. For the month of January, the partnership earned a net income of $750.00. Their distribution of net income statement is shown in Figure 22-10.

Preparing a distribution of net income statement showing a deficit

1. Calculate the monthly amounts due to each partner: *$550.00* for Ford and *$450.00* for Pope.

2. Determine the deficit amount, *$200.00* ($950.00 due to both partners − $750.00 net income).

3. Calculate each partner's share of the deficit, *120.00* for Ford and *80.00* for Pope.

4. Prepare the distribution of net income statement showing the deficit.

OWNERS' EQUITY STATEMENT

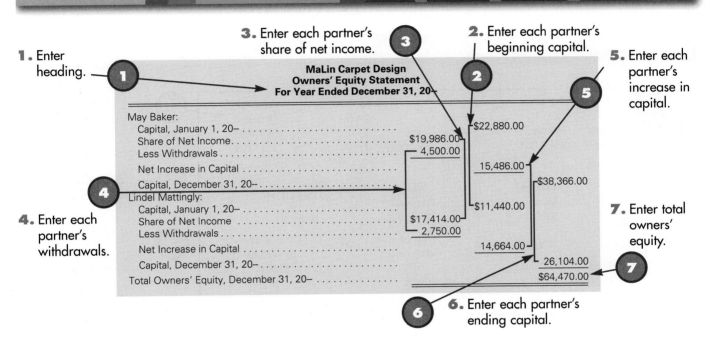

Figure 22-11

A corporation's equity is reported on a statement of stockholders' equity. A similar statement is prepared for a partnership. A financial statement that summarizes the changes in owners' equity during a fiscal period is called an **owners' equity statement**. The owners' equity statement shows the changes occurring in equity as shown in Figure 22-11.

Preparing an owner's equity statement

1. Enter the 3-line heading, *MaLin Carpet Design, Owners' Equity Statement, For Year Ended December 31, 20--*.

2. Enter each partner's capital at the beginning of the fiscal period, *$22,880.00* and *$11,440.00*. This balance is found in each partner's capital account in the general ledger.

3. Enter each partner's total share of net income, *$19,986.00* and *$17,414.00*. These amounts are obtained from the distribution of net income statement.

4. Enter each partner's withdrawals during the fiscal period, *$4,500.00* and *$2,750.00*. These amounts are found on the work sheet.

5. Enter each partner's net increase in capital during the fiscal period, *$15,486.00* and *$14,664.00*.

6. Enter each partner's capital on the last day of the fiscal period, *$38,366.00* and *$26,104.00*.

7. Enter the partnership's total owners' equity on the last day of the fiscal period, *$64,470.00*.

MaLin Carpet Design
Balance Sheet
December 31, 20--

ASSETS			
Current Assets:			
Cash		$42,802.47	
Petty Cash		200.00	
Accounts Receivable	$11,992.51		
Less Allowance for Uncollectible Accounts	139.47	11,853.04	
Supplies—Carpet		1,628.50	
Supplies—Office.		425.00	
Prepaid Insurance		846.50	
Total Current Assets			$57,755.51
Plant Assets:			
Equipment	$12,504.97		
Less Accumulated Depreciation—Equipment	1,250.50	$11,254.47	
Truck	4,900.00		
Less Accumulated Depreciation—Truck	$ 918.75	3,981.25	
Total Plant Assets			15,235.72
Total Assets			$72,991.23
LIABILITIES			
Accounts Payable			$ 8,521.23
OWNERS' EQUITY			
May Baker, Capital		$38,366.00	
Lindel Mattingly, Capital		26,104.00	
Total Owners' Equity			64,470.00
Total Liabilities and Owners' Equity			$72,991.23

Figure 22-12

On a partnership balance sheet, each partner's ending capital is reported under the heading *Owners' Equity* as shown in Figure 22-12.

ADJUSTING ENTRIES

1. Adjusting entry for uncollectible accounts.

2. Adjusting entries for supplies.

3. Adjusting entry for insurance.

4. Adjusting entries for depreciation.

	DATE		ACCOUNT TITLE	DOC. NO.	POST. REF.	DEBIT	CREDIT	
1			*Adjusting Entries*					1
2	*Dec.*²⁰⁻⁻	31	*Uncollectible Accounts Expense*			1 1 9 55		2
3			*Allowance for Uncoll. Accts.*				1 1 9 55	3
4		31	*Supplies Expense—Carpet*			7 6 7 6 50		4
5			*Supplies—Carpet*				7 6 7 6 50	5
6		31	*Supplies Expense—Office*			1 4 2 0 00		6
7			*Supplies—Office*				1 4 2 0 00	7
8		31	*Insurance Expense*			5 0 3 20		8
9			*Prepaid Insurance*				5 0 3 20	9
10		31	*Depreciation Expense—Equipment*			1 2 5 0 50		10
11			*Accum. Depreciation—Equipment*				1 2 5 0 50	11
12		31	*Depreciation Expense—Truck*			9 1 8 75		12
13			*Accum. Depreciation—Truck*				9 1 8 75	13

GENERAL JOURNAL PAGE *12*

Figure 22-13

MaLin's adjusting entries, shown in Figure 22-13, are made to record expenses in the fiscal period to which they apply. (*CONCEPT: Matching Expenses with Revenue*)

CLOSING ENTRIES

1. Close income statement accounts with credit balances.

2. Close income statement accounts with debit balances.

3. Close Income Summary.

4. Close partners' drawing accounts.

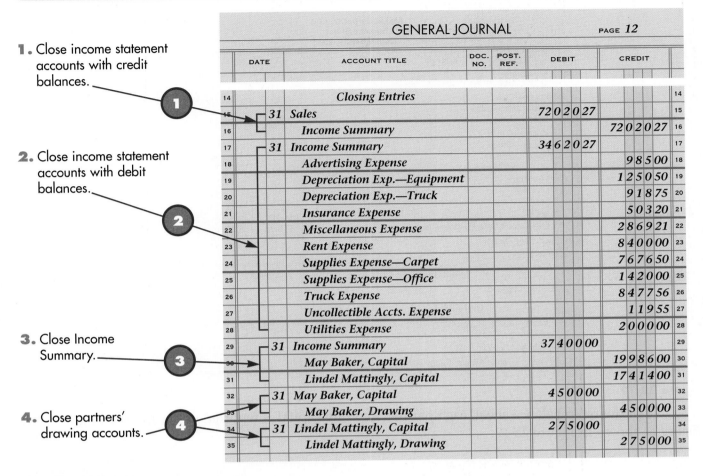

	DATE	ACCOUNT TITLE	DOC. NO.	POST. REF.	DEBIT	CREDIT	
14		*Closing Entries*					14
15	31	Sales			7202027		15
16		Income Summary				7202027	16
17	31	Income Summary			3462027		17
18		*Advertising Expense*				98500	18
19		*Depreciation Exp.—Equipment*				125050	19
20		*Depreciation Exp.—Truck*				91875	20
21		*Insurance Expense*				50320	21
22		*Miscellaneous Expense*				286921	22
23		*Rent Expense*				840000	23
24		*Supplies Expense—Carpet*				767650	24
25		*Supplies Expense—Office*				142000	25
26		*Truck Expense*				847756	26
27		*Uncollectible Accts. Expense*				11955	27
28		*Utilities Expense*				200000	28
29	31	Income Summary			3740000		29
30		*May Baker, Capital*				1998600	30
31		*Lindel Mattingly, Capital*				1741400	31
32	31	May Baker, Capital			450000		32
33		*May Baker, Drawing*				450000	33
34	31	Lindel Mattingly, Capital			275000		34
35		*Lindel Mattingly, Drawing*				275000	35

GENERAL JOURNAL   PAGE *12*

Figure 22-14

Closing entries for a partnership are similar to those of a corporation. The major difference is in recording distribution of earnings to the partners as shown in Figure 22-14.

FEDERAL INCOME TAXES OF A PARTNERSHIP

MaLin's distribution of net income statement shows salaries for each of the partners. However, the Internal Revenue Service does not consider partners to be employees of the partnership they own. The IRS classifies the partners as self-employed persons whose salaries are not an expense of the partnership. Therefore, partners' salaries are considered to be withdrawals of partnership earnings, not expenses.

A partnership does not pay income tax on its earnings. However, a partnership does submit to the IRS a partnership tax return that reports the earnings distributed to each partner. This type of return is known as an information return. In addition, partners include their respective share of the partnership net income or net loss on their personal income tax returns.

As self-employed persons, partners are entitled to old-age, survivors, disability, and hospitalization insurance benefits known collectively as social security and Medicare. Each partner personally pays a self-employment tax to qualify for social security and Medicare coverage. Therefore, the self-employment tax rate is double that of an employed individual's social security and Medicare tax rates. Thus, the same total amount of social security and Medicare taxes are paid for both self-employed persons and employees. The self-employment taxes are personal expenses of the partners, not of the partnership. Therefore, partners' self-employment social security and Medicare taxes are not recorded on partnership records. (CONCEPT: Business Entity)

The business entity concept states that financial information is recorded and reported separately from the owner's personal financial information. A business' records must not be mixed with an owner's personal records and reports. For example, a business owner may buy insurance to protect the business and insurance to protect the owner's home. Only the insurance obtained for the business is recorded in the business' financial records. The insurance purchased for the owner's personal home is recorded in the owner's personal financial records. One bank account is used for the business and another for the owner. A business exists separately from its owners.

POST-CLOSING TRIAL BALANCE

MaLin Carpet Design
Post-Closing Trial Balance
December 31, 20--

Account Title	Debit	Credit
Cash	$42,802.47	
Petty Cash	200.00	
Accounts Receivable	11,992.51	
Allowance for Uncollectible Accounts		$ 139.47
Supplies—Carpet	1,628.50	
Supplies—Office	425.00	
Prepaid Insurance	846.50	
Equipment	12,504.97	
Accumulated Depreciation—Equipment		1,250.50
Truck	4,900.00	
Accumulated Depreciation—Truck		918.75
Accounts Payable		8,521.23
May Baker, Capital		38,366.00
Lindel Mattingly, Capital		26,104.00
	$75,299.95	$75,299.95

Figure 22-15

After adjusting and closing entries have been posted, MaLin prepares a post-closing trial balance as shown in Figure 22-15. MaLin's post-closing trial balance is similar to that of a corporation with the exception of the capital accounts.

F.Y.I.

Partners pay self-employment tax on their share of net income.

REMEMBER

The post-closing trial balance indicates that the accounting records are ready for the next fiscal period.

AUDIT YOUR UNDERSTANDING

1. Why is an adjustment for accrued federal income tax never planned on a partnership work sheet?

2. When does a deficit occur?

3. What is the purpose of the owners' equity statement?

WORK TOGETHER

End-of-fiscal-period-work for a partnership

Maria Delgado and Oren Kelso are partners in a business. Statement paper, page 15 of a general journal, and a portion of the partnership's completed work sheet for the year ended December 31 of the current year are provided in the *Working Papers*. Your instructor will guide you through the following examples.

4. Prepare an income statement. Calculate and record the component percentages for total operating expenses and net income. Round percentage calculations to the nearest 0.1%.

5. Prepare a distribution of net income statement. Each partner is to receive 8% interest on January 1 equity. Also, partners' salaries are Maria, $15,000.00 and Oren, $14,000.00. The remaining net income, net loss, or deficit is shared equally.

6. Prepare an owners' equity statement.

7. Journalize the closing entries.

ON YOUR OWN

End-of-fiscal-period work for a partnership

Jeffrey Lowe and Mona Ray are partners in a business. Statement paper, page 12 of a general journal, and a portion of the partnership's completed work sheet for the year ended December 31 of the current year are provided in the *Working Papers*. Work independently to complete the following problem.

8. Prepare an income statement. Calculate and record the component percentages for total operating expenses and net income. Round percentage calculations to the nearest 0.1%.

9. Prepare a distribution of net income statement. Each partner is to receive 8% interest on January 1 equity. Also, partners' salaries are Jeffrey, $12,000.00 and Mona, $16,000.00. The remaining net income, net loss, or deficit is shared equally.

10. Prepare an owners' equity statement.

11. Journalize the closing entries.

ACCOUNT BALANCES BEFORE REALIZATION

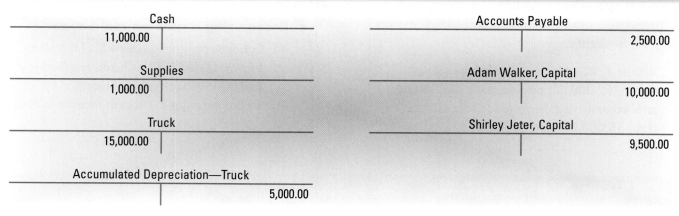

Cash	
11,000.00	

Supplies	
1,000.00	

Truck	
15,000.00	

Accumulated Depreciation—Truck	
	5,000.00

Accounts Payable	
	2,500.00

Adam Walker, Capital	
	10,000.00

Shirley Jeter, Capital	
	9,500.00

Figure 22-16

If a partnership goes out of business, its assets are distributed to the creditors and partners. The process of paying a partnership's liabilities and distributing remaining assets to the partners is called **liquidation of a partnership**.

Cash received from the sale of assets during liquidation of a partnership is called **realization**. Typically, when a partnership is liquidated, the noncash assets are sold, and the available cash is used to pay the creditors. Any remaining cash is

distributed to the partners according to each partner's total equity.

On July 31, Adam Walker and Shirley Jeter liquidated their partnership. At that time, financial statements were prepared and adjusting and closing entries were journalized and posted. After the end-of-fiscal-period work was completed, the partnership had account balances as shown in Figure 22-16.

GAIN ON REALIZATION

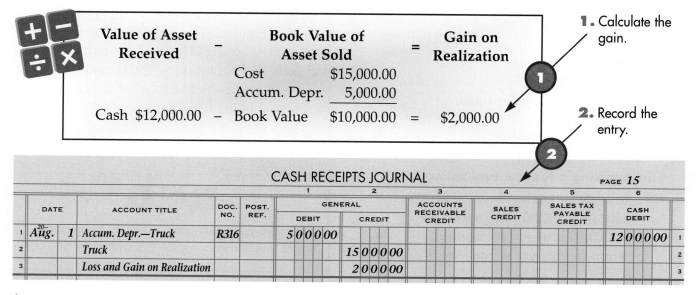

Value of Asset Received	−	Book Value of Asset Sold	=	Gain on Realization
		Cost $15,000.00		
		Accum. Depr. 5,000.00		
Cash $12,000.00	−	Book Value $10,000.00	=	$2,000.00

1. Calculate the gain.

2. Record the entry.

CASH RECEIPTS JOURNAL
PAGE 15

	DATE	ACCOUNT TITLE	DOC. NO.	POST. REF.	GENERAL DEBIT	GENERAL CREDIT	ACCOUNTS RECEIVABLE CREDIT	SALES CREDIT	SALES TAX PAYABLE CREDIT	CASH DEBIT	
1	20-- Aug. 1	Accum. Depr.—Truck	R316		5000 00					12000 00	1
2		Truck				15000 00					2
3		Loss and Gain on Realization				2000 00					3

Figure 22-17

Noncash assets might be sold for more than the recorded book value. When this happens, the amount received in excess of the book value is recorded as a gain on realization. The gain is recorded as a credit in an account titled Loss and Gain on Realization.

August 1, 20--. Received cash from sale of truck, $12,000.00: original cost, $15,000.00; total accumulated depreciation recorded to date, $5,000.00. Receipt No. 316.

The partnership's gain on the sale of the truck is calculated as shown in Figure 22-17.

S **Recognizing a gain on realization**
T
E **1.** Calculate the gain on the sale of the asset, $2,000.00 ($12,000.00 cash received – $10,000.00 book value of asset).
P **2.** Record the entry in the cash receipts journal.
S

LOSS ON REALIZATION

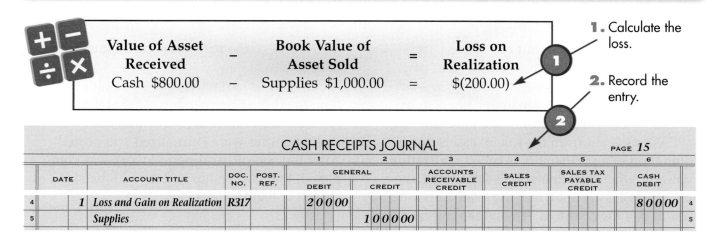

	Value of Asset Received	–	Book Value of Asset Sold	=	Loss on Realization
	Cash $800.00	–	Supplies $1,000.00	=	$(200.00)

1. Calculate the loss.

2. Record the entry.

			CASH RECEIPTS JOURNAL								PAGE 15
						1	2	3	4	5	6
	DATE	ACCOUNT TITLE	DOC. NO.	POST. REF.	GENERAL DEBIT	GENERAL CREDIT	ACCOUNTS RECEIVABLE CREDIT	SALES CREDIT	SALES TAX PAYABLE CREDIT	CASH DEBIT	
4	1	Loss and Gain on Realization	R317		2 0 0 00					8 0 0 00	4
5		Supplies				1 0 0 0 00					5

Figure 22-18

Sometimes during liquidation, the sale of an asset brings in less cash than the recorded book value.

August 1. Received cash from sale of supplies, $800.00; balance of supplies account, $1,000.00. Receipt No. 317.

S **Recognizing a loss on realization**
T
E **1.** Calculate the loss on the sale of the asset, $200.00 ($800.00 cash received – $1,000.00 book value of supplies).
P **2.** Record the entry in the cash receipts journal.
S

The journal entry to record this transaction is shown in Figure 22-18. After both liquidation entries have been journalized, the balance of Loss and Gain on Realization, $1,800.00, is the amount received in excess of the value of the truck and supplies combined.

F.Y.I.

A partnership usually tries to sell the business before it begins the process of liquidation.

CASH PAYMENTS JOURNAL

PAGE 15

	DATE	ACCOUNT TITLE	CK. NO.	POST. REF.	GENERAL DEBIT	GENERAL CREDIT	ACCOUNTS PAYABLE DEBIT	CASH CREDIT	
1	Aug. 4	Accounts Payable	422		2 5 0 0 00			2 5 0 0 00	1

Figure 22-19

The partnership's available cash is used to pay creditors. The entry is recorded in the cash payments journal as shown in Figure 22-19.

August 4, 20--. Paid cash to all creditors for the amounts owed, $2,500.00. Check No. 422.

ACCOUNT BALANCES AFTER LIQUIDATION OF NONCASH ASSETS AND PAYMENT OF LIABILITIES

Cash		Shirley Jeter, Capital	
Bal. 21,300.00			Bal. 9,500.00

Adam Walker, Capital		Loss and Gain on Realization	
	Bal. 10,000.00		Bal. 1,800.00

Figure 22-20

When this transaction has been journalized and posted, the partnership has only four general ledger accounts with balances as shown in Figure 22-20.

TECHNOLOGY FOR BUSINESS

SPREADSHEET ACTIVITY— DISTRIBUTION OF PARTNERSHIP EARNINGS

All Season Golf Center is an indoor golf facility with six computerized golf simulators. The partnership is owned by Arthur Wilson and Pamela Kim. According to the partnership agreement, Arthur receives 8% interest on equity and a salary of $22,000.00. Pamela receives 8% interest on equity and a salary of $18,000.00. The remainder of net income is divided equally. For the current year, net income for All Season Golf Center is $52,000.00.

Required:

1. Create a distribution of partnership earnings spreadsheet. Use Figure 22-4 as a model. Write formulas to calculate interest on equity, salary, division of remaining income, and the total distribution. Save the spreadsheet. Print a copy of the distribution of partnership earnings.
2. Use the spreadsheet to calculate the distribution of partnership earnings for the next year assuming net income is $66,000.00.

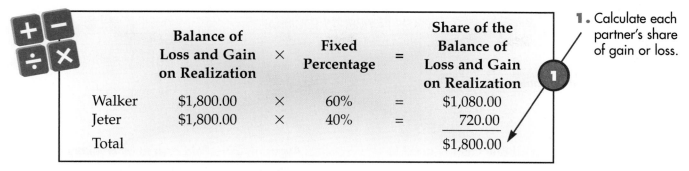

1. Calculate each partner's share of gain or loss.

	Balance of Loss and Gain on Realization	×	Fixed Percentage	=	Share of the Balance of Loss and Gain on Realization
Walker	$1,800.00	×	60%	=	$1,080.00
Jeter	$1,800.00	×	40%	=	720.00
Total					$1,800.00

2. Record entry to distribute gain or loss.

GENERAL JOURNAL PAGE 8

	DATE		ACCOUNT TITLE	DOC. NO.	POST. REF.	DEBIT	CREDIT	
1	Aug. 20--	6	Loss and Gain on Realization	M412		1 8 0 0 00		1
2			Adam Walker, Capital				1 0 8 0 00	2
3			Shirley Jeter, Capital				7 2 0 00	3

Figure 22-21

When all creditors have been paid, the balance of Loss and Gain on Realization is distributed to the partners. A credit balance indicates a gain on realization. A debit balance indicates a loss. The distribution is based on the method of distributing net income or net loss as stated in the partnership agreement. The percentages for the Walker and Jeter partnership are Adam, 60%, and Shirley, 40%. The distribution of the balance of Loss and Gain on Realization is calculated as shown in Figure 22-21.

August 6, 20--. Recorded distribution of gain on realization: to Adam Walker, $1,080.00; to Shirley Jeter, $720.00. Memorandum No. 412.

If a loss on realization is distributed to the partners, Loss and Gain on Realization is credited to close the account. Each partner's capital account is debited for the partner's share of the loss on realization.

CASH PAYMENTS JOURNAL PAGE 15

		DATE	ACCOUNT TITLE	CK. NO.	POST. REF.	1 GENERAL DEBIT	2 GENERAL CREDIT	3 ACCOUNTS PAYABLE DEBIT	4 CASH CREDIT	
2		6	Adam Walker, Capital	423		11 0 8 0 00			21 3 0 0 00	2
3			Shirley Jeter, Capital	424		10 2 2 0 00				3

Figure 22-22

Any remaining cash is distributed to the partners. The cash is distributed according to each partner's capital account balance regardless of the method used to distribute net income or net loss.

August 6. Recorded final distribution of remaining cash to partners: to Adam Walker,

$11,080.00; to Shirley Jeter, $10,220.00. Check Nos. 423 and 424.

After this journal entry is journalized, as shown in Figure 22-22, and posted, all of the partnership's general ledger accounts will have zero balances. The partnership is liquidated.

liquidation of a
  partnership
realization

1. What is meant by the term "realization"?
2. What accounts are debited when distributing remaining cash to partners during liquidation?

Liquidation of a partnership

Jason Edson and Peggy Karam agreed to liquidate their partnership on April 30 of the current year. On that date, after financial statements were prepared and closing entries were posted, the general ledger accounts had the balances shown in the *Working Papers*.

A cash receipts journal, page 6, a cash payments journal, page 8, and a general journal, page 4, are provided in the *Working Papers*. Your instructor will guide you through the following examples.

May 1. Received cash from sale of office equipment, $6,000.00. R86.
    1. Received cash from sale of supplies, $950.00. R87.
    3. Received cash from sale of truck, $7,500.00. R88.
    5. Paid cash to all creditors for amounts owed. C116.
    6. Distributed loss or gain to Jason Edson, 60%; to Peggy Karam, 40%. M21.
    6. Distributed remaining cash to partners. C117 and C118.

3. Journalize the transactions.

Liquidation of a partnership

Denise Oxley and Charles Tatum agreed to liquidate their partnership on May 31 of the current year. On that date, after financial statements were prepared and closing entries were posted, the general ledger accounts had the balances shown in the *Working Papers*.

A cash receipts journal, page 8, a cash payments journal, page 10, and a general journal, page 5, are provided in the *Working Papers*. Work independently to complete the following problem.

June 1. Received cash from sale of office equipment, $6,200.00. R96.
    1. Received cash from sale of supplies. $900.00. R97.
    3. Received cash from sale of truck, $9,000.00. R98.
    5. Paid cash to all creditors for amounts owed. C125.
    6. Distributed loss or gain to Denise Oxley, 60%; to Charles Tatum, 40%. M29.
    6. Distributed remaining cash to partners. C126 and C127.

4. Journalize the transactions.

CHAPTER SUMMARY

After completing this chapter, you can

1. Define accounting terms related to distributing earnings and completing end-of-fiscal-period work for a partnership

2. Identify accounting concepts and practices related to distributing earnings and completing end-of-fiscal-period work for a partnership.

3. Calculate the distribution of partnership earnings.

4. Journalize entries for withdrawal of partnership earnings.

5. Complete end-of-fiscal-period work for a partnership

6. Prepare a distribution of net income statement for a partnership.

7. Journalize entries for liquidating a partnership.

EXPLORE ACCOUNTING

DETERMINING VALUE OF PARTNERSHIP

When a partnership decides to add another partner or an existing partner wants to withdraw, the value of a partnership must be determined. The book value of a partnership is not necessarily an equitable value to the new or existing partners. Therefore, before admitting a new partner or retiring one, a current equitable value should be determined for the partnership. Three common methods used to value a partnership are (1) comparable sales, (2) appraisal, and (3) income capitalization.

Comparable sales method. This method attempts to compare other comparable businesses that have been sold recently with the partnership business being valued. Factors to be considered in selecting comparable businesses are type, size, and location of the business. If a comparable business recently sold for $500,000.00, this provides a sound basis for valuing the partnership at $500,000.00 regardless of the book value of the partnership.

Appraisal method. This method estimates the current fair market value of each of the assets and liabilities. A professional appraiser would be employed to determine the value of the assets and liabilities of the business.

Income capitalization method. This method places most emphasis on the expected future earnings capacity of the business. The buyer of a business or share of a partnership probably is making the investment for the anticipated future earnings of the business. This method places a value on the business based on those expected future earnings.

REQUIRED:

Assume that you are a doctor. You have been offered a one-quarter interest in a growing medical practice located in a growing area. Which method of valuing the existing partnership would you prefer? Explain the reason for your choice.

APPLICATION PROBLEM
Calculating partnership earnings

Jill Fargo and Sheila Kain are partners in a business called Fargo and Kain. On December 31 of the current year, the partners' equities are Jill, $80,000.00 and Sheila, $120,000.00. The net income for the year is $80,000.00.

Instructions:
For each of the following independent cases, calculate how the $80,000.00 net income will be distributed to the two partners.

1. Each partner receives a fixed percentage of 50% of net income.
2. Each partner receives a percentage of net income based on the percentage of total equity.
3. Each partner receives 12% interest on equity. The partners share remaining net income, net loss, or deficit equally.
4. Jill receives a salary of $24,000.00; Sheila receives a salary of $30,000.00. The partners share remaining net income, net loss, or deficit on a fixed percentage of Jill, 40% and Sheila, 60%.
5. Jill is to receive 10% interest on equity and a salary of $24,000.00. Sheila is to receive 8% interest on equity and a salary of $30,000.00. The partners share remaining net income, net loss, or deficit equally.
6. Jill is to receive 15% interest on equity and a salary of $30,000.00. Sheila is to receive 15% interest on equity and a salary of $36,000.00. The partners share remaining net income, net loss, or deficit equally.

 APPLICATION PROBLEM
Journalizing partners' withdrawals

Janet Agnew and Buford Franco are partners in a business. Each partner withdraws assets during May of the current year.

Transactions:
June 5. Janet Agnew, partner, withdrew office supplies for personal use, $400.00. M46.
26. Buford Franco, partner, withdrew cash for personal use, $600.00. C284.

Instructions:
Journalize the transactions using page 12 of a cash payments journal and page 6 of a general journal.

 APPLICATION PROBLEM
Completing end-of-fiscal-period work for a partnership

Susan Poole and Ann Dodd are partners in a business called Plantasia. The partnership's work sheet for the year ended December 31 of the current year is provided in the *Working Papers*.

Instructions:
1. Prepare an income statement. Calculate and record the component percentages for total operating expenses and net income. Round percentage calculations to the nearest 0.1%.

continued

2. Prepare a distribution of net income statement. The partners share in net income, net loss, or deficit according to each partner's percentage of total equity. The January 1 equity is Susan, $23,400.00 and Ann, $12,600.00. Round percentage calculations to the nearest 0.1%.

3. Prepare an owners' equity statement.

4. Prepare a balance sheet.

5. Journalize the adjusting entries using page 12 of a general journal.

6. Journalize the closing entries on the same general journal page.

APPLICATION PROBLEM
Liquidating a partnership

Donald Winn and Judy Reed agreed to liquidate their partnership on June 30 of the current year. On that date, after financial statements were prepared and closing entries were posted, the general ledger accounts had the following balances.

Cash	$ 5,000.00
Supplies	500.00
Office Equipment	10,000.00
Accumulated Depreciation—Office Equipment	5,500.00
Truck	17,000.00
Accumulated Depreciation—Truck	12,200.00
Accounts Payable	500.00
Donald Winn, Capital	7,300.00
Judy Reed, Capital	7,000.00

The following transactions occurred during July of the current year.

Transactions:

July 1. Received cash from sale of office equipment, $4,000.00. R114.

1. Received cash from sale of supplies, $200.00. R115.

3. Received cash from sale of truck, $5,000.00. R116.

5. Paid cash to all creditors for amounts owed. C156.

6. Distributed balance of Loss and Gain on Realization to Donald Winn, 65%; to Judy Reed, 35%. M34.

6. Distributed remaining cash to partners. C157 and C158.

Instructions:
Journalize the transactions. Use page 13 of a cash receipts journal, page 13 of a cash payments journal, and page 7 of a general journal.

MASTERY PROBLEM
Completing end-of-fiscal-period work for a partnership

22-5

Sarah Saxon and Jane Rolf are partners in a business called J & L Service. The partnership's work sheet for the year ended December 31 of the current year is provided in the *Working Papers.*

Instructions:

1. Prepare an income statement. Calculate and record the component percentage for total operating expenses and net income. Round percentage computations to the nearest 0.1%.

2. Prepare a distribution of net income statement. Each partner is to receive 10% interest on January 1 equity. The January 1 equity is Sarah, $15,000.00 and Jane, $12,000.00. Also, partners' salaries are Sarah, $10,000.00 and Jane, $15,000.00. The partners share remaining net income, net loss, or deficit equally.

3. Prepare an owners' equity statement.

4. Prepare a balance sheet.

5. Journalize the adjusting entries using page 12 of a general journal.

6. Journalize the closing entries on the same general journal page.

CHALLENGE PROBLEM
Completing end-of-fiscal-period work for a partnership

22-6

Theresa Doran and Roy Eden are partners in a business called D & E Sales. The partnership's work sheet for the year ended December 31 of the current year is provided in the *Working Papers.*

Instructions:

1. Prepare an income statement. Calculate and record the component percentages for cost of merchandise sold, gross profit on operations, total operating expenses, and net income or net loss. Round percentage calculations to the nearest 0.1%. If there is a net loss, use a minus sign with the component percentage.

2. Prepare a distribution of net income statement. Each partner is to receive 10% interest on January 1 equity. The January 1 equity is Theresa, $24,250.00 and Roy, $21,500.00. Also, partners' salaries are Theresa, $12,000.00 and Roy, $10,000.00. The remaining net income, net loss, or deficit is shared as follows: Theresa, 55%; Roy, 45%.

3. Prepare an owners' equity statement.

4. Prepare a balance sheet.

INTERNET ACTIVITY

Point your browser to

http://accounting.swpco.com

Choose **Advanced Course**, choose **Activities**, and complete the activity for Chapter 22.

Point your browser to http://accounting.swpco.com Choose Advanced Course, choose Activities, and complete the activity for Chapter 22.

Applied Communication

Brian Hughes and Wendy Perez formed a partnership five years ago. The partnership has been very successful and is growing rapidly. The partners are evaluating future actions for the next five years. They are projecting continued growth of their business. Brian and Wendy are trying to decide whether they should incorporate their business.

Required:

Write a short report explaining the advantages and disadvantages of a partnership versus a corporation that Brian and Wendy can use in making their decision.

Cases for Critical Thinking

Case 1

Lola Stroud invests $30,000.00 in a partnership. Her partner, Juan Santo, invests $50,000.00. Miss Stroud has 10 years' experience in a similar business; Mr. Santo has no experience. Miss Stroud is to spend about 20 hours a week working for the partnership. Mr. Santo is to work full-time. Which method of distributing partnership earnings would you suggest for this partnership? Explain your answer.

Case 2

The P & A partnership does not prepare a distribution of net income statement or an owners' equity statement at the end of a fiscal period. Instead, the information is all reported in detail on the partnership's balance sheet. Is this an acceptable practice? Explain your answer.

AUTOMATED ACCOUNTING

GENERATING FINANCIAL REPORTS FOR A PARTNERSHIP

Financial statements for partnerships are similar to the statements prepared for other types of business organizations. The primary difference is the distribution of net income or loss to the partners.

Partnership with Equal Distribution

When the Company Info. tab of the Customize Accounting System window specifies the business organization as Partnership Equal Distribution, *Automated Accounting 7.0* will perform all closing entries needed at the end of the fiscal period.

Partnership with Unequal Distribution

When the Company Info. tab specifies the business organization as Partnership Unequal Distribution, *Automated Accounting 7.0* will close revenue and expense accounts. However, journal entries must be entered to distribute the income or loss to the partners' accounts. The journal entries required to complete the closing process are:

1. Closing the amount in Income Summary to the partners' capital accounts.

2. Closing the partners' drawing accounts to their capital accounts.

Income Statement

The software will display net income or loss in two formats. The format is specified in the Company Info. tab of the Customize Accounting System window.

Report by Fiscal Period

This format shows the profitability of the business from the beginning of the fiscal year until the time when the income statement is displayed.

Report by Month and Year

This format shows profitability for the current month and for the year to date.

AUTOMATING MASTERY PROBLEM 22-5

Instructions:

1. Load *Automated Accounting 7.0* or higher software.

2. Select database A22-5 (Advanced Course Mastery Problem 22-5) from the accounting template disk.

3. Select File from the menu bar and choose the Save As menu command. Key the path to the drive and directory that contains your data files. Save the database with a file name of XXX225 (where XXX are your initials).

4. Access Problem Instructions through the Help menu. Read the Problem Instruction screen.

5. Refer to page 627 for data used in this problem.

6. Exit the Automated Accounting software.

AUTOMATING CHALLENGE PROBLEM 22-6

Instructions:

1. Load *Automated Accounting 7.0* or higher software.

2. Select database A22-6 (Advanced Course Mastery Problem 22-6) from the accounting template disk.

3. Select File from the menu bar and choose the Save As menu command. Key the path to the drive and directory that contains your data files. Save the database with a file name of XXX226 (where XXX are your initials).

4. Access Problem Instructions through the Help menu. Read the Problem Instruction screen.

5. Refer to page 627 for data used in this problem.

6. Exit the Automated Accounting software.

23

Budgeting and Accounting for a Not-for-Profit Organization

AFTER STUDYING CHAPTER 23, YOU WILL BE ABLE TO:

1. Define accounting terms related to budgeting and accounting for a not-for-profit governmental organization.

2. Identify accounting concepts and practices related to budgeting and accounting for a not-for-profit governmental organization.

3. Describe the process used to develop an operating budget.

4. Journalize budget transactions for a not-for-profit organization.

5. Journalize revenues for a not-for-profit organization.

6. Journalize expenditures, encumbrances, and other transactions for a not-for-profit organization.

All businesses, whether organized as proprietorships, partnerships, or corporations, have a common objective—to earn a profit. Some organizations are formed for purposes other than earning a profit. An organization providing goods or services with neither a conscious motive nor expectation of earning a profit is called a **not-for-profit organization**. Not-for-profit organizations are also referred to as non-profit organizations.

Both businesses and not-for-profit organizations provide goods and/or services. Business owners generally invest in a business for the purpose of earning a profit. Not-for-profit organizations, however, are formed to provide needed goods or services to a group of individuals without regard to earning a profit. The primary purpose of the organization is to make available the needed goods or services that may not be available otherwise.

TERMS PREVIEW

not-for-profit
   organization
fund
expenditure
operating budget
appropriations
tax levy
encumbrance
general fixed assets
certificate of deposit

F.Y.I.

GASB has proposed a new statement. If this new statement is adopted, governmental entities would be required to prepare financial statements from an entity-wide perspective and a fund perspective. Governmental entities would be required to place a value on all infrastructure assets, such as roads and curbs, and to set up depreciation schedules for these assets.

ACCOUNTING
IN YOUR CAREER

BUILDING A NEW STADIUM

The town of Amity is planning to build a new stadium for the high school. Last year's budget approved funds for acquiring land and obtaining plans from an architect, money that has been spent. The land has been purchased. The architect has completed building plans, and an artist's rendering of the new stadium is displayed in the high school lobby.

This year's budget approved by the legislature has a revenue amount for proceeds from a tax levy for building the new stadium and an expenditures account for the new stadium. The expenditure is contingent on voter approval of the tax levy.

A major employer has announced plans to leave Amity and widespread unemployment is expected. Citizens are not optimistic about the economic situation in the town and the levy for the new stadium is defeated in the special election. Students and staff at the high school are disappointed that the new stadium cannot be built.

John Rutherford, superintendent of schools, and Joan Tarsus, chair of the board of education, meet to discuss the situation. They review the year's education budget, looking for ways to economize so that they can still proceed with the building of the new stadium. They discover that they can afford the new stadium if they cut the staff by 10%, delay budgeted new employees until next year, postpone budgeted new textbook purchases, and cancel all planned building maintenance.

They know that the stadium issue is popular in Amity and that with better economic conditions the voters would have approved the levy. Therefore, they decide to implement the budget cuts they have planned and hire a contractor to break ground for the new stadium.

Critical Thinking

1. What are the sources of revenue in your state and city?
2. Have John Rutherford and Joan Tarsus made an appropriate decision in going ahead with the stadium construction?

NATURE OF NOT-FOR-PROFIT ORGANIZATIONS

Figure 23-1

Types of Not-for-Profit Organizations

Not-for-profit organizations may differ as to the types of goods or services they provide, their sources of revenues, or the procedures they use to select their leaders or managers. Major types of not-for-profit organizations are as follows.

1. Governmental, such as federal, state, county, city, town, and village.

2. Educational, such as elementary, secondary, and post-secondary schools.

3. Health, such as hospitals and nursing homes.

4. Charitable, such as United Way, United Fund, and American Red Cross.

5. Foundational, including trusts and corporations organized for charitable and educational purposes, such as the Carnegie Foundation and the Ford Foundation.

6. Religious, such as churches and other religious organizations.

Since not-for-profit organizations have a common objective, they share many of the same needs for financial information. Thus, the accounting system and many of the financial reports are similar for all not-for-profit organizations. However, because of differences in goods or services provided, sources of revenues, or methods of leadership selection, their accounting procedures and reports are modified for the specific type of organization.

Purpose of Governmental Organizations

All individuals are affected by or are members of one or more governmental organizations. Also, more individuals are employed by governmental organizations than any other type of not-for-profit organization. Therefore, Chapters 23 and 24 emphasize accounting for local governmental organizations.

A governmental organization's purpose is normally to provide needed goods or services that would be impossible for individuals to provide for themselves. For example, the federal government provides national defense for all citizens of the nation. Individual states and cities would find it difficult and very inefficient to provide for their own defense from foreign pressures. Similarly, cities provide police and fire protection that would be very expensive and inefficient for individuals to provide for themselves.

A governmental organization has four major characteristics that affect the accounting system.

1. *No profit motive exists.* A business' success can be measured by whether or not it earns a profit. A business that is inefficient, or not competitive, will not earn a profit. Without profits, a business will soon be unable to continue operations. However, since a governmental organization does not intend to earn a profit, success is much more difficult to measure. As long as money is available, a governmental organization can continue to operate regardless of its efficiency or inefficiency.

2. *Leadership is subject to frequent change.* Policy-making bodies of governmental organizations are generally elected by popular vote of the group's members. Thus, the leadership depends on the political process and may change frequently. Therefore, policies and long-range goals may change when the leadership changes. These frequent changes make effective long-range planning difficult.

3. *Users of services do not necessarily pay for the services.* Revenues for governmental organizations are provided primarily by taxation on property, retail sales, or income. Organization members who have the greatest amount of property or income provide the greatest amount of revenues. However, the goods or services are normally provided to all members of the organization based on need. The amount that individuals pay is not directly related to the benefits they receive. Therefore, individuals have decreased incentive for ensuring that services are administered efficiently.

4. *Conflicting pressures for differing objectives exist.* No direct relationship exists between who pays for and who receives the services provided by a governmental organization. Therefore, individuals generally support the organizational objective most advantageous to themselves. For example, some citizens of a city may place the construction of a city library high on their list of priorities. Others, who seldom use a library, may place this project low on their list of priorities. Consequently, services provided by a governmental organization are usually determined through negotiation and compromise among the different interest groups. This procedure does not necessarily provide for the best services or the most efficiency.

The characteristics of governmental organizations have affected the development of governmental accounting systems. Therefore, numerous financial and legal regulations for determining the source and amount of revenues and for planning and executing expenditures of funds are required.

Characteristics of Governmental Accounting Systems

Six accounting practices are similar for business and governmental organizations.

1. The accounting equation (assets equal liabilities plus equities) is applied.

2. An appropriate chart of accounts is prepared.

3. Transactions are analyzed into debit and credit elements.

4. Transactions are journalized and posted to ledgers.

5. Financial statements are prepared for each fiscal period.

6. Most of the same accounting concepts are applied.

The characteristics of governmental organizations and the conditions in which they operate create information and control requirements that differ from those of businesses. Because of these differences, governmental accounting and financial reporting differ in several ways from business accounting and financial reporting.

Eastfield
General Fund

ASSETS

Cash	$350,000.00
Taxes Receivable	50,000.00
Total Assets	$400,000.00

LIABILITIES AND FUND EQUITY

Liabilities:	
Accounts Payable	$ 60,000.00
Fund Equity:	
Fund Balance	340,000.00
Total Liabilities and Fund Equity	$400,000.00

Eastfield
Library Fund

ASSETS

Cash	$70,000.00

LIABILITIES AND FUND EQUITY

Liabilities:	
Accounts Payable	$ 5,000.00
Fund Equity:	
Fund Balance	65,000.00
Total Liabilities and Fund Equity	$70,000.00

Figure 23-2

The accounting system for a business includes a single accounting entity. That is, all accounts used to record accounting transactions for the entire business are part of a single set of accounts. Within this set of accounts, assets must equal liabilities plus equities. A governmental accounting entity with a set of accounts in which assets always equal liabilities plus equities is called a **fund**. A governmental unit, such as a city, may have several different funds.

A fund accounting system emphasizes strong controls on the use of funds. The amount in a fund can be spent only for the specified purpose of the fund. Different funds may be created for different purposes. For example, the town of Eastfield has two funds: (1) a general fund and (2) a library fund. Balance sheets for the two funds are shown in Figure 23-2.

The town of Eastfield has total assets of $470,000.00 (general fund, $400,00.00, *plus* library fund, $70,000.00). However, the assets are accounted for separately. Assets in the library fund may be used only for library purposes. General fund assets may be used for other authorized town expenditures. Each fund is kept as a separate set of accounts.

The fund equity, similar to owners' equity for a business, is the net amount of assets available for use. For example, Eastfield's library fund equity is $65,000.00 (assets, $70,000.00, *less* liabilities, $5,000.00). If $6,000.00 cash is spent for library salaries, total assets available for spending would be reduced to $64,000.00 ($70,000.00 *less* $6,000.00). The fund equity account, **Fund Balance**, would be reduced to $59,000.00 (assets, $64,000.00, *less* liabilities, $5,000.00). After this transaction, the fund remains in balance. The governmental accounting equation, assets equal liabilities plus fund equity, is in balance.

Types of funds vary with the type of not-for-profit organization and the types of goods or services provided. A unique set of funds normally is used for each type of organization—federal government, state and local governments, hospitals, schools, etc.

Modified Accrual Accounting

Most businesses use accrual accounting so that revenue and expenses incurred during a fiscal period determine the resulting net income for the period. (CONCEPT: *Matching Expenses with Revenue*) In governmental accounting, modified accrual accounting is used. In modified accrual accounting, revenues are recorded in the accounting period in which they become measurable and available. For example, property taxes become measurable and available as soon as the amount is determined and tax statements are sent to property owners. However, sales taxes cannot be determined until sales are made. Thus, sales tax revenue is recognized when the taxes are received from merchants.

DIFFERENCE BETWEEN EXPENSES AND EXPENDITURES

Cash disbursements and liabilities incurred for the cost of goods delivered or services rendered are called **expenditures**. In modified accrual accounting, expenditures are generally recognized when a liability is incurred. Therefore, governmental organizations record expenditures rather than expenses. An important distinction is made between expenditures and expenses. Businesses emphasize matching expenses with revenue in each fiscal period. However, governmental accounting emphasizes determining and controlling revenues and expenditures during a fiscal period. For example, if a business buys a truck, **Plant Asset** or **Truck** is debited and **Cash** or **Notes Payable** is credited. No expense is incurred until the truck is used. If a governmental organization buys a truck, **Expenditure** is debited and **Cash** or **Notes Payable** is credited. The amount of money spent or liability incurred is recorded, not the expense. Thus, expenditures are decreases in net financial resources. Emphasis is placed on control of the net financial resources, not on matching expenses with revenue. Thus, modified accrual accounting is used for measuring financial position and operating results of governmental organizations.

FINANCIAL REPORTING EMPHASIS

Both business and governmental organizations prepare financial statements at the end of a fiscal period. *(CONCEPT: Accounting Period Cycle)* However, because the organizations have different objectives, their charts of accounts and statements differ. The chart of accounts for Sparta appears in Figure 23-3.

The two most common financial statements prepared by businesses are an income statement and a balance sheet. The two most common financial statements prepared by governmental organizations are a statement of revenues, expenditures, and changes in fund balance and a balance sheet (described in Chapter 24).

Businesses prepare income statements to report the amount of net income earned during a fiscal period. Earning a net income is not an objective of governmental organizations. However, identifying and controlling the sources of revenues and the expenditure of funds are emphasized as part of the control process. Therefore, a statement of revenues, expenditures, and changes in fund balance is prepared.

A business' balance sheet reports the assets, liabilities, and owners' equity of the business at the end of a fiscal period. A governmental organization's balance sheet also reports the current assets and liabilities of the organization at the end of a fiscal period. However, no specific ownership of a governmental organization exists. Therefore, assets less liabilities is reported as fund equity.

BUDGETING

Both businesses and governmental organizations prepare budgets. The primary purpose of all budgets is planning and control. For businesses, planning is required to prepare the budget. During the fiscal period, budgeted amounts are compared with actual amounts to provide information to management about the effectiveness of cost control. Planning is also required to prepare a budget for a governmental organization. However, an approved governmental budget becomes (1) a legal authorization to spend and (2) a legal limit on the amount that can be spent.

TOWN OF SPARTA GENERAL FUND CHART OF ACCOUNTS

Balance Sheet Accounts

(1000) Assets
1010	Cash
1020	Taxes Receivable—Current
1030	Allowance for Uncollectible Taxes—Current
1040	Taxes Receivable—Delinquent
1050	Allowance for Uncollectible Taxes—Delinquent
1060	Interest Receivable
1070	Allowance for Uncollectible Interest
1080	Inventory of Supplies
1090	Investments—Short Term

(2000) Liabilities
2010	Accounts Payable
2020	Notes Payable

(3000) Fund Equity
3010	Unreserved Fund Balance
3020	Reserve for Encumbrances—Current Year
3030	Reserve for Encumbrances—Prior Year
3040	Reserve for Inventory of Supplies

Revenue and Expenditure Accounts

(4000) Revenues
4010	Property Tax Revenue
4020	Interest Revenue
4030	Other Revenue

(5000) Expenditures

5100 GENERAL GOVERNMENT
5110	Expenditure—Personnel, General Government
5120	Expenditure—Supplies, General Government
5130	Expenditure—Other Charges, General Government
5140	Expenditure—Capital Outlays, General Government

5200 PUBLIC SAFETY
5210	Expenditure—Personnel, Public Safety
5220	Expenditure—Supplies, Public Safety
5230	Expenditure—Other Charges, Public Safety
5240	Expenditure—Capital Outlays, Public Safety

5300 PUBLIC WORKS
5310	Expenditure—Personnel, Public Works
5320	Expenditure—Supplies, Public Works
5330	Expenditure—Other Charges, Public Works
5340	Expenditure—Capital Outlays, Public Works

5400 RECREATION
5410	Expenditure—Personnel, Recreation
5420	Expenditure—Supplies, Recreation
5430	Expenditure—Other Charges, Recreation
5440	Expenditure—Capital Outlays, Recreation

Budgetary Accounts

(6000) Budgetary
6010	Estimated Revenues
6020	Appropriations
6030	Budgetary Fund Balance

6100 GENERAL GOVERNMENT
6110	Encumbrance—Personnel, General Government
6120	Encumbrance—Supplies, General Government
6130	Encumbrance—Other Charges, General Government
6140	Encumbrance—Capital Outlays, General Government

6200 PUBLIC SAFETY
6210	Encumbrance—Personnel, Public Safety
6220	Encumbrance—Supplies, Public Safety
6230	Encumbrance—Other Charges, Public Safety
6240	Encumbrance—Capital Outlays, Public Safety

6300 PUBLIC WORKS
6310	Encumbrance—Personnel, Public Works
6320	Encumbrance—Supplies, Public Works
6330	Encumbrance—Other Charges, Public Works
6340	Encumbrance—Capital Outlays, Public Works

6400 RECREATION
6410	Encumbrance—Personnel, Recreation
6420	Encumbrance—Supplies, Recreation
6430	Encumbrance—Other Charges, Recreation
6440	Encumbrance—Capital Outlays, Recreation

The chart of accounts for Sparta is illustrated above for ready reference as you study Chapters 23 and 24 of this textbook.

Figure 23-3

REMEMBER

Governmental organizations record expenditures rather than expenses.

Town of Sparta
Annual Operating Budget—General Fund
For Year Ended December 31, 20--

ESTIMATED REVENUES		
Property Tax	$1,594,000.00	
Interest	10,000.00	
Other	2,500.00	
Total Estimated Revenues		$1,606,500.00
ESTIMATED EXPENDITURES AND BUDGETARY FUND BALANCE		
General Government:		
Personnel	$ 263,280.00	
Supplies	12,150.00	
Other Charges	113,400.00	
Capital Outlays	16,220.00	
Total General Government		$ 405,050.00
Public Safety:		
Personnel	$ 589,200.00	
Supplies	20,000.00	
Other Charges	153,150.00	
Capital Outlays	90,300.00	
Total Public Safety		852,650.00
Public Works:		
Personnel	$ 113,400.00	
Supplies	5,600.00	
Other Charges	47,500.00	
Capital Outlays	51,500.00	
Total Public Works		218,000.00
Recreation:		
Personnel	$ 58,260.00	
Supplies	1,970.00	
Other Charges	25,250.00	
Capital Outlays	11,620.00	
Total Recreation		97,100.00
Total Estimated Expenditures		$1,572,800.00
Budgetary Fund Balance		33,700.00
Total Estimated Expenditures and Budgetary Fund Balance		$1,606,500.00

Figure 23-4

A plan of current expenditures and the proposed means of financing those expenditures is called an **operating budget**. A governmental fund's annual operating budget authorizes and provides the basis for control of financial operations during a fiscal year. Since each governmental fund is a separate accounting entity, an operating budget is normally prepared to show the estimated revenues, estimated expenditures, and budgetary fund balance for each fund. The operating budget in Figure 23-4 was prepared for the general fund of the town of Sparta.

Sparta organizes revenue accounts by source of revenue. Expenditure accounts are organized by department and type of expenditure. Some organizations maintain subsidiary accounts for each of the general ledger accounts to provide more detail about the sources of revenues and types of expenditures. Because of its small size, Sparta maintains only the general ledger accounts listed in its chart of accounts, Figure 23-3.

Some basic procedures are followed to prepare an annual governmental operating budget.

1. Departments of the governmental organization submit budget requests to the chief executive of the organization. Requests are based on an analysis of expenditures for the previous year and expected changes in expenditures for the coming year.

2. The chief executive reviews budget requests with department heads. When budget requests are acceptable to the chief executive, departmental requests are consolidated into a single budget request for the organization. The chief executive then submits the operating budget to the legislative body. The legislative body is a group of persons normally elected by the citizens/members of the organization and granted authority to make laws for the organization.

3. The legislative body approves the operating budget. The approved operating budget becomes an authorization to spend the amounts listed in the budget. Before the operating budget can be approved, revenues plus the available amount of fund equity must be at least as great as the expenditures. If the expenditures are more than the total of expected revenues and available fund equity, the expected sources of revenue must be increased or expenditures decreased.

Sparta is a small town with a town manager and five town council members. The council members are elected to their positions. One member of the council serves as mayor. The council serves as the legislative body for Sparta. The council appoints the town manager who works full time as chief executive of the town. Sparta has three department heads: public safety director, public works director, and recreation director. Because Sparta is small and most of its revenues come from property taxes, the accounting system contains only one fund—a general fund.

At the request of the town manager, Sparta's three department heads analyze the current year's expenditures and expected changes, and then prepare budget requests for the next year. The town manager reviews the budget requests and prepares a single operating budget for Sparta's general fund for next year. The operating budget is submitted to the town council.

The town council represents the interests of all the town's citizens. Thus, the council should evaluate the operating budget from at least four perspectives. (1) Are adequate services being provided? (2) Are the services desired by a majority of citizens? (3) Are the amounts requested essential to provide the desired level of services? (4) Does the city have the financial capacity to support the budget?

The approved operating budget determines the amount of revenues needed for the year. The town's tax rate necessary to provide the needed funds for the approved operating budget is then determined.

After completing its review, the Sparta council formally approves next year's governmental operating budget. The approved governmental operating budget becomes authorization for the town manager and department heads to make expenditures as specified in the budget.

Approval of an annual governmental operating budget by the proper authorities provides legal authorization to make expenditures in accordance with the approved budget. Authorizations to make expenditures for specified purposes are called **appropriations**. Sparta's approved operating budget has appropriations that authorize expenditures up to the amounts stated in the budget. The tax rate is then set at a rate that will raise at least enough revenue to cover the appropriations.

Many governmental organizations have restrictions as to the amount that taxes can be increased. Public hearings may be required before taxes can be increased. A formal vote in an election may also be required. If a proposed operating budget exceeds the amount of taxes and other estimated revenue, the budget may need to be reduced to the level of available revenues.

	DATE		ACCOUNT TITLE	DOC. NO.	POST. REF.	GENERAL				CASH				
---	---	---	---	---	---	DEBIT	CREDIT			DEBIT		CREDIT		
1	Jan.²⁰⁻⁻	2	Estimated Revenues	M35		1606 5 0 0 00								1
2			Appropriations				1572 8 0 0 00							2
3			Budgetary Fund Balance				33 7 0 0 00							3

JOURNAL — PAGE 1

Figure 23-5

As an additional control measure, Sparta journalizes its approved operating budget as shown in Figure 23-5. Budgetary accounts are for control purposes and are closed at the end of a fiscal period.

Governmental organizations, like businesses, record accounting transactions initially in a journal. Source documents are the basis for the journal entries. Governmental organizations may use a multi-column journal, a general journal, or special journals adapted to the organization's needs. Sparta uses a multi-column journal.

January 2. Recorded Sparta's approved operating budget: estimated revenues, $1,606,500.00; appropriations, $1,572,800.00; budgetary fund balance, $33,700.00. Memorandum No. 35.

Estimated Revenues is increased by a debit for the amount of budgeted revenues, *$1,606,500.00*. Estimated Revenues has a normal debit balance, opposite the normal credit balance of an actual revenue account. Appropriations is increased by a credit for the amount of Sparta's budgeted expenditures, *$1,572,800.00*. Appropriations has a normal credit balance, opposite the normal debit balance of the actual expenditure accounts. Budgetary Fund Balance is increased by a credit, *$33,700.00* (estimated revenues, $1,606,500.00, *less* appropriations, $1,572,800.00).

A separate revenue account will be credited as revenues are earned. Balances of the two accounts, Estimated Revenues and Revenues, can be reviewed to compare the amount of actual revenues earned and the amount of revenues estimated to be earned. If actual revenues are not as great as expected, expenditures may need

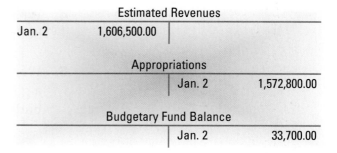

to be reduced to avoid exceeding available funds. Recording the estimated revenues in the budgetary account Estimated Revenues provides this planning and control information.

Separate expenditure accounts will be debited as actual expenditures are made. Ensuring that expenditures do not exceed the appropriations (budgeted expenditures) is essential for governmental organizations. Periodically, the appropriations account balance can be compared with the total of expenditure account balances to avoid overspending appropriations. Appropriations less total expenditures is the amount still available for spending. Recording appropriations in the budgetary account Appropriations provides this additional control information. Each department also keeps records of its appropriated and expended amounts to ensure that no department exceeds its appropriation amounts.

If appropriations exceed estimated revenues, Budgetary Fund Balance is debited to make the total debits equal the total credits. However, most governmental organizations normally set their revenue sources slightly above appropriations to avoid exceeding appropriations.

TERMS REVIEW

not-for-profit organization
fund
expenditure
operating budget
appropriations

AUDIT YOUR UNDERSTANDING

1. What four characteristics affect the accounting system for a governmental organization?

2. List the accounting practices that are similar for businesses and governmental organizations.

3. What is a fund?

4. What is the purpose of a governmental operating budget?

5. What accounts are debited and credited to journalize a governmental organization's approved operating budget?

WORK TOGETHER

Journalizing governmental operating budgets

The town of Powell approved its annual general fund operating budgets effective January 1 of the current year. Your instructor will guide you through the following example.

6. Journalize the entry to record the following operating budget for the town of Powell.

Estimated Revenues	Appropriations	Budgetary Fund Balance
$843,000.00	$836,800.00	$6,200.00

ON YOUR OWN

Journalizing governmental operating budgets

The town of Worthington approved its annual general fund operating budgets effective January 1 of the current year. Work independently to complete the following problem.

7. Journalize the entry to record the following operating budget for the town of Worthington.

Estimated Revenues	Appropriations	Budgetary Fund Balance
$2,461,000.00	$2,423,000.00	$38,000.00

JOURNALIZING CURRENT PROPERTY TAX REVENUES

1. Total taxes levied.

DATE	ACCOUNT TITLE	DOC. NO.	POST. REF.	GENERAL DEBIT	GENERAL CREDIT	CASH DEBIT	CASH CREDIT	
4	2 Taxes Receivable—Current	M36		1610 00 0 00				4
5	Allowance for Uncollectible Taxes—Current				16 0 00 00			5
6	Property Tax Revenue				1594 00 0 00			6

JOURNAL PAGE *1*

2. Estimated losses for taxes not collected.

3. Revenue recognized from tax levy.

Figure 23-6

Governmental fund revenues are recorded in the accounting period in which the revenues become measurable and available.

When property tax rates have been set and tax amounts calculated, taxes are levied on all taxable property. Authorized action taken by a governmental organization to collect taxes by legal authority is called a **tax levy**. Levied property taxes are considered measurable and available because they become a legal obligation of property owners. Therefore, when the levy is made, a journal entry is made to record property tax revenue as shown in Figure 23-6. Although tax levies are legal obligations of property owners, some property owners do not pay their taxes. Legal action may eventually be taken against these property owners in an effort to collect the taxes. Even with these actions, a government generally does not collect all the taxes

levied. On January 2, Sparta authorized its tax levy and sent out property tax statements to property owners. Sparta estimated that $16,000.00 of property taxes will not be collected.

> *January 2. Recorded property tax levy: taxes receivable—current, $1,610,000.00; allowance for uncollectible taxes—current, $16,000.00; property tax revenue, $1,594,000.00. Memorandum No. 36.*

Taxes Receivable—Current	
Jan. 2 1,610,000.00	

Allowance for Uncollectible Taxes—Current	
	Jan. 2 16,000.00

Property Tax Revenue	
	Jan. 2 1,594,000.00

S T E P S **Journalizing current property tax revenue**

1. Debit *Taxes Receivable—Current* for the total amount of tax levied, $1,610,000.00. This amount is the total of the tax statements sent to taxpayers.

2. Credit the contra asset account, *Allowance for Uncollectible Taxes—Current*, for the amount of estimated loss, $16,000.00.

3. Credit the revenue account, *Property Tax Revenue*, for the amount of revenue recognized, $1,594,000.00. This amount is the total tax levy, $1,610,000.00, *less* the allowance for current uncollectible taxes, $16,000.00.

	DATE	ACCOUNT TITLE	DOC. NO.	POST. REF.	GENERAL		CASH	
					DEBIT	CREDIT	DEBIT	CREDIT
12	10	Taxes Receivable—Current	R371			194 0 0 0 00	194 0 0 0 00		12

JOURNAL — PAGE 3

Figure 23-7

Cash received for property taxes reduces the taxes receivable account as shown in Figure 23-7.

> **January 10. Received cash for current taxes receivable, $194,000.00. Receipt No. 371.**

Cash is increased by a debit for the amount of cash received, $194,000.00. Taxes Receivable—

Current is decreased by a credit for the same amount, $194,000.00.

Cash	
Jan. 10 194,000.00	

Taxes Receivable—Current	
Bal. 1,610,000.00	Jan. 10 194,000.00

OTHER REVENUE

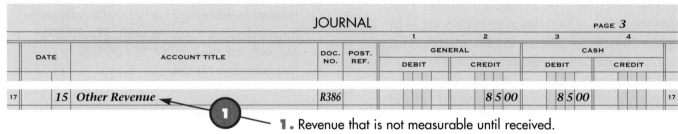

JOURNAL — PAGE 3

	DATE	ACCOUNT TITLE	DOC. NO.	POST. REF.	GENERAL		CASH	
					DEBIT	CREDIT	DEBIT	CREDIT
17	15	Other Revenue	R386			8 5 00	8 5 00		17

1. Revenue that is not measurable until received.

Figure 23-8

Some revenues, such as fines, inspection charges, parking meter receipts, and penalties, are normally not known and, thus, are not measurable until cash is received. A journal entry to record such revenues, therefore, is generally made only when cash is received as shown in Figure 23-8.

> **January 15. Received cash from traffic fines, $85.00. Receipt No. 386.**

Cash is increased by a debit for the amount of cash received, $85.00. Other Revenue is increased by a credit for the same amount, $85.00.

Cash	
Jan. 15 85.00	

Other Revenue	
	Jan. 15 85.00

F.Y.I.

In some states, the operating budget is not officially approved until it is reviewed by tax committees at the county and state level.

					GENERAL		CASH	
DATE		ACCOUNT TITLE	DOC. NO.	POST. REF.	DEBIT	CREDIT	DEBIT	CREDIT
Mar.	1	Taxes Receivable—Delinquent	M65		64 2 0 0 00			
		Allowance for Uncollectible Taxes—Current			16 0 0 0 00			
		Taxes Receivable—Current				64 2 0 0 00		
		Allowance for Uncollectible Taxes—Delinquent				16 0 0 0 00		
	20	Taxes Receivable—Delinquent	R420			12 0 0 0 00	12 0 0 0 00	

JOURNAL — PAGE 21

1. Entry to record delinquent property taxes.

2. Entry to record collection of delinquent property taxes.

Figure 23-9

Tax payments specify the date that property taxes are due and payable. Taxes not paid by the specified date are reclassified as delinquent. Sparta's property taxes are due on February 28. On March 1, taxes not paid are considered delinquent. On that date, a journal entry is made to transfer uncollected taxes from current to delinquent status as shown in Figure 23-9.

Taxes that Sparta expects to collect are accounted for by using two accounts, **Taxes Receivable—Current** and **Allowance for Uncollectible Taxes—Current**. Delinquent taxes are accounted for using two accounts, **Taxes Receivable—Delinquent** and **Allowance for Uncollectible Taxes—Delinquent**. A journal entry transfers the balances of the two current accounts to the two delinquent accounts.

March 1. Recorded reclassification of current taxes receivable to delinquent status, $64,200.00, and the accompanying allowance for uncollectible accounts, $16,000.00. Memorandum No. 65.

Taxes Receivable—Delinquent	
Mar. 1 64,200.00	

Allowance for Uncollectible Taxes—Current	
Mar. 1 16,000.00	Bal. 16,000.00

Taxes Receivable—Current	
Bal. 64,200.00	Mar. 1 64,200.00

Allowance for Uncollectible Taxes—Delinquent	
	Mar. 1 16,000.00

S T E P S — **Journalizing entry to record delinquent property taxes**

1. Debit *Taxes Receivable—Delinquent* for the amount of current taxes becoming delinquent, $64,200.00. Debit the contra asset account, *Allowance for Uncollectible Taxes—Current*, for the balance in that account, $16,000.00.

2. Credit *Taxes Receivable—Current* for the amount of current taxes becoming delinquent, $64,200.00. Credit *Allowance for Uncollectible Taxes—Delinquent* for the amount of allowance on the delinquent taxes, $16,000.00.

Collection of Delinquent Property Taxes

Although some taxes become delinquent, Sparta continues efforts to collect these taxes. Cash received for delinquent taxes reduces **Taxes Receivable—Delinquent** as shown in Figure 23-9.

March 20. Received cash for delinquent taxes receivable, $12,000.00. Receipt No. 420.

Cash is increased by a debit for the amount received, $12,000.00. Taxes Receivable—Delinquent is decreased by a credit for the same amount, $12,000.00.

 **TERM REVIEW**

tax levy

 **AUDIT YOUR UNDERSTANDING**

1. When is a journal entry made to record property tax revenue?

2. What accounts are affected, and how, when a taxpayer pays current property taxes?

3. What accounts are affected, and how, when a taxpayer pays property taxes two months after the due date?

 **WORK TOGETHER**

Journalizing governmental revenue transactions

Groveport's town council recently approved the town's general fund operating budget for the current year. Use page 1 of the journal provided in the *Working Papers*. Your instructor will guide you through the following examples.

Jan. 1. Recorded property tax levy: taxes receivable—current, $2,400,000.00; allowance for uncollectible taxes—current, $24,000.00; property tax revenue, $2,376,000.00. M34.

14. Received cash from traffic fines, $1,354.00. R84. (Other Revenue)

Feb. 11. Received cash for current taxes receivable, $973,000.00. R113.

Mar. 1. Recorded reclassification of current taxes receivable to delinquent status, $96,200.00, and the accompanying allowance for uncollectible accounts, $24,000.00. M68.

12. Received cash for delinquent taxes receivable, $30,300.00. R157.

4. Journalize the selected transactions.

 **ON YOUR OWN**

Journalizing governmental revenue transactions

Centuria's town council recently approved the town's general fund operating budget for the current year. Use page 1 of the journal provided in the *Working Papers*. Work independently to complete the following problem.

Jan. 1. Recorded property tax levy: taxes receivable—current, $1,200,000.00; allowance for uncollectible taxes—current, $12,000.00; property tax revenue, $1,188,000.00. M163.

20. Received cash from parking meter receipts, $894.00. R541. (Other Revenue)

Feb. 11. Received cash for current taxes receivable, $485,200.00. R596.

Mar. 1. Recorded reclassification of current taxes receivable to delinquent status, $48,100.00, and the accompanying allowance for uncollectible accounts, $12,000.00. M225.

15. Received cash for delinquent taxes receivable, $15,150.00. R628.

5. Journalize the selected transactions.

JOURNALIZING EXPENDITURES

	DATE	ACCOUNT TITLE	DOC. NO.	POST. REF.	GENERAL DEBIT	GENERAL CREDIT	CASH DEBIT	CASH CREDIT	
1	20-- Jan. 10	Expenditure—Other Charges, Public Safety	C355		2 9 0 00			2 9 0 00	1

Figure 23-10

A primary objective of governmental accounting is to control the financial resources. Governmental accounting focuses on measuring changes in financial resources rather than determining net income. Therefore, in governmental accounting, expenditures rather than expenses are recorded. The use of two special accounting procedures enhances the control of expenditures.

1. Expenditures are classified into categories to assign specific responsibility for the expenditure and to analyze the purpose of the expenditure. For example, Expenditure—Personnel, Public Safety is one of Sparta's expenditure accounts. Personnel indicates the type of expenditure (salaries for personnel). Public Safety indicates the department for which the personnel expenditures were made.

2. Budgetary accounts are used to record estimated amounts of expenditures to protect against overspending the budgeted amounts. To accomplish this control procedure, encumbrance accounts are used. A commitment to pay for goods or services that have been ordered but not yet provided is called an **encumbrance**. When an order that will require a future expenditure is placed, a budgetary encumbrance account is debited for the estimated amount. This entry reduces the fund balance and ensures that commitments and expenditures will not be greater than funds available.

Exact amounts of some expenditures are known as soon as the obligation is determined.

For example, the amount and due date of payment for utility costs is known when the utility statement is received. The entry to record the expenditure is shown in Figure 23-10.

January 10. Paid cash for electrical service in public safety department, $290.00. Check No. 355.

Expenditure—Other Charges, Public Safety is increased by a debit for the cost of the electrical service, $290.00. Cash is decreased by a credit for the same amount, $290.00.

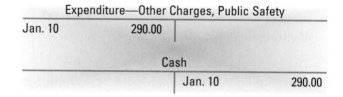

The major control of expenditures is achieved by holding department heads accountable for expenditures in their department. Classification of expenditures is used to analyze major types of expenditures within each department. For Sparta, each department's expenditures are recorded in one of four classifications: personnel, supplies, other charges, or capital outlays. The other charges classification is used for all expenditures except salaries and related personnel expenditures, supplies expenditures, and capital outlays. Capital outlays is used for expenditures that will benefit future years.

						GENERAL		CASH	
	DATE	ACCOUNT TITLE	DOC. NO.	POST. REF.	DEBIT	CREDIT	DEBIT	CREDIT	
12	12	Encumbrance—Supplies, Public Works	M40		380 00				12
13		Reserve for Encumbrances—Current Year				380 00			13

JOURNAL — PAGE 3

Figure 23-11

To avoid spending more resources than are available, encumbrance accounts are used. When goods or services are ordered that will be provided at a later date, an obligation for a future expenditure is made. Resources have not yet been used, but there is a promise to give up those resources when ordered goods or services are delivered. Encumbering resources is a way of setting aside the amount estimated to be needed to pay for the ordered goods or services. When the goods or services are delivered, the estimated amount is removed from the encumbrance account and the exact amount of the expenditure is journalized in an expenditure account.

> *January 12. Encumbered estimated amount for supplies in public works department, $380.00. Memorandum No. 40.*

The budgetary account Encumbrance—Supplies, Public Works is increased by a debit for the amount of the order, *$380.00*. The fund equity account Reserve for Encumbrances—Current Year is increased by a credit for the amount of the supplies order, *$380.00* as shown in Figure 23-11. This account serves as an offsetting account for the encumbrance account and shows that this amount of the fund equity is reserved for an encumbrance.

Expenditures plus encumbrances for a specific account equal the total commitment that has been made against the appropriated amount for that account. The appropriated amount less

Encumbrance—Supplies, Public Works	
Jan. 12 380.00	

Reserve for Encumbrance—Current Year	
	Jan. 12 380.00

the encumbrances and expenditures equals the amount that can still be spent. For example, Sparta appropriated $5,600.00 for supplies for the public works department. If expenditures are $900.00 and encumbrances are $380.00, then $4,320.00 is still available for public works supplies expenditures.

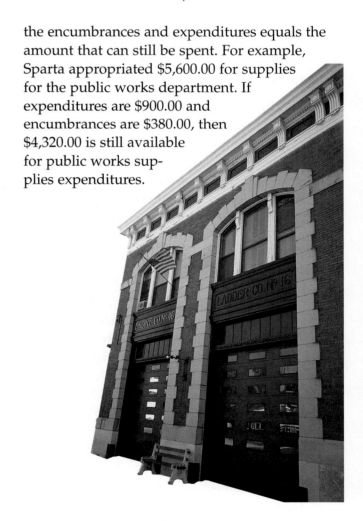

Appropriated for Supplies	–	Expenditures	–	Encumbrances	=	Amount Still Available
$5,600.00	–	$900.00	–	$380.00	=	$4,320.00

JOURNAL   PAGE 6

	DATE	ACCOUNT TITLE	DOC. NO.	POST. REF.	GENERAL DEBIT	GENERAL CREDIT	CASH DEBIT	CASH CREDIT	
10	25	Reserve for Encumbrances—Current Year	M46		380 00				10
11		Encumbrance—Supplies, Public Works				380 00			11
12	25	Expenditure—Supplies, Public Works	C362		375 00			375 00	12
13									13

1. ① Entry to cancel encumbrance.   **2.** ② Entry to record expenditure.

Figure 23-12

When goods or services that have been encumbered are received, two entries must be made.

1. The encumbrance entry is reversed to remove the estimated amount from the encumbrance and reserve for encumbrance accounts.

2. The expenditure is recorded.

These entries are illustrated in Figure 23-12.

January 25. Paid cash for public works department supplies, $375.00, encumbered January 12 per Memorandum No. 40. Memorandum No. 46 and Check No. 362.

Effect of first entry

Reserve for Encumbrances—Current Year

Jan. 25	380.00	Jan. 12	380.00
		(New Bal. zero)	

Encumbrance—Supplies, Public Works

Jan. 12	380.00	Jan. 25	380.00
(New Bal. zero)			

Effect of second entry

Expenditure—Supplies, Public Works

Jan. 25	375.00

Cash

Jan. 25	375.00

S T E P S

Journalizing expenditures for amount encumbered

1. Debit *Reserve for Encumbrances—Current Year* and credit *Encumbrance—Supplies, Public Works* for *380.00.* The entry cancels the encumbrance entry by removing the estimated amount from the encumbrance and reserve for encumbrance accounts. The encumbrance is no longer needed since it is no longer outstanding. The encumbrance was for an estimated amount, *$380.00.* When the supplies were delivered, the actual cost was $375.00. The actual amount of an expenditure sometimes differs from the amount estimated when an order is placed.

2. Debit *Expenditure—Supplies, Public Works* and credit *Cash* for the actual cost of supplies, *$375.00.*

JOURNAL PAGE 21

	DATE	ACCOUNT TITLE	DOC. NO.	POST. REF.	GENERAL DEBIT	GENERAL CREDIT	CASH DEBIT	CASH CREDIT	
17	10	Expenditure—Capital Outlays, Gen. Gov't.	C400		90000			90000	17

Figure 23-13

Governmental organizations are formed to provide services that their members need, not to earn a profit. A business records the cost of property, such as a computer, as an asset. The business then depreciates the asset over its useful life. The depreciation expense is matched with revenue earned in each fiscal period. Since governmental organizations do not earn net income, they have no need for expense information. However, controlling the expenditure of funds is important. When money is spent for capital outlays, the amount is recorded as an expenditure in the period spent even though the item may benefit several accounting periods.

On March 10, Sparta's general government department bought a new computer.

March 10. Paid cash for a computer for general government department, $900.00. Check No. 400.

Expenditure—Capital Outlays, General Government is increased by a debit for the cost of the computer, $900.00. Cash is decreased by a credit for the same amount, $900.00. The journal entry is shown in Figure 23-13.

Governmental properties that benefit future periods are called **general fixed assets**. Most governmental organizations keep a record of general fixed assets. This record helps to safeguard the government's ownership of the property. Sparta keeps a card file with information about each general fixed asset.

JOURNAL PAGE 1

	DATE	ACCOUNT TITLE	DOC. NO.	POST. REF.	GENERAL DEBIT	GENERAL CREDIT	CASH DEBIT	CASH CREDIT	
15	4	Notes Payable	NP26			10000000	10000000		15

Figure 23-14

Governmental organizations may need to borrow cash for short periods until tax money is received. At other times, these organizations have cash to invest for short periods until the cash is needed to pay expenditures. Sparta sends tax statements to property owners on January 1 each year. Taxes can be paid anytime from January 1 through February 28. Consequently, the town may need to borrow cash until taxes are received.

January 4. Issued a 1-month, 9% note, $100,000.00. Note Payable No. 26.

Cash is increased by a debit for the amount received, $100,000.00. Notes Payable is increased by a credit for the same amount, $100,000.00. The journal entry to record this transaction is shown in Figure 23-14.

JOURNALIZING THE PAYMENT OF LIABILITIES

JOURNAL   PAGE 8

	DATE	ACCOUNT TITLE	DOC. NO.	POST. REF.	GENERAL DEBIT	GENERAL CREDIT	CASH DEBIT	CASH CREDIT	
22	4	Notes Payable	C370		100 00 0 00			100 75 0 00	22
23		Expenditure—Other Charges, Gen. Gov't.			7 5 0 00				23
24									24

Figure 23-15

When Sparta's note payable is due on February 4, the amount of the note plus interest expense is paid to the bank.

> **February 4. Paid cash for the maturity value of NP26: principal, $100,000.00, plus interest, $750.00; total, $100,750.00. Check No. 370.**

Notes Payable is decreased by a debit, $100,000.00. Expenditure—Other Charges, General Government is increased by a debit for the amount of interest expense, $750.00. Cash is decreased by a credit for the total amount paid, $100,750.00. The journal entry is shown in Figure 23-15.

INVESTING IN SHORT-TERM INVESTMENTS

JOURNAL   PAGE 21

	DATE	ACCOUNT TITLE	DOC. NO.	POST. REF.	GENERAL DEBIT	GENERAL CREDIT	CASH DEBIT	CASH CREDIT	
19	1	Investments—Short Term	C385		300 00 0 00			300 00 0 00	19
20									20

Figure 23-16

Most of Sparta's property taxes, the major portion of the town's revenue, are collected by March 1 each year. Cash that will not be needed for several months is placed in short-term investments. Interest on these investments provides additional revenue.

> **March 1. Paid cash for a 4-month, 8% certificate of deposit, $300,000.00. Check No. 385.**

A document issued by a bank as evidence of money invested with the bank is called a **certificate of deposit**. The time and interest rate to be paid are included on the certificate.

Investments—Short Term is increased by a debit for the amount of the certificate, $300,000.00. Cash is decreased by a credit for the same amount, $300,000.00. The journal entry is shown in Figure 23-16.

REMEMBER

The interest rate of a certificate of deposit usually increases as the time period increases. Interest rates of certificates are frequently tied to the prime rate.

	DATE	ACCOUNT TITLE	DOC. NO.	POST. REF.	GENERAL		CASH	
					DEBIT	CREDIT	DEBIT	CREDIT
22	1	*Investments—Short Term*	R572			300 00 00 00	308 00 00 00		22
23		*Interest Revenue*				8 00 00 00			23

Figure 23-17

When the certificate of deposit is due on July 1, cash is received for the original cost of the investment plus interest revenue earned.

> *July 1. Received cash for the maturity value of certificate of deposit due today: principal, $300,000.00, plus interest, $8,000.00; total, $308,000.00. Receipt No. 572.*

Cash is increased by a debit for the amount of cash received, $308,000.00. Investments—Short Term is decreased by a credit for the certificate of deposit's original cost, $300,000.00. Interest Revenue is increased by a credit for the amount of interest earned, $8,000.00. The journal entry is shown in Figure 23-17.

INTERNATIONAL TRAVEL

International travel usually requires a passport. A passport is a formal document that allows exit from and reentry into a country. It proves citizenship and provides identity for the traveler.

First-time passport applicants must complete an application, which may be obtained from a United States Postal Service office. The application must be submitted with the following:
1. Proof of U.S. citizenship (usually a certified birth certificate).
2. Proof of identity (typically a document such as a driver's license).
3. Two identical 2" x 2" photographs (These photos must meet certain criteria. Many local photo studios advertise passport photo service.)
4. Fee. (The applicable fee when this textbook was written was $65.)

This information must be sent to a designated postal service office; a clerk of a federal or state court of records or a judge or clerk of a pro-bate court who accepts applications; a U.S. consular official; or an agent at a passport agency in Boston, Chicago, Honolulu, Houston, Los Angeles, Miami, New Orleans, New York, Philadelphia, San Francisco, Seattle, Stamford, or Washington, D.C.

Required:

Complete the following information that will be transferable to a passport application.

NAME: first, middle, and last name
ADDRESS: street, city, state, zip, country
PLACE OF BIRTH: city, state, country
DATE OF BIRTH: month, day, year
PERSONAL: Social Security number, height, color of hair, color of eyes
PHONE NUMBER: area code and home phone
FAMILY: father's name, birthplace, birth date, U.S. citizen (yes or no), mother's name, birthplace, birth date, U.S. citizen (yes or no)

GLOBAL PERSPECTIVE

encumbrance

general fund assets

certificate of deposit

1. What is an encumbrance?

2. What two entries are required when goods or services that have been encumbered are received?

3. Why does a governmental organization not record depreciation expense?

4. What is a certificate of deposit?

WORK
TOGETHER

Journalizing governmental encumbrances, expenditures, and other transactions

The town of River Falls uses a general fund for all financial transactions. Expenditures are recorded by type of expenditure and by department. The four categories of expenditures are personnel, supplies, other charges, and capital outlays. Departments are General Government, Public Safety, Public Works, and Recreation.

Page 1 of a journal is provided in the *Working Papers*. Source documents are abbreviated as follows: memorandum, M; check, C; notes payable, NP. Your instructor will guide you through the following examples.

Jan. 11. Paid cash for electrical service in public works department, $238.00. C482.

16. Encumbered estimated amount for supplies in public safety department, $155.00. M111.

19. Issued a one-month, 12% note, $200,000.00. NP15.

27. Paid cash for public safety department supplies, $151.00, encumbered January 16 per M111. M125 and C497.

Feb. 6. Paid cash for printer for general government department, $395.00. C520. (Capital Outlays)

19. Paid cash for the maturity value of NP15: principal, $200,00.00, plus interest, $2,000.00; total $202,000.00. C538.

Mar. 16. Paid cash for a 3-month, 10% certificate of deposit, $150,000.00. C567.

June 16. Received cash for the maturity value of certificate of deposit due today; principal, $150,000.00, plus interest, $3,750.00; total, $153,750.00. R312.

5. Journalize the transactions completed during the current year.

ON YOUR OWN

Journalizing governmental encumbrances, expenditures, and other transactions

The town of Annandale uses a general fund for all financial transactions. Expenditures are recorded by type of expenditure and by department. The four categories of expenditures are personnel, supplies, other charges, and capital outlays. Departments are General Government, Public Safety, Public Works, and Recreation.

Page 1 of a journal is provided in the *Working Papers*. Source documents are abbreviated as follows: memorandum, M; check, C; notes payable, NP. Work independently to complete the following problem.

Jan. 12. Paid cash for consultant's services in recreation department, $500.00. C267. (Personnel)

17. Encumbered estimated amount for supplies in public works department, $215.00. M88.

20. Issued a one-month, 10% note, $50,000.00. NP10.

28. Paid cash for public works department supplies, $211.00, encumbered January 17 per M88. M95 and C282.

Feb. 7. Paid cash for desk for public safety department, $375.00. C294. (Capital Outlays)

20. Paid cash for the maturity value of NP10: principal, $50,00.00, plus interest, $416.67; total $50,416.67. C322.

Mar. 17. Paid cash for a 3-month, 12% certificate of deposit, $75,000.00. C351.

June 17. Received cash for the maturity value of certificate of deposit due today; principal, $75,000.00, plus interest, $750.00; total, $75,750.00. R101.

6. Journalize the transactions completed during the current year.

After completing this chapter, you can

1. Define accounting terms related to budgeting and accounting for a not-for-profit governmental organization.

2. Identify accounting concepts and practices related to budgeting and accounting for a not-for-profit governmental organization.

3. Describe the process used to develop an operating budget.

4. Journalize budget transactions for a not-for-profit organization.

5. Journalize revenues for a not-for-profit organization.

6. Journalize expenditures, encumbrances, and other transactions for a not-for-profit organization.

EXPLORE ACCOUNTING

ACCOUNTING IN NOT-FOR-PROFIT ORGANIZATIONS

When asked to think about accounting careers available in the not-for-profit sector, most people think about city, county, and state positions. Most often, these positions involve completing the accounting and reporting tasks required by these governmental agencies. However, there are other accounting-related careers in the not-for-profit sector that offer the opportunity for exciting and challenging positions. These opportunities include working for the Federal Bureau of Investigation (FBI), the Internal Revenue Service (IRS), and/or insurance companies in an area called "forensic accounting."

Forensic accounting is the investigation of accounting records and reports when fraud and/or embezzlement is suspected. Forensic accountants may help investigate crimes such as extortion, fraud, and embezzlement.

FBI agents may use interview and research techniques to investigate crimes. Requirements for employment as an FBI agent working in the accounting field include a four-year accounting degree from an accredited school and at least one year of experience in accounting or auditing. In addition, an agent must be a citizen of the U.S. between the ages of 23 and 35 and in good physical condition.

The IRS also employs accountants in various areas. Internal revenue agents are accountants who, by looking at the accounting records and tax returns of a business, determine if the business owes taxes and, if so, how much.

The IRS also employs internal auditors who examine the procedures and operations used with the IRS itself. A third position within the IRS is that of special agent. Special agents investigate tax fraud cases. Requirements for employment within the IRS vary, but most do include a four-year degree with some experience in the accounting field.

Insurance companies also hire accountants to assist in investigating cases involving suspected insurance fraud.

REQUIRED:

Contact the director of the FBI or a local IRS recruitment office, to request more detailed information on job opportunities, requirements, and application procedures. Report your findings in written form.

23-1 APPLICATION PROBLEM

Journalizing governmental operating budgets

Three towns, Appleton, Milltown, and Wilson, approved their annual general fund operating budgets effective January 1 of the current year. The available information about the budgets is as follows.

	Estimated Revenues	Budgetary Appropriations	Fund Balance
Appleton	$2,050,000.00	$2,009,000.00	$41,000.00
Milltown	794,500.00	789,200.00	5,300.00
Wilson	1,754,000.00	1,722,500.00	31,500.00

Instructions:

Journalize the entry to record the operating budgets for each of the three towns for the current year. Use page 1 of a journal.

23-2 APPLICATION PROBLEM

Journalizing governmental revenue transactions

Dalton's town council recently approved the town's general fund operating budget for the current year.

Transactions:

Jan. 1. Recorded property tax levy: taxes receivable—current, $1,100,000.00; allowance for uncollectible taxes—current, $11,000.00; property tax revenue, $1,089,000.00. M88.
8. Received cash for current taxes receivable, $97,600.00. R134.
14. Received cash from traffic fines, $56.00. R147. (Other Revenue)
Feb. 11. Received cash for current taxes receivable, $172,350.00. R194.
16. Received cash from parking meter receipts, $274.50. R212. (Other Revenue)
Mar. 1. Recorded reclassification of current taxes receivable to delinquent status, $56,800.00, and the accompanying allowance for uncollectible accounts, $11,000.00. M107.
12. Received cash for delinquent taxes receivable, $10,700.00. R259.

Instructions:

Journalize the transactions for the current year. Use page 1 of a journal.

23-3 APPLICATION PROBLEM

Journalizing governmental encumbrances, expenditures, and other transactions

The town of Templeton uses a general fund for all financial transactions. Expenditures are recorded by type of expenditure and by department. The four categories of expenditures are personnel, supplies, other charges, and capital outlays. Departments are: General Government, Public Safety, Public Works, and Recreation.

Transactions:

Jan. 11. Paid cash for supplies in public works department, $205.00. C244.
15. Encumbered estimated amount for supplies in public safety department, $235.00. M33.

Jan. 16. Issued a one-month, 10% note, $150,000.00. NP6.

28. Paid cash for public safety department supplies, $232.00, encumbered January 15 per M33. M40 and C258.

Feb. 5. Paid cash for calculator for general government department, $255.00. C267. (Capital Outlays)

16. Paid cash for the maturity value of NP6: principal, $150,000.00, plus interest, $1,250.00; total, $151,250.00. C279.

28. Encumbered estimated amount for supplies in public works department, $276.00. M49.

Mar. 15. Paid cash for a 3-month, 8% certificate of deposit, $200,000.00. C296.

18. Paid cash for public works department supplies, $278.00, encumbered February 28 per M49. M58 and C315.

21. Paid cash for consultant's services in recreation department, $360.00. C322. (Personnel)

June 15. Received cash for the maturity value of certificate of deposit due today: principal, $200,000.00, plus interest, $4,000.00; total, $204,000.00. R184.

Instructions:
Journalize the transactions for the current year. Use page 1 of a journal.

MASTERY PROBLEM
Journalizing governmental transactions

The town of Ingalls uses a general fund for all financial transactions. Expenditures are recorded by type of expenditure and by department. The four categories of expenditures are personnel, supplies, other charges, and capital outlays. Departments are: General Government, Public Safety, Public Works, and Recreation.

Transactions:

Jan. 2. Recorded current year's approved operating budget: estimated revenues, $1,270,000.00; appropriations, $1,224,000.00; budgetary fund balance, $46,000.00. M42.

2. Recorded current year's property tax levy: taxes receivable—current, $1,220,000.00; allowance for uncollectible taxes—current, $12,200.00; property tax revenue, $1,207,800.00. M43.

9. Received cash for current taxes receivable, $57,300.00. R105.

11. Paid cash for gas utility service in general government department, $234.00. C168.

12. Issued a 2-month, 9% note, $200,000.00. NP7.

16. Encumbered estimated amount for supplies in public works department, $165.00. M54.

20. Received cash from traffic fines, $225.00. R111. (Other Revenue)

30. Paid cash for lawn mower for public works department, $450.00. (Capital Outlays) C182.

Feb. 6. Paid cash for public works department supplies, $170.00, encumbered January 16 per M54. M58 and C190.

24. Encumbered estimated amount for supplies in recreation department, $133.00. M69.

Mar. 1. Recorded reclassification of current taxes receivable to delinquent status, $51,400.00, and the accompanying allowance for uncollectible accounts, $12,200.00. M76.

12. Paid cash for the maturity value of NP7: principal, $200,000.00, plus interest, $3,000.00; total, $203,000.00. C222.

20. Paid cash for a 3-month, 8% certificate of deposit, $400,000.00. C234.

22. Paid cash for recreation department supplies, $131.00, encumbered February 24 per M69. M88 and C241.

continued

Apr. 10. Received cash for delinquent taxes receivable, $21,000.00. R355.
  25. Paid cash for consultant's services in recreation department, $500.00. C266. (Personnel)
June 20. Received cash for the maturity value of certificate of deposit due today: principal, $400,000.00, plus interest, $8,000.00; total, $408,000.00. R497.

Instructions:
Journalize the transactions for the current year. Use page 1 of a journal.

23-5 CHALLENGE PROBLEM
Journalizing governmental transactions

The town of Mabank uses a general fund for all financial transactions. Expenditures are recorded by type of expenditure and by department. The four categories of expenditures are personnel, supplies, other charges, and capital outlays. Departments are General Government, Public Safety, Public Works, and Recreation.

Transactions:
Jan. 2. Recorded current year's approved operating budget: estimated revenues, $1,528,000.00; appropriations, $1,542,100.00; budgetary fund balance, $14,100.00. M88.

> (Note: Most towns prohibit deficit spending. In this case, a town would be prohibited from having a debit balance in the budgetary fund balance account. However, if sufficient fund equity is available at the beginning of a year, a town council may choose to appropriate more than the estimated revenues. The available fund equity would then be used for the amount that expenditures exceed revenues for the current period.)

  2. Recorded current year's property tax levy: total amount of tax statements sent, $1,452,000.00; uncollectible taxes estimated at 1% of total tax levy. M89.
  9. Received cash for current taxes receivable, $64,700.00. R111.
  17. Paid cash for electric utility service in public works department, $286.00. C131.
  20. Issued a 2-month, 12% note, $175,000.00. NP14.
  25. Encumbered estimated amount for supplies in public safety department, $170.00. M102.
Feb. 3. Received cash from parking meter receipts, $1,158.00. R152.
  10. Paid cash for public safety department supplies, $162.00, encumbered January 25 per M102. M130 and C188.
  21. Paid cash for swing set for recreation department, $575.00. C199. (Capital Outlays)
Mar. 1. Recorded reclassification of current taxes receivable to delinquent status, $158,100.00, and the accompanying allowance for uncollectible accounts. M154.
Mar. 15. Paid cash for a 4-month, 9% certificate of deposit, $500,000.00. C220.
  20. Paid cash for the maturity value of NP14: principal, $175,000.00, plus interest. C230.
  21. Received cash for delinquent taxes receivable, $22,500.00. R206.
Apr. 4. Encumbered estimated amount for printer in general government department, $880.00. M178. (Capital Outlays)
  16. Paid cash for general government department printer, $898.00, encumbered April 4 per M178. M190 and C267.
July 15. Received cash for the maturity value of certificate of deposit due today, $500,000.00, plus interest. R289.

Instructions:
Journalize the transactions for the current year. Use page 1 of a journal.

INTERNET ACTIVITY

Point your browser to

http://accounting.swpco.com

Choose **Advanced Course**, choose **Activities**, and complete the activity for Chapter 23.

Applied Communication

When property taxes become delinquent, the city for which you work issues a Notice of Delinquency to the property owner. The notice is a form letter that includes:

- The address of the property

- The census tract number

- The name and address of the property owner

- The total tax due

- The amount of the tax that is delinquent

Required:

You have been asked to create a new form for the Notice of Delinquency. The form should be created to allow data to be merged into the form. Use the mail merge or similar feature of your word processor to create a suitable form letter.

Cases for Critical Thinking

Case 1

The town of Oneida has three funds in its accounting system: general, library, and recreation. Oneida's new town manager, Donna Ward, has questioned the necessity of having three separate governmental funds. Ms. Ward suggests combining all the funds into a single general fund. What do you recommend? Explain your answer.

Case 2

Edwin Mansky, a new accounting clerk with the town of Thornton, has been struggling with accounting entries involving encumbrances. He suggests that no entries be made until goods or services are received. When goods are received, an expenditure would be recorded. Encumbrances would not be necessary and the final results would be the same. What is your response to Mr. Mansky's suggestion? Explain your answer.

AUTOMATED ACCOUNTING

USING AUTOMATED REPORTS FOR ANALYZING BUDGET TO ACTUAL BUSINESS ACTIVITY

Businesses develop budgets as part of their planning processes. Budgets define in number terms the plans and expectations for the coming year. Budgets may be prepared by one or more managers or owners of the business. However, some businesses include all levels of management in their budgeting process. By including more people in the process, businesses expect greater success in meeting the goals established in the budgets.

The most common type of budget shows expected revenues and expenses for the coming year. Other types of budgets assist in planning for capital expenditures and cash management.

Entering Budget Data

Automated Accounting 7.0 and higher allows yearly budget amounts to be entered for all revenue and expense accounts. The data are entered using the Budgets tab of the Other Activities window. The complete list of revenue and expense accounts appears in the window as shown in Figure AA23-1. Amounts are keyed for each account. The amounts should be the total planned revenue or expenditure for the year. (Note that accounts may not be added from this screen.)

Budgeted amounts can be changed as often as necessary. However, the amounts are generally updated only once a year. In many companies, budgets are prepared in November and December of the current year. The new budget amounts can then be entered into the software at the first of the year.

Using Budgets to Prepare Performance Reports

Before budgets can be used, two steps must be taken:

1. The Budgeting feature must be active. To activate this feature, click the check box beside Budgeting. This option is one of the features available in the Company Info. tab of the Customize Accounting System window as shown in Figure AA23-2.

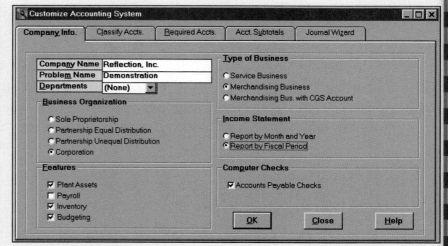

Figure AA23-1

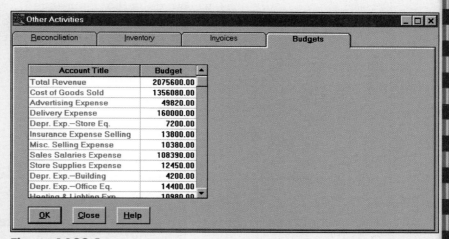

Figure AA23-2

2. Budget amounts must be entered for all revenue and expense accounts as described above.

When these steps have been taken, performance reports can be displayed as shown in Figure 23-3. The performance report compares the budgeted amount to the actual amount for each revenue and expense. The report has four columns:

1. Budget. Shows the budgeted amount for the appropriate period.

2. Actual. Shows the amount reported for the revenue or expense on the income statement.

3. Diff. from Budget. Shows the difference between the budgeted amount and the actual amount.

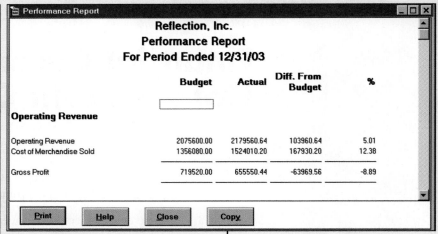

Figure AA23-3

4. %. Displays the difference from budget expressed as a percentage.

The performance report is accessed through the Report Selection window. The report may be displayed or printed in the same manner as other financial reports.

Evaluating Performance Reports

Managers and business owners use performance reports to spot trends and to identify potential problem areas. If revenues are falling below budget, action can be taken to increase sales. If an expense category substantially exceeds budget, action may be needed to control the expenditure.

Financial Reporting for a Not-for-Profit Organization

AFTER STUDYING CHAPTER 24, YOU WILL BE ABLE TO:

1. Identify accounting concepts and practices related to financial reporting for a not-for-profit governmental organization.

2. Prepare a worksheet for a governmental organization.

3. Prepare financial statements for a governmental organization.

4. Record adjusting and closing entries for a governmental organization.

Both businesses and not-for-profit organizations prepare financial statements periodically to report the results of financial activities. *(CONCEPT: Accounting Period Cycle)* However, financial information needed for not-for-profit organizations differs from that needed for businesses. A business measures performance primarily through determining the amount of net income. Thus, the accounting records are designed to emphasize the measurement of net income. In addition, the purpose of the income statement is to report the net income of the business. However, a not-for-profit organization's performance is measured primarily by the services provided and the efficiency with which resources are used. A not-for-profit organization does not prepare an income statement. Instead, it prepares a statement of revenues, expenditures, and changes in fund balance. A not-for-profit organization's financial statements are designed to provide information for the following purposes.

1. To make decisions about the use of resources.

2. To assess services provided and the ability to provide those services.

3. To assess management's financial accountability and performance.

4. To determine the assets, liabilities, and fund equity of the organization.

ACCOUNTING
IN YOUR CAREER

SPENDING THE BUDGET

Robin Anderson manages the Parks Department of the city of Columbia. In the tenth month of the fiscal year, her department is well under its budget. Robin realizes that if expenditures proceed at the current pace, she will finish the period with expenditures 25% under her budget for the year.

She considers ending significantly under budget to be a disadvantage for several reasons. From her many years of experience with the city, she knows that when a new budget is prepared the legislature reviews the past year's experience. The legislature examines the variance reported on the statement of revenues, expenditures, and changes in fund balance—budget and actual. When a department has not spent its entire budget, the next year's budget is cut back to the actual expenditures of the previous year. It is very difficult to get an increase over this reduced amount. Secondly, her performance is usually evaluated based on whether she has spent her budgeted amounts, without closely examining the individual expenditures.

Robin's department is under budget this year because a number of planned and budgeted projects could not be undertaken for various reasons. Therefore, she begins a program of spending her budgeted amounts on unplanned projects so that she finishes the year closer to her actual budget.

Critical Thinking

1. What is your opinion of the way the legislature arrives at the amounts for a year's budget?
2. What is your opinion of the way department managers are evaluated?
3. Is Robin's plan for spending the rest of her budget for the year appropriate?

RECORDING A TRIAL BALANCE ON A WORK SHEET

Town of Sparta General Fund Work Sheet For Year Ended December 31, 20--		
	1	2
ACCOUNT TITLE	TRIAL BALANCE	
	DEBIT	CREDIT
1 Cash	7836000	
2 Taxes Receivable—Current		
3 Allow. for Uncoll. Taxes—Cur.		
4 Taxes Receivable—Delinquent	1564000	
5 Allow. for Uncoll. Taxes—Delin.		875000
6 Interest Receivable		
7 Allow. for Uncoll. Interest		
8 Inventory of Supplies		
9 Investments—Short Term		
10 Accounts Payable		3612500
11 Notes Payable		
12 Unreserved Fund Balance		1170500
13 Res. for Encum.—Current Year		164000
14 Res. for Encum.—Prior Year		
15 Reserve for Inv. of Supplies		
16 Property Tax Revenue		159400000
17 Interest Revenue		878500
18 Other Revenue		262500
19 Expend.—Personnel, Gen. Gov't.	26317500	
20 Expend.—Supplies, Gen. Gov't.	1194000	
21 Expend.—Other Chgs., Gen. Gov't.	11238000	
22 Expend.—Cap. Outlays, Gen. Gov't.	1600000	
23 Expend.—Personnel, Public Safety	58865000	
24 Expend.—Supplies, Public Safety	1979000	
25 Expend.—Other Chgs., Pub. Safety	15263500	
26 Expend.—Cap. Outlays, Pub. Safety	8935000	
27 Expend.—Personnel, Public Works	11330000	
28 Expend.—Supplies, Public Works	554000	
29 Expend.—Other Chgs., Pub. Works	4734000	
30 Expend.—Cap. Outlays, Pub. Works	5117500	
31 Expend.—Personnel, Recreation	5811000	
32 Expend.—Supplies, Recreation	196000	
33 Expend.—Other Chgs., Recreation	2510500	
34 Expend.—Cap. Outlays, Recreation	1154000	
35 Estimated Revenues	160650000	
36 Appropriations		157280000
37 Budgetary Fund Balance		3370000
38 Encum.—Supplies, Public Safety	164000	
39	327013000	327013000
40 Excess of Revenues Over Expend.		

Figure 24-1

1. List all General Ledger accounts—except Encumbrances.

2. List encumbrance account with a balance.

3. Calculate totals.

The town of Sparta uses an eight-column work sheet similar to the one used by LampLight, Inc., in Part 5. However, the work sheets differ in one set of columns. Sparta's work sheet has Revenues/Expenditures Debit and Credit columns. LampLight's work sheet has Income Statement Debit and Credit columns.

A trial balance is entered in the Trial Balance columns as the first step in preparing a work sheet. All general ledger accounts except encumbrances are listed in the Account Title column in the same order as they appear in the general ledger, as shown in Figure 24-1. Only encumbrance accounts with balances are listed. The Trial Balance columns are totaled to prove the equality of debits and credits.

S T E P S Recording a trial balance on a work sheet

1. List all general ledger accounts except encumbrances in the Account Title column in the same order as they appear in the general ledger.

2. List only those encumbrance accounts with a balance in the Account Title column.

3. Total the trial balance columns. Compare totals to verify that the totals are equal.

F.Y.I.

Governments often issue bonds to pay for large projects, such as building schools and highways. Investors are not required to pay federal income tax on the interest income on these bonds.

	Town of Sparta General Fund							
	Work Sheet							
	For Year Ended December 31, 20--							
	1	2	3	4	5	6	7	8
ACCOUNT TITLE	TRIAL BALANCE		ADJUSTMENTS		REVENUES/EXPENDITURES		BALANCE SHEET	
	DEBIT	CREDIT	DEBIT	CREDIT	DEBIT	CREDIT	DEBIT	CREDIT
6 Interest Receivable								
7 Allow. for Uncoll. Interest								
8 Inventory of Supplies			(a)2 8 2 0 00					
9 Investments—Short Term								
10 Accounts Payable		36 1 2 5 00						
11 Notes Payable								
12 Unreserved Fund Balance		11 7 0 5 00						
13 Res. for Encum.—Current Year		1 6 4 0 00						
14 Res. for Encum.—Prior Year								
15 Reserve for Inv. of Supplies				(a)2 8 2 0 00				
16 Property Tax Revenue		1594 0 0 0 00						
17 Interest Revenue		8 7 8 5 00						

Figure 24-2

Some general ledger accounts for governmental funds need to be brought up to date before financial statements are prepared. However, since governmental funds report expenditures and not expenses, no adjustments are needed for expense accounts. The actual amounts that have been spent and recorded as expenditures are the amounts reported.

Since governmental funds recognize revenues when the revenues become measurable and available, an adjustment may be needed to record some revenues.

Adjustments are planned on a work sheet. Sparta makes adjustments to three accounts. (1) Inventory of Supplies. (2) Interest Revenue. (3) Reserve for Encumbrances—Current Year.

Inventory of Supplies Adjustment

When supplies are bought, an expenditure account is debited. Some supplies may be unused at the end of a fiscal period. These unused supplies should be reported as an asset. (CONCEPT: Adequate Disclosure) Thus, an adjustment is made at the end of a fiscal period to record the remaining amount of supplies inventory as an asset, as shown in Figure 24-2. Expenditure accounts debited when supplies

were bought are not adjusted. When an expenditure is made during a fiscal period, the expenditure is reported regardless of the purpose.

The total account balances of a governmental fund represent the equity of that fund. Thus, assets *less* liabilities *equals* total fund equity, which, unless reserved for a specified purpose, should represent resources that are available for appropriations and spending. The inventory of supplies, however, will be used by the organization. Therefore, this asset is not available for spending. To show that this asset, Inventory of Supplies, is not available for other uses, an equal amount of fund equity is reserved. Thus, the amount is credited to a restricted fund equity account titled Reserve for Inventory of Supplies.

Inventory of Supplies, an asset account, is increased by a debit for the amount of supplies on hand, $2,820.00. Reserve for Inventory of Supplies is increased by a credit for the same amount, $2,820.00.

Inventory of Supplies	
Adj. (a) 2,820.00	

Reserve for Inventory of Supplies	
	Adj. (a) 2,820.00

Town of Sparta General Fund

Work Sheet

For Year Ended December 31, 20--

	ACCOUNT TITLE	1 TRIAL BALANCE DEBIT	2 TRIAL BALANCE CREDIT	3 ADJUSTMENTS DEBIT	4 ADJUSTMENTS CREDIT	5 REVENUES/EXPENDITURES DEBIT	6 REVENUES/EXPENDITURES CREDIT	7 BALANCE SHEET DEBIT	8 BALANCE SHEET CREDIT	
6	Interest Receivable			(b) 2565 00						6
7	Allow. for Uncoll. Interest				(b) 513 00					7
8	Inventory of Supplies			(a) 2820 00						8
9	Investments—Short Term									9
10	Accounts Payable		36125 00							10
11	Notes Payable									11
12	Unreserved Fund Balance		11705 00							12
13	Res. for Encum.—Current Year		1640 00	(c) 1640 00						13
14	Res. for Encum.—Prior Year				(c) 1640 00					14
15	Reserve for Inv. of Supplies				(a) 2820 00					15
16	Property Tax Revenue		1594000 00							16
17	Interest Revenue		8785 00		(b) 2052 00					17
38	Encum.—Supplies, Public Safety	1640 00								38
39		3270130 00	3270130 00	7025 00	7025 00					39

Figure 24-3

Interest is assessed on all delinquent taxes. Interest on delinquent taxes becomes measurable and available when it is assessed. Thus, to bring the accounts up to date and record revenue earned but not collected at the end of the year, an adjustment is made, as shown in Figure 24-3.

Sparta's interest due but not yet collected on December 31 is $2,565.00. Experience has shown that approximately 20% of this amount, *$513.00* ($2,565.00 × 20%), will not be collected. Thus, the amount expected to be collected, *$2,052.00* ($2,565.00 – $513.00), is recorded as revenue.

At the end of a fiscal year, a governmental organization may have outstanding encumbrances—orders that have not yet been delivered. When goods are delivered that were encumbered against the preceding year's appropriations, the amount should not be recorded as an expenditure of the current period. Therefore, at the end of a fiscal period, the balance of Reserve for Encumbrances—Current Year, the amount of encumbrances outstanding, should be reclassified to prior year status. Then, when the prior year's orders arrive, they can be debited to Reserve for Encumbrances—Prior Year, rather than current year's expenditures. This procedure prevents charging expenditures of one year to another year's appropriations.

Interest Receivable	
Adj. *(b)* 2,565.00	

Allowance for Uncollectible Interest	
	Adj. *(b)* 513.00

Interest Revenue	
	Adj. *(b)* 2,052.00

Reserve for Encumbrances—Current Year	
Adj. *(c)* 1,640.00	Bal. 1,640.00
	(*New Bal. zero*)

Reserve for Encumbrances—Prior Year	
	Adj. *(c)* 1,640.00

Town of Sparta General Fund

Work Sheet

For Year Ended December 31, 20--

	ACCOUNT TITLE	TRIAL BALANCE DEBIT	TRIAL BALANCE CREDIT	ADJUSTMENTS DEBIT	ADJUSTMENTS CREDIT	REVENUES/EXPENDITURES DEBIT	REVENUES/EXPENDITURES CREDIT	BALANCE SHEET DEBIT	BALANCE SHEET CREDIT	
1	Cash	78 360 00						78 360 00		1
2	Taxes Receivable—Current									2
3	Allow. for Uncoll. Taxes—Cur.									3
4	Taxes Receivable—Delinquent	15 640 00						15 640 00		4
5	Allow. for Uncoll. Taxes—Delin.		8 750 00						8 750 00	5
6	Interest Receivable			(b)2 565 00				2 565 00		6
7	Allow. for Uncoll. Interest				(b) 513 00				513 00	7
8	Inventory of Supplies			(a)2 820 00				2 820 00		8
9	Investments—Short Term									9
10	Accounts Payable		36 125 00						36 125 00	10
11	Notes Payable									11
12	Unreserved Fund Balance		11 705 00						11 705 00	12
13	Res. for Encum.—Current Year		1 640 00	(c)1 640 00						13
14	Res. for Encum.—Prior Year				(c)1 640 00		1 640 00			14
15	Reserve for Inv. of Supplies				(a)2 820 00				2 820 00	15
16	Property Tax Revenue		1594 000 00				1594 000 00			16
17	Interest Revenue		8 785 00		(b)2 052 00		10 837 00			17
18	Other Revenue		2 625 00				2 625 00			18
19	Expend.—Personnel, Gen. Gov't.	263 175 00				263 175 00				19
20	Expend.—Supplies, Gen. Gov't.	11 940 00				11 940 00				20
21	Expend.—Other Chgs., Gen. Gov't.	112 380 00				112 380 00				21
22	Expend.—Cap. Outlays, Gen. Gov't.	16 000 00				16 000 00				22
23	Expend.—Personnel, Public Safety	588 650 00				403 495 00 / 588 650 00				23
24	Expend.—Supplies, Public Safety	19 790 00				19 790 00				24
25	Expend.—Other Chgs., Pub. Safety	152 635 00				152 635 00				25
26	Expend.—Cap. Outlays, Pub. Safety	89 350 00				89 350 00				26
27	Expend.—Personnel, Public Works	113 300 00				850 425 00 / 113 300 00				27
28	Expend.—Supplies, Public Works	5 540 00				5 540 00				28
29	Expend.—Other Chgs., Pub. Works	47 340 00				47 340 00				29
30	Expend.—Cap. Outlays, Pub. Works	51 175 00				51 175 00				30
31	Expend.—Personnel, Recreation	58 110 00				217 355 00 / 58 110 00				31
32	Expend.—Supplies, Recreation	1 960 00				1 960 00				32
33	Expend.—Other Chgs., Recreation	25 105 00				25 105 00				33
34	Expend.—Cap. Outlays, Recreation	11 540 00				11 540 00				34
35	Estimated Revenues	1606 500 00				967 150 00 / 1606 500 00				35
36	Appropriations		1572 800 00				1572 800 00			36
37	Budgetary Fund Balance		33 700 00				33 700 00			37
38	Encum.—Supplies, Public Safety	1 640 00				1 640 00				38
39		3270 130 00	3270 130 00	7 025 00	7 025 00	3176 130 00	3215 602 00	99 385 00	59 913 00	39
40	Excess of Revenues Over Expend.					39 472 00			39 472 00	40
41						3215 602 00	3215 602 00	99 385 00	99 385 00	41

Figure 24-4

All asset, liability and fund equity account balances except Reserve for Encumbrances—Prior Year are extended to the Balance Sheet columns on the work sheet.

The reserve for encumbrances accounts are listed as balance sheet accounts in the chart of accounts. During a fiscal period, the current year reserve for encumbrances account is used as a balancing account for the encumbrance accounts. Fund equity is not actually reduced when encumbrances are recorded. Therefore, the current year's reserve for encumbrances account is considered to be a budgetary account until accounts are closed at the end of a fiscal period.

Therefore, the balance of **Reserve for Encumbrances—Prior Year** is extended to the Revenues/Expenditures columns of the work sheet, as shown in Figure 24-4.

The balances of all temporary accounts are also extended to the work sheet's Revenues/Expenditures columns. Temporary accounts are closed at the end of each fiscal period. Temporary accounts include all revenue, expenditure, and budgetary accounts.

CALCULATING THE EXCESS OF REVENUES OVER EXPENDITURES

	Revenues/Expenditures Credit column total (line 39)	$3,215,602.00
Less	Revenues/Expenditures Debit column total (line 39)	3,176,130.00
Equals	Excess of revenues over expenditures	$ 39,472.00

Figure 24-5

The Revenues/Expenditures and Balance Sheet columns are totaled. Totals are written as shown on line 39 of the work sheet shown in Figure 24-4. The difference between the Revenues/Expenditures Credit column total and the Debit column total is the excess of revenues

over expenditures. If the Debit column total is larger, the difference is the excess of expenditures over revenues. Sparta's excess of revenues over expenditures is calculated as shown in Figure 24-5.

COMPLETING THE WORK SHEET

The excess of revenues over expenditures, *$39,472.00*, is written under the work sheet's Revenues/Expenditures Debit column total on line 40 to make the two Revenues/Expenditures columns balance. The words *Excess of Revenues Over Expend.* are written in the Account Title column on the same line.

Sparta's excess of revenues over expenditures, *$39,472.00*, is also written under the Balance Sheet Credit column total on line 40 to make the two Balance Sheet columns balance.

When there is an excess of expenditures over revenues, the excess amount is written on a work sheet in the Revenues/Expenditures Credit and Balance Sheet Debit columns.

After the excess of revenues over expenditures is recorded on the work sheet, the last four columns are totaled again and ruled. Both pairs of Sparta's totals are the same, as shown in

Figure 24-4. When the totals of each pair of columns are the same, the work sheet is assumed to be correct.

After the work sheet is completed, expenditures in the Revenues/Expenditures Debit column are totaled for each department. These totals are used in the preparation of financial statements. Departmental totals are written in small numbers below the amount of the last listed expenditure for the department. For General Government, lines 19 through 22, the total, *$403,495.00*, is written below line 22. For Public Safety, lines 23 through 26, the total, *$850,425.00*, is written below line 26. For Public Works, lines 27 through 30, the total, *$217,355.00*, is written below line 30. For Recreation, lines 31 through 34, the total, *$96,715.00*, is written below line 34.

AUDIT YOUR UNDERSTANDING

1. What columns on a governmental organization's work sheet replace the Income Statement columns on a business' work sheet?

2. What accounts are affected, and how, when an interest revenue adjustment is recorded for a governmental organization?

3. To which column of a work sheet is the balance of Reserve for Encumbrances—Prior Year extended?

4. How is the excess of revenues over expenditures calculated on the work sheet?

WORK TOGETHER

Preparing a work sheet for a governmental organization

The town of Anoka uses a general fund. The trial balance for December 31 of the current year is recorded on a work sheet in the *Working Papers*. Your instructor will guide you through the following examples.

5. Analyze the following adjustment information and record the adjustments on the work sheet.

Supplies Inventory	$2,925.00
Interest Revenue Due but not Collected	2,490.00

An estimated 20% of the interest revenue due will not be collected.

The reserve for encumbrances for the current year is reclassified to prior year status.

6. Complete the work sheet. Save your work to complete the Work Together on pages 671 and 674.

ON YOUR OWN

Preparing a work sheet for a governmental organization

The town of Annandale uses a general fund. The trial balance for December 31 of the current year is recorded on a work sheet in the *Working Papers*. Work independently to complete the following problem.

7. Analyze the following adjustment information and record the adjustments on the work sheet.

Supplies Inventory	$1,870.00
Interest Revenue Due but not Collected	2,180.00

An estimated 20% of the interest revenue due will not be collected.

The reserve for encumbrances for the current year is reclassified to prior year status.

8. Complete the work sheet. Save your work to complete the On Your Own on pages 671 and 674.

STATEMENT OF REVENUES, EXPENDITURES, AND CHANGES IN FUND BALANCE—BUDGET AND ACTUAL

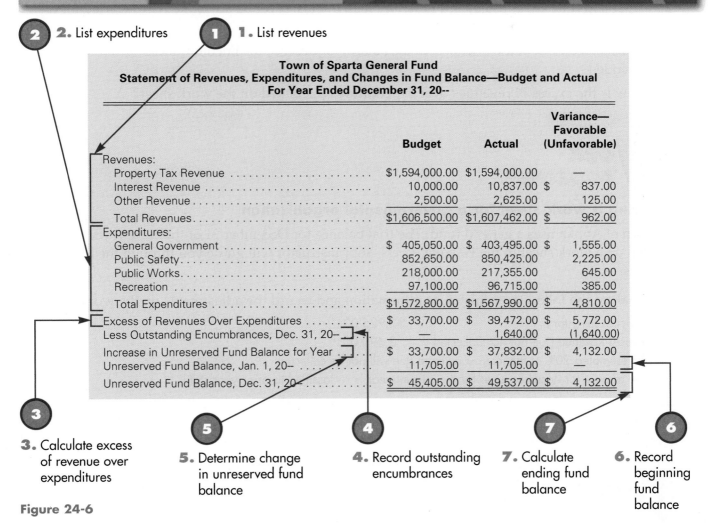

2. List expenditures   **1.** List revenues

Town of Sparta General Fund
Statement of Revenues, Expenditures, and Changes in Fund Balance—Budget and Actual
For Year Ended December 31, 20--

	Budget	Actual	Variance—Favorable (Unfavorable)
Revenues:			
Property Tax Revenue	$1,594,000.00	$1,594,000.00	—
Interest Revenue	10,000.00	10,837.00	$ 837.00
Other Revenue	2,500.00	2,625.00	125.00
Total Revenues	$1,606,500.00	$1,607,462.00	$ 962.00
Expenditures:			
General Government	$ 405,050.00	$ 403,495.00	$ 1,555.00
Public Safety	852,650.00	850,425.00	2,225.00
Public Works	218,000.00	217,355.00	645.00
Recreation	97,100.00	96,715.00	385.00
Total Expenditures	$1,572,800.00	$1,567,990.00	$ 4,810.00
Excess of Revenues Over Expenditures	$ 33,700.00	$ 39,472.00	$ 5,772.00
Less Outstanding Encumbrances, Dec. 31, 20--	—	1,640.00	(1,640.00)
Increase in Unreserved Fund Balance for Year	$ 33,700.00	$ 37,832.00	$ 4,132.00
Unreserved Fund Balance, Jan. 1, 20--	11,705.00	11,705.00	—
Unreserved Fund Balance, Dec. 31, 20--	$ 45,405.00	$ 49,537.00	$ 4,132.00

3. Calculate excess of revenue over expenditures

5. Determine change in unreserved fund balance

4. Record outstanding encumbrances

7. Calculate ending fund balance

6. Record beginning fund balance

Figure 24-6

Financial statements are prepared for each governmental fund. (*CONCEPT: Adequate Disclosure*) Sparta prepares two financial statements for its general fund. (1) Statement of revenues, expenditures, and changes in fund balance—budget and actual. (2) Balance sheet.

A statement of revenues, expenditures, and changes in fund balance—budget and actual reports the amount of revenues earned and expenditures made for a fiscal period. The changes in the unreserved fund balance from the beginning to the end of the fiscal period are also reported. In addition, actual revenues, expenditures, and unreserved fund balance are compared with budgeted amounts for a fiscal period. (*CONCEPT: Accounting Period Cycle*)

Sparta's general fund statement of revenues, expenditures, and changes in fund balance—budget and actual for the fiscal year ended December 31 is shown in Figure 24-6.

Information used to prepare the Budget column is obtained from the annual operating budget shown in Chapter 23, page 637. Information needed to prepare the Actual column is obtained from the work sheet's Revenues/Expenditures columns. The beginning fund balance that is used in both the Budget and Actual columns is obtained from the prior year's balance sheet.

Preparing the statement of revenues, expenditures, and changes in fund balance—budget and actual

1. List revenues by source. Sparta has three sources of revenues: property taxes, interest, and other. The total of all three sources of revenues is also shown.

2. List expenditures as totals for each department. Departments are responsible for controlling expenditures through budgeting and appropriations of specific amounts for each department. Thus, to aid the control process, amounts actually spent are reported for each responsible department. The total expenditures for the whole fund are also shown on the statement.

3. Calculate the excess of revenues over expenditures. If expenditures exceed revenues, the difference is labeled "excess of expenditures over revenues."

4. Record any outstanding encumbrances for the current year. Outstanding encumbrances are not deducted in figuring excess of revenues over expenditures. However, funds will be required in the future when the goods for which the encumbrances were made are delivered. Therefore, current year's encumbrances should be reported as a reduction in the current year's excess of revenues rather than in the next year when goods are paid for. Because no amount is budgeted for the encumbrances, the amount shown in the budget column is zero.

5. Deduct outstanding encumbrances from excess of revenues over expenditures to determine the change in the unreserved fund balance for the year. The remaining excess of revenues over expenditures is an increase in the unreserved fund balance for the current year.

6. Record the beginning unreserved fund balance. This January 1 balance is obtained from the prior year's balance sheet.

7. Calculate the ending unreserved fund balance. The increase in the unreserved fund balance for the year plus the beginning unreserved fund balance equals the ending unreserved fund balance.

Each amount recorded in the Variance column is the difference between the budget and actual amounts for the item. For example, the variance for other revenue is $125.00 (actual, $2,625.00, *less* budget, $2,500.00). Variances are considered favorable if actual results are better than the amount budgeted for that item. When actual revenues are more than budgeted revenues, variances are favorable. When actual revenues are less than budgeted revenues, variances are unfavorable. When actual expenditures are less than budgeted expenditures, variances are favorable. When actual expenditures are more than budgeted expenditures, variances are unfavorable. A reserve for encumbrances variance has the same effect as an expenditure variance. Because encumbrances are not budgeted, any variance will be unfavorable since an actual encumbrance will cause an increase. Unfavorable variances are indicated by placing the amounts in parentheses.

F.Y.I.

Governmental financial statements are often published in local newspapers.

REMEMBER

Parentheses are placed around unfavorable variances to show negative results.

Town of Sparta General Fund
Balance Sheet
December 31, 20--

ASSETS		
Cash		$78,360.00
Taxes Receivable—Delinquent	$15,640.00	
Less Allowance for Uncollectible Taxes—Delinquent	8,750.00	6,890.00
Interest Receivable	$ 2,565.00	
Less Allowance for Uncollectible Interest	513.00	2,052.00
Inventory of Supplies		2,820.00
Total Assets		$90,122.00
LIABILITIES AND FUND EQUITY		
Liabilities:		
Accounts Payable		$36,125.00
Fund Equity:		
Unreserved Fund Balance	$49,537.00	
Reserve for Encumbrances—Prior Year	1,640.00	
Reserve for Inventory of Supplies	2,820.00	
Total Fund Equity		53,997.00
Total Liabilities and Fund Equity		$90,122.00

Figure 24-7

A governmental fund balance sheet reports information about assets, liabilities, and fund equity for a specific date, usually the last day of a fiscal period. *(CONCEPT: Adequate Disclosure)* Assets and liabilities on a governmental fund balance sheet have characteristics similar to those on a corporation's balance sheet. However, a governmental fund does not have specific owners. Therefore, a governmental fund has no owners' equity section. Instead, the difference between assets and liabilities is reported as fund equity. Thus, unless restricted, fund equity represents the amount that is available for expenditures or encumbrances.

On December 31, Sparta's fund equity, consisting of three fund equity account balances, is $53,997.00. The Unreserved Fund Balance, *$49,537.00*, represents equity in the fund that has no restrictions (Total fund equity, $53,997.00, less Reserve for Encumbrances—Prior Year, $1,640.00, and less Reserve for Inventory of Supplies, $2,820.00). With proper authorization, Sparta may appropriate this amount for expenditures.

The other two fund equity account balances are reserved for specific purposes. The Reserve for Encumbrances—Prior Year, *$1,640.00*, is an amount of equity set aside for an encumbrance outstanding on December 31 of the prior year. When the goods arrive and are paid for in the current year for an order that was encumbered in a prior year, Reserve for Encumbrances—Prior Year is debited rather than Expenditures. Payment of the prior year's order closes the reserve for encumbrances account. The entry also avoids recording an expenditure in the current year for goods ordered in a prior year.

The Reserve for Inventory of Supplies, *$2,820.00*, represents the equity in inventory of supplies. Although supplies are assets, they are available for use, not spending. Therefore, part of the fund equity is reserved for the amount of supplies on hand. This reserve avoids appropriating the amount of equity that is represented by the asset supplies.

On a governmental fund balance sheet, total assets must equal total liabilities and fund equity. Sparta's balance sheet has total assets of $90,122.00. The total liabilities and fund equity is the same amount. The balance sheet is in balance and assumed to be correct.

AUDIT YOUR UNDERSTANDING

1. What are the three columns found on a statement of revenues, expenditures, and changes in fund balance—budget and actual?

2. Where is the information obtained to prepare the Actual column of the statement of revenues, expenditures, and changes in fund balance—budget and actual?

3. When actual expenditures are less than budgeted expenditures, is the variance favorable or unfavorable?

4. What must total assets equal on a governmental fund balance sheet?

Preparing financial statements for a governmental organization

Use the working papers from the Work Together on page 667. The town of Anoka's general fund operating budget for the current year is given in the *Working Papers*. Your instructor will guide you through the following examples.

5. Prepare a statement of revenues, expenditures, and changes in fund balance—budget and actual for the year ended December 31 of the current year.

6. Prepare a balance sheet for December 31 of the current year.

ON YOUR OWN

Preparing financial statements for a governmental organization

Use the working papers from the On Your Own on page 667. The town of Annandale's general fund operating budget for the current year is given in the *Working Papers*. Work independently to complete the following problem.

7. Prepare a statement of revenues, expenditures, and changes in fund balance—budget and actual for the year ended December 31 of the current year.

8. Prepare a balance sheet for December 31 of the current year.

ADJUSTING AND CLOSING ENTRIES

JOURNAL

PAGE 48

	DATE	ACCOUNT TITLE	DOC. NO.	POST. REF.	GENERAL DEBIT	GENERAL CREDIT	CASH DEBIT	CASH CREDIT	
1		*Adjusting Entries*							1
2	Dec. 31	Inventory of Supplies			2820 00				2
3		Reserve for Inventory of Supplies				2820 00			3
4	31	Interest Receivable			2565 00				4
5		Allowance for Uncollectible Interest				513 00			5
6		Interest Revenue				2052 00			6
7	31	Reserve for Encumbrances—Current Year			1640 00				7
8		Reserve for Encumbrances—Prior Year				1640 00			8
9		*Closing Entries*							9
10	31	Property Tax Revenue			1594000 00				10
11		Interest Revenue			10837 00				11
12		Other Revenue			2625 00				12
13		Unreserved Fund Balance				1607462 00			13
14	31	Unreserved Fund Balance			1567990 00				14
15		Expenditure—Personnel, General Government				263175 00			15
16		Expenditure—Supplies, General Government				11940 00			16
17		Expenditure—Other Charges, General Government				112380 00			17
18		Expenditure—Capital Outlays, General Government				16000 00			18
19		Expenditure—Personnel, Public Safety				588650 00			19
20		Expenditure—Supplies, Public Safety				19790 00			20
21		Expenditure—Other Charges, Public Safety				152635 00			21
22		Expenditure—Capital Outlays, Public Safety				89350 00			22
23		Expenditure—Personnel, Public Works				113300 00			23
24		Expenditure—Supplies, Public Works				5540 00			24
25		Expenditure—Other Charges, Public Works				47340 00			25
26		Expenditure—Capital Outlays, Public Works				51175 00			26
27		Expenditure—Personnel, Recreation				58110 00			27
28		Expenditure—Supplies, Recreation				1960 00			28
29		Expenditure—Other Charges, Recreation				25105 00			29
30		Expenditure—Capital Outlays, Recreation				11540 00			30
31		Appropriations			1572800 00				31
32	31	Budgetary Fund Balance			33700 00				32
33		Estimated Revenues				1606500 00			33
34		Unreserved Fund Balance			1640 00				34
35	31	Encumbrance—Supplies, Public Safety				1640 00			35

Figure 24-8

Sparta's adjusting entries are recorded on December 31, as shown in Figure 24-8. Information needed for Sparta's adjusting entries is obtained from the work sheet's Adjustment columns.

REMEMBER

Governmental budgetary accounts are temporary accounts that are extended to the work sheet Revenue/Expenditures columns and closed at the end of the fiscal year.

Sparta's closing entries are also recorded on December 31, as shown in Figure 24-8. Information needed for the closing entries is obtained from the work sheet's Revenues/Expenditures columns. The following four entries are made:

1. Close all revenue accounts to the unreserved fund balance account.

2. Close all expenditure accounts to the unreserved fund balance account.

3. Close the budgetary accounts. At the beginning of the fiscal year, estimated revenues and appropriations were recorded based on the approved operating budget. At the end of the fiscal year, these budgetary accounts are closed. This entry is the opposite of the original entry to record the operating budget.

4. Close the outstanding encumbrance accounts to the unreserved fund balance account. This entry reduces the unreserved fund balance account by the amount of the outstanding encumbrance for supplies, public safety, $1,640.00.

The balance of **Reserve for Encumbrances—Prior Year**, *$1,640.00*, has been a budgetary account balance. Thus, the account balance is listed in the work sheet's Revenues/Expenditures Credit column. However, after the outstanding encumbrance account is closed to **Unreserved Fund Balance, Reserve for Encumbrances—Prior Year** is considered a fund equity account. The account, therefore, is not closed. This account balance now is the amount of total fund equity that is reserved for outstanding encumbrances.

After posting the closing entries, all temporary accounts have zero balances and are prepared for a new fiscal period. The difference between revenues and expenditures has been transferred to the unreserved fund balance account. Fund equity amounts that are not available for appropriations are recorded in reserve accounts.

PREPARING A POST-CLOSING TRIAL BALANCE FOR A GOVERNMENTAL ORGANIZATION

Town of Sparta General Fund
Post-Closing Trial Balance
December 31, 20--

Cash	$78,360.00	
Taxes Receivable—Delinquent	15,640.00	
Allowance for Uncollectible Taxes—Delinquent		$ 8,750.00
Interest Receivable	2,565.00	
Allowance for Uncollectible Interest		513.00
Inventory of Supplies	2,820.00	
Accounts Payable		36,125.00
Reserve for Encumbrances—Prior Year		1,640.00
Reserve for Inventory of Supplies		2,820.00
Unreserved Fund Balance		49,537.00
Totals	$99,385.00	$99,385.00

Figure 24-9

After all end-of-fiscal-period activities are complete, a post-closing trial balance is prepared to prove the equality of debits and credits in the account balances, as shown in Figure 24-9.

Because the debit and credit balance totals equal, the general ledger accounts are ready for the new fiscal period. (*CONCEPT: Accounting Period Cycle*)

1. What are the sources of information for a governmental organization's adjusting entries?

2. Into what account are revenue and expenditure accounts closed?

3. What accounts are debited and credited to close the budgetary accounts?

4. Which of the following accounts will appear on a post-closing trial balance?

   Appropriations

   Reserve for Encumbrances—Prior Year

   Property Tax Revenue

   Taxes Receivable—Delinquent

   Budgetary Fund Balance

   Unreserved Fund Balance

WORK
TOGETHER

Journalizing adjusting and closing entries for a governmental organization

Use the working papers from the Work Together on page 667. Page 40 of a journal form is provided in the *Working Papers*. Your instructor will guide you through the following examples.

5. Journalize the adjusting entries.

6. Journalize the closing entries.

ON YOUR
OWN

Journalizing adjusting and closing entries for a governmental organization

Use the working papers from the On Your Own on page 667. Page 52 of a journal form is provided in the *Working Papers*. Work independently to complete the following problem.

7. Journalize the adjusting entries.

8. Journalize the closing entries.

After completing this chapter, you can

1. Identify accounting concepts and practices related to financial reporting for a not-for-profit governmental organization.

2. Prepare a worksheet for a governmental organization.

3. Prepare financial statements for a governmental organization.

4. Record adjusting and closing entries for a governmental organization.

EXPLORE ACCOUNTING

GOVERNMENTAL ACCOUNTING STANDARDS BOARD

Governmental accounting is governed by the Governmental Accounting Standards Board (GASB). GASB was organized in 1984 to establish standards of financial accounting and reporting for governmental entities. These standards cover the preparation of external financial reports.

GASB's mission is "to establish and improve standards of state and local governmental accounting and financial reporting that will: (1) Result in useful information for users of financial reports and (2) Guide and educate the public, including issuers, auditors, and users of those financial reports."

When developing a new standard, GASB follows a process that permits input from individuals and groups. A task force studies a topic, seeks advice of experts, and may write a Discussion Memorandum. This Discussion Memorandum defines the problem, discusses the issue, and presents alternative solutions and the arguments and implications of each alternative solution.

A public hearing is then held to allow interested individuals or groups to give input relative to the issue and to suggest alternative solutions. Written input is also accepted. Board members study the comments made during the open hearing period and discuss the issue until they have reached a conclusion.

An Exposure Draft is written and voted on by the Board. If a majority of the seven-member board approves the Exposure Draft, it is issued. Generally, a period of 60 days or more is allowed for written comments on the draft. After this public comment period is over, the Board will again study the comments received and issue a final Statement.

This Statement, when issued, will explain the new statement, its effective date, background information, and the basis for the Board's decision.

The seven members of the Board are selected from government, public accounting, and accounting education associations. Each member serves on a part-time basis.

REQUIRED:

Using your local library or the Internet, find the most recent Statement of Standard that has been issued by GASB. Report your findings in written form. Include the name and the effective date of the new Standard.

APPLICATION PROBLEM
Preparing a work sheet for a governmental organization

The town of Winona uses a general fund. The trial balance for December 31 of the current year is recorded on a work sheet in the *Working Papers*. The following adjustment information is available.

Adjustment Information, December 31

Supplies Inventory	$3,534.00
Interest Revenue Due but not Collected	2,900.00

An estimated 20% of the interest revenue due will not be collected.
The reserve for encumbrances for the current year is reclassified to prior year status.

Instructions:

1. Analyze the adjustment information and record the adjustments on the work sheet.

2. Complete the work sheet. Save your work to complete Application Problems 24-2 and 24-3.

APPLICATION PROBLEM
Preparing financial statements for a governmental organization

Use the work sheet prepared in Application Problem 24-1 to complete this problem.

The town of Winona's general fund operating budget for the current year is shown on page 677.

Instructions:

1. Prepare a statement of revenues, expenditures, and changes in fund balance—budget and actual for the year ended December 31 of the current year. The unreserved fund balance on January 1 was $41,244.00.

2. Prepare a balance sheet for December 31 of the current year.

APPLICATION PROBLEM
Journalizing adjusting and closing entries for a governmental organization

Use the work sheet prepared in Application Problem 24-1 to complete this problem.

Instructions:

1. Use page 23 of a journal. Journalize the adjusting entries.

2. Continue using page 23 of a journal. Journalize the closing entries.

Town of Winona
Annual Operating Budget—General Fund
For Year Ended December 31, 20--

ESTIMATED REVENUES

Property Tax	$1,459,000.00	
Interest	8,950.00	
Other	9,000.00	
Total Estimated Revenues		$1,476,950.00

ESTIMATED EXPENDITURES AND BUDGETARY FUND BALANCE

General Government:		
Personnel	$ 250,250.00	
Supplies	13,230.00	
Other Charges	124,740.00	
Capital Outlays	14,600.00	
Total General Government		$ 402,820.00
Public Safety:		
Personnel	$ 414,740.00	
Supplies	22,000.00	
Other Charges	168,460.00	
Capital Outlays	81,270.00	
Total Public Safety		686,470.00
Public Works:		
Personnel	$ 157,730.00	
Supplies	6,160.00	
Other Charges	52,250.00	
Capital Outlays	46,350.00	
Total Public Works		262,490.00
Recreation:		
Personnel	$ 55,350.00	
Supplies	22,170.00	
Other Charges	27,780.00	
Capital Outlays	10,460.00	
Total Recreation		115,760.00
Total Estimated Expenditures		$1,467,540.00
Budgetary Fund Balance		9,410.00
Total Estimated Expenditures and Budgetary Fund Balance		$1,476,950.00

MASTERY PROBLEM
Completing the end-of-fiscal-period work for a governmental organization

The town of Duluth uses a general fund. The trial balance for December 31 of the current year is recorded on a work sheet in the *Working Papers*. The following adjustment information is available.

Adjustment Information, December 31

Supplies Inventory	$2,900.00
Interest Revenue Due but not Collected	2,350.00

An estimated 20% of the interest revenue due will not be collected.

The reserve for encumbrances for the current year is reclassified to prior year status.

continued

Instructions:

1. Analyze the adjustment information and record the adjustments on the work sheet.

2. Complete the work sheet.

Duluth's general fund operating budget for the current fiscal year is as follows.

Town of Duluth
Annual Operating Budget—General Fund
For Year Ended December 31, 20--

ESTIMATED REVENUES

Property Tax	$1,265,000.00	
Interest	7,250.00	
Other	7,750.00	
Total Estimated Revenues		$1,280,000.00

ESTIMATED EXPENDITURES AND BUDGETARY FUND BALANCE

General Government:		
Personnel	$ 211,750.00	
Supplies	11,360.00	
Other Charges	106,700.00	
Capital Outlays	12,390.00	
Total General Government		$ 342,200.00
Public Safety:		
Personnel	$ 397,590.00	
Supplies	18,900.00	
Other Charges	144,290.00	
Capital Outlays	72,320.00	
Total Public Safety		633,100.00
Public Works:		
Personnel	$ 92,270.00	
Supplies	5,280.00	
Other Charges	44,770.00	
Capital Outlays	39,680.00	
Total Public Works		182,000.00
Recreation:		
Personnel	$ 48,220.00	
Supplies	1,880.00	
Other Charges	23,690.00	
Capital Outlays	8,910.00	
Total Recreation		82,700.00
Total Estimated Expenditures		$1,240,000.00
Budgetary Fund Balance		40,000.00
Total Estimated Expenditures and Budgetary Fund Balance		$1,280,000.00

3. Prepare a statement of revenues, expenditures, and changes in fund balance—budget and actual for the year ended December 31 of the current year. The unreserved fund balance on January 1 was $35,550.00.

4. Prepare a balance sheet for December 31 of the current year.

5. Use page 42 of a journal. Journalize the adjusting entries.

6. Continue using page 42 of the journal. Journalize the closing entries.

CHALLENGE PROBLEM
Completing end-of-fiscal-period work for a governmental organization

The town of Plymouth uses a general fund. The trial balance for December 31 of the current year is recorded on a work sheet in the *Working Papers*. The following adjustment information is available.

Adjustment Information, December 31

Supplies Inventory	$3,382.00
Interest Revenue Due but not Collected	6,080.00

An estimated 20% of the interest revenue due will not be collected.
The reserve for encumbrances for the current year is reclassified to prior year status.

Plymouth's general fund operating budget for the current fiscal year is shown as follows.

Town of Plymouth
Annual Operating Budget—General Fund
For Year Ended December 31, 20--

ESTIMATED REVENUES AND BUDGETARY FUND BALANCE

Property Tax	$1,455,900.00	
Interest	13,360.00	
Other	16,580.00	
Total Estimated Revenues		$1,485,840.00
Budgetary Fund Balance		25,320.00
Estimated Revenues and Budgetary Fund Balance		$1,511,160.00

ESTIMATED EXPENDITURES

General Government:		
Personnel	$ 260,480.00	
Supplies	14,280.00	
Other Charges	130,240.00	
Capital Outlays	15,130.00	
Total General Government		$ 420,130.00
Public Safety:		
Personnel	$ 484,610.00	
Supplies	23,080.00	
Other Charges	176,920.00	
Capital Outlays	84,920.00	
Total Public Safety		769,530.00
Public Works:		
Personnel	$ 113,300.00	
Supplies	6,660.00	
Other Charges	53,120.00	
Capital Outlays	48,875.00	
Total Public Works		221,955.00
Recreation:		
Personnel	$ 56,855.00	
Supplies	2,790.00	
Other Charges	28,925.00	
Capital Outlays	10,975.00	
Total Recreation		99,545.00
Total Estimated Expenditures		$1,511,160.00

Plymouth's town council permits departmental managers to exceed budgeted amounts for supplies, other charges, and capital outlays. However, total amounts expended for these three types of expenditure must be within the total budget amounts for these three items within each department.

Plymouth is prohibited from deficit spending. However, if sufficient funds are on hand at the beginning of a year, the town council may choose to appropriate more than the estimated revenues. Sufficient funds are on hand when the beginning fund balance plus estimated revenues equals or exceeds appropriations.

Instructions:

1. Analyze the adjustment information and record the adjustments on the work sheet.

2. Complete the work sheet.

3. Prepare a statement of revenues, expenditures, and changes in fund balance—budget and actual for the year ended December 31 of the current year. The unreserved fund balance on January 1 was $63,450.00.

4. Prepare a balance sheet for December 31 of the current year.

5. Use page 40 of a journal. Journalize the adjusting entries.

6. Continue using page 40 of the journal. Journalize the closing entries.

INTERNET ACTIVITY

Point your browser to
http://accounting.swpco.com
Choose **Advanced Course**, choose **Activities**, and complete the activity for Chapter 24.

Applied Communication

As you complete this text, review the book's objectives stated in the Introduction, page xiv.

Required:

Prepare a written self-assessment. For Objectives 2 through 8 list at least two specific concepts or practices you have learned. Then rate your overall performance in this course as excellent, good, fair, or poor.

Cases for Critical Thinking

Case 1

The town of Spearman's statement of revenue, expenditures, and changes in fund balance—budget and actual lists expenditures by type. Expenditures listed are personnel, supplies, other charges, and capital outlays. Charles Lambert, a new accountant, suggested that expenditures be reported on this statement by departmental organization. Do you agree with Mr. Lambert? Explain your response.

Case 2

Vicki Bonilla, a new accounting clerk for the town of Evergreen, recorded the closing entries for the current year. Miss Bonilla questions the necessity of making a closing entry for encumbrance accounts with balances. She suggests not closing the encumbrances. Then when items are received for which the encumbrances were recorded, make the regular journal entries. That is, (1) reverse the encumbrance entry and (2) debit Expenditures and credit Cash. Do you agree with Miss Bonilla? Explain your response.

AUTOMATED ACCOUNTING

USING THE JOURNAL WIZARD TO CUSTOMIZE THE APPEARANCE OF JOURNALS

Automated Accounting 7.0 and higher includes a utility that allows the user to define the amount columns to be included in the various journals. This utility is the Journal Wizard. A wizard is simply a step-by-step guide created by the programmer to help the user easily modify some aspect of the software or to easily complete a complex task.

The Journal Wizard is a tab located on the Customize Accounting System window. Before it can be used, a company must be set up. Modifications to journals should be made before any data are entered into the journals.

The control buttons for the wizard are located at the right of the tab. The buttons direct the user through the process. The user can move to the next screen, back a screen, finish the process, close the wizard without completing the task, or get help. (In *Automated Accounting 8.0,* the Journal Wizard control buttons are located at the bottom of the Journal Wizard tab.)

For each screen of the wizard, the user must carefully read the screen and make the appropriate choice. The screens contained in the wizard are described in the following paragraphs.

Select Journal

Only one journal at a time may be modified. If General Journal is selected, the next two screens do not appear.

Establish Offsetting Account

In most cases, the default account that appears with this screen will be the correct choice.

However, the user may modify the account, the column type, and the column heading.

General Debit and Credit

This screen allows the user to include a General Debit and General Credit column in the journal. The default choice of the software is generally correct.

Special Journal Columns

This screen is used to identify all special columns in the journal. The user enters the account title, the header, and checks whether the account will be debited or credited. The header may have two lines. Each line is limited to 7 to 9 characters depending upon the font and the letters used.

After all items have been specified, click the Finish button. The Journal Wizard will complete the process. The modified journal will be available each time the company and problem are used. This journal is associated with the open company and problem. No other companies or problems are affected.

USING JOURNAL WIZARD

(Note: This template does not use data from a problem in the text.)

Instructions:

1. Load *Automated Accounting 7.0* or higher software.

2. Select database ARA-2 from the accounting template disk.

3. Select File from the menu bar and choose the Save As menu command. Key the path to the drive and directory that contains your data

files. Save the database with a file name of XXX241 (where XXX are your initials).

4. Do not refer to the Problem Instructions.

5. Click the Custom tool and change the Company Info. to two departments.

6. Change the chart of accounts so that there are two purchases accounts: Purchases-Dept. 1 and Purchases-Dept. 2.

7. Use the Journal Wizard to change the purchases journal. Replace the Purch. Debit column with a Debit column for each of the two new purchases accounts.

8. Create a purchase on account transaction for each department and enter each in the purchases journal to test whether the journal has been changed properly.

9. Repeat the process for the sales journal and the cash receipts journal if time permits. Note that you will first need to change the chart of accounts so that there is a Sales account for each deparment. Note: To be a complete departmentalized accounting system, it would also be necessary to depart-mentalize the purchases and sales discount and returns and allowances account. However the purpose of this problem is to experiment with the Journal Wizard.

10. Exit the Automated Accounting software.

Accounting Concepts

Accountants follow concepts commonly accepted by the profession as guides for reporting and interpreting accounting information. The accounting procedures described in this textbook are based on the application of accepted concepts. Eleven commonly accepted concepts are described in this appendix and referenced throughout the textbook.

CONCEPT: ACCOUNTING PERIOD CYCLE

Changes in financial information are reported for a specific period of time in the form of financial statements.

Financial statements summarize the financial information that a business records. The time period for which financial statements are prepared depends on the needs of the business. An accounting period may be one month, three months, six months, or one year. For tax purposes, every business prepares financial statements at the end of each year.

CONCEPT: ADEQUATE DISCLOSURE

Financial statements contain all information necessary to understand a business' financial condition.

Owners, managers, lenders, and investors rely on financial statements to make informed decisions. All relevant financial information must be adequately and completely disclosed on financial statements.

A business reports only the total liabilities of $200,000.00 on its balance sheet. However, the total liabilities include $75,000.00 in current liabilities and $125,000.00 in long-term liabilities. Therefore, the balance sheet does not adequately disclose the nature of the liabilities. The critical information not disclosed is that $75,000.00 is current and due within a few months.

CONCEPT: BUSINESS ENTITY

Financial information is recorded and reported separately from the owner's personal financial information.

A business' records must not be mixed with an owner's personal records and reports. For example, a business owner may buy insurance to protect the business and insurance to protect the owner's home. Only the insurance obtained for the business is recorded in the business' financial records. The insurance purchased for the owner's personal home is recorded in the owner's personal financial records. One bank account is used for the business and another for the owner. A business exists separately from its owners.

CONCEPT: CONSISTENT REPORTING

The same accounting procedures must be followed in the same way in each accounting period.

Business decisions are based on the financial information reported on financial statements. Some decisions require a comparison of current financial statements with previous financial statements. If accounting information is recorded and reported differently each accounting period, comparisons from one accounting period to another may not be possible. For example, in one period a business reports $170,000.00 for total operating expenses and in the next period it reports $120,000 as cost of merchandise sold and $50,000 as operating expenses. A user of this information cannot adequately compare the two accounting periods. Therefore, unless a change is necessary to make information more easily understood, accounting information is reported in a consistent way for each accounting period.

CONCEPT: GOING CONCERN

Financial statements are prepared with the expectation that a business will remain in operation indefinitely.

New businesses are started with the expectation that they will be successful. Accounting records and financial statements are designed as though businesses will continue indefinitely.

A business bought store equipment for $30,000.00. The store equipment is expected to last 10 years. Yearly depreciation, therefore, is recorded and reported based on the expected life of the equipment. After six years of the expected 10-year life, the equipment's book value (cost less accumulated depreciation) is $13,200.00. If the business ended operations and the equipment had to be sold, the amount received may be less than the $13,200.00. However, accounting records are maintained with the expectation that the business will remain in operation indefinitely and that the cost will be allocated over the useful life of the equipment. The equipment value, therefore, remains $13,200.00 on the records regardless of what the equipment may be worth when sold.

CONCEPT: HISTORICAL COST

The actual amount paid for merchandise or other items bought is recorded.

The actual amount paid for an item in a business transaction may be different from the value. For example, OfficeMart purchased a delivery truck valued at $20,000.00 and advertised at a sale price of $18,000.00. OfficeMart negotiated to purchase the delivery truck for $17,000.00. The amount recorded in accounting records for the delivery truck is the historical cost, $17,000.00—the actual amount paid.

Six months later, OfficeMart sells the delivery truck to Flowers by Giverney for $15,000.00. For Flowers by Giverney, the historical cost of the delivery truck is $15,000.00.

CONCEPT: MATCHING EXPENSES WITH REVENUE

The revenue from business activities and the expenses associated with earning that revenue are recorded in the same accounting period.

Business activities for an accounting period are summarized in financial statements. To adequately report how a business performed during an accounting period, all revenue earned as a result of business operations must be reported. Likewise, all expenses incurred in producing the revenue during the same accounting period must be reported. Matching expenses with revenue gives a true picture of business operations for an accounting period.

For example, a business had sales of $100,000.00 in December. Expenses before adjustments were $80,000.00. Adjustments for items such as uncollectible accounts expense, supplies expense, and depreciation expense totaled $5,000.00. Therefore, total expenses for December should be reported as $85,000.00. The matching of expenses with revenues results in an accurate report of net income of $15,000.00. By including all expenses, readers of the financial statements have a more complete picture of the financial condition of the business.

CONCEPT: MATERIALITY

Business activities creating dollar amounts large enough to affect business decisions should be recorded and reported as separate items in accounting records and financial statements.

Business transactions are recorded in accounting records and reported in financial statements in dollar amounts. How the amounts are recorded and reported depends on the amount involved and the relative importance of the item in making business decisions. Dollar amounts that are large will generally be considered in making decisions about future operations. A separate accounting record is kept for items with dollar amounts large enough to be considered in making decisions about future operations. Dollar amounts that are small and not considered important in decision making may be combined with other amounts in the accounting records and financial statements.

For example, modems and print motors used to manufacture fax machines are considered direct materials and accounted for separately. Connectors and gears used in the manufacture of fax machines are parts with a small enough dollar value that they are grouped together and their total value is recorded in the accounting records as indirect material.

CONCEPT: OBJECTIVE EVIDENCE

A source document is prepared for each transaction.

The source document is the original business paper indicating that the transaction did occur and that the amounts recorded in the accounting records are accurate and true. For example, a check is the original business paper for cash payments. The original business paper for purchases on account is the purchase invoice. When accounting information reported on the financial statements needs to be verified, an accountant will first check the accounting record. If the details of an entry need further checking, an accountant will then check the business papers as objective evidence that the transaction did occur.

CONCEPT: REALIZATION OF REVENUE

Revenue is recorded at the time goods or services are sold.

A business may sell either goods or services. Cash may be received at the time of sale or an agreement may be made to receive payment at a later date. Regardless of when cash is actually received, the sale amount is recorded in the accounting records at the time of sale. For example, a business sells office furniture for $2,000.00. The business agrees to an initial payment of $400.00 with the remaining balance to be divided in four monthly payments of $400.00 each. The full $2,000.00 of revenue is recorded at the time of sale even though $1,600.00 will be paid later.

CONCEPT: UNIT OF MEASUREMENT

Business transactions are reported in numbers that have common values—that is, using a common unit of measurement.

All transactions are recorded in accounting records in terms of money. Useful nonfinancial information may also be recorded to describe the nature of a business transaction.

If part of the information in the accounting records is financial and part is nonfinancial, the financial statements will not be clear. For example, if MasterSport states its sales in number of units sold (nonfinancial) and its expenses in dollars (financial), net profit cannot be calculated. Instead, total expenses (financial) subtracted from money taken in through sales (financial) equals profit.

Using a Calculator and Computer Keypad

KINDS OF CALCULATORS

Many different models of calculators, both desktop and hand held, are available. All calculators have their own features and particular placement of operating keys. Therefore, it is necessary to refer to the operator's manual for specific instructions and locations of the operating keys for the calculator being used. A typical keyboard of a desktop calculator is shown in Illustration B-1.

DESKTOP CALCULATOR SETTINGS

Several operating switches on a desktop calculator must be engaged before the calculator will produce the desired results.

The *decimal selector* sets the appropriate decimal places necessary for the numbers that will be entered. For example, if the decimal selector is set at 2, both the numbers entered and the answer will have two decimal places. If the decimal selector is set at F, the calculator automatically sets the decimal places. The F setting allows the answer to be unrounded and carried out to the maximum number of decimal places possible.

The *decimal rounding* selector rounds the answers. The down arrow position will drop any digits beyond the last digit desired. The up arrow position will drop any digits beyond the last digit desired and round the last digit up. In the 5/4 position, the calculator rounds the last desired digit up only when the following digit is 5 or greater. If the following digit is less than 5, the last desired digit remains unchanged.

The *GT* or *grand total* switch in the on position accumulates totals.

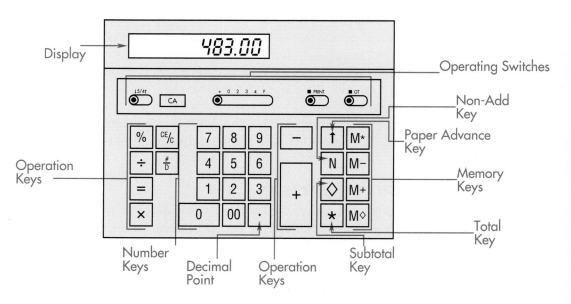

Figure B-1

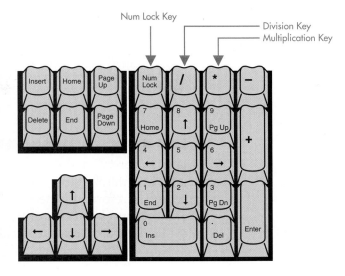

Standard
Keyboard Layout

Enhanced
Keyboard Layout

Figure B-2

KINDS OF COMPUTER KEYBOARDS

The computer has a keypad on the right side of the keyboard called the **numeric keypad**. Even though several styles of keyboards for the IBM® and compatible computers are found, there are two basic layouts for the numeric keypad. The standard layout and enhanced layout are shown in Illustration B-2 on page B-3. On the standard keyboard the directional arrow keys are found on the number keys. To use the numbers, press the key called **Num Lock**. (This key is found above the "7" key.) When the Num Lock is turned on, numbers are entered when the keys on the keypad are pressed. When the Num Lock is off, the arrow, Home, Page Up, Page Down, End, Insert, and Delete keys can be used.

The enhanced keyboards have the arrow keys and the other directional keys mentioned above to the left of the numeric keypad. When using the keypad on an enhanced keyboard, Num Lock can remain on.

The asterisk (*) performs a different function on the computer than the calculator. The asterisk on the calculator is used for the total while the computer uses it for multiplication.

Another difference is the division key. The computer key is the forward slash key (/). The calculator key uses the division key (÷).

TEN-KEY TOUCH SYSTEM

Striking the numbers 0 to 9 on a calculator or numeric keypad without looking at the keyboard is called the **touch system**. Using the touch system develops both speed and accuracy.

The 4, 5, and 6 keys are called the **home row**. If the right hand is used for the keyboard, the index finger is placed on the 4 key, the middle finger on the 5 key, and the ring finger on the 6 key. If the left hand is used, the ring finger is placed on the 4 key, the middle finger on the 5 key, and the index finger on the 6 key.

Place the fingers on the home row keys. Curve the fingers and keep the wrist straight. These keys may feel slightly concaved or the 5 key may have a raised dot. The differences in the home row allow the operator to recognize the home row by touch rather than by sight.

Maintain the position of the fingers on the home row. The finger used to strike the 4 key will also strike the 7 key and the 1 key. Stretch the finger up to reach the 7; then stretch the finger down to reach the 1 key. Visualize the position of these keys.

Again, place the fingers on the home row. Stretch the finger that strikes the 5 key up to reach the 8 key, then down to reach the 2 key. Likewise, stretch the finger that strikes the 6 key up to strike the 9 and down to strike the 3 key. This same finger will stretch down again to hit the decimal point.

If the right hand is used, the thumb will be used to strike the 0 and 00 keys and the little finger to strike the addition key. If the left hand is used, the little finger will be used to strike the 0 and 00 keys and the thumb to strike the addition key.

HAND-HELD CALCULATORS

Hand-held calculators are slightly different from desktop calculators, not only in their size and features but also in their operation. Refer to the operator's manual for specific instructions for the calculator being used.

On a hand-held calculator, the numeric keys are usually very close together. In addition, the keys do not respond to touch as easily as on a desktop calculator. Therefore, the touch system is usually not used on a hand-held calculator.

PERFORMING MATHEMATICAL OPERATIONS ON DESKTOP CALCULATORS

Mathematical operations can be performed on a calculator both quickly and efficiently. The basic operations of addition, subtraction, multiplication, and division are used frequently on a calculator.

Addition

Each number to be added is called an **addend**. The answer to an addition problem is called the **sum**.

Addition is performed by entering an addend and striking the addition key (+). All numbers are entered on a calculator in the exact order they are given. To enter the number 4,455.65, strike the 4, 4, 5, 5, decimal, 6, and 5 keys in that order, and then strike the addition key. Do not enter commas. Continue in this manner until all addends have been entered. To obtain the sum, strike the total key on the calculator.

Subtraction

The top number or first number of a subtraction problem is called the **minuend.** The number to be subtracted from the minuend is called the **subtrahend**. The answer to a subtraction problem is called the **difference**.

Subtraction is performed by first entering the minuend and striking the addition key (1). The subtrahend is then entered, followed by the minus key (2), followed by the total key.

Multiplication

The number to be multiplied is called the **multiplicand**. The number of times the multiplicand will be multiplied is called the **multiplier**. The answer to a multiplication problem is called the **product**.

Multiplication is performed by entering the multiplicand and striking the multiplication key (3). The multiplier is then entered, followed by the equals key (5). The calculator will automatically multiply and give the product.

Division

The number to be divided is called the **dividend**. The number the dividend will be divided by is called the **divisor**. The answer to a division problem is called the **quotient**.

Division is performed by entering the dividend and striking the division key (÷). The divisor is then entered, followed by the equals key (=). The calculator will automatically divide and give the quotient.

Correcting Errors

If an error is made while using a calculator, several methods of correction may be used. If an incorrect number has been entered and the addition key or equals key has not yet been struck, strike the clear entry (CE) key one time. This key will clear only the last number that was entered. However, if the clear entry key is depressed more than one time, the entire problem will be cleared on some calculators. If an incorrect number has been entered and the addition key has been struck, strike the minus key one time only. This will automatically subtract the last number added, thus removing it from the total.

PERFORMING MATHEMATICAL OPERATIONS ON COMPUTERS AND HAND-HELD CALCULATORS

On a computer keypad or a hand-held calculator, addition is performed in much the same way as on a desktop calculator. However, after the 1 key is depressed, the display usually shows the accumulated total. Therefore, the total key is not found. Some computer programs will not calculate the total until Enter is pressed.

Subtraction is performed differently on many computer keypads and hand-held calculators. The minuend is usually entered, followed by the minus (–) key. Then the subtrahend is entered. Pressing either the 1 key or the 5 key will display the difference. Some computer programs will not calculate the difference until Enter is pressed.

Multiplication and division are performed the same way on a computer keypad and hand-held calculator as on a desktop calculator. Keep in mind that computers use the * for multiplication and / for division.

SAFETY CONCERNS

Whenever electrical equipment such as a calculator or computer is being operated in a classroom or office, several safety rules apply. These rules protect the operator of the equipment, other persons in the environment, and the equipment itself.

1. Do not unplug equipment by pulling on the electrical cord. Instead, grasp the plug at the outlet and remove it.

2. Do not stretch electrical cords across an aisle where someone might trip over them.

3. Avoid food and beverages near the equipment where a spill might result in an electrical short.

4. Do not attempt to remove the cover of a calculator, computer, or keyboard for any reason while the power is turned on.

5. Do not attempt to repair equipment while it is plugged in.

6. Always turn the power off or unplug equipment when finished using it.

CALCULATION DRILLS

Instructions for Desktop Calculators:

Complete each drill using the touch method. Set the decimal selector at the setting indicated in each drill. Compare the answer on the calculator to the answer in the book. If the two are the same, progress to the next problem. It is not necessary to enter 00 in the cents column if the decimal selector is set at 0-F. However, digits other than zeros in the cents column must be entered preceded by a decimal point.

Instructions for Computer Keypads:

Complete each drill using the touch method. There is no decimal selector on computer keypads. Set the number of decimal places as directed in the instructions for the computer program. In spreadsheets, for example, use the formatting options to set the number of decimal places. When the drill indicates "F" for floating, leave the computer application in its default format. Compare the answer on the computer monitor to the answer in the book. If the two are the same, progress to the next problem. It is not necessary to enter 00 in the cents column. However, digits other than zeros in the cents column must be entered preceded by a decimal point.

DRILL D-1   Performing addition using the home row keys
             Decimal Selector—2

4.00	44.00	444.00	4,444.00	44,444.00
5.00	55.00	555.00	5,555.00	55,555.00
6.00	66.00	666.00	6,666.00	66,666.00
5.00	45.00	455.00	4,455.00	44,556.00
4.00	46.00	466.00	4,466.00	44,565.00
5.00	54.00	544.00	5,544.00	55,446.00
6.00	56.00	566.00	5,566.00	55,664.00
5.00	65.00	655.00	6,655.00	66,554.00
4.00	64.00	644.00	6,644.00	66,555.00
5.00	66.00	654.00	6,545.00	65,465.00
49.00	561.00	5,649.00	56,540.00	565,470.00

DRILL D-2   Performing addition using the 0, 1, 4, and 7 keys
             Decimal Selector—2

4.00	11.00	444.00	4,440.00	44,000.00
7.00	44.00	777.00	7,770.00	77,000.00
4.00	74.00	111.00	1,110.00	11,000.00
1.00	71.00	741.00	4,400.00	41,000.00
4.00	70.00	740.00	1,100.00	71,000.00
7.00	10.00	101.00	4,007.00	10,000.00
4.00	14.00	140.00	7,001.00	10,100.00
1.00	17.00	701.00	1,007.00	40,100.00
4.00	40.00	700.00	1,004.00	70,100.00
7.00	77.00	407.00	7,700.00	74,100.00
43.00	428.00	4,862.00	39,539.00	448,400.00

DRILL D-3 Performing addition using the 2, 5, and 8 keys
Decimal Selector—2

5.00	58.00	588.00	8,888.00	88,855.00
8.00	52.00	522.00	5,555.00	88,822.00
5.00	85.00	888.00	2,222.00	88,852.00
2.00	52.00	222.00	8,525.00	88,222.00
5.00	25.00	258.00	2,585.00	85,258.00
8.00	58.00	852.00	8,258.00	22,255.00
5.00	82.00	225.00	8,585.00	22,288.00
2.00	28.00	885.00	5,258.00	22,258.00
5.00	88.00	882.00	2,852.00	22,888.00
8.00	22.00	228.00	2,288.00	25,852.00
53.00	550.00	5,550.00	55,016.00	555,550.00

DRILL D-4 Performing addition using the 3, 6, 9, and decimal point keys
Decimal Selector—2

6.00	66.66	666.66	6,666.99	66,699.33
9.00	99.99	999.99	9,999.66	99,966.66
6.00	33.33	333.33	3,333.99	33,366.33
3.00	33.66	666.99	3,366.99	36,963.36
6.36	33.99	999.66	6,699.33	69,636.36
3.36	99.66	333.66	9,966.33	33,333.66
9.36	99.33	696.36	9,636.69	66,666.99
9.63	33.36	369.63	3,696.36	99,999.33
6.33	33.69	336.69	6,963.99	96,369.63
9.93	69.63	963.36	6,699.33	36,963.36
68.97	603.30	6,366.33	67,029.66	639,965.01

DRILL D-5 Performing subtraction using all number keys
Decimal Selector—F

456.73	789.01	741.00	852.55	987.98
−123.21	−456.00	−258.10	−369.88	−102.55
333.52	333.01	482.90	482.67	885.43

DRILL D-6 Performing multiplication using all number keys
Decimal Selector—F

654.05	975.01	487.10	123.56	803.75
× 12.66	× 27.19	× 30.21	× 50.09	× 1.45
8,280.273	26,510.5219	14,715.291	6,189.1204	1,165.4375

DRILL D-7 Performing division using all number keys
Decimal Selector—F

900.56	4	450.28	5	2.
500.25	4	100.05	5	5.
135.66	4	6.65	5	20.4
269.155	4	105.55	5	2.550023685*
985.66	4	22.66	5	43.49779346*

*Number of decimal places may vary due to machine capacity.

Recycling Problems

RECYCLING PROBLEM 1-R1
Performing file maintenance activities; journalizing departmental purchases and cash payments

The Floor Store has two departments: Carpeting and Linoleum. The following is Floor Store's partial general ledger chart of accounts.

6105	Advertising Expense
6110	Depreciation Expense—Store Equipment
6115-1	Salary Expense—Carpet
6115-2	Salary Expense—Linoleum

Transactions:

Nov. 1. Paid cash for office supplies, $62.50. C301.
2. Paid cash for rent, $1,000.00. C302.
4. Paid cash on account to Lyndale Linoleum, $2,763.60, covering P176 for linoleum for $2,820.00, less discount, $56.40. C303.
5. Purchased carpeting on account from King Carpets, $3,740.00. P178.
7. Paid cash on account to Floors and More, $1,651.30, covering P177 for linoleum for $1,685.00, less discount, $33.70. C304.
8. Returned carpeting to King Carpets, $186.00, from P178. DM19.
10. Purchased linoleum on account from Mercury Floors, $2,680.00. P179.
12. Paid cash on account to King Carpets, $3,482.92, covering P178 for carpeting for $3,740.00, less DM19 for $186.00, and less discount, $71.08. C305.
14. Purchased carpeting on account from Carpet Distributors, $2,670.00. P180.
14. Paid cash for advertising, $82.50. C306.
15. Returned linoleum to Floors and More, $212.40, from P177. DM20.
15. Returned carpeting to Carpet Distributors, $450.00, from P180. DM21.
17. Paid cash on account to Mercury Floors, $2,626.40, covering P179 for linoleum for $2,680.00, less discount, $53.60. C307.
18. Purchased linoleum on account from Mercury Floors, $1,360.00. P181.
19. Paid cash for store supplies, $62.75. C308.
21. Paid cash on account to Carpet Distributors, $2,175.60, covering P180 for carpeting for $2,670.00, less DM21 for $450.00, and less discount, $44.40. C309.
24. Purchased carpeting on account from King Carpets, $1,925.00. P182.
25. Paid cash on account to Mercury Floors, $1,332.80, covering P181 for linoleum for $1,360.00, less discount, $27.20. C310.
28. Purchased linoleum on account from Lyndale Linoleum, $4,340.00. P183.
30. Paid cash to replenish the petty cash fund, $214.00: office supplies, $65.50; advertising, $87.30; miscellaneous, $61.20. C311.
30. Received bank statement showing November bank service charge, $21.20. M22.
30. Recorded credit card fee expense for November, $567.50. M23.

Instructions:

1. Add Credit Card Fee Expense and Supplies Expense—Store to the general ledger chart of accounts using the unused middle number method described in this chapter.

continued

2. Journalize the following transactions completed during November of the current year. Page 11 of a purchases journal and a purchases returns and allowances journal and page 21 of a cash payments journal are provided in the *Recycling Problems Working Papers*. All vendors documents are abbreviated as follows: check, C; debit memorandum, DM; purchase invoice, P.

3. Prove and rule the journals.

RECYCLING PROBLEM 1-R2
Reconciling a bank statement

On September 30 of the current year, Boone, Inc., received a bank statement dated September 28. The following information is obtained from the bank statement and from the records of the business.

Bank statement balance	$27,160.00
Bank service charge	10.40
Bank credit card charge	393.80
Outstanding deposit: September 29	3,157.20
Outstanding checks:	
No. 231	1,221.00
No. 232	860.40
Checkbook balance on Check Stub No. 233	28,640.00

Instructions:
Prepare a bank statement reconciliation using the form provided in the *Recycling Problem Working Papers*. Use September 30 of the current year as the date.

RECYCLING PROBLEM 2-R
Journalizing department sales, sales returns and allowances, and cash receipts

Highcrest Computers, Inc., has two departments: Hardware and Software.

Transactions:
Apr. 1. Sold hardware on account to Allen Davis, $1,640.00, plus sales tax. S119.
　　 2. Recorded cash and credit card sales: hardware, $3,170.00; software, $2,690.00; plus sales tax. T2.
　　 5. Received cash on account from Western Co., covering S116 for software ($168.00 plus sales tax), less discount and less sales tax. R72.
　　 5. Granted credit to Gloria Odum for software returned, $30.00, plus sales tax, from S118. CM21.
　　 8. Sold software on account to Geig Enterprises, $680.00, plus sales tax. S120.
　　 8. Received cash on account from Travis O'Leary, covering S117 for hardware ($850.00 plus sales tax), less discount and less sales tax. R73.
　　 9. Received cash on account from Gloria Odum, covering S118 for software ($168.00 plus sales tax), less CM21 ($30.00 plus sales tax), less discount and less sales tax. R74.
　　 9. Recorded cash and credit card sales: hardware, $5,780.00; software, $4,620.00; plus sales tax. T9.
　　11. Received cash on account from Allen Davis, covering S119 for hardware ($1,640.00 plus sales tax), less discount and less sales tax. R75.
　　13. Sold software on account to Susan Newman, $75.00, plus sales tax. S121.
　　15. Sold hardware on account to Travis O'Leary, $480.00, plus sales tax. S122.

Apr. 16. Recorded cash and credit card sales: hardware, $6,210.00; software, $5,030.00; plus sales tax. T16.
18. Received cash on account from Geig Enterprises, covering S120 for software ($680.00 plus sales tax), less discount and less sales tax. R76.
19. Granted credit to Susan Newman for software returned, $18.00, plus sales tax, from S121. CM22.
22. Sold hardware on account to Melrose Schools, $1,640.00; no sales tax. S123.
23. Received cash on account from Susan Newman, covering S121 for software ($75.00 plus sales tax), less CM22 ($18.00 plus sales tax), less discount and less sales tax. R77.
23. Recorded cash and credit card sales: hardware, $6,630.00; software, $4,720.00; plus sales tax. T23.
25. Received cash on account from Travis O'Leary, covering S122 for hardware ($480.00 plus sales tax), less discount and less sales tax. R78.
27. Sold software on account to Gloria Odum, $100.00; plus sales tax. S124.
30. Recorded cash and credit card sales: hardware, $3,890.00; software, $3,930.00; plus sales tax. T30.

Instructions:

1. Journalize the transactions completed during April of the current year. Calculate and record sales tax on all sales and sales returns and allowances as described in this chapter. Page 4 of a sales journal and a sales returns and allowances journal and page 7 of a cash receipts journal are provided in the *Recycling Problems Working Papers*. Highcrest offers its customers terms of 2/10, n/30. The sales tax rate is 5%. Source documents are abbreviated as follows: credit memorandum, CM; receipt, R; sales invoice, S; cash register tape, T.

2. Prove and rule the sales journal and the sales returns and allowances journal.

3. Prove and rule the cash receipts journal.

RECYCLING PROBLEM 3-R
Completing payroll records, journalizing payment of a payroll, and journalizing payroll taxes

Sheridan Shoes has two departments: Men's Shoes and Women's Shoes. A biweekly payroll system of 26 pay periods per year is used. Salesclerks and employees in the accounting department are paid on an hourly basis and receive 1-1/2 times the regular hourly rate for all hours worked over 80 each pay period. A time card is used for hourly employees to record hours worked. Departmental supervisors are paid a biweekly salary and receive monthly commissions of 1% of net sales. Commissions are paid in the first pay period of the following month.

Sheridan Shoes provides the same employee benefits as MasterSport in Chapter 3. The employee benefits provided are in the employee benefits schedule shown in Figure 3-1.

Instructions:

1. Prepare Joan Aldrich's benefits record for the first four biweekly pay periods of the current year using the form provided in the *Recycling Papers Working Problems*. Use the information at the top of the next page.

2. Prepare the commissions record for each departmental supervisor for the month ended January 31 of the current year. Use the basic payroll information given in the table on the next page. The following additional information is needed to complete the commissions records.
   a. Men's Shoes department: sales on account, $5,143.77; cash and credit card sales, $9,656.04; sales discount, $115.17; sales returns and allowances, $389.94.
   b. Women's Shoes department: sales on account, $6,712.50; cash and credit card sales, $9,320.40; sales discount, $124.30; sales returns and allowances, $517.60.

continued

Employee No.: 1
Department: Women's Shoes

Employee Name: Joan J. Aldrich
Date of Initial Employment: February 15, 1997

Pay Period	Regular Hours	Employee Benefits Available			Employee Benefits Used		
1/2	80	V66	S41	P19	V8	S0	P2
1/16	80	_____	_____	_____	V0	S3	P4
1/30	80	_____	_____	_____	V24	S4	P0
2/13	80	_____	_____	_____	V4	S0	P3

V = Vacation time; S = Sick leave time; P = Personal leave time

Employee No.	Employee Name	Position	Dept.	Marital Status	Allow.	Total Hours	Regular Pay	Overtime Pay
1	Aldrich, Joan J.	Salesclerk	W	M	2	83	$520.00	$29.25
2	Bryant, Mark K.	Supervisor	M	S	1	—	525.00	—
3	Colfax, Mary D.	Clerk	A	S	2	82	520.00	19.50
4	Emerson, Theodore A.	Salesclerk	M	M	3	80	464.00	—
5	James, Kelly A.	Salesclerk	W	M	2	84	432.00	32.40
6	Newton, Loretta M.	Supervisor	W	M	4	—	550.00	—
7	Penn, Joseph P.	Clerk	A	M	3	82	448.00	16.80
8	Russell, Eileen R.	Salesclerk	M	S	1	84	440.00	33.00
9	Thomas, Emily R.	Salesclerk	M	S	1	83	456.00	25.65
10	Washburn, Mark S.	Salesclerk	W	M	2	83	448.00	25.20

Departments: Men's Shoes, M; Women's Shoes, W; Administrative, A

3. Prepare Sheridan Shoes' payroll register for the biweekly pay period ended February 13 and paid February 20 of the current year. The following additional data are needed to complete the payroll register.
   a. A deduction for federal tax is to be made from each employee's total earnings. Use the appropriate income tax withholding tables shown in Chapter 3, Figure 3-8.
   b. A deduction of 4.5% for state income tax is to be made from each employee's total earnings.
   c. A deduction of 6.5% for social security tax and 1.5% for Medicare tax is to be made from each employee's total earnings.
   d. All employees have dental insurance, $9.10, and health insurance, $13.40, deducted from their pay each biweekly pay period. The letter D is to be written in front of the dental insurance deduction. The letter H is to be written in front of the health insurance deduction.

4. Complete Joan Aldrich's employee earnings record for the fourth pay period ended February 13 of the current year. The following data about Joan Aldrich are needed to complete the record.
   a. Hourly rate, $6.50.
   b. Social security number, 514-30-2258.
   c. Accumulated earnings for the first three payroll periods, $1,503.00.

5. Journalize the February 20 payroll payment using page 4 of a cash payments journal. The source document is Check No. 125.

6. Journalize the employer payroll taxes using page 4 of a general journal. Use February 20 of the current year as the date. The source document is Memorandum No. 10. Employer tax rates are: Social Security, 6.5%; Medicare, 1.5%; federal unemployment, 0.8%; and state unemployment, 5.4%.

RECYCLING PROBLEM 4-R1
Estimating ending merchandise inventory; preparing an interim departmental statement of gross profit; calculating and recording component percentages

Shoreline Shoes has two departments: Men's Shoes and Women's Shoes. The following data were obtained from the accounting records on March 31 of the current year.

	Men's Shoes	Women's Shoes
Beginning Inventory, January 1	$65,340.30	$58,120.50
Estimated Beginning Inventory, March 1	65,144.59	60,154.72
Net Purchases, January 1 to February 28	22,178.40	25,420.60
Net Sales, January 1 to February 28	40,680.20	42,520.70
Net Purchases for March	9,746.00	6,270.60
Net Sales for March	14,480.00	16,200.00
Gross Profit on Operations as a Percent of Sales	45.0%	45.0%

Instructions:

1. Prepare an estimated merchandise inventory sheet using the form provided in the *Recycling Problems Working Papers* for each department for the month ended March 31 of the current year.

2. Prepare an interim departmental statement of gross profit. Calculate and enter departmental and total component percentages for cost of merchandise sold and gross profit on operations. Round percentage calculations to the nearest 0.1%.

RECYCLING PROBLEM 4-R2
Preparing end-of-fiscal-period work for a departmentalized business

Deluxe Decorating, Inc., has two departments: Paint and Wallpaper. The trial balance on December 31 of the current year is provided in the Trial Balance columns of the work sheet in the *Recycling Problems Working Papers*. Statement paper is also provided in the *Recycling Problems Working Papers*.

Instructions:

1. Complete the departmental work sheet. Use the following information to prepare the adjustments.

Adjustment Information, December 31
Uncollectible accounts expense estimated as 1.0% of sales on account.
Sales on account for year, $214,060.00.

Merchandise Inventory—Paint	$186,740.20
Merchandise Inventory—Wallpaper	165,460.70
Office Supplies Inventory	1,610.30
Store Supplies Inventory	3,260.20
Value of Prepaid Insurance	2,520.00
Annual Depreciation Expense—Office Equipment	1,320.00
Annual Depreciation Expense—Store Equipment	1,480.00
Federal Income Tax Expense for the Year	11,995.95

2. Prepare a departmental statement of gross profit. Calculate and record component percentages for cost of merchandise sold and gross profit on operations. Round percentage calculations to the nearest 0.1%.

3. Prepare an income statement. Record the component percentages for cost of merchandise sold and gross profit on operations from the departmental statement of gross profit. Calculate and record the component percentages for total operating expenses and net income before and after federal income tax. Round percentage calculations to the nearest 0.1%.

4. Prepare a statement of stockholders' equity. Use the following additional information.

January 1 balance of capital stock account	$200,000.00
(2,000 shares issued for $100.00 per share)	
No additional capital stock issued.	
January 1 balance of retained earnings account	182,181.92
Dividends declared during the current year	40,000.00

continued

5. Prepare a balance sheet.

6. Journalize the adjusting entries. Page 14 of a general journal is provided in the *Recycling Problems Working Papers*.

7. Journalize the closing entries. Continue using page 14 of a general journal. Do not skip a line between the adjusting and closing entries.

RECYCLING PROBLEM 5-R
Journalizing transactions in a voucher system

Walston Company uses a voucher system, including a voucher register and a check register, similar to those described in Chapter 5.

Transactions:

May 1. Purchased merchandise on account from Moraska Company, $790.00. V30.
2. Bought sales supplies on account from Waldoch Supplies, $159.78. V31.
4. Bought store equipment on account from Murphy Equipment, $1,449.77. V32.
8. Purchased merchandise on account from Westhaven Company, $1,278.00. V33.
8. Paid cash to Moraska Company, $774.20, covering V30 for $790.00, less 2% discount, $15.80. C19.
10. Made a deposit in the checking account, $2,957.50.
14. Received invoice for delivery service from Davis Delivery, $29.50. V34.
14. Paid cash to Davis Delivery, $29.50, covering V34. C20.
14. Issued DM5 to Westhaven Company for return of merchandise purchased, $170.00. Cancel V33. V35.
15. Paid cash to Westhaven Company, $1,085.84, covering V35 for $1,108.00, less 2% discount, $22.16. C21.
16. Recorded voucher for semimonthly payroll for period ended May 15, $1,396.47 (total payroll: sales, $1,116.00; administrative, $744.00; less deductions: employee income tax payable—federal, $280.50; employee income tax payable—state, $34.23; social security tax payable, $120.90; Medicare tax payable, $27.90). V36.
16. Paid cash for semimonthly payroll, $1,396.47, covering V36. C22.
22. Paid cash to Waldoch Supplies, $159.78, covering V31. C23.
25. Bought office equipment on account from Yurik Company, $1,979.99. V37.
29. Made a deposit in the checking account, $1,279.51.
30. Purchased merchandise on account from Moraska Company, $1,875.95. V38.

Instructions:

1. Page 7 of a check register is provided in the *Recycling Problems Working Papers*. Record the bank balance brought forward on May 1 of the current year, $6,597.66.

2. Journalize the transactions completed during May of the current year. Use page 8 of a voucher register and page 7 of a check register. When a voucher is paid or canceled, make appropriate notations in the voucher register. Source documents are abbreviated as follows: check, C; debit memorandum, DM; voucher, V.

3. Prove and rule both the voucher register and the check register.

RECYCLING PROBLEM 6-R
Determining cost of merchandise inventory; estimating cost of merchandise using estimating methods; calculating merchandise inventory turnover ratio and average number of days' sales in merchandise inventory

On December 31 of the current year, Rackley, Inc., took a periodic inventory. Selected information about the inventory is provided in the *Recycling Problems Working Papers*.

Instructions:

1. Calculate the total inventory costs using the fifo, lifo, and weighted-average inventory costing methods, using the form provided in the *Recycling Problems Working Papers*.

2. Rackley uses the weighted-average costing method to determine the cost of inventory. Use the market price to determine the cost of inventory using the lower of cost or market method. Total the Lower of Cost or Market column.

3. Calculate the corporation's estimated ending inventory using the gross profit method of estimating inventory. The gross profit percentage is 40%. The following information is obtained from the corporation's records on December 31 of the current year:

Item	Cost	Retail
Beginning merchandise inventory	$ 400.00	$ 670.00
Net purchases to date	3,000.00	5,080.00
Net sales to date	—	4,600.00

4. Calculate the corporation's estimated ending inventory using the retail method of estimating inventory. Round the percentage to the nearest 0.1%.

5. Use the information and the estimated inventory calculated in Instruction 4. Calculate the corporation's merchandise inventory turnover ratio. Round the ratio to the nearest 0.1%.

6. Calculate the corporation's average number of days' sales in merchandise inventory. Round the amount to the nearest day.

RECYCLING PROBLEM 7-R

Estimating and journalizing uncollectible accounts using a percentage of net sales—allowance method; calculating and journalizing the adjusting entry for uncollectible accounts expense

Motion, Inc., uses the allowance method of recording uncollectible accounts expense.

Transactions:

Jan. 18. Wrote off Judith Tessman's past-due account as uncollectible, $43.96. M25.

Mar. 4. Wrote off James York's past-due account as uncollectible, $80.85. M34.

Mar. 28. Received cash in full payment of Judith Tessman's account, previously written off as uncollectible, $43.96. M45 and R83.

June 20. Wrote off Beverly Axel's past-due account as uncollectible, $17.16. M63.

Oct. 7. Wrote off Tanya Wadsworth's past-due account as uncollectible, $108.15. M79.

Dec. 11. Received cash in full payment of James York's account, previously written off as uncollectible, $80.85. M87 and R97.

Instructions:

1. Journalize the transactions completed during the current year. Page 1 of a general journal and page 1 of a cash receipts journal are provided in the *Recycling Problems Working Papers*.

2. Journalize the adjusting entry for uncollectible accounts expense on December 31 of the current year. Motion, Inc., has the following account balances on December 31 before adjusting entries are recorded.

Accounts Receivable	$ 19,768.25
Sales	104,463.79
Sales Discount	1,573.58
Sales Returns and Allowances	901.42

Motion, Inc., estimates that the amount of uncollectible accounts expense is equal to 0.5% of net sales.

continued

3. If all the entries recorded in the general journal and cash receipts journal were posted, including the adjusting entry, what would be the new balance of Allowance for Uncollectible Accounts? The January 1 balance of Allowance for Uncollectible Accounts, before the transactions for the year were recorded, was $1,434.61.

RECYCLING PROBLEM 8-R1
Journalizing transactions for plant assets

Ludden, Inc., uses the straight-line method of calculating depreciation expense. Ludden uses one plant asset account, Office Equipment.

Transactions:

Jan. 5, 20X1.   Paid cash for chair, $200.00: estimated salvage value, none; estimated useful life, 2 years; Serial No., none. C30.

Mar. 3, 20X1.   Paid cash for desk, $650.00: estimated salvage value, $150.00; estimated useful life, 4 years; Serial No., D125. C45.

Jan. 5, 20X2.   Paid cash for file cabinet, $300.00: estimated salvage value, $75.00; estimated useful life, 5 years; Serial No., F325. C115.

July 3, 20X2.   Paid cash for table, $270.00: estimated salvage value, $20.00; estimated useful life, 10 years; Serial No., none. C170.

Jan. 3, 20X3.   Discarded chair bought in 20X1. M50.

Mar. 5, 20X3.   Received cash for sale of desk, Serial No., D125, $300.00. M55 and R50.

June 29, 20X3. Paid cash, $200.00, plus old file cabinet, Serial No. F325, for new file cabinet: estimated salvage value of new cabinet, $80.00; estimated useful life of new cabinet, 5 years; Serial No. of new cabinet, F915. M70 and C200.

July 1, 20X3.   Paid cash for typewriter, $1,000.00: estimated salvage value, $200.00; estimated useful life, 5 years; Serial No., A6501M341. C230.

Instructions:
Journalize the transactions. Journalize an entry for additional depreciation expense if needed. Page 1 of a general journal, page 5 of a cash receipts journal, and page 5 of a cash payments journal are provided in the *Recycling Problems Working Papers*.

RECYCLING PROBLEM 8-R2
Calculating depreciation expense

On January 5 of the current year, Burdick, Inc., paid cash for a new company car, $15,000.00: estimated salvage value, $1,500.00; estimated useful life, 5 years. Forms used to prepare the depreciation tables are provided in the *Recycling Problems Working Papers*.

Instructions:

1. Prepare a depreciation table, similar to Figure 8-15, showing depreciation expense calculated using the straight-line, declining-balance, and sum-of-the-years-digits methods.

2. Assume that Burdick's car has an estimated useful life of 100,000 miles. Also assume that the car is driven the following number of miles: 1st year, 27,000; 2d year, 23,000; 3d year, 15,000; 4th year, 20,000; 5th year, 15,000. Prepare a depreciation table, similar to Figure 8-16, using the production-unit method of calculating depreciation expense.

RECYCLING PROBLEM 8-R3
Calculating and journalizing property tax

Amluxson, Inc., has real property with an assessed value of $400,000.00. The tax rate in the city where the property is located is 5% of assessed value. Property tax is paid in two installments.

Instructions:

1. Calculate Amluxson's total annual property tax for the current year.

2. Journalize the payment of the first installment of property tax on May 1. Page 9 of a cash payments journal is provided in the *Recycling Problems Working Papers*. Check No. 142.

RECYCLING PROBLEM 9-R
Journalizing adjusting and reversing entries for prepaid expenses initially recorded as expenses and for accrued expenses

Sutton, Inc., completed the following transactions during the current year. Sutton initially records prepaid expenses as expenses. Source documents are abbreviated as follows: check, C; note payable, NP.

Transactions:

Aug.	1.	Issued a 1-month, 10% note, $700.00. NP1.
Sept.	1.	Paid cash for the maturity value of NP1: principal, $700.00, plus interest, $5.83; total, $705.83. C95.
Sept.	1.	Issued a 150-day, 10% note, $1,300.00. NP2.
Oct.	1.	Issued a 120-day, 12% note, $1,500.00. NP3.
Dec.	1.	Discounted at 12% a 60-day non-interest-bearing note, $800.00; proceeds, $784.00, interest, $16.00. NP4.

Instructions:

1. Calculate the maturity dates for Notes Payable Nos. 2, 3, and 4.

2. Journalize the transactions. Page 15 of a cash receipts journal and page 17 of a cash payments journal are provided in the *Recycling Problems Working Papers*.

3. Sutton, Inc., has the following general ledger balances on December 31 of the current year before adjusting entries are recorded.

Supplies Expense—Administrative	$600.00
Supplies Expense—Sales	900.00
Insurance Expense	800.00

Using the following adjustment information, journalize the adjusting entries for prepaid and accrued expenses on December 31. Use page 13 of a general journal.

Adjustment Information, December 31	
Administrative Supplies Inventory	$300.00
Sales Supplies Inventory	350.00
Value of Prepaid Insurance	400.00
Remaining Prepaid Interest	8.00
Accrued Interest on Notes Payable	89.19
Accrued Salaries—Administrative	250.00
Accrued Salaries—Sales	215.00
Accrued Payroll Taxes—Social Security Tax	30.23
Accrued Payroll Taxes—Medicare Tax	6.97
Accrued Payroll Taxes—Federal Unemployment Tax	3.72
Accrued Payroll Taxes—State Unemployment Tax	25.11
Accrued Federal Income Tax	400.00

4. Journalize the reversing entries on January 1 of the next year. Use page 1 of a general journal.

RECYCLING PROBLEM 10-R
Journalizing notes receivable, unearned revenue, and accrued revenue initially recorded as revenue transactions

Marastreet, Inc., completed the following transactions during the current year. Marastreet initially records unearned items as revenue.

Transactions:

July 1. Received a 60-day, 10% note from Juan Beldoza for an extension of time on his account, $200.00. NR20.

July 5. Received a 2-month, 12% note from David Symanski for an extension of time on his account, $400.00. NR21.

Aug. 30. Juan Beldoza dishonored NR20, a 60-day, 10% note, maturity value due today: principal, $200.00; interest $3.33; total, $203.33. M39.

Sept. 5. Received cash for the maturity value of NR21: principal, $400.00, plus interest, $8.00; total, $408.00. R70.

Nov. 1. Received cash for three months' rent in advance from Clarkson, Inc., $1,800.00. R75.

Nov. 29. Received cash from Juan Beldoza for dishonored NR20: maturity value, $203.33, plus additional interest, $5.14; total, $208.47. R90.

Instructions:

1. Journalize the transactions. Page 7 of a general journal and page 17 of a cash receipts journal are provided in the *Recycling Problems Working Papers*. Source documents are abbreviated as follows: memorandum, M; note receivable, NR; receipt, R.

2. Continue using page 7 of the general journal. Journalize the adjusting entries using the following information.

Adjustment Information, December 31	
Accrued Interest on Notes Receivable	$ 17.57
Rent Received in Advance and Still Unearned	600.00

3. Journalize the reversing entries on January 1 of the next year. Use page 8 of a general journal.

RECYCLING PROBLEM 11-R
Journalizing transactions for starting a corporation, paying dividends, and preparing a balance sheet

Hillcrest, Inc., received its charter on July 1 of the current year. The corporation is authorized to issue 500,000 shares of $1.00 stated-value common stock and 1,000 shares of 8%, $50.00 par-value preferred stock.

Transactions:

July 5. Received cash from five incorporators for 300,000 shares of $1.00 stated-value common stock, $300,000.00. R1-5.

July 8. Paid cash to George Quitman as reimbursement for organization costs, $4,000.00. C1.

July 12. Received a subscription from Angela Smith for 50,000 shares of $1.00 stated-value common stock, $50,000.00. M1.

July 25. Received a subscription from Dayne Wilson for 5,000 shares of $1.00 stated-value common stock, $5,000.00. M2.

Aug. 10. Received cash from Dayne Wilson in payment of stock subscription, $5,000.00. R6.

Aug. 10. Issued Stock Certificate No. 6 to Dayne Wilson for 5,000 shares of $1.00 stated-value common stock, $5,000.00. M3.

Oct.   1.   Received cash from Angela Smith in partial payment of stock subscription, $25,000.00. R7.

Oct.   15.   Received a subscription from Lance Mosier for 30,000 shares of $1.00 stated-value common stock, $30,000.00. M4.

Nov.   1.   Received cash from Angela Smith in final payment of stock subscription, $25,000.00. R8.

Nov.   1.   Issued Stock Certificate No. 7 to Angela Smith for 50,000 shares of $1.00 stated-value common stock, $50,000.00. M5.

Instructions:

1. Journalize the transactions. Page 1 of a cash receipts journal, a cash payments journal, and a general journal are provided in the *Recycling Problems Working Papers*.

2. Prepare a balance sheet for Hillcrest, Inc., as of November 2 of the current year.

3. Journalize the following transactions completed during the following two years to record the declaration and payment of the dividends. Continue using page 1 of the general journal and the cash payments journal.

Nov.   24.   Hillcrest's board of directors declared an annual dividend of $50,000.00. Preferred stock issued is $250,000.00 of 8%, $50.00 par-value preferred stock. Common stock issued is $400,000.00 of $1.00 stated-value common stock. Date of payment is January 15. M106.

Jan.   15.   Paid cash for annual dividend declared November 24, $50,000.00. C257.

RECYCLING PROBLEM 12-R
Journalizing stocks and bonds transactions

Fleming, Inc. is authorized to issue 200,000 shares of $20.00 stated-value common stock and 50,000 shares of 12%, $200.00 par-value preferred stock.

Transactions:

Jan. 1, 20X1.   Received cash for the face value of a 5-year, 10%, $1,000.00 par-value bond issue, $100,000.00. R104.

Jan. 8, 20X1.   Received cash from Mary Brooker for 800 shares of $20.00 stated-value common stock at $20.00 per share, $16,000.00. R110.

Feb. 15, 20X1.   Paid cash to Alfred Clark for 800 shares of $20.00 stated-value common stock at $21.00 per share, $16,800.00. C124.

Feb. 27, 20X1.   Received cash from Connie Boyle for 300 shares of $200.00 par-value preferred stock at $198.00 per share, $59,400.00. R127.

Mar. 13, 20X1.   Received cash from Edward Timmell for 100 shares of $20.00 stated-value common stock at $21.00 per share, $2,100.00. R143.

Mar. 22, 20X1.   Received cash from Carol Petre for 200 shares of treasury stock at $21.00 per share, $4,200.00. Treasury stock was bought on February 15 at $21.00 per share. R149.

Apr. 15, 20X1.   Received cash from Dennis Cochran for 100 shares of treasury stock at $22.00 per share, $2,200.00. Treasury stock was bought on February 15 at $21.00 per share. R155.

Apr. 21, 20X1.   Received cash from David Vassel for 300 shares of $200.00 par-value preferred stock at $202.00 per share, $60,600.00. R156.

July 1, 20X1.   Paid cash to bond trustee for semiannual interest on bond issue, $5,000.00. C308.

July 1, 20X1.   Paid cash to bond trustee for semiannual deposit to bond sinking fund, $10,000.00. C309.

July 12, 20X1.   Received store equipment from Jake Smith at an agreed value of $50,000.00 for 250 shares of $200.00 par-value preferred stock. M361.

continued

July 30, 20X1. Received cash from Lester Branch for 100 shares of treasury stock at $20.50 per share, $2,050.00. Treasury stock was bought on February 15 at $21.00 per share. R215.

Jan. 1, 20X2. Paid cash to bond trustee for semiannual interest on bond issue, $5,000.00. C519.

Jan. 1, 20X2. Paid cash to bond trustee for semiannual deposit to bond sinking fund, $9,700.00, and recorded interest earned on bond sinking fund, $300.00. C520.

Jan. 5, 20X6. Received notice from bond trustee that bond issue was retired using bond sinking fund, $100,000.00. M491.

Instructions:

Journalize the following transactions. Page 1 of a cash receipts journal, page 2 of a cash payments journal, and page 7 of a general journal are provided in the *Recycling Problems Working Papers.*

RECYCLING PROBLEM 13-R
End-of-fiscal-period work for a corporation

The trial balance of Nichol, Inc., on December 31 of the current year is provided in the Trial Balance columns of the work sheet in the *Recycling Problems Working Papers.* Statement paper is also provided in the *Recycling Problems Working Papers.*

Instructions:

1. Complete the work sheet. Use the following information to prepare the adjustments.

Adjustment Information, December 31

Accrued Interest Income	$ 122.33
Uncollectible accounts expense estimated as 1.0% of sales on account.	
Sales on account for year, $277,474.00.	
Merchandise Inventory	110,939.29
Sales Supplies Inventory	4,951.42
Administrative Supplies Inventory	6,106.97
Value of Prepaid Insurance	3,153.46
Prepaid Interest	4.06
Annual Depreciation Expense—Store Equipment	6,626.28
Annual Depreciation Expense—Office Equipment	8,965.31
Organization Expense	100.00
Accrued Interest Expense	9,005.64
Accrued Salaries—Sales	488.36
Accrued Salaries—Administrative	1,302.77
Accrued Payroll Taxes—Social Security Tax	116.42
Accrued Payroll Taxes—Medicare Tax	26.87
Accrued Payroll Taxes—Federal Unemployment Tax	1.69
Accrued Payroll Taxes—State Unemployment Tax	11.39

Use the tax rates listed on page 351 in Chapter 13 to calculate the federal income tax for the year.

2. Prepare an income statement. Calculate and record the following component percentages. (a) Cost of merchandise sold. (b) Gross profit on operations. (c) Total selling expenses. (d) Total administrative expenses. (e) Total operating expenses. (f) Income from operations. (g) Net addition or deduction resulting from other revenue and expenses. (h) Net income before federal income tax. (i) Federal income tax expense. (j) Net income after federal income tax. Round percentage calculations to the nearest 0.1%.

3. Analyze Nichol's income statement by determining if component percentages are within acceptable levels. If any component percentage is not within an acceptable level, suggest steps that the company should take. Nichol considers the following component percentages acceptable.

Cost of merchandise sold	Not more than 43.0%
Gross profit on operations	Not less than 57.0%
Total administrative expenses	Not more than 18.0%
Total operating expenses	Not more than 31.0%
Income from operations	Not less than 26.0%
Net deduction from other revenue and expenses	Not more than 8.0%
Net income before federal income tax	Not less than 18.0%

4. Calculate earnings per share. Nichol's has 24,000 shares of $4.00 stated-value common stock issued and 940 shares of $100.00 par-value preferred stock issued. Treasury stock consists of 160 shares of common stock. The dividend rate on preferred stock is 10.0%.

5. Prepare a statement of stockholders' equity for the year ended December 31 of the current year. Use the following additional information.

	January 1 Balance	Issued During the Year	December 31 Balance
Common stock:			
No. of shares	20,000	4,000	24,000
Amount	$100,000.00	$20,000.00	$120,000.00
Preferred stock:			
No. of shares	900	40	940
Amount	$90,000.00	$4,000.00	$94,000.00

The January 1 balance of Retained Earnings was $29,439.29.

6. Calculate the following items based on information from the statement of stockholders' equity. (a) Equity per share of stock. (b) Price-earnings ratio. The market price of common stock on December 31 is $24.25.

7. Prepare a balance sheet for December 31 of the current year.

8. Calculate the following items based on information from the balance sheet. Net sales on account are $277,474.00. (a) Accounts receivable turnover ratio. Accounts receivable and allowance for uncollectible accounts on January 1 were $64,984.46 and $2,482.57, respectively. (b) Rate earned on average stockholders' equity. Total stockholders' equity on January 1 was $216,559,29. (c) Rate earned on average total assets. Total assets on January 1 were $421,689.57.

9. Journalize the adjusting entries. Use page 13 of a general journal.

10. Journalize the closing entries. Use page 14 of a general journal.

11. Journalize the reversing entries. Use page 15 of a general journal. Use January 1 of the following year as the date.

RECYCLING PROBLEM 14-R
Preparing a budgeted income statement and a cash budget with supporting budget schedules

On December 31, 20X2, the accounting records of Reilly Corporation show the following unit sales for 20X2.

1st quarter	20,600 units	3d quarter	22,800 units
2d quarter	21,500 units	4th quarter	35,100 units

continued

The following are additional actual amounts for the 4th quarter of 20X2.

Sales (35,100 units @ $5.00)	$175,500
Purchases (29,400 units @ $2.60)	76,440
Ending inventory	11,500 units

Management has established a unit sales goal of 120,000 units for 20X3 and 25,000 units for the first quarter of 20X4. The sales manager, after reviewing price trends and checking with the company's merchandise suppliers, projects the unit cost of merchandise will increase from $2.60 to $2.80 in the first quarter of 20X3. Because of the increase in costs, the company will need to increase its unit sales price from $5.00 to $5.20 in the first quarter of 20X3. After considering the time required to reorder merchandise, the sales manager requests that 50.0% of each quarter's unit sales be available in the prior quarter's ending inventory. Expenses are projected as follows. Except where noted, percentages are based on quarterly projected net sales. For these items, calculate each quarter's amount by multiplying the percentage times that quarter's net sales. Calculate the annual total by adding the four quarterly amounts. When a dollar amount is given, the total amount should be divided equally among the four quarters.

Selling Expenses

Advertising Expense	1.2%
Delivery Expense	0.7%
Depreciation Expense—Delivery Equipment	$4,200
Depreciation Expense—Store Equipment	$1,800
Miscellaneous Expense—Sales	0.2%
Salary Expense—Sales	5.4%
Supplies Expense—Sales	0.8%

Administrative Expenses

Depreciation Expense—Office Equipment	$1,440
Insurance Expense	$3,640
Miscellaneous Expense—Administrative	$2,400
Payroll Taxes Expense	12.0% of salaries
Rent Expense	$6,640
Salary Expense—Administrative	$26,000
Supplies Expense—Administrative	$1,800
Uncollectible Accounts Expense	0.5%
Utilities Expense	1.5%

Interest expense for each quarter is projected to be $450.

Federal income taxes are calculated using the tax rates listed on page 351 in Chapter 13. Equal quarterly income tax payments are based on the projected annual federal income tax expense.

Additional information is listed as follows.
a.   The balance of cash on hand on January 1, 20X3, is $22,540.
b.   In each quarter, cash sales are 20.0% and collections of accounts receivable are 25.0% of the projected net sales for the current quarter. Collections from the preceding quarter's net sales are 54.5% of that quarter. Uncollectible accounts expense is 0.5% of net sales.
c.   In each quarter, cash payments for cash purchases are 10.0% and for accounts payable 50.0% of the purchases for the current quarter. Cash payments for purchases of the preceding quarter are 40.0% of that quarter.
d.   In the first quarter, $12,000 will be borrowed on a promissory note, and equipment costing $17,500 will be purchased for cash. In each quarter, dividends of $15,000 will be paid in cash. In the fourth quarter, the promissory note plus interest will be paid in cash, $13,800.

Instructions:

Prepare the following budget schedules for the year ended December 31, 20X3. Use the forms provided in the *Recycling Problems Working Papers*. Round percentage amounts to the nearest 0.1%, unit amounts to the nearest 100 units, and dollar amounts to the nearest $10.

1. Prepare a sales budget schedule (Schedule 1).

2. Prepare a purchases budget schedule (Schedule 2).

3. Prepare a selling expenses budget schedule (Schedule 3).

4. Prepare an administrative expenses budget schedule (Schedule 4).

5. Prepare another revenue and expenses budget schedule (Schedule 5).

6. Prepare a budgeted income statement.

7. Prepare a cash receipts budget schedule (Schedule A).

8. Prepare a cash payments budget schedule (Schedule B).

9. Prepare a cash budget.

RECYCLING PROBLEM 15-R
Calculating contribution margin and breakeven point; calculating sales dollars and unit sales for planned net income

NewWave Cycle, Inc., manufactures and sells racing bicycles. The company's income statement for January of the current year appears in the *Recycling Problems Working Papers*.

Instructions:

1. Prepare NewWave Cycle's January income statement reporting contribution margin using the form provided in the *Recycling Problems Working Papers*.

2. Calculate the contribution margin rate.

3. Calculate the sales dollar breakeven point.

4. Calculate the unit sales breakeven point.

5. If an $18,000.00 monthly net income is planned, calculate the required (a) sales dollars and (b) number of cycles to be sold.

6. NewWave Cycle currently produces one of the components of its cycles. However, the company can also purchase the component from another company, reducing fixed costs by $5,000.00 per month, but increasing variable costs by $25.00 per cycle. Calculate the projected net income assuming NewWave Cycle sells 180 cycles per month. Should NewWave Cycle purchase the component from another company? Explain your answer.

RECYCLING PROBLEM 16-R
Preparing and analyzing comparative financial statements

Information taken from the financial records of Reardon Corporation for two fiscal years ended December 31 are provided in the *Recycling Problems Working Papers*.

The following additional information is known:

Dividends Declared	$25,000.00	$25,000.00
Shares of Capital Stock Outstanding	3,000	3,000
Accounts Receivable (Book Value), January 1	62,430.00	59,480.00

continued

Merchandise Inventory, January 1	$229,690.00	$120,830.00
Total Assets, January 1	493,180.00	421,200.00
Capital Stock, January 1	300,000.00	300,000.00
Retained Earnings, January 1	49,860.00	43,220.00
Market Price per Share of Stock, December 31	112.50	123.00

Instructions:

1. Prepare the following comparative financial statements using trend analysis. Use the forms provided in the *Recycling Problems Working Papers*. Round percentage calculations to the nearest 0.1%.
   a. Comparative income statement.
   b. Comparative stockholders' equity statement.
   c. Comparative balance sheet

2. Use the financial statements' trend analysis to determine if the trend from the prior to current year for each of the following items appears to be favorable or unfavorable. Give reasons for these trends.
   a. Net sales
   b. Net income
   c. Total stockholders' equity
   d. Total assets

3. Prepare a comparative income statement using component percentage analysis. Round percentage calculations to the nearest 0.1%.

4. Record from the statement prepared in Instruction 3 or calculate the component percentages for each of the following. Determine if the current year's results, compared with the prior year, appear to be favorable or unfavorable. Give reasons for your responses.
   a. As a percentage of net sales:
      1. Cost of merchandise sold
      2. Gross profit on operations
      3. Total operating expenses
      4. Net income after federal income tax
   b. As a percentage of total stockholders' equity:
      1. Retained earnings
      2. Capital stock
   c. As a percentage of total assets or total liabilities and stockholders' equity:
      1. Current assets
      2. Current liabilities

5. Based on Reardon's comparative financial statements, calculate the following ratios for each year.
   a. Profitability ratios:
      1. Rate earned on average total assets
      2. Rate earned on average stockholders' equity
      3. Rate earned on net sales
      4. Earnings per share
      5. Price-earnings ratio
   b. Efficiency ratios:
      1. Accounts receivable turnover ratio
      2. Merchandise inventory turnover ratio
   c. Short-term financial strength ratios:
      1. Working capital
      2. Current ratio
      3. Acid-test ratio
   d. Long-term financial strength ratios:
      1. Debt ratio
      2. Equity ratio
      3. Equity per share

6. For each of the items in Instruction 5, indicate if there appears to be a favorable or an unfavorable trend from the prior to current year. Give reasons for these trends.

RECYCLING PROBLEM 17-R
Preparing a statement of cash flows

An analysis of the annual income statement and comparative balance sheet of Cascade Trucking Supply, Inc., reveals the following net income, depreciation expense, amortization costs, and changes in current assets and current liabilities:

Net Income	$122,370.00
Amortized Organization Costs	10,000.00
Depreciation Expense	51,500.00
Increase in Notes Receivable	5,100.00
Decrease in Accounts Receivable	35,600.00
Increase in Supplies	3,300.00
Increase in Merchandise Inventory	68,200.00
Decrease in Notes Payable	8,700.00
Increase in Accounts Payable	14,000.00
Decrease in Salaries Payable	1,200.00

Instructions:

1. Prepare the cash flows from operating activities section of the statement of cash flows for the current year ending December 31. Use the form provided in the *Recycling Problems Working Papers.*

An analysis of the current comparative balance sheet of Cascade Trucking Supply, Inc., shows the following changes in long-term assets:

Increase in Office Equipment	$30,200.00	Increase in Building	$154,000.00
Increase in Office Furniture	12,340.00	Decrease in Land Due to Sale	75,000.00

2. Prepare the cash flows from investing activities section.

An examination of the comparative balance sheet and statement of stockholders' equity of Cascade Trucking Supply, Inc., reveals the following changes in long-term liabilities and stockholders' equity:

Increase in Mortgage Payable	$40,000.00
Sale of Common Stock	20,000.00
Payment of Cash Dividend	25,500.00

3. Prepare the cash flows from financing activities section.

4. Compute the net increase or decrease in cash resulting from the operating, investing, and financing activities of the business.

5. Enter a beginning cash balance of $98,700.00 on the statement of cash flows.

6. Complete the statement of cash flows for Cascade Trucking Supply, Inc., by computing the ending cash balance for the fiscal year ending December 31.

7. Verify the accuracy of the statement of cash flows by comparing its ending cash balance with the cash balance of $158,630.00 listed for the current year on Cascade Trucking Supply's comparative balance sheet.

RECYCLING PROBLEM 18-R
Completing end-of-fiscal-period work for a merchandising business using departmental margins

Lawn Care is a merchandising business that specializes in lawn mowers and mower parts. The trial balance on December 31 of the current year is provided in the Trial Balance columns of

continued

the work sheet in the *Recycling Problems Working Papers*. Statement paper is also provided in the *Recycling Problems Working Papers*.

Instructions:

1. Complete the 12-column work sheet for the year ended December 31 of the current year. The following adjusting information is available. Extend amounts to the proper debit and credit columns for Departmental Margin Statement—Mowers, Departmental Margin Statement—Parts, Income Statement, and Balance Sheet. Accounts on trial balance lines 55-63 are classified as indirect expenses.

Adjustment Information, December 31

Uncollectible accounts expense—mowers estimated as
1.0% of sales on account.
   Sales on account for year, $78,000.00.

Merchandise Inventory—Mowers	$67,623.30
Merchandise Inventory—Parts	52,611.10
Supplies Used—Mowers	2,413.80
Supplies Used—Parts	4,023.00
Supplies Used—Administrative	1,609.20
Insurance Expired—Mowers	2,220.00
Insurance Expired—Parts	2,775.00
Insurance Expired—Administrative	555.00
Depreciation Expense—Office Equipment	123.90
Depreciation Expense—Store Equipment, Mowers	896.10
Depreciation Expense—Store Equipment, Parts	232.30
Federal Income Tax Expense for the Year	5,401.80

2. Prepare a departmental margin statement for each department. Calculate and record the component percentages for each item on the statements. Round percentage calculations to the nearest 0.1%.

3. Prepare an income statement. Calculate and record the component percentages for each item on the statements. Round percentage calculations to the nearest 0.1%.

RECYCLING PROBLEM 19-R
Preparing cost records

Air Wave, Inc., manufactures CB (citizen band) radios. The company records manufacturing costs by job number and uses a factory overhead applied rate to charge overhead costs to its products. The company estimates it will manufacture 5,000 radios next year. For this amount of production, total factory overhead is estimated to be $198,000.00. Estimated direct labor costs for next year are $220,000.00. On November 6, Air Wave began work on Job No. 753. The order is for 30 No. LR75 CB radios for stock, date wanted November 21.

Transactions:

Nov.   6.   Direct materials, $762.00. materials Requisition No. 524.
      6.   Direct labor, $120.00. Daily summary of job-time records.
      7.   Direct labor, $180.00. Daily summary of job-time records.
      8.   Direct materials, $230.00. Materials Requisition No. 535.
      8.   Direct labor, $136.00. Daily summary of job-time records.
      9.   Direct labor, $126.00. Daily summary of job-time records.
     10.   Direct materials, $185.00. Materials Requisition No. 542.
     10.   Direct labor, $210.00. Daily summary of job-time records.
     13.   Direct materials, $156.00. Materials Requisition No. 548.
     13.   Direct labor, $198.00. Daily summary of job-time records.

Nov. 14. Direct materials, $112.00. Materials Requisition No. 556.
14. Direct labor, $186.00. Daily summary of job-time records.
15. Direct materials, $145.00. Materials Requisition No. 563.
15. Direct labor, $112.00. Daily summary of job-time records.
16. Direct labor, $52.00. Daily summary of job-time records.

Instructions:

1. Calculate Air Wave's factory overhead applied rate for next year as a percentage of direct labor cost.

2. Open a cost sheet for job No. 753 and record the transactions. Use the job cost sheet provided in the *Recycling Problems Working Papers*.

3. Complete the cost sheet, recording factory overhead at the rate calculated in Instruction 1.

4. Prepare a finished goods ledger card for Stock No. LR75 CB radio. Minimum quantity is set at 10. Inventory location is Area B-11.

5. Record on the finished goods ledger card the beginning balance on November 1. The November 1 balance of LR75 CB radios is 20 units at a unit cost of $133.50. Air Wave uses the first-in, first-out method to record inventory costs.

6. Record the following transactions on the finished goods ledger card for LR75 CB radios.

Nov. 10. Sold 8 LR75 CB radios. Sales Invoice No. 743.
16. Received 30 LR75 CB radios. Record cost from cost sheet for Job No. 753.
21. Sold 20 LR75 CB radios. Sales Invoice No. 757.

RECYCLING PROBLEM 20-R
Journalizing entries that summarize cost records at the end of a fiscal period; preparing statement of cost of goods manufactured

The following information is taken from the records of Bartley Company on January 31 of the current year.

a. The various general ledger accounts used in recording actual factory overhead expenses during the month have the following balances on January 31.

5510	Depreciation Expense—Factory Equipment	$ 2,885.12
5515	Depreciation Expense—Building	1,411.20
5520	Heat, Light, and Power Expense	4,527.60
5525	Insurance Expense—Factory	752.64
5530	Miscellaneous Expense—Factory	6,890.24
5535	Payroll Taxes Expense—Factory	21,868.00
5540	Property Tax Expense—Factory	3,044.16
5545	Supplies Expense—Factory	9,031.68

b. Inventory accounts have the following balances on January 1.

Account No. 1125 Materials	$272,244.00
Account No. 1130 Work in Process	95,961.60
Account No. 1135 Finished Goods	71,442.00

c. The following accounts are needed for completing the posting. No beginning balances are needed.

2110	Employee Income Tax Payable		3120	Income Summary
2120	Social Security Tax Payable		5105	Cost of Goods Sold
2125	Medicare Tax Payable		5505	Factory Overhead

continued

d. The total factory payroll for the month according to the payroll register is $154,000.00, distributed as follows.

Work in Process	$114,520.00	Employee Income Tax Payable	$16,940.00
Factory Overhead	39,480.00	Social Security Tax Payable	10,010.00
Cash	124,740.00	Medicare Tax Payable	2,310.00

e. The total of all requisitions of direct materials issued during the month is $126,115.00. The total of all requisitions of indirect materials issued during the month is $10,085.00.

f. The factory overhead to be charged to Work in Process is 87% of the direct labor cost.

g. The total of all cost sheets completed during the month is $314,440.00.

h. The total of costs recorded on all sales invoices for January is $327,026.00.

Instructions:

1. Open ledger accounts and record balances for information items in (a), (b), and (c). Use the accounts provided in the *Recycling Problems Working Papers*.

2. Journalize the factory payroll entry on page 2 of a cash payments journal. C1012. Post the general debit and general credit amounts.

3. Journalize the following entries on page 1 of a general journal. Post the entries.
   a. An entry to transfer the total of all direct materials requisitions to Work in Process and indirect materials to Factory Overhead. M844.
   b. An entry to close all individual manufacturing expense accounts to Factory Overhead. M845.
   c. An entry to record applied factory overhead to Work in Process. M846.

4. Continue using page 1 of the general journal. Journalize and post the entry to close the balance of the factory overhead account to Income Summary. M847.

5. Journalize and post the entry to transfer the total of all cost sheets completed from Work in Process to Finished Goods. M848.

6. Journalize and post the entry to transfer the cost of products sold from Finished Goods to Cost of Goods Sold. M849.

7. Prepare for Bartley Company a statement of cost of goods manufactured for the month ended January 31 of the current year.

RECYCLING PROBLEM 21-R
Forming and expanding a partnership

On January 1 of the current year, Richard Meyer and Susan Rusk form a partnership. The partnership accepts the assets and liabilities of Mr. Meyer's existing business. Miss Rusk invests cash equal to Mr. Meyers' investment. The partners share equally in all changes in equity. The January 1 balance sheet for Mr. Meyer's existing business is provided in the *Recycling Problems Working Papers*.

Transactions:

Jan. 1. Received cash from partner, Susan Rusk, as an initial investment, $6,000.00. R1.
1. Accepted assets and liabilities of Richard Meyer's existing business as an initial investment, $6,000.00. R2.
Mar. 1. Journalized personal sale of equity to new partner, Luke Chin, $4,000.00, distributed as follows: from Richard Meyer, $2,000.00; from Susan Rusk, $2,000.00. M18.

Aug. 1. Received cash from new partner, Penney Cory, for a one-fourth equity in the business, $4,000.00. R92.

Sept. 2. Received cash from new partner, Chad Breslau, for a one-fifth equity in the business, $3,600.00. Existing equity is redistributed as follows: from Richard Meyer, $80.00; from Susan Rusk, $80.00; from Luke Chin, $80.00; from Penney Cory, $80.00. R121 and M32.

Nov. 1. Received cash from new partner, Sharon Logan, for a one-sixth equity in the business, $4,200.00. Goodwill, $1,400.00, is distributed as follows: Richard Meyer, $280.00; Susan Rusk, $280.00; Luke Chin, $280.00; Penney Cory, $280.00; Chad Breslau, $280.00. R181 and M42.

Instructions:
Journalize the transactions. Page 1 of a cash receipts journal and page 1 of a general journal are provided in the *Recycling Problems Working Papers*. Source documents are abbreviated as follows: memorandum, M; receipt, R.

RECYCLING PROBLEM 22-R
Completing end-of-fiscal-period work for a partnership

James Dyson and Gerald Nickle are partners in a partnership called Fast Service Plumbing. The partnership's work sheet for the year ended December 31 of the current year is provided in the *Recycling Problems Working Papers*. Statement paper is also provided in the *Recycling Problems Working Papers*.

Instructions:

1. Prepare an income statement. Calculate and record the component percentages for total operating expenses and for net income. Round percentage calculations to the nearest 0.1%.

2. Prepare a distribution of net income statement. Each partner is to receive 8% interest on January 1 equity. The January 1 equity is: Mr. Dyson, $22,000.00; Mr. Nickle, $20,000.00. Also, the partners' salaries are: Mr. Dyson, $10,000.00; Mr. Nickle, $8,000.00. The partners share remaining net income, net loss, or deficit equally.

3. Prepare an owners' equity statement.

4. Prepare a balance sheet.

5. Journalize the adjusting entries. Use page 12 of a general journal.

6. Continue using page 12 of the general journal. Journalize the closing entries.

RECYCLING PROBLEM 23-R
Journalizing governmental transactions

The town of Osage uses a general fund for all financial transactions. Expenditures are recorded by type of expenditure and by department. The four categories of expenditures are: personnel, supplies, other charges, and capital outlays. Departments are: General Government, Public Safety, Public Works, and Recreation.

Transactions:

Jan. 2. Recorded current year's approved operating budget: estimated revenues, $1,148,500.00; appropriations, $1,113,000.00; budgetary fund balance, $35,500.00. M35.

2. Recorded current year's property tax levy: taxes receivable—current, $1,033,000.00; allowance for uncollectible taxes—current, $15,500.00; property tax revenue, $1,017,500.00. M36.

9. Paid cash for gas utility service in recreation department, $182.00. C134.

continued

Jan. 15. Issued a 1-month, 9% note, $100,000.00. NP7.
16. Received cash for current taxes receivable, $61,200.00. R85.
19. Encumbered estimated amount for supplies in general government department, $120.00. M52.
31. Received cash from traffic fines, $490.00. R100. (Other Revenue)
Feb. 3. Paid cash for general government department supplies, $117.00, encumbered January 19 per M52. M61 and C155.
15. Paid cash for the maturity value of NP7: principal, $100,000.00, plus interest, $750.00; total, $100,750.00. C189.
22. Paid cash for library books for recreation department, $450.00. C192. (Capital Outlays)
Mar. 1. Recorded reclassification of current taxes receivable to delinquent status, $72,000.00, and the accompanying allowance for uncollectible accounts, $15,500.00. M73.
15. Paid cash for a 4-month, 8% certificate of deposit, $300,000.00. C209.
Apr. 5. Encumbered estimated amount for supplies in public safety department, $250.00. M94.
18. Received cash for delinquent taxes receivable, $34,500.00. R255.
26. Paid cash for public safety department supplies, $254.00, encumbered April 5 per M94. M102 and C244.
May 8. Paid cash for consultant's services in general government department, $500.00. C265. (Personnel)
July 15. Received cash for the maturity value of certificate of deposit due today: principal, $300,000.00, plus interest, $8,000.00; total $308,000.00. R314.

Instructions:
Journalize the transactions completed during the current year. Page 1 of a journal is provided in the *Recycling Problems Working Papers*.

RECYCLING PROBLEM 24-R
Completing end-of-fiscal-period work for a governmental organization

The town of Weston uses a general fund. The trial balance on December 31 of the current year is provided in the Trial Balance columns of the work sheet in the *Recycling Problems Working Papers*. Statement paper is also provided in the *Recycling Problems Working Papers*.

Instructions:
1. Analyze the following adjustment information and record the adjustments on the work sheet.

Adjustment Information, December 31
Supplies inventory $3,380.00
Interest revenue due but not collected   3,650.00
An estimated 20% of the interest revenue due will not be collected.
The reserve for encumbrances for the current year is reclassified to prior year status.

2. Complete the work sheet.

Weston's general fund operating budget for the current fiscal year is provided in the *Recycling Problems Working Papers*.

3. Prepare a statement of revenues, expenditures, and changes in fund balance—budget and actual for the year ended December 31 of the current year. The unreserved fund balance on January 1 was $47,610.00.

4. Prepare a balance sheet for December 31 of the current year.

5. Journalize the adjusting and closing entries. Use page 48 of a journal.

Answers to Audit Your Understanding

CHAPTER 1, PAGE 11
1. Assets = Liabilities + Owner's Equity
2. An asset account has a normal debit balance; a revenue account has a normal credit balance.
3. a. A separate numeric listing is provided for each ledger division.
   b. A predesigned arrangement of numbers is provided within each ledger division.
   c. Enough account number digits are provided to allow the addition of new accounts.

CHAPTER 1, PAGE 19
1. Purchases—Tennis is debited; Accounts Payable is credited.
2. Accounts Payable is debited; Purchases Returns and Allowances—Tennis is credited.

CHAPTER 1, PAGE 27
1. Accounts Payable is debited; Cash and Purchases Discounts—Tennis are credited.
2. To assure that all expenses are recorded during the fiscal period in which they occurred.
3. Memorandum.

CHAPTER 2, PAGE 47
1. A tax-exempt customer is not required to pay sales tax. Examples include federal, state, and local government agencies; nonprofit educational institutions; and certain religious and charitable organizations.
2. A credit memorandum is issued by a vendor to show the amount deducted from the customer's account for returns and allowances.

CHAPTER 2, PAGE 54
1. A 2% sales discount may be deducted if sales on account are paid within 10 days of the invoice date. All sales on account must be paid within 30 days of the invoice date.
2. Both cash sales and credit card sales result in an immediate increase in the bank account balance.

CHAPTER 3, PAGE 69
1. Because taxes represent a business transaction with dollar amounts large enough to affect business decisions.
2. As a reward for continuous service.
3. $60.00 if paid a 1-1/2 times regular pay (5 hours × $8.00 × 1.5)

CHAPTER 3, PAGE 77
1. Federal income tax, social security tax, and Medicare tax.
2. By consulting withholding tax tables provided by the Internal Revenue Service.
3. Total Earnings minus Total Deductions equals Net Pay.
4. Total earnings for the pay period.

CHAPTER 3, PAGE 84
1. Cash
2. a. Employer social security tax.
   b. Employer Medicare tax.
   c. Federal unemployment tax
   d. State unemployment tax

CHAPTER 4, PAGE 100
1. Interim departmental statement of gross profit, departmental statement of gross profit, estimated merchandise inventory sheet.
2. Periodic inventory and perpetual inventory.
3. Operating Revenue, Cost of Merchandise Sold, and Gross Profit on Operations.

CHAPTER 4, PAGE 111
1. Schedule of accounts receivable and schedule of accounts payable
2. To bring certain general ledger accounts up to date.
3. Asset, liability, and stockholders' equity accounts.

CHAPTER 4, PAGE 118
1. Departmental statement of gross profit, income statement, statement of stockholders' equity, balance sheet.
2. Total operating expenses divided by net sales equals total operating expenses component percentage.
3. Capital Stock and Retained Earnings.

CHAPTER 4, PAGE 124
1. To update general ledger accounts at the end of a fiscal period.
2. All temporary accounts or all income statement accounts and the dividends account.
3. To prove that debit equal credits in the general ledger after closing entries have been prepared.
4. a. Prepare schedules of accounts receivable and accounts payable.
   b. Prepare a trial balance on the work sheet, and complete the work sheet.

c. Prepare financial statements.
d. Journalize and post adjusting and closing entries.
e. Prepare a post-closing trial balance.

CHAPTER 5, PAGE 150
1. Vouchers Payable.
2. To serve as an additional control: all vouchers can be accounted for.
3. Purchases journal.

CHAPTER 5, PAGE 154
1. Cash payments journal.
2. According to the name of the vendor.
3. Vouchers Payable.

CHAPTER 5, PAGE 158
1. Vouchers Payable is debited; Purchases Returns and Allowances is credited.
2. Remove the voucher from the unpaid voucher file and write Canceled across Section 5.
3. A payroll register.

CHAPTER 6, PAGE 172
1. a. Cost of beginning merchandise inventory.
   b. Cost of the net purchases added to the inventory during the fiscal period.
2. Understated.
3. a. By physically counting the items.
   b. By keeping a continuous record showing the number purchased and sold for each item.

CHAPTER 6, PAGE 178
1. A method that best matches the revenue and costs for that business during the fiscal period.
2. The last-in, first-out (lifo) method
3. The first-in, first-out (fifo) method.
4. a. The cost of the inventory using the fifo, lifo, or weighted-average method.
   b. The current market price of the inventory.

CHAPTER 6, PAGE 183
1. That a continuing relationship exists between gross profit and net sales.
2. Separate records of both cost and retail prices for net purchases, net sales, and beginning merchandise inventory.
3. That the business sold the average merchandise inventory five times during the current year.
4. Days in year (365) divided by merchandise inventory turnover ratio equals average number of days' sales in merchandise inventory.

CHAPTER 7, PAGE 198
1. When a customer's account is believed to be uncollectible, it should be written off because it is no longer an asset of the business.
2. Uncollectible Accounts Expense is debited; Accounts Receivable is credited. The cus-

tomer's account in the accounts receivable ledger is also credited.
3. To provide a complete history of a customer's credit activities.

CHAPTER 7, PAGE 205
1. a. Percentage of sales method.
   b. Percentage of accounts receivable method.
2. Net sales times the percentage expected to be uncollectible equals the estimated uncollectible accounts expense.
3. a. Compute an estimate for each age group.
   b. Compute the total estimate.
   c. Subtract the current balance of Allowance for Uncollectible Accounts
   d. Compute the addition to the allowance account.

CHAPTER 7, PAGE 208
1. Net sales on account divided by average book value of accounts receivable equals accounts receivable turnover ratio.
2. Customers are taking about 60 days to pay their accounts. The business needs to encourage more prompt payment in order reduce the number of days to receive payment to 30 days.
3. Business can be lost as some customers may buy from competitors with less restrictive credit terms.

CHAPTER 8, PAGE 221
1. a. General information completed when the asset is bought.
   b. Disposal section completed when the asset is discarded, sold, or traded.
   c. Section to record annual depreciation expense.
2. The entry does not involve the purchase of merchandise.
3. Property Tax Expense is debited; Cash is credited.

CHAPTER 8, PAGE 226
1. Over the useful life of the plant asset.
2. Matching Expenses with Revenue.
3. Because of its permanent nature, depreciation is not recorded for land.
4. Original cost, estimated salvage value, and estimated useful life.
5. A calendar month.

CHAPTER 8, PAGE 233
1. The date, type, and amount of disposal.
2. Depreciation Expense will be debited; Accumulated Depreciation will be credited to bring the accounts up to date before disposal.

3. Cash received minus the book value of the asset sold.
4. Cash plus the book value of the store equipment traded equals the book value of the new store equipment.

CHAPTER 8, PAGE 240
1. Declining balance.
2. The amount of use the asset receives.
3. Tons of mineral mined times the depletion rate equals the annual depletion expense. The depletion rate is calculated by dividing the estimated total value of the mineral resource by the estimated number of tons of the mineral to be recovered.

CHAPTER 9, PAGE 255
1. Principal times interest rate times fraction of a year equals the interest to be paid on a note.
2. As an annual rate.
3. Principal and interest expense.

CHAPTER 9, PAGE 261
1. Matching Expenses with Revenue.
2. To record the amount of supplies used during the period as an expense.
3. If an adjusting entry creates a balance in an asset or a liability account, the adjusting entry is reversed.

CHAPTER 9, PAGE 268
1 a. Accrued interest expense.
   b. Accrued salary expense.
   c. Accrued employer payroll taxes expense.
   d. Accrued federal income tax.
2. Interest Expense is debited; Interest Payable is credited.
3. Salaries Payable, Employee Income Tax Payable, Social Security Tax Payable, and Medicare Tax Payable are debited; Salary Expense (for each department) is credited.

CHAPTER 10, PAGE 282
1. To provide an extension of time to pay on account.
2. Accounts Receivable is debited; Notes Receivable and Interest Income are credited.
3. The additional interest is charged from maturity date to payment date.

CHAPTER 10, PAGE 287
1. Cash is debited; Rent Income is credited.
2. If the adjusting entry creates a balance in an asset or liability account.
3. Unearned Rent is debited; Rent Income is credited.
4. Interest Receivable is debited; Interest Income is credited.
5. Interest Income is debited; Interest Receivable is credited.

CHAPTER 11, PAGE 304
1. Determine corporate policies and select corporate officers to supervise the day-to-day management of the corporation.
2. a. The right to vote at stockholders' meetings.
   b. The right to share in the corporation's earnings.
   c. The right to share in the distribution of a corporation's assets if a corporation ceases operations and sells its assets.

CHAPTER 11, PAGE 309
1. Stock Subscribed is debited; Capital Stock is credited. (The kind of stock issued will be included in the account title.)
2. Under the heading Intangible Assets, as the last subdivision of the Assets section.
3. A single summary general ledger capital account is used for each kind of stock issued.
4. Cash is debited; Capital Stock—Common is credited.
5. a. An incorporation fee paid to the state when the articles of incorporation are submitted.
   b. Attorney fees for legal services during the process of incorporation.
   c. Other incidental expenses incurred prior to receiving a charter.

CHAPTER 11, PAGE 313
1. The board of directors.
2. The corporation is obligated to pay the dividend.
3. a. To avoid a large number of entries in the corporation's cash payments journal.
   b. To reserve cash specifically for paying dividends.

CHAPTER 12, PAGE 327
1. Selling stock to investors and borrowing money.
2. Cash is debited; Capital Stock—Preferred is credited.
3. Cash is debited; Capital Stock—Preferred and Paid-in Capital in Excess of Par Value—Preferred are credited.
4. Cash and Discount on Sale of Preferred Stock are debited; Capital Stock—Preferred is credited.
5. May be assigned to no-par value stock, and it serves the same function as par value.

CHAPTER 12, PAGE 333
1. Stock that has been issued and reacquired by a corporation.
2. Cash is debited; Treasury Stock and Paid-in Capital from Sale of Treasury Stock are credited.
3. Historical Cost

CHAPTER 12, PAGE 339

1. a. Additional capital becomes part of a corporation's permanent capital.
   b. Dividends do not have to be paid unless earnings are sufficient.
2. Stockholders' equity is not spread over additional shares of stock.
3. Interest must be paid on the loan, which decreases net income.
4. Bond Sinking Fund is debited; Cash and Interest Income are credited.

CHAPTER 13, PAGE 354

Recognizing a portion of an intangible expense over a period of years.
Quarterly.

CHAPTER 13, PAGE 362

1. The amount of net income belonging to a single share of stock.
2. The relationship between the market value per share and earnings per share.
3. Total assets at the beginning and end of the fiscal period and net income after federal income tax.

CHAPTER 13, PAGE 369

1. a. Closing entry for income statement accounts with credit balances.
   b. Closing entry for income statement accounts with debit balances.
   c. Closing entry to record net income or net loss in the retained earnings account and close the income summary account.
   d. Closing entry for the dividends account.
2. Form 1120.
3. The gains and losses on the sale of noncash assets are subject to taxation. Thus, additional tax reports for the corporation must be filed.

CHAPTER 14, PAGE 392

1. A business can control expenses by comparing actual expenses with projected expenses. The comparison identifies differences where costs are higher than projected. The business can then take action to correct the differences.
2. One year.
3. Net income will increase. If net sales increase at a higher percentage than cost and expense items, net income will be favorably affected.

CHAPTER 14, PAGE 401

1. Establish targets to work toward in the coming year. Help coordinate the efforts of all areas toward a common direction.
2. Previous net sales and the trend in net sales for a period of several years, general economic conditions, consumer buying trends, competition, new products on the market, and such activities as planned special sales.

CHAPTER 14, PAGE 408

1. Good cash management requires the planning and controlling of cash so that cash will be available to meet obligations when due.
2. Projected beginning cash balance, cash receipts, cash payments, and ending cash balance.
3. A performance report compares actual amounts with projected amounts for the same fiscal period. A comparative income statement compares actual amounts of one fiscal period with actual amounts of a prior fiscal period.

CHAPTER 15, PAGE 422

1. The line would be straight, parallel to the base. The line is straight because fixed costs are exactly the same for each month.
2. Gross profit is determined by subtracting only the cost of merchandise sold from net sales. Contribution margin is determined by subtracting all variable costs from net sales.

CHAPTER 15, PAGE 426

1. In sales dollars or unit sales.
2. As an alternative method to calculate the breakeven point when no financial statements exist.
3. Prepare an income statement using the breakeven point numbers. If the breakeven point is accurate, net income will be zero.

CHAPTER 15, PAGE 434

1. Fixed costs and variable costs.
2. Total fixed costs plus planned net income.

CHAPTER 16, PAGE 451

1. To assist in decision making. For managers: to identify areas for improving profitability. For lenders: to decide whether to loan money to a business. For owners and potential owners: to decide whether to buy, sell, or keep their investment.
2. Determine (a) profitability, (b) efficiency, (c) short-term financial strength, and (d) long-term financial strength.
3. Adequate disclosure.
4. Prior company performance and comparison with published trade performance standards.

CHAPTER 16, PAGE 460

1. How well a business is using its assets to earn net income.
2. How much net income stockholders' investment is earning.
3. Accounts are being collected 9.1 times a year.

CHAPTER 16, PAGE 465

1. a. Owners' investments and retained earnings.
   b. Loans.
2. a. Working capital.
   b. Current ratio.
   c. Acid-test ratio.
3. Quick assets include all current assets except merchandise inventory and prepaid expenses.
4. Total quick assets divided by total current liabilities equals the acid-test ratio.
5. The debt ratio, equity ratio, and equity per share.
6. Total liabilities divided by total assets equals the debt ratio.
7. Total stockholders' equity divided by shares of capital stock outstanding equals equity per share.

CHAPTER 17, PAGE 481

1. The accrual basis of accounting recognizes revenue when it is earned and expenses when they are incurred.
2. The cash basis of accounting recognizes revenue when cash is received and expenses when cash is paid out.
3. a. Operating activities.
   b. Investing activities.
   c. Financing activities.

CHAPTER 17, PAGE 487

1. The actual cash outflow occurred in a prior fiscal period when the asset was bought.
2. A company made more credit sales than it collected during the year.
3. A company owes more to its vendors at the end of the year than at the beginning of the year.
4. Net income (net loss).

CHAPTER 17, PAGE 493

1. By analyzing the changes in long-term assets (plant assets) on the comparative balance sheet.
2. The increase in accumulated depreciation matches the depreciation expense that was recorded on the income statement. The effect on cash flows due to depreciation expense was already accounted for under operating activities.
3. By examining the changes in long-term liabilities on the balance sheet and reviewing the statement of stockholders' equity.
4. If the Cash Balance, End of Period shown on the statement of cash flows equals the current year's cash balance reported on the comparative balance sheet.

CHAPTER 18, PAGE 511

1. a. Each manager is assigned responsibility for those revenues, costs, and expenses for which the manager can make decisions and affect the outcome.
   b. The revenues, costs, and expenses must be readily identifiable with the manager's unit.
2. Revenue, cost of merchandise sold, and direct expenses.
3. The departmental margin statement for each department.

CHAPTER 18, PAGE 516

1. The departmental margin statements.
2. Departmental margin divided by departmental net sales equals component percentage for departmental margin.
3. a. Current period's departmental margin component percentage compared with a company-assigned goal.
   b. Current period's departmental margin component percentage compared with previous periods' departmental margin component percentages.
4. The Income Statement columns of the work sheet.

CHAPTER 19, PAGE 530

1. a. Direct materials.
   b. Direct labor.
   c. Factory overhead.
2. Work in process.
3. To keep a record of all charges for direct materials, direct labor, and factory overhead for each specific job.

CHAPTER 19, PAGE 538

1. Ordered, received, issued, and balance.
2. Purchase order.
3. To authorize transfer of items from the storeroom to the factory.
4. Estimated factory overhead divided by estimated direct labor cost equals factory overhead applied rate.
5. Because the unit costs of each job frequently are different.

CHAPTER 20, PAGE 555

1. On cost sheets.
2. Overapplied overhead.
3. Applied factory overhead is only an estimate used to assign factory overhead to jobs. The amount of actual factory overhead is determined at the end of the period; it consists of the actual costs for indirect labor, indirect materials, and other factory expenses.

CHAPTER 20, PAGE 563
1. Income Statement Debit column.
2. Underapplied overhead is added to the cost of goods sold.
3. Current Assets.

CHAPTER 21, PAGE 586
1. To avoid misunderstandings. Some states require that partnership agreements be in writing.
2. The existing partnership is terminated.
3. The right of all partners to contract for a partnership.

CHAPTER 21, PAGE 592
1. The existing partnership is terminated.
2. Total equity (including investment by new partner) multiplied by new partner's share of equity equals the new partner's equity.
3. Goodwill is debited; existing partners' capital accounts are credited.

CHAPTER 22, PAGE 608
1. In the partnership agreement.
2. a. Fixed percentage.
   b. Percentage of total equity.
   c. Interest on equity.
   d. Salaries.
   e. Combination of methods.
3. The partner's drawing account.
4. The partner's drawing account.

CHAPTER 22, PAGE 618
1. Because a partnership does not pay federal income tax.
2. When the allowances to partners exceed net income.
3. To summarize the changes in owners' equity during the fiscal period.

CHAPTER 22, PAGE 623
1. Cash received from the sale of assets during liquidation of a partnership.
2. The partners' capital accounts.

CHAPTER 23, PAGE 640
1. a. No profit motive exists.
   b. Leadership is subject to frequent change.
   c. Users of services do not necessarily pay for the services.
   d. Conflicting pressures for differing objectives exist.
2. a. The accounting equation is applied.
   b. An appropriate chart of accounts is prepared.
   c. Transactions are analyzed into debit and credit elements.
   d. Transactions are journalized and posted to ledgers.
   e. Financial statements are prepared for each fiscal period.

   f. Most of the same accounting concepts are applied.
3. A governmental accounting entity with a set of accounts in which assets always equal liabilities plus equities.
4. To authorize and provide the basis for control of financial operations during a fiscal year.
5. Estimated Revenues is debited; Appropriations and Budgetary Fund Balance are credited.

CHAPTER 23, PAGE 644
1. When property taxes are levied.
2. Cash is debited; Taxes Receivable—Current is credited.
3. Cash is debited; Taxes Receivable—Delinquent is credited.

CHAPTER 23, PAGE 651
1. A commitment to pay for goods or services which have been ordered but not yet provided.
2. a. The encumbrance entry is reversed to remove the estimated amount from the encumbrance and reserve for encumbrance accounts.
   b. The expenditure is recorded.
3. Because the organization does not earn a net income and, therefore, has no need for expense information.
4. A document issued by a bank as evidence of money invested with the bank.

CHAPTER 24, PAGE 667
1. Revenues/Expenditures
2. Interest Receivable is debited; Allowance for Uncollectible Interest and Interest Revenue are credited.
3. Revenues/Expenditures Credit column
4. Revenues/Expenditures Credit column total less Revenues/Expenditures Debit column total equals excess of revenues over expenditures.

CHAPTER 24, PAGE 671
1. a. Revenues
   b. Expenditures
   c. Changes in unreserved fund balance.
2. The work sheet
3. Favorable
4. Total assets must equal total liabilities and fund equity.

CHAPTER 24, PAGE 674
1. Work sheet's Adjustments columns.
2. Unreserved Fund Balance
3. Appropriations and Budgetary Fund Balance are debited; Estimated Revenues is credited.
4. Reserve for Encumbrances—Prior Year; Taxes Receivable—Delinquent; Unreserved Fund Balance

Account: a record summarizing all the information pertaining to a single item in the accounting equation. (p. 8)

Accounting: planning, recording, analyzing, and interpreting financial information. (p. xvi)

Accounting cycle: the series of accounting activities included in recording financial information for a fiscal period. (p. 123)

Accounting equation: an equation showing the relationship among assets, liabilities, and owner's equity. (p. 6)

Accounting records: organized summaries of a business' financial activities. (p. xvi)

Accounting system: a planned process for providing financial information that will be useful to management. (p. xvi)

Accounts receivable turnover ratio: the number of times the average amount of accounts receivable is collected during a specified period. (p 206)

Accrual basis of accounting: The accounting method that records revenues when they are earned and expenses when they are incurred. (p. 474)

Accrued expenses: expenses incurred in one fiscal period but not paid until a later fiscal period. (p. 262)

Accrued revenue: revenue earned in one fiscal period but not received until a later fiscal period. (p. 285)

Acid-test ratio: a ratio that shows the numeric relationship of quick assets to current liabilities. (p. 462)

Adjusting entries: journal entries recorded to update general ledger accounts at the end of a fiscal period. (p. 119)

Administrative expenses budget schedule: a statement that shows the projected expenses for all operating expenses not directly related to selling operations. (p. 398)

Aging accounts receivable: analyzing accounts receivable according to when they are due. (p. 201)

Amortization: recognizing a portion of an expense in each of several years. (p. 350)

Appropriations: authorizations to make expenditures for specified purposes. (p. 638)

Articles of incorporation: a written application requesting permission to form a corporation. (p. 298)

Assessed value: the value of an asset determined by tax authorities for the purpose of calculating taxes. (p. 220)

Asset: anything of value that is owned. (p. 6)

Auditing: the independent reviewing and issuing of an opinion on the reliability of accounting records. (p. xvii)

Auditor: a person who examines the records that support the financial records of a business to assure that generally accepted accounting principles (GAAP) are being followed. (p. xvii)

Automatic check deposit: depositing payroll checks directly to an employee's checking or savings account in a specific bank. (p. 79)

Average number of days' sales in merchandise inventory: the period of time needed to sell an average amount of merchandise inventory. (p. 181)

Bad debts: see *uncollectible accounts.*

Balance sheet: a financial statement that reports assets, liabilities, and owner's equity on a specific date. (p. 117)

Bank statement: a report of deposits, withdrawals, and bank balance sent to a depositor by a bank. (p. 25)

Board of directors: a group of persons elected by the stockholders to manage a corporation. (p. 298)

Bond: a printed, long-term promise to pay a specified amount on a specified date and to pay interest at stated intervals. (p. 334)

Bond issue: all the bonds representing the total amount of a loan. (p. 334)

Bond sinking fund: an amount set aside to pay a bond issue when due. (p. 336)

Book inventory: see *perpetual inventory.*

Book value of accounts receivable: the difference between the balance of Accounts Receivable and its contra account, Allowance for Uncollectible Accounts. (p. 206)

Book value of a plant asset: the original cost of a plant asset minus accumulated depreciation. (p. 224)

Book value per share: see *equity per share.*

Breakeven point: the amount of sales at which net sales is exactly the same as total costs. (p. 423)

Budget: a written financial plan of a business for a specific period of time, expressed in dollars. (p. 386)

Budgeted income statement: a statement that shows a company's projected sales, costs, expenses, and net income. (p. 400)

Budgeting: planning the financial operations of a business. (p. 386)

Budget period: the length of time covered by a budget. (p. 388)

Capital stock: total shares of ownership in a corporation. (p. 116)

Cash basis of accounting: the accounting method that records revenues when they are received and expenses when they are paid. (p. 474)

Cash budget: a statement that shows for each month or quarter a projection of a company's beginning cash balance, cash receipts, cash payments, and ending cash balance. (p. 405)

Cash discount: a deduction that a vendor allows on the invoice amount to encourage prompt payment. (p. 20)

Cash flows: the cash receipts and cash payments of a company. (p. 477)

Cash payments budget schedule: projected cash payments (p. 404)

Cash receipts budget schedule: projected cash receipts (p. 402)

Certificate of deposit: a document issued by a bank as evidence of money invested with the bank. (p. 649)

Charter: the approved articles of incorporation. (p. 298)

Check register: a journal used in a voucher system to record cash payments. (p. 152)

Closing entries: journal entries used to prepare temporary accounts for a new fiscal period. (p. 120)

Common stock: stock that does not give stockholders any special preferences. (p. 299)

Comparative income statement: an income statement containing sales, cost, and expense information for two or more years. (p. 390)

Component percentage: the percentage relationship between one financial statement item and the total that includes that item. (p. 98)

Consignee: the person or business who receives goods on consignment. (p. 169)

Consignment: goods that are given to a business to sell, but for which title to the goods remains with the vendor. (p. 169)

Consignor: the person or business who gives goods on consignment. (p. 169)

Contra account: an account that reduces a related account on a financial statement. (p. 16)

Contra balance: an account balance that is opposite the normal balance. (p. 18)

Contribution margin: income determined by subtracting all variable costs from net sales. (p. 420)

Controlling account: an account in a general ledger that summarizes all accounts in a subsidiary ledger. (p. 9)

Corporation: an organization with the legal rights of a person and which may be owned by many persons. (p. 296)

Cost accounting: the determination and control of costs of a business enterprise. (p. xvii)

Cost ledger: a ledger containing all cost sheets for products in the process of being manufactured. (p. 528)

Credit memorandum: a form prepared by the vendor showing the amount deducted for returns and allowances. (p. 44)

Current ratio: a ratio that shows the numeric relationship of current assets to current liabilities. (p. 462)

Date of a note: the day a note is issued. (p. 252)

Date of declaration: the date on which a board of directors votes to distribute a dividend. (p. 310)

Date of payment: the date on which dividends are actually to be paid to stockholders. (p. 310)

Debit memorandum: a form prepared by the customer showing the price deduction taken by the customer for returns and allowances. (p. 16)

Debt ratio: the ratio found by dividing total liabilities by total assets. (p. 463)

Declaring a dividend: action by a board of directors to distribute corporate earnings to stockholders. (p. 310)

Declining-balance method of depreciation: multiplying the book value at the end of each fiscal period by a constant depreciation rate. (p. 234)

Deferred revenue: see *unearned revenue.*

Deficit: the amount by which allowances to partners exceed net income. (p. 613)

Departmental accounting system: an accounting system showing accounting information for two or more departments. (p. 12)

Departmental margin: the revenue earned by a department less its cost of merchandise sold and less its direct expenses. (p. 504)

Departmental margin statement: a statement that reports departmental margin for a specific department. (p. 504)

Departmental statement of gross profit: a statement prepared at the end of a fiscal period showing the gross profit for each department. (p. 96)

Depletion: the decrease in the value of a plant asset because of the removal of a natural resource. (p. 239)

Depreciation expense: the portion of a plant asset's cost that is transferred to an expense account in each fiscal period during a plant asset's useful life. (p. 107)

Direct expense: an operating expense identifiable with and chargeable to the operation of a specific department. (p. 504)

Direct labor: salaries of factory workers who make a product. (p. 526)

Direct materials: materials that are of significant value in the cost of and that become an identifiable part of a finished product. (p. 526)

Direct write-off method of recording losses from uncollectible accounts: recording uncollectible accounts expense only when an amount is actually known to be uncollectible. (p. 196)

Discount on capital stock: an amount less than par or stated value at which capital stock is sold. (p. 324)

Dishonored note: a note that is not paid when due. (p. 280)

Distribution of net income statement: a partnership financial statement showing distribution of net income or net loss to partners. (p. 612)

Dividends: earnings distributed to stockholders. (p. 116)

Double-entry accounting: the recording of debit and credit parts of a transaction. (p. 7)

Earnings per share: the amount of net income belonging to a single share of stock. (p. 357)

Electronic funds transfer (EFT): transferring payroll accounts electronically from the employer's account directly to the employee's bank account. (p. 79)

Employee benefits: payments to employees for non-working hours and to insurance and retirement programs. (p. 64)

Employee earnings record: a business form used to record details affecting payments made to an employee. (p. 76)

Encumbrance: a commitment to pay for goods or services that have been ordered but not yet provided. (p. 645)

Equities: financial rights to the assets of a business. (p. 6)

Equity per share: the amount of total stockholders' equity belonging to a single share of stock. (p. 358)

Equity ratio: the ratio found by dividing stockholders' equity by total assets. (p. 464)

Ethics: the principles of right and wrong that guide an individual in making decisions. (p. xxii)

Expenditures: cash disbursements and liabilities incurred for the cost of goods delivered or services rendered. (p. 635)

Factory overhead: all expenses other than direct materials and direct labor that apply to the making of products. (p. 526)

Fifo: see *first-in, first-out inventory costing method.*

File maintenance: the procedure for arranging accounts in a general ledger, assigning account numbers, and keeping records current. (pp. 9, 54)

Financial accounting: the recording of a business' financial activities and the periodic preparation of financial reports. (p. xvii)

Financing activities: cash receipts and payments involving debt or equity transactions. (p. 480)

Finished goods: manufactured products that are fully completed. (p. 527)

Finished goods ledger: a ledger containing records of all finished goods on hand. (p. 528)

First-in, first-out inventory costing method: using the price of merchandise purchased first to calculate the cost of merchandise sold first. (p. 173)

Fiscal period: the length of time for which a business summarizes and reports financial information. (p. 94)

Fixed assets: see *plant assets.*

Fixed costs: total costs that remain constant regardless of change in business activity. (p. 419)

Fund: a governmental accounting entity with a set of accounts in which assets always equal liabilities plus equities. (p. 634)

General fixed assets: governmental properties that benefit future periods. (p. 648)

General ledger: a ledger that contains all accounts needed to prepare financial statements. (p. 9)

Goodwill: the value of a business in excess of the total investment of owners. (p. 590)

Gross profit method of estimating an inventory: estimating inventory by using the previous year's percentage of gross profit on operations. (p. 96)

Horizontal analysis: see *trend analysis.*

Income statement: a financial statement showing the revenue and expenses for a fiscal period. (p. 114)

Indirect expense: an operating expense chargeable to overall business operations and not identifiable with a specific department. (p. 504)

Indirect labor: salaries paid to factory workers who are not actually making products. (p. 526)

Indirect materials: materials used in the completion of a product that are of insignificant value to justify accounting for separately. (p. 526)

Intangible assets: assets of a non-physical nature that have value for a business. (p. 308)

Interest: an amount paid for the use of money for a period of time. (p. 252)

Interest expense: the interest accrued on money borrowed. (p. 254)

Interest rate of a note: the percentage of the principal that is paid for use of the money. (p. 252)

Interim departmental statement of gross profit: a statement showing gross profit for each department for a portion of a fiscal period. (p. 96)

Internal auditor: see *auditor.*

Inventory record: a form used during a periodic inventory to record information about each item of merchandise on hand. (p. 171)

Investing activities: cash receipts and cash payments involving the sale or purchase of assets used to earn revenue over a period of time. (p. 479)

Journal: a form for recording transactions in chronological order. (p. 7)

Last-in, first-out inventory costing method: using the price of merchandise purchased last to calculate the cost of merchandise sold first. (p. 174)

Ledger: a group of accounts. (p. 9)

Liability: an amount owed by a business. (p. 6)

Lifo: see *last-in, first-out inventory costing method.*

Liquidation of a partnership: the process of paying a partnership's liabilities and distributing remaining assets to the partners. (p. 619)

Long-term assets: see *plant assets.*

Lower of cost or market inventory costing method: using the lower of cost or market price to calculate the cost of ending merchandise inventory. (p. 177)

MACRS: see *Modified Accelerated Cost Recovery System.*

Management advisory services: management advice provided to an organization by a private accountant. (p. xix)

Managerial accounting: the analysis, measurement, and interpretation of financial accounting information. (p. xvii)

Marginal income: see *contribution margin.*

Market value: the price at which a share of stock may be sold on the stock market. (p. 358)

Materials ledger: a ledger containing all records of materials. (p. 528)

Maturity date of a note: the date a note is due. (p. 252)

Maturity value: the amount that is due on the maturity date of a note. (p. 254)

Merchandise inventory turnover ratio: the number of times the average amount of merchandise inventory is sold during a specific period of time. (p. 181)

Merchandising business: a business that purchases and sells goods. (p. 12)

Modified Accelerated Cost Recovery System: a depreciation method required by the Internal Revenue Service to be used for income tax calculation purposes for most plant assets placed in service after 1986. (p. 238)

Mutual agency: the right of all partners to contract for a partnership. (p. 583)

Nonprofit organization: see *not-for-profit organization.*

No-par-value stock: a share of stock that has no authorized value printed on the stock certificate. (p. 300)

Note: see *promissory note.*

Notes payable: promissory notes that a business issues to creditors. (p. 252)

Notes receivable: promissory notes that a business accepts from customers. (p. 278)

Not-for-profit organization: an organization providing goods or services with neither a conscious motive nor expectation of earning a profit. (p. 630)

Operating activities: the cash receipts and payments necessary to operate a business on a day-to-day basis. (p. 479)

Operating budget: a plan of current expenditures and the proposed means of financing those expenditures. (p. 637)

Organization costs: fees and other expenses of organizing a corporation. (p. 303)

Other revenue and expenses budget schedule: budgeted revenue and expenses from activities other than normal operations. (p. 399)

Overapplied overhead: the amount by which applied factory overhead is more than actual factory overhead. (p. 552)

Overhead: see *factory overhead.*

Owner's equity: the amount remaining after the value of all liabilities is subtracted from the value of all assets. (p. 6)

Owners' equity statement: a financial statement that summarizes the changes in owners' equity during a fiscal period. (p. 614)

Partnership: a business in which two or more persons combine their assets and skills. (p. 13)

Partnership agreement: a written agreement setting forth the conditions under which a partnership is to operate. (p. 583)

Par value: a value assigned to a share of stock and printed on the stock certificate. (p. 300)

Par-value stock: a share of stock that has an authorized value printed on the stock certificate. (p. 300)

Pay period: the period covered by a salary payment. (p. 62)

Payroll: the total amount earned by all employees for a pay period. (p. 62)

Payroll register: a business form used to record payroll information. (p. 72)

Payroll taxes: taxes based on the payroll of a business. (p. 62)

Performance report: a report showing a comparison of projected and actual amounts for a specific period of time. (p. 407)

Periodic inventory: a merchandise inventory determined by counting, weighing, or measuring items of merchandise on hand. (p. 96)

Perpetual inventory: a merchandise inventory determined by keeping a continuous record of increases, decreases, and balance on hand. (p. 96)

Personal financial planning: assisting individuals in managing their personal investments. (p. xvii)

Personal property: all property not classified as real property. (p. 220)

Petty cash: an amount of cash kept on hand and used for making small payments. (p. 24)

Physical inventory: see *periodic inventory*.

Plant asset record: an accounting form on which a business records information about each plant asset. (p. 218)

Plant assets: assets that will be used for a number of years in the operation of a business. (p. 107)

Post-closing trial balance: a trial balance prepared after the closing entries are posted. (p. 122)

Posting: transferring information from a journal entry to a ledger account. (p. 14)

Preferred stock: stock that gives stockholders preference in earnings and other rights. (p. 299)

Prepaid expenses: expenses paid in one fiscal period but not reported as expenses until a later fiscal period. (p. 256)

Price-earnings ratio: the relationship between the market value per share and earnings per share of a stock. (p. 358)

Principal of a note: the original amount of a note. (p. 252)

Production-unit method of depreciation: calculating estimated annual depreciation expense based on the amount of production expected from a plant asset. (p. 237)

Promissory note: a written and signed promise to pay a sum of money at a specified time. (p. 252)

Purchase order: a completed form authorizing a seller to deliver goods with payment to be made later. (p. 170)

Purchases budget schedule: a statement prepared to show the projected amount of purchases that will be required during a budget period. (p. 395)

Purchases discount: a cash discount on purchases taken by a customer. (p. 20)

Quick assets: those current assets that are cash or that can be quickly turned into cash. (p. 462)

Rate earned on average stockholders' equity: the relationship between net income and average stockholders' equity. (p. 361)

Rate earned on average total assets: the relationship between net income and average total assets. (p. 361)

Rate earned on net sales: the rate found by dividing net income after federal income tax by net sales. (p. 455)

Ratio: a comparison between two numbers showing how many times one number exceeds the other. (p. 444)

Real estate: see *real property*.

Realization: cash received from the sale of assets during liquidation of a partnership. (p. 619)

Real property: land and anything attached to the land. (p. 220)

Responsibility accounting: assigning control of business revenues, costs, and expenses as a responsibility of a specific manager. (p. 504)

Responsibility statements: financial statements reporting revenue, costs, and direct expenses under a specific department's control. (p. 512)

Retail method of estimating inventory: estimating inventory by using a percentage based on both cost and retail prices. (p. 180)

Retained earnings: an amount earned by a corporation and not yet distributed to stockholders. (p. 116)

Retiring a bond issue: paying the amounts owed to bondholders for a bond issue. (p. 337)

Reversing entry: an entry made at the beginning of one fiscal period to reverse an adjusting entry made in the previous fiscal period. (p. 259)

Salary: the money paid for employee services. (p. 62)

Sales budget schedule: a statement that shows the projected net sales for a budget period. (p. 394)

Sales discount: a cash discount on sales. (p. 48)

Sales mix: relative distribution of sales among various products. (p. 432)

Schedule of accounts payable: a listing of vendor accounts, account balances, and total amount due all vendors. (p. 102)

Schedule of accounts receivable: a listing of customer accounts, account balances, and total amount due from all customers. (p. 102)

Selling expenses budget schedule: a statement prepared to show projected expenditures related directly to the selling operations. (p. 396)

Serial bonds: portions of a bond issue that mature on different dates. (p. 337)

Share of stock: each unit of ownership in a corporation. (p. 13)

Source document: a business paper from which information is obtained for a journal entry. (p. 6)

Special journal: a journal used to record only one kind of transaction. (p. 7)

Stated-value stock: no-par-value stock that is assigned a value by a corporation. (p. 300)

Statement of cash flows: a statement that summarizes cash receipts and cash payments resulting from business activities during a fiscal period. (p. 477)

Statement of cost of goods manufactured: a statement showing details about the cost of finished goods. (p. 560)

Statement of stockholders' equity: a financial statement that shows changes in a corporation's ownership for a fiscal period. (p. 116)

Stock certificate: written evidence of the number of shares each stockholder owns in a corporation. (p. 300)

Stockholder: an owner of one or more shares of a corporation. (p. 14)

Stockholder's equity: value of the owner's equity in a corporation. (p. 135)

Stock ledger: a file of stock records for all merchandise on hand. (p. 170)

Stock record: a form used to show the kind of merchandise, quantity received, quantity sold, and balance on hand. (p. 170)

Straight-line method of depreciation: charging an equal amount of depreciation expense for a plant asset in each year of useful life. (p. 223)

Subscribing for capital stock: entering into an agreement with a corporation to buy capital stock and pay at a later date. (p. 306)

Subsidiary ledger: a ledger that is summarized in a single general ledger account. (p. 9)

Sum-of-the-years-digits method of depreciation: using fractions based on years of a plant asset's useful life. (p. 235)

Taking an inventory: see *periodic inventory.*

Tax accounting: the preparation of tax returns as well as tax planning. (p. xvii)

Tax base: the maximum amount of earnings on which a tax is calculated. (p. 71)

Tax levy: authorized action taken by a governmental organization to collect taxes by legal authority. (p. 641)

Term bonds: bonds that all mature on the same date. (p. 337)

Total costs: all costs for a specific period of time. (p. 418)

Treasury stock: a corporation's own stock that has been issued and reacquired. (p. 329)

Trend analysis: a comparison of the relationship between one item on a financial statement and the same item on a previous fiscal period's financial statement. (p. 445)

Trial balance: a proof of the equality of debits and credits in a general ledger. (p. 103)

Trustee: a person or institution, usually a bank, who is given legal authorization to administer property for the benefit of property owners. (p. 335)

Uncollectible accounts: accounts receivable that cannot be collected. (p. 194)

Underapplied overhead: the amount by which applied factory overhead is less than actual factory overhead. (p. 552)

Unearned revenue: revenue received in one fiscal period but not earned until the next fiscal period. (p. 283)

Unit cost: an amount spent for one of a specific product or service. (p. 418)

Variable costs: total costs that change in direct proportion to a change in the number of units. (p. 419)

Vertical analysis: see *component percentage.*

Voucher: a business form used to show an authorized person's approval for a cash payment. (p. 144)

Voucher check: a check with space for writing details about a cash payment. (p. 151)

Voucher jacket: see *voucher.*

Voucher register: a journal used to record vouchers. (p. 148)

Voucher system: a set of procedures for controlling cash payments by preparing and approving vouchers before payments are made. (p. 144)

Weighted-average inventory costing method: using the average cost of beginning inventory plus merchandise purchased during a fiscal period to calculate the cost of merchandise sold. (p. 175)

Withholding allowance: a deduction from total earnings for each person legally supported by a taxpayer. (p. 71)

Working capital: the amount of total current assets less total current liabilities. (p. 461)

Work in process: products that are being manufactured but are not yet complete. (p. 527)

Work sheet: a columnar accounting form used to summarize the general ledger information needed to prepare financial statements. (p. 103)

Writing off an account: canceling the balance of a customer account because the customer does not pay. (p. 194)

Photo Credits